EPISTEMOLOGY OF PERCEPTION

GAṄGEŚA'S TATTVACINTĀMAṆI

THE PERCEPTION CHAPTER

EPISTEMOLOGY OF PERCEPTION

Transliterated Text, Translation, and Philosophical Commentary of **Gaṅgeśa's** *Tattvacintāmaṇi* (Jewel of Reflection on the Truth)

PRATYAKṢA-KHAṆḌA

The Perception Chapter

STEPHEN H. PHILLIPS
N.S. RAMANUJA TATACHARYA

MOTILAL BANARSIDASS PUBLISHERS
PRIVATE LIMITED • DELHI

*First Indian Edition : Delhi, **2009***
*Earlier published by **American Institute of Buddhist Studies,***
Columbia University, and Co-published with Columbia University's
Center for Buddhist Studies and Tibet House US

ISBN : 978-81-208-3332-6

MOTILAL BANARSIDASS
41 U.A. Bungalow Road, Jawahar Nagar, Delhi 110 007
8 Mahalaxmi Chamber, 22 Bhulabhai Desai Road, Mumbai 400 026
203 Royapettah High Road, Mylapore, Chennai 600 004
236, 9th Main III Block, Jayanagar, Bangalore 560 011
Sanas Plaza, 1302 Baji Rao Road, Pune 411 002
8 Camac Street, Kolkata 700 017
Ashok Rajpath, Patna 800 004
Chowk, Varanasi 221 001

PRINTED IN INDIA
BY JAINENDRA PRAKASH JAIN AT SHRI JAINENDRA PRESS,
A-45, NARAINA, PHASE-I, NEW DELHI 110 028
AND PUBLISHED BY NARENDRA PRAKASH JAIN FOR
MOTILAL BANARSIDASS PUBLISHERS PRIVATE LIMITED,
BUNGALOW ROAD, DELHI 110 007

To

the memory of

Jagannatha Vedalankara

CONTENTS

PREFACE TO THE INDIAN EDITION

This edition is largely the same as that published by the American Institute of Buddhist Studies, New York, 2004. A few corrections have been made, one due to Arindam Chakrabarti. The first part of the introduction, on Nyāya epistemology in broad perspective, has been expanded in connection with a talk I presented at Jadavpur University, Kolkata, January 2008: "Internalism as well as Externalism in Nyāya Epistemology." My thanks to the Jadavpur Philosophy Department for excellent discussion that has led to several improvements.

Special thanks are also due to Shri N.P. Jain, who has made this publication occur in part from support provided long ago when I was deciding to concentrate on Nyāya and Gaṅgeśa. I am happy now to have a second book with Motilal Banarsidass, and thank everyone who has aided production. N.S. Ramanuja Tatacharya and I feel strongly that an Indian edition is important so that our work can reach a broader audience.

Stephen Phillips

Austin, Texas
January 2008

PREFACE AND ACKNOWLEDGMENTS (American Edition)

N. S. Ramanuja Tatacharya and I are collaborators in this effort. We wish first of all to thank Arindam Chakrabarti, Professor of Philosophy, University of Hawaii, who edited a late draft. Professor Chakrabarti has made the translations and comments of practically every page more exact and readable. I am fortunate to be flanked by two such able Naiyāyikas!

Let me explain the contribution of Shri Ramanuja Tatacharya. Gaṅgeśa's style is highly elliptical, and my teacher, who is a great master of Nyāya, filled in gaps and provided background with explanations and glosses in Sanskrit. Although the English sentences and commentary have been written by me, his expertise accounts for their accuracy. Formerly Vice Chancellor, Rashtriya Sanskrit Vidyapeetha, Tirupati, N. S. Ramanuja Tatacharya holds many traditional degrees and titles. He is editor of *Tattvacintāmaṇi* (1972), which includes the text translated here (and occasionally improved, as explained in "preliminaries"), as well as editor of two volumes covering Gaṅgeśa's inference chapter (1982, 1999), part of which we translated, *Gaṅgeśa on the Upādhi* (2002). Among his books and papers in Sanskrit is, notably, *Pratyakṣatattvacintāmaṇi Vimarśa: A Comprehensive and Evaluative Study of the Pratyakṣakhaṇḍa of the Tattvacintāmaṇi* (1992). He worked with me for long stretches in 1991, 1995, 1996, 1997, 1998, and 1999, a few matters being ironed out in February 2000. I humbly thank him for all his good will: *śrīmadrāmānujatātācāryebhyaḥ praṇāmāñjalir iyam vākyamālā.*

Robert Thurman and Thomas Yarnall of the American Institute of Buddhist Studies and Columbia University have played a crucial role in this book's appearance. The interdependence of the Indian schools—including, to be sure, the Bauddha and the Naiyāyika—should be reflected in modern scholarship, as Professor Thurman suggests in his preface. Especially in logic and epistemology, partisans sharing the medium of Sanskrit learned from one another, as philosophy moved to new heights. Hopefully now there can be reëngagement from all sides. I speak for Shri Ramanuja Tatacharya in saying that we are proud to launch this series of translations of classical Indian thought.

The Centre d'Indologie, École Française d'Extrême Orient, Pondicherry, was integral to the project. François Grimal, Directeur, hosted our sittings, and made available bibliographic resources and the supportive atmosphere of a center for spoken Sanskrit as well as scholarship. The American Institute of Indian Studies funded two trips of mine to India. I thank Dr. Pradeep Mahirendatta and his staff. The Center for Asian Studies, University of Texas at Austin, helped fund other trips; the Philosophy Department provided a semester of leave. The University of Texas Research Institute funded another semester of leave and assumed other expenses. I am grateful to the University of Texas Coöperative Society Bookstore here in Austin for a subvention awarded as part of a program that supports Texas faculty publications, as well as to Rajiv Malhotra whose Infinity Foundation also provided a generous grant.

Among current and former graduate students in either Philosophy or Asian Studies at Texas (some now professors elsewhere) whose comments and questions have made this a better book are Alex Catlin, Joel Feldman, Megan Nowell-Kaufman, Eric Loomis, and Ellen Briggs. Professors Karl Potter, Rama Rao Pappu, Daniel Bonevac, Patrick Olivelle, Sibajiban Bhattacharyya, J. N. Mohanty, and Kisor Chakrabarti read one or more sections, making suggestions for which I am grateful. In Pondicherry, Pandit S. L. P. Anjaneya Sarma often talked with me about Nyāya and Indian philosophy, as did my long-standing mentor, Professor Arabinda Basu. I should like to acknowledge their help—as well as that of the broader community of Sanskrit speakers in Pondicherry.

This volume is dedicated to the memory of Shri Jagannatha Vedalankara, Sri Aurobindo Ashram, who worked with me with great kindness in the seventies. For more than forty years he was the leader of a group of dedicated Sanskrit teachers at the Sri Aurobindo International Centre for Education. May the centuries-old tradition of Sanskrit pandits that Shri Jagannatha represents flourish in future centuries!

Stephen Phillips — Austin, Texas
June 2004

PRELIMINARIES

1. For Philosophers

Scholars of Indic philosophies are not, I imagine, this book's only audience. Gaṅgeśa's reasoning deserves to be accessible to those who know almost nothing about Indian thought. It is high time the best of non-Western philosophy be incorporated into the curriculum of philosophy as an academic discipline. At present, however, few professional philosophers are familiar with Eastern systems, and specialists tend to write for other specialists. Here a wider audience is addressed, with considerable context supplied to make some passages clear. Philosophy had flourished for more than a thousand years in the Indian subcontinent prior to Gaṅgeśa who lived around 1325 CE. Furthermore, Gaṅgeśa presumes that his readers know not only his own Nyāya school but Nyāya's principal rivals. Fortunately, Gaṅgeśa is a great thinker, and many of his arguments transcend his culture. His central issues, moreover, will be familiar to all students of philosophic theories of knowledge. But in some cases quite a long commentary is supplied in an effort to set Gaṅgeśa's views within the right ideative space. In this way, a broad span of philosophy can be learned piecemeal.

Appended is a glossary that explains every Sanskrit word used in English. Brief characterizations of persons and schools are also presented there. An index references Gaṅgeśa's main topics. An introduction provides the essentials of theory and history.

With regard to translative style, I have employed a maximalist strategy that is also in a way minimalist. Gaṅgeśa's sentences are rendered in sentences with ellipses restored, propositional anaphora filled in with the propositions referred to, and background assumptions provided (in parentheses). My aim has been to translate Gaṅgeśa in sentences that read fluidly on the principle that as little as possible should be filled in (the minimalism) so long as a sentence is readable and makes plain Gaṅgeśa's sense (the maximalism). Parentheses are used generously to indicate that a word or phrase has no explicit correlate in the Sanskrit or to supply a presupposition or to allow a quick gloss or rewording, not directly translating the text. If these practices are distracting or hard to keep in mind, please ignore the parentheses and treat their content as part of the text.

This is sound advice because everything provided in English under the headings, "Text and Translation," including the longest expressions in parentheses, is to be understood as meant by Gaṅgeśa's Sanskrit sentences. Admittedly, in some cases the line is hard to draw between the truly implicit—which is so closely presupposed that without it a sentence could not be read, and which I take to be subject to restoration in English—and elaboration and exegesis appropriate to commentary. As indicated, a running commentary is provided under the headings, "Comments," where more extensive explanations of background theories are presented as well as reconstructions of arguments. Sometimes I try to make Gaṅgeśa's reasoning come alive in the context of current issues. Or, especially with difficult passages, explanations by Ramanuja Tatacharya drawing on the later classical tradition are given at length. But the goal has been to make the translation intelligible without comments. One should be able to read the translation by itself, without relying on comments at all.

A conceptual introduction to Gaṅgeśa and his Nyāya school provides general background. An overview of his epistemology is supplied, but much of Gaṅgeśa's genius lies in details of his reasoning. There are, however, two matters explained in the introduction that have to be learned. First, one must have a rudimentary understanding of the Nyāya concept of "cognition," *jñāna*. Second, one must learn a pattern of inference along with certain words used to talk about inference, i.e., five or six technical terms of logic (which are also explained in the glossary).

Mastering the pattern of inference is clearly a precondition for reading this book, since Gaṅgeśa employs it continuously. That is to say, Gaṅgeśa often formalizes his arguments by using a standard inferential pattern that the introduction explains. The explanation of cognition is less essential in fact, since the topic is elaborated and refined throughout the entire volume, whereas Gaṅgeśa assumes that everyone knows the inference form. On the other hand, the topic of cognition is so important it is a good idea to have a hold on it, too, from the start. Other positions and arguments are introduced only in broad overview, particularly in the first subsection where I place Nyāya within the spectrum of Western epistemology.

2. For Sanskritists

Several "liberal" translative practices are utilized, such as squeezing verbs out of nominalizations, turning passive into active constructions, and rendering a single Sanskrit adjective with a pair of English adjectives or an adjectival phrase. Moreover, ellipsis is commonly restored, and antecedents commonly substituted in place of anaphoric pronouns. Gaṅgeśa's Sanskrit can, nevertheless, be reconstructed or at least traced from the English. Thus, probably not much needs to be said in justification of these practices—all done in the interest of *intelligibility* and *readability*. However, the *discourse structure* of classical philosophic texts, such as Gaṅgeśa's, which I make explicit by labelling speakers, may require defending for some. Attributing views by name and concordant paragraph breaks are not stylistic features of Gaṅgeśa's Sanskrit.[1]

The structure of the *TCM* centers on a series of philosophic topics examined within certain formal constraints of textual division the most important of which is the segmentation of opponents' views—or *pūrva-pakṣa*, the prior or *prima facie* position or an objection—in relation to Gaṅgeśa's own views—*siddhânta*, the final, established position answering the *pūrva-pakṣa*. Readers have to be acutely mindful of this textual division including *pūrva-pakṣa* within *pūrva-pakṣa* and sometimes another level down. Without appreciating this discourse structure of Gaṅgeśa's text, no one could understand more than an isolated sentence or two, though sometimes Gaṅgeśa does not himself explicitly identify discourse divisions.

A *pūrva-pakṣa* is, to give a definition, topically unified exposition, complete with supporting arguments, of an opposed position or of an attack correlate to a *siddhânta*, which is itself unified exposition of an accepted position, complete with supporting arguments or correlate responses.

Hand in hand with the discourse segmentations of *pūrva-pakṣa* and *siddhânta*, there are further conventions of the philosophic genre that we must be mindful of, conventions that are drawn on but are not typically stated. They are instantiated but not expressed. The reply provided in a *siddhânta* is related to a preceding *pūrva-pakṣa* by what I call, following recent linguistic literature, a *discourse relation*. Discourse relations bind together *pūrva-pakṣa* and *siddhânta* sections as well as separate them. Furthermore, the discourse relations that Gaṅgeśa employs have a certain logic. In general, each is a debate rule or principle, a rule of refutation or right response.

The thesis that principles of debate structure the *TCM* has several ramifications, what we might call entailments of the genre. One is that the segment labelling used below, the emboldening of names, **Gaṅgeśa**, etc., is called for. Gaṅgeśa expected his immediate audience to be able to identify views by proponents and practically hear in the language he uses the voices of individual advocates. We would like to hear these, too, in English. Sometimes the labelling can be, however, no more specific than a nondescript "objector" versus Gaṅgeśa expressing his own view. Still, as far as is clear to us names have been supplied.

Principles that apply to the relations of *pūrva-pakṣa*s and *siddhânta*s are the principles that structure debate among philosophic disputants in general. These include all well-known argument patterns, debate rules (such as winning through pointing out well-known fallacies in an opponent's arguments), and principles of epistemology such as the power of perceptual evidence to trump testimony. All such principles are candidates for a type of intimate presupposition that, though unstated in the source, structures a response and is thus available for express indication in English—or whatever target language is employed. For example, in sections devoted to defining terms, the Nyāya theory of definition and, in particular, a Nyāya list of commonly occurring fallacies of definition—underextension, overextension, and non-applicability—are, though unstated, discourse relators or principles of response. These, then, can be made explicit, as they are here typically, in translation, and with or without parentheses, as they are part of the text. The text could not be read by anyone unmindful of them, including Gaṅgeśa himself. Another example is the case of a *reductio* pattern of argument, called in the traditional debate theory, *tarka*, ''counterfactual reasoning'' or ''indirect proof,'' which is sometimes set up by a, let us say, *pūrva-pakṣa* anaphor—an anaphor whose antecedent is an immediately preceding wrong view—and the phrase, *tathā sati*: *If* you hold such and such, then you are faced with the following untoward ramification, *āpatti* or *prasaṅga*. We might say that these are part of the *surface* semantics of a text. Actually, they are not on the surface, but are so barely submerged as to be seen when we look.

Identification of discourse segments—the breaks of voice—is usually not difficult. Though Gaṅgeśa does not employ the conventions used here, normally he does use segmentation cues, which I call *discourse markers*. A straightforward textual cue marking the beginning of a *pūrva-pakṣa* occurs in adverbial discourse markers, in particular, the paragraph adverbs, *nanu* and *atha*. Such terms need not be directly translated as their meaning may be absorbed into English paragraph breaks and disputant labelling. Gaṅgeśa typically uses a discourse marker to signal the beginning of a passage that is answered later, and our labelling does the same in the translation.

This style is appropriate, we believe, but it cannot be denied that there is an interpretive element in discerning discourse structure, particularly in some instances.[2] In others, the precise boundary is pellucidly clear. Yet doubtless some decisions Ramanuja Tatacharya and I have made are flawed, and can be improved upon, especially when discourse relators are suppressed.

Nevertheless, there is probably less distortion with our revealing discourse structure than with our labellings. Gaṅgeśa uses expressions such as *mama tu*, ''My view, in contrast,'' as discourse markers, a practice that we may generalize, attributing *siddhânta* sections to Gaṅgeśa himself, as we do, using his name. But such ascription does not suggest as much as it should. A *siddhânta* is normally more than Gaṅgeśa's own view; it is supposed to be the view of Nyāya tradition, a view that Gaṅgeśa is interpreting as well as asserting anew (*atra brūmaḥ* also occurs as a discourse marker: ''To this, *we* respond''). Furthermore, a *siddhânta* indicator is not meant to introduce a perspective or way things might be, but a view arrived at by careful considerations and asserted as true. The considerations that comprise *siddhânta* text are asserted both as true and as definitive of traditional Nyāya even when they are original.

The emboldened labelling of Gaṅgeśa's name is, then, best understood as signaling text where Gaṅgeśa gives his own views while taking himself to speak for the school. To be sure, rival Naiyāyika positions are sometimes aired, and often he distinguishes his contemporary or "New" (*navya*) Nyāya from that of "Old" Nyāya. Nevertheless, *siddhânta*s are asserted as expressing the positions of a school, not only of an individual philosopher.

There are three other rules of translative and interpretive practice that we might briefly rehearse.

(1) The principle of *intelligibility*: a translator should not render what is intelligible in a source language as unintelligible in a target language. Different languages have different thresholds of tolerance for ellipsis, presupposition, anaphoric reference, and the like. Thus adherence to this principle often requires target constructions that are innovative.

(2) The principle of *readability*: between two expressions with the same meaning, a translator should choose the more readable. This principle trumps any merit there might be in trying to mirror the syntax of the source or to use words in one-to-one correspondence. That is to say, this principle trumps what we might call misguided literalness.

(3) The principle of *charity*: A translator should choose the best interpretation, which is, for starters, a *non-contradictory* interpretation. We assume in conversation, debate, and so on, that a speaker would not, except in special circumstances, contradict himself or herself. Thus, without being able to provide a special explanation, we should not settle for an interpretation that is contradictory. An apparent contradiction makes us look for another interpretation, just as in everyday conversation we would either understand an apparent contradiction as a figure of speech or ask our interlocutor just what he or she means. The principle of charity also demands we assume the sincerity of our author as a philosopher, a sense on his part of relevance, as well as, beyond non-contradiction, a sense of overall coherence. Indeed, we interpret a philosopher as trying, in any particular instance, to say something true and warranted as well as coherent with his or her overall view. Of course, such granting of trustworthiness to Gaṅgeśa has to be contextualized. This means that with respect to his own times he would not deny, for example, a bit of world knowledge commonly assumed. At least we may presume he would not do so without somehow signaling the fact. Thus, to make a similar point, we may presume that inherited positions of Gaṅgeśa's own Nyāya tradition count, without explicit evidence to the contrary, as views endorsed by him. Sometimes we are told that Old Nyāya needs to be revised. But, as pointed out, Gaṅgeśa normally takes himself to speak for the school.

Finally about transliteration and a few conventions adopted. The transliterated text is taken from the Tirupati edition of the perception chapter of the *Tattvacintāmaṇi* which Ramanuja Tatacharya has edited (1972) along with the commentary of Rucidatta (c. 1500) and subcommentary by Rāmakṛṣṇādhvarin (c. 1650). Compounds are indicated by hyphens, and *saṃdhi* is broken but letters dropped or changed are not restored. A circumflex indicates a vowel *saṃdhi* at the word junction of a compound, overriding the usual hyphen. Beyond indicating *saṃdhi* breaks, no effort has been made to improve the representation of *saṃdhi*. The Tirupati edition is practically mirrored, and violations of *saṃdhi* are left as they appear. (For example, Ramanuja Tatacharya has often failed to convert a final 't' to 'd' although apparently called for. This can usually be viewed as a kind of punctuation, marking pauses like commas.) Some punctuation has been simplified, and there are no paragraph indentations or designations other than the big breaks for translation and comment. In this way our transliterated text is an edition distinct from the Tirupati edition, representing how Ramanuja Tatacharya and I read Gaṅgeśa. All non-punctuation emendations are indicated in notes.

Again, the transliteration represents how Ramanuja Tatacharya and I understand the text. We acknowledge that it is an interpretation. But at this basic level it is an interpretation almost wholly determined by Ramanuja Tatacharya as editor of the Tirupati edition. We do in a few instances made textual emendations. We try to take into account textual variants in the Calcutta edition (1884) edited by Kamakhyanath Tarkavagish complete with a famous commentary by Mathurānātha (c. 1650) and notes by Jayadeva (c. 1500). Several of our emendations are due to the justly renowned *Māthurī*. Nevertheless, excepting paragraph breaks and so forth as listed above, all departures from the Tirupati edition are flagged by numbered notes; the Calcutta edition is not similarly improved. The two editions differ only occasionally, however, and for the convenience of those who want to see the Devanāgarī, we provide page numbers for both editions.

Parentheses in the translation have a variety of functions, none unfamiliar. Primarily they bracket meanings so closely presupposed that a passage would be unintelligible without them—meanings directly implicated, that is, without being designated on the surface in Sanskrit. In plainer words, sometimes a sentence or phrase is unintelligible without a brief gloss, a rewording or a presupposition supplied. These are placed in parentheses.

INTRODUCTION

Gaṅgeśa and Nyāya Philosophy

1. An Epistemology of *pramāṇa*, "Knowledge Sources"

Gaṅgeśa Upādhyāya (c. 1325 CE) solidified the "New" (*navya*) phase of the long-running school of epistemology and metaphysics known in Sanskrit as Nyāya. Or, it is really two schools, Nyāya and Vaiśeṣika, that comprise Gaṅgeśa's inheritance. These words may be translated "Logic" and "Particularism," but we shall use the Sanskrit names. Each school is a complex tradition of philosophy, with distinct literatures until Udayana (c. 1000) who combines them as Nyāya.

Gaṅgeśa lived in Mithilā, in northern India, where he was a prominent teacher. He had two wives and two sons and a daughter. One of his sons, Vardhamāna, was a famous philosopher in his own right. Gaṅgeśa has left us a single composition, the *Tattva-cintā-maṇi* (*TCM*), "Jewel of Reflection on the Truth (about Epistemology)."

The *TCM* is Navya Nyāya's—"New Logic's"—root text. It contains reflection distilled from generations of earlier philosophy both within Nyāya and Vaiśeṣika and outside. Gaṅgeśa's originality is in fact less than traditionally implied. Udayana innovates several of the positions characteristic of the New Logic movement, as Gaṅgeśa himself acknowledges. Nevertheless, Gaṅgeśa refines and polishes Nyāya theories, developing new lines of argument. Clearly, he is recognized as the founder of New Logic, and his text stands at the center of subsequent centuries of philosophy in the Nyāya school.

Gaṅgeśa defends a realist view of everyday objects and a causal view of learning about them. "Knowledge sources," *pramāṇa*, the most important of which are perception, inference, and testimony, reveal objects that not only exist independently of cognition but also cause it. There are, furthermore, *pramāṇa* subvarieties whose operations involve specific rules, as well as a fourth "source," analogy, restricted to acquisition of vocabulary (i.e., learning a word through someone's drawing an analogy). But all "knowledge generators" are viewed as natural processes, as part of the universe's causal web. The veridical cognitions generated and their indications are, to be sure, identified from the inside, from a first-person perspective, and it is possible to know cognitive origin by a kind of introspection ("I see that I am *inferring* that *a* is F"). Nevertheless, the *pramāṇa* are worldly processes, common among all perceivers, inferrers, and so on, and are described from an impersonal point of view.

A veridical cognition, no matter what its source, hits a fact, or, more properly, an object (*viṣaya*), its object, and there can be cognitions that are accidentally veridical. For instance, a fire-cognition produced from a person's mistaking dust for smoke on a mountain where there is actually fire is veridical but is not *pramāṇa*-generated. A veridical cognition is a cognition of an object as it is. The pseudo-inferential cognition of fire from seeing dust is veridical though by accident. Veridicality is typically best *explained* by a cognition-producing process, but veridicality itself is a relation from cognition to object that is independent of cognitive origin.

Gaṅgeśa embraces what we may call a *correspondence* theory of truth, though about the equivalent term in Sanskrit, *yathârthatva*, he expresses some unhappiness (below, p. 218). This is due to his sense that the term is thought to imply a kind of similarity, and there is, he says, little similarity between, for example, a pot and a cognition of a pot. The relation between cognitions and their objects is called *having-an-object* (from the side of cognition) and *objecthood* (from the side of the cognized), and we shall come back to and focus on these crucial terms in the next subsection.

Nyāya's "knowledge sources," *pramāṇa*, like their results, have a truth logic. No non-veridical cognition is *source*-generated. Here the English word "perception" used for Nyāya's *pramāṇa* is to be understood as an infallible process: *perception in optimal circumstances* is a roughly equivalent concept from a Cartesian perspective that would admit the possibility of fallible perception as Nyāya does not. Nyāya takes a factive point of view, such that no non-veridical cognition could have been *pramāṇa*-produced. There must have been a deviation from the genuine process, while only the genuine deserves the name. Similarly, the result, a genuinely *perceptual* awareness, is by definition veridical, being distinguished from a *pseudo*-perception (or "perception-appearance," *pratyakṣâbhāsa*) that is in fact non-veridical although a subject takes it to be veridical when it occurs. A pseudo-perception is not *pramāṇa*-generated. Mistaking a rope for a snake is not, properly speaking, perceptual but only pseudo-perceptual. A process—or "method," as identified subjectively—has to be working perfectly, with no defects, to deserve *pramāṇa* status. Defects are multifarious, including environmental factors and sensory functioning. Perception as a causal process includes, importantly, the object cognized as standing appropriately in the causal chain or complex of causal factors that results in its being cognized.

Source individuation is an issue throughout the *TCM*. What are the salient types of cognitive process? For example, are sight and hearing separate knowledge sources? How do we know psychological properties such as pleasure and pain? Is there a special source of knowledge for absential awareness (e.g., "There is no pot on the floor")? Is postulation a source different from inference? These and similar questions threaten to undermine the Nyāya project which depends on discernible source types. A fundamental concern of Gaṅgeśa's throughout the *TCM* is defense of Nyāya's thesis that veridical cognitions fall into groups as results of perception and other sources considered as types. Special requirements govern subtypes such as awarenesses of absences and other cognitions according to what they are about, their objects or "objecthoods," as will be explained.

Alignment of cognitions with their sources has epistemic consequences. A *pramāṇa* recognized by intrinsic features and in relation to a particular result would make that result "*pramāṇa*-certified." That is, a cognition known as knowledge-source-generated becomes "source-certified"—one of three ways a cognition can be known to be true, according to Nyāya. A cognition can also be certified with respect to its fruit, success of effort and action. Historically, the official Nyāya position is that inference from success of effort is the way certification proceeds; *pramāṇa* identification is implied but unacknowledged. A third procedure, which seems like self-certification but is not, Gaṅgeśa argues (below, p. 127), involves typing. Once a type of cognition as specified by its "objecthood" has been certified, a later cognition known to be a token of the type becomes certified, too. In debate, to try to prove what is already known (*siddha-sādhana*) is censured. Nyāya focuses on first-time cognitive occurrences assuming that the mental vehicles for prompting speech and later effort and action (called *saṃskāra*s, "dispositions" or "memory impressions") will be properly formed only by cognitions that are veridical. But it is fully realized that, although serial, cognitions fall into types, and that certification blocks doubt without new evidence.

Thus *justification*—or, more properly, *conscious justification*—amounts to certification, which can happen in these three ways, all of which involve inference. The operation of a knowledge source, in contrast, provides a non-inferential bottom level of implicit, unconscious justification, or, in the case of inference as a *pramāṇa*, a bottom level of justification that is inferential but also about the world, i.e., about something other than the veridicality of the cognition C generated by inference. The veridicality of C is inferred on the meta-level of certification.

In other words, knowledge *per se* does not require certification according to Nyāya. Knowledge does not require conscious justification in the sense explained. It requires only the proper tie between cognition and fact, which amounts to a cognition's being *pramāṇa*-generated.

Perception, inference, and testimony generate cognitions whose truth we take for granted as shown by our speech and other acts, Naiyāyikas argue.

The justification required for knowledge—i.e., "knowledge" as explained by Western epistemologists—is according to Nyāya the causal link to the truth. Bottom-level justification consists in a cognition's being *pramāṇa*-generated in fact, whether or not the subject knows that it is *pramāṇa*-generated. (Translating in reverse direction, I would render 'knowledge' by Nyāya's lights as a *jñāna*, "cognition," that is *pramāṇa-ja*, "source-generated," i.e., as a "veridical cognition," *pramā*, that is so in virtue of being *pramāṇa*-generated.)

The decisive consideration is that normally people act—and act successfully—on the basis of a perceptual or inferential awareness without worrying about veridicality, which is assumed. A cognition that was only accidentally truth-hitting in a certain instance would belong to a type that could not be relied on, since similar cognitions would frustrate effort and action. Our memories of what to trust are reinforced by unceasing streams of feedback. We learn, for example, not to trust a person known to lie or exaggerate, or to rely on vision when there is not enough light. Gaṅgeśa is interested in veridical cognitions that are by type veridical, by law veridical, such that the law may be invoked to resolve disputes—and all the deep concerns of philosophy surely require justification, all being hotly disputed—and arrive at right views. His project is to specify the connections between the world and cognizers that result nomologically in cognitions that are true. Then when there is doubt or dispute we have methods to follow (in particular, paradigm inferences).

In other words, conscious justification is not just important but thematic for Gaṅgeśa and Nyāya. When a doubt, dispute, or desire to know arises, then turning to knowledge sources as best we can is our method of resolving it. (The role of knowledge sources in inquiry is stressed in the *Nyāya-sūtra*, the school's oldest text, c. 200 CE.) Certification with reference to a recognized knowledge source elevates, moreover, a learner's level of confidence, and presents a higher barrier to doubt and dispute than there would be otherwise. Bits of inferential knowledge—just as perceptual awarenesses and knowledge from testimony—become more secure through checking to make sure they are true. But though knowledge can be coupled with degrees of certainty, a bottom level of, so to say, sense certainty (without being actually certified) naturally accompanies cognitions purporting to present the world. Otherwise, there would not be sustained what Western philosophers call belief, or, as Gaṅgeśa would say, trust in cognition as shown in action.

Nyāya's (largely) externalist epistemology marches hand in hand with a many-sided realism. The objects about which we speak—on the basis of cognitions and the "memory impressions" (*saṃskāra*) they create—exist independently of our consciousnesses. In other words, the way something is shapes the mental occurrences and instruments that cause speech and other acts with respect to the thing. Perception is the chief or original *pramāṇa* according to Nyāya. It is implicated in the operation of inference and the rest. Thus Nyāya's realism depends heavily on its theory of perception. Perceptual awareness of something as F originates in an F-qualified object connected to a sense organ. We perceive Bessie as a cow because she is a cow in fact, and the *pramāṇa* of perception connects us to that reality.

Nyāya's commitment to entities that exist independently of consciousness causing its content leads Gaṅgeśa and other Naiyāyikas to embrace fallibilism about cognitions of practically all varieties. The knowledge-generators are conceived of as infallible, but from a first-person perspective a subject may have a cognition that seems to be genuinely perceptual, for example, whereas it is non-veridical in fact and thus only pseudo-perceptual. An object's existence apart from the activities of the instruments of right cognition means that the possibility of error about it cannot be eliminated, except in some cases of apperception. An apperceived object—for example, an immediately previous cognition—is internal and may be entirely accessible to the cognizer with no possibility of causal defect (though Gaṅgeśa does not think that apperception is in every respect infallible, as will be discussed). But other types of object exist independently of our consciousnesses; as causes of and objects of different individuals' truth-hitting mental events, they are external to anyone's individual awareness. Furthermore, objects have properties some of which on any given occasion typically go uncognized, and most processes of cognitive generation are not open to direct cognitive grasp. At least some factors in the generational process are not directly cognizable. Such transcendence, in sum, of objects to consciousness leads Naiyāyikas to embrace cognitive fallibilism. The whole range of cognition that is truth-directed has as its normal nature to be veridical in fact. But (non-apperceptive) cognitive processes sometimes get disrupted without our knowing or having any evidence of the disruption, and there is generated a cognition that we assume is veridical but is not, as sometimes we find out.

And so here again we run into an internalist side of Nyāya epistemology. Our fallibilism makes us keen to know the nature of justification, or certification, and to use our findings to shore up a whole range of positions in our philosophy, from atoms and their properties to the nature of the self, *ātman*, and the supreme personal good, *parama-puruṣârtha*. Knowledge sources become methods, which we employ (especially inference) to prove our positions in philosophy.

Finally, note that despite all the talk of causal processes, there are special epistemic properties called *excellences* and *faults* whose identification, given doubt or desire to know, are signs of the operation of *pramāṇa* or of their absence, and are thus key to learning and the establishing of right positions in philosophy as in everyday life. Now these properties have to be cognized.

They are labelled from an epistemic perspective; they are "excellences" and "deficiencies" from an epistemic point of view. For instance, one may make an immediate inference and act on its basis, but to certify that the conclusion drawn is the result of inference as a *pramāṇa* is to check the process to make sure that it is based on a *pervasion* of F-hood by G-hood, considering an inference from F*a* to G*a*. Such pervasion would be confirmed with reference to positive correlations—other things both F and G—and negative correlations—things not-G and not-F. Nevertheless, the epistemic excellences—awareness of pervasion and the like—are themselves externally described. Excellences are supposed to have causal relevance, even in inference. Thus they are both properties figuring prominently in causal laws and signs of knowledge sources. We do have to keep in mind that epistemology does not begin for Nyāya with (Cartesian) doubt or the (Socratic) intellectualist requirement that a genuine knower of *p* must be able to articulate a good reason for believing *p*. According to Nyāya, people do not normally distrust their cognitions, nor need they be able to say why they have knowledge when they have it. For, as has been explained, one has a veridical cognition and follows it in action if it is *pramāṇa*-generated whether or not the subject is aware of the fact. But disagreement is one of several conditions leading to real doubt, and real questions can arise. Then identification of knowledge sources and "excellences" as epistemic properties becomes relevant, answering questions, restoring confidence, removing doubt, and ending dispute.

Meta-epistemology is enjoined by Gaṅgeśa throughout his treatise. He combats Buddhists and other theorists who have different views about *pramāṇa* and the world they reveal. According to Gaṅgeśa and Nyāya, all candidate sources for whatever type of veridical cognition either reduce to perception, inference, analogy, and/or testimony or are not genuine. The causal stories told about each of these types of knowledge process—and about each of the candidates put up by Nyāya's adversaries—show that these are *pramāṇa* and that there are only these four.

Gaṅgeśa is mainly concerned to unroll his Naiyāyika views from a Naiyāyika perspective, probably himself using his work as a textbook. But the *inter*school controversy over *pramāṇa*—which is as historically central as any other issue in the whole long course of philosophy written in Sanskrit—informs Gaṅgeśa's discussion. He rehearses the positions and arguments of other schools as well as Nyāya's answers. The *pramāṇa* debate, we may note, influenced jurisprudence, literary criticism, and other genre, and of course other areas of philosophy. For this reason, the *TCM* is arguably the most important work of the whole of late classical literature in that it is the most important work of epistemology.

Gaṅgeśa's *TCM* has four chapters, a chapter for each *pramāṇa*, three long ones for perception, inference, and testimony, and a short one on analogy.

Along with a preamble to the book as a whole, the perception chapter is translated here. Within it, there are clearly delineated sections on various subtopics, as well as remarks about cognition and veridicality in general.

2. Cognition

Cognition (*jñāna*), its varieties and causes as well as its intrinsic properties, is of fundamental concern to Gaṅgeśa. Ontologically, a cognition is a short-lived, episodic quality of an individual self. Strictly speaking, a cognition is a mental event and a short-lived state rather than an act. But an act may be among a cognition's causes, as in focusing on something in particular. Cognitions are intentional; they are invariably *of* some object or objects. For example, a pot is an object (*viṣaya*) of a cognition just when and insofar as it is cognized. Unlike Western epistemology, Nyāya focuses not on beliefs but on cognitions that are identified by their objects or "objecthood" (*viṣayatā*), and to this crucial notion we now turn.

Nyāya holds that the simplest verbalizable cognition has as object something qualified by a qualifier. That is, a verbalizable cognition's object has minimally the structure of a qualificandum qualified by a qualifier (*viśiṣṭa-jñāna*). For example, the perception, "That's a pot," indicates an entity qualified by pothood or being-a-pot. "That's a pot" verbalizes an occurrent cognition, which is roughly equivalent to an "occurrent belief" as discussed in Western epistemology. "Non-occurrent belief" is not Nyāya's focus, though "dispositions," *saṃskāra*, which are formed by perceptions and other cognitive occurrences, do maintain cognitive continuity. Roughly, the theory is that a perception indicating *a* as F—whose objecthood is F*a*—produces a disposition that when aroused helps to bring about a remembering, an effort, or another psychological event whose objecthood is F*a*.

Objecthood, which is also called having-an-object, is the relation between cognitions and their objects. It is a direct relation between cognitions and things. No realm of sense data, platonic forms, or "intentional inexistents" comes between a cognition and what it is about or of. Strictly speaking, cognitions do not have content; they have intentionality which by its very nature is the hitting of things. Again, the relation between a cognition and its object is talked about in two ways, as objecthood, which is a relational property of an object cognized with the cognizing cognition as the "successor" or second term, and having-an-object, which is a relational property of a cognition with the object cognized as the "successor" term.

Gaṅgeśa and his fellow Naiyāyikas recognize that some cognitions are non-veridical. Thus, it would seem that at best only veridical cognitions could have objecthood understood in Nyāya fashion, that is, as indicating something's being some way that it is in fact. The objecthood of non-veridical cognitions, whose indications do not hit the facts, would have to be understood differently. But according to Gaṅgeśa, non-veridical cognitions too have reality-directed intentionality. When we misperceive a rope as a snake, taking *a* to be F when it is not F, the F-hood bit of objecthood, which originates in previous experience of Fs—of snakes in our example—directs one towards that property, which is thoroughly real, among the world's furniture, though it is not experienced where it exists in fact, which is in snakes, not in the rope at hand. At work would be a memory disposition which under normal conditions would prompt a remembering but which in the deviant conditions of perceptual error retrieves and fuses a snakehood bit of intentionality into a current pseudo-perception. A non-veridical cognition may be said to have misplaced intentionality; it presents something (the rope) not as what it is. But what it presents it as is something that exists elsewhere full-blooded, and as its object under normal circumstances is intended also in the abnormal circumstances of error. It is the real-world locus of part of the objecthood whose second term is the cognition whose object it is.

Technically, the relation considered from the side of the cognition is having-an-object (*viṣayitā*). It is said to have three "parts": (i) a qualificandum portion (*viśeṣyatā*), (ii) a qualifier portion (*viśeṣaṇatā*)--also referred to as the *prakāra*, the "way" something is appearing—and (iii) a portion of qualificative relationality (*vaiśiṣṭya*). These match parts of an object's objecthood (*viṣayatā*): (i) its being a property-bearer and mere object cognized (*a*), (ii) its having a property that is being cognized (F), and (iii) its being related to that property by an ontologically qualificative relation. Again, the cognition-object relation itself may be considered in either direction, and we shall uniformly call it objecthood, as is Gaṅgeśa's own practice usually. Note that a pseudo-perception's qualificandum portion, the "*a*" part in "*a* is F," would successfully hit the object in front, the rope, as were someone to say "That's a snake," pointing to a rope, correct that there is something there, ontologically a qualificandum cognized as qualified by a qualifier, though the qualifier is "misplaced." This hitting of the *a* makes the error pseudo-*perceptual*, i.e., a result of a process that generates belief in the fashion of perception, although it is not the true *pramāṇa*.

Abstracting the objecthood of types of cognition makes it possible to talk about two subjects S and T having the same cognition. But having-an-object is itself nothing other than a (quasi-) property of cognitions, a relational property whose second term, I repeat, is the object cognized. Thus cognitions are all the mental entities needed. A person's conscious life is comprised of a series of cognition tokens the types of which as specified by their having-an-object Naiyāyikas discuss in the ways Western philosophers discuss propositions and people having the same belief. It is the public nature of cognized objects, their intersubjective accessibility, that allows one to verbalize the indications of cognition and do logic and epistemology. Again, there is no realm of either propositions or sense data.

Cognitions divide most broadly into awarenesses and rememberings, with several varieties of awareness. "Awareness" is a makeshift translation of the Sanskrit *anubhava* which connotes "presentation of new information" as opposed to presentation of old information in a remembering. Thus there are inferential awarenesses and word-generated awarenesses as well as perceptual awarenesses in the sense that the cognitive event is an acquisition of fresh news. There is technically, then, no *awareness* of that which has been experienced in the past, though there is the cognition. A current cognition of something as past is a *remembering*.

Perceptual awarenesses are causally continuous with physical realities, excepting perceptions of psychological properties such as pleasures and pains which are mediated solely by a posited "internal (sensory) organ," *manas*. External objects are perceived through a sense-organ/object connection that varies according to what is perceived and sensory modality. An entire causal complex is responsible for any given perception, a complex in which a sense organ will be chief among a cast including the object perceived and a variable sensory connection. More about this in the next section.

A perceptual awareness is a perceiving expressible, minimally, as something *a* being qualified by a qualifier F (F*a*). We should note that the word *pratyakṣa*, "perception," is used, unfortunately, in two different senses: (1) as the cognition that is the result of a sense-mediated causal process and (2) as the process itself, the *pramāṇa*. So, perception as a *pramāṇa* generates a *perceptual awareness*, let us say, an immediate cognition ("F*a*") of an entity as qualified by a qualifier (F) that the sense-contacted object (*a*) possesses in fact. This holds, by the way, whether the sense organ is externally oriented such as in the sight of a pot or internally such as with experiences of pleasure and pain through the internal graspings of the *manas*.

There are *indeterminate* perceptions, we shall learn, which grasp nothing but a qualifier and are unverbalizable and non-introspectible and neither veridical nor non-veridical. They are posited, we shall see, for systematic needs, and are controversial even among Naiyāyikas. *Determinate* perceptual awarenesses, which are verbalizable, are in any case key epistemically.

In Sanskrit, the predicative copula (*is*, etc.) is usually elliptically understood. Thus, a perceptual cognition verbalized as "A pot" (*ghaṭaḥ iti*, in Sanskrit, with the nominative suffix indicating an understood copula and the *iti* as quotational, indicating the cognition as opposed to what it is about) may be interpreted as the perceptual awareness, "The thing in front of me now is a pot." (This is Gaṅgeśa's favorite example.)

Ontologically, the objecthood relation gets its structure from the relational property of "qualification" that obtains in the world. The simplest veridical perceptual awareness has as its object an individual cognized (the qualificandum) as related to a qualifier by this relation. With the veridical perceptual awareness, "A pot," for example, we would have a particular pot-**inherence**-potness as the objective complex cognized as something appearing as a pot. Since the cognitive relation is direct, the inherence, or whatever the tie between qualifier and qualificandum, must be part of the cognition's object or "objecthood." It also has to be real, Gaṅgeśa will argue.

As mentioned, a cognition's "predication content," *prakāra*, which is a "qualifier," *viśeṣaṇa*, as appearing in consciousness, is said to be the predicate (F) portion of a cognition's objecthood (*a*-as-F). The perception, "(A) pot," has potness as its "predication content." The qualifier presented in consciousness is the basis of our saying (in the appropriate circumstances) the "pot" portion of "That's a pot." "Predication content" is the closest Gaṅgeśa comes to a purely phenomenological notion in his system, and its ontology is hotly disputed. It is central to the explanation of illusion.

A few more words about illusion. Gaṅgeśa analyzes non-veridical sensory awareness as a cognition whose predication content does not qualify the object connected to the sense organ. A causal story is to be told why there is such a foul-up, why something appears as other than what it is. The story is not always the same. Sometimes something is wrong with the sense organ; sometimes causal auxiliaries such as light or the distortions of water into which a perceived object is immersed give rise to "error." But while error-causing circumstances (*doṣa*) vary, there are invariable factors such as, for perceptual error, the role of memory which provides material from previous experiences for projection into current experience. That is, in explaining perceptual illusion Gaṅgeśa finds a constant in memory providing the predication content, the qualificational material, so to say, for the illusion, which, he argues, is to be construed as a single cognition of an entity as qualified. Our author devotes much effort (in the section, "Presentation of Something as Other Than What It Is," pp. 250ff) to showing that this view is to be preferred over an alternative two-cognition theory (a perceiving and a remembering and a not noticing the difference) championed by a rival faction of realists.

3. Inference[1]

Naiyāyikas view inference as a knowledge source, a *pramāṇa*, that results in veridical cognitions called *anumiti*, "inferential awareness." Inference as a generator of veridical cognition—inference as a *pramāṇa*—is in Sanskrit known by the word *anumāna*. Thus, unlike the word *pratyakṣa*, "perception," used for both process and result, the common terms for inferential process and result are different.

As mentioned, Gaṅgeśa, like all Nyāya philosophers, views perception as our principal cognitive link with external objects. All other knowledge sources are said to depend on perception in one or another manner, including, to be sure, inference. Any general rule, or "pervasion" (*vyāpti*), upon which a genuine inference would depend—what is F, that is G—is thought of as known through wide perceptual experience forming a memory-impression of the association of F and G. Such a memory-impression, *saṃskāra*, would be a causal factor in an inferential process running from a cognition "F*a*" to another "G*a*." Paradigmatically, perceptual awareness is thought to inform inference in another way, too. The model inference is launched by perceptual awareness, sight of smoke rising from a mountain, for instance, sparking an inference to fire at the same place. Such an inference-prompting awareness—or premise—could be provided by testimony, it is realized, or by another inference, but at some earlier point in a series of information transfers a perceptual awareness—the result of the chief or "eldest," *jyeṣṭha*, knowledge source—would be required, says Nyāya. Gaṅgeśa opens his inference chapter by saying that inference is treated by him after perception because of this dependence. For us, the dependence means, most importantly, that from a subject's own point of view inference is defeasible, as will be explained.

Although an extrapolative pattern is said sometimes to be obvious, e.g., verbal equivalences or *a priori* tautologies ("A pot is distinct from everything that is not a pot, *since* it has pothood, unlike a cloth"), Gaṅgeśa explains inference with reference to a paradigm case where extrapolation is fallible. An inferential awareness (*anumiti*) comes about through a locus or object—a mountain, for instance, called the inferential subject (*pakṣa*)—being cognized as exhibiting one property as pervaded (*vyāpya*) by another. That is, the subject is cognized as exhibiting a prover property (*sādhana*), e.g., smoke or, more precisely, smokiness, as pervaded by another property called technically the probandum, the property to be proved (*sādhya*), fieriness. Such a cognition is said to be informed by a memory of the prover in relation to the probandum, a memory formed by the inferrer's previous experiences. The memory would in the standard case have resulted from "wide experience" (*bhūyo-darśana*) of correlations positive (G*a*, F*a*; G*b*, F*b*; G*c*, F*c* . . .) and negative (~G*d*, ~F*d*; ~G*e*, ~F*e*; ~G*f*, ~F*f* . . .). Pervasion is an asymmetrical relation (pervasion of F by G) such that there may be instances of the pervader (the probandum, G) where the pervaded (the prover, F) is not (e.g., Gg, ~Fg), but no instances of the pervaded without the pervader. By extrapolation, what possesses the prover, that possesses the probandum ("What has smokiness, that has fieriness")—including a given instance cognition of which launches for a particular subject the process that results in inferential awareness ("The mountain has fieriness," which is equivalent to, "The mountain is fiery").

Throughout New Logic, the nature of the relation called pervasion (*vyāpti*) is the main focus of reflection under the general rubric of inference—

pervasion, that is to say, insofar as knowledge of it is a causal factor in generating inferential awareness. In his inference chapter, Gaṅgeśa rejects more than twenty definitions of pervasion, *vyāpti*, and accepts eight.

Gaṅgeśa employs regularly, whatever the topic, a three-part inferential statement form that he assumes his readers can reconstruct as a five-step argument form standardized throughout classical philosophical discourse. In the perception chapter, he never uses the five-step argument form. But it is helpful for learning Nyāya's logical system.

First, the logical terms, which are also for the most part common across schools, their technical meanings not being confined to Nyāya:

pakṣa	the inferential subject; the mountain in the stock example
sādhana	the prover or prover property (*hetu* and *liṅga* are synonyms); smokiness
sādhya	the probandum, the property to be proved; fieriness
vyāpti	the inference-grounding pervasion; ''wherever smoke, there fire''

Inductive support is presumed, a basis for the proper formation of the inference-informing *saṃskāra*, which is called the ''example.''

dṛṣṭânta	a pervasion-supportive example, a locus that is known to exhibit both the prover and the probandum; a kitchen hearth.

Gaṅgeśa considers both ''inference for oneself'' and ''inference for others.'' The latter is, as mentioned, a five-step presentation (*nyāya*) of information for the purpose of generating a veridical cognition in another person:

1. That mountain is fiery. (The proposition to be proved, that is, that the *pakṣa*, the inferential subject, is qualified by the *sādhya*, the probandum; i.e., the subject has the probandum property. This is called the *pratijñā*, the ''proposition.'')

2. That mountain is smokey. (The inferential subject is qualified by the probandum's prover; the *pakṣa* has the *sādhana*, the prover property. This is called the *hetu*, the ''reason.'')

3. What is smokey, that is fiery. (The statement of the general rule or inference-grounding *vyāpti*, pervasion: what has the prover property, that has the probandum property.) Like a kitchen hearth, and unlike a lake. (There is this extrapolative basis. This is called the *udāharaṇa*, the ''example'' generating the general rule.)

4. And this is likewise. (The mountain is an instance of the general rule. This is called the *upanayana*, the ''application.'')

5. Therefore, that mountain is fiery. (This is the same information as in step one except—taking now as defeasible default that nothing already known stands in contradiction as well as that there is no equally well-evidenced counterprobandum—the proposition is proved. This is called the *nigamana*, the "conclusion.")

The five steps are to be construed as a single statement governed by grammatical and semantic rules. Gaṅgeśa elaborately defends this view in his inference chapter, in the section, "The members of a formal presentation of an inference for others," *avaya-prakaraṇa* (*TCM* II, pp. 540–76).

The three-part statement form:

> An inferential subject *a* is qualified by S a probandum (part one: S*a*), *since* that same subject *a* is qualified by H a prover (part two: H*a*), like *b* an example (part three: H*b* and S*b*).

Here the putatively inference-supporting pervasion is (in Sanskrit) discerned from the order of the terms in the statement form. Gaṅgeśa's use of the three-part form is signaled in translation by italicization of the word *since*—a convention adopted throughout. (This mountain is fiery, *since* it is smokey, like a kitchen hearth.)

One does not need logical symbols to understand Gaṅgeśa's inferences in the perception chapter, though one does indeed need to understand pervasion, *vyāpti*. Still I shall employ a few symbols as expositional aids. The following reconstruction is not adequate to every dimension of Gaṅgeśa's thought about pervasion. In particular, pervasions are interpreted as causal relations, and logical complexities attend differentiation of types of causality. The difference between a factor necessary for an effect and a set of factors together sufficient is also crucial, as will be explained.

1. H*a* (the subject, *a*, possesses H, the *sādhana* or *hetu* property). And
2. (x) (Hx $\rightarrow$ Sx) (what has the H property, that has the S property). Therefore,
3. S*a* (the subject, *a*, possesses S).

Schematically, a pervasion *by* a probandum S *of* a prover H suggests a conditional relationship: if an H, then an S. If a mountain is smokey, then it is also fiery, because there is a general relation, captured by a universally quantified conditional, between smokiness and fieriness. Whatever has the one has the other—as the point is put by Naiyāyikas who are not concerned with relations among sentences or propositions but among terms, property-possession standing stead for the copula.

This pattern of reasoning comprises an inductive procedure that is much discussed, a way of discerning pervasion by knowing, or examining, cases other than that at issue: similar instances, *sapakṣa*, which are known to exhibit the probandum and thus should also, at least in one case, exhibit the prover (e.g., H*b* and S*b*)—and dissimilar instances, *vipakṣa*, which are known not to exhibit the probandum and should lack the prover, too (e.g., ~S*c* and ~H*c*). The "example," *dṛṣṭânta*, is a single instance of *sapakṣa* where the prover also occurs (H*b* and S*b*), its citing in part three of the three-part form (see above) indicating that there is inductive support. More generally, by reference to cases that are *sapakṣa*—i.e., known instances of the probandum—where the prover is also found, we marshall positive evidence supporting an inference-underpinning pervasion (the method of agreement, *anvaya*, "positive correlation"). And by reference to cases that are *vipakṣa*—i.e., known instances of the absence of the probandum—we garner support by not finding the prover (the method of disagreement, *vyatireka*, "negative correlation"). Citing an example is shorthand to indicate that such a procedure supports assertion of a *vyāpti*, "pervasion" or the general rule.

Each line of the reconstruction could be prefixed by an epistemic operator "(K)"—to be read, "A person P has defeasible cognition (i.e., knows) that." As a singular inference, the argument would be:

$$(K)(S^{p}Ha) \rightarrow (K)Sa$$

"If P knows that H-as-qualified-by-being-pervaded-by-S qualifies *a*, then P knows that S*a*." However, since Gaṅgeśa denies that cognition is self-aware (he denies the KK thesis, K*p* → KK*p*: see below, pp. 132–33), representation of the grasping cognition is probably best suppressed, though it is understood.

The broader picture is clear. For Gaṅgeśa, knowledge is not closed under deduction considered in abstraction from "consideration," *parāmarśa*, which is the psychological event of the information in the two premises being put together, so to say. Through such consideration, warrant—or "certainty" (*niścayatā*)—passes from premises to conclusion, and we act unhesitatingly, for example, to put a fire outl. And we *know* that there is a fire over there, given that the cognition is true.

However, if we are aware of a defeater, a counterexample or another fallacy, no new knowledge is acquired and we do not unhesitatingly act. Awareness of an inferential defeater prevents inferential awareness. In sum, there is no inferential conclusion resulting no matter what else is known—to parties in a debate or, with respect to inference for oneself, what later comes to be known. Correct inference is not simply a matter of formally valid patterns of symbol conversions, though the standard pattern is indeed valid. In other words, Naiyāyika fallibilism extends to apparent inferential awareness—indeed, to all cognition, except some apperception as will be explained.

Historically, the theory of inference developed not only within broader epistemology (*pramāṇa-śāstra*) but also within theory and practice of debate. Buddhists, Naiyāyikas, and disputants from all the schools had recognized by Gaṅgeśa's time a common list of fallacies and defeaters, struggling together to capture the requirements of winning arguments.

4. Ontological Categories

Gaṅgeśa is ontologically "realist" in the sense of being committed to entities whose existence is independent of consciousness. As already mentioned, realism leads Nyāya philosophers to embrace fallibilism. Gaṅgeśa's realism is also evident in his definitional projects, which are philosophic "characterizations" of worldly realities, not explanations of linguistic usages. Furthermore, individuals of whatever type (substances, qualities, universals, and so on) are all real in the sense of being causes or (in the case of universals) implicated in causal relations (as fire causes smoke in being an instance of firehood not as an instance of substancehood).

Let us review the traditional list of "categories," *padârtha*, "types of things to which words refer," to translate more perspicaciously the Sanskrit word. In some places, Gaṅgeśa expresses a sense of the list's inadequacy to comprehend all the things we experience and talk about, especially those posited in explanations. But unlike several later Naiyāyikas, he is an ontological conservative and loathe to admit additional categories. He is not loathe to show us temptations.

(1) *Substances*, (2) *qualities*, and (3) *motions* or actions are the most basic types of existent. There are non-composite substances, such as atoms of earth, water, fire, and air, and non-atomic, non-composite substances, namely, ether (the medium of sound), time, space, minds, and selves (a mind, i.e., an internal organ or *manas*, is a controversial substance to which there is devoted an entire section, below, pp. 537ff). There are also composite substances, such as rocks, trees, houses, and persons. Qualities are color, size, weight, shape, and so on, features that always occur in or as qualifying individual substances. Examples of motions are moving straight ahead, upwards, and so on. Motions are like qualities in that they occur in substances, but they have causal effects that qualities by themselves do not have, bringing about conjunctions and disjunctions, for example. Conjunctions ("contacts," *saṃyoga*) are relational properties qualifying at once two individual substances.

There are also (4) *universals*, or natural kinds, which occur in substances, qualities, and motions, and which are responsible for recurrent experience of a single type of thing. Western ontologists are accustomed to think of qualities as universals, since qualities are presumed to recur. But according to Nyāya, a quality, such as the blue of a pot, is an individual, though there is also the natural class, or universal, to which the blue belongs. Because opponents of

Nyāya, Buddhists in particular, deny the reality of universals from early in the history of Indian thought, this area of Naiyāyika theory is much developed prior to Gaṅgeśa but is far from unproblematic in Gaṅgeśa's theorizing. We shall encounter four or five lines of argument in support of universals, as well as find Gaṅgeśa using universals to handle various problems.

A few further features of the view. Naiyāyikas are not platonists (and for this reason the translation "natural kind" may be preferable to "universal," though both are used here): there are no uninstanced universals dwelling apart from the individuals that are their instances, nor a hierarchy of universals except in a certain sense. Universals do not qualify universals, but a lower or narrower kind may be said to be included in a higher, broader kind in the sense of an extensional inclusion, that all residences of the narrower universal are also residences of the broader, waterhood and substancehood, for instance (everything that is water is also a substance). If universals occurred in universals, there would be an infinite regress. Universals are given directly in perception insofar as their loci are perceived. Indeed, we come to know individuals only through general, repeatable characteristics. And a universal is "locus-pervading"; cowhood, for example, exists throughout Bessie and every individual cow.[2]

Another basic category is (5) *individualizer*. In the earliest texts, individualizers are considered correlate to universals: thus together a species-genus relation. Later, a reason for positing individualizers as a separate type of thing appears to be that otherwise individual atoms all of the same type (water, for example) would be identical: a better translation is probably "numeralizer." Gaṅgeśa rarely mentions this category.

Gaṅgeśa does, however, devote an entire section of the perception chapter to the next category on the traditional list, (6) *inherence*, the relation that binds qualities and motions to substances, universals to their residences, an a substance to its parts. A piece of cloth inheres in its threads; cowhood inheres in a cow; blue and motion inhere in a blue bird aloft. A central problem for Gaṅgeśa concerns the relation between a qualificandum perceived (a) and a qualifier perceived (F) in a cognition of an entity as qualified ("Fa"), e.g., "This is a pot." The cognition's object, the pot, is so cognized insofar as it is related to pothood in a certain way. Thus inherence underpins the cognitive relatedness of qualifier and qualificandum. But with absential cognitions, "There is no pot on the floor," the relation of the missing pot to the floor is not inherence, says Gaṅgeśa; absence-of-pot is related to the floor by what he calls a self-linking relation. So just what is inherence, and how is it known?

A entire section is also devoted to (7) *absences* and our knowledge of absences. Absences underpin true negations and give rise to negative perceptions, such as, to use again Gaṅgeśa's favorite example, a perceiving the absence of a pot on a floor. Absences are relational. An absentee, or countercorrelate, e.g., the pot, is related to a locus, the floor, by the absential relation of being *not* there.

Depending on what is cognized—an individual substance, a universal, an absence, a previous cognition (in what is called apperception), and so on—the relationality between the cognizing and the cognized varies. The different sense organs also connect with objects differently. Sensory relationality is an important topic to which an entire section is devoted (and parts of other sections, too). Unlike several later Naiyāyikas, Gaṅgeśa does not see here a need for an additional category (to wit, "objecthood"). Generalizable causal principles of perception, expressed in terms of just these items and including laws not governing all perception but restricted to a consistent subtype, are to be identified and woven into a unified theory, as we shall see.

5. Causality

Preceding conditions that are regulative (*niyāmaka*) are the causes that Gaṅgeśa identifies in explaining varieties of perception. That is, a cause is for him a factor F that is necessary to the arising of an effect G. And its being necessary amounts to no G arising without being preceded by an F so long as the F cannot be counted "irrelevant" (*anyathā-siddha*). The stock example of precedence that is irrelevant is an ass that just happens always to be used to bring the clay out of which a particular kind of pot is made. The ass is not regulative. A modern example would be a barometric change that invariably precedes a storm.

The presence of an effect, in sum, entails the prior occurrence of all its true (non-irrelevant) causal factors. The presence of one such cause, however, does not entail the occurrence of the effect. Other factors may well be necessary, too, and typically are. For example, the presence of smoke entails the occurrence of fire, a necessary factor. But fires can be smokeless, for instance, the fire in molten metal. So fire does not entail smoke. Gaṅgeśa does talk about sufficient causality, about a set of causal conditions, *sāmagrī*, whose being in place unfailingly brings about an effect of a particular type. But the causal principles formulated involve only necessary factors, not an entire *sāmagrī*.

In the terms of traditional Nyāya-Vaiśeṣika, such necessary factors are considered *instrumental* causes, *nimitta-kāraṇa*, which are distinguished from two other types. Gaṅgeśa inherits a division of causality into *inherent* (*samavāyin*) and *emergent* (*a-samavāyin*) causes in addition to the instrumental (*nimitta*), which is sometimes said to be the pre-eminent sense of "cause" as reflected in ordinary usage. An inherent cause is a substratum of a superstratum related to it by inherence. For example, in the case of a blue pot, the pot is the inherent cause of the blue color. A cow is an inherent cause of cowhood. The inherent cause of a cloth are the threads in which it is nested. And so on. Note that substances are not the only inherent causes, since universals inhere in qualities and in motions as well as in substances. Thus, a cognition, itself a quality whose inherent cause is an individual self, is an inherent cause of the universal, cognitionhood, which has multiple inherent causes, all the cognitions in the universe. An emergent cause, in contrast, is always a quality or a motion. Recall that a whole is said to inhere in its parts. A quality that inheres in the inherent causes of something *x*, a whole, can emerge as, or "cause" (in this sense) a quality of *x* itself, and is thus said to be its emergent cause. For example, the blue color of the threads of a blue piece of cloth is the emergent cause of the blue of the cloth. Finally, whereas inherent causes are important in a variety of contexts, Gaṅgeśa talks about emergent causes very rarely. Only in one section does the notion figure prominently (p. 540, below, where two varieties of emergent cause are distinguished).

Within a set of necessary conditions—causes of all three types—that together are sufficient for an effect, that instrumental cause called the *karaṇa* gets special attention, for the *karaṇa* is the unique condition which, on being met—after it comes along and, so to say, adds itself *in operation* to a heap of enabling conditions already in place—the effect necessarily comes about. The word could be translated "trigger" or sometimes "proximate instrumental cause," but "chief instrumental cause" is our usual rendering.

The requirement that a *karaṇa* must be in operation, or employed, is controversial. A category dispute rears its head as philosophers try to be precise in identifying the *karaṇa*s of effects, particularly, as with Gaṅgeśa, the effects that are our veridical and non-veridical cognitions. To be sure, these are results of perceptual, inferential, and other cognitive processes. But what precisely is the *karaṇa*, or type of *karaṇa*, for each type of cognitive effect, veridical perception and so on? We may remark that the word *karaṇa* is used in grammar as the sense of the instrumental case, and there may be a presumption operative that an instrumental cause worth mentioning (there are always very many) would be somehow special ("He cut down the tree *with an axe*,"where the axe is the *karaṇa* although the forester's arm and other implements are clearly also instrumental causes).

Gaṅgeśa appears to be of two minds about the nature of cognitive *karaṇa*. The *karaṇa* of a sense perception is, he holds, the appropriate sense organ, which is a substance *in operation*, that is to say, in sensory connection to an object perceived. Such a connection would be a physical contact or a more complex relation qualifying a physical contact according to what is perceived. But in the case of inference, the *karaṇa* is viewed as a cognition (*parāmarśa*, "consideration"), which is a psychological quality. Furthermore, with inference the *karaṇa* does not have to have an operation but rather would immediately bring about an inferential cognition as its effect, although commentators disagree about this. Gaṅgeśa's views of the *karaṇa* of analogical and word-generated knowledge are still something else: they are cognitions, as with inference, but they also, in a sense, have operations. Thus it appears that he is not to be taken to mean that a *karaṇa* has to be the absolutely last factor before its effect's occurrence. Within the perception chapter at least, he holds that a true *karaṇa* has to have an employment, or "operation" (*vyāpāra*), that in a sense stands between it and the effect. For example, an axe has to be employed in action to fell a tree. The translation "proximate instrumental cause" is sometimes used, but it is really the "*nearly* proximate instrumental cause," since it is understood that the *karaṇa* has to be employed. (See also the discussion of the *karaṇa* of perception in comments on the definition of perception labelled D^{11}, below, p. 335.)

Determining causality is often a contentious topic, and not only in contexts where precise identification of necessary factors is at issue. Causal relevance as determined by the properties through which something is identified (a pot's being cognized as a pot has different causes than the same thing's being cognized as a substance), parsimony regarding causal explanations, the question of the causal status of universals, and other general issues are addressed.

6. Predecessors and Opponents

Gaṅgeśa may be presumed to have had a livelihood as a teacher of Nyāya. He may also have been a teacher of Mīmāṃsā, another school flourishing at his time. There is considerable evidence, especially among later writers, of philosophic academicism in classical India, that is, the teaching of positions without advocacy. Furthermore, though Mīmāṃsaka positions and arguments are attacked throughout the *TCM*, Gaṅgeśa has an impressive knowledge of them. He understands Mīmāṃsā like a Mīmāṃsaka.

Gaṅgeśa belonged to what would now be called a Hindu intellectual circle—more properly, the late classical culture of the Indian subcontinent—with a rich intellectual heritage in which Mīmāṃsā, as the most religiously conservative school, had a central place. It is also probably the classical school that has been the least studied by modern scholars. As we scan a few high points of cultural history, we need to pay particular attention to Mīmāṃsā.

6.1. Mīmāṃsā, Vedānta, and Bauddha philosophy

By Gaṅgeśa's time, the oldest and most revered text within Hinduism, the Veda (c. 1200 BCE in its oldest portions), was no longer commonly read. The Sanskrit was archaic and difficult. But the Veda was commonly revered as the source of right religious practices—birth, marriage, and death ceremonies and all the rites and rituals that provided, or were thought to provide, social cohesion and right relations throughout the universe. Mīmāṃsā, "Exegesis," the oldest of the philosophical schools (the *Mīmāṃsā-sūtra* dates to the first century BCE), entrusted itself with the proper interpretation not only of the Veda but of a vast Vedic literature appended during a thousand years following the oldest Vedic composition.

The Mīmāṃsaka outlook is organized around the concept of *dharma*, "right (religious) practice," and the meaning of injunctions about what we should do. Throughout the course of classical philosophy, Mīmāṃsakas refine views within philosophy of language in particular. But they take positions on nearly every topic of classical interest. In early centuries, Mīmāṃsā is allied in a realist outlook with Nyāya against the Buddhist "Consciousness Only" school (Vijñāna-vāda). The great Mīmāṃsakas become renowned for painstakingly dismantling Buddhist arguments. Buddhists, we should note, rejected not only, let us say, Vedic philosophies, but also the rites, rituals, and social practices of Vedic society. Of course, as philosophers sharing the medium of Sanskrit partisans of all stripes learned from one another, especially in logic and epistemology. But Mīmāṃsakas tend to see the meaning of Vedic injunctions as beyond reproach, and their epistemological differences with Gaṅgeśa may in broad overview be connected to their concern to justify Vedic practices (which, at least at the time of the core elaborations of Mīmāṃsaka epistemology, were presumably under Buddhist attack).

Within Hinduism, or Vedic society, there was, however, no little ambiguity about the true Veda (the word means "knowledge" or "revelation" in Sanskrit), whether it was to be construed, for example, as including, to mention the most prominent controversy, the mystical teachings of treatises called Upaniṣads (c. 800 - 300 BCE and later). Upaniṣads were in early years passed along in the same oral traditions responsible for preserving the Veda, or Vedas, proper. Proclaiming a mystical experience as the supreme goal of life and of a series of lives (rebirth continuing until a "liberating" experience), early Upaniṣads are a more important source for classical philosophy than the Vedas. Systemizing Upaniṣadic philosophy became the province of the prolific *Vedānta* school through its many branches and hundreds of texts.

But Upaniṣads are not, concerning Gaṅgeśa's Nyāya and Vaiśeṣika, nearly so important as the typical modern exposition makes out. The development of Nyāya represents a distinct, non-mystical, in effect non-religious, approach to philosophy (despite Gaṅgeśa's affinity for Mīmāṃsā), an approach forged in conjunction with the development of grammatical analyses and rhetoric and strategies of oral debate. Upaniṣadic mysticism is not entirely ignored or rejected. Like many previous Naiyāyikas, Gaṅgeśa writes at some length about *mukti*, the liberating mystical experience—not in the perception chapter but in the chapter on inference. But neither that reflection of his nor the thoughts of earlier Naiyāyikas on *mukti* is well integrated into Nyāya as a whole. Gaṅgeśa's embrace of *mukti* shows social conservatism, not a mystical philosophy.

In later centuries, Gaṅgeśa's Nyāya is borrowed from by theistic Vedāntins opposed to a monistic Advaita Vedānta whose metaphysics is illusionist (all is the Absolute Brahman, diversity is illusion). Though no branch of Vedānta gets much attention in early Naiyāyika literature, both Udayana and Gaṅgeśa attack Advaita positions and arguments, and still later Naiyāyikas join theistic Vedāntins in an all-out polemical war on the illusionist philosophy.[3]

Nyāya is theistic, though the term is a little misleading. God is, to be sure, a concern of increasing prominence in Nyāya literature, whose treatment reaches a plinth of philosophic excellence (both in the judgment of the tradition and of modern critics) in Udayana's *Nyāyakusumāñjali* (c. 1000). In this long book, several proofs of God's existence are defended against Buddhist attack. Nevertheless, Nyāya theism is closer to what is called deism in the West than it is to a robust theism, and the topic of God is hardly all-consuming. Especially compared to the all-powerful God of theistic Vedānta, Nyāya's God is limited—in its cosmological status and as a topic for philosophy. A supreme being is proposed mainly to answer the question of how things began; he/she creates under constraints; and God is rarely referred to in explanations of worldly processes. Even morality, or the ineluctably moral nature of the universe, is accepted and explained by Naiyāyikas, as by atheistic schools, mainly with reference to human *karman*.

Gaṅgeśa presents a view of the world that by and large does not resort to religious explanation, with one major exception and a few minor ones. The major exception is that he provides a semantics for Vedic injunctions—mainly in the fourth and final chapter of the *TCM*. A telling discussion of the transmission of Vedic meaning occurs her in the perception chapter within a stretch of text concerned with what is required for a testimonial statement to produce a veridical cognition in a hearer (below, pp. 177–93). Gaṅgeśa argues against a traditional Naiyāyika inference to the existence of God that proceeds from the assumption that the Veda must have an author. Like a Mīmāṃsaka, he attacks the premise that hearer's meaning presupposes a causal role for a correct cognition on the part of the speaker. Thus, he says, there is no need to suppose that God is the Veda's author.

Now a few words about the *TCM*'s opening section. It is not part of the perception chapter—it does not concern perception at all—but is traditionally treated as part of Gaṅgeśa's first chapter and so is included here. Some readers may want to begin with the section entitled, "Knowing Veridicality," which is where the perception chapter proper begins (below, p. 69). In the preamble, Gaṅgeśa, socially conservative, upholds the practice of doing something ritually auspicious (*maṅgala*) at the beginning of an enterprise such as writing a book. He also questions (in a playful mood) whether there is gain in doing so. But his final position is that there is. The entire discussion can be construed as Gaṅgeśa doing something right here ritually auspicious, as any good Mīmāṃsaka would do. Again, one cannot miss Gaṅgeśa's sympathy for Mīmāṃsā in certain instances. But those who would read Gaṅgeśa solely for his epistemology need not be apprehensive: Vedic practices command little attention except here.

We shall come back to subcamps of Mīmāṃsā after reviewing the history of Gaṅgeśa's open affinities, Nyāya and Vaiśeṣika.

6.2 Nyāya and Vaiśeṣika

A comprehensive Sanskrit grammar was composed by Pāṇini (c. 450 BCE), who established the earliest grammarian tradition the world over, earlier than the Graeco-Roman. Among the important topics for Nyāya first broached in this literature are universals as the meaning of common nouns. The entire categorial system that scholars usually say Nyāya borrows from its sister school, Vaiśeṣika, can be traced to distinctions made by grammarians. Since Sanskrit had ceased to be anyone's mother tongue long before the second century CE—the approximate time of the final redaction of the earliest Nyāya and Vaiśeṣika texts—learning Sanskrit as a second language meant learning its grammar. Thus grammarians were positioned for a broad intellectual influence, as several scholars now contend. Sanskrit came to be the intellectual idiom of vast amounts of culture in all parts of the Indian subcontinent over more than twenty-five hundred years, the language of thousands of texts, of jurisprudence, court poetry, major and minor epics, (long) religious didactic verse, crafts, and sciences (including philosophy), among other genre. This was made possible by the standardization achieved by grammarians. To learn Sanskrit was to learn Pāṇinian grammar, for Gaṅgeśa and all earlier and later classical Naiyāyikas and for authors within more than a dozen comparable schools. Pāṇinian *sūtra*s are explicitly referred to by Gaṅgeśa in the perception chapter, as they are by philosophers throughout the long history of Sanskrit composition. Tibetan and Chinese scholars translated Sanskrit texts, carrying on traditions of Buddhist philosophy. Sanskrit, we may note, was only partially supplanted as the subcontinent's lingua franca by Muslim invaders and their Persian, late in classical times, and continued to be prominently used and spoken in the nineteenth century. Eventually it was eclipsed by English and regional vernaculars.

The direct influence of grammarians in philosophy is better evident in early Vaiśeṣika than early Nyāya. The latter seems to grow less out of grammarian concerns than out of the interests of public speakers, debaters who would win over an audience, in rather formal settings, we might add. The *Nyāya-sūtra* itself (c. 200 CE), the founding document of the Nyāya school and the oldest extant Nyāya text, has an entire chapter (out of five) devoted to listing fallacies and "clinchers" in a debate context. Furthermore, in Upaniṣads and other very early Sanskrit literature, there is evidence of debates held on philosophic and religious topics by kings and wealthy ministers. Scholars have argued that the larger text of the *Nyāya-sūtra* grew out of a handbook on how to do well in public debate. On this reconstruction of the work's history, the text was expanded to include principles of informal logic, epistemology, and finally ontology and metaphysics, as the sequence of *sūtra*s took its final shape as propounding a many-sided philosophy.

Like other *sūtra* texts outlining trades and practices of Indian society—dramatic dance, sexual love, courtly advice, yoga—the *Nyāya-sūtra* is preceded by a long tradition of reflection and controversy, and of framing principles and findings succinctly in definitions and aphorisms (*sūtra*s) easily committed to memory. These "threads" or *sūtra*s are terse, and typically cannot be understood without a commentary. Doubtless, oral commentaries were the stock-in-trade of early Naiyāyika teachers. The oldest extant *Nyāya-sūtra* commentary is by Vātsyāyana (c. 450), who refers to Naiyāyikas preceding him. A series of subcommentaries ensued over the centuries, as well as independent treatises heavily dependent on the *Nyāya-sūtra* and a core commentary literature.

Details of Nyāya theory and argument will be given by Gaṅgeśa, who will be our Nyāya spokesperson, and we shall move quickly now to an overview of two Mīmāṃsaka subcamps, his principal opponents. But we do need to know a little more about the person most closely followed by Gaṅgeśa, Udayana (c. 1000), especially about Udayana and Vaiśeṣika. Gaṅgeśa refers to Udayana as his revered teacher, and, as mentioned, this same Udayana is responsible for turning Nyāya and Vaiśeṣika into a single philosophical stream. Furthermore, despite Gaṅgeśa's reverence, the division between the views of Udayana and Gaṅgeśa is taken traditionally to constitute the break between an Old Nyāya and a "New" (*navya*). What this division amounts to is hardly resolved in these pages. But we take up the question at various places in comments, in particular to passages where Gaṅgeśa mentions Udayana. Let us look quickly at the Vaiśeṣika side of Udayana's legacy.

The *Vaiśeṣika-sūtra* (c. 150 CE), Praśastapāda's restructuring and commentary (c. 650), and Udayana's commentary on Praśastapāda, together with certain non-commentary Vaiśeṣika writings by Udayana, constitute the major swells in the stream of ontological and causal reflection that Gaṅgeśa knows as Vaiśeṣika. The relation between Nyāya and Vaiśeṣika is historically rich and complex. Vātsyāyana is familiar with Vaiśeṣika views, declaring that the Vaiśeṣika categories (*padârtha*s) can be included in the list of knowables mentioned at the opening of the *Nyāya-sūtra*. Other Naiyāyikas prior to Udayana show both familiarity and sympathy for Vaiśeṣika atomism in particular. Praśastapāda, conversely, shows both familiarity and influence from the Nyāya tradition, and subcommentaries draw further upon Naiyāyika works. Thus, by the last of these, Udayana's long *Kiraṇāvalī* commentary on Praśastapāda, it is practically pointless to talk of two separate schools. Udayana also wrote an extensive subcommentary on the *Nyāya-sūtra* and its core commentaries, and all his works, despite their titles, show the dual inheritance. Finally, somewhat as Gaṅgeśa will be our single spokesperson for what is a school and tradition of philosophy, Udayana seems to have served as the tradition's spokesperson for Gaṅgeśa. Our author does, however, sometimes draw our attention to other authors and texts.

Udayana is an innovator, no mere expositor. But the question of just who is responsible for which innovation is dealt with by us only sporadically. There is much scholarship still to be done (though doubtless Ramanuja Tatacharya knows more about the differences between Old and New Nyāya than is presented here). For practical purposes, "New Logic," *navya nyāya*, is to be taken by traditional fiat, including Gaṅgeśa's own way of speaking, to place Udayana as the last important Naiyāyika of the *Old* school.[4]

6.3 Mīmāṃsaka subcamps

Two principal branches of Mīmāṃsā trace to two giants of philosophy, Kumārila Bhaṭṭa (c. 650) and Prabhākara (c. 700), both of whom wrote long commentaries on the *Mīmāṃsā-sūtra*. Followers of Kumārila are customarily called Bhāṭṭas, and followers of Prabhākara, Prābhākaras (first vowel strengthened). The voice most commonly given to a philosophic perspective other than the Naiyāyika is given, throughout the *TCM*, to the Prābhākara. This Mīmāṃsaka faction is typically, in the structure of Gaṅgeśa's writing, expressed in a section's *pūrva-pakṣa*, with which, normally, a section opens. A *pūrva-pakṣa* is, as explained above (p. 3), text where an opponent's position is expressed along with arguments against a traditional Nyāya theory. A *pūrva-pakṣa* is correlative to text where Gaṅgeśa presents his own final and definitive view, the *siddhânta*. So by saying that Prābhākara positions dominate Gaṅgeśa's *pūrva-pakṣa*s, we mean that that Prābhākara views are usually taken as competing head-to-head with Nyāya on whatever topic of Nyāya's concerns, epistemology, ontology, even ethics. Thus, we shall learn much about Prābhākara theories—those of the Bhāṭṭa camp as well, though less comprehensively—as we proceed.

In advance we need to know only that both Bhāṭṭas and Prābhākaras are realists who hold ontological positions similar to Naiyāyikas'. The most major differences occur in epistemology, as we shall see.

śrīr astu

Tattvacintāmaṇi

JEWEL OF REFLECTION ON THE TRUTH (ABOUT EPISTEMOLOGY)

PREAMBLE

maṅgala-vādaḥ

DISCOURSE ON AUSPICIOUS PERFORMANCE

Text and Translation

guṇâtīto 'pi īśas tri-guṇa-sacivas try-akṣara-mayas
tri-mūrtir yaḥ sṛṣṭi-sthiti-vilaya-karmāṇi tanute |
kṛpā-pārâvāraḥ parama-gatir ekas tri-jagatām
namas tasmai kasmaicid a-mita-mahimne pura-bhide || 1 ||

Though beyond quality, served by three qualities, Īśa, made of the three imperishables (and signified by the three-lettered *aum*),
Who, taking three forms, performs the (sacred) actions of creation, preservation, and destruction;
Who is the near and further shore, the sea of compassion, the supreme way (to felicity) for the three worlds, the One —
Honor to that someone, whose greatness is unmeasured, the (triple-)fortress-smasher (Śiva). || 1 ||

Comments

This introductory verse is an example of Gaṅgeśa's own "doing something auspicious," *maṅgala*, here praising his "chosen deity" (*iṣṭa-devatā*), Śiva. The "Lord," Īśa, though for present purposes described, is also considered indescribable (thus referred to by the indefinite "someone"). Śiva is the One, the Absolute Brahman.

Mathurānātha explains the "three qualities" as knowledge, will, and action necessary for the Lord's creation, preservation, and destruction of the universe. A literary trope of apparent contradiction is thus set up since the idea flies in the face of the *beyond quality* with which the verse begins. The word for quality is *guṇa*, a word that suggests the triad of *sattva*, *rajas*, and *tamas*—"light/intelligence," "action/passion," and "darkness/inertia"—proclaimed by the Sāṃkhya school as the fundamental constituents of nature. The Lord, in Gaṅgeśa's conception, does transcend nature. But, on the other hand, God is in the Divine nature qualified by the qualities of knowledge, will, and action. This opposition also contributes to the trope (called in Sanskrit poetics "apparent contradiction," *virodhâbhāsa*, or simply *virodha*).

Other tropes, such as a double meaning (*śleṣa*) rendered by the expression in parentheses in the first line, are employed as well.

The "three forms" are Brahmā, the Creator, Viṣṇu, the Preserver, and Śiva, the Destroyer, though God is commonly thought of in Hinduism as manifesting in many forms. The compound translated "the supreme way" (*parama-gati*) implies attainment and mystical knowledge as well as the path thereto. The three worlds are heaven, an "intermediate realm," and earth. Śiva is apparently Gaṅgeśa's "preferred divinity," *iṣṭa-devatā*, who destroyed the demon-inhabited cities of gold, silver, and iron in the ether, air, and earth.

The next verse states the name of the work, its purpose, and who the author is, as is common with texts of late classical philosophy.

Text and Translation

anvīkṣā-nayam ākalyya gurubhir jñātvā gurūṇāṃ matam
cintā-divya-vilocanena ca tayoḥ sāraṃ vilokya a-khilam |
tantre doṣa-gaṇena durgamatare siddhânta-dīkṣā-gurur
gaṅgeśas tanute mitena vacasā śrī-tattva-cintā-maṇim || 2 ||

Having examined the principles of critical investigation (Nyāya) with teachers, knowing the thought of the (so-called) "Teachers" (the Prābhākara Mīmāṃsakas or "*guru*s"),
With a divine (illumined) eye of reflection, seeing entirely the essence of both,
This teacher (*guru*) who initiates into the right, the established positions, in a difficult system made by the errors (of earlier teachers) more difficult,
Gaṅgeśa lays forth the blessed *Tattva-cintā-maṇi* ("Jewel of Reflection on the Truth") in measured (true) words. || 2 ||

Comments

A *cintā-maṇi* is a wish-fulfilling jewel. It helps to provide something desired, something worried about (*cintā*). Śiva's heaven is sometimes said to be made of thousands of such gems. The word *cintā-maṇi* is not uncommon in religious and literary works, though it is in philosophy. By itself *cintā* can mean "thoughtful reflection."

The word *anvīkṣā*, "critical investigation," is etymologically similar to the *ānvīkṣikī* that appears in Kauṭilya's *Artha-śāstra* (the core portion, c. 300 BCE) in reference to a type of training a good minister of state should have. It also appears in a usage we might call self-referential in the *Nyāya-sūtra* commentaries (beginning with Vātsyāyana, c. 450). Although *anvīkṣā* can mean simply "inference," or the "science of inference," here the word could appropriately be translated "philosophy," signifying a tradition of thought to be understood more as "critical investigation" than as the "enlightened seeing," or *darśana*, for which ancient and classical Indian philosophy is perhaps better known. On the other hand, Gaṅgeśa also invokes the idea that what he is doing is *darśana*, with the expression, "divine eye."

Our author does indeed know thoroughly the philosophy of the Prābhākara branch of Mīmāṃsā, as well as that of his own Nyāya school. The book is filled with refutations of Prābhākara positions, which are usually followed by subtle reworkings of traditional Naiyāyika views, and arguments establishing them, as we shall see.

The title of the Gaṅgeśa's book presents some difficulty in the word *tattva*, rendered as "Truth." The natural question to ask upon hearing about reflection on the truth is: the truth about what? The answer is: epistemology, *pramāṇa-śāstra*, a term elliptically understood. Alternatively, the ellipsis may be taken to be of the four words for the four *pramāṇa* recognized by Nyāya, the "means of knowledge," perception, inference, analogy, and testimony, to which Gaṅgeśa devotes a chapter each. Book titles are meant to have poetic virtue as well as to be descriptive of contents. To have said *pramāṇa-śāstra-tattva-cintā-maṇi*, or to have listed the separate means, perception and so on, would have been leaden. There is elegance as well as a hint of presumption in Gaṅgeśa's ellipsis. There is also the double meaning of "whatever truths you wish to know" that resounds because of the common use of the compound, *cintā-maṇi*, to mean "wish-fulfilling gem," as explained.

Text and Translation

yato maṇeḥ paṇḍita-maṇḍana-kriyā
pracaṇḍa-pāṣaṇḍa-tamas-tiras-kriyā |
vipakṣa-pakṣe na vicāra-cāturī
na ca sva-siddhânta-vaco-daridratā || 3 ||

Because a jewel's action as an ornament of learning
Is the action of removing darkness (of ignorance) in bold heretics (Buddhists and others),
There is no cleverness in the thought on the opponent's side (that is not cut through),

Nor poverty in the statements on one's own side (that is not made rich hereby). || 3 ||

Comments

Gaṅgeśa develops a metaphor based on a jewel's attributes of sharpness and of light (some jewels are thought to be self-luminous) as well as of financial value.

The word *sva* in the last line means "property" as well as "own" or "belonging to oneself"—a double meaning that almost comes across in English. The line can also be read: "And there is no lack of words to increase (our) property (i.e., make us rich)." Also suggested is: "However poor in speech we may be, we shall be enriched." The implication is that the magical jewel will continue to enrich those who keep it nearby.

• •

Now, what follows is traditionally identified and commented upon by later Navya Nyāya philosophers as the first section of the *TCM*, the *maṅgala-vāda*, "Discourse on the Doing of Something Auspicious." Gaurinath Sastri argues pretty persuasively, however, that the section constitutes an independent work by Gaṅgeśa, that it is not part of the *TCM*.[1] Clearly, it is not part of the perception chapter.

In addition to several rather formal textual arguments, Gaurinath points out, entirely rightly, that the substantive reflection of the *TCM* begins with the next section, on knowledge of the veridicality of cognition (the *prāmāṇya-jñapti-vāda*). Some may therefore want to begin reading at that point (below, pp. 69ff). Nothing essential by way of background theses or arguments introduced—either in Gaṅgeśa's text or in comments made—would be missed. As explained in the introduction, the section is not concerned with perception. It is a preamble to the whole book, not just to this chapter, if it is a preamble at all.

Nevertheless, whether Gaurinath is right or not (and his arguments have not convinced Ramanuja Tatacharya), it is the better judgment to treat the section as integral to the *TCM*. Not only would this be the only other work by Gaṅgeśa that we know of, there is merit in following the classical identification. Moreover, while there may not be so much of philosophic value at stake in the issues considered and positions advanced, epistemological principles are employed and major themes advanced, such as, in particular, how a causal relation is discerned. And there is one strong internal textual point favoring a view of the section's integrality to the *TCM*: at the end of the section, Gaṅgeśa makes a forward reference ("we shall answer later") that is presumably to the final chapter of the *TCM* where a similar topic is discussed. Still, there is nothing, or not much, about perception here.

This opening section is also one in which Gaṅgeśa often seems playful, establishing his views by arguments that sometimes do not tie in, contentwise, very tightly with the rest of his philosophy. But the style, especially the argument constructions, are inimitably Gaṅgeśa's: clear and precise.

Text (p. 6, Tirupati, and p. 5, Calcutta) and Translation

iha khalu sakala-śiṣṭa-eka-vākyatayā abhimata-karmârambha-samaye tat-samāpti-kāmā maṅgalam ācaranti | tatra yady api maṅgalasya kāraṇatā na anvaya-vyatireka-gamyā, maṅgalaṃ vinā api pramattânuṣṭhita-samāpteḥ | na ca tatra janmântarīya-tat-kalpanam, anyonyâśrayāt, lokâvagata-kāraṇena anyathā-siddheś ca |

Pūrvapakṣin (voicing a position other than Gaṅgeśa's own, a position that Gaṅgeśa will later refute, correct, or modify): Here indeed inasmuch as the (Vedically) cultured speak with a single voice, those wanting to complete an undertaking do something, on the occasion of commencing an intended work, auspicious (*maṅgala*). With regard to this, the doing of something auspicious is, as a causal factor for the completion of the work, not to be known by the method of positive and negative correlation, since even without such action sometimes what has been undertaken by someone heedless of the practice is completed. Moreover, it is no good to imagine that auspicious action has in those instances been undertaken in a previous birth, for that would beg the question, and, since the causes of completion are commonly known, positing as a cause the doing of something auspicious would be superfluous.

Comments

Though, as suggested, the topic of *maṅgala* is far from central to Gaṅgeśa's philosophy, this section does introduce some important themes and make use of key concepts and theses of Navya Nyāya. For example, in this opening passage we have mentioned the inductive procedure of correlation, positive (checking things F to make sure that they are G) and negative (checking things not G to make sure that they are not F), used to establish a causal relation, a pervasion (*vyāpti*), that would provide underpinnings for a correct inference.

If the question is whether doing something auspicious is necessary to complete a work, it is no good to imagine that the counterexamples are explained away by the theory that such action has been undertaken in a previous birth, for it is only by supposing that *maṅgala* is indeed a causal factor that one would imagine such action to have been undertaken in a previous birth.

The term *anyathā-siddhi*, translated "superfluous," is used for occasional or fortuitous causal factors that are not strictly necessary to the bringing about of an effect of a particular type. An example commonly given is a potter's ass that has carried the clay used to make a pot.

Text (p. 10, Tirupati) and Translation

na api maṅgalaṃ saphalam, a-vigīta-śiṣṭâcāra-viṣayatvād darśa-vad iti, phala-siddhau prāripsita-samāptes tadānīm apekṣitatvena niyamena upasthitatvāt phalântarasya a-tathâ-bhāvāt viśva-jin-nyāyena phala-kalpane gauravāt pariśeṣânumānena tat-kāraṇatā-grahaḥ | vyabhicāreṇa kāraṇatvasya a-bhāvāt upāya-sahasreṇa api grahītum a-śakyatvāt |

(The **pūrvapakṣin** continues:) Nor (does the following reasoning go through).

Objection: Doing something auspicious is efficacious, *since* it is an object of the (Vedically) cultured's effort that is not contradicted (by scripture), like a *darśa* (new-moon) sacrifice. Given that it is efficacious, we have a further argument to show what it is efficacious for, namely, the completion of what has been intended as an undertaking, which is, then, what it depends on. Such an intention is invariably presented first and set in memory (*upasthitatvāt*). An intention for a different fruit would not be like this. It would be needlessly cumbersome to imagine a different fruit by the rule (i.e., were we benightedly to assume an application of the Mīmāṃsaka rule) *viśva-jit* (where there is not an explicitly stated purpose). (Thus) the causal efficacy of doing something auspicious is apprehended by an eliminative argument.

Pūrvapakṣin: (The above reasoning is wrong) since, because of deviation (between *maṅgala* and completion of a work), there is no causality. (Given deviation) even a thousand such stratagems cannot make a causal relation grasped.

Comments

There has to be an *inference* to a scriptural injunction because there is no explicit Vedic injunction on the topic. The idea is that an unknown Veda—not all of the sacred authority has been discovered by humans and transmitted—contains such an injunction and that the Vedically cultured have somehow internalized it through the diligence of their practices in accordance with the known Veda.

According to Mīmāṃsā, a sacrifice that has no fruit scripturally specified is to be understood as undertaken for the sake of winning heaven. The rule is named after the *viśva-jit* sacrifice, and is discussed at *Mīmāṃsā-sūtra* 4.3.15-16 and commentaries.

The next passage presents the reasoning of an advocate of *maṅgala*, who himself considers and answers still other objections. The advocate is not Gaṅgeśa asserting his own views. This is a second-order *pūrvapakṣin*, who will not be answered by the first-order *pūrvapakṣin* for several pages, beginning p. 48, below.

Text (p. 20, Tirupati) and Translation

tathā api tathā-vidha-śiṣṭâcārânumita-śrutir eva maṅgalasya abhimata-hetutve mānam | na ca vyabhiçāraḥ | niṣparipanthi-śrutyā maṅgalaṃ samāpti-sādhanam iti pramāpite tatra api tayā eva liṅgena janmântarīya-tad-anumānāt | tac ca idam ārabdha-karmâṅgam, karmârthitayā śiṣṭais tat-pūrvaṃ kriyamānatvāt, phalântarâbhāve sati phalavat-karmâripsamānena niyamatas tat-pūrvaṃ kriyamānatvāc ca, darśe prayājâdi-vat | ācāra-mūlaka-śruty-anumānābhyāṃ tad-arthitayā tat-kartavyatva-bodhanāt tat-phalakatva-bodhanāc ca | darśârambha-samaye niyamena kriyamānāyā apy ārambhanīyāyās tad-arthitayā a-kriyamānatvāt phalântara-śravaṇāc ca pradhānatvam iti na tayā vyabhicāraḥ |

Advocate (of *maṅgala*, against the *pūrvapakṣin*): Nevertheless, there is a well-founded reason to accept that doing something auspicious is a cause of the desired result (viz., completion). It is an *inferred scriptural text*, inferred from the sort of behavior of (Vedically) cultured people suggested above.

And there is no deviation (undermining supposition of a causal relation). That doing something auspicious is a means to completion is made known by a scriptural declaration without opposition. And with respect to a case (where nothing auspicious has been performed and there is completion all the same), just by that mark (namely, the completion) should a doing of that in another lifetime be inferred.

And that (being made known by an inferred Vedic injunction), which is this (doing something auspicious, *maṅgala*), is a *subordinate instrument* (*aṅga*) to the action undertaken. It is such an instrument, *since* the (Vedically) cultured, as intent on the chief end (namely, completion), are engaged in doing it before undertaking an enterprise. Furthermore, given that there is no other intended fruit (i.e., none other than the chief end), *maṅgala* is a subordinate instrument, *since* one desiring to undertake a fruitful action invariably performs prior *maṅgala*. (For both of these arguments concerning *maṅgala*'s instrumental status, the confirming example is) like the preliminary sacrifices done before a *darśa* (new-moon) sacrifice.

The behavior-founding scriptural injunction and the inference (concerning the doing of something auspicious in a previous birth) make it known that *maṅgala* should be performed and that it is fruitful insofar as one is intent on that (chief end, e.g., the completion of a book). On the occasion of commencing a *darśa* sacrifice, although an *ārambhanīya* sacrifice is being performed, it is invariably not being performed by one intent on that (chief end of the *darśa* sacrifice). Furthermore, there is a scriptural statement declaring another fruit. Thus, it (is not a subordinate instrument but) has its own chief end. Therefore (i.e., because it is not being performed by one intent on the chief end of the *darśa* sacrifice), there is, in its case, no counterexample (undermining our argument).

Comments

Again, not all of the Veda has been heard and memorized or written down. The behavior of Vedically cultured persons, who perform *maṅgala* on the occasion of commencing an enterprise, such as writing a book, comprises grounds for inferring that there is a Vedic injunction to that effect. The injunction would in turn serve as proof that doing something auspicious is a cause of the intended completion.

In the paradigm case of inference—from sight of smoke rising above a mountain to the presence of fire there—the reasoning proceeds from something directly experienced to something not directly experienced. So here too one goes from the directly experienced to the not directly experienced—in inferring from a work's completion that a person who has evidently not performed something auspicious in this lifetime has done so in a previous lifetime.

Two arguments are given by the advocate of *maṅgala*—against the overall thrust of this *pūrva-pakṣa* section—to establish that doing something auspicious is a subordinate instrument to the completion of an enterprise such as writing a book. First, the Vedically cultured perform *maṅgala*. Second, performing *maṅgala* is for no other purpose than the chief end of the enterprise to be undertaken, e.g., completion of a book. There seems to be an exception to the confirming example, "like the preliminary sacrifices done before a *darśa* sacrifice." It is an *ārambhanīyā* sacrifice, which is done preliminary to a *darśa* sacrifice and which has its own chief end, whereas a true "subordinate instrument" has to have the same goal as the principal action. But there was a qualification given in the original argument, namely, "by one intent on that (chief end)," which qualification is not fulfilled by a performance of an *ārambhanīyā* sacrifice. Therefore, that is no counterexample undermining the reasons given for regarding *maṅgala* as a subordinate instrument to the completion of an enterprise such as writing a book.

Text (p. 33, Tirupati, and p. 27, Calcutta) and Translation

> nanu maṅgalam a-laukikaṃ laukike na aṅgaṃ bhavati, lokâvagata-kāraṇata eva tad-upapatteḥ | ata eva gṛha-rathâdāv "āre bhagne indra-bāhur baddhavyaḥ" "pāyasaṃ brāhmaṇo bhojayitavyaḥ" ity atra tad ubhayaṃ na aṅgaṃ, kiṃ tu naimittikaṃ | tad-vad idam apy ārambha-samaya-nimittakam astu, viśva-jit-nyāyāt svargaḥ phalam iti cet, na |

Objection (against the *maṅgala* advocate): Doing something auspicious is other-worldly. With regard to something worldly (such as completion of a book), it is no "subordinate instrument" (as with a Vedic sacrifice). For, simply from commonly understood (i.e., worldly) causes is completion possible.

Just for this reason, the (sacrificial) situation of a spoke of the household sacrificial chariot or the like being broken, "An iron stake ("the arm of Indra," i.e., an "iron crow") is to be bound," and "A Brāhmin should eat a milk-sweet," are (Vedically enjoined) actions that are not subordinate instruments but rather *occasionals* (*naimittika*). So this too is, let us say, an occasional (action) on the strength of the rule, *viśva-jit*, where heaven is the fruit (i.e., the understood intention of the sacrifice).

Advocate: No.

Comments

Mathurānātha glosses "the arm of Indra" as "iron crow." The point here is that the Vedically enjoined actions involving the iron stake and milk-sweet are *conditional* to the otherwise unfortunate occurrence of a spoke on a wheel of a sacrificial chariot being broken. Similarly, the objection runs, doing something auspicious is not, as the object of an (inferred) Vedic injunction, a subordinate instrument but rather an *occasional* or conditional act. In this way, the objection that doing something auspicious, which is other-worldly, cannot be a subordinate instrument to an action that involves a worldly goal can be met: the *maṅgala* is an occasional or conditional act, not a subordinate instrument.

But the advocate does not accept the suggestion.

Text (p. 35, Tirupati, and p. 30, Calcutta) and Translation

tasya a-pūrva-rūpôpakāra-janakâṅga-viṣayatvāt | ayaṃ tu pratibandhakâ-bhāva-rūpa upakāraḥ | tasya ca lokâvagata-kāraṇa-sahakāritā eva, pratibandhake sati tasmāt tad-an-upapatteḥ | a-pūrvan tu na tathā | vighna-dhvaṃsa-dvārā ca idam aṅgaṃ, na tv "iḍo yajati" ity-ādi-vidhi-bodhita-prayājâdy-aṅga-yāga-vad a-dṛṣṭa-dvārā | maṅgala-janyâ-dṛṣṭaṃ vinā api svataḥ-siddha-vighna-virahavata ārabdha-nirvāhāt | na ca evaṃ vighna-dhvaṃsa-dvārā api na idam aṅgaṃ, tatra eva vyabhicārād iti vācyam | sati vighne tad-dhvaṃsa-dvārā tasya aṅgatvāt | na ca evaṃ prayājâder api durita-dhvaṃsa eva dvāram, kalpya-durita-dhvaṃsataḥ a-pūrvasya laghutvāt |

(The **advocate** of *maṅgala* continues:) The topic of that (maxim you cite ruling out the status of subordinate instrument) is the subordinate instrument insofar as its effect would be produced by unseen force (*a-pūrva* = *a-dṛṣṭa*, viz., *karman* or "karma") as auxiliary cause. But this auxiliary cause (i.e., the doing of something auspicious) takes the form of effecting an absence of hindrances. And its auxiliary status is with respect to commonly understood causes (such as, in the case of writing a book, mental effort, command of the topic, etc.). If there is (effective) hindrance, for that reason this (the completion of the enterprise) would not be possible.

But unseen force is not like that (i.e., does not operate in co-operation with commonly understood causes). This (*maṅgala*) is a subordinate instrument by way of its destruction of obstacles, not by way of unseen force, as with sacrifices that are subordinate instruments such as the preliminary sacrifice that the injunction, *iḍo yajati*, declares. Even without any unseen force produced by doing something auspicious, a person who is free of hindrances—a freedom self-accomplished—finds success in action begun.

Objection: Since there exists an exception (to what it takes to be a subordinate instrument) in that very person (who is free from obstacles by nature and not by *maṅgala*), this is not a subordinate instrument, although it is effective by way of destruction of obstacles.

Advocate: That should not be alleged. For, when there are obstacles, this is a subordinate instrument by way of their destruction.

And not like this are the preliminary Vedic sacrifices; even the preliminary sacrifices, etc., are subordinate instruments by way of the destruction of sin. For it is simpler to hold that imaginable sin is destroyed by unseen force.

Comments

This is an abstruse passage, at least for those unfamiliar, as Gaṅgeśa was not, with Brāhminical sacrifices.

There are five preliminary sacrifices for a *darśa* (new-moon) sacrifice.

Sacrifices achieve their intended results by way of creating good karma, that is to say, unseen force, which is considered other-worldly. Obstacles to completion of a project, such as writing a book, appear to be thoroughly worldly, in contrast, and the destruction of such obstacles as well. Thus, something's causality by way of destruction of obstacles would be a *worldly* causality, not the kind of causality attributable to Vedic sacrifices and enjoined rituals. A pretty good case seems, then, to be made against regarding doing something auspicious as a subordinate instrument in the sacrificial sense. However, there are other types of subordinate instrument, the advocate claims.

Text (p. 38, Tirupati) and Translation

vastutas tu prāyaṣo vighna-saṃśaye tan-niścaye vā niyamena śiṣṭānāṃ maṅgalâcaraṇe vighnâ-bhāva eva dvāratvena abhimataḥ | nirvighnaṃ samāpyatām iti kāmanayā tat-karaṇa-pakṣe śrutita eva dvāratva-nirṇayaḥ | kiṃ ca a-pūrva-dvāratve laukikâṅgatva-virodhaḥ, kḷpta-kāraṇād eva tad-utpatter indra-bāhu-bandhana-vat | nanu vighna-sandehe kathaṃ tan-nāśârthaṃ pravṛttiḥ, durita-dhvaṃsârthi-pravṛttau tan-niścayasya hetutvāt prāyaś-citta-vad iti cet, na | vighna-saṃśaye niścaye vā niyamena śiṣṭānāṃ maṅgalâcārāt vighna-jñānaṃ pravarttakam | tādṛśâcārânumita-vidhinā api vighna-jñānavān ārabdha-samāpti-kāmo adhikārī bodhyate |

(The **advocate** of *maṅgala* continues:) But, in reality, it is generally the case that, whether there is doubt about obstacles or certainty, the (Vedically) cultured as a rule perform *maṅgala*. Just the absence of obstacles is considered the way the *maṅgala* is effective. On an occasion of doing it with the desire, "Without obstacles, may this be completed," an (inferred) scriptural text itself (inferred on the occasion) renders the conclusion about the way (*maṅgala* is effective, namely, securing an absence of hindrances).

Moreover, if the *maṅgala* were effective by way of unseen force, then there would be incompatibility with its being a worldly subordinate instrument. For, just from well-established causes is that (a worldly effect) produced, as with the binding of "Indra's arm" (which would be incompatible with its being a worldly subordinate instrument).

Objection: If there is doubt about whether there are obstacles, how can there be effort for their destruction? When someone makes an effort, intent on the destruction of sin, certainty about the existence of sin is a cause (i.e., motivator), as in the case of expiational acts.

Advocate: No. Whether there is doubt or certainty about obstacles, the (Vedically) cultured as a rule perform *maṅgala*. Thus *cognition* of obstacles (whether they really exist or not) is the instigator. And the (Vedic) injunction inferred from such behavior makes it known that the person fit (to do something auspicious) is someone cognizing a possibility of obstacles who desires to complete an enterprise begun.

Comments

And surely we would all be aware of such a mere possibility! And not knowing just what obstacles there are, one would be wise to take precautions.

A would-be sacrificer has to be meet various requirements, depending on the sacrifice, to be "fit" to undertake the sacrifice, *adhikārin*. Here it is said that the only requirement for performing *maṅgala* is cognizing a possibility of obstacles while desiring completion.

Text (p. 41, Tirupati, and p. 37, Calcutta) and Translation

> prāyaścitte tu tan-niścayavān, tathā eva vidhi-bodhanāt | ata eva adhikāri-viśeṣaṇaṃ vighna iti tat-sandehe kathaṃ pravṛttiḥ vaidike 'dhikāra-niścayād eva pravṛtter ity apāstam | yataḥ pradhānâdhikāriṇa eva aṅge 'dhikāro na sva-tantraḥ aṅgatva-bhaṅga-prasaṅgāt | na ca pradhāne prāripsite duritam adhikāri-viśeṣaṇaṃ, virodhāt | kiṃ tu samāpti-kāmanā, sā tu niścitā eva |

(The **advocate** of *maṅgala* continues:) But in the case of expiational acts, the fit person is someone certain about that (the presence of sin). For scriptural injunction makes it known that such indeed is the case.

Objection: Since with respect to Vedic sacrifices effort to act comes from certainty about what it takes to be fit, (there is the insuperable problem) how can there be effort (for doing something auspicious) when there is doubt about obstacles?

Advocate: This worry is rejected for the reason just given, namely, that (the cognition) "(Possible) obstacles" is the condition governing what it takes to be fit to perform *maṅgala*.

Since to be fit for acting toward the chief end is precisely to be fit with regard to an instrument subordinate to that end, there is no independence here. For, (otherwise) there would be the difficulty that being a *subordinate* instrument would be meaningless.

And the existence of sin is not a condition for being fit for the chief end for which the action is to be undertaken, since that would be contradictory. Rather, desire for completion is what is certain (considering the issue of fitness).

Comments

Surely one doesn't *need* to be sinful to complete a book. Fitness to perform *maṅgala* is just a matter of desiring completion and being aware of possible obstacles. Certainty is not required concerning obstacles, but apparently one should not waver in one's desire for completion.

Text (p. 42, Tirupati) and Translation

yat tv anyatra niścitâdhikāra-kartṛkatve 'pi maṅgalaṃ sandigdhâdhikāra-kartṛkatvam eva, vighna-sandehavatāṃ śiṣṭānām ācārânumita-vedena tathā eva bodhanād iti | tan na | vighnavattvena adhikārâ-bhāvāt | kvacit tan-niścaye 'pi pravṛtteś ca | api ca śaṅkitân-iṣṭa-vāraṇârtham api pravartante parīkṣakāḥ, yathā sarpâdi-daṃśa-janya-viṣa-saṃśaye tan-nāśāya bheṣa-ja-pānâdau | kiṃ ca phalasya saṃśaye 'py upāyatva-niścayād yathā kṛṣy-ādau pravṛttiḥ tathā maṅgale 'pi | yadi ca vṛṣṭy-ādau sati kṛṣy-ādito '-vaśyaṃ phalam iti tarkāt tatra pravṛttis tadā sati vighne maṅgalād a-vaśyaṃ phalam iti tarkāt tatra api pravṛttiḥ |

Objection: But whereas elsewhere the fitness conditions for agency are certain, doing something auspicious involves only an agency whereof the fitness conditions are doubtful. The scripture (that you say is) inferred from behavior of the (Vedically) cultured, who are doubtful about the existence of obstacles, would make known just this (namely, that someone has to be doubtful, etc., to be fit to perform *maṅgala*, which, of course, scripture does not do).

Advocate: That's wrong. For there is no fitness understood as being faced with obstacles, and sometimes there is effort of performing *maṅgala* when there is certainty about that (namely, being faced with obstacles).

Furthermore, to avoid something dubious but unwanted, thoughtful persons also make effort, as, for example, with the drinking of a medicine when there is doubt whether there is poison produced from a snake's bite or the like—to destroy it. Moreover, though there is doubt about a result, there may be certainty about the means. As there is effort regarding preparation of a field, etc. (with doubt about the resulting crops), so also regarding doing something auspicious. And if the effort there stems from the reasoning, "Given rain, etc., necessarily will there be result from preparation of the field, etc.," then also effort here stems from the reasoning, "Given obstacles, necessarily will there be result from doing something auspicious."

Comments

The prescribed sacrifice for rain proves that doubt about the result—namely, in that instance, rain—does not rule out the doubter as fit to undertake the sacrifice.

Text (p. 44, Tirupati, and p. 43, Calcutta) and Translation

nanu sphyasya bhaktâśleṣa-nimittakêjyāyām iṣṭatvena darśa-dharma-grahe saty atideśâgata-pūrva-dina-kartavya-devatâvāhanasya aṅgasya sphyâśleṣa-dvāra-saṃśaye an-anuṣṭhānam uktaṃ, yathā kṛṣṇale dvāra-bādhe | ato vighna-saṃśayāt tad-dhvaṃsa-dvāra-saṃśaye kathaṃ maṅgalânuṣṭhānam iti cet, na |

Objection: Regarding the (derivative) sacrifice whose instrument is slicing a half-ripened food-offering with a wooden sacrificial sword, which is a (derivative) sacrifice when a *darśa* (new-moon) sacrifice (as the root sacrifice) is in mind, it is said (by Mīmāṃsakas) that the (normally enjoined) part about invoking the divinity on the previous day is not to be performed: the previous day now has come and gone, regarding extension of the sacrificial action. (So) given that there is on that previous day doubt about the means (to carry out the root sacrifice, here whether there will be, namely), slicing with a wooden sword (etc.), the situation is like the overriding of the means with regard to the golden bean (*kṛṣṇala*, which, unlike the rice ordinarily used sacrificially, does not have to be husked).

So, since there is doubt about the existence of obstacles, why should *maṅgala* be performed, given that there would be doubt about the means of destruction of obstacles?

Advocate: No.

Comments

If the existence of hindrances is doubtful, so too will be the destruction of hindrances.

According to the *Mīmāṃsā-sūtra*,[2] if there is doubt about the *dvāra*, the "means" to carry out an intention, there will be no instigation of action.

A *vikṛti*, or derivative sacrifice, is called for under certain circumstances that cannot be foreseen. Thus, though ordinarily invocation of the presiding deity is enjoined, in some cases that action cannot be carried out and thus is not enjoined (cf., Immanuel Kant's "ought implies can").

The golden bean provides a nice analogue, because, unlike rice, etc., it has no husk. Therefore, husking, which is normally enjoined, is overridden by that impossibility.

Text (p. 48, Tirupati) and Translation

naimittike hi nimittavān adhikārī yathā bhinne juhoti ity atra pātra-bhedavān | tathā iha āśleṣavān adhikārī iti pūrva-dine āśleṣa-niścayâ-bhāvāt yuktam an-anuṣṭhānaṃ | api ca ijyā-kartavyatā-niścaye tad-aṅgânuṣṭhānaṃ | na ca āśleṣa-saṃśaye tan-niścayaḥ pūrva-dine | ataḥ pradhāne 'dhikārâ-bhāvān na aṅge 'dhikāra iti na āvāhanaṃ pūrva-dine | yadi ca yadi na syād iti nyāyena kuryāt tadā an-adhikṛta-kartṛkatvena niṣphalaṃ syāt | sphyâśleṣe sati ijyā-kartavyatā-niścaye 'pi na āvāhanaṃ, pūrva-dinasya aṅgasya a-bhāvād iti ijyāyām āvāhana-bādha eva | maṅgale tu vighna-dhvaṃsa-jñānavān adhikārī ity uktaṃ | tac ca saṃśaye 'pi asti | pradhāne kartavyatā-niścayo 'sty eva iti dvāra-sandehe 'pi yuktam anuṣṭhānam | bhaviṣyad-vivāhâdāv ābhyudayike 'pi taj-jñānavān adhikārī, tathā eva ācārāt |

(The **advocate** of *maṅgala* continues:) For, with regard to an instrumental action, the person who carries it out is (by that very act) the fit person: as with the injunction, "He makes an oblation into the broken bit," the one who has broken the dish is there the one who is fit, so here (with your example) the one doing the slicing is fit. Since on the previous day there is no certainty about (such) slicing, it is appropriate not to do the usual invocation of the presiding deity. (But that is not the situation with *maṅgala*.)

Furthermore, if there is certainty about a sacrifice to be performed, then its subordinates *are* to be performed. And given doubt about the slicing, there is no such certainty, on the previous day. For this reason, according to the rule, "There is no fitness for the subordinate, if there is no fitness for the chief sacrifice," there is no invocation on the previous day. And if one is (to go ahead on the previous day and do the invocation although it is not with certainty called for, and thus benightedly) to follow the maxim, "If there is no (heaven, then what's the loss)," then, inasmuch as there would be no fit actor, the invocation would be fruitless.

Given the slicing with the wooden sword, there is no invocation even though there is certainty about the sacrifice to be performed, because there was no subordinate sacrifice on the previous day—thus in fact a block to the sacrificial invocation. Regarding doing something auspicious, however, the person who is aware of the possibility of obstacles is the *adhikārin*, "fit person"—this has been said, and it should hold even if there is doubt.

"About the chief goal (e.g., completion of a book, or a principal sacrificial action), there is nothing less than certainty"—in that case, though there be doubt about the means, it is appropriate to carry out the action.

On such occasions as an upcoming wedding, a "prosperity-granting" (*ābhyudayika*, i.e., a preliminary) sacrifice is underway, too (though there is not certainty about the marriage). The person aware of that (the possible marriage) is fit (for the preliminary sacrifice). Just like that is there the practice of *maṅgala*.

Comments

Mathurānātha fills out the maxim above about the possibility of there being no heaven. Ramanuja Tatacharya, let me report, an accomplished Mīmāṃsā scholar, laughed heartily when we read this passage together. (If there is no heaven, then in vain are sacrifices performed. But also, if there is no heaven, all is meaningless, and so what's the harm in performing sacrifices?—so goes the joke.) He also cites a maxim by Kumārila: *na asti cen na asti no hāniḥ, asti cen nâstiko hataḥ*, "If there is no heaven, what's the loss to us (of performing sacrifices); if there is heaven, the non-performer is lost." This version is similar to "Pascal's wager" in Western thought.

Text (p. 53, Tirupati) and Translation

> nanv aṅgānāṃ pradhāna-vidhi-vidheyatvaṃ | na ca granthâdi-samāptau pradhāna-vidhir asti | na ca tat-kartavyatā-bodhakasya laukikam a-pramāṇasya śāstram eka-deśo yujyate | tasya tan-nirapekṣatvād iti cet, na | a-pūrva-janakâṅgānāṃ tathātvāt ācārânumita-śrutyā pradhāna-vidhiṃ vinā api tad-aṅgatva-vidhānāc ca |

Objection: Subordinate sacrificial actions are known as enjoined through (combinations with Vedic) injunctions about primary sacrificial actions. And there is no injunction about a primary act for anything like completion of a book! (Therefore, there could be no injunction to do *maṅgala*.) And it is not the case that a worldly authority (or, knowledge source, *pramāṇa*), were it to make known that this (e.g., completion of a book) should be done, could appropriately be a part with a (Vedic) teaching. For, it (a Vedic teaching) is independent of that.

Advocate: No. What you say applies (only) to subordinate actions that generate an "unseen force" (*a-pūrva*, that accomplishes the end in view). And through the scriptural pronouncement that is inferred from the behavior (of the Vedically cultured), even without an injunction about a primary action (e.g., writing a a book), there can be prescription to do what is subordinate (e.g., performing *maṅgala*).

Comments

Mīmāṃsā interprets any statement enjoining a subordinate sacrificial act as forming a single sentence with an injunction to perform the correlate primary sacrifice.

The advocate views the completion of a book not to require "unseen force" as a cause, which would effect only the removal of obstacles. Doing something auspicious would be, then, a kind of prophylactic. Thus, such a combination of the worldly and the other-worldly would be legitimate.

Text (p. 54, Tirupati, and p. 51, Calcutta) and Translation

> api ca pradhāna-kartavyatā-bodhaka-bodhya-kartavyatākatvaṃ prayojakaṃ, tac ca iha apy asti, pratibandhakâ-bhāvasya sakala-kārya-hetutvena laukika-pramāṇasya api tat-sāpekṣatvāt | nanu yāgâdi-vat pradhāna-deśa-kālânvayas tad-aṅge maṅgale syād iti cet, na | a-sādhāraṇe '-pūrva-janake ca aṅge tad-anvayāt |

(The **advocate** of *maṅgala* continues:) Moreover, a statement that makes known that a primary action is to be done is itself to be made known by (the totality of) of that statement which has such duty as content (namely, the conjunct statement making known a subordinate dutiful act as well as the primary act). It is the "impeller" (*prayojaka*). And that is here, too (namely, concerning (a) completion of a book and (b) performing *maṅgala*). For, inasmuch as the causes of the entire effect do not face insuperable blocking, the worldly authority (for writing a book) is also dependent on that (the inferred scriptural injunction that one should do something auspicious).

Objection: As with the *yāga* subordinate sacrifice, a connection with the same place and time as the principal sacrificial action is required, and this rule should apply to the doing of something auspicious as a subordinate to that (principal action).

Advocate: No, not for a subordinate action that is not a special cause (special for the chief end in view, e.g., completion of a book) and that does not generate unseen force (that accomplishes the end in view). A different connection for that applies.

Comments

No requirement about a set time or place applies to doing something auspicious on the occasion of beginning a book. One might, for instance, perform *maṅgala* in one country and complete the book in another!

Text (p. 59, Tirupati) and Translation

> ata eva baddha-śikhatvâdau na pradhāna-deśa-kālânvayaḥ | na ca duritâ-bhāve

svataḥ siddhe sāṅga-maṅgalânuṣṭhānaṃ niṣphalam iti tad-vedâ-prāmāṇyaṃ | lokâvagata-kāraṇe hi durite sati vedena tasya tad-dhvaṃsa-janakatvaṃ bodhyate, na tu tad-ullaṅghya | ata eva tattva-jñānavato bhogârthaṃ niṣiddhânuṣṭhānaṃ doṣâ-bhāvān na a-dharma-janakam iti na tad-vedâ-prāmāṇyam | pramāṇântarāt svataḥ-siddha-duritâ-bhāvâvagatau maṅgalâ-karaṇe nitya-vad-anuṣṭhānaṃ śiṣṭānāṃ bhajyeta iti cet, na | vighna-jñānavato nitya-vad-anuṣṭhānād iti sampradāyaḥ |

(The **advocate** of *maṅgala* continues:) Just for this reason, there is, in the case of binding the toplock of hair, no required connection to the time and place of the principal sacrifice.

And regarding the person for whom there are no obstacles because of his own accomplishments, it is not the case that doing something auspicious, as subordinate (to a primary action, e.g., writing a book), would be fruitless (i.e., unnecessary), and therefore the (inferred injunction of the) Veda (to do *maṅgala*) would be non-authoritative (or non-veridical). For, (even) given that there are obstacles whose causes are those commonly understood, that some would be destroyed by doing something auspicious is made known by (the inferred injunction of) the Veda. There is no overstepping that.

Just for this reason, doing something prohibited for the sake of enjoyment by someone who is aware of the true principles (of the self or soul, i.e., who is spiritually enlightened) does not generate *a-dharma*, "evil," since there is no imperfection. Therefore, that (inferred injunction of the) Veda is not non-authoritative.

Objection: If there is someone who has learned from another knowledge source that he faces no obstacles on account of his own accomplishments, and who does not perform *maṅgala*, (well) he should participate in the practice of the (Vedically) cultured, (in that it is) like the constant(ly ordained) actions (such as the five daily ritual acts).

Advocate: No, because, like the constant actions, performance is by someone aware of the possibility of obstacles—this is the traditional teaching.

Comments

Binding the hair into a toplock is a subordinate sacrificial action and a "common cause" for all Vedic sacrifices.

There are no obstacles to completing a work "whose causes are those commonly understood" for a knower of the self, a knower who has transcended the moral force and payback of *karman* or action. Thus, the inferred Vedic injunction holds only for those for whom there could be such obstacles.

Several early Upaniṣads, along with the *Bhagavad-Gītā*, say that no action, whether good or bad, calls for karmic payback for a knower of the self (*ātman*). For example, in the *Gītā* the phrase is repeated several times (with slightly different wording), *ātmā na upalipyate*, "the true Self is not stained (by sin or works or being embodied)."[3]

With the next passage, we return to the voice of the first-level *pūrvapakṣin*, who rebuts the advocate.

Text (p. 60, Tirupati, and p. 57, Calcutta) and Translation

mā evam maṅgalaṃ vinā api pramattânuṣṭhita-samāpteḥ | na ca tena vinā api sidhyatas tad-aṅgam | na ca janmântarīyaṃ tat, janmântarīya-granthâdikam uddiśya śiṣṭais tad-a-karaṇāt | nanu putrêṣṭau karma-sādguṇye aihika-phalâ-bhāve āmuṣmikaṃ phalaṃ sāṅge 'pi maṅgale yatra na phalam tatra āmuṣmika-phalam iti cet, na | tatra putra-mātrasya kāmanâśravaṇāt | iha tu prāripsita-samāpti-kāmanayā maṅgalâcāra iti tathā eva vedânumānāt kārīrī-vad āsanna-samayârabdha-samāptiḥ phalam |

Pūrvapakṣin: Don't think like that. Even without doing anything auspicious, there is completion of what has been undertaken (books, etc.) by those negligent of the practice. And doing something auspicious is not a subordinate action to something that is accomplished strictly without it.

Furthermore, that was not performed in another birth. For, regarding the likes of books written in another birth, the cultured may *not* have done *maṅgala* then.

Objection: As (Mīmāṃsakas put forth the following principle:) when sacrificial actions have been properly carried out in connection with the rite for the birth of a son without the desired result in this lifetime, the result will be in the next lifetime. So, similarly, where doing something auspicious has been performed complete with auxiliaries and no fruit occurs, there the fruit will occur in the next lifetime.

Pūrvapakṣin: No. For, the (scriptural) injunction is directed to one who is desirous of a son generally (without specification of whether the son will be born during the sacrificer's current lifetime or another). But the performance of *maṅgala* is done by those desirous of completion here of a work begun; just accordingly would there be an inference to a Vedic injunction from which, like the *kārīrī* sacrifice (done by farmers for rain), the fruit would be completion (i.e., rain, or finishing a book) *near* the time it was begun.

Comments

Rain the next year is not what the sacrificing farmer wants. And an author performing *maṅgala* would like the book completed within the author's current lifetime.

Text (p. 61, Tirupati) and Translation

nanv āsanna-samayas tat-sambandhe vā na maṅgala-janya iti samāpti-mātraṃ janyam | tac ca aihikâmuṣmika-sādhāraṇam iti cet, na | āsanna-samayasya sva-vṛtti-samāpty-upalakṣakatvāt | anyathā kārīry api na āsanna-samaya-phalā syāt | tasmād vyabhicārān na tad-aṅgam iti |

Objection: What is produced by doing something auspicious is not (necessarily) near-term, nor (necessarily) tied to the near term. Therefore, only completion is what is generated. And that is common to this lifetime and the next.

Pūrvapakṣin: No. For, completion in the near term is indirectly indicated for that whose term is near. Otherwise, the *kārīrī* sacrifice (for rain) would also not have its (intended) fruit in the near term (and rain the following year would suffice).

Therefore, because of deviation (i.e., counterexamples, as pointed out from the beginning), doing something auspicious is not a subordinate action to that (completion of, e.g., a book).

Comments

The implication behind the objection is that the inferred Vedic injunction does not have to be formulated with explicit mention of the term of completion. The *pūrvapakṣin* replies that the near term is at least indirectly indicated by the very nature of the desire of the Vedically cultured, i.e., by the intended fruit of those who practice *maṅgala*.

The distinction between indirect indication and true qualification—a distinction that Gaṅgeśa takes up near the end of this first chapter—involves a causal dimension: there is no causal relation between the crows above Devadatta's house, mention of which serves a merely referential purpose—in the standard example of indication (*upalakṣaṇa*)—as opposed to a true qualifier or property, e.g., being-a-house, which would help to generate a perception of what the thing essentially is (see below, pp. 642-43). The advocate of efficacy for *maṅgala* can claim that there need be no causal relationship to the *time* of completion. The advocate would in this way weaken his claim. Still, the *pūrvapakṣin* responds, there would be an indirect indication to the near term, which, moreover, would be sufficient to defeat the advocate's attempt to wriggle out from under the weight of the clear counterexamples to a need for doing something auspicious.

Text (p. 62, Tirupati, and p. 60, Calcutta) and Translation

anye tu maṅgalaṃ pradhānam, a-dṛṣṭa-dvārā ārabdha-karma-samāptiḥ phalaṃ, tat-kāmo 'dhikārī | kvacit tu phalâ-bhāvaḥ karmâdi-vaikalyāt kārīrī-vat | na ca anyadā api karaṇam | niyata-kālīna-tādṛśâcāreṇa phalavat-karmâripsamānas tat-samāpti-kāmī maṅgalam ācared iti śrutyā ārambha-samaya-kartavyatā-bodhanāt | yathā "āgnā-vaiṣṇavam ekādaśa-kapālam caruṃ nirvaped darśa-pūrṇa-māsāv āripsamānaḥ" iti śrutyā ārambhaṇīyêṣṭeḥ pradhānāyāḥ darśârambha-samaya-kartavyatvam | kāmanôpadhi-kāryatve 'py ārambha-samaye nityam anuṣṭhānam |

ārabdha-karma-samāpty-arthinā upāyatvena a-vaśyan tad-anuṣṭhānāt | na ca kāmyatve parisamāpti-kāmanāṃ vinā phalavat-karmârambhe 'pi tad-anuṣṭhānaṃ na syād iti vācyam | samāptaṃ karma phalāya alam iti phalârthinaḥ samāptau kāmanâ-vaśyaṃ-bhāvād iti |

Others, however (hold the following view).

(Second) **advocate** (of *maṅgala*, against the *pūrvapakṣin*): Doing something auspicious is (not a subordinate rite but rather) a principal sacrificial action. Completion of work begun is the fruit (but) by means of unseen force (not by means of destruction of obstacles). The person desiring completion is the person "fit" to do the rite. But, in some cases, there is no fruit—due to a defect or deficiency in the work or the like, as in the case of the *kārīrī* sacrifice (for rain).

And there is (on this view) no instrumentality proposed by way of another lifetime. The (inferred) scriptural injunction, (inferred) from such practice (of the Vedically cultured) as is tied to a particular time-frame, is: "Practice *maṅgala*, you who desiring to undertake a fruitful work desire its completion." (Thus another lifetime is ruled out because) it explicitly makes known that that which is to be done is to be done within the time-frame of the beginning of the undertaking. For example, there is the scriptural injunction: "Make a separate oblation, to Agni and Viṣṇu, into eleven clay-pot bits, you who desire to undertake a new and full-moon sacrifice." This is an *ārambhanīyā* sacrifice that is to be done within the time-frame of the beginning of the *darśa* (new-moon) sacrifice, which is the principal sacrificial action.

Although the desire is an adventitious qualifier of the duty (such that it is not at the time of the desire that the action is to be undertaken), the practice is lawfully bound up with the time-frame of the beginning of the action, since (in the case of the question on the table, namely, *maṅgala*), necessarily is it that such is practiced as a means, on the part of a person seeking completion of a work begun.

And it should not be said that (on our view) there would be, even on the occasion of the beginning of a fruitful work, no practice of *maṅgala* in the instance of something being desired but without a desire for an utterly entire completion. For, such desire is necessarily for completion, on the part of anyone seeking the fruit of the work, as (the thought) "A completed work is sufficient to get the fruit" (guides his effort).

Comments

According to Mīmāṃsā and other schools, unseen force, or "karma," is generated by sacrificial acts, force that, given other factors, may be said to bring about a desired result.

A writer wants fame, etc., from writing a book, and aims at its completion to get those fruits. Obviously the completion brings the fruits. Thus, anyone who desires such fruits desires the completion of the action that would bring them about.

Text (Tirupati, p. 63) and Translation

tan na | kārīrī-janyâtiśaya-vad vihita-pradhāna-janyâtiśayatvāt maṅgala-janyâ-pūrvasya api phalâ-sampādakâ-śeṣa-kāraṇa-sampādakatayā ārabdha-karma-samāpty-a-vaśyam-bhāvâpatteḥ phalâ-vaśyam-bhāva-niścayaṃ vinā vaidika-karmân-anuṣṭhānāt | na ca evam, bhūyasi sāṅge 'pi maṅgale kvacid ārabdha-samāpty-a-bhāvāt | na ca tatra āmuṣmikaṃ phalam, aihika-mātra-phalatvāt | vaidika-karmanaḥ phalâ-vaśyam-bhāvena āgantuka-duritena apy a-pratibandhāt |

Pūrvapakṣin: This view is wrong. As in the case of an excess of good *karman* generated by the *kārīrī* sacrifice (for rain), the scripturally enjoined principal sacrificial action generates such excess. Thus, the difficulty (that defeats the view just put forward) is that necessarily would there have to be completion of a work begun (when *maṅgala* has been performed), inasmuch as unseen force generated by the *maṅgala* would, too, bring about an entirety of causal factors that would (in turn) bring about the result. For, without certainty about the results necessarily coming about, Vedic sacrifices would not be performed. And such is not the case. Even when *maṅgala* has been performed many times, there is sometimes no completion of something begun.

And in those cases where there is no completion, the result is not in the next lifetime, since (it was explicitly said in the initial statement of the position) that the result is only here in this lifetime. (Is there any other way out? No.) As Vedic sacrificial actions necessarily bring results, there would be no blocking of completion even by future, adventitious obstacles.

Comments

The Mīmāṃsaka supposition is that Vedic sacrifices always bring results, through workings of unseen force, so long as there is no defect or deficiency (variously defined).

Text (p. 68, Tirupati) and Translation

kiṃ ca ā kārīry-ādikam agrima-puruṣa-vyāpāraṃ vinā eva phala-hetuḥ, tathā maṅgalam api tena vinā eva hetuḥ syāt | na ca evaṃ | lokâvagata-kāraṇatvāt tad-apekṣā iti cet, tarhi sa eva hetur astu kim anena | ārabdha-karma-janakâ-dṛṣṭa-kāraṇa-sampattau putrêṣṭi-vat tat-samāpti-sādhanatvaṃ śrutyā bodhyata iti cet, na | tatra dṛṣṭa-kāraṇa-sampattau putrân-utpādād a-dṛṣṭa-dvārā putrêṣṭes taj-janakatvam astu | na ca karma-nirvāhe dṛṣṭa-sakala-hetu-sampattau vilambaḥ, yena maṅgala-janyâ-dṛṣṭâpekṣā syāt | api ca maṅgalaṃ vinā api pramatta-nāstikânuṣṭhita-samāpter na tat tatra kāraṇam | janmântarīya-puṇya-sampattis tatra hetur iti cet, na | tathā api vyabhicārāt | kvacit puṇya-sampattiḥ kvacin maṅgalaṃ hetur iti vrīhi-yava-vad vikalpa eva iti cet, tarhi tat-sambhāvanayā niyataṃ maṅgalânuṣṭhānaṃ na syāt, yava-prayoge vrīher iva | vikalpe ca ubhayasya a-śāstârthatvāt |

(The **pūrvapakṣin** continues:) Moreover, as with the likes of the *kārīrī* sacrifice (for rain), where the causes of the result (clouds, etc.) work totally without further exertion on the part of the person who has done the sacrifice, so doing something auspicious would, too, totally without further exertion be such a cause. But it is not so!

Objection: Since there are the commonly known causes, there would be dependence on them.

Pūrvapakṣin: If you can think that, let them alone be considered causal! What would be the use of doing something auspicious?

Objection: Regarding cases where known (worldly) causes productive of a work begun are all present, what is made known by scripture is that doing something auspicious is a factor within the (total) instrumentality.

Pūrvapakṣin: No. There (concerning the example of a sacrifice performed for a son), given the complete presence of the known causes, sometimes a son does not come forth. So let it be accepted that by means of the unseen force of the sacrifice for a son there is such generation. And (yet here) regarding completion of a work (such as writing a book), given the complete presence of all the known causes, there is no delay in the appearance of the effect whereby there could be any dependence on unseen force produced by doing something auspicious.

Furthermore, even without doing something auspicious, those negligent of the practice and those who reject Vedic culture complete what they have begun. Thus, doing something auspicious is not a cause there.

Objection: The acquisition of religious merit acquired in a previous birth (through practicing *maṅgala*, etc.) is there (in the seemingly contrary examples) a cause.

Pūrvapakṣin: No, since there would be similarly deviation.

Objection: This is simply a case of alternates (if X is not a causal factor, then Y is, and vice-versa). That is, sometimes acquisition of merit is a cause, sometimes doing something auspicious, like rice or barley (alternatives allowed in the performance of some sacrifices).

Pūrvapakṣin: Then performance of *maṅgala* would not be required for the possibility of completion of work undertaken, like rice when barley is used (rice being proscribed after a choice of barley). And if this is to be a situation for alternatives, then the two together would not be the teaching.

Comments

Unlike the *kārīrī* sacrifice done for rain, where the rain has its worldly causes in clouds and so on, causes that work independently of human exertion, a sacrifice for a son requires further human participation to bring about the desired result, and still it may not come about. So this may seem the pertinent comparison regarding *maṅgala* and completing a book, since some perform *maṅgala* and work diligently but their book is not completed. However, books are completed when all the worldly causal factors are assembled, as is shown by those who complete them but who have not performed *maṅgala*.

Well, then, it must have been a surfeit of religious merit in those cases. (Religious merit, *puṇya*, or good *karman*, we may note, is not acquired only through performance of *maṅgala*, but through in general living righteously and through many specific observances.) A problem is, then, that people with no discernible religious merit do start and even finish books! Another is that on the traditional view both *puṇya* and *maṅgala* are required.

The *pūrvapakṣin* spends small effort in dispelling the objector's suggestions—in the last case, about alternatives, with quips. There is no role for rice in a sacrifice prescribing a choice between rice and barley once the sacrifice has been undertaken with a selection of barley. And so, strictly speaking, neither barley nor rice is a necessary factor, and the two together are expressly not, in such situations, taught.

Rucidatta mentions a well-known example of alternative causality. Straw used to start a fire is an alternative causal factor that is necessary to one set of conditions sufficient to produce fire although straw need not be present in an alternative set of factors that would also be sufficient to produce fire.

Text (p. 71, Tirupati, and p. 71, Calcutta) and Translation

> nanu vidhi-vākyaṃ na phala-niyata-pūrva-sattvaṃ bodhayati, kiṃ tu maṅgalāt phalâ-vaśyam-bhāvam iti cet, na | iṣṭa-sādhanatvasya vidhy-arthatvāt | atha anvaya-vyatirekābhyāṃ tad-grahe vyabhicāro doṣāya, na tv āgamena tad-grahe | tad uktam "āgama-mūlatvāc ca asya arthasya vyabhicāro na doṣāya" iti | ata eva yāgâdeḥ, svarga-sādhanatā iti cet, na | niyata-pūrva-sattvasya grāhyasya a-bhāvād āgamena api bodhayitum a-śakyatvāt | yāga-janita-svarge kārīrī-janita-vṛṣṭau ca jāti-viśeṣa eva asti |

Objection: The (inferred) injunctive statement does not make known that there is invariably antecedence (of *maṅgala* for completion of an enterprise). Rather, it makes known that from doing something auspicious the result inevitably comes about (whether here or somewhere else).

Pūrvapakṣin: No, since the meaning of an injunction is to refer to a means of accomplishing something desired (and completion is desired here, not somewhere else).

Objection: Then, with respect to positive and negative correlation, if there is understanding of it (that way, that is, as a necessary antecedent implied by the inferred Vedic injunction to perform *maṅgala*), then deviation would be a fault, but not with respect to sacred tradition (i.e., the Veda) if there is understanding of it (this way, that is, as one way completion could be guaranteed). So it has been said (by Udayana): "If a meaning is rooted in sacred tradition, deviation does not make for fault." Just for this reason, sacrifices and the like are (considered, severally, each) the means to heaven.

Pūrvapakṣin: No. From a lack of something's being invariably antecedent to an effect, even sacred tradition cannot make it known (as a cause). Regarding the heaven secured by a particular sacrifice and the rain produced by a *kārīrī* sacrifice, there is a particular type (of heaven and of rain) only.

Comments

According to the first objection, *maṅgala* would not be a necessary condition for completion of work begun—we find counterexamples in the case of the negligent, etc.—but would be, apparently, a sufficient condition though the fruit would sometimes not be in the current lifetime. The *pūrvapakṣin* responds that this is not the way an injunction is to be understood. And there would still be the set of counterexamples of those who have done something auspicious but who have not completed something undertaken.

The *pūrvapakṣin*'s second response recalls the opening of the section where it was said that deviation—i.e., a counterexample to a rule—means no causal principle, and "even a thousand stratagems cannot make one grasped." We have now firmly in mind counterexamples to two different senses of *cause*: (a) that doing something auspicious is *necessary* to completion is ruled out by counterexample of those completing their works without practicing *maṅgala*, and (b) that doing something auspicious is *sufficient* for completion is ruled out by counterexample of people who have practiced *maṅgala* but who have not completed their enterprises.

Nevertheless, it seems the advocate of a causal role for *maṅgala* might have a case if a weaker understanding of cause were in place—say, as one factor contributing to one of many possible causal complexes, each sufficient to bring about a particular effect. Similarly, different sacrifices help to win heaven, and there are other activities, such as charity, that are also helpful for that end. And not all rain is produced by a *kārīrī* sacrifice, though, given other factors (perhaps themselves necessary), that might help. The *pūrvapakṣin* responds by claiming that the heavens secured by distinct sacrifices are themselves distinct; similarly, there are distinct rains.

The quotation from Udayana is from his *Kiraṇāvalī*, the opening section, where he himself addresses the question of the usefulness of *maṅgala*.[4]

Text (p. 72, Tirupati) and Translation

> apare tu maṅgalasya ārabdha-nirvāhakatvaṃ vighna-saṃsargâ-bhāva-dvārā, tathā eva pratibandhakâ-bhāvasya hetutvāt | sa ca a-bhāvaḥ sato vighnasya dhvaṃso 'n-āgatasya an-utpādaś ca karma-nirvāha-samaya-sthāyī | vighna-kāraṇa-vināśa-dvārā prāg-a-bhāvasya sādhyatvam | yasmin saty agrima-kṣaṇe yasya sattvaṃ yad-vyatireke ca a-sattvam, tad eva tasya taj-janyatvaṃ na tv a-sataḥ sattvaṃ gauravāt | asti ca vighna-kāraṇa-nāśe sati vighna-prāg-a-bhāvasya tathātvam | tāvati samaye duritân-utpādaś ca na sākṣān maṅgala-janya ity a-dṛṣṭa-dvārā tathā | evaṃ nirvighnaṃ samāpyatām iti kāmanayā tad-ācāro 'pi saṅgacchate | ata eva yatra vighnâ-bhāvaḥ svataḥ siddhaḥ tatra maṅgalasya a-kiṃcit-karatvena vedâ-prāmāṇyam iti nirastam | an-āgata-vighnâ-bhāvasya tatra api sādhyatvāt | "sarve vighnāḥ śamaṃ yānti" iti yatra vināyaka-stava-pāṭâdau śrutam asti tatra tata eva pramattânuṣṭhita-samāpteḥ an-ādau saṃsāre '-vaśyaṃ tad-ācārāt | tathā ca tena samaṃ maṅgalasya vikalpa eva | yatra ca sāṅge maṅgale saty api na phalaṃ tatra vighna-bhūyastvād iti |

Others, however, hold the following view.

(Third) **advocate** (of *maṅgala*): Doing something auspicious is a cause of completion (not simply by way of destruction of obstacles, or of unseen force, but) by way of bringing about relational absence (prior absence, destructional absence, and constant absence) of obstacles to completion. So, in fact, absence of blockers is a cause, and this absence is the destruction of present obstacles as well as a non-arising of future obstacles through the time of a work's completion.

Prior absence is established as a means of destruction of causes of obstacles. (But how can a prior absence be itself brought about, since it is beginningless up to the time of its destruction?) Given an *x* (a cause, e.g., doing something auspicious, or a stick and so forth used to make a pot) in relation to a *y* (an effect, e.g., a prior absence of obstacles, or of a presence of a pot) that would exist at the next instant, and given that its negation is accompanied by (the *y*'s) non-existence, that *x* is in fact for the *y* its generator. But something that does not exist is not the generator for something existent, because that is a cumbersome conception. And given that doing something auspicious destroys causes of obstacles, it is such (i.e., it is an example of the principle just stated) for a prior absence of obstacles.

And for so long a period of time as there is no arising of obstacles the absence is generated by the doing of something auspicious, but not directly. Thus, it is so (i.e., a generator) by way of unseen force (that is, through unseen force as intermediary).

In this way, "May this be completed without obstacles," is a desire that is in harmony, moreover, with the practice of doing something auspicious.

Objection: In cases where an absence of obstacles is established by oneself (by one's own nature, due to good *karman* built up in previous lifetimes), there doing something auspicious, as not having any point, would mean that the (inferred) Vedic injunction lacked authority.

Advocate: By the reasoning just given this is thrown out. For, there, too, doing something auspicious would establish an absence of future obstacles.

"All obstacles go to rest"—where this has been (at a minimum only) heard in readings and so on of hymns to Gaṇeśa, there just from such hearing is there completion of what has been undertaken on the part of those negligent (of the practice of *maṅgala*), since in beginningless transmigration necessarily has that been practiced (that is to say, necessarily must there be religious merit built up in previous births). And so there are alternatives: doing something auspicious is on par with that (meritorious practice in a previous life, with regard to generating an absence of obstacles).

And where *maṅgala* has been practiced as a (ritually) subordinate act, but without result, there the reason must be that the obstacles were too many (or too large).

Comments

Naiyāyikas view absences as falling into two main divisions: (a) relational absences and (b) distinctness or mutual exclusion. Relational absences comprise, in turn, three types: prior absences (e.g., of a pot before it is produced), posterior or destructional absences (e.g., of a pot after it has been broken into shards), and absolute or constant absences (e.g., of color in air). We shall often encounter these notions in pages to follow, and an entire section of this first chapter of the *TCM* is devoted to absences, in particular to how they are known.

The destruction of a prior absence of, let us say, a pot is equivalent to the production of a pot. If one does something auspicious, then at the next instant there is a prior absence of obstacles to a work's completion. But if one does not do something auspicious, then at the next instant the prior absence of obstacles disappears, that is to say, obstacles arise. Thus, doing something auspicious would generate a prior absence of obstacles.

In the next passage, the original *pūrvapakṣin* rejects the advocate's attempt to tie the effectiveness of doing something auspicious to bringing about an absence. He does so by drawing out the nature of an "operation" of an instrumental cause, *vyāpāra*. A stock example is an axe's (repeated) contact with a tree, causing it to be felled. Such an operation, or employment, stands between, so to say, an efficient and otherwise proximate instrumental cause (*karaṇa*), such as the axe in the stock example, and its effect, the felling. In other words, the axe is the proximate instrumental cause only in employment.

The *pūrvapakṣin* will contend that an absolute absence cannot play the role of an employment or operation because it itself is, by nature, constant and uncaused, whereas a true operation must be brought into play.

Text (p. 78, Tirupati) and Translation

tan na | vighnân-utpādasya vyāpāratve mānâ-bhāvāt | saṃsargâ-bhāvatvena hetutvāt tathā eva vyāpāratvaṃ, tac ca prāg-a-bhāve 'py asti iti cet na | atyantâ-bhāvasya api vyāpāratvâpatteḥ | svataḥ siddhasya na hetutvaṃ yadi, tadā prāg-a-bhāve 'pi tulyam | kiṃ ca yatra maṅgalaṃ na tatra niyamena vighna-kāraṇam asti, yena tan-nāśa-dvārā prāg-a-bhāvasya sādhyatvam | evam api yatra vighnân-utpādo 'pi svataḥ siddhas tatra maṅgalam a-kiñcit-karam eva | vighna-dhvaṃsân-utpādayor ārabdha-nirvāha-kālâvastāyinor maṅgalād eva utpatter na tad-artham a-dṛṣṭa-dvāratā | maṅgalasya vikalpena anvaye śiṣṭair niyamato maṅgalânuṣṭhānaṃ na syād ity uktam | kiṃ ca pradhānatve sāṅga-maṅgala-mātraṃ na samāpti-hetuḥ, tasmin saty api tad-a-bhāvāt | pracitaṃ tathā iti cet, na | a-pracitād api phala-sattvāt | na ubhayam, an-anugamāt | guru-karmârambhe pracitam alpa-karmârambhe 'lpam iti cet, na | kvacit tādṛśād api phalâ-sattvāt vaiparītye 'pi phala-sattvāc ca | etena bahu-vighna-śaṅkayā bahutaram, alpa-vighna-śaṅkayā alpataraṃ ca hetuḥ, tādṛśa-śruty-unnayanād iti nirastam | tādṛśād api prāripsitâ-samāpteḥ vaiparītye 'pi samāpteś ca | bahutvasya tri-catur-ādi-bhāvena alpatvasya ca eka-dvy-ādi-rūpatayā an-anugamena tādṛśa-śiṣṭâcāreṇa tādṛśa-śrutyā bodhayitum a-śakyatvāc ca | tasmān maṅgalaṃ na aṅgaṃ na vā pradhānam iti pūrva-pakṣa-saṃkṣepaḥ |

Pūrvapakṣin: That's wrong. There is no argument showing that a non-arising of obstacles functions as the operation (of *maṅgala* as an instrumental cause). If it is thought that a relational absence is a cause (of completion) and so in fact an operation while including a prior absence, too—that's wrong. For, this would provoke the difficulty of an absolute absence also being an operation (of an instrumental cause). If that which is self-established cannot be a cause (in the sense of an operation, as, for example, an absolute absence is no such cause), then the same holds for a prior absence, too (since all prior absences are beginningless and self-established).

Moreover, (you propose the rule that) where *maṅgala* is practiced, there no causes of obstacles obtain—this is such that by means of destruction of those (causes) a prior absence would be established. Even so, where obstacles do not in fact arise—as a state effected by someone through his own nature—there *maṅgala* would be thoroughly pointless and ineffective.

Both a destruction of and a non-arising of obstacles obtain during the period of completion of what has been begun. If both are produced just from doing something auspicious, still it is not, for that purpose, by means of (generation of) unseen force. The positive causal status of doing something auspicious is (furthermore, only) one alternative: practice of *maṅgala* by the (Vedically) cultured would then not be a matter of invariable principle—so it has been said (above, i.e., by you expressly admitted).

Furthermore, regarding the principal action (e.g., completing a book), merely doing something auspicious as a subordinate (ritual) act is not a cause of completion, since that is absent sometimes even when doing something auspicious is present.

Objection: Accumulation of more *maṅgala* is needed in those cases.

Pūrvapakṣin: That's wrong. For, even from no accumulation, the result comes about (in other cases). Nor is it both (with the causality varying with the cases), since that is not uniform (and true causes are uniform: like effects, like causes).

Objection: To begin a weighty enterprise (e.g., writing a long book), a significant accumulation (of *maṅgala*); to begin a slight enterprise, slight accumulation.

Pūrvapakṣin: That's also wrong. For, sometimes though there is such significant accumulation, there is no result. And in the reverse situation, sometimes there is result.

Objection: With regard to a worry that there may be many (or great) obstacles, many (*maṅgala*) would be a cause, while with regard to a worry that there may be only few (or slight) obstacles, fewer (*maṅgala*) would be a cause—from such behavior (of the Vedically cultured) would there be inference of such a scripture, from which (such behavior would be called for).

Pūrvapakṣin: This is rejected by the reasoning already given. For, again, even from such behavior, sometimes there is no completion of what was desired to be undertaken, and, in the reverse situation, sometimes there is completion. Furthermore, since "many" would be three, four, and so on, while "few" would be one or two—in such forms of practicing *maṅgala* no uniformity would obtain with the behavior of the cultured. Such a scripture (inferred from such behavior) could not possibly make all this known.

Therefore, doing something auspicious is neither a subordinate (sacrificial) act nor a principal one—such is, in sum, the *prima facie* position (*pūrva-pakṣa*).

Comments

Just below as well as in other contexts, Gaṅgeśa does find absences to be causal factors. But there are no circumstances in which an absence could be an operation or employment of a "proximate instrumental cause," *karaṇa*, (see the discussion of *karaṇa* in the introduction, above, pp. 24–5).

The *pūrvapakṣin* not only takes up and refutes the principal points of the immediately preceding view and its supporting arguments, he concludes with a summary statement of the reasons for rejecting any conception of *maṅgala* as an effective rite. Thus, by implication, he rejects the position that it has any causal role whatsoever regarding completion of an enterprise. Now comes Gaṅgeśa's own stance, as we begin a *siddhânta* section.

atha maṅgala-vāda-siddhânta

NOW, THE RIGHT VIEW, WITHIN THE DISCOURSE ON AUSPICIOUS PERFORMANCE

Text (p. 81, Tirupati, and p. 88, Calcutta) and Translation

siddhântas tu | ārabdha-karma-samāptau maṅgalaṃ na aṅgaṃ, na vā pradhānam, a-hetutvāt | kiṃ tu prāyascitta-vat pradhānaṃ vighna-dhvaṃsaḥ phalam | ārabdha-karma-nirvāhe vighno mā bhūd iti kāmanayā tad-anuṣṭhānāt | vighnasya saṃśaye niścaye vā śiṣṭānāṃ tad-ācaraṇād vighnâ-bhāvasya ākāṅkṣitatvāc ca | yadi ca nirvighnaṃ samāpyatām iti kāmanayā tad-ācaraṇaṃ, tadā api na a-gṛhīta-viśeṣaṇa-nyāyena ahaṃ svargī syām ity atra svarga iva vighnâ-bhāvá eva phalaṃ na samāptiḥ, ubhayato vyabhicārāt | samāptis tu vighna-rūpa-pratibandhakâ-bhāve sati lokâvagata-sva-kāraṇād eva |

Gaṅgeśa: But the right position is as follows. With respect to completion of work begun, doing something auspicious is neither a subordinate (ritual) act nor the principal act, since it is *not* a cause of completion. Rather, like an expiational act, it is a principal (ritual) act, but the result is (not completion but rather) destruction of obstacles. For, "In completing the work begun, may there be no obstacles," with such a desire, *maṅgala* is performed. Given doubt about obstacles, or certainty, the (Vedically) cultured engage in the practice. And they expect that there will be no obstacles.

And if its practice is accompanied by the desire, "May this, free of obstacles, be completed," then, too, by the maxim, "Without a qualifier being grasped (there is no grasping of a qualificandum)," (and in accordance with the example) "May I be one who has heaven"—as here *heaven* being the intended result (the qualifier, with *I* as the qualificandum: "May I be *heaven*-having," *svargī*)—so, just an absence of obstacles is the intended result, since (if we take completion to be the result, then) there would be deviation in both ways (both in positive correlation—sometimes when *maṅgala* is performed there is no completion—and in negative correlation—sometimes when *maṅgala* is not performed there is completion). Yet completion—given no blockers in the form of insuperable obstacles—results from its own commonly known (or worldly) causes only.

Comments

According to Ramanuja Tatacharya, the quotation of the maxim in the second paragraph is from Kumārila, "Without a qualifier being grasped, there is no grasping of a qualificandum" (*na a-gṛhīta-viśeṣaṇā buddhir viśiṣṭeṣu upajāyate*). I have been unable to locate it.

Gaṅgeśa's view is that completion results from the commonly known causes, not from *maṅgala*. Doing something auspicious does, however, destroy obstacles or prevent insuperable obstacles from arising. In this way he upholds the practice.

The question is, then, the precise relation of such destruction, and prevention, to the desired result. But Gaṅgeśa does not seem interested in spelling this out. He simply affirms, in the next passage, the causal status of relational absences without elaborating. The point appears to be to provide a minimal sketch of the efficacy of doing something auspicious, and thereby to defend the practice without being unnecessarily precise.

Text (p. 94, Tirupati) and Translation

pracitâ-pracita-devatā-stuty-ādi-sāṅga-maṅgalāt pratyekaṃ vighna-dhvaṃso bhavaty eva | ato vaidike phala-niścayān maṅgale pravṛttiḥ | na ca vedâ-prāmāṇyam | samāpty-a-bhāvaś ca kvacit prācīna-vighna-bhūyastvāt, kvacin maṅgalân-antarôtpanna-vighnāt, kvacil lokâvagata-kāraṇâ-bhāvāt | prāripsita-vighna-dhvaṃsaś ca na maṅgalaṃ vinā | na ca prāyaścittena śaṅkita-vighna-vināśaḥ | vighna-saṃśaye tad-an-upadeśāt | na ca kāmanôpādhi-kartavyatve niyatam anuṣṭhānaṃ na syād iti vācyam | ārabdha-karma-kāraṇa-pratibandhakâ-bhāvôpāyatvena a-vaśyaṃ tad-anuṣṭhānāt | tena vinā pratibandhakâ-bhāvâ-bhāvāt karmân-utpatteḥ | na ca pradhānatvena anyadā api tat-karaṇam | niyata-samaya-śiṣṭâcārânumita-śrutyā karmârambha-samaye tat-kartavyatva-bodhanāt darśârambha-samaye ārambhaṇīyā-vat | vighna-saṃsargâ-bhāvaś ca samāpti-hetuḥ | sa ca kvacit svataḥ-siddhaḥ kvacin maṅgala-sādhyaḥ | ata eva maṅgalaṃ vinā api janmântarânuvartamāna-vighnâtyantâ-bhāvāt pramatta-nāstikânuṣṭhita-samāptiḥ | na ca an-adhyavasāyaḥ | śaṅkita-vighna-vāraṇârthaṃ pravṛttir ato yāvad-vighna-śaṅkaṃ tad-ācaraṇāt | ata eva tac-chaṅkayā madhye 'pi tad ācaranti | gurv-ārambhe 'pi bahu-vighna-śaṅkayā bahu-maṅgalâcaraṇam | yathā ca vighna-saṃśaye 'pi pravṛttis tathā uktam eva |

(**Gaṅgeśa** continues:) From each and every *maṅgala*, whether large (or long) or not, together with such auxiliaries as praising a divinity, there is in fact destruction of obstacles. Hence, performing *maṅgala* is a Vedic act (i.e., proclaimed by the Veda, albeit by the "unheard" Veda, there being an inference thereto), effort toward which proceeds from certainty about the result. And it is not the case that the Veda would prove unauthoritative here.

And lack of completion is due sometimes to the extent of the obstacles that already existed, sometimes to an obstacle that arises after the doing of something auspicious, sometimes to lack of some commonly known causal factor (necessary to a work's completion). And without *maṅgala*, what is desired to be begun would face obstacles that would not be destroyed. Furthermore, expiational acts do not destroy dubious obstacles, since we have received no teaching concerning doubt about obstacles.

And it should not be said that what is to be done is qualified by a certain desire ("May there be no obstacle"), such that the practice would not be universally called for. Inasmuch as it is a means to achieve an absence of blockers, which *is* a cause of the proceeding of work begun, necessarily is it to be practiced. Without it, because of an absence of an absence of blockers, the work would not be produced.

And it is not the case that as the principal act it is being performed at other times as well (in addition to the beginning of an undertaking). For, the governing scripture is inferred from the (Vedically) cultured's behavior, behavior occurring at a fixed time. Scripture makes it known that it should be performed at the time of commencing a work. Similarly, on the occasion of a *darśa* (new-moon) sacrifice, the *ārambhaṇīyā* sacrifice (is to be performed first and only at the beginning).

Furthermore, relational absence of obstacles is a cause of completion.

And such relational absence is sometimes established by someone's own nature; sometimes it is accomplished by doing something auspicious. Just for this reason, even without doing something auspicious, because of an absolute absence of obstacles remaining in force from a previous birth, there is completion of what has been undertaken by those heedless of *maṅgala* or by those who reject Vedic culture.

And there need be no lack of resolution. Effort proceeds for the purpose of avoiding (even) dubious obstacles; hence so long as (or, as much as) there is worry about possible obstacles, that is to be performed.

Just for this reason, some perform it even in the middle of an undertaking (and not only at the beginning), because of doubt about such possible obstacles. Also, upon commencing something weighty (a proposed thick book, for instance), one performs many *maṅgala*s, out of worry about there being many obstacles. And as even in the face of worry about obstacles effort proceeds, so (too with *maṅgala*)—this has already this been explained.

Comments

If performing *maṅgala* were the principal act with respect to completing, e.g., a book, it would be done throughout the process instead of, presumably, making effort at writing, etc.

See above, p. 56, for a discussion of relational absence in this context. Here the main point is that while doing something auspicious is not itself a direct cause of completion, it helps to put into place all the factors—including certain relational absences—that together cause completion. In other words, *maṅgala* helps to bring about an entire relational absence of obstacles which is, along with commonly known, worldly factors, necessary and sufficient to a result. Such relational absence is, we should note, a richer notion than a mere destruction, which would amount to, even if the destruction were entire, only a posterior absence, to use the technical terms of Gaṅgeśa's system. We shall learn more about the causal roles of absences as we proceed.

Mathurānātha elaborates "lack of resolution" as wondering how much *maṅgala* to perform or what kind of *maṅgala*.

Gaṅgeśa refers to an earlier explanation of effort in the face of such worry (above, p. 42, explained by the "advocate"). Elsewhere he says, however, that doubt or worry normally does indeed block effort.

Text (p. 96, Tirupati) and Translation

syād etat | maṅgalam ācared iti vidhau kiṃ maṅgalatvam | na tāvad devatā-stuty-āditvam, an-anugamāt | na api prāripsita-pratibandhaka-vighnôpaśama-hetu-kriyātvam, vighnôtsāraṇâ-sādhāraṇa-kāraṇatvaṃ vā | kriyā-viśeṣasya tad-a-sādhāraṇa-kāraṇasya vā stuty-āder vedād viśiṣṭâ-paricaye pravṛtti-viṣayâ-lābhāt | na api nirvighnaṃ samāpyatām iti kāmanayā śiṣṭācāra-viṣayatvam, vedasya ācārân-upajīvakatvāt, vedād ādyâcārân-upapatteś ca, anyonyâśrayāt | na api tat-kāmanayā veda-vihitatvam, prāripsita-karma-nirvāhakatve sati karmârambha-kāle vihita-vaidika-karmatvaṃ vā, tādṛśa-vedântarâ-bhāvāt | na api smṛty-ādau maṅgalatvena utkīrtitatvam | vedasya smṛty-an-upajīvakatvāt | smṛti-kartur eva vedād ādyâcārân-upapatteś ca | ucyate | maṅgalam ācared iti na vidhiḥ | kiṃ tu nirvighna-samāpti-kāmo devatā-stutim ācared ity-ādi pratyekam eva vidhiḥ | tathā eva śiṣṭācārāt | tad-upajīvya nirvighnam ārabdhaṃ parisamāpyatām iti kāmanayā tad-vighnôpaśama-hetutvena vā veda-vihitatvaṃ maṅgalatvam ity adhigamya devatā-stuti-namaskārâdiṣu maṅgala-vyavahāraḥ śiṣṭānām iti | ata eva durita-nāśakam api gaṅgā-snānâdi na maṅgalaṃ | tathā a-vidhānāt | "maṅgalâcāra-yuktānām nityaṃ ca prayatâtmanām | japatāṃ juhvatāṃ ca eva vinipāto na vidyate ||" ity anena bodhita-ādarśa-darśanâdeḥ pṛthag eva maṅgalatvam, na tu vighna-nivartakatayā, tatra nānârthatā eva | anyathā granthârambhe namaskāra-tulyatayā tat-karaṇa-prasaṅgaḥ |

Objection: That may be. But with respect to the (inferred) injunction, "May *maṅgala* be performed," what is it to be *maṅgala*?

It is not, first of all, (D^1) to be a hymn to a divinity and so forth, since that would not be uniform.

Nor is it (D^2) to be an activity that brings to rest obstacles that would block what is desired to be begun; nor (D^3) to be the "uncommon cause" (the proximate instrumental cause when employed) of driving away obstacles. For, as a particular type of activity, or as the uncommon cause of that (destruction of obstacles), a hymn and so forth are (unknown; i.e., are) outside the acquaintance of what is characterized in the Veda, and so they could not be known as the object of effort (as you suppose they are with your inferred Vedic injunction).

Nor is it (D^4) to be the object of behavior of the (Vedically) cultured as expressed by the desire, "Free of obstacles, may this be completed." For, the Veda is not dependent on behavior, and no original behavior (founding the practice of *maṅgala*) could possibly be drawn from the Veda, because of (an impossible) mutual dependence.

Nor is it (D^5) to be what is enjoined by the Veda with respect to a person having a desire for destruction of obstacles; nor (D^6) Vedic acts enjoined for the time of beginning a work, given that there is motivation to complete the work desired to be begun. For (that would presuppose that there is such a Vedic injunction but) there is no such additional Veda.

Nor (D^7) to be what is proclaimed as *maṅgala* in (secondarily authoritative) *smṛti* texts (the laws of Manu, the epics, and so on), for the Veda is not dependent on *smṛti*, and no original behavior (founding the practice of *maṅgala*) could possibly be drawn from the Veda by the authors of *smṛti*.

Gaṅgeśa: We answer. "Let *maṅgala* be performed," is not the injunction. Rather (there is no common form of *maṅgala*, which, if there were, we would need to define, but) "Let one who desires a completion free from obstacles make a hymn to a divinity" and the like, is each, individually, the injunction. Just so (is there inference) from the behavior of the (Vedically) cultured. Depending on that (the inferred specific Vedic injunction, that is to say, given that a person has comprehended a specific injunction), to be *maṅgala* is to be what has been enjoined by the (inferred) Veda—either (as held by earlier Naiyāyikas) in accordance with the desire, "May what has been begun be entirely completed, free from obstacles," or (as is the view endorsed here) in the form of a cause of the death of obstacles to that. With such understanding, there is the common practice of the (Vedically) cultured in making a hymn to a divinity, honoring one, and the like.

Just for this reason, bathing in the Gaṅgā (Ganges) and the like, although destructive of sins, are not *maṅgala*, since they are not similarly enjoined.

"And for those constantly engaged in the practice of *maṅgala*, whose minds are disciplined, who do *japa* (recitation of mantras and prayers), and indeed who make oblations, calamity does not occur." This (*smṛti* text) declares that looking at a divine image and so forth are, just individually, doing something auspicious—but not *as* bringing an end to obstacles. There *maṅgala* has in fact a variety of meanings. Otherwise (if *maṅgala* were to be understood univocally as bringing about an end to obstacles, then performing it would be) the same as doing honor to a divinity and those acts would be done (too)—this is the difficulty.

Comments

In addition to reciting or composing a hymn to a divinity, some activities that by common practice are taken to be *maṅgala* are: bowing to a divinity, offering flowers, etc., and repeating certain sacred words such as *om*.

The notion of the "uncommon cause," or "proximate instrumental cause (in employment)" (*a-sādhāraṇa-kāraṇa* = *karaṇa*), is crucial to explanatory projects, as noted in the introduction (above, p. 24).

The problem expressed concerning D^2 and D^3 trades on a need to have a prior acquaintance with *maṅgala*. To know that to do something auspicious is to do something that destroys obstacles does not tell us at all concretely what sort of action this might be.

D^4 would appear to address the problem, but the circularity involved in inferring a Vedic injunction from behavior, and in turn, viewing the behavior as Vedically enjoined, rears its head. Furthermore, the meaning of the Veda is not determined by people's behavior.

D^5 and D^6 assume known Vedic injunctions, but, as Rucidatta points out, there is no evidence for such.

The quoted *smṛti* text is the *Mānava-dharma-śāstra*.[5]

Gaṅgeśa's main point appears to be that only certain actions called *maṅgala* are performed—and are appropriately performed—on the occasion of beginning an enterprise such as writing a book. Other activities are, however, also designated *maṅgala*, but they are not to be regarded as universally having the effect of removing obstacles.

Text (p. 101, Tirupati) and Translation

atha-śabdo vighna-nivartakatvān maṅgalam eva | "oṃ-kāraś ca atha-śabdaś ca dvāv etau brahmaṇaḥ purā | kaṇṭhaṃ bhittvā viniryātau tena māṅgalikāv ubhau |" iti smṛteḥ | na ca śubha-sūcakatvam eva tasya, śāstrârambhe mah-arṣinā tad-an-upādāna-prasaṅgāt | guṇavattayā jñāpanaṃ stutiḥ | yam uddiśya yasya svâpakarṣa-bodhanânukūlo vyāpāra-viśeṣaḥ sa tasya namas-kāraḥ | vyāpāre ca kāyika-vācika-mānasika-rūpe viśeṣo jāti-viśeṣa eva anubhava-sākṣikaḥ | kara-śiras-saṃyoga-mātre tad-a-vyavahārāt, bhavato 'ham apakṛṣṭa ity-ādi-vacane tad-a-vyavahārāc ca |

(**Gaṅgeśa** continues:) The word, *atha* ("now"), is in fact a *maṅgala* in that it brings an end to obstacles. "The syllable, *oṃ*, and the word, *atha*, these two were the Absolute Brahman's in the beginning. Splitting the throat, the two emerged. Therefore, both are *maṅgala*." So says *smṛti*.

And the word *atha* is not used only to express happiness (or a wish for good fortune and not also to destroy obstacles). For, that would have the contrary ramification that the great seer-sage (Kaṇāda, the author of the *Vaiśeṣika-sūtra*) would not have used it at the beginning of his textbook.

Hymning (*stuti*) is the making known (of a divinity) as having positive qualities.

Doing honor (*namas-kāra*) is a particular action (or "exertion," *vyāpāra*), expressly directed to that divinity to whom it is directed in conformity with showing inferior position. As a particular, the action is directly experienced as of a particular type taking bodily, verbal, and mental forms. For, merely touching the head with the hands is not the practice of doing honor; and saying, "I am your inferior," is not the practice of that.

Comments

The *Vaiśeṣika-sūtra* begins: *atha ato dharmaṃ vyākhyāsyāmaḥ.*

A textual reason to regard this section as a separate treatise by Gaṅgeśa, distinct from the *TCM*, is that the first word in the following section, on veridicality—which would be the true beginning of the *TCM*, as discussed above—is *atha*. Here we would have a separate explanation of such an opening.

Text (p. 104, Tirupati, and p. 104, Calcutta) and Translation

yad vā kāyikâdau pratyekam eva vidhi-kalpanam ato nānârthatā eva | yat tu, buddhi-viśeṣa-pūrvakatva-jñānaṃ vinā kāyikâdau na tad-vyavahāra iti sa eva vācyo 'nyatra lakṣaṇā iti, tan na | kāyikâdi-vyāpāra-viśeṣam an-avagamya buddhi-viśeṣa-pūrvakatvâ-jñānāt |

(**Gaṅgeśa** continues:) Alternatively, with respect to the bodily and so on (ways of doing honor), each one is in fact (to be imagined as enjoined if it is being practiced). Therefore, indeed, is a variety of meanings possible.

Objection: But without a cognition that is the particular thought (of inferiority with respect to a divinity honored) preceding any action, the bodily and so on are not the practice of doing honor. Therefore, that alone should be said (when a definition is given). The other is a matter of secondary meaning.

Gaṅgeśa: No. For, without having first comprehended the particular action, i.e., the bodily action and so on (that is doing honor), there would be no awareness of a particular preceding thought.

Comments

The thought is to be inferred from the sight of someone performing the particular actions of bowing, etc. Gaṅgeśa is insisting on a third-person or externalist approach.

Text (p. 106, Calcutta) and Translation

svīkṛta-veda-pramāṇa-bhāvaḥ śiṣṭaḥ | ācāre ca vedâ-niṣiddhatvam a-vigītatvaṃ viśeṣaṇaṃ deyam | yad vā a-laukika-viṣaya-śiṣṭâcāratvam eva hetuḥ | śiṣṭâcāratvaṃ ca bhramâ-janyâcāratvam | āstika-nāstikayor a-gamyâgamana-caitya-vandanâdāv ācāra-janaka-jñānasya bhramatvāt balavad an-iṣṭânubandhitvād iṣṭâ-sādhanatvāc ca | loke ca pākhaṇḍa-vyāvṛtta-śiṣṭa-vyavahāro veda-prāmāṇyâbhyupagama-nibandhanaḥ | tairthikatve 'pi śiṣṭâ-śiṣṭa-vyavahāro veda-niṣiddhâ-kartṛtva-tat-kartṛtva-nibandhanaḥ | yad vā veda-prāmāṇyâbhyupagantṛtve sati yo yadā veda-niṣiddhâ-kartā sa tadā śiṣṭaḥ tat-kartā tv a-śiṣṭaḥ | ata eva veda-niṣiddhâ-kartṛtve 'pi bauddho na śiṣṭaḥ | pāpa-janakatva-jñānaṃ vinā veda-niṣiddha-kartṛtvaṃ yasya na asti sa śiṣṭa iti tu na | tairthikasya api kasyacit pāpa-janaka-jñānaṃ vinā veda-niṣiddha-kartṛtvāt |

(**Gaṅgeśa** continues:) To be "(Vedically) cultured" is to accept the Veda as an authority.

And concerning the behavior (of the Vedically cultured, from which a Vedic injunction about doing something auspicious is inferred), a qualification has to be given: behavior that is not (expressly) prohibited by the Veda, that is, not (expressly) contradicted.

Alternatively, the prover (in the inference to the Vedic injunction) is just "being behavior of the (Vedically) cultured whose object is other-worldly (*a-laukika*)."

And behavior of the (Vedically) cultured is behavior that is not produced by error. Since, for example, approaching a woman who is not to be approached, stupa worship, or the like, whether on the part of those who accept the Veda or those who do not, is behavior produced by erroneous cognition, it is connected with what we ardently do not want and would not establish what we want (by way of inferring Vedic injunctions).

And in everyday discourse, behavior of the cultured excludes that of heretics; that is to say, it is behavior grounded in an acceptance of the Veda as an authority. Even in the discourse of those who know sacred texts, whether behavior is of the cultured or of the non-cultured is grounded in whether the agency has been prohibited or not by the Veda.

Alternatively, among those who accept the Veda as an authority, someone in doing something not prohibited by the Veda, then in that instance is he cultured, but when he does something prohibited, he is not cultured. By these lights, a Buddhist, although not doing anything prohibited by the Veda, is not cultured.

But the following (definition) is wrong: the cultured is a person who, without an awareness of an action's producing sin, does not do what is prohibited by the Veda. For, just anyone who happens to know sacred texts and who, without an awareness of an action's producing sin, does not (in fact) do what is prohibited by the Veda would count as cultured.

Comments

A Jaina or a Buddhist might know some of the sacred texts, and might not do anything prohibited by the Veda, and might never act thinking that the particular type of action produces sin. Nevertheless, such a heretic would not count as "cultured."

Text (p. 111, Tirupati) and Translation

yat tu rāga-dveṣa-hīnaḥ śiṣṭaḥ | sa ca sarvajñatvān manv-ādir eva | a-vigīta-tad-ācārād eva vedânumānam iti | tan na | evaṃ hi manv-ādy-ācārâ-darśinām ādhunikānāṃ maṅgale pravṛttir na syāt | ādhunikānām ācāreṇa manv-ādy-ācāram anumāya tena ca vedam anumāya bālaḥ pravartata iti cet, tarhi yādṛśâcāreṇa manv-ādyâcārânumānaṃ sa eva vedânumāpako 'stu, kim anumitânumānena | ādhunikānām api śiṣṭatvena vyavahriyamānatvāc ca | tathā ca smṛtiḥ, "yasmin deśe ya ācāraḥ pāraṃparya-kramâgataḥ | śruti-smṛty-a-virodhena sad-ācāraḥ sa ucyate ||" sarvajñasya maṅgalâcāre mānâ-bhāvāc ca | manv-ādi-praṇīta-smṛtau maṅgalaṃ dṛśyata iti cet, tan na | smṛti-kartur a-sarvajñatve 'pi vedād arthaṃ pratītya smṛti-praṇaya-saṃbhavāt | yat tu śiṣṭâcāratvena kartavyatā eva anumīyatāṃ kiṃ vedena iti tatra vakṣyāmaḥ |

Objection: But to be cultured is to be free of passion and hatred. And such a one is so because of knowledge of all (true principles, or, the self), like Manu and company. Just from their uncontradicted behavior is there inference to a Vedic injunction to do *maṅgala*.

Gaṅgeśa: Wrong. For, if so, since people living now have not witnessed the behavior of Manu and company, they would not make effort to do *maṅgala*.

Objection: From the behavior of people living now the behavior of Manu and company is inferred, and through that inferred behavior the Vedic injunction to do *maṅgala* is inferred. So a child can make effort (to do *maṅgala*).

Gaṅgeśa: Then (what you are claiming is that) by such behavior as founds the inference to the behavior of Manu and company would there be in fact a basis for inferring the Vedic injunction to do *maṅgala*. So what would be the point of (the extra inference, i.e., of) an inference to what is (anyhow) inferred? Moreover, some people living now are cultured according to identification in everyday life (i.e., some are commonly referred to as cultured).

And so there is the *smṛti* verse: "That behavior in whatever place that has come down in uninterrupted succession and that is not contradicted by the Veda (*śruti*) or *smṛti* is known as right behavior."

Furthermore, there is no evidence for the assumption that anyone knows all (true principles) with respect to the practice of *maṅgala*.

Objection: Yes, there is, in the *smṛti* composed by Manu and company.

Gaṅgeśa: Wrong. Even without the authors of *smṛti* knowing all (true principles), they were able to compose *smṛti* in comprehending meanings from the Veda.

Objection: But, given (as you have said, the express injunction) "May what is to be done be inferred from the behavior of the (Vedically) cultured," what's the use of an (inferred) Vedic injunction?

Gaṅgeśa: We shall answer this later (in the fourth and final chapter of the *TCM*).

Comments

Several early Upaniṣads declare that a person who knows the true self knows everything and is free of passion and hatred.[6]

We have been unable to identify the *smṛti*. But the phrase quoted in it, "that has come down in uninterrupted succession," can be interpreted as "proven by experience." Compare what John Stuart Mill says in *Utilitarianism*, "During all that time mankind have been learning by experience the tendencies of actions; on which experience all the prudence as well as the morality of life are dependent."[7]

The answer to the last objection—which Gaṅgeśa says he will deal with later (namely, in the *śabda-khaṇḍa*)—hinges on the other-worldly medium of *maṅgala*'s causality. This is, by the way, the passage that is the best evidence, as mentioned earlier, for the thesis that the *maṅgala-vāda* is integral to the *TCM*.

pratyakṣa-khaṇḍaḥ

THE PERCEPTION CHAPTER[1]

atha prāmāṇya-vādaḥ

NOW, ON VERIDICALITY

tatra jñapti-vādaḥ

WITHIN THAT DISCOURSE, **DISCOURSE ON KNOWING VERIDICALITY**

Text (p. 114, Tirupati, and p. 114, Calcutta) and Translation

atha jagad eva duḥkha-paṅka-nimagnam uddidhīrṣur aṣṭādaśa-vidyā-sthāneṣv abhyarhitatamām ānvīkṣikīṃ parama-kāruṇiko muniḥ praṇināya | tatra prekṣāvat-pravṛtty-arthaṃ pramāṇâdi-ṣoḍaśa-padārthānāṃ tattva-jñānān niḥśreyasâdhigamaḥ ity-ādāv asūtrayat | teṣv api pramāṇâdhīnā sarveṣāṃ vyavasthitir iti pramāṇa-tattvam atra vivicyate |

Gaṅgeśa: Now, intending to raise up the world itself, which is mired in the mud of suffering, the supremely compassionate sage (Gautama, the author of the *Nyāya-sūtra*) established the most honored of the eighteen sciences, critical philosophy (*ānvīkṣikī*, i.e., Nyāya).

To that end, he composed a *sūtra*, an instructive aphorism, in order to motivate the astute, at the beginning (of his text): "From knowledge of the nature of the sixteen (aforementioned) topics, beginning with *sources of knowledge* (*pramāṇa*), comes the supreme good." Determination of each and every one of those topics depends on sources of knowledge. Therefore, the nature of the sources is examined here.

Comments[2]

The compassionate sage referred to in the opening sentence is Gautama, the author of the *Nyāya-sūtra*, Nyāya's root text. The eighteen sciences are explained by Mathurānātha as: the four Vedas, the six auxiliaries to the Vedas (*vedâṅga*: the science of grammatical elements, rules on ritual, grammar, etymology, prosody, and astronomy), the four sub-auxiliaries (*upāṅga*: Mīmāṃsā, Nyāya, Dharma-śāstra, and Purāṇa), and then medicine, archery, music, and politics.

The quotation is an abridgment of *Nyāya-sūtra* 1.1.1, which also lists the sixteen principal topics of the text. In identifying sources of knowledge as "foundational" in an extended sense of the term, Gaṅgeśa follows Vātsyāyana (c. 450), whose *Nyāya-sūtra* commentary is the oldest extant.

Text (p. 115, Tirupati) and Translation

nanu pramāṇâdīnāṃ tattvaṃ pratipādayac chāstraṃ param-parayā niḥśreyasena sambadhyate iti na yuktaṃ, pramāṇa-tattvâvadhāraṇasya a-śakyatvāt | tad dhi pramā-tattvâvadhāraraṇâdhīnam | tac ca svataḥ parato vā na sambhavati, vakṣyamāṇa-dūṣaṇa-gaṇa-grāsāt |

Objector.1: That a scientific text (*śāstra*) propounding the nature of sources of knowledge, etc., is connected as a link in a causal sequence to the supreme good is not correct, since the nature of such sources cannot be determined. For that would depend on determining the nature of veridical cognition, and that (in turn) is not possible, either intrinsically (i.e., within a given cognition, as Mīmāṃsakas say) or extrinsically (by another cognition, as Naiyāyikas hold), because one would be eaten up (like the moon by Rāhu) by hordes of faults, as will be explained.

Comments

Both Rucidatta and Mathurānātha say that objector.1 is a Mādhyamika Buddhist, a skeptic about veridicality and epistemological projects in general. But whether a Mādhyamika or not, the objector is not immediately answered. In fact, Gaṅgeśa's response could be taken to occupy the section as a whole.

Now as explained in the introduction, the word "knowledge" in English can render only in a rough and colloquial way Sanskrit *pramā*; normally, "veridical cognition" is a better rendering, and likewise, "sources of veridical cognition" better than "knowledge sources." Nevertheless, to speak of knowledge sources, etc., is often convenient, and this translation aims at a mix of the colloquial and technical. When English "knowledge" is used, however, one must not fail to keep in mind that the chief issue is the nature of veridicality—paradigmatically, a perceptual awareness's characterizing its object as it is in fact—not of the truth of a proposition believed in.

Another translational difficulty is that often the term, *jñāna*, "cognition," is used where *anubhava*, "awareness," would seem better. In Gaṅgeśa's view, all awarenesses are cognitions. Rememberings are cognitions but not awarenesses. An inferential veridical cognition is an awareness, as indeed is every type of cognition that is a candidate for veridicality, in Gaṅgeśa's view. Rememberings require a distinct epistemological analysis, as we learn at the very end of the chapter. Every veridical cognition is a veridical awareness.

Correct rememberings are not as reliable as right awarenesses, and thus do not qualify for veridicality though they can be "in conformity with the object." However, in *pūrva-pakṣa* sections Gaṅgeśa's conceptual divisions are not to be taken as presupposed. Here usually the term, *jñāna*, is translated "cognition," and, for the time being, *pramā* as "veridical cognition," since, at least in this early section, *jñāna* is Gaṅgeśa's term for that which can be veridical or non-veridical. In the section on defining veridicality, he switches to *anubhava*, "awareness."

Text (p. 116, Tirupati) and Translation

atha kiṃ prāmāṇya-jñānena | pravṛtti-mātre tasya vyabhicārāt bahu-vitta-vyayāyāsa-sādhye pravṛttiś ca āvaśyakârtha-niścayād eva | na ca yat-saṃśaya-vyatireka-niścayau yasya pravṛtti-bandhakau tan-niścayas tad-dhetur anumitau vyāpter iva iti vācyam | tat-sandehe saty artha-sandehena arthâ-niścayād eva a-pravṛtteḥ tatra tayor a-pratibandhakatvād iti cet, na | prāmāṇya-saṃśayân-antaraṃ idaṃ ittham eva ity avadhāraṇasya niṣkampa-pravṛtty-aṅgasya prāmāṇya-niścayâdhīnatvāt |

Objector.2: Now, what is the point of cognizing veridicality? Simply with respect to making effort to act, there is no invariable connection with veridicality being cognized (i.e., some actions are undertaken without such cognition). Further, activity to accomplish something with expenditure of much wealth and effort does come from certainty about the necessary *object* (but not about veridicality).

Objection (against objector.2): If it is true that either doubt about some cognition x or certainty about its negation means that effort toward something y is blocked, then certainty about the x is a reason for effort concerning the y, like an inference occurring from (cognition of) a pervasion.

Answer (by objector.2): That should not be said. For, given doubt about that (the cognition's veridicality) because of doubt about its object, it is only uncertainty about the object that accounts for a lack of effort to act; the two together (uncertainty about the object and uncertainty about the cognition's veridicality) are not what block the effort.

Gaṅgeśa: No. Following doubt about veridicality, that there be the ascertainment, "This is in fact such and such," which is a component of unhesitating effort to act, depends on certainty about veridicality.

Comments

Objector.2, whom Rucidatta says is neutral (*taṭa-stha*), not a disputant with a particular position to defend, fails from Gaṅgeśa's perspective to see the importance of certainty about veridicality to one's making effort after there has been doubt. The objection may be taken as a second standing challenge that Gaṅgeśa will answer by the end of the section. Though Gaṅgeśa does reply in this case right away, the position is not elaborated quite yet. And argumentwise the claim that once we have doubt we need certainty about veridicality to proceed unhesitatingly will show itself to have decisive phenomenological clout against Mīmāṃsakas.

But Gaṅgeśa does not wield the weapon until the next half section, the *siddhânta* (beginning on p. 86, below), where the focus is on his own views, not in this half, which is a *pūrva-pakṣa* (see the glossary entry), although there are a few sentences with Gaṅgeśa speaking in his own voice.

Next, we encounter the true *pūrvapakṣin*, the dominant voice of the subsection, a Mīmāṃsaka who advocates the view that knowledge of veridicality is intrinsic to the knowledge that a cognition has occurred, or is occurring, as opposed to a Naiyāyika extrinsicality view.

Historically, the intrinsicality/extrinsicality controversy flows from the issue of Vedic authority. If the information cognized upon understanding a Vedic sentence—a kind of testimonial cognition like a perceptual cognition, etc.—can be established as intrinsically veridical, then the Mīmāṃsaka gains his fundamental point: the Veda has authority. This, in turns, sanctions the priestly—i.e., Vedic—teaching of *dharma*, "right religious practice," the right conduct of life. In the current section, the issue of Vedic authority never surfaces. But it does in the next even though the main topic is production of veridical perception, not knowledge from testimony. This shows that Gaṅgeśa has not himself lost sight of the dispute about scripture. Nevertheless, in this section the intrinsicality/extrinsicality debate is fought out with no mention of testimony or the Veda. The paradigmatic veridical cognition is an awareness that is the result of perception as the knowledge means.

Text (p. 124, Tirupati) and Translation

nanu svataḥ eva astu tan-nirūpaṇam |

Pūrvapakṣin: Let the determination of that (veridicality) be just from itself (i.e., intrinsically to the occurrence of a cognition).

Comments

This is the core of the Mīmāṃsaka position, common, as will be explained, to three subcamps. That is, the *pūrvapakṣin* will defend each of three variations of the position, and he is not to be identified with any single Mīmāṃsaka faction. He keeps all three in view.

Next comes what is famed as the "five options," questions used by Gaṅgeśa to engage debate between the various Mīmāṃsaka intrinsicality theorists, on the one hand, and the extrinsicality view of the Nyāya that he has inherited and will champion (and modify), on the other. Here it is immaterial to identify a voice or perspective since the passage is comprised mainly of questions, though, if we wish, we may take the voice to be Gaṅgeśa's, alternatively, the *pūrvapakṣin*'s.

Text (Tirupati, p. 124, and p. 121, Calcutta) and Translation

tathā hi vipratipattayaḥ | jñāna-prāmāṇyam tad-a-prāmāṇyâ-grāhaka-yāvaj-jñāna-grāhaka-sāmagrī-grāhyaṃ na vā | tad-jñāna-viṣayaka-jñānâ-janya-jñāna-grāhyaṃ na vā | parataḥ pakṣe jñāta eva jñāne prāmāṇya-grahaḥ svataṣtve prāmāṇyavata eva jñānasya grahāt |

For so there are the mutually exclusive options: (a) Is a cognition's veridicality to be grasped, or not, invariably (*yāvat*) through the collection of causal conditions that gives rise to a grasping of the cognition and not to a grasping of non-veridicality? (b) Is it (i.e., the veridicality of a first cognition) to be grasped, or not, by a cognition that is not produced by a cognition whose object is that (first) cognition? On the view (that a cognition's veridicality is cognized) by another (cognition), veridicality is grasped only when the cognition itself is cognized. On the intrinsicality view, cognition is grasped by itself as possessing veridicality.

Comments

Five such incompatible options (or even seven by a different count) are stated by way of spelling out what is at stake in the dispute over veridicality between Mīmāṃsā and Nyāya. J. N. Mohanty (1989) explains the alternatives, drawing on the commentaries of Raghunātha, Gadādhara, and others, and differentiating among three Mīmāṃsaka theories of intrinsicality: the Prābhākara, the Bhāṭṭa, and the less well-known view of Murāri Miśra (whom Gaṅgeśa does not mention by name).[3] Mohanty's discussion is excellent. It is commonly acknowledged, however, that the classical commentators sometimes overinterpret Gaṅgeśa's questions. Much in their long discussions is *innovative* philosophically. In any case, a few of the more salient points are as follows.

The first two questions address the heart of the Mīmāṃsā view: despite important differences, all the Mīmāṃsaka theorists uphold the thesis that the causal conditions giving rise to awareness of a cognition x also give rise to awareness of x's veridicality. That is to say, to register a cognition is to register it as correct. Cognition is by nature veridical (error requires special explanation), and however a cognition comes to be itself known (here there are divergencies within Mīmāṃsā), its veridicality is known in the same way, indeed, in the same event, as that in which the cognition itself is known. Naiyāyikas deny this.

The second question further sharpens the issue between Mīmāṃsā and Nyāya. According to Nyāya, the standard way that a cognition's veridicality is grasped is by an inference from success of effort based on the cognition. Such an inference requires that the cognition itself be cognized—by another cognition. But it does not require that the target be cognized as veridical. That would be the result not of the target's being cognized but of the inference. A noticing cognition of a target cognition is called an apperception (*anuvyavasāya*). An apperception, according to Nyāya, is produced in part by the target cognition that is its object. Mainstream Mīmāṃsaka views have it that veridicality is grasped by a cognition that is *not* produced by a target cognition. That is to say, within the two more prominent Mīmāṃsaka camps, those of Kumārila and Prabhākara, apperception is deemed irrelevant. Again, Nyāya does not hold that an apperception need be the grasper of veridicality, but only that an apperception is required for the very question of a cognition's veridicality to arise—that is, again, in the standard way veridicality is known (in another way, as will be explained, apperception is involved more crucially). The third Mīmāṃsaka camp, that of Murāri Miśra, agrees with the Naiyāyika here that apperception is called for, but disagrees that an inference could be necessary, too.

To help us keep in mind the four views, the following table is offered in the spirit of Gaṅgeśa's questions. The aim is to highlight differences among the three Mīmāṃsaka positions perhaps better than his questions.[4] (Gaṅgeśa is mainly concerned with contrasts with Nyāya, not so much with differences among the other views.) (1) Only Nyāya denies that the cognition whereby a cognition is known need grasp it as veridical. (2) Nyāya is joined by the Murāri faction in holding that the cognition that takes a cognition as object is another cognition, an apperception. (3) Nyāya disagrees with the Murāri camp and joins with the others in denying that an apperception is necessary to know a cognition as veridical, although, from the Nyāya perspective, usually the knowledge source (inference) would presuppose apperception (an exception is the inferential knowledge "Every cognition is knowable" which is self-inclusive with no need of apperception). (4) Only the Prābhākara asserts that every cognition is self-known as veridical. (5) Only the Bhāṭṭas (followers of Kumārila) assert that a cognition is known to occur only through an inference that concurrently knows it as veridical. (6) Only the Naiyāyika claims that the standard way a cognition is known to be veridical is by an inference from success of effort prompted by the cognition (although there are also other inferential ways that veridicality can be grasped, Gaṅgeśa argues, as will be explained).

proponent →	Prābhākara	Bhāṭṭa	Murāri M.	Naiyāyika
(1) Does the cognition that grasps a cognition (whether itself or another) grasp it as veridical?	Y	Y	Y	N
(2) Is a cognition grasped by a second apperceptive awareness?	N	N	Y	Y
(3) To be known as veridical does a cognition require an apperception that grasps it as veridical?	N	N	Y	N
(4) Does every cognition grasp itself and its own veridicality?	Y	N	N	N
(5) Is a cognition grasped by an inference and thereby known to be veridical?	N	Y	N	N
(6) Is a veridical cognition normally so known by an inference based on successful effort?	N	N	N	Y

Text (p. 166, Tirupati) and Translation

> svâśraya-grāhakeṇa gṛhyata eva na vā, svâśrayeṇa gṛhyata eva na vā iti pratyekam eva vā |

(c) Is veridicality just grasped, or not, by (a cognition's) grasping its (the veridicality's) locus? (d) Is it just grasped, or not, by its own locus? Would this hold in every case or not?

Comments

The next two options concern the locus of veridicality conceived as an entity, viz., the cognition that is veridical by way of being that in which veridicality resides. The Murāri Miśra view is that an apperception grasps both a target cognition and its veridicality. The Bhāṭṭas hold that the very inference that cognizes the occurrence of a target cognition also cognizes that cognition's veridicality. And on the Prābhākara view a cognition takes itself and its own veridicality as object as well as a thing in the world.

The third question, or option, engages the Murāri Miśra view by asking whether veridicality is known just by a cognition that takes the veridicality's locus as object. Naiyāyikas of course deny that veridicality can be so straightforwardly known, except in certain cases (more about which below).

The fourth question (or option, comprised of two questions) engages the Prābhākara position: Does a cognition grasp itself and its veridicality by its own locus? And is this true in every instance? Note that the Prābhākara case would appear stronger in instances of self-awareness, awareness of desire, and so on, than in instances of awareness of external objects.

Text (p. 171, Tirupati) and Translation

> yat tu yogaja-dharma-sāmānya-lakṣaṇa-pratyāsattyā svâśraya-prāmāṇyaṃ tena eva gṛhyata ity aṃśataḥ siddha-sādhanam ato yogaja-dharmâdy-a-janyatvaṃ viśeṣaṇam iti | tan na | paraṃ praty a-siddheḥ prāmāṇya-mātra-pakṣatve prāmāṇyaṃ svâśrayeṇa gṛhyata eva ity uddeśya-pratīter a-siddheś ca na aṃśataḥ siddha-sādhanam |

Objection: Whether through the ("extraordinary") relationality characteristic of yogic merit or of (unperceived instances of) universals, a cognition's veridicality is (sometimes) grasped (you Naiyāyikas yourselves say) in its own locus, just by itself—(inasmuch as you say as much) there would be, in part, the fallacy of "proving what is admitted" (i.e., Naiyāyikas advancing the Mīmāṃsaka thesis, *siddha-sādhana*). Thus, the qualification, "not through yogic merit, etc.," should be added.

Gaṅgeśa: That is wrong. For, with regard to the others (the Mīmāṃsakas) this is not admitted. Furthermore, veridicality in general (*mātra*) being the scope (of the Mīmāṃsā thesis), the proposition to be shown is not established (not admitted on all sides), namely, that veridicality is only grasped by its own locus. (Thus) there is not even in part a fallacy of trying to prove what is already admitted.

Comments

Naiyāyikas recognize (a) yogic perceptions that include themselves as object or content, as well as (b) cognitions such as "Cognition is knowable," which, as a token of the type, cognitionhood, is known in a self-referential, "self-illuminating" way. Furthermore, any future token of a confirmed cognition (as specified by its objecthood) would appear to be known to be veridical without extrinsic verification. An example would be my perceptual awareness of a garden hose coiled in the barn, which I have previously verified not to be a snake. (The first time I thought it looked like one I cautiously checked and now know immediately that my hose-cognition is veridical.) Thus because of endorsement of self-veridicality by Naiyāyikas, the issue about how veridicality is known needs, it seems, to be redrawn. However, Mīmāṃsakas do not themselves accept these views, Gaṅgeśa responds. Moreover, the thesis at issue is the position that *all* veridicality is cognized intrinsically. The Naiyāyika admissions fall far short of the Mīmāṃsaka universalist view. Thus, there is not the *siddha-sādhana* fallacy.

Text (p. 174, Tirupati) and Translation

yad vā ghaṭo 'yam iti jñāna-prāmāṇyaṃ etaj-jñāna-grāhyaṃ na vā | etaj-jñāna-grāhaka-mātra-grāhyaṃ na vā iti |

(Furthermore, there are the following questions:) (e) Whether or not the veridicality of a cognition, (e.g.) "This is a pot," is to be grasped by that cognition itself; (and) whether or not the veridicality is to be grasped solely by (the cognition) grasping that cognition (i.e., the one bearing the veridicality).

Comments

The first of this last set of incompatible options sharpens the issue between the Prābhākara and the Naiyāyika, the second between the Naiyāyika and the Murāri Miśra camp. Again, the Prābhākara position is that every cognition is self-aware and aware of its own veridicality within that self-awareness. The Murāri view posits an apperception that is aware of both a target cognition and its veridicality. Now, Naiyāyikas admit in certain cases an apperception does grasp both a target cognition and its veridicality: this happens, as explained, in yogic perceptions and in cases of generalizations of cognitions already discerned to be veridical. But these instances are exceptional. Gaṅgeśa formulates the dispute with the Murāri Miśra camp by asking whether it is *solely*, i.e., in all cases, that a cognition's veridicality is to be known by an apperceptive cognition grasping the cognition that is veridical.

Next, we are treated to what may be construed as a Naiyāyika attack on the possibility of the Mīmāṃsaka position in any of its forms: no definition of a veridical cognition accords with the intrinsicality view. As translated below, the Mīmāṃsaka *pūrvapakṣin* answers a long objection with a long response, but, in Sanskrit, the entire passage—three paragraphs in English—is connected as a single long sentence: "Although . . . , still . . . ." More specifically, the point is: these the following difficulties notwithstanding, veridicality can be defined so that the intrinsicality view is not so far ruled out.

Text (p. 174, Tirupati, and p. 126, Calcutta) and Translation

tatra yady api viśeṣyâ-vṛtty-a-prakārakatvaṃ a-gṛhīta-grāhitaṃ vā, sarva-dhī-yathârthatva-pakṣe 'nubhavatva-jāter a-bhāvena smaraṇânya-jñānatvaṃ viśiṣṭa-jñānatvaṃ vā prāmāṇyaṃ svasya na tena eva na vā anuvyavasāyena grahaṇa-yogyam | viśeṣyâ-vṛtty-a-prakārakatvâder viśeṣaṇasya prāg an-upastitau tad-vaiśiṣṭyasya jñātum a-śakyatvāt | na api jñānâtīndriyatve jñānânumityā tad gṛhyate |

jñāna-mātra-liṅgasya prākaṭyâdes tad-vyabhicārāt | na api pramā-hita-jñātatā-viśeṣāt, tasya prathamaṃ durnirūpatvāt | anyathā a-pramā-hita-jñātatayā a-prāmāṇyasya api svato grahâpattir iti | tathā api tadvati tat-prakāraka-jñānatvaṃ tadvati tad-vaiśiṣṭya-jñānatvaṃ vā prāmāṇyam | tan-niścayād eva niṣkampa-vyavahārāt, lāghavāt | na anyat gauravāt | tac ca jñāna-grāhaka-sāmagrī-grāhyam eva | tathā hi viśeṣye tad-dharmavattvam tad-dharma-prakārakatvaṃ ca vyavasāyasya anuvyavasāyena anumityā sva-prakāśena vā gṛhyate | viṣaya-nirūpyaṃ hi jñānam | ato jñāna-vitta-vedyo viṣaya iti vyavasâye bhāsamāne dharma-dharmi-vat tad-vaiśiṣṭyam api viṣayaḥ | vyavasāya-rūpa-pratyāsattes tulyatvāt |

Objection (against the Mīmāṃsaka *pūrvapakṣin*): In this regard (veridicality cannot be defined in accordance with an intrinsicality view of how it might be known) whether as (D^1) "being that (viz., a cognition) which does not have predication content (i.e., a presentation of something as *such and such*) that does not reside in the qualificandum (that a cognition determines, namely, the thing cognized)" or as (D^2) "being that (viz., a cognition) which grasps what has not been grasped previously," or, on the view that all cognition is "as things are" (*yathârtha*), (D^3) "being a cognition that is other than memory"—assuming that being an awareness is not a universal—(or, D^4) "being a cognition of an entity as qualified." (On all these definitions) veridicality would not be suitable for an intrinsic grasping, nor indeed by an apperception (that is posited by some). For, it would be impossible to cognize the relationality (that these definitions involve) beginning with (D^1) "being that (viz., a cognition) which does not have predication content that does not exist in the qualificandum," given that the qualifier has not been presented previously.

Nor on the assumption that cognition is supra-sensible would veridicality be grasped by an inference that grasped the cognition (that is veridical). For, there would be an (inference-undermining) deviation from veridicality on the part of the mark (or prover) of such cognition in general being manifest (i.e., the set of cognitions is wider than the set of veridical cognitions).

Nor would the inference proceed from a special kind of *cognizedness* (a putative basis for an inference to an occurrence of a target cognition) restricted to veridical cognitions. First, it would be difficult to determine that there is this special cognizedness. Moreover, assuming otherwise (i.e., that there is the special cognizedness), non-veridicality, too, as cognized through a cognizedness not restricted to veridical cognitions, would be grasped intrinsically—such would be the unfortunate ramification.

Pūrvapakṣin: Although (there are the problems mentioned with the definitions surveyed), nevertheless, veridicality is either (D^5), "to be a cognition with predication content about a ϕ-object as ϕ," or (D^6) "to be a cognition with a ϕ-relationality to a ϕ-object." For, just from certainty about this (i.e., veridicality so defined) is there unhesitating effort and activity in the everyday world; it is the parsimonious view; and any other would be (in comparison) cumbersome.

And veridicality is in fact grasped through the same collection of causal factors that produces a grasping of a cognition (that is veridical). In particular, (on all three Mīmāṃsaka views, whether) by an apperception of a target cognition, or by an inference, or by self-illumination, a fact of having that (ϕ) property respecting a qualificandum (viz., a ϕ-object) and the fact of the cognition's having predication content as that (ϕ) property are grasped. For, cognition is determined by its object. Hence, the object is known in the awareness of the cognition that is grasped.

Thus, like a property and property-bearer appearing in an original cognition (or target cognition), the relationality (between them) is also a cognitive object. For, through a sensory relation operative for a target cognition, the relationality is cognized in just the same way (that the qualificandum and qualifier of a target cognition are cognized).

Comments

The terms of cognitive analysis, "predication content" (*prakāra*), "qualifier" (*viśeṣaṇa*), and "qualificandum" (*viśeṣya*), were briefly explained in the introduction (above, pp. 14–16). The objector's opening argument hinges on lhe principle that a qualificandum is always known through a qualifier; for instance, the thing that is a pot is known as a pot through the qualifier, "being a pot." This is a principle that Gaṅgeśa defends in the section below on indeterminate perception, and it is presumed to be endorsed by all parties (Kumārila's statement of it was quoted above in the *maṅgala-vāda*, p. 59). But this cognitive law makes it impossible for veridicality—so defined—to be known intrinsically, or to be known by the apperception posited by certain Mīmāṃsakas, or by the inference posited by others. That may be right, the *pūrvapakṣin* responds, but there are definitions available to us that are not subject to this problem.

The distinction between awareness and remembering is crucial to D^3, but it does not command attention until later.

On the Bhāṭṭa view, cognition of a pot creates a special property, namely, cognizedness, that resides in the pot and that, being grasped by an ensuing cognition, is the spur to an inference to the occurrence of the previous, veridical pot-cognition. The Naiyāyika objector points out that this special property is not generally admitted. Gaṅgeśa in fact will present arguments against it in almost every section of this the first chapter of the *TCM*. Furthermore, the Naiyāyika objector adds here, a non-veridical cognition should create the special cognizedness as well, such that it would be wrong to conclude that any previous cognition was veridical.

D^5, by the way, is practically the same definition as the definitive one Gaṅgeśa gives in the section on defining veridicality (see D^{26}, below, pp. 236–38, including the comments).

It is important to keep in mind that on all three Mīmāṃsaka views the veridicality of a cognition is grasped by the process through which the cognition itself is grasped, though the three differ on what that way amounts to.

The heart of the *pūrvapakṣin*'s response is that, on all the Mīmāṃsaka views, a cognition is known complete with its full intentionality, that is to say, qualificandum and qualifier in qualificative relation. The qualificative relation is part of the cognition's ''objecthood'' (*viṣayatva*) just as much as the qualifier and qualificandum.

Text (p. 179, Tirupati, and p. 173, Calcutta) and Translation

sambandhitâvacchedaka-rūpavattayā jñāyamāne sambandhini sasambandhika-padârtha-nirūpaṇam ity anuvyavasāyasya rajatatvâvacchinnatvena puro-varti-viṣayatvāc ca | anyathā puro-vartinaṃ rajataṃ ca tad-ākāraḥ syān na rajatatvena puro-vartinam iti |

(The **pūrvapakṣin** continues:) Moreover, given that one of the terms of a relation is being cognized as specifying the relation, the thing (the relation) that has terms in relation is determined, and so the apperception has as (part of) its objecthood (or intentionality) the thing in front (e.g., silver) as specified by silverhood. Otherwise, the apperception would have the form, ''I am aware of an object in front (of me) *and* of silver,'' but not the object in front *as* silver.

Comments

If, as from the Murāri Miśra perspective, an apperception makes a target cognition known, all the ''components'' of the target—the qualificandum (or presentation of an object in front), the qualifier (or presentation of silverhood), and the relation of the two—are known, the *pūrvapakṣin* claims. In other words, an apperception grasps a qualificandum and qualifier *in relation*, not as separate elements.

The Mīmāṃsaka view faces a difficulty in that an apperception of a veridical cognition would seem to be the same as an apperception of a non-veridical cognition. The example of silver and silverhood is used because the *error* of mother-of-pearl misperceived as silver is a standard one in philosophic discussions: Gaṅgeśa wants us to see that such an apperception as the *pūrvapakṣin* describes could be of a target cognition that is *non-veridical*. The current point is, however, simply that the Murāri Miśra view is committed to apperception of an integrated cognition of a thing cognized as qualified by a qualifier.

Text (p. 180, Tirupati) and Translation

ata eva a-pramā api pramā ity eva gṛhyate | anuvyavasāyasya bhrama-viṣaya-vaiśiṣṭya-viṣayatvāt | na ca na prāmāṇyaṃ prathamato na tad-āropaḥ syād iti vācyam | prāmāṇyasya jñāna-grāhaka-sāmagrī-grāhyatvena jñāna-vitti-vedyatvāt | a-bhāva-pratītau pratiyogitvâ-bhāvayor iva |

(The **pūrvapakṣin** continues:) Just for this reason, a non-veridical awareness is in fact grasped as veridical. For, the apperception has the relatedness in the object of an error as (part of) its objecthood.

Objection (against the Murāri Miśra view): Since veridicality is not cognized from the first (i.e., in the occurrence of a target cognition), it could not be attributed.

Pūrvapakṣin: That should not be said. For, veridicality, as grasped through the same collection of causal factors that produce a grasping of the cognition (that is veridical), is known in the knowing of the cognition—like, with an awareness of an absence, awareness of both the absentee (i.e., what is absent) and the fact of its absence.

Comments

An apperception would grasp, according to the Murāri Mīmāṃsaka view, both a target cognition and its veridicality. According to Nyāya, in contrast, an apperception, in the standard case, would not cognize its target as veridical, but only as having such-and-such an object. Thus, according to Nyāya, too, would the relatedness in the intentionality or objecthood of a non-veridical awareness (or, indeed, of a veridical awareness) be apperceived, but an awareness need not be apperceived as veridical.

Text (p. 181, Tirupati) and Translation

tad-a-bhāvavati tat-prakāraka-jñānatvam a-prāmāṇyaṃ parato jñāyate | tad-a-bhāvavattvasya bhramân-ullikhitatvena anuvyavasāyâ-viṣayatvāt | na ca evam anuvyavasāyasya yāvad-vyavasāya-viṣaya-viṣayakatve bhrānta-bhrānti-jña-saṃkara iti vācyam | bādhân-avatāra-daśāyāṃ tasya iṣṭatvāt | tad-avatāre tasya eva pratibandhakatvāt upanāyaka-bhrānter a-bhāvāc ca | ata eva anya-bhrānti-jñasya na bhramaḥ |

(The **pūrvapakṣin** continues:) Non-veridicality, which is to be a cognition with ϕ predication content about something that does not exhibit ϕ, is cognized extrinsically. For, the fact that something cognized does not exhibit that (ϕ, the predication content) is not (part of the) objecthood (or intentionality) of the apperception, inasmuch as it is not explicitly presented (and is not mentioned in a verbalization) of an error.

Objection (against the Murāri Miśra Mīmāṃsaka view): Given that an apperception has as its object the full extent of the target cognition's object, a conflation of what has been erroneously cognized and the error (itself) would occur.

Pūrvapakṣin: That should not be said. For, that is the consequence we want so long as a correcting negation has not set in. When one does set in, it itself would block the conflation.

And there is no "cognition-mediated" (*upanāyaka*) error.

Just for this reason, the knower of another person's error is not in that error.

Comments

On the Murāri Mīmāṃsaka view that posits an apperception as knowing a previous cognition, the apperception would not know a non-veridical cognition as non-veridical, although the veridicality of a veridical cognition would be known apperceptively. Thus, in an apperception of an error there would be conflation of what is factwise erroneous, that is to say, of (a) the object of the target cognition and of (b) the erroneous target itself. The *pūrvapakṣin* replies that such is just what he wants, that is, until a correcting cognition has occurred. Then the facts are separated out and the cognition is known as an error.

By "cognition-mediated error" is meant information "presented extraordinarily," as the smell of sandalwood seen at a distance (see, below, p. 125, and the glossary entry, p. 685). The view that information can be presented perceptually through the mediation of memory is key to Nyāya's explanation of illusion. Forms of the verbal root *nī* conjoined with the verbal prefix *upa* are used to allude to the theory of mentally-mediated, or cognition-mediated, perceptual presentation, as in the statement of the *pūrvapakṣin* here.

Text (p. 182, Tirupati) and Translation

> atha tadvattvaṃ na dharma-dharmi-vaiśiṣṭya-mātram, kiṃ tu tasya viśeṣaṇatā-viśeṣaḥ | sa ca vyavasāye bhāsate na anuvyavasāye, manaso bahir-a-svātantryā iti cet, na | vyavasāyôpanītatvena viśeṣaṇa-viśeṣyayor iva viśeṣaṇatā-viśeṣasya api tad-viṣayatvāt, viśeṣaṇatāyā nirākariṣyamāṇatvāc ca |

Objection: The fact of having that (i.e., of exhibiting whatever property ϕ) is not merely the relatedness of a property and a property-bearer, but it is, rather, a special qualifierhood belonging to that. And this appears in the original (non-apperceptive) cognition, not in the apperception. For, the internal organ (*manas*) has no independent ability concerning what is outside (the body: that is, it has no ability independent of the operation of the external senses to perceive an external object).

Pūrvapakṣin: No. Like the qualifier and the qualificandum, the special qualifierhood, too, is the apperception's object, inasmuch as it (too, just like the other two) is presented extraordinarily through (the previous cognition, i.e., in) the original (non-apperceptive) cognition. Moreover, the qualifierhood (which is not accepted by us as a real entity) is, below, (rightly) rejected (as will be explained).

Comments

Mohanty does a particularly excellent job of explaining this passage, and I shall only rephrase what he says.[5] The special property of being veridical of some object belongs to a first-level cognition. It is special in its relationality, which belongs to the cognition but also depends on the nature of the thing cognized. The objection is that an apperception is incapable of picking up such a relation as part of its intentionality, since such intentionality would have to involve facts about external objects whereas an apperception cannot independently ascertain such facts. Any facts that go beyond the nature of a strictly cognitive presentation, that is to say, that go beyond what its target cognition would be independently of such a relation, would be beyond its ken.

To look at the mechanics of the situation, the internal organ, or "mind," *manas*, is responsible for apperception, the objector points out. It grasps a target cognition and re-presents it. This it does independently of the external senses. But in perception of worldly things, things outside the body, the *manas* depends in its operations on the workings of the external sense faculties, sight, hearing, and so on.

The *pūrvapakṣin*'s response is simply that there is no reason why the special relationality that qualifies a target cognition cannot be an apperception's object any less than the target's qualificandum, qualifier, or the relation between them. The mode of presentation is, as with the three, the extraordinary type of sensory connection that depends on a previous cognition, in this case the target cognition itself. (See below, p. 125, on "extraordinary sensory presentation.")

Mīmāṃsaka arguments for rejecting "qualifierhood" as a category appear in another section (below, pp. 245–48).

Text (p. 178, Calcutta) and Translation

> etena a-sva-prakāśe na svataḥ prāmāṇya-grahaḥ, dharmy-a-grahe tad-dharmâ-grahāt | śabda-gandha-vad yogyatvāt tad-grahe 'pi jñānaṃ pramāṇam iti dhīr na syāt | sva-prakāśe 'pi sva-mātra-sākṣiṇaḥ sva-dharma-grahe '-sāmarthyāt | sāmarthye vā a-prāmāṇyam api gṛhṇīyāt | para-prakāśe liṅgena manasā vā jāyamānaṃ jñānaṃ na bhrama-vyāvṛttaṃ prāmāṇyaṃ gṛhṇīyāt vyabhicārāt |

na ca yatra yad asti tatra tad gṛhyate, a-prāmāṇyasya api svato grahâpatteḥ, anuvyavasāyasya anumiter vā viṣayâ-janyatvāc ca iti nirastam |

(The **pūrvapakṣin** continues:) By this reasoning, the following objections are thrown out.

(1) If there is no self-illumination, there can be no *intrinsically grasped* veridicality, since if the property-bearer is not grasped, there can be no grasping of its property. While veridicality can be grasped—there is a capacity to do so, as with sound and smell—still, there can be no cognition (of the form), "The cognition is (in itself) a veridical source (of knowing itself)."

(2) Even if there is self-illumination, no witnessing *merely* of itself would have the capacity to grasp any of its properties (and veridicality would be one of its properties). Or, if there is the capacity, non-veridicality would be grasped, too (when the self-illumining cognition happened to be non-veridical).

(3) If there is illumination of cognition through another cognition—whether (that second cognition comes about) by an inferential mark (viz., a cognizedness being apprehended) or by (activity of) the internal organ (viz., in an apperception)—the (second) cognition coming about would not grasp (the first's) veridicality as excluding error, because there are counterexamples.

(4) And what (property) is where (i.e., in which object) would not be grasped (i.e., a cognition as veridical would not be grasped), unless you embrace the untoward consequence of non-veridicality being grasped of itself, too. Moreover, neither (on one view) the apperception, nor (on another view) the inference would be generated by (the nature of) the object.

Comments

On the Murāri view of an apperception grasping a cognition and its veridicality, there would be an intrinsically grasped veridicality even though cognition is not held to be self-illumining. Thus, the property-bearer (the target cognition) and its property (veridicality) would be grasped together, by the apperception. The cognition would be a veridical source of knowing itself in the sense that, on this Mīmāṃsaka view, it would be in virtue of the target cognition's being grasped that its veridicality would be grasped, too.

The second objection engages the Prābhākara view according to which every cognition has itself as object as well as something external to itself (and indeed the cognizer or self). The other objections engage both the Murāri apperception view and the Bhāṭṭa view of cognition as apprehended through a property—an inferential mark—created in the object, its cognizedness.

The *pūrvapakṣin* claims that these objections are answered by the point, made previously, that through the "extraordinary" cognitive relatedness any property (save non-veridicality) can be picked up by the cognition-grasping cognition, no matter in which of the three Mīmāṃsaka ways "cognition-grasping cognition" is understood.

Text (p. 185, Tirupati) and Translation

tadvati tat-prakāraka-jñānatvaṃ tadvati tad-vaiśiṣṭya-jñānatvaṃ vā prāmāṇyaṃ vyavasāyasya iti svena anuvyavasāyena anumityā vā tad-grahāt, tad-viṣayatvasya tat-prakārakatvasya ca jñāna-grāhaka-sāmagrī-grāhyatvāt | yadi ca prāmāṇyaṃ parato jñāyeta tadā prāmāṇya-jñāne 'pi tad-anumāpaka-liṅga-pakṣa-vyāpty-ādi-jñāneṣu ca sva-viṣaya-niścayârthaṃ prāmāṇyasya parato phala-mukhī kāraṇa-mukhī ca an-avasthā syād iti prāmāṇyaṃ na jñāyeta eva iti pariśeṣād api svataḥ prāmāṇya-grahaḥ ||

(The **pūrvapakṣin** continues:) Whether the veridicality of an original cognition be "to be a cognition with predication content about a ϕ-object as ϕ" or "to be a cognition with a ϕ-relationality to a ϕ-object," through that cognition itself or through an apperception or through an inference is veridicality grasped. For, having veridicality as object and having it as predication content are grasped through the same collection of causal factors that produce grasping of the original cognition.

And if veridicality were to be known by something else (namely, a cognition other than the one that grasps the veridical cognition itself, as Naiyāyikas claim), then there would be an infinite regress. An infinite regress would obtain with respect to cognition of veridicality and with respect to cognition of an inferential mark, that is, of its location, its pervasion (by the property to be proved, veridicality), or the like, which would make veridicality known inferentially. A regress would obtain in the seeking of certainty about each (proving) cognition's own object. The regress would be both in the direction of the result (veridicality ascertained) and in the direction of the cause (the ascertaining)—if (to repeat) veridicality were to be cognized by something else. Therefore, by elimination, too (in addition to other arguments), veridicality is grasped intrinsically.

Comments

The *pūrva-pakṣa* ends here with Mīmāṃsā's best argument, an alleged infinite regress on the alternative view of veridicality as grasped extrinsically. Note that the key supposition is that a second cognition that grasped a first's veridicality would itself have to be grasped as veridical, requiring a third and so on. Gaṅgeśa challenges this assumption, below, p. 90.

atha siddhântaḥ

NOW, THE RIGHT VIEW

Text (p. 187, Tirupati, and p. 184, Calcutta) and Translation

siddhântas tu, prāmāṇyasya svato grahe 'n-abhyāsa-daśôtpanna-jñāne tat-saṃśayo na syāt, jñāna-grahe prāmāṇya-niścayāt | a-niścaye vā na svataḥ prāmāṇya-grahaḥ | jñānâ-grahe dharmi-jñānâ-bhāvān na saṃśayaḥ |

Gaṅgeśa: But the right position is as follows. If veridicality were grasped intrinsically, then there would be no doubt about veridicality with a cognition arising in unfamiliar circumstances, since, given that the cognition is grasped, there would be certainty about its veridicality. Or, if there were not certainty, there would be no intrinsically grasped veridicality. (And) if the cognition were not grasped, then there could not be doubt (about its veridicality), since there would be no cognition (of the cognition that exhibited, or not, veridicality, that is, no cognition) of the property-bearer. (However, such doubt occurs.)

Comments

Gaṅgeśa's refutation seems on target. A cognition arising in unfamiliar circumstances is typically doubted whether in fact it is veridical or non-veridical. Assume a veridical cognition. Then, doubt about it would be incompatible with the cognition's veridicality being cognized at the same time. But the intrinsicality view entails that the veridicality would be cognized at the same time.

Ramanuja Tatacharya gives the following example of a cognition arising in unfamiliar circumstances. In a strange country, one is walking and sees what is apparently a river in the distance. The cognition is in fact veridical, but at the time one has doubts. One knows that it is possible, from the heat of summer, to be tricked about such a distant appearance of water. The apparent stream could be a mirage. So one might well doubt: Is my cognition of water veridical? In contrast, after approaching the river, bathing in it, etc., and then, a second time, days later, walking toward it from the same direction and seeing it in the distance such that the appearance is the same as on the first occasion, one would typically *not* wonder whether the cognition is veridical, since the type of cognition would have been verified.

Text (p. 187, Tirupati) and Translation

nanu koṭi-smaraṇâdinā saṃśaya-pūrva-kṣaṇe vyavasāya-vināśān na tad-viśeṣyako mānasaḥ saṃśaya iti cet, na | jñānôpanīte vyavasāye prāmāṇya-saṃśayāt | nanu dharmi-jñānaṃ na saṃśaya-hetuḥ, koṭi-jñāna-viśeṣâ-darśana-dharmîndriya-saṃnikarṣaiḥ prāmāṇya-saṃśaya-rūpa eva jñāna-graha utpadyata iti cet, na | jñānâtīndriyatvena taj-jñānaṃ vinā tad-dharmaka-mānasa-saṃśayân-upapatteḥ | liṅgaṃ ca na saṃśaya-janakam, tasya niścāyakatvāt | jñānasya mānasatve ca prāmāṇya-jñāna-vat tat-sāmagry api saṃśaya-pratibandhakā, tan-niścāyakatvāt | anyathā viśeṣa-darśana-kāle 'pi saṃśayâpatteḥ |

Objection: There can be no such doubt, no mentally mediated doubt (i.e., none mediated by the internal organ), whose qualificandum would be some original cognition, since the original cognition would be destroyed the instant before the doubt arose—given that doubt arises through memory, etc., of alternatives.

Gaṅgeśa: No, since doubt about veridicality does occur with respect to an original cognition brought back through memory.

Objection: Cognition of a property-bearer (i.e., cognition of a cognition bearing or not bearing veridicality) is not a cause of doubt. Doubt arises from cognition of alternatives (e.g., ''Is it a post or a person''), non-perception of particulars (such as hands and feet), and sensory connection with the property-bearer (that is not known clearly). This, which is in fact the form any doubt about veridicality would have to take, is the way (the required) grasping of a cognition would be produced.

Gaṅgeśa: No. Inasmuch as cognition is beyond the sphere of the (external) senses, without cognition of a cognition (i.e., of an original cognition as property-bearer) there could be no mentally mediated doubt which was about a cognition as its qualificandum (and such doubt does of course occur). Furthermore, no inferential mark generates doubt, since an inferential mark is a cause of certainty. And if cognition is mental (i.e., mentally grasped in an apperception), the very collection of causal factors that produces cognition of veridicality would—as does cognition of veridicality—block doubt, since such a collection causes certainty. Otherwise, we would be faced with the unfortunate consequence that there would be doubt even at the time of experience of (doubt-resolving) particulars (such as hands and feet in the case of a doubt whether something is a post or a person).

Comments

According to the first objection, a perceptual cognition could not be the direct object of a doubt, because the mind's very holding forth of alternatives would destroy it. All cognitions endure only a couple of brief moments. Moreover, the internal organ, the mind or *manas*, is capable of presenting at most one cognition at a time (except in special circumstances that are irrelevant here). Gaṅgeśa's answer draws on, without explanation, the thorny area of Naiyāyika theory concerning the mental processes at work in doubt, though he will expand on this shortly. (See also, below, p. 125, comments on "extraordinary sensory presentation.") His main point, however, is simply that doubt about the veridicality of a veridical cognition does sometimes occur.

Gaṅgeśa's response to the second objection is again to insist that, phenomenologically, the doubt occurs. He also mounts a counterattack, first, according to Mathurānātha, against the Bhāṭṭa theory—according to which a cognition is known to have occurred by way of an inference—then against the apperception view of Murāri Miśra.

Text (p. 190, Tirupati, and p. 199, Calcutta) and Translation

atha dharmiṇi viśeṣâ-darśana-daśāyāṃ eka-koṭi-smaraṇe tad-āropaḥ koṭi-dvaya-smaraṇe saṃśaya iti niścaya-sāmagrītaḥ saṃśaya-sāmagrī balavatī iti koṭi-dvaya-smaraṇe saṃśaya eva syāt na tu niścaya iti cet, na | viruddhôbhayâropa-sāmagrī-dvaya-samājād ubhayâropa eka eva bhavati | sa eva saṃśayaḥ | na tv ekâropa-sāmagryā aparâropa-sāmagrī-pratibandhaḥ, a-virodhāt | na ca ubhayâropa-sāmagryā eka-niścaya-sāmagrī-pratibandhaḥ iti vācyam | pratyekâropa-sāmagry-atiriktāyās tasyā a-bhāvāt | na ca sāmagrī-dvayāt kārya-dvayam | samūhâlambana-vad upapatteḥ | tasmāt prāmāṇya-niścaya-sāmagrī-sattvān na tat-saṃśayaḥ syāt | dharmi-jñānaṃ ca saṃśaya-hetuḥ | anyathā saṃśaye dharmi-niyamaḥ koṭy-utkaṭatvaṃ ca na syāt |

Objection: If a single possibility is remembered when no details about a property-bearer are experienced, then that possibility is attributed. But if a pair of possibilities is remembered, there is doubt. In this way, a collection of causal factors producing doubt would be stronger than a collection producing certainty. So, given a remembering of a pair of possibilities, there would be doubt alone, not certainty.

Gaṅgeśa: No. From an assembly of two sets of causal conditions sufficient each for one of two incompatibilities, there can be attribution of both to a single thing, which attribution would be doubt. But it is not the case that because of the set of causal conditions sufficient for the one attribution the set sufficient for the other attribution would be blocked, since the acts of attribution are not incompatible (in that doubt does occur).

Nor should it be said that the set of causal conditions responsible for the certainty of one of the pair is blocked by the combined set of causal conditions responsible for attribution of both possibilities. For, there is nothing (i.e., no set of causal conditions) over and above each set of causal conditions responsible for an attribution (i.e., that would be responsible for this certainty). Furthermore, a pair of effects does not result from such a pair of sets of causal conditions. For, the possibility (of a single effect is illustrated: it) is like cognition of a group of things. Therefore, from the presence of a collection of causal conditions sufficient for certainty about a cognition's veridicality, doubt about that would not be.

Moreover, cognition of a property-bearer is (as we have said) a cause of (a necessary condition, a causal condition for) doubt. Otherwise, there would be neither the rule, respecting doubt, of the property-bearer (i.e., that a property-bearer must be cognized), nor the possibility that one alternative could be weightier.

Comments

Why does Gaṅgeśa seem to imply that the set of causal conditions that would be responsible for the certainty is the same as one of the two sets of causal conditions which when both are in place would cause the incompatible attributions? In the next section, he argues that a special causal excellence is responsible for the veridicality of an awareness, i.e., a causal condition that is over and above those responsible for generating either a mere cognition or a doubt (which is, technically, a non-veridical cognition). What, perhaps, he means in the passage at hand is, then, that if there is a set of causal conditions sufficient for certainty, doubt will not occur. In other words, what is chiefly wrong with the objection is the presupposition that there could be a set of causal conditions sufficient for certainty and certainty not occur because of some kind of blockage. Thus, a set sufficient for true certainty is not the same as a set that helps to cause doubt. Gaṅgeśa is clarifying how the word *sāmagrī* is used, "set of causal factors sufficient to produce *x*," or, what such a set's being in place entails, namely, *x*'s occurrence.

As Mohanty elaborates, some Naiyāyikas disagree with Gaṅgeśa about there being a possibility, respecting doubt, of a weightier alternative.[6] Gaṅgeśa's point is that something about a property-bearer invariably is comprehended, something that may be sufficient to weight one alternative over another but not necessarily to provide certainty.

Text (p. 198, Tirupati) and Translation

> atha pītaḥ śaṅkhaḥ ādarśe mukham ity-ādi-bhramo viśeṣa-darśane 'pi yathā doṣântarāt, tathā niścaye 'pi prāmāṇye doṣântarāt tat-saṃśaya iti cet, na | tad-vad eva atra api pravṛtti-prasaṅgāt | sākṣāt-kāri-bhrame sākṣāt-kāry eva viparīta-niścayaḥ pratibandhakaḥ na tv ānumānikâdiḥ |

Objection: Errors, such as a yellow conch (that is really white) and a face in a mirror, occur in spite of experience of distinguishing features. As this must be because of another defect, so in spite of veridicality being known with certainty doubt can occur because of another defect (than the veridicality not being known with certainty).

Gaṅgeśa: No. If it were like that here too, then there would be effort (as there is toward a "yellow" conch on the part of a person wanting it, but in the case of doubt there is no effort)—this is the difficulty. An error of immediate experience (i.e., a perceptual error) is blocked just by another immediate experience, one that amounts to certainty about an opposite (or opposed, state of affairs, e.g., a *white* conch), but not by inferential considerations or the like.

Comments

Gaṅgeśa's reply occurs in the context of rebutting the view that veridicality can be known with certainty and doubt still occur. Later, he himself will acknowledge that, in the case of some perceptual errors, inferential considerations are correcting. Here his point is that the occurrence of doubt about a cognition's veridicality is not comparable to perceptual error, nor is cognition of veridicality. A different logic applies in each situation.

Text (p. 201, Tirupati) and Translation

> saṃśaye tu niścaya-sāmānyam | anumānâdinā tan-niścaye kadācid api tasya an-utpādāt, diṅ-mohâdau tathā darśanāt | tac ca na, pittâdinā pratibandhāt | na ca jātyā eva kaścid doṣo 'sti | na ca prāmāṇya-saṃśayād viṣaya-saṃśaya-vat prāmāṇya-jñāne prāmāṇya-saṃśayād prāmāṇya-saṃśaya iti vācyam | prāmāṇya-jñāne 'pi svataḥ prāmāṇya-grahe tat-saṃśayân-upapatteḥ |

(**Gaṅgeśa** continues:) But doubt is blocked by certainty in general. For, given certainty about veridicality through inference or the like, doubt never arises. And this is not similar to what is experienced in the case of (such an illusion as) confusion about direction, since (in such cases of illusion, veridicality's) blockage occurs through the likes of bile.

Furthermore, a cognitive defect does not belong to whatsoever natural kind (there is no true universal comprising all possibilities of cognitive error).

Objection: As doubt about an object results from doubt about the veridicality of a cognition *x* (about that object), so too with cognition of veridicality: from doubt about the veridicality of a cognition of *x*'s veridicality there results doubt about *x*'s veridicality.

Gaṅgeśa: That should not be said. For, if a cognition's veridicality is grasped intrinsically, there would be no possibility—no matter its being a cognition of *x*'s veridicality—of doubt concerning it (and again we know such does occur).

Comments

Gaṅgeśa gives here, implicitly, a response to the charge of an infinite regress: given certainty, doubt does not arise. There is no infinite regress in that certainty blocks doubt. A bit of certainty may well not last forever, as cognitive conditions change. But there can be no simultaneous doubt and certainty about the same thing, nor even, explains Ramanuja Tatacharya, a direct cognitive succession. Awareness of additional evidence would have to intervene in the flow of cognitions that comprises one's mental life. Thus, the Mīmāṃsaka alternative view is wrong because, however the Mīmāṃsaka might try to wriggle out of the difficulty, it remains true that, on all versions of the intrinsicality theory, doubt about the veridicality of a veridical cognition could not arise immediately on the heels of of the cognition's occurrence, whereas in fact there are situations where we do immediately question the veridicality of a veridical cognition.

Text (p. 202, Tirupati, and p. 222, Calcutta) and Translation

> nanu jñāna-mātraṃ na virodhi-buddhi-nivartakam, bhramôttaraṃ bādhaka-jñānôdayāt, kiṃ tv an-anyathā-siddham | ata eva tena vinā api taj-jñānaṃ saṃbhavati iti anyathā-siddhatayā śaṅkitaṃ tan-niścayaṃ paribhūya jñāna-viṣayatvād viṣaye yathā saṃśayas tathā prāmāṇye tan-niścayasya anyathā-siddhi-śaṅkayā taṃ paribhūya bhavati saṃśayaḥ | na ca vyavasāyasya jñānatve ghaṭa-viṣayakatve ca yathā anuvyavasāya-viṣayatvān na saṃśayas tathā prāmāṇye 'pi na syāt, anuvyavasāyasya pramātva-niyamād iti vācyam | a-jñāne a-viṣaye ca jñānatva-viṣayatvayor anuvyavasāyena a-grahaṇa-niyamāt tad-viṣayatvam an-anyathā-siddhaṃ prāmāṇya-viṣayatvaṃ ca tena vinā api saṃbhavati iti tatra saṃśaya iti cet, mā evam | bhramatvam anyathā-siddhatvam | tataś ca prāmāṇya-niścaye bhramatva-saṃśayena tad-viṣaye prāmāṇya-saṃśaya iti phalito 'rthaḥ | bhramatva-saṃśayaś ca taj-jñānâ-jñānābhyāṃ na saṃbhavati ity uktatvāt | evam anyatra api bhramatva-saṃśayān na viṣaye saṃśayaḥ, svataḥ-prāmāṇya-grahe bhramatva-saṃśayâ-bhāvāt |

Objection.1 (by a Mīmāṃsaka): Cognition does not in general (absolutely) close off an opposed cognition (thus, coghition of veridicality does not exclude doubt), since following an error a negating and correcting cognition sometimes arises (which would not be possible if a given cognition absolutely excluded what it was opposed to). Rather, not being "something that is known (in context) as other than a strictly necessary (or relevant) causal factor," *anyathā-siddha* (is a cognition that prevents doubt). Just for this reason, a cognition ("F*a*") doubted as not resulting from a strictly necessary factor (i.e., *a*'s being F)—"This cognition of F*a* could come about without F*a* (being a reality)," overcomes (natural) certainty about F*a*. As there can be doubt about an object on the basis of its being (no more than) the object of a cognition, so there can be doubt about veridicality through a doubt that (a cognition's having F*a* objecthood) is due to something that is not a strictly necessary (or relevant) causal factor (for the cognition "F*a*" to arise), the doubt thus overcoming the certainty.

Objection.2 (against objector.1, the Mīmāṃsaka): Since apperception is by rule veridical, doubt does not occur about an original cognition's being a cognition, nor about its having as object a pot (when it does indicate a pot). Hence, inasmuch as all this would be the object of an apperception, so, too (on your view, doubt could not occur, contrary to what happens in fact), about an original cognition's veridicality.

Answer (by objector.1): That should not be alleged. For, the rule is that an apperception does not determine that something is a cognition when there is no cognition, or that something is a cognitive object when there is no such object. These objects (of an apperception) could not be known as not strictly necessary (or relevant) causally (the reality of the corresponding objects *is* strictly required), whereas veridicality as an object (of an apperception) could come about without that (veridicality in fact obtaining). Therefore, there can be doubt about it.

Gaṅgeśa: Don't think like that. "Something known as other than a strictly necessary causal factor" (as you use the phrase) amounts to "being an error." And so (what you are really saying, i.e.) the resulting meaning is: by means of a doubt about the certainty of a cognition's being veridical, a doubt about veridicality occurs *with respect to* the original cognition's object. (You would thus smuggle in the possibility of doubt.) And yet doubt about a cognition's being an error (an illusion, *bhrama*) cannot occur (according to you), whether there is cognition or not of that (original cognition, in apperception), since this is what (by you) has been said. In this way (you face the untoward ramification of your position that) doubt could not occur concerning other matters, too, based on doubt about error, since, if veridicality is grasped intrinsically, doubt could not occur about a cognition's being an error.

Comments

According to the Mīmāṃsaka objector, there would be no absolute rule that everything apprehended in an apperception would be correctly apprehended. Objector.2, who is a Naiyāyika, retorts by citing a standard view about apperceptive veridicality being immune from doubt on two counts: (a) with respect to a target's being-a-cognition and (b) with respect to the target's having the objecthood that it in fact has. Thus if the Mīmāṃsaka holds that an apperception scopes a target as veridical, then it should be impossible to doubt that the target's objecthood holds in fact. The Mīmāṃsaka agrees with the Naiyāyika's view of apperceptive infallibility but stresses that it is limited to (a) and (b), not including (c) scoped veridicality. And he analyzes the distinction in terms of strictly necessary causal factors. Thus an apperception scoping a target cognition as (a) a cognition could not come about without the target actually being a cognition, and scoping it as (b) having a certain objecthood could not come about without its having that objecthood. It could, however, grasp the target as (c) veridical without the target's actual veridicality being responsible for the apperception.

Gaṅgeśa chides the Mīmāṃsaka for finding veridicality to be invariably an apperceptive object without admitting what the position entails. No cleverness about "strctly necessary factors" can save the Mīmāṃsaka intrinsicality view from its fundamental failure in precluding the possibility of doubt about a cognition's being an error. If a target is cognized as veridical, then doubt—no matter how it is analyzed—will be blocked.

A few more words about the supposed infallibility of apperception are, however, in order. Gaṅgeśa has not revealed at this point in the text precisely what he thinks about cognition of cognition and the limits of doubt. Much later in the chapter—at the end of the section on *manas*, the mind or "internal organ," which, to repeat, is the organ responsible for generating an apperception of a previous cognition as object (below, pp. 568ff)—he shows how delicate a subject he regards apperception. The prevailing (unrefined) Naiyāyika opinion is, as presented here by objector.2, that a target's objecthood lies infallibly within apperceptive grasp—also the target's cognitionhood—but not its veridicality. However, a cognition is sometimes grasped in apperception as veridical, Gaṅgeśa points out at the end of this section (pp. 137–40). The point against the Mīmāṃsaka is, rather, that in grasping a cognition apperceptively the target is not *ipso facto* known as veridical. Furthermore, though Gaṅgeśa does accept (a) that a target's being-a-cognition would be grasped infallibly, cognitive subtype is grasped apperceptibly but fallibly, in his view. That is, one could be mistaken about whether a target's predication content is perceptual or retrieved through memory, etc. Also, a target's extent or duration could be erroneously grasped. For example, we can be wrong about whether a bit of objecthood belongs to an immediately preceding perception or one happening moments before, although it seems perceptual. Thus, "I am (simultaneously) seeing, tasting, smelling, and touching a pastry" could be an illusion in that the feel, for example, of the pastry being seen may be projected into visual experience by memory and not veritably by the organ of touch. An apperception that something has been cognized as a pastry with a certain taste, etc., would block doubt that there may not have been a cognition with such an objecthood. But other types of doubt could occur on the heals of the cognition that prompts such a verbalization. Thus the Mīmāṃsaka here is on the right track in finding limits to apperceptive infallibility. His mistake is to take apperception as invariably grasping a target as veridical and then to try to account for the doubt that sometimes occurs about it by way of a ruse.

On the notion of "causal irrelevance" or "being known (in the context) as other than a strictly necessary causal factor," *anyathā-siddha*, see the introduction, above, p. 23.

Text (p. 206, Tirupati) and Translation

na ca vācyaṃ prāmāṇya-saṃśayān na viṣaye saṃśayaḥ, mānâ-bhāvāt | jñāna-viṣayatvāt samāna-dharmād eva tad-upapatteḥ | na ca evaṃ sarvatra viṣaya-saṃśaye tan-niścayôcchedaḥ, prāmāṇya-saṃśaye 'pi tulyatvād iti | tasya a-sārvatrikatvāt | bhramatva-saṃśayaṃ vinā niścita-viṣaye saṃśayân-utpatter ānubhavikatvāc ca |

Objection (by the Mīmāṃsaka): Doubt about a cognition's object does not result from doubt about its veridicality, because of lack of proof. For, doubt about an object can be accounted for just from a common property (shared by all cognized objects, i.e.) in virtue of their being (simply) objects of cognition. And it is not the case that there would be, in this way, doubt everywhere about objects such that all certitude about things would be altogether extinct, since the same reasoning would apply, too, to doubt about veridicality.

Gaṅgeśa: That should not be said. For, doubt about veridicality is not universal. Moreover, experience shows that, without a cognition being doubted as erroneous, doubt does not arise with respect to an object that has been with certainty ascertained.

Comments

The Mīmāṃsaka tries a different strategy to avert the difficulty. The Naiyāyika in denying that veridicality is grasped intrinsically would embrace the view that every cognition is a potential subject for doubt. But the truth here can be accounted for differently. All agree that every cognition has an object. Doubt, then, would arise from the commonness of the property, having-an-object, and this would be why it seems that every cognition is a subject for doubt in spite of the truth of intrinsic veridicality.

Such an insight does not entail universal skepticism, since by Nyāya's own lights the same reasoning would apply to a cognition's veridicality. If Mīmāṃsakas are skeptics because they view doubt as arising out of the common property of having-an-object, then so too are Naiyāyikas skeptics because they view veridicality as a common property subject to doubt. For the Mīmāṃsaka, veridicality is a mere honorific; doubt concerns objects not cognitions. For the Naiyāyika, in contrast, veridicality is a significant determination, and a certification of veridicality blocks doubt just as doubt about an object cognized implies doubt about the cognizing's veridicality.

Gaṅgeśa has, presumably, opened this line of inquiry to remind us that doubt about veridicality is, as he says, *not* universal. Veridicality not being intrinsically grasped does not entail that in all circumstances doubt about veridicality is called for. Normally things are known with certainty, whether that certainty is itself grasped or not. Doubt arises only in specific circumstances, so experience shows. And we do not doubt something we have cognized unless we realize that we were in error. A default certitude is undermined by evidence that makes us realize that we were wrong.

To fill out the picture, note that for the Mīmāṃsaka there is no meta-level of certitude, whereas for the Naiyāyika certitude about a cognition's veridicality is distinct from a lower-order default certitude that a cognition provides about its object. Higher-order certitude normally blocks doubt whereas the lower does not. Gaṅgeśa, we shall see, says explicitly at the end of the section that once a cognition has been certified as veridical, there is erected a higher barrier to doubt; default certitude gets reinforced and much more is required for an undermining. Conversely, doubt at the lower level itself precludes higher-level confidence unless the doubt is eliminated. But the main point is that default certitude that has not been reinforced is much more readily subject to doubt. The problem with the Mīmāṃsaka view is that the higher barrier would seem to be in place all the time such that it becomes difficult to understand how doubt could occur.

Text (p. 207, Tirupati, and p. 226, Çalcutta) and Translation

atha tadvati tat-prakārakatvaṃ prāmāṇyam, tac ca jñāna-grāhakeṇa gṛhītam eva iti na tat-saṃśayaḥ | na ca asmin niścite 'pi prāmāṇya-saṃśayāt na tat-prāmāṇyam iti vācyam | etan-niścayād eva niṣkampa-vyavahārād iti ced, astu tāvad idaṃ prāmāṇyam, tathā apy anuvyavasāyân-antaraṃ vyavasāyasya prāmāṇye arthasya tadvattve ca saṃśayasya anubhava-siddhatvān na artha-tadvattvaṃ tasya viṣayaḥ |

Objection (by the Mīmāṃsaka): Veridicality (we grant) is a cognition's having of a predication content that is exhibited by that (the cognition's object qua qualificandum). And this (we hold) is in fact grasped by the grasper of the cognition (that is veridical). Thus (you say that on our view) no doubt can occur concerning the cognition. And yet it should not be said (this is where you go wrong) that even though a cognition's veridicality is known with certainty doubt about the veridicality means that the cognition is not veridical (that is, a cognition can be veridical and there be doubt about its veridicality at the same time). For, just from certainty about it (i.e., the cognition's being veridical) is there unhesitating action.

Gaṅgeśa: Let it be granted, first of all, that this is the right view of veridicality. Still, immediately following an apperception there is sometimes doubt concerning whether the original cognition is veridical and whether the object (of the original cognition) possesses that (predication content presented in the original cognition), as is established by experience. The object's possessing that in fact is not the apperception's object.

Comments

An apperception may grasp infallibly the presentational object of its target cognition. But it does not grasp whether that presentational object actually holds for the object in the world that the target cognized. Doubt sometimes follows apperception, and sometimes cognitions apperceived are discovered, on the basis of evidence later acquired, to be non-veridical.

Text (p. 208, Tirupati) and Translation

nanu vyavasāyasya idaṃtva-rajatatva-viśiṣṭêdaṃ-viṣayatve 'nuvyavasāya eva mānam | tathā ca yāvad-vyavasāyôllikhita-prakāra-viśiṣṭa eva dharmī anuvyavasāye bhāsate | anyathā viṣayâṃśe tasya nirvikalpakatve idaṃ rajataṃ jānāmi iti tad-ākāro na syāt | ato dharmiṇi idaṃtva-rajatatva-vaiśiṣṭyam anuvyavasāyena gṛhītam iti dharmiṇi svataḥ-prāmāṇya-graha-vad rajatatva-vaiśiṣṭye 'pi svataḥ-prāmāṇya-jñānam a-varjanīyam | ata eva dharmy-aṃśe na kadâpi prāmāṇya-saṃśaya iti cet, mā evam | idaṃ rajataṃ ca jānāmi iti na anuvyavasāyaḥ, bahir-viśeṣyake manaso '-svātantryāt | kiṃ tv idaṃ idaṃtvena rajatatvena jānāmi iti | tatra idaṃtva-rajatatve prakāratvena bhāsate tat-prakāraka-jñānavattvaṃ ca ātmani bhāsate, anyathā prakāra-vāci-tṛtīyârthâ-saṃbhavaḥ | rajatatva-vaiśiṣṭyasya tad-arthatve vyavasāye 'pi tṛtīyârthôllekhâpattiḥ |

Objection (by the Mīmāṃsaka): An apperception alone is what shows that an original cognition has as its object a ''this'' as qualified (e.g.) by ''being a this'' and ''being silver'' (in the case of an original cognition verbalized as ''This is silver''). And so the property-bearer appears in the apperception precisely as qualified by only such predication content as is explicit (and directly verbalizable) in the original cognition. Otherwise, the apperception would be indeterminate (and unverbalizable) with respect to its object portion (as distinct from its ''I cognize'' portion): ''I cognize this to be silver'' would not be its form (and of course it is). Hence, the relationality between the thisness and the silverhood in the property-bearer is grasped by the apperception. Thus, like a grasping of intrinsic veridicality with respect to a property-bearer (or, object cognized), so too is there, unavoidably, cognition of intrinsic veridicality with respect to a relationality with silverhood. Just for this reason, there is never doubt about veridicality with respect to the property-bearer portion (or qualificandum, of a cognition).

Gaṅgeśa: Don't think that way. ''I cognize this *and* (I cognize) silver'' is not the form the apperception takes, since the internal organ (*manas*) has no independent capacity (i.e., independent of the external senses) to grasp an external qualificandum. Rather, the apperception is ''I cognize this *as* a this, *as* silver.'' There the two, ''thisness'' and ''silverhood,'' would appear as predication content.

And the having of the (target) cognition with such predication content (all as the apperception's object) appears in a self; otherwise, the use of the instrumental case (in the sense of the predicative instrumental, or an appearing *as*, i.e.) to express predication content would not be possible. If (factual) relatedness to being silver were the the meaning of the instrumental case, there would be the unfortunate ramification that even the original (target) cognition would also be verbalized by the instrumental case (but one does not normally express ''This is silver'' as ''This by means of silverness'').

Comments

Gaṅgeśa's grammatical argument is perhaps a little misleading, because his point is cogent. An apperception taking a prior cognition as object is indifferent to the target cognition's veridicality. As Gaṅgeśa mentions in several other places, an erroneous cognition, "This is silver," and a veridical cognition, "This is silver," are identical as apperceptive object. What is known is the prior cognition as having such-and-such predication content, not as veridical or non-veridical. Letting 'Q' stand for the qualificative relation implicit in any cognition of an entity as qualified, we may represent a first-order, non-apperceptive cognition of silver: Q(this, silver). The apperception, in contrast, would be: Q(I, awareness-of-Q(this, silver).

Gaṅgeśa implies that normal usage in expressing an apperception is neutral with regard to the question of its target's veridicality. That is why the *predicative instrumental* is used, which makes explicit that the apperception's first-order object is a cognition, a cognition in which the apperception's second-order object—corresponding to the terms expressed in the instrumental case—is known as having been cognized in relation to something. First-order objecthood, in contrast, is normally expressed as an assertion about a "this" *being* a "that" ("This *is* a that," e.g., "This *is* a pot," as opposed to, "Something is appearing *as* a pot"), where not the instrumental but the nominative ("This is a that") would be used. In other words, a first-order, non-apperceptive perception is expressed *committally*, "This is silver," whereas a second-order apperceptive awareness is verbalized *non-committally*, "Something *by* thisness, *by* silverness," where the instrumental case is used. Or, to make explicit the cognized qualificative relation that would be asserted, namely, that between the cognizer's self and the target cognition, we may construct a verbalization also using the instrumental case: "*I* have *awareness* of something *by means of* the qualifiers, thisness and silverness."

Text (p. 210, Tirupati) and Translation

tathā ca dharmiṇi idaṃtva-rajatatva-prakāraka-jñāna-viṣayatve tādṛsa-jñānavattve ca ātmano 'nuvyavasāya eva mānam iti na viṣaye tasya nirvikalpakatvam | ata idaṃtva-rajatatva-vaiśiṣṭyaṃ puro-vartini na anuvyavasāya-viṣaya iti na svataḥ prāmāṇya-grahaḥ | tasmād an-abhyāsa-daśâpanna-jñāna-prāmāṇyaṃ parato jñāyate sāṃśayikatvād a-prāmāṇya-vad ity ācāryāḥ |

(**Gaṅgeśa** continues:) And so an apperception is not indeterminate with respect to its object: a self's apperception is alone the proof for an object being an original cognition with (e.g.) "thisness" and "silverhood" as predication content with respect to a property-bearer, as well as the proof for the having of such a cognition as object. Hence, factual relatedness of thisness and silverhood to a thing in front (of a perceiver) is *not* an object of apperception. Thus, grasping of veridicality is *not* intrinsic. Therefore, the veridicality of a cognition occurring in unfamiliar circumstances is known extrinsically (i.e., from later evidence), *since* such a cognition is subject to doubt, like non-veridicality—so has reasoned our revered teacher (Udayana).

Comments

Apperception shows us precisely what the object of a target cognition has been, as well as that the target has occurred. Thus, it counts as the justification for such statements as "I am cognizing this to be such-and-such"; the apperception would be that which prompted the speech act. But no factual relation to an external object is revealed therein, and veridicality consists in the factuality of the predicated relation. Thus, such a factual relation must be shown extrinsically, by other evidence. Moreover, this view can account for the phenomenon that cognition arising in unfamiliar circumstances is often regarded as dubious—"Is that really an elephant in the highway?"—after apperceiving that one has seen something *as* an elephant in a highway.

The reference to Udayana is to his *Nyāyakusumāñjali*, where Gaṅgeśa's teacher, too, argues that a veridical cognition "arising in unfamiliar circumstances" being subject to doubt proves that its veridicality is known extrinsically.[7]

Text (Calcutta, p. 233) and Translation

nanu sva-grāhyatve 'pi kadācit para-grāhyatvāt svasya apy anyâpekṣayā paratvāt bhaṭṭa-mate ca para-grāhyatvāt siddha-sādhanam | na ca grāhya-prāmāṇyâpekṣayā paratvam | grāhakasya api grāhya-prāmāṇyatvena tad-apekṣayā paratvâ-bhāvāt | a-grāhya-prāmāṇyâpekṣayā paratve a-prāmāṇya-prasaṅgāt |

Objection: Even given intrinsic grasping (of veridicality, as a general rule), sometimes (we admit) it is grasped by something else. And since an "itself" (the intrinsic) is a "something else" relative to another, you are committing the fallacy, from the perspective of the Bhāṭṭa view, of trying to prove what is already admitted, because of your insistence on veridicality being grasped by something else.

And "to be something else" is not relative to the veridicality to be grasped (and so you should not try that way of nominally saving your position). For, even that cognition x which grasps the veridicality of another cognition y is (on your view), as (itself) something veridical to be grasped, not a "something else" relative to that, since, relative to something veridical that is not grasped, to be "other" would involve you in the difficulty of the non-veridicality of x.

Comments

The Bhāṭṭas (Mīmāṃsakas who follow Kumārila Bhaṭṭa) hold, we should recall, that an inference is what grasps both an original cognition and its veridicality. Such an inference would be, of course, "something else" relative to what it grasped. (The theory is nevertheless an *intrinsic* view of the way veridicality is known, because, in contrast with the Naiyāyika position, it is the same inference that grasps both the cognition and its veridicality.)

Gaṅgeśa will not answer this rather trivial objection (mostly mere wordplay) for several sentences. First, he develops objections to the overall Mīmāṃsaka stance, objections still centering on doubt about veridicality. Unfortunately, he uses some highly elliptical language.

Text (p. 211, Tirupati) and Translation

ucyate | an-abhyāsa-daśâpanna-jñāna-prāmāṇyaṃ na svâśraya-grāhyam svâśrayâtirikta-grāhyaṃ vā | svâśraye saty api tad-uttara-tṛtīya-kṣaṇa-vṛtti-saṃśaya-viṣayatvāt, a-prāmāṇya-saṃśayâ-janya-saṃśaya-viṣayatvād[8] vā, a-prāmāṇya-vat | arthe niścite 'pi na tan-niścayân-antara-tṛtīya-kṣaṇe artha-saṃśayo na vā prāmāṇya-saṃśayaṃ vinā iti na arthe vyabhicāraḥ | vivāda-padaṃ na yāvat-svâśraya-grāhaka-grāhyam, svâśraya-niścaye sati tat-tad-uttara-tṛtīya-kṣaṇe a-prāmāṇya-saṃśayaṃ vinā vā saṃdihyamānatvāt a-prāmāṇya-vat | yad vā an-abhyāsa-daśâpanna-etaj-jñāna-prāmāṇyam etat-prāmāṇya-saṃśaya-pūrva-kālīna-etaj-jñāna-niścayâ-viṣayaḥ, etaj-jñāna-niścayân-antaraṃ saṃdihyamānatvāt a-prāmāṇya-vat | na ca sva-padasya prāmāṇya-mātra-paratvāt tad-āśrayâ-grāhyatve[9] bādhaḥ | sva-padasya saṃbandhi-paratvena samabhivyāhṛta-paratvāt | anyathā svasya paratvāt parasya ca svatvāt tad-etattvasya tad-etad-anyatvasya ca sva-para-sādhāraṇatvāt svataḥ parato vā iti saṃśayo na syāt | prāmāṇyasya sva-grāhyatve bādhāt pariśeṣeṇa anyathā-grāhyatvaṃ parato grāhyatvam iti kaścit |

Gaṅgeśa: We answer. (Here is a cogent inference.) The veridicality of a cognition occurring in unfamiliar circumstances (the *pakṣa* of our inference) is not grasped by what stands as *its own* substratum (namely, the cognition itself, the unfamiliar cognition that is veridical). Nor (we now give a second *sādhya*:) is it grasped (at the time) by something over and above its own substratum. (Our view is, in contrast, that no veridicality is, in these circumstances, grasped.) *Since* (and now we give our "reason," our *hetu*) although a cognition's very own substratum is present, veridicality sometimes comes to be the object of a doubt occurring (immediately after the cognition, that is to say, while its substratum is still occurrent, within) the third instant after it, *or*, it comes to be the object of a doubt that is not generated by doubt about *non*-veridicality—*like* the non-veridicality (of a non-veridical cognition arising in such circumstances).

If an object is apprehended with certainty, in contrast, doubt about the object does not occur within the third instant immediately following the certainty about it. Nor without doubt about its veridicality does doubt occur at all. Thus (it is normal for there to be) no deviation from the object (as cognized).

The word that we are disputing ("veridicality," well, it) is rarely grasped by that which grasps its substratum (though there are cases, God's cognitions, for instance). *Since*, there may be certainty about the substratum (that is, certainty that the cognition has occurred, in an apperception) while within the third instant after that—or, without doubt about *non*-veridicality occurring—veridicality becomes doubted—*like* the non-veridicality (of non-veridical cognitions arising in similar circumstances).

Alternatively, the veridicality of this cognition *x* occurring in unfamiliar circumstances does not become the object of certainty about this cognition *x*, that is, not of any certainty that precedes doubt about veridicality, *since* immediately following any certain apprehension whose object is this cognition *x*, *x*'s veridicality is (in our example of cognition arising in unfamiliar circumstances) doubted—*like* the non-veridicality (of a non-veridical cognition arising in unfamiliar circumstances).

Objection: (The *sādhya* of the first inference above is defeated.) It is not true that the veridicality of a cognition occurring in unfamiliar circumstances *is not grasped by what stands as* ***its own*** *substratum*, inasmuch as the locution, "its own," means only veridical cognition.

Gaṅgeśa: There is no defeating of our claim in that way, since the locution, "its own" (in the above inference), which implies a correlate, has meaning according to what it is in relation to. Otherwise, since (considered in general, the meanings of words like) "itself" can be a "something else" and a "something else" an "itself," and since both an "itself" and a "something else" can in common be a "that" which is a "this" and a "that" which is "other than a this," then there could be no disputing about the *of-itself* or the *through-something-other* (that is to say, if the above argument were right, then our dispute about intrinsically or extrinsically known veridicality would be nonsense). Given that (as we have now shown) the view that veridicality can be known intrinsically has been refuted, veridicality is known, by elimination—either *by some other means* or *by something else*. (At least, we may so conclude for the moment, or, let us say) so someone (may well conclude: further elaboration is still ahead).

Comments

In his subcommentary (Tirupati, p. 234), Rāmakṛṣṇa identifies the "someone" that Gaṅgeśa mentions in the last line as called Jayadeva, but precisely who this Jayadeva is is unclear. Mathuranātha says that the "someone" is simply Gaṅgeśa's signal that this is not his final position.

Cognition is practically momentary. The smallest appreciable increment of time is the "instant" or "moment," *kṣaṇa*. By the third instant after arising, a cognition will have passed away. Of course, a cognition can be preserved in memory, and the veridicality of a cognition can be doubted, or known with certainty, at a much later time through the operation of memory. But with memory operative, the *substratum* of the veridicality, the cognition itself, will have passed away. So, if a cognition's veridicality is to be known instrinsically through a grasping of the cognition itself, i.e., through a grasping of the substratum of the veridicality, that would have to occur while that substratum is available, i.e., before the cognition passes away. However, one finds that doubt, in certain circumstances, occurs immediately: as soon as one sees water in the distance, one doubts not only whether it is real but the veridicality of the cognitive presentation.

Do not let Gaṅgeśa's quaint cognitive psychology obscure the fact that in a general form his argument is sound. A cognition arising in unfamiliar circumstances may be in fact veridical and fail to be trusted nevertheless. This proves the falsity of the thesis that any cognition is known to be veridical by whatever makes the cognition itself known. When we see strange things, we are not sure whether we should believe our eyes. This presents, Gaṅgeśa shows, an insurmountable problem for the Mīmāṃsakas, whatever the particular version of the intrinsicality theory.

The passage here, however, is directed principally against the Prābhākara camp's view of self-illumining cognition. And, in that context, the cognitive psychology is important. For, the Prābhākara himself acknowledges laws of cognitive psychology, one of which is crucial here, namely, that within a certain tiny time-span anything cognized as ϕ cannot, within that time-span, be cognized as not-ϕ. But to doubt a cognition's veridicality is to cognize the cognition as presenting something ϕ as possibly non-veridical, that is, as possibly non-ϕ precisely within the time-span disallowed by the Prābhākara. So, on the Prābhākara thesis no doubt could occur about an immediately preceding cognition's veridicality. Yet such doubt is found.

Another Mīmāṃsaka opponent raises the objection, near the end of the passage, that Gaṅgeśa's inference uses a self-contradictory probandum. For, on the Mīmāṃsaka view, there are no non-veridical cognitions (error is to be explained away, as we shall see in another section). Therefore, what Gaṅgeśa is trying to prove cannot be proven, since there are no instances of the *sādhya*, the "property to be proved." Gaṅgeśa retorts, in effect, that usage of an indexical expression depends on context of usage. It is, then, no argument against the Naiyāyika that the Mīmāṃsaka would understand an indexical in a different way, a way that the Naiyāyika denies explicitly.

Text (p. 243, Tirupati, and p. 246, Calcutta) and Translation

prathamaṃ ca prāmāṇya-jñānaṃ vyatirekiṇā | nanu prāmāṇya-prasiddhiṃ vinā vyāpty-a-grahāt kathaṃ anumānam | atha vyāghāta-daṇḍa-bhayena pramā-tad-viṣaya-siddhau tad-dṛṣṭântena jñeyatvâdinā vahneḥ pramā-viṣayatvam anumeyam | tataś ca sāmānyatas tat-siddhau na sādhyâ-prasiddhiḥ | viśiṣyâ-nirṇayān na anvayitvâ-sādhāraṇye |

(**Gaṅgeśa** continues:) And, at first (i.e., when in a set of circumstances for the very first time), the cognition of the veridicality (of a guiding cognition, e.g., of water at a certain place) is by means of an inference based on negative correlations (where no S, there no H: where no veridical cognition, there no successful effort: or, more precisely, if that cognition had been non-veridical, this effort would not have been successful, e.g., drinking water).

Objection: Since the veridicality (of that type of cognition) is not known (the circumstances being absolutely unfamiliar), a pervasion (involving it) cannot be grasped. So, how can there be the inference?

Gaṅgeśa: Now, since *some* veridical cognition and its object has to be admitted, on pain of pragmatic self-refutation, that a fire (or anything) is the object of a veridical cognition is to be inferred from that case by the likes of the object's being cognizable. And, then, given that veridicality has in general been established (i.e., that one knows what in general is the difference between the veridical and the non-veridical), there is no fallacy of an unexampled probandum. Since (with the veridicality of a veridical cognition that arose in unfamiliar circumstances) there is no definite ascertainment of things similar to the qualified (i.e., to the first-time cognition that is veridical), the inference whereby the veridicality is known is not an inference based on positive correlations nor does it commit the no-similar-instance fallacy.

Comments

The stock Naiyāyika answer about how the veridicality of (an object-specified) cognition would be known is that it would be inferred on the basis of its having produced successful effort appropriate to that kind of cognition. An inference based on positive correlations to a given instance of veridicality would be, for example: "That fire-cognition is veridical, *since* it cognitively produced successful effort of an appropriate type (where cognitive production of successful effort, there veridicality), as in the case of cognition of edible fruit." The inference could be based on both positive and negative correlations, as we can see with the following expression of the pervasion in negative terms: "That fire-cognition is veridical, *since* it cognitively produced successful effort of an appropriate type (and where no veridicality, there no cognitive production of successful effort), as with erroneous cognition of silver (i.e., when the object-in-front is mother-of-pearl)." More problematic are pervasions that are known only by positive correlations or only by negative correlations; the latter is mentioned here.

Gaṅgeśa is answering not just the general question of how veridicality is known but specifically how it could be known in the case of the veridical, but also dubitable, cognition that he has used as an example—i.e., as a phenomenological fact—with which to batter the Mīmāṃsaka intrinsicality theory, namely, a cognition arising in unfamiliar circumstances that is in fact veridical. According to Gaṅgeśa, we can find out that such a cognition is veridical. And we can find it out pretty quickly (though not so quickly as on the Mīmāṃsaka view). It is imaginable that a person make a (technically termed, *kevala-vyatirekin*) inference, based, as will be explained, only on negative correlations (instances of non-S and non-H). This would be appropriate since there would be no positive comparison class in that no similar cognitions have been had before by the individual in the thought experiment. Nevertheless, successfully drinking water discovered by trusting a first-time presentation of, for instance, water in the distance, is the way one knows that the cognition is veridical. The person realizes that had the cognition *not* been veridical, he would *not* now be drinking water. A *modus tollens* step then completes his reasoning: he is drinking water and so the cognition is, or was, veridical. His success is the inferential mark of the veridicality of the cognition that guided his action even though he has not known such success coupled with this type of cognition before. He does know, as Gaṅgeśa says, what veridicality is in general and also non-veridicality. But he does not know, prior to the inference, the veridicality of this type of cognition. Negative correlation (no veridicality, no success) allows him to focus on the pertinent evidence (thirst-quenching), and infer veridicality by *modus tollens*. The veridicality is thus established *by something else*, namely, by the said "negative only" (*kevala-vyatirekin*) inference.

Against Mohanty,[10] the issue is not "Meno's paradox": If something is unknown, how can instances of it be recognized so that knowledge of it can be acquired? According to this logic, if veridicality is not already established, it seems impossible that it be inferred. However, the main problem is not how veridicality in general can be found out (indeed, this is explained by the fire example) but rather how there can be known the veridicality that is the particular attribute of a cognition whose object is unfamiliar—both factwise and cognitionwise in that the object has not been encountered before and no similar cognition has occurred before.[11] Gaṅgeśa does touch upon the Platonic concern below—mainly by way of refuting those who take the problem to entail memories from previous births (à la Plato indeed!). But this is not the issue in focus here, which is, rather, how the veridicality of a cognition arising in unfamiliar circumstances can be found out.[12]

Gaṅgeśa provides a simple bit of *tarka*, counterfactual reasoning, to show that we can assume that there is at least a single instance of a veridical cognition and of its object somewhere. Otherwise, even a denial would be nonsense. (He elaborates this response in the next passage as well as in refuting skepticism about inference at the very beginning of the next chapter and in the section on *tarka*, "counterfactual reasoning": see my discussion, *Classical Indian Metaphysics*, pp. 158–64.) A universal denial of veridicality has to be false because it presupposes what it would deny. (Is the denial supposed to be veridical? If so, veridicality is established. If not, the denial does not have to be taken seriously. In other words, unlimited skepticism is nonsense, since it is parasitic on what it would eliminate.) So we have every right to assume that something somewhere, a fire, for instance, has been cognized veridically. (This is why, by the way, Gaṅgeśa mentions such a universally available example of veridicality in something's, a fire's, say, being nothing more than *cognizable*.)

Then the question is: How do we know about some specific thing and some specific cognition that the one is cognized veridically and the other is a veridical cognition, and how could this be known for a first-time occurrence of a particular type of veridical cognition (e.g., of water in the distance) when the circumstances are unfamiliar, that is to say, where there are no other known instances of the type of cognition as specified by its object? This is, again to stress, the very example with which Gaṅgeśa has refuted the *pūrvapakṣin*, his Mīmāṃsaka adversary. And Gaṅgeśa's answer is: an inference based on negative correlations only, *kevala-vyatirekin*, an inference that is "only negative." The last sentence of the passage is meant to explain why this is so and why the inference is to be regarded as cogent. But understanding Gaṅgeśa's remarks requires some rather complex background concerning the "negative only" inference.

A long discussion of this type of inference in the next chapter centers on a *tri*-lemma, three apparently exhaustive alternatives, none of which appears unobjectionable.[13] (1) There are other known instances of the probandum—in which case the inference would be either (a) based on positive correlations (and thus not be "negative only") or (b) fallacious as committing the "no-similar-instance" fallacy. This fallacy is committed when there is no known example of the prover in the *sapakṣa*, i.e., the set of things where the probandum is known to occur. "Sound is eternal, since it has soundhood" is a commonly cited example: the prover, soundhood, is not found in the *sapakṣa*, ether, atoms, and other things known to be eternal. (It is also not found in the *vipakṣa*, i.e., the set of things where the probandum is known *not* to occur; this is what makes it seem to be a good prover.) (2) There are no known instances of the probandum—in which case the probandum term cannot be available for inference of any variety. One cannot make an inference where one does not understand the terms it trades on. (3) The probandum is known to occur on the subject or *pakṣa* itself—in which case there would be no point to the inference. No one takes the trouble to prove what is already known. To solve the trilemma, Gaṅgeśa fiddles with (2), the familiarity requirement. He accepts (1) and (3). He does concede with respect to (1) that, in some cases, a negative-only inference need not have been *only* negative, there being available positive correlations that were, for some reason or other, simply not cognized, while the negative inference remains correct. In other circumstances, one might have made an inference based on both types of evidence. Presumably, here, too, with a veridicality-inference, a cognizer might have, under appropriately different circumstances, have based his inference also on positive correlations. Nevertheless, it is Gaṅgeśa's qualifying of (2)—the requirement that the probandum be exampled—that is his core response overall and that is salient here concerning the negative-only inference to the veridicality of a cognition not had by the cognizer previously.

Gaṅgeśa says that in the case of such a first-time cognition "there is no definite ascertainment of things similar to the qualified." An inference based on positive correlations could possibly commit the "no-similar-instance" fallacy. But where there is no *sapakṣa*, the fallacy cannot occur. The point in the current context is that there is no known example of the veridicality specific to the particular type of cognition in question. How then is veridicality a term available for inference? The answer lies in the difference between veridicality in general and veridicality in particular.

Veridicality is not a universal; it varies with particular cognitions. The veridicality of the cognition, "This fire is hot," is the fire's being hot, as, to use A. Tarski's example, the veridicality of "Snow is white" is snow's being white. Since our subject has never before had the cognition, "This is a river," there is unavailable to him positive correlations, things (both H and S) both prover-exhibiting and probandum-exhibiting in the specific sense of the veridicality of the particular cognition in focus, the fact perceived by him for the very first time. Veridicality and non-veridicality are known by him in general. Indeed Gaṅgeśa defines both in general, with suitable variables, in spite of insisting that veridicality is not a universal (below, pp. 236ff). To make an inference based only on negative correlations, things both not-S and not-H, familiarity with things S and not-S is required only in general. Our subject understands that the success of his effort to drink water as he is now doing would not have come about had the guiding cognition been non-veridical, like what happens when seeking silver one picks up mother-of-pearl. His effort, in drinking water, etc., is not frustrated, and he makes the negative-only inference.

Text (p. 246, Tirupati) and Translation

na ca prāmāṇyaṃ na anugatam, kiṃ tu prati-jñānaṃ viṣaya-prakāra-bhedāt bhinnam, tathā ca vahni-jñānasya vahny-a-vṛtti-prakārân-avacchinnatvâdikaṃ sādhyaṃ tac ca a-prasiddham iti vācyam | vahni-jñānasya viśeṣyâ-vṛtti-prakārân-avacchinnatvâdikaṃ sādhyamānaṃ pakṣa-dharmatā-balena vahni-viṣayaka-pramātve paryavasyati iti cet, tarhi prathamaṃ kasya api svârthaṃ prāmāṇyânumānaṃ na syāt | prāmāṇya-niṣedha-rūpasya parakīya-vyāghātasya tadā an-upasthiteḥ | svayaṃ prāmāṇya-niṣedhasya tad-dhī-pūrvakatvāt prāmāṇyam a-parijñāya prāmāṇya-niṣedhena parakīya-vyāghātasya apy a-jñānāc ca | pravṛtti-saṃvāda-visaṃvādābhyāṃ tad-dhetu-jñāna-vaicitryânumāne 'pi yathôkta-rūpa-prāmāṇyasya viśiṣyâ-pratītir iti |

Objection: Veridicality is not uniform but is, rather, for every cognition distinct, since each has a distinct object and distinct predication content. (Thus, veridicality in general cannot be defined, unlike what you implied.) And so (the inference you gave to show how veridicality in general becomes comprehended is misstated:) the probandum should be for the cognition of fire that there *not* be the likes of a specifying of the cognition's predication content that is not present *in the fire*, or whatever, and this is not exampled (outside the given cognition of fire).

Gaṅgeśa: That should not be said. If on the strength of the subject (the fire-cognition) exhibiting the property (that is the prover, here, as above, being-cognizable or the like) one were to draw conclusions while taking the probandum to be (as you have it), namely, that there be *no* likes of a specifying of that cognition of fire by predication content that does not rest in the qualificandum—if in these terms one were to draw conclusions concerning the veridicality of a cognition whose object is fire—then (you would be right but) there could be no first inference (since there could be no comparison class), on the part of anyone, reasoning for himself, that a cognition is veridical (which is absurd). For, at the time a contradiction made by another, taking the form of a denial of veridicality, is not set in awareness (according to the terms of the thought experiment). To deny veridicality requires a prior understanding of it, and without oneself having comprehended what it is to be veridical, another's contradiction, too, would not be known as a denial of veridicality. Even though from the success and failure of effort a diversity of the cognitions that are the causes may be inferred, veridicality so defined (as in your inferential formulation) could not be understood as belonging to what is qualified (by the prover term).

Comments

The problem that the variability of veridicality presents for the definitional project will be dealt with by Gaṅgeśa in a later section. Here the objection is that since veridicality has been said to vary according to what is cognized, one needs target a specific cognition and its object. This means that an inference to veridicality cannot be based on a suitable comparison class, that the probandum cannot be exampled outside the case at issue, and thus that there can be no evidence for its pervading the prover term.

Gaṅgeśa replies that the probandum is wrongly formulated by the objector, who takes too seriously the need for specificity, though it will remain an issue whether the objector's formulation is an acceptable definition of veridicality.

Against the objector's formulation, Gaṅgeśa is not saying that it is impossible to deny anything because to mention it is to accept its existence. Rather, he applies the principle that anything that is meaningfully denied must in general be comprehended. And, so understood, his argument about a need for an appreciation of veridicality appears cogent. Non-veridicality, like veridicality, is to be understood in more general terms than those proposed by the objector. Just what those might be he now tells us in firming up his position overall.

Text (p. 251, Tirupati, and p. 252, Calcutta) and Translation

> ucyate | prāg-bhavīya-saṃskārād viśeṣyâ-vṛtty-a-prakāratvaṃ tadvati tat-prakāraka-jñānatvaṃ vā prāmāṇya-mātraṃ smṛtaṃ vahni-jñānâdau sādhyamānaṃ sarva-nāma-mahimnā pakṣa-dharmatā-balād vahni-jñānasya viśeṣyâ-vṛtty-a-prakārakâdau paryavasyati | svataḥ-prāmāṇya-niṣedhe prāthamika-prāmāṇya-jñānasya anyathôpapādayitum a-śakyatvād iti sampradāya-vidaḥ | vayaṃ tu brūmaḥ, prathamam a-prāmāṇyâ-bhāva eva prāmāṇyaṃ vyatirekiṇā sādhyam | tata eva niṣkampa-pravṛtter upapatteḥ | tad eva vā sidhyat pakṣa-dharmatā-balena tadvati tat-prakārakatvâdikam ādāya sidhyati | tad-an-antaram arthād vā sidhyati iti vakṣyate | tathā hi, ayaṃ vahnitvena anubhavaḥ na vahnitvâ-bhāvavati vahnitva-prakārakaḥ, a-vahni-vṛtti-prakārako na, viśeṣyâ-vṛtti-prakārako na, vahnitva-prakārakatve sati vahny-a-viśeṣyako na, vahnitva-vyadhikaraṇa-prakārâvacchinno na, vahny-a-vṛtti-prakārako na vā, dāha-samartha-viṣayaka-prayatna-janakatve sati vahnitve-prakāraka-niścayatvāt, dāha-samartha-viśeṣyaka-vahnitva-prakāraka-niścayatvād vā, yan na evaṃ tan na evaṃ yathā vahny-a-pramā |

(**Gaṅgeśa** continues:) Whether veridicality is (a) not to have predication content that does not exist in the qualificandum or (b) to be a cognition having ϕ predication content about a ϕ object, it is said (by some Naiyāyikas) that in general it is remembered as the result of a memory-impression formed in a previous birth: that being what is to be proved, it is, with respect to cognition of fire and so on, conclusively proved by the force of the pronouns (in the definition being appropriately substituted for and) on the strength of the inferential subject exhibiting the prover property concerning the likes of there being no exhibiting of predication content that does not exist in the qualificandum, for a cognition of fire. (This supposing of a memory-impression from a previous birth is required) because, given a denial of intrinsic veridicality, it would otherwise be impossible to account for cognition of the veridicality of a first-time cognition (i.e., the known veridicality of a first-time cognition, a cognition arising in unfamiliar circumstances)—so say some knowers of (Nyāya) tradition.

However, we say that, on such an occasion of a first-time cognition being known as veridical, the veridicality, which is precisely the absence of non-veridicality, is to be proved by an inference based on negative correlations. For, just from veridicality being known is the possibility of unhesitating effort explained (e.g., the unhesitating effort when one sees the water a second time). Or, proving precisely that (veridicality), one can (on one view, directly) prove it, taking it to be the having of ϕ predication content about a ϕ object, or the like, on the strength of the subject exhibiting the prover. Or (on another view), immediately after that (proving that the cognition is not non-veridical), one could prove its veridicality, by force of the meaning (of what is first proved)—as will be explained.

For example, this awareness (of something) as fire, which has firehood as its predication content, is not of something that does not exhibit firehood. Nor does it have predication content that exists in what is not fire. Nor does it have predication content that does not exist in the qualificandum. Nor, given that its predication content is firehood, does it determine a qualificandum other than fire. Nor is it specified by predication content that belongs to a different locus than that of firehood. Nor does it have predication content that does not exist in fire. *For* (or *since*), given that it (the cognition of fire) *produces (and guides) effort* directed toward an object (viz., fire) capable of burning fuel, it is an ascertainment whose predication content is firehood; alternatively, it is an ascertainment whose predication content is firehood determining a qualificandum (viz., fire) that is capable of burning fuel. What is not so, is not so, as (for example) a non-veridical cognition of fire.

Comments

The various terms used in the alternative formulations of the veridicality of a cognition of fire will be examined by Gaṅgeśa in the section on defining veridicality. Gaṅgeśa apparently does not want to discuss right now the best way to define or characterize veridicality; he wants instead to argue that we need not postulate possession of the concept of veridicality in a previous birth and preserved by a memory-impression in the current one to understand how it is possible to find out inferentially (i.e., extrinsically) a cognition's being veridical, even in the case of an initially dubitable cognition that turns out to be—we discover upon having success in action guided by it—veridical. Fire is capable of burning fuel, and if we want to burn something and are successful in doing so, then the veridicality of the cognition is proved by the success of our effort guided by, indeed, in part produced by, cognition of fire.

Gaṅgeśa distinguishes his own view about how the veridicality of such a first-time cognition is known—namely, directly—by saying that it is veridicality "which is precisely the absence of non-veridicality" that is proved by the inference based on negative correlations. The pervasion rule is transpositional and a key step in the reasoning is *modus tollens*: all non-S are non-H, and this thing *a* is not a non-H, so it's not a non-S. According to some Naiyāyikas, another inference converts a double absence (*a* is not a non-S) into a presence (*a* is S). But Gaṅgeśa apparently believes that a single-stepped inference will do. Apparently, this is connected with his ideas about "negative only" inferences, which will be explained in greater detail in comments to the following passage (the rule is, he says, all S are non-H—considering non-veridicality to be a positive property—with this cognition *a* as not a non-H and therefore a non-S, i.e., veridical: see below). But that there is according to him simply a single-stepped inference could also be interpreted as connected with assumptions about "internal definitional equivalences" (*antar-vyāpti*, to use the term of later Naiyāyikas) embedded in inferential formulations. These, too, seem not to be counted by Gaṅgeśa as true inferential steps. In other words, knowing that something is capable of burning fuel is intrinsic to our understanding of it as fire. Gaṅgeśa makes a similar point below in using the expression *arthāt*, "in effect," that is, something F may in effect be considered as G since the two properties are in effect definitionally identical: p. 122.

Text (p. 266, Tirupati) and Translation

> tatra bādhân-antaraṃ smṛty-upanīte bhrame vahnitvâ-bhāvavati vahnitvena mama jñānaṃ vṛttam ity a-prāmāṇyaṃ manasā eva paricchidyate mānântareṇa vā sarva-siddham | evaṃ vahny-a-pramāyāṃ vahnitvâ-bhāvavati vahnitva-prakārakatvâdi-samartha-pravṛtti-janakatvâ-bhāvayor vyāpti-grahe '-prāmāṇya-vyāpaka-hetv-a-bhāvâ-bhāva-rūpād dhetor a-prāmāṇyâ-bhāva-rūpam sādhyaṃ sidhyati | yad-vyāpakatayā hetv-a-bhāvo gṛhītas tad-a-bhāva eva hetunā sādhyate | yatra tv a-bhāvasya vyāpakatā hetv-a-bhāvasya jñāyate tatra sādhya-prasiddhir aṅgam, tāṃ vinā tad-a-jñānāt | yatra tu bhāva-vyāpakatā hetv-a-bhāvasya tasya na tad-aṅgam | tena vinā api vyatireka-vyāpter grahāt | ata eva itara-vyāpakatā ākāśatvâ-bhāvasya gṛhītā ity ākāśatvena a-prasiddha eva itarânyonyâ-bhāvaḥ sidhyati |

(**Gaṅgeśa** continues:) There (in the case of detection of a non-veridical cognition of fire), the error is presented through memory immediately following a cancelling corrective cognition. Its non-veridicality is known in the following manner: "My cognition, which occurred as of something as fire, was about something that lacks firehood"—just by the mind (or internal organ, *manas*, retrieving, *upanīta*, the cognition that was about something). Or, it is known by another means (also distinct from the non-veridical cognition itself). So much is admitted by all.

In this way, the pervasion is grasped (that makes possible the inference to the veridicality of a first-time cognition): with respect to (an instance of the *vipakṣa*, something where the probandum definitely does not occur, for example) a non-veridical cognition of fire, a correlation is grasped between (a) the likes of that which has firehood as predication content while being about something that lacks firehood and (b) a lack of production of effort (directed toward something really) capable (of burning fuel). Here the prover property (such capability) takes the form of an absence of an absence of itself (non-non-H), and this latter (lack of such capability, non-H) pervades non-veridicality (non-S): from it, the probandum property in the form of an absence—namely, an absence of non-veridicality—is proved.

That whose absence is the means whereby an absence of the prover is grasped as a pervader (wherever no S, no H) is just what is proved by the prover. (Now) where an absence of the prover is cognized as pervading an absence (an absence of things S), there the probandum property (things S) must be known well (enough for the inference to proceed, *prasiddha*)—this is part of the inference—for without that the absence (something as not an S) could not be cognized. Where, in contrast, an absence of the prover is cognized as pervading a presence (wherever S, there no H), there that (cognition of an absentee as informing a cognition of the probandum, S as not non-S) is not part of the inference. For, even without it, a pervasion according to negative correlations can be grasped.

Just for this reason, an absence of etherhood as pervading what is other than ether can be grasped. Thus is ether proved to be mutually distinct from that which is other than it by (the prover) etherhood, although the mutual distinctness is not known (outside of the inferential subject, ether).

Comments

Gaṅgeśa opens by declaring that a non-veridical cognition can be known apperceptively through retrieval of a cognition—kept alive in memory—that is cancelled or defeated by later evidence. In some cases, an inference may be required (''Or, it is known by another means''). The reason he says that this ''is admitted by all'' is that the Mīmāṃsakas who accept the possibility of non-veridicality admit that it is known through a cognition distinct from the non-veridical cognition itself. Furthermore, on the Prābhākara ''omission'' analysis (where there is no cognitive non-veridicality), what people say is non-veridical is *by another cognition* exposed (as a failure to distinguish a concurrent perceiving and remembering, as explained in a later section).

Cognition of an absence requires prior cognition of the absentee. (To see that my glasses are not on the table I have to have prior acquaintance of them.) But the crucial veridicality inference is ''negative only'': the correlations run between (a) cognitions known to be non-veridical and (b) successful efforts being generated. That is, the pervasion is grasped only with respect to cognitions known to be non-veridical. Now, each non-veridical cognition is a positive presence, and its non-veridicality—which is a ''surplus property,'' *upādhi*, an imposed or titular property, not a true universal—is nevertheless something positive, too, the property N, let us say. The prover, generating successful effort (G), is not found in things that are N such that N is pervaded by such a lack (N → ~G). Then, with our veridicality inference, knowledge of the pervasion is not of a prover whose absence pervades the absence of the probandum—this would require that the probandum be known previously—but rather a positive property. The *modus tollens* step renders a negation of this property (i.e., given that *a* is not a ~G—where G is the prover—*a* is not an N). This means that the first-time veridical cognition (*a*) is proved to be not non-veridical (not an N). But then knowing the general definition of the non-veridical—and indeed the veridical in general (here the contrasting definitions *are* understood together)—we realize that the cognition is veridical without offending the absential cognition rule.

The *kevala-vyatirekin* ("negative only") inference is crucial to a certain type of definition. Even ether can be defined in this way, "Ether is distinct from things that are not ether, *since* it has etherhood." (The question of the ontological status of ether*hood* is irrelevant in this context. The standard example is earth, whose earthhood is, by the way, a true universal, a classification that is also irrelevant.) Ether is the inferential subject and thus bracketed in the inferential context. There is nothing outside of ether that is distinct from things that are not ether; there is thus no *sapakṣa*. Since there is no *sapakṣa*, there can be no discovery of a pervasion by the method of "positive correlation," *anvaya*, which requires finding cases of the prover and probandum together. But there is very good negative evidence: everything that we look at both does not exhibit etherhood and is not distinct-from-things-that-are-not-ether. The trick with "negative only" inferences is how the probandum term is familiar enough for the inference to proceed, given that the inferential subject is not known to possess the probandum prior to the inference. And if the probandum term is known outside the inferential subject, there would be no point to a "negative only" method. An inference could proceed based on positive as well as negative correlations, as discussed above. (To repeat, Gaṅgeśa addresses what I call a trilemma in a section of the next chapter.[14]) A pot, for example, is something that possesses the positive property (albeit a "surplus property," *upādhi*), not-being-distinct-from-things-that-are-other-than-ether (S) and also (is not-H, i.e.) does not exhibit etherhood (thus S and not-H). In fact, everything we look at outside of the inferential subject is like this, such we may say that there is a pervasion (to wit, S → ~H). The inferential subject, ether (*a*), however, does exhibit etherhood (*a* is not ~H). Thus by *modus tollens* we get a negation of (S) not-being-distinct-from-things-that-are-other-than-ether, which is (*arthāt*) equivalent to being-distinct-from-things-that-are-other-than-ether. Thus is this proved of ether. Other definitions—such as earth as distinct from all those things that are other than earth since it has earthhood or the property being-smelly (only earthen things are thought to have smell)—can be reconstructed on precisely parallel lines.

All the parts of the picture are now in place, but elaboration of an example considered in tedious detail in the *kevala-vyatirekin* section of the inference chapter may help us better appreciate how the problem of an unexampled probandum is solved here. We have explained that the veridicality of a first-time cognition is not known, prior to the inference, as the specific property that it is. But veridicality is known in general, and in general can be defined. Likewise, non-veridicality. This situation is precisely the reverse of that resolving the exampling or availability problem in the case of the stock inference later so laboriously discussed: ''Earth is distinct from the other things (on the traditional ontological list, viz., water and the other substances as well as qualities and things belonging to non-substance categories), *since* it is smelly; what is not so is not so, like a pond.'' In the terms of our trilemma, (1) there is no example of *is-distinct-from-the-other-things* outside of earth, the inferential subject, but (2) this probandum is known prior to the inference *in particular*—for instance, a pot, something earthen, is so known—and (3) the probandum is not known *in general* to apply to all of earth prior to the ''negative only'' inference and so the *siddha-sādhana* fallacy is not committed. The inference makes something new known through a generalization that proceeds on the basis of negative evidence (this pond is both not-distinct-etc. and not smelly). In the case of our veridicality inference, conversely, the new thing known is something absolutely particular and the property in general is what known previously.

Text (p. 268, Tirupati, and p. 257, Calcutta) and Translation

viśeṣaṇa-jñānaṃ vinā kathaṃ prāmāṇya-viśiṣṭânumitir iti cet, prathamaṃ na kathaṃcit | jñāne prāmāṇyam ity anumity-an-antaraṃ tena eva hetunā tatra eva prāmāṇya-viśiṣṭânumitiḥ, a-bhāva-viśeṣyaka-pratīty-an-antaram a-bhāvavad-bhūtalam iti jñāna-vat | evaṃ ca idaṃ vahni-prakāraka-jñānaṃ tadvati tad-a-bhāvavati vā iti saṃśayân-antaraṃ tad-a-bhāvavati tat-prakārakatva-vyatirekaḥ sidhyan tat-prakārakatām ādāya sidhyati | tṛtīya-prakārâ-bhāvena vinā sādhyasya upasaṃhartum a-śakyatvāt, jñāna-nityatva-vat | yad vā idaṃ vahnitva-prakāraka-jñānaṃ vahnitvavad-viṣayakaṃ, vahnitvâ-bhāva-vad-a-viṣayakatve sati saviṣayakatvāt, yan na evaṃ tan na evaṃ yathā vahny-a-pramā iti vyatireky-antarāt tat-siddhiḥ |

(**Gaṅgeśa** continues:) How, without (prior) cognition of the qualifier (i.e., the particular veridicality of a first-of-its-kind cognition), can there be an inference to what is qualified by veridicality? (Well) that is not cognized at the (very) first moment (in the relevant process), by any means. Immediately following an inference that there is veridicality in a cognition, by that (the same) prover, with regard to that (the same) subject, there is an inference to what is qualified by veridicality (*the* particular cognition). This is comparable to (the situation with) the cognition, "The floor is possessed of (is qualified by) an absence," that follows immediately a cognition whose qualificandum is the absence.

And, in this way, immediately following a doubt whether this cognition with firehood as its predication content is about something really possessing firehood or about something not possessing it, an absence of what has such predication content is proved with respect to what does not exhibit such firehood (by a "negative only" inference). Then, taking the having of such predication content in general, the veridicality (of the cognition) is proved. For, it is impossible to suppress an establishing of the probandum without some third type of absence. This is like (the inference to) the eternity of the cognition (that God uses in creating the universe).

Alternatively, this cognition with firehood as its predication content has as its object something that exhibits firehood, *since* it is something whose object does not exhibit an absence of firehood and it has an object. What is not so, is not so, as, for example, a non-veridical cognition of fire. Here veridicality is proved by another inference based on negative correlations.

Comments

A third type of absence would be one the absence of which would not be equivalent to a presence, and, Gaṅgeśa is implying, there is none: (1) a simple absence, (2) an absence of an absence, that is, a presence, and (3) something that does not obey the logic of, let us say, double negation.

To cognize a floor as qualified by an absence, first we have to cognize the the floor as a qualifier of the absence as qualificandum. Otherwise, as we shall learn, the rule that a cognition of an entity as qualified requires a prior cognition of the qualifier would not hold for absential cognitions in that invariably the absence would be the qualifier and would have to have been cognized previously. A quick or one-step inference converts the terms—the qualifier (the floor) and the qualificandum (the absence) swap places cognitively—and we say that the floor is qualified by the absence. The principle here is deep, and is involved in the posit of indeterminate perception (*nirvikalpaka-pratyakṣa*) as a first stage of perception, where a qualifier is independently cognized, not, as in a second stage, in determinate perception, as qualifying a qualificandum. See below, pp. 407ff, for details about cognition of absences.

Mathurānātha fills in the ellipsis in the comparison to eternal cognition. Since the universe is an effect of effort, cognition must have guided its production. The cognition must be eternal, for there are only the two possibilities, the eternal and the non-eternal, and we have reasons for ruling out the latter.

The final inference has a conjunct prover term, being-something-that-has-an-object coupled with not-having-an-object-that-exhibits-an-absence-of-firehood. Perhaps someone is worried that a cognition that is proved not to be about what lacks firehood does not have an object at all. The worry would be relieved by this inference where it is given (as captured in the prover term) that the cognition has an object in the sense of a qualificandum, here, an individual fire.

Text (p. 276, Tirupati, and p. 259, Calcutta) and Translation

atirikta-viṣayatā-pakṣe ayaṃ vahnitvena anubhavo '-vahni-vṛtti-vahnitva-prakāraka-viṣayatāko na, vahnitvâ-samānâdhikaraṇa-vahnitva-prakāraka-viṣayatāko na, viṣayâśrayâ-vṛtti-prakārakatvaṃ vā arthāt sidhyati, na tu prathamaṃ sādhyâ-prasiddheḥ |

(**Gaṅgeśa** continues with an inference framed in questionable terms:) On the view of objecthood as a (distinct category and) reality over and above (the commonly recognized categories of Nyāya-Vaiśeṣika ontology), this experience of something as fire does not have (or determine) an objecthood whose predication content is a firehood that exists in what is not fire, nor an objecthood whose predication content is a firehood that does not have the same locus (or substratum) as firehood, nor a predication content that does not exist in the same substratum as its objecthood—such is the property to be proved (the *sādhya*, the probandum in the current inference). That is to say, an experience's determining an objecthood whose predication content is a firehood that exists in fire—alternatively, whose predication content exists in the substratum of its objecthood—would be proved (let us say, for example)—but not for a first-time cognition whose veridicality is known, because the probandum would be unfamiliar.

Comments

Here an understood prover has to be supplied from preceding parallel inferences already stated (above, p. 108) without use of the controversial term *objecthood*: "given that the experience of fire produces (and guides) effort directed toward an object (viz., fire) capable of burning fuel, it is an ascertainment whose predication content is firehood; alternatively, it is an ascertainment whose predication content is firehood determining a qualificandum (viz., fire) that is capable of burning fuel."

Now to understand the passage at hand one has to understand some background theory and discussion concerning "objecthood" or "cognitive-objecthood" (*viṣayatā*). Objecthood is an ontological posit made by Naiyāyikas of a camp rival to Gaṅgeśa's. Gaṅgeśa does not himself subscribe to the position that there is such a separate real. He is, nevertheless, often willing to consider epistemic questions from perspectives that find objecthood a distinct and legitimate division of the real.

Objecthood exists only in an epistemic context; it exists in an object cognized only so long and insofar as it is cognized. To be an object, *viṣaya*, is to be an object of a particular cognition. The relation between the cognition and its object can be considered from the side of the object or from the side of consciousness. In the former case, it is called objecthood, which is said to reside in the object. In the latter, it is "the property of having an object," which, as a property, resides in the cognition. So far, even Gaṅgeśa would agree.

But further details about objecthood are disputed among Naiyāyikas, and not only its ontological status. Here Gaṅgeśa, according to Mathurānātha (as Mohanty explains[15]), refers to the particular view that three components normally identified—qualificandumhood, predication-contenthood, and qualificative-relationality—are not exhaustive, that there is an additional, more primitive objecthood that is principally a matter of being-a-qualificandum. And, indeed, the two properties, being-predication-content and qualificative-relationality, are properties not directly of the object but of this additional objecthood, or qualificandumhood, which is impregnated with them, so to say. As Mohanty constructs the debate, the point is "to rehabilitate the importance of the substance-attribute category in epistemological analysis, an importance which had suffered greatly: hence the attempt to locate the additional *viṣayatā* in the substantival component."[16]

The inferences framed are good ones though the probandum term would not be available for a first-time inference (without previous fire cognition we could hardly have previous cognition of firehood). Once we have become familiar with fire, these would be available—if we can swallow the theory of objecthood.

Text (p. 277, Tirupati) and Translation

vahni-bhrame ca viṣayatâśrayo na vahniḥ, viṣayatāyā viśeṣya-vṛttitvād iti bhramatvena na siddha-sādhanam | anye tu vahni-bhrame yā viśeṣaṇa-vṛttir viṣayatā sā viśeṣya-vṛtti-viṣayatāyā a-bhinnā iti na sā vahnitvâ-samānâdhikaraṇa-dharmân-avacchinnā iti na siddha-sādhanam iti |

(**Gaṅgeśa** continues:) And in the case of an erroneous cognition of fire, fire is not the substratum of the objecthood (that the cognition determines), since the objecthood rests in the qualificandum (and so the probandum terms given just above are successful in distinguishing the veridical from the non-veridical). Thus (you cannot allege that) in the case of error (we commit a mistake in proving what you accept; that is to say, there is with the inferences) no fallacy of "trying to prove what is admitted," *siddha-sādhana*.

Others, however, hold that in the case of an erroneous cognition of fire (the matter should be viewed differently, in that, on this view) the objecthood that resides in the qualifier is not distinct from the objecthood that exists in the qualificandum. As such, it is not specified by a property (whether *qua* qualifier or *qua* qualificandum) whose locus is not the same as that of firehood. Here, too, there would be no fallacy of trying to prove what is admitted.

Comments

An example of a non-veridical cognition as understood in terms of the first version of "objecthood" is straightforward: if something *x* perceived as fire is not fire, then the objecthood that exists in *x*—an objecthood established there, or determined, by the experience—does not exist in fire. Readers are invited to think through the other formulations on their own.

Ramanuja Tatacharya explains the avoidance of the *siddha-sādhana* fallacy, following Mathurānātha (pp. 262–63). From the Mīmāṃsaka perspective, the subject term of the inference at the top of page 276 of the Vidyapeetha edition (above, p. 114), "this experience (of something) as fire," applies to what Naiyāyikas see as both veridical and non-veridical cognitions. The worry is, then, that the probandum terms (to focus on the first, namely, "does not have an objecthood whose predication content is a firehood that exists in what is not fire") may also apply to what Naiyāyikas see as error. Thus the inference would establish what Mīmāṃsakas admit, namely, that all experiences, *qua* experiences, are veridical.

The seriousness of the worry becomes sharper when one sees, as Ramanuja Tatacharya explains, that disputants find two distinct types of error, (a) where a qualifier is projected, so to say, onto a thing in front with which one is in sensory contact, and (b) where something else's identity is projected. The first type would be an error by way of a false inherence, or "resting-in" relation, between a property and a property-bearer, the second by way of a false identity between two property-bearers. Almost any example can be viewed in both ways. An example of the first type would be mother-of-pearl misperceived as silver, where silverhood is a projected qualifier (seeing *a* as possessing F when *a* lacks F). An example of the second type would be mother-of-pearl mistaken for silver, where silver itself, not silverhood, is projected (seeing *a* as *b* when *a* is not *b*). The latter would be a mistake of identity, *tādātmya*. With this type of error, the experience would meet the stipulations of the probandum term, the first probandum term given on p. 276, since, to change examples, not firehood but fire itself would be the predication content. Thus, the probandum would fail to exclude error—in that a projection of fire as opposed to firehood would indeed be an experience that "does not determine an objecthood whose predication content is a *firehood* that exists in what is not fire''—and would be an example of the fallacy, ''proving what is admitted (by the other side).'' So, Gaṅgeśa draws our attention away from the probandum and points out that the subject term, ''experience of something *as fire*''—where in Sanskrit the term *firehood* is used in the predicative instrumental (that is, experience of something as recognized by its *firehood*)—excludes errors of the identity type. Since the objecthood that the experience determines is supposed to *rest in* the property-bearer, the identity type of error is excluded, and the inference does not commit the fallacy of ''proving what is already admitted.''

The ''others'' Gaṅgeśa mentions here, who do not distinguish an objecthood determined by a qualifier from an objecthood determined by a qualificandum, also have no problem distinguishing error and veridical cognition, in that, were one so to understand objecthood, then by means of a new probandum that Gaṅgeśa provides—viz., ''is not specified by a property (whether qua qualifier or qua qualificandum) whose locus (or substratum) is not the same as that of firehood''—one would also successfully exclude error. In error, the property ''thisness'' would specify an objecthood whose locus is not the same as that of firehood.

Text (p. 278, Tirupati) and Translation

> na ca maṇi-jñānasya prāmāṇyânumāne maṇi-pramāyāṃ maṇi-bhrameṇa pravṛttasya maṇi-prāptau maṇi-gocara-prayatna-janaka-maṇitva-prakāraka-niścayatvam an-aikāntikam iti vācyam | maṇi-prabhā-viṣayaka-jñānena bhinna-viṣayatayā maṇi-gocara-prayatnân-utpādāt | maṇi-prāptis tu na antarīyakatvāt | jñāna-prayatnayor a-samāna-kālatve 'py anubhava-smaraṇayor iva kāraṇa-kārya-bhāva-graha iti na a-siddhiḥ |

Objection: Given (a person's successful effort in) acquiring a jewel by (let us suppose) mistaking the jewel's lustre for the jewel itself, an inference to the veridicality of a cognition of a jewel (faces the following problem): the certainty would be ambiguous in its generating effort whose object is such a jewel—certainty whose predication content would be jewelhood.

Gaṅgeśa: That should not be said. For, a cognition whose object is a jewel's lustre does not (strictly speaking) give rise to effort directed toward a jewel (but rather toward a jewel's lustre): the objects (the lustre, on the one hand, and the jewel, on the other) are distinct. The acquisition of the jewel would not be intimate (to the effort, i.e., would be accidental). Although cognition and effort do not occur at the same time, a cause-and-effect relationship is grasped by the mind (the internal organ, *manas*), as it does in the case of a (memory-forming) awareness and a remembering. Thus, there is no failure (of the general pattern of inference to veridicality in that here its terms are not met).

Comments

Gaṅgeśa's dismantling of the objection disambiguates "cognizing an object," which here would be perceiving a qualificandum, on the one hand, and perceiving it as having a property, on the other. And then he rejoins the two in his theory of effort. An object perceived as F simply does not provoke effort toward another perceived as G. This view ties in tightly with the Naiyāyika understanding of error as having predication content that in fact does not qualify the object cognized. The error, "Silver," in the face of mother-of-pearl has the mother-of-pearl, which is what is reached for, as its object qua qualificandum. But the effort is guided by the cognition's predication content. Here the deep point is that success and failure are explainable, Gaṅgeśa says, without abandoning this picture of the relation between cognition and the will to act. Also, this is a supposition that is reinforced, he points out at the end, by an analogy to awareness of something and a later remembering of the same thing.

Text (p. 282, Tirupati) and Translation

a-bhāva-sādhyake ca nirvikalpakasya prathamaṃ sapakṣatvena a-niścayān na a-sādhāraṇam |

(**Gaṅgeśa** continues:) And when the probandum is the absence (of non-veridicality, as in the above inference stated from the perspective of those who accept objecthood as a distinct and separate category of the real), there is no fallacy of no-similar-instance since, with a first-time cognition, an indeterminate perception (which might be thought to be a comparison class, and, as not a case of the current inference's prover, would suggest that the no-similar-instance fallacy has been committed. But it) is not definitely known to be a case like the subject in question.

Comments

The no-similar-instance fallacy, *a-sādhāraṇya*, is technically not where there is no known example of the probandum—this would be *sādhyâ-prasiddhi* (mentioned p. 243, Tirupati, above, p. 102), an "unexampled probandum"—but where there is no example of the probandum and prover together presuming that there is a *sapakṣa*, at least one instance of the probandum other than the (bracketed) case of the inferential subject itself. The prover does not have to be found in every instance of the probandum since the required pervading is the other way around, namely, *of* the prover *by* the probandum, not the reverse. Nevertheless, normally some cases where the probandum and prover occur together have to be known, and if we know of a *sapakṣa* we need to find the prover somewhere there. That is to say, if there is a *sapakṣa*, then there has to be at least one known case of the prover qualifying something in that set of probandum instances.

Given that a person's inference to the veridicality of a first-time cognition uses a general rule, however, that is, as explained, based on negative correlations, there need be no positive comparison class. All we have to do is recognize that the cognition is *unlike* any cognition that had led to failure. Now one might think that a cognition arising in unfamiliar circumstances would be similar to an indeterminate perception, that is to say, to a cognition that directly grasps a qualifier but not as related to a qualificandum, a cognition that is not verbalizable because it is *niṣprakāraka*, "without predication content." Cognitions of this type would constitute a comparison class, in that, as Gaṅgeśa will later explain (below, pp. 238–39), indeterminate perceptions are neither veridical nor non-veridical. Since both veridicality and non-veridicality presuppose predication content while they do not have any, they fall outside the division. Thus they would seem to fit the description of the probandum given on p. 276 (Tirupati)—above, p. 114—since as not non-veridical they would "*not* determine an objecthood whose predication content, etc." And as instances of the probandum, we would expect the general rule, or pervasion, to be supported by some occurrences of the prover there and, likewise, an inference that is based on positive correlations. And if the prover were not found, there would be the fallacy of no-similar-instance. There would be other instances of the probandum but not of the probandum and prover together. For, indeed, in no indeterminate cognition is there the prover for the current inference. However, since the subject at issue is a first-time cognition, whether indeterminate cognition is comparable is not definitely known. So there is no positive comparison class.

Text (p. 264, Calcutta) and Translation

tathā ayaṃ pṛthivī ity anubhavaḥ pṛthivītvâ-bhāvavati pṛthivītva-prakārako na, a-pṛthivī-vṛtti-prakārako na, viśeṣyâ-vṛtti-prakārako na, pṛthivītva-prakārakatve sati pṛthivy-a-viśeṣyako na, pṛthivītva-vyadhikaraṇa-prakārakâvacchinno na, pṛthivy-a-vṛtti-prakārako na vā, gandhavad-viśeṣyaka-pṛthivītva-prakāraka-niścayatvād iti vyatirekī | pṛthivītva-bhramaḥ pṛthivītvâ-bhāvavati pṛthivītva-prakāraka iti na bhramatvena siddha-sādhanam, na vā gandhavad-viśeṣyaka iti na vyabhicāraḥ | pṛthivītvavati pṛthivītva-prakārakatvâdikam arthāt sidhyati | viṣayatā-pakṣe ayaṃ pṛthivītvena anubhavaḥ pṛthivī-vṛtti-pṛthivītva-prakāraka-viṣayatāko na, pṛthivy-a-vṛtti-pṛthivītva-prakāraka-viṣayatāko na, pṛthivītvâ-samānâdhikaraṇa-pṛthivītva-prakāraka-viṣayatāko na, viṣayatâśrayâ-vṛtti-prakārako na vā iti sādhyam | pṛthivītva-samānâdhikaraṇa-pṛthivītva-prakāraka-viṣayatākatvâdikam arthāt sidhyati | anye tu pṛthivītvâ-samānâdhikaraṇa-prakārâvacchinna-viṣayatākatvâ-bhāvaḥ sādhyaḥ, gandhâ-samānâdhikaraṇâ-prakāraka-gandha-samānâdhikaraṇa-prakāraka-viṣayatā-pratiyogi-jñānatvāt | tena saṃśaya-vyavacchedaḥ | niścayatvaṃ vā tad-viśeṣaṇam ity āhuḥ | śītā pṛthivī ity anubhavaḥ pṛthivy-aṃśe pramā eva | pramā-bhrama-rūpe ca samūhâlambane na vyabhicāraḥ | aṃśe tasya api pramātvāt, viśeṣya-bhedena viṣayatā-bhedāc ca | na ca prakāra-bhedena viṣayatā-bhedaḥ mānâ-bhāvāt |

(**Gaṅgeśa** continues:) Similarly, the awareness, "This is earth," is (when the awareness is indeed of earth) not something with earthhood predication content about that which does not exhibit earthhood, nor something whose predication content exists in what is not earth, nor something whose predication content does not exist in the qualificandum, nor, given that its predication content is earthhood, is it something that does not have as its qualificandum earth, nor something specified by a predication content that has a different locus from that of earthhood, nor something whose predication content does not exist in earth, *since* it is an ascertainment whose qualificandum exhibits (the property of) odor and whose predication content is earthhood—this is an inference based on negative correlations.

An erroneous cognition of earthhood, with earthhood as its predication content, is with respect to something that does not exhibit earthhood. Thus (you cannot allege that) in the case of error (we commit a mistake in proving what you accept; that is to say, there is with the inference) no fallacy of trying to prove what is admitted (by the other side). Nor does the cognition have as its qualificandum that which exhibits earth. Thus, there is no fallacy of deviation (i.e., of a counterexample to a general rule or pervasion). By implication, the likes of having earthhood as predication content about a qualificandum that does exhibit earth (in other words, veridicality) is proved.

On the view of those who see objecthood as an independent real, this awareness of something as earth does not determine an objecthood whose predication content is an earthhood that exists in what is not earth, nor does it determine an objecthood whose predication content is an earthhood that does not exist in earth, nor does it determine an objecthood whose predication content is an earthhood that does not reside in the same locus as that of earthhood, nor does it have predication content that does not exist in the substratum of the objecthood (that the cognition determines)—such is the probandum. By implication, the likes of determining an objecthood whose predication content is an earthhood having the same locus as earthhood is proved.

Others, however, hold that the probandum is: an absence of a determining of an objecthood specified by predication content that does not reside in the same locus as earthhood. (The prover would be:) *since* it is a cognition that is correlate to an objecthood (that it determines) having as predication content odor that exists in the same locus (as the objecthood) and not having as predication content odor that does not exist in its same locus. By this, doubt would be excluded. Or, that this is an ascertainment is (added as) a qualification to that (that is, added as a qualification to the prover, "a cognition that is correlate, etc.")—so they (these others) say.

The awareness, "Cold is this earth," is simply veridical in the portion about earth (when earth indeed is cognized). And so there is no deviation with respect to a cognition based on a group of things in the form of something being veridically cognized and something else erroneously. For, it is also, in the part, veridical, and a distinctness between two qualificanda means a distinctness between two objecthoods (that the group cognition determines). And distinct predication contents do not mean distinct objecthoods, since there is no argument.

Comments

See the comments just above, pp. 114ff, on objecthood.

Being cold is not a property of earth, according to the physics that Gaṅgeśa inherits from his Nyāya-Vaiśeṣika tradition. Thus, "Cold is this earth," would appear to be a non-veridical cognition, and to be as well, unfortunately, a cognition that meets the definitions of a veridical cognition in the inferences just above. However, that cognition is veridical in its portion concerning earth, Gaṅgeśa points out. He also says that it involves two distinct qualificanda, which is perplexing, since the cognition does not appear to refer to two distinct things, but to one, known as both earth and cold. Yet, according to Gaṅgeśa's physics, cold is a property of water, and the proper causal analysis of the error is that undetected water mixed in with earth has produced a sensation of cold. So, in fact the cognition would have two qualificanda, earth and water, though of course they (or one of them) may be unrecognized at the time—the cognition is, after all, an error in part. But it is an error only in part. Thus, the previous inference, which relies on certain characterizations of veridicality, can stand.

Those definitions, by the way, command more attention in the section, "Characterizing Veridicality," the *pramā-lakṣaṇa-vāda*.

Finally, it is worth keeping in mind that, as Gaṅgeśa says here, distinct predication contents do not correspond to distinct objecthoods, according to the rival ontological position centering on objecthood. Distinct qualificanda, on the other hand, do correspond to distinct objecthoods. This seems right in that a single thing typically would have multiple properties, and could be cognized as exhibiting more than one property, whereas distinct qualificanda are simply distinct things. The proper analysis of the cold-earth cognition is, according to Gaṅgeśa, not "This is cold and earthen" but "This is cold" and "This is earthen."

Text (p. 288, Tirupati) and Translation

yat tu iyaṃ pṛthivī ity anubhavaḥ pṛthivītva-samānâdhikaraṇa-dharmâvacchinna-pṛthivī-viśeṣayaka-viṣayatākaḥ, pṛthivītva-vyadhikaraṇa-dharmân-avacchinna-pṛthivī-viśeṣyaka-viṣayatākaḥ, pṛthivy-a-vṛtti-dharmân-avacchinna-pṛthivī-vṛtti-

viṣayatāko vā, gandhâ-samānâdhikaraṇa-dharmâ-prakāraka-viṣayatā-pratiyogi-jñānatvāt, a-gandhavad-vṛtti-pṛthivītva-prakāraka-viṣayatākatvāt, gandha-samānâdhikaraṇa-viṣayatā-pratiyogi-jñānatvād iti | tan na | sādhyâ-prasiddheḥ | kiṃ tv arthād eva tat sidhyati | evaṃ yat-prakāra-vyāpyatayā yad-gandha-sneha-samartha-pravṛtti-janakatva-kara-caraṇâdikam avagataṃ tadvati tat-prakāraka-jñānatvam eva prāmāṇye liṅgam |

(**Gaṅgeśa** continues:) But the following inference (for the veridicality of a first-time cognition) would be wrong: An awareness, "This is earth" (when indeed earth is cognized), determines an objecthood whose qualificandum is earth, a qualificandum specified by a property that has the same locus as earth-hood, or it determines an objecthood whose qualificandum is earth, a qualificandum not specified by a property having a different locus than earth-hood, or it determines an objecthood that exists in earth and that is not specified by a property that does not exist in earth, *since* it is a cognition correlate to an objecthood that does not have as its predication content a property not having the same locus as odor, or *since* it determines an objecthood having as its predication content an earthhood that does not exist in that which does not exhibit odor, or *since* it is a cognition correlate to an objecthood having the same locus as odor. (The reason it would be wrong to take such an inference as a prover of the veridicality of a first-time cognition is that) the probandum property would be unexampled (outside the current case). However, simply by force of the meaning (of what can be proved), this could be proved.

Thus, a property that is understood as pervaded by a (property appearing in a cognition as its) predication content, such as odor, fluidity, a generating-of-effort-toward-something-capable (of producing an appropriate sensory quality), or a having of hands and feet, is an inferential mark of veridicality: it (what is so understood) is just the fact that the cognition has ϕ predication content about a ϕ object.

Comments

In the passage's first paragraph, the probandum property is, in each case, so formulated that the probandum could not be previously known in an instance of a first-time cognition of a certain type (as before, without previous earth-cognition we could hardly have previous cognition of earthhood). However, such inferences as these, Gaṅgeśa says, could be teased out simply by appreciating the meaning of that which has legitimately been proved.

"Teasing out" may not be quite the right way to express what Gaṅgeśa means by the expression *arthāt*, translated here as, "by force of the meaning," and earlier as, "by implication," and generally as "in effect." He himself explains what he means in the second paragraph. Given that we cognize something—Gaṅgeśa's implicit examples are earth, water, veridical cognition (in apperception), and a human body—as exhibiting a property S that itself we know to be invariably indicated by another property H (H as pervaded by S: where an H, there an S), then cognition of the latter, H, as exhibited by the same qualificandum as that determined by a cognition of S, shows that the cognition of S is veridical. In fact, knowledge of such pervasions make possible confirmation of a cognition by the success of effort based thereon. We know, for example, that a cognition of earth is veridical by having a later cognition of odor, and by knowing (as a matter of definition, *arthāt*, though a definition that is in a way perceptually given, as will be explained) that whatever exhibits odor also exhibits earthhood. Similarly, for a cognition of a human body by a cognition of hands and feet and so on. I hazard the interpretation that by *arthāt* Gaṅgeśa indicates what philosophers have called the *a priori* and what Ludwig Wittgenstein would call a grammatical rule. For Wittgenstein, it would be a grammatical remark—a providing of a definition—to say that fire is capable of burning fuel, that earthen things have smell, and so on.

It would of course be wrong, however, to take a thoroughly apriorist view of knowledge of such enabling definitions, since, for Gaṅgeśa and the entire Nyāya tradition, the definitions have perceptual roots, as we shall see in the next passage.

On a related matter, the pragmatic test of veridicality, we should keep in mind, is unnecessary to all confirmation. Veridicality can be confirmed by knowing the type of thing perceived such that no real effort or action (or not much) may be required—once one had seen that an object in the distance does in fact possess hands and feet—in that through apperception one can know that a perception of one property confirms the perception of another, given that the two cognized properties are perceived as exhibited by the same thing. There would be a pervaded property, e.g., possessing hands and feet, etc., as pervaded by a pervader, being a human body. Thus, a perception of the former could confirm the veridicality of a perception of the latter—without effort or action.

In the next passage, Gaṅgeśa explains these "enabling definitions" as perceptually given. There is also an analogy drawn to inference, and the causal processes similarly involve a role for the mind in retrieving the content of previous perceptions through provocation of memory. The move makes veridicality inferences seem awfully immediate, and thus it seems at least a step towards the Mīmāṃsaka intrinsicality stance. The objector in the next passage makes this point as he wraps up his challenge to Gaṅgeśa's reliance on such so-to-say self-evident truths, "Fire is capable of burning fuel" and so on.

Text (p. 289, Tirupati) and Translation

nanu vahni-jñānasya dāha-samartha-viṣayatvaṃ na dāha-samartho 'yam iti vyavasāya-gamyam, jñāna-viṣayatayos tad-a-viṣayatvāt | na api tad-

anuvyavasāya-gamyam, puro-varti-dāha-sāmarthyasya tad-a-gocaratvāt | vyavasāyôpanīta-dāha-sāmarthyasya ca bhāne tad-a-sāmarthyāt | anyathā vyavasāyôpanītasya puro-vartini vahnitvasya anuvyavasāya-viṣayatve svataḥ prāmāṇya-grahâpatteḥ | evaṃ pṛthivī-jala-jñānayor gandha-snehavad-viṣayakatva-grahe 'py an-upapanna iti | ucyate | vahnitva-prakāraka-jñānânuvyavasāye sati tatra viṣaye dāha-sāmarthya-jñānân-antaraṃ tat-smṛty-upanīte vahni-vyavasāye smṛty-upanīta-dāha-samartha-viṣayakatvam | evaṃ jala-pṛthivī-jñānayoḥ smṛty-upanītayoḥ jñānôpanīta-sneha-gandhavad-viṣayakatvaṃ manasā paricchidyate | gandhâdimaty eva mama pṛthivītvâdy-anubhava iti gandhâdimattva-paricchedân-antaram anubhavāt | smṛty-upanīte dhūmâdau vyāpti-pariccheda-vat cakṣuṣā candane saurabha-jñāna-vac ca |

Objection: That a cognition of fire has as its object something capable of burning fuel is not known from an original (non-apperceptive) cognition, "This is capable of burning fuel," since neither such a cognition nor such an object (i.e., capacity for burning) figures as object of the cognition of fire. Nor is it known from an apperception (that takes the original cognition of fire as its object), since the capacity of the thing in front (the fire) for burning fuel is not within its scope (either). Moreover, such an apperception is not capable of presenting a capacity for burning as set in the original cognition. Otherwise, if the object of the apperception comprised the firehood (not only) as presented in the original awareness (but as really) *in the thing in front*, then there would be the unfortunate ramification (unfortunate, that is, from your Naiyāyika point of view) of a grasping of veridicality intrinsically. In this way, too, that cognitions of earth and of water grasp as their objects (respectively) an exhibiting of odor and of fluidity would be impossible (that is, on your view).

Gaṅgeśa: We answer. Immediately after an apperception of a cognition having firehood as its predication content, there occurs (in appropriate circumstances) a cognition of a capacity for burning fuel with respect to that very object (i.e., the object of the original cognition, fire, namely). Given an original cognition of fire brought back into perceptual content through a memory that is of that, the fact that the object is capable of burning fuel is (also) brought back through memory.

In this way, the fact that cognitions of water and of earth, as perceptually brought back through memory (*upanīta*), have objects that exhibit (respectively) fluidity and odor (which are properties themselves) brought back by other cognitions (i.e., through connections that are "mentally mediated," *jñāna-lakṣaṇa-saṃnikarṣa*), is apprehended by the mind (by the internal organ, *manas*, in apperception). For, there is immediately afterwards a concluding that something has odor and so on, an awareness (expressed as follows): "My experience of earthhood and so on is (was) in fact about something exhibiting odor and so on." This is like an apprehension of pervasion in smoke and so on, which are brought back through memory, and like a cognition of fragrance in sandalwood presented by the visual organ.

Comments

The mind has an extraordinary capacity for synthesis of elements presented in experience: so long as the fragrance, for example, of sandalwood has been previously experienced, even the visual organ can provoke an awareness of it, through a mentalized sensory connection, called by Naiyāyikas a *jñāna-lakṣaṇā-pratyāsatti*.

As we shall see in the section on perceptual illusion, a theory of "extraordinary sensory connection," is appealed to to explain an infusion of memory content (of course acquired perceptually) into a current perception, to explain, for example, the "silverness" portion of an erroneous seeing of mother-of-pearl, "This is silver." Naiyāyikas distinguish "common" (*laukika*) and "extraordinary" (*a-laukika*) sensory connections according to how directly a sense organ is involved in the causal process that results in the given bit of perceptual or predication content. There is extraordinary breadth, it seems, to the theory of mentally mediated perceptual objects.

The visual perception, "A piece of *fragrant* sandalwood," is cited as a non-illusory example of the phenomenon. This would involve an "extraordinary" sensory connection in that the fragrance is said to be visually presented—to speak of the most immediate role of a sense organ—although, of course, the experience of the fragrance is of a smell. A memory created by a previous smelling experience gets fused, "extraordinarily," and becomes a perceptual object, although there is no current contact of the smelling organ with the sandalwood. Apparently this is borne out phenomenologically: people sometimes report the pleasure of smelling a piece of sandalwood that, in a physical sense, they only see. Thus, as in error, a memory-impression would play a crucial causal role.

The theory of extraordinary sensory connection has wider application still. It is invoked to explain recognitions (e.g., "This is that Devadatta I saw yesterday"), as we shall see. It is also invoked in answer to the question of how pervasions are known, as Gaṅgeśa points out here.

The objector targets the claim that a fire that is presented perceptually would also be presented perceptually as "capable of burning fuel." The certificational inferences that Gaṅgeśa has sketched depend on water being known as quenching thirst, fire as capable of burning fuel, and so on. Apperception can trigger, Gaṅgeśa says in reply, a retrieving of previous perceptual content such that a fire is known in the way that other fires have been known, to wit, as "capable of burning fuel," a bit of predication content enlivened and fused into current perception, so to say. With knowledge of such truths, certificational inferences can proceed—confirming one bit of content by later cognition of the other or coming to see the non-veridicality of a cognition with the one bit of content through a cognition of an absence of the other with respect to the same qualificandum.

Text (p. 290, Tirupati, and p. 271, Calcutta) and Translation

tarhi pṛthivītva-jñāne gandhavad-viśeṣyakatvavat cakṣuṣā gandhavati pṛthivītvôpanayân-antaram iyam pṛthivī iti pṛthivītva-prakārakânubhave upanīte pṛthivītvavati pṛthivītva-prakārakatvam | tathā tatra eva jñāne ghaṭatva-prakāratā-virahavat pṛthivy-a-vṛtti-prakārâ-bhāvavattvaṃ viśeṣyâ-vṛtti-prakārâ-bhāvavattvaṃ vā prāmāṇyaṃ manasā eva paricchidyatām iti svata eva prāmāṇya-graha iti cet, na | jñānântarôpasthāpita-jñāna-vṛtti-prāmāṇya-grahe paratastvân-apāyāt | yāvaj-jñāna-grāhaka-sāmagrī-grāhyatvam, yāvat-svâśraya-grāhaka-grāhyatvam, taj-jñāna-viṣayaka-janya-jñānâ-janya-janya-jñāna-grāhyatvaṃ vā svatastvam | tad-anyathā-grāhyatvaṃ tu paratastvam | manasā ca evaṃ prāmāṇya-grahasya abhyupagame taj-jñāna-viṣayaka-janya-jñāna-janya-jñāna-grāhyatvān na parastva-hāniḥ | vyatireky-an-antaraṃ taj-jātīyatvena anvayinā[17] prāmāṇyânumānam | yathā idaṃ śarīra-jñānaṃ pramā kara-caraṇa-vati śarīra-jñānatvāt sva-śarīra-jñāna-vat | na ca kara-caraṇântaravati kara-caraṇântaravattva-jñāne vyabhicāraḥ, śarīrâṃśe tasya pramātvāt |

Objection: Then, like the fact of a qualificandum exhibiting odor being apprehended in a cognition of earthhood, (there would be the following cognitive sequence: first) earthhood being retrieved from memory by means of (an awareness involving) the visual organ about something exhibiting odor would be immediately followed by (second) an awareness having earthhood as its predication content and retrieved by memory, "This is earth"—(given all this, there would be apprehended, third) the fact of a having of earthhood as predication content, a having that is about something that exhibits earthhood. Similarly, in that same (third, apperceptive) cognition, like a lack of pothood as predication content, let there be apprehended, just by the mind (by the internal organ, *manas*), a fact of an exhibiting of an absence of predication content that does not exist in earth, or a fact of an exhibiting of an absence of predication content that does not exist in the qualificandum, (which amounts to) veridicality! Thus would there be a grasping of veridicality instrinsically only!

Gaṅgeśa: No. For, if veridicality is grasped as existing in one cognition as presented by another cognition, there is no avoiding of an extrinsicality view (of how veridicality is cognized).

The *intrinsicality* view amounts to veridicality being grasped through just that collection of causal conditions responsible for the grasping of the target cognition, or veridicality being grasped by just that which grasps its own substratum (the substratum being the cognition that is veridical), or veridicality being grasped by a generated cognition that is not generated by a generated cognition whose object is that cognition (i.e., the cognition that is veridical). But veridicality viewed as being grasped in another way than these is an *extrinsicality* position. And, in this way, if a grasping of veridicality by the mind (the internal organ, *manas*) is accepted, then, since it would be grasped by a cognition generated by a generated cognition whose object is that cognition (i.e., the cognition that is veridical), there is no relinquishing of an extrinsicality view.

Following an inference based on negative correlations, there can be an inference to veridicality according to the method of positive correlations *to the same type of cognition*, as, for example, there is with, "This cognition of a human body is veridical, *since* it is a human-body cognition with respect to something exhibiting hands and feet, like a cognition of one's own body."

And there is no deviation in the case of a cognition of something as exhibiting hands and feet with respect to something else exhibiting hands and feet, for it would be veridical in its portion concerning a human body (though it got another portion wrong).

Comments

Gaṅgeśa's analysis of intrinsicality in his second paragraph of response is perhaps too compact. An apperception is generated in part by its target cognition. Thus an apperception whose target is veridical would be generated in part by a cognition the grasping of whose veridicality is at issue. And such an apperception would itself be in part responsible for generating the inference which shows the target cognition to be veridical, on the Nyāya view. So the veridicality is not as an intrinsicality view would have it; the veridicality is grasped by a generated cognition that *is* "generated by a generated cognition whose object is that cognition" that is veridical.

Once we are familiar with a type of cognition and know other instances to be veridical—e.g., of something exhibiting hands and feet, or, of the appearance of water in a certain environment—we can be sure of a later instance's veridicality *without* checking. The second time we see the river in the distance, we need not bathe and so on to know that the river cognition is veridical. Thus, while pragmatic verification is the ultimate touchstone, it is not the only way we can know veridicality.

Text (p. 292, Tirupati) and Translation

etena kara-caraṇavati śarīra-jñānatvād ity atra kara-caraṇavattvaṃ na upalakṣaṇam, vyāvṛttôpalakṣyâ-bhāvāt | na ca viṣayatayā jñāna-viśeṣaṇam, kara-caraṇavattva-prakāraka-śarīra-jñānatvasya vyabhicārāt, śarīram iti jñāne tad-a-siddheś ca | viṣaya-viśeṣaṇatve kara-caraṇavad-viṣayaka-śarīra-jñānasya vyabhicārāt | śarīra-bhramasya vastutaḥ karâdimad-viṣayakatvāt | na api kara-caraṇâdi-śūnye yac-charīratvena jñānaṃ tad-anyatve sati iti vivakṣitam | śūnya ity atra viṣayatvaṃ saptamy-artha iti kara-caraṇa-śūnya-viṣayaka-śarīra-jñānânya-śarīra-jñānatvād ity arthaḥ | tathā ca a-siddhiḥ | śarīra-jñānasya tac-chūnya-śarīratvâdi-viṣayakatva-niyamāt | na vā kara-caraṇa-śūnye yac-charīratvena jñānaṃ na bhavati iti vivakṣitam | tṛtīyârthasya viṣayatve ukta-doṣāt anyasya a-saṃbhavād iti nirastam | kara-caraṇavad-viśeṣyaka-śarīratva-prakāraka-jñānatvasya hetutvāt | śarīra-bhrame ca kara-caraṇavataḥ śarīrasya viśeṣaṇatvāt | viṣayatā-pakṣe kara-caraṇâdi-śūnya-niṣṭha-śarīratva-prakāraka-viṣayatā-pratiyogitva-śūnyatve sati śarīra-jñānatvād iti hetuḥ |

(**Gaṅgeśa** continues:) By this reasoning are rejected the following objections.

Objection: The prover term (in the example of an inference based on positive correlations, "This cognition of a human body is veridical, *since* it is a cognition of a human body with respect to something exhibiting hands and feet, like a cognition of one's own body," the prover, namely) *being a cognition of a human body with respect to something exhibiting hands and feet*, here the *something exhibiting hands and feet* is not a designator, because there is nothing designated as excluded. And it is (not only not a designator, it is also) not a qualifier (and presumably the term must be either a designator or a qualifier) of the cognition through an objecthood (that the cognition determines), since there would be deviation (from the set of things exhibiting the property to be proved, veridicality, namely) on the part of some human-body cognitions with predication content as an exhibiting of hands and feet (in that there could be an erroneous cognition presenting a human body and hands and feet), and since that (something exhibiting hands and feet) is not (necessarily) known in the case of a cognition, "This is a human body."

If it is taken to be a qualifier of the object, there would (still) be deviation on the part of some human-body cognitions whose object exhibited hands and feet, since an erroneous cognition of a human body really has, too, as its object (in the sense of predication content) something exhibiting hands, etc. Nor could the intended meaning be "cognition of something as a human body, given that it is other than that which lacks hands, feet, and so on." The meaning would amount to: "*since* it is a cognition of a human body that is other than a cognition of a human body whose object lacks hands and feet," in that here (with the last proposal) the word, "lacks" (or "lacking," in the locative case) is to be taken in the sense of a cognitive object, which is the meaning of the locative case, and as such the object would be unexampled (there being no object *qua* cognitive presentation that either has or does not have hands and feet: these belong to things in the world). It is a general principle that any human-body cognition has as its cognitive object the likes of human-body-*hood* that lacks that (i.e., real hands and feet)! Nor is the intended meaning, "a cognition of something as some human body that does not come to be with respect to something that lacks hands and feet." For, since the meaning (here) of the instrumental case (something as recognized *by* . . .) is (also) the cognitive object, there is the fault already stated, another meaning being impossible.

Gaṅgeśa: All these are misinterpretations in that the prover term is *being a cognition that has* ***as its qualificandum*** *something exhibiting hands and feet* and as its predication content *human-body-hood* (or, *being a human body*). And in the case of an erroneous cognition of a human body, the qualifier (presented in cognition as predication content) is a human body *as* possessing hands and feet (as opposed to being about something that really exhibits hands and feet).

On the view of objecthood (as an independent category), the prover property is: *being a human-body cognition, given that the there is no cognitively correlate objecthood whose predication content is a human-body-hood that rests in something lacking hands, feet, etc.*

Comments

The objections hinge on an ambiguity of the word, *viṣaya*, "object," an ambiguity matched in use of the English word: (a) cognitive presentation, the object of a cognition in the sense of a presentation whether veridical or non-veridical, and (b) thing in the world, an object of cognition in the sense of a real thing in the world being cognized. There is the same ambiguity in the senses, referred to in the text, of the locative and instrumental cases in Sanskrit. Gaṅgeśa, in his response, makes it clear that he means an object in the sense of a cognition's qualificandum, that is to say, the thing in the world that the cognition is about, not its predication content, which is separately specified.

Text (p. 293, Tirupati, and p. 276, Calcutta) and Translation

> nanu na anya-gṛhīta-prāmāṇyaṃ jñānaṃ para-prāmāṇya-niścaya-rūpam an-avasthānāt | na api sva-jñāyamāna-prāmāṇyam, svataḥ-prāmāṇya-grahâpatteḥ | ato '-gṛhīta-prāmāṇyam eva jñānaṃ para-prāmāṇya-niścaya-rūpam āstheyam | tathā ca vyavasāyo 'py a-gṛhīta-prāmāṇya eva sva-viṣayaṃ niścāyayatu | kiṃ viṣaya-niścayârthaṃ tat-prāmāṇya-niścayena | atha vyavasāyasya a-prāmāṇya-darśanān na tan-mātrād artha-niścayaḥ | tarhi prāmāṇyânumiter apy a-prāmāṇya-darśanān na tato 'pi prāmāṇya-niścaya iti cet, na brūmo jñāna-prāmāṇya-niścayād eva artha-niścaya iti | kiṃ tu yatra a-prāmāṇya-śaṅkā na asti kara-talâmalakâdi-jñāne tatra vyavasāya eva artha-niścaya iti tata eva pravṛttir niṣkampā | yatra an-abhyāsa-daśāyāṃ prāmāṇya-saṃśayena artha-niścayaṃ paribhūya artha-saṃśayaḥ tatra prāmāṇya-niścayâdhīna-jñānād arthaṃ niścitya niṣkampaṃ pravartate na anyathā iti sarvânubhava-siddham |

Objection: A cognition whose veridicality is grasped by another cognition could not assume the form of an ascertainment of (still) another's veridicality, because of (fear of) an infinite series. Nor would its veridicality be self-cognized, since this would incur the unfortunate consequence (i.e., unfortunate for Naiyāyikas) of veridicality being grasped intrinsically. Therefore, let a cognition whose veridicality is in fact *not* grasped (either by itself or by another cognition) assume the form of an ascertainment of another's veridicality. And so an original (non-apperceptive) cognition, though its veridicality would indeed not be grasped, let it be thought of as an ascertainment of its own object. (In this way) for the purpose of being certain about an *object* (i.e., what it is central to be certain about), what would be the point of (worrying about) certainty about the *cognition's* veridicality?

If it were objected that, since an original (non-apperceptive) cognition is seen to be non-veridical sometimes, certainty about an object results from just that (namely, a later determination of veridicality), then (we say in response that you Naiyāyikas face the same problem, that is), since an inference to veridicality is seen to be non-veridical sometimes, certainty about (the original cognition's) veridicality is also not to be had thereby.

Gaṅgeśa: We do not hold that only from certainty about a cognition's veridicality is there certainty about an object. Rather, where doubt does not occur concerning (veridicality or) non-veridicality, there an original cognition itself is an *ascertainment* of an object (i.e., is itself a bit of certitude), for example, a cognition about an *āmalaka* fruit in the palm of one's hand. Just from that (i.e., not from a cognition of veridicality) is there unhesitating effort.

But where, in (e.g.) unfamiliar circumstances, doubt about an object occurs—defeating any certainty—through doubt about veridicality, there one makes unhesitating effort to proceed only after having become certain about the object from a cognition dependent on certainty about veridicality, not otherwise—so everyone's experience proves.

Comments

The infinite series mentioned at the beginning of the objection would be in the reverse direction than is usually thought: a veridical cognition C_1 whose veridicality would be grasped by another cognition C_2 would be a grasper of the veridicality of still another cognition, an earlier cognition C_0, and so on, C_{-1}, *ad infinitum*.

The objector's challenge and Gaṅgeśa's response make this an important passage for several of Gaṅgeśa's central epistemological theses, including, in the first paragraph, (1) certainty as a cognitive default, and, in the second, (2) the rule that certainty has to be restored before there can be, normally, unhesitating effort to act. Implicit in the second thesis is a, let us say, accessibility view concerning defeasibility that was suggested above. This is the view that any undermining of a bit of certainty works through one's realizing that one's previous cognition was in error or may well have been in error, through one's realizing, by acquisition of new information, that it was false or at least dubious.

On the first front of certainty as a cognitive default, Gaṅgeśa points out that normally we do not need a determination of veridicality to be certain about something, for instance, a piece of fruit in the palm of one's own hand. There is no call to apperceive the perception and worry about its veridicality, especially if we want to eat.

About the second thesis, perhaps most interesting is its tie to the view that defeaters are accessible (we are ourselves aware of the process of a bit of certainty becoming doubted and undermined or, indeed, restored). What Gaṅgeśa argues is that just because a bit of certainty comes to be doubted, and doubted legitimately, there is no reason why the certainty may not be restored. It all depends on the new evidence or investigation, we may elaborate, evidence of which we become aware or an investigation we carry out or hear about from an authority.

Gaṅgeśa's own stress has to be understood against the background of the views of his Mīmāṃsaka opponent who tries to argue here that doubt and certainty are restricted to being about first-order objects, not about cognitions that have objects, and who, while concurring that certainty is the cognitive default, concludes that there is no point in concerning oneself with certainty about a cognition, i.e., a second-order object. Gaṅgeśa's reply is that once doubt has arisen (legitimately), we have to determine whether an original awareness is veridical or not to be sufficiently confident to make unhesitating effort to act, as happens in fact. Unhesitating effort to act is, we should keep in mind, the public mark of certainty.

Text (p. 294, Tirupati, and p. 278, Calcutta) and Translation

ata eva a-gṛhīta-prāmāṇyam eva jñānaṃ para-prāmāṇyaṃ niścāyayati | a-prāmāṇya-śaṅkā-kalaṅkâ-bhāvāt | yatra tu prāmāṇya-jñāne a-prāmāṇya-śaṅkayā prāmāṇya-saṃśayas tatra prāmāṇya-jñāne prāmāṇya-niścayād eva prāmāṇya-niścayaḥ | evaṃ yāvad-a-prāmāṇya-saṅkaṃ taj-jñāna-prāmāṇya-niścayād eva tan-niścayaḥ | na ca evam an-avasthā | carama-jñāna-prāmāṇyasya jñānâ-bhāvena koṭi-smaraṇâ-bhāvena viṣayântara-saṃcāreṇa vā prāmāṇya-saṃśayân-a-vaśyaṃ-bhāvāt | anyathā bhaṭṭa-mate prāmāṇyasya jñānânumiti-grāhyatvena an-avasthā syāt | guru-mate 'pi prāmāṇyasya sva-grāhyatvaṃ na sva-grāhyaṃ, sva-rūpa-prāmāṇyābhyāṃ bahir-bhūtatvāt, para-grāhyatve an-avasthānāt | kiṃ tu pariśeṣânumānena prāmāṇyântareṇa vā grāhyam | tathā ca tat-prāmāṇyasya api sva-grāhyatvam anyena eva ity an-avasthā eva |

(**Gaṅgeśa** continues:) Just for this reason, a cognition whose own veridicality is in fact not grasped makes certain another's veridicality, since it is itself not blemished by any suspicion about its non-veridicality. But where doubt about veridicality occurs through suspicion about the non-veridicality of a cognition of veridicality (e.g., suspicion about the correctness of an inference whereby a cognition has been determined to be veridical), there only from a (later determination of) certainty about the cognition of veridicality would there be certainty about the veridicality of the original cognition. In this way, inasmuch as there is suspicion of non-veridicality, there would be certainty about something only from certainty about the veridicality of the cognition of it.

And there would not in this way be an infinite series (or infinite regress). For, whether by way of no cognition occurring whose object would be a last cognition's veridicality, or by way of a lack of memory of options, or by way of transference of attention to another object, there is no necessity of doubt about veridicality.

Otherwise, on the Bhāṭṭa view, there would be an infinite regress, inasmuch as veridicality has to be grasped through an inference to a cognition (whereby both its occurrence and its veridicality would be cognized). On the Guru's view, too (i.e., on the Prābhākara view), the self-grasping character of veridicality would not be self-grasped, since the self-grasping would be external to (i.e., other than) both the thing itself (i.e., the cognition) and its veridicality. Rather, it would be grasped either by an eliminative inference or by another verificational means. And so the self-grasping character of its veridicality would be confirmed by something else indeed; hence, an infinite regress indeed.

Comments

Once we have good grounds for doubting whether an awareness is presenting a fact, we need to determine, by an outside means, that the cognition is veridical before putting our highest confidence in it and proceeding unhesitatingly. And, unless there are good grounds for doubt about the confirmational power of the outside means, the confirmation it achieves is sufficient to eliminate the original doubt.

So, typically, even when we are moved to take the trouble to confirm the veridicality of an awareness, or even, at a further extreme of abnormality, to confirm the confirmational power of the outside means, at some point we simply trust—since we have no reason to doubt—the last prover's power to prove. In this way, the default position of assuming an original cognition's veridicality (unless there are grounds for doubt) transfers to the confirmers. As Gaṅgeśa suggests in his first sentence, a certifier of veridicality does not bring along a further certifier for its own certitude not because it is self-certified—no cognition is—but because its own certitude is untainted by any reason to doubt.

It is a ramification of this view, as Gaṅgeśa also suggests in the first paragraph, that a bit of knowledge does not entail that it itself is known. In contemporary epistemological terms, the thesis,

> $\mathrm{K}p \rightarrow \mathrm{KK}p$ (knowledge that p entails knowledge that knowledge that p)

is denied by Gaṅgeśa. Thus he denies, too, the contrapositive,

> $\sim\mathrm{KK}p \rightarrow \sim\mathrm{K}p$ (if there is no knowledge that knowledge that p, then there is no knowledge that p)

These denials are central to his answer to the regress charge. A bit of certainty about an object (which if veridical would be a bit of knowledge) does not require certainty about itself.

Other blockers of a regress of a search for sure grounds are: no memory of a possibility of a way a confirmer (or indeed an original cognition) could be misleading, and loss of interest in the topic through greater interest in something else.

Gaṅgeśa also points out that if his opponent insists that potentiality for an infinite regress of confirmers is a problem, it will not be easy to avoid it on the alternatives, indeed, on the very alternatives advanced by those prone to make the infinite-regress charge against Nyāya. What, we may ask, confirms the veridicality of the inference that, according to the Bhāṭṭa Mīmāṃsakas, grasps both the occurrence of a target cognition and its veridicality? Even on the Prābhākara view, which stipulates that every cognition grasps itself (is self-grasping) as well as its veridicality, what confirms this self-grasping? Since the self-grasping is mentioned, it is distinguishable from—is other than—the cognition and its veridicality. So what confirms it? Thus, the only real option is to admit that default certainty does not call for confirmation unless there are grounds for suspecting non-veridicality.

Text (p. 295, Tirupati, and p. 279, Calcutta) and Translation

> yat tu vyavasāyasya prāmāṇya-niścayād eva pravṛtter na tasya api prāmāṇyânusaraṇam iti na an-avasthā | na ca prāmāṇya-saṃśayād aucityâ-varjito viṣaya-saṃśaya iti vācyam | niścite saṃśayâ-bhāvāt | anyathā svato grahe 'pi tat-saṃśaye 'n-avasthā iti | tad a-sat | yadi prāmāṇya-saṃśayān na viṣaye saṃśayo niścitatvât tadā viṣaya-niścayârthaṃ prāmāṇya-niścaya vyarthaḥ | prāthamika-viṣaya-niścayād eva niṣkampa-pravṛtty-upapatteḥ | na hi viṣaya-saṃśayam an-ādṛtya prāmāṇya-niścayaḥ pravṛtti-hetur ity uktam | anya-saṃśayād anyatra niścite kathaṃ saṃśaya iti cet, anubhavaṃ pṛccha | yena sva-sākṣikam eva prāmāṇya-saṃśayasya viṣaya-saṃśaya-hetutvam anumatam | jñāna-viṣayatvam api prāmāṇya-saṃśayam āsādya viṣaya-saṃśāyakam |

Objection (by a Prābhākara): But just from certainty about the veridicality of an orginal (non-apperceptive) cognition is there effort. So no ensuing determination of the certainty's veridicality, too, is called for. Hence there is no regress (for this reason, not for the reason you alleged).

And it should not be said (against our view) that doubt about an object occurs as unavoidably appropriate from doubt about veridicality. For, given that something is cognized with a sense of certainty, doubt does not occur. Otherwise, even given an intrinsic grasping, doubt about anything could not come to a halt (i.e., there would be an infinite regress).

Gaṅgeśa: That (what you say) is false. If it is to follow from the fact that an object has been cognized with a sense of certainty that it could not be doubted as a result of doubt about the veridicality of the cognition of it, then, for the purpose of becoming certain about an object, certainty about veridicality would be meaningless. Just from a cognition with a sense of certainty about an original object would (all) possibility of unhesitating effort be accounted for (doubt being invariably precluded, as also all resolution of doubt, which is nonsense).

For people do not say (or behave in such a fashion) that without heeding doubt about the object (of an original, non-apperceptive cognition), there can be certainty about its veridicality, which then would cause (or motivate) effort (toward that object).

If it be asked how there can be doubt about one thing x that has been cognized with a sense of certainty, doubt about x resulting from another thing y, we say, consult your experience. Thereby the fact that doubt about a cognition's veridicality is a cause of doubt about its object would be approved as simply *self-witnessed* (i.e., by experience paying attention to experience).

Moreover, being an object of a cognition gives rise to doubt about the object (only) on account of doubt about the cognition's veridicality.

Comments

Note the mocking irony in Gaṅgeśa's referring to experience as "self-witnessed."

The key idea of the passage is fallibility. No certainty guarantees the veridicality of an awareness. Indeed, the word *niścaya* should not be thought of as "certainty"—at least as Gaṅgeśa uses it—if one insists that certainty does entail truth. Of course, Wittgenstein has taught us not to be ashamed of certainty, and, despite the heavy load of Cartesian connotation borne by Western epistemological terminology, "certainty" does seem the right translation. The point is that even given that we are initially certain that such and such is the case on the basis of an immediate perception, grounds may later arise for doubting that such and such is the case, including grounds for questioning the cognition that appeared to show that such and such is the case with whatever degree of surety. A sense of certainty that there is a piece of fruit in my hand is sufficient for me to proceed to eat it, if I am hungry. But if, after appearing to see a piece of fruit, I were to find out that I had had electrodes fastened to my brain causing me to hallucinate, then I would doubt both the veridicality of the perception and its object's reality.

The last sentence is addressed to a Prābhākara suggestion voiced above. Realizing that an object is an object of cognition is not sufficient for doubt unless one has an independent reason, e.g., knowing that the subject or perceiver has an impaired sense organ, or labors under severe mental delusion, for a routine doubt about whatever happens to be his cognitive object, his cognition's objecthood in general.

Text (p. 297, Tirupati, and p. 281, Calcutta) and Translation

nanu liṅga-pakṣa-vyāpty-ādinām jñānasya prāmāṇyâvadhāraṇe 'n-avasthā, an-avadhāraṇe hetv-a-siddhiḥ | atha liṅgâdi-jñānaṃ sva-viṣayâvadhāraṇe kartavye sva-prāmāṇya-jñānaṃ na apekṣate, anumāna-mātrôccheda-prasaṅgāt | liṅgâdi-niścayasya ca sva-kāraṇâdhīnasya sarva-siddhatvād iti cet, na | prāmāṇya-saṃśayena liṅgasya api saṃdehāt | na hi na liṅga-jñāne prāmāṇya-saṃśayaḥ, a-virodhād iti | ucyate | a-prāmāṇya-śaṅkā-kalaṅkâ-bhāve liṅgâdi-jñānasya eva artha-niścāyakatvāt, tat-kalaṅke tu uktā eva gatiḥ |

Objection.1 (attacking the Nyāya position): There is an infinite regress, in the determination of the veridicality of the cognition of an (appropriate) inferential mark (or prover), the subject (qualified by it), pervasion, etc. (whereby some other cognition's veridicality is supposed to be known), since, if that is not determined, the reason (or prover for considering the original cognition to be veridical) will not be established.

Objection.2 (attacking objector.1): Cognition of an inferential mark, etc., is not dependent on a cognition of its own veridicality in doing what it does, namely, determining its own object, since (otherwise) we would land in the predicament of implosion of inference in general. Moreover, it is universally accepted that certainty about an inferential mark and so on is dependent on its own causes.

Answer (by objector.1): No. For, doubt about the veridicality of a cognition of an inferential mark results in doubt about the inferential mark. For, it is not the case that, given a cognition of an inferential mark, there can be no doubt about its veridicality, since the two are not (inherently) opposed.

Gaṅgeśa: We answer. If there is no taint of suspicion of non-veridicality, a cognition of an inferential mark, etc., is itself a cause of a bit of certainty about an object. But if there is such a blemish, the way one proceeds is precisely as has been stated (above).

Comments

The objector tries to hurl Gaṅgeśa's argument back into his face, the argument, that is, that doubt about a cognition's veridicality spreads to its object or indication. Gaṅgeśa counters by insisting on the default status of an assumption of certainty. There have to be reasons for bringing into question the default certainty a cognition has for what it indicates. This applies, too, to a restoration of certainty by determining a doubted cognition's actual veridicality through an inference.

Text (p. 298, Tirupati) and Translation

yat tu vyavasāye kvacid a-prāmāṇya-saṅkā bhavati kvacin na iti tvayā api vācyam | evaṃ bahu-vitta-vyayâyāsa-sādhye svarga-sādhanaṃ yāga iti jñānaṃ na gṛhīta-

prāmāṇyaṃ pravartakam, prāmāṇyânumiteḥ pūrvam eva vināśāt | kiṃ tu taj-jñāna-samāna-viṣayakam a-prāmāṇya-śaṅkā-śūnyaṃ jñānântaram eva | nanv evaṃ bahu-vitta-vyayâyāsa-sādhye niṣkampa-pravṛttāv an-upayogitvāt niṣphalaṃ prāmāṇya-jñānam iti kiṃ tad-upāyânusaraṇena iti cet, na | svarga-sādhanaṃ yāga iti jñāna-prāmāṇye niścite tat-samāna-viṣayaka-jñānântare a-prāmāṇya-śaṅkā na bhavati iti jñānântaram a-gṛhītam-prāmāṇyam api svârtha-niścaya-rūpaṃ niṣkampa-pravṛttiṃ janayati ity a-prāmāṇya-śaṅkā-pratibandha-dvārā niṣkampa-pravṛttāv upayujyate prāmāṇya-jñānam iti na niṣphalam |

(**Gaṅgeśa** continues:) But what is alleged (as a fault of our view), namely, that with regard to an original (non-apperceptive) cognition, sometimes there is suspicion of non-veridicality, sometimes not—this by you (Mīmāṃsakas), too, has to be admitted. In this way, given that carrying out a sacrifice requires much expenditure of wealth and much exertion, the cognition, "A sacrifice is a means to heaven," whose veridicality has been grasped, does not motivate (or guide) the effort. For, prior indeed to an inference to veridicality, it (such a motivating cognition) has been destroyed (and is gone). Rather, another cognition in fact, one whose object is the same as that cognition (whose veridicality has been grasped), and one about which there is no suspicion of its not being veridical (is the motivator of the effort).

Objection: In this way (the way you have specified) there would be unhesitating effort toward something whose accomplishment requires much expenditure of wealth and much exertion (i.e., without a determination of a guiding cognition's veridicality). So since cognition of veridicality would not play a role in prompting unhesitating effort, determination of veridicality would be fruitless. Hence, what is the point of pursuing the means whereby such a determination would proceed?

Gaṅgeśa: No. If the veridicality of a cognition has been determined with certainty, (e.g.) "A sacrifice is a means to heaven," then suspicion of the non-veridicality of another cognition with the same object as that does not come to be (normally). Hence, although that other cognition is one whose veridicality has not been grasped, it generates unhesitating effort in assuming the form of an ascertainment of its own object. Thus, by way of blocking suspicion of non-veridicality, a cognition of veridicality is useful with respect to unhesitating effort. Hence, these concerns are not without fruit.

Comments

Gaṅgeśa sometimes seems to imply that no cognition, or only those that are almost immediately verified, could have their own veridicality known, since a cognition lasts only for a brief moment. However, earlier he said that the verificational process operates through apperception and presentation through memory. And this is a view that he develops here, as well as in lines just below, at the end of the section.

But there is an interpretational problem in that Gaṅgeśa can be read as saying that a determination of a cognition's veridicality absolutely blocks suspicion of the non-veridicality of similar cognitions, and so such a determination would, in effect, guarantee their correctness. This seems in general correct; it is clearly an important position of Gaṅgeśa's that once the veridicality of a certain *type* of cognition is known by an inference based on successful effort other cognitions of that type can be known to be veridical without a pragmatic test. But, I take it, grounds could, in principle, appear that drew into question any veridicality determination, and thus also the veridicality of similar cognitions. Thus, such a determination would not be an absolute block.

Of course, Gaṅgeśa's main point is to show the relevance of a determination of veridicality to the domain of effort and action, given his fallibilism and insistence that many cognitions that rightfully motivate and guide effort have not been, and need not be, determined to be veridical. And he seems right that, other things being equal, such a determination does erect a higher threshold for reasonable doubt than the default position—where the question of a cognition's veridicality has not arisen—which is itself doubt-free.

Text (p. 299, Tirupati, and p. 283, Calcutta) and Translation

> yat tv anumānasya nirasta-samasta-vibhramâ-śaṅkasya svata eva prāmāṇya-graha ity uktam | tat dhūmavati vahni-jñānatvam anumiteḥ prāmāṇya-niyatam anuvyavasāyôpanītam | ato viśeṣa-darśanān na tatra a-prāmāṇya-śaṅkā iti prāmāṇya-niścayād eva a-prāmāṇya-śaṅkā-virahād arthaṃ niścitya niṣkampa-vyavahāra ity abhiprāyaḥ | vastutas tu parataḥ-pakṣe na kvacid api prāmāṇya-grahaḥ iti | evam anuvyavasāyasya prāmāṇya-niyatatvān na prāmāṇya-śaṅkā | na hy a-jānan jānāmi iti pratyeti | na vā ghaṭa-jñāne paṭaṃ jānāmi iti | bhrame 'py anuvyavasāyena rajatatvâdikaṃ vyavasāya-prakāratvena ullikhyate tac ca tathā eva |

(**Gaṅgeśa** continues:) The view that the veridicality of a (veridicality-proving) inferring cognition is grasped intrinsically (in that the same collection of causal factors that produce the concluding would produce knowledge of its rightness) has been stated (by Vācaspati Miśra in his "Notes" on the *Nyāya-sūtra*): the inferential cognition is (as he says) "free of suspicion, with all (possibility of) error banished." But the position intended is as follows. Apperception presents the fact that (e.g.) a cognition of fire regarding that which exhibits smoke (with exhibiting-smoke known to be a property *pervaded by* exhibiting-fire) is *in principle* connected with such an inferential cognition's veridicality. Hence, because of something special being known (namely, that a cognition being of a certain type *is pervaded by* an exhibiting of veridicality, like smoke by fire), no suspicion of non-veridicality occurs there. Thus, just from certainty about the inferential cognition's veridicality, which amounts to a lack of suspicion about non-veridicality, the (original) object is cognized with a sense of certainty, and unhesitating activity ensues—this is his intended meaning (not that even such an inferential cognition is known to be veridical intrinsically).

But in fact, on the extrinsicality position, an intrinsic grasping of veridicality is never a motivator of effort. Thus, since apperception is in principle veridical, suspicion about veridicality does not occur. For, "Not cognizing, I am cognizing," is not cognized. Nor (does the cognition occur), "I am cognizing (what I take to be) a cloth with my pot-cognition." Even when an apperception is of an error (as its target cognition), it makes explicit the silverhood, etc., as the predication content of the original cognition. And, that (Vācaspati's position on the veridicality-proving inferential cognition) is just so (i.e., that an apperception indubitably presents the type of inferring as veridical).

Comments

The reference is to Vācaspati Miśra's "Notes" (c. 900) on the first sentence of Vātsyāyana's *Nyāya-sūtra-bhāṣya* (c. 450).[18] Vātsyāyana says that success of effort depends on understanding an object in accordance with sources of right cognition (*pramāṇa*), and implies that success of effort is the inferential mark or prover of a right cognition (*pramā*). Vācaspati, pondering how a veridicality-proving inference is itself known to be right, says: "But the (veridicality-proving) inference that comes from success of effort is an inference from which all suspicion of counterexamples has been banished. ... It is known as veridical just in itself. For, it arises out of an inferential mark that undeviatingly shows the inferendum."[19] This view seems to contradict Gaṅgeśa's own. However, one must appreciate the factual nature of veridicality. Veridicality is a property that some cognitions wear and can be known as wearing through an appreciation of the type of cognition they are. Thus, the type of inference that shows a cognition to be veridical can itself be presented in apperception along with the crucial property, a high-order (or self-) veridicality. The position is similar to that, in recent philosophy, of inductive generalization being bootstrapped, or self-supported. For Gaṅgeśa, however, there may well be no suspicion about the veridicality-proving inference in the first place. An apperception can apprehend that a particular veridicality-proof is the same as other veridicality-proofs.

But the certainty that motivates effort to act does not originate in the apperception but in the original cognition or, if that has been brought into doubt, in the proof of its veridicality.

Text (p. 303, Tirupati) and Translation

yat tu abhyāsa-daśāyāṃ jhaṭiti pracuratara-niṣkampa-pravṛtti-darśanāt prāmāṇyaṃ

svata eva gṛhyate, anyatra tu parata iti | tan na | viśeṣya-niṣṭhâtyantâ-bhāva-pratiyogi-prakārân-avacchinnatvâdikaṃ prāmāṇyaṃ svato grahītum a-śakyam iti parata eva gṛhyate | jhaṭiti pravṛttis tu kara-caraṇâdimati śarīra-jñānatvâder viśeṣasya anuvyavasāyena grahād a-prāmāṇya-śaṅkā-śūnyāt vyavasāyād eva, na prāmāṇya-jñānaṃ pravartakam ity uktam | jhaṭiti tat-samavadhānaṃ tu sva-kārâdhīnam | na hi pipāsūnāṃ jhaṭiti pracuratarā samarthā ca pravṛttir ambhasi iti pipāsôpaśamana-śaktir asya pratyakṣā iti |

Objection: The veridicality of a cognition arising in *familiar* circumstances is grasped intrinsically, since effort that is exceptionally unhesitating is seen to flow from it rather swiftly. But in other cases it is known extrinsically.

Gaṅgeśa: That's wrong. Veridicality—which is something like the property of not having as predication content anything that is the absentee of an absolute absence resting in the qualificandum (i.e., an absolute absence resting in the thing cognized)—cannot be grasped intrinsically. (Veridicality by its factual nature is incapable of being intrinsically grasped.) Hence, it is grasped extrinsically only.

But (to consider your example) effort that occurs at once (without, apparently, the time necessary for an inferential determination of veridicality of the cognition that motivates it) results from an original (non-apperceptive) cognition that is devoid of suspicion of non-veridicality. The effort results *simply* from the original cognition—a cognition of its veridicality is not the motivator, as has been explained—even though (as has also been explained) the reason that some particular cognition is devoid of such suspicion is that an apperception has grasped it as a cognition of (veridicality-confirming) detail, like a human-body cognition of something known as possessing hands and feet (i.e., it has been grasped as the type of cognition that has been shown to be veridical, and that resolves and blocks doubt, as sight of hands and feet—known marks of a human being—resolves and blocks further doubt about whether an object in the distance is a human being in fact).

But the quick appearance—in association with the cognition—of a complex that produces an instantaneous inference to the cognition's veridicality is based on its own causes. From the fact that the effort of the thirsty toward water is quick—i.e., exceptionally unhesitating and fruitful—it should not be concluded that water's power to quench thirst is perceptually given (in the motivating perception of water).

Comments

An apperception can show veridicality, as has been indicated. An apperception of a cognition of, for instance, a human being, with the dual predication content, "being a human being" and "exhibiting hands and feet and so on" (thus, "I am cognizing a human being as having hands and feet and so on"), blocks doubt by confirming veridicality, as can be seen in the reformulation,

"It's a human that I am cognizing because it has hands and feet and so on"). An exhibiting of hands, feet, and so on is not an exhibiting of just any property, but of a particular detail that is confirmational of something's being a human being, in that each and every human being possesses hands, feet, and so on (the *and so on* allows inclusion of amputees). In apperception, we are capable of noticing that two properties exist in a pervaded-pervader relationship, such that we can be sure that we are perceiving something that exhibits the pervader property by noticing that we are perceiving the same thing as exhibiting the pervaded property.

Earlier, Gaṅgeśa said that confirmational cognitions could be motivators of unhesitating effort to act. Here he might be taken to say the opposite. But the earlier declaration was made with respect to situations where doubt had, for some reason, arisen. In such cases, cognition of veridicality would be doubt-*resolving* (as well as doubt-*blocking*, blocking further doubt), and thus a motivator of effort to act. If, on the other hand, doubt has not arisen, then, even if there is doubt-*blocking* (but not doubt-*resolving*) apperception of the veridicality of a certain type of cognition, the unhesitating effort is to be regarded as flowing directly from the original, non-apperceptive cognition, not from the confirmation.

This explains the example about water and thirst. That water quenches thirst is not provided perceptually when we first reach out for water. There is instead a cognitive presentation working through memory of a pervasion between wateriness and thirst-quenchingness. If we quickly realize this by reflecting on our success in getting our thirst quenched, or even before we make effort to act, that would have its own causes. Our success flows from the first-order cognition about water. We do not need to be conscious of the cognition's veridicality.

atha prāmāṇya-vāde utpatti-vādaḥ

NOW, WITHIN THE DISCOURSE ON VERIDICALITY,
DISCOURSE ON PRODUCTION (OF A VERIDICAL COGNITION)

Text (p. 306, Tirupati, and p. 287, Calcutta) and Translation

utpadyate 'pi pramā parato na tu svataḥ jñāna-sāmagrī-mātrāt | taj-janyatvena a-pramā api pramā syāt | anyathā jñānam api sā na syāt | jñāna-sāmagryāṃ dośânupraveśād a-pramā iti cet, tarhi jñāna-viśeṣa-vad a-pramā pramā-viśeṣaḥ syāt jñāna-sāmagrī-janyatvāt | tasmāt pramâ-pramāyor vaicitryāt guṇa-doṣa-janyatvam |

Gaṅgeśa: A veridical cognition is (not only known but) produced, too, from something extrinsic, not "of itself," i.e., not from a collection of causes sufficient to produce just any cognition. If a veridical cognition were produced from the same collection of causes as is sufficient to produce just any cognition, a non-veridical cognition would be a veridical cognition. Otherwise, a non-veridical cognition would not be a cognition at all.

Objection: A non-veridical cognition results from a defect entering into a causal complex (otherwise) sufficient to produce a (veridical) cognition.

Gaṅgeśa: Then, like the different kinds of cognition (perceptual, inferential, etc.), a non-veridical cognition would be a special variety of veridical cognition, since it would be produced by a causal complex (otherwise) sufficient to produce a (veridical) cognition. Therefore, because of the difference between a veridical and a non-veridical cognition, the two are (in part) produced, respectively, by an epistemic excellence and an epistemic defect.

Comments

Gaṅgeśa begins this section by forthrightly stating his view against the backdrop of a Mīmāṃsaka theory that is not developed right away and that is most completely filled out—along Prābhākara lines—in the section on error (below, pp. 250ff). But we may say that the Mīmāṃsaka holds not only an intrinsicality view of how veridicality is known, he finds veridicality to be the natural intrinsic property of cognition itself because a cognition and its veridicality are born of the same set of causal conditions. According to the Prābhākara, every cognition is veridical and error or illusion is a matter of behavior (resulting from a *failure* to cognize). Here the behavioral aspect of the Prābhākara view is not brought out, and Gaṅgeśa's opponent, who

Mathurānātha says is either a Bhāṭṭa or a follower of the Murāri Miśra view, appears to admit that non-veridical cognition is possible. The point now is to challenge Gaṅgeśa's extrinsicality view only with respect to causal conditions. For our current Mīmāṃsaka, the causal complex that must be in place for any cognition to arise is sufficient to produce a veridical cognition. Non-veridicality results from an additional factor entering an otherwise standard causal complex, abnormalizing the causal process.

Now, Gaṅgeśa, though he does not have a Prābhākara opponent at this point, does let us see here that an admission of non-veridical cognition crucially supports the Naiyāyika picture. In brief, both a veridical and a non-veridical cognition involve causal factors that are over and above those common to every cognition. Veridical cognitions result from epistemic excellences and non-veridical cognitions from epistemic defects.

Gaṅgeśa's argument is that, without identifying differentiating causal factors for veridical as well as for non-veridical cognitions, the right slice between the veridical and the non-veridical could not be secured. Only by supposing that any veridical cognition results in part from an epistemic excellence, and any that is non-veridical from an epistemic defect, can the difference be accounted for.

Text (p. 307, Tirupati) and Translation

atha yatra guṇa-doṣau vinā tayor a-bhāvasya jñāna-sāmagrī na asti tat-sattve jñāna-mātrôtpatti-prasaṅgād iti cet, na | viśeṣa-vinākṛta-sāmānya-kāryâ-bhāvāt | tat-sāmagrīm ādāya eva hi sāmānya-sāmagrī tāṃ vinā na asty eva vā | anyathā kārya-viśeṣe kāraṇa-viśeṣôcchedaḥ |

Objection: Where the veridical and the non-veridical do not exist—no (veridicality-producing) excellence nor (non-veridicality-producing) defect being in place—there no causal complex sufficient to produce any cognition would be present. If such were present, the difficulty would be that (a third—neither true nor false—kind of cognition) a *mere* cognition would be produced.

Gaṅgeśa: No, because there is no generic effect divorced from particulars. For, considering just that causal complex (sufficient to produce a particular), we have a causal complex sufficient to produce the generality (that inheres in a particular). Or, without that, there is none (i.e., no effect, neither particular nor general). Otherwise, there would be a break in the rule of a specific effect having its specific causes.

Comments

The objector says that the non-veridical and the veridical exhaust the class of cognitions: every cognition is either veridical or non-veridical. Gaṅgeśa does not reject the point but only the further opinion that the Nyāya view entails a third kind of cognition, a cognition in general that would be neither veridical nor non-veridical. Later Gaṅgeśa will in fact identify indeterminate perception as neither veridical nor non-veridical. But for the moment he accepts the division as exhaustive, and implies that whereas a veridical and a non-veridical cognition have a set of causal factors in common, there is no particular cognition that results from such a pared-down set alone.

Beginning with the next passage, the principal voice becomes that of a Mīmāṃsaka *pūrvapakṣin*.

Text (p. 308, Tirupati, and p. 289, Calcutta) and Translation

nanu yathā eka-jātiya-sāmagrī-sattve 'pi ghaṭayor bhedo yamajayor vaidharmyaṃ ca tathā pramâ-pramāyor bhedo vaidharmyaṃ ca bhaviśyati | atha anugata-vyavahārāt pramātvam anugatam iti pramā-mātre hetur vācyaḥ, anugata-kāryasya an-anugatād an-utpatter iti cet, na | pramātvasya upādhitvena kāryatâvacchedakatve mānâ-bhāvāt | kārya-mātra-vṛtti-dharmatvasya nīla-ghaṭatva-ghaṭa-jñānatvâdau vyabhicārāt |

Pūrvapakṣin (a Mīmāṃsaka): As from the presence of strictly a single type of causal complex, two distinct pots are produced, and two different twins (and so on), so the distinctness and qualitative difference of the veridical and the non-veridical (are produced from a single type of causal complex).

Objection (by a Naiyāyika against the *pūrvapakṣin*): On the basis of uniform experience and linguistic practice (*vyavahāra*), veridicality is uniform. Therefore, a uniform cause with respect to the veridical in general is to be stated, since uniform effects do not arise from non-uniform causes.

Pūrvapakṣin: No. Veridicality, which is a surplus property (*upādhi*, not a universal), does not specify what kind of effect (a cognition is), because there is no evidence. (Moreover) there is deviation (with respect to the claim that there is a uniform effect over and above cognition in general, i.e., deviation) of the property that (you say) rests in (and therefore specifies) the generic being-an-effect: (the deviation occurs) in such phenomena as being-a-blue-pot (which results from the same general causal complex as being-a-pot) and being-a-cognition-of-a-pot (which results from the same general causal complex as any other cognition).

Comments

The Mīmāṃsaka *pūrvapakṣin* puts forth the view that insofar as we identify causal laws involving causal complexes there is no difficulty with the idea that distinct individuals of the same type arise as effects from one and the same type of causal complex. So, as cognitions, the veridical and the non-veridical can arise from the same type of causal complex.

The objector—who may be taken to be a Naiyāyika but who does not necessarily voice Gaṅgeśa's own views—demurs, saying that we mean the same thing when we say that this cognition A is veridical and that that one B is veridical, too, that the cognition of one person at a certain time is veridical and that the cognition of another at another time is also veridical. Admittedly, the cognitions are distinct, but there must be a way of identifying and stating what is common in the causal complexes that gives rise to the commonality in the effects. Similarly, for the non-veridical. The implication is that the veridical and non-veridical are salient differences among cognitions and so must be accounted for with respect to causal complexes. The *pūrvapakṣin*, the Mīmāṃsaka, denies the relevance.

A second reason given in support of the denial draws on a theory of causality according to which the blue of a blue pot is irrelevant to the production of the pot. That is to say, whether a blue or a white pot is the effect, the causal factors responsible for the thing as a pot would be the same. All pots are indeed colored, but a particular color is irrelevant in the causal process productive of a pot. Similarly regarding cognitions: the economical, or most elegantly formulated, causal law would not differentiate between cognitions of pots and cognitions of other things. Or, as any pot will be colored, so any cognition will be of an object. A causal law could be formulated such that according to what the color is, or what the cognitive object, there could be appropriate substitution for a variable (expressible in Sanskrit by correlative pronouns, *yat . . .* , *tat . . .*).

The *pūrvapakṣin*'s saying, in the first line of his response, that veridicality is a "surplus property," *upādhi* (see the glossary, the second or ontological sense of the word), touches a subject that is more important in the following section, on defining veridicality. As explained in my *Classical Indian Metaphysics*, the term *upādhi* is used for properties that do not conform to the rules in place for the accepted ontological categories of substance, quality, and so on, and as problematic they stand at the center of much on-going ontological work.[1] Here and later with respect to veridicality being an *upādhi*, the core idea is simply that veridicality is not a universal. See below, pp. 210–11 and 238–42.

Text (p. 309, Tirupati, and p. 291, Calcutta) and Translation

> atha pramā jñāna-hetv-atirikta-hetu-janyā janya-jñānatvāt a-pramā-vad iti cet, na | pramāyā jñānatve tad-dhetu-janyatayā sādhye bādhāt, jñānâ-janakatve virodhāt, a-pramāyāṃ tad-a-siddheḥ, vyartha-viśeṣaṇatvāt vyāvarttyâ-prasiddheḥ | kiṃ ca yat-kiñcit-jñāna-hetv-apekṣayā sarva-tad-dhetv-apekṣayā vā atiriktatve indriyâdibhiḥ siddha-sādhanāt |

Objection (by a Naiyāyika putting forth an inference): A veridical cognition is produced by a cause over and above the (common) causes for cognition, *since* it is a generated cognition, like a non-veridical cognition.

Pūrvapakṣin: No. Your inference leads to a "patent falsehood" (*bādha*) with respect to the probandum, inasmuch as a veridical cognition, given that it is a cognition, is considered produced by the causes of cognition (and nothing besides). (Moreover) there is incompatibility with respect to your thesis that veridical cognition is produced by something other than that which produces cognition. (And) that (being produced by an additional cause) is not established in (your confirming example, namely) a non-veridical cognition. (Furthermore) the qualification (that you give in the prover portion of your inference, namely, "generated") is nonsense, since what is to be excluded thereby (to wit, the cognitions of God, which, according to you, are not generated) is not universally agreed to.

Furthermore, whether the being over and above (you allege for a cause of veridicality) be taken with respect to the causes of just any cognition or with respect to the causes of all, you commit the fallacy of trying to prove what is admitted, as that holds with the sense organs, etc.

Comments

The inference is attributable to Udayana. A similar one occurs in his *Nyāya-kusumâñjali*.[2]

The first fallacy mentioned is *bādha*, "patent falsehood," where the probandum is known in advance *not* to qualify the inferential subject, e.g., "Fire is cold, *since* it is a substance, like water." The subject (*pakṣa*) of the proposed inference is *veridical cognition*, the prover (*sādhana*) is *being a generated cognition*, and the probandum (*sādhya*), *being produced by a cause over and above the (common) causes for cognition*. The Mīmāṃsaka holds that a veridical cognition is *not* produced by a cause over and above the (common) causes of cognition and that this is something, as it were, known in advance, like fire's being not cold.

Second, there is incompatibility, from the Mīmāṃsaka perspective, between the prover and the probandum, in that a generated cognition is produced by nothing other than the causal complex that generates it. The Naiyāyika inference involves the sort of contradiction typical of the fallacy, *virodha*, "incompatibility," where the prover proves the very opposite, or absence, of the probandum, e.g. "Sound is eternal, *since* it is produced."

The Mīmāṃsaka *pūrvapakṣin*'s third complaint—about the confirming example, "like a non-veridical cognition"—seems mysterious in that we presume that he, too, holds that a non-veridical cognition has as a cause something that is over and above the causal complex sufficient to produce just any cognition. But if we could assume a Prābhākara perspective, the point could be that qua cognition what Naiyāyikas call a non-veridical cognition is not like that. Non-veridicality is not a matter of cognition at all although there are cognitive constituents. These constituents are themselves veridical. And even if this is not a Prābhākara, all Mīmāṃsakas find the tie between cognition and veridicality to be exceedingly tight.

With regard to the penultimate rebuttal, Mīmāṃsā does not accept the existence of God, much less the view that God has ungenerated cognitions. Thus, from the Mīmāṃsaka perspective, there is no reason to make the qualification "generated" with respect to cognitions in the context of trying to determine their causes. All cognitions are generated.

Finally, everyone admits that every cognition has special causes. For example, a visual perception has the visual organ as a cause over and above the causes common to all cognitions. A Prābhākara would see the term *veridical* as superfluous in the statement of the inferential subject. Then to say simply that a cognition has causes over and above the causes common to all cognitions is not to say anything we did not already know and agree to.

Now in what follows the Mīmāṃsaka *pūrvapakṣin* will often claim that a proposal commits the fallacy of trying to prove the obvious or already known. That way of framing the matter, however, will not usually reveal the entire problem, which typically involves ambiguity. The Mīmāṃsaka, in each case, will find a way of interpreting the Naiyāyika's statement in a sense different from that intended, and in such a way that he can admit the proposal without concurring that a veridical cognition results from an epistemic excellence.

Text (p. 310, Tirupati) and Translation

> na api jñāna-sāmānya-sāmagry-atirikta-sāmagrī-janyā iti sādhyam | pūrva-vat siddha-sādhanāt virodhāc ca | na ca sāmānya-viśeṣayoḥ sāmagrī-dvayam, pramāyā jñāna-bhinnatvâpatteḥ anyathā sāmagrī-bhedâ-siddhiḥ tasya kārya-bheda-kalpyatvāt | etena jñāna-sāmānya-hetv-atirikta-hetu-janyā iti sādhyaṃ pratyuktaṃ | sakala-jñānâbhiprāye ca indriyâdibhiḥ siddha-sādhanaṃ | jñānatvâbhiprāye hetv-a-siddhiḥ | na api jñānatvâvacchinna-kāryatvânya-kāryatva-pratiyogika-kāraṇa-janyā iti sādhyam | jñānatvasya nitya-vṛttitayā kāryatvân-avacchedakatvāt |

Objection (by the Naiyāyika): (Let me patch up the problem with a qualification so that) what is to be shown—the probandum—would be (that a veridical cognition) is produced out of a causal complex over and above the causal complex sufficient for what is common to cognitions (*since*, as before, it is a generated cognition, like a non-veridical cognition).

Pūrvapakṣin: No, because, as before, this would commit the fallacy of trying to prove what is admitted, and also because there would be incompatibility.

And it is not the case that there are two types of causal complex, one for the generic and one for the particular, since that would land us in the predicament of viewing a veridical cognition as distinct from cognition. Otherwise, in that we are forced to imagine that distinct types of causal complex issue in distinct types of effect, distinct causal complexes would be unknown.

By this reasoning, your probandum is refuted, the probandum, namely, (that a veridical cognition) is produced by causes over and above the common causes of cognition.

And if (by "what is common to cognitions") you mean all cognitions, you commit the fallacy to trying to prove what is admitted, as with the sense organs, etc. If (by this phrase) you mean the universal cognitionhood, then no causal complex can be found for that (since universals are not caused).

Objection (by the Naiyāyika): The probandum should be (that a veridical cognition) is produced by causes that are causes in relation to effects that are other than those effects that are specified by (a mere) cognitionhood (*since*, as before, it is a generated cognition, like a non-veridical cognition).

Pūrvapakṣin: Wrong. For, cognitionhood, which resides in eternal cognition as well (that is, on your view that there is a God whose cognition is eternal), cannot be the specifier of the effects.

Comments

The structure of the *pūrvapakṣin*'s first response is a little obscure. There are two parts. First, he alleges that if the fault of incompatibility, previously pointed out, would be avoided by adding that it is something over and above the causal complex sufficient for *what is common* to cognitions, then the fallacy would be proving what is admitted, since every cognition is slightly different from every other and results from some one or another peculiar cause. Alternatively, the incompatibility between being-a-cognition and not-being-produced-by-the-causes-of-cognition would not be avoided at all.

The *pūrvapakṣin*'s rejection of the Naiyāyika's final formulation of the probandum of the inference centers on "cognitionhood" as incapable of specifying the relevant set of effects—according to Nyāya, God's cognitions are eternal. A correction follows.

Text (p. 312, Tirupati, and p. 294, Calcutta) and Translation

> atha yad-dharmâśrayasya a-sataḥ sattvaṃ hetv-adhīnaṃ tat kāryatâvacchedakaṃ, jñānatvaṃ ca tathā | na ca a-sata ity adhikaṃ, vyomâdi-sādhāraṇa-sattva-mātrasya hetv-a-niyamyatvād iti cet, na | yad-āliṅgitasya sva-rūpaṃ hetv-adhīnaṃ tat-kāryatâvacchedakaṃ lāghavāt jñānatvaṃ tu na tathā | a-nitya-jñānatve iti karaṇe indriyâdibhir yathāyathaṃ siddha-sādhanaṃ | teṣāṃ pratyekaṃ jñāna-mātrâ-hetutvāt | etena pramātvaṃ jñānatvâvacchinna-kāryatā-nirūpita-kāraṇatā-bhinna-kāraṇatā-pratiyogika-kāryatâvacchedakaṃ jñānatva-sākṣāt-vyāpya-dharmatvāt a-

pramātva-vad iti nirastam | pramātvasya nitya-vṛttitvāt | a-nitya-pramātvaṃ tathā kārya-mātra-vṛtti-dharmatvād ity api nīla-ghaṭatvâdinā vyabhicārī |

Objection (by the Naiyāyika): Okay, then, whatever property (F) whose substratum as (previously) non-existent comes to be depending on a cause, that (F) is the specifier of the type of effect. Cognitionhood is such.

And it is not the case that (the word) "non-existent" commits us to something more, since ether (an eternal element) and so on, which also exist, are not regulated by (or dependent on) any cause.

Pūrvapakṣin: No. It is simpler to hold that a specifier of a type of effect is that whose substratum's essence is dependent on a cause. But cognitionhood is not like that (particularly on your view, since you say that God's cognitions are eternal).

If you try the qualification, "*non-eternal*-cognitionhood," you (still) commit the fallacy of trying to prove what we all admit, because the sense organs, etc., are to be taken in their proper function. For none of them is a cause of cognition in general.

Objection: (Then consider the following:) veridicality specifies a type of effect (veridical cognitions) in relation to causes that are distinct from those causes which are causes in relation to effects specified by a (mere) cognitionhood, *since* it is a property entirely pervaded by cognitionhood, like non-veridicality (which is also a property entirely pervaded by cognitionhood).

Pūrvapakṣin: By the reasoning just given that inference is rejected, too. For, veridicality (is a property residing in something) eternal (that is, in the case of God's cognitions, on your view).

(If you were to change the subject of the inference to say) *non-eternal* veridicality (and continue with the probandum) as stated (namely, that it specifies a type of effect in relation to causes that are distinct from those causes which are causes in relation to effects specified by a mere cognitionhood), *since* it is a property that exists only in effects, then there would be deviation (vitiating this new inference) in such cases as blue-pot-hood.

Comments

The Naiyāyika gives a definition of what it is to be a specifier (*avacchedaka*) of a class of effects such that cognitionhood would qualify to be such a specifier. The Mīmāṃsaka rejects the definition and gives another whereby cognitionhood is no such specifier. What is at issue, from the Naiyāyika perspective, is to get clear about the limitations of cognitionhood as specifying a class of effects, so that we may see how veridical and and non-veridical cognitions as effects require something extra.

But against the Mīmāṃsaka, the Naiyāyika's characterization of cognitionhood does not help. First of all, God's cognitions are not effects according to

Nyāya. If the Naiyāyika adds the qualifier "non-eternal" to rule these out, then the Mīmāṃsaka would find not only another superfluous word (in reality all cognitions are non-eternal) but also the objection, previously stated, that everyone agrees that any cognition has peculiar causes.

The final inference considered is to be reconstructed as follows. The subject is: *non-eternal veridicality*. The probandum is: *specifies a type of effect in relation to causes that are distinct from those causes which are causes in relation to effects specified by a mere cognitionhood*. And the prover is: *being a property that exists only in effects*. The *pūrvapakṣin* purports to find deviation, which would be an occurrence of the putative prover without an occurrence of its probandum. Blue-pot-hood is just that, that is to say, it is a property that exists only in effects but does not specify what is claimed in that it does not specify any *single* type of effect. This is so because while it is accepted that there is a causal complex responsible for things that are blue, and one responsible for things that are pots, there is no distinct causal complex specified by blue-pot-hood. We have here an artificial compound, so to say, an analyzable "surplus property" existing in effects (*upādhi* in the ontological sense of the term: see the glossary). Or, to put the point a little differently, the causal conditions responsible for something's being blue are irrelevant, as explained earlier, to something's being a pot. The most elegant formulation of the causal laws involved in production of pots would not take color into consideration.

Text (p. 316, Tirupati) and Translation

a-nitya-pramā pramâ-pramôbhaya-hetu-bhinna-hetu-janyā janyatvāt a-pramā-vad iti cet, na | doṣasya pittâdeḥ sva-viṣaya-pramā-hetutvena a-pramāyāṃ sādhyâ-prasiddheḥ | ghaṭa-dṛṣṭāntatve tayā eva vyabhicārāt | śaṅkhâdy-aṃśe pītaḥ śaṅkha iti jñānasya api pramātvāt, kāraṇa-vyakti-bheda-janyatvena siddha-sādhanāc ca |

Objection (another proposal by the Naiyāyika supported by another inference): A non-eternal veridical cognition is produced by a cause that is distinct from the causes that produce both veridical and non-veridical cognitions, *since* it is produced, like a non-veridical cognition.

Pūrvapakṣin: No. Here the probandum is unknown (in your confirming example, namely) in any non-veridical cognition, since a fault such as bile (making white things appear to be yellow) can be a cause of a veridical cognition with respect to its own object (as in, "I am seeing the conch *as* yellow").

If you try as the confirming example, "(like) a pot," there would (still) be deviation in virtue of that alone (to wit, the non-veridical, since the non-veridical is produced but not by a cause that is distinct in the way claimed).

Moreover, there would also be the fallacy of trying to prove what is admitted, since the cognition, "The conch is yellow," would be veridical with respect to the conch portion, etc., as it would be produced by a distinct individual as cause.

Comments

The non-veridical awareness, "The conch is yellow," is veridical in its "conch portion" when, as is presumed, there is in fact a conch in front the person misperceiving it. Though the conch is erroneously appearing to be yellow, the conch portion of the cognition is produced by the conch. The Mīmāṃsaka, too, sees the cognition as veridical in presenting a conch. He holds, as mentioned, that the non-veridical has to be accounted for by something additional in a causal complex that would otherwise produce, in the standard fashion, a cognition, that is, a veridical cognition. Thus, the Naiyāyika proposal would commit the *siddha-sādhana* fallacy ("trying to prove what is admitted").

Perhaps a more telling counter, however, is the first one that the Mīmāṃsaka makes, namely, that causes of a non-veridical cognition can also be causes of a veridical cognition, as with the apperception, "I am seeing the conch *as* yellow."

Text (p. 316, Tirupati) and Translation

> atha pramā a-pramā-vyāvṛtta-dharmâvacchinna-kāryatva-pratiyogika-kāraṇa-janyā a-pramā-vijātīya-kāryatvāt ghaṭa-vat | yadi pramā a-pramātvâ-samānâdhikaraṇa-rūpa-nirūpita-kāryatva-pratiyogika-kāraṇa-janyā na syāt a-pramā syād iti cet, na | a-pramā-vyāvṛtta-dharmâvacchinna-kāryatvaṃ saṃyogasya tat-pratiyogika-kāraṇam indriyâdi iti taj-janyatvena siddha-sādhanāt | a-pramâ-sādhāraṇa-vyakti-janyatvaṃ ca agre '-pramā-tādātmye prayojakam iti tarko apy a-prayojakaḥ |

Objection (another proposal by the Naiyāyika supported by still another inference and then by *tarka*, counterfactual reasoning): A veridical cognition is produced by a cause that is a cause in relation to a set of effects specified by a property (veridicality) that excludes the non-veridical, *since* it is an effect of a different type than a non-veridical cognition, like a pot. If a veridical cognition were not produced by a cause that is a cause in relation to a set of effects specified by something that belongs to a different locus than (the property) non-veridicality, then a veridical cognition would be non-veridical!

Pūrvapakṣin: No. This commits the fallacy of trying to prove what is admitted (in the following way): contact belongs to a set of effects specified by a property (contacthood) that excludes the non-veridical (in that a veridical perception is generated by a contact between a sense organ and an object and the contact itself is an effect as well as a property of both the sense organ and the object). A cause in relation to that is, for example, a sense organ. Thus, a veridical cognition is produced by that (we both agree).

Furthermore, your counterfactual reasoning is also ineffective: a veridical cognition's being produced by an individual that is (a cause but) not a common cause of a non-veridical cognition (unlike, that is, time, space, etc., that are causes of every effect) would demonstrate its identity with the non-veridical from the beginning.

Comments

The Naiyāyika's counterfactual reasoning, *tarka*, denies that the probandum qualifies the inferential subject and then draws an untoward implication. However, that implication, properly framed, is not unwanted by the Mīmāṃsaka, who sees both veridical and non-veridical cognition as dependent on an individual distinct from the common causes of, well, yes, non-veridical cognition but also of veridical cognition, too.

The first Mīmāṃsaka rejoinder is similar to the reasoning we have seen before though filled out this time by the example of contact. The *pūrvapakṣin* can readily agree that the causal complex that produces a veridical cognition excludes the non-veridical. Connection between sense organ and object perceived is one of many details of a causal picture that are affirmed in common. It is foremost in the analysis of non-veridicality where there is difference.

Text (p. 318, Tirupati) and Translation

atha a-nitya-pramā pramâ-pramânyatara-pratibandhaka-janyā, pramâ-pramânyataratvāt a-pramā-vat, cākṣuṣa-pramā cākṣuṣa-bhramâ-janaka-janyā a-nitya-pramātvāt rāsana-pramā-vad iti cet, na | pramā-janakâ-sādhāraṇa-vyakti-bhedasya a-pramā-pratibandhakatvena cākṣuṣa-bhramâ-janakatvena ca siddha-sādhanāt | etena pramā sva-virodhy-anubhava-pratibandhaka-janyā a-nityânubhavatvāt a-pramā-vat | dūrāt puruṣasya sthāṇutayā jñāne saṃnidhau ca bhūyo-'vayavêndriya-saṃnikarṣasya virodhi-sthāṇv-anubhava-pratibandhakatvaṃ puruṣa-jñāna-janakatvaṃ ca dṛṣṭam, a-pramāyāṃ pittâder liṅgâdi-bhramasya ca tathātvam iti nirastaṃ | pramā-janaka-viśeṣasya a-pramā-pratibandhakatvaṃ pramā-janakatvaṃ ca asti iti siddha-sādhanād iti na pramāyām atirikta-guṇa-siddhiḥ |

Objection (another proposal by the Naiyāyika and two more inferences): A non-eternal veridical cognition is produced by that which blocks either the veridical or the non-veridical, *since* it is either veridical or non-veridical, like a non-veridical cognition. A visual veridical cognition is produced by that which does not produce a visual error, *since* it is a non-eternal veridical cognition, like a veridical cognition of taste.

Pūrvapakṣin: No. This (again) commits the fallacy of trying to prove what is admitted: a distinct particular (e.g., a contact between a sense organ and an object) can be the uncommon cause (i.e., the proximate cause, *karaṇa*) producing a veridical cognition, and is (thus) a blocker of a non-veridical cognition; (likewise) with not producing a visual error.

Naiyāyika: A veridical cognition is produced by that which blocks whatever is in opposition to itself, *since* it is a non-eternal awareness, like a non-veridical cognition.

Pūrvapakṣin: By the reasoning just given this is rejected, too. Blockage is seen (for example) regarding a cognition (had by someone) from afar of a person (misperceived) as a stump: when one is near, connection of the visual organ with many parts (of the object) blocks experience of the incompatible stump, and the thing is ascertained to be a person.

And, similarly, in the case of a "non-veridical cognition," such as (a perceptual error arising) from bile, or (an inferential error) from a mistaken inferential mark (e.g., dust rising from a mountain leading to a mistaken inference of fire). That (too) would commit the fallacy of trying to prove what is admitted: a particular producing a veridical cognition can be a blocker of a non-veridical cognition, as well as a generator of a veridical cognition.

Therefore, there is no proof of an additional epistemic excellence (over and above the causal complex common to cognition in general) in the case of a veridical cognition.

Comments

The point of the odd probandum "produced by that which blocks etc." is that the Naiyāyika holds that there is something additional in the causal complex for a veridical cognition that *prevents* error, as there is something additional in the causal complex for a non-veridical cognition that prevents veridical awareness. Thus the presence of a person properly perceived is not only a causal factor for the veridical person perception but helps block error too. This is borne out in that once the object formerly viewed as possibly a stump is perceived as a person in fact, the perceiver has his stump worry blocked.

Of course, from the *pūrvapakṣin*'s perspective, it is unnecessary to posit an additional cause to explain either veridical cognition or blockage of the non-veridical. All that is needed is to find particular causes for particular effects. Such parsimony, or theoretic modesty, is perhaps the strongest consideration in favor of the Mīmāṃsaka stance.

The theory of the visual organ as contacting its object directly is alluded to here. See, in this volume, p. 346.

Text (p. 319, Tirupati) and Translation

kiṃ ca pratyakṣa-pramâdau anugatasya arthântarasya guṇasya a-bhāvaḥ indriya-saṃnikarṣâdīnāṃ ca an-anugamaḥ | na ca jātyā eva guṇa-doṣau, pramā-janakatvaṃ guṇatvaṃ bhrama-janakatvaṃ ca doṣatvam atiprasaktaṃ | tan-mātra-janakatvaṃ ca a-siddham iti |

(The **pūrvapakṣin** continues:) Moreover, there is no "excellence" that is some other thing (beyond the admitted causes and) that (somehow) is uniform, with regard to a perceptual veridical cognition and so on. And there is no uniformity (period) in such (causal factors) as the connection to a sense organ. Furthermore, "excellence" and "defect" could hardly be universals (as though as inherent in instances of veridical and non-veridical cognitions they would be causal factors of that sort). You implausibly stretch applicability in viewing being-an-excellence as generating veridical cognitions, and being-a-defect as generating errors. And (finally) the generating of just that (the veridical or the non-veridical) is (simply) not established.

Comments

The *pūrvapakṣin* wraps up his presentation by identifying a few other places where the Naiyāyika goes wrong. There are no uniform excellences or deficiencies that have perceptually a causal role. Uniformity is required of causal principles as well as in identifying true universals. So, the Naiyāyika cannot say that the way an excellence is a causal factor is like cowhood in relation to a cow. And without showing uniformity—along with all the failed inferences—the Naiyāyika simply has not provided an argument why we should believe in the mysterious properties.

Regarding the last sentence, Mathurānātha provides the gloss of "that" (*tat*) as either the veridical or the non-veridical. While our Mīmāṃsaka *pūrvapakṣin* does accept an additional causal factor for the non-veridical, he rejects such a dual thesis, which is the Naiyāyika view.

atha utpatti-vāda-siddhântaḥ

NOW, THE RIGHT VIEW, WITHIN THE DISCOURSE ON PRODUCTION (OF A VERIDICAL COGNITION)

Text (p. 321, Tirupati, and p. 307, Calcutta) and Translation

ucyate | evam a-pramā api svata eva syān na tu parataḥ, pramā-vad a-sādhāraṇa-kāraṇād eva tad-utpattau doṣasya tatra a-hetutvāt | atha jñāna-sāmagrī-sattve 'pi viśeṣâ-darśanādi-pittâder anuvidhānād a-pramāyāṃ doṣo hetur iti cet, tarhi viśeṣa-darśana-pittâdy-a-bhāvâditas tatra eva viṣaye pramā tad-a-bhāvān na iti pramāyām āgantuka-kāraṇâpekṣā iti kathaṃ na paratastvam | api ca niyama-garbhaḥ kārya-kāraṇa-bhāvaḥ | niyamaś ca na vyaktor eva, vyabhicārād atiprasaṅgāc ca iti niyama-nirūpakam anuguṇam anugatam āstheyam | evaṃ ca a-pramāyām iva pramāyām api tad-vyāvṛttaṃ kāraṇam anugatam āstheyam |

Gaṅgeśa: We answer. Following your way of thinking, a non-veridical cognition would also be produced just "from itself," not (as you Mīmāṃsakas admit) from something else (i.e., something other than the causes common to all cognition). If (as you say) a non-veridical cognition arises like a veridical cognition through (the activity) of a proximate instrumental cause (in every case), then a defect (contrary to what you hold) would not be a cause of a non-veridical cognition.

Objection: If, even though the causal conditions sufficient for a cognition are present, there is—because of a lack of experience of particulars, bile, and so on, according to the situation—a non-veridical cognition whereof the (extra) causal factor is a defect (*dośa*), then, just there, with regard to the (same) object—from experience of particulars, an absence of bile, and so on—there is a veridical cognition, because of an *absence* of defect.

Gaṅgeśa: No. Considering a veridical cognition, (you have told us again and again that there is) dependence on some adventitious cause (the basis of your claim that many Naiyāyika inferences fall to the fallacy of "trying to prove the admitted"). So why not (a view of) extrinsicality (i.e., extrinsic causality)?

Moreover, the relation of cause and effect falls within (the realm of) principle (i.e., is lawful), and a principle (or law) does not hold only between two particulars, because of deviation (from what it is to be a principle) and because of wrong application. Thus, the relation is governed by principle, in conformity (with the nature of the effect produced); (that is to say) its uniformity is to be vigorously held. And, in this way, as with a non-veridical cognition, so with a veridical cognition, too, that there is a uniform cause excluding that (the other of the pair) is to be vigorously held onto.

Comments

The principle, "similar effect, similar cause," is a foundation stone of a systematic understanding of things. Gaṅgeśa often evokes it as a type of fundamental justification, finding causal relations underpinning possibilities of veridical perception, inference, and so on.

Gaṅgeśa argues that consistency demands the Mīmāṃsaka to accept the Naiyāyika picture. For, the Mīmāṃsaka does identify an additional causal factor in the case of non-veridical cognition—at least the Mīmāṃsaka *pūrvapakṣin* did, who we may think of as a Bhāṭṭa or a follower of Murāri Miśra. Later, we will meet Prābhākaras who, denying that any cognition is non-veridical, do not embrace the "additional causal factor" view that is and has been in focus (though, of course, what people say when they have been cognitively misled does require, according to the Prābhākara, an explaining that mentions something more than the normal cognitive causes).

Gaṅgeśa also contends here that there is sufficient uniformity among the processes that lead to veridical cognitions to identify excellences as in general necessary. Thus do we theorize on the appropriate level of abstraction. The nature of the relevant excellences and defects may vary according to the situation and the nature of the knowledge acquired. But in every case there is to be identified either an epistemic excellence or deficiency.

The objector's argument opens the thorny issue of the causal role of absences, which will be thoroughly aired in several upcoming sections.

Text (p. 323, Tirupati, and p. 308, Calcutta) and Translation

kiṃ ca yat kāryaṃ yat-kārya-vijātīyaṃ tat tat-kāraṇa-vijātīya-kāraṇa-janyaṃ[3] yathā ghaṭa-vijātīyaḥ paṭaḥ | anyathā kārya-vaijātyasya a-kasmikatâpatteḥ | ghaṭa-jñāna-jātīyam api kāryaṃ tad-vijātīya-kārya-kāraṇa-vijātīya-ghaṭêndriya-saṃnikarṣâdi-janyam iti na vyabhicāraḥ |

(**Gaṅgeśa** continues:) Furthermore, whatever effect is of a different type with respect to another effect, that effect is produced by a cause that is of a different type with respect to the causes of the other effect, as, for example, a cloth is of a different type with respect to a pot. Otherwise, there would be the unfortunate difficulty that a difference of effect would occur without a reason.

(So) also the effect that is of the type to which belongs a cognition of a pot is produced by a sensory connection to a pot, etc., (a causal collection) that is of a different type from (that accounting for) a cause and effect relationship that is of a different type. Therefore, there is no deviation.

Comments

Not only is a pot a different type of thing than a cloth, a pot cognition is a different type of thing than a cloth cognition, and results from a distinct causal complex, though of course there are causal factors in common, for example, a sensory connection.

The theorist's task is to formulate relevant as well as economical causal explanations. That an epistemic excellence is invariably part of a causal complex that results in veridical cognition is relevant to explaining the distinction between veridical and non-veridical cognition, like, Gaṅgeśa suggests, the relevance of pots and cloths as cognitive causes to explaining the difference between pot and cloth cognitions.

The example should not lead one into thinking that formulating general principles, economical and elegant, having both explanatory simplicity and breadth, would be a practical impossibility. After all, the main issue here is the very general principle endorsed by Gaṅgeśa that every veridical cognition, no matter what its proximate cause, the visual organ, the auditory sense, inferential calculation, and so on, has among its causes an epistemic excellence. That epistemic excellences vary is of course presumed. They vary from sense faculty to sense faculty but, we shall learn, nevertheless uniformly within each of four distinct knowledge processes, perception, inference, and the rest.

Indeed, Gaṅgeśa finds no significant similarities in the causal processes that result in veridical perceptions as opposed to veridical inferences, veridical analogical cognitions, and veridical bits of testimony *other than* the supervenience, let us say, of the epistemically evaluative "excellence" that is attributed to each process because of its result. The next several passages are among many where we see Gaṅgeśa exploring the right levels of generality—though he also, in the very next bit of text, is able to deal in a swoop with a main line of complaint against the earlier Naiyāyika inferences made by the *pūrvapakṣin*.

Text (p. 324, Tirupati) and Translation

evaṃ ca a-nitya-pramā a-pramā-kāraṇa-vijātīya-kāraṇa-janyā a-pramā-vijātīya-kāryatvāt, ghaṭa-vat | evaṃ ca anugatasya pramā-hetutve pramā sva-virodhy-anubhava-pratibandhaka-jātīya-janyā janyânubhavatvāt a-pramā-vat ity-ādāv api na siddha-sādhanam |

(**Gaṅgeśa** continues:) And in this way of thinking (there is the cogent inference against you:) a non-eternal veridical cognition is produced from a cause that is of a different type than the causes of a non-veridical cognition, *since* it is an effect of a different type than a non-veridical cognition, like a pot.

Furthermore, in this way (there is another inference:) given something uniform (an excellence) as a cause of veridical cognition, a veridical cognition is produced by something that is of the type that blocks awareness opposed to it, *since* it is a generated cognition, like a non-veridical cognition.

Thus, with respect to this (formulation) and others like it, there is no fallacy of trying to prove what is admitted.

Comments

By specifying two distinct types of effect, veridical cognitions as opposed to non-veridical cognitions, Gaṅgeśa eliminates the ambiguity that plagued previous inferential formulations establishing the Nyāya view: the difference between the types of effect shows that there are both epistemic excellences and deficiencies as causal factors. The former is not admitted by the Mīmāṃsaka of whatever subcamp. Thus, there is now no fallacy of "trying to prove what is admitted" by Mīmāṃsā.

Text (p. 325, Tirupati) and Translation

api ca a-nitya-pramātvaṃ kāryatâvacchedakaṃ, bādhakaṃ vinā kārya-mātra-vṛtti-dharmatvāt, a-pramātva-vat | nīla-ghaṭatvaṃ tu viśiṣṭaṃ na kāryatâvacchedakaṃ, pratyekânugata-prayojaka-dvayād eva viśiṣṭa-siddher ārthaḥ samājaḥ | ghaṭa-jñānatvâdau tu bādhakaṃ | astu vā tatra apy anugata-bhojakâ-dṛṣṭa-hetukatvam | anyathā kārya-mātre na a-dṛṣṭaṃ hetuḥ syāt |

(**Gaṅgeśa** continues:) Furthermore, being-a-non-eternal-veridical-cognition does specify a set of effects, *since* it is a property that is present in just that (type of effect) without a counterconsideration prevailing, like being-a-non-veridical-cognition. But being-a-blue-pot is not a specifier of a set of effects, because from exactly two uniform (sets of) causes, one for each (the being-blue and the being-a-pot, there comes to be) an objective assembly resulting in a qualified thing (a blue pot).

Yet there is (also) a counterconsideration with respect to the likes of being-a-cognition-of-a-pot('s being a specifier of a set of effects). Or, let there be such a specifier there, too: the cause would be unseen force which is (a common cause of every experience and thus) a uniform cause of the enjoyment experience (that is to say, of all cognitions, all cognitions being enjoyments). Otherwise, unseen force would not be a cause of effects in general.

Comments

The confirming example of the inference, to wit, being-a-non-veridical-cognition, does not require the qualification, "non-eternal," because, unlike veridical cognitions some of which—God's—are not generated, all non-veridical cognitions are generated.

A cognition of a pot can result from perception, from inference, or from someone's testimony, as well as from remembering. So the property, being-a-cognition-of-a-pot, does not specify a set of effects in relation to a uniform type of cause.

Unseen force, or *karman*, is considered a cause of any effect, or at least of any involving a human being, among which of course cognitions are to be counted. The allusion is to the ancient doctrine that no human experience occurs unless it is deserved and earned by the experiencer.

Text (p. 338, Tirupati, and p. 311, Calcutta) and Translation

evam a-nitya-pramātvam a-nitya-jñānatvâvacchinna-kāryatva-pratiyogika-kāraṇatā-bhinna-kāraṇatā-pratiyogika-kāryatâvacchedakam a-nitya-jñānatva-vyāpya-kāryatâvacchedaka-dharmatvād a-pramātva-vat ity a-nitya-pramāyām a-pramā-vyāvṛttânugata-hetu-siddhiḥ | anyathā anugata-kāryatân-upapatteḥ | tathā a-nitya-pramātvaṃ a-pramā-kāraṇatân-avacchedaka-rūpâvacchinna-kāraṇatā-pratiyogika-kāryatâvacchedakaṃ, bhramâ-vṛtti-kāryatâvacchedakatvāt ghaṭatva-vat | cākṣuṣa-pramātvaṃ cākṣuṣâ-pramā-kāraṇatân-avacchedaka-rūpâvacchinna-kāraṇatā-pratiyogika-kāryatâvacchedakaṃ, cākṣuṣa-bhramâ-vṛtti-kāryatâvacchedakatvāt ghaṭatva-vat | a-nitya-rajata-pramātvaṃ rajatâ-pramā-kāraṇatân-avacchedaka-rūpân-avacchinna-kāraṇatā-pratiyogika-kāryatâvacchedakaṃ, rajata-bhramâ-vṛtti-kāryatâvacchedakatvāt ghaṭatva-vat | anyathā niyāmakaṃ vinā cākṣuṣâdi-rajata-jñānaṃ kiñcid rajata-vṛtti-prakārakaṃ kiñcid rajatâ-vṛtti-prakārakam iti niyamo na syāt | jñāna-sāmagryās tulyatvāt |

(**Gaṅgeśa** continues:) In this way, being-a-non-eternal-*veridical*-cognition specifies a set of effects in relation to causes that are distinct from causes that are causes in relation to a set of effects specified by (mere) being-a-non-eternal-cognition, *since* it is a property specifying a set of effects that are pervaded by (the property) being-a-non-eternal-cognition, like being-a-non-veridical-cognition.

So is established, with respect to the non-eternally veridical, a uniform cause that excludes the non-veridical. Otherwise, the uniform effects (here) would not be possible.

Similarly, being-a-non-eternal-veridical-cognition specifies a set of effects (non-eternal veridical cognitions) in relation to causes specified by something of a form (being-an-epistemic-excellence) that does not specify causes of non-veridical cognitions, *since* it specifies a set of effects that are not errors, like pothood (being-a-pot).

Being-a-visual-veridical-cognition specifies a set of effects (veridical visual cognitions) in relation to causes specified by something of a form (being-an-epistemic-excellence, as in a sight of hands, feet, etc., in the perception of a human being) that does not specify causes of non-veridical visual cognitions, *since* it specifies a set of effects that are not visual errors, like pothood.

Being-a-non-eternal-veridical-cognition-of-silver specifies a set of effects (non-eternal veridical cognitions of silver) in relation to causes not specified by something of a form that specifies causes of non-veridical cognitions of silver, *since* it specifies a set of effects that are not errors concerning silver, like pothood.

Otherwise, without such regulation, there would be no law: some one or another visual, etc., silver (etc.), cognition would be a cognition whose predication content would be present in silver (that is right under one's nose) while some other one or another would be a cognition whose predication content would not be present in silver (but we would not make the distinction). For, the cognitions' causal complexes would be all alike.

Comments

The first set of effects mentioned is of course the set of veridical cognitions other than God's.

Gaṅgeśa is aiming for the right level of generality in his causal principles. There are several fundamental types of epistemic excellence. For example, the excellence responsible for a veridical visual cognition is both uniform among visual experiences and quite different from that responsible for a veridical taste experience. Even veridical cognitions of distinct types of thing, such as silver, may well require their own special law, Gaṅgeśa seems to suggest here. Nevertheless, appropriate generality can be defended, it must be stressed. Again, all veridical visual cognitions will have sufficiently similar excellences in their causal complexes that they may appropriately be specified as a set of effects in relation to uniform causal complexes. And without a causal law governing the difference between veridical and non-veridical cognitions, Gaṅgeśa repeats, there would be no difference between a veridical experience of silver and a silver illusion when the object is mother-of-pearl.

Nevertheless, we have to be careful in generalizing. Gaṅgeśa's final position is, as we shall see, that beyond all being excellences the factors that account for the veridicality of perceptions and those that account for the veridicality of inferences, analogical knowledge, and the testimonial differ fundamentally. The causal processes are not very much alike, except in their issue presenting what occurs in fact.

Text (p. 339, Tirupati) and Translation

yat tu pramāyā a-sādhāraṇa-kāraṇa-janyatve sādhye pramânyatvam upādhiḥ | na ca pakṣêtaratvam | tava īśvara-jñānasya pramātvāt pakṣasya vyāvartyatvāt | ubhaya-siddha-vyāvartakatvaṃ tantram, na tu vyāvartyasya ubhaya-siddhiḥ, gauravāt | vyatireke '-sādhāraṇatvaṃ ca pakṣêtaratvasya an-upādhitve bījaṃ | tac ca atra na asti | bhagavaj-jñānasya tvat-sammatasya sapakṣatvād iti | tan na | vipakṣa-bādhaka-bālena hetoḥ sādhya-vyāpyatvena upādheḥ sādhyâ-vyāpakatvāt |

Objection (by a Mīmāṃsaka): But being-other-than-a-veridical-cognition is an "undercutter," *upādhi* (a vitiator of your inference given above, to wit, "a non-eternal veridical cognition is produced from a cause that is of a different type than the causes of a non-veridical cognition, *since* it is an effect of a different type than a non-veridical cognition, like a pot") given that a (non-eternal) veridical cognition is to be proved to be produced-by-a-cause-that-is-not-shared(-by-non-veridical-cognition).

And this is not an instance of being-other-than-the-inferential-subject (*pakṣêtaratva*, when that fails to be a true undercutter). For, you yourself exclude the veridicality of the cognitions of God from the inferential subject (given that the *pakṣa*, the inferential subject, is "a *non-eternal* veridical cognition," thus excluding the eternal cognitions of God, according to you; we of course deny the existence of God and eternal cognitions).

We both agree that a true principle (governing what counts as an undercutter) is exclusion (of the probandum from loci where the undercutter is absent: otherwise the undercutter would not pervade the probandum). But not (i.e., the principle does not depend) on our both taking the same things to be excluded, because that would be cumbersome.

And the fact that the "no similar instance" fallacy of the prover appears to hold with respect to the requirement of dual absence (where the undercutter is absent, the probandum must be absent, and being-other-than-a-veridical-cognition would appear to be absent only in the inferential subject, namely, in veridical cognitions, which are things, you claim, where the probandum occurs) is a seed (we admit) for suspecting that the being-other-than-the-subject type of undercutter is not a true undercutter (in that it would not vitiate in some cases). Yet that would be wrong in this case. For, the cognitions of God, you yourself say, are common (to both the absence of the undercutter and the absence of the probandum, since God's cognitions are not non-eternal).

Gaṅgeśa: That's wrong. For, the (putative) undercutter does not pervade the probandum, in that the prover (of our original inference) *is* pervaded by its probandum, on the strength of its being blocked out of counterinstances (i.e., places where the probandum is not).

Comments

The objector phrases his point using Naiyāyika logical terms (most of which are common across the schools of classical philosophy), and thus makes the structure of his argument apparent. So, we have to know, in particular, what an inferential "undercutter" is (*upādhi*), as well as why the putative *upādhi*, being-other-than-the-subject (*pakṣêtaratva*), is sometimes a true undercutter and sometimes not. We also have to follow some rather complicated argumentation.

Although in his chapter on inference Gaṅgeśa does not accept a standard definition (D^u) of an *upādhi* found in several schools, and although he provides replacements, the two conditions set out in D^u are sufficient to illumine the passage at hand.

> An *upādhi* is (D^u): a property U such that (1) U pervades the probandum, the *sādhya*, S (i.e., anything that is an S is a U), and (2) U does not pervade the prover, the *sādhana or hetu*, H (i.e., there is something that is an H but not a U).
>
> (1) $(x)\,(Sx \rightarrow Ux)$
> (2) $(\exists x)\,(Hx \cdot {\sim}Ux)$

It follows then that

> (3) $(\exists x)\,(Hx \cdot {\sim}Sx)$. (There is something that exhibits the prover without exhibiting the probandum.)

Thus, there is "deviation" and no relation of pervasion:

(4)~(x) (Hx → Sx)

And so an original inference fails: that the inferential subject (*a*) exhibits the probandum (S*a*) is not shown.

To elaborate, an S's pervading an H is supposed to be the crucial enabling condition for an original inference, such that wherever an H there an S. But an *upādhi* shows that with a target inference an S's pervading the H does not obtain. Thus it blocks an inference; no longer do we have confidence in the pervasion relationship on which the inference was based.

To run through the terms of a stock example, an occurrence of fire does not guarantee an occurrence of smoke. Wet fuel is an *upādhi* for an inference of smoke from a perception of fire. All occurrences of smoke are occurrences of wet fuel (U pervades S), and there is fire in some cases, for instance, molten metal, where there is no wet fuel (U does not pervade H). (Fire occurs in molten metal accounting for the heat.) Thus, an *upādhi* undercuts an inference, since it would show that there are occurrences of the prover where there are not occurrences of the probandum, and the case at issue might be one of these.

Now, one problem with the standard definition, D^u, appears to be that invariably a property designatable as "being-other-than-the-inferential-subject," *pakṣêtaratva*, would fulfill the conditions of D^u but would sometimes be a true *upādhi* and sometimes not. The property is cooked up to exploit the legitimate concern in an epistemic context not to beg the question concerning the subject or case at issue, and a third condition seems to be needed.

The *pakṣa*, the "inferential subject," is paradigmatically designated by a singular term; it is normally a particular. Thus, everything in the universe other than a given inferential subject will exhibit the property being-other-than-the-subject. So, since the case at issue, the inferential subject, is bracketed for the purposes of examining the cogency of a proposed inference, any example of this variable property (varying according to inferential subject) will pervade the probandum (outside, to repeat, the case at issue: looked at inductively, the inferential subject is the next case, one we know to be an H but not as an S or as a non-S). Being-other-than-the-inferential-subject will also always not pervade the prover, since the case at issue is not bracketed concerning exhibition of the prover: perception of smoke rising from a mountain—the inferential subject—is, roughly speaking, what launches an inference to fire. Thus, being-other-than-the-subject in every instance will meet the standard definition, D^u. However, it is obviously not always a true undercutter, since it would vitiate good inferences.

Gaṅgeśa observes within the *upādhi-prakaraṇa* of the next chapter that when a probandum is known definitely not to occur on an inferential subject, that is, when a proposed inference is "defeated in advance" (falling to a variety of the fallacy, *bādha*, "patent falsehood," as were someone to try to prove "Fire is not hot"), then a property that is "other-than-the-subject" turns out to be a true *upādhi*; otherwise, it is not.[4] In other words, it is mainly a fallacious *upādhi*, and fails to vitiate. This is suggested by the fact, Gaṅgeśa also observes, that in a counterinference a proposed undercutter sets up, *pakṣêtaratva* would be, according to D[u]—and some other definitions, too—not widely enough instantiated to permit the inference, or, more precisely, to permit an inductive leap to the pervasion required by an *upādhi*-constituted inference. That is, an inference based on a pervasion of the probandum expressed in transposition—"where the *upādhi* is not, there the probandum also fails to occur"—would fall to the fallacy, "no similar instance," in that since everything in the universe is other-than-the-inferential-subject save the inferential subject itself there would be no instance of "where the *upādhi* is not" in those things where there is an absence of the probandum, the *sapakṣa* for the transposited inference. This explains why the Mīmāṃsaka objector says here that the "no similar instance" fallacy "is a seed (we admit) for suspecting that a being-other-than-the-subject type of undercutter is not a true undercutter."

To backtrack a bit, the Mīmāṃsaka claims that there is an undercutter facing the inference that was put forth above, p. 156: a (non-eternal) veridical cognition (the inferential subject) is produced by a cause that is not shared by a non-veridical cognition (the probandum), *since* it is an effect of a different type than a non-veridical cognition (the prover). The putative undercutter is: being-other-than-a-veridical-cognition.

The putative *upādhi* appears to be of the being-other-than-the-subject type. However, the objector points out, God's cognitions, at least according to Nyāya, are things that do not exhibit the property, being-other-than-a-veridical-cognition, and since these are excluded from the inferential subject of the original inference, the *upādhi* is not of the *pakṣêtara* type. The counterinference it sets up (where the *upādhi* is not, there the probandum is not) does not fall to the "no similar instance" fallacy, since being-other-than-a-veridical-cognition is indeed absent from God's cognitions, all of which are veridical. It is not an example of the cooked-up undercutter, and yet it still appears to pervade the inference's probandum (since wherever the property produced-by-a-cause-that-is-not-shared-by-a-non-veridical-cognition occurs so does the putative *upādhi*, given that the case at issue is bracketed), while failing to pervade the prover in the instance of the inferential subject itself (where, to repeat, the case at issue is not bracketed).

Gaṅgeśa does not analyze why the Mīmāṃsaka's putative *upādhi* appears to pass the tests and still fails to be a true *upādhi*, a true "undercutter." He says simply that his original inference is cogent. If an original probandum pervades its original prover, then no "undercutter" can both pervade the probandum and fail to pervade the prover.

Text (p. 340, Tirupati, and p. 316, Calcutta) and Translation

> nanv astu pramāyāṃ doṣâ-bhāvo hetuḥ, āgantuka-bhāvân-apekṣya-jñāna-sāmagrī-janyatvaṃ svatastvaṃ | yat tv a-bhāvo na kāraṇaṃ | kiṃ tu daṇḍatvâdi-vat-kāraṇatâvacchedakatvena sāmagrī-bhedôpalakṣaka iti | tan na | japā-kusumâdi-saṃnidhau na pramā, tad-a-saṃnidhau sphaṭikâdau pramôtpatter an-anyathā-siddhatvena hetutvād iti cet, na | bhūyo-'vayavêndriya-saṃnikarṣa-viśeṣa-darśanâdi-samavadhāne pramā tad-a-bhāve tv a-pramā iti pramāyāṃ guṇaḥ, a-pramāyāṃ tad-a-bhāvo hetur ity eva kiṃ na syāt |

Objection.1 (by a Mīmāṃsaka): Let *absence of defects* be a cause of veridical cognition. Being produced by a causal complex sufficient for cognition free of dependence on anything positive and adventitious (i.e., something extra other than an absence) is (what we mean by) intrinsicality (with respect to causes of veridicality).

Objection.2 (against objector.1): An absence is not a cause. Rather, like being-a-stick (i.e., the universal, stickhood), etc., an absence is, as a specifier of the type of cause, indirectly indicated as distinct from (i.e., as something over and above) the causal complex.

Answer (by objector.1): That's wrong. There is no veridical cognition in the case of, e.g., a red rose next to a crystal (making the crystal appear red). The fact that when that rose, etc., is not there, a veridical cognition arises of the crystal, etc., shows that the absence of the rose, etc., *is* a cause, insofar as without it the effect would not be.

Gaṅgeśa: No. Veridical cognition occurs when such (excellences) occur as a sensory connection with many parts (of an object perceived) and experience of particulars (e.g., of hands and feet in the case of a visual perception of a human body). But in the absence of these, non-veridical cognition occurs. Thus, an excellence is a cause of a veridical cognition, and an absence of that, of a non-veridical cognition. Why not just this view?

Comments

Both Mathurānātha and Rucidatta identify the objector as belonging to the Murāri Miśra branch of Mīmāṃsā. And indeed there may be middle ground between the Naiyāyika position that a veridical cognition arises out of a causal complex that includes an epistemic excellence and the Prābhākara position that no excellence is required: veridicality is produced by the conditions sufficient to produce a cognition *plus* an absence of epistemic defect. The Prābhākara, as we shall learn, views an absence as an ontological free lunch, i.e., as reducing to its locus. But it is not clear that the Mīmāṃsaka here is a reductionist about absences. Indeed, he argues that an absence can be a cause of a positive epistemic effect in his response to objector.2. The rose causes a non-veridical cognition of the color of the crystal, and its being taken away accounts for the ensuing veridical perception.

Gaṅgeśa, it should be noted, finds positive epistemic defects in addition to absences of excellences, bile, for example, that causes a person to see white things as yellow. Sometimes an absence of an excellence, such as *not* being able to discern the parts of an object in the distance, is the defect that accounts for a non-veridical experience. Other situations involve positive defects, defects that are not absences. In other words, some errors are explained simply by lack of an excellence, while other errors occur when the factors that would otherwise be viewed as excellences are playing their causal role. In these latter cases, a positive epistemic defect abnormalizing the causal process carries the explanatory load. But the simplest approach, so goes Gaṅgeśa's implication at the end, is to identify excellences as causes of veridical cognitions, excellences whose absence means non-veridical cognition.

Text (p. 340, Tirupati) and Translation

atha a-sad-artha-viṣayakatve sad-artha-viṣayaka-hetv-a-bhāvo na prayojakaḥ, jñāne sad-artha-viṣayatā-niyamena tad-a-sambhavāt | sad-artha-viṣayakatve '-sad-artha-viṣaya-kāraṇâ-bhāvo hetuḥ sambhavati | pramāyāḥ sad-artha-mātra-viṣayatva-vad a-pramāyām a-sad-artha-mātra-viṣayatvâ-bhāvād iti cet, tarhy a-pramāyāḥ sad-artha-viṣayatā na syāt, hetv-a-bhāvāt | sad-artha-mātra-viṣayatve a-sad-artha-viṣaya-hetv-a-bhāvo hetur iti cet, tarhi guṇa eva tatra hetuḥ | tad-a-bhāvas tv a-sad-artha-viṣayatve prayojaka ity astu |

Objection: (What you say misrepresents our position.) An absence of a cause of a cognition whose object is an existent object is not a cause of (what we call errors, i.e.) cognitions whose object is not an existent object. For, by the rule that all cognitions have an existent object as object, such is impossible.

An absence of a cause of a non-existent as object is possible as a cause of (errors and veridical cognitions alike, understood as) having an existent as object. For, like the objects of veridical cognitions—namely, existent objects only—there is, in the case of a non-veridical cognition, (a cognition resulting from) an absence of just a non-existent object as cognitive object.

Gaṅgeśa: Then, a non-veridical cognition could not have as its object an existent object, since there could be no cause (of anything like that). If you say that, since cognitive objects are restricted to existent objects, an absence of a cause of non-existing object is a cause, then it would be precisely an "excellence" (*guṇa*) that would be a cause there. An absence of that (*guṇa*), in contrast, would be a cause of the having of a non-existent object as cognitive object—let this view be.

Comments

Mīmāṃsakas of all stripes accept the principle that all cognition has only the existent as object, as does Nyāya and Gaṅgeśa in a sense to be carefully articulated. (The Bhāṭṭa, who is closest here to the Naiyāyika, holds that something about the relationality of the qualificandum and qualifier may be non-existent, but the qualificandum and qualifier presented are invariably existent and real.) Thus, an absence of a cause of a cognition's having the non-existent as object may be said to be always causally operative in the generation of a veridical cognition, if you like, says the current Mīmāṃsaka objector, who stands his ground and refuses to admit special excellences but offers the Naiyāyika a sop.

Gaṅgeśa takes absences seriously and invokes their logic in his response. It is impossible to cognize an absence of *x* without previous cognition of *x*. To talk of an absence of an absolutely non-existent object is nonsense, e.g., an absence of a rabbit's horn. Since there is no experience of the non-existent, there can be no cognition of an absence of that. But despite this refutation, Gaṅgeśa goes on to use the Mīmāṃsaka claim to lead *him* to the right view, extending his own conciliation. He says that the admission of a causal role for "an absence of a cause of a non-existent as cognitive object" is equivalent to admitting a causal role for a positive epistemic excellence. The term "absence" and the term "non-existent" in effect cancel each other out, leaving a positive cause, an excellence, to account for a cognition's being veridical.

Text (p. 342, Tirupati) and Translation

> nanu guṇâ-bhāvasya sādhāraṇatvāt tad eva satyam a-satyaṃ ca na syāt, guṇa-tad-a-bhāvayor ekatra a-sattvād iti cet | na | doṣâ-bhāve 'pi tulyatvāt kvacit kaścit doṣa iti guṇe 'pi samānam | guṇâ-bhāvād a-san-mātra-viṣayakam api jñānaṃ syād iti cet, na | doṣād apy a-san-mātra-viṣayaka-jñānâpatteḥ | sarvatra viṣaye doṣo na sambhaviti iti guṇâ-bhāve 'pi tulyam |

Objection: Since (according to you) an absence of epistemic excellence is a common cause (of errors), therefore indeed would there be (in an error) no conjunction of the true and the untrue (contrary to the Nyāya explanation of error as a mixture of truth and untruth, e.g., "This is silver," which presents what sparks truth in its "thisness" portion and what sparks untruth in its "silverness" portion, when the object in front is mother-of-pearl). For, an epistemic excellence and its absence could not both be present with respect to a single thing (because of incompatibility).

Gaṅgeśa: No. For, the same reasoning would hold as much for an absence of defects as it would for (a presence of) an excellence: it would be the same (either way) when somewhere a defect is operative (i.e., there is no advantage to your account).

Objection: From an absence of an epistemic excellence would result cognition with an object as precisely that which does not exist!

Gaṅgeśa: No. For (if so) from a defect, too, would result cognition with an object as precisely that which does not exist—this is the difficulty. If you say that no defect is possible anywhere concerning cognitive objects, then that would hold for an absence of excellence, too—(again) the same reasoning.

Comments

All parties agree that something is veridically cognized in a typical case of error. Thus since the Mīmāṃsaka objector is willing to admit that an absence of defects is a cause, Gaṅgeśa is able to hurl his objections back as applying to his view, too. This may appear to commit the fallacy of *tu quoque*, "two wrongs don't make a right," *pratibandhī* in Sanskrit, which is a defeater in certain contexts. But that would be on the presumption that there is indeed something wrong with Gaṅgeśa's view in the first place. So, the structure of his response is: "If what you point out is a problem (and I do not believe that it is), then it is also a problem for your view."

Text (p. 343, Tirupati, and p. 319, Calcutta) and Translation

atha viśeṣa-darśanâdi-guṇas tad-a-bhāvaś ca an-anugata iti na tau pramā-a-pramā-hetū, kiṃ tu doṣa-tad-a-bhāvāv iti cet, tarhi pittâdir doṣas tad-a-bhāvaś ca an-anugata iti tāv api na tatra hetū | sva-pramāyāṃ svâ-bhāvasya vyabhicāraś ca | atha doṣatvaṃ na ekam | na hi tat-tad-bhrama-hetutvaṃ tat, ātmâdau gatatvād an-anugamāc ca | na api bhrama-mātra-hetutvaṃ, pittâder an-anugatatvena tad-a-bhāvād a-saṃbhavāc ca | na api pramā-hetv-a-bhāva-pratiyogitvam, anyonyâśrayāt, pittâdeḥ sva-pramā-hetutvāc ca | na api sva-pramā-bhinna-pramā-pratibandhakatvam | evaṃ hi pratyakṣa-pratibandhakasya sal-liṅga-parāmarśasya doṣatvād anumitiḥ pramā na syāt bhramaś ca syāt | tasmāt kvacit kaścid doṣa iti cet, tarhi guṇe 'pi tulyam |

Objection: Experience of particulars (hands and feet, for example, in the case of perception of a human body) and so on, as (your) epistemic excellence and its absence (as your defect) are not uniform. Thus, the two are not causes of veridical and non-veridical cognition (since a cause has to be uniform). The two causes are, rather, defect and its absence.

Gaṅgeśa: Then, a defect, such as the likes of bile, and its absence are not uniform. Thus, the two (i.e., your two) also would not be causes there. Furthermore, in the case of a defect itself as veridically cognized (e.g., "This yellow presentation is due to bile"), there would be deviation: an absence of itself (would not be a cause in such an instance of veridicality).

Objection: Being a defect is no single thing. For, it is not a cause of this and that error, since it would apply to (cognitions of) a self and so on (which are not errors), and since it is not uniform. Nor is it a cause of error in general, since that is non-existent (i.e., there is no cause in general of error) inasmuch as bile and so on are not uniform, and since that is impossible (for the same reason). Nor is it the absentee of (or correlate in relation to) an absence of a cause of a veridical cognition, because that would beg the question, and because bile and so on (as defects) are causes of veridical cognitions of themselves.

Nor is being a defect to be a blocker of veridical cognitions distinct from veridical cognitions of itself (as a defect). For, in this way, a mental appreciation of a true inferential mark (e.g., smoke), which blocks a perception (e.g., of fire, in that it is followed by an *inferential* awareness, not a perception, in the stream of cognitions that comprise a person's consciousness), would be a defect whereby the inference (or inferential awareness, e.g., that there is fire on a mountain) would not be a veridical cognition but would be an error (though it presented fire that is actually there). Therefore (error is to be understood as follows:) with respect to something there is some defect (but that cannot be spelled out more precisely without reference to particular cases).

Gaṅgeśa: Then, the same reasoning would hold with an epistemic excellence.

Comments

A cognition of self, as in ''I am perceiving this thing as yellow,'' is no error, especially not with respect to the ''self'' portion of the cognition, even when the cognition itself is in part due to a ''defect,'' namely bile.

The objector in his long statement appears to be rejecting plausible definitions of what it is to be a defect in an epistemic context. The proposal, ''to be a blocker of veridical cognitions distinct from veridical cognitions of itself (as a defect),'' is offered to avoid the overextention that vitiates the immediately previous proposal in the case of such cognitions as, ''This yellow presentation is due to bile.'' But the new proposal is too wide in a different way. A principle, or law, of cognitive psychology, according to Gaṅgeśa and Mīmāṃsakas alike, is that a mental appreciation of one property—the inferential mark or prover—as pervaded by another—the property to be proved—blocks perception in the next moment, prompting instead, in the stream of cognitions that make up a person's conscious life, an inferential cognition. (This picture will be greatly elaborated in the *TCM*'s next chapter.) Thus, as a blocker of a (presumably) veridical perception, such mental appreciation would be counted a defect, though it gives rise to a veridical cognition of the inferential variety.

Overall, Gaṅgeśa is using the objector to air issues concerning relevant uniformity in the causes of veridical and non-veridical cognitions. Argumentwise, his particular response here is, as before, that no comparative advantage has been discovered for the ''absence of defect view.''

Text (p. 344, Tirupati) and Translation

syād etat, pramāṃ bhramaṃ ca ākurvati jñāna-hetu-stome maṇḍūka-vasâñjana-dośāt vaṃśôraga-vibhramaḥ, tad-a-bhāve vaṃśa-pramā iti tatra doṣā-bhāvaḥ pramā-hetur ity anyatra api tathā, kḷptatvāt | maṇḍūka-vasā nayana eva doṣaḥ na tvaci iti tatra doṣâ-bhāvāt tvacā vaṃśa-pramā eva | gauro 'ham ity a-bheda-bhrama-hetu-doṣa-saṃskāra-sattve 'pi mama śarīram iti pramā iti cet, na | viśeṣâ-darśanasya tatra hetutvam, na tu saṃskārasya, tad-a-sattve tad-a-siddheḥ | na ca dūre cakṣuṣaḥ saṃnikarṣe 'pi keśâdau sajātīya-saṃyoge pramā, tad-a-bhāve na iti tatra saṃyoga-rūpo guṇaḥ pramā-hetur ity anyatra api guṇa-janyatā iti vācyam | tāvad-deśa-varti-keśa-sākṣātkāre sa hetuḥ, tena vinā tad-a-bhāvāt | tava api tāvad-dūra-pramāyāṃ sa hetuḥ saṃnikṛṣṭa-keśa-pramāyās tena vinā api bhāvāt | tatra api doṣâ-bhāvaḥ kalpyo doṣa-janyatve a-pramātvâpātāt |

Objection.1: That may be. A mistaking of bamboo for a snake due to the defect of applying an ointment of frog membrane (to the eyes) assumes the form of a veridical cognition and of an error; in the absence of that, a veridical cognition of bamboo occurs. Thus, an absence of the defect is a cause there of the veridical cognition; elsewhere, too, it's like that, since this is established (and no further cause need be identified).

The (ointment of) frog membrane is a defect only with respect to the eye, not to the skin. Thus occurs just a veridical cognition of bamboo through the organ of touch because of an absence of defect.

Objection.2 (against objector.1): "My body" (i.e., a body as belonging to me as a self) is a veridical cognition that occurs although a subliminal impression is present as a defect causing (on other occasions) an error of non-distinctness (expressible as, e.g.) "I am fat" (where the referent of "I" is erroneously taken to be the body).

Answer (by objector.1): No. A cause in that case is lack of experience of particulars (differentiating self and body), not a subliminal impression, since if the former is not present, that (the false identification) does not occur.

Objector.2 (against objector.1): In a case of something far away like a hair, a veridical cognition occurs (only) if there is a conjunction with (many hairs, i.e.) others of the same kind, although the (single) hair be connected with the visual organ. In the absence of such conjunction, no (veridical cognition occurs)—thus an epistemic excellence in the form of the conjunction would be a cause of the veridical cognition. Thus, in other cases, too, would it be generated by an excellence.

Answer (by objector.1): That should not be said. For, such conjunction is a cause (only) of a perception of (e.g.) hair present at such a distance, since without it the perception would not be. For you (you Naiyāyikas), too, it is a cause of a veridical cognition of something at such a distance (but not in general), since without it a veridical cognition of hair contacted (visually, close-by) does occur. Alternatively, there, too (i.e., in the case of the distant hair, too), a absence of defect is to be imagined, since, if a defect were causal, a non-veridical cognition would occur.

Comments

According to Nyāya, all erroneous perception is veridical in part, specifically in the part that indicates a "this," a qualificandum. Thus, "This is a snake," when there is really only bamboo, would be partly veridical in that there is something, a "this," perceived in front.

The objector—objector.1, a Mīmāṃsaka—is arguing that an absence of defect is sufficient to account for veridicality. No special excellence, *guṇa*, need be postulated when a well-established causal category explains all instances of veridical cognition. A minimally uniform "defect" is the key factor governing error. This line of thought continues to be developed through the next passage. Gaṅgeśa gives his definitive rebuttal after that (beginning with *ucyate*, p. 172, below).

The error of false identification of body and self is usually taken, across schools (insofar as the position is subscribed to), to be due to *saṃskāra*s, "subliminal impressions," that cause the error to endure. The problem mentioned in the passage at hand is that these are present even in the case of a veridical cognition such as "My body" (implying, in the use of the genitive personal pronoun, that the self is distinct from the body).

The Mīmāṃsaka (objector.1), however, insists on another explanation common in classical spiritual theorizing (Vedānta, etc.): a lack of awareness of differentiating factors—a kind of defect—is the cause. Presumably, in the case of "My body" an absence of such a lack would be causal in that the cognition is veridical.

Against the assumption that a special excellence would be called for to perceive hair at a distance—the presence of *many* hairs with which the visual organ would be connected—the Mīmāṃsaka claims that the instance is anomalous, or that there, too, an absence of defect could and should be imagined as causal.

Text (p. 347, Tirupati, and p. 323, Calcutta) and Translation

nanu viśeṣa-darśanaṃ pramā-hetuḥ viśeṣâ-darśanasya doṣatve tad-a-bhāvasya hetutvād iti cet, tarhi doṣâ-bhāvatvena sa hetuḥ na tu guṇatvena bhāvatvena vā | kiṃ ca viśeṣa-darśana-pratibandhakāḥ pittâdayo doṣāḥ āvaśyakatvāt, na viśeṣâ-darśanam | na ca teṣām an-anugatatvena viśeṣa-darśana-pratibandhakatayā anugame lāghavād viśeṣâ-darśanam eva hetur iti vācyam | kvacit kaścit doṣa ity anugamāt | anyathā pittâdito 'py a-pramā syāt | an-anugamāt | maṇy-āder iva an-anugame 'pi a-doṣatvāc ca | tad-a-bhāva-kūṭasya hetutvāt | sarvatra viśeṣâ-darśanam eva hetuḥ, pittâder an-anugamena tatra upakṣayād iti cet, na | pittâdy-utkarṣeṇa bhramôtkarṣāt | pittâder a-doṣatve ca viśeṣa-pramā eva kuto na bhavati | viśeṣasya viśeṣântarâ-darśanād iti yadā tadā an-avasthā eva | kiṃ ca viśeṣa-darśanaṃ na pramā-mātre na vā pratyakṣa-pramāyāṃ hetur vyabhicārāt | tatra eva tad-dhetutve 'n-avasthâpātāc ca | atha pratyakṣe indriya-saṃnikarṣo guṇaḥ a-pramâṃśe tad-arthasya a-sattvena saṃnikarṣâ-bhāvāt doṣo hetuḥ | na ca pramâṃśe 'pi sa hetuḥ, a-doṣatva-prasaṅgāt, pramâṃśasya a-pramātva-prasaṅgāc ca | sākṣātkāritvaṃ ca indriya-saṃnikarṣa-janyatvād iti cet, na | jñāne viṣaya-rūpasya aṃśasya indriya-tad-doṣâ-janyatvāt a-pramâṃśe ca indriya-saṃnikarśâ-bhāvena sākṣātkāritvaṃ na syāt | doṣasya tad-dhetutve 'tiprasaṅgo 'n-anugamaś ca | pramāyāṃ pramâ-pramāyāṃ ca yāthârtha-prayojakam asti a-pramāyāṃ doṣa-vad iti cet, na | doṣâ-bhāvasya sattvād iti |

Objection (by objector.2, a Naiyāyika, against objector.1, the Mīmāṃsaka): Experience of distinguishing features is a cause of veridical cognition, since, if lack of experience of features that distinguish is a (veridicality-undermining) defect, absence of that would be (for you, too) a cause.

Answer (by objector.1, the Mīmāṃsaka): Then, a cause (of a veridical cognition) is to be recognized as an absence of defect, but not as an epistemic excellence or a (special) presence. Furthermore, bile and so forth, which block (in a positive way) experience of distinguishing features, are necessarily (to be considered) defects, not (your) no-experience-of-distinguishing-features (which is an absence and negative and thus not preferred by you in *your* causal explanations).

Objection (by objector.2, the Naiyāyika): Inasmuch as they (bile and so forth) are not uniform as blockers of experience of distinguishing features, lack of experience of distinguishing features is indeed a cause on the grounds that it is simpler (i.e., is the "lighter" property).

Answer (by objector.1, the Mīmāṃsaka): That should not be said. For, there is (this minimal) uniformity (in the causes of all errors): with respect to something there is some defect. Otherwise, although due to bile or the like, a cognition would not be a non-veridical cognition, since there would be no uniformity (and hence no cause), and since, even given that some causes are not uniform, like a jewel and so forth (i.e., a magical jewel, a mantra, drugs, and so on, considered as preventers or blockers of getting burned although their causal operations are in no other way alike), they (bile and company) would not be defects. For, a collection of absences of such is a cause (of veridical cognitions).

Objection (by objector.2, the Naiyāyika): Everywhere a cause (of error) is simply lack of experience of distinguishing features, since bile and the like pale into insignificance here because of their non-uniformity.

Answer (by objector.1, the Mīmāṃsaka): No, since with an increase of bile and the like, there is increase in error (e.g., white things seem yellow*er* through the influence of more bile).

And if bile and so on were not defects, why should a veridical cognition of a detail (e.g., something as white) not come to be? If it is answered that it would be because of lack of experience of another detail (for instance, more white or, in another example, toes of the feet of a human body) belonging to the one detail (e.g., the feet), then we face an infinite regress.

Furthermore, experience of distinguishing features is not a cause of veridical cognition in general, nor of perceptual veridical cognition (in general), since there is deviation (in that experience of distinguishing features is such a cause only in cases of preceding doubt, as in "Is that a stump or a human?") And if it were a cause there, too (i.e., for all veridical perceptual awareness), then an infinite regress would again be incurred.

Objection (by objector.2, the Naiyāyika): Regarding perception (in general), the excellence is a sensory connection. Regarding (in general) the erroneous portion (of an erroneous perception, i.e., not the portion presenting a qualificandum), a defect is a cause, in that there is lack of a (normal) sensory connection inasmuch as the cognition's object (*qua* qualifier) is not present. And that is not a cause of the veridical portion, too, since the consequences would be (a) it would cease to be a defect and (b) the veridical portion would not be veridical—these are the difficulties. Moreover (concerning the qualificandum, whether of an erroneous or veridical perception) there is perceptual immediacy, because of its being generated by a sensory connection.

Answer (by objector.1, the Mīmāṃsaka): No. Neither the senses nor sensory defects generate, in a cognition, the object portion. Furthermore (if your view were right) there would be no perceptual immediacy with respect to the non-veridical portion (of an erroneous perception) since there would be no sensory connection.

Objection (by objector.2, the Naiyāyika): If a defect is (considered) a cause of every non-veridical cognition, then the problem is that the applicability (of your implicit thesis) is too wide, as well as that there is no uniformity (in what it is to be a defect).

Regarding veridical cognitions and cognitions that are both veridical and non-veridical, there is something that occasions the conformity with fact, like a defect regarding non-veridical cognitions.

Answer (by objector.1, the Mīmāṃsaka): No, because there is (simply) a lack of defect.

Comments

The property, *being a blocker of the awareness of details necessary for veridical perception*, would appear to be the theoretically simpler, or lighter (*lāghava*), property in comparison with the multiple properties involved in each and every defect posited on the Mīmāṃsaka view, because this blockage property would bring that diversity into the unity needed to formulate a causal law. The Mīmāṃsaka replies that the uniformity that is needed—and that is appropriate, given the diversity in errors—is no more than "some defect somewhere."

"Lightness," or parsimony, *lāghavatva*, is a theoretic virtue in identifying relevant properties, properties that specify the type of causality operative for a particular type of effect. Such "simplicity" (let us say) is a virtue in other contexts as well. Indeed, the applicability of considerations of theoretic simplicity and cumbersomeness ("heaviness," *gauravatva*) is itself an important issue, discussed at various points (see in particular, below, pp. 178–79).

The current *pūrva-pakṣa* closes with a good summary of the opposed positions, the Naiyāyika holding that there is an identifiable factor—appropriately general or uniform, an excellence—responsible for any veridical cognition's conforming with fact. That factor is, according to the Mīmāṃsaka, nothing other than an *absence* of veridicality-undermining defects. The issue will not be closed even after this entire section, but will be rejoined in several that follow, particularly in the next one on defining veridicality and in the section on absence. But now Gaṅgeśa gives us the main lines of his rebuttal, which involve a shift, relative to his Naiyāyika predecessors, on the question of uniformity.

Text (p. 353, Tirupati, and p. 327, Calcutta) and Translation

ucyate | pramā-mātre na anugato guṇaḥ kiṃ tu tat-tat-pramāyāṃ bhūyo-'vayavêndriya-saṃnikarṣa-yathârtha-liṅga-sādṛśya-vākyârtha-jñānānāṃ yathā-yathaṃ pratyekam eva guṇatvam, anvaya-vyatirekāt | tat-tad-a-pramāyāṃ pittâdi-liṅga-bhramâdīnāṃ doṣatva-vat pratyakṣe viśeṣa-darśanam api guṇaḥ, tad-anuvidhānāt |

Gaṅgeśa: We answer. *There is no uniform excellence for veridical cognitions in general.* Rather, for this and that veridical cognition (there is a specific excellence), (1) a sensory connection with many parts (of the object perceived, for perceptual awareness), (2) cognition of a true inferential mark (for inferential awareness), (3) cognition of similarity (for an analogical understanding), and (4) cognition of the meaning of a sentence (for testimonial awareness) are, as the case may be, severally, excellences. This is shown by positive and negative correlations.

In the case of perception, experience of distinguishing features (etc.) is also an excellence, according to the perceptual circumstances, as, for this and that non-veridical cognition, bile, etc., and errors about an inferential mark, etc., are defects.

Comments

The four epistemically supervenient meritorious properties, i.e., excellences, that Gaṅgeśa lists correspond to the four basic types of veridical cognition to which he devotes a chapter each. Now, though these may be said to be the excellences responsible for the veridicality of, in each case, a broad type of cognition, they apparently are not thought to be absolutely uniform within their special domains—at least this is true of perception, Gaṅgeśa suggests in his second paragraph. Observation, according to the principles of positive and negative correlation, may show the regularity of the four excellences listed, but Gaṅgeśa seems to have in mind special cases where the standard perceptual excellence is, if not abrogated, modified and supplemented according to the nature of what is known and circumstances surrounding the knowing. In other words, "a sensory connection with many parts" can, under a broad interpretation, be viewed as a causal factor of (almost) any veridical perception. But other excellences are also crucial in various cases. For example, there may be circumstances, so Gaṅgeśa suggests, where experience of distinguishing features would be an excellence, too. This may seem to differ only marginally from "a sensory connection with many parts," but the analogy drawn with epistemic defects, which are quite diverse—there are many distinct types of cause of perceptual and inferential error—drives home the point about variability.

A prime example of a special excellence is elaborated in the next passage, where the epistemically relevant circumstances include sense-based doubt.

Text (p. 360, Tirupati) and Translation

nanu viśeṣa-darśana-hetur eva tad-dhetur astu, tad-vyatirekād eva tad-a-bhāvôpapatteḥ | anyathā viśeṣa-darśanam eva tatra kuto na syāt | tatra api tad-apekṣāyām an-avasthānād iti cet, evaṃ vyāpya-viṣaya-vyāpaka-pratyakṣa-niyame anumitāv iva puruṣa-pratyakṣe prāmāṇya-saṃśayo na syāt, karâdimati puruṣa-jñānatvasya anuvyavasāyena niścayāt | tava api viśeṣa-darśanaṃ vinā kathaṃ vyāpaka-pratyakṣam iti cet, na | saṃśaya-viparyayôttara-pramāyāṃ tasya hetutvāt | mama api tad-dhetus tatra eva hetur iti cet, na | kara-caraṇa-cibukâdīnāṃ pratyekaṃ viśeṣatvena tad-dhetūnām an-anugatatayā tādṛśa-pratyakṣe a-hetutvāt | tad-darśaneṣu ca vyāpya-darśanatvam anugatam asti |

Objection: Let what causes experience of distinguishing features (rather than the experience itself) stand as a cause of veridical perceptual awareness, since from a lack of the one an absence of the other would be produced. Otherwise, why should there not simply be experience of distinguishing features (as opposed to the veridical cognition for which experience of distinguishing features is supposed to stand as a cause)?

Even if experience of distinguishing features occurs, there will be an infinite regress if (to have a veridical cognition) there is dependence on that (experience of distinguishing features, i.e., further details, fingers, etc., needing to be experienced to achieve experience of first-order features, hands, etc., on to fingernails, tips of fingernails, *ad infinitum*).

Gaṅgeśa: (No, there is no infinite regress in the following way.) The rule is that (doubt-resolving) perception is of a pervader property in relation to a (confirmed) cognition's object as a pervaded property, as with inference. Thus there would be no doubt about the veridicality of a perception of a person on account of the certainty (that results, following doubt, from perception of a property that is pervaded by a property cognized previously with respect to the same thing, as is) grasped by an apperception of the fact that (for instance) the cognition of a person concerns something that possesses hands, etc. (i.e., a property that is pervaded by the property being-a-person).

Objection: How, for you, too, is there to be perception of a pervader property (e.g., being-a-person) except through experience of distinguishing features (e.g., hands and feet, etc.)?

Gaṅgeśa: No. It is a cause (only) for such veridical cognition that follows doubt or a wrong awareness (not for veridical cognitions, or even veridical perceptual awarenesses, in general).

Objection: For me, too, what causes that (experience of distinguishing features) is a cause there indeed.

Gaṅgeśa: No. For, as (relevant doubt-resolving) details, hands, feet, chin, and so on, have, each of them, as their causes (i.e., as their perceptions' causes), causes that are not uniform, which (as such) are not causes of the perception (that follows doubt or a wrong awareness). Moreover, the fact of experience of a pervaded (property) *is* uniform in such cases of perception.

Comments

Mathurānātha glosses the "otherwise" (*anyathā*) that occurs early in the passage as an *absence of a lack* of what causes experience of distinguishing features, which, of course, amounts to an occurrence of the cause. Rucidatta provides a similar gloss. The objector's point is that the middle term can be eliminated, that there is no reason to identify experience of distinguishing features as an excellence responsible for veridical perception, since, the implication is, what causes that (namely, from the Mīmāṃsaka perspective, lack of defect) will be uniformly responsible for veridical cognition—as opposed to the piecemeal approach of Gaṅgeśa. Moreover, the objector continues, there is with "experience of *distinguishing features*" the special problem of an infinite regress.

Gaṅgeśa responds to the latter problem first. The right way to understand "experience of distinguishing features" is according to the rule that requires a doubt-resolving perception to be, with regard to one and same thing, of a property, such as possessing-hands-and-feet-etc., that is pervaded by another property that is thus confirmed, such as being-a-human-being. As we saw in the last section, such a confirmational pervasion can be grasped in an apperception that results in certainty that the thing seen is a person. Thus, the doubt-blocking certainty, and the epistemic excellence in such circumstances, is perception of not just any detail—requiring for confirmation perception of some further detail, *ad infinitum*—but rather of a detail, such as a possessing of hands and feet, etc., that is really an inferential mark ("as with inference") of the object's being a person, in that it is pervaded by the property, being-a-person.

Having responded in this way to the charge of an infinite regress, Gaṅgeśa has the weaponry needed to respond to the implied charge that his special excellence, "experience of (relevant) features," should be dispensed with in favor of a true cause of each and every veridical perception, namely, the (minimally uniform) "lack of defect" of Mīmāṃsā (or, more precisely, non-Prābhākara Mīmāṃsā: the subtly different Prābhākara position will shortly come into focus). Here it becomes pellucidly clear that experience of distinguishing features—relevant details, involving, as explained, pervader and pervaded properties—is a uniform epistemic excellence only in certain circumstances, those, for instance, of prior, perception-based doubt.

In support of Gaṅgeśa's position we may observe that, although in an extended sense "sensory connection with many parts" may be thought to cover such a situation of sensory doubt, there does seem to be a phenomenological difference between (a) seeing something as a whole, e.g., a human being, without noticing, without attending to, such parts as the hands and feet, and (b) seeing an object as a human being by way of noticing its having hands and feet, in particular *after* one has wondered about it, i.e., doubted whether the object spotted (in the distance) is a person or a stump.

Text (p. 370, Tirupati) and Translation

> nanv evaṃ saṃśayôttaraṃ vyāpya-jñāne saty anumitiḥ syāt na pratyakṣam anumiti-sāmagryā balavattvād iti cet, na | anyatra tathātve 'py atra pratyakṣa-sāmagryā balavattvāt | tatra puruṣaṃ paśyāmi ity anuvyavasāyāt | ata eva viśeṣa-darśana-janyatvena jñātaṃ bādhakam | tad-darśanâ-janyaṃ[5] bādhyam | anyathā bādhya-bādhaka-vyavasthā na syāt |

Objection: If you were right, there would be, following doubt, inferential awareness, not perceptual awareness—given that there is cognition of something (a property) as pervaded. For, the collection of causal factors for inferential awareness would be dominant.

Gaṅgeśa: No. Even though elsewhere the conditions you describe obtain, here the collection of causal conditions for perception would be dominant. (Moreover) there is the evidence of the apperception, "I am seeing a person there" (not, "I am inferring a person there"). Just for this reason, what is cognized through the cognition generated by experience of distinguishing features is a defeater (i.e., blocks the erroneous alternative with the doubt, "Is that a stump or a person?"). What is not generated by such experience (e.g., cognition of a stump) is defeated (or blocked). Otherwise, the relationship of defeater and defeated would not be.

Comments

A cognition of ~*p* is a blocker of a cognition of *p* in that an occurrence of the former would prevent, as a causal factor in certain circumstances, an occurrence of the latter—as an occurrence of the latter would also prevent the former from occurring. But it is not appropriate to talk about just any cognition as such a blocker. The circumstances have to be appropriate. There would have to be a cognition to block, as there would be in the case of the prior doubt, "Stump or person?" This is emphasized by Gaṅgeśa in his next statement.

Text (p. 339, Calcutta) and Translation

na ca pramā bādhikā, kara-bhrama-janya-puruṣa-jñānasya api sthāṇu-jñāna-bādhakatvāt | na api viparīta-bodhakatvena bādhakatvam, bādhya-tulyatvāt | an-anyathā-siddhaṃ bādhakaṃ cet, na | viśeṣa-darśana-janyatvasya eva tad-arthatvāt | na ca pītaḥ śaṅkha ity atra viśeṣa-darśane 'pi śvaitya-pramā na iti tad-dhetuḥ | yad-viśeṣa-darśanaṃ hi bhrama-virodhi tad-bhāvaḥ pramā-hetuḥ | pratyakṣa-bhrame ca pratyakṣa-viśeṣa-darśanaṃ virodhi | diṅ-mohe gauro 'ham iti bhrame ca tathā darśanāt | tac ca tatra doṣān na asti |

(**Gaṅgeśa** continues:) And a veridical cognition is not (*per se*) a defeater, since a cognition (for instance) of a person generated by an erroneous perception of hands defeats a cognition of a stump (not every veridical cognition). Nor is a defeater to be understood as the making known of an opposite, since there has to be something to be defeated.

Objection: A defeater is what is not otherwise established (what is not causally irrelevant).

Gaṅgeśa: Wrong, since the meaning of that (term, "not being otherwise established," i.e., being causally relevant) is just (in this context) generation by experience of distinguishing features.

Objection: In the case of (the erroneous perception) "The conch is yellow," there is no veridical cognition of the white, although experience of distinguishing features there is. Therefore, no cause (of veridical cognition) lies in the experience.

Gaṅgeśa: And that's wrong, too. For, experience of distinguishing features that at the same time is opposed to error, its presence is a cause of a veridical cognition (not experience of distinguishing features in just any circumstances). Furthermore, experience of perceptible detail is opposed to perceptual error (not errors of inference and so on). For, such perception of detail is found in (some non-perceptual) cases (for instance) of confusion about direction and in the error, "I am light-complexioned" (the referent of "I," the self, not having complexion). And the perception occurs in these cases not because of a defect.

Comments

One knows the error of, "The conch is yellow," on the basis of previous experience of the conch as white, or, perhaps, by a voice of authority ("It's white, and you are ill.") In any case, experience of detail does not eliminate the error.

The defect of which Gaṅgeśa speaks in the last sentence of the passage would be one that puts the error out of the domain of what can be known perceptually. For example, just looking about will not correct confusion about directions. One has to have a fixed reference point, to be provided, presumably, by an authority. And the defect of false identification of self with body is not part of a perceptual causal complex presumably, since saints who no longer so identify have perceptions like everyone else.

Text (p. 373, Tirupati) and Translation

api ca liṅga-sādṛśya-vākyârtha-bhrama-dośâ-bhāva-mātrān na anumity-ādir iti satya-parāmarśâdi-guṇa-siddhiḥ | evaṃ pramāyāḥ guṇa-janyatvena vede 'pi pramā vākyârtha-yathârtha-jñāna-guṇa-janyā iti tad-āśrayêśvara-siddhiḥ | nanu pratyakṣâdāv astu guṇa-janyatvam | vede tu bhramâdy-a-bhāva-catuṣṭayaṃ pramā-hetuḥ | loke bhramâdy-a-bhāva eva pramôtpatter iti cet, na | tatra lāghavād vākyârtha-yathârtha-jñānasya hetutvena bhramâdy-a-bhāvānām anyathā-siddhatvāt | āptasya bhramâdy-a-bhāva-mātreṇa vākyârtha-jñānaṃ vinā tādṛśa-vākyâ-bhāvāc ca | anyathā tava api tatra vaktṛ-jñānânumānaṃ na syāt tasya a-hetutvāt | astu vā ubhayam api hetuḥ vinigamakâ-bhāvāt | tathā api vede guṇa-siddhiḥ | na ca nitya-nirdoṣatvād dṛṣṭād eva vede prāmāṇyôpapattau na a-paridṛṣṭa-nitya-jñānâdi-sarva-jña-kalpanā gauravād iti vācyam | pramāṇavataḥ phala-mukha-gauravasya api svargâdāv iva a-doṣatvāt | pūrvaṃ kāraṇatā-graha-samaye phalân-upasthityā gauravâ-jñānāt loke nityatvâ-bhāvāc ca |

(**Gaṅgeśa** continues:) Further, inferential awareness and so on (as veridical cognitions) do not result just from a lack of defect regarding errors of an inferential mark, of similarity, and of a statement's meaning (since they result, in part, from positive excellences). In this way the epistemic excellences of correct consideration (of an inferential mark) and the others are established.

So, too, are veridical cognitions in the case of the Veda—*inasmuch as any veridical cognition is generated by some epistemic excellence*—generated by the excellence that is cognition of facts expressed in the meaning of statements.

In this way is established (according to Old Nyāya) the (existence of the) Lord as the locus of those (statements, i.e., as their author).

Objection: Let's say that generation by an excellence does apply to perception and so on. But in the case of the Veda, a quadruplet of absences of (the speaker's being in) error and so forth causes a veridical cognition. For, in the everyday world, given an absence of (a speaker's being in) error and so on, (testimonial) veridical cognition is produced.

Gaṅgeśa: No. There (concerning the everyday world) to view cognition of facts expressed in the meaning of statements (not the absences) as the cause is simpler, since the absences of error (on the part of the speaker) and so on are causally irrelevant (*anyathā-siddha*, i.e., a testimonial veridical cognition could occur while an error on the part of the speaker or the like occurred, too). Moreover, without cognition of the meaning of a statement, there would be no such statement made brought about by absence of error on the part of an authoritative speaker, etc., alone. Otherwise, for you (the Mīmāṃsaka), too, there could be no inference to a speaker's cognition, because it would have no basis (or cause).

Alternatively, let the two (the quadruplet of absences and a cognition of facts as expressed in the meaning of statements) both be causes, because there is no clear choice. Nevertheless, an excellence with respect to (veridical cognition deriving from) the Veda does occur.

Objection (by the Mīmāṃsaka, who is atheistic): If the veridicality of the Veda can be explained by the thesis that it is eternally free of faults (or defects, *doṣa*), as is indeed witnessed (by us), then we are not to imagine an omniscient being (as the author of the Veda) whose cognitions are eternal, etc., (all as) *un*witnessed (by us), since such is cumbersome.

Gaṅgeśa: That is not to be alleged. For, there is no fault even in (adopting) the cumbersome (as the right view) before the effect (i.e., before the cause-effect relationship has been ascertained), if it is supported by evidence, as is the case with (views about) heaven and so on.

Since the (precise nature of an) effect is not set in awareness prior to the time that the causal relationship is grasped, cumbersomeness is not known. Moreover, eternality is absent in the everyday world (all causes known in the everyday world are non-eternal).

Comments

Mathurānātha lists the quadruplet of error-causing defect with respect to testimonial comprehension (knowledge based on what someone says): (a) the speaker's being in error, (b) carelessness (on the part of the speaker or hearer), (c) desire to deceive, and (d) weakness in the instruments (slur of speech, etc.).

This is an interesting passage mainly because of its focus on another fundamental type of epistemic excellence, that pertaining to knowledge gained from testimony or "trustfully understood words." But there is also much deep context concerning several thorny areas of Nyāya theory, including the theoretic evil of cumbersomeness—which sometimes but not always is pitted against the theoretic virtue of parsimony—as well as an argument for the existence of God.

The standard example of cumbersomeness in understanding a causal relationship targets a property of the effect, not the cause, and in this way is unlike the example in the current passage. It may prove helpful nevertheless: to identify *blue* smoke as an effect in relation to fire as a cause is "cumbersome," *gaurava*, albeit such smoke is invariably preceded by fire. And only by knowing that all smoke is caused by fire are we able to see that identification of blue smoke as the effect in the formulation of the causal law is cumbersome. Similarly, there are properties of causes that are irrelevant to the production of a particular effect, but that irrelevance can be known only after the precise causal relationship has been ascertained.

In the passage at hand, Gaṅgeśa points out, first of all, that there is other evidence to establish the existence of the Lord along with the supreme being's properties of omniscience and so on. (Arguments for the existence of God are thoroughly aired at the end of the next chapter, on inference.) Second, imagination of such an author may seem cumbersome in comparison with Mīmāṃsā's view of the Veda's veridicality as derivative from a more basic property, "being eternally free of faults." Nevertheless, the precise causal relationship has not been ascertained by us—since we belong to this world, and the Veda, or at least its origination or foundations, to another. We cannot say, therefore, what is cumbersome and what is not.

Gaṅgeśa also disputes the contention that the property, "being eternally free of faults," is really witnessed by us: "eternality is absent in the everyday world." The example of heaven is given in this same vein of thought: since heaven has not been experienced by us the living, the precise nature of the causal status of the performance of sacrifices, etc., is not known by us, though we may be confident that they do secure heaven.

A few pages below, Gaṅgeśa explicitly renounces a "Veda-explanational" proof of the existence of God advanced by earlier Naiyāyikas. The view expressed at the opening of the current passage is, then, best understood as preliminary airing of theological positions, not as Gaṅgeśa's final stand on the score—nor, indeed, on the nature of the epistemic excellence responsible for testimonial knowledge to which he devotes a chapter about as long as this one. However, we are treated to quite an extended discussion of testimonial knowledge beginning with the second passage to follow; the next is focused on the Veda.

In overview, any Mīmāṃsaka is first and foremost intent upon defending Vedic authority. If the only requirement for veridicality is negative (absence of defect), then so long as defects are absent testimony would be a source of veridical cognition. And if a bit of testimony is speakerless, it automatically would be defectless speakerwise. So the Mīmāṃsaka would have a successful defense of scriptural authority were he to show that veridicality is intrinsic to cognition in the sense of being the causal default. Old Nyāya will not let this pass. The veridicality of Vedic testimony runs through the additional, positive property—the epistemic excellence—of the omniscience of its source or speaker, namely, God. Testimony's veridicality requires more than an absence of defects.

Text (p. 376, Tirupati, and p. 344, Calcutta) and Translation

> atha vede kartr-a-smaraṇâder bādhakāt loke 'pi nirdoṣatvena eva pramā-hetutvam, vede tu nityatvena eva vaktur a-bhāve 'pi nirdoṣatvam avadhāryata iti cet, na | bādhakasya bahuśo nirākariṣyamāṇatvāt bhrānta-pratāraka-vākye ghaṭo 'sti iti vākye paṭo asti iti doṣa-janya-vākye ca saṃvādāt[6] pramāṇe tad-a-bhāvāc ca | kiṃ ca daiva-vaśa-sampannaṃ caityaṃ vandeta ity-ādikaṃ śuka-bālâdi-vākyam apy evaṃ pramāṇaṃ syāt, vaktṛ-doṣâ-bhāvāt pramāṇân-apekṣatvena veda-tulyatvāt |

Objection (by a Mīmāṃsaka): That *smṛti* (the "remembering" that comprises a second-order of sacred texts) makes no mention of a maker (i.e., of an author of the Veda) defeats (your view and postulation of a Lord). So, in the everyday world, too, a veridical cognition should be recognized as having a cause in simply the fact of (a statement's) being fault-free. In the case of the Veda, however, although a speaker that is eternal is just the sort of speaker that there is not, being (eternally) fault-free is clearly determined (to apply).

Gaṅgeśa: No. For, many instances defeating (your contention that *smṛti* does not mention a Lord as author of the Veda, etc.) will be given in refutation (later). Moreover (your overall view of the foundations of the veridicality of testimonial cognition is wrong) because that (not being generated by a defect) is absent in (some) sources of veridical cognition. It is absent, for instance, in the statement of a perceptually deluded deceiver saying, "It's a pot" (when there really is a pot present), and in the statement generated out of a defect, "It's a cloth" (when there really is a cloth present), in that there would be conformity (i.e., the resulting veridical cognition on the part of a hearer would not be defeated by unsuccessful effort).

Furthermore, the likes of, "One should perform stupa worship," as well as the statements of parrots, children, and so on, which occur by force of chance (i.e., without cognition, on the part of the speaker, of the meaning of the utterance), would on your view (that veridical cognition is due to lack of defect) be sources of veridical cognition (an untoward consequence for your position). For, (in such cases) there need be no defect on the part of a speaker. Moreover, such statements need have no dependence on (another) source of veridical awareness. (Thus) they would be on a par with (your view of) the Veda.

Comments

Gaṅgeśa will later citẹ many passages in sacred texts as proof texts for the existence of God—in the *TCM*'s final chapter, on knowledge through testimony.

A speaker such as a parrot, a child, or a Buddhist, none of whom intend to deceive or, indeed, possess any of the faults that the Mīmāṃsaka identifies as leading to apparent but non-veridical testimonial cognition, could make statements that would generate veridical awareness that would have to be given the highest epistemic endorsement. This point contrasts with another made where, *despite* exhibiting the Mīmāṃsaka's ''faults,'' a speaker utters a statement that generates a hearer's veridical awareness. Thus, the Mīmāṃsaka view is refuted by counterexamples both in the method of agreement and in that of disagreement. (Accidental generating of a veridical cognition on the part of a hearer is not, however, an easy example for Gaṅgeśa himself to handle, as shortly will be evident.)

According to Mīmāṃsā, the Veda's authoritativeness does not rest on anything, not on the omniscience of God or any extrinsic property. In this way, the Veda's statements would be like the statements of parrots, children, and so on that occur by chance and by chance hit the truth or not.

A perceptually deluded deceiver, a person intending to lie, would tell the truth, .e.g., ''That's a snake,'' though he thinks it's not. This could be, then, the way that a hearer comes to know about an actual snake though veridical cognition of the snake is not the basis for the statement of the speaker. This is theoretically a tough nut to crack. The ''knowledge source'' here does not appear to be generalizable.

Text (p. 378, Tirupati) and Translation

nanu tava api śukâdi-bhrānta-pratāraka-vākyaṃ kathaṃ pramāṇaṃ, guṇâ-janyatvāt | na ca guṇâ-janyatvāt vaktṛ-tātparyâ-viṣayatvāc ca tad-a-pramāṇam | saṃvādena sādhye bādhāt | yat tu bhrānta-pratāraka-vākye yogyatā eva na asti | vaktṛ-jñāta-vākyârthâ-bādho hi yogyatā | bhrama-viṣayaś ca bādhita iti | tan na | ghaṭavati ghaṭo na asti iti bhinna-viṣayatayā bhramasya a-hetutvāt | kiṃ ca vākyârthâ-bādho yogyatā lāghavāt | vākyârthaś ca tatra a-bādhita eva | na ca śuka-bālâdi-vākyād artha-bodha eva na bhavati, kiṃ tv evam ayaṃ vadati ity evaṃ-prakārā pratītir iti vācyam | ākāṅkṣâder anvaya-bodha-sāmagryāḥ sattve 'nubhavân-apalāpāt | saṃvādena yathârthatvânubhavāc ca | evaṃ dhūma-bhramād vahni-maty eva vahny-anumitir na pramā syāt yathârtha-liṅga-jñānâ-janyatvāt | na ca vahny-antaram eva tatra viṣayaḥ pratyabhijñānāt gotvâdy-eka-vyaktike tad-a-bhāvāc ca | na api tatra anya-tādātmyâropaḥ, saṃsargâropāt liṅgôpadhānâṃśe bhramatve 'pi sādhyâṃśe pramātvād iti |

Objection.1: For you, too, how can a statement on the part of the likes of a parrot or of a perceptually deluded deceiver be a source of veridical cognition, in that there would be no production by (as you have it) an epistemic excellence? And it is not open to you to respond as follows, that the statement would not be a knowledge source because it would not be produced by an excellence and the resulting cognition would not have as its object what was intended by the speaker. For, that move is ruled out by what is to be proved (namely, according to you, that the resulting cognition would be non-veridical) in that there *would be* conformity (that is to say, as before, the resulting cognition on the part of the hearer would not be defeated by unsuccessful effort).

Objection.2 (against objector.1, by a Naiyāyika giving a preliminary response): But then there would be no semantic fitness (a requirement, according to Nyāya, for meaningfulness) in the statement of a perceptually deluded deceiver. For, semantic fitness consists in the undefeatedness of what is known by the speaker to be the meaning of his own statement, whereas the content of the statement of someone who is perceptually deluded *is* defeated (*ipso facto*).

Answer (by objector.1): That's wrong. For, "There is no pot" (as the cognition of a deluded person who expresses it in a corresponding statement), when there really is a pot, is a cognition with distinct intentionality or objecthood (from that of the veridical cognition accidentally generated in the hearer). It is an error that is not a cause (of the hearer's veridical awareness).

Furthermore, semantic fitness is that which is not defeated with respect to the meaning of a statement, because this is the simpler view (compared to, "a *speaker's* having cognized his statement's meaning"). Moreover, the meaning of the statement (as comprehended by the hearer who is provoked thereby to a veridical awareness) is here (with each example) not in fact defeated. (Thus, as examples of veridical awareness, our examples are indeed problems for your view.)

Objection (by objector.2, the Naiyāyika): An understanding of meaning does not result from a statement of a parrot, a child, and so on, but rather the resulting cognition has the following predication content, "*He is saying* such and such is the case" (as opposed to, "Such and such is the case").

Answer (by objector.1): That response should not be tried. For, there is no denying a (veridical testimonial) awareness its occurrence once there is present a collection of causal factors—syntactic expectation and so forth—sufficient to produce an understanding of grammatical connection among the words. Furthermore, the resulting awareness is of how something actually is (that is to say, the awareness is veridical) inasmuch as it conforms (and would not be defeated).

If you were correct, then, from an erroneous perception of smoke, an inference of fire concerning something that actually exhibits fire would not be a veridical awareness, since (according to you) it would not be produced from (the distinctive epistemic excellence for good inferences) cognition of a correct inferential mark. Furthermore, the object (of the inference) would not be, in such a case, simply another fire (distinct from the one that is actually there), because of the evidence of recognition ("This is that fire which I inferred"). And there is another reason: if (universals such as) cowhood and so on (including a *firehood* that is being inferred and attributed, in the present example) are singular entities, that (a different fire) could not be.

Nor is (it a way out for you to find) a superimposition of the identity of another (fire) there. For, the (wrong) relation would be superimposed (that is to say, firehood would be presented as related to its exhibitor by inherence, whereas identity would be the relation between two entities superimposed). And the cognition would be veridical concerning the probandum (namely, fire), although in the prover portion error occurred.

Comments

If there were no semantic fitness, there would be no veridical testimonial awareness, according to the standard Naiyāyika account. Semantic fitness or appropriateness rules out such nonsense as "He is watering with fire." However, cases can be imagined where a hearer's cognition is veridical albeit its etiology includes an erroneous cognition on the part of the speaker. For, it is the true *statement* of a speaker, not his cognition, that provokes a veridical awareness on the part of a hearer.

Or, one could say that the problem for the Naiyāyika is the unlikely prospect of being able to spell out uniform epistemic excellences for such examples of veridical awareness.

Syntactic expectation, appropriate pausing (avoidance of inordinately long pauses between the words), and semantic fitness are viewed by Naiyāyikas as invariably necessary conditions for a statement to be comprehensible. Thus *each* is a necessary condition—and an epistemic excellence—for knowledge from testimony.

As may be surmised from the current discussion, another candidate condition, speaker's intention, is controversial. Some Naiyāyikas accept it as a fourth condition, but others do not. As a topic it looms large, in particular with resolving ambiguity. Gaṅgeśa has a long discussion of speaker's intention in his last chapter. He does not see it as in general an excellence for veridical testimonial cognition—as he also makes plain in the (shorter) discussion that follows here.

Next we need to think about an important topic in the context of contemporary epistemology, especially of so-called "Gettier problems." It is also hermeneutically important. Not only a testimonial awareness of questionable origin but also an inference from an erroneous perception of smoke (e.g., a line of dust, mistaken for smoke, seen rising from a mountain) apparently can result in a veridical awareness of fire when there really is fire at the place where the mistaken mark or prover is seen. However, the Naiyāyika would not count this as a veritable inference and would rule out not veridicality but the "knowledge source" status of the generator of the veridical result: the cognition has not been produced in the right way. But how can there be this kind of misalignment? And, in particular, how is this case of falsely arrived-at veridical cognition of fire any different from the case of a perceptually deceived liar whose true statement generates a veridical cognition in a hearer? How can there be a "knowledge source" in the one case and not in the other? Note that the problem is not simply translational since the pseudo-inference based on dust instead of smoke provokes a cognition that fits Gaṅgeśa's preferred definition of a veridical cognition, "awareness with predication content about a ϕ-object as ϕ" (*tadvati tad-prakārakânubhavaḥ*, below, p. 236). Though there is some dispute about this, the resultant fire-cognition fits the definition.

Considering the contemporary debate about the nature of knowledge, we may repeat a point made in the introduction: cognitive origin plays for Nyāya the role that Western epistemologists usually give to justification. Knowledge has to have been formed in the right way, that is, through cognitive means that invariably produce veridical awarenesses. Of course, there can be defects in cognitive processes, which result in awarenesses that are only apparently inferential, perceptual, etc., not results of veritable *pramāṇa*. Cognitions having the right pedigree is a crucial epistemic standard since cognitions form "dispositions" in memory (*samskāra*) that are necessary to act successfully. that is to say, have to have been formed through *truth-sensitive* processes. Furthermore, in a context of debate or inquiry we are interested in cognitions as belonging to types, a veridical cognition that is by type veridical, by law veridical, such that we, or anyone, at any time, may act confidently on its basis. An example that just happens the one time to be veridical—not true in its type—would not be *pramāṇa*-generated and while it itself might not be unreliable others of its type would be. With such reflection might we try to firm up Naiyāyika intuitions about the "non-veridicality" of a true but pseudo-inferential result brought about by false evidence. It may be veridical but it does not get the epistemic endorsement of being *pramāṇa*-generated. It does not have *prāmāṇya*, "veridicality," in the sense at issue here is this section, namely, to be the result of an epistemic excellence.

An etymological point is also relevant. The word *prāmāṇya*, "veridicality," has two senses attaching to two distinct derivations: (a) as an abstraction formed from *pramā*, "veridical cognition," and (b) as an abstraction formed from *pramāṇa*, "truth-generating cognitive means." The true cognition resulting from reasoning from false evidence would have veridicality only in the first sense. The cognition would not have veridicality if we mean by that having been produced by a cognitive means that infallibly produces cognitions that capture the facts. Of course, we should hasten to add, a person may not be able to identify in a particular instance whether the cognitive generator is in fact a *pramāṇa*. Thus is the overall direction of Gaṅgeśa's response. But then why is the deceived-liar case not to be analyzed in the same way, as a veridical cognition nevertheless to be downgraded for its pedigree?

A caveat and qualification concerning the above remarks about veridicality. For us the adjective "veridical" will continue to be used in the weak sense spelled out by Gaṅgeśa in his definition of a veridical cognition. Thus we should keep sharply in mind the Naiyāyika's contrasting problems: (a) regarding veridical cognitions that are not *pramāṇa*-generated, such as the true inferential awareness resulting from a bad inference, and (b) regarding the questionable *pramāṇa* status of a cognitive means that seems flawed and would not invariably produce veridical awarenesses, as with the true statements of the deluded liar.

A few more words are in order now to help us appreciate the Naiyāyika point of view. Consider how readily the inference with the bad origin would be defeated though it does indicate a fact. One might well notice that the presumed smoke is really dust before finding the fire. The point is that veridicality in the second sense involves a much tighter tie to the facts than simply something like fact-hitting intentionality, as is implied by saying that a cognitive process is in general truth-generating. The falsely inferred, true cognition of fire would be rather easily challenged and the subject's certainty undermined by closer inspection, whereas a *pramāṇa*-generated inferential cognition is not nearly so readily knocked out—though of course in principle we could be misled by new evidence. We may quarrel about details of appropriate classification, but Naiyāyikas do tend to see the fire-cognition as an inferential error although it is technically a *pramā*. And so, again, why not say the same about the statements of the truth-telling liar?

The deceived-liar case makes it tempting to the Naiyāyika somehow to count both it and the pseudo-inferential case as not instances of *pramāṇa*-generation, as both cognitive processes involving an epistemic defect resulting in non-veridical cognitions. The easiest way to accomplish this is to find of way of viewing the results as themselves non-veridical. But the objector shows a couple of routes whereby one might try that move to be in fact closed. Since a good inference would make a subject know that some bit of fire or other is on the mountain, i.e., since it would work through apprehension of the universal firehood, not through apprehension of exactly one fire as opposed to another, one cannot say that the apparent but false inferential awareness has a different object than a veritable one would have. Furthermore, such wrongly motivated inferring would present firehood as related to what exhibits it by way of the relation of inherence. But a superimposition of a second fire on a first would be a presentation by way of identity, not by way of inherence. One cannot say that the awareness is non-veridical for such reasons.

Text (p. 380, Tirupati, and p. 349, Calcutta) and Translation

> ucyate | bhrānta-pratāraka-vākye śukâdi-vākye ca pramāṇa-śabdatvena āptôktatvāt veda-vad īśvarasya eva yathârtha-vākyârtha-jñānaṃ janakam, tasya kārya-mātre kartṛtvāt | śukâdi-vākyasya ca veda-tulyatā doṣâ-bhāva-vādinā api vācyā |

Old Nyāya: We answer. Regarding a statement of a perceptually deluded deceiver and a statement of the likes of a parrot as well, just the Lord's correct cognition of the meaning of the statement (that is comprehended by the hearer) is, as with the Veda, the generator (of the hearer's veridical awareness), inasmuch as the words would be a source of veridical cognition by having been spoken (as it were) by (the Lord as) an authority. For, just he brings about effects that otherwise would not have a cause.

Moreover, that a statement by the likes of a parrot is on a par with the Veda is to be embraced by those (you Mīmāṃsakas) who advocate the (Veda's) lack of faults.

Comments

Good fortune is strictly due to God, and the examples cited are not cases of veridicality by chance. Here we see the depth of the Naiyāyika commitment to the supervenience on the process resulting in a veridical cognition (in the weak sense) of an epistemic excellence.

In the context of the debate with Mīmāṃsā, the Naiyāyika cannot resist a dig, making out the examples as each a two-edged sword. A parrot is not really the "author," in the everyday sense, of a statement it utters that happens to be true. On the Mīmāṃsā account, the Veda would be similarly authorless. Gaṅgeśa himself, by the way, has sympathies here that are as much in line Mīmāṃsā as with Old Nyāya, as becomes clear in the following passage.

Text (p. 381, Tirupati) and Translation

> nanv evaṃ śabdâbhāsôcchedaḥ tasya api īśvara-vaktṛkatvād iti cet, na | tad-vākyârthasya a-sattvena bhagavaj-jñānâ-gocaratvāt | evaṃ liṅgâbhāsa-janya-pramāyām api vahni-vyāpyavattva-jñānam īśvarasya eva janakam iti saṃpradāya-vidaḥ | atra brūmaḥ | śābda-pramāyāṃ loke vaktur yathârtha-jñānaṃ na guṇaḥ, kiṃ tu yogyatâdikaṃ yathârtha-taj-jñānaṃ vā | lāghavād āvaśyakatvāc ca | bhrama-pramāda-vipralipsā-janye vākye visaṃvādini na yathârtha-yogyatā-jñānam, vākyârthasya bādhitatvāt | evaṃ karaṇâ-pāṭavād anyasmin vaktavye 'nyâbhidhāne visaṃvādini, saṃvādini tu pramāṇam eva | yogyatâdi-jñānam eva kvacin na asti |

Objection: If your view were right, erroneous word-generated awareness (an apparently testimony-generated cognition that is false but credible) would be a shattered notion, since it, too, would have the Lord as its speaker.

Answer (by philosophers of **Old Nyāya**): No. For, inasmuch as what such a statement means would not be the case, it would be outside the scope of the Lord's cognition.

So too does it hold for a veridical (inferential) cognition generated by an apparent inferential mark: the generator would be the Lord's cognition of the fact that something is being pervaded by fire—so say those who know the (Nyāya) tradition.

Gaṅgeśa: But we say the following. In the everyday world, a true cognition on the part of a speaker is not an epistemic excellence with respect to veridical testimonial cognition. Rather, a (vehicle statement's) semantic fitness and the rest and a correct cognition (on the part of the hearer) of that (semantic fitness, syntactic expectancy, etc.) are such excellences. For, this is the simpler position, and it is necessary (i.e., the Old school's alternative is not acceptable).

A statement generated out of perceptual delusion, carelessness, or a desire to deceive is (generally) a (false) statement that fails to conform (in that statements of the type are found to be defeated by lack of success of effort undertaken on their promptings). Such is (in general) not cognized (by a hearer) according to the standards of semantic fitness (etc.), since the statement's indication could be defeated (and readily shown to be false). The same holds for a reference to one thing (e.g., a pot, with the statement "A pot," *ghaṭaḥ*) when what should be said is something else ("A cloth," *paṭaḥ*) out of impairment of an organ. But if what is said conforms (to what is, in that it would not be defeated), then it is indeed a source of veridical cognition, *pramāṇa*. Sometimes (on the other hand, let us stress) cognition of semantic fitness, etc., does not in fact occur (and then there is no veridical word-generated awareness).

Comments

On the Old Nyāya view, the orderly arrangement of the world due to the Lord is the reason why a parrot's statement might prompt in a hearer a veridical cognition. This would not be due to chance. So far, Gaṅgeśa is sympathetic.

But he gives up the theological inference advanced by earlier Naiyāyikas that postulating an excellence to explain the veridicality of cognitions deriving from the Veda would mean to postulate God as the infallible author of scripture. Gaṅgeśa finds other proofs for the existence of God. Word-generated veridical awareness need not have an excellence pertaining to an author or speaker but rather just to the statement itself and the hearer's comprehension. The point is repeated in the next passage as well.

Gaṅgeśa's remarks here signal a shift in the Naiyāyika problem space concerning testimony-generated knowledge. The Old Nyāya problem concerned the speaker, how his being knowledgeable, non-deceiving, communicative, and so on could ensure the veridicality of the awareness that his statement would generate. Gaṅgeśa and New Nyāya concern themselves with the hearer, how his uptake would be correct on the basis of a syntactically well-formed, semantically fit sentence.

Nevertheless, Gaṅgeśa agrees with Old Nyāya that *pramāṇa*-generation does not occur by accident, that there must be a generalizable success story when *pramāṇa*-generation occurs. Note that in Gaṅgeśa's assertion, "But if what is said conforms (to what is, in that it would not be defeated), then it is indeed a *source of veridical cognition*, *pramāṇa*," the word *pramāṇa* occurs, not *pramā*, "knowledge source" as opposed to "veridical cognition" in the weak sense. To be *pramāṇa*-generated is to receive the highest epistemic endorsement.

An excellence ties an awareness to a fact that is its indication or object. Conversely, there must be a failure—such as of semantic fitness or of another of the excellences for word-generated cognition—when a word-generated cognition is generated on the basis of a false statement. (Just how we understand false statements is a different matter, a subject taken up in the *TCM*'s final chapter.) For, in general these are not to be trusted; statements of the type prove to be unreliable. Thus, an epistemic defect is to be identified, the precise nature of which need not be discussed now.

Gaṅgeśa does not deal directly with the example of the pseudo-inference resulting in a fire cognition with respect to a mountain that is indeed fiery. But his outlook may be reconstructed. Reasoning from a mistake about a property of an inferential subject, as when one "sees" a mountain as fiery from a line of dust in the distance, leads generally to *mis*directed effort and action. Thus, though in a particular case such a cognition be truth-hitting, cognitions of the type are unreliable. Furthermore, even the seemingly chance veridicality of the pseudo-inferential result may well have an explanation, it seems Gaṅgeśa would likely say if pressed, though he remains silent about Old Nyāya's resort to God. Human karma, i.e., "unseen force," *a-dṛṣṭa*, seems a likely alternative candidate in his own view. Or, maybe he is silent because he thinks such anomalies may be ignored.

In any case, the heart of Gaṅgeśa's resolution of the deluded-liar case is to focus on the causal story and to suggest the "irrelevance" (*anyathā-siddhatva*) of factors very far back in the causal chain. The speaker's intention (etc.) is causally irrelevant. Thus it is not an epistemic excellence with respect to veridical testimonial cognition. Semantic fitness and the other conditions on a statement's meaningfulness along with correct cognition on the part of the hearer are the excellences here. He says in the current passage that this position is to be preferred over the Old Nyāya view because of its simplicity.

Text (p. 382, Tirupati) and Translation

nanv evaṃ nānârthād anya-parāt tātparya-bhrame taṃ vinā eva vā yathârtha-yogyatâdi-jñāne sati saṃvādy-apara-śakya-jñānam api pramā iti tatra api tad-vākyaṃ pramāṇaṃ syād iti cet, na | iṣṭatvād | tātparya-viṣaye ca tad-vākyaṃ na tadā pramā-janakaṁ iti na pramāṇam | evaṃ vede 'pi yathârtha-yogyatā-jñānam eva guṇa iti na vaidika-pramāyāṃ guṇa-janyatvena īśvara-siddhiḥ |

Objection (by a Naiyāyika of the Old school): Because of (some words having) multiple meanings, error can be occasioned about a speaker's intended meaning in that it refers to one thing (and the hearer understands something else). With or without such (an error), if what you say were true, given a correct cognition of semantic fitness, etc., even a (word-generated) cognition that referred to something else (than what its speaker intended in uttering the statement that prompts it) would be a veridical cognition so long as it conformed. Thus there, too, the statement (that is misunderstood) would be a source of veridical cognition.

Gaṅgeśa: No, in that this (your conclusion) is what we want (that is, in part). Moreover, the statement in its (original) intended meaning would not, in the case you imagine, generate the veridical cognition. Thus, it would not be a source of veridical cognition.

In this way, concerning the Veda, too, correct cognition of semantic fitness (etc.) is an excellence. Thus, the Lord is *not* established with respect to Vedically derived veridical awareness through its being generated through Him as an excellence.

Comments

The word *hari* means a monkey, the sun, Viṣṇu, and so on, depending on context. Thus, it could be understood by a hearer differently from a speaker's intention in using it, and the hearer would have a correct word-generated awareness so long as a monkey (or whatever) was present. Gaṅgeśa says that this is acceptable to him. The statement under the interpretation of the speaker would not be a source of veridical cognition, but rather only under the interpretation of the hearer. The reason for this move is more fully explained in the next passage.

As mentioned, Gaṅgeśa is willing to give up one of Old Nyāya's inferences to the existence of God.

Text (p. 383, Tirupati) and Translation

syād etat | vede vaktur yathârtha-vākyârtha-jñānam api guṇaḥ | loke pramāṇa-śabdaṃ prati tādṛśasya jñānasya hetutvāt | ata eva tava loke vaktṛ-jñānânumānam | evaṃ ca vedo vākyârtha-gocara-yathârtha-jñāna-vat-sva-tantra-puruṣa-praṇītaḥ pramāṇa-śabdatvāt gām ānaya iti vākya-vad iti īśvara-siddhiḥ | mā evam | pramāṇa-śabdatvaṃ hi vākyârtha-yathârtha-jñāna-pūrvakatāṃ vinā api saṃbhavati, āvaśyaka-yogyatâdi-sattvāt yathârtha-taj-jñānād vā ity upapāditam, ato '-prayojakam etad iti | tathā api loke vākyârtha-jñānaṃ pramāṇa-vākye kāraṇaṃ gṛhītam iti tena vinā kathaṃ tad iti cet, na | pravṛtty-ādy-arthaṃ hi prayojyasya hi vākyârtha-jñānam uddiśya etādṛśa-padebhyo vākyârthaṃ jñāsyati iti buddhyā vākya-prayoga ity anyathā-siddhaṃ prathamaṃ vaktur vākyârtha-jñānam, na tu tādṛśa-padâvalī-prayoge tasya hetutvam | tādṛśa-pada-samūhasya pratyeka-pada-hetor eva śukâdi-vad upapatteḥ |

Objection (Old Nyāya): That may be. (But) in the case of the Veda, the speaker's (i.e., the Lord's) correct cognition of a statement's meaning is also an excellence. For, in the everyday world such a cognition is a cause of testimonial speech that is a source of veridical cognition.

Just for this reason one is able to infer the cognition, in the world, that a speaker has.

And in this way (there is the following inference:) the Veda is authored by an independent person within whose correct cognitions are the meanings of (Vedic) statements, *since* the Veda is testimonial speech that is a source of veridical cognition, like the statement, "Bring the cow." Thus the establishment of (the existence of) the Lord.

Gaṅgeśa: Don't think like that. For, even without being preceded by (on the part of the speaker) a correct cognition of a statement's meaning, testimonial speech that is a source of veridical cognition is possible. That has already been established as due to the presence of (a statement's) semantic fitness and so on, which *are* necessary, or from a correct cognition (on the part of a hearer) of that (semantic fitness, etc.). Hence, your inference is unsupported (and ineffective).

Objection (Old Nyāya): Nevertheless, in the everyday world cognition of a statement's meaning (on the part of the speaker) is understood to be a cause of an utterance that is a source of veridical cognition. Thus, without that, how could it be?

Gaṅgeśa: No. For, considering a cognition of a statement's meaning on the part of someone urged to make an effort (e.g, to bring a cow), etc. (e.g., to cease from doing something), he will understand the meaning of the statement from such words (as "Bring the cow"). Thus, through his cognition the statement is put to use. Thus, the original cognition, on the part of the speaker, of the meaning of the statement is *causally irrelevant* (*anyathā-siddha*).

But that (a hearer's cognition) does not have a cause in just such a string of words that is employed (by the speaker). For, it is possible that such a collection of words have the same cause as each word (individually), as with the likes of (the sounds of) a parrot.

Comments

Denying that the speaker's string of words causes the hearer's cognition, Gaṅgeśa apparently means that it is instead the words under a particular interpretation that play the causal role. Thus, the words not as a string of individual sounds but as components of a statement marked by semantic fitness et cetera under the interpretation of the hearer cause the hearer's veridical awareness. Wholes, we may note, for Nyāya from the very beginning of the school, are considered more than collections, more than sums of their parts, having certain properties that the parts do not have. Similar is this view of a statement having a semantic fitness that the words that comprise it do not possess. And given that there can be a difference between speaker's and hearer's meaning, it is the statement under the interpretation of the hearer that is the relevant cause.

The hinge argument differentiating Gaṅgeśa's from the Old Nyāya's view is the "causal irrelevance," *anyathā-siddha*, i.e., explanatory irrelevance, of factors at a distance from an effect that is to be explained. A potter's ass used to carry the clay out of which a pot is made is not to be listed among the relevant causes of a new pot. Similarly, a speaker's intention may be just a bit behind in the causal chain that leads to a hearer's veridical cognition, and the statement itself under the construal of the speaker may be even closer. But the hearer's veridical cognition does not require them explanationally. Furthermore, there are the counterexamples of the parrot and so on mentioned above.

To Gaṅgeśa's citing parsimony, we might add that verbal communication is a common but also complex phenomenon. We had better stick to trying to trace the more immediate causes if we wish to make explanatory progress. (On *anyathā-siddha*, see above, p. 23.)

Text (p. 385, Tirupati) and Translation

atha tātparya-viṣaye vedaḥ pramāṇam | tātparyaṃ ca tat-pratīticchayā uccāraṇam | na ca asmad-āder vedaṃ vinā atīndriya-vedârtha-gocara-jñānaṃ, yena tat-pratīticchayā uccāraṇam bhavet | na ca vedād eva tat, anyonyâśrayāt | ataḥ sakala-veda-vedârtha-darśinā yasya vedasya yad-artha-tat-pratīticchayā uccāraṇam kṛtaṃ sa tatra pramāṇam iti tādṛśecchā eva guṇaḥ taj-janyā vedârtha-pramā iti tad-āśraya-sva-tantra-puruṣa-dhaureya-siddhir iti cet, mā evam | mīmāṃsâdi-sakalâṅga-sācivyād veda-vākyârtha-jñānavatā adhyāpakena tat-tad-artha-pratīticchayā vedasya uccāraṇam iti vedârtha-yathârtha-vidas tat-tad-arthe tātparyam asty eva | evaṃ pūrva-pūrva-tādṛśâdhyāpakena tat-tad-artha-pratīticchayā uccaritatvaṃ tat-paratvam avagamya uttarôttareṣāṃ vedârtha-pratyaya ity an-ādis tātparya-paraṃ-parā iti kim īśvareṇa | tarhi vedârthânabhijñâdhyāpakena uccārita-vedasya na tad-artha-pratītîcchayā uccāraṇam iti tātparyâ-bhāvān na pramāṇaṃ na vā tato 'rtha-niścaya iti cet, na | an-ādau saṃsāre tasya vedasya kadācit kenacit mīmāṃsâdy-adhīna-vedârtha-jñānavatā tat-pratītîcchayā uccāraṇaṃ kṛtam, tāvatā eva tat-paratvam iti |

Objection (Old Nyāya): About its intended subject matter (*tātparya*), the Veda is a source of veridical cognition. To be intended is to be uttered with the desire to generate a cognition of that (in a hearer). And without the Veda, those such as we would not have—within the domain of Vedic meaning, which is beyond the realm of the senses—cognition whereby there could be (a speaker's) utterance according to his desire to generate a cognition (in us). And that could not come just from the Veda, because of the fallacy of mutual dependence. Hence, by one who sees the meaning of the entire Veda has there been an utterance according to his desire to generate a cognition (in us) of that meaning belonging to the Veda. He is in that regard a source of veridical cognition. Thus, such a desire (to communicate) is an epistemic excellence. Veridical cognition of Vedic meaning is produced by that. Thus is established the (existence of the) foremost of persons, who is independent and the locus of that (desire).

Gaṅgeśa: Don't think like that. By a teacher who has the help of all the (Vedic) auxiliaries, the science of interpretation (*mīmāṃsā*) and so on (grammar and the like), and who knows the meaning of Vedic statements, there is utterance of the Veda according to his desire to generate (in pupils) cognition of this and that meaning. Thus, there is indeed an intended subject matter in this and that (statement's) meaning, with the intention belonging to one who correctly knows Vedic meanings. In this way, through (a line of successive or) earlier and earlier such teachers has it been uttered according to this and that one's desire to generate cognition of this and that meaning. Having understood one of these (teachers') intended meanings, later and later (teachers) have cognized Vedic meanings. Thus is there a beginningless succession of intended subject matter. Therefore, what is the point of postulating the Lord (in this regard)?

Objection (Old Nyāya): Then the Veda as uttered by a teacher unfamiliar with Vedic meanings would not be uttered according to his desire to generate cognition of Vedic meaning. Thus since this would not be the intended subject matter, the Veda would not be a source of veridical cognition, nor, therefore, would there be certainty about its meaning.

Gaṅgeśa: No. Within beginningless transmigratory existence (*saṃsāra*), the Veda has been uttered at some time by someone who knows Vedic meanings through depending on the (Vedic auxiliaries of) the science of interpretation and the like—(and) uttered according to his desire to generate a cognition of it. In simply just such a way there is such an intended meaning.

Comments

Gaṅgeśa further corrects the reasoning of the Old school on the topic of how Vedic statements have intended significance. One does not have to resort to the cumbersome task of postulating desires of the Lord. Here, as remarked in the introduction, he shows a certain affinity for the views of Mīmāṃsā.

Text (p. 386, Tirupati, and p. 356, Calcutta) and Translation

prābhākarās tu prāmāṇyaṃ svata eva utpadyate jñāyate ca iti | tathā hi, niṣkampa-pravṛtty-aṅgaṃ smṛty-anubhava-sādhāraṇaṃ yathârthatvam eva prāmāṇyam | tac ca jñāna-mātra-sāmagrī-janyam, na tu guṇaṃ doṣâ-bhāvaṃ vā apekṣate | sarva-jñānānāṃ yathârthatvena a-vyabhicārāt | a-yathârthas tu vyavahāraḥ tasya eva bādhyatvāt | jñānaṃ tu na bādhyate | bādhakâbhimata-jñāna-tulyatvāt | jñāne ca a-yathârthatva-vyapadeśaḥ viparīta-vyavahāra-jananôpādhikaḥ |

(**Gaṅgeśa** continues:) But the Prābhākaras hold the following.

Prābhākara: Veridicality is both produced and known just intrinsically. For, as a constituent cause of unhesitating effort common to both memory and awareness, veridicality is simply conformity to fact. And it is produced by a collection of causal conditions common to cognition in general; it is not dependent on an excellence or on an absence of defects. For, there is no deviation from the rule that all cognitions conform to fact.

But that which (sometimes) fails to conform to fact is (not cognition but) everyday action, since it alone is what is defeated (and corrected). Cognition, in contrast, is not defeated (and corrected). For, as defeaters (two contradictory) cognitions are equal. Furthermore, the linguistic application of the phrase "not in conformity with fact" to some cognitions is a superimposition (a transferred epithet) that applies to occasions when contrary *speech* is produced.

Comments

In the Prābhākara view, every cognition grasps (a) an object, (b) itself the cognition, and (c) an "I," a knower or self. Here it is added that neither an epistemic excellence nor an absence of defect (contrary to the Mīmāṃsaka view considered earlier) is to be identified as a cause. Most importantly, cognition as intrinsically veridical is never defeated. No error in cognition really occurs. Error is a matter of motivation or of a certain type of lack or of certain speech behavior, according to various Prābhākara subfactions. And whether motivation or speech prompted by failed effort et cetera, error has of course peculiar causes including cognition. But a non-veridical cognition is not among them since there is no such critter.

There are not only faults intrinsic to the opposite view—the view that there are cognitive defeaters—such as how to tell which of two opposed cognitions defeat, we can explain why it is sometimes said that a cognition is not in conformity with fact. Saying of some cognitions that they are non-veridical, using the phrase "not in confórmity with fact," is to transfer the description of the speech behavior to the other subject. This typically occurs when someone says something contrary to fact.

Text (p. 387, Tirupati) and Translation

atha yathârthatvasya prāmāṇyatve ràjata-jñānaṃ śuktau katham a-prāmāṇam, a-prāmāṇyaṃ ca kathaṃ parata utpadyata iti cet, na | a-yathârthatvaṃ prāmāṇyam, sarva-dhiyāṃ yathârthatvāt | kiṃ tu viparīta-vyavahāra-pravartakatvam | tac ca jñāna-sāmagryām adhika-doṣânupraveśāt doṣa-hetukâ-saṃsargâ-grahād vā utpanne jñāne doṣa-sahakārād vā dharma-dharmiṇos a-saṃsargâ-graha-rūpam ekatvâ-saṃsargâ-graha-sahitaṃ parata utpadyate, na tu jñāna-mātra-sāmagrītaḥ, pramāyām atiprasaṅgāt |

Objection: If to be in conformity with fact is to be veridical, how is it that a cognition of silver with respect to mother-of-pearl is non-veridical, and how is it that the non-veridical arises extrinsically?

Prābhākara: No. Not to be in conformity with fact is not what it is to be non-veridical, since all cognition is in conformity with fact. Rather, the non-veridical is the motivating of effort that is proved wrong in everyday action. And that comes about from the entering of an extraneous defect into a collection of causal conditions that produces cognition, or (more precisely) from a *non*-grasping of a non-relation, a non-grasping that is caused by a defect, or from (we might say) a defect as a causal auxiliary, auxiliary to a produced cognition (which is also a cause of the failed effort). The accompaniment (to a produced cognition) of a non-grasping of a lack of a relation of unity is an accompaniment that takes the form of a non-grasping of a non-relation between a property and a property-bearer. It is produced extrinsically, not from a collection of causal conditions common to cognition in general. For (otherwise), there would be an unfortunate overapplication to veridical cognition.

Comments

We can now see more clearly the affinity between the Mīmāṃsaka *pūrvapakṣin* and the Prābhākara. The *pūrvapakṣin* maintained an extrinsicality position with respect to the production of non-veridical cognitions. We see now that the Prābhākara does, too, though he denies that there are cognitions that are non-veridical. We fail to notice that a memory of silver is not different from a perception of mother-of-pearl, and that trigger is itself caused by something extrinsic to the conditions that would produce simply a cognition (i.e., a veridical cognition). We *say* there is error when there is failed effort. Failed effort comes about from a defect extrinsic to the common causes of cognition, an epistemic defect that makes us not notice a non-relation between—a distinctness between—a remembering of silver and a perception of mother-of-pearl, for instance, as expressed in the statement, "This is silver," when the object in front is mother-of-pearl.

Text (p. 390, Tirupati) and Translation

unnīyate ca viparīta-vyvahāra-janakatvaṃ bādhakāt | tasya tena tad-anuvyavasāyena vā ġrahītum a-śakyatvāt | jñāna-sva-rūpe ca na doṣa-tad-a-bhāvau hetū, vyabhicārāt | jñānâ-yathârthatve 'pi yathârthatvaṃ jñāna-sāmagrī-janyam eva | na tu guṇāt doṣâ-bhāvād vā, viparyayâder api dharmy-aṃśe yathârthatvāt, a-sad-artha-viṣayatā doṣāt indriyāṇām a-saṃnihite '-sad-arthe sāmarthyâ-bhāvāt | nanu doṣa-mātraṃ na kāraṇam, kiṃ tu tad-apekṣā jñāna-sāmagrī iti yathârthatve doṣâ-bhāva-sāpekṣā sā hetur iti cet, na | sā eva sāmagrī a-sad-arthâṃśe doṣa-sāpekṣā iti tad-aṃśe jñānam a-yathârtham | sad-arthâṃśe doṣa-nirapekṣā iti tad-aṃśe yathârtham | na tu sā eva tatra eva jñāne doṣa-tad-a-bhāva-sāpekṣā, virodhāt | yathârthatve[7] doṣa-tad-a-bhāvau na antarīyakau | yathârthatvaṃ ca jñānôllikhita-prakāravattvam arthasya, yad-dharmavattvam arthasya tat-prakāraka-jñānatvaṃ vā |

(The **Prābhākara** continues:) Furthermore, the fact that a cognition has helped produce the misdirected effort and everyday action is inferred from the (subsequent) defeater. For, this (the fact of unsuccessful effort) cannot be grasped either by that (viz., cognition) or by an apperception of that.

Furthermore, neither defect nor absence of defect is a cause of cognition in its intrinsic nature, since there are counterexamples.

Even if there were cognition that was not in conformity with fact, conformity with fact would be produced only by the causal conditions sufficient for a cognition (in general), not from an excellence or from an absence of defect. For, there is also, with (what you Naiyāyikas call an error or) contrary cognition, conformity with fact regarding the property-bearer portion (of the cognition, as you yourselves say). (On your view) an objecthood (or, the fact of being a cognitive object) whose object is unreal is what results from a defect, since the sense organs (you yourselves admit) are not capable of coming into connection with an object that is unreal.

Objection: Defect in general is not a cause (of non-veridical cognition), but rather in connection with that (i.e., in connection with some particular defect or other) there is a collection of causal conditions sufficient to produce a cognition. Thus, with regard to (a cognition's) being in conformity with fact, the causes include an *absence* of defect.

Prābhākara: No. That very collection of causes responsible for the portion about an unreal object would work in connection with a defect. Thus, the cognition would not be in conformity with fact in that portion. (And at the same time, the same collection working) independently of defect (would be responsible) for the portion about a real object. Thus, it would be in conformity with fact in that portion. However, nothing such (i.e., no such causal collection) works both in connection with defect and with no defect regarding just that (i.e., one and the same) cognition, because of incompatibility.

(But, in fact) defect and its absence are *not internal to* (i.e., have nothing to do with, cognitions') being in conformity with fact.

And to be in conformity with fact is an object's having (as a property) what is explicit predication content, or it is to be a cognition whose predication content is a property that the object has.

Comments

The Prābhākara is denying the coherence of the Naiyāyika view that one and the same cognition can be both veridical and non-veridical, veridical in presenting something, e.g., mother-of-pearl, as being where it is, right in front of a perceiver, and non-veridical in presenting it as silver. To avoid such incoherence, it is better to look for the bearer of error elsewhere.

Mathurānātha interprets "not internal to" (*na antarīyakau*) as "otherwise established"; thus, defect and its absence would be causally irrelevant.

Two definitions are given of "being in conformity with fact," one interpreting it as a property of the object cognized, the other as a property of the cognition. Thus we have a clear statement of veridicality's two faces, (a) an *object's* having the property that appears in cognition as explicit predication content and (b) a *cognition's* predication content being a property that the object has.

Text (p. 361, Calcutta) and Translation

idaṃ rajatam iti jñānam arthasya rajatatvaṃ svasya rajatatvâśraya-viṣayakatvaṃ yathârthatva-rūpaṃ prāmāṇyaṃ sva-prakāśatvena svayam eva paricchindat svârtha-niścaya-rūpam | tad-atiriktaṃ ca na prāmāṇyaṃ mānâ-bhāvāt | astu vā tad api svato jñāyatāṃ parato vā mā vā jñāyi kiṃ tan-nirūpaṇena | pravṛttāv an-upayogāt | arthaṃ hi niścitya pravartata ity āvaśyakârtha-niścayād eva pravṛtty-upapatteḥ | atha artha-niścayād eva pravṛttir iti satyam | kiṃ tv evaṃ-rūpo 'yam artha iti niścayo jñāna-prāmāṇya-grahâdhīna iti cet, na | sarvaṃ hi jñānaṃ rajata-rūpo 'yam artha ity-ādy-ākāraṃ svârtha-niścaya-rūpam eva utpadyate | kā tatra parâpekṣā | ata eva artha-tathātvaṃ svayam eva paricchidyata iti svataḥ prāmāṇya-grahaḥ | yadi ca taj-jñānaṃ na svârtha-niścaya-rūpaṃ tadā prāmāṇya-jñānam api na prāmāṇya-niścaya-rūpaṃ, na vā tad-adhīnaṃ jñānântaram api svârtha-niścaya-rūpam iti vyartham artha-niścayârthaṃ prāmāṇya-nirūpaṇam | prāmāṇya-jñāne 'pi sva-viṣaya-niścayârtham anyâpekṣāyām an-avasthā |

(The **Prābhākara** continues:) (Consider) the cognition, "This is silver."

(The cognition's) silverhood, which belongs to the object, is its own having of silverhood's substratum as object, a having that takes the form of conformity with fact, (in short) veridicality—which is known self-illuminatingly, that is, by itself alone. Cognizing, the cognition takes the form of a bit of certainty about itself and its own object (including its veridicality). And anything additional to this is not veridicality, since there is no argument.

Or, let there be something like that, too. Or, let it be cognized intrinsically or extrinsically. Or, don't let it be so. What would be the point of determining it, since such a determination would be useless when it comes to effort (and action)?

For, cognizing an object with a sense of certainty, one makes effort (and acts). Thus is effort possible (i.e., explained) as resulting from required certainty about an object.

Objection: It is true that effort results just from certainty about an object. However, a bit of certainty, (e.g.) "This object has such and such a form," can be dependent on the cognition's veridicality being grasped.

Prābhākara: No. For, all cognition is produced in such shape as, "This object has the form of silver," such that all cognition takes the form of a bit of certainty about its own object. Where is there dependence on something else?

Just for this reason, an object's being such and such is cognized by the cognition alone. Thus is there grasping of veridicality intrinsically.

And if a cognition of that (silver) did not take the form of a bit of certainty about its own object, then a cognition of veridicality, too, would not take the form of a bit of certainty about veridicality. Nor depending on that (certainty about veridicality) would there be the other cognition (the original cognition of silver), too, as taking the form of a bit of certainty about its own object. Thus useless would be a determining of veridicality for the sake of certainty about the object. If a bit of certainty, albeit a cognition of veridicality, depended on another (cognition of veridicality) for its certainty about its own object, then there would be an infinite regress.

Comments

By making fun of the very dispute about what veridicality is and how it is known, and by declaring that only certainty about the object, and not a grasping of veridicality, is what prompts (unhesitating) effort, the Prābhākara makes dramatically the point that effort flows from a first-order cognition. This is the heart of his argument, his central argument that ends, we see here, with a charge of infinite regress befalling one who adopts an extrinsic view of how veridicality is known and produced. The horror of that regress depends on the assumption that certainty about an object requires a determination of veridicality: a cognition's veridicality would have to be known if we are to be certain about a first-order object, e.g., silver. Again, the main force of the passage flows from the position that a first-order cognition has within itself all that is necessary for a cognizer to get along in the world.

It is important to keep in mind that the expression that the Prābhākara uses to gloss veridicality, namely, "an object's being such and such," is to be interpreted as what is knowable within a given cognition, that is to say, without an external relation to fact being determined. Thus, the idea is favorable to an idealist metaphysics, though the Prābhākara is, like Gaṅgeśa, a realist. Just below, in the voice of a Mīmāṃsaka of a rival camp, Gaṅgeśa will crucially point out that "an object's being such and such," *artha-tathātva*, as the Prābhākara uses and understands the expression, is common both to cognitions that capture and those that fail to capture a fact. An error presents its object as being such and such just as much as a cognition that is veridical. Thus on the Prābhākara view it seems veridical cognition need not be produced by a bit of reality that is independent of consciousness. Thus, the Mīmāṃsaka's *artha-tathātva*, "an object's being such and such," needs to be emended, since only a presentation of something as such and such, e.g., of something as silver, is what it is whether or not it presents such and such in fact.

Text (p. 394, Tirupati) and Translation

> kiṃ ca parataḥ-pakṣe gṛhīta-prāmāṇyasya parasya prāmāṇya-niścāyakatve 'n-avasthā | ato yathā jñānāntaram a-gṛhīta-prāmāṇyam eva para-prāmāṇya-niścaya-rūpam, yadā tu tat-prāmāṇya-jijñāsā tadā tasya api prāmāṇya-gṛhīta-prāmāṇyena eva pareṇa niścīyate iti na an-avasthā, tathā artha-jñānam api a-niścita-prāmāṇyam eva artha-niścaya-rūpam a-viśeṣāt | na hy utpanne jñāne artha-saṃśayaḥ kim evam an-evaṃ vā iti | atha jñānam artha-niścaya-rūpam api svam a-gṛhṇat kathaṃ sva-prāmāṇyaṃ gṛhṇīyād iti cet, tarhi sva-prakāśatve vivādaḥ | arthasya tathā-bhāva-rūpaṃ prāmāṇyaṃ svata eva gṛhyata iti tava apy anumatam |

(The **Prābhākara** continues:) Moreover, on the extrinsicality view, there would be an infinite regress in an ascertaining of (a first-order) veridicality by "another" whose veridicality is grasped. Hence (let us assume that) the other cognition, which takes the form of a bit of certainty about the veridicality (of a first-order cognition), is just one whose own veridicality is *not* grasped (so that there would be no infinite regress). If, on the other hand, there arises a desire to know its veridicality, then its veridicality, too, could be ascertained by another whose own veridicality remains in fact *un*grasped. So there (still) need be no infinite regress. Given this, so too the (first-order) cognition of an object, which takes the form of a bit of certainty about the object, might as well be the one whose veridicality remains *un*ascertained, since there is no difference (among the candidate cognitions and so let us settle on the first). For, with respect to a cognition that has already arisen, doubt about its object,

"Is it such and such or not such and such?" does not occur.

Objection: Though a cognition occurs in the form of a bit of certainty about its object, how in not grasping itself would it grasp its own veridicality?

Prābhākara: So then (you see see the reason for) the debate about self-illumination. The object's having such a form, which *is* (a cognition's) veridicality, is simply intrinsically grasped—you, too, accept as much.

Comments

If it were true that doubt did not occur with respect to the object of a cognition that has arisen, "Is it such and such or not," then the Prābhākara would have a strong case. That each occurrent cognition is a bit of certainty is the linchpin of his position. The dispute about veridicality is not really so central, from his perspective. What he wants is intrinsic certainty. Only a person who wants to ask a question about the veridicality of cognition (and the Prābhākara does not want to, since for him all cognition is veridical) needs the reply that veridicality is intrinsically grasped. In other words, if one assumes that certainty can be undermined with worry about veridicality, then one needs to see that veridicality is intrinsically grasped—on pain of infinite regress or the untoward ramification that there would be no certainty about a (first-order) object.

Text (p. 396, Tirupati, and p. 364, Calcutta) and Translation

> atha svataḥ prāmāṇya-grahe an-abhyāsa-daśâpanna-jñāne idaṃ pramā na vā iti saṃśayo na syāt | niścite tad-a-bhāvāt | ata eva a-pramātva-śaṅkayā arthe 'pi kim evam an-evaṃ vā iti saṃśayāt na jñāna-mātrāt kara-talâmalakâdāv apy artha-niścayo vyabhicārād iti cet, na | na hy atra jñāne satyatvâ-satyatva-saṃśayaḥ, sarva-jñānānāṃ satyatvāt | kiṃ tu a-gṛhīta-bhedaṃ jñāna-dvayam ekaṃ vā jñānam ity ākāro jñānaṃ pramā na vā iti saṃśayaḥ | sa ca kāraṇa-doṣa-saṃśayāt | sa ca jñānântarān nivartate | nanv anubhūtitvaṃ pramātvam | tac ca smṛty-anya-jñānatvam | smṛtitvaṃ ca saṃskārâ-sādhāraṇa-kāraṇakatvam iti svato na gṛhyate | saṃskārâder a-grahāt | ata eva na svata eva utpadyate, smṛti-sādhāraṇatvād iti cet, na | pravṛtty-aupayikaṃ hi prāmāṇyam artha-tathātva-niścayatvam | tac ca svata eva gṛhyate utpadyate ca | na tv anubhūtitva-sahitam, gauravāt | tava api saṃvādâdinā pravṛtteḥ prāmāṇyaṃ yathârthatvam eva anumīyate, na tv anubhūtitve sati, smṛtau vyabhicārāt | smṛty-anubhavayor a-pramā-pramā-vyapadeśas tāntrikāṇāṃ sāpekṣatva-nirapekṣatva-nibandhanaḥ | "yathârthânubhavo mānam an-apekṣatayā iṣyate" iti tair abhidhānād iti |

Objection: If veridicality is grasped intrinsically, then the doubt would not occur, "Is this veridical or not," (not even) with respect to a cognition that has occurred in unfamiliar circumstances. For, if its veridicality has been ascertained, doubt about it is absent. Just for this reason, by way of suspicion about non-veridicality, there would be doubt about the object, too, "Is it such and such or not such and such," and so there would not be certainty about the object, even in such a case as a piece of *āmalaka* fruit in the palm of one's hand insofar as there would be just a cognition (of it), because of deviation (i.e., counterexamples to the supposition that all cognition carries with it a sense of certainty understood as excluding the possibility of doubt).

Prābhākara: No. For, here, doubt with respect to cognition is not really about whether it is true or not true, since all cognitions are true. Rather, the doubt, "Is the cognition veridical or not," assumes the following form, "Is the cognition a (disguised) pair of cognitions, with their distinctness not grasped, or a single (cognition)?" And the doubt results from doubt about a (possible) epistemic defect. And it ceases as a result of another cognition (that grasps the distinctness or in another way settles on one alternative).

Objection: (Then according to you) being a veridical awareness amounts to *being an awareness.* And this (being an awareness) is to be a cognition other than a remembering. Further, being a remembering is to have as proximate cause a memory impression (*saṃskāra*). Thus, a remembering is not grasped intrinsically, since the memory impression, etc., are not grasped. Just for this reason, cognition in general is not intrinsically produced, since the causal conditions (common to all cognitions) are common to remembering (in that a remembering is a cognition).

Prābhākara: No. For, veridicality, which is the motivator of effort, is certainty about an object being such and such (*artha-tathātva*). And it is both grasped and produced intrinsically. It is not united with being-an-awareness, for that would be (theoretically) cumbersome. For you (Naiyāyikas), too, veridicality, which just amounts to conformity with fact, is inferred from effectiveness, etc., of effort. It does not occur given the occurrence of just any awareness, since remembering is (for you) a counterexample.

Remembering and awareness, which are conventionally spoken of (respectively) as not a veridical cognition and as a veridical cognition, are, according to professional teachers (or knowers of inherited systems, *tāntrika*), (respectively) causally dependent (i.e., depending on a previous awareness) and independent.

(**Another Mīmāṃsaka**:) "Awareness in conformity with fact is accepted as an independent prover," so by them (by the Prābhākaras) is it designated.

Comments

See above, p. 86, for discussion of cognition arising in unfamiliar circumstances. It was this example, it may be recalled, that was key to Gaṅgeśa's argument in the last section. The cognition is veridical but also doubted, and its veridicality is discovered later. Here in the current passage, the Prābhākara tries to explain such doubt as not really about the veridical cognition but about whether there is one cognition or two, an awareness and a remembering, with their difference not grasped. (The single cognition by Naiyāyika lights would be veridical but the two would be a single non-veridical cognition.) This Prābhākara view is not refuted by Gaṅgeśa right away, but is the focus of the section following the next, on error. Instead, we have some preliminary sniping concerning awareness (*anubhava*) and remembering (*smṛti*).

As explained in the introduction, everyday usage restricts the word "veridical" to awarenesses, excluding rememberings. Rememberings and awarenesses are the two broadest types of cognition according to the standard Naiyāyika schema. The division informs the final objection that the Prābhākara answers; his reply shows how he views it. The full weight of the exchange is difficult to appreciate without already knowing issues aired in the final section of the chapter—in particular the "thatness" problem facing the epistemic credentials of memory and other reasons for downgrading it in comparison to perception. (See, below, pp. 658ff.) The upshot of the objection is that the Prābhākara must too radically distinguish perceiving and remembering, since obviously a remembering arises from something extrinsic, viz., a memory-impression which is not something directly or intrinsically cognized. The response argues that rememberings and perceivings are not so far apart without disputing that a perception-formed *saṃskāra* ("memory-impression") has with rememberings a causal role.

One would expect a minor reformulation by the Prābhākara, attuning his thesis to the remembering/awareness distinction. Instead, he takes all rememberings to be veridical cognitions, too, such that rememberings are not counterexamples to his thesis. Being veridical and being an awareness are not equivalent. The supporting argument seems to be that it is only a matter of conventional designation to regard rememberings and awarenesses as distinct. Systemizers make a sorting on the basis of whether there is dependence on a previous awareness, but, apparently, that has no relevance. Gaṅgeśa leaves the Prābhākara response incomplete, suggesting that Prābhākaras approve of the view that awareness is independent (and, by implication, that remembering is not).

After this long exploration of Prābhākara positions, we come now, not to Gaṅgeśa's own views, but to those of another faction of Mīmāṃsā. Mathurānātha explicitly says that the following text still presents a Mīmāṃsaka stance, and the evidence of what views are espoused do support his attribution—although this is not a classical Mīmāṃsā and we do get positions that come closer to Gaṅgeśa's own theories. Gaṅgeśa in fact appears to be leading those attached to traditional Mīmāṃsā gradually away from the standard views, and gradually closer to Nyāya, by keeping some planks and altering others.

Or—and this seems the better interpretation—Gaṅgeśa is patiently preparing his *coup de grâce*, his final refutation of the mainstream Mīmāṃsā theory of intrinsic production of veridicality, which then leaves its rival commanding the field, namely, his own view. On this reading, Gaṅgeśa would be conveniently setting the factions of Mīmāṃsā against one another, as he prepares his final moves. These come near the very end of the section.

Text (p. 399, Tirupati) and Translation

atra brūmaḥ | prāmāṇya-niścayo niṣkampa-pravṛtti-hetur na tat-saṃśaya ity anubhava-siddhaṃ tvad-anumataṃ ca | tac ca prāmāṇyaṃ na artha-tathātva-niścaya-rūpaṃ | an-abhyāsa-daśâpanna-jñānasya sva-prakāśena anuvyavasāyena vā artha-tathātva-niścaya-grahe 'pi niṣkampa-pravṛtty-a-bhāvāt, prāmāṇya-saṃśayāc ca | sarva-dhiyāṃ yathârthatva-niyamena artha-tathātva-niścayatvasya sva-rūpato viṣayataś ca a-gṛhīta-bheda-jñāna-dvaya-rūpa-bhrama-sādhāraṇatvāt | tasmān na bhrama-samānâkārād idaṃ rajatam iti jñānān niṣkampa-pravṛttiḥ, kiṃ tu tad-vyāvṛttâkārāt | atha tatra prāmāṇye na saṃśayas tasya artha-tathātva-niścayatva-rūpasya niścayāt | kiṃ tv a-gṛhīta-bhedaṃ jñāna-dvayaṃ viśiṣṭa-jñānaṃ vā iti saṃśayaḥ | sa eva niṣkampa-pravṛtti-pratibandhako 'pi | atas tasya jñānântarān nivṛttau niṣkampa-pravṛttir iti cet, tarhi yasya saṃśayo vyatireka-niścayaś ca yat-pratibandhakas tan-niścayas tad-dhetur iti vyāpteḥ bhrama-vyāvṛttasya viśiṣṭa-jñānatvasya niścayaḥ pravṛtti-hetuḥ na tv artha-tathātvasya, bhrama-sādhāraṇyāt, tasmin saty a-pravṛtteś ca | tat-saṃśayâ-bhāva-sahitasya artha-tathātva-niścayasya pravartakatve gauravāt |

Another **Mīmāṃsaka** (not a Prābhākara): Here we say (the following). (The thesis) that certainty about veridicality is a cause of unhesitating effort—that such effort does not occur when there is doubt about veridicality—is established by experience and is (in effect) agreed to by you (the Prābhākara).

And such veridicality does not take the form of a bit of certainty about an object being such and such (or, an object's being just as it is presented to be, *artha-tathātva*, as you say). For, although there be a grasping of a bit of certainty about an object's being such and such—whether by self-illumination or by an apperception—unhesitating effort does not occur for a cognition arising in unfamiliar circumstances. Furthermore, there would be doubt about the cognition's veridicality. By the rule that all cognition is in conformity with fact, the certainty that an object is such and such would, both intrinsically and objectwise, be common to error—error that takes the form of a pair of cognitions whose distinctness is not grasped. Therefore, unhesitating effort does not result from a cognition, "This is silver," which takes the same form as an error. Rather, it results from (a cognition in) a form that excludes that (namely, error).

Objection: There (in the case of error) doubt does not (really) occur concerning veridicality, since there is certainty about the veridicality which itself takes the form of a bit of certainty about an "object being such and such" (*artha-tathātva*). Rather, doubt occurs over whether there is a pair of cognitions whose distinctness is not grasped, or a (single, veridical) cognition of an entity as qualified. Just that (namely, doubt) is the blocker, furthermore, of unhesitating effort. Hence, when it ceases on account of another cognition (that grasps the distinctness, or in another way eliminates the option), unhesitating effort occurs.

The (non-Prābhākara) **Mīmāṃsaka**: Then, where a doubt about something, or certainty about its non-occurrence, blocks an effort, there certainty about it (would eliminate the block and the certainty) *would be* a cause of effort—this pervasion means that a bit of certainty that there is a cognition of an entity as qualified (and not a pair of cognitions, etc.), which excludes error, is a cause of effort, but not certainty that there is an object as such and such (*artha-tathātva*), since that is common to error and when it occurs effort sometimes does not. (Moreover) it is cumbersome to view the motivator of effort as certainty about an object's being such and such, with an absence of such doubt as its accompaniment.

Comments

Rucidatta says that the mention of apperception is to include the Murāri Miśra Mīmāṃsaka view. See the discussion in the previous section, pp. 73–5.

Apparently, the Mīmāṃsaka who is now speaking sees that we can know that we are prone to error even in such a case as seeing real silver, such that we would not immediately reach out to pick up what might be mother-of-pearl. In other places Gaṅgeśa says, in voicing his own views, that a cognition of silver, though an illusion, is sufficient to prompt unhesitating effort—to pick up what is apparently silver. The two positions could be compatible in that in the cases Gaṅgeśa cites the person could be imagined not to have had evidence sufficient to suspect a false presentation whereas in other cases there would be. On the other hand, Gaṅgeśa probably intends here to present a view that is incompatible with his own.

The Mīmāṃsaka, who is opposed to the Prābhākara account of veridicality as an object being presented as such and such, but who accepts the account of error as "a pair of cognitions whose distinctness is not grasped," himself wrongly assumes that certainty not only blocks doubt but also the possibility of error. Certainty excludes or prevents doubt but does not prevent error. Similarly, doubt may stop short of effort, at least of unhesitating effort, but erroneous certainty issues in effort just as much as veridical certainty. Otherwise, there would be no frustrated effort. Here the Mīmāṃsaka sees that the Prābhākara account of veridicality fails to exclude error, and so he reasons that certainty must be of the form of a single cognition of an entity as qualified as well as that it must not be an error, that is to say, that it must not be a pair of cognitions with their distinctness unnoticed.

The problem with his view, we might repeat though Gaṅgeśa is silent, is that no such certainty is available. A fact of a cognition being veridical excludes the possibility of its being an error, but not "certainty" about a cognition's object or about its veridicality. We can just about always be wrong.

Text (p. 402, Tirupati, and p. 368, Calcutta) and Translation

kiṃ ca pravṛtti-hetu-jñānaṃ vighaṭayata eva jñānasya tatra pratibandhakatvam | na ca iha tathā, saṃśaye saty api tasya sattvāt | api ca viśiṣṭa-jñānatvam eva prāmāṇyaṃ bhrama-vyāvṛttatvāt | na tv artha-tathātva-niścayatvam, bhrama-sādhāraṇatvāt | laukika-parīkṣakāṇāṃ bhrama-vyāvṛtte prāmāṇya-vyavahārāt | tad-atikrame pramātvasya pāribhāṣikatvâpatteḥ | tasmāt bhrama-vyāvṛttatvāt niṣkampa-pravṛtti-hetutvāt prāmāṇya-saṃśaya-nivartakatvāc ca viśiṣṭa-jñānatvam eva prāmāṇyam | nanv astu tathā, tad eva svato gṛhyata iti cet, na | a-gṛhītâ-saṃsarga-dharma-dharmi-viṣaya-eka-jñānatvaṃ bhrama-vyāvṛttaṃ viśiṣṭa-jñānatvam | tat tu svato grahītuṃ na śakyate | a-gṛhītâ-saṃsargâdeḥ prāg an-upasthiteḥ sāmagrī-virahāt | sva-prakāśatā hi sva-mātra-sākṣiṇī | anyathā an-abhyāsa-daśâpanne 'pi tasya svato-grahād a-prāmāṇya-saṃśayo na syāt | ata eva na jñāna-sāmagrīta eva prāmāṇyam utpadyate | bhramasya api tathātvâpatteḥ |

(The **Mīmāṃsaka** continues:) Furthermore, a cognition (viz., a doubt) that in fact displaces a cognition that would cause effort is a blocker of it. And that does not happen here (on your view of veridicality understood as certainty about an object being presented as such and such), since such (certainty) occurs even when doubt occurs.

And, moreover, being a cognition of an entity as qualified is in fact veridicality, since it excludes error—not certainty about an object's being such and such, since that is common to error (and veridical cognition alike). For, both everyday speakers and (epistemological) investigators talk of veridicality as excluding error. If that (practice) is transgressed, the predicament is that veridicality (would be defined for the sake of definition within a system, i.e.) would become a technical term. Therefore, because of excluding error, causing unhesitating effort, and causing doubt about veridicality to cease, being a cognition of an entity as qualified is in fact what it is to be veridical.

Objection (by a more traditional Mīmāṃsaka): Let it be so. Veridicality is grasped indeed intrinsically.

The **Mīmāṃsaka**: No. To be a cognition of an entity as qualified, which excludes error, is to be a single cognition whose object is a property and a property-bearer whose non-relation is not grasped. But that cannot be grasped intrinsically, since, inasmuch as a non-relation that is not grasped and so on would not be set in awareness previously, the collection of causal conditions (required for cognition of veridicality) would be lacking (at the time of the occurrence of the veridical cognition itself). For, self-illumination is (to be understood as) a witnessing by and of itself alone. Otherwise, since veridicality would be intrinsically grasped, there could be no doubt concerning the (possible) non-veridicality of even that which has occurred in unfamiliar circumstances. Just for this reason, it not the case (too) that veridicality is produced from the same collection of causes responsible for a cognition (that is veridical). For, error, too, would be such (namely, veridical)—this is the difficulty.

Comments

An error is still to be analyzed as two cognitions, and certainty as certainty that there is a single cognition of an entity as qualified, according to this renegade brand of Mīmāṃsā. But he understands veridicality differently from the Prābhākara, although both find veridicality to occur when there is a single cognition. But the renegade takes a step in the Naiyāyika direction adding that to be a cognition of an entity as qualified is to be veridical, for example, "This is silver," with silverness as ontologically qualifying a thing in front and reflected in a cognitive presentation of it as qualifying the thing in front. Error, in accordance with a more traditional Mīmāṃsā and in contrast with Nyāya, is a failure to notice a distinction between a perceptual awareness and a remembering.

Gaṅgeśa portrays the new Mīmāṃsaka as willing to give up the intrinsicality thesis in part because of his view of veridicality—both regarding cognition of veridicality and a veridical cognition's production. And at the end of the section, where Gaṅgeśa states one last time his own views, he elaborates the argument given here that centers on the impossibility that the conditions for veridicality could be comprehended at the time of the occurrence of the cognition that is veridical. There he expands the argument by including other accounts of the nature of veridicality, arguing that on no account could it be intrinsically grasped. The argument against veridicality being intrinsically produced is also repeated, and continues to trade on, as here, the possibility of doubt, indeed, its likelihood given unfamiliar circumstances and certain other conditions.

Gaṅgeśa does not respond to the renegade Mīmāṃsaka's position. The text continues with views of philosophers who may more clearly be labelled, namely, new Prābhākaras. Thus the renegade seems a mere pawn in Gaṅgeśa's rebuttal strategy.

Text (p. 403, Tirupati) and Translation

navyās tu, a-vidyamāna-bhedasya a-grahaḥ prāmāṇyam | sa ca atyantâ-bhāvaḥ | kadā api tasya jñānâ-bhāvād atyantâ-bhāva-rūpatayā svataḥ siddhatvena prāmāṇyaṃ svata ity ucyate | vidyamāna-bhedasya a-graho '-prāmāṇyam | sa ca a-grahaḥ prāg-a-bhāvaḥ | agre bhedasya grahāt | bheda-grahe prasakte na sa jāyate doṣād ity uttara-kāla-saṃsarga-rūpasya tat-paripālanasya doṣa-janyatvena a-prāmāṇyaṃ parata utpadyate | visaṃvādi-saṃvādi-vicitra-vyavahāro 'pi vidyamānâ-vidyamāna-bhedâ-graha-rūpa-vilakṣaṇa-hetuka eva | vyavahārôpayuktaṃ tu prāmāṇyaṃ yathârthatvam eva | tac ca jñāna-hetu-mātra-hetukam | a-prāmāṇyaṃ doṣāt | an-abhyāsa-daśâpanne prāmāṇya-saṃśayo 'pi vidyamānâ-vidyamāna-bhedâ-graha-koṭi-dvayâvalambī, sa eva niṣkampa-pravṛtti-pratibandhaka iti |

But new (Prābhākaras say the following).

New Prābhākaras: Veridicality is a non-grasping of a non-existing distinctness. And such a non-grasping is (to be understood as) an absolute absence (of grasping). Sometimes, through lack of cognition of a non-existing distinctness, which (also) takes the form of an absolute absence, veridicality comes about intrinsically, inasmuch as it is established of itself—so it is said. Non-veridicality is a non-grasping of an existing distinctness. And this non-grasping is a prior absence (of grasping, in that the error can be corrected by a later grasping of the distinctness. Furthermore) at first, the distinctness is grasped. So long as the distinctness as grasped is kept in view, the non-grasping does not arise. From a defect it arises. Thus, inasmuch as maintenance of that (non-grasping of an existing distinctness) would be generated by a defect—that is, a maintenance in relation to a later time (when the distinctness would be grasped)—the non-veridical is produced from another (namely, a defect, that is to say, is produced extrinsically).

Furthermore, everyday behavior as varied—as non-effective and effective—is caused just by a (crucial) difference in the form of a distinctness that is not grasped, that is, whether it is existing (as with what is called non-veridical cognition) or non-existing (as with what is called veridical cognition). But everyday speech practice finds it useful to talk of veridicality as simply conformity with fact. And that conformity with fact is caused by the same causes responsible for cognition (in general).

The non-veridical results from an epistemic defect. Furthermore, a doubt about the veridicality of that which arises in unfamiliar circumstances would rest on a pair of alternative non-graspings, of an existing or of a non-existing distinctness. It alone would block unhesitating effort.

Comments

"This is silver," when the object cognized is in fact silver, involves no distinctness between the "this" and silver; furthermore, the non-existing distinctness is not grasped. There is thus just a single cognition, whose predication-content factor and qualificandum are related by identity. The cognizer is ignorant of both distinctness between them and non-distinctness between them, though they are non-distinct. A non-veridical cognition, "This is silver," in contrast, involves ignorance of an actual distinctness between the this (if "the this" is a permissible English locution) and silver, there being actually two cognitions, one a perception whose object is the this, the other a memory whose object is silver.

An absolute absence is considered constant or eternal (*nitya*). Thus, it is "self-established." And so veridicality understood as a type of absolute absence would be self-established as well—according to these new Prābhākaras.

Text (p. 405, Tirupati, and p. 370, Calcutta) and Translation

tan na | niṣkampa-pravṛtti-hetur hi prāmāṇyaṃ grahyaṃ na tv anyat | niṣprayojanatvāt | tac ca yady api a-vidyamāna-bedâ-graha-rūpaṃ tadā tan na svato jñātuṃ śakyate | a-vidyamāna-bheda-grahasya tat-pratiyogino '-sattvāt, prāg-an-upasthiteś ca | an-abhyāsa-daśāyāṃ jñāne jñāte 'py a-vidyamāna-bhedâ-grahe saṃśayāc ca | etena autsargikaḥ saṃsarga-graha eva prāmāṇyam, a-saṃsargâ-graha eva a-prāmāṇyam iti nirastam | saṃsarga-grahatvasya svena grahītum a-śakyatvāt | śakyatve vā an-abhyāsa-daśāyām api tad-grahe tat-saṃśayo na syāt | tasmāt bhrama-vyāvṛttaṃ niṣkampa-pravṛtti-hetuḥ prāmāṇyam a-gṛhītâ-saṃsarga-[8] dharma-dharmi-viṣayaka-eka-jñānatva-rūpaṃ viśiṣṭa-jñānatvaṃ, saṃsarga-jñānatvaṃ vā, a-vidyamāna-bhedâgrahatvaṃ vā svato jñātuṃ na śakyate | kiṃ tu viśeṣa-darśanâdi-janya-jñānād avadhāryata iti vajra-lepāyitaṃ parataḥ-prāmāṇyam ity utpatti-vādaḥ |

Gaṅgeśa: That is wrong. For, veridicality as grasped (not as something not grasped) is a cause of unhesitating effort (when it is such a cause), not something else, since there is no call for it.

And that, even if it did take the form of a non-grasping of a non-existing distinctness, could not, in that case, be known intrinsically. For, there is no absentee (or countercorrelate, *pratiyogin*) for it, namely, a *grasping* of a non-existing distinctness. Nor would that be previously set in memory. Moreover, even if a cognition arising in unfamiliar circumstances is itself cognized (by itself or by an apperception), doubt may well occur though there be no grasping of a non-existing distinctness.

By this (reasoning it is shown that) the following view is thrown out: that the normal situation of a grasping of a relation is just what it is to be veridical, (and) that just a non-grasping of a non-relation is what it is to be non-veridical. For, it is impossible that a fact of a grasping of a relation could be grasped by the grasping itself. Or, if it is possible, that should be grasped even when the circumstances are unfamiliar, so that doubt concerning it should not occur. Therefore, whether veridicality be understood as a cognition of an entity as qualified—i.e., a cognition that takes the form of a single cognition that has as object a property and a property-bearer whose non-relation is not grasped—or as a cognition of a relation, or as a non-grasping of a non-existing distinctness, it cannot, as excluding error and as causing unhesitating effort, be known intrinsically. Rather, it is ascertained from cognition generated by such (epistemic excellences) as experience of distinguishing features. Thus, the view of extrinsically (produced and known) veridicality is set in stone as hard as diamond (*vajra-lepāyita*).

Here (ends) the *utpatti-vāda*, "discourse on the production (of a veridical cognition)."

Comments

Any veritable absence has a countercorrelate, or absentee, what it is an absence *of.* This is an ontological requirement. Epistemologically, a person has to have previously cognized an absence's absentee in order to be able to have an absential cognition. A memory-impression furnishes the absentee term.

Gaṅgeśa closes the section by concluding that however Mīmāṃsakas may want to analyze veridicality—and on any plausible analysis, that is, on any that is not "systematically definitional" (*pāribhāṣika*)—veridicality cannot be known or produced intrinsically. His own view, whose independent supports were given previously, can now be seen as without serious rival.

In sum, a human being's veridical cognitions are effects, and each one of them is the outcome of a complicated causal process. The processes that generate veridical cognitions fall into four natural types, although there are important variations within a type having to do with what is cognized, prior doubt, and other circumstances. The processes are infallible, but there do occur non-veridical cognitions as the result of sometimes very similar processes easily mistaken for *pramāṇa*s as well as by other routes. Thus there is a call for epistemologists to explain the relevant differences between the causal factors that lead to veridical cognition and those that lead to non-veridical cognition, that is to say, to find indicators of a process's being a *pramāṇa*, causal excellences, marks of veritable perceptionhood, inferencehood, and so on, and likewise at least the most general causal defects (fallacies, etc.). A factor generally can be identified that accounts for veridicality or non-veridicality. In the case of veridical cognitions, we see this factor as an epistemic excellence, which is, then, an epistemic property—very different in nature depending on particular circumstances—supervenient upon something within the causal processes, or, more precisely, within the set of conditions (*sāmagrī*) sufficient to generate such an effect. Similarly, an epistemic defect is to be identified in cases of non-veridical cognition. And the causal factor to be so designated in a particular case is of course to be a factor necessary to the outcome, to the production of the one type of cognition or the other. Explanationally, necessary conditions are what we look for, even if none is by itself sufficient to bring about the type of effect that we are interested in. Having reflected on a wide range of cognitions, cognitions arising in various circumstances and by various means, we do indeed find such excellences, whose nature we can and will spell out (albeit occasionally with some difficulty). We may ignore accidentally veridical cognitions or leave them for later inquiry. Therefore, the veridicality of a veridical cognition is not only known extrinsically, as has been argued, but also produced extrinsically. A typical veridical cognition would result, in part, from an epistemic excellence, whereas a complex sufficient for a non-veridical cognition would contain an epistemic defect instead. And the excellence is not simply the absence of defect.

Our opponents try to rearrange the important points of our arguments, and offer confusing views about the relation between certainty and action in particular. The right view is that both veridical and non-veridical cognitions occur taken as certain; certainty is an epistemic default and it is normally a factor in prompting and guiding an effort to act. But once a cognition's veridicality has been brought into doubt, a determination of veridicality is needed, generally speaking, before a person will proceed unhesitatingly to act. That determination, by the way, can be according to cognitive type, where identification of typical excellences and defects is relevant.

atha pramā-lakṣaṇa-vāda

NOW, **DISCOURSE ON CHARACTERIZING VERIDICAL AWARENESS**

Text (p. 409, Tirupati, and p. 372, Calcutta) and Translation

atha kim tat prāmāṇyam | na tāvaj jātiḥ | yogya-vyakti-vṛttitvena pratyakṣatve pramātva-saṃśayân-upapatteḥ, pramātvasya anumeyatvāc ca | sākṣāttvâdinā saṃkarâpatteś ca | bīja-sāmyena guṇe 'pi tasya doṣatvāt | tāratvâder utkarṣa-rūpatayā jātitva-niyame ca an-anya-gatikatayā ca nānātvāt | pramātva-nānātve tv an-anugamaḥ |

Gaṅgeśa: Now what is this veridicality? First of all, it is not a real universal, *jāti*. (If it were, then it would be perceptible in veridical cognitions, and) if it were perceived when its individual instances were perceived, then it would be impossible to doubt the veridicality (of perceptual awarenesses). (However, such doubt occurs.) Moreover, veridicality is known by inference.

Also (veridicality is not a universal) because that would involve a cross classification with (other characteristics of awarenesses such as) "immediacy," for example.

Although veridicality concerns a quality (not a substance such that the criticism of "cross classification" does not apply, some argue), the reason this is to be avoided holds here just as it does there (with substances). For example, if the shrillness of a sound (a quality) as loud (as opposed to soft) were accepted as a universal, then to retain a fixed rule for what it is to be a universal, *jāti*, we would have to embrace a manifold of *jāti*s here (with the letter-sounds "ka," "kha," etc., according to shrillness). But if veridicality were to be viewed (similarly) as manifold (varying with each veridical awareness), then there would be no recurrent, unifying character, *anugama* (another criterion for a true *jāti*).

Comments[1]

The opening question is whether veridicality is a universal, *jāti*, in the sense of *prāmāṇya* that derives from *pramā*, "veridical cognition" as opposed to *pramāṇa*, "source of veridical cognition." This is important for the definitional project, as Gaṅgeśa himself will explain in his *siddhânta* (below, pp. 236ff). Insofar as an individual is perceptible, the universals which inhere in it are also perceptible, according to inherited theory. But, Gaṅgeśa points out, we cannot merely read off of cognitions their veridicality or non-veridicality (except in special cases). We can tell from a perceptual awareness of, e.g., an individual cow that she is a cow. We are directly aware of "cowness," a universal nested in the individual. But with an awareness arising in unfamiliar circumstances (above, pp. 86ff), for example, we may well doubt whether the cognition is veridical though in fact it is veridical. We can perceive (by apperception) a veridical cognition while also questioning its veridicality. Such doubt shows that veridicality is not a universal, *jāti*.

Moreover, Gaṅgeśa says, the veridicality of an awareness is known by inference, as has been shown.

Although veridical perceptual awareness is both immediate and veridical, cogent inference (*anumāna*) is not immediate but is veridical, and perceptual illusion is immediate but not veridical. That there would be such cross-classification (*jāti-saṃkara*, "cross-sectioning") is another reason why veridicality is not a universal. Universals slice nature at her joints such that the extension of a lower-order or narrower universal must fall entirely within that of a higher or broader kind. The Nyāya-Vaiśeṣika theory of universals (see above, pp. 21–22) was sharpened by Udayana proposing six "blockers of universals," *jāti-bādhaka*, of which "cross-sectioning" is one.[2]

One might think that the cross-sectioning test would eliminate only putative universals of substance, whereas universals of qualities, such as shrillness, could obtain with overlap. Shrillness would obtain in the sound "ka" when that sound is shrill, but the abstract property "ka-ness" would also obtain, which lies in cases of shrillness and of non-shrillness alike. The "ka" sound is sometimes uttered in a low voice, sometimes in a shrill voice. Similarly, a "kha" sound can also be uttered in both a low and a shrill voice. But "ka-ness" obviously does not inhere in a "kha" sound, and so there would be "confusion of class." Gaṅgeśa cites a contemporary Naiyāyika opinion that there is no special difficulty with such examples because they concern classification of qualities, and qualities, as opposed to substances, do not fall into neat, non-overlapping classes. But this move will not work for the defender of veridicality as a universal. Unlike shrill "kha"s where the abstract property shrillness pulls all the instances together under a common character, veridicality once admitted to be multiple would fail to unify anything. There is no point in talking about a universal (*jāti* = *sāmānya*) that does not bring at least two particulars into the unity of a class. (This requirement is also on Udayana's list: see again note 2, pp. 700–701.)

Text (p. 414, Tirupati) and Translation

kiṃ ca evam a-pramāyā aṃśe pramātvaṃ na syāt, jāter vyāpya-vṛttitā-niyamāt | na ca iṣṭâpattiḥ | aṃśe saṃvādini visaṃvādini ca samūhâlambane pramātvâ-pramātvayor anubhūyamānatvena eka-śeṣasya kartum a-śakyatvāt | atha viparyayasya aṃśe na pramātvam, kiṃ tu smṛti-vad yathârthatvam eva iti cet, tarhi yathârthânubhavatvam eva prāmāṇyam, āvaśyakatvāt | na ca tad api iti vakṣyate |

(**Gaṅgeśa** continues:) Moreover, if veridicality were a universal, then there could be no veridicality in a part of a non-veridical awareness. Universals are invariably "locus-pervading" (*vyāpya-vṛtti*).

Do not say that the above criticism is the fallacy of "maligning what is desired" (*iṣṭâpatti*), i.e., that it would be all right to rule out the possibility of partial veridical awareness. Consider a cognition of a group of two things, one of which is veridically perceived, the other not (e.g., a piece of tin and a piece of silver seen as two pieces of silver). Since here we experience both veridicality and non-veridicality, we cannot make a single determination.

Objection: Then it is wrong to hold that in a portion of an erroneous awareness there can be veridicality. Rather, let us say, like memory, there is "conformity with the object" (in the right part of the erroneous awareness, but not veridicality).

Gaṅgeśa: Then to be veridical would be simply "to be awareness in conformity with the object," as would be the necessary consequence of your suggestion. But that, too, is not correct, as will be explained.

Comments

Cowhood is present throughout each and every cow. It is not the case that some parts of a cow exhibit the universal while others do not. An awareness, however, can exhibit partial veridicality. For example, the awareness "This is silver" in the face of mother-of-pearl would be veridical in the "thisness" part, as previously remarked. Mathurānātha uses the example of a group cognition (*samūha-ālambana-jñāna*) of two pieces of silver when in reality the two things are a piece of silver and a piece of tin.

As noted, Naiyāyikas hold that a moment of memory, a remembering, cannot be a veridical awareness, since a remembering is not an experience or awareness, *anubhava*, although it is a cognition, *jñāna*. All awarenesses, *anubhava*, are, like rememberings, cognitions, *jñāna*, but only awarenesses can be veridical awarenesses, *pramā*. Thus a right remembering would be "in conformity with the object" remembered but would not be a veridical *awareness*. Gaṅgeśa draws out the consequence of the opponent's suggestion: veridicality in all cases, not just cases of partially veridical awareness, would be this conformity with the object. He says that he will explain his objections to this view below, and he does in examining the characterization labelled D^3.

Text (p. 415, Tirupati) and Translation

atha yathā bhāvo '-bhāvo vā na a-vyāpya-vṛttir iti niyamaṃ tiraskṛtya a-bādhitânubhava-balāt saṃyoga-tad-a-bhāvayor a-vyāpya-vṛttitvaṃ, tathā jātir vyāpya-vṛttir eva iti vyāptim abhibhūya anubhava-balād eva pramātva-tad-a-bhāvayor a-vyāpya-vṛttitvam astu | na ca yad a-vyāpya-vṛtti tan na vyāpya-vṛtti, yac ca vyāpya-vṛtti na tad a-vyāpya-vṛtti iti vyāpteḥ pramātvasya na ubhaya-rūpatvam iti vācyam | saṃyogâtyantâ-bhāve vyabhicārāt | na ca tasya a-bhāva-dvayaṃ mānâ-bhāvāt | guṇa-doṣayor ekatra sattve a-vyāpya-vṛttitvam, guṇa-mātra-sattve vyāpya-vṛttitvam ity anyathôpapatteś ca | anyathā pramātvasya upādher apy atyantâ-bhāva-sāmānâdhikaraṇyaṃ[3] na syāt sāmānyatvāt na syāc ca ubhaya-rūpatvam iti | mā evam | avacchedaka-bhedaṃ vinā viruddhayor ekatra a-samāveśāt a-pratīteś ca | na ca viṣaya eva aṃśa-rūpaḥ pramātva-vṛttāv avacchedakaḥ | tad-viṣayatvasya bhrame 'pi sattvāt |

Objection: Rejecting the rule that a presence or absence (need exclude the other, i.e.) is locus-pervading, one must accept through uncontroverted experience that contact, for example, is non-locus-pervading, as is an absence of contact. (A contact, *saṃyoga*, can be present and absent at the same time with respect to a single thing; for example, with "A monkey is in the tree," we have an awareness of a contact between a monkey and a tree—specifically, in its branches—a tree that is devoid of the contact at its roots.) Similarly, overcoming the false assumption of concomitance, let us accept on the force of uncontroverted experience that a universal need not be locus-pervading, so that neither veridicality nor absence of veridicality would be expected to be locus-pervading. It should not be said that there is a concomitance, namely, that what is non-locus-pervading is not locus-pervading and conversely, such that veridicality could not have both forms, since a clear exception is absolute absence of contact (which is pervasive only in some instances). And there are not two types of absence (of contact), since there is no reason (to assume two; there is only one, sometimes locus-pervading and sometimes not).

Furthermore (if we try to save the concomitance by restricting it to presences such that for any existent or presence, as opposed to an absence, if it is locus-pervading it would not be non-locus-pervading and conversely, then) what is in fact the case would be impossible, namely, that when with regard to a single *existent* (awareness) there are both an epistemic excellence and a defect veridicality would not be locus-pervading, but when there is only an excellence, veridicality would be locus-pervading. (Thus veridicality with regard to a veridical awareness, e.g., "This is silver," when it is indeed silver in one's hand, would be locus-pervading, but in the erroneous awareness, "This is silver," when it is mother-of-pearl, the veridicality would be non-locus-pervading, being confined to the "this" portion.) Otherwise (if the concomitance holds as restricted to presences), veridicality, even though considered (your way) as an accidental or surplus property, *upādhi* (not a *jāti*, universal), will not be present in the same locus (an awareness) along with its absolute absence (that is to say, non-veridicality) because the same considerations hold. Nor (even as an surplus property) could it have both forms (the locus-pervading and the non-locus-pervading).

Gaṅgeśa: This is wrong. Without a difference of specification (or delimiter, *avacchedaka*), two opposed (properties) cannot be present in the same thing. Nor are they ever so experienced.

Moreover, it should not be said that the relevant specification of where or how veridicality is present takes the form of a part only with respect to the object (indicated by an awareness). ''Having that as object'' is also present in cognitive error (and so it would have to be counted veridical).

Comments

Some things pervade the loci that they qualify. Others do not. A tree is qualified by contact-with-a-monkey when a monkey is sitting in its branches. But the same tree would also be qualified by absence-of-monkey-contact—at its roots. The property, contact-with-a-monkey, is not locus-pervading, being restricted to the place in the tree where it occurs. Similarly, an awareness may be veridical only in part. When it is, its veridicality would be non-locus-pervading, so goes the current proposal. But when an awareness is entirely veridical, the veridicality would be locus-pervading. Other universals would be likewise locus-pervading or not only under certain conditions. The objector says that on Gaṅgeśa's view of veridicality as an accidental or surplus property, *upādhi*, one has to adopt these same principles, and so, he implies, uniformity among veridical awarenesses demands that veridicality be recognized as the universal it indeed is.

Mathurānātha explains two two types of absence of contact or conjunction: one applicable to (a) substances, things that sometimes exhibit ''contact,'' *saṃyoga*, the other to (b) qualities, etc., things that never exhibit it since they categorially exclude the possibility. In other words, an absolute absence of contact of a pot and a floor at a particular time and spot is not pervasive of the floor at all its spots and throughout its period of existence, whereas an absolute absence of a contact in a sound is ''locus-pervading,'' since as a quality it is categorially guaranteed not to be in contact with anything. In plainer English, no sound could be conjoined with anything, whereas a floor might or might not be conjoined with a pot.

In reply, Gaṅgeśa uses the important *avacchedaka* concept, which proves valuable in a variety of contexts (and especially in formulation of causal principles, as we shall see). ''Specifiers,'' *avacchedaka* s, make abstractions precise. They help to eliminate vagueness. For example, the apparent contradiction of a tree possessing both a monkey-contact and an absence of monkey-contact is eliminated through specifying precisely where in the tree the monkey-contact is occurrent and where it is not. Spatial specification is required. In the case of a pot black before baking and red afterwards, temporal specification is called for. In cases of cognitions whose veridicality is partial, we need to specify how we make the cut—rather than abandon the rule that a true universal is locus-pervading. Thus, Gaṅgeśa implies, the previous arguments against veridicality as a real universal still hold.

Veridical awarenesses are where veridicality dwells; they are its loci. And so the specification required in the case of a partially veridical awareness has to be with respect to the awareness, not to the object presented, since illusions also have objects in this sense. Thus the thesis that veridicality is a universal cannot be saved in this way.

Text (p. 416, Tirupati) and Translation

nanu viśeṣyâ-vṛtty-a-prakārakatvaṃ viśeṣyâ-vṛtti-prakārakatvaṃ ca pramātva-tad-a-bhāvayor vṛttāv avacchedakam asti iti cet, tarhi tayor eva pramâ-pramā-vyavahāra-janakatvam astu, āvaśyakatvāt prathamôpasthitatvāc ca, kiṃ jātyā | na ca tad api iti vakṣyate |

Objection: Veridicality is to be understood as (D^1) "lack of such predication content, *prakāra*, as is not located in the qualificandum"; non-veridicality is (D^{1c}) "presence of such predication content as is not located in the qualificandum." Thus the occurrence is specified in the relevant way (while the definition shows the uniformity of a real universal).

Gaṅgeśa: Well, if this is your view, then you should say that these two (lack or presence of such content as the appropriate specifiers) are by themselves responsible for everyday speech about the veridical and non-veridical. Let them be so conceived. Then since one of the two would be indispensable (to identify the veridical or the non-veridical in every instance) and since one of the two would be what is established in awareness first, what would be the point of a univeral? (That is, there is no need to suppose that this role is played by veridicality as a universal.)

Furthermore, we do not accept the definitions, as will be explained.

Comments

Vātsyāyana commenting on *Nyāya-sūtra* 1.1.3 explains that a good definition specifies a property that differentiates one type of thing from other types. This is then properly "characterization," since the definiendum is a set of objects, not a word (e.g., having a dewlap characterizes cows). Proper characterization can be a basis for linguistic reform or usages that are "technical" (*pāribhāṣika*). Another sense of suitable definition simply targets "conventional usage," *vyavahāra*. Here a universal or another recurrent property is thought of as the ground for proper employment (e.g., cowhood is the ground for use of the word "cow").[4]

A cognition's qualificandum is a bearer or possessor of properties, the subject to which "predication contents" are ascribed. With the veridical awareness, "A pot," a particular pot is the qualificandum and possesses factwise the cognition's predication content in the property of potness.

Gaṅgeśa rejects D^1, but it is not too far from his own D^{26} (see below).

To plug in the example of the awareness "A pot" occurring in the presence of a pot, we see that it would not have predication content that did not exist in the individual pot cognized, the cognition's qualificandum. Similarly, the awareness "Silver" in the presence of mother-of-pearl would have predication content not existing factwise in the mother-of-pearl cognized, which would be that cognition's qualificandum.

However, the adequacy of D^1 is not Gaṅgeśa's primary concern at this point. His intent is to nail shut the coffin of the veridicality-as-a-universal thesis. A specifier makes known the specified, as in general, according to Nyāya, the general makes known the particular. Since a specifier—here in effect D^1 or D^{1c}—would guide identification of an awareness as veridical or not, no universal would be needed to play that role. Specifiers, *avacchedaka*s, are not themselves universals. They are needed to solve problems of vagueness, and we shall see that Gaṅgeśa uses them to make his own definitions work.

We may remark that the ontological status of specifiers remains a live issue in Navya Nyāya long past Gaṅgeśa occupying the school's best minds.

Gaṅgeśa also has qualms about the definitions uncoupled from the veridicality-as-a-universal thesis. He says he will inform us about that later.

Text (p. 416, Tirupati) and Translation

na api yathârthâ-gṛhīta-grāhitvaṃ loka-siddha-pramātvam, dhārā-vāhika-buddhy-a-vyâpteḥ | na ca pratyakṣasya vartamānârtha-grāhitvena svâśraya-kṣaṇa-viśiṣṭa-stambhâdi-grāhakatvena a-gṛhīta-grāhitvaṃ loka-siddham, anyathā eka-samaye jñāna-yaugapadya-prasaṅga iti vācyam | kṣaṇānām atīndriyatvāt sthūlôpādhim ādāya vartamānatva-grahāt sva-rūpa-sat-kramika-kṣaṇôtpattikatvena jñānâ-yaugapadyāt | na ca stambhâdiṣu prati-kṣaṇaṃ guṇa-karmâdy-utpattir asti, yena tad ādāya a-gṛhīta-grāhitvaṃ syāt | vedāt kramôtpanna-vedârtha-gocara-dhārā-vāhika-buddhy-a-vyāpteś ca |

(**Gaṅgeśa** continues:) Nor is it correct to hold (with Bhāṭṭa Mīmāṃsakas) that veridicality as it is known in everyday speech belongs to (D^2) "an awareness that grasps what has not been grasped (previously) concerning an object as it is." This putative characterization is no good because it would exclude veridical awarenesses that form a continual stream of awareness of one and the same thing (e.g., "This is a pot" cognized at time t_1 and "This is a pot" cognized immediately subsequently at time t_2).

Objection: A perceptual awareness as the grasper of a current object—as the grasper, say, of a stump in its role as the possessor of a distinct time qualification—is commonly accepted as veridical. Otherwise, we would face the difficulty that more than one awareness would occur at a single instant (if each were independent of qualification by time).

Gaṅgeśa: That should not be said. For, instants of time are not graspable in sense perception. The present is grasped only with respect to (crude measures of time, i.e.,) "thick" or "gross" properties (*upādhi*). Non-simultaneity of cognition is due to a cognition's nature as produced serially.

(Moreover) you cannot say that there is "grasping of what has not been grasped previously" (D^2) on the grounds that in a stump, etc., qualities, motions, etc., arise every instant. (For there is no such production.)

Furthermore, because it fails to cover veridical awareness due to scripture, D^2 is no good; that is to say, the definition is no good because it fails to include such serial awareness as of the meaning of a scriptural statement whose cause is the scriptural statement.

Comments

Rucidatta attributes D^2 to the Bhāṭṭa, i.e., Kumārila or a followers.

Gaṅgeśa points out that the later members in a series of awarenesses veridically cognizing the same thing would not be covered. The objector replies that things change at every instance specifically with respect to qualification by time. Gaṅgeśa thinks of the unincluded awarenesses as distinct members of a series in virtue of temporal qualifiers; so too then other things, such as stumps. That is, without thinking of cognitions as each occurring at a time—as temporally qualified or indexed—we could not think of them as occurring in a series. But it is a phenomenological fact that awarenesses occur in a series. Gaṅgeśa retorts that it possible that two cognitions occur at different times having an object that has not changed.

Gaṅgeśa's response relies on an understanding of time as a single, unitary container. Temporal divisions are "accidental" or "imposed properties," *upādhi*, "surplus," as explained, in the sense of falling outside the "accomplished" ontology, the core theory of seven categories. By inferential reasoning, Naiyāyikas have decided that the smallest division of time is the "point instant" (*kṣaṇa*). Awarenesses do indeed form uninterrupted series, as is also established by inference. Nothing enduring only for such an instant is perceptible. Again, it is only with reference to divisions of time imposed in a "gross" or "thick" fashion, i.e., that endure for more than an instant, that we are aware of a cognition or anything else as "in the present." (The point is made against Buddhists who would turn the momentariness of cognition into a momentariness of everything.) The fact remains that some things by nature do not change instantly, do not form series. Many things with their full array of properties endure through successive moments of perception. Each perception is nonetheless veridical and not to be ruled out.

Similarly, the same scriptural text may be read and correctly understood by person S at time t_1 and at time t_2. According to the definition proposed, the later cognition would not be veridical.

Text (p. 419, Tirupati) and Translation

na api yathârthânubhavatvam, jñāne ghaṭatvâdinā yathā-śabdârtha-sādṛśyâ-bhāvāt | sādṛśya-mātrasya bhrame 'pi gatatvāt |

(**Gaṅgeśa** continues:) Nor is the abstraction (D^3) "awareness matching the object" (or, alternatively, "as is the object, so is the awareness") the right abstract with which to characterize veridicality. The word *yathā* ("matching" or "as") means similarity, and there is no similarity between, for example, potness and a cognition of a pot. (Potness exists in pots, and cognition is a quality of a self.) Further, if it is similarity in general that is proposed (or, just any similarity), that would also obtain with non-veridical awareness.

Comments

Both an awareness, as a quality of an individual self, and an object of awareness, e.g., a pot, *exist*. There would invariably be this much similarity. But a non-veridical awareness would also *exist*, as would an object erroneously cognized, e.g., mother-of-pearl cognized as silver. Thus such similarity is not relevant to characterizing veridicality.

Text (p. 419, Tirupati) and Translation

na ca guṇa-janyânubhavatvam, doṣâ-bhāva-janyânubhavatvaṃ vā | tayor an-anugatatvāt pramâ-pramā-nirūpyatvāc ca |

(**Gaṅgeśa** continues:) Nor is (D^4) "awareness produced by an epistemic excellence" any better, or (its equivalent, D^{4a}) "awareness not produced by any epistemic defect." Neither of these terms applies unequivocally to all instances of veridical awareness. Also, (there is circularity in that) "produced by an excellence" and "produced not by a defect" are determined by whether it is a veridical awareness or not that has been produced.

Comments

"Produced by an excellence" means one thing with veridical perceptions, another with veridical inferential awarenesses, and still something else with analogical acquisitions of vocabulary and with bits of knowledge based on testimony, whereas the reigning assumption, for the moment at least, is that a definition of veridicality must be univocal. Later, in explicating his own definitions, Gaṅgeśa will qualify this requirement.

Furthermore, there is the problem mentioned earlier of veridical awarenesses where no epistemic excellence is apparent, e.g., an inference from a mistaken perception of smoke to fire on a mountain that is indeed fiery. There are veridical awarenesses that have not been produced by a *pramāṇa*.

And, Gaṅgeśa suggests in the last sentence, identification of epistemic excellences presupposes an epistemic point of view where we are aware of cognitions as veridical. The defiens would presuppose the definiendum as well as the reverse relationship, whereas one should be able to instruct another and teach a new word by way of a definition. Circularity violates a learnability constraint on a good definition.

Text (p. 419, Tirupati) and Translation

na apy a-bādhitânubhavatvam | bādhasya viparīta-pramātvāt |

(Gaṅgeśa continues:) Nor (D^5) "awareness that is undefeated." (This definition exhibits the fault of "self-dependence") in that a defeating awareness is an opposed, confuting awareness that is itself veridical.

Comments

Since veridicality is what we are endeavoring to define, it will not help to talk in terms of defeated awarenesses, since an awareness is determined to count as defeated only through the occurrence of what is regarded as veridical. Thus, D^5 is culpably circular.

"Defeating" is an internalist term, having to do with certainty from a first-person perspective and its being undermined. But of course all cognitions of which a person is certain are regarded by him as veridical, whether they are veridical or not. So, certainty and related ideas such as "defeating" do not provide leverage on what it is *to be* veridical as opposed to *to be regarded as* veridical.

Text and Translation

na api saṃvādy-anubhavatvam | jñānântareṇa tathôllikhyamānatvasya saṃvāditvasya bhrama-sādhāraṇatvāt |

(Gaṅgeśa continues:) Nor (D^6) "awareness that agrees with another cognition." Agreement or conformity with another cognition insofar as it is made explicit is (potentially) common to error.

Comments

Two people can both see mother-of-pearl erroneously as silver and say in agreement erroneously, "This is silver." Or, the conformity could be with another of one's own awarenesses, also erroneous. D^6 is thus too wide.

The eleventh-century Advaitin Śrīharṣa, whom Gaṅgeśa appears to be following through this stretch of text, argues that even such confirmational cognitions as those Naiyāyikas tout as showing veridicality (through showing success of action) can be illusory: desire can be satisfied in a dream.[5]

Text and Translation

na api samartha-pravṛtti-janakânubhavatvam | upekṣā-pramāyām a-vyāpteḥ | tad-yogyatāyāḥ pramā-nirūpyatvāt |

(**Gaṅgeśa** continues:) Nor (D^7) "awareness that leads to successful activity." This would not include those veridical awarenesses which result in an attitude of indifference (that are not acted upon). Furthermore (this characterization exhibits the fault of "self-dependence" in that) the potentiality here (for successful activity) presupposes veridical awareness.

Comments

D^7 is commonly considered the contribution of Yogācāra Buddhist philosophers, especially Dharmakīrti (c. 640). But it is also in accord with the pragmatism that Vātsyāyana expresses in his introductory commentary to *Nyāya-sūtra* 1.1.1: successful activity depends on veridical awareness.[6]

Three cognitive attitudes are distinguished by Vātsyāyana and Nyāya tradition: embracing cognitions (*upādāna-buddhi*), avoiding or rejecting cognitions (*hāna-buddhi*), and ignoring cognitions (*upekṣā-buddhi*). Ignoring cognitions lead to indifference towards their objects, and are not acted upon.

Gaṅgeśa's rejection of D^7 shows that he distinguishes between—to use a different terminology—a test of truth and the nature of truth. Success in action shows that a cognition is veridical, but it is not what it is to be veridical.

Text and Translation

na api tattvânubhavatvam, a-vastuno '-bhānāt | bhāne vā bhrama-sādhāraṇyāt |

Nor (D^8) "awareness of a reality." What is not a real object does not appear. Or if it does appear, then D^8 would apply also to erroneous awareness.

Comments

Nothing absolutely unreal even appears. To hallucinate what one takes to be an elephant requires prior acquaintance with an elephant. Or, if what is meant is the reality of appearance itself, that is common to non-veridical awareness.

Udayana puts forth D^8 in his *Lakṣaṇamālā*.[7]

Text (p. 420, Tirupati, and p. 383, Calcutta) and Translation

> na api viśeṣya-niṣṭhâtyantâ-bhāvâ-pratiyogi-dharma-prakārakânubhavatvam | samyogâdi-pramâ-vyāpteḥ | a-bhāve vyāpya-vṛttitva-viśeṣaṇe saṃyoga-bhrame 'tivyāptiḥ | tad-atyantâ-bhāvasya ekatvāt |

(**Gaṅgeśa** continues:) Nor (D^9) "awareness having as predication content a property that is not the countercorrelate (*pratiyogin*, the "absentee") of an absolute absence resident in the cognized thing."

This fails to include veridical awareness of contact and the like (qualities that are non-locus-pervading; for example, "The tree has a monkey in it," is an awareness of something, a tree, where there is an absolute absence of what is predicated, namely, a contact with a monkey; that is, such an absence obtains at the tree's roots). If you would qualify the term "absence" in the definition to require that it be locus-pervading, then too much would be let in. Errors about contacts would have to be counted veridical in that there is just one kind of absolute absence of contact.

Comments

For example, the awareness "(This is) a pot" would be veridical when the thing cognized is a pot since the awareness's predication content, potness, would not be (properly speaking, the specifier of) the *pratiyogin*(-ness) of an absolute absence resident in the pot. (Gaṅgeśa introduces the "specification" refinement with the next definition considered, D^{10}.) An example of such an absolute absence would be an absence of a cloth, where a cloth would be the *pratiyogin* (and clothness the property specifier of the *pratiyogin*-ness). On the other hand, the awareness "Silver" when one is looking at mother-of-pearl would be non-veridical according to D^9, because there would be an absolute absence of silverness in the thing cognized, so that silverness would be both a predication content and the ruled-out (specifier of) *pratiyogin*(-ness).

An absolute absence is a constant non-occurrence of something F in something G, with, again, the F as the countercorrelate or absentee, *pratiyogin*, of the absence.

Absolute absences are constant, ever present in what they qualify, and an absolute absence of a contact or conjunction in a substance is, like a conjunction, non-locus-pervading. So the only possible non-veridical awareness about a contact would be, e.g., "The quality exhibits a contact"—because, in fact, no quality ever exhibits a contact (qualities like color and desire cannot conceivably *touch* any surface; hence contacts are categorially excluded from qualifying qualities such that this absence *is* locus-pervading). By setting the standard for the pertinent absence too high, we would make the requirement for veridicality too weak. An error about any possible contact whatsoever (i.e., with regard to any substance) would have to be counted veridical since there would *not* be a constant, locus-pervading absence of a monkey, say, anywhere such a contact might be.

Thus no definition that employs in this way the notion of a countercorrelate to an absolute absence will be able to get around the difficulty Gaṅgeśa cites regarding awareness of a contact, unless we have reason to suppose that there is not only one kind of absolute absence of contact. The rule there seems to be that a difference concerning type of locus is not enough to secure a difference of absence.

Text (p. 384, Calcutta) and Translation

na api viśeṣya-vṛtty-anyonyâ-bhāva-pratiyogitâvacchedaka-dharmâ-prakārakânubhavatvam, a-vyāpya-vṛtti-pramân-upagrahāt | mūle vṛkṣaḥ kapi-saṃyogavān na agre ity a-bādhitânubhavāt saṃyogavad-anyonyâ-bhāvasya a-vyāpya-vṛttitvāt | bhedâ-bheda evaṃ syāt iti cet, anubhavam upālambhasva, yad-balād avaccheda-bhedena atyantâ-bhāva-vad anyonyâ-bhāvasya apy a-vyāpya-vṛttitvam upeyam | ata eva pakve idānīṃ na śyāma iti dhīḥ samaya-bhedād a-viruddhā tatra eva tad-anyonyâ-bhāvam avalambate |

(**Gaṅgeśa** continues:) Nor (D^{10}) "awareness that does not have as its predication content a property that specifies a countercorrelate-ness (*pratiyogi-tā*) of a mutual exclusion resident in the thing cognized." This also fails to include veridical awarenesses about properties that are not locus-pervading.

A tree, for example, does not have a contact with a monkey at its roots while it does in its branches. (The tree would be the locus of a quality, a monkey-conjunction, that would be the countercorrelate of an exclusion, an exclusion of monkey conjunction, of which it would also be the locus.) This is a common, uncontroverted experience. Exhibiting a contact and not exhibiting a contact, though mutually exclusive, are not locus-pervading.

"So in this way there would be both distinctness and non-distinctness." If you are prone to think this, then we say, "Blame your experience." Experience shows that a mutual exclusion should also be accepted as non-locus-pervading—that is, so long as there is distinct specification—just as in the case of an absolute absence. In this way, the judgment, "Having been baked, the pot is not now black," is not self-contradictory, because of a distinctness of occasion (black before baking, red afterwards). There is experience that both sides of a mutual exclusion can be present in this way in just a single thing.

Comments

A *pratiyogitā-avacchedaka* property is a property that specifies, ties down, or delimits a countercorrelate-ness that is pertinent to a distinctness or mutual exclusion (*anyonyâ-bhāva*, "mutual absence"). For example, a pot is distinct from a cloth, with the cloth as the countercorrelate of a distinctness resident in the pot. Thus clothness is the property that delimits the relevant countercorrelate-ness. With the veridical awareness, "A pot," this property is not predication content.

D^{10} falls to the same argument that felled D^9, since the logic of mutual exclusion is not significantly different from that of absolute absence. The general difference between the two is that of an F's not being a G (mutual exclusion) as opposed to an F's never being in a G (absolute or constant absence). But in the present context, both would require *ad hoc* specification according to particular circumstances, e.g., awareness of a contact. Thus both definitions fail to be sufficiently general.

Gaṅgeśa's example is suggestive. Recognition is a primary topic of this chapter, and the possibility of recognition requires an object that endures long enough to be recognized as the same from one to another time. Some objects have to have temporal spread. This means that with temporal indexing, objects can be the loci of what would be contemporaneously incompatibles.

Text (p. 422, Tirupati) and Translation

> na api viśeṣyâ-vṛtty-a-prakārakânubhavatvam | eka-eka-viśeṣyâ-vṛtti-nānā-prakāraka-samūhâlambanâ-vyāpteḥ | na ca prakārasya eka-viśeṣya-vṛttitayā na viśeṣyâ-vṛttitvam iti vācyam | pramâ-pramā-rūpa-samūhâlambanâtivyāpteḥ | na ca yāvad-viśeṣyâ-vṛttitvaṃ vivakṣitam | eka-eka-viśeṣya-vṛtter yāvad-viśeṣyâ-vṛttitvena samūhâlambanâ-vyāpteḥ | eka-viśeṣyake yāvad-arthâ-bhāvāc ca |

(**Gaṅgeśa** continues:) Nor (D^{11}) "awareness without predication content that does not exist in the thing cognized." This characterization is no good because it fails to apply to a veridical awareness of a group of things (pot, cloth) cognized under various predicates (potness, clothness) that do not apply to each and every individual in the group.

Objection: But "non-existence in the cognized" is not to be taken without qualification. It is to be understood with respect to the predication content residing in each individual item singly.

Gaṅgeśa: No, this response is patchwork that should not be tried. The definition would still fail because then it would include too much. It would include, namely, a non-veridical awareness of a group of things where some of the items are veridically cognized and some not.

Objection: With respect to however many items are cognized (is how D^{11} should be extended).

Gaṅgeśa: That also should not be tried. For, it would fail to include veridical awareness of a group in that each item could exhibit something that does not exist in the cognized "with respect to however many items are cognized." Moreover, a veridical awareness of a single thing does not include a notion of "however many."

Comments

D[11] would allow an awareness of a group to be veridical if any single item were veridically cognized although other items were erroneously cognized, with the result that—according to common usage and supposition—the group cognition would be non-veridical. An example is an awareness of a piece of tin and a piece of silver as both silver. D[11], along with the variations suggested, patently suffers from ambiguity: the one lets in too little and the others too much. Nevertheless, Gaṅgeśa is honing in on the right way to characterize veridicality.

Text (p. 387, Calcutta) and Translation

atha viṣayatāyā āśrayo viśeṣyaḥ, jñānaṃ tat-pratiyogi | bhrame ca śukti-vṛttir viṣayatā vyadhikaraṇena rajatatvena avacchidyate | rajata-vṛttis tu samānâdhikaraṇena rajatatvena | viṣayatā ca viṣaye na jñānâhitā jñātatā-rūpā vivakṣitā | apasiddhāntād a-siddheḥ, atītân-āgata-pramāyāṃ tad-a-bhāvāc ca |

(**Gaṅgeśa** continues:) The locus of objecthood (*viṣayatā*) is the qualificandum (the thing cognized); cognition is the determining correlate (*pratiyogin*) of that. And with erroneous awareness, objecthood exists in, for example, the mother-of-pearl—objecthood, that is, as specified by silverness, which is something not present in that same locus. (In veridical awareness) silverness is present in the same locus as the objecthood that exists in (some bit of) silver (when it is cognized).

And objecthood should not be taken as a "cognizedness" produced in the object by cognition. Not only would such an unproved view depart from Naiyāyika theory, but also with veridical awareness of things that are past or future, "cognizedness" could not arise.

Comments

An awareness of a table has the table as its object. Thus objecthood is located in the table, and it is an objecthood with respect to that specific awareness. In the technical terms employed, the objecthood has a locus (the table) and a determining correlate (the cognition).

In other words, objecthood exists only in an epistemic context. It exists in an object cognized only so long and insofar as it is cognized. So *viṣayatā-pratiyogitā*, "countercorrelateness to objecthood," is an abstract property of cognitions correlate to objects whose objecthoods—whose being objects—they determine. An object cognized, the *viśeṣya* (or *dharmin*), is the *anuyogin*, or "supercorrelate," of objecthood, i.e., its locus. (For our previous discussion of objecthood, see above, pp. 114–15.)

In the passage at hand, Gaṅgeśa is, in part, disputing a position belonging to Bhāṭṭa Mīmāṃsakas, namely, that cognition creates a property in a cognized object, "cognizedness," which is very similar to Nyāya's own "objecthood." According to Kumārila's school, this property becomes the basis for an inference to the occurrence of our own cognition. Gaṅgeśa points out that awareness cannot change objects that are past, nor just by itself (presumably) things to come.

But the main point here is not to get clear on how we know our own awareness, or to dispute a Mīmāṃsaka position, but rather to get clear about ontological concepts crucial, according to some, to the project of characterizing veridical awareness, in particular, objecthood. Gaṅgeśa is warning us not to confuse objecthood with a property of awareness nor, most importantly, with a "cognizedness" as understood by the Bhāṭṭas. Cognizedness, after all, makes a real difference to the object it qualifies, being a positive property useful for the purposes of inference. Objecthood, on the other hand, tends to be seen as either a "surplus property," *upādhi*, that is nothing other than a special way of talking about an object, or some special category not mentioned on the traditional list. Those who take it at all seriously posit it only to make sense of the relation between a cognition and its worldly object. In the next passage, the view gets aired further, and we shall focus again on *viṣayatā*, "objecthood," in the comments.

Text (p. 388, Calcutta) and Translation

> kiṃ tu jñānasya viṣaye viśeṣaṇatā-viśeṣaḥ kaścit | para-jñānaṃ jñānatvena tad-viṣayaṃ ca ghaṭatvena jānato ghaṭam ayaṃ jānāti na vā iti saṃśayād viṣaya-jñāna-sva-rūpâtiriktasya svâśraya-svâ-bhāvâdi-viśeṣaṇatā-viśeṣasya āvaśyaṃ svīkārāt | anyathā ghaṭatvena jñāto 'rtha iti tṛtīyârthâ-saṃbhavaḥ | prakāratvam api viṣayasya jñāne viśeṣaṇatā-viśeṣa eva, na tu viṣayatvam atiprasaṅgāt |

(**Gaṅgeśa** continues:) (For the reasons mentioned, we Naiyāyikas understand objecthood differently:) objecthood is a particular type of attribution, or qualifier (*viśeṣaṇatā*), that resides in a cognition's object. Another person's cognition—cognized as cognition—and its object, a pot, can become the object of a doubt, "Is he cognizing the pot or not?" The fact that such a doubt can occur shows that (i.e., according to some Naiyāyikas) objecthood is something ontologically over and above both the object cognized and the cognizing awareness. Objecthood is a particular type of attribution, or qualifier, *viśeṣaṇatā*, that is distinct from such qualifiers as (a) the cognition whose locus is the person and (b) an absence of that cognition (whose locus would also be the person).

Otherwise (if objecthood were not a particular type of qualifier ontologically over and above both a cognition and its object), it would not be possible to use the instrumental case to convey that an object is cognized *as* (e.g.) a pot.

Being a predication content (or predication-contenthood, *prakāratva*) is also a specific type of qualifier (*viśeṣaṇatā*), one that (in contrast with objecthood) is *of* the object but is *in* cognition. It is that only. It is not equivalent to objecthood (which qualifies, or resides in, the object). To suppose it is equivalent would be to suppose too much.

Comments

According to the reasoning and the example of a doubt given here, the property *viṣayatā*, the objecthood that S's doubt determines, rests in another person's cognition—in T's cognition, let us say—since T's cognition is the object of S's doubt. But it is not just an occurrence of cognition that is doubted: T may be presumed to have awareness of something or other. S's doubt is whether T is cognizing a particular pot. A certain pot-intentionality is, at least in part, the doubt's object. Also, it is not just the pot that is doubted. Thus the doubt's object must be something over and above both T's cognition and the pot—that is, according to certain Naiyāyikas whom Gaṅgeśa will answer (in text following D^{36e} below). The cognition is known and the pot can be ruled out, so the object of the doubt has to be something else. The proposal here is that it is an objecthood as an ineliminable property.

As mentioned in the section on how veridicality is known, Gaṅgeśa does not himself subscribe to the theory that objecthood is an additional real, and, again, he eventually counters this argument. But it seems that he has no terribly strong feelings on the point, because often he takes into consideration this rival Naiyāyika view. Even in the following *siddhānta* section, he formulates several characterizations of veridical awareness in which he follows the contours of the rival Naiyāyika ontological position, as we shall see. And in this *pūrvapakṣa* section, the notion of objecthood as an additional real is not among the faults that Gaṅgeśa targets in the definitions he rejects.

According to the rival ontological view, cognition is only *indirectly* related to an object cognized and to its properties; that is, it is related by way of an objecthood that it determines. Thus predication content, *prakāra*, would belong to a peculiar objecthood that occurs in a thing cognized when it is cognized—at one remove from the cognition itself. The predication content would occur within, so to say, the objecthood that an awareness determines. Objecthood (or "intentionality," *viṣayatā*) has predication content, although an objecthood correlate to an experience and impregnated with a certain content can fail to *reside in* the same locus as its predication content (as in error). Moreover, the object cognized would be directly related to the objecthood, which then would stand between—would stand ontologically between—an awareness and its qualificandum.

Thus the relation is a (tertiary) property or attribution, whose precise ontological status, we may assume, was much debated among Navya-Nyāya philosophers of Gaṅgeśa's time. Later Naiyāyikas take up the topic as of prime philosophic interest, for example, Gadādhara.[8]

Doubt (*saṃśaya*) figures crucially in the argument of the rival ontological camp. Epistemologically, no Navya-Nyāya philosopher sees doubt as other than a species of non-veridical awareness. But the ontological status of a doubt's object is much disputed and discussed. Gaṅgeśa shows below (see the text following D^{36e}) something of how he understands the ontological underpinnings of doubt. Here we get Gaṅgeśa's Nyāya mixed in with a rival camp's views.

The argument hinges on a use of the instrumental case in Sanskrit, the "predicative instrumental." The example is of the instrumental case used to express the notion "*as* a pot." If objecthood as an additional real were not a qualifier of the object, then the object, the thing cognized, could not be predicated of in this way.

If objecthood were not an independent qualifier qualifying the object, the thing cognized, then the object could not be rightly predicated of by means of a noun in the instrumental case. In contrast with a predicative copula, which is understood to express a relation of *identity*, two nouns used predicatively in different cases, nominative and instrumental—not the usual pair of nominatives—imply *distinctness*. The instrumental case used predicatively (as opposed to the usual pattern of double nominatives and an expressed or understood copula) requires an objective link, a thick link, something ontologically substantial, not something ontologically flimsy and eliminable like the relation of identity. This is objecthood, the objecthood that links together a qualificandum and a qualifier. A bit of objecthood is determined by a cognition, as we can see in such attribution. But it objectively real. That is, whatever we see something *as* is in part determined by cognition (by focusing, etc.). But the unity of cognition is reflected in a triadic fact, or otherwise we could not know, to use Gaṅgeśa's example, a pot by its potness, i.e., *as* a pot. We could not know that complex object.

At the end of the passage, Gaṅgeśa contrasts "being a predication content," *prakāratā*, with objecthood. Specifying the predication content of an awareness vis-à-vis the objecthood an awareness determines is crucial to several of Gaṅgeśa's own characterizations of veridicality, as well as to his ability to say precisely what an illusion is.

Of course, the ontological status of an awareness's predication content is tricky business because of illusion. Ontologically, a veridical cognition is to be analyzed solely in terms of (1) awareness, an episodic quality of a self, and

(2) intentional objects. But a qualifier presented in awareness does not necessarily belong to the object cognized; otherwise erroneous awareness would be impossible. "Being a predication content" is a notion that cuts across the veridical/non-veridical distinction. Ontologically, where does predication content reside? According to the current passage—within an exploration of faulty definitions including ones proposed by good Naiyāyikas—*being* a predication content (*prakāratā*) is an abstract property of an awareness-of-an-object (as a quality of a self), an abstract property most directly related to—or residing in—cognition, as opposed to the cognition's object.

This account presents a problem in that any particular bit of predication content Gaṅgeśa consistently treats as ontologically a qualifier obtaining somewhere in the world. The view expressed at the end is not that of the Naiyāyika camp that sees predication content as belonging to the objecthood that an awareness determines. The text says that "being a predication content" belongs to, or rests in, cognition. But any given bit of predication content is simply a (world-residing) qualifier appearing in cognition. So probably what is meant is that it is in virtue of appearing in cognition that a qualifier is called a predication content.

One way, then, to read the current statement as consistent with Gaṅgeśa's view that ontologically a predication content belongs to an object concerns a point about qualifiers taken in abstraction (*viśeṣaṇa-tā*). As Sibajiban Bhattacharyya points out, there are two ways to abstract from qualifiers to capture the relation between cognition and its objects, objectwise and cognitionwise.[9] Objecthood is a relational abstraction in the former direction; predication-contenthood goes in the latter direction. Thus to say that predication-contenthood is *in* cognition does not mean that particular bits of predication content rest ontologically in cognition. All particular bits of predication content are qualifiers of objects in the world—in illusion, they are misperceived with regard to their actual loci. A qualifier appearing in cognition is the predication content of the cognition, and predication-content*hood* is a relational abstraction in the direction of cognition.

Note that for Gaṅgeśa neither of the abstracts is an independent real. But in the present context, both of these key relational notions are presumably taken to be independent reals, and—this seems to be the main point—predication-contenthood is not to be viewed as equivalent to objecthood: one is an independent real preëminently bound up with the object (although "determined," *nirūpaka*, by cognition) and the other a real preëminently bound up with cognition (wherever the loci of the particular bits of predication content may be). Or the point is that we need the distinction in order to do our epistemology and logic and will later worry about how precisely to view these ontologically: we are now ready to review some veritable contenders for an adequate characterization of veridical awareness.

Text (p. 424, Tirupati) and Translation

evaṃ ca viṣayatā-samānâdhikaraṇa-prakārakânubhavaḥ, prakāra-samānâdhikaraṇa-viṣayatā-pratiyogy-anubhavo vā sva-samānâdhikaraṇa-dharma-prakāraka-viṣayatā-pratiyogy-anubhavo vā sva-samānâdhikaraṇa-dharmâvacchinna-viṣayatā-pratiyogy-anubhavo vā pramā iti cet, na | nirvikalpakâ-vyāpteḥ, viṣayatā-samānâdhikaraṇêdantva-prakāraka-bhramasya api pramātva-prasaṅgāc ca | bhramas tatra aṃśe pramā eva iti cet, tarhi anubhavatvam eva pramātvam, vyartham adhikam | anubhava eva kvacid aṃśe pramâ-pramā ca iti cet, na | ukta-lakṣaṇe tādṛśâ-lābhāt |

Objection: And in this way the following characterizations of veridical awareness are arrived at: (D^{12}) "awareness whose predication content has the same locus as the objecthood," (D^{13}) "awareness correlate to an objecthood that has the same locus as the predication content," (D^{14}) "awareness correlate to an objecthood with a predication content in the form of a property that has the same locus as the objecthood," and (D^{15}) "awareness correlate to an objecthood that is specified by a property that has the same locus as the objecthood."

Gaṅgeśa: No, these are wrong. For, (a) they fail to include indeterminate perception, and (b) an erroneous awareness can have as predication content a "thisness" having the same locus as the objecthood correlate to the awareness and so would have to be counted veridical.

If it is objected that erroneous cognition *is* in that portion veridical, then (having equated the veridical and the non-veridical) one would say simply that "to be an awareness" is "to be veridical." To say more would be pointless.

If it be contended that awareness in some part is veridical and in some part not, we respond that the definitions on the table do not yield that view.

Comments

Armed with a technical apparatus, Gaṅgeśa presents a series of rival Naiyāyika definitions. Note the increasing complexity of the definitions, which may be read as formulated in accordance with the views of the rival ontological camp. But they are not, according to Gaṅgeśa, the best definitions that that camp might propose. Later, with definitions D^{28} through D^{36e}, Gaṅgeśa puts forth what he sees as, in contrast, acceptable definitions according to the view that objecthood is an additional real.

"Indeterminate cognition," *nirvikalpaka jñāna*, has no *predication* content (*prakāratva*). It has bits of objecthood, but they are unrelated in the qualificandum-relation-qualifier structure (a-R-b) that all determinate awareness has. Here the assumption is that a *nirvikalpaka* cognition could be veridical. Later Gaṅgeśa will argue that indeterminate perception is neither veridical nor non-veridical, but that is not the assumption here. (As will be explained, this section probably should not be counted a true *pūrva-pakṣa*.

Nevertheless, the definitive views come later. And according to the Asiatic Society edition this is a *pūrva-pakṣa* and the examining voice other than Gaṅgeśa's own. This would account for the inconsistency.)

"This is silver" cognized in the presence of mother-of-pearl includes "thisness" as predication content, a thisness that does indeed reside in the object cognized, the mother-of-pearl.

The erroneous awareness, "This is silver," when the object cognized is mother-of-pearl, is veridical in its thisness bit of objecthood. The problem, then, with the current definitions is that they do not differentiate bits of objecthood perspicaciously. A successful characterization must be capable of capturing both the overall non-veridicality of an erroneous awareness and the veridicality of whatever bit of objecthood is correctly cognized.

Text (p. 426, Tirupati) and Translation

> atha sva-vyadhikaraṇa-prakārân-avacchinna-viṣayatā-pratiyogy-anubhavaḥ pramā | samūhâlambane ca prati-viśeṣyaṃ viṣayatā-bhedād eka-vṛttir viṣayatā na apara-vṛttinā avacchidyate | ato na a-vyāptir iti cet, na | bhramâṃśa-pramāyām a-vyāpteḥ | na hi yā viṣayatā vyadhikaraṇa-dharmeṇa avacchidyate sā tad-an-avacchinnā, virodhāt |

Objection: Then veridical awareness is (D^{16}) "awareness correlate to an objecthood that is *not* specified by a predication content that belongs to a different locus than its own." (This characterization does not fall to the criticism previously made, against D^{11}, of failing to include veridical cognition of a group of things.) In veridical awareness of a group, the criterion applies to each cognized thing, since there is in the case of each item a distinct objecthood. So objecthood would reside in each thing separately, not (as in the previous faulty characterization) in the other things, too.

Gaṅgeśa: No, you are wrong again. The current candidate fails because it does not apply to the veridical part of a partly erroneous awareness. For, an objecthood (correlate to the awareness, e.g., tin) that is specified by a property (e.g., silverness) that does not have the same locus as the objecthood is not equivalent to an objecthood that is not specified like that, because of incompatibility.

Comments

With a person S's veridical awareness, "This is a book," the objecthood correlate to the awareness is specified by the predication content "bookness," which as a property does indeed reside in the book of which S is aware. The locus of the bookness, namely, the book, is the locus of the objecthood correlate to the awareness. In the terms of D^{16}, the awareness is correlate to an objecthood that is not specified by a predication content, e.g., potness, that does not have the same locus as the objecthood; potness is indeed located not in the book of which S is aware but in pots. With the veridical awareness of a group of things—for example, ''A book and a pot''—the definition would fit since each object is known under the separate specification that is true of it. Two distinct objecthoods correlate to the awareness are specified by two distinct bits of predication content.

Gaṅgeśa's rebuttal suggests a partially veridical awareness of silver when a person is confronted with silver and tin, ''This and that are silver.'' Silverness would be an example of ''predication content not present in the same locus as that of the objecthood'' that would be present in the tin. The problem is that ''silver'' would be correct with respect to the piece of silver but would not be counted correct by this definition. According to D^{16}, then, an awareness that was erroneous with regard to any objecthood correlate to the awareness would have to be counted as entirely erroneous, even though one thing, for example, silver of the pair silver and tin, was veridically cognized.

Text (p. 393, Calcutta) and Translation

na api prakāra-vyadhikaraṇa-viṣayatvâ-pratiyogy-anubhavaḥ pramā | prakāra-vyadhikaraṇa-viṣayatā-pratiyogini tad-a-pratiyogitvasya a-bhāvena bhramâṃśa-pramâ-vyāpteḥ | na api sva-vyadhikaraṇa-dharmâvacchinna-viṣayatvâ-pratiyogy-anubhavaḥ, svâdhikaraṇâ-vṛtty-a-prakāraka-viṣayatā-pratiyogy-anubhavo vā pramā, tata eva | bhrame viṣayatāyāḥ sva-vyadhikaraṇa-prakārâvacchinnatvāt svâdhikaraṇâ-vṛtti-prakārakatvāc ca | na api sva-samānâdhikaraṇânyonyâ-bhāva-pratiyogitâvacchedaka-dharmân-avacchinna-viṣayatā-pratiyogy-anubhavaḥ pramā | bhramâṃśa-pramâ-vyāpteḥ | anyonyâ-bhāvasya a-vyāpya-vṛttitvena a-vyāpya-vṛtti-pramāyām a-vyāpteś ca | yat tu pramātvâ-pramātvayor virodha eva bhramo na pramā iti, tat tuccham | aṃśa-bhedam ādāya ubhayasya anubhavāt | anyathā bhramasya ubhaya-bahir-bhāvâpatteḥ | etena sva-vyadhikaraṇa-prakārakaṃ jñānaṃ bhramas tad-anyo 'nubhavaḥ pramā, bhramo dharmy-aṃśe na pramā iti nirastam |

(**Gaṅgeśa** continues:) Nor is it correct to characterize veridical awareness as (D^{17}) ''awareness not correlate to an objecthood not present in the same locus as the predication content.'' This fails to handle the veridical in a partially erroneous awareness (e.g., silver and tin cognized as only silver) in the right way, since in that case there is a correlate to an objecthood (namely, the tin's objecthood) not present in the same locus as the predication content. But (with the veridically cognized object) a non-correlation with that (objecthood not present in the same locus with the predication content) does not occur.

Nor, for the same reason, should veridical awareness be characterized as (D^{18}) ''awareness not correlate to an objecthood specified by a property present in a locus not the same as that of the objecthood,'' nor as (D^{19})

"awareness correlate to an objecthood without predication content that does not reside in the same locus with the objecthood." With erroneous awareness there is (such) objecthood that is specified by a predication content residing in a locus different than its own, while there is also such predication content (in the veridical portion of an erroneous awareness), not residing, that is, in the same locus with an objecthood (not correlate to the awareness).

Nor should veridical awareness be characterized as (D^{20}) "awareness correlate to an objecthood not specified by a property that specifies a counter-correlateness of a distinctness (or mutual exclusion) resident in the same locus with the objecthood." For, this too fails to cover correctly the veridical in a partially erroneous awareness. Furthermore, since the relation of mutual exclusion (or distinctness) is not locus-pervading, the definition fails to cover veridical awareness of the non-locus-pervading.

Objection: Then given that veridicality and non-veridicality are mutually opposed, an erroneous awareness is not (contrary to your assumption) veridical (in any portion).

Gaṅgeśa: No, that is an empty proposal. It is a common experience to realize with respect to the part both what was veridical and what was not (i.e., to know that what one was aware of as a "this" is indeed a this while the portion that had it as "silver" is known as non-veridical). If it were otherwise, an erroneous awareness would be neither veridical nor non-veridical.

Therefore, according to the definition of erroneous awareness as (D^{21c}) "cognition whose predication content does not reside in the same locus as that of the objecthood (that the cognition determines)," and the definition of veridical awareness (D^{21}) "awareness that is not like that (namely, having predication content not residing in the same locus as that of the objecthood)," should the thesis be thrown out that erroneous awareness cannot be veridical even in the portion concerning the (cognized) object as a possessor of properties (*dharmin*).

Comments

"Silver" as object of an awareness of silver and tin as only silver is predication content that both resides in and does not reside in a locus that is the same as that of an objecthood not correlate to the experience. The problem is that D^{17} fails to differentiate what is and what is not veridically cognized here.

An example of D^{20} would be the veridical awareness "A pot" had on the part of a person S such that S's awareness would be correlate to an objecthood resident in the pot which is not qualified by a property, such as clothness, that is excluded, as is clothness, by a distinctness that resides in the cognized pot, namely, the distinctness of the pot from a cloth.

Gaṅgeśa's second objection to D^{20} runs as follows. The definition as tied to the logic of distinctness, i.e., mutual exclusion, is incapable of capturing correctly veridical awareness of facts that do not exhibit that logic. For example, a "contact with a monkey" can be veridically cognized as qualifying a tree. But since the logic of mutual exclusion is not sensitive to the fact that the contact does not reside in the roots of a tree (being limited to the branches), such an awareness would be counted by D^{20} as non-veridical. That is to say, the tree would be the locus (a) of an objecthood correlate to the awareness, an objecthood specified by a property, absence of the monkey-contact (i.e., at the roots), that specifies the countercorrelateness of a distinctness, i.e., a property that is excluded by a distinctness, that (b) resides in that same locus, the tree (i.e., the distinctness from non-monkey-contact that resides in the tree's branches).

At the end of the passage, Gaṅgeśa tips his hand and gives a definition (D^{21}) that is almost identical to one he accepts, with qualification, as we shall see. The point is to stress that a cognition can be veridical concerning a qualificandum while being non-veridical concerning what it presents it as, e.g., "That shiny thing is a piece of silver" when the thing is indeed shiny but not a piece of silver.

Text (p. 427, Tirupati) and Translation

> na api prakārâdhikaraṇâ-vṛtty-a-prakāraka-viṣayatā-pratiyogy-anubhavaḥ, prakārân-adhikaraṇâ-vṛtti-viṣayatā-pratiyogy-anubhavo vā pramā | prameyam idam iti jñāne prakārân-adhikaraṇasya a-prasiddheḥ | kiṃ ca rajatatva-prakāraka-viṣayatāyā rajata-vṛttitva-niyamāt rajatatvâvacchinnā eva rajata-bhrame rajata-vṛtti-viṣayatā | ato rajata-bhramo 'pi rajate pramā syāt | atha rajata-purovartinor ekā eva viṣayatā | sā ca prakārân-adhikaraṇa-vṛtti-dharmâvacchinnā eva iti cet, tarhi dharmy-aṃśe 'pi taj-jñānaṃ pramā na syāt, vyadhikaraṇa-prakārakatvasya tulyatvāt | dharmy-aṃśe tu pramātve rajate 'pi pramā syāt | atha rajatâṃśe dharmy-aṃśe ca taj-jñānaṃ pramā eva | vaiśiṣṭyâṃśe na pramā iti cet, na | vaiśiṣṭyasya pūrva-jñānâ-viṣayatvena a-prakāratvāt | vaiśiṣṭya-vṛtti-viṣayatāyāṃ rajatatva-purovartinoḥ prakāratvena bhramasya vaiśiṣṭyâṃśe pramātvâ-pramātvâpātāt |

(**Gaṅgeśa** continues:) Nor (D^{22}) "awareness correlate to an objecthood not resident in the same locus with a predication content that it does not have"; nor (D^{23}) "awareness correlate to an objecthood that does not reside in the same locus with the predication content." Both these definitions fail because with the cognition, "This thing is knowable," there is no instance where the predication content does not have a locus.

Moreover, the definitions fail because in an erroneous awareness of silver the objecthood that exists in (real) silver is indeed specified by silverness. The rule is that an objecthood having silverness as predication content exists in silver. Therefore, on these definitions an erroneous awareness of silver would have to be counted veridical (not only in the "thisness" portion but) also concerning the silver (since there are real pieces of silver in the world).

Objection: Then silver and "being in front" (or "thisness") have only a single objecthood. And that objecthood is indeed specified by a property that does not have the same locus as the predication content. (So an awareness of silver in the face of mother-of-pearl would be erroneous and the definitions may stand.)

Gaṅgeśa: (No.) Then even with the object as simply a bearer of properties, the cognition would not be veridical, since there would still be a having of predication content not residing in the same locus. But if the portion concerning the object as simply a bearer of properties is to be considered veridical, then the silver portion as well would have to be veridical (since there would be only a single objecthood according to the current proposal).

Objection: Then in both the portion concerning silverness and that concerning the bearer of properties, cognition should be regarded as veridical only. (That is to say, silverness exists in the real silver in the world, and "silverness" picks it out; thisness exists in the object in front, and "thisness" picks it out.) But in the portion that relates the two the cognition is not veridical.

Gaṅgeśa: No. The relationality—the relating of the two—not being an object in the preceding (indeterminate, *nirvikalpaka*) perception—is not a bit of predication content. Moreover, if the objecthood that would reside in the relationality would be determined by both the "silverness" and the "being in front" as predication content, then there would be both veridicality and non-veridicality in the relational portion of an erroneous awareness.

Comments

Everything is knowable, *prameya*. Therefore, both definitions rely on a potentially empty expression: given "being knowable" as the predication content, there would be no locus where it did not reside.

Gaṅgeśa is firmly committed to the rule that no illusion is non-veridical in all respects. In particular, every awareness is veridical with regard to an object cognized as a mere "bearer of properties" (*dharmin*), i.e., a something in some respect. Thus an erroneous awareness must be correlate to more than one objecthood.

A *savikalpaka* awareness, a relational or determinate awareness of an entity as qualified, is preceded and in part caused by a non-relational, indeterminate perception where a qualifier of an object is directly presented though not as related to the thing cognized. Erroneous awareness involves putting together a qualifier with a qualificandum to which it does not belong—a position that Gaṅgeśa will elaborate in the next section. A presentation of a misplaced qualifier arises, it may seem, in a non-relational cognitive moment. A non-relational awareness seems a good candidate for the origin of the data, so to say, that is put together in relational awareness. But whereas even relations, such as contact and inherence, are cognized in the non-relational stage, the relationality—the actual togetherness—is not, according to Gaṅgeśa. Thus, relationality cannot explain the non-veridical portion of an erroneous awareness.

Furthermore, it is impossible, Gaṅgeśa says, for a single relationality to be both veridical and non-veridical.

Text (p. 431, Tirupati) and Translation

> na api sva-vyadhikaraṇa-prakārân-avacchinna-viṣayatā-pratiyogy-anubhavaḥ pramā | prameyam idam iti jñāne prameyatva-prakāraka-viṣayatân-āśrayasya a-prasiddhyā a-vyāpteḥ | na ca saṃyogitvâdinā prameyatva-prakāraka-viṣayatā-vyatireko ghaṭâdau prasiddha iti vācyam | pratiyogitâvacchedaka-rūpavattvena pratiyogi-jñānasya a-bhāva-dhī-hetutvāt | kiṃ ca yat kiṃcid-vyadhikaraṇa-prakārân-avacchinnatvaṃ bhrama-sādhāraṇam, prakṛta-jñāna-vyadhikaraṇa-prakārân-avacchinnatvaṃ nirvikalpakâ-vyāptam, tasya niṣprakārakatvād iti |

(**Gaṅgeśa** continues:) Nor is veridical awareness to be characterized as (D^{24}) "awareness correlate to an objecthood that is not specified by a predication content that belongs to a different locus than its own." The definition fails to cover the cognition, "This thing can be known." Nothing is found to have a different locus than that of (the objecthood determined by a cognition whose predication content is "knowability," or, simply, than that of) the objecthood whose predication content is "knowability."

Objection: In a pot and the like, the (required) absence of the objecthood whose predication content is knowability is exampled, that is, knowability as determined by a relation such as being-in-contact-with (since knowability does not qualify things knowable by the relation of contact or touch).

Gaṅgeśa: No, that should not be said. For, (prior) cognition of the absentee or countercorrelate is a cause (a necessary condition) of an absential cognition in virtue of the cognition's being determined by the (property and relational) specifiers of what makes the absentee the absentee (and being-in-contact-with cannot figure as such a specifier in the case of knowability as the absentee).

Furthermore, whatever would meet the stipulation "not specified by predication content present in a locus that is not the same as . . ." would include erroneous awareness.

And it (D^{24}) fails to cover indeterminate perception, since indeterminate perception does not have predication content. Your definition states that the objecthood has to be not specified by predication content present in a locus that is not the same as (that of the objecthood determined by) the cognition in question. (But that is impossible in the case of *nirvikalpaka* awareness.)

Comments

D^{24} fails because one of its terms would fail to refer if the particular bit of veridical awareness, "This thing is knowable," were plugged in. There is nothing that is "a locus that is not the same as that of the objecthood" if the objecthood is that having the predication content "knowability."

The objector tries a trick to handle this case: knowability as "in the relation of contact" with an object gives us the required absence in that nothing knowable is qualified by knowability through the relation of contact (or "conjunction," *saṃyoga*, "touch"). But this does not fit the causal analysis of absential cognition just because such a relation could not specify what it is to be an absentee or countercorrelate in this case, Gaṅgeśa says. Something is known as absent at a particular spot by the same relation that its presence would be known there.

As already remarked, later we get Gaṅgeśa's ruling that indeterminate perception falls outside the veridical/non-veridical distinction. (Indeterminate awareness does not have predication content—there no qualifier appears as qualifying a qualificandum—and both veridical and non-veridical awareness presuppose predication content.) At the end of the current passage, he again prepares that move by pointing out that D^{24} fails to cover indeterminate perception.

Here ends Gaṅgeśa's rejection of faulty definitions. Beginning with D^{25}, he defends the definitions he puts forth. Accordingly, the Asiatic Society edition labels the previous text as a *pūrva-pakṣa*, contrasting with a following *siddhânta*. However, the preceding text contained several long expatiations crucial to understanding the upcoming right characterizations of veridical awareness. And in Ramanuja Tatacharya's judgment, it has been exposited in Gaṅgeśa's own voice. The Vidyapeetha edition indicates a discourse division, but does not label the preceding section as a *pūrva-pakṣa* but rather as "inquiry," *vāda*. (According to the *Nyāya-sūtra*, "inquiry" is undertaken among friends. It is not debate.) The word *ucyate*, "we answer," does, nevertheless, signal us to be ready for definitions with Gaṅgeśa's endorsement.

Text (p. 434, Tirupati, and p. 401, Calcutta) and Translation

> ucyate | yatra yad asti tatra tasya anubhavaḥ pramā | tadvati tat-prakārakânubhavo vā | yatra yan na asti tatra tasya jñānaṃ, tad-a-bhāvavati tat-prakāraka-jñānaṃ vā a-pramā |

Gaṅgeśa: We answer. (The right way to characterize veridical awareness is as follows:) veridical awareness is (D^{25}) "awareness of something there where it is."

Or, (D^{26}) "awareness with ϕ as predication content about an object that is ϕ."

Non-veridical awareness (conversely) is (D^{25c}) "cognition of something there where it is not." Or, (D^{26c}) "cognition with ϕ as predication content about an object that is not ϕ."

Comments

D^{25c} is close to a definition Udayana gives in his *Nyāya-kusumâñjali.*[10]

According to D^{25}, an awareness of a pot as a pot with the pot's being a pot would be a veridical awareness. The "there where" expression may be taken to represent a subject of predication, a qualificandum or *viśeṣya* (i.e., a bearer of properties, *dharmin*), and the "of something" as predication content. Note that in Sanskrit, first, only correlative pronouns are used and, second, the use of the locative case suggests presence or absence of properties at a location. But the "there" and "where" are broader in sense, representing in context any possible *dharmin*, "bearer of properties," in relation to any property possibly appearing as predication content. Another translation: veridical awareness is "an awareness that ϕ*x* only if ϕ*x*," in other words, an awareness that an object is ϕ only if it is indeed ϕ.

According to D^{26}, awareness with predication content about a pot as a pot would be a veridical awareness. According to D^{25c}, awareness of mother-of-pearl as silver would be a non-veridical awareness. Or, according to D^{26c}, awareness with predication content about something (mother-of-pearl) that is not silver as silver would be a non-veridical awareness.

Text (p. 438, Tirupati) and Translation

> tad-anyatve sati anubhavatvam eva vā pramātvam | tat-prakārakatvaṃ ca tad-vaiśiṣṭya-viṣayakatvaṃ tad-viśeṣaṇa-jñāna-janyatvaṃ vā | īśvarasya tad-viśiṣṭa-viṣayaṃ jñānaṃ na tu tat-prakārakam | pramâ-pramā-bahir-bhūtam eva, vyavahārân-aṅgatvāt | a-vyapadeśya-padena tad-upagrahasya nāma-jāty-ādi-yojanā-rahitam api pratyakṣam asti iti atra tâtparyam | idaṃ rajatam iti jñānam idantvavati tad-anubhavatvāt pramā, rajatatvâ-bhāvavati tat-prakāraka-jñānatvād a-pramā | aṃśe samūhâlambanaṃ ca na a-pramā | eka-prakārâ-bhāvavaty api tad-a-pratīteḥ |

(**Gaṅgeśa** continues:) Alternatively, simply being an awareness that is other than the non-veridical is to be a veridical awareness (that is to say, the veridical and the non-veridical are mutually exclusive and their definitions are linked).

(What is it to have "predication content," *prakāra*?) Having ϕ as predication content is to have "being qualified by ϕ" as object. Or, it is to be capable of being generated by a cognition of ϕ as a qualifier.

"Having an object qualified by ϕ" applies to God's cognition, but not "having ϕ as predication content" (insofar as this is understood as being generated by a preceding indeterminate perception, since God's cognition is not generated).

Indeterminate cognition is outside the scope of the "veridical/non-veridical" distinction; these terms do not apply. (Veridicality and non-veridicality fall within the province of linguistic practice, and) indeterminate perception is not linguistic. The word *a-vyapadeśya* (in the *Nyāya-sūtra*'s characterization of perception, *NyS* 1.1.4), "non-verbal," is used to include the indeterminate as a type of perception, according to the *Tātparya-ṭīkā* commentary (of Vācaspati Miśra): (unlike cognition of an entity as qualified) it is devoid of the binding (to a cognized object) of name, universal, etc. (that makes a determinate cognition have predication content).

The cognition "This is silver" (when faced with mother-of-pearl) is veridical concerning the "thisness," since the cognized object is a this, and the this is presented in the awareness. The "silver" portion is not veridical since the cognized object is not silver (or, possesses the absence of silverness) while the cognition has that as predication content.

A cognition of a group of things need not be non-veridical concerning each item. Although some bit of predication content may be lacking (with regard to the group or to a particular individual item while some other individual item has it), that (right bit) need not appear (to qualify the whole or the items that lack it).

Comments

In this passage, Gaṅgeśa makes several clarificational remarks.

Although veridicality is a "surplus property" that varies according to what there is veridical cognition *of*, there is the uniformity among veridical cognitions that the definitions capture. How this is to be interpreted will become clear within the next couple of passages. But, above all, Gaṅgeśa points out first, there is the uniformity of the contrast of the veridical and the non-veridical. There is no middle ground—that is, for determinate awarenesses. We also learn here that the distinction does not hold for the indeterminate, *nirvikalpaka*, "cognitions without predication content."

Only the first of the two explanations of what it is to have predication content applies to God's cognition; "being generated by a cognition of ϕ" does not apply, since God's cognition is ungenerated.

Next we have an explicit statement that indeterminate perception falls outside the veridical/non-veridical distinction, and Gaṅgeśa goes on to say a few words about how he understands this type of cognition. The *Nyāya-sūtra* appears to define "perception" (*pratyakṣa*) as "cognition produced through a sensory connection with an object, a cognition that is non-verbal, non-deviating, and determinate'' (*NyS* 1.1.4). But Vācaspati Miśra in his *Tātparya-ṭīkā* commentary argues that two words in the string are not meant to help define perception but to distinguish two types, *nirvikalpaka* (''indeterminate'') perception as opposed to *savikalpaka* (''determinate'').[11] As we shall see in the section on defining perception (below, pp. 327ff), Gaṅgeśa follows Vācaspati. Consonantly, here he uses the word ''non-verbal'' to refer to indeterminate perception. And taking off from a gloss of that resonant term, he explains why indeterminate cognition is neither veridical nor non-veridical. This type of perception is ''non-verbal'' precisely because it lacks the binding to a name, universal, etc., characteristic of (determinate) cognition of an entity as qualified. Verbalizable cognitions attribute, so to say, a property to a property-bearer, and judgments of veridicality and non-veridicality presuppose that an entity has been cognized as qualified by a property presented as predication content. But no universal et cetera appears as predication content in *nirvikalpaka pratyakṣa*.

Finally, Gaṅgeśa takes up the topic of dual or multiple intentionality, asserting, again, the doctrine of partial veridicality. This applies to a cognition of a group of things, ''A pot and a cloth,'' for example. If one were to have such a perception when there is instead a pot and a piece of paper, the awareness would be veridical in the ''pot'' portion alone.

Text (p. 442, Tirupati) and Translation

> nanu evam a-vyāpya-vṛtti-bhāvâ-bhāvayor ekatra pramâ-pramā ca syāt tad-a-bhāvavati tat-prakāraka-jñānatvād iti cet, na | bhinna-bhinnâvacchedena hi vṛkṣe saṃyoga-tad-a-bhāvau, na vṛkṣa-mātre, virodhād an-anubhavāc ca | tathā ca yatra vṛkṣe saṃyogo na tatra tad-a-bhāvaḥ | yad-avacchedena yatra yad asti iti vā vivakṣitam |

Objection: According to your definitions, an awareness of a single object (e.g., a tree) both as having a property (e.g., a monkey-contact) that is non-locus-pervading and at the same time lacking it would be both veridical and non-veridical. The object would in fact exhibit an absence of the property, but the cognition would have the property as predication content.

Gaṅgeśa: No. For, only according to distinct specification (*avaccheda*) would there be both the presence and absence of a contact in a tree (for example). The two would not exist merely in the tree (i.e., throughout the tree); that would be contradictory and is not experienced.

For example, (D^{25} would hold with regard to a monkey-contact and a tree in this way:) the contact (that is cognized) there where it is, in the tree, (secures a veridical awareness). It is not cognized where it is not. Or we should say (veridical awareness is D^{27}), ''(awareness of) something where it is according to the relevant specification.''

Comments

Gaṅgeśa considers the case of an awareness of a qualifier that is non-locus-pervading with respect to its qualificandum, using the stock example of a monkey-contact qualifying a tree. Such cases, it will be recalled, were the straits through which several of the definitions considered earlier could not sail. Gaṅgeśa is exceedingly casual here, given how serious the problem was taken to be earlier. But this just shows how important is the notion of specification with respect to presences and absences (or assertions and denials, F*a* and not F*a*). No property ϕ and its opposite not-ϕ can qualify the same qualificandum except through a difference of specification. This, we should keep in mind, applies also to cognitions that are partially veridical and partially not. Such specification would be required there, too.

Text (p. 451, Tirupati) and Translation

gotvâder api sāsnâdy-avacchedena vṛtteḥ | pāka-rakte śyāmo 'yam iti dhīḥ pramā eva | kadācit tatra tat-sattvāt | idānīṃ śyāma iti tv a-pramā eva | na ca yat-tadbhyāṃ lakṣaṇân-anugamaḥ, na hi pramā sarvatra pramā, kiṃ tu kvacit | tathā ca kiṃ jñānaṃ kutra pramā iti tat-tad-viśeṣasya lakṣyatvena yat-tadbhyām eva lakṣaṇaṃ yuktam |

(**Objection**: But in the case of some veridical cognitions, e.g., "That's a cow," where cowhood is the predication content, no mention of specification is necessary since cowhood is locus-pervading. Thus D^{27} cannot be right.)

Gaṅgeśa: (No.) Even with cowhood, etc., specification could be relevant concerning the individual perceived as having a dewlap, etc. (The cowhood part might be mistaken as shown by the thing's not having a dewlap.) The cognition, "This (was) black," with regard to a pot now red from baking, would be veridical. At one time it was like that. But "Now it is black" would be non-veridical indeed.

Moreover, the correlative pronouns used in the definitions do not make the definitions equivocal (although the objects to which they may refer vary), since veridical awarenesses are not alike in all respects but only in some. For example, the question "Which cognition is veridical in what respect?" can be relevant to the sense in which the pronouns are to be taken when the characterization is correct concerning this or that particular (type of veridical awareness) to be characterized.

Comments

The particularization move made with D^{27}, Gaṅgeśa now suggests, would be irrelevant to awarenesses of locus-pervading properties such as cowhood. So a cognition of Bessie as a cow would have to be simply right or wrong.

Nothing can be in a specified part a cow and in another part not a cow. Cowhood, like all universals, is locus-pervading. But, Gaṅgeśa points out, specification is always potentially relevant with perceptual awarenesses. There is always, as remarked, the veridicality of the qualificandum part, the veridical "thisness" in, for example, "This is silver," when we have an erroneous perception of mother-of-pearl. If it turned out that the object perceived were not Bessie (we walked up closer and found the thing didn't have a dewlap), we could specify that the cow cognition was non-veridical in the cowhood portion but veridical in its qualificandum part.

The last paragraph of the passage prompts us to take an overview. Although veridical awarenesses vary uniformly according to their means of production—perceptions, inferences, and so on are definable by means of regularities in the causal processes—veridicality itself varies according to objects. Thus correlative pronouns have to be used whose meaning varies with substitution. D^{27} is thus doubly sensitive to differences reflected in cognition according to the object cognized. Cognition has no form of its own; it is *nirākāra*. Thus one cannot say so much that is significant about veridical awareness in abstraction from what there is veridical awareness *of*. Gaṅgeśa may be said to endorse a "disquotational view" of truth where the truth of "Snow is white" differs from the truth of "The pot is blue" just in virtue of the difference between snow's being white and the pot's being blue (though we must keep in mind that he is talking about a property of awarenesses, not a property of propositions or sentences). Nevertheless, a very abstract kind of correspondence view is embraced, too, as is captured by his definitions. A veridical cognition is an awareness where the qualifier presented as predication content, no matter what it is, must qualify the awareness's object qua qualificandum. Furthermore, there are first, second, and so on occurrences of the same type of cognition as determined by object, such that, as was emphasized in the section on knowing veridicality, we may infer the veridicality of a cognition C_2 discerned to be like a prior cognition with the same object C_1 on the basis of already knowing C_1 to be veridical without verifying C_2 through action.

In other words, the pronouns *yat* and *tat* in Gaṅgeśa's definitions, "which *x*" and "that *x*," univocally refer to one and the same object as cognized; the pronouns are true correlatives and function logically like a single variable. But the objects to be substituted according to the various cognitions that are veridical are not uniform. Thus the pronouns are not univocal in the sense that the nature of the objects over which they range and which they would refer to in a particular case varies irregularly. Veridical awarenesses vary according to the particular natures of their objects, and there may be veridicality in one respect while there is non-veridicality in another. However, to consider veridicality in general, there is precisely the degree of commonality that

Gaṅgeśa's definitions state there is. The sort of *anugama*, "uniformity," or "consecutive character," which indicates a true universal, does not occur here. But that does not matter. The definitions are restricted appropriately.

Text (p. 452, Tirupati, and p. 413, Calcutta) and Translation

anye tu, anubhavatvam eva prāmāṇyam, bhrame 'py aṃśam ādāya pramā-vyavahārāt | rajatâdi-pramâ-pramā ca viśiṣya lakṣaṇīyā, rajatatvavati tad-anubhavaḥ tad-a-bhāvavati tad-anubhavo vā ity-ādinā | nanv anubhavatvasya pramâ-pramā-sādhāraṇyena taj-jñānasya na niṣkampa-pravṛtty-aṅgatvam iti cet, satyam | viśeṣa-viṣaya-pramāyā eva pravartakatvāt |

(**Gaṅgeśa** continues:) Some say, on the other hand, that to be veridical is simply to be an awareness, for, they say, one speaks of veridical awareness even with respect to erroneous awareness, focusing on the (veridical) part. And while (this is wrong in that) veridical and non-veridical awareness of silver and so on are to be distinguished, the two are to be characterized in relation to one another: e.g., (as has been done here) "awareness of *x* as silver, with *x*'s being silver," and "awareness of it as that, without its being that."

Objection: Awareness as what is common between veridical and non-veridical awareness does not cause unhesitating effort to act (with regard to *x*) when there is cognition of *x*.

Gaṅgeśa: That is true. It is veridical awareness (not *qua* awareness nor even *qua* veridical, but rather) with a particular as its object that is the impeller.

Comments

Again Gaṅgeśa emphasizes the uniformity in the contrast between the veridical and the non-veridical. See the discussion above.

The cash value of awareness is paid out in human action. Various objects of awareness, in their peculiar natures, are what we work to acquire or avoid. We reach out to pick up what we regard as silver—on the basis of a presentation of silverhood predication content—whether the thing reached for is really silver or mother-of-pearl mistaken for silver. A bit of content as taken to be exhibited by an individual cognized is the impeller in both instances. Thus, such impelling is irrelevant to distinguishing the veridical from the non-veridical. It may underline the epistemic default of an assumption of veridicality, but it is not relevant to the characterization project.

Text (p. 454, Tirupati) and Translation

atirikta-viṣayatā-pakṣe viṣayatâśrayâ-vṛtty-a-prakārakânubhavaḥ pramā |

kevalânvayini viṣayatâśrayâ-vṛttir a-vṛttir eva prasiddhaḥ | yad vā yat-prakārikā yā viṣayatā tat-prakāra-samānâdhikaraṇa-viṣayatākaḥ, sva-prakāra-samānâdhikaraṇa-viṣayatāko vā anubhavaḥ pramā | yat-prakārikā yā viṣayatā tat-prakāra-vyadhikaraṇa-viṣayatākaṃ sva-prakāra-vyadhikaraṇa-viṣayatākaṃ vā jñānaṃ bhramaḥ | prakāra-bhedena ekatra viṣayatā-bheda iti lakṣaṇa-dvaya-samāveśāt pramā-bhrama-saṃkaraḥ | yad vā viśeṣya-niṣṭhâtyantâ-bhāvâ-pratiyogi-prakāraka-viṣayatā-pratiyogī, viśeṣya-niṣṭhâtyantâ-bhāva-pratiyogi-prakārân-avacchinna-viṣayatva-pratiyogī vā, viṣayatā-samānâdhikaraṇâtyantâ-bhāva-pratiyogi-prakāraka-viṣayatvâ-pratiyogī vā, viṣayatā-samānâdhikaraṇâtyantâ-bhāva-pratiyogi-prakārân-avacchinna-viṣayatâ-pratiyogī vā anubhavaḥ pramā | sva-samānâdhikaraṇa-prakārân-avacchinna-viṣayatā-pratiyogi jñānaṃ, sva-vyadhikaraṇa-prakārâvacchinna-viṣayatā-pratiyogi jñānaṃ vā bhramaḥ | idaṃ rajatam iti bhrame ca viṣayatā-dvaye vyadhikaraṇa-prakārâvacchinnatva-tad-an-avacchinnatvayoḥ viṣayatva-pratiyogitva-tad-a-pratiyogitvayor a-virodhāt | samūhâlambane ca viṣayatā-bhedān na pramâ-pramā-lakṣaṇe '-vyāpty-ativyāptī |

(**Gaṅgeśa** continues:) According to the view (held by some Navya Naiyāyikas) that objecthood (*viṣayatā*) is something ontologically over and above (the cognized object as well as awareness), veridical awareness would be (D^{28}) "awareness that does not have predication content not located in the substratum of the objecthood." With regard to a claim that has no counterinstance (*kevala-anvayin*, e.g., "This is knowable"), the non-existence (required by the definition) of something not located in the substratum of the objecthood is well-known (according to this Naiyāyika faction).

Or, veridical awareness is (D^{29}) "awareness with a corresponding objecthood that has the same locus with that predication content which is the predication content had by the objecthood." Or, (D^{30}) "awareness with a corresponding objecthood that has the same locus as the awareness's predication content."

Erroneous awareness is (D^{29e}) "cognition (*jñāna*) with a corresponding objecthood that does not have the same locus as that of the predication content, which predication content is that had by the objecthood." Or, (D^{30e}) "cognition with a corresponding objecthood that does not have the same locus as that of its predication content." The mixture of veridical and erroneous awareness (that occurs, e.g., with "This is silver" when the cognized object is mother-of-pearl) is explained through the co-operation of two characterizations (one of the error, one of the right awareness), since there will be distinct objecthoods (one determined by "silverness," the other by "thisness") in the case of the awareness, along with distinct predication content.

Or, veridical awareness is (D^{31}) "awareness correlate to an objecthood with predication content that is not the countercorrelate of an absolute absence resident in the thing cognized." Or, (D^{32}) "awareness correlate to an objecthood not specified by a predication content that is the countercorrelate of an absolute absence resident in the thing cognized." Or, (D^{33}) "awareness that is not correlate to an objecthood with a predication content that is the countercorrelate of an absolute absence that shares the same locus with the objecthood.'' Or, (D^{34}) ''awareness correlate to an objecthood not specified by predication content that is the countercorrelate of an absolute absence sharing the same locus with the objecthood.''

Erroneous awareness is (D^{35e}) ''awareness correlate to an objecthood not specified by predication content sharing the same locus with the objecthood.'' Or, (D^{36c}) ''awareness correlate to an objecthood specified by predication content that does not have the same locus as that of the objecthood.'' The erroneous awareness ''This is silver'' determines two objecthoods. There is no essential opposition between (a) correlation to an objecthood that is specified by predication content that does not have the same locus—or to one not specified like that—and (b) non-correlation to an objecthood so specified or not so specified (in one and the same awareness). Moreover, since there can be distinct objecthoods, there is no problem (for these definitions) presented by the example of a cognition of a group of things: the characterizations of veridical and non-veridical awareness cover neither too much nor too little.

Comments

Bracketing the ontological question, Gaṅgeśa gives characterizations utilizing the relational abstract, objecthood.

First note that by mentioning objecthood, Gaṅgeśa does not need correlative pronouns, and presumably a more traditional, i.e., ontological, type of *anugama* (uniformity or consecutive character) would be preserved. This gain, however, would be outweighed, apparently, by a corresponding ontological cost, namely, objecthood as an additional, irreducible real.

Moreover, Gaṅgeśa rejected D^{22} and D^{23} because each contained a term that was potentially empty; each contained a term that would be empty with respect to the veridical awareness, ''This is knowable'' (occurring in the presence of anything whatsoever). Such a determinate awareness has no counterinstance (*kevala-anvayin*, more literally, ''is exclusively positive,'' i.e., present everywhere). The problem pointed out with the two rejected definitions—and, it would seem, with D^{28} as well—is that they are formulated negatively and thus cannot capture the veridicality of an exclusively positive cognition.

But with D^{28}, Gaṅgeśa can be read as suggesting that there is something—according to Rucidatta, *gagana*, the sky or space—which is an example of the counterinstance required by the definitions when an ''exclusively positive'' predicate is plugged in. To take up Rucidatta's example, the sky can be only a container, not a contained. It itself has no substratum. Thus all the terms of the definition would be exampled even with the awareness, ''This is knowable.'' However, as we shall see with an explicit statement that comes next, probably Gaṅgeśa is not to be understood as endorsing this view but as explaining it according to its best advocates.

Such Naiyāyikas rely on a multiplicity of objecthoods correlate to an awareness in order to explain erroneous cognition that is veridical in part. "A pot and a cloth" is a cognition determining two objecthoods. The analysis of such a cognition of a group of things is parallel to that of an erroneous awareness veridical in its "thisness" part, since an erroneous awareness would also determine (at least) two objecthoods.

Text (p. 456, Tirupati, and p. 422, Calcutta) and Translation

vastutas tu viśeṣaṇatā-viśeṣo na asti eva, mānâ-bhāvāt |

(**Gaṅgeśa continues**:) But in fact, objecthood is not a special qualifierhood, *viśeṣaṇatā* (ontologically over and above cognition and the object), for there is no argument.

Comments

There appeared to be an argument, which was rehearsed, pp. 225ff, above. Gaṅgeśa is saying that the argument is indecisive. The argument is that if I doubt whether a person T is aware of a particular pot or not, the object of my doubt must be something over and above both T's awareness and the particular pot. Thus objecthood would have to be a distinct and irreducible real. If objecthood were not ontologically something over and above both cognition and its object, such doubt could not occur. Gaṅgeśa proceeds to refute this reasoning.

Text and Translation

sāmānyato jñāne jñāte tasya kvacid-viśeṣaṇatā iti sāmānyato viśeṣaṇatā-jñāne 'pi ghaṭam ayaṃ jānāti na vā iti saṃdeha-tādavasthyāt |

(**Gaṅgeśa continues**:) A cognition can be cognized in general simply as a cognition. In other words, a cognition can be cognized in general with its qualificative predicate as (simply) about something in some regard. Although the cognition would have (and would be known as having) such predicationhood in general, doubt can occur (for example) whether a particular person is cognizing or not a particular pot.

Comments

Gaṅgeśa makes a phenomenological appeal in resisting the ontological posit of the rival camp. Apparently he presumes that the rival Naiyāyikas see the object of the doubt as something definite, which cannot, however, be pinned down precisely to one of the accepted categories. Thus they are motivated to make a posit of objecthood as an additional real. Gaṅgeśa denies that the object of the doubt is definite. To be sure, in the example it is about a cognition, but what the cognition is about is undetermined. As about a cognition with undetermined predication content, the object of the doubt does not need to be further specified as this type of thing or that. Doubt has an object, but the object in some instances may not be specifiable other than very generally as "something in some regard."

Text (p. 457, Tirupati) and Translation

tasmāt ghaṭa-taj-jñānayoḥ sva-rūpa-grahe 'pi tadīyatvaṃ na gṛhītam iti tad-viṣayatve saṃdehaḥ | tadīyatvaṃ ca saṃbandhaṃ vinā tat-saṃbandha-svabhāvatvam | tad uktam, "prakāśasya satas tadīyatā-mātra-nibandhanaḥ sva-bhāva-viśeṣaḥ tad-viṣayatvam" iti |

(**Gaṅgeśa continues**:) Therefore, even when the very nature of a pot and of a cognition of it have been grasped, the state of "belonging to that" (*tadīyatva*, or, "relating to that")—i.e., whether it is *that object's* objecthood (as determined by a particular cognition)—need not be grasped. So the doubt could occur whether the objecthood belongs to a particular thing (as determined by a particular cognition).

And the state of "belonging to that" is to be understood as the very nature of a relation to that (i.e., as a self-linking relation), without a (further) relation. Thus has it been said, "A thing's objecthood is a self-linking relation that ties the awareness (determining the objecthood) to a state of belonging to that (thing)."

Comments

Here we are treated to reflection about self-linkage, which is developed in a later section, on *samavāya*, "inherence." Self-linkage is viewed by Gaṅgeśa as accomplished by the second term in a relational complex a-R-b, namely, -R-b. In cases of self-linkage, -R-b is to be taken ontologically as a single thing, a single qualifier-cum-relational-tie with respect to a qualificandum, *viśeṣya*, although we may speak of each of the three separately. Here with objecthood, the qualifier is just cognition itself, which by nature is relational, having an intrinsic, though open-ended, coupler, so to say. Objecthood (*viṣayatā*) is the name of the abstracted relationality, abstracted objectwise; its first term is an object, its second, a cognition. It is matched by another abstracted relationality, subjecthood (*viṣayitā*), which resides in the cognition and has the object cognized as its second term. There is in the cognitive episode, considered in general, nothing real in addition to the cognition and its object. Thus, objecthood, which is one way of talking about the relationship, has to be self-linking, in Gaṅgeśa's view. Later Navya-Nyāya philosophers, for example, Gadādhara, depart from him on the point, agreeing apparently with the rival Naiyāyika camp that Gaṅgeśa has referred to.

It is not hard to appreciate the other side, for ontologically Gaṅgeśa seems to try to have his cake and eat it too. He identifies the relationality of objecthood as what the doubt is about. In this way, he would keep the cake. But he would eat it too in that ontologically this relationality disappears: a self-linking relation is no additional real. Gaṅgeśa is ontologically a conservative, and is loathe to depart from views inherited from Udayana.

The quotation, which is slightly altered from the original, is from Udayana's *Ātma-tattva-viveka*.[12]

Text (p. 458, Tirupati) and Translation

> saṃbandhaṃ vinā kathaṃ tadīyatvam, saṃbandhasya eva svabhāvatvāt, yathā tava eva viśeṣaṇatāyām | anyathā an-avasthānāt | anyatra api sva-rūpa-saṃbandhe eṣā eva gatiḥ | anyathā sāmānyena a-bhāva-samavāyayor jñāne 'dhikaraṇe jñāte tayoḥ saṃśayo na syāt, adhikaraṇa-tad-ubhaya-sva-rūpāṇāṃ jñātatvāt | tatra apy a-bhāva-samavāyayor viśeṣaṇatā-viśeṣo na gṛhīta iti cet, na | sāmānyatas tad-grahe 'pi saṃśayāt |

(**Gaṅgeśa continues**:) If it is asked (by you who advocate the view that objecthood is something ontologically over and above the cognition and its object) how without a (further) relation there can be the state of "belonging to that," we say that it is the self-linking nature of the relation itself, as you yourself accept with "qualifierhood" (*viśeṣaṇatā*). Otherwise, there would be an infinite regress. There are other cases as well where, without understanding the relations involved to be self-linking, an impasse would ensue.

If this move were ruled out, there could be no doubt in general concerning an absence nor about inherence when there is cognition of a locus, since the locus and the general nature of either (the absence or the inherence) would be known.

Objection: There, too, i.e., in a case of an absence or of inherence (as in other cases of doubt), the particular instance of a qualifier would also not be grasped (and thus doubt could occur).

Gaṅgeśa: No. For, that (particular qualifier) is grasped in the doubt but only in general (as something in some regard).

Comments

Gaṅgeśa holds that a cognition and its object, an absence and its locus, and inherence in relation to those things related by it are related through self-linkage. His view is that self-linkage varies with each particular instance, such that no individual cognition is immune to doubt in virtue of having an object. Thus this is unlike the knowledge of cowhood implicit in the veridical awareness, "A cow." We can generalize about cows from the example of Bessie, but we cannot generalize from the objecthood relation which is self-linking. Doubt rules out inherence, which is single and uniform (*anugama*), as the relator. Self-linkage, in contrast, is unique in all its occurrences.

There is further advantage to the self-linkage notion. Self-linkage allows us to talk about relations while avoiding an infinite regress. To speak of self-linkage with respect to a self-linking term is to abstract the (open-ended) relational hook that is considered intrinsic to a qualifier without committing oneself to the existence of a relation as an additional real.

Another argument is that since we have to invoke self-linkage to solve other problems, there is no harm in invoking it with respect to objecthood. Absential qualifierhood is held, in Nyāya, to be self-linking (see below, pp. 385ff). Abstraction is possible without ontological commitment. Abstracting objecthood (qualifierhood, etc.) allows us to talk about cognitions in general and thus to do our epistemology and logic.

Text (p. 459, Tirupati) and Translation

> yat tu samūhâlambana-viśiṣṭa-jñānayor viśeṣânubhavād viśiṣṭa-jñāne viśeṣaṇatām ādāya api samūhâlambana-saṃbhavāt | tatra api viśeṣaṇatântara-svīkāre an-avasthā | samūhâlambanāt tu viśiṣṭa-jñānasya viśeṣaḥ kāraṇa-kṛtaḥ kārya-kṛtaḥ prakāra-kṛto vā | prakāro 'pi viśeṣaṇatā-viśeṣaḥ sa ca dharmiṇy eva astv iti cet, na | tam ādāya api samūhâlambana-saṃbhavāt |

Objection: Since a difference is experienced between a cognition of a group of things and a cognition of an entity as qualified (as just a single thing), in the case of the latter the cognition's object has to be considered a different type of qualifier (than those in a cognition of a group).

Gaṅgeśa: No. Even considering the qualifierhood (to be no more than what pertains to individuals), cognition of a group of things is possible. Furthermore, if another type of qualifierhood were postulated, there would be an infinite regress.

The difference between cognition of a group of things and a cognition of an entity as qualified is attributable to different causes, to different effects, or to different predication content (not to an ontologically distinct type of qualifier).

Objection: Predication content (*prakāra*) is also a distinct type of qualifier. And it exists just in the thing cognized (in the *dharmin*, the bearer of properties). (So you need not worry about accepting an ontologically distinct type of qualifier, which is, again, what you need to explain cognition of a group of things.)

Gaṅgeśa: No. Cognition of a group of things is possible although we take that (*prakāra*) as we have explained it.

Comments

The question is whether a cognition of a group of things, e.g., of a pot and a cloth, can be analyzed in the same way as a cognition of a single qualified thing, i.e., invoking the schema a-R-b. Gaṅgeśa avers that it can be, that there is no essential difference. Indeed, if one required an additional tool of analysis to handle a cognition of a group of two things, then there would be no end to the additional tools needed for analyzing awareness of three things, four, and so on. A cognition of a group of things has more than one bit of predication content. But while predication contents can vary, the differences do not force us to accept fundamentally distinct types of qualification.

Predication content is a distinct type of qualifier; it is a qualifier that appears as an object of awareness. Not all qualifiers so appear, since everything is not cognized in its full array of properties (except by God). We have no problem analyzing a cognition of a group of things using the notion of predication content as we have explained it.

anyathā-khyāti-vāda

DISCOURSE ON PERCEPTUAL PRESENTATION OF SOMETHING AS OTHER THAN WHAT IT IS

Text (p. 463, Tirupati, and p. 430, Calcutta) and Translation

nanu sarva-jñānānāṃ yathârthatvāt pramā-lakṣaṇe viśeṣaṇasya vyāvartyâ-prasiddher viśeṣaṇa-vaiyarthyam, anyathā-khyātau mānâ-bhāvāt | tathā hi, rajatârthi-pravṛtti-viṣayatvaṃ rajatatva-prakārakânubhava-viṣayatva-vyāpyaṃ rajatârthi-pravṛtti-viṣaya-mātra-vṛtti-dharmatvāt rajata-mātra-vṛtti-dharma-vad ity anyathā-khyāti-vyāpyaṃ siddhyati ity a-prāpta-kālatvaṃ, rajata-mātra-vṛttitvaṃ ca upādhiḥ |

Pūrvapakṣin (a Prābhākara): All cognitions are in conformity with their objects (*yathârthatva*). Thus, regarding the definition of veridical cognition (that you have defended above), the qualification (*tadvati tat-prakāraka*, "having ϕ predication content about an object that is ϕ") is useless, in that the qualification fails to exclude what you want to exclude (namely, non-veridical cognition), since there is no argument to show that *anyathā-khyāti*, "a cognitive presentation of something as other than what it is," ever takes place.

For example, the following argument suffers from the fallacy "being mistimed," since one would prove something pervaded by (i.e., entailing) the doctrine of *anyathā-khyāti*, "a cognitive presentation of something as other than what it is" (instead of proving *anyathā-khyāti* itself in the proper argument order). (The argument is) being the object of effort of a silver-seeking person (*a*) is (S) pervaded by being the object of an awareness whose predication content is silverness, *since* it (*a*) is (H) a property that exists only in the objects of effort of silver-seeking persons, like (*b*) the property of existing only in silver (viz., silverhood).

It also is vitiated by the undercutter (*upādhi*), existing-only-in-silver (U).

Comments[1]

The Naiyāyika view of perceptual illusion—called "error" (*bhrama*) in philosophic shorthand—is that something with which a sense organ is in relation, a qualificandum, is presented as "other than what it is," as having a qualifier it does not in fact have. In other words, a perceptual awareness's predication content does not reside in the qualificandum.

Considering how intricately views and arguments about perceptual illusion connect with other areas of theory, this section, which is dominated by hair-splitting exchanges between Nyāya and Prābhākara Mīmāṃsā, is tedious. Illusion is philosophically exciting, and I think that Gaṅgeśa expects that we bring excitement to the text. Since we are not told why the debate is so important, I sense that he assumes his audience to be familiar with the centrality of illusion to earlier (Indian) philosophy. Throughout the centuries of classical Indian philosophy, Buddhists and Advaita Vedāntins use arguments about illusion to attack Nyāya and Mīmāṃsā and to establish an anti-realist metaphysics. In the larger context, it's as though Gaṅgeśa's quarrel with Prābhākara Mīmāṃsā is about which realist theory better serves the overall realist cause.[2]

By flatly denying that any cognition could be non-veridical, the Prābhākara meets head-on the argument of the subjectivists and anti-realists that illusion shows a perception's object not to be a feature of the world but to be contributed somehow from the side of the subject. If, according to the Buddhists and others, a rope can be perceived as a snake, with no difference, from the perspective of the perceiver, between the illusion and a veridical snake perception, all our experience could be illusory in relation to a *nirvāṇa* experience, a mystical experience of a transcendent reality (or "Nothingness," *śūnyatā*). But if the way people act and talk can be explained while maintaining that all cognition is veridical, that possibility is undermined. Gaṅgeśa, however, holds that the subjectivists are right to this extent: sometimes a person does perceive *a* to be F when *a* is not in fact F and cannot discern (at that time) from her own first-person perspective that she is having a perception that is non-veridical. But the predication content, the presentation of F-hood, nevertheless originates in things' really being F, through previous veridical experience of F-hood. Here we touch the heart of Nyāya's realism. Snakehood is available to become illusory predication content through previous veridical experience of snakes. It gets fused into a current perception by means of a foul-up in the normal causal process through the arousing of a snakehood memory-impression formed by previous experience of snakes. The content of an illusion is to be explained causally as generated by real features of real things just as veridical perception is too, though illusion involves the projection into current perception of predication content preserved in memory whereas at least in some cases (for example, those where an indeterminate perception furnishes the qualifier) veridical perception need not be shaped by memory (as explained in the section, "Indeterminate Perception," below). Illusion is a perceptual (mis)taking something to be what it is not, a seeing or perceiving it through a misplaced qualifier.

Thus a key difference between Gaṅgeśa and the Prābhākara concerns the possibility—denied by the Prābhākara and affirmed by the Naiyāyika—of perceptual presentation of a qualifier furnished by memory. The Naiyāyika takes snakehood, for example, to be fused into the perceptual presentation verbalized as "This is a snake" when the object sensorily contacted is a rope, whereas the Prābhākara holds that the rope alone is perceived and the snakehood is *separately* cognized in a remembering albeit the separation goes unnoticed. Indeed, it is that ignorance—the separation going unnoticed, a lack of cognition of the remembering and the perceiving as distinct—that is responsible for error—which is itself not cognitive but a matter of acting on the ignorance. The Naiyāyika insists, in contrast, that the snakehood is presented perceptually, that illusion is something positive and cognitive, being a "presentation otherwise," a perceiving of an object in some way that it is not in fact.

In the opening stretch of text, a Prābhākara *pūrvapakṣin* attacks various inferences that have been put forth by Gaṅgeśa's predecessors purporting to prove the Naiyāyika view. A first argument is purported to fail to target the real conclusion and thus to invite the censure of "being mistimed." The mistimed is a fallacy—more precisely, a *nigraha-sthāna*, a defeater and point of censure—according to conventional debate rules. The inference does not directly establish the Naiyāyika view in that a supplementary inference would be required. This seems, however, a quibble. The point of the inference is that a person intent on silver but whose effort results in the obtaining of mother-of-pearl would be someone whose guiding cognition presented the thing sought *as* silver, i.e., as qualified by silverhood, which would be a presentation of mother-of-pearl as other than what it is.

But this first inference is also said to face an "undercutter," *upādhi*, a more serious charge. And in that context it is important to see that the Naiyāyika's is a two-step argument, as will be explained. Below, there are a string of undercutters put forth to undercut or block a string of *prima facie* inferences for the Nyāya view. So let us examine this first one carefully, using a simplified predicate logic (see also, above, pp. 160–61, on the logic of the *upādhi*).

The subject of the inference, or *pakṣa*, here an abstract individual, *a*, is:

a: being the object of effort of a silver-seeker.

The probandum, that which is to be proved, or *sādhya*, S, is:

S: being pervaded by being the object of an awareness whose predication content is silverness.

The prover, the *sādhana* or *hetu*, H, is:

H: existing only in the objects of effort of silver-seekers.

And the confirming example, *b*, a known locus of both S and H, again here an abstract individual:

b: the property of existing only in silver.

To review the inferential pattern, all instances of a prover property have to be instances of a probandum property, that is to say, the prover has be *pervaded by* the probandum, such that an H entails an S (the S set has to have the H set as a subset), and there has to be an inferential subject known to possess the prover, as well as a known example of the prover and the probandum occurring together (other than the inferential subject), if an inference is cogent. A successful undercutter (U), on the other hand, has to pervade the S, such that an S entails a U (the U set has to have the S set as a subset, at least according to a standard definition that Gaṅgeśa is apparently using) while not pervading the H (the H set is not a subset of the U set). The undercutter (*upādhi*) here is:

U: existing only in silver.

The effort of a person intent on picking up a piece of silver has a certain "object" in two senses of the term, (a) what he thinks he is about to pick up, which is definitely silver, based on the silverhood predication content of a prompting cognition, and (b) what he is actually about to pick up, which is possibly silver, possibly mother-of-pearl or something else that looks like silver. Or, this is how things seem from the Naiyāyika perspective, where the object mentioned in the inference is understood in both senses such that the object about to be picked up could be mother-of-pearl appearing as "other than what it is." From the Mīmāṃsaka perspective, the object is understood only in the second sense, which is, he claims, the thing perceived, the thing with which there is current perceptual connection. For the Naiyāyika, every instance of effort so defined will be guided by an awareness having as its object something appearing as silver available to pick up, i.e., something appearing to be qualified by silverness whether or not silverness is there in fact (S*a*). Why? Because wherever H, there S, and *a* is an H. And it does seem as though, like *b*, which is both an H and an S, wherever there is the property that is defined as existing only in things that are sought by people seeking silver (whether the objects they pick up are silver or things that look like silver), we will also find an S, namely, something that is sought on the basis of the predication content, silverness, in the awareness that directs the seeking of silver. In other words, such predication content is invariably silverness, the something awareness of which guides the effort whether or not there is silver in fact. Let *a* be instantiated by a piece of mother-of-pearl (here is the second step). Thus would be established the Naiyāyika view.

However, according to the *pūrvapakṣin*, it is not the case that wherever H there S, because wherever S there U, and some things H are not U. To elaborate, the object of a silver presentation itself exists in silver, to speak ontologically. Silverness exists only in silver. So S is pervaded by U. But some H are not U. Indeed, the subject of the inference itself, *a*, is an H but need not be a U, and its not being a U is crucial, as we noted, to a second inference needed to establish the doctrine of *anyathā-khyāti* (where we assume *a* is a piece of mother-of-pearl, more precisely, being-mother-of-pearl).

The undercutter makes a distinction. The property of being mother-of-pearl, mother-of-pearl-hood, does not exist only in silver. But it is an H, it is sometimes a property of that which is sought by a person seeking silver. In this way, the inference is undermined.

The undercutter is also an element in an inference whose conclusion is in line with the Prābhākara Mīmāṃsaka view. For, if we suppose that U (existing only in silver) occurs on or qualifies this subject (being the object of effort of a silver-seeker), then the Naiyāyika's subject and crucial example, mother-of-pearl, will be excluded. The Naiyāyika's second step will be blocked. Then those cases where U is exhibited along with H will indeed be cases of S (being pervaded by being the object of an awareness whose predication content is silverness). All cognition is veridical, but the object of effort may be furnished by a remembering whose difference from a perceiving is not noticed, according to Prābhākara Mīmāṃsā.

In other words, while it seems that sometimes people do reach out to pick up a piece of mother-of-pearl believing on an experiential basis that it is silver, this description is contested. The Naiyāyika inference presupposes that the silverness that exists only in silver can be presented experientially in cases where the object reached out for is mother-of-pearl, since Nyāya holds that the guiding experience could be a cognitive error, an awareness of mother-of-pearl as "other than what it is." The Prābhākara, who does not accept cognitive error, counters by saying that it is not shown that such silverhood, silverhood so interpreted, is being *experientially* presented in cases where silver is sought but the object reached out for is mother-of-pearl. The Prābhākara holds, in contrast, that the mother-of-pearl is all that is being presented perceptually, and that the silverness is smuggled in by a separate remembering.

Or, the issue is perhaps better framed as whether or not the erroneous presentation of silver is a single, relational cognition (of something as qualified by silverhood)—the Naiyāyika view—or two cognitions, a perception and a memory, with the difference between them unnoticed—the Prābhākara position.

With the following arguments, I attempt to reconstruct the inferences only in informal, intuitive terms, better to keep in front of us the main issues.

Text (p. 468, Tirupati) and Translation

śukti-vṛtti-jñāna-viṣayatā rajatatva-prakārikā rajatârthitā-janya-pravṛtti-viṣaya-vṛtti-viṣayatātvāt rajata-vṛtti-viṣayatā-vad ity atra rajata-vṛttitvam upādhiḥ |

(The **pūrvapakṣin** continues:) The cognitive objecthood that exists in mother-of-pearl is in its predication content portion silverhood, *since* it is an objecthood that exists in the object of the effort of those intent on silver, like the objecthood that exists in silver. Here the undercutter (*upādhi*) is: being that which exists in silver.

Comments

That which exists in silver, the undercutter, pervades the probandum since the silverhood presented by a cognition as its predication content exists (objectwise) in silver (both parties agree). And it also does not pervade the prover since the actual object of people intent on silver is sometimes not silver but mother-of-pearl.

The first inference focused on the object desired. This second inference focuses on the cognitive object in its qualificandum portion, the "being-a-this" or "being-in-front," which exists in the object that is in sensory connection but is somehow erroneously cognized. From the Naiyāyika perspective, the argument looks good since it captures our intuition about the silver/mother-of-pearl example that we see, in the physical sense, mother-of-pearl, such that it is the object of our seeing, but also that we see it in such a fashion that its being an object for us involves its appearing as silver. However, this only appears to be a good inference, says the Prābhākara *pūrvapakṣin*, because the Naiyāyika fails to realize the ramification of the fact that silverhood exists only in silver. The objecthood that exists in mother-of-pearl does not somehow contain as predication content silverhood, which belongs to a different cognition altogther.

The next two inferences focus on the cognitive presentation in its predication content portion.

Text and Translation

rajatatvam a-rajata-vṛtti-jñāna-viṣayatâvacchedakam a-rajata-viṣaya-pravṛtti-hetu-jñāna-prakāratvāt śuktitva-vad ity atra rajatâ-vṛttitvam upādhiḥ |

(The **pūrvapakṣin** continues by anticipating and undercutting another inference in favor of *anyathā-khyāti*:) Silverhood specifies a cognitive objecthood that exists in things that are not silver, *since* it is the predication content (portion of a cognitive objecthood) of a cognition that causes effort directed toward things that are not silver, like mother-of-pearl-hood. Here the undercutter is: being that which does not exist in silver.

Comments

The Prābhākara *pūrvapakṣin* denies that silverhood could do what is claimed. Nothing that specifies a cognitive objecthood existing objectwise in things that are not silver could exist in silver. Such abstracts, *avacchedaka*s, have themselves ontological loci. The issue is whether (e.g.) silverhood, which exists objectwise only in silver, could specify a cognitive objecthood that exists subjectwise in a perceptual presentation of mother-of-pearl with which a sense organ is in connection.

Text and Translation

rajata-prakārikā jñāna-viṣayatā a-rajata-vṛttiḥ a-rajata-niṣṭhâtyantâ-bhāvâ-pratiyoginī vā a-rajata-viṣaya-pravṛtti-hetu-jñāna-viṣayatātvāt śukti-vṛtti-viṣayatā-vad ity atra rajatâ-vṛttitvam upādhiḥ |

(The **pūrvapakṣin** continues:) The cognitive objecthood whose predication content portion is silverhood exists in that which is not silver, or, it is not the absentee of an absolute absence that rests in that which is not silver, *since* it is the objecthood of a cognition that causes effort directed toward objects that are not silver, like the objecthood that exists in mother-of-pearl. Here the undercutter is: not existing in silver.

Comments

The inference has a disjunctive probandum, but the undercutter pervades both options: the property of not-existing-in-silver determines a set U that pervades—in being coterminous with—the set of things that are not silver (the first disjunct), and it is also coterminous with the set of things that are not the absentee, etc. (the second disjunct—which expression reduces to the first anyhow). But the inferential subject itself is something not not-existing-in-silver (not U); thus the undercutter fails to pervade the prover in that the prover is known to qualify the inferential subject. The objecthood (mentioned in the description of the inferential subject) exists, from the Prābhākara perspective, in silver, indeed in silver alone!

Text (p. 470, Tirupati) and Translation

viṣayatāyā nirastatvāc ca | vivāda-padaṃ rajata-jñānaṃ śukti-viṣayakaṃ śuktau pravartaka-jñānatvāt śukti-jñāna-vad ity atra jñānamānêṣṭa-bhedâ-grahe kāraṇatâvacchedakaṃ rajata-jñānaṃ na pravartakam ity a-siddhiḥ |

(The **pūrvapakṣin** continues:) And since (inferences focused on) objecthood have been thrown out, (let us try as the subject of an inference) the putative cognition of silver: this is a cognition whose object is mother-of-pearl, *since* it is a cognition motivating effort toward mother-of-pearl, like a cognition of mother-of-pearl. Here the fallacy is that of an "unestablished prover" (a prover's failing to qualify its purported subject), in that, when there is no grasping of the distinctness between that which is being cognized and that which is desired, what specifies the causality is not a cognition of silver. A cognition of silver does not motivate the effort (but rather a cognition of mother-of-pearl along with a memory of silver, that is, as is said, with the distinction not grasped).

Comments

The Naiyāyika view of error as "something appearing as other than what it is" would be established, we should keep in mind, with the establishment of an error as a cognition of an entity as qualified. The object misperceived would be the cognition's qualificandum and what it is misperceived as the cognition's predication content. The Naiyāyika tries to establish this view by making us attend to the effort of mistakingly reaching for mother-of-pearl. What other than a cognition of an entity as so qualified could cause that effort?

The *pūrvapakṣin* himself is well aware that the dispute centers on whether there can be a cognition whose predication content is silverhood while the object perceived is mother-of-pearl, and he denies the possibility. He has an alternative theory, and from his perspective the Naiyāyika prover is a non-entity unable to qualify the subject of his inference.

Text (p. 472, Tirupati, and p. 437, Calcutta) and Translation

> śuktī rajata-jñāna-viṣayatâśrayaḥ rajatârthi-pravṛtti-viṣayatvāt rajata-vad ity atra rajatatvam upādhiḥ |

(The **pūrvapakṣin** continues:) Mother-of-pearl is the locus of a silver cognition's objecthood, *since* it is the object of the effort of the silver-seeker, like silver. Here the undercutter (*upādhi*) is: silverhood.

Comments

According to the Prābhākara *pūrvapakṣin*, any locus of a silver cognition's objecthood would be silver, i.e., a locus of silverhood. No mother-of-pearl could be such.

From the Naiyāyika perspective, the inference is also no good, since, as is pointed out, silverhood could itself be the locus of the predication content portion of a cognition's objecthood, and silverhood pervades the probandum—through the vaguenes of the term "objecthood" in the description of the probandum ("is the locus of a silver cognition's objecthood"). But it does not pervade the prover, since in some cases of error the object of effort is mother-of-pearl.

Next a final inference rejected by the *pūrvapakṣin*.

Text and Translation

> śuktau rajatârthi-pravṛttiḥ sva-dharmi-dharmika-rajatatva-prakāraka-jñāna-sādhyā rajatârthi-pravṛttitvāt rajata-pravṛtti-vad ity atra rajata-viṣayatvam upādhiḥ sva-padârthân-anugamaś ca | tat-parityāge tu rajatârthi-pravṛtti-dharmi-dharmika-rajatatva-prakāraka-jñānena ubhaya-siddhena rajata-smaraṇena arthântaram |

(The **pūrvapakṣin** continues:) An effort, directed toward mother-of-pearl, of someone seeking silver is produced by a cognition whose predication content is silverhood and whose qualificandum is the object, qua qualificandum, of itself (the effort), *since* it is effort of someone seeking silver, like effort directed toward (real) silver. Here the undercutter (*upādhi*) is: silver's being the object (of effort). And (this inference is no good for a further reason, namely) because the word "itself" (*sva*) is ambiguous.

But if, to avoid that (the problem of ambiguity), (the probandum is explicitly said to be "is produced) by a cognition whose predication content is silverhood and whose qualificandum is the object, qua qualificandum, of the effort of someone seeking silver," then, inasmuch as that cognition is accepted by both of us as a memory of silver, there is the fallacy of another meaning (or "irrelevance," *arthântara*).

Comments

An effort's qualificandum is the object that it is directed to. Efforts also have predication content, but that is not relevant at this point.

This final rejected inference focuses on another factor that the Naiyāyika finds involved in the chain that starts with an erroneous cognition and ends with unsuccessful effort, the effort, for instance, of a person seeking silver and reaching out for mother-of-pearl. The problem is still, of course, the nature of the cognition, or dual cognitions (in the Prābhākara view), responsible for motivating effort directed toward silver when the object in front is mother-of-pearl. The Naiyāyika does accept, as is pointed out here, that a memory—or at least a memory transmitter, or impression, *saṃskāra*—is responsible for furnishing the candidate predication content, silverhood. In the Nyāya view, presented silverhood is veritably fused with the qualificandum presentation, through an "extraordinary sensory connection," *a-laukika-saṃnikarṣa*, resulting in a single cognition that has the real mother-of-pearl (under the aspect of a "this") as the qualificandum portion of its objecthood and silverhood as its predication content. The Prābhākara holds, in contrast, that there is no such fusion, but rather two cognitions, with the distinctness between them unrecognized.

So, from the *pūrvapakṣin*'s perspective, "silver's being the object" is a successful undercutter, since any cognition whose predication content is silverhood will have silver as object. Moreover, there is also the problem that such effort as is referred to in the statement of the probandum is not just to be assumed to be motivated by a cognition understood according to the Naiyāyika position. The statement suffers from an ambiguity that is made explicit at the end of the passage.

Text (p. 472, Tirupati) and Translation

ucyate | rajatârthitā-janyā śuktau pravṛttir iṣṭa-viṣaya-viśiṣṭa-jñāna-sādhyā pravṛttitvāt śuktau śukty-arthi-pravṛtti-vat | na ca iṣṭa-viṣaya-pravṛttitvam upādhiḥ, sādhana-viśeṣitatvāt |

Gaṅgeśa: We answer. An effort, directed toward mother-of-pearl, generated by a desire for silver, is produced by a cognition of an entity as qualified, a cognition whose object is that of the effort directed toward what is wanted, *since* it is an effort, like an effort directed toward mother-of-pearl on the part of someone seeking mother-of-pearl.

And being-effort-directed-toward-a-desired-object is not an undercutter (*upādhi*), for that is (just) the prover qualified.

Comments

That which is to be proved as qualifying the misdirected effort is "being produced by a cognition of an entity as qualified"—not by two cognitions with the difference between them unnoticed—a cognition, that is to say, "that has the same object as that of the effort it produces." This probandum, the set of things, namely, that are productions of this type, includes the set determined by the reason or prover, the set of things that are efforts, since desires, as well as efforts, are productions falling within the probandum set. The series of causes runs in the following order: cognition, desire, effort, activity. The putative undercutter, the set of things that are efforts directed toward a desired object, meets the second requirement for a true undercutter (according to the standard definition of an *upādhi* that is to be assumed as the working definition at this point in the text: see above, p. 160), that is, it does not pervade the prover set (all efforts), because it is itself included in that set, being narrower in extension. But for that very reason it does not pervade the probandum set, according to Gaṅgeśa who of course sees the probandum set as pervading the prover set and thus as necessarily pervading it, too. Thus he says that the putative undercutter is simply a qualified form of the prover.

Text (p. 477, Tirupati, and p. 443, Calcutta) and Translation

yad vā rajatêcchā-janya-śukti-viṣaya-pravṛtti-janaka-rajatatva-prakārakaṃ jñānaṃ śukti-viśeṣyakaṃ śukti-pravṛtti-prayojaka-jñānatvāt śuktau śukty-arthi-pravṛtti-janaka-jñāna-vat | avacchedakatve 'pi prayojakatvān na a-siddhiḥ | hetutvam api tasya sādhayiṣyāmaḥ |

(**Gaṅgeśa** continues:) Alternatively, a cognition (1) whose predication content is silverhood and (2) which generates effort toward an object, mother-of-pearl—effort that is (also) generated by desire for silver—is a cognition whose qualificandum is mother-of-pearl, *since* it is a cognition motivating effort directed toward mother-of-pearl, like a cognition which is about a bit of mother-of-pearl and which generates effort (directed toward it) in a person seeking mother-of-pearl.

Although a specifier may be suspected (such that silverhood would not itself be a cause, but only a specifier of a type of causality, with the true cause as the particular, the cognition), silverhood is the motivator (*prayojaka*, and a motivator is a true cause). Therefore, there is no fault of an ''unestablished prover'' (i.e., the prover not qualifying the subject).

(Just how) it is a cause, we shall show (in what follows).

Comments

Naiyāyikas generally maintain that causal relations are fundamentally relations among particulars. So silverhood as a universal appearing as a cognition's predication content could only specify a set of particular cognitions that are causes, and not itself be a cause. But, Gaṅgeśa says, there is a sense, namely, that of the motivator, *prayojaka*, in which such predication content can be considered a cause. This is explained just below (p. 484, Tirupati).

Gaṅgeśa's argument may be reconstructed as follows. Any cognition that prompts a person to reach out for a piece of mother-of-pearl thinking that it is silver has the piece of mother-of-pearl as its object qua qualificandum. The reason is that the cognition prompts effort toward the piece of mother-of-pearl, which is its qualificandum. In this way it is like a cognition having mother-of-pearl-hood as predication content that prompts the effort of a person who wants a piece of mother-of-pearl to pick up a veritable piece mother-of-pearl. Thus, it becomes obvious that *anyathā-khyāti* does occur.

Text (p. 478, Tirupati) and Translation

tathā-vidham idaṃ jñānam vā rajatatva-prakārakaṃ rajatêcchā-janya-pravṛtti-hetu-jñānatvāt satya-rajata-jñāna-vat | na ca grahana-smaraṇayor viśiṣṭasya jñānasya vā pakṣatve bādha āśrayâ-siddhir vā, ubhaya-siddhena śukti-niṣṭha-pravṛtti-hetutvena pakṣatvāt | anyathā sādhya-tad-a-bhāvavataḥ pakṣatvena anumānôcchedaḥ |

(**Gaṅgeśa** continues:) Or, this cognition that is of such a type (i.e., generating effort toward mother-of-pearl) has as its predication content silverhood, *since* it is a cognition that is a cause of effort that is (also) generated by a desire for silver, like a cognition of real silver.

And there is neither the fault of patent falsehood, with respect to the prover's qualifying the subject, nor of the subject not being known, whether the subject be considered a cognition of an entity as qualified (our view) or a perceptual grasping and remembering (your view). For, the subject (whether taken the one way or the other) is accepted by both of us as a cause with respect to the effort attaining mother-of-pearl. Otherwise (i.e., if a subject could not be only partly agreed to) such that it could be known neither as possessing a probandum nor as not possessing it, inference (as a general possibility) would be destroyed.

Comments

As indicated, effort is directed toward something, its qualificandum, under a certain predication content. So, like a cognition, its intentionality is to be understood as impregnated with a qualifier-qualificandum relationality.

From the Prābhākara perspective, the inference appears subject to the fallacies mentioned, since there is no such cognition of an entity as qualified. But the opponent does accept, Gaṅgeśa tells us, the prover's qualifying some such subject, a subject sufficiently agreed upon to allow the inference. Using inferences in debate would be impossible if everything had to be agreed to in advance.

Next, Gaṅgeśa directs an argument against Vaiśeṣikas, who hold that inherence, which is often the ontological tie between a qualifier and a qualificandum, is not itself perceptually grasped.

Text (p. 480, Tirupati, and p. 446, Calcutta) and Translation

samavāyâtīndriyatva-vādinaṃ prati a-gṛhītâ-saṃsarga-dharma-dharmi-viṣayakam ekaṃ jñānam eva viśiṣṭa-jñānaṃ siddhyati | na ca evam ubhaya-khyātiḥ na anyathā-khātir iti vācyaṃ | vyadhikaraṇa-prakāraka-jñānasya tattvāt | na ca visaṃvādi-pravṛtty-a-janakam upādhiḥ | tathā-vidhe idaṃ-jñāne rajata-jñāne ca tvan-mate sādhyâ-vyāpakatvāt | na api doṣâ-janyatvaṃ, parasya jñāna-mātre tathātvāt | anyathā tayor eva sādhyâ-vyāpakatvāt | na ca a-prayojakatvaṃ | iṣṭa-puro-varti-viśiṣṭa-jñānasya pravṛtti-hetutvāt |

(**Gaṅgeśa** continues:) (Now) to those who hold that inherence transcends (what is graspable by) the senses: (we say) a single cognition, whose object is a property and a property-bearer with their unrelatedness not grasped, simply proves (our view of error as) a cognition of an entity as qualified.

And it should not be said that in this way (error would be) a presentation of both (a qualifier and a qualificandum separately), not a "presentation otherwise" (*anyathā-khyāti*). For, otherwise-presentation (error) is a cognition whose predication content belongs (objectwise) to a different locus (than the qualificandum that the cognition determines).

Further, the (putative) undercutter, *upādhi*, not-producing-ineffective-effort, is not a true undercutter. For, on your view (too, i.e., on the Prābhākara view) it fails to pervade the probandum (in the inference, above, where the probandum is "is a cognition whose qualificandum is mother-of-pearl"). The pervasion fails concerning (the subject, viz.,) "the type of cognition (that generates effort directed toward mother-of-pearl) that is this cognition (i.e., whose qualificandum is mother-of-pearl)," and concerning "cognition of silver" as well.

Nor is not-being-produced-by-an-epistemic-defect an undercutter, since, for the other (view, too, i.e., the Prābhākara view), with respect to the (two) cognition(s), error is so conceived (and thus the putative undercutter fails to exclude an instance of the prover property). Otherwise (if error is not accepted as due to a defect), both the two (putative undercutters) will fail to pervade the probandum.

Nor (are the inferences examples of) the fallacy "ineffectual" (i.e., where the prover fails to be pervaded by the probandum, as is shown by consideration of counterfactual cases), since the effort is caused by a cognition of an entity as qualified, the thing that is both desired and is in front.

Comments

According to Vaiśeṣika, the relation between a property and its bearer is not perceptually grasped. Thus, error would have to be a cognition of an entity as qualified, because there could be no relational absence known whereby the two could be cognized as separated.

The view that error is "a presentation of both" would apply to our standard example in this way: "Silver *and* mother-of-pearl," where two things would each be perceived correctly through a property each actually possesses. Thus there would be no error. In rejecting the view, Gaṅgeśa in effect gives us a definition of *anyathā-khyāti*, error as a "cognition whose predication content belongs (objectwise) to a different locus (than the qualificandum that the cognition determines)."

However error is conceived—whether in the Naiyāyika manner or the Prābhākara—not-generating-ineffective-effort is not an undercutter for Gaṅgeśa's inferences, since both parties hold that a cognition—or the Prābhākara's double cognitions—sometimes generate ineffective effort.

The final point is a general one summarizing the Naiyāyika case as one of successful inferences supported by the reasoning given. In other words, Gaṅgeśa's inferences do not commit the "ineffectual" fallacy (*a-prayojaka*). This would be failing to support a claim of pervasion through failing to consider counterinstances (where the probandum is not, there the prover must fail to be too).

Here ends the examination of inferences purporting to establish a non-veridical perception as a cognition of an entity as qualified. We now come to another long Prābhākara *pūrva-pakṣa*, but, fortunately, to arguments that are not advanced in such formal, some might say, tortuous terms.

Text (p. 484, Tirupati, and p. 448, Calcutta) and Translation

atra prābhākarāḥ, a-prayojakam idam | sva-tantrôpasthitêṣṭa-bhedâ-grahād eva pravṛtty-upapatteḥ kiṃ viśiṣṭa-jñānena | pareṇa apy āropa-niyamârthaṃ tad-abhyupagamāt | na ca rajate pravṛttiṃ prati viśiṣṭa-jñānasya hetutvād iha api tat-siddhiḥ | pravṛtti-mātre bhedâ-grahe sati iṣṭa-puro-varti-jñānasya lāghavena hetutvāt, na tu sad api viśiṣṭa-jñānaṃ tantraṃ gauravāt |

(**Gaṅgeśa** continues:) Here are Prābhākara views.

Prābhākara: This (your inference) does commit the "ineffectual" fallacy. For, since the effort (you mention) is possible just on account of (as we have it) a non-grasping of a distinctness between (a cognition of) a thing desired and something independently established in memory, what's the use of (postulating your) cognition of an entity as qualified? For, on the strength of the rule of superimposition (which governs error on all accounts), this (our view) is (in effect) accepted by our opponents, too.

And it is not the case that—granting that a cognition of an entity as qualified causes effort directed toward (real) silver—here, too (with error and misdirected effort), a cognition of an entity as qualified is established (as a cause). For, given no grasping of distinctness, it is simpler to hold that a cognition of a desired thing in front causes effort, not, even if it occurs, a cognition of an entity as qualified, because that is the more cumbersome view.

Comments

The Prābhākara, we need to keep in mind, sees error as two separately produced cognitions, (a) a perceptual cognition of a "this," of a particular thing out there that is, erroneously, an object of desire, e.g., a piece of mother-of-pearl, and (b) a memory cognition of silver.

The Naiyāyika accepts superimposition in the form of a qualifier appearing to be tied to a qualificandum by the inherence relation—in the example of the silver illusion and others, too—whereas the Prābhākara sees the superimposition as a matter of apparent, though false, identity. Thus the relation, in the Nyāya view, is between a class concept, so to say, a type term, and the designatum of a name, whereas, in the Prābhākara view, the relation is between two particulars, a bit of mother-of-pearl perceived and a bit of silver remembered.

Now, not just anything will be misperceived as anything else. The law of superimposition that the Prābhākara cites includes a plank about similarity: mother-of-pearl and silver can be confused, but *not* mother-of-pearl and a pot.

An advantage of the Prābhākara view is the plausibility of an associative theory of memory, which would account for why mother-of-pearl is mistaken for silver—it looks a lot like silver.

The argument from simplicity is also a strong one, and does appear to favor the Prābhākara position, since a single type of causality is posited. However, Gaṅgeśa meets the argument head-on—at the beginning of the following *siddhânta*, below, pp. 282ff. The Prābhākara *pūrvapakṣin* has first a few more points to make and some objections to disarm.

Text (p. 490, Tirupati) and Translation

na ca rajate puro-varti-bheda-grahasya a-prasiddhyā kathaṃ tad-a-bhāva iti vācyaṃ | puro-varti-niṣṭhe bhede rajata-pratiyogitva-jñāna-viṣayatvâ-bhāvasya puro-vartini iṣṭa-bhinnatva-prakāraka-jñāna-viṣayatvâ-bhāvasya vā hetutvāt | na ca a-bheda-vyavahāro vyavahartavya-dhī-sādhyo na tu tad-a-bhāvâ-grahāt, anyathā bhedâ-grahād bheda-vyavahārâpattir iti vācyam | icchâdīnāṃ jñāta-puro-varti-mātra-viṣayatvāt | a-bhedâbhilāpo 'pi jñāta-bhedasya[3] a-saṃsargâ-grahād iti na a-jñāte vyavahāraḥ |

Objection: Since with (real) silver no grasping of a distinctness between it and a desired thing in front is known, how can there be an absence of that (known)? (No absence can be known whose countercorrelate or absentee is unknown.)

Prābhākara: That should not be asked. For, the cause (of such a prior cognition of the countercorrelate or absentee) could be either (a) silver's not being the object of a cognition in being the countercorrelate (or absentee) of a distinctness (a mutual absence) resting in the thing in front (i.e., a piece of silver's not being cognized as that from which the thing in front is distinct) or (b) something's not being the object of a cognition whose predication content is a being-distinct from that which is desired with respect to a thing in front.

Objection: Whereas everyday talk about non-distinctness is founded on a cognition of what is to be talked about (as non-distinct), such cognition does *not* result from a *non*-grasping of an absence. For, otherwise, there would be the difficulty that, from a *non*-grasping of a distinctness, talk of distinctness would ensue.

Prābhākara: That should not be said. For, desire and the like have as their intentionality (or objecthood) just the cognized object in front. Although there is talk of non-distinctness, something cognized (viz., the thing in front, that is to say), something distinct, is that with which there is a non-relation that is not grasped (resulting in such talk). Thus speech does not occur (on our view) about something not cognized.

Comments

When we fail to cognize that a piece of mother-of-pearl right in front of us is not silver—in other words, that it is distinct from silver—we make an error. A distinctness from silver is present, but we fail to notice it. Thus, we talk as though there were a non-distinctness from silver, i.e., as though the mother-of-pearl were silver.

An error is not due to a cognition of an entity as qualified, but comes about from a failure to grasp such a distinctness. This view is not subject to the criticism that effort, including speech behavior, results from positive cognition, not from any *non*-grasping. For, on our Prābhākara view, the thing in front is cognized, and its cognition sparks effort including effort to speak. And the absentees that we mention as part of our overall explanation are generally known. Of course, due to an epistemic defect, distinctness from, e.g., silver, is sometimes not grasped. But, to repeat, effort and speech are grounded in something as cognized, the thing in front, namely, which is presented perceptually.

Moreover, this holds whether the talk of something as silver, that is, as non-distinct from silver, is not frustrated or, in what is termed an error, is frustrated. In the former case, the thing is non-distinct from silver, and is said to be so because no relation to silver as something distinct is grasped, and in the latter case the same story is to be told. That is, it is said to be so because no relation to silver as something distinct is grasped, although there is in fact a distinctness. But in each case the speech is about the thing presented perceptually, which is what prompts it.

Text (p. 492, Tirupati, and p. 452, Calcutta) and Translation

> nanu pītaḥ śaṅkho na śveta iti bheda-jñāne 'pi śvetâ-bhedânumityā śvetârthi-pravṛtter a-bheda-dhīs tad-dhetur iti cet, na | tava api pītaḥ śaṅkha ity a-bheda-jñānāt pītârthī na pravartate bhedânumiter iti bhedâ-graha eva tad-dhetuḥ syāt | bhramatvena jñātam a-bheda-jñānam a-kiñcit-karam iti yadi tadā bhramatvena jñātaṃ bheda-jñānam api tathā |

Objection: Even with a cognition of distinctness (like), "The shell seems yellow, not white," effort by someone intent on the white thing can come about by means of an inference to non-distinctness ("But it is really white"). That effort is caused by a cognition of a non-distinctness (not a *non*-cognition of distinctness).

Prābhākara: No. For you, too, someone who was intent on something yellow (nevertheless) would not make effort on the basis of a cognition of a non-distinctness, (e.g.) "The shell is yellow." For he would make an inference to a distinctness. Therefore (if one were to make effort), just a non-grasping of a distinctness would be a cause.

If a cognition of a non-distinctness were known to be an error without a result, then a cognition of a distinctness known as an error should be likewise, too.

Comments

Non-distinctness is equivalent to identity. "The shell is white," is, according to the Prābhākara analysis, a cognition of a non-distinctness between a shell and something white. (Naiyāyikas, in contrast, claim that the relation cognized is not identity but inherence, a color quality inhering in the shell.)

The dominant issue continues to be the role of an absence of cognition in error. How, on the Prābhākara view, can the fact be explained that when someone knows, by way of an inference, a *non*-distinctness, his effort may well be successful? The Prābhākara replies that no ice is cut by the difference between making effort and not making effort. In each case, both presence and absence of cognition figure in the causal complex. Furthermore, there is no rule that cognition always causes effort and non-cognition is responsible for inactivity. There can be inactivity from cognition and activity from non-cognition (of distinctness).

Text and Translation

yad vā iṣṭa-bhedâ-viṣayakaṃ jñānaṃ pravartakam | na ca a-bhedânumitāv iṣṭa-bhedo viṣayaḥ | ata eva pūrvaṃ bheda-pratyaye 'pi sa pratyayo na bheda-grāhī iti diṅ-moha-pratibimbâdi-pratyayāḥ |

(The **Prābhākara** continues:) Alternatively, a cognition that does not have as object a distinctness from a thing desired causes effort (directed toward, e.g., the white thing). And the object is not a distinctness between the thing desired (and something yellow) in an inference to a non-distinctness ("But it is really white"). Just for this reason, there being a cognition of a distinctness ("This is not white") before (the inference), the (inferential) cognition does not grasp a distinctness.

Similar cognitive occurrences are found in confusion about directions (which is followed, for example, by an inference that such a direction is east) and reflections (in mirrors, etc., where the difference between the glass and the image is not noticed, and later an inference is made that they are identical, or have the same locus).

Comments

Under the sway of a non-grasping of a distinctness between something yellow and a shell, one does not make effort, given that one wants a white shell (though the shell is really white). But when there emerges—by means of an inference—a cognition of a non-distinctness between something white and a shell, still a non-grasping of a distinctness is part of what stirs effort and ensuing activity. (And one is surely indeed not grasping a distinctness, one is not aware of any, in the example.) That's why the Prābhākara says that, alternatively, one may take the effort to be caused by a cognition *without distinctness as object*. Either (a) a non-grasping of a distinctness or (b) a grasping without any distinctness as object—the Prābhākara is happy with either view of the effort's cause.

Text (p. 494, Tirupati, and p. 457, Calcutta) and Translation

> nanv evaṃ rajate 'pi viśiṣṭa-jñānaṃ na siddhyet pravṛtter bhedâ-grahād eva upapatteḥ | idaṃ rajatatayā jānāmi rajatatayā jñātam ity anubhavaḥ śuktāv api tulyaḥ | na ca śuktau rajatatva-bādhāt so 'py a-saṃsargâ-grahaḥ, bādhasya api viśiṣṭa-jñānatve mānâ-bhāvād iti cet, na | tatra hi rajatasya na smṛtiḥ prāg-an-anubhavāt | grahanaṃ ca tasya dharmi-viṣayakaṃ yogya-dharmi-yogena rajatatva-jāti-grahād ity artha-siddhaṃ dharma-dharmi-viṣayakam ekaṃ jñānam | na ca rajatatvasya śukty-anubhava-viṣayatve hetur asti | na ca pratyabhijñāna-vat saṃskārêndriye hetū | tayor atra bhinna-viṣayakatvāt | ekadā sva-tantrôpasthita-viruddhân-eka-bhedâ-grahe saṃśayaḥ |

Objection (by a Naiyāyika): In this way, with regard to (real) silver, too, a cognition of an entity as qualified would not be established (contrary to what you yourself say), for just from a non-grasping of a distinctness (between a thing in front and silverhood, as in the case of error on your view) would effort be possible.

(Moreover) "This I know *as* silver; it is known through its silverhood," such an experience (i.e., an apperception) would equally apply to a mother-of-pearl case, too.

Furthermore, since silverhood is negated through a correcting cognition with respect to a (real) piece of mother-of-pearl ("It is not silver"), that experience (the apperception through which one becomes apprised of the error) would not be a *non*-grasping of a non-relation too. For, given that the correcting cognition would be a cognition of an entity as qualified, there would be no proof (that there was such a non-grasping: the non-relation is instead *grasped*).

Prābhākara: No. (We accept that there are cognitions of entities as qualified in the instances you cite.) For, there (in the case of veridical experience of silver) there is no memory of silver (or, there need not be), since it is not experienced before (i.e., it comes, or could come, into awareness now, in perceptual experience). And the (perceptual) grasping of it includes a property-bearer as object. Through a relation with a suitable property-bearer there is a grasping of the universal, silverhood. Therefore, the cognition establishing the object is single (i.e., relational) with a property and a property-bearer as object. And (this does not obtain with error:) there is no cause of silverhood as an experience's object that is also a cause of mother-of-pearl (as object, i.e., error is not a single cognition).

Further, a memory-impression (*saṃskāra*) and a sense organ do not, as with (the phenomenon of) recognition, serve as two causes, since the two in this case would have distinct objects.

(Moreover) doubt (which is a kind of non-veridical cognition) occurs when there is a non-grasping, all at once, of a distinct, mutually opposed plurality where each object is independently set in consciousness.

Comments

Nyāya sees apperception as capable of showing that a target cognition is a cognition of an entity as qualified, for there its being relational is supposed to be plainly apparent, as is indicated in the example. Moreover, an apperception of a mother-of-pearl illusion would have the same object as the cited example of an apperception of a veridical cognition of silver, viz., "This I am cognizing as silver." Finally, an apperception of a defeating or correcting cognition ("I see now that it is not silver") shows clearly that the correcting cognition cannot be understood in the Prābhākara fashion, because there a grasping (not a non-grasping) of the non-relation between silverness and the mother-of-pearl is itself grasped.

Gaṅgeśa takes up the topic of recognition in the last section of the chapter, the *savikalpaka-jñāna-vāda*. Recognition ("This is that Devadatta whom I saw yesterday") is a single perception with a single qualificandum and (minimally) two qualifiers, one furnished "extraordinarily" by way of a memory-impression and the other in the normal fashion by a sense organ. The Prābhākara's view of recognition is that, like error, it is two cognitions, a perception and a memory.

The Prābhākara points out that perception does not require a memory-impression as a cause. This is a position with which Naiyāyikas agree in that, they say, many perceptions are like that (though others—absential perceptions, recognitions, seeing a pot as the thing that one has just touched—do have memory-impressions as causes, says Nyāya). Thus, the explanation of speech behavior that indicates that an error has occurred does not undermine other parts of the Prābhākara cognitive psychology, Gaṅgeśa's opponent claims. Indeed, the positions shared with Nyāya support the position on error. The best example is perhaps doubt, which the Naiyāyika also sees as a kind of non-veridical cognition. And since doubt is viewed by both parties in this way, the question, in the next passage, is whether doubt is a variety of a "presentation of something as other than what it is," or, as the Prābhākara holds, a certain type of lack of cognition.

Text (p. 497, Tirupati) and Translation

> na ca krameṇa upasthitân-eka-bhedâ-grahe yena sa kramika-viparyaya-dvaya-rūpaḥ syāt | anyathā tava apy a-pratīkārāt | na ca saṃśayân-antaraṃ viparyaya-daśāyām ubhaya-bhedâ-grahe saṃśayaḥ, eka-bhedâ-grahe anyathā-khyātiḥ, doṣa-mahimnā hy ekasya na svâtantryeṇa upasthitiḥ, kiṃ tv a-bhāva-viśeṣaṇatayā iti tad-a-bhedâ-graho 'py a-kiṃcit-karaḥ |

(The **Prābhākara** continues:) And it is not the case that a non-grasping of a distinct plurality is serially set in awareness, whereby doubt (e.g., "A stump or a person?") would be a dual form of serial wrong cognition. Otherwise, for you, too, doubt would be impossible.

Furthermore, immediately following one doubt another doubt does not, on the occasion of a wrong cognition (i.e., a wrong resolution of the alternatives), arise concerning a non-grasping of the two as distinct, and so there is not in the non-grasping of a distinctness (an instance of) "presentation of something as other than what it is" (*anyathā-khyāti*). For, through the predominance of an epistemic defect, no single thing is (alone) independently set in awareness. Rather, there is (with the wrong cognition, "It's not a stump but a person," not another doubt, but) an absential qualifier. So (on your interpretation), albeit there would be a non-grasping of a distinctness (i.e., no grasping of a non-existent distinctness of a stump as distinct from itself), it (the non-grasping) would not bring about doubt.

Comments

The reason why doubt would be impossible for the Naiyāyika on the serial conception is, according to Mathurānātha, that for Nyāya a later cognition able to take an immediately previous cognition as object (i.e., in apperception) but not any others, that is, not without the aid of memory. Doubt serially conceived would require three cognitions: first, a stump as object, second, a person, and third, a combinatory cognition, "Is it a stump or a person?" However, the third cognition could not take the first directly as object, on the Nyāya view, without help from memory.

One might be tempted to say that, so long as doubt is conceived as having only a *single* object, there would be "presentation of something as other than what it is," even in a non-grasping of a distinctness between, e.g., a stump and a person. Thus the doubt would have to be understood as a relational cognition, with its object mispresented. However, the Prābhākara retorts, if a single thing were all by itself independently established in awareness (for example, a stump as a stump), then, whereas no grasping of something as distinct from itself might well occur, clearly *doubt* would not occur. Doubt requires two cognitions, each with an absential qualifier.

Text (p. 460, Calcutta) and Translation

na ca saṃśayân-antaraṃ dhūma-bhramād asti kvacid vahny-arthi-pravṛttir na tu tena vinā | na ca tasya sva-tantrôpasthita-vahny-a-saṃsargâ-graho dvāraṃ, saṃśayânurodhena tasya prāg api sattvād vahny-anumitir dvāram iti vācyam | liṅga-bhramasya hi nirvahnitvasya svātantryeṇa upasthiti-pratibandhakatvena niyamataḥ sva-tantra-vahni-smṛtir dvāram iti na saṃśayânyathā-khyātī | na ca parvatasya pratyakṣatve vahneś ca smaraṇe pratyakṣa-bhramān na viśeṣa iti sākṣāt-karomi iti syāt na tv anuminomi iti vācyam | liṅga-jñānân-antara-bhāvitva-pratisandhānâ-pratisandhānābhyām ubhaya-sambhavāt |

(The **Prābhākara** continues, anticipating an objection:) And it is not true that on an occasion following a doubt (about, e.g., whether or not there is fire on a mountain) sometimes effort is made by the fire-seeker because of an error about smoke, an error without which (in that situation) there would be no effort (so that it might seem that a non-grasping would not be a cause but only the perceptual mistaking, e.g., dust for smoke. But in fact there would be a non-grasping, because there would be no grasping of the cognition of smoke as being a memory.)

Objection: Since, *qua* means, a non-grasping of a lack of relation to fire as independently set in awareness would be there beforehand in the case of such a situation of doubt, an inference to fire would have to be the means (causing the effort).

Prābhākara: That should not be said. For (an effort-guiding awareness) that something is without fire is (in such a case) blocked by an erroneous inferential mark (viz., the error that there is smoke)—a blocker that is independently set in awareness (through a memory-impression). From this rule, it follows that the means (causing such misdirected effort toward fire) is a remembering wherein fire has been independently set. Therefore, such a doubt would not be a case of "presentation of something as other than what it is."

Objection: (On your view) when a mountain is seen (as possessing smoke) and fire is remembered, there would be no difference from the case of a perceptual error (regarding the inferential mark). Therefore (on your view), (the apperception would be) "I am directly aware (of fire)," not (as is of course correct) "I am inferring fire."

Prābhākara: That should not be alleged. For, it is possible that either of the following two could occur just after a cognition of an inferential mark: (a) a mental reflection (a remembering) and (b) a cognition that is not such a mental reflection. (Thus, no ice is cut by your so-called apperceptive evidence.)

Comments

The hypothetical case being discussed is an instance of misdirected effort following doubt. One is not sure whether or not there is fire on a mountain, and then making a mistaken inference proceeds as if there were. Here, because the Prābhākara's non-grasping would be there in the prior stage when there is doubt, such non-grasping does not appear to spark the misdirected effort.

To this objection, the Prābhākara replies that it is a remembering—an association of smoke with fire set in memory being revived because of an epistemic defect—that blocks the course of action, or inaction, that one would have taken on the basis of there being no evidence of fire. Thus, again, the effort is to be analyzed as resulting from a failure to distinguish something as presented through memory and something—an absence of evidence of fire—as presented perceptually.

But, then, mistaking fire on the basis of an inference would seem to be the same psychologically as a perceptual *mis*-taking. An apperceptive report of the hypothetical case being discussed would seem to be, "I am directly aware of fire," according to the Prābhākara account, since, just as with perceptual error, what something is being mistaken as, namely, as fire-possessing, is furnished by an unnoticed remembering. The Prābhākara's reply to this second objection draws on his view that every cognition is self-aware; the Prābhākara denies the need for a separate and subsequent apperception. He says that a remembering and an awareness of a remembering might or might not occur following the failure to notice the memory nature of a presentation of an inferential mark, depending on other circumstances. Thus, there is no counter-consideration from so-called apperception.

Text (p. 499, Tirupati, and p. 462, Calcutta) and Translation

> evaṃ sva-tantrôpasthitân-iṣṭa-bhedâ-graho 'pi nivartakaḥ | tena idaṃ rajataṃ na śuktir ity a-bhāva-pratiyogitvena an-iṣṭôpasthites tad-bhedâ-graho na nivartakaḥ | śukty-a-bhāvâ-saṃsargâ-grahaś ca na-kārasya artha iti na anyathā-khyāti | an-iṣṭâ-bheda-grahasya nivartakatve ca rajata eva na idaṃ rajatam iti kṛtvā na vivarteta, anyathā anyathā-khyāty-āpatteḥ | ata eva rajata eva na idaṃ rajatam iti jñāne 'pi na pravṛtty-anyathā-khyātī rajata-bhedâ-saṃsargâ-grahāt |

(The **Prābhākara** continues:) In this way, a non-grasping of distinctness between something not desired and something independently set in memory motivates, moreover, effort to desist (or refrain from action or avoid). Thus, a non-grasping of a such a distinction—as in "This is silver, not mother-of-pearl," where being the absential countercorrelate is the thing (the mother-of-pearl) not desired set in awareness—does not motivate effort to desist (since, in this case, a person desiring silver would make effort on the positive basis of cognition of silver, not on cognition of the negation of mother-of-pearl). And because a non-grasping of a non-relation to an absence of mother-of-pearl is the meaning of the term "not" (in "This is silver, *not* mother-of-pearl"), there is no "presentation of something as other than what it is."

Moreover, if a grasping (not, as we have it, a *non*-grasping) of a *non*-

distinctness with the thing not desired (viz., an identity with mother-of-pearl) were the motivator of effort to desist, (then) cognizing "This is not silver" when it is silver in fact, a person would not make effort to desist (whereas, of course, he would), because you would have landed in the predicament of the "presentation otherwise view" being (itself) otherwise!

Just for this reason, though "This is not silver" is cognized when there is silver in fact, there is neither effort (to pick it up) nor "presentation otherwise"—because of (the true motivator of the person's not making effort to pick up the silver, namely) a non-grasping of a non-relation to a distinctness from silver (in that, as we said earlier, a non-grasping of a non-distinctness with the thing not desired motivates effort to act).

Comments

Effort is of two kinds, effort to act and effort to stop or check oneself and hold back, effort, so to say, not to act. The former seems motivated by an awareness of identity, or non-distinctness ("This is silver"), between (a) something presented—a qualificandum—and (b) what it is presented as—a qualifier—as something desired. But is this the right analysis? Is it an awareness of a *non*-distinctness that is the motivator, or a non-awareness of distinctness? Similar perplexity attends our reflection on effort to desist or refrain from acting. Is it awareness of a distinctness with what is desired, or non-awareness of an identity, that motivates effort not to act? The Prābhākara cleverly plays on the perplexity generated by the scope of the negative particle.

If, in the case of "This is silver, not mother-of-pearl," the "not" meant a distinctness—as Naiyāyikas would say—between silver and mother-of-pearl, then the cognition would be veridical even in a situation where what is cognized is not silver but mother-of-pearl (since mother-of-pearl is in all cases distinct from silver). Thus, it is better to construe the meaning in the Prābhākara way, so goes the argument.

In the situation where we are to imagine that an object perceived really is silver but the perceiver's cognition is "This is not silver," the cognition fails to grasp a non-distinctness with something not desired, in that it grasps a distinctness between what gets expressed as "this" and silver, i.e., a distinctness with something desired. But it is wrong to hold that *because* it so fails, the person would fail to desist (and desiring silver would reach out to pick up the silver prompted by the cognition "This is not silver"). Thus the Naiyāyika view of "presentation otherwise" would be manifest, in the example, in the "this" appearing otherwise, namely, as not silver . But the Naiyāyika view is shown not to be the right one here concerning the crucial touchstone, namely, prompting effort to act or not to act toward something. Thus, the untoward ramifications show it itself to be "otherwise"!

Text (p. 501, Tirupati) and Translation

nanu rajata-raṅgayor ime raṅga-rajate ity atra pratyekam ubhaya-bhedâ-grahe yugapat pravṛtti-nivṛttī syātām iti cet, na | evaṃ-vidha-bhrame mānâ-bhāvāt | kāryônneya-dharmāṇām yathā-kāryam unnayanāt | kramôtpanna-jñānayor bhedâ-grahād ekatvâbhimānaḥ | anyathā tava api sva-tantrôbhaya-bhedâ-grahāt pratyekaṃ rajataṃ raṅgaṃ vā iti saṃśayaḥ syāt | yad eva vā tatra viparyaya-niyāmakaṃ tata eva pravṛtti-nivṛttī syātāṃ tad-dhetor eva iti nyāyāt |

Objection: If, regarding silver and tin, (the cognition, getting each wrong) "Tin and silver," is due to a non-grasping of a distinctness of both (a memory and a perception) in each case, then, simultaneously would there be effort to act and effort not to act (toward the same things).

Prābhākara: No, because there is no proof that such an error occurs. One gets the impression that here there is (error of) a single type because the non-grasping of a distinctness is with respect to two (sets of) cognitions produced serially (perception and memory of, respectively, tin and silver, and perception and memory of, respectively, silver and tin): properties (hypothesized or) inferred on the basis of their effects must be inferred according to the nature of the effect. Otherwise, for you, too, (there would be the difficulty that not an error but) a doubt, "Is it silver or tin," would result for each from a non-grasping of the distinctness which for both would be independently set in awareness.

Or, there is the rule of error (i.e., governing the range of possible superimposition resulting in error): just what on what. According to that rule, (certain types of) effort to act and effort not to act come to be—by the principle of "just from that cause (comes just this effect)."

Comments

An error of seeing two things wrongly has to be due to four cognitions, on the Prābhākara theory. Thus, one pair and then another would have to be serially ordered in the stream of consciousness. But this presents no theoretical difficulty for the Prābhākara, so the passage argues. The four-cognition analysis of the dual error of "Tin and silver" (given two objects that are in fact silver and tin) is not only endorsed but expanded to explain the dual motivation of effort to act (toward the tin) and not to act (toward the silver). However, we shall see that this example continues to plague the Prābhākara. The distinctness of the one from the other appears to be given perceptually, not "independently set in awareness" in a remembering, as the Prābhākara implies.

In the next passage, the Prābhākara counterattacks, arguing that the Naiyāyika account would not differentiate the non-veridical from the veridical, because the mutual opposition proposed would not differentiate which one of an opposed pair was right and which wrong. The Prābhākara view that finds no awareness to be non-veridical, analyzing error as a matter of behavior, not of perception, is said to avoid the problem and to be simpler to boot.

Text (p. 502, Tirupati, and p. 465, Calcutta) and Translation

> yat tu "prasakta-pratiṣedhâtmā bādho '-khyātau na yujyate | sādhayaty anyathā-khyātiṃ bādha eva hi naḥ sphuṭam" || iti | tad-viparītaṃ | paraspara-viruddhatvâ-viśeṣeṇa bādhyatvâ-vyavasthiteḥ | viruddhârthakatayā utpannatvaṃ ca tulyam | pūrveṇa api kvacit-parasya bādhāt | tasmād bhedâ-grahāt[4] prasañjito vyavahāro bheda-grahād bādhyata iti yuktam |

(The **Prābhākara** continues:) But (what is claimed by your camp in a slogan) that is contrary to fact. (The slogan is) "The fact that a correcting negation ('This is not silver' when there is indeed no silver in front) consists in repudiation of what is first assumed does not match the (Prābhākara) view of (error as) 'non-presentation' (i.e., non-cognition of a distinctness); rather it establishes (error as) 'presentation otherwise.' For, with respect to (such) negation (or defeating, *bādhyatva*) alone, it's perfectly clear that our view is right." (This is contrary to the real fact of the matter.) For, since there is no partiality in mutual opposition (*virodha*), what's to be negated (which of the pair is the defeated) cannot be determined.

And it's all the same with production, so far as having opposed objects is concerned. In some cases, an earlier cognition can also negate a later.

Therefore, because of a non-grasping of a distinctness, there are the everyday statements that we are talking about (i.e., false statements), which are negated by a grasping of a distinctness—this is the appropriate view.

Comments

According to the Prābhākara, cognition is invariably veridical. Thus, what gets shown to be wrong, or negated, are certain statements spoken out of a non-grasping of a distinctness. Cognitions do not get negated. For example, a person does not notice a snake. Asked why he does not move, he replies, "Why should I? It's not a snake." The force of this statement gets negated when the snake is seen, and his behavior changes.

We have not found the source of the Naiyāyika verse that Gaṅgeśa has his Prābhākara opponent ridicule. There is much mutual punning and irony in the passage, underpinned by the logic of correction. What shows which of an opposed pair of cognitions is correct? Temporal ordering does not cut the ice since sometimes people have it right at first ("Oh, it's only mother-of-pearl") and later make an error ("Why, it's silver!"). The presumption that the later cognition has to be the one that is right is not borne out by the logic of opposition.[5]

The point made about mutual opposition (*virodha*) is a good one. However, there is more to be said, and Gaṅgeśa, below, takes the argument to support the Naiyāyika pragmatic test of veridicality. So we may as well wait and try to analyze "defeater" (*bādhaka*) more fully after we see what he says. The Prābhākara has other arrows in his quiver, moreover, and the arguments keep piling up. Fortunately, relief comes with the *siddhânta*, not too far below (p. 282).

Text (p. 503, Tirupati and Translation

upekṣā-bhrame ca śabda-prayogo bādhyaḥ | tadīyatā-mātra-sva-bhāvatvāt tad-viṣayatvasya | kathaṃ rajatīya-mātra-jñānam a-rajatīyaṃ sva-bhāva-vyāghātāt | na ca ubhayīyam, samūhâlambanâpatteḥ | tad uktam, "anyasya hy anyathā bhānaṃ prati ity eva parāhatam | parasmin bhāsamāne tu na param bhāsate yataḥ ||" iti | viṣayaṃ vinā eva tad-ākāraṃ jñānam iti sākāra-vādaḥ | jñānâ-yathārthatve ca jñāna-mātrasya tac-chaṅkayā na niṣkampa-pravṛttiḥ | na ca dośâ-janyatvâdinā viśvāsaḥ | bhramād a-viśvāse pravṛtty-a-bhāvâpatteḥ | na api taj-jñānāt | jñānatvena tatra apy a-viśvāsāt | tad ucyate, "aho bata mahān eṣa pramādo dhīmatām api | jñānasya vyabhicāritve viśvāsaḥ kiṃ nibandhanaḥ ||" iti |

(The **Prābhākara** continues:) And with regard to errors to which we are indifferent (i.e., that do not provoke effort to act or not to act), it is verbal expressions that are negated.

(Moreover) since objects of a certain type have just that type of essential nature, how can a cognition of precisely the silvery be non-silvery, in that such a cognition would deny its essential nature? And it is not "bothly" (i.e., not of both types), for that provokes the difficulty of (i.e., that a single error "Silver" would have to be understood as) cognition of a group ("Silver *and* mother-of-pearl").

Thus it is said: "The appearance of one thing otherwise—by that notion itself (is the view) defeated, since in the one thing that is appearing the other does not appear."

The (Buddhist) view (of cognition as) "having form within itself" is (the thesis that) a cognition has, without an (external) object, some form (of its own). (So you Naiyāyikas hold the same view as those heretics.)

And if for cognition in general there were not (accepted) a cognition's conformity with its object, then through doubt about it there would not be unhesitating effort to act (ever at all).

Moreover, it is false that reliance (trust, belief) comes about by an absence of epistemic defect, etc., since this would land you in the difficulty that error, resulting in no trust, would mean no effort to act. Nor (does trust come about) from cognition of such (an absence of defect), since there, too (about the possibility of knowledge of an absence of defect), there would no relying on cognition.

Thus is it said, "Oh my, what a great folly this is, even of (you Naiyāyikas who are apparently) intelligent men! If cognition wanders from its mark, on what ground can we trust it?"

Comments

The argument about indifference is clear. The second argument captures the heart of the Prābhākara position. Cognitions are what they are: they prompt and guide action by presenting bits of the world. A cognition of the silvery has the silvery as its object. A cognition of mother-of-pearl has as its object mother-of-pearl. The cognitions do not change their nature. Mistaken action results from ignorance; what is needed is not different but more knowledge. The deluded needs to see that his remembering of silver is distinct from his perception of mother-of-pearl.

Nyāya holds that in itself cognition has "no form," and that it takes its form from objects—sometimes through a perceptually "extraordinary" causal process involving memory retrieval and sometimes without memory as a causal factor at all. Prābhākaras also subscribe to a "no form" thesis, but do not have to distinguish "extraordinary" and "ordinary" causal processes. Buddhist Yogācārins hold that cognition has an internal form: there are no objects "external" to consciousness. The Prābhākara accuses the Naiyāyika of joining the camp of the heretic in holding that a silvery presentation could possibly not be about what is silvery in fact. "Predication contents" in illusions look, on the Nyāya analysis, a lot like cognitions' taking form and content independently of what the cognized object is in fact and thus to be subjectively determined entities. Once one admits such determination from the side of the subject what check will one have against the worry that all perceptual presentations are like that—so runs the charge.

Mathurānātha glosses "reliance" (*viśvāsa*, "trust," sometimes translated "belief") as "certainty about veridicality."

The Prābhākara trades on the difference between an actual error and a known or realized error. It is only the latter that blocks an effort to act. The deluded silver-seeker acts; the one who realizes his failure is the one who does not reach out to pick up the mother-of-pearl.

Finally, we do trust cognition, and on what is this trust based if not its nature of presenting things as they are? Skepticism if set loose would spread and fly off with trust in cognition, which, then, could not be tied back down. Our action would be infected with hesitation and uncertainty. Admitting the possibility of erroneous cognition, how can the Naiyāyika show that trust in cognition should be restored?

Text (p. 505, Tirupati, and p. 470, Calcutta) and Translation

bhramasya ca san-mātra-viṣayakatve na a-yathārthatā | a-sad-viṣayakatve '-sat-khyātiḥ | na ca tatra hetur asti | śabdasya āptôktasya nirdoṣasya liṅgasya ca a-hetutvāt | na ca śabdânumānâbhāsāt sā | yogyatâdimattayā śabdasya liṅgavattayā pakṣasya jñānāc chābdânumitī | na ca ābhāse taj-jñānam asti, hetv-a-bhāvād eva, kin tv a-gṛhitâ-saṃsarga-jñāna-dvayam | tatra indriyasya sambaddha-grāhakatvāt na ca pratyabhijñāna-vat, uktôttaratvāt |

(The **Prābhākara** continues:) And if error has as its object only that which really exists, then there is no "not being in conformity with the object" (i.e., there is no non-veridicality and the Nyāya view is wrong). If (on the other hand) error has as its object something not existing, then (correct is the Mādhyamika Buddhist view) "presentation of the non-existent."

Moreover, there is no reason for that ("presentation otherwise" view). The testimony spoken by an authority and a faultless inferential mark constitute no such reason. Nor from *apparent* testimony, nor from *apparent* inference, do we get that (view of error as "presentation otherwise"). Verbal and inferential knowledge result from a cognition (in the first case) of speech as possessed with (the veridicality-grounding attributes of) semantic appropriateness, etc., or (in the second case) of an inferential subject as possessed with a (veritable) inferential mark. And in (what you Naiyāyikas see as) apparent cases, there is no cognition of such, for precisely the reason that there is no reason (to regard them that way). Rather (with what you see as only apparently veridical cognitions) we have (in each case) a pair of cognitions whose non-relation is not grasped.

Since in those cases grasped is what is in connection with a sense organ, there is no similarity with recognition (where presentations of perception and of memory are both known to function, e.g., "This is that Devadatta whom I saw yesterday"), because of an answer that has been given above.

Comments

Authoritative verbal testimony cannot be support for the Nyāya view, since it generates only veridical cognitions. Similarly faultless inference. What Naiyāyikas call cases of non-veridical, or only apparently veridical, awareness is best explained in our Prābhākara way.

Recognition involves a single property-bearer—with "This is that Devadatta," it would be Devadatta—whereas error, on the Naiyāyika view, does not. The "silver" presentation, for instance, has its actual locus elsewhere. According to the Prābhākara, recognition is like what Naiyāyikas call error, except that we do notice the functioning of memory.

Text (p. 506, Tirupati, and p. 473, Calcutta) and Translation

na ca doṣa-vaśād a-sambaddhe 'pi vijātīyaṃ kāryam | doṣasya a-janakatvāt | na hi duṣṭāt kuṭaja-bījād yavâṅkuraḥ | bhasmakaṃ ca na doṣaḥ | kiṃ tu vahner udbhavaḥ | tasya ca dāha-sāmarthyaṃ dṛṣṭam eva | rasârjanaṃ tu na bhavati, bhakṣya-dāhāt | dava-dahana-dagdha-vetra-bījaṃ ca naṣṭam eva | tad-bhasmanaḥ kadalī-janakatvam | tad uktam, "sākāra-vādād a-sato na bhānāt saṃvid-virodhād atha hetv-a-bhāvāt | dhiyām an-āśvāsa-bhayāc ca na iṣṭā yato 'nyathā-khātir ato yathârthā ||"

(The **Prābhākara** continues:) And it is wrong to hold that a sense organ gives rise to a heterogenous effect (i.e., a categorially distinct effect, a *non*-veridical as opposed to a veridical cognition), albeit a defect is the reason that a sense organ is not in connection (with an object remembered). For, a defect does not produce (such an effect). For, from a defective seed of the *kuṭaja* plant, no shoot of barley or the like arises. And (if we followed your reasoning) the *bhasmaka* stomach disorder is not a defect; rather, it's the rising up of (real) fire and its ability to burn is witnessed in fact! Taste is not acquired from cooked food, and bamboo seed burned by a forest fire is in fact (thereby) destroyed! From its ashes, a banana tree is produced!

Thus is it said,

> (A) Because of (falling into) the position (on cognition as) "having form of itself," (B) because of the non-existent's not appearing, (C) because of opposition to common opinion, (D) because of lack of causal explanation, and (E) because of (inciting) the fear of no trust (at all in cognition), "presentation otherwise" is not to be accepted (as a possibility); therefore, (all awareness is) "in conformity with its object."

Comments

The ridiculous counterfactuals have greater literary unity than comes across in English, because they make use of etymological derivatives of a Sanskrit word for fire (from the root, *dah*, "to burn") and another for ashes, and are thus a mass of puns as well as laughable ramifications of a wrong position.

A defective bamboo seed does not produce a banana tree. It does not produce a tree at all. Likewise, a defective perceptual process does not produce a cognition that mispresents the world; it produces a *failure*, a lack, a failure to notice the difference between a perception and a simultaneous remembering.

The verse, which is presumably from Prabhākara but which we have not found, sums up not just the immediately preceding argument but in all five reasons why the Naiyāyika position is impossible. The alternative is to view all awareness as "in conformity with its object" (*yathârtha*).[6] (A) The Naiyāyika admits a realm of mental objects, and surrenders his realism, by proposing that cognition is shaped subjectively, taking "a form of itself," not caused by the object. (B) The Naiyāyika opens the door to the pan-illusionist polemic by allowing cognition to present the non-existent. If the non-existent can appear, then all our experience could be (as claimed by the Buddhist, alternatively, the Advaita Vedāntin) nothing but a dream. (C) The Naiyāyika denies the common assumption that a cognition has a single or uniform nature which is to present something as it is, not as what it is not. (D) There is no causal explanation available to the Naiyāyika why a cognition should become so disformed as to present something as what it is not. Ignorance is the cause of failed effort, not a mangled positive cause. (E) Cognitions presenting what there is in fact ground our confidence and trust and prompt action. The Naiyāyika would incite the fear comprised of universal skepticism, and we would act only with hesitation and uncertainty.

Text (p. 507, Tirupati) and Translation

> tasmād vivāda-padaṃ jñānaṃ na vyadhikaraṇa-prakārakaṃ jñānatvāt satya-jñāna-vat | bhedâ-graha-janya-rajatatva-prakāraka-śuktîcchāyāṃ pratiyogi-prasiddhiḥ | jñānatvaṃ sva-vyadhikaraṇa-prakārâvacchinna-viṣayatā-pratiyogi-vṛtti na bhavati jñāna-mātra-vṛtti-dharmatvāt pramātva-vat | na ca cakṣuś cākṣuṣa-satya-jñānâtirikta-jñāna-janakaṃ, indriyatvāt rasana-vad iti pratirodhaḥ, a-prayojakatvāt | cākṣuṣa-satya-jñānâtirikta-jñāna-janakatvôpādheḥ anyathā-khyāter api dharmy-aṃśe satyatvāt tulya-nyāyatayā vyāpake 'pi vyartha-viśeṣaṇatvāc ca |

(The **Prābhākara** continues:) Therefore, a cognition, the topic of our dispute, does not have (misplaced) predication content that exists (objectwise) in a different locus (than the one in front), *since* it is a cognition, like (what you call) a cognition of something real (silver, for instance).

The countercorrelate (mentioned in the probandum) is exampled in a desire for mother-of-pearl (i.e., a desire whose qualificandum is mother-of-pearl), a desire having silverhood as predication content generated by a non-grasping of a distinctness.

Being-a-cognition correlate to an objecthood as specified by predication content belonging to a different locus than the objecthood does not occur, *since* being-a-cognition is a property that obtains only with cognition, like veridicality.

Objection (by a Naiyāyika putting forth a counterinference): The visual organ can generate cognition different from that which reveals a visual reality, *since* it is a sense organ, like the organ of taste.

Prābhākara: No, that counterinference too is wrong. For, it is "ineffective" (or, has a "misleading prover," *a-prayojaka*, because sense organs other than the visual organ could reveal a visual reality if the visual organ could do what is alleged). And there is an undercutter (*upādhi*), namely (your very probandum), generating-cognition-different-from-that-which-reveals-a-visual-reality. A "presentation otherwise" would be true (not only with respect to the cognition's qualifier portion but) also with respect to the property-bearer portion by your same reasoning, and although there would be a pervading, the qualification, "different from that which reveals a visual reality," would be meaningless.

Comments

Desires as well as cognitions and efforts are considered to have objects, both predication contents and qualificanda. Thus a desire can have an intentionality that hits a qualificandum (e.g., mother-of-pearl) that a predication content (silverhood) appears to qualify. A mistaken desire is an example of what cognition is not, and thus the Prābhākara's inference whose probandum characterizes cognition as excluding such a countercorrelate cannot be faulted for relying on an unexampled term.

The opponent is a Naiyāyika who realizes that his view requires an "extraordinary" sensory relation that is like the case of the visual organ provoking an experience of fragrant sandalwood when the sandalwood is seen only at a distance and the olfactory organ is inoperative. His inference would establish an analogue for what happens in perceptual illusion: in both cases, a memory-impression would be an auxiliary cause of a revival and projection into current perception of previous experience.

The objector's proposed counterinference provokes a refutation that is difficult to unpack. The undercutter property clearly pervades the objector's probandum, because they are the same term. Does it fail to pervade the prover? This may be the point of calling the prover "misleading" (*a-prayojaka*), as the Prābhākara does to open his remarks. But what, then, is the counterexample, the known locus of the prover (being-a-sense-organ) without the probandum (in effect, generating-veridical-non-visual-cognition)? Rather obviously that would be the visual organ itself. However, the visual organ is the *pakṣa*, the "inferential subject," of the opponent's inference, and it is bracketed in the inferential context. So the Prābhākara tries to bring out the "patent falsehood" (*bādha*) of the objector's conclusion (as is appropriate with this type of cooked-up inference; cf., above, pp. 161–62, on *pakṣetaratva*). According to both Mathurānātha and Rucidatta, the Prābhākara does this by shifting our focus to the qualificandum of the cognition generated. Patently, the visual organ does not generate a cognition whose qualificandum is "different from that which reveals a visual reality" where, that is to say, the "visual reality" would be a property-bearer, a qualificandum. The sandalwood in the Naiyāyika's example is indeed what is made known, qua qualificandum, by the visual organ. Thus the qualification "different from that which reveals a visual reality" will not fly, being "meaningless" in the sense of "contradictory."

Text (p. 475, Calcutta) and Translation

evaṃ sva-rūpato viṣayataś ca a-grahīta-bhedaṃ jñāna-dvayam eva visaṃvādi-pravṛtti-hetuḥ | tad uktam, "sannihita-rajata-śakale rajata-matir bhavati yādṛśī satyā | bhedân-adhyavasāyād iyam api tādṛk parisphurati ||" iti | vyavahāra-

mātrasya bhedâ-graha-janyatve 'pi tasya saṃvāda-tad-a-bhāvābhyāṃ jñāne yathārthatvâ-yathārthatva-vyapadeśaḥ | ata eva loke uṣṇaṃ jalam iti jñāne na a-yathārthatva-vyapadeśaḥ | upekṣā-jñāne tu tad-vyapadeśas tad-yogyatvāt |

(The **Prābhākara** continues:) In this way, (we conclude) from what something is in itself, and from (the nature of all) cognitive objecthood, that just a pair of cognitions, with their distinctness unnoticed, causes unsuccessful effort. Thus is it said, "Such true mental presentation of silver as results from silver that is right nearby is this (apparent error), too, (which occurs) because of a non-awareness of a distinctness—so it sparkles with clarity."

It is a non-grasping of a distinctness (that is crucial causally). But verbal behavior alone is that to which everyday talk (of error) applies—the talk of a cognition's conformity, or lack of conformity, with its object—as is indicated by success or the absence of it. Just for this reason, in everyday life, regarding a cognition, "Hot water," there is no talk of lack of conformity (though there is a kind of error in fact).

But talk of such (conformity and lack of conformity) does occur with respect to cognitions to which we are indifferent, since they are capable of provoking effort (that is successful or unsuccessful depending on whether or not there is, concomitantly, a failure to cognize a distinctness).

Comments

The citation appears in Śālīkanātha's *Prakaraṇapañcikā*.[7]

According to Nyāya—and other classical philosophies cum science—the reason water sometimes feels hot is that fiery atoms have become conjoined, invisibly, to a greater mass of watery atoms on which the hot character of the former is nonetheless superimposed. The Prābhākara points out that, given this state of things, people should, if Nyāya were right in its analysis of error, say that a cognition of hot water is *not* in conformity with its object (i.e., *a-yathârtha*). The reason they do not is that the criterion of error talk in everyday life is success or failure of effort. Therefore, he implies, the Mīmāṃsaka analysis is right to focus on speech behavior, showing why people *say* that there is error, not on cognitions as erroneous. In fact, no cognition is erroneous. Talk of error is, in sum, something that is to be analyzed as brought about by a non-grasping of a distinction between two occurrent cognitions, a perceiving and a remembering.

Here ends the Prābhākara *pūrva-pakṣa*. Next comes Gaṅgeśa's *siddhânta*, with a Prābhākara now in the role of skeptical opponent and challenger.

atha anyathā-khyāti-vāda-siddhânta

NOW, THE RIGHT VIEW ON (ERROR AS) PRESENTATION AS OTHERWISE

Text (p. 510, Tirupati, and p. 477, Calcutta) and Translation

siddhântas tu, satya-sthale pravṛtti-mātraṃ prati iṣṭa-purovarti-jñāne hetutayā vyavasthite 'tiprasaṅga-vāraṇârthaṃ viṣayatayā vaiśiṣṭyam eva kāraṇatâvacchedakaṃ kalpyate lāghavāt | kāraṇatā-graha-samaye jñāna-vitti-vedyatayā śīghrôpasthitikatvāt bādhakâ-bhāvāc ca | na tu sva-tantrôpasthitêṣṭa-bhedâ-grahaḥ kāraṇam, tādṛśa-bhedâ-grahatvaṃ ca kāraṇatâvacchedakaṃ, gauravāt kalpanīyôpasthitikatvāc ca | viśiṣṭa-jñāne 'pi hetutvena āvaśyakatvād bhedâ-graha eva hetur iti cet, na | viśiṣṭa-jñāne tad-dhetutvasya tat-kalpanôttara-kalpyatvena pravṛtti-kāraṇatā-graha-samaye tad-an-upastiteḥ | na ca evaṃ mithyā-jñāna-kalpane gauravaṃ | pramāṇa-pravṛtti-samaye siddhy-a-siddhi-parāhatatvena phala-mukha-gauravasya a-doṣatvāt | pramāṇavatas tasya nyāyatvāt |

Gaṅgeśa: The right view, however, is that, on an occasion of experience of a reality, a cognition of a desired thing in front is a cause of any effort to act. Given this order of things, just qualificative relationality, as (part of) the cognitive object, is to be posited—to avoid unwanted cases—as the specifier of the type of cause (operative with effort), because that is simpler. Furthermore, at the time when such causality is grasped in an apperception (i.e., when we apperceive a cognition's provoking effort), the qualificative relationality has been set in awareness. Moreover, there are no obstacles (to such a view).

There is not a cause, however, in a non-grasping of a distinctness independently set in awareness. For, it is cumbersome to view the specifier of the causality as a non-grasping of such distinctness (a non-existing distinctness in the case of successful effort). And that which is to be posited (as the specifier) should be set in awareness (on the occasion of the causal operation in question, as is our "qualificative relationality").

Objection: (Your theory of) a cognition of an entity as qualified, too (faces a charge of cumbersomeness). For, whatever is necessary is to be understood as a cause. (So) a *non-grasping of a distinctness* is indeed a cause (of effort, since it is cumbersome to talk about a cognition of an entity as qualified as standing in the middle).

Gaṅgeśa: No. For, that (your "non-grasping of a distinctness") as a cause of the cognition of an entity as qualified would be a construction posited later. It could not be set in awareness at the time when the causes of the effort are operative.

And there is not in this way theoretical cumbersomeness concerning the way false cognition is imagined. Given that on occasions of effort guided by a veridical cognitive means it is there (i.e., a cognition of an entity as qualified is a cause on those occasions, according to both our parties), aside from whether the effort turns out to be successful (as you would have it because a *non-*

existing distinctness was not grasped) or unsuccessful (because an *existing* distinctness was not grasped). So no fault of cumbersomeness is to be alleged with respect to what comes afterwards, after fruition (or failure of the effort). For, (only) that (e.g., a claim of cumbersomeness) is warranted which is backed up by a source of right cognition.

Comments

Gaṅgeśa's point that a posit of qualificative relationality is simpler in comparison with the Mīmāṃsaka thesis trades on the cumbersomeness of the notion that it is a *non-existing* distinctness that is not grasped in the case of successful effort.

Now, Gaṅgeśa has much to say about Nyāya's thesis of qualificative relationality in the next three sections of the *TCM*. Here we need to know that both parties agree that in the case of a veridical cognition a qualifier and a qualificandum are presented in relation. What Gaṅgeśa is rejecting is the cumbersome theory—put forth to maintain uniform causality between cases of success and failure of effort—of a non-grasping of a distinctness, whether non-existing or existing, as the specifier of the type of causality operative. On Gaṅgeśa's view, a cognition as a particular, as an individual, is the pertinent cause, a cognition, furthermore, whose qualificative relationality specifies what type of causality is operative, a cognition of an entity as qualified, to be precise. This relationality is evident apperceptively. When we apperceive a cognition that provokes effort (the effort and the apperception occurring concurrently), we see in place a qualifier presented as qualifying a qualificandum, so Gaṅgeśa contends.

Moreover, Gaṅgeśa argues, any non-grasping of such a distinctness as is dear to the Prābhākara is to be inferred with respect to what happens later if it is is to be inferred at all. It is simpler to identify causes that are already required—required in this case, that is, to explain provocation of effort regardless how it turns out—as opposed to reinventing a whole new causal sequence with respect to what comes later, namely, the failure or success of the effort and act.

The unwanted cases that Gaṅgeśa says—at the beginning of the passage—he wants to avoid Mathurānātha elaborates as graspings of a thing in front as distinct from a thing desired where there would be no effort to act. Such cases are important, as we shall see.

Text (p. 517, Tirupati) and Translation

> **evaṃ ca visaṃvādi-pravṛttir api viśiṣṭa-jñāna-sādhyā pravṛttitvāt satya-pravṛtti-vat | kḷpta-kāraṇaṃ vinā an-upapatteḥ an-anyathā-siddhatayā pravṛttyā samānīta-viśiṣṭa-jñāna-balāt tat-kāraṇaṃ sadoṣam indriyâdy eva | sarvato balavatī hy**

anyathā-an-upapattiḥ | na ca bhedâ-grahāt pravṛtty-upapattir api | viparīta-catuṣke yugapat pravṛtti-nivṛtty-āpatteḥ | na ca mānâ-bhāvaḥ | ime raṅga-rajate iti satya-jñāna-vat rajata-raṅgayoḥ pratyeka-bhrama-sāmagryor ekadā sattvena tādṛśa-bhramôtpatter ānubhavikatvāt | anyathā samūhâlambanôcchede dvitvâdy-a-pratyakṣatâpatteḥ | ime raṅga-rajate iti śabdâbhāsād evaṃ-vidha-bhrama-sambhavāc ca | mama doṣa-mahimnā rajata-raṅgayoḥ rajata-raṅga-bheda-grahān na saṃśayaḥ | tava ca ekatra sva-tantrôbhaya-bhedâ-grahāt pratyekaṃ raṅgaṃ rajataṃ vā iti saṃśayaḥ syāt |

(**Gaṅgeśa** continues:) And in this way also effort that proves ineffective is caused by a cognition of an entity as qualified, *since* it is effort, like effort directed toward a reality. Without this known cause, ineffective effort would not happen. On the strength of a cognition of an entity as qualified, a cognition that is inferred on the basis of effort that requires it, the (special) cause of ineffective effort is just a defective sense organ, etc. For, that something would otherwise be impossible (or, be inexplicable, *anyathā-an-upapatti*) is, universally, the forceful consideration (the consideration that carries the day).

And, furthermore, it is not possible that there be effort to act resulting from a non-grasping of a distinctness. For, (on that view) one lands in the difficulty that there would be simultaneously effort to act and to refrain from acting with respect to four opposed possibilities (regarding cognition of silver and tin).

And it (what you said before) is wrong, (namely) that there is no proof for the occurrence of this (type of error). Like the (veridical) cognition of a fact, (viz.) "These two are tin and silver," the possibility of such an error is known by experience, by the obtaining of, at the same time, two causal complexes sufficient to produce each error. Otherwise, one would, concerning the perception of a pair, etc., land in the unfortunate difficulty of the shattering (of all possibility) of cognition of a group of things. Furthermore, "These two are tin and silver" (given that the pair is silver and tin) is a type of error that can (also) occur from misleading testimony.

By way of gross error on my part, (say) I grasp distinctnesses from silver and from tin, in silver and tin (whereas no distinctness from silver lies in silver and no distinctness from tin lies in tin). Then (by my lights) doubt does not occur (and in fact none occurs, although of course there is error). Yet, according to you, since there would be, concerning each single item, a non-grasping of a distinctness between two presentations independently set in awareness, a doubt should occur in both cases concerning the single item(s), i.e., with each "Is it tin or silver?"

Comments

This is an important passage where Gaṅgeśa both gives an inference that establishes the Naiyāyika position and presents his centralmost objection to the Prābhākara account. The subject of his inference is ineffective effort, which the Prābhākara sees as caused by a certain ignorance, a lack of cognition, but which Gaṅgeśa sees as resulting from a perceptual illusion understood as a single cognition of an entity as qualified (by a qualifier that it does not possess in fact). The nub of his argument is that it is better to extend the applicability of a known causal relationship than to dream up another. Successful effort has a qualificative cognition, a cognition of an entity as qualified, as a cause, and so it is reasonable to presume that unsuccessful effort also has a cognition of an entity as qualified as a cause.

The statement about the forcefulness of reasoning that otherwise something actual would be impossible—also called "postulation," *arthâpatti*—is from Kumārila, and is often quoted in philosophical texts.

Not only is the Naiyāyika account supported by cogent inference, the Prābhākara account faces counterexamples, Gaṅgeśa says. The Prābhākara is embarrassed in particular by error about a group of things. Imagine a piece of silver adjacent to a piece of tin, with someone mistaking the tin for silver and the silver for tin. Such an error would provoke, on the Prābhākara analysis, four instances of effort to act or not to act toward the two objects. That is, "Silver and tin," occurring with respect to tin and silver, gives us: (a) a perceptual presentation of tin, and thus (1) motivation for effort not to act, to refrain from acting, toward the tin, on the part of one desiring silver, (b) a memory of silver, undistinguished, and thus (2) motivation for effort to act toward the tin, (c) a perceptual presentation of silver, and thus (3) motivation for effort to act toward it, and (d) a memory of tin, undistinguished, and thus (4) motivation for effort not to act toward the silver. (Effort, like cognition, is considered to have intentionality.) Gaṅgeśa may be interpreted as saying that such simultaneous effort to act and not to act toward the same object is impossible. However, *arthâpatti*, "postulation," may also be understood as involving only the weaker standard of explicability. Thus, Gaṅgeśa's point may be that the Prābhākara's view is implausible because of its complexity. The debate henceforth will center on whether there is such a fourfold possibility or not and, later, on whose account is on the whole simpler.

According to Gaṅgeśa, a telling untoward ramification of the Prābhākara's position is that doubt should occur in the case of the fourfold cognitive occurrence, since the factors sufficient for such a doubt—"Is it tin or silver?"—would be in place (twice). However, not doubt but error occurs—as shown by unsuccessful effort to act with a piece of tin picked up, and by even more unfortunate effort not to act with a piece of silver left lying undisturbed.

Text (p. 519, Tirupati, and p. 459, Calcutta) and Translation

atha yad-dharma-jñānād yad-upasthitis tatra tad-bhedâ-grahāt pravṛtti-nivṛttī | raṅga-rajata-dharmeṇa rajata-raṅge smārite na tu raṅga-rajate | māṣa-rāśi-sthamasī-viṣaye māṣârthi-pravṛttiḥ masī-nīlima-smārita-māṣa-bhedâ-grahāt |

anubhūyamānâropo '-siddha eva | anyathā tava api pratyekam ubhaya-jñānaṃ syād iti cet, mā evam | śabdâbhāsāt pratyakṣād vā iṣṭân-iṣṭôpasthitau tad-a-bhāvāt | mama tv eka-dharmād ubhayôpasthitāv api rajata-raṅgayos tattayā na jñānaṃ doṣād ity ubhaya-ṣiddhaṃ viparīta-jñānaṃ ca doṣāt | na ca evam āvaśyaka-doṣād eva pravṛtti-nivṛttī, satya-sthale tad-a-bhāvāt | na ca visaṃvādinī doṣāt, indriya-liṅga-śabdâdi-doṣāṇām an-anugatatvāt | taj-janya-jñāne ca jāti-bhedāt |

Objection (by a Prābhākara): Effort to act and not to act result from a non-grasping of a distinctness (that is to be understood in the following manner, a distinctness) from something F that exists in something G, where the F is set in memory because of a cognition of the something as possessing that property. (So) by a property that exists in tin and in silver, tin and silver are remembered, but not (in the way they really are, namely) as silver and tin.

(Similarly) there would be effort on the part of someone intent on (picking up) a *māṣa* bean (a kind of unhusked dal), effort (erroneously) directed toward a bit of ink powder in the midst of a pile of *māṣa* beans, because of a non-grasping of a distinctness in the *māṣa* beans, which are remembered by the dark color of ink powder (a color they have in common with ink powder). Superimposition of something being experienced (on something else being experienced) is entirely unknown. Otherwise (i.e., if there were not a single shared property), for you, too, each (distinct property) would be (a provoker of) cognition of both.

Gaṅgeśa: Don't think like that. For, from apparent (but false) testimony (pointing to silver as tin and tin as silver) or from perception, what's desired or what's not desired can be set in awareness *without that* (memory of a property as a causal factor).

I, on the other hand, hold that a single property (perceived, e.g., silver*i*ness) can set both (of two distinct types of thing, e.g., silver and tin) in awareness.

Even so, we agree that it's because of an epistemic defect in cases where silver and tin are not cognized as silver and tin. Yet the defect results in (not as you say a non-grasping of a distinctness, but in an erroneous, a) contrary awareness.

Moreover, it is not the case that inasmuch as a defect is required one would be entirely responsible for the effort to act or not to act. For, in situations of a reality (being known), no defect is found (but there is effort to act or not to act). Nor is it (enough to say) that ineffective effort to act or not to act results from a defect (leaving out the role of cognition), since defects are not uniform but vary according to (whether an erroneous cognition has been generated by a) sense organ, inferential mark, testimony, etc. Furthermore, there are distinct universals with regard to cognitions' causes (i.e., they fall into natural kinds).

Comments

Contrary to what the Prābhākara claims, superimposition of something currently being experienced on something else currently being experienced is a phenomenon that is not unknown within classical philosophic discussions: a red flower behind a crystal makes the crystal seem red without a need for a superimposition of something remembered. Nor does the bean-ink example that the Prābhākara gives appear apt, since it, like the red-crystal illusion, dubiously requires a remembering. The point is to answer Gaṅgeśa's refutation, namely, that a double mistake concerning silver and tin would give rise, on the Prābhākara account, to doubt. In each case, a non-grasping of a distinctness between a perception of a thing in front and a memory of the second of a pair (tin or silver)—four occurrent cognitions in all—would provoke in their simultaneity nothing but confusion, i.e., doubt, specifically about which item is tin and which silver. However, the everyday practice is to speak of the situation as one of error, not doubt. Gaṅgeśa will repeatedly mention the difficulty.

Now, if there were only a single property remembered that tin and silver share, as the Prābhākara claims here, then the difficulty of the doubt might be avoided. There would be no cognitive error but only a failure to notice the difference of the one from the other because of the shared property. The Prābhākara contends, moreover, that if the Naiyāyika does not accept that a single property in both cases—a property furnished by memory—is what gets superimposed, then he would be forced into a similar predicament, namely, that two distinct properties would provoke doubt in each case. Gaṅgeśa's rejection of this counterargument targets the supposition that the superimposed property has to be furnished by memory, which seems indeed the weak plank in the Prābhākara's stance. In the example of the double mistake of tin and silver, we can readily imagine that a presumed authority S could point to the tin and say to T "Silver" and point to the silver and say "Tin." A memory need not play a causal role at all, as it would not in this example of a bit of false but apparent testimony. (Imagine that T had never before experienced tin or silver.)

There are, furthermore, the significant regularities that Gaṅgeśa points out. Though epistemic defects are not uniform overall, ineffective acts can be usefully grouped according to the type of erroneous cognition that has generated them, and these, in turn, he suggests at the end, can be sorted naturally, at least according to type of apparent source—apparent perception, apparent inference, and so on—that is defective as an epistemic process.

The example of testimony that Gaṅgeśa cites does not, however, appear pertinent in that the error then would seem not to be perception-like but rather a mistake concerning what something is called—along with an association with value in the case of that called silver and a contrary association in the case of that called tin. This would not be a case of something *appearing* as other than it is. On the other hand, Gaṅgeśa, for the moment at least, may be understood to be pointing out merely that the Prābhākara's insistence on a remembering to explain misdirected effort faces counterexamples. Gaṅgeśa does continue to cite the example, but whether he misconstrues it remains to be seen.

Text (p. 522, Tirupati, and p. 494, Calcutta) and Translation

navyās tu, raṅga-vṛttitayā jñāta-dharmasya rajate utkaṭâkāṅkṣā, tena saha bhūyas-sahacāra-darśanāt, na raṅge alpa-tathātvād iti tatra an-utkaṭā sā | evaṃ rajata-vṛttitayā jñāta-dharmasya api | ataḥ utkaṭâkāṅkṣayā an-utkaṭâkāṅkṣā-pratibandhān na raṅge nivṛttiḥ | evaṃ rajate na pravṛttir iti | tan na | ime raṅga-rajate iti śabdâbhāsād yugapat pravṛtti-nivṛtti-prasaṅgāt śabdād upasthitau ākāṅkṣāyās tulyatvāt | kiṃ ca evaṃ dharmayor bhuyo-'lpa-sahacārâvagamād utkaṭân-utkaṭa-koṭiko raṅgaṃ rajataṃ vā iti saṃśayaḥ syāt | utkaṭân-utkaṭâkāṅkṣā-kalpane mānâbhāvāt utkaṭatvâ-niruktes ca |

(**Gaṅgeśa** continues:) But the new (Prābhākaras reason as follows).

New Prābhākaras: A property (e.g., a certain glitter) known as present in tin (nevertheless) arouses an acute expectation of silver, because it is seen to be in abundance associated with silver. In the case of tin, there is no such acute expectation, because in small quantities is it so (i.e., seen to be associated with tin). Thus, in the case of tin, the expectation is not acute. In this way, although the property is known to be present in silver, there is, therefore, no effort to refrain from acting toward misperceived tin, because by an *acute* expectation (of silver) the *slack* expectation of tin is blocked. Thus (also) is there no effort directed toward the silver.

Gaṅgeśa: That's wrong. (The cognition) "These two are tin and silver" (when in reality the two are silver and tin) could come about from apparent (false) testimony, such that there would be simultaneously effort to act and not to act (toward each thing)—this is the difficulty. When from testimony the two are set in awareness, the expectations would be the same.

Furthermore, if you were right, two properties in association (with one or the other of two things) according to a presence in abundance or in a small quantity would give rise to doubt (and not to error, doubt) whose alternatives would be expectation that is acute or not acute, "Is it tin or silver?" (Moreover) there is no reason to imagine acute and non-acute expectations. And no explanation of (such) acuteness (is available).

Comments

Mathurānātha gives the example of *cākacakya*, "a certain glitter."

According to the New Prābhākaras here, not precisely a remembering—

though memory-impressions are surely involved—but an expectation, such as occurs with inference (e.g., an expectation of fire from sight of smoke), explains error, i.e., erroneous behavior. A property, such as the lustre of tin, excites an expectation of a certain property-bearer, tin, one that is defined by the universal, tinhood. But the same property in greater abundance excites an expectation of a distinct property-bearer, silver, defined by a distinct universal, silverhood. All cognition is veridical, but somehow something goes wrong with an expectation excited. In the case of tin mistaken for silver, the strength of an expectation excited—an expectation presumably built up through memory-impressions formed by previous experiences—blocks a normal expectation of tin. We are not told, however, how the reverse illusion occurs, how silver could be mistaken for tin.

Gaṅgeśa's response is straightforward. The explanation does not apply to the case where S *says* to T, pointing at two items in front, "Silver and tin"—switching the order—the two being in reality tin and silver. T's mistake does not occur through the force of an expectation excited. And again, though the mistake would apparently not be an example of perceptual illusion according to Nyāya, Gaṅgeśa's point is to give a counterexample to the account of misdirected effort. And that he does.

Furthermore, the New Prābhākara faces the same problem as the Old Prābhākara faced, to wit, that doubt would occur upon expectations of tin and silver—in the dual illusion—being simultaneously raised. Finally, Gaṅgeśa says that the postulation of such an acuteness, or lack of it, is unsupported by experience.

Text (p. 524, Tirupati) and Translation

syād etat | saṃvādi-visaṃvādi-pravṛttyor vaicittrye viśiṣṭa-jñāna-bhedâ-grahau hetū kḷptatvāt, na tu viśiṣṭa-jñāna-satyatvâ-satyatve gauravād | a-siddheś ca | pravṛtti-nivṛtti-mātre ca iṣṭân-iṣṭa-purovarti-jñānaṃ hetur iti na an-anugamaḥ | na tu viśiṣṭa-jñānaṃ gauravāt | na ca bheda-grahe 'tiprasaṅgaḥ | viśiṣṭa-jñānaṃ bhedâ-grahaṃ ca viśeṣa-dvaya-hetuṃ vinā sāmānya-hetoḥ kāryân-utpādāt | na hi nirviśeṣaṃ sāmānyaṃ nāma | anyathā andhasya tvak-sambandhe mahaty udbhūta-rūpavati candra-mahasi pratyakṣatâpattiḥ | dravya-sākṣātkāra-hetoḥ sattvāt | evaṃ raṅge rajate ca visaṃvādinyau bhavataḥ bhedâ-grahāt | na ca saṃvādinyau, viśiṣṭa-jñānâ-bhāvāt |

New Prābhākaras: That may be. (However) a cognition of an entity as qualified and a non-grasping of distinctness are two causes for (respectively) effective and non-effective effort to act as distinct phenomena, since the two causes are both well-known. True and untrue cognitions of entities as qualified are not the causes, since that (hypothesis) is theoretically cumbersome as well as unevidenced. (To say) that a cause of effort to act, or of effort not to act, taken by itself, is cognition of a desired, or an unwanted, object in front, is not to posit something that is non-uniform. The cause is not, however, cognition *of an entity as qualified* (adding the qualification, "of an entity as qualified"), since that would (again) be cumbersome.

Nor do we face a defeating difficulty by including too much (namely, predicting effort to act) when there is grasping of a distinctness (e.g., mother-of-pearl perceived and silver remembered, along with a correctional grasping of the distinctness of mother-of-pearl from the silver that is perceptually grasped). Without (distinct) causes for two different particular effects—(here, namely) cognition of an entity as qualified and a non-grasping of a distinctness—the applicable general causes would not produce the effects (that we are all well aware of). For, there is never generality (as a cause) divorced from particulars. Otherwise, a blind person would, through contact of touch, perceive the light of the moon, which has a materially manifest color—this is the difficulty—since the (relevant) cause, namely, direct contact with a substance, would be occurring.

In this way, effort that is ineffective, both toward tin and silver, but not effective effort, comes to be from a non-grasping of a distinctness, because no cognition of an entity as qualified is occurring.

Comments

Compared to the Prābhākara theory, the Naiyāyika theory adds an additional entity, non-veridical cognition of an entity as qualified. Thus is it said to be cumbersome in explaining ineffective effort to act. The Nyāya view is unevidenced in that regard, too, being concocted just to play that explanatory role. If the New Prābhākara theory seems to posit non-uniform causes, the response is that the effects to be explained are not uniform. Concerning simply effort to act or not to act, there is a uniform cause but not for the *abnormal* result of ineffective effort. Distinct effects require distinct causes. Both the sense of sight and the sense of touch work by, in general, sensory connection. But further particulars are relevant. Otherwise, a blind person would sense a pot's color (or the color of moonlight) from touching a pot (moonlight, the Prābhākara's example, is similarly thought to be tangible).

The Prābhākara's postulated *non*-grasping is, by the way, not viewed as an additional entity, in that, from the Prābhākara perspective, an absence does not belong to a separate category but is reducible to its locus. Thus, a non-grasping is ontologically eliminable, being nothing other than the person that fails so to grasp. (This position on negation will be argued at length by a Prābhākara *pūrvapakṣin*, below, in the section on absence, *a-bhāva-vāda*.)

Text (p. 527, Tirupati, and p. 499, Calcutta) and Translation

atha rajata-raṅgayoḥ rajata-raṅga-bhedâ-grahāt visaṃvādinyau balāt syātām, tat-sāmagrī-sattvāt | visaṃvādinī tatra satya-rajate na sambhavati iti cet, ata eva bhedâ-graho na tad-dhetuḥ, tat-sattve 'pi tad-a-bhāvāt | na ca pravṛtti-nivṛtti-gataṃ visaṃvāditvaṃ saṃvāditvam apekṣya tad-dhetunā te janyete | kāraṇasya kāryân-apekṣaṇād iti | mā evam | pravṛtter an-iṣṭa-viṣayatvaṃ nivṛtter iṣṭa-viṣayatvaṃ ca visaṃvādaḥ | tathā ca an-iṣṭa-pravṛttāv iṣṭa-viṣaya-nivṛttau ca bhedâ-graho hetur iti kathaṃ tata iṣṭân-iṣṭa-pravṛtti-nivṛttī syātām, tatra tasya a-sāmarthyād iti |

Objection (by a Naiyāyika against the New Prābhākara view): (According to your theory) there may be (in reality) silver and tin, but because of a non-grasping of a distinctness (a non-existing distinctness between, say, silver and silver, any) effort to act should be, willy-nilly (*balāt*), ineffective, because (on your view) such a causal complex would be present. If (you say that) the two bits of ineffective effort (ineffective effort not to act toward tin as well as ineffective effort to act toward silver) would not occur in the case of real silver (etc.), then just for this reason a non-grasping of a distinctness would not be a cause (in general of ineffective effort) in that, although a non-grasping occurs, ineffective effort would not be. Moreover, depending on ineffectiveness or effectiveness residing in an effort to act or an effort not to act, the two (effort to act and effort not to act) would not be produced from that cause (namely, a non-grasping of a distinctness), since a cause is not dependent on its effect (but rather vice-versa).

New Prābhākaras: Don't think that way. (You misunderstand what we mean by ineffective effort.) Effort to act, whose object is (really) unwanted, and effort not to act (to stop oneself or refrain from acting), whose object is (really) wanted, is (what we mean by) the ineffective. And, similarly, a non-grasping of a distinctness *is* a cause with respect to an effort to act whose object is (really) unwanted, and with respect to an effort not to act whose object is (really) desired. Given this, how would there be, therefrom, effort both to act and not to act, toward the desired and undesired? For there would be no capacity there of that (non-grasping of a distinctness).

Comments

The objection depends on a supposition that Gaṅgeśa will later elaborate and stress, the contention that non-graspings of distinctnesses are very common. In the case of anything veridically perceived, for example, a non-existing distinctness from itself is not grasped. Moreover, the distinctness of a pot from a cloth may well not be grasped and the pot still be veridically perceived. Thus since such non-grasping is supposed the crucially differentiating factor, the New Prābhākara view would entail the ineffectiveness of all effort: such a non-grasping would obtain whenever all the other necessary conditions for effort were present. And if the causal status of a non-grasping is denied with respect to effective effort, then it should be denied, too, with ineffective effort, for it is there in both instances.

In response, a clarification of ineffective effort to act and not to act is presented. The clarification does not, however, neutralize the objection, and Gaṅgeśa goes on, in the next passage, to offer a better way to understand the causal processes involved.

Text (p. 501, Calcutta) and Translation

atra brūmaḥ | jñānaṃ sva-viṣaye pravartakam ity ādya-pravṛttau saṃvādi-pravṛttau ca sarvair avadhāritam, lāghavād bhādhakâ-bhāvāc ca | tata iṣṭa-jñānaṃ śuktau pravartakaṃ tad-viṣayakaṃ tad-vyavahāra-hetutvāt svâ-viṣaye tasya a-sāmārthyāt |

Gaṅgeśa: Here we respond as follows. A cognition causes effort to act toward that which is its object. Thus is it definitely determined by all with regard to the first effort to act (in a person's lifetime), and with regard to *effective* effort (in general), because of simplicity and lack of any contrary reason. Therefore (the same holds with *ineffective* effort:) cognition of something desired (e.g., silver) causes effort to act toward (cases like) mother-of-pearl (which is not desired), effort whose intentional content includes that same object (mother-of-pearl), since it is a cause of actual conduct (*vyavahāra*) directed toward that (mother-of-pearl). For, it has no capacity (to cause effort) toward something that is not its object or intentional content.

Comments

Gaṅgeśa' argument is that, since *effective* effort to act, such as reaching out to pick something up, is guided by a cognition whose object is the thing desired which is to be picked up, so *ineffective* effort to act is to be, in the simplest fashion, understood too as guided by a cognition whose object is both (a) something desired and (b) the object in front that is actually picked up. But then the cognition has to be a cognition of an entity as qualified, with the desire prompted by (a) non-veridical predication content, toward (b) something real in front, the object qua qualificandum.

Mathurānātha gives the standard example of a first effort to act, a newborn baby's reaching for its mother's breast. According to Gaṅgeśa, this would be an effort guided by a cognition of an entity as qualified.

In the next passage, a Prābhākara challenges the claim that the Naiyāyika theory is simpler.

Text (p. 529, Tirupati, and p. 502, Calcutta) and Translation

atha bhedâ-grahāt grahaṇa-smaraṇāc ca āvaśyakād visaṃvādi-pravṛtty-upapatter viśiṣṭa-jñāna-kalpane gauravāc ca svâ-viṣaye 'pi jñānaṃ pravartakam iti kalpanāt sarvaiḥ prathamam avadhāritam api tyajyatām iti cet, na | prathama-pravṛtta-pramāṇa-balena tatra api viśiṣṭa-jñāna-kalpanāt | tatra bādhakaṃ vinā tad-virodhena kalpanântarân-udayāc ca phala-mukha-gauravasya a-doṣatvāt | anyathā prathamaṃ sarvair gṛhītā api kāryânvite śaktiḥ siddhârtha-darśanāt gauravāc ca parityajyeta iti sādhu samarthitaṃ guru-matam |

Objection (by a Prābhākara): From a non-grasping of a distinctness, and from a (perceptual) grasping along with a remembering—all as necessary—an ineffective effort can come to be. Positing a cognition of an entity as qualified (to explain ineffective effort) is cumbersome, needless. Thus because of the rule that a cognition can cause effort to act toward that which is *not* its object, *give up* (what you said about) it being from the first (effort in a person's lifetime) definitely determined by all, too!

Gaṅgeśa: No. On the strength of its being first established veridically that effective effort exercised has a cognition of an entity as qualified (as a cause), there, too (regarding ineffective effort), a cognition of an entity as qualified is to be posited (as a cause).

Thus, there, without a reason to the contrary, and without an alternative notion arising in opposition to that (which is already established as a cause), a (charge of) cumbersomeness—coming after and directed toward what has already born fruit—is (to identify) no fault (and thus your attack is disarmed).

If this were not so, the designating force (of a word), although grasped by everyone from the earliest (moment of learning what the word means, precisely as you Prābhākaras hold) in connection with an action (i.e., in connection with something to be accomplished, such as a child's seeing a cow being brought after the words "Bring a cow" have been uttered—well, *you* should have to *give up* this your theory of meaning when you say to us), "Give it up," (for the very reason we Naiyāyikas cite your theory of meaning, namely) because a thing (referred to) is already established (without being connected to an action, as in "That is a cow there"), and because of cumbersomeness—oh, well considered is the view of the Guru (Prabhākara)!

Comments

Gaṅgeśa's charge is that the Prābhākara view is inconsistent. The Prābhākara cannot (a) hold that words are learned and retain their meaning in a person's own speech acts throughout his/her lifetime only in connection with action (e.g., a bringing of a cow), a connection that is, then, never lost even when a word learned is used merely for something factive unconnected to action (such as "There is a cow there"), and at the same time (b) recommend rejecting a cause—which is first and definitely determined with respect to effective effort—regarding ineffective effort. In his theory of meaning, he proceeds in the way that he is criticizing.

Near the beginning of Gaṅgeśa's response, a literary trope seems to occur in the words, "the heaviness (*gaurava*) of the first fruit (*phala-mukha*) is no fault.'' But of course the point is that the objection that the Naiyāyika theory is cumbersome falls flat, not strictly because the positing of a cognition of an entity as qualified is simpler than the Mīmāṃsaka view of a lack of awareness of a distinctness, but because, given that the Naiyāyika posit works elsewhere—has borne fruit elsewhere, concerning effective effort—cumbersomeness is outweighed by theoretical success and unity.

Text (p. 530, Tirupati, and p. 505, Calcutta) and Translation

nanu sva-viṣaye jñānaṃ pravartakam iti satyaṃ | kiṃ tu visaṃvādi-pravṛttāv idaṃ-jñānam eva pravartakaṃ na tv iṣṭa-jñānam api | tad dhi jñāyamānêṣṭa-bhedâ-grahe kāraṇatâvacchedakaṃ lāghavād iti daṇḍatva-vad anyathā-siddhaṃ | evaṃ hi tat-pratibaddha-vyavahārânukūlakatvaṃ tad-viṣayatvaṃ rajata-jñānasya śuktau na asti | anyathā rajata-jñānasya śukti-viṣayatvâpatteḥ | saṃvādi-pravṛttau ca iṣṭa-jñānaṃ pravartakam, tasya viśiṣṭa-jñānatvāt a-bhedena avacchedakatvâ-bhāvād iti mama siddhânta-sāra iti cet, ucyate | sva-tantrânvaya-vyatirekād iṣṭa-jñānaṃ hetur eva na tv itara-hetutâvacchedakam anyathā-siddhaṃ vā | na hi iṣṭa-jñānam ādāya eva iṣṭa-bhedâ-grahasya anvaya-vyatirekau yena daṇḍatva-vat tad-avacchedakam | na api iṣṭa-jñānasya bhedâ-graha-garbhatvena anvaya-vyatirekau, yena daṇḍa-rūpa-vat tad-anyathā-siddham | anyathā a-gṛhīta-bhedêṣṭa-jñānaṃ hetur avacchedako bhedâ-graha ity eva kiṃ na syāt | tasmāt sva-tantrânvaya-vyatirekād ubhayor api hetutvam |

Objection (by the Prābhākara:) Concerning its own object, a cognition is indeed a cause of effort to act—this is true. But concerning ineffective effort, cognition of a ''this'' is alone a cause, not (as you say) cognition of what's desired, too. For, then, in a non-grasping of a (presented thing's) distinctness from something desired that is being cognized (too, i.e., that is being remembered) is there specification of the type of cause (that is to say, the non-grasping qualifies the motivating cognition in its causal role), since this is the economical position. (The non-grasping is not itself a cause, but only a specifier of the type of cause since) it, like being-a-stick (vis-à-vis a pot as an effect) is not strictly necessary (*anyathā-siddha*, ''is present other than as a cause'').

For, in this way is there no cognition of silver in mother-of-pearl, no cognition that has that (mother-of-pearl) as its object in conformity with conduct blocked by cognition of silver. Otherwise, we would land in the unfortunate difficulty of a cognition of silver having mother-of-pearl as its object.

And concerning effective effort, cognition of a thing desired is the instigator, since that (in that case) is a cognition of an entity as qualified. For (there, in cases of successful effort) there is no qualification by a (cognitive) non-distinctness—such is the heart of our position.

Gaṅgeśa: We answer. By positive and negative correlations independently ascertained, we arrive at the position that cognition of a thing desired is indeed a cause (in all instances of effort); it is not the specifier of a type of cause (but is itself a cause). Nor is it not strictly necessary (*anyathā-siddha*).

For, regarding precisely a cognition of something desired, there is no correlation, positive or negative, with a non-grasping of a distinctness with what is desired whereby, like being-a-stick (a universal inhering in a stick used to make a pot), that would be a specifier (of a type of cause). Nor is there correlation, positive or negative, between cognition of what is desired and an internalization (a cognitive internalization) of a non-grasping of a distinctness such that, like the color of a stick (which is *not* necessary to the production of a pot but that is internal to a veritable cause of the production of a pot), that would not be strictly necessary.

Otherwise, why indeed shouldn't a cognition of something desired as possessing a distinctness (from whatever) that is not grasped be a cause? Then (what you say would be right:) a non-grasping of a distinctness would be a specifier (i.e., specifying a type of cognition that is a cause of effort to act).

Therefore, by positive and negative correlations independently ascertained, (we arrive at) the causality for both (effective and ineffective effort).

Comments

The Prābhākara sees the object of a cognition—qua qualificandum, that is—as presenting something in front, as presenting a "this," which in all instances is a cause of effort to act, whether effective or ineffective. In the case of ineffective effort, another necessary factor is the non-grasping that has been explained, but not a perceptual cognition's predication content. The Naiyāyika, in contrast, views perceptual predication content as causally crucial with respect to whatever effort, and seeing it that way allows us to understand why a person desiring silver sometimes reaches out to pick up a piece of mother-of-pearl.

At the end of the objection, the shorthand, "qualification by a (cognitive) non-distinctness," amounts to the same thing as a non-grasping of a distinctness. According to the Prābhākara, when a remembering and a perceiving are not seen to be distinct, there obtains such a cognitive non-distinctness. In the case of cognitions that motivate successful effort, on the other hand, no such qualification is required.

The heart of Gaṅgeśa's response is that where there is effort there is desire, and where there is no desire there is no effort. Thus, the "silver" content of an erroneous cognition is required just as much as the cognition's qualificandum, all as presented perceptually, to understand why a person desiring silver sometimes reaches out to pick up a piece of mother-of-pearl.

The Prābhākara variation involving specifiers does not confuse Gaṅgeśa, who shows that such a refinement is uncalled for. In the next passage, Gaṅgeśa says that at the level of such specifiers what the Prābhākara proposes is flatly wrong.

Text (p. 507, Calcutta) and Translation

kiṃ ca iṣṭa-viṣaya-pravṛtti-sthale pravṛtti-mātraṃ prati iṣṭa-jñānasya hetutvād iyam api pravṛttis taj-janyā kḷpta-hetuṃ vinā kāryân-utpatteḥ | na ca iṣṭa-jñāna-janyatve iṣṭa-viṣaya-pravṛttitvam avacchedakaṃ gauravāt | bādhakaṃ vinā sāmānyayoḥ kārya-kāraṇa-bhāva-niyamāt | ata eva tan na upādhir api |

(**Gaṅgeśa** continues:) Moreover, in the case of effort to act toward an object that is desired, a cognition of what is desired is a cause of the effort. The effort, we might add, is produced by that (we hold), because, without its known cause, an effect (simply) does not arise.

And we deny that being-effort-to-act-toward-the-object-that-is-desired shows what kind of causality there is with respect to a cognition's responsibility for achieving something desired. For, that is cumbersome (that is, in comparison with, simply, being-effort-to-act). Without considerations to the contrary, the (default) rule of the cause-effect relationship is that the relationship applies to pairs as considered *in general.*

Just for this reason, that (being-effort-to-act-toward-the-object-that-is-desired) is not, furthermore, an undercutter, *upādhi* (with respect to the inference, suggested above: cognition of something desired is a cause of effort to act in cases of undesired mother-of-pearl, *since* it is a cause of actual conduct directed toward such things, like effort directed toward desired realities).

Comments

In the first paragraph, Gaṅgeśa says that once we see a particular causal relationship we are justified in assuming, according to the causal law, that without that cause the effect would not arise, and thus here that without a cognition of something desired there would be no effort to act.

The disagreement over the specifier of the type of cause reflects the heart of the dispute over error. For, Gaṅgeśa includes instances of error and veridical cognition alike as causes of effort to act, whereas the Prābhākara will so interpret "object" in his proposed causal specifier that instances of ineffective effort—namely, error, on his view—are excluded. Gaṅgeśa sees simply being-effort-to-act as the specifier. The Prābhākara, on the other hand, does not view, it is worth repeating, perceptual cognition of desired silver as motivating someone to reach to pick up what is actually mother-of-pearl.

The default rule, Gaṅgeśa points out, is that the cause-effect relationship applies to pairs as considered in general, that is, without counterconsiderations. In other words, a consideration could lead to a need to specify a special causal factor, but that is not the default position. Nor are we mindful of any such counterconsideration.

The reason the Prābhākara specifier is not an *upādhi* for the inference suggested is that, though it pervades the probandum—here, being a cause of effort directed toward such things as undesired mother-of-pearl—it also pervades the prover—being a cause of actual conduct directed toward such things. Therefore, the inference is not undermined.

Text (p. 532, Tirupati, and p. 508, Calcutta) and Translation

atha tatra api idaṃ-jñānam[8] pravartakaṃ, daivâdhīnaṃ tasya iṣṭa-viṣayatvam api iti cet, tarhi iṣṭe idam iti jñānād eva pravṛttiḥ syāt | na hy atra iva tatra api jñāyamānêṣṭa-bhedâ-grahaḥ pravartakaḥ | etena na rajata-jñānaṃ śukti-viṣayakaṃ tat-pratibaddha-vyavahārâ-hetutvād iti nirastam | a-siddheḥ |

Objection: There (regarding desired silver), too, a cognition of a "this" causes effort to act. It, too, has the thing desired as object; (however, that objecthood is negligible in that) it depends on chance (i.e., it is fortuitously additional to the causal complex responsible for the effort to act).

Gaṅgeśa: If that were right, then, just from a cognition "This" with respect to something desired there would be effort to act. (In other words, cognition of it as, e.g., silver would not be necessary, while of course it is.) For, it is not the case that, as it is here (with respect to error), there, too (with veridical cognition), the instigator is a *non-grasping* of a distinctness between (a) a thing being cognized and (b) something desired.

Thus is the view thrown out that since a cognition of silver does not cause behavior opposed to itself, it cannot have as its object mother-of-pearl. For that is unestablished.

Comments

The glaring failure of the Prābhākara position is that no silver-seeker is moved to pick up something that is cognized as a mere "this." Thus, the Naiyāyika, but not the Prābhākara, is able to maintain a cognitive parallelism with both successful and unsuccessful effort, namely, in finding a cognition of an entity as qualified to be in both instances a cause. Thus, the view has to be discarded that a cognition whose object is, in one sense (i.e., qua predication content), silver, cannot have, in another sense (i.e., qua qualificandum), an object in mother-of-pearl.

Text (p. 532, Tirupati) and Translation

nanu jñānaṃ yathârtham eva iti vyāptir eva tad-bādhikā | ata eva pravṛtti-mātre viśiṣṭa-jñānam iṣṭa-jñānaṃ ca hetur lāghavāt sva-viṣaye jñānaṃ pravartakam, sarvair eva ādya-pravṛttau tathâvagamāt | a-satya-sthale iṣṭa-jñānam api pravartakaṃ, na tu bhedâ-grahe hetutâvacchedakam ity anyathā-khyāti-sādhanaṃ na bhavati iti cet, na | teṣām an-anyathā-siddhāv[9] anvaya-vyatirekâvadhārita-kāraṇatā-mūlakatvena tair eva vyāpti-bādhāt | kḷpta-hetuṃ vinā kāryân-utpatteḥ vipakṣe bādhakâ-bhāvāc ca | jñānâ-yathārthatve 'pi niṣkampa-pravṛtty-ādyupāyasya vakṣyamāṇatvāt | etena saṃskārêndriyābhyāṃ pratyabhijñāna-vac chabdâbhāsād ito vā paras-paraṃ saṃbandha-virahiṇi ekaṃ jñānaṃ na bhavati iti jñānaṃ yathârtham eva iti vyāptir iti nirastam | vyāpty-ādy-a-siddheḥ sāmagrī-sattve kāryâvaśayakatvāc ca |

Objection (by the Prābhākara): Cognition conforms to its object in every instance—such is a pervasion (wherever there is cognitionhood, there is conformity to the object) defeating that (the view that a silver-cognition can have mother-of-pearl as its qualificandum, *anyathā-khyāti*).

Just for this reason is there no establishing of (your) "presentation otherwise" theory as follows (let me rehearse it): that since it is simpler to hold that effort to act is caused both by a cognition of an entity as qualified and a cognition of a thing desired, (no absence, no *non*-grasping, but rather a presence, namely) a cognition instigates effort toward its own object. For, (as you say) so it is understood by everyone concerning an original effort (e.g., a baby's reaching for its mother's breast). On the occasion of experience of a (as you say) unreality, cognition of something desired is (you also say) still the motivator of effort to act. (You say) it is not (as we say) the specifier of the causality with respect to a non-grasping of a distinctness.

Gaṅgeśa: No. For, these (our arguments)—as rooted in causality ascertained by finding positive and negative correlations with respect to that which is not (causally) irrelevant—just these defeat (your supposed) pervasion (viz., wherever there is cognitionhood, there is conformity to the object). For, without the cause that is well known to exist, there is no arising of the effect.

Moreover, our view faces no counterconsideration. (And) we shall explain how, although cognition is not (invariably) in conformity with its object, it is the instrument of unhesitating effort (and trust in it may be rightly placed).

Objection: That there is a pervasion—such that a cognition *is* invariably in conformity with its object—is shown by the fact that here, from a bit of apparent (but false) testimony, like a recognition that arises from (the activity of) a memory-impression and a sense organ, a single cognition does *not* occur with respect to something lacking the mutual relationship (of qualifier and qualificandum).

Gaṅgeśa: By reasoning already given is this thrown out. For, such a pervasion has not been established, and, given an entire causal complex sufficient for an effect, the effect does occur necessarily.

Comments

The central plank of the Prābhākara position is that all cognition is veridical. A naturally occurring pervasion—between a cognition and a presenting of an object as it is—is said here to be sufficient just by itself to block Naiyāyika reasoning to a contrary conclusion. Gaṅgeśa's response is to deny the pervasion—principally on the grounds that unhesitating effort, which is an effect, has to have, whether frustrated or satisfied, a positive instigator. Such a positive instigator is a cognition of an entity as qualified in the case of frustration just as in the case of successful effort and satisfaction. Positive and negative correlations show as much.

The Prābhākara insists, question-beggingly, that since, e.g., a piece of tin is not ontologically a qualificandum relative to silverhood as qualifier, S's testifying to T, as they both look down at what is really a piece of tin, "This is silver," cannot spark, on T's part, a single cognition. The case is like a recognition, which the Prābhākara analyzes as two cognitions, but which, as we shall see in the last section of the chapter, Gaṅgeśa views as, like an error, a single perception informed by a memory-impression, that is to say, a perception with previous perceptual content retrieved through the activation of a latent memory-impression. On the Prābhākara view, the difference between a recognition and a situation of error is that in the former case we are aware that the remembering is a remembering and is distinct from the perception, whereas in the latter we are not.

Although Gaṅgeśa also views a memory-impression as having a causal role in both illusion and recognition, he does not capitulate concerning the latter. As he holds that effort-prompting error could be entirely perceptual, so he will also argue that a recognition as an occurrent cognition is to be viewed as entirely perceptual too. Arguments for such a view of recognition dominate that final section of the chapter. But some will be considered in the current section, a few pages below, as the discussion hones in on the role of memory-impressions in illusion.

Text (p. 533, Tirupati, and p. 512, Calcutta) and Translation

eka-deśinas tu, rajata-raṅgayo rajata-raṅga-bhedâ-grahān na yugapat pravṛtti-nivṛttī | na ca anyathā-khyātiḥ, doṣa-vaśāt puro-vartinaṃ vihāya smṛta-rajata-raṅgābhyāṃ puro-vartini bheda-grahāt | na ca rajatatvena smṛtiḥ saṃskāra-gocara-sarva-rajata-viṣayā syāt sāmānya-pratyâsattes tulyatvād iti vācyam | tattâṃśe rajatatve ca pratyāsattāv api doṣāt smṛty-anubhava-pratibandha-vad upapatteḥ | kiṃ ca pratyakṣe sāmānyaṃ pratyāsattiḥ, smaraṇe tu manaḥ karaṇaṃ saṃskāraḥ pratyāsattiḥ, na tu tasya sāmānyaṃ pratyāsattir a-karaṇatvāt | tan na | eka-raṅga-rajata-mātra-jñānântaraṃ tayor eva yamajayor vā viparīta-catuṣke 'tiprasaṅgād anyathā-khyāter vā |

(**Gaṅgeśa** continues:) But a faction (of Prābhākaras reasons as follows).

Prābhākara faction: Because the distinctness between silver and tin is not grasped with respect to silver and tin, effort to act and effort not to act would not (as was objected earlier) occur simultaneously. And this is not a case of "presentation otherwise," since, with the thing in front being ignored because of a defect, a distinctness *is* grasped between what's in front and remembered silver (on the one hand) and between what's in front and remembered tin (on the other).

Objection: Inasmuch as the memory would be of silverhood (if what's in front is ignored), it would have as its object all the pieces of silver (in the universe). The memory-impression would take them as its range, since the same sensory relation that obtains with (unexperienced instances of) universals would be operative.

Prābhākara faction: That should not be said. For, it is possible, as with a blocking of remembering by immediate experience, that the defect would block both the "that" portion (of the memory) and silverhood as well.

Furthermore, in the case of a perception, a universal is the operative relation, whereas in the case of a memory, the internal organ (*manas*) is the chief instrumental cause (in appropriate employment), a memory-impression being the operative relation. It is definitely false that a universal is the operative relation in the case of a memory, since it is not its chief instrumental cause.

Gaṅgeśa: That's wrong. For, *either* you get more than you want in an incompatible quatrad (as explained earlier) immediately following simply a cognition of a single bit of tin and of a single bit of silver, just with regard to the two (things in front), as with twins, *or* it is a case of "presentation otherwise."

Comments

Given the presence of a piece of tin and a piece of silver, a non-grasping, with respect to the tin, of its distinctness from silver blocks effort not to act, according to the Prābhākara faction, and a non-grasping, with respect to the silver, of its distinctness from tin blocks effort to act. Thus the objection put forth earlier against the Prābhākara position that there would be simultaneously effort to act and not to act would miss its mark. Apparently, on this view, there would be only effort to act, as unblocked, directed toward the tin, and effort not to act (or to refrain from acting), as unblocked, directed toward the silver—in the example of the dual error concerning silver and tin. We are not told, however, what the instigator of this effort would be. Gaṅgeśa's response draws on that failure.

The Prābhākara faction also maintains that the example would not be a case of "presentation otherwise" (also as earlier alleged)—silver and tin cognized as *qualified*, respectively, by an absence of a distinctness from tin and by an absence of distinctness from silver—because there would be a grasping of a distinctness between the thing-in-front, e.g., the silver, and *remembered* silver, and similarly for the tin: such memory is not taken to *qualify* the thing in front.

Gaṅgeśa's response is that if there is no such qualification, then the impossible foursome sinks the proposal. The point is that, with no instance of qualification, each cognition—(1) perception of tin and (2) memory of silver, along with (3) perception of silver and (4) memory of tin—would occur independently, like twins who are separate individuals. Since, as explained earlier, the memories would not be known as memories, they would motivate effort to act and not to act, like the two perceptions—thus the impossible quatrad. If the four are in any way reduced to two, with their intentionalities integrated—Gaṅgeśa says spelling out the second horn of the fatal dilemma—we would have a version of the Naiyāyika "presentation otherwise" view.

Another problem is that a memory of a qualifier divorced from a particular qualificandum would be of a universal (or the like), such as silverhood. But then silverhood exists in all the bits of silver there are in the world. And so the Prābhākara, who sees a remembering as constituting what the Naiyāyika sees as predication content, must explain why the deceived perceiver makes effort to act toward a particular bit of stuff as opposed to that kind of stuff in general. The reply is that a defect can carry this explanatory load. Gaṅgeśa, however, will bring up the problem again, indicating that he does not think that such a response is adequate, though he lets it pass here.

Text (p. 536, Tirupati, and p. 514, Calcutta) and Translation

> anye tu, rajate na idaṃ rajatam iti jñānaṃ rajatatvâ-saṃsargâ-saṃsargâ-graha-rūpaṃ[10] rajata-bhedâ-saṃsargâ-graha-rūpaṃ pravṛtti-pratibandhakam iti | tan na | anya-vṛttitayā upasthitasya rajatatvâ-saṃsargasya rajata-bhedasya ca raṅge '-saṃsargâ-grahāt nivṛtti-prasaṅgāt raṅge ca tayor a-saṃsarga-grahe anyathā-khyātiḥ |

(**Gaṅgeśa** continues:) But others (Prābhākaras) say the following.

Another **Prābhākara faction**: The cognition, with respect to silver, "This is not silver," is to be analyzed as a non-grasping of the non-relation of silverhood's non-relation (to the "this"), that is, a non-grasping of the (thing-in-front's) non-relation of distinctness from silver (since there really is a non-relation of distinctness from silver). As such, it is what blocks effort to act.

Gaṅgeśa: That's wrong. For, a non-relation to silverhood and a distinctness from silver as well are established in memory as qualifiers of something else (e.g., mother-of-pearl). Since they are not grasped as *not* related to the tin (in the example of the dual error, "Silver and tin," when, instead, tin and silver are there—they are not so grasped when tin is grasped as silver), you land in the predicament that there would be effort to desist (although a person desiring silver would in fact reach out to pick up the tin). And if their non-relation with respect to the tin *is* grasped, there is "presentation otherwise."

Comments

The proposal of (1) a *non*-grasping of (2) a *non*-relation of silverhood's (3) *non*-relation to the "this"—as an analysis of the error verbalized as "This is not silver'' (when there is silver in fact)—is based on the fact that a piece of silver *is* related to silverhood (the second and third negations cancel each other out but are needed to gloss the statement). Thus there is in fact no non-relation of silverhood to the this, or a non-relation of silverhood's non-relation to the this. The non-grasping of this fact is a bit of ignorance informing the error.

In other words, this latest proposal from within the Prābhākara camp focuses on a failure to grasp an absence of a distinctness that is informing a perceptual cognition of a thing-in-front. But whereas in fact a person would make effort directed toward a piece of misperceived tin, the current proposal would mean blockage not only of effort to act toward the silver but also of effort to act toward the tin, since it is not grasped as not related to silverhood, etc. If, on the other hand, a grasping of the non-relation is identified, we would have a view of a cognition of an entity as qualified—a cognition of a ''this'' as qualified by a non-relation to a distinctness from silver—and a version of ''presentation otherwise,'' *anyathā-khyāti*.

Next we are treated to Prābhākara obfuscation by a further piling up of negatives.

Text (p. 537, Tirupati) and Translation

rajate rajata-bhedâ-saṃsargâ-saṃsargasya a-saṃsargâ-grahān nivṛttir iti cet, na | bhedâ-saṃsargâ-saṃsargasya bheda-saṃsarga-rūpatvena rajata-bheda-saṃsargâ-saṃsargâ-grahād[11] raṅge nivṛtti-prasaṅgāt | rajata-bheda-saṃsargâ-saṃsarga-grahe ca anyathā-khyātiḥ | rajata-vṛttitayā upasthite bhede rajata-bhedena saha bhedâ-grahaḥ pravṛtti-pratibandhakaḥ, evaṃ raṅge nivṛttāv api iti cet, na | evam api śabdâbhāsāt yugapat pravṛtti-nivṛtty-āpatteḥ pravṛtti-nivṛtti-viṣaya-niṣṭa-bhedayo raṅga-rajata-bhedayoś ca śabdāt an-upasthityā pratibandhakâ-bhāvāt |

Objection: Effort to refrain from acting toward the (real) silver stems from a non-grasping of the non-relation of a non-relation's non-relation to distinctness from silver.

Gaṅgeśa: No. For, that involves the difficulty that there would be effort not to act toward the tin, since there would be no grasping (as you say) of the non-relation of a non-relation's non-relation to distinctness from silver, inasmuch as the non-relation of a non-relation to distinctness from silver is *the same as* a relation to the distinctness. And if (on the other hand), a grasping of a non-relation to a relation to a distinctness from silver occurs, we have a case there of ''presentation otherwise.''

Objection: The blocker of effort to act is a non-grasping of the distinctness between (two further distinctnesses, namely) the distinctness (from mother-of-pearl) that is established in memory as a qualifier of silver, and the distinctness from silver (that is established in memory as a qualifier of mother-of-pearl). Similarly, too, with respect to (blocking of) effort not to act toward the tin.

Gaṅgeśa: No. If this were so, we would have the predicament of simultaneously both effort to act and not to act (toward the same thing) resulting from apparent (i.e., false but credible) testimony (e.g., "Silver and tin," with respect to two things that are really tin and silver). The testimony would not set in awareness the distinctnesses—distinctnesses that reside in the objects of both the effort to act and the effort not to act, as well as distinctnesses in the tin and the silver (which, in the case we are imagining, would be perceptually presented). Thus there would be not be the blockage (you allege).

Comments

However subtly the Prābhākara tries to formulate his view of the centrality of a non-grasping, proposing a string of absences or non-relations as what is not grasped, he fails—concerning the example of the dual error, "Tin and silver"—to avoid the problem of simultaneous effort to act and to refrain from acting toward each object. If he, on the other hand, admits a grasping, the absences or non-relations count as qualifiers and we have what the Naiyāyika wants, namely, "presentation otherwise."

The example of dual error resulting from false testimony is also a perceptual situation. A person T sees two things that are silver and tin, but does not notice perceptually which is which. S, a mistaken testifier, says the one on the left is tin and the other silver whereas the opposite is true. The point of the example is that the *distinctness* the one thing exhibits in relation to the other (and vice-versa: we are imagining two distinct things, a piece of silver and a piece of tin) is given perceptually, not by the false testimony. The false testimony sets in awareness only tinhood and silverhood. Although testimony is capable of setting in awareness two things as distinct from one another, in the example the distinctnesses would be given perceptually. The cognition of these would guide effort to act toward the mistaken tin and effort not to act toward the mistaken silver.

Text (p. 538, Tirupati) and Translation

apare tu purovarti-niṣṭhatayā jñāte bhede iṣṭân-iṣṭa-pratiyogitvâ-bhāva-grahāt pravṛtti-nivṛttī | tathā hi, raṅge rajata-bhedaḥ sann api doṣān na bhāsate 'nyasmād bhāsata eva | tathā ca raṅga-vṛttitayā jñāte bhede rajata-pratiyogitvâ-bhāva-grahād yathârthād eva raṅge pravṛttiḥ, raṅga-pratiyogitvâ-bhāvaḥ sann api doṣān na bhāsata iti tatra na nivartate | evaṃ rajata-niṣṭhatayā upasthite bhede raṅga-pratiyogitvâ-bhāva-grahāt rajate nivartate | rajata-pratiyogitvâ-bhāvaḥ sann api doṣān na gṛhyata iti na yugapat pravṛtti-nivṛttī | na ca raṅga-vṛtti-bhedatvaṃ rajata-bhede 'py asti iti tena rūpeṇa so 'pi bhāsate sāmānya-buddheḥ sarva-viśeṣa-viṣayatvāt | tathā ca rajata-bhede 'pi tat-pratiyoginitvâ-bhāva-grahe 'nyathā-khyātir iti vācyam | pratyāsattāv api raṅga-vṛtti-bhedatvena rajata-bhedasya doṣeṇa a-grahād iti |

(**Gaṅgeśa** continues:) Still others (Prābhākaras) say the following.

Another **Prābhākara faction**: When a distinctness is known as residing in a thing in front, effort to act or not to act arises (in a case of error, not from a non-grasping but) from a grasping that lacks in its correlation either the desired or the not-desired as what is excluded. For example, although there is in tin distinctness from silver, it fails, due to a defect, to appear; a distinctness from something else alone appears. And so effort to act toward (undesired) tin arises just from a grasping, which is in conformity with its object, that lacks in its correlation silver as what is excluded, given that a distinctness is known as residing in the tin (the thing really in front). Although there is an absence of an exclusion of tin (in the real tin), it does not, because of a defect, appear. Thus, one does not make effort not to act (toward it). (Moreover) in this way, one does make effort not to act toward (desired) silver because of a grasping that lacks in its correlation tin as what is excluded, given a distinctness set in awareness as residing in (what is really in front, namely) silver. Although there is an absence of an exclusion of silver (in the real silver), it is not grasped because of a defect. Thus, there is no simultaneous effort to act and not to act (toward the same object).

Objection: (There *are* the standing problems.) The "being distinct" that occurs in the tin also occurs in the silver. So in that form too does it appear inasmuch as a cognition of a universal has as its range all the particulars (that exhibit it). (Second) in your way of thinking, there would also be "presentation otherwise" concerning distinctness from silver, in the grasping that lacks that in its correlation.

Prābhākara faction: That should not be said. For, because of a defect there is no grasping of distinctness from silver *as* the distinctness that exists in (the thing in front) the tin, although a cognitive connection (with the thing in front as distinct) obtains.

Comments

Gaṅgeśa has put forth a dilemma: either there is simultaneous effort to act and not to act toward the same thing (in fact, an impossibility), or the error as a cognition of an entity as qualified is a presentation of something as other than what it is. We should keep in mind that, as always, the current Prābhākara proposal to pass through the dilemma's horns would preserve the central thesis that the seemingly perceptual error of taking a piece of tin to be silver is to be analyzed as two *veridical* cognitions, one a perception, the other a remembering, with something about their relation, or non-relation, going unnoticed. In the example of perception of two things—silver as tin and tin as silver—there would be, according to the Prābhākara, a veridical perception of each. And the tin that is veridically perceived is distinct from many other things, including silver. However, although there is in the real piece of tin a real distinctness from silver, because of a defect it goes unnoticed and what gets noticed instead—triggered by a remembering of the distinctness's countercorrelate or *pratiyogin* (what there is distinctness *from*)—is something else, something not silver: "a distinctness from something else alone appears."

Gaṅgeśa responds, in the next passage, not by insisting on the dilemma, but by citing "experience," by which he means apperception. A further reason given is theoretical economy. The various Prābhākara factions have put forth a series of increasingly convoluted qualifications to save their core positions. Gaṅgeśa points out that the Nyāya view is a simple expansion of a theory that works in other cases, that is, in cases of experience of realities. Finally, the current proposal fails to apply to instances of false testimony about which of two items presented perceptually is silver and which is tin, since the *distinctnesses* would be presented perceptually.

Text (p. 539, Tirupati, and p. 518, Calcutta) and Translation

> mā evam | idaṃ rajatam iti jñānam anvaya-vyatirekābhyāṃ pravartakam ity anubhava-siddham | tac ca satya-sthale viśiṣṭa-jñānam anyatra jñāna-dvayam ekaṃ vā jñānam iti vivādaḥ | tatra taj-jñānaṃ na pravartakam ity anubhava-bādhitam | tad api hetur ity api na | tasya satya-sthale '-siddhatvāt | viśiṣṭa-jñānâpekṣayā gurutvāt śabdâbhāsāt pravṛttau bhedâdi-jñānâ-bhāvāc ca | evaṃ nivṛttāv api |

Gaṅgeśa: Don't think like that. The instigator of effort to act is shown to be—by the method of agreement and disagreement (where F, there G; where no G, there no F)—the cognition, "This is silver" (even when the thing in front is tin)—so much does experience establish. And on an occasion of an experience of a reality, it is a cognition of an entity as qualified (that is the instigator). Our disagreement is whether in other cases (namely, in cases of error) there is dual cognition or a single cognition. (And) to hold that a cognition of something is not the instigator of effort to act toward that something is to contradict experience.

It is wrong to say that that (your dual cognition), too, is such a cause. For, it is not known (as such) on any occasion of experience of a reality. In comparison with (the theory of) a (single) cognition of an entity as qualified, (positing) dual cognition is heavier (or theoretically cumbersome).

Furthermore, from apparent (but false) testimony (in the case of the error, "Silver and tin," occurring regarding tin and silver), no cognition of a distinctness, etc., arises with respect to the effort to act (rather, the items as distinct from one another is a matter furnished by perception). All this holds for the effort to refrain from acting, too.

Comments

That unity is simpler than duality is apparently the reason that Gaṅgeśa sees his theory of a single cognition as the instigator of effort as simpler than the Prābhākara view of a dual cognition. But the fact that Nyāya finds the same motivation to act in cases of error and veridical experience alike would also seem to make it the simpler of the two candidates.

Text (p. 540, Tirupati, and p. 520, Calcutta) and Translation

> anye tu, iṣṭa-vṛttitayā gṛhyamāṇo 'n-iṣṭa-vṛttitayā ca a-gṛhyamāṇo dharmaḥ svâśraye pravartaka iti sa ca dharmo rajate rajatatvaṃ raṅge rajata-sādṛśyam | evaṃ nivṛttāv api iti na yugapat pravṛtti-nivṛttī iti | tan na | evaṃ hi ime raṅga-rajate iti śabdâbhāsāt raṅga-rajatayoḥ pravṛtti-nivṛttī na syātām | rajata-vṛtti-dharmasya ca raṅge raṅga-vṛtti-dharmasya rajate śabdād an-upasthiteḥ | na ca śabdân-antaraṃ pratyakṣeṇa tayor upasthitiḥ, tatra hetur na śabda iti vācyam | an-anyathā-siddha-śabdânuvidhānāt ime rajata-raṅge iti svakīyaṃ yathârtha-jñānam an-ādṛtya tatra eva ime raṅga-rajate iti pratāraka-vākye viśvāsena pravṛtti-nivṛtti-darśanāc ca |

(**Gaṅgeśa** continues:) Still others (Prābhākaras) say the following.

Another **Prābhākara faction**: A property that is being grasped as qualifying something desired and that is not being grasped as qualifying something not-desired motivates effort to act toward *its own substratum*. Thus (in accordance with this rule) the property of the silver is silverhood (when one makes effort to pick up silver); it is *similarity* to silver as found in tin (when one makes effort to pick up tin regarded as silver). Effort to refrain from acting, too, is to be understood in this manner. Therefore, there is no simultaneous effort to act and not to act (toward the same thing).

Gaṅgeśa: That's wrong. For, in this way there would be neither effort to act nor not to act toward the tin and silver (whereas in fact one would reach out to pick up what is regarded as silver and make effort to avoid what is regarded as tin) on the basis of a bit of apparent (but false) testimony, "These two are tin and silver," since the testimony would not set in awareness the property resident in silver as in the tin, and the property resident in tin as in the silver.

Objection: Immediately following the testimony, the two would, through a perception, be set in awareness. And thus the cause (of the effort) in this case would not be the testimony (but the perception instead).

Gaṅgeśa: That should not be said. For, the case conforms to cases where testimony is causally relevant (the person acts on the basis of the testimony, reaching out to pick up tin), and (moreover) we do find effort to act and not to act prompted by trust in (what turns out to be) a deceiver's statement just about those two (the silver and tin of our example), "These two are tin and silver"—when (as sometimes happens) one ignores one's own right (perceptual) awareness, "These two are silver and tin."

Comments

Mathurānātha points out that while similarity to silver does indeed rest in tin, that is not a property that could motivate effort to pick up silver. When a poet says that his beloved's face is like the moon, he may be taken to assert that there is similarity to the moon in his beloved's face, but not in the moon. So, the current proposal faces ontological objections, at least from the Naiyāyika perspective. However, the Prābhākara, who sees similarity as a distinct category of the real, views the property in question, which is the instigator of the effort of a deluded person to pick up tin, as "similarity to some bit or other of silver," so Mathurānātha says, a similarity that exists in a bit of silver at hand as well as in the tin. Thus, on the current proposal, memory would not have a role, and there would not be the impossibility of simultaneous effort to act and not to act toward the same thing.

Gaṅgeśa's response is that in the case of an awareness generated by testimony the required properties would not be set in awareness—since the testifier may be presumed to make no mention of any similarity but rather of tin and silver alone. Furthermore, sometimes people disregard their own perception and make effort to act on the basis of what another person tells them, even though that person is, in fact, a deceiver.

Text (p. 540, Tirupati) and Translation

itare tu, rajate rajatatvaṃ na gṛhyate doṣāt | tathā ca rajata-vṛttitayā yāvad upasthita-dharmasya rajatatvena bheda-grahān[12] na pravartate | raṅga-vṛttitayā upastitasya ca kasyacid dharmasya rajatatvena bhedâ-grahād raṅge pravartate | evaṃ nivṛttāv api | yathā tava a-bheda-grahe 'pi mānântarāt bheda-grahaḥ pravṛtti-pratibandhakaḥ tathā rajate rajata-bhedâ-grahe[13] 'pi rajata-vṛttitayā yāvad upasthitasya rajatatvena mama bheda-grahaḥ pravṛtti-pratibandhaka iti | tan na | etad-apekṣayā viśiṣṭa-jñānasya laghutvena anvaya-vyatirekhābhyāṃ ca hetutvāt | na ca hetv-a-bhāvaḥ | pratyabhijñāna-vat saṃskārêndriyābhyāṃ viśiṣṭa-dhī-saṃbhavāt | tasya jñāna-dvayatve '-bhedôcchedaḥ, tasya tad-eka-mānatvāt | na ca eka-viṣayatvena tayoḥ paras-para-sahakāritā | nāma-viśiṣṭa-nāmi-pratyakṣe tattâṃśe ca tad-a-bhāvāt gauravāc ca | na ca atiprasaṅgaḥ | bhedâ-grahasya api tad-dhetutvāt |

(**Gaṅgeśa** continues:) But still others (Prābhākaras) say the following.

Another **Prābhākara faction**: Silverhood is not grasped as existing in silver because of a defect. And so, one does not make effort to act (toward a real bit of silver) because the property that is set in awareness as existing in (a real bit of) silver is, insofar as it is so set, grasped as distinct from silverhood. And (likewise) because of a failure to grasp that a certain property that is set in awareness as existing in (a real bit of) tin is distinct from silverhood, one makes effort toward the tin. Effort to refrain from acting is to be understood in this way (too).

On your (Naiyāyika) view, although a non-distinctness is grasped (erroneously, e.g., a non-distinctness between a shell that is really white and the color yellow) there can be a grasping of a distinctness (of yellow from the shell) from another source (of information, e.g., inference or testimony), a grasping that would block effort to act (on the part of someone desiring a yellow shell). Similarly, there can be, on our view, a grasping of a distinctness that would block effort to act toward silver although there be no grasping of a distinctness from the silver. This grasping would be of a distinctness from silver*hood* regarding the property set in awareness as existing in the silver so long as it is so set.

Gaṅgeśa: That's wrong. Compared to that (i.e., what you have just said), it is simpler to view a cognition of an entity as qualified (as a cause in cases of error). Furthermore, it is shown to be such a cause by positive and negative correlations (in cases of experience of realities as well as of errors). And it is not the case that it is not a cause (here). As with a recognition (e.g., "This is that Devadatta whom I saw yesterday"), it is possible that a cognition of an entity as qualified result from both a memory impression (*saṃskāra*) and a sense organ('s current activity).

If a recognition were two cognitions, destroyed would be the non-distinctness (that one does in fact thereby grasp, "This is that Devadatta"), since the non-distinctness is made known by a single instance.

Furthermore, it is false that the two (a memory impression and a perception) are mutually assistant causes with respect to a single objecthood (as opposed to a complex content). For, that does not happen in the case of a perception of a name-bearer as qualified by a name, nor in the case of the "thatness" portion (of a recognition). Moreover, the view is cumbersome.

And (our) view is not an example of (fallacious) overextension (such that we could be charged with failing to distinguish veridical awarenesses of distinctnesses from cases of error). For (while a veridical awareness of a distinctness may indeed be informed by memory as well as by perception) a non-grasping of a distinctness (as you put it, i.e., an error) may also have the same as a cause.

Comments

If recognition can be established as a qualificative cognition that is perceptual in nature, then it can provide a model—an appropriate analogy—for error on the Nyāya account. The contrast is between (a) a single (perceptual) cognition with complex intentionality (the Nyāya view) and (b) two cognitions each with, in effect, simple intentionality. (On the Mīmāṃsā view, cognitions actually have complex content, but our noticing some of it gets suppressed or "stolen away"). In this passage, Gaṅgeśa gives another analogue: perception of a name-bearer (e.g., Devadatta) as the person who has the name ("Devadatta"). The point is that the whole complex is perceptual, with the name evidently supplied by a memory-impression fusing into a perceptual presentation and not provoking a remembering.

Just how there is such suffusion concerns the "extraordinary sensory connection," which was explained above, p. 125. And as mentioned, the chapter closes with further combatting of the Prābhākara view of recognition. But some of the most interesting arguments occur in the next couple of passages.

Mathurānātha provides the elaboration required to make sense of the last paragraph of the current passage. The point is that the difference in causal factors responsible for veridical and non-veridical cognition does not involve a role, or lack thereof, for a memory-impression. Rather, on the Nyāya view, the difference is, as has been stated, between the presence of an epistemically relevant "excellence" (*guṇa*) or of a similarly relevant "defect" (*doṣa*).

Text (p. 542, Tirupati, and p. 524, Calcutta) and Translation

atha pratyabhijñāyā ekatve 'pi tattâṃśe na sākṣātkāritvam | tatra indriyâ-saṃnikarṣāt taj-jñāna-janyatvāc ca | kiṃ tu smṛtitvam | purovarty-a-bhedâṃśe ca sākṣāttvaṃ smṛtitvam anubhūtitvaṃ ca na jātir a-vyāpya-vṛttir vā iti cet, tarhi saṃskārād a-saṃnikṛṣṭam api bhāsata iti tava apy anumatam | tathā ca tava eva rītyā pratyabhijñāna-vad idaṃ rajatam ity ekaṃ jñānam astu, tat-sāmagrī-sattvāt | mama tv indriya-janyatvāt jaty-a-saṃkarāc ca sākṣātkāritvam eva ubhayatra |

Objection (by a Prābhākara): Although recognition is unitary (i.e., the "thisness" portion and the "thatness" portion, with "This is that," refer to the same thing), the thatness portion is not (perceptual, i.e., not) a matter of immediate experience. For, there is no sensory connection (with the object) and it (the thatness portion) is generated by a (previous) cognition of a that. The thatness portion is, instead, a matter of memory.

While there is immediacy concerning the portion that captures non-distinctness with the thing in front (the thing recognized), being-a-matter-of-memory and being-a-matter-of-experience (or of-awareness, *anubhava*) are not universals (*jāti*, "natural kinds"). (Unlike universals) they are not locus-pervading (as, e.g., cowhood pervades the whole of Bessie; they are non-locus-pervading precisely in the case of a recognition, which can be, then, partially an awareness and partially not an awareness).

Gaṅgeśa: (If your theory were right) then a recognition would result from a memory-impression even when there was no sense/object connection. You would be committed to such a view.

And so, in just your own way and manner, (the error) "This is silver" (when faced with mother-of-pearl), well, let it, like a recognition, be discerned as (what it is, namely, not two cognitions but) a single cognition. For, it occurs when the causal conditions sufficient for a single cognition occur.

Urged by the fact that a recognition is sensory in origin and by the fact that universals do not cross-sect (while awarenesshood and memoryhood *are* universals), my view, in contrast, is that there is indeed immediacy (awarenesshood but not memoryhood) in both (portions, the "thisness" and the "thatness").

Comments

"A cognition that is not generated by a cognition" is a Naiyāyika definition of perception that Gaṅgeśa defends below (p. 335). In the *Nyāya-sūtra* itself, perception is in part defined as a cognition resulting from sense/object connection. The Prābhākara objector argues that recognition is not entirely perceptual on the grounds that a recognition is *not* generated by sense/object connection in its "thatness" portion. Something would be recognized when it is experienced *and* realized as the same thing that was experienced previously. The "thatness" would be grounded in the previous experience as preserved in memory. Furthermore, he says, a recognition *is* "generated by a cognition" (the previous experience of Devadatta).

The Prābhākara also anticipates a Naiyāyika argument when he says that awarenesshood or experiencehood ("being-a-matter-of-experience") and memoryhood are not universals, suggesting they are "surplus properties" (*upādhi*) instead. Thus it is possible that they, unlike universals, be only partly present in a locus, such as in a recognition.

Again, Gaṅgeśa does not lay out his full understanding of recognition until the last section of this first chapter of the *TCM*. Precisely how to understand recognition is a central problem of the entire chapter. Naiyāyikas traditionally see recognition as a perception. But a recognition would seem to be closely informed by—or even, as Prābhākaras hold, constituted in part by—a remembering. Gaṅgeśa's view is that a recognition is not even in part an act of remembering, nor is it even in part caused by a remembering. Rather, it is in part caused by a *memory-impression* (*saṃskāra*). And considering the instrumental causes, the memory-impression is not the chief instrumental cause, which is the sense organ, but only an "auxiliary cause" (*sahakārin*). A memory-impression is an auxiliary cause of a recognition's "thatness" portion. Perhaps counterintuitively, Gaṅgeśa also says that the thatness portion is somehow itself properly perceptual. This view he now has to defend from Mīmāṃsaka attack.

Concerning the view that genuine universals never *cross-sect* or intersect in their extensions, see, in this text, pp. 700–701.

Text (p. 543, Tirupati) and Translation

nanu yo yat-sākṣātkāraḥ sa tad-indriya-saṃnikarṣa-janyaḥ | na ca rajate sa iha asti iti cet, na | pratyabhijñāyā indriya-janyatayā sākṣātkāritvena tattāyāṃ nāmni ca vyabhicārāt | saṃskārasya smṛter vā saṃnikarṣatvāc ca | na ca rajatatva-pratyakṣe saṃyukta-samavāyasya pratyāsattitvena hetutvāt taṃ vinā tad iti vācyam | tad-viśiṣṭa-jñāne viśeṣaṇa-jñānôpakṣīṇatvena tasya a-hetutvāt | na hi viśiṣṭa-dhī-sāmagrī-sattve tena vinā tad-vilambaḥ |

Objection: (There is the rule:) Whatever (cognitive element) is immediate, that (cognitive element) is sensory in origin. And immediacy does not occur here concerning silver (i.e., in the error).

Gaṅgeśa: No. For, there are counterexamples concerning (a) the thatness of a recognition that as sensory in origin is (indeed) immediate, and concerning (b) a name-bearer (in connection with its name). Moreover, the (sensory) connection can be made by (or through) either a memory-impression or a memory.

Objection: Since a perception of silverhood would have a cause in a sensory connection, (viz.) "inherence in what is in contact (with a sense organ)," none would occur without that operative connection.

Gaṅgeśa: That should not be said. For, inherence-in-what-is-in-contact is not a cause of the (erroneous) cognition of an entity as qualified ("This is silver") inasmuch as cognition of the qualifier (that does exist by the relation of inherence in what the sense organ is in contact with) has been quieted (because of a defect). For, given an occurrence of the causal complex sufficient to bring about the (erroneous) cognition of an entity as qualified ("This is silver"), it is not the case that it would be delayed without that (connection holding).

Comments

Nyāya maintains that perceptual cognitive content is invariably sensory in origin. How can this be asserted alongside the insistence that a recognition's "thatness" is perceptual? or an illusion's "silverhood?" What is the sensory connection? The answer is, as explained, that memory is capable of projecting contents of previous perceptions into a current perception. This projecting capability—or revival of previous contents—is evident in phenomena ranging from illusion to perception of a name-bearer to recognition. The process is perceptual, we may say, in three mutually reinforcing ways. A memory cannot revive what has not been perceived (perception is responsible for the data, so to say, retrieved by memory). A current sensory connection triggers the revival in the first place. And the result of the whole process is a perception. That is to say, the process (a) begins with a sensory connection, (b) works through perception-dependent memory, and (c) results in a perception of an entity as qualified, a cognition all of whose objecthood is perceptually given as shown phenomenologically in apperception. For example, sometimes current sight of sandalwood triggers through memory the pleasing smell which appears to belong to that very sighted sandalwood as we can tell apperceptively, "I am perceiving the sandalwood as fragrant."

The next section of the *TCM*, a short one, is on defining perception. In it as well as in the following section, Gaṅgeśa takes up the general topic of what it is to be "sensory in origin." Following Uddyotakara, he lays out six types of common or "ordinary" (*laukika*) sensory connection, one of which is mentioned in the passage above, inherence-in-what-is-in-contact.

But, to repeat, to explain error we must talk about "extraordinary" (*a-laukika*) sensory connections. An illusory presentation of something as silver is considered perceptual—phenomenologically as well as upon analysis—even in its "silverhood" portion, like the fragrance of a piece of sandalwood contacted only by sight.

Mother-of-pearl-hood inheres in a piece of mother-of-pearl to which, let us imagine, a sense organ is connected. But because of a defect that qualifier is not perceived but rather silverhood. Thus, the sensory connection of "inhering in what is in contact" is not strictly necessary for a perception of something as silver.

Text (p. 546, Tirupati, and p. 526, Calcutta) and Translation

kiṃ ca viśeṣaṇa-jñānaṃ viśeṣya-saṃbandhas tayor a-saṃsargâ-graha iti pratyabhijñā-satya-pratyakṣa-sādhāraṇasya viśiṣṭa-pratyakṣa-hetor bhrame 'pi saṃbhavāt | rajata-sākṣātkāre rajata-saṃyogasya hetutve 'pi viśeṣya-saṃnikarṣatvena hetutā, na tu rajata-saṃyogatvena | yat-sāmānye yat-sāmānyaṃ hetus tad-viśeṣasya hetutva-niyamāt | saṃyogasya viśeṣya-bhāna-sāmagry-antaritatvena anyathā-siddhatayā viśeṣa-sāmagry-antarâ-kalpanāt gauravāc ca | pratyakṣa-hetutvena kḷpta-viśeṣya-saṃbandhād eva tad-upapatteḥ | api ca pravṛttau sva-tantrôpasthitêṣṭa-bhedâ-graha-kāraṇatvâpekṣayā rajata-sākṣātkāre viśeṣya-saṃnikarṣatvena hetutvasya laghutvāt |

(**Gaṅgeśa** continues:) Moreover (we are talking about) a cognition of a qualifier and a (sensory) relation with a qualificandum. That there be no grasping of a non-relatedness of these two (qualifier and qualificandum) is possible in error, just as a non-grasping of their non-relatedness is a cause of any perception of an entity as qualified, common (as well) to both recognition ("this" and "that" are taken to pick out the same thing: there is no grasping of their being distinct) and perception of a reality ("this" and "silver," when there really is silver in front, are taken to pick out the same thing: there is no grasping of their being distinct). Although in a (veridical) case of an immediate experience of silver a contact with silver would be a cause (of silverhood appearing as predication content), the causality would work by way of the sensory connection to the qualificandum, not by way of contact with silver (*per se*). For there is the rule: a cause with respect to something general is (or, has to be identified as) something general; something as a particular is (or, has to be identified as) a cause of something particular.

For, (sensory) contact, which is necessarily included in a collection of causes sufficient to produce an appearance of a qualificandum, is not to be considered as necessarily included in a collection of causes sufficient to produce (an appearance of) a particular (qualifier). And to consider it necessary would be theoretically cumbersome. As to perceptual causes, that is possible (i.e., the appearance of a misplaced qualifier is possible) just from the well-known (and generally accepted, sensory) contact with a qualificandum.

And, furthermore, in comparison with the (Prābhākara) view that a cause of effort to act (in the case of what is called error) is a failure to grasp the distinctness between (the thing in front and) something (e.g., silver) that is independently set in awareness (through remembering) and is desired, (in comparison with such a view) it is theoretically simpler to consider a cause of an immediate presentation of silver to be a sensory connection to the qualificandum (which would be mother-of-pearl, for instance, in the case of the error).

Comments

Gaṅgeśa's claim, at the beginning of the passage, that there is "no grasping of a non-relatedness" stands in tension with what he says below in the section on inherence (the *samavāya-vāda*), where he insists on a sense in which a qualifier and a qualificandum are grasped as distinct.

Here Gaṅgeśa argues that the principle that a perceptual appearance of silver has as its relational cause "sensory connection with silver" cannot stand unqualified. The true principle is, rather, that a perceptual appearance of silver has "sensory connection with silver" as the operative relation *insofar as the silver is understood as a qualificandum*, a bearer of properties. In other words, the rule is that while sensory connection to *x* (something perceived) is necessary for a perception of *x* as a qualificandum, such connection is not necessary with respect to what *x* is appearing *as* qua qualifier. Rucidatta adds that otherwise contact with one bit of silver could cause perception of some other bit of silver somewhere else.

In contemporary epistemology, two senses of "see" are sometimes identified. In one sense, "to see" implies success vis-à-vis an intersubjectively accessible object. Thus, if I see a book on a table, then there is a book there. A second sense is phenomenalist and does not imply that kind of success. Thus, Macbeth sees a daggar floating in the air, though there is there no intersubjectively perceptible dagger. Gaṅgeśa's point is different but can be understood by way of the two usages: If we see *x*, then *x*, qua qualificandum, exists, but what we take ourselves to see *x as*—namely, as an F, or as having F-hood, what in Sanskrit is called a qualifier (*viśeṣaṇa*)—need not exist where we take it to be. Whatever we see, qua qualificandum, must be related to our sense faculties in the standard ways, but not whatever we see as a qualifier.

Text (p. 549, Tirupati) and Translation

vastutas tu, doṣād bhrama ity ubhaya-siddham, tatra bhramo na a-saṃsarga-grahâbhāvaḥ | tasya adhikaraṇa-rūpatve a-sādhyatvāt | taj-jñāna-rūpatve ca tasya pramātvena doṣâ-janyatvāt | bhrama-sthānâbhiṣikta-pramā doṣa-janyā eva iti cet, na | tasyāḥ kḷpta-sāmagry-antara-janyatvād iti bhramo '-satya-jñānam ity a-saṃnikṛṣṭam api doṣāt bhāsata ity abhyupeyam | api ca doṣasya viśiṣṭam eva jñānaṃ vyāpāraḥ, pravṛttau tad-dhetutvasya kḷptatvāt | na ca bhedâ-grahaḥ, kalpanīya-kāraṇa-bhāvatvāt | yat tu duṣṭāt kāryaṃ na iti tatra bījêndriya-sādhāraṇaṃ na duṣṭatvam ekam asti |

(**Gaṅgeśa** continues:) But now the heart of the matter. Both parties accept that error occurs because of an epistemic defect. (However, contrary to your view) error is not a failure to grasp a non-relation.

(For, both alternatives of a dilemma are closed for you on the issue of the nature of such failure, i.e., given the Prābhākara view that absence—and what is the failure but an *absence* of grasping?—is not a separate category, as Nyāya holds, but is reducible, ontologically, to something else. First) on the alternative (that the failure is ontologically just) its (the failure's, the non-grasping's) locus, it (the locus, viz., the person or self failing so to grasp) is not something that is *done* or *committed* (i.e., a self, unlike a failure, is not something that is *committed*). And (second) on the alternative (that the failure is ontologically just) the cognition of that very absence (or the failure itself), it (the cognition), as a veridical cognition (in accordance with the Prābhākara view that all cognition is veridical) would not be produced by a *defect* (and, as I have just said, we both agree that it *is* produced by a defect).

Objection: (Our) veridical cognition that takes the place of error could indeed be defect-generated.

Gaṅgeśa: Wrong. For, such is produced only within the range of the known and established components of a causal complex.

Therefore, an error is a false (*a-satya*) cognition. It has to be accepted that something (a predication content) not produced from a current sensory connection can, nevertheless, because of a defect, appear.

Moreover, it is (as we say) a cognition of an entity as qualified (not, as you say, two cognitions) that is the operation of the chief instrumental cause when an error (is playing a causal role) with respect to unsuccessful effort to act, since the causes of unsuccessful effort are *well-known* (*kḷpta*, i.e., they are the same as those established for successful effort). And a non-grasping of a distinctness is not (a cause of such effort), since that has to be *postulated* as a cause.

But as for the objection that no effect comes about from a defective cause (put forth in the *pūrva-pakṣa* challenging our position that an error as an effect comes about from a defect), the objection takes a seed (which when defective simply fails to produce a sprout) and a sense organ to be alike. (However) what it is to be defective is not something single (or uniform).

Comments

Below, in the section on absence, Gaṅgeśa combats the Prābhākara view that absence is not a separate category, as Nyāya holds, but is reducible, ontologically, to something else: when, for instance, an absence of a pot is cognized on a floor, either (a) the absence is simply the *locus* of the absential cognition, the (mere) floor, or (b) simply the *cognition* of the (mere) floor. Both views are mentioned in the current passage. Concerning (a), the non-grasping's locus would be the self who fails so to grasp. However, whereas such non-grasping would be something committed—as we say a failure is committed—the self is not like that. And so the ontological reduction suffers from a mismatch. With (b), the cognition would have to be veridical in accordance with the Prābhākara view, but would also be produced by a defect.

Gaṅgeśa's argument about the greater economy of his view is clear, although whether it is cogent is not so clear. Gaṅgeśa does, after all, have two kinds of perception, veridical and non-veridical, whereas the Prābhākara has only one.

When a sense organ is defective, as is the vision of a person who has hepatitis, a sense perception may occur that has the sense organ as a cause but that also mispresents what there is—something white is seen as yellow. A seed when defective, in contrast, may simply fail to produce a sprout at all. Depending on the nature of what is defective, the outcome of the presence of defects varies. There is no universal or natural kind, defectiveness. This is Gaṅgeśa's response to the line of argument introduced by the *pūrvapakṣin* (above, p. 278) that ridiculed the Naiyāyika by saying that by his lights a defective bamboo seed should produce a banana tree and so forth.

Text (p. 550, Tirupati) and Translation

> evaṃ pratyakṣam apy anyathā-khyātau mānaṃ kāraṇa-bādhâ-bhāvāt | tathā hi, idaṃ rajatayā jānāmi ity anuvyavasāya-sākṣikam eva anyasya anyathā bhānam | na hi viṣayatve 'nuvyavasāyād anyat pramāṇam | na hy a-tad-viṣayas taj-jñāna-viṣayatvena na vā tad-a-viṣayakaṃ tad-viṣayakatvena anuvyavasīyate | anuvyavasāyasya pramātva-niyamāt | anyathā ghaṭa-jñāne 'pi kadācit paṭaṃ jānāmi iti syāt | na ca bhedâ-graha-daśāyāṃ rajata-jñāna-viṣayatvâ-saṃsargâ-grahaḥ | śuktau bheda-grahe 'pi śuktī rajatatvena mayā jñātā śuktau rajata-jñānaṃ me vṛttam ity anuvyavasāyāt |

(**Gaṅgeśa** continues:) In this way, perception, too (and not only inferential argument, as above), shows the truth of (our view of error as) "appearance otherwise," since nothing blocks its doing so. To be precise, that there can be an appearing of something as other than what it is is shown simply by the apperception, "I know this (as silver) by its silverhood." For, on the issue of what counts as a bit of objecthood, there is no authority (*pramāṇa*) other than apperception. For, no object *not*-ϕ occurs (in apperception) as an object in virtue of the (apperception's target) cognition having ϕ as object. Nor does anyone ever apperceive, by way of a (target cognition's) having ϕ as object, a cognition as *not* having as object ϕ.

Apperception is by rule veridical. Otherwise, even when someone is cognizing a pot, he would sometimes apperceive, "I am cognizing a cloth."

And it is wrong to hold that on an occasion when (as you Prābhākaras would have it) there is a "non-grasping of a distinctness" there would (also) be (the equivalent of an apperception founded in) a non-grasping of a non-relation between an object (qua qualificandum) and a cognition (a remembering) of silver. For, regarding mother-of-pearl, once a distinctness (between it and silver) had been grasped, there would be the apperception, "The mother-of-pearl was cognized by me as silver"; (or) "To me a silver cognition occurred with respect to mother-of-pearl."

Comments

How do we know what phenomenologically we seem to be perceiving? According to Nyāya, we know it infallibly through apperception, although some qualifications come into focus below. That is, I know by apperception not a pot but a cognition that indicates a pot. And once we identify the target cognition to be an error, we know something—the target's qualificandum—as having appeared otherwise than as it is, Gaṅgeśa says here. In other words, apperception attests to the truth of Nyāya's account of error as *anyathā-khyāti*.

The view of apperception that Gaṅgeśa attributes to the Prābhākara is not as outlandish as it might seem. The Prābhākara holds that every awareness is self-aware, that there is no meaningful distinction between a first-level, object awareness (as the Naiyāyika would put it) and a second-level awareness of a previous awareness. Thus, self-awareness would be simultaneous with "a non-grasping of a non-relation between an object (qua qualificandum) and a cognition (a remembering) of silver." And so error could not be known in apperception—a consequence in accordance with the position that all cognition is veridical. Error is not a matter of cognition but of behavior, behavior to be analyzed as rooted in a non-grasping. Gaṅgeśa responds by insisting that sometimes we do directly cognize a previous cognition as an error, although exactly how in that successive moment of cognition it could *already* be known that the previous cognition was an error is not explained.

Text (p. 552, Tirupati, and p. 530, Calcutta) and Translation

atha vicāra-sādhyâ-saṃsarga-graha-bādhyo 'yam a-saṃsargâ-grahaḥ, tena vicāraṃ vinā bheda-grahe 'py avatiṣṭhata iti cet, na | idaṃ rajatatayā jānāmi ity atra śukti-karmaka-rajatatva-prakāraka-jñānâ-saṃsargâ-grahasya ātmany a-saṃbhavāt tādṛśya-jñānâ-prasiddheḥ |

Objection (by a Prābhākara): That which is to be corrected (or defeated, *bādhya*) is so by a *grasping* of a non-relation that is brought about by reflection (i.e., by making an inference, not through apperception), "This is (an error) a non-grasping of a non-relation." Without such reflection, it (the non-grasping, the error) would continue even if there were awareness of distinctness.

Gaṅgeśa: Wrong for the following reason. Here with (the apperception) "I am cognizing this as silver," it is not possible that there be (your) "non-grasping," occurring to a self (or person). For, that would have to be a non-grasping of a non-relation in a cognition having as qualificandum mother-of-pearl and as predication content silverhood. Such a cognition (such a *grasping*, the negatum in your "*non*-grasping") is not known.

Comments

Gaṅgeśa's response draws on the tenet that an absence is parasitic on what it is an absence of. An absence is the absence *at* a particular spot *of* an absentee, e.g., "My pen is not on the table," where the absentee is my pen and the table the spot where it is not. Any cognition of an absence makes explicit the absentee, and, indeed, it is nonsense to talk about an absence without mentioning the absentee. As we shall have many occasions to remark, Gaṅgeśa holds firmly to the precept that an absentee is determined by a particular person's absential cognition and that a candidate absentee must have been previously experienced by the person. So, given that Gaṅgeśa's Prābhākara opponent postulates an absence—a *non*-grasping, an absence of grasping—to explain error-provoked behavior, what would the *grasping* be? What would be the absentee? If nothing such could have occurred in the experience of a cognizer prior to an occasion of error, then the proposal to understand error in that way has to be wrong.

Text (p. 530, Calcutta) and Translation

na idaṃ jānāmi iti rajataṃ jānāmi iti tad-ākāraḥ, tṛtīyârthasya prakāratvena prakāriṇo '-bhāne '-bhāna-prasaṅgāt | viśiṣṭa-jñānaṃ ca sarvatra viśeṣaṇa-viśeṣyīyam ity anyathā-bhānam api tathā | jñāne rajatatvân-abhyupagamād viṣeṣaṇa-viśeṣya-viṣayakatvāc ca na sākāra-vādaḥ |

(**Gaṅgeśa** continues:) And an apperception does not take the following (conjunctive) form: "I am cognizing this" (and) "I am cognizing silver." For (in that case), given (*ex hypothesi*) no appearance of that which the predication content would qualify, we would—according to the way the instrumental case is used to express a predication content ("I know this *by* its silverhood" ≡ "I know this *as* silver")—land in the predicament of no appearance of predication content.

Furthermore, all cognitions of an entity as qualified have both a qualifier and a qualificandum as object. Therefore (an error) an "appearance otherwise" (*anyathā-bhāna*) is this way, too.

And (our view is) not (Buddhist) *sākāra-vāda* (the position that cognition has "its own form" internal to it and independent of any so-called external object), since we do not accept that silverhood (for example, as a universal) exists in cognition and since (on our view, unlike the Buddhists') cognition has an object (structured) as qualifier and qualificandum.

Comments

Gaṅgeśa's argument centering on the predicative instrumental is designed to show the unity of an apperception. In Sanskrit, "*idam* (this) *rajatatvena* (by its silverhood) *jñānāmi* (I am cognizing)," is a single sentence, with a unified sense, namely, the cognition being apperceived, which shows a qualifier and qualificandum in qualificational relation.

One reason why Gaṅgeśa might have brought up a very different view of cognition—the Yogācāra Buddhist view—right at this point in his argument is that once error is seen as a (tightly) unified, single cognition of an entity as qualified, the qualifier would seem to be contributed internally, from cognition itself. And, indeed, it is contributed internally, through a memory-impression, according to Nyāya. But the memory-impression is, in the Nyāya view, formed by a cognitive contact with something extra-cognitive in the first place and in the second awakened by a current object/organ connection. So even though the erroneous cognition is a single unified whole, each of its parts comes from outside the cognition. They are together in the error, though not together in the world—they are *severally* out there in the world rather than being intrinsic to cognition.

Text (p. 553, Tirupati, and p. 532, Calcutta) and Translation

yat tu jñāna-mithyātve bādhya-bādhaka-vyavasthā na syād a-viśeṣād iti | tan na | an-anyathā-siddhāyā dhiyo bādhakatvāt | tathā hi yatra duṣṭâ-duṣṭêndriya-janyaṃ paras-para-nirapekṣam ekatra viruddhaṃ jñāna-dvayam utpadyate, tatra prathamam an-upajāta-virodhitvān na āgataṃ bādhate, tasya a-prāptatvāt | uttaraṃ tu sva-kāraṇād utpadyamānam upajāta-virodhitayā na an-upamṛdya pūrva-bādhâtmakam[14] utpadyate anyathā na utpadyeta eva | na ca evam eva iti vācyam | anubhava-virodhāt | yad āhuḥ, "pūrvāt para-balīyastvaṃ tatra nāma pratīyate | anyonya-nirapekṣāṇāṃ yatra janma dhiyāṃ bhavet ||" iti | yatra pūrvâpekṣam uttaraṃ jñānam utpattum unmukhaṃ tatra upajīvya-pūrva-virodhena uttaraṃ na utpadyate | ato '-jātaṃ sat pūrvaṃ kathaṃ bādhatām | yathā pratyakṣâdi-viruddhânumitiḥ | nanu bhramasya kiṃ bādhyate | na sva-rūpaṃ tasya sattvāt | na api rajatatva-prakārakatvaṃ śukti-viṣayatvaṃ vā, tayor apanetum a-śakyatvāt |

jātaṃ hi tad rajatatvena śuktiṃ viṣayī-kṛtya | na api vyavahāraḥ, pravṛtty-āder vṛttatvāt | na apy an-āgata-vyavahāra-janakatvam, tasya kāraṇâ-bhāvād eva a-saṃbhavāt | ucyate | bādhakena bhramasya bhramatva-buddhir eva bādhaḥ |

Objection: If cognition can be false, then there can be no relation of (cognitive) defeaters and defeated (as when "This is mother-of-pearl" defeats "This is silver"), since there would be no difference (between the two cognitions: either could be false).

Gaṅgeśa: That's wrong. For, a cognition that is a defeater would be (invariably) causally relevant (or, not "causally irrelevant" to the defeating). For example, in all cases where a defective and a non-defective sense organ have given rise to, regarding a single thing, a pair of opposed (or incompatible) cognitions that are mutually independent, there the first to occur does not defeat the other that has not yet occurred—the incompatibility of the two is not (yet) evident—(simply) because it is not (yet) occurrent. The one occurring later, however, produced from its own (distinct) causes (including a non-defective sense organ)—with the incompatibility of the two (now) evident—is, without itself being ground down (and defeated), incapable of being produced *as* a cognition whose nature is that of (a cognition that is) *prior and defeated*. Otherwise, it simply would not occur.

Objection: (Then) it would indeed occur like that.

Gaṅgeśa: Such a rejoinder should not be tried, since that would be contrary to experience.

So they say (this verse), "Overpowering by another (i.e., by an incompatible) of a previous (cognition) is cognized just there where (incompatible and) mutually independent cognitions would arise."

In all cases where a later cognition about to be produced is dependent on an earlier, there the later is not produced if it is opposed (*virodha*) to the earlier on which it depends. (That's why the verse says "mutually independent.") Therefore, how (do you propose to allow, i.e., how) could a later cognition that is not produced defeat an earlier (on which its very occurrence would depend)? Similar is the case of an inference that would oppose perception, etc. (on which it depended).

Objection: What, belonging to an error, is "defeated" (in your sense)? Not its essence (*sva-rūpa*), for that is real (i.e., the occurrence of an error is a reality). Nor a having of silver as predication content, nor of mother-of-pearl as (qualificandum) object, since those two cannot be denied (i.e., they occur, too). For, it (such an erroneous cognition) is born taking mother-of-pearl as object (qua qualificandum), mother-of-pearl (cognized) as silver. Nor is it a bit of behavior (that is defeated), since effort to act, etc., occurs. Nor is it production of some bit of future behavior, since, if it is not to be caused, that would not be possible.

Gaṅgeśa: We answer. A defeater (cognition) showing the erroneousness of an error—just this is a defeating.

Comments

This is an important passage for Gaṅgeśa's externalist and objectivist view of what a defeater is: "a defeater undefeated by any undefeated defeater relative to the set of all truths"—to quote John Pollock, *Contemporary Theories of Knowledge*[15]—seems to be what he has in mind. (Pollock may be rightly counted an internalist in holding that a defeater is a reason for a belief that is first-person privileged, but in trying to solve Gettier problems with the notion of an "undefeated defeater *relative to the set of all truths*"—emphasis mine—he assumes an externalist stance.) Gaṅgeśa supposes that only a veridical cognition can be a defeater. How then do we know that a given cognition is a defeater? Well, we may not, but that is beside the point, according to Gaṅgeśa's argument about temporal ordering. In this way a ramification of what a defeater is is developed independently of how we recognize one. An apparent but factually false defeater could occur at a later time relative to a (veridical) cognition that it appears to defeat but does not. But no true defeater could occur earlier than the defeated, since it would have no cognition to defeat. Furthermore, a cognition that is in fact veridical cannot in reality be defeated. Defeating entails true success.

Both veridicality and epistemic success, then, are insured in virtue of a cognition's being a defeater. A defeater is a veridical cognition that *shows* a non-veridical cognition to be non-veridical. A defeater defeats both from a first-person perspective and in a factual sense.

As no inference that was launched from a perceptual cognition P could show P to be in error, an absential cognition, e.g., "Mary's pot is not on the floor," which is dependent on a previous cognition of the absentee, Mary's pot, could not show that Mary's pot never existed. There could be no defeating in such cases. True defeating entails two cognitions that are mutually independent.

The quoted statement is from Kumārila.[16]

The next passage presents an objection challenging Gaṅgeśa's combination of fallibilism and objectivism: we could never be sure we were not wrong and thus we would lose faith in our own perceptions.

Text (p. 553, Tirupati, and p. 533, Calcutta) and Translation

yat tu dhiyām a-yathārthtve katham āśvāsa iti | tan na | prāmāṇya-grahôpāyasya darśitatvāt | satyatva-niyame 'pi sad-a-saṃsargâ-grahasya a-gṛhītâ-saṃsargasya jñāna-dvayasya ca bahuṣu darśanāt katham āśvāsaḥ | atha sad-a-saṃsargâ-grahasya pratisandhānaṃ vilambitam | sad-viṣayatvaṃ ca śīghrôpasthitam ity autsargikasad-viṣayatva-jñānād viśvāsaḥ | yatra tu kadācit saṃśayas tatra jñānântarād eva saṃśaya-nivṛttir iti cet, mama api autsargikaṃ dhiyāṃ satyatvaṃ bādhakena apanodyata iti tad-an-avatārāt satyatva-viśvāsaḥ | kiṃ ca tava jñānântare 'py a-viśvāsaḥ | viśeṣa-darśanād viśvāsas tulya eva | yathā ca tatra api na saṃdehas tathā uktaṃ parataḥ-prāmāṇye |

Objection (by a Prābhākara): But if cognition can fail to conform, how is there to be trust (in perception and so on)?

Gaṅgeśa: That's misguided. For, there are known means leading to a grasping of veridicality (e.g., inference from successful effort).

Even if truth were the (absolute) law (for cognitions), there would still be found many instances of (error, i.e., what you Prābhākaras call) non-grasping a non-relation with a real thing (in front) and a pair of cognitions whose non-relation is not grasped. Thus, how (on your view, too, according to your argument) is there to be trust (in the possibility that such non-grasping does not obtain)?

Prābhākara: The (cognitive) joining up (i.e., the realization) of a (previous) non-grasping of a non-relation with a real thing (in front) is slow to occur, while a having of a real thing as object is quickly established in awareness. Thus, from cognition as generally having a real thing as object comes trust (in cognition). But where doubt sometimes arises, there a cessation of doubt comes about just from some other (confirming) cognition.

Gaṅgeśa: For me, too, (an assumption of) truth is the condition of cognitions in general, (an assumption of) truth that can be driven away by a defeater. Thus, so long as none presents itself, we have trust that a cognition is true.

Moreover (on your theory) there would be no trust in the other (confirming) cognition, too. (And it is open to me) just the same (as it is open to you to hold) that trust would come from (such cognitions as) sight of particulars (e.g., hands and feet, resolving a doubt whether an object in the distance is a stump or a person). And why there would not be doubt there too (and thus *not* a problem of an infinite regress of doubts) has already been explained (here in this book) in connection with our treatment of (our view of how veridicality is known, the doctrine called) "extrinsically known veridicality."

Comments

This passage is one of the clearest statements Gaṅgeśa makes of his fallibilism and, best of all, of his stance on faith in cognition in the face of possible doubt. The default attitude with a cognition whose veridicality has not been confirmed is that it is veridical.

Gaṅgeśa's first retort to the objector's worry of universal skepticism is *tu quoque*: well, on your (Prābhākara) view of error, too, there would be the problem. This is not a fallacious rejoinder in that Gaṅgeśa also argues that the problem is bogus. The heart of his response draws on the tie between cognition and action.

There are known ways, Gaṅgeśa points out, to confirm a cognition's veridicality, as were explained in previous sections. But also, he says succinctly, without counterevidence, without at least the appearance of a defeater, human beings take the attitude that any given cognition is veridical, although, of course, some are defeated and shown to be non-veridical. How otherwise could they act? As Wittgenstein also has taught us, practices begin in action and not in doubt.

Legitimate doubt arises only in specifiable circumstances and usually can be resolved through known procedures. To the question of the possibility of an infinite series of doubt-eliminators, Gaṅgeśa says he has already provided an answer and gives a cross-reference to the section on knowing veridicality. More precisely, the reference is to Tirupati, p. 293, Calcutta, p. 276, and in this book, p. 130. See also the comments made there. The main point is that not every veridical cognition's veridicality needs to be shown in order for us to be certain and make unhesitating effort to act on the basis of what we take to be fact, as with cognition of a piece of *āmalaka* fruit in the palm of one's hand. And our practice of proceeding to make unwavering effort when doubt is put to rest by sight of particulars and the like would not occur were we to require further grounds not to doubt such doubt-resolvers.

Text (p. 558, Tirupati) and Translation

> anye tu, smṛta-yogya-vaidharmyâ-bhāvo 'dhikaraṇaṃ taj-jñānaṃ vā | tac ca pratyakṣata eva gṛhītam iti yukto viśvāsaḥ | a-yogye bhedake 'dhikaraṇe ca bheda-saṃśaye jñānântarād viśvāsa iti | tan na | ubhayatra api jñānântarād viśvāsa-tulyatvena śiṣya-dandhana-mātratvāt | vastutas tu bhedâ-grahād eva a-bheda-vyavahārôpapattāv a-bheda-viṣayatvaṃ kva api na siddham asti iti kathaṃ sad-viṣayatva-siddhiḥ |

(**Gaṅgeśa** continues:) But others (other Prābhākaras) say the following.

Prābhākara faction: Trust (in cognition) is appropriate in that by perception is grasped an absence of an incompatible property (e.g., being-tin with respect to silver), a property remembered but that could be perceived. The absence is nothing but a substratum (real silver, for instance), or a cognition of that. And if a substratum whose distinctness (from an incompatible) is not capable of being perceived (in that the substratum is not distinctly perceived, for instance as a stump or a person)—if such a substratum were the target of a doubt about the distinctness, then trust would have to come from another cognition.

Gaṅgeśa: That's wrong. Since equally for you as well as for me, trust would come from another cognition, your answer is nothing but a ruse to mislead students!

But, in reality (i.e., what is really wrong with your view, is that), since conventional talk of non-distinctness (e.g., ''The lotus is blue'') can be accounted for as occurring just from (as you say) a lack of grasping of a distinctness (no distinctness between a lotus and a blue thing would be grasped in the case of ''The lotus is blue''), so (on your view) a cognition with object as non-distinctness is not thought of as occurring anywhere. Thus, how could there be established (what you have claimed concerning trust, namely) a cognition with such an object? (That is, how could an absence of a distinctness—an absence of an incompatible property—be, as you say, grasped as the way that we know that we are not being deceived?)

Comments

The principal Prābhākara position on absence is that an absence is nothing other than the *bare* substratum. But another view, espoused by some Prābhākaras, is that an absence is ontologically nothing other than the cognition that grasps it. Both views are mentioned here, as they were earlier. Again, they occupy much space in the upcoming section on absence.

The Prābhākara proposal here should be taken not just against the background of the question about how we can have faith in cognition but also in the face of Gaṅgeśa's *tu quoque* challenge put forth above: if universal skepticism would obtain on the Naiyāyika view sketched, then also no one could be sure that we are not in what the Prābhākara calls a condition of a not-grasping-a-non-relation (etc.). Here a Prābhākara faction proposes that we can be sure, to wit, through a perceptually given absence of an incompatible property. For example, an absence of tinhood would be perceptually presented not *in* silver but *as* silver, an absence, that is to say, that would seem not really to be there or to be cognized, given the Prābhākara view of absences. This would happen in all situations in which we take ourselves to be certain. But if, the free-thinking Prābhākara disciple admits, there is not certainty but rather doubt, such that what the incompatible property is could not be pinned down, then another cognition would be required, for example, of hands and feet resolving doubt about an object in the distance as a person (where then an incompatible property could again be pinned down). In other words, by force of ''another cognition'' would trust be restored.

Note, first of all, how similar this is to Gaṅgeśa's own account of how the veridicality of cognitions of a certain type can be known, not, as here, perceptually, but by an inference. The view is also similar to Gaṅgeśa's position on how given prior doubt certainty arises, as he himself points out opening his rejoinder.

Gaṅgeśa responds also by alluding to the Prābhākara doctrine of intrinsic veridicality. Intrinsic veridicality is in tension with the free-thinker's admission that "trust would come from another cognition." Thus, deception of students (*śiṣya*, correlative to *guru*, "teacher," and the original Prabhākara is called *guru*) is all the disciple's answer seems made for.

The remainder of Gaṅgeśa's rebuttal is abstruse, depending on views of predication and on ontological doctrines about the relation between a property and its bearer that cannot be explained adequately in a brief space. See the section on inherence (pp. 368ff) for more on both Prābhākara and Naiyāyika positions on predication and a thing's fundamental identity in relation to the properties (qualifiers) it has. And we get a little more on identity in the next passage.

In rough outline, then, on the Prābhākara view no awareness can present merely a non-distinctness, an identity, which is instead a matter of a distinctness not being grasped. Predication, we may say (i.e., in the case of the simplest verbalizable awareness verbalized), is understood by Prābhākaras as involving no awareness of a distinctness between a subject and a predicate term. But the proposal that cognitive trust is secured by an awareness of an absence of an incompatible property presupposes an awareness of an identity, the identity between that absence and the thing cognized (alternatively, the cognition), for example, a bit of cognized silver's being identical with the absence of tinhood presumed simultaneously perceived.

Text (p. 561, Tirupati, and p. 535, Calcutta) and Translation

> yat tu doṣo na hetur iti, tan na | phala-balena tathātvāt | atha idaṃ rajatam iti jñānaṃ katham a-yathârtham, idaṃ-rajatayoḥ sattvāt | na ca tad-ubhaya-tādātmyam a-sat, ubhayaṃ tādātmyam ca ity ato 'dhikasya a-bhāvāt | tayoś ca sattvāt | a-sattve vā a-sat-khyātiḥ | evaṃ saṃsargâropo 'pi iti | ucyate | san-mātra-viṣayatve 'pi tad-a-bhāvavati tat-prakārakatvaṃ prakāra-vyadhikaraṇa-viṣayatākatvaṃ vā a-yathârthatvam |

Objection: But a defect is not a cause (in your fashion, as I said above).

Gaṅgeśa: No. It is so, by force of (our experience of) actual effects (as I said earlier).

Objection: How can a cognition (e.g.), "This is silver," fail to present things as they are? Both the "this" and the silver exist.

And it would be wrong to say that the identity of the two does not exist. The two of them and the identity (i.e., each's identity), therefore, are there, since there is no more (identity to be had than what a thing has) and since the two exist. Or, if the identity is held not to exist, then (yours is the position on error called) "appearance of the non-existent." Also, it would be (the view of error called) "relational superimposition."

Gaṅgeśa: We answer. (We do not hold that the non-existent is the object of an illusion.) We hold that only the existent appears as an object. Although only the existent appears, a failure to present things as they are (i.e., non-veridicality) is (as was earlier spelled out) "cognition with ϕ as predication content about an object that is not ϕ" or "cognition whose objecthood does not have the same locus as its predication content."

Comments

Mādhyamika Buddhists are commonly associated with the view of error called "appearance of the non-existent." The second view mentioned, called "relational superimposition," is espoused by grammarians and others as the sole type of superimposition. Naiyāyikas, in contrast, accept both relational superimposition and superimposition by way of identity. The Mādhyamikas are viewed as saying that error involves the appearance of something actually non-existent. The upholders of "relational superimposition" say that only the relation between a qualificandum and what it is perceived as would be non-existent. In the terms of the stock example ("This is silver"), the "this" would exist and the silver would exist, but a superimposed relation would not exist, whereas according to the objector holding identity not to exist would amount to saying that the qualificandum and the qualifier as well as the relation do not exist.

Gaṅgeśa, ignoring the obfuscation about identity, reaffirms the Nyāya commitment to the view that only the existent appears as cognitive object, and then repeats, in shortened form, a couple of definitions given earlier of non-veridical cognition. (See, in this book, definitions D^{26c} and D^{29c}, pp. 237 and 243.) Gaṅgeśa takes himself to have already explained (in talking about how veridical and non-veridical cognitions typically arise) how it is possible for a single cognition to fail to present something as it is in fact.

Text (p. 563, Tirupati, and p. 536, Calcutta) and Translation

prāñcas tu, tādātmya-saṃsargayor a-sator eva manyante viṣayatvam | na ca evam a-sat-khyātiḥ, sad-uparaktasya atyantâ-sataḥ khyāty-abhyupagamāt | sat-an-uparaktasya a-khaṇḍasya atyantâ-sataḥ khyātir a-sat-khyātir na abhyupeyate kāraṇâ-bhāvāt | tad-an-upapattis tulyā eva iti cet, na | atra viśiṣṭa-jñāna-sāmagryā darśitatvāt | tad uktaṃ vācaspati-miśraiḥ, "tasmād yad anyathā santam anyathā pratipadyate | tan-nirālambanaṃ jñānam a-sad-ālambanaṃ matam ||" iti ||

(**Gaṅgeśa** continues:) But the older (**Naiyāyikas**) think that an identity and a relation that simply do not exist can be cognitive object (i.e., in error). And their view (of error) is not in this way "appearance of the non-existent," since they hold that appearance of (even) an absolutely non-existent will be of something *tinged* with the existent. Appearance of a wholly and absolutely non-existent not tinged with the existent is not accepted, for (they say) there is no cause (of anything like that).

Objection (against the Old Nyāya view): That (a cause of an appearance of a non-existent tinged with the existent) is just as impossible.

Old Nyāya: No. For such is seen to occur—through a collection of causes sufficient for a cognition of an entity as qualified.

So it is said by Vācaspati Miśra: "Therefore, something that exists one way but that is cognized another—(well, we commonly say) the cognition does not have it as its object. Such a cognition is considered to have as its object something *non-existent*."

Comments

From Gaṅgeśa's perspective, the main point is that a memory-impression can form part of "a collection of causes sufficient for a cognition of an entity as qualified," and does so in the case of a perceptual error. But a memory-impression is invariably formed by something existent, not something non-existent tinged with the existent.

The citation of Vācaspati is from his *Tātparya-ṭīka* commentary on *Nyāya-sūtra* 1.1.2.[17]

atha pratyakṣa-lakṣaṇa-vāda

NOW, DISCOURSE ON CHARACTERIZING PERCEPTION

Text (p. 567, Tirupati, and p. 538, Calcutta) and Translation

sā ca pramā catur-vidhā pratyakṣânumity-upamiti-śābdī-bhedāt | evaṃ catasṛṇāṃ tāsāṃ karaṇaṃ pramāṇam api catur-vidhaṃ pratyakṣânumānôpamāna-śabda-bhedāt | anyeṣāṃ yathā-yathaṃ eṣv eva antar-bhāvāt | tathā ca vakṣyāmaḥ |

Gaṅgeśa: And such veridical cognition occurs in four varieties, in that the perceptual, the inferential, the analogical, and the verbal are distinct. In this way, there are proximate instrumental causes for the four—i.e., "means to veridical cognition," *pramāṇa*—in four varieties, in that perception, inference, analogy, and testimony are distinct. Others (claimed as further varieties) are included in these, just (in which) as the case may be. And we shall say how so (below).

Comments

The *Nyāya-sūtra* commentators discuss how other candidate sources of veridical cognition are included in Nyāya's four, perception, etc. Later in this chapter, Gaṅgeśa will show how "non-cognition," *an-upalabdhi*, is included in perception, and in the next chapter how "postulation," *arthâpatti*, is included in inference.

Text (p. 568, Tirupati) and Translation

nanu na pratyakṣaṃ tāvad indriyârtha-saṃnikarṣôtpannaṃ jñānam a-vyabhicāri | ātmânumiti-smṛtyor jñāna-mātre ca ativyāpteḥ | ātmano 'rthasya manasā indriyeṇa saṃyogād utpatteḥ | īśvara-pratyakṣâ-vyāpteś ca | saṃnikarṣasya ca saṃyogâdi-rūpatvena an-anugamāc ca | saṃyogâdy-anyatamasya ca a-nirdhārita-eka-paratve bhāgâ-siddhir itara-bheda-sādhane, vyartha-viśeṣaṇatvaṃ ca | indriyârthayor eka-janyatvasya lakṣaṇatve vyartha-viśeṣaṇatvam | na ca tayor eka-eka-janyatvam eva lakṣaṇaṃ, ātma-mano-janyatvena jñāna-mātre gatatvāt | indriyasya pratyakṣa-nirūpyatvāc ca |

Objection (against the *Nyāya-sūtra* definition of perception): Perception is not as follows: (D^1) "cognition produced from sense organ/object connection that does not deviate (from the cognized fact)." For, that definition suffers from overcoverage: inference to self, memory, and (indeed) any cognition (would fall under D^1), in that a cognition's production is (invariably in part) from a contact of an object—viz., a self—with a sense organ—viz., the internal organ (*manas*, the "mind").

Furthermore, God's perceptions are not covered (so it suffers from undercoverage as well).

Moreover, the connection, which takes the form of contact, etc., is not sufficiently uniform. And whereas a good definition would establish distinctness from the other (i.e., from all those things that are not that which is to be defined), here there is the fallacy of "non-establishment in a part," in that whichever one of the connections—contact and so on—is operative in a given instance of perception, it fails to be definitely ascertained as integrative. And a qualification (added to correct this fault) would be to no avail.

(Furthermore) there is a single productive process defined (here) by two (factors mentioned in the definition), the "object" and the "sense organ." The qualification (in mentioning both) is pointless. And a definition that had the production as through each one of the two would still be wrong, since cognition in general would fall within the scope of the definition inasmuch as every cognition is produced by a self and internal organ in relation.

Moreover, a sense organ (a term used in the definition) is determined by its role in perception (and thus there is circularity).

Comments

As noted earlier, the *Nyāya-sūtra* definition of perception (1.1.4) was given a new interpretation by Vācaspati Miśra (c. 950) who reads the two words *a-vyapadeśyam* ("non-verbal") and *vyavasāyâtmakam* ("definite") as indicating two fundamental types of perception—indeterminate and determinate—and so as not part of the definition itself.[1] Gaṅgeśa follows Vācaspati here and so quotes the *sūtra* leaving out the extraneous words.

An inference to a self is made based on perception of such psychological properties as desire, pleasure, pain, and volition: as qualities they must have a substratum or locus. Such an inference would fall within the scope of definition D^1 in that these properties are grasped by an internal organ, *manas*, coming into contact with their locus, namely, a self. Memory is also thought to occur through self/*manas* contact: a self is the locus of impressions, *saṃskāra*s, that carry the information retrieved by the *manas* in rememberings.

Furthermore, the definition would apply to all cognitions on account of the fact that any cognition is caused in part by a connection between *manas* and self. (The idea appears to be that that every cognition requires attention, so to say, and thus connection of the inner sense with the self.) And God's perceptions, which a good definition should cover, fall outside the scope of D^1 in that they are eternal and thus not produced.

See, above, pp. 215 and 240ff, for Gaṅgeśa's sense of the requirements that must be met by a good definition, or "characterization," *lakṣaṇa*, and, in particular, p. 215 on the difference between citing a differentiating characteristic versus citing a relevant universal. Both types of definition occur in this section. Note that sometimes I am a bit free in rendering the word *lakṣaṇa* where it means strictly a differentiating characteristic. I provide full definitional statements (D^1, D^2, and so on) by supplying the definiendum ("Perception is . . . ").

Text (p. 569, Tirupati) and Translation

na api jñāta-karaṇâ-janyatve sati satyo 'nubhavaḥ pratyakṣaṃ | liṅgâder a-janakatayā jñānasya a-jñātasya karaṇatve anumity-ādau gatatvāt | jñānâ-janyo 'nubhavaḥ satya ity api na | viśiṣṭa-pratyakṣâ-vyāpteḥ tasya viśeṣaṇa-jñāna-janyatvāt | na api satyatve sati sākṣāt-kāritvaṃ, niyata-vyañjakâ-bhāvena grahītum a-śakyatayā tasya jātitvâ-siddheḥ | sattve vā tad eva lakṣaṇaṃ vyavahāra-nimittaṃ ca astu kiṃ jātyā |

(The **objector** continues:) Nor (is the following definition correct, D^2:) perception is "true experience that is not produced by a chief instrumental cause (i.e., a sense organ) being cognized (in that sense organs are not cognized but are the triggers for cognitions of other things)." For it would overextend to inference, etc., inasmuch as the chief instrumentality in the case of an inferential mark, etc., is a cognition that is not cognized.

(D^3) "True experience that is not produced by cognition" is also not right. For it fails to cover perception of an entity as qualified since perception of an entity as qualified (i.e., determinate perception) is generated by (a preceding indeterminate) cognition of a qualifier.

Nor (D^4) "True experience that is immediate acquaintance." Since this is impossible to grasp without a clear manifester, it is not established as the (pertinent) universal. Or, if there is a manifester, let that stand instead. And (by the way) this is how the definitional purpose is served in everyday discourse. (So) what would be the use of a universal?

Comments

According to Navya Naiyāyikas, not smoke, for example, but a certain cognition of smoke is the chief instrumental cause—the trigger—of a veridical inferential cognition of fire. But the cognition of the prover is itself not cognized, not apperceived, at least not in standard cases. So D^2 fails to exclude what it should.

Gaṅgeśa's position on the causal role of indeterminate perception is treated in detail below in a separate section (pp. 609ff).

A definition has to be useful from a first-person perspective, even if it is technical. If a universal is pointed out, there must be a way it is known. There must be recurrent experience. So what is the evidence here? What manifests the recurrent character proposed by D⁴? Having a dewlap indicates a certain class of animals, cows, namely, and is a manifester of the universal, cowhood, without under or overextension. Thus to mention having a dewlap would be a correct way to characterize or define cows. The problem with "immediate acquaintance" as the defining property of perception is that it has no manifester, so it is said. Or, if there is a manifester, why not let that stand as the definer? Why try to come up with something else? Postulating a universal seems pointless. And pointing out class manifesters is how people explain the meaning of words in everyday life.

Text (p. 570, Tirupati) and Translation

ucyate | pratyakṣasya sākṣātkāritvaṃ lakṣaṇaṃ | cākṣuṣâdi-jñāne sāṣkāt-karomi ity anugata-buddher bādhakaṃ vinā jāti-viṣayatvāt | na ca indriya-janyatvaṃ tathā | anyonyâśrayād indriyasya atīndriyatvāc ca | na ca niyata-vyañjakâ-bhāvān na jātiḥ | gotvâdau sāsnâder iva an-anugatasya api cakṣuḥ-karaṇaka-vyañjaka-niyamaḥ, jñānêcchā-prayatna-sukha-duḥkhâdes tad-a-bhāvāt | pratyuta niyata-vyañjaka-sattve jāty-a-siddher eva | tata eva anugata-tad-buddhy-upapatteḥ | nirvikalpakêśvara-yogi-pratyakṣe ca pratyakṣatvaṃ dharmi-grāhaka-māna-siddhaṃ | yogaja-dharmâ-janya-janya-sva-viṣayaka-savikalpakâ-janya-sāmānya-lakṣaṇa-pratyāsatty-a-janya-janya-pratyakṣasya lakṣaṇam an-āgata-gocara-sākṣātkāra-hetu-pratyāsatty-a-janya-janya-sākṣātkāratvam |

Gaṅgeśa: We answer. (D⁵) "Cognitive immediacy" does define perception. (What's the evidence?) The cognition (i.e., the apperception), "I am immediately aware," which is recurrent regarding visual perceptions and so on, is to be taken as having this universal (cognitive immediacy) as its object, in that there are no counterconsiderations.

And (D⁶) "being produced by a sense organ" is not like this. For, that (as a definition) would incur the censure of "mutual dependency." Also, sense organs are imperceptible (and could not appear in apperception, which is a type of perception).

Furthermore, (the criticism) that cognitive immediacy is not to be accepted as a universal because of lack of a clear manifester is wrong. For, being-an-experience and so on, whose instrumental cause is (e.g.) a visual organ, is (indeed) a manifester (here), although, like a dewlap and so on with respect to cowhood and so on, the manifester can fail to be perfectly recurrent (some cows are presumably bereft of a dewlap). Moreover, there is no rule that a manifester of a universal has to be perfectly recurrent (or co-extensive and uniform, *anugata*), since that is not the case with cognition, desire, volition, pleasure, pain, and the like (as manifesters of being-a-self as a universal). On the contrary, if a fixed manifester were present, a universal might well not be established (in that the manifester itself would be considered such). (For) the recurrent presentation would be explained just by the fixed manifester (that is to say, the evidence would be explained with no need to posit a distinct universal).

And the same evidence that shows the existence of the property-bearer establishes perceptionhood (the universal of perception) in cases of indeterminate perceptions, God's perceptions, and yogins' perceptions (i.e., the evidence that establishes indeterminate perceptions, God and God's perceptions, and yogic perceptions, in the first place).

An (acceptable) definition of (ordinary) perception, which is (not "extraordinary," *a-laukika*, i.e.) not produced by merit born of yoga, nor by a determinate cognition whose own object is productive, nor by the operative connection characteristic (of cognition) of universals (in unobserved instances), is (D^7): "cognitive immediacy that is not produced by an operative connection that brings about immediate cognition of the future."

Comments

Gaṅgeśa has given an objectivist or externalist account of both the production of veridicality and how it is known. And his entire treatise of epistemology is organized around spelling out the nature of four processes that generate veridical cognitions, perception and the rest. Ontological issues, the question of error, memory, recognition, and so on are increments, so to say, on a largely externalist journey through the principles and terms of epistemology. But a few typically internalist theses and elements are also endorsed. D^5's "cognitive immediacy" connects with these, since nothing more is required to know what a perception is than a kind of self-inspection.

D^{11}, on the other hand, which is another definition that Gaṅgeśa endorses, is externalist, targeting the process that engenders perception, as do also other definitions to be taken up. Gaṅgeśa also uses basic features of his causal picture—such as that every perception is sensory in origin—to refute a rival Prābhākara definition, as we shall see,

Cognitive immediacy (D^5) would seem to be a defining characteristic of perception in the way that a dewlap is a defining characteristic of a cow. However, cognitive immediacy is, Gaṅgeśa says, a universal, like cowhood.

Recurrent presentation, *anugata-buddhi*, is taken from as early as Praśastapāda (c. 600) to be evidence for a universal. Recurrence concerning perceptions as objects occurs in apperception, which finds them to be uniformly immediate. Note that this apperceptive evidence is not said to be infallible. Rather, it is decisive because it is in fact undefeated, not because it is indefeasible.

D^6, "being produced by a sense organ," could not be, Gaṅgeśa says, similarly evidenced in apperception for two reasons. First, a sense organ is imperceptible and could not be apperceptively grasped. Second, as argued just previously, being a sense organ is to be defined in relation to perception—thus a fault of "mutual dependence" (*anyonyâśraya*).

Since no ordinary apperception takes indeterminate perceptions, God's perceptions, or yogic perceptions as its target, the question arises: What is the argument in these cases for D^5? Gaṅgeśa's answer is that the argument for indeterminate perception (which will be given at the end of the chapter), the teleological argument for God (which is to be spelled out in the next), and so on, count in these cases as evidence for cognitive immediacy, too.

In the definition given of everyday, ordinary perception, D^7, God's perceptions are excluded by the term, "produced." There are three types of extraordinary human perception that are to be excluded as well: (a) yogic perception, which can take future occurrences as somehow immediate objects, (b) direct perception through non-standard media that involve a special cognitive link, e.g., the fragrance of sandalwood through the agency of the visual organ assisted by previous experience of the fragrance, and (c) perception of instances of universals, which is extraordinary in that future instances, for example—cows still to be born—are known only in their common aspect, as exhibiting the universal, e.g., cowhood. Also note that to perceive a universal its *extension* need not be perceived. Perception of a universal does not entail perception of all its instances.

Text (p. 580, Tirupati, and p. 547, Calcutta) and Translation

> anye tu sāmānya-jñāna-pratyāsattyor indriya-saṃbaddha-viśeṣaṇatântar-bhāvāt taj-janyaṃ pratyakṣaṃ saṃgrāhyam eva iti | yad vā viṣayatvena sva-viśeṣya-janyaṃ jñānaṃ janya-pratyakṣam | ātma-viśeṣyakânumiti-śābda-smṛtiṣu viśeṣyatvena tasya na hetutvaṃ, viśeṣyaṃ vinā api tāsām utpatteḥ kiṃ tu samavāyitvena | yad vā indriya-janyaṃ jñānaṃ janya-pratyakṣam | indriyatvena janakatvaṃ vivakṣitam | janya-pratyakṣa-mātre indriyatvena cakṣur-ādīnāṃ kāraṇatā | anugata-hetuṃ vinā anugata-kāryasya a-kasmikatvâpatteḥ | smṛty-anumity-ādau ca manaso na indriyatvena hetutvam, kiṃ tu manastvena | anyathā smṛty-ādeḥ sākṣātkāratvâpatteḥ |

(**Gaṅgeśa** continues:) But others hold that perception is to be understood more comprehensively to include that generated through the connection operative with perception of universals (in unobserved instances) and that generated through (the other extraordinary) cognitive connections. These are covered by (the abstract) being-a-qualifier-of-what-is-related-to-a-sense-organ, such that (perception would be, D^8) "that generated by that (being-a-qualifier-etc.)."

Alternatively, generated perception is (D^9) "cognition produced by that which has, as its object, the qualificandum." Regarding inferences to a self as the (inferences') qualificandum, bits of verbal knowledge (with a self as content), and memories (with the self as object), the cognition is not caused by the qualificandum. For, they are produced without the qualificandum (having a causal role). Rather, the qualificandum has (in those cases) a role as that in which they inhere (since they are among a self's qualities).

Alternatively, generated perception is (D^{10}) "cognition produced by a sense organ." The productiveness of what it is to be a sense organ is to be explained as the causality of the visual organ and the like as sense organs with regard to generated perception in general. For, without (positing) a uniform cause, we would fall into the predicament of effects' being uniform without any reason. And with respect to memory, inference, and the like, the internal organ (*manas*) is a cause not as a sense organ but as the internal organ. Otherwise, memory and so forth would, unfortunately, have to be counted as cognitively immediate (and they are not).

Comments

Rāmakṛṣṇa in his subcommentary elaborates that it is a qualificandum qua existing here and now that generates perception. But no such qualificandum generates inferences to a self and so on. With the inferences and other cognitions that Gaṅgeśa refers to, what a cognition is about is not one of its causes.

Earlier, the *Nyāya-sūtra* definition of perception, D^1, was faulted for mentioning sense organs, the criticism being that what it is to be a sense organ is determined in relation to perception. Thus would be committed the definitional fallacy of "mutual dependence." But just below Gaṅgeśa defines what it is to be a sense organ without mentioning perception. And here he suggests an enumerative list, "the visual organ *and the like*."

Another worry is that of over-extension through the fact that the mind or internal organ, *manas*, is considered a sense organ in Nyāya (and in other schools). This organ is thought to be involved in all cognitive activity. Overextension is avoided by the stipulation that *manas* is to be counted a sense organ only when it works like one. Thus Gaṅgeśa makes a break with the Naiyāyika tradition of viewing *manas* as simply another sense faculty. It is one in the perception of psychological qualities, pleasure, pain, and so forth, but not in its role in inferential processes, rememberings, and the like.

Text (p. 587, Tirupati) and Translation

> indriyatvaṃ ca smṛty-a-janaka-jñāna-hetu-manaḥ-saṃyogâśrayatvam | prāṇa-śarīrâtmānaś ca smṛti-janaka-manaḥ-saṃyogavantaḥ | śabdêtarôdbhūta-viśeṣa-guṇân-āśrayatve sati jñāna-hetu-manas-saṃyogâśrayatvaṃ vā |

(Gaṅgeśa continues:) And what it is to be a sense organ is to be a substratum of contact with the internal organ, a contact that does not produce memory and is a cause of cognition (perception, namely). Furthermore, breath, the body, and the self possess (i.e., are the locus or substratum of) contact with the internal organ that does produce memory (and thus the definition excludes them).

Or, given that the (relevant) substratum is not that of a manifest specific quality that is other than sound, what it is to be a sense organ is to be a substratum of a contact with the internal organ that is a cause of cognition.

Comments

According to Nyāya psychology, *manas*, the internal organ, channels all sensory information to a self. Thus, organ/*manas* contact is a cause of whatsoever perception, of all sensory information being delivered to an individual self.

Apparently, Gaṅgeśa believes that there is a practically continual internal detecting of breath, which is a cause of other ordinary perceptions in the sense that to be alive is a necessary condition for any awareness on our parts; similarly, concerning *manas*'s contact with a person's body.

The convoluted qualification that begins "given that the (relevant) substratum" is put forth to exclude, again, contact with self, with breath, and with a person's body. One then might expect Gaṅgeśa to say, "distinct from that which is the substratum of a contact with self, with breath, and with the body," but compared to this locution the one he uses is shorter (at least in Sanskrit). An adage about grammarians and definitions is that the happiness produced in saving a syllable is greater than that of the birth of a child. Gaṅgeśa seems to have the same tastes.

Another point of background theory alluded to here is the view that, except for the auditory organ (which is the element ether delimited by the ear canal), the sense organs do not exhibit in a manifest way the "specific quality" that is typical of the element of which they are made. That is, while the organs are considered to be made out of the elements that are the media for conduit of the various types of sensory informational flow—the visual organ out of fiery element (*tejas*), the organ of taste out of water, and so on—the organs themselves are imperceptible.

Text (p. 595, Tirupati) and Translation

jñānâ-karaṇakaṃ jñānam iti tu vayam | viśiṣṭa-pratyakṣe ca viśeṣaṇa-jñānaṃ na karaṇaṃ vyāpārâ-bhāvāt | viśiṣṭa-vaiśiṣṭya-pratyakṣe ca viśeṣaṇa-jñānaṃ hetur na tu viśeṣaṇa-viśeṣaṇa-dhīr api viśeṣaṇa-dhī-dvārā karaṇam, mānâ-bhāvāt | pratyabhijñāyāṃ tu tattā-smṛtiḥ kāraṇaṃ na tu saṃskāra-dvārā anubhavaḥ karaṇam | tasyāḥ saṃskāra-janyatve smṛtitvâpatteḥ | smṛtitve lāghavena saṃskāra-janyatvasya tantratvāt | tad-dhetutvena eva tat-siddheś ca |

(**Gaṅgeśa** continues:) But we (endorse the following definition of perception,

D[11]): "cognition that does not have a cognition as its chief instrumental cause (*karaṇa*, "trigger")."

And cognition of a qualifier is not the chief instrumental cause of a perception of an entity as qualified (by that qualifier although a preceding cognition of the qualifier is a causal factor including sometimes indeterminate cognition), because it (indeterminate cognition and all such causally efficacious prior cognition of the qualifier) has no employment in its causal operation (that is, no *vyāpāra*, no "operation," and a true chief cause or trigger has to be employed).

Furthermore, a cognition of a qualifier is a cause with respect to a cognition of something doubly qualified (e.g., "The lotus is blue," with the blue qualifying the something that is also qualified by lotushood or being-a-lotus). But it is not the case that a cognition of a qualifier of a qualifier is also, by means of a cognition of a qualifier (as its employment in the causal process), the chief instrumental cause. For, there is no argument.

Concerning a recognition (as in "This is that Devadatta whom I saw yesterday"), however, a memory of thatness is a cause. But an awareness is not, by means of a memory impression, the chief instrumental cause, since that would have the untoward ramification of a recognition's being produced by a memory impression (as chief instrumental cause) and (indeed) of its *being* a memory (whereas it is a perception). It is simpler to accept that whatever is produced by a memory impression is a memory, since the one does bring the other about and since memory impressions are known just by being the (chief instrumental) cause of memory.

Comments

The "employment in its causal operation" that is the *vyāpāra* of a chief instrumental cause is usually illustrated by an axe—the chief instrumental cause of the action of a tree being felled—which is employed in the action of (repeated) contact with the tree.

As mentioned in the introduction, Gaṅgeśa appears to be of two minds about *karaṇa* in the cognitive context. The appropriate sense organ in operation, that is to say, in sensory connection with an object perceived, is the *karaṇa* of a perception. But with inference a different view of what is required to be a *karaṇa* seems to be in place The current passage probably should be taken as marking a transition within Nyāya, and Gaṅgeśa's inconsistency either a spur to or a reflection of a process of change in theory. Mathurānātha, Rucidatta, and other classical commentators have much to say on the score.

D[11] is only part of the characterization that Udayana gives in his *Lakṣaṇa-mālā*, two further defining marks being, "sense-organ-produced" and "veridical cognition": "A perception is a sense-organ-produced veridical cognition whose chief instrumental cause is not a cognition."[2]

Though Gaṅgeśa in using the term *vayam* ("we") appears to endorse D^{11}, it is possible that he is simply stating that his school, and in particular his revered teacher Udayana, embrace it (and the supporting argument) while we are supposed to know from other signals that he himself has qualms. But it seems better to read Gaṅgeśa as himself endorsing D^{11} and the positions about this kind of causality. The tension with views expressed in the inference chapter, however, remain, and press one to look for an alternative reading.

As mentioned, debate about recognition—its nature and causes—will be developed until the end of this, the *TCM*'s first chapter. And below, in this very section, Gaṅgeśa disputes the Prābhākara view that the "thatness" portion of a recognition is not perceptual. Here in the passage at hand he tells us that a memory-impression of course is one causal factor within a causal complex sufficient to bring a recognition about. A recognition is not, however, a memory, and would not have a memory-impression as proximate cause, as would indeed a remembering.

The next two passages delineate several central areas of theory, the first in a Prābhākara voice, the second in Gaṅgeśa's own. The two parties have the same or similar commitments on several topics, but not, most notably here, about self-awareness and recognition. Subtle differences on recurrence and the perception of universals occur, too.

Text (p. 607, Tirupati, and p. 556, Calcutta) and Translation

> prābhākarās tu, sākṣād-dhīḥ pratyakṣam | sākṣāttvaṃ ca na jātiḥ, niyata-vyañjakâbhāvāt | na api savikalpakân-apekṣa-jñānatvam, pratyabhijñā-sādṛśya-dvitvâdi-pratyakṣâ-vyāpanāt | kiṃ tu yaj-jñānaṃ yad-viṣayatve savikalpakâ-janyaṃ tat tatra sākṣād-dhīḥ | miti-mātṛ-prakāśe ca sarvam eva jñānaṃ pratyakṣaṃ jñānâ-janyatvāt | jātāv anugata-dhīr api pratyakṣā jāti-vyakti-nirvikalpaka-janyatvāt | sādṛśyatvâdi-viśiṣṭa-vaiśiṣṭya-pratyakṣe ca na viśeṣaṇa-jñānaṃ hetuḥ, tena vinā api yugapad-indriya-saṃnikṛṣṭe viśiṣṭa-pratyayôdayāt | dīrgâdi-pratyakṣe ca na hrasvâdi-jñānâpekṣā, kiṃ tu tad-vyavahāre | anumity-āder meyâṃśe pratyibhijñāyāś ca tattâṃśe jñāna-janyatvān na pratyakṣatvam, kiṃ tu parokṣatvam eva | miti-mātr-aṃśe idantâṃśe ca dvayor eva pratyakṣatvam | yat tu tattā-prakāśe na tattā-savikalpakatvena kāraṇatā, kiṃ tu tattā-jñānatvena | tan na | anumity-ādāv api liṅgâdi-jñānatvena anumeyâdi-tulyatvād iti |

(**Gaṅgeśa** continues:) But the Prābhākaras (defend the following definition).

Prābhākara: Perception is (D^{12}) "immediate cognition." And (cognitive) immediacy is not (as you hold with D^{5}) a universal, since there is no manifester of it. Nor is it "to be a cognition that is (causally) independent of determinate cognition," for that would fail to cover recognition, perception of similarity, and (counting or) perception of duality and so on. Rather, whatever cognition with *x* as its object is not generated by a determinate cognition, that cognition as about x is an immediate cognition.

And indeed every cognition in its illumination (of itself, i.e.) of the "measuring" and of (the "I," i.e.) its "mother" is a perception, since there is no production by a (determinate) cognition.

Recurrent cognition indicating a universal is also perceptual, since (in a determinate perception of an entity as qualified the factors of) the universal and the particular are produced by (a preceding) indeterminate cognition.

And a cognition of a qualifier is not a cause of a perception of anything that is relational in virtue of being qualified by similarity and so forth (e.g., a face that is similar to the moon). For, a cognition of an entity as qualified (e.g., of a face as similar to the moon) arises without such a cognition so long as there obtains a simultaneous connection with a sense organ (on the part of both the individual qualificandum—the face—and the qualifier—being similar to the moon).

And with perception of something long and the like, there is no dependence on cognition of something short and the like. Rather, this is matter of conventional speech.

Perception does not include the object portion of an inference or the like, nor the "thatness" portion of a recognition, because they are generated by a (determinate) cognition. These are, instead, simply non-immediate. The cognition and "I" portions, as well as the "thisness" portion, of just those two (inference and the like, along with recognition) are included as perceptual.

Objection: But concerning awareness of the "thatness" (in a recognition), the causality does not involve a determinate cognition of thatness but rather (just) a cognition of thatness.

Prābhākara: That's wrong. For, with regard to inference and so on, too, the same reasoning would apply to what is (known, i.e.) inferred and so on, inasmuch as it is known through a cognition of the inferential mark and so on.

Comments

Prābhākaras hold that a complete verbalization of the content of any cognition would include self-reference both to the cognizer and to the cognition itself, thus not "A pot" but "I am aware of a pot," where the terms "I" and "aware of" express contents of the awareness. (And the awareness nevertheless is not, in Naiyāyika terms, an apperception, but rather a first-order perception.) Thus even with inferences and other types of veridical cognition that are non-immediate—e.g., "I am inferring fire from smoke"—the "I" factor and the self-awareness, i.e., awareness of awareness, are considered perceptually given. Only the "fire" factor is not.

Again, Prābhākaras share with Naiyāyikas the view that indeterminate cognition has in perception a causal role. But there are disagreements, as

Gaṅgeśa will make plain, on universals and relational cognitions such as of something short or long as well as on the thatness of a recognition, although on relational cognitions the telling engagement does not come until the section on absence, and the other topics are also not settled here. In the following response, Gaṅgeśa focuses mainly on the Prābhākara's definition.

Text (p. 609, Tirupati) and Translation

atra ucyate | yadi tattāyāṃ pratyabhijñā parokṣânubhava-rūpā tadā na utpadyeta, tad-dhetu-liṅgâder a-bhāvāt | tattā-jñāna-sahitam indriyaṃ janakam iti cet, tarhi indriya-janyatvāt tatra sākṣād-dhīr eva syāt | na ca jñānân-apekṣêndriya-janyatvaṃ tatra tantram, gauravāt | jñāna-sahitêndriya-janyatvena idantâṃśe 'py a-pratyakṣatva-prasaṅgāc ca | na hy ekasmin jñāne janayitavye tad-apekṣā tad-an-apekṣā ca sambhavati | aṃśe tad ubhayam api iti cet, na | jñāne aṃśasya viṣayatvena tad-a-janyatvāt | evaṃ miti-mātr-aṃśe ca sarvaṃ jñānaṃ na pratyakṣam indriyâ-janyatvāt sākṣātkāre tasya kāraṇatvāt | mano-janyatve anumeyâṃśe 'pi tattva-prasaṅgaḥ | na ca jñāna-mātra-sāmagrī-janyatvaṃ pratyakṣatve tantram, gauravāt | jñāna-mātraṃ ca na jñānatvaṃ, tasya a-janyatvāt | na api sarvaṃ jñānaṃ, pratyakṣa-jñāne pratyekaṃ sarva-jñāna-sāmagry-a-janyatvāt sarva-jñāna-sāmagry-a-prasiddheś ca | api ca jñāne avayavâ-bhāvena aṃśo viṣaya eva | viṣaye ca jñānaṃ na kāraṇam | ato 'numiti-pratyabhijñayoḥ sva-viṣaye 'numeye tattāyāṃ ca pratyakṣatvaṃ syāt | viṣayasya savikalpakâ-janyatvāt |

Gaṅgeśa: Here we answer. If a recognition took the form of a *non*-immediate awareness in the thatness (it presents), then no such thing would arise, since there would be (no cause, i.e.) no inferential mark, etc., which are causes for that (type of cognition, the non-immediate).

Objection: A sense organ produces a recognition (like that indeed) aided by a cognition of thatness.

Gaṅgeśa: Then just because it would be produced by a sense organ, it would be an immediate cognition!

And there (concerning cognitive immediacy), being-generated-*independently*-of-cognition is not the causal principle. For, that's too cumbersome, and it would provoke the difficulty that the "thisness" portion (of a recognition), too, as generated by a sense organ *aided by a cognition* (i.e., an indeterminate cognition) would not be perceptual. For, it is not possible that a single cognition is producible both depending on and not depending on the same thing.

Objection: Taking the part into account, then both can be.

Gaṅgeśa: Incorrect, since the part as cognitive presentation would not be generated by that same thing.

And so your thesis is wrong that all cognitions in their portions of cognition and of the cognizer are perceptual: (some such cognitions and cognitive portions are not perceptual in that) they are not produced by a sense organ. With the cognitively immediate, a sense organ is a cause. To hold that these cognitive portions are produced by the internal organ (*manas*) gets you into the difficulty that (with an inference) the part about the object inferred would be like that, too (i.e., it would be perceptual, too).

And the causal principle concerning what it is to be a perception is not (as follows): to be produced by a causal complex responsible for "cognition in general." For, that is cumbersome, and (your) "cognition in general" is not (the universal) cognitionhood, since that is not produced (no universal is produced). Nor can (your) "cognition in general" be every cognition, since it is not the case that every time a perceptual cognition occurs it occurs produced by a causal complex *responsible for every cognition*. Nor is a "causal complex responsible for every cognition" an established fact.

Furthermore, because there are no parts (*avayava*) to a cognition, (to talk of) a portion (*aṃśa*) is with respect to an object only. And a cognition is not a cause of its object!

Therefore, inference and recognition would be perceptual (on your view, as well as on ours), each with respect to its own object, (the former) to the inferable (e.g., a mountain as fiery) and (the latter) to the "thatness" (as well as the thisness it presents), on account of their presentations not being produced by a determinate awareness.

Comments

Gaṅgeśa is here primarily intent on undermining one Prābhākara position by presuming another—albeit his own views are sometimes similar. Concerning the head-to-head controversy, keep in mind that the "thatness" presented by a recognition is not considered perceptual by the Prābhākara, though by Gaṅgeśa it is.

Cognitions do not have parts in the way a physical object has, but illusion forces us to talk of "factors" (*ghaṭaka*) of cognitions—the qualifier factor, the qualificandum factor, and the relational factor—also called parts or portions, and by Gaṅgeśa himself, as we have often seen. But Naiyāyikas are usually careful about insisting, as does Gaṅgeśa here, that these have to be understood in regard to objects cognized. A qualificandum has multiple properties or qualifiers, and even universals which cannot be lost by their exhibitors are distinct from a qualificandum conceived merely as a property-bearer. The causal role of a memory-impression in perception is restricted to the qualifier "portion" of an awareness, Gaṅgeśa contends.

Except for the unreal objects of imaginings and the like, a cognition is surely indeed not a cause of its object, as though imagining a mountain could make a real one appear! But precisely why does Gaṅgeśa say, "And cognition is not a cause of its object," as though the Prābhākara position were a metaphysical idealism? Here the answer is unclear, but we learn, just below, that this line of criticism is directed at the Prābhākara plank that any cognition takes itself as object (the "measurer").

Text (p. 610, Tirupati) and Translation

> atha pratyabhijñāyāṃ tattā-viṣayatve na taj-jñānaṃ kāraṇam | evam anumity-ādau meya-viṣayatve 'pi | miti-mātr-idantā-dharmi-viṣayatve ca na jñānaṃ kāraṇam, kiṃ tu jñāna-sāmagrī iti cet, na | tad-viṣayatvaṃ hi jñāne sva-kāraṇâdhīnaṃ tadīya-sva-bhāvatvaṃ sva-rūpa-viṣayaḥ | sa ca jñānâ-janya eva | daṇḍi-jñānâdau ca a-vyāptiḥ | tasya anumity-ādi-vad viśiṣṭa-jñānatvena viśeṣaṇa-jñāna-janyatvāt | na ca parokṣatvam upādhiḥ | pratyabhijñāyāṃ prathamôtpanna-jāti-vyakti-jñāna-janye jāter anugata-pratyakṣe ca sādhyâ-vyāpakatvāt | pūrva-vyakti-vṛttitve saty etad-vyakti-vyakti-vṛttitvam anugatatvam iti tatra pūrvânubhūta-vyakter viśeṣaṇatvena taj[3]-jñānasya anugatatva-pratyakṣe kāraṇatvāt | anyathā prathamam apy anugata-dhī-prasaṅgaḥ |

Objection (by the Prābhākara): No cognition of a "that" is a cause of recognition, of its thatness presentation; so, too, with inference and the like, regarding the inferred object as presentation. Moreover, cognition does not cause a "presentation" to include cognition (i.e., itself, the "measure"), the cognizer (the "mother"), and "thisness" as the property-bearer. Rather, it's the causal complex sufficient to produce a cognition.

Gaṅgeśa: No. For, having *x* as object is, regarding cognition, dependent on a cognition's own (particular causes including *x*, as a pot is in part responsible for a cognition's having it as object). (A cognition's) essential nature as being such-and-such (or "thatly," *tadīyatva*) is essentially a particular, and it is not at all generated by cognition (but rather by pots and other objects in the world).

Moreover, your view suffers from failure to include (as perceptual) the likes of cognition of a staff-bearer (which, like "A blue lotus," is a cognition of a doubly qualified entity). For, like inference and so on, such a cognition is produced by a cognition of a qualifier (cognition of a staff, that is to say,) by a cognition that is a cognition of an entity as qualified.

And being-(cognitively)-non-immediate is not an "undercutter," *upādhi*, (for the inference: "The cognition, 'This is a staff-bearer,' is generated by a cognition of a qualifier, *since* it is a cognition of an entity as qualified"). For (in two types of case) the (putative) undercutter fails to pervade the probandum—with recognition as well as with recurrent cognition of a universal, the latter being generated by an (indeterminate) cognition produced first, where the universal and the individual are first grasped.

(What do I mean by "recurrent?") Given a prior individual as in a particular way present (and cognized), to be recurrent is the presence (and cognition, a second time, with respect to something else) of the way the (prior) individual was present (and cognized). Thus, in such a case, an individual first experienced as such and such a qualifier is a cause of a perception where there is cognitive recurrence. Otherwise, there would be the unfortunate ramification that even a first-time cognition would be a recurrent one.

Comments

The Prābhākara has put forth two definitions of perception: "cognitive immediacy," and, relevant to the present context, "whatever cognition with *x* as object is not generated by a determinate cognition, that (cognition) as about *x*" is a perception. Here the main problem is that some perceptual cognitions do appear to be generated by determinate, not just indeterminate, cognitions. For example, a person cognized as holding a staff, viz., "A staff-bearer," is cognized by way of a determinate cognition of a staff, i.e., a cognition of something as qualified by staffhood. The staff has to be determinately perceived before the person bearing the staff can be perceived as a staff-bearer.

An example of a recurrent cognition is "A cow," and then later, "A cow," and so on, where one individual after another is cognized as a cow. This is an important passage for elaboration of cognitive recurrence, which is the principal way—we are told throughout Nyāya-Vaiśeṣika—that a universal is known.

Text (p. 570, Calcutta) and Translation

ata eva jñāna-sākṣād-a-janyaṃ pratyakṣam | pratyabhijñāyāṃ saṃskāra eva sākṣāj-janakaḥ | jātāv anugata-dhīr api saṃskāra-janyā | evaṃ sādṛśyâdi-pratyakṣe 'pi pratiyogi-saṃskāra-janyā, evaṃ sādṛśyâdi-pratyakṣe 'pi pratiyogi-saṃskāra eva kāraṇam iti nirastam | daṇḍânubhava-janya-daṇḍi-pratyakṣe dhārā-vāhika-pratyakṣe ca a-vyāpanāt | uttara-viśiṣṭa-jñāne pūrva-viśiṣṭânubhavasya eva viśeṣaṇa-jñānatvena hetutvāt saṃskārasya smaraṇêtarâ-janakatvāc ca | anyathā pratyabhijñâdeḥ saṃskāra-janyatvena smṛtitvaṃ syād ity uktatvāt |

(**Gaṅgeśa** continues:) Just for this reason the following (definition) is rejected.

(An alternative **Prābhākara** definition, one moving closer to the Nyāya point of view:) Perception is (D^{13}) "cognition that is not generated directly by (another) cognition." A memory-impression (which is not a cognition) directly generates a recognition (so the definition fits, insofar as recognition is regarded as perceptual). A recurrent cognition of a universal is also generated by a memory-impression. In this way, too, just a memory-impression of an absentee causes perception of similarity and the like.

Gaṅgeśa: The definition (D^{13}) fails (this time, too) to include (a) perception of a staff-bearer as generated by experience of a staff, as well as (b) a series of perceptions (of the same thing). (In both cases) the previous cognition itself (e.g., of a staff) is, as a cognition of a qualifier, a cause of the later cognition (e.g., of a staff-bearer). Moreover, a memory-impression does not generate (as proximate instrumental cause) anything other than a memory. Otherwise, a recognition, etc., as (in your view) generated by a memory-impression, would be a memory, as has been said.

Comments

The point of the new definition, D^{13}, is that by the qualification, "directly," overapplications would be avoided that vitiated definitions advanced earlier by the Prābhākara camp.

With a series of perceptions of the same thing, an earlier member is considered a direct causal factor for an immediately subsequent member.

We can now see that Gaṅgeśa is willing to take the broader view of the conditions necessary for a perception to occur, and would count, according to the particular type of perception, a variety of cognitive factors as causes including memory-impressions and immediately preceding perceptions. Thus, Gaṅgeśa's endorsement of D^{11}—"cognition that does not have a cognition as its proximate instrumental cause"—makes the distinction between an ordinary necessary factor, so to say, and the proximate instrumental cause (*karaṇa*) all the more important. "Sensory connection," we may say, is what is most central to the causal process that results in perception. And sensory connection is what Gaṅgeśa takes up next.

So here ends Gaṅgeśa's reflection on defining perception. The next topic is one of the most problematic areas of Naiyāyika theory—by Gaṅgeśa's own lights, or struggles, if we may say, almost as much as by our own perspective informed by science and its radically different views of sensory processes. The main problem for Gaṅgeśa is the variable nature of the operative sensory connection, since not only do the several sense faculties differ significantly in how they relate to objects perceived, so too do objects themselves differ significantly in how they are perceptible.

atha saṃnikarṣa-vāda

NOW, **DISCOURSE ON SENSORY CONNECTION**

Text (p. 613, Tirupati, and p. 572, Calcutta) and Translation

pratyakṣa-viśeṣe saṃnikarṣa-viśeṣo hetur anugata[1] eva | saṃyogena dravya-grahaḥ saṃyukta-samavāyena rūpa-karmaṇor grahaṇaṃ, saṃyukta-samaveta-samavāyena rūpatvâdeḥ, samavāyena śabdasya, samaveta-samavāyena śabdatvâdeḥ, viśeṣaṇatayā śabdâ-bhāvasya, indriya-sambaddha-viśeṣaṇatayā samavāya-ghaṭâ-bhāvâder yogya-saṃnikarṣād eva graho na saṃnikarṣa-mātrāt |

Gaṅgeśa: For different types of perception, different sensory connections are indeed required as uniform causal conditions. (1) Substances are grasped through a contact (between a sense organ and the object perceived). (2) Through inherence-in-what-is-in-contact, colors (and other qualities) and motions are grasped. (3) Through inherence-in-what-is-inhering-in-what-is-in-contact, colorhood (the universal of color) and the like are grasped. (4) Through inherence, sound is grasped. (5) Through inherence-in-what-is-inhering, soundhood (the universal of sound) and the like are grasped. (6a) Through being-a-qualifier, absence of sound is grasped. (6b) Through being-a-qualifier-of-what-is-in-relation-to-a-sense-organ, inherence and such absences as of a pot are grasped. The grasping (in each case) results from the *appropriate* sensory connection, not from sensory connection in general.

Comments

"Appropriate" is used not only to underscore that there are the different relations but also to exclude atoms and other things that are "unfit" (*a-yogya*) to be perceived. Sensory contact is not specified on the level of atoms.

Gaṅgeśa mentions colorhood and soundhood, and indicates that other universals are cognized similarly. But still other universals are considered known through inherence-in-what-is-in-contact, joining qualities (colors, etc.) and motions, though Gaṅgeśa fails to state this here. Note that sensory relationality with unperceived instances of universals falls into the "extraordinary" category, also not mentioned. These are the six "ordinary" sensory relations, which are not mentally mediated, etc.—the glossary entry for *a-laukika-saṃnikarśa* (p. 685) lists the "extraordinary" relations.

Text and Translation

atha sūkṣmâvayavâvacchedena avayavi-saṃyoge 'pi na tad-graha iti mahâvayavâvacchedena saṃyogo hetuḥ | tathā ca avayavêndriya-saṃyoga eva hetuḥ | na ca grāhya-saṃyogâvacchedakâvayava-saṃyogâpekṣayā grāhya-saṃyogasya laghutvāt sa eva hetuḥ | tasya atiprasaktatvāt | etena svâvayava-saṃyogâpekṣayā sva-saṃyogasya laghutvāt sa eva hetur iti nirastam | na apy avacchedaka-saṃyogena anyathā-siddhau tatra apy avacchedakântara-saṃyogena anyathā-siddhir iti saṃyogo hetur eva na syād iti vācyam | alpataratama-bhāgâvacchedena saṃyogasya hetutve 'tiprasaṅgād iti | mā evam | dravya-grahe avayavi-mātra-grahe vā sthūlâvayavâvacchedena saṃyogo na hetuḥ, ātma-trasa-reṇu-sūkṣma-bhāga-grahe vyabhicārāt | kiṃ tu ghaṭâdi-grahe sa hetuḥ | evaṃ ca ātmâdi-dravya-graho grāhya-saṃyoga-janya iti ghaṭâdi-graho 'pi tad-vad eva sva-grāhya-saṃyoga-janya iti | tasmin saty api ghaṭâdi-graho na asti iti yadi tadā sthūlâvayava-saṃyogo 'vacchedako 'stu tat-saṃyogo 'pi vā hetuḥ | na tu kḷpta-hetu-parityāgaḥ |

Objection.1: There may be contact (of a sense organ) with an object as a whole, specifically in its very small parts, while the whole is *not* grasped (e.g., one sees a part of an object behind a door and cannot identify it). Therefore, contact with the whole object specifically *in the large parts* causes perception. And, similarly, (specification is required) for a sensory contact with the parts as a cause.

And it is not the case that "contact with the thing grasped" is simpler (theoretically) in comparison with "contact with parts" made specific by (the qualification) "contact with the whole thing grasped" such that just contact with the thing grasped should be considered causal. For in application that would be too wide.

Thus is rejected the view that, because of simplicity in comparison with "contact with the whole's parts," "contact with the whole" is causal.

Objection.2 (against objector.1): That no contact is in fact a cause of perception is true for the following reason. Contact specified is causally irrelevant, in that however the contact would be specified there would have to be further specification (e.g., parts of the parts of the thing with which the sense organ is in contact).

Answer (by objector.1): That should not be said. For, too wide an application of the causal role of contact would be entailed by (trying as) the specifier whatever smaller or smallest portion (whereas this is not true of contact thought of as restricted to a thing's *gross* parts).

Gaṅgeśa: Don't think like that. In grasping a substance—that is, in grasping a thing simply as a whole—contact specifically restricted to the gross parts is not a cause. For, that would leave out perceptions of self, of a mote in a sunbeam, and of very small parts.

Rather, in graspings of pots and the like, contact *tout court* is causal.

And, in this way, grasping of substances, such as a self, *is* generated by contact with the thing grasped. Thus, grasping of pots and the like, too, is just like that, namely, generated by a contact with a sense organ.

If it is argued that, though a contact be present, a grasping of a pot and the like might not occur (that is, say, if the contact is with a very small part, and this even though the remainder of a causal complex is present), then, let there be a specifier: contact-with-the-*gross*-parts. (Thus the right view is: *either* the causality has to be specified like that) *or* contact with the thing grasped is causal. One does not, however, throw out a known cause.

Comments

One may see a very small part of something—less than a centimeter of the bottom of a pot, let us say—without identifying the thing as a pot, while indeed there would be "contact with the thing grasped," according to the Nyāya view of how sight works. The main issue is how much of an object—a substance—must be in contact with our senses in order for us to perceive it. Since there is a broad range of cases including perception of partless substances, Gaṅgeśa does not want a strict rule about this.

The objector holds that a contact is a cause of perception of a substance only insofar as it is thought of as restricted to the gross parts of the thing grasped. Gaṅgeśa points to counterexamples. A self—which is a substance, a *partless* substance—is grasped by way of a contact with the internal organ, *manas*, as reflected in apperception, e.g., "*I* am cognizing a pot." We do not see the parts of a mote in a sunbeam, which is considered the smallest thing graspable in perception. If one were divided, it would become imperceptible.

Gaṅgeśa appears to prefer the view that contact unspecified is causal, but he admits at the end that in some cases we would want to understand a contact as a cause only if it is with the gross parts of a thing perceived.

The central problem in this area of theory is, apparently, cumbersomeness, having to invoke special qualification for special circumstances.

Text (p. 616, Tirupati) and Translation

> nanu saṃyukta-samavāyena avayavi-graho 'stu, na tu saṃyogâdis tatra hetuḥ, tasya rūpâdi-grahe kḷptatvāt | na ca lāghavāt saṃyoga eva tathā | tasya kalpanīya-kāraṇatvāt iti cet, na | ātma-grahe indriya-saṃyogasya kāraṇatvād anyatra api dravya-sākṣātkāratvena tathā kalpanāt | na ca bahir-indriya-dravya-grahe avayavi-grahe vā saṃyukta-samavāyaḥ kāraṇam | lāghavena saṃyogasya eva kāraṇatvena kalpanāt |

Objection: (Then) let grasping of a whole be through inherence-in-what-is-in-contact (with a sense organ); contact and your special specifier do not cause perceptions of substances. For, in the case of a grasping of color or the like, inherence-in-what-is-in-contact *is* known to be a cause.

And it is not to be held on the basis of simplicity that contact *tout court* is like that (i.e., is a known cause), since its causality has to be imagined (dreamed up).

Gaṅgeśa: No. Since in the case of a grasping of a self contact with a sense organ (the *manas*) is (known to be) a cause, so elsewhere, too, is it to be imagined as that, to wit, with the cognitive immediacy of substances.

And in the case of a substance being grasped by an external organ (i.e., not by the *manas* as in a perception of self), or in the case of a grasping of a whole, inherence-in-what-is-in-contact is not a cause, since it is simpler to imagine contact alone as the cause.

Comments

The organs of sight and touch are *prāpya-kārin*, ''reaching'' the thing perceived; that is, they are thought to contact objects outside the body, in the space where the objects themselves are stationed. Other sense organs, in contrast, remain in their own location, and perceive at an internal location: in the ear, in the case of hearing, in the mouth, in the case of taste, and in the nose, with smell. The organ of smell, by the way, is not thought to perceive substances but only qualities that inhere in substances, odors, namely. These are carried to the nose in small particles of flowers and other earthen substances floating in the air.

The objector's suggestion that inherence-in-what-is-in-contact be counted the connectional cause instead of contact (etc.) in the case of substances is motivated in part by the long-standing Naiyāyika position that a whole inheres in its parts. Thus, a sense organ in contact with something's parts would grasp the whole that is inhering in them through the connection, inherence-in-what-is-in-contact.

Gaṅgeśa rests his case on the fact that contact is a known cause of self perception. It is both irrelevant and uneconomical to imagine a more complicated cause, so goes his argument.

Text (p. 619, Tirupati, and p. 589, Calcutta) and Translation

> nanu saṃyukta-samavāyo na gandha-grāhakaḥ, kiṃ tv āśraya-saṃyogaḥ | evaṃ gandhatva-graho 'py āśrayâśraya-saṃyogād iti saṃyukta-samaveta-samavāyo 'pi na hetuḥ | na ca gandhe sati gandha-samavāyaṃ vinā gandhâ-graho 'sti | na ca evaṃ saṃyukta-ghaṭe bhāvi-gandha-grahaḥ syāt, gandhasya api sva-grahe hetutvāt | na ca gandhasya pratyakṣatvena indriya-saṃnikarṣâśrayatvam anumeyam | śabda-pratyakṣa-hetoḥ samavāyasya gandhe 'pi sattvāt, gandhêndriya-saṃnikarṣa-sādhane sādhyâ-prasiddhiḥ |

Objection: Inherence-in-what-is-in-contact is not a cause of grasping an odor; the (relevant) cause is, rather, contact-with-a-substratum. In this way, grasping odorhood, too, is from contact-with-a-substratum's-substratum (in that odorhood has odors as its substrata, which, in turn, have earthen substances as their substrata). Thus (your) inherence-in-what-is-inhering-in-what-is-in-contact is also not a cause.

Further, given the presence of an odor, it is false that there is no perception of the odor without an *inherence* on the part of the odor.

And (unlike the difficulty concerning inherence, which is conceived as one and same relation everywhere) there would not be in this way a grasping of a future odor in (for example) a pot in (sensory) contact (i.e., small bits of which are in contact with the organ of smell), since the odor (itself) would be a cause with respect to a grasping of it (not the relation of inherence).

Furthermore, it is not a matter of inferring that an odor has a substratum that stands in a sensory connection because the odor is perceived (thus turning our view into yours, in that the sensory connection would be inherence-in-what-is-in-contact). For, inherence, which is (on your view) a cause of the perception of sound, would be present regarding odor, too (and so we would smell sounds!). (Moreover) if you are trying to prove a sensory connection with odor, then there is the fallacy of the probandum being unexampled.

Comments

The worry addressed in the next to last paragraph above and again in the last concerns the phenomenon of a change of property while a property-bearer remains unchanged, for example, a pot's change in color from red to black through baking. Similarly there could be a change of odor.

Now, inherence, according to Nyāya-Vaiśeṣika, is a single, uniform relation. This plank of the ontology comes under attack in the current passage, and, as we shall see, there are pretty good reasons for pulling it up and using smaller boards in replacement. In any case, it is as a single and uniform relation that inherence is a necessary condition for perception of odor, etc. But then all the qualities, future as well as present and past, of odor (etc.) that tie to a property-bearer by that relation would have to be perceived at once. This problem is dealt with more thoroughly by Gaṅgeśa in the following section, on inherence. But he does say something now in response, in the very next passage.

The inference suggested in the objection would seem to be as follows: An odor has a substratum that stands in a sensory connection, *since* it is perceptible, like a pot. Thus the probandum would be: *has a substratum that stands in a sensory connection*. So the inference would seem to commit the fallacy of trying to prove what is already admitted, since both sides accept that the sensory connection in odor perception is contact-with-a-substratum. But the objector says that the fallacy is not this but that of an "unexampled probandum." Therefore, the inference must be as follows: An odor stands in a sensory connection, *since* it is perceptible, like a pot.

Text (Tirupati, p. 620) and Translation

mā evam | gandha-samavāyi-saṃyogasya hetutve hi yadi gandha-samavāyasya viśeṣaṇatā tadā sa hetur eva | upalakṣaṇatve ca saṃyukta-dravya-mātram upalakṣyam | tathā ca ghaṭa-saṃyogāt paṭa-gandha-graha-prasaṅgaḥ | atha sva-samavāyi-saṃyogo hetuḥ | tatra samavāyo 'vacchedaka iti cet, tarhi saṃyogi-samavāyasya hetutve saṃyogo 'vacchedakaḥ samavāyo hetur iti tulyam | tad etat parivartya kṣauma-paridhānam iti ucyate |

Gaṅgeśa: Don't think like that. The (relevant) cause is a contact with that in which odor inheres. For, if an odor's inherence is the qualifier (as indeed is the case), then indeed it is (also) a cause.

Further, if (this were not a true qualifier but only) an indicator (*upalakṣaṇa*, a differentiator that merely helps to pick something out as opposed to an attributed property), then, in general, any substance in contact could be the indicator target. And so from contact with a pot there could be grasped a cloth's odor—this is the difficulty.

Objection: Contact with what it inheres *in* is the (relevant) cause. Inherence is (only) a specifier.

Gaṅgeśa: Then, given that it would be inherence-in-what-is-in-a-contact-relation that is the cause, (why not say) contact is the specifier (and) inherence is the cause—it amounts to the same position. Changing this to that should be said to be like wrapping a linen cloth (around the body in the opposite way).

Comments

A perception of odor is caused in part by contact between the organ of smell and a smelly substance. Thus the contact would be qualified by the odor's inherence. An odor as inherent is the key qualifier of an object or substance in a case of odor perception; or, more precisely, inherence-in-what-is-in-contact (with a sense organ).

Merely indicational marks, *upalakṣaṇa*, which are treated in detail in a later section of the chapter, can have the loosest of relationships to what they are indications of, unlike properties tied by inherence. So inherence is required to block the unwanted counterfactuals of a cloth's odor being smelled when a pot is being perceptually grasped and so on.

In the last paragraph, Gaṅgeśa appears to be in substantial agreement with the objector's proposal. There is small difference, qua cause of the phenomenon, between contact-with-the-thing-in-which-an-odor-inheres and inherence-in-what-is-in-the-contact-relation. The objector presents an essentially equivalent formulation, Gaṅgeśa points out.

Text (p. 621, Tirupati, and p. 594, Calcutta) and Translation

nanu saṃyukta-samavāyo na saṃyogaḥ na vā samavāyaḥ na ubhau vā, gandhe indriye ca a-vṛtteḥ | na ca indriyeṇa gandhasya param-parā-saṃbandhaḥ | param-parā hi saṃyoga-samavāyāv eva | tatra virodha eva na adhiko 'pasiddhântād iti cet, na | indriya-tat-saṃyoga-tad-āśraya-samavāyānām eva param-parā-sambandhatvāt | anyathā nīlatva-jāteḥ param-parā-sambandhena vastra-carma-kambaleṣv anugata-vyavahārôcchedaḥ |

Objection: (Concerning perception of odor) inherence in the contacted (is your view of the operative sensory connection), not contact, nor inherence, nor both, in that none of these exist in both the odor and the sense organ. Moreover, (with perception of odor) there is no serial relation of the odor to the sense organ. For, the series would run precisely in the order of contact and inherence—which is an impossibility. Nor is there an additional (relation, the "serial," whereby the two could be sequentially related without opposition), since that would go beyond (your) accepted positions.

Gaṅgeśa: No. The sense organ, the contact, the substratum (or locus) of the contact (i.e., the contact's second term, the object contacted), and inherence are, in fact, related serially. Otherwise, there would be a break in the uniform (and recurrent) speech practice that depends on the presence of blueness as a universal in a serial relation with respect to (for example, all things blue, e.g.) a piece of clothing, a piece of leather, a woolen blanket (i.e., the relation is serially stepped: blue substances such as a cloth, particular blues as qualities (*guṇa*), and blueness, the universal, which, then, is not directly related to the cloth).

Comments

According to Gaṅgeśa's Nyāya, inherence-in-what-is-in-contact is a necessary factor in a causal complex responsible for producing an awareness of a smell. But what is related to what in precisely what order in the case of this operative sensory connection responsible for a smelling? An odor, the object, inheres in something smelly that comes to be in contact with a sense organ is the thesis in the background. But this would seem to imply that the object, the odor, is related to the grasping sense organ through an ordering that would have inherence together with contact—dropping out the intermediary term, the substance (apparently because including it the organ and the object would be too far apart). Gaṅgeśa in his response identifies a model for the disputed ordering: universals of qualities such as blueness do not directly qualify substances such as a cloth but rather particular bits of blue that inhere in substances such as a cloth.

Nevertheless, the epistemic and ontological status of such serial stepping is hardly pellucid—in the case of perceptions of smells and some other objects. The discussion comes to center on four factors with a fifth, the *quality perceived*, suggested implicitly: (1) the organ of smell, (2) a substance's *contact* with it, (3) the *substance* in contact, and (4) the *inherence* (of the odor, etc.) that qualifies the substance in contact.

But that discussion is not enjoined again until later sections. For the remainder of this one, we move on to objections to other items on Nyāya's sensory-relator list, and next to an attack that includes bombardment of the

Nyāya theory of universals. The objector is pretty clearly a Prābhākara. For, Gaṅgeśa's response is in part a counterattack on an alternative theory commonly attributed to the Prābhākara camp.

Text (p. 596, Calcutta) and Translation

nanu saṃyukta-samaveta-samavāyāt na rūpatvâdi-grahaḥ tad-a-bhāvād iti cet, na | tad-an-abhyupagame 'pi rūpâdi-sādṛśyasya tato grahāt | na ca dravya-sādṛśyād eva tad-vyavahāraḥ, bādhakaṃ vinā pratīty-a-viśeṣād vaiparītyâ-patteḥ | āśraya-vaisādṛśye 'pi rūpa-rasâdeḥ sādṛśyânubhavāc ca | rasatva-madhuratva-gandhatva-surabhitvâdiś ca jātiḥ anugata-pratyayāt | rūpe ca yady api idaṃ nīlam ity anubhavo na tv idaṃ rūpam idaṃ rūpam iti, tathā api pīto varṇaḥ nīlo varṇa iti varṇâkārânugata-buddhir asti rūpatve mānam | na ca cakṣur-ādy-ekaikêndriya-grāhyatvaṃ rūpatvâdikam | bādhakaṃ vinā anugata-buddher jāti-viṣayatvāt | indriyâtīndriyatvena cakṣur-ādy-a-grahe 'pi rūpatvâdi-pratīteḥ | na hy an-anusaṃhitôpādher upahita-pratyayaḥ | atīndriya-rūpa-rasa-gandhân-anumānâpatteś ca | yogyatāyā rūpatvâdi-jāti-nirūpyatvāt |

Objection (by a Prābhākara): Grasping of colorhood and the like does not result from inherence-in-what-is-inhering-in-what-is-in-contact, since that (colorhood, as you understand it, as a universal) does not exist.

Gaṅgeśa: No. Even not accepting it as a universal, you (Prābhākaras) see it as *similarity* comprising colorhood and the like, a similarity that would be a similarity grasped (only) therefrom (i.e., from the obtaining of the relation, inherence-in-what-is-inhering-in-what-is-in-contact).

And do not say that the speech practice on this score results simply from similarity among *substances* (as opposed to qualities). For, with no prevailing counterconsiderations, there is no difference between the notions (of similarity among substances, and similarity among qualities, such as color); so you would incur the untoward ramification of reversal (from what you want: in rejecting similarity among qualities you might as well be rejecting similarity among substances, too). Moreover, even when the substrata are dissimilar, color, taste, and so on are experienced as similar.

Tastehood, sweetness, odorhood, pleasant-fragrance-hood, and so on are universals, on the strength of recurrent cognition.

And, concerning color (*rūpa*), even if the (common and recurrent) experience is, "This is blue," not, "This is color," "This is color" (and so on), still recurrent cognition in the form of (particular) colors is evidence for colorhood.

And it is not the case that (as you Prābhākaras say) colorhood and the like are to be analyzed as (various ways) the perceptible is grasped by the visual organ and the like, by one sense organ alone. For, unless there are prevailing counterconsiderations, recurrent experience is to be understood as having a universal as object.

(Furthermore) the sense organs are not sensory objects; they are not grasped by the visual organ or the like. Still, we know them to be colored, etc.

(which should be impossible if to be colored is, as you say, a way something perceptible is grasped by a sense organ). For, no one has a cognition of something as qualified (even) by a "surplus property" if the property cannot be ascertained, and (on your view) the color, taste, smell (etc.) of things that are beyond the grasp of the sense organs could not be inferred—this is the unfortunate consequence. (Just the reverse of what you say is true:) suitability for perception is determined by the presence of a universal such as colorhood (not the reverse; i.e., the presence of such a universal is a necessary though not a sufficient condition for perceptibility).

Comments

Udayana lists six counterconsiderations that would rule out a candidate universal, i.e., an abstract whose candidacy is secured by recurrent experience. See, in this book, pp. 700–701.

The Nyāya-Vaiśeṣika distinction between universals of substance and universals of quality contrasts with the Prābhākara view according to which there are only substance universals. The Prābhākara also denies the Nyāya-Vaiśeṣika view that recurrent experience is the primary evidence for universals.

Naiyāyikas of several periods struggle, as does Gaṅgeśa here, to understand color in the terms of the ontological inheritance. What is the relation between colorhood and bluehood? of degrees of blue? of a particular shade of blue to the universal of that particular shade, and so on? We shall see, just a bit below, a Prābhākara opponent continuing to exploit these problems.

Atoms have color and other qualities. This is known by inference. But if the Prābhākara position on the generality involved in qualities were accepted, there could be no such inference. Atoms, the sense organs, and other realities are not grasped by our sense organs, but we know their existence and some of their properties by inference. More generally, we may infer that there are things and properties out there that we do not experience, and any view that disallows this has a count against it.

Text (p. 624, Tirupati, and p. 602, Calcutta) and Translation

yady api tan-mate nīla-pītâdy-ekaikam eva nityaṃ na atīndriyam, tathā api cakṣur-ghrāṇâdi-rūpasya āloka-pṛthivy-ādi-rūpâ-bhinnatvena pratyakṣatva-prasaṅgaḥ | na ca ekam eva rūpam udbhūtam an-udbhūtañ ca iti | virodhāt |
rūpatvâdinā paras-para-vyāvṛttatayā jñātasya rūpâder upalabdhyā tat-karaṇatvena paras-para-vyāvṛtta-cakṣur-ādy-anumitiḥ, paras-para-vyāvṛtta-cakṣur-ādy-anumitau ca cakṣur-grāhyatvâdinā rūpâdi-paras-para-vyāvṛtta-dhīr ity anyonyâśrayāc ca |
nīla-pītâdi-pratītau bhinna-bhinna-karaṇatva-siddhāv api tat-tat-karaṇa-grāhyatvasya sarva-rūpeṣv a-siddhīḥ |

(**Gaṅgeśa** continues:) Even if it is, as on your view, that blue, yellow, and the other colors are individual, eternal, and not ever themselves beyond perceptible range, still, inasmuch as the color of the visual organ, the organ of smell, and so on would not be distinct from the color of light, earth, and so on, you would land in the unfortunate situation of endorsing the perceptibility (of the color of the visual organ and so on, which no one is known to have perceived).

Furthermore, it is wrong to hold that a color as simply single or individual is manifest and unmanifest (in its various occurrences). For, there is incompatibility (between the two).

Moreover, your inference that concludes that the visual organ and company are mutually distinct is based on the view that experiences of color and company are caused by colorhood and so on, color and company that (themselves) are known as mutually distinct by means of colorhood and so on. And in holding that color and company are mutually exclusive on the basis of the inference that the visual organ and company are mutually distinct because of (colorhood and so on being understood as) being-graspable-by-the-visual-organ-etc., you commit the fallacy of circular reasoning (or, "mutual dependence," *anyonyâśraya*).

Even if cognition of blue, yellow, and so on were to establish this and that distinct instrumental cause, then what the apprehensional instrumentality is would remain (nevertheless) unestablished with respect to each color (i.e., the whole range of color—as though there were a distinct sense organ for each distinguishable band!).

Comments

We shall hear much more about the possibility that things have an unmanifest color in the section on the perceptibility of air, below, pp. 489ff.

As several times remarked, the fallacy, *anyonyâśraya*, "mutual dependence," can be translated sometimes as "begging the question." Here, however, Gaṅgeśa should say that the problem is, technically, the fallacy, *cakraka*, "circular reasoning." The two are similar and often not distinguished. Circular reasoning involves more than two elements in the circle, whereas mutual dependence involves only two.

How do we know that we have distinct sense organs? If objects perceived establish distinct instrumental causes in perceptual processes, then we had best be very careful about distinctions among things perceived—lest we be forced to admit an organ for the experience of blue and a hoard of other peculiar faculties. Clearly, a particular sense organ is chief among the necessary factors, but what precisely is the way a sense organ is known and what additionally might that imply?

Text (p. 625, Tirupati) and Translation

nanu nīla-pītâdy-upalabdhi-karaṇeṣu gandha-rasa-sparśâ-vyanjakatve sati nīlâdi-vyañjakatvāt āloka-vad iti taijasatvaṃ prasādhya taijasêndriya-grāhyatvena nīlādau rūpâkārânugata-dhīr evaṃ gandhâdāv api iti cet, na | evaṃ-praṇālī-jñānâ-bhāve 'pi rūpa-rasâdāv anugata-pratyayāt nīlâkārânugata-buddheś ca nīlatvaṃ jātiḥ | na ca cakṣur-grāhyatvaṃ tat, pītâdau gatatvāt | nanu ekaikā eva nīlâruṇâdi-vyaktayaḥ, nānâ-masī-nīlimni masī-bheda-grahe 'pi tattvena pratyabhijñānāt | na ca an-eka-vyakti-vṛttitve nityatve jātitvâpattiḥ | jāteḥ saṃsthāna-mātra-vyaṅgyatvāt, avavayâvayavi-vṛttitvāt, gotvâdinā parâpara-bhāvân-upapatteś ca | nīlatarâdi-pratītiś ca tad-anya-rūpâ-sambhedād iti cet, na | pākena śyāmaṃ naṣṭaṃ raktam utpannam iti pratyayāt | na ca asau bhramaḥ, bhādhâ-bhāvāt | na ca utpāda-vināśa-pratyayasya samavāyo viṣayaḥ, tad-ullekhāt | evaṃ ca madhurâdi-rasānāṃ saurabhâ-saurabhāṇāṃ ca gandhānām eka-ekatvaṃ syāt nīlâdi-tulyatvāt | evam astu iti cet, na | teṣām utpāda-vināśânubhavāt | eka-ekatve madhuratarатvâdy-an-upapatteś ca |

Objection (by a Prābhākara): Given (the inference) that instrumental causes of such experiences as blue and yellow are not indicated by (experiences of) odor, taste, and touch, *since* they are indicated by (visual experiences of) blue and so on, like light—so is it proved that the materiality (of the visual organ) is the element, *tejas*, the fiery element. (Thus) a recurrent cognition in the form of color—blue and so on—would be due to (not your universal, color-hood, but to) being-graspable-by-the-fiery-sense-organ. Similarly, for odor and so on.

Gaṅgeśa: Wrong. Though there be no recurrent cognition in that way sufficiently extensive (to prove your proposal about the materiality of the visual organ), there would be recurrent cognition with respect to color, taste, and so on, recurrent cognition, furthermore, that taking the form of blue establishes bluehood as a universal.

And that (bluehood) is not (equivalent to) being-graspable-by-the-visual-organ. For (to name another problem), that (your proposal) would include the yellow and so on (that are graspable by the visual organ but are patently not instances of bluehood).

Prābhākara: Just single, unitary are the individuals, blue, ruddy, and so on. Although distinct bits of ink are grasped in various blue inks, they are grasped *as* that (namely, blue, which is unitary). Recognition shows this (i.e., the recognizing of one and the same blue everywhere, like the unitariness of Devadatta as known in "This is that Devadatta").

And it is not the case that we fall into (what would be for us) the unfortunate straits of having to admit a universal on the basis of our blue's residing in multiple individuals and its being eternal (positions that we do in fact subscribe to but that are not to be interpreted your way). For (according to you) a universal is supposed to be indicated by configuration of parts, i.e., structure, alone (but while cowhood may be indicated by something's having a dewlap there is no such indication of bluehood). And since a universal is supposed to exist in (all) the parts of a whole, it would be impossible that bluehood find its place in a hierarchy (of universals) along with cowhood and the rest. Moreover, there is cognition of the bluer, etc., because of non-mixture with other colors (i.e., the bluer it is the less blended it is with other colors like white, the bluest being pure blue alone).

Gaṅgeśa: No. "Through baking, the black is destroyed and the red is produced," because of this (and other such) cognition (your view is wrong). Moreover, this is no error, since there are no counterconsiderations prevailing.

Nor is it that a cognition of such production and destruction (of qualifiers while a qualificandum remains the same) takes as its object inherence, because that is not explicitly presented (or mentioned in the cognition's verbalization).

And there would be unity in this way in the case of tastes, such as sweetness, as well as with odors, such as the pleasantly-fragrant and the foul-smelling, since they are like bluehood.

"Then let it be," if so (you were to object, implying that such unity is just what you, not we, want), then (we say) no (that's not our position), since there is experience of qualifiers' production and destruction. And if the unity (were as you understand it, namely, as of the qualifier itself), then there would be no being sweeter, et cetera.

Comments

The reason that Gaṅgeśa says, to open his response, that no sufficiently extensive cognition (*praṇālī*, a long stream) would prove the Prābhākara proposal is that the Prābhākara view precludes the possibility that there be unsensible qualities of the sense organs. No direct experience, much less a long stream of experience, of the sense organs takes place.

Naiyāyikas define a universal as "that which, though unitary and eternal, exists in multiple individuals." A central problem alluded to here is that universals are recognized by recurrent experiences of the same shapes, or structures, etc., as, for instance, having a dewlap in the case of cowhood. But such indicators are absent in the case of bluehood, so Gaṅgeśa's Prābhākara opponent says. So though Naiyāyikas may claim they accept bluehood and the like as universals, it is hard to understand how they can. For, furthermore, Naiyāyikas say that cowhood, like all universals, exists in every part of those things that exhibit it. But something blue is not necessarily blue all over. Finally, blue according to the Prābhākara is forever a single color, and on this view the cognitions "bluer" and so on are easy to explain, i.e., as indicating the presence of another individual color. Only "bluest" would be a cognition of blue alone.

Gaṅgeśa's counterarguments are for the most part clear. The Prābhākara response that he has in mind when he says that inherence is not an object of a cognition of destruction and production of a quality is the clever view that not a quality or qualifier such as red but rather inherence between a qualifier and a qualificandum is what is produced and destroyed. This view is elaborated in the next section, on inherence.

Text (p. 629, Tirupati) and Translation

nanu śrotreṇa samavāyena śabda-grahe sarva-śabdôpalabdhiḥ syāt | na ca karṇa-śaṣkuly-avacchedena utpanno gṛhyate | avacchedyasya ākāśatvena a-viśeṣāt | tad-anyatve śabdasya tatra a-samavāyāt | tasmād yaḥ śabdo yaṃ prati yogyaḥ sa tena gṛhyate na anyaḥ | na ca puruṣa-viśeṣaṃ prati yogyatvaṃ na sva-rūpam, an-anugamāt, na ca jātiḥ, tasyāḥ niṣpratiyogikatvāt, na hi gauḥ kiṃcit praty a-gaur iti vācyam | sapratiyogikatvaṃ hi na sāvadhitvaṃ dīrghatvâdi-vat | na api itara-dhī-nirūpyatvam a-bhāva-vat | kiṃ tu śabda-grahe sā jātiḥ kāraṇaṃ tad-avacchedikā vā | ata eva na kurvad-rūpatva-praveśaḥ, sahakāritā-svīkārāt | sarva-sādhāraṇatvam iṣṭam eva, sarvais tathā vyavahriyamāṇatvāt | gotve 'pi tad eva tat | śabda-mātrasya yogyatvam an-anugatam eva, guṇa-yogyatva-vad iti |

Objection (by the Prābhākara): If grasping of sound is by means of inherence (as the operative sensory connection) along with the auditory organ, then every sound should be perceived (by everyone, since both the substratum of the inherence, ether, namely, and inherence are single and unitary, according to you). And it is not the case that (as you hold) sound as produced is grasped by a delimitation (of the ether) to the ear canal, since the ether, which is what is to be delimited (on your view), is without distinctions (or parts). (Moreover) in what is other than ether (namely, air and so on), sound (by your own admission) does not inhere.

Therefore, whatever sound *x* is fit (to be heard) with respect to a person S, that *x* is grasped by S and not another.

And it is not the case that the fitness (of a sound to be heard), which is relative to each particular person, is not self-linking (rather, the relation is self-linking, that is to say, it varies with each particular instance). And it is not a universal, because a universal is a phenomenon that does not require a countercorrelate. For, it should not be said that a cow is in relation to someone or other not a cow (i.e., cowhood is an independent reality, not perceiver-relative). For, having-a-countercorrelate is not the same as having a limit (or point of reference or contrast), as, for example, in the case of being-long (that has a point of contrast in being-short). Nor is it (i.e., the person-relative fitness-to-be-heard of a sound) determined, like an absence, with respect to cognition of something else (as an absence is determined by cognition of what it is an absence of). Instead, it is either a universal as a cause or as a specifier of that (the relevant causality).

Just for this reason, there is (contrary to what Buddhists hold) no utilization of a (special property accounting for change of causal circumstance, viz.)

"operational form" (*kurvad-rūpa*), in that we accept (that the fitness is causally efficient along with) auxiliary causes.

That the fitness would be common to everyone (presents no difficulty; for us, it) is in fact the desired position. Likewise, by everyone (within hearing range) something being spoken conversationally (is in fact heard). With respect to cowhood, too, it's just that (that is, cowhood is known in common by people).

(Although a universal to our way of thinking) the fitness is in fact not uniform considering sounds generally. (Instead) it is like the fitness of qualities (with respect to what they qualify, e.g., intelligence, of persons, having a dewlap, of cows, and so on).

Comments

To be told that the fitness is not a universal and, later, that it is a universal makes this Prābhākara passage difficult to understand. Probably the first statement should be construed as the assertion that it is not a universal in the Naiyāyika sense. On the other hand, Gaṅgeśa may be letting his opponent ramble at cross purposes. Still, Gaṅgeśa rarely sets up an obvious strawman.

Buddhists posit a special "operational form" (*kurvad-rūpa*) to explain why a seed, a momentary reality, produces in a granary another seed the next instant, whereas a seed in the field produces a sprout. The latter case occurs through conjunction with another momentary property, the "operational form."

In brief, the Prābhākara's position is that inherence is not the sensory connection in perceptions of sound. Rather, that relation is a certain "fitness," as is elaborated.

Text (p. 630, Tirupati, and p. 612, Calcutta) and Translation

mā evam | śabdasya pratyakṣatvena pratyāsatti-sādhanāt | na ca samavāyo 'tiprasakto 'nyo 'n-abhyupagata iti vācyam | karṇa-saṃyogâvacchinna-samavāyasya pratyāsattitvāt | karṇa-saṃyoga hi samavāya-vṛttyā śabdâdhāratāyāṃ paricāyakaḥ | evaṃ ca iha śabdo na iha śabda ity anubhavāt śabdasya a-vyāpya-vṛtttve siddhe yasya śabdasya samavāya-vṛttyā ādhāratā karṇa-saṃyogena avacchidyate sa gṛhyate, yasya tu tad-atyantâ-bhāvena avacchidyate sa na gṛhyate | tathā saṃyogasya samavāyena ādhāratā hasta-saṃyogena avacchidyate na tad-a-bhāvena iti hasta-saṃyogâvacchedena gṛhyate na anyatra, anyathā hasta-saṃyogasya an-avacchedakatve sarvam idaṃ samānam iti saṃyogasya api sarvatra upalabdhiḥ syāt | na ca evaṃ samavāyo 'pi a-vyāpya-vṛttiḥ | samavāyena vṛttyā tasya ādhārâ-vṛttitvāt | a-bhāvas tu viśeṣaṇatayā vyāpya-vṛttir eva | na ca evaṃ sarvatra sarva-śabdôpalabdhiḥ syāt | śabda-samavāyasya sattve 'py anyatra śabdâtyantâ-bhāva-sattvāt |

Gaṅgeśa: Don't think like that. Sound inasmuch as it is perceived proves a (special) sensory connection (inherence, namely).

And it should not be said that inherence has here too wide an application, that it is something else, or that is not accepted (by us as applicable to sound): (our view is that a sound's) inherence (in ether) is specified by a conjunction of ether with the ear canal—this is the operative sensory connection. For, a conjunction with the ear canal—by way of inherence as the connection—in the substratum of a sound is what makes the sound perceived.

And in this way (is explained our experience of) one sound here, another sound not here—which is our experience.

Given that a sound (as a quality) has been proved not to pervade the locus it qualifies, whatever sound has a locus that is specified by a conjunction with the ear canal, that sound is perceived—by way of inherence as the connection. But whatever sound has a locus that is specified by an absolute absence of conjunction with the ear canal, that sound is not perceived.

Similar is the case of a conjunction (e.g., a contact between a book and a hand) that has a locus—by way of inherence—that is specified by contact with the hand, not by an absence of that, such that the thing (the book) is grasped specifically through contact with the hand, not elsewhere (such as in the foot). Otherwise, if contact with the hand did not delimit (the precise locus), all this would be the same. Thus, the contact, too, would be perceived throughout (the body).

And it is not the case that in this way inherence would be non-locus-pervading (in that a sound as a quality is non-locus-pervading and there must be a match with the relation whereby a sound hooks up to its property-bearer). (Inherence is in fact locus-pervading) for inherence does not occur in a substratum by way of inherence (rather, it occurs by way of self-linkage, which need not itself be locus-pervading, being unique in each case).

An absence (of inherence by the relation of inherence would then have to be everywhere inherence occurs; yes, it) is in fact locus-pervading (this is our position), through the relation, being-a-qualifier (*viśeṣaṇatā*).

And it is not the case that in this way a sound would be experienced everywhere. For, although the inherence of a sound occurs (in one place), there would be an absolute absence of the sound at other places.

Comments

An unmentioned reason why inherence must not relate to either of its relata by the relation inherence is fear of infinite regress. Inherence is itself tied down uniquely wherever it occurs and does its relational work.

Inherence is one and same everywhere, and a sound is tied to its locus by inherence. Nevertheless, a sound is not heard everywhere because an absolute absence of that sound blocks such an occurrence. Presumably, this absolute absence—a fundamental silence considering all sounds—would be the default, itself removed by the causes responsible for the production of something of a certain type. Thus, drawing on the logic of natural blockage (where a G, there no F), Gaṅgeśa is able to maintain the uniformity of inherence. Similarly, air is not colored—though other qualities do *inhere* there—because of a natural blockage. The thesis that an absence can be thus a causal factor comes into focus below, near the end of the section.

Text (p. 636, Tirupati, and p. 617, Calcutta) and Translation

atha vīṇâdau śabda ity a-bādhitânubhava-balāt tad-avacchinnaṃ nabhaḥ śrotraṃ na tu karṇâvacchinnam eva | karṇe na śabdaḥ kiṃ tu vīṇāyām ity anubhavāt | anyathā karṇe śabda iti dhīḥ syāt | na ca an-anta-vīṇâdy-avacchedakatvena an-anta-śrotra-svīkāre gauravam, śabda-deśatvena ekatve ca atiprasaṅgaḥ, sarva-deśānāṃ śabdâvacchedakatvād iti vācyam | vīṇâdi-deśatā-grahasya bādhakaṃ vinā pramāṇatve gauravasya nyāyatvāt | pratyuta sarvato dikṣu an-anta-śabda-saṃtānôtpāda-krameṇa karṇôtpāde kalpanā-gauravaṃ mānâ-bhāvāt | na ca dūra-saṃnidhānayoḥ śabdānām a-bādhita-tāra-mandatvâdi-vaidharmya-pratītyā bheda-siddheḥ saṃtāna-siddhiḥ | dūratvâdi-doṣāt tāratvâ-grahe mandatvâropāt tad-upapatteḥ | vyavahita-karṇe śabdân-utpāda-vat vyavahita-śabdân-upalabdhiḥ | nimitta-vāyu-saṃyogâ-bhāvāt | na tu vyavadhānâ-bhāvasya hetutvāt tasya saṃnidhy-upakṣīṇatvāt karṇân-upaghāto 'pi hetur iti na tad-upaghāte śabda-graha iti |

Prābhākara: On the strength of undefeated experience, "The sound is in the veena (the stringed instrument) or the like," the organ of hearing should be regarded as the ether (*nabhas*) delimited just by that (i.e., by whatever produces the sound). For, sound does not occur in the ear but rather in the veena—so says experience. Otherwise, we would cognize, "The sound is in the ear" (but we don't).

Objection (by a Naiyāyika): In accepting that the organ of hearing is infinite on the grounds that the veena and so on that delimit it are infinitely numerous, you embrace an overly cumbersome view, and in finding (the sense organ's) unity in specification according to a sound's location (a veena and so on where sounds are produced), you have a view that extends too far, in that every location is capable of sound.

Prābhākara: That should not be alleged. For, there is the maxim that cumbersomeness should be discounted when there is an authority (as there is here) of a grasping (i.e., of a perceptual experience)—according to the location of a veena or its equivalent. On the contrary, cumbersomeness of conception belongs to (your view of) production (of sound) in the ear serially according to production of streams of infinite sounds (streams originating in a veena and so on but heard in the ear), because (in that case, unlike with our view) there is no (cumbersomeness-countering, experiential) authority.

And there is not (contrary to what you say) establishment of a stream (or a series) of sounds on the basis of establishment of distinct individual sounds through undefeated experience of incompatible properties—loudness and softness—experience had by two (perceivers), one far away (from the origin) and the other near (i.e., perceived sound changes according to whether one is close or far away, and there must therefore be a series of distinct sounds). For, that can be explained (on our unitive view): when (true) loudness is not grasped, it is due to such a defect as being far away, which brings about a superimposition of softness. Like (your view of) no production of sound (i.e., sound heard) when (passage to) the ear is obstructed, (so we say) there is no experience of obstructed sound when there is no conjunction with *enabling* air.

We, however, do not say that absence of obstruction is (in general) a cause of perception of sound, as do those who reason that when such absence disappears there is a sensory presence—although it is true that we do not say that not being afflicted earwise (i.e., an absence of that particular kind of obstruction) *is* a cause of hearing: when someone is so afflicted, there is no grasping of sound.

Comments

The Prābhākara position is not, in the classical context, as implausible as it may seem. The issue is whether a particular sense organ—here, the organ of hearing—is *prāpya-kāri*, "works by reaching" or not, that is, whether the sense organ grasps its object where the object is located as opposed to a grasping that occurs within the body. The topic is widely debated for each sense faculty. Naiyāyikas hold that the visual organ is *prāpya-kāri*, that it travels out of the eyes, collects visual information on the spot, so to say, and conveys it by way of the *manas* to the individual embodied self. Light is an enabling medium, a "carrier" (*vāhaka*) of the organ. So, similarly, with respect to hearing, both parties hold that air is an auxiliary cause (*vāhaka*). Thus the resources are in place to construct a reaching-out theory of hearing.

Moreover, phenomenologically sounds do seem to be heard where they occur—as we do seem to see things not in our heads but out in the world.

Gaṅgeśa, however, will be able to make a stronger case overall for his non-reaching theory, citing, as we shall see, overriding evidence.

Text (p. 637, Tirupati) and Translation

mā evam | karṇâvacchedena api śabda-grahāt karṇa-śaṣkuly apy avacchedikā iti karṇâvacchinnam eva nabhaḥ śrotram, āvaśyakatvāt lāghavāc ca | śabda-mātra-grahe tad-anuvidhānāt, śarīra-saṃyuktasya sataḥ sākṣāt-pratīti-sādhanasya indriyatvāt, karṇena vīṇā-śabdaṃ śṛṇomi iti tat-karaṇatvena[2] a-bādhitânubhavāc ca | na tu vīṇâdikam, an-antatvāt, śabda-mātra-grahe tad-an-anuvidhānāt, vīṇâdy-avacchinnasya nabhasaḥ śarīrâ-saṃyuktatvena an-indriyatvāt vīṇayā śabdaṃ śṛṇomi ity an-anubhavāc ca | kathaṃ tarhi vīṇāyāṃ śabda iti jñānam, śrūyamāṇasya śabdasya tad-an-adhikaraṇatvād iti cet, na | na hi sarvatra śabde mṛdaṅgâdy-adhikaraṇa-graha-niyamaḥ | anyathā kvacid api deśe saṃdeha-viparyaya-tad-an-ullekhānām an-upapatteḥ | yatra apy asti tatra śarīre sukham iti-vat utpattaye param-parayā vīṇâdy-apekṣaṇāt tad-adhikaraṇatvam | tava api vīṇāyāḥ śabdân-āśrayatvena tathā eva adhikaraṇatvāt |

Gaṅgeśa: Don't think like that. Sound is indeed heard within the ear, and so the ear canal is also a specifier (or delimiter, of the sense organ): ether precisely as delimited by the ear is the organ of hearing. For this is both the necessary and the economical position. Moreover, (a) only sound is grasped in accordance with that (the operation of the organ of hearing), (b) an instrument giving rise to an immediate experience is a sense organ only insofar as it is conjoined to the body, and (c) "With my ear, I am hearing the sound of a veena," such is an undefeated experience of the ear as chief instrumental cause. A veena or the like, however, is not the chief instrumental cause, because (d) such things are infinitely numerous, (e) it is not the case that only sound would be grasped in accordance with that, (f) ether as delimited by a veena or the like is not a sense organ in that no such thing is conjoined to the body, and (g) there is no experience, "With my veena, I am hearing the sound."

Objection: How, then, is there the cognition, "The sound is *in* the veena?" For, the ear is not the locus of a sound being heard.

Gaṅgeśa: Wrong. There is no general rule that sound is grasped in all instances along with such things as drums as the locus. Otherwise, it would be impossible to have doubt about precisely at which place (a sound is heard), and it would be impossible to have an erroneous experience of the location—such cognitions, which do not expressly indicate that (a drum or the equivalent as locus) would be impossible. Even where there is (experience of sound in a veena, for instance), there, like (the cognition) "Pleasure *in* the body" (with the pleasure residing in fact in an individual self, *ātman*), there is dependence on a veena or the like for the purpose of sequential production (of sound heard): (in this way) those (a veena and the like) are the locus. (Finally) for you, too, a veena is not the substratum of a sound (the substratum, you say, is ether, ether delimited by a veena and so on), and so just in that way is it (for you) the locus.

Comments

Gaṅgeśa sees his view as the more economical because he posits delimitation by the two ear canals, whereas the Prābhākara posits delimitation by a potentially infinite number of things.

Among the excellent arguments made here particularly telling is Gaṅgeśa's indirect proof that a certain kind of doubt and a certain kind of error would be impossible on the Prābhākara view. Phenomenologically, the doubt and the error occur. But they should not occur, given the Prābhākara theory.

As the veena is necessary to produce the first in a series of sounds that results in a distinctive type of hearing in the ear canal, so the body is necessary to experience pleasure although, strictly speaking, the pleasure is *in* the self.

Text (p. 638, Tirupati, and p. 625, Calcutta) and Translation

nanv evaṃ karṇe an-eka-ga-kārôtpāde an-eka-grahaṇa-prasaṅgaḥ | na ca eka-grahe anya-graha-sāmagrī pratibandhikā | kolāhale tathā a-darśanād iti cet, na | tāreṇa mandâbhibhavāt | tulyatve vā an-eka-grahasya iṣṭatvāt | bhedâ-grahas tu atyanta-sārūpyāt | evaṃ ca vīṇâder a-śrotratve maitreṇa aham anuvākam adhyāpito yad gītaṃ tvayā śrutaṃ tan mayā api ity-ādi-pratītīnāṃ tad-uccāraṇâdi-prayojya-jātīyatvaṃ viṣayaḥ | śabde hi kāraṇa-viśeṣa-prayojyā jātir a-vaśyaṃ vācyā | anyathā śabda-viśeṣeṇa putrâdy-anumānaṃ na syāt, jātiṃ vinā viśeṣântarâ-bhāvāt | evaṃ ca karṇâvacchinnasya nabhasaḥ śrotratve tena vīṇâdi-prabhava-śabda-graho na tatra saṃtāna-krameṇa utpādaṃ vinā ity an-anya-gatikatayā tat-kalpanā api prāmāṇikī |

Objection: If it were the way you say, there would be, upon the production of many *ga* sounds in the ear, the unfortunate consequence of a grasping of a plurality (however, only a single sound is heard). And it would be wrong to hold that, given a grasping of (just) one (*ga* sound when many have been simultaneously uttered by, let us say, many singers), it would prevent the others from being grasped, since that is not experienced, for example, with a tumultuous clamor (where one sound does not block others out).

Gaṅgeśa: No. For, a loud sound drowns out a soft one. Or, if there is to be equality (of loudness) and a plurality of sounds grasped—such is something we accept. But when a situation of no grasping of distinctness (among sounds) occurs, it is due to an extreme similarity (among them).

And so, given that a veena and the like are not the organ of hearing (but rather ether delimited by the ear canal), "I have been taught by Maitra an *anuvāka* (a Vedic chapter-section for recitation)," "What has been recited by you has also been heard by me," and other such cognitions rely on—as their objects—the universals (or types) of the utterables in such pronouncings and so forth.

For, regarding sounds (the thesis) that what is utterable by distinct agents is a universal is necessarily to be proclaimed. Otherwise, it could not be inferred (by a father) that the utterer must be his son on the basis of particular sounds (uttered and heard, although the utterer be out of sight and among many children who are shouting simultaneously), since, without a universal, there would be no further particulars (of the type).

And so, given that the organ of hearing is the ether delimited by the ear, a grasping of a sound produced by the likes of a veena, therefore, could not occur without a serial production (of sounds): that this is the only way such grasping can be understood proves that thesis, too (the thesis of a series of sounds produced one after the other reaching the ear).

Comments

Gaṅgeśa is imagining situations that make it plain that sounds have type character as words grasped on occasions of out-loud speech. Sound-types or word-types are universals; audible utterances are made up of particulars which are tokens. Otherwise, when a *guru* has said out loud a Vedic statement and a student (*śiṣya*) has repeated it, it would be hard to say what is common between the two utterances since the individual sounds made by the two persons are distinct. (Such repetition was and still is in India a standard first step in teaching a scriptural text.)

Gaṅgeśa also shows that sound travels by a series of distinct qualities being produced, with a universal "sense," so to say, riding piggyback on the individual tokens.

The first problem raised in the objection with which the passage begins would appear to be how a plurality of sounds can remain distinct within the small space of the ear canal. If this is the right reading, then Gaṅgeśa does not really address the difficulty. He simply agrees with the objector that we do hear distinct sounds simultaneously. Gaṅgeśa does not elaborate the mechanics of the operation of the hearing organ (called not the "ear" but the "hearing," *śrotra*, in Sanskrit). But we are about to be treated to several further dimensions of his physical theory.

Text (p. 628, Calcutta) and Translation

śabdena ca a-vyavahita-paramâṇu-deśôtpāda-krameṇa na śabdârambho yena meghajâdi-śabdānāṃ bhū-loka-prāptir yugântare 'pi na syāt | kiṃ tu meghâdy-abhihita-sarvato-gāmi-mahā-vāyoḥ mahati deśe saṃyoga-nimittam āsādya ādya-śabdena sarva-dig-vartī śabda eka eva janyate | nimitta-saṃyogânurodhitvāt vibhu-kāryāṇāṃ uttarôttareṇa api adhikâdhika-deśataḥ sarvatra eka-eka eva śabdo vīcī-taraṅga-vad udpādyate | ata eva sarvair eka-śabda-grahaḥ | vāyoś ca nayana-van mahā-vegatayā śīghra-gāmitvena agrima-śabdârambhād ādya-śabdân-antaram a-cireṇa eva śabdôpalambhaḥ | vāyor eva ca mandataratamâdi-krameṇa mandâdi-śabdôtpattiḥ | yad vā ādya-śabdena kadamba-golaka-vat daśa daśi daśa śabdā ārabhyante taiś ca daśa śabda-saṃtānā iti |

(**Gaṅgeśa** continues:) Furthermore, sound does not originate (and travel in the following manner) by means of a series of sounds whose order of production is according to the location of an uninterrupted series of ultimate atoms (viz., a continuous atomic sound stream). If so, sounds such as thunder would not be heard on the ground until another *yuga* (a very long period of time).

On the contrary, there are series of instrumental causes which are contacts, contacts in measurable places with *gross* particles of all-traversing air. These gross particles are struck by the likes of (the thunder-creating action of) clouds. Thus results an original sound that gives rise to streams of sound going in all directions—(thus) sound that is just single (of one kind) arises (and is heard by people in different locations). For, the widespread effects that occur are in accord with such contacts being the instrumental causes, one right after the other, and in more and more (i.e., a wider spread of) locations: everywhere each individual sound is produced, like a series of large or small waves. Just like this is there grasping by everyone of "one and the same" sound.

And air, like the visual organ, travels quickly because of its great velocity: from the start of the next sound, immediately following a first sound, it is (typically) not at all a long time to a sound perception. And uniquely aerial series, whether slower or slowest and so on, produce sounds that are low and so on.

Or, we might say, from a first sound, like (the expansion or opening of) the ball of the *kadamba* flower, ten (each) in a direction, (so) ten sounds originate; and from them, ten streams of sound.

Comments

There are four *yuga*s in a larger cycle of time. A *yuga* ranges from almost two million years in length for the first in a cycle to about a half a million for the last.

If a series of sounds were to qualify a series of ultimate atoms of air, then not only would sounds be infinite (not an undesired ramification in itself) but an infinite series of atoms would have to be crossed, taking a long time, whereas sound is heard quickly following production. Thus, avoidance of a problem similar to the paradoxes of Zeno in ancient Greek philosophy informs Gaṅgeśa's conclusions here about the grossness and measurableness of the increments of sound propagation. It seems that according to him sound travels in a wave-like rather than in a particle-like fashion. The airy atoms move, but sound series are not merely patterns of atoms.

If the enabling air moves quickly, shrill or high sounds are heard; if slowly, low sounds are heard. Presumably, a shrill utterance would make the air move quickly (though none of this seems confirmed by touch).

On the option that Gaṅgeśa mentions at the end, sound would travel in ten directions for the smallest increment of a measurable distance, and then ten new sounds would be created, forming ten streams of sound, multiplied to a hundred and a thousand and so on with each successive moment of gross time.

Text (p. 640, Tirupati, and p. 630, Calcutta) and Translation

nanv eka-śabdena katham an-eka-śabdârambhaḥ sāmagrī-bhedād iti cet, na | sarvato-'n-eka-vāyv-ādi-sahakārāt prāg-a-bhāva-bhedād vā | na ca itara-hetu-sākalye tad-bhedān na kārya-bhedaḥ tathā a-darśanād iti vācyam | kārya-bhedo hi sāmagrī-bhedāt | sa ca hetv-antara-bhedād iva prāg-a-bhāva-bhedād api | anyathā samavāyy-ādi-bhede 'pi kārya-vaijātyam na syāt | ghaṭa-vyaktiṣu tathā a-darśanāt | pākaje rūpâdau hetv-antarâ-bhede 'pi prāg-a-bhāva-pūrva-rūpâdi-dhvaṃsa-bhedena bhedāc ca | atha rūpâdy-eka-prāg-a-bhāva-dhvaṃsayoḥ sarvatra tulyatve kiṃ vinigamakam, gandhâdi-prāg-a-bhāvānāṃ rasâdau vyabhicāre 'pi gandhâdau rasâdi-prāg-a-bhāvānām a-vyabhicārād iti cet, na | vāyu-sparśe gandha-rasa-rūpa-prāg-a-bhāva-pradhvaṃsānām, tejo-rūpe gandha-rasâ-bhāvayoḥ, jala-rase gandha-prāg-a-bhāvasya vyabhicāreṇa a-hetutve sva-prāg-a-bhāva-hetutāyā āvaśyakatvāt | pākajeṣu rūpa-rasa-sparśeṣu gandhâdi-prāg-a-bhāvānām anyathā-siddhatvāc ca | rūpâdiṣu tathâ-darśanāt | gandhe 'pi sva-prāg-a-bhāvasya a-vaśya-hetutvāt a-bhāvântarāṇām anyathā-siddhatvam | yad vā rūpa-rasa-sparśa-tulyatve 'pi agni-saṃyoga-viśeṣāt kvacit saurabham a-saurabhaṃ ca utpadyate | na ca agni-saṃyogo rūpâdi-mātre kāraṇaṃ, vyabhicārāt | evaṃ rasâdāv api |

Objection: When a single sound is heard (by different people), how (according to you) could a plurality of sounds originate (from a source, spreading like waves), since there are no distinct collections of causal factors?

Gaṅgeśa: No—because the auxiliary causes include multiple air-packets that are all-traversing, or, because there are distinct prior absences (accounting for the fact that different people hear the same sound).

Objection: Given an entire collection of causal factors excepting a prior absence, no distinct effects would arise out of distinct prior absences (as though from ten distinct locations of a pot's prior absence ten distinct pots would be produced given an otherwise identical collection of causal factors). So likewise (here), since there is no experience (of production like that).

Gaṅgeśa: That should not be said. For, there are distinct effects from distinct collections of causal factors. And, as from distinct causes come effects in cases of causes other than prior absence, so too from distinct prior absences (in that had the absentee been present, something else would have occurred). Otherwise, even when there are distinct substrata and the like (as causes), there would not be differences in the effects (e.g., a cloth could be made out of clay and a pot of threads). Similarly, such is not found with individual pots. Moreover, although (other) causes are not distinct in the case of the color and so on (smell, taste, and touch) of something heated, there is distinctness (of color and taste as well as of changes of color and taste) by means of (1) distinct prior absences and (2) the destruction of the former color and so on.

Objection: Since (on your view) each prior absence and destruction of color and so on (smell, taste, and touch) would be everywhere the same, how could an alternative be settled upon (as causing changes of color, etc.)? For, even if taste and the like deviate from prior absences of smell and the like (regarding water, for instance, which has no smell), the smell and the like (of something earthen) would not deviate from prior absences of taste and the like (since everything earthen has a taste).

Gaṅgeśa: No. Because of counterexamples the following are not causes: (a) prior absences and destructions of smell, taste, and color for air's touch, (b) absences of smell and taste for fire's color, and (c) prior absence of smell for water's taste, inasmuch as the causality is necessarily restricted to (a quality's) own prior absence. Moreover, prior absences of smell and so on are causally irrelevant (*anyathā-siddha*, "known in context as something other than a strictly necessary causal factor") regarding colors, tastes, and touches changed through baking. For, such are not seen with respect to color, etc., though with respect to smell (for instance) a smell's own type of prior absence is necessarily a cause. Other absences are causally irrelevant.

Alternatively, although from a particular type of contact with fire (on the part of something earthen), color, taste, and touch change in common, in some cases good fragrance is produced and in some cases foul fragrance (depending on other causal factors including different prior absences of smell, i.e., of the precise smell that could in a particular case be present). And contact with fire is not the only cause of (change of) color and the like, because of counterexamples. This holds for taste et cetera, too.

Comments

Gaṅgeśa responds to the opening objection by denying, implicitly, that there is a single effect in different people hearing the same sound. The problem is to account for a sameness of object in auditory experience among different people. Here Gaṅgeśa seems forced to utilize the conception of prior absences to defend his theory of propagation of multiple sounds from a single source. But note that this is only one of a pair of explanations advanced, though it is the only one developed. The other, concerning all-traversing air-packets, is left obscure.

Prior absences are identified by their absenteees, and are important for the formulation of natural laws. They would help, for example, to account for differences in perceiver, location, etc., when the same sound is heard. A universal, in contrast, would account for the sameness.

The objector attacks the thesis that distinct prior absences can be decisive in producing distinct effects. In other words, two distinct prior absences, he says, do not result, by rule, in two distinct effects, all other causal factors being the same. Gaṅgeśa counterattacks by alluding to examples. The causes of change of taste of a ripening mango are not distinct from the causes of its change of color, except for distinct prior absences, one of color, the other of taste. Prior absences help us target the appropriate dimensions of things in the formulation of natural laws. Similarly, posterior absences sometimes play a causal role. When baking changes the color of a pot from black to red, the destruction of the black is a cause of—it makes room for, so to say—the appearance of the red. Thus both types of absence are crucial for for formulating rules about the relevant dimensions of change.

We follow Mathurānātha in changing the placement, in effect, of the word "only" (*mātra*) in the next to the last sentence.

Text (p. 643, Tirupati, and p. 636, Calcutta) and Translation

nanu kārya-mātre prāg-a-bhāva-mātraṃ na hetuḥ, tayor vyatireka-kālân-avagamāt | sarva-muktāv itara-hetv-a-bhāvād eva kāryân-utpādād iti cet, na | hetv-antara-sattve 'py utpannasya punar an-utpādena prāg-a-bhāvasya hetutvāt | ekā sāmagrī ekam eva kāryaṃ janayati sva-bhāvād iti cet, na | kāryân-utpādasya sāmagrī-viraha-prayojyatva-niyamāt | na ca kārya-saha-bhāvena kāraṇatvam, gauravāt | na ca vinaśyad-avasthe samavāyini kāryân-utpattes tathātvam iti vācyam | tāvatā samavāyi-kāraṇasya eva tathātvāt, kāraṇa-mātre mānâ-bhāvena tasya a-prayojakatvāt | nanu samaveta-samavāyo na grāhakaḥ śabdatvâdi-jāter a-bhāvād iti cet, na | rūpatvâdi-nyāyena tat-sādhanāt |

Objection: A mere prior absence is not a cause of any effect, since a time when both are not is not found (i.e., if something F is a cause of something G, then there should be a time when there is no F and no G). For, when everything is liberated (i.e., at the time of a *pralaya* or universal destruction), there is no arising of effects (i.e., of a new creation) just from an absence of another cause (of a new creation)!

Gaṅgeśa: No. For, although given a (continued) presence of all other causes (i.e., other than a prior absence), that which has been produced does not arise a second time because the prior absence *is* a cause.

Objection: A single set of causal factors sufficient for an effect generates, by its very nature, a single effect.

Gaṅgeśa: No. For, the rule is that non-production is dependent on a lack of a set of sufficient causal factors.

And it is not the case that a prior absence is a cause inasmuch as it occurs *along with* an effect, since that is a cumbersome thesis.

Objection: It is such (namely, a cause in virtue of occurring along with an effect) in that an effect is not produced in the case of something inherent if its locus is destroyed.

Gaṅgeśa: That should not be said. For, only an inherent cause is like that insofar as anything is (whereas instrumental causes are not like that at all). Since there is no evidence (for this view) concerning causality in general, there is no reason to adopt it.

Objection: Inherence-in-something-inherent (which you have said is the operative sensory connection with perception of the universal of sound, soundhood) is not a generator of perception, since there is no universal, soundhood, or the like.

Gaṅgeśa: No. By the rule governing colorhood and the like, there is proof of it (viz., by experience of recurrence, *anugama*, without prevailing counter-considerations).

Comments

A pot comes about when a set of necessary conditions together sufficient to bring it about is in place. A true cause—a truly necessary condition—would be a member of such a set, a member whose absence would mean the effect would not come about. So an absence can be a causal factor. "I would have produced a pot but I ran out of clay," is a causal explanation of a potter's failure to produce a pot. Prior absences are crucial, we repeat, for the formulation of natural laws, in that the presence of the absences' absentees would comprise strictly necessary causal factors.

Puzzles, however, can be generated as we consider the peculiar nature of these non-entities. An absence of a prior absence would appear to be a presence. But is such an absence also a cause? And does an absence produce only another absence or a presence? We seem to need special rules for causes that are absences as opposed to presences.

Gaṅgeśa's response to the first puzzle mentioned above clarifies the logic of causal formulations involving prior absences: a set of conditions sufficient for an effect E includes a prior absence of E inasmuch as the set minus the prior absence of E does not produce E a second time.

Gaṅgeśa's cumbersomeness charge is directed against the thesis that a prior absence is a cause in virtue of occurring *along with* an effect. Gaṅgeśa's own view is that the blockage an absence of a prior absence accomplishes begins when the effect occurs. Mathurānātha adds that the "along with" thesis is not borne out by experience: a prior absence simply does not occur along with an effect but rather before an effect. Gaṅgeśa's point is that there is no need for such an additional principle of causality, but perhaps he should have said, "That is a cumbersome thesis and worse!"

Finally, we should recall that the entire discussion here of prior absence was launched by the problem of the operative connection in the sensory experience of sound. Gaṅgeśa closes the section by taking up the next sensory relator, in the usual order, after that which is operative with sound, namely, inherence-in-something-inherent, which he sees as required because, as he argues here, soundhood is a true universal.

atha samavāya-vādaḥ

NOW, DISCOURSE ON INHERENCE

Text (p. 645, Tirupati, and p. 640, Calcutta) and Translation

nanu samavāyâ-siddheḥ na sā pratyāsattiḥ | vipratipattiś ca śuklaḥ paṭa iti pratītiḥ viśeṣaṇa-viśeṣya-saṃbandha-viṣayā na vā iti |

Pūrvapakṣin: Since inherence is not established as real, it is not a sensory connection. (Clearly it is not established) for there is dissension whether with such a cognition as "The cloth is white" the relation is an object or not in addition to the qualifier (white) and what it qualifies (a piece of cloth).

Comments[1]

As is his usual practice, Gaṅgeśa begins his treatment of a new topic by outlining and defending a *pūrva-pakṣa* position to be answered later in text traditionally labelled *siddhânta*, the "right view." The *pūrvapakṣin* for this section may be supposed to be a free-thinking Naiyāyika opposed to positing inherence as a separate category; alternatively, a Bhāṭṭa Mīmāṃsaka (Kumārila is well-known to have rejected inherence).

If the relation between the white and the cloth is an object of cognition, then inherence should be accepted, the *pūrvapakṣin* implies. But if it is not, inherence need not be supposed. The very debate among philosophers—within and outside Nyāya-Vaiśeṣika—shows that the relation is problematic. Śaṅkara, the Advaitin, denies its reality. Kumārila, though embracing a realist ontology similar to Nyāya's, does not allow the qualificative relation cognized in cognitions of entities as qualified the status of a distinct primitive but reduces it to its terms. The Prābhākara sees it as independent, but not, contra Udayana, as eternal. Praśastapāda views inherence as inferred. Most of the Early Logicians, in contrast, take it to be perceptible. Clearly, then, there is no consensus.

Text (p. 640, Calcutta) and Translation

atha jāti-guṇa-kriyā-tadvantau mithaḥ saṃbaddhāv anubhūyete | na hi a-saṃbaddha-sva-rūpa-dvaye viśiṣṭa-dhī-vyapadeśāv iti cet, na | saṃbaddhânubhavena hi saṃbandho na viśeṣaṇam bhāsate, tasya prathamam a-jñānāt, saṃyogināv imāv iti-vat samavāyināv ity an-anubhavāc ca | na api viśeṣyaḥ, anayoḥ samavāya ity an-anubhavāt | na api sva-rūpeṇa bhāsate | samavāyaṃ jānāmi iti viṣayatân-anubhavāt |

Objection (against the *pūrvapakṣin* by a traditional Naiyāyika): It is as related to one another that these are experienced: (i) a universal (*jāti*) and what possesses it, (ii) a motion and what possesses it, and (iii) a quality and what possesses it. For unless the pair appeared as essentially related there could not be (a) cognition of an entity as qualified or (b) linguistic usage (referring to an entitied as qualified).

Pūrvapakṣin: No. In the experience of these relata, the relation does not appear as a qualifier. There are two considerations in support of this: there is no awareness of the relation at first (i.e., when the relata are experienced), and there is no experience of a pair as related by inherence as there is of a pair conjoined.

Moreover, inherence is not experienced as a qualificandum (i.e., as the bearer of properties), since there is no awareness of the form, "Inherence holds between the two" (with the inherence expressed linguistically in the nominative case, reflecting its status as the qualificandum factor in the awareness and the qualificandum in nature). Nor does inherence appear just in itself (rather than implicitly through its relata appearing). There is no experience that has as its content, "I am aware of *inherence*."

Comments

An example of an awareness of a universal exhibited by a particular is the awareness "A cow," which is to be analyzed as "*a* has cowhood"; "*a* is moving up" illustrates an awareness of a motion and its possessor in relation, and "*a* is blue," of a quality and its possessor.

As noted, Praśastapāda regards inherence as inferred, while others, for example, Advaitins and Bhāṭṭa Mīmāṃsakas, deny its separate reality altogether. Gaṅgeśa's view, as we shall see in the *siddhānta*, is that inherence is perceived when its relata are perceived. The main point now is that it is at least not commonly admitted that any relation other than contact is known perceptually.

Text (p. 646, Tirupati) and Translation

> nanu nīlo ghaṭa ity-ādy-anubhavo viśeṣaṇa-viśeṣya-saṃbandha-viṣayaḥ viśiṣṭa-pratītitvāt daṇḍi-jñāna-vad iti cet, na | a-ghaṭaṃ bhūtalaṃ jñātam iṣṭaṃ kṛtaṃ ca ity atra vyabhicārāt |

Objection: There is the following inference (A^1): an awareness such as "The pot is blue" has the relation along with (the relata) the qualifier and the qualificandum as object, *since* it is a cognition of an entity as qualified, like awareness of a staff-bearer.

Pūrvapakṣin: No. There are awarenesses that are cognitions of entities as qualified where there is (according to accepted Nyāya theory) no relation as part of the object as indicated: for example, "The floor has no pot," "Something is known," "Something is desired," and "Something has been done."

Comments

With awareness of a staff-bearer, the relation tying together a qualificandum (a person bearing a staff) and a qualifier (the staff) is conjunction, *saṃyoga*, which is not a matter of dispute in realist camps. Conjunction, or contact, is a worldly object, a quality, and is known perceptually.

According to inherited Nyāya theory, in some instances of cognition of an entity as qualified, the relation is to be analyzed away ontologically. For example, "The floor has no pot" (i.e., "There is no pot on the floor") is to be analyzed as floor-self-linkage-absence of pot. The absence is a "self-linking" term; similarly *mutatis mutandi* with the other examples.

Thus the *pūrvapakṣin*'s point is that there has to be a special story told to justify positing inherence as an additional real. The fact that cognitions have contents with relational structure is insufficient.

Text (p. 641, Calcutta) and Translation

> saṃbandha-viṣayatve bādhakaṃ vinā iti viśeṣaṇam iti cet, na | bādhakâ-bhāvasya eva samarthatve śeṣa-vaiyarthyāt sādhakâ-bhāvena sat-pratipakṣāc ca | bādhakâ-bhāvasya sādhakatva-vat sādhakâ-bhāvasya bādhakatvāt | tasmād ubhayâ-bhāve saṃśayaḥ syāt | na ca pratītir eva samavāya-sādhikā, tasyās tad-viṣayatvâ-siddheḥ | anyathā anyonyâśrayāt |

Objection: My inference (A^1) needs to be modified by adding a qualification (to the prover given, to wit) "without a counterconsideration (ruling out the possibility of objective indication)." (In the case of each of your counterexamples, "The floor has no pot," etc., there is such a counterconsideration, but not with "The pot is blue" and other cognitions of entities as qualified) where the relation should be considered a part of the object as indicated (*viṣayatva*, "objecthood").

Pūrvapakṣin: No. If the efficacy of "lack of a counterconsideration" were accepted, the rest of the argument could be pointless. (There would be no need to put forth as the prover, "it is a cognition of an entity as qualified"; "lack of a counterconsideration" by itself would be decisive.) Moreover, by the same token the opposite position would be established, with the prover being "absence of a positive consideration." Lack of a counterconsideration is like having a positive consideration; lack of a positive consideration is itself a counterconsideration. Therefore, when we have neither, doubt cannot be resolved.

Furthermore, the cognition by itself ("The pot is blue," for example) does not establish the objective reality of inherence. That inherence is at all an object there is not shown.

If another route (than what has already been tried and rejected, namely, inference) be ventured to establish the reality of inherence, there would be "begging the question" (*anyonyâśraya*).

Comments

The counterconsideration is not spelled out, but Gaṅgeśa could refer to places in his book (for instance, the end of the section on absences, below, p. 469) where a reason is given against relational reification. However, to Gaṅgeśa this formulation apparently seems sloppy, as the *pūrvapakṣin* dismisses it almost with a sneer. If there were no counterconsideration in a strong sense, then there would be a cogent consideration in favor of the conclusion, the *pūrvapakṣin* retorts. But, so far, no *cogent* consideration has been put forth on either side. Thus doubt cannot be resolved.

In Sanskrit, there is no predicative copula with the expression translated, "The pot is blue"; that no term designating inherence occurs in the linguistic usage expressing the cognition helps to motivate the *pūrvapakṣin*'s position.

Rucidatta suggests how there would be "begging the question," assuming that we take the "other route" to inherence—mentioned in the last paragraph—to be inference. Let the prover for inferring the reality of inherence be: "*since* they are cognitions of an entity as qualified." But with this premise, we presuppose that relations such as inherence are real, since, on this proposal, such is what being *qualified* amounts to. That there be a single veridical cognition of an entity as qualified entails that there be an entity qualified in a "thick" sense (i.e., as not simply reflecting the self-linkage of self-linking terms). From this it follows that there must be relations, such as inherence, that are real.

Text (p. 647, Tirupati, and p. 642, Calcutta) and Translation

> atha a-ghaṭaṃ bhūtalaṃ jñātam ity-ādy api viśiṣṭa-dhīḥ saṃbandha-viṣayā, kiṃ tu bhrāntā, bādhaka-sattvād iti cet, tarhi bhūtale '-ghaṭatvasya jñātatvâdeś ca a-bhāvaḥ syāt | tathā ca vyavahāra-vilopaḥ | saṃbandhaś ca na saṃyogaḥ samavāyo vā anyataro vā bādhād a-siddher vā | na api saṃbandha-mātram, jñāpakatvâdinā siddha-sādhanāt | na apy a-viśiṣṭa-vyāvṛtta-viśiṣṭa-jñāna-niyāmakaḥ | a-bhāva-jñānâdāv iva sva-rūpa-saṃbandhena arthântaratvāt | na ca saṃbandhi-bhinnatvaṃ sādhye viśeṣaṇam | a-bhāva-jñānâdinā vyabhicārāt | bādhakâ-bhāvasya ca viśeṣaṇatvaṃ hetau nirastam eva | vinā api bhinna-saṃbandham a-bhāva-jñānâdāv iva viśiṣṭa-dhī-saṃbhavena a-prayojakatvāc ca | viśeṣaṇatā-viśeṣa-rūpaḥ prakārâdi-kṛto vā viśeṣaḥ saṃbandhâ-viṣayatve 'pi tulyaḥ |

Objection: Then let us say that cognitions of an entity as qualified such as "The floor is cognized as potless" are cognitions with the relation as part of the object as indicated (its *viṣayatva*, "objecthood"). However, they are erroneous, since counterconsiderations rule out the objective reality of the relation.

Pūrvapakṣin: In that case (if, for example, the cognition, "The floor is cognized as potless," were non-veridical), for the floor there would be no not having of a pot (even when a pot is absent there) and such a fact would not be cognized (though of course sometimes it is). And thus linguistic practice would be a mess (since we do sometimes say, "The floor is cognized as potless").

The relation (cognized in these types of awareness) is not contact, nor is it inherence, nor is it contact in some cases while in others it is inherence. Counterconsiderations rule out the possibility of contact, while inherence is not established as a possibility.

Nor should it be held that we have here "relation in general," for if this amounts to a "making known, etc.," you would commit the fallacy of "establishing what is already admitted" (since you and I agree a qualifier presented as related to a qualificandum makes the qualificandum known).

Nor should it be held that inherence is a relation that secures cognition of an entity as qualified as invariably distinct from cognition that is not like that. Concerning cognition of an absence, etc., there would be the fallacy of the argument establishing just what you do not want, because in these cases the relation is (you yourself say) that of a self-linking term (not inherence).

Nor should you add the qualification concerning what you want to prove, the qualification, namely, that the relation be distinct from the relata. (Again) the examples of cognition of an absence, etc., would be counterexamples.

Any attempt to patch up the prover in the argument that would add the qualification "without counterconsiderations" has already been rejected. Also, the argument in this case would suffer from the fallacy of a "misleading prover," since indeed (as you hold) concerning awareness of an absence, etc., there is the possibility of cognition of an entity as qualified even without a distinct relation.

Or let us say you try to differentiate (between cognitions of an entity as qualified through self-linkage and as qualified through inherence) by proposing either that the distinction takes the form of a distinct qualifierhood or that it is secured by the predication content, etc. Then note that the same distinction would hold on the view that relations are not part of a cognition's object (or indication, *viṣayatva*, "objecthood.")

Comments

The *pūrvapakṣin*'s response to the inference A^1 that cognitions of an entity as qualified establish the reality of inherence was that there are cognitions of an entity as qualified without an ontologically distinct relation over and above the relata. The proponent of A[1] now argues that that response does not cut the ice since the counterexamples can be ruled out as errors.

The *pūrvapakṣin* points out an untoward ramification of the error proposal. Many obvious truths would have to be false, e.g., "There is no pot on the floor," when indeed there is none, and "The floor is cognized as potless." (Gaṅgeśa cleverly brings in two examples of relations other than inherence in citing a single cognition: the relation between an absence-of-pot and a floor where there are no pots and the relation between being-cognized-as-F and a floor that is cognized as F.)

The *pūrvapakṣin* continues to insist that while it is not in dispute that all awareness presupposes some kind of hook-up between a qualifier and a qualificandum, this need not be an ontologically distinct relation. The opponent's task—the Naiyāyika task—is to establish the reality of inherence without reifying relations in all cases of cognition of an entity as qualified.

Both sides also agree that a qualifier invariably makes a qualificandum known. For example, in the case of "A pot," the qualifier "potness" as related to a qualificandum makes it known as a particular pot. So if this is all the proponent of the reality of inherence is claiming, then he would commit the fallacy of trying to prove what is already granted.

At the end, the contention is in effect that nothing about a cognition as viewed internally, from a first-person perspective, secures a view of the reality of inherence over and against the alternative view that what is called inherence is nothing but forms of a self-linking being-a-qualifier. Evidence has to be either (a) a matter of predication content or (b) a (theoretically suspect) objectification (a "distinct qualifierhood") of the way that a bit of predication content qualifies whatever it makes known. The *pūrvapakṣin*'s assertion is that his alternative view handles every consideration that can be offered under either head equally or better than the inherence theory.

Text (p. 649, Tirupati) and Translation

> syād etat | avayava-guṇa-kriyā-jāti-tadvatāṃ iha tantuṣu paṭaḥ, iha paṭe śauklyaṃ, iha calanaṃ paṭatvaṃ ca iti iha-pratyayaḥ ādhārâdheya-saṃbandha-nimittakaḥ yathârthêha-pratyayatvād iha kuṇḍe badaram iti pratyaya-vad iti cet, na | iha bhūtale ghaṭâ-bhāvo jñānaṃ ca ity-ādau vyabhicārāt, bādhakaṃ vinā ity asya nirastatvāt, tathā eva ādhārâdheya-bhāvād eva upapatteś ca | utpattaye sthitaye jñaptaye ca apekṣaṇīyasya ādhāratvāt |

Objection: Some of what you say may be true. But there is the following argument that establishes the reality of inherence. A cognition of "being here" that applies to the relation of a whole to its parts, a quality to what has it, a motion to what exhibits it, and a universal or natural kind to its instances—for example, "The cloth is *here* in the threads," "The color white is *here* in the cloth," "The movement is *here* (in this thing)," and "Clothness (is *here* in this cloth)"—secures (as ontologically distinct) the relation as that between a locus and a located. The prover: *since* it is both a cognition that matches reality and a cognition of "being here." The confirming example: like a cognition (that establishes the reality of the relation, contact), "The jujube fruit is in the bowl."

Pūrvapakṣin: No. There are clear counterexamples to your prover, namely, the cognition, "*Here* on the floor there is an absence of a pot." And again, do not try the patchwork qualification, "without counterconsiderations," for that move has already been ruled out. In sum, your argument is no good because the relations you cite are possible without a "locus/located" relation that is ontologically something over and above the relata. All we need say about "locatedhood" in the case of production (as a cloth from threads), of maintenance (as a cloth in the threads that make it up after it has been produced), and in making known (as a pot helping to cause an awareness of itself) is that there is a necessary dependence (a self-linking relation): that's what it is to be a "locus" (in this sense).

Comments

The argument for inherence is put forth by Praśastapāda (c. 575), the Vaiśeṣika luminary.[2]

The *pūrvapakṣin*'s reply relies on the assumption, presumed acceptable to all parties, that with an awareness of an absence the relation in the complex a-R-b is not a distinct entity. The factor -R-b—the absence—is taken to be self-linking. His argument here is that the factor, -(necessary-dependence)-located, need not be viewed otherwise.

Text (p. 649, Tirupati, and p. 644, Calcutta) and Translation

> anye tu, śabda-jāti-rūpâdir indriya-saṃbaddhaḥ pratyakṣatvād ghaṭa-vad ity-anumānāt saṃyoga-bādhe indriya-saṃbandha-ghaṭakatayā samavāya-siddhiḥ, indriyasya saṃbaddha-grāhakatvāt | ata eva samavāyo na pratyakṣaḥ indriyeṇa a-saṃbandhāt | na ca saṃbandhatvena tat-siddhiḥ | an-avasthānāt, sva-bhāvād eva jñāna-vat sva-saṃbaddha-vyavahāra-kāritvāc ca | samavāyo hi saṃbandhaṃ vinā eva sva-bhāvād eva kasyacit | na ca jāty-āder api sva-bhāvād eva sva-saṃbaddha-vyavahāra-kāritve samavāya-vilopaḥ | jāty-ādeḥ indriyâ-saṃbandhe samavāya-vad a-pratyakṣatvâpātād iti |

Pūrvapakṣin: Others offer the following inference in favor of positing inherence.

Objection: A sound, a universal, a color, or the like is related to a sense organ, *since* it is perceived, like a pot. Accordingly is it established that the relation is inherence when contact is not the factor accomplishing the relation to the sense organ.

A sense organ grasps what is related to it. Thus, inherence is not directly perceptible because (as the relation or relator) it is not what is *in* relation to a sense organ.

Further, it is not just as a relation that it is established. (If inherence were inferred as doing nothing but bringing two terms together) there would be an infinite regress. Like an awareness (and its intentionality, *viṣayitva*), inherence must be self-linking, not only because of the threat otherwise of an infinite regress, but because it grounds linguistic practices that reflect self-linkage. In order that inherence indeed be without a further relation, it has to link itself by its own nature to something.

The same reasoning does not hold with respect to universals and so on, such that they themselves would be what ground the linguistic practices of self-linkage (when they are involved) without a role for inherence. If universals and so on did not stand (as non-self-linking terms) in relation to a sense organ, then like inherence they would be imperceptible—an implication that is contrary to fact.

Comments

An infinite regress of relations can be avoided only by supposing self-linkage at some step. Simply to suppose inherence to be the relator would not avoid the problem, since there would have to be inferred another relation to relate inherence itself to each of the terms, another relation to relate that new relation, *ad infinitum*. The key question is, then, why inherence should be admitted at all, since, as the *pūrvapakṣin* has pointed out, there are qualificative cognitions whose relational content it does not underpin, and in any case inherence itself has to be viewed as self-linking with its terms. Considerations of ontological parsimony would appear to demand its pruning.

The argument here is that in the specified cases, which are patently not cases where an object perceived is in direct relation with a grasping sense organ, there nevertheless has to be a real relator, since we do perceive universals, et cetera. The *pūrvapakṣin* now shows that this argument is inadequate because of the inadequacy of the defensive move, expressed at the end, that would rule out self-linkage as the way universals, etc., hook up with particulars standing in direct relation with a sense organ.

Text (p. 650, Tirupati, and p. 646, Calcutta) and Translation

tan na | samavāya-svīkāre 'pi sva-rūpa-saṃbandhasya āvaśyakatvāt | ghaṭa-jñānayoḥ bhūtalâ-bhāvayor iva vā dravyeṇa guṇa-jāty-ādibhiḥ sva-rūpam eva saṃbandho 'stu | tathā ca śabdasya indriya-viśeṣaṇatayā, śabdatvasya viśeṣaṇa-viśeṣaṇatayā, rūpâdi-jāty-āder indriya-saṃbaddha-viśeṣaṇatayā, rūpatvâder indriya-saṃbaddha-viśeṣaṇa-viśeṣaṇatayā sva-bhāva-saṃbandha-rūpayā grahaṇa-saṃbhave kiṃ samavāyena | dravye sva-bhāva-saṃbandhād na indriyeṇa grahaṇam iti kathaṃ guṇâdes tena graha iti cet, samavāyena api na dravya-grahaṇam iti tulyam |

Pūrvapakṣin: This is the wrong approach. Even were we to accept inherence as a real, the notion of self-linkage would have to be used. (So why bother postulating inherence?)

So let us say that a substance is related to a quality or to a universal and so on by, in each case, the latter's own nature as a self-linking term, like (the clear examples of) the relation between a cognition of a pot and the pot or between the floor and an absence (when there is no pot there).

And so sound (which is a quality) would be related to the auditory sense organ by the (self-linking) relation "qualifierhood" (or "being a qualifier"). (Other examples of self-linking relations in the processes of perception by means of the sense organs include) the universal "soundhood" (being related to the sense organ) by the relation of a "second-order qualifierhood" (another self-linking relation); color, etc., and (some) universals, etc., by the relation of "qualifying what is related to the sense organ"; abstracts or the natural kinds of color, etc., by the relation of a "second-order qualifying of what is related to the sense organ." Since perceptual cognition can be explained in each of these cases taking the relation to be self-linking, what's the point of positing inherence?

Objection: On this view, since the operative perceptual relation would be self-linking, perception (even) in the case of a substance would be (somehow direct, i.e.) unmediated by (a relation with) a sense organ. So how could qualities, etc., be grasped by a sense organ?

Pūrvapakṣin: Even in postulating inherence there would be equally the problem that a perception of a substance (would remain distinct from perceptions of other sorts of objects, that it) would not occur by means of inherence (but rather by a different relation, contact).

Comments

The proposal is not self-linkage of a relation but of a term. To talk of self-linking relations would be to focus on the coupling aspect of the term, to abstract its hook, so to say. Thus would one avoid reification and achieve ontological parsimony. A variety of the self-linking relation "qualifierhood," not inherence, would be the relation in each case where the *pūrvapakṣin* proposes a replacements for an item on the Naiyāyika's list of sensory connections.

Both sides admit that there has to be a relation of some sort between each sense faculty and each object perceived. The project is to explain what the natures of the various connections. Again, the argument rejected by the *pūrvapakṣin* is that inherence must be ontologically distinct in order for sound to be perceptible and so on.

To take up an example, according to Nyāya theory the visual organ travels like a ray out of the eye and comes into contact with substances having color and shape. So, for example, the sensory connection in a perception of color would be a *qualifying* of what is related to the sense organ by contact, i.e., there would be contact between (a) a substance perceived and *qualified* by color and (b) the sense organ. Thus this and the other relations that the *pūrvapakṣin* lists—and not that of an *inhering* in what is related to the sense organ by contact, etc.—would perform the required theoretical role. Thus we would maintain an ontological economy.

A problem with the *pūrvapakṣin*'s view is that no reason has been given why the sensory relation to substances should be any different whereas it is difficult to imagine a sense organ *self-linking* to a substance perceived. The point is parried by the argument that even in accepting inherence we have to view contact as the basic relation between a sense organ and an object perceived. Inherence would not replace sensory contact in its fundamental role, whereas secondary differences can, as has been explained, be handled by varieties of the relation, qualifierhood.

Text (p. 650, Tirupati) and Translation

> apare tu, ekatra ghaṭe āma-pāka-daśāyāṃ krameṇa śyāma-rakta-rūpôpalambho 'sti | sa ca na tad-ubhaya-nibandhanaḥ, rūpasya nityatvena ekadā upalambhâpatteḥ | nityatvād eva ca na tayor utpāda-vināśau | tasmāt tayoḥ saṃbandhasya tau syātām, sa eva samavāya iti | tan na | śyāmaṃ naṣṭam, raktam utpannam, ity-ādy-a-bādhitânubhavāt samavāyasya utpāda-vināśân-ullekhāc ca | tvan-mate tasya atīndriyatvāt | anyathā avayavi-jñāna-gandha-rasâder api nityatvaṃ samavāyasya utpāda-vināśāv iti kiṃ na rocayet | na hy utpāda-vināśa-pratītir a-prāmāṇikī bādhakaṃ vinā iti ||

Pūrvapakṣin: But others (Prābhākaras) argue as follows.

Objection: In one and the same pot, which has the color of raw earth at the time of its baking, we experience a gradual change from black to red. And this experience (according to our view) could not be based on its *being* both colors, since a color is an unchanging entity. Thus there is the difficulty that an experience of color at one time would forever fix that quality (such that a pot would be forever black). And because of the unchangingness, there could be no arising nor destruction of either of the two colors. Therefore, in order that there be such a possibility, the arising and destruction must be *of a relation* between the two. That relation is inherence.

Pūrvapakṣin: This also is wrong. "The black is destroyed; the red is produced," such is an uncontroverted experience. But here (to express the predication content) there need be no mention of either an arising or destruction of inherence. On your view, inherence would have to be imperceptible. So on other matters as well—with a whole having parts, cognition, smell, taste, etc.—why shouldn't a view of unchangingness find favor with you, with the arising and destruction confined to the inherence? For it is no option to hold that an appearance of arising or destruction is not veridical, unless you can put forth definite considerations against its veridicality.

Comments

We say "The color has changed" when the clay pot is baked to become reddish. But the color itself does not change. Black is always black, and red always red. Thus the suggestion is that the relation with one color replaces the relation with another, the replacement explaining the change of color.

Rucidatta identifies the objector's position as belonging to the Prābhākara camp. Color and all class characters are eternal, according to the Prābhākara. Change of property is analyzed as a relation appearing or disappearing.

The *pūrvapakṣin*'s rebuttal is forceful and clear. Our experience is not of the destruction of *inherence* but rather of *colors*. An imperceptible inherence would have to arise and disappear. But why assume imperceptibles in the first place, especially when another theory is able to account for the phenomenon without such contortions? Also, to be consistent the Prābhākara would have to give a similar analysis of other types of change. And all talk of error on *his* part would be empty, as we have already learned (in the long discussion, above, on error).

Text (p. 651, Tirupati, and p. 648, Calcutta) and Translation

ucyate | guṇa-kriyā-jāti-viśiṣṭa-buddhayo viśeṣaṇa-saṃbandha-viṣayāḥ viśiṣṭa-buddhitvāt, daṇḍī iti buddhi-vat |

Gaṅgeśa: We answer. Cognitions of an entity as qualified by a quality, motion, or universal have both the qualifier and the relation as object, *since* they are cognitions of an entity as qualified, like the cognition, "A staff-bearer."

Comments

A staff-bearer is a person holding a staff. The person and the staff are in conjunction or contact, *saṃyoga*. Contact is a quality that inheres in two substances simultaneously, here the person and the staff. Like other qualities that inhere in perceptible things, it itself is perceptible; it is perceived riding piggy-back on the substances in which it inheres. Thus the objective complex, person-contact-staff, gives rise to the perceptual cognition, "Staff-bearer," where the person is the qualificandum, the staff is the qualifier, and contact the relation between them. In this cognition of an entity as qualified, the relation is patently presented as an object, as part of the "objecthood" or thing as indicated by the cognition. Gaṅgeśa's argument is that cognitions of entities as qualified by qualities, motions, or universals are pertinently all the same type of cognition, and that, like contact in the confirming example, inherence is shown thereby to be an objective reality.

In other words, there is the following generalization: all qualificative cognitions have a triadic indication, qualifier, qualified, and the binding relation, all three as "object" (*viṣaya*). In accord with Nyāya's overall causal realism, this shows that the relation is objectively real. Then the question is whether the relation is to be taken as a separate reality, like the contact perceived between a person and a staff.

Text (p. 653, Tirupati) and Translation

na ca vyabhicāraḥ | a-bhāvâdi-viśiṣṭa-buddher api sva-rūpa-saṃbandha-viṣayatvāt |

(**Gaṅgeśa** continues:) The prover in this argument does not admit of counterexamples (unlike the arguments put forth previously). Cognitions of entities as qualified by an absence and so on also *have* the relation as object (or part of the "objecthood"), the relation, namely, of self-linkage.

Comments

A dramatic reversal comes with the statement that the self-linking aspect of a self-linking term is indicated, part of an appropriate cognition's indication or "objecthood." Of course, Gaṅgeśa is not conceding that self-linkage is an *independent* real. The argument so far is thus only a first step; a second follows. That is to say, first Gaṅgeśa establishes that cognitions of an entity as qualified have the relation as object. This shows that as a fundamental tie between a qualificandum and a qualifier both inherence and self-linking terms are realities in the world. Although self-linkage is not an independent real, self-linking things are reals, and self-linkage, as an abstraction based in their nature, shares in their reality, so to say. Now Gaṅgeśa is ready for a second step, to distinguish inherence from self-linkage.

Text (p. 648, Calcutta) and Translation

na ca evam atra api tena eva arthântaram, yato guṇa-kriyā-jāti-viśiṣṭa-buddhīnāṃ pakṣa-dharmatā-balena viṣayaḥ saṃbandhaḥ sidhyan lāghavād eka eva sidhyati | sa eva samavāyaḥ, na tu sva-rūpa-saṃbandhaḥ, tat-tat-sva-rūpāṇām an-antatvāt saṃbandhatvena a-kḷptatvāc ca |

(**Gaṅgeśa** continues:) And do not object that in this way we would be reasoning to counterpurposes, establishing just what we do not want. In our argument, the prover (being a cognition of an entity as qualified) is a property of the inferential subject, namely, any cognition of an entity as qualified by a quality, motion, or universal. The argument establishes that the relation is a cognitive object (*viṣaya*). Then that it is single, uniform, is established on the basis of parsimony. So the relation is indeed inherence, not self-linkage. The self-linkage of self-linking terms is infinitely varied according to the particular natures of the infinitely many things that are related by self-linkage. Furthermore, self-linkage as a relation is not a (separate) existing thing.

Comments

Since Gaṅgeśa admits that the self-linkage of self-linking terms also falls within the domain of the argument which constitutes step one of his two-step strategy to establish inherence, there is also no fallacy of "deviation," i.e., the prover admitting of counterexamples. This is how he undercuts the main line of objection expressed earlier. Self-linkage is a part of a cognition's indication or object, but is not a distinct real, according to Gaṅgeśa. To secure inherence as truly a distinct real, there is now further argument, to wit, parsimony (*lāghava*), as step two. The relation in the case of cognitions of qualities, etc., must be regarded as inherence because that is the economical view, in that self-linkage varies according to the infinitely many things that are so related. Self-linkage is as varied as all the instances of qualification in which it is the relation linking a qualifier with a qualificandum.

Parsimony would seem to favor the *pūrvapakṣin*'s view, since inherence would be the additional category. However, Gaṅgeśa's response centers on the economy of the inherence posit. Parsimony is what secures inherence over self-linkage in that inherence allows a more refined sorting, along causal lines, of the indications of qualificative awarenesses. By section end we shall have details about just what this superiority amounts to. And the next passage begins to spell it out by formulating a causal rule along with another inference.

Text (p. 654, Tirupati) and Translation

athavā viśeṣaṇa-saṃbandha-nimittikā iti sādhyam | hetau tu satyatvaṃ viśeṣaṇam | viśeṣaṇa-saṃbandhaś ca kāraṇatvena eka eva sidhyati | lāghavād anugata-kāryasya anugata-kāraṇa-niyamyatvāc ca | na tu sva-rūpa-saṃbandhaḥ, teṣām an-anugatatvād an-antatvāc ca | na ca ubhayam apy a-prayojakam | viśiṣṭa-sākṣātkārasya saṃbandhâ-viṣayatve tad-a-janyatve vā gavâśvâdāv api viśiṣṭa-buddhi-prasaṅgāt |

(**Gaṅgeśa** continues:) Or, there is another inference. The probandum is the property of having a relation with a qualifier as a cause (which is predicated of cognitions of an entity as qualified by a quality, etc.).

To the prover in this argument, a qualification has to be added: (cognitions of an entity as qualified by a quality, etc., have a relation with a qualifier as a cause insofar as) they are *veridical* cognitions of an entity as qualified.

Moreover, the relation with a qualifier is proved to be—as a cause—single or uniform on the basis of parsimony and the rule to be maintained, "Effects of the same type, causes of the same type." These requirements exclude self-linkage, because self-linking terms are not identical through multiple instances but are infinitely various.

Furthermore, with neither of these two arguments is the fallacy "misleading prover" committed. If an experience of an entity as qualified were to occur either without having the relation as (part of) its object (or objecthood) or without having been caused (in part) by the relation with the qualifier, then it would be possible to be aware of a cow as a horse and other absurdities.

Comments

Cognitions of an entity as qualified have the relation between the entity qualified and its qualifier as a cause. They would not occur without it. A relation with a qualificandum (e.g., Bessie the cow) must be so tight that it causes its reflection in awareness. Otherwise, we might see her as a horse.

The relation stands as such a cause, Gaṅgeśa hurriedly points out, only in the case of veridical cognitions, not with non-veridical. Non-veridical cognitions involve misperceiving a qualifier and relational tie vis-à-vis a qualificandum. There is then a second step as with the previous argument, namely, parsimony supplemented by the causal rule, "Like effects, like causes."

Now these considerations—parsimony and the causal principle—seem inseparable in that maintaining the causal principle would be one way parsimony would be achieved. Nor is it clear that Gaṅgeśa regards the two as two independent criteria. In any case, self-linkage is excluded on both counts in that self-linkage is infinitely various. In contrast, cognitions of an entity as qualified by, for example, qualities (*guṇa*), are all alike in the way that qualities are all alike, and thus these cognitions must have an identical cause. Inherence-in-a-substance-in-relation-to-a-sensory-organ is a relation that occurs in every case of cognition of an entity as qualified by a quality.

Text (p. 660, Tirupati, and p. 651, Calcutta) and Translation

> navyās tu, guṇa-kriyā-jāti-viśiṣṭa-buddhiḥ saṃbandhi-bhinna-viśeṣaṇa-saṃbandha-viṣayā nirviṣayaka-bhāva-viśeṣaṇaka-viśiṣṭa-buddhitvāt |

(**Gaṅgeśa** continues:) There are, however, Navya Nyāya philosophers who reason differently.

Navya Nyāya faction: Cognitions of an entity as qualified by a quality, motion, or universal have the relation with the qualifier as object such that the relation is distinct from the relata (and thus not self-linkage). The prover: *since* they are cognitions of an entity as qualified by a qualifier (a) that is a presence (not an absence) and (b) that itself does not have an object.

Comments

The cases excluded in the prover are cognitions of absences and cognitions of cognitions. Since they involve self-linking relations (absential qualification and objecthood, respectively), their inclusion would make the prover deviate. An absence self-links with what it qualifies, and an apperception scopes a prior cognition whose objecthood qualifies it by self-linkage.

Text (p. 663, Tirupati) and Translation

itara-nirūpaṇâ-nirūpya-viśeṣaṇaka-viśiṣṭa-buddhitvād vā | ato '-bhāvâdi-viśiṣṭa-buddhau na vyabhicāraḥ | na ca a-prayojakam, nirupādhi-saṃbandha-śâlitvāt | saṃbandhaś ca a-viśiṣṭa-vyāvṛtta-viśiṣṭa-dhī-niyāmakaḥ |

(The **Navya Nyāya** faction continues:) Or (the prover may be formulated still differently:) *since* they are cognitions of an entity as qualified not having a qualifier that is further determined by another determining (or qualification, expressed by another "of . . ." or "about . . . " clause). Thus, there is no deviation with regard to cognitions of an entity as qualified by an absence, et cetera.

Moreover, the fault of a "misleading prover" cannot be alleged, because this is an inference that admits no exceptions in the relating of the two (that is to say, there is pervasion, *vyāpti*). And the relation unfailingly secures a distinction between (a) cognitions of an entity as qualified and (b) cognitions that are not of a qualified entity (i.e., indeterminate awarenesses).

Comments

An absence of *x* has *x* as its *pratiyogin*, countercorrelate or absentee. The *pratiyogin* is said to *determine* the absence as its qualifier. Thus, since an absence is determined by its absentee, cognitions of an absence are excluded.

Further, cognition has, according to Nyāya, no intrinsic shape or content of its own. It is *nirākāra*, "formless." The object alone shapes cognition and provides form and "objecthood," on the Nyāya view. So here *nirūpaṇa*, "determining," is also used to exclude apperception, which cognizes a previous cognition determined by its objecthood. An apperception's qualificative objecthood is determined by further qualification, and apperception is thus excluded from the extension of the prover in the argument.

The task is to find a prover that would sift out the cases of self-linkage so that only inherence would be left. Absential cognitions, e.g., a cognition of a floor as qualified by (through a self-linking relation) an absence of a pot, and apperceptions, e.g., a cognition of a cognition as qualified by (through a self-linking relation) being-about-a-pot, are cognitions of an entity as qualified by a qualifier Q that is itself qualified by a further qualification (of-a-pot or about-a-pot). Hence the new formulation.

All cognition of an entity as qualified presupposes a relation as object or part of the objecthood that a cognition determines. But in non-relational, indeterminate awareness, no relation is cognized as doing relational work. Hence indeterminate cognition, which does not have inherence as object, is not a cognition of an entity as qualified.

Text (p. 664, Tirupati, and p. 642, Calcutta) and Translation

yad vā indriya-pratyāsattitvena samavāya-siddhiḥ | tathā hi guṇa-kriyā-jāti-sākṣātkāraḥ indriya-saṃbandha-sādhyaḥ janya-pratyakṣatvāt daṇḍi-jñāna-vad ity ataḥ sākṣāt-saṃbandha-bādha-kāraṇatvena indriya-saṃyukte saṃbandhaḥ sidhyan pakṣa-dharmatā-balāl lāghavena anugataḥ samavāya eka eva sidhyati, anugata-kāryasya anugata-kāraṇa-janyatvāt | na tu saṃyukta-viśeṣaṇatā-rūpa-sva-rūpa-saṃbandhaḥ, tasya ca tat-tad-rūpādi-rūpatvena an-anugatatvāt |

Gaṅgeśa: Or, there is another inference. Inherence is established because it is a variety of operative connection with a sense organ. That is to say, an awareness of a quality, motion, or universal is brought about by a relation with a sense organ, *since* it is a generated perception, like a cognition of a staff-bearer. According to this inference, a relation other than the direct relation (between an object grasped and a grasping sense organ), a relation that is operative *through* (the direct relation, through the sensory) contact is established, since we are talking about qualities, motions, and universals as cognitive objects (none of which is ever in direct contact with a sense organ). Then that this relation is continuous (*anugata*), single (and thus) inherence is established on the basis of parsimony. (Again) we have the rule that effects of the same type are to be considered produced by the same type of cause.

The relation cannot be (as postulated by the *pūrvapakṣin*) the self-linking relation, "qualifying that which stands in a relation of contact" (*saṃyukta-viśeṣaṇatā*), because that relation (as an example of self-linkage) takes this, that, and the other form. It is not continuous or uniform.

Comments

This fourth formal argument, which will be given by far the greatest elaboration, focuses on the relation between sense organs and objects perceived. Contact is a relation restricted to perception of substances; the sense organs do not come into contact with qualities, motions, or universals. The weight of a pot is known *through* a tactile contact with the pot as a substance. The sense organ is in contact with the pot, but its weight is known by inhering in the pot.

A problem then would seem to be just as Gaṅgeśa's own *pūrvapakṣin* has stated: in some cases of sensory connection self-linkage is the relator. Thus, it is parsimony and the economy governing causal suppositions that here, as before, demands inherence rather than self-linkage. Gaṅgeśa elaborates the point in subsequent text.

The qualification "generated" excludes God's cognition from the extension of the prover in the inference. God's cognition is not generated.

Text (p. 665, Tirupati) and Translation

> evaṃ rūpatva-rasatva-sākṣātkāre 'pi kāraṇatvena indriya-saṃbandhaḥ samavāya eva anugataḥ sidhyati lāghavāt | na tu indriya-saṃbaddha-viśeṣaṇa-viśeṣaṇatā[3], tasyā rūpatvâdi-sva-rūpatvena an-anugatatvāt | ata eva saṃyogo viśeṣaṇatā ca pratyāsattir astu, na tu samavāyâdi-catuṣṭayam iti nirastam | tasyās tat-tat-sva-rūpatvena an-anugatatvāt | pratyāsattitvena abhyupagate ca samavāye pratyakṣatā saṃbandhi-dvaya-pratyakṣatvāt |

(**Gaṅgeśa** continues:) In this way, in the case of direct perceptual awareness of colorness (a quality universal), or tastehood as well, the relation to the sense organ is just inherence, because it stands as a cause.

Inherence, which is uniform and continuous (*anugata*), is established on the basis of parsimony. The relation is not (as the *pūrvapakṣin* proposed earlier, that of) "qualifying a qualifier of what is in relation with a sense organ." This would be to link colorness and the like by a self-linking relation, which, as such, would not be uniform and continuous.

Hence let us accept that contact and "qualifierhood" are types of operative connection in sensory awareness. But this move does not exclude the view that there are four others that in one way or another involve inherence. (If we followed the *pūrvapakṣin* in his proposal of four alternative relations—all variations on "qualifierhood" and all self-linking—then) the operative connection in each of these cases would be, as self-linking, not uniform and continuous.

Further, since inherence is to be accepted as sometimes itself the sensory connection (that is, when we have a case of sound or soundhood), inherence must be perceptible in certain cases, namely, in those cases where both relata are perceptible.

Comments

The argument is that although viewing inherence as an additional real means including it on the list of ontological primitives, better that for maintaining an economy with the relationality of universals and so on than to admit the infinitely various relations of self-linkage. Analogously, to accept cowhood as a universal commits one to an additional real over and above all cows. But this is the parsimonious position—literally "lighter" (*lāghava*)—in the sense of "more orderly," in that the unity of the kind reduces complexity. Indeed, the same term, *anugata*, "continuous, uniform," is used as is used for justifying including universals in our ontology, *recurrent* cognition.

Recall once more the six types of operative connection in sense perception: (1) contact (for example, in perception of a pot as a substance); (2) inherence-in-the-conjoined (for example, in perception of blue which inheres in a pot in conjunction with the sense organ); (3) inherence-in-the-inherent-in-the-conjoined (for example, in perception of bluehood); (4) inherence (in the case of sound); (5) inherence-in-the-inherent (in perception of soundhood); and (6) qualifierhood (in perception of an absence). Gaṅgeśa does accept that absences self-link with the loci they qualify and thus that the relation in this one type of case is the self-linking "being-a-qualifier." His objections to viewing it as a single, uniform "qualifiedness" (equivalent to inherence) are explained a few sentences below.

On the issue of how inherence is known, Gaṅgeśa lines himself up with the early Naiyāyika position as opposed to the Vaiśeṣika. Inherence is perceptible when its relata are perceptible. Note that he takes a similar stance with respect to universals, which are perceptible when their instances are perceptible.

Text (p. 666, Tirupati, and p. 653, Calcutta) and Translation

nanv evam a-bhāva-viśiṣṭa-pratyakṣe 'pi viśiṣṭa-buddhitvāt saṃyoga-samavāya-bādhe 'nugataṃ vaiśiṣṭyaṃ saṃbandho viṣayaḥ nimittaṃ ca bhaved iti cet, na | tasya hi samavāya-vad ekatve ghaṭâ-bhāvavati paṭavati paṭâ-bhāva-dhī-prasaṅgaḥ | ghaṭâ-bhāva-vaiśiṣṭyam eva hi paṭâ-bhāva-vaiśiṣṭyam | paṭâ-bhāva-vaiśiṣṭya-sattve 'pi paṭâ-bhāvo na asti tataḥ tasya bhinnatvād iti cet, na | paṭâ-bhāvâ-bhāvasya a-bhāvatve so 'pi vaiśiṣṭyena saṃbandhena tatra asti, vaiśiṣṭyasya ekatvāt | paṭâ-bhāvâ-bhāvasya bhāvatve ca paṭa eva pratibandhako vācyaḥ | evaṃ paṭâ-bhāvaḥ paṭâ-bhāva-dhī-hetuḥ syāt | paṭâ-bhāvasya vaiśiṣṭyena saṃbandhena tatra asty eva | vaiśiṣṭyasya praty-a-bhāva-vyakti nānātve ca a-bhāva-viśiṣṭa-buddhau na ekaḥ saṃbandhaḥ kāraṇaṃ viṣayo vā iti tad-a-bhāva-pratyakṣe 'n-anugatam eva vaiśiṣṭyaṃ viṣayaḥ kāraṇaṃ ca vācyam | tathā ca 'n-anugata-tat-tat-sva-rūpa-rūpā viśeṣaṇatā eva astu kḷptatvāt kiṃ an-anta-vaiśiṣṭyena | samavāyasya vaiśiṣṭyasya ca pratyakṣatve tvayā api indriya-saṃbaddha-viśeṣaṇatā-svīkārāt |

Objection: In this way, with regard to a perception of an entity as qualified by an absence, the relation called qualifiedness, *vaiśiṣṭya* ("being-qualified"), would be established for the (same) reason, namely, that it is a cognition of an entity as qualified. Contact and inherence can in this case be ruled out. Thus we would have left this qualifiedness. It is uniform and continuous. It is a cognitive object, and it is a cause (of perceptions of absences).

Gaṅgeśa: No, for were this "qualifiedness" single like inherence, then when one locus exhibited both an absence of a pot and the presence of a cloth, we would have to say that the cloth was also absent. This is the difficulty. The being-qualified of a *pot's* absence would be equivalent to the being-qualified of a *cloth's* absence.

Objection: Given the reality of the qualifiedness of a cloth's absence, it is not necessarily so that an absence of a pot would have to be there, too, since the two (the qualifiedness and the absence) are distinct.

Gaṅgeśa: Wrong. Since the qualifiedness would be one and the same, an absence of an absence of a cloth, as itself an absence, would have to be there, too, by this relation, being-qualified. (So we would have both an absence of a cloth and an absence of an absence of a cloth in one and the same place.)

And it has to be held that (with regard to an awareness of a cloth's absence) the cloth itself (when perceived) is a "preventer," *pratibandhaka* (blocking the possibility of awareness of such an absence). In this way, an absence of a cloth gives rise to a cognition of a cloth's absence. An absence of a cloth is related to its locus by the relation of qualifiedness (but qualifiedness is not like inherence but varies with each occurrence).

Being-qualified is distinct according to each particular absence (that it relates to a locus). Moreover, with regard to cognitions of an entity as qualified by an absence, being-qualified is not single and uniform as a relation or as a cause of the cognition or as its object. Thus, we hold that qualifiedness is non-continuous and non-uniform as both content of an awareness and as a ground.

And so let us say that it is just a type of qualifier and self-linking with each of its diverse and discontinuous instances. Since "being-a-qualifier" (*viśeṣaṇatā*) is a notion we are already working with, what's the point of postulating an (additional) infinitely varied "being-qualified?"

Therefore, with regard to (the whole range of) perception, we have to accept both inherence and qualifiedness as types of qualifiers qualifying what is in relation to a sense organ.

Comments

By the same reasoning that Gaṅgeśa would establish inherence, an objector now urges that another relation, the qualifiedness obtaining between absences and their loci, should be viewed as a separate real.

Note the use of the term, *pratibandhaka*, "preventer," which is used by Gaṅgeśa to express what he takes to be natural opposition. An absence and an absence of the absence do not occur together at the same spot at the same time.

Again, the unique character of any absence is what urges that the relationality that binds it to its locus is neither inherence nor another separate real. Absences are non-repeating particulars. Every absence is determined by a unique cognitive act, in that the cognizer's memory supplies the absentee portion of the objecthood.

"Being-a-qualifier" includes both inherence and self-linking qualifiedness. There is no point in introducing additional conceptual apparatus when that we are using is working fine. Economy is to be maintained along every dimension of theory so long as our system is capable of explaining our experiences and linguistic practices.

Having in this way established that his position is better than the *pūrvapakṣin*'s, Gaṅgeśa next turns his attention to various conundra surrounding the inherence posit.

Text (p. 672, Tirupati, and p. 654, Calcutta) and Translation

> nanu samavāyasya ekatve kathaṃ rūpi-nīrūpa-vyavasthā | ghaṭena saha rūpa-saṃbandha-rūpatvaṃ samavāyasya na vāyunā iti cet, na | rūpa-saṃbandha-rūpatvaṃ hi samavāyasya sva-rūpam eva yadi, tadā rasa-saṃbandha-rūpatvaṃ na syāt tayor virodhāt, anyac ca durvacam iti cet, ucyate | vāyau rūpa-samavāya-sattve 'pi rūpâtyantâ-bhāvo 'sti na ghaṭe | katham evam, adhikaraṇa-sva-bhāvād a-bādhita-rūpi-nīrūpa-pratīteś ca |

Objection: If inherence is single and uniform, how can there be a clear separation of colored things from the non-colored? If you were to respond that in the case of a pot, but not in the case of air, inherence would constitute the relation tying down the color, that view can be rebutted. For if inherence performing its function of tying down *color* would do so (in a single and uniform way) as part of its intrinsic nature, then it could not constitute the relation that ties down *taste* to what has it, since the two qualities are in some instances (naturally) opposed to one another (like an absence and a presence) and how they could be otherwise would be difficult to say.

Gaṅgeśa: We answer. In the case of air, there is, we admit, inherence to be understood as (by its intrinsic nature) tying down color. Nevertheless, there is also present in air an *absolute* absence of color. This is not the case with a pot (which is invariably colored). You ask, how can this be? It is due to the intrinsic nature of the particular substratum. And this view is in accordance with uncontroverted experience concerning the colored and the non-colored.

Comments

The quality of touch perceived in air is thought of as tied down by inherence. But if inherence is single and uniform and is what ties down color to colored things as well as touch to air, air would have to be colored, it seems.

Similarly, the relation tying down taste cannot be the same as that which ties down color, particularly since there is in some cases a natural opposition (or natural correlation), for example, between *green* in the case of a mango and a *sweet* taste (green mangoes taste bitter). Inherence as single and invariable cannot do the work it is purported to do, because of the variable natures of the items it is supposed to link up.

Gaṅgeśa answers that indeed these natures are variable. Air is simply by nature never colored. Thus we can happily say that the inherence that ties touch to air is the same inherence that ties color to a pot. But air by its intrinsic nature *blocks* the color-tying function of inherence. The natural absolute absence of color in air overpowers, so to say, the natural color-tying function of inherence.

Text (p. 673, Tirupati) and Translation

> nanv evaṃ jñāto ghaṭa iti pratīteḥ jñātatā api syāt vartamāne bādhakâ-bhāvāt | atītân-āgatayoś ca tad-dhīḥ bhrāntā iti cet, na | atītân-āgatayoḥ jñātatāyā a-bhāve vyavahārâ-bhāvâpatteḥ, tasya jñātatā-sādhyatvāt | na ca jñātatā-jñānam eva vyavahāra-hetuḥ | gauravāt | atītâdau jñāna-tad-viṣayāv eva jñātatā-dhī-gocarāv iti cet, tarhi vartamāne tāv eva tad-viṣayau | na hy atīta-vartamānayoḥ jñātatā-pratītyoḥ viṣaya-vailakṣaṇyam īkṣāmahe |

Objection (by a Bhāṭṭa Mīmāṃsaka): In this way (i.e., on the grounds whereby you support inherence), cognizedness would stand as a real and distinct property (inhering in things cognized). The reason to accept it would be the occurrence of, for example, the cognition, "A pot is cognized." Further, there is no counterconsideration that would rule it out in the present. Concerning something now past (i.e., destroyed) or something in the future (i.e., not yet produced), the thought that it possesses the property would be an error.

Gaṅgeśa: No. Since there would be no property "cognizedness" in things that are no longer or are still to come, there should be no practice of speaking of past things as having been cognized or of cognizing things yet to be produced. But this is a common practice rendered possible by cognizedness (and thus no error).

Moreover, the ground for the linguistic usage is not simply cognition of "cognizedness." That would be too cumbersome an explanation. If you were to expand your view to say that concerning a past object, etc., both cognition and its object that are what an awareness of "cognizedness" would be about, then concerning something in the present the same two should be what it is about, too. (But in the present, what cognizedness is about, you yourself say, is just the cognized thing.) For we do not see an essential difference of content between something past and something present when both are conceived as cognized.

Comments

The peculiar logic of inherence and of the considerations that motivate its ontological listing invites dormant proposals to rear their heads in the hope of profit from the admissions. The debate about cognizedness may be a digression in the current context, but there is also this wider point about Nyāya vulnerability with the inherence posit.

Concerning the particulars of the passage, a current remembering could hardly be said to create a property of an object that is no longer. Similarly, cognitions, or plans, about objects we intend to create, as a potter planning a pot in the future, do not create properties in objects that do not yet exist. In his last sentence, the objector, a Bhāṭṭa Mīmāṃsaka (perhaps the selfsame *pūrvapakṣin* of the section, see above, p. 369), tries to skirt the difficulty by claiming that attributing cognizedness to objects past or future would be erroneous. The crux of the argument is that in the present the form of the cognition, "The pot is cognized," is parallel to those which Gaṅgeśa identifies as the prover in his inference to the objective reality of the inherence that binds qualities et cetera to their loci. Thus would another unwanted ramification be teased out of Gaṅgeśa's view.

In response, Gaṅgeśa points out that in the case of something non-existent "cognizedness" could hardly be *in* that thing. However, we do talk in such a fashion. If the Bhāṭṭa tries to minimalize the ontological commitment, the same attitude should be taken regarding cognizedness and currently existing things, too. This the Bhāṭṭa will not do, committed, as he is, to the importance of the property for an inference to self-awareness among other closely held positions.

Throughout the next stretch of text, it is definitely a Bhāṭṭa, and perhaps the original *pūrvapakṣin* of the section himself, who presents an elaborate argument against Gaṅgeśa's view. Again, the Bhāṭṭa, the disciple of Kumārila, recognizes such real relata as (a) Nyāya's qualities and (b) the substances they qualify but not (c) the relation, at least not as anything other than the self-linkage of one or the other term.

Text (p. 675, Tirupati, and p. 656, Calcutta) and Translation

nanu rūpa-ghaṭayor na samavāyaḥ, kiṃ tu a-bhedaḥ | daṇḍī puruṣa ity atra daṇḍi-puruṣayor iva nīlo ghaṭa ity atra api nīla-ghaṭayor a-bādhitâ-bhedânubhavāt | nīlo ghaṭaḥ daṇḍī puruṣa iti buddhyoḥ viśeṣaṇa-saṃbandha-mātra-gocaratve nīlo ghaṭa iti-vat daṇḍaḥ puruṣaḥ, daṇḍī puruṣa iti-vat nīlī ghaṭa ity api syāt | tasmād ekatra a-bhedo viṣayaḥ aparatra viśeṣaṇa-saṃbandhaḥ, viṣayeṇa eva dhiyāṃ viśeṣāt | athavā viśeṣaṇatā-viśeṣyatâvacchedakayor nīlatva-ghaṭatvayoḥ eka-vṛttitvaṃ jñāyate, daṇḍitva-puruṣatvayor iva puruṣe | evaṃ nīla-ghaṭa-padayoḥ śābdam api sāmānâdhikaraṇyaṃ yujyate | nīlatva-ghaṭatvābhyāṃ bhinna-pravṛtti-nimittābhyāṃ tayor eka-pravṛtteḥ | na ca matupo lopāt a-bhedôpacārād vā nīla-padaṃ nīlavatparaṃ iti vācyam | na hi prayogaṃ sādhakaṃ brūmaḥ, kiṃ tu nīla-ghaṭayor a-bheda-pratītim | pade 'pi na upacārâdi-kalpanā, gauravāt mukhye bādhakâ-bhāvāc ca iti |

Bhāṭṭa: The relation between blue and a pot, for example, is not inherence but *non-distinctness*. As with, "The man is a staff-bearer," so also with, "The pot is blue": there is uncontroverted experience of non-distinctness between the staff-bearer and the man, on the one hand, and the blue and the pot, on the other.

If, to consider the two cognitions, "The pot is blue" and "The man is a staff-bearer," the mere relation with the qualifier were objectively indicated, then, like "The pot is blue," we would say, "The man is a staff"; alternatively, like "The man is a staff-bearer," we would say, "The pot is a blue-bearer." Therefore, in the one case (i.e., "The pot is blue"), the object is non-distinctness; in the other (i.e., "A staff-bearer"), there is a relation with a qualifier (namely, contact between the man and the staff). We make this distinction on the basis of the respective cognitions' indications or objects.

In other words (in the case of the cognition, "The pot is blue") a single entity is cognized by way of specifiers (delimiters, *avacchedaka*), namely, (1) a qualifier specified by bluehood and (2) a qualificandum specified by pothood. It is one entity that is cognized (nevertheless), just as it is a single man that is cognized (with the cognition "The man is a staff-bearer"), with "staff-bearingness" and "manness" (as the specifiers). In this way, the cognition is expressed verbally with the words *nīla*, "blue," and *ghaṭa*, "pot," used in the same case (the nominative case), appositively. Although the abstracts, blueness and pothood, give rise to distinct verbal expressions, they are invoked for a single meaning, a single intention.

Nor should it be said that there is ellipsis here, with a dropping of an implicit possessive suffix, or that the non-distinctness is figurative such that the word "blue" would mean "having blue." We do not say that the verbal usage is what establishes non-distinctness. It is, rather, *appearance* of the blue and a pot as non-distinct (the appearance is the reason why we say that a pot and its blue are non-distinct, "It's a blue pot" or "The blue pot," pointing it out). Nevertheless, concerning (precisely) the words used (our case is reinforced:) it should not be imagined that there is any figurative meaning, etc. Not only would that be a cumbersome explanation, there is no consideration against taking the expression in its primary, denotative sense.

Comments

The Bhāṭṭa position constitutes a tough challenge to Gaṅgeśa's view, and with this objection Gaṅgeśa launches an extended treatment, first exploring and then rebutting the notion that non-distinctness is the relational tie.

In Sanskrit, the word for "blue" is an adjective in the nominative case agreeing with "pot"; thus with an awareness of a blue pot verbalized as "The pot is blue," the word for "blue" is, just as in English, a predicate adjective. The word for "staff-bearer," in contrast, is a nominal derivative, a noun, "staff," transformed into an adjective by a possessive suffix, "-bearer," or, to better reflect the Sanskrit, "-bearing." The Bhāṭṭa is taking the possessive suffix to indicate a real relation, contact, which is evident perceptually in the man's holding a staff. The lack of a term or suffix indicating a relation with "The pot is blue" (the predicative copula is omitted in Sanskrit), the Bhāṭṭa interprets as reflecting an ontological identity. There is only a single reality, expressed by different terms, "pot" and "blue."

This is not a linguistic argument, though it is presumed that the linguistic evidence reflects veridical experience, as is mentioned in the last paragraph, and background linguistic theories seem to bolster the Bhāṭṭa stance. Even Naiyāyikas in their semantics take the terms "blue" and "pot" as used in "The pot is blue" to have the same reference (though distinct "senses"). And, again, if perceptually the "pot" and "blue" indications are the same thing, there would no need to postulate inherence. Furthermore, there are perceptions, and usages, of "blue" as in "The blue (color)" where there is simply a single thing, blue.

The Bhāṭṭa says explicitly that were some such relator doing real work, we would say that the pot *has* blue instead of that the pot is blue; in Sanskrit, the possessive suffix would be used. To suppose that such usage, or any metaphorical sense, is implicit is unreasonable when a usage can be straightforwardly interpreted in its primary, denotative sense. Thus it is non-distinctness, and not inherence, that plays the relational role with cognitions such as "The pot is blue."

Gaṅgeśa holds that ontologically a blue pot is indeed non-distinct from the pot *simpliciter*. But the blue and the pot have to be themselves different.

Text (p. 676, Tirupati) and Translation

> ucyate | śukla-paṭa-śabdayoḥ ekârthatve ghaṭaḥ kumbha iti-vat śuklaḥ paṭa iti saha-prayogo na syāt | andhasya paṭa-graha-vat rūpa-grahaḥ, rūpâ-graha-vat paṭâ-graho 'pi vā syāt | mahārajata-rakte paṭa-graha-vat śukla-grahaḥ, śuklâ-graha-vat paṭâ-graho 'pi bhavet | paṭam ānaya ity ukte yaṃ kaṃcit śuklam ānayet | a-paṭaḥ paṭa iti-vad a-śuklaḥ paṭa iti virudhyeta, paṭa-śuklayor a-bhedāt | agni-saṃyogād ekatra śyāma-raktayoḥ vināśôtpāde ghaṭasya tau syātām, ghaṭa-sattve vā tayor api na syātām |

Gaṅgeśa: We answer. If (with the verbalized cognition, "The cloth is white") the word "white" and the word "cloth" meant one and the same thing, then like *ghaṭa* ("pot") and *kumbha* ("pot") (which are synonyms), the two would not be used together. Furthermore, a blind person in apprehending a cloth (in his hand by the sense of touch) would apprehend its color; or in not apprehending its color would not apprehend the cloth. And after a white cloth had been dyed with turmeric, white still would be apprehended when the cloth is apprehended; or with the white not grasped, the cloth would not be grasped. When "Bring a cloth" is said, anything white would be brought. Further, like "The cloth is not a cloth," to say "The cloth is not white" would be self-contradictory, since there would be no distinctness between the cloth and the white. Once a pot has been baked in fire, the arising and destruction of the black and of the red—both colors (simultaneously)—would belong to the pot. Or, we would have to say that neither (the arising nor the destruction) of the two concerns what the pot is.

Comments

According to Nyāya, "Cattle are cows," is not a proper sentence, because of the repetitive character of use of the two synonyms. But the judgment "The cloth (is) white" is obviously unlike "A pot (*ghaṭa*) (is) a pot (*kumbha*)." This is the first of Gaṅgeśa's counterarguments.

There are, by my count, seven additional arguments, which are all clear and apparently cogent. The non-distinctness view has other advantages, however, and Gaṅgeśa's upholding inherence faces further difficulties, as we shall see.

Gaṅgeśa is defending an ontological hierarchy and layeredness. A pot can be both red and black at different times, remaining the same through a change of properties. And since a blue pot is something capable of subsisting through a change of color, its blue is something distinct, a superstratum that is related to the pot as substratum by the relation of inherence.

Text (p. 676, Tirupati, and p. 658, Calcutta) and Translation

> atha śuklatvâdīnāṃ dravya-bhedāt tad-bodhârthaṃ saha-prayogaḥ | andhâdinā śuklâdi-grahe śuklatvâdīnām a-graha upapadyate | śuklatvâdi-jāteś ca dravyeṇa a-bhedo na samavāyaḥ, kiṃ tu sva-rūpa-saṃbandha iti cet, na | śuklatva-madhuratva-surabhitvôṣṇatvâdīnāṃ dravya-vṛttitve dravya-grāhaka-tvag-ādibhiḥ grahaṇa-prasaṅgāt | rūpatvâdīnāṃ dravya-vṛttitve pratiniyatêndriya-grāhyatā eva na syāt, yogya-vṛttitvena jāter grahaṇa-yogyatvāt | tat-taj-jātitvena yogyatve 'n-anugamāt | tasmād rūpatvâdīnāṃ pratiniyatêndriya-grāhyatā api guṇa-guṇi-bhede mānam | a-bhede ca kathaṃ paṭasya śuklaṃ rūpam iti bheda-buddhiḥ | paṭo nīlimā iti buddhi-prasaṅgaś ca |

Bhāṭṭa: Universals such as whiteness do differ from substances (but qualities such as white do not differ from substances). In the examples you gave, the usage of terms together (that you showed were not synonyms) is to make such difference known. Non-apprehension of whiteness, etc., by a blind person, etc., is possible though there is apprehension of white, etc. Moreover, there is a sense in which there is non-distinctness (even) between a substance and universals such as whiteness. It is not (as you say) inherence; rather, it is self-linkage.

Gaṅgeśa: No. If whiteness, sweetness, fragrance, hotness, etc., resided (directly) in substances (as opposed to in the white, sweet and so on qualities that do reside directly in substances), then when a substance is apprehended by any sense organ—the organ of touch, for example—there would be apprehension (of all of these). This is the difficulty. If colorness, etc., resided (directly) in substances, then there would not be cognizability according to a specific sense organ (but there is). A universal is capable of being apprehended according to the fittingness to be apprehended of that in which it exists (i.e., colorness, for example, resides in colors and will be apprehended only when a color is apprehended). The fittingness of this and that universal to be apprehended is not uniform. Therefore, the fact that colorness and other universals are cognizable only by specific sense organs is further proof of the distinction between quality and quality-possessor.

And if they were non-distinct, how could the cognition of distinctness in "The cloth *has* a white color" be explained? Moreover, there would be the difficulty that (in the case of a blue cloth) we would cognize "The cloth is blueness" (as opposed to "The cloth is blue").

Comments

The Bhāṭṭa is claiming that a white thing would be grasped by a blind person by the organ of touch, for example, but the thing *as* white would not be grasped because the universal whiteness would not be grasped. Apparently, it would be a grasping of the universal that would bring the color into consciousness. The Bhāṭṭa seems to want to collapse the distinction between (a) bare or thin particulars and (b) particular qualities (though what the text says is substances and qualities) but not that between universals and their instances. Moreover, the Bhāṭṭa says that even with an admission of that distinction, no relation as an additional real need be supposed in that the two terms are self-linking.

According to Gaṅgeśa's Nyāya, the universal colorness is cognizable only by the sense organ capable of apprehending color, the visual organ. In more general terms, the cognizability of a universal depends on the cognizability of that in which it rests, as colorness in color. But if there is no distinctness between a universal and a substance contacted by a sense organ, something as white, sweet, fragrant, etc., should be perceived when there is any perception whatsoever—by whichever organ—of the substance.

The view that there is an ontological layeredness—a firm distinction between the property-bearer and its properties, and, a level up, between the first-level properties and their further properties (as sweetness is the universal of sweet tastes which are properties of pastries and other sweets)—has several advantages, not the least of which is its ability to explain differences of sense presentation, an ability not shared by the non-distinctness view.

In response to the Bhāṭṭa's grammatical argument, Gaṅgeśa implies that it is perfectly good usage to say "The cloth *has* a white color," making verbally explicit the relational tie.

Text (p. 677, Tirupati) and Translation

> nanv ekântâ-bhede sarvam idaṃ dūṣaṇam | vayaṃ tu bhedâ-bheda-vādinaḥ | tathā ca bhedam ādāya apaunarukty-ādi | bhedâ-bhede ca uktam eva pramāṇaṃ pratyakṣam | atha vā ubhaya-siddha-bhede sāmānâdhikaraṇya-dhīr a-bhede pramāṇam | yad vā atyantam a-bhede bhede ca na sāmānâdhikaraṇyam iti tata eva bhedâ-bheda-siddhiḥ | na ca bhedâ-bhedayoḥ paraspara-viraha-rūpatayā viruddhayoḥ katham ekatra samāveśa iti vācyam | saṃyoga-tad-a-bhāvayor iva a-virodhāt | pākân-antaraṃ rakto 'yaṃ na śyāma ity a-bādhitânubhava-balāt tatra eva tad-anyonyâ-bhāva-siddheḥ tvayā api bhedâ-bheda-svīkārāt | anyonyâ-bhāvatvam a-vyāpya-vṛtti-vṛtti[4] nityâ-bhāva-vṛtty-a-bhāvatva-sākṣād-vyāpya-dharmatvāt[5] atyantâ-bhāvatva-vat | nitya iti vā na viśeṣaṇam a-vyāpya-vṛtti-pratiyogika-prāg-a-bhāva-pradhvaṃsayor a-vyāpya-vṛttitvāt ity ato 'pi bhedâ-bheda-siddhiḥ |

Bhāṭṭa: If we held strictly to a position of non-distinctness, you would be right: all this we have said would fail. But we (Bhāṭṭa Mīmāṃsakas) hold the position of *distinctness within non-distinctness* (between properties and property-possessors). And so by accepting the distinctness, use of terms non-repetitiously, etc., can be explained. Just as we claimed, moreover, the proof of our position of distinctness within non-distinctness is perception. Or, given that both of us accept the distinctness plank, let us present an argument only for non-distinctness: use of terms appositively in the same case to express certain cognitions demands it (in the case of "The pot (is) blue," for example, "blue" and "pot" are both nominatives). Alternatively, note that in the case of a complete non-distinctness (as with the synonyms *ghaṭa* and *kumbha*, both of which mean "pot") and in the case of a complete distinctness (as with the meanings of "horse" and "cow"), use of appositives does not occur (to avoid repetition). Therefore, just for this reason our position of distinctness within non-distinctness is proved.

Nor should it be asked how it is possible for distinctness and non-distinctness—understood as mutually opposed, each entailing the absence of the other—to occur together in one thing. The possibility is shown by the fact that a contact and its absence can so occur. (For example, a monkey can be in contact with a tree while in the same tree there is also absence of the contact.)

You (Naiyāyikas) also accept this our (Bhāṭṭa) "distinctness within non-distinctness" position: it is an uncontroverted experience (you often say) that after baking a pot is red and no longer black, and you accept that a red thing and a black thing are mutually exclusive.

Consider another inference. The property of mutual exclusion (*anyonyâ-bhāva*, "mutual absence") resides in things (or properties) that are non-locus-pervading. The prover: *since* it is a property that is thoroughly pervaded by the type of absence that is constant (and a constant absence is non-locus-pervading). The confirming example: like an absolute absence. Alternatively, the qualification in the prover that mutual exclusion is a *constant* absence is unnecessary. (Thus the prover would be that the property of mutual exclusion is a type of absence, with all absences as non-locus-pervading.) The absence of x before its production (*prāg-a-bhāva*) and the absence of x after its destruction (*dhvaṃsâ-bhāva*) involve absentees that are not locus-pervading; hence, they too are not locus-pervading (and thus need not be excluded by the qualification, "constant," in the prover given). Therefore, because of this inference as well, our view of distinctness within non-distinctness is established.

Comments

That it is one and the same pot, at one time black and later red, would secure the non-distinctness. The change from black to red would secure the distinctness. In general, continuity would manifest a thing's non-distinctness, its identity. Change would manifest the distinctness between property and bearer.

The mention of synonyms is, perhaps, opaque, although we have seen the argument already. In English, it is perfectly permissible to use a synonym to explain a term, "The dish requires coriander, cilantro," but in Sanskrit, "Coriander (is) cilantro," is disallowed. Similarly, no one says, "A cow (is) not a horse" (see the end of the first paragraph of text: "in the case of a complete distinctness . . ."). Definition by giving a synonym would require a kind of punctuation mark in the use of *iti*, roughly in this usage a quotation mark or separator of the synonymous terms: *kumbha iti ghaṭaḥ*, " 'Pot_k' means the same as 'pot_g'."

The inference given by the Bhāṭṭa presupposes that the relation distinctness (holding between any two things that are distinct), which is technically termed "mutual exclusion" (*anyonyâ-bhāva*), is not locus-pervading. Thus it would not rule out the non-distinctness, the sense in which the pot is the one and the same thing.

In other words, distinctness and non-distinctness would mark different sides of the ontological tie between something and its properties. The thing would not be what it is without the property, and the property would be distinct from the property-bearer in that it would not *exhaust* what the qualificandum is. Note that this distinctness is itself an absence. Absences are non-locus-pervading, thus clearly not exhausting what a thing is. Distinctness is a mutual absence, *anyonyâ-bhāva*, two things' not having the same identity.

Text (p. 679, Tirupati) and Translation

ucyate | tasya eva tatra a-bhāvo 'vaccheda-bhedena vartate jñāyate ca yathā saṃyogâdy-a-bhāvaḥ | śyāmâvacchinnasya tasya eva anyonyâ-bhāvas tatra eva raktâvacchinne | tad-anyonyâ-bhāvâ-bhāvaś ca śyāmâvacchedena | tad iha api nīlasya anyonyâ-bhāvo ghaṭatvâvacchedena iti nīlāt ghaṭasya bhedo 'stu | a-bhedas tu nīlânyonyâ-bhāvâ-bhāva-rūpo na ghaṭe ghaṭatvâvacchedena eva, virodhāt | ekâvacchedena bhāvâ-bhāvayoḥ ekatra a-vṛtter a-jñānāc ca | na apy avacchedakântareṇa | ghaṭatvâvacchinne ghaṭe tad-a-bhāvāt tad-a-jñāne 'pi nīlo ghaṭa ity anubhavāc ca | na ca anyonyâ-bhāva-rūpo bhedo 'stu, a-bhedas tu na bhedâ-bhāvaḥ kiṃ tv anya eva iti vācyam | a-bheda-vyavahāre tasya a-hetutvāt | tasmāt nīlo ghaṭa ity atra nīla-saṃbandha eva bhāsate |

Gaṅgeśa: We answer. When there is an absence of x in y, the absence both exists and is known by way of a distinctness of specification (determining, e.g., a part of y), as, for example, an absence of contact (of a monkey in a part of a tree conjoined with a monkey elsewhere). A mutual exclusion specified by black (as what is excluded) obtains precisely in the case of a pot as specified in color as red. Further, an absence of mutual exclusion has to be precisely specified as well, as, for example, with regard to the black (of the pot at the earlier time). So (to consider your distinctness within non-distinctness view), we will accept that there is distinctness between a pot and its blue, a distinctness understood as a mutual exclusion *of* blue specified *by* potness. However, we take a different attitude toward the non-distinctness you claim. There is no non-distinctness understood as an absence of mutual exclusion of blue in a pot specified indeed by potness, since that would be contradictory. There does not occur at a single locus both a presence and an absence with one and the same (precise) specification (*avaccheda*). Nor is such ever cognized ("A cow is not a cow," for instance, is not cognized.)

Nor is there a presence and an absence at a single locus secured by another specifier. First, in a pot specified by potness (or, regarding a pot cognized as a pot), there is no other specifier. Second, although the thing could be cognized in a way that it is not cognized currently, the point is that a current awareness may be just "The pot is blue."

Nor should it be said that in accepting distinctness as mutual exclusion, we should see non-distinctness not as the absence of distinctness but as something else. In that case, there would be no reason for employing the term "*non*-distinctness."

Therefore, here with the awareness, "The pot is blue," a relation with the blue is indeed manifest.

Comments

The distinctness within non-distinctness view would require that the counter-correlate of the mutual exclusion cognized in, e.g., "The pot is blue"—which would be the property blue as distinct from the thing as a pot—be present in the qualificandum specified in the same way (viz., as a pot) as it could be specified when the property blue is cognized as excluded or absent. This is contradictory, Gaṅgeśa maintains. A pot cannot be both blue and not-blue and is not cognized like that—so long, that is, as we are talking about the thing *as a pot* and not about its parts where it might have both the one color and its absence. In the case of something both having and not having a certain property, there is a change of specification, a monkey in a tree at a precise location or of a pot at one time black and another red. We never say that a currently blue pot is not now blue.

Now Gaṅgeśa had already shown that the thing cognized, the qualificandum, has to be distinct from a qualifier such as blue. It could be another color, a blind person could know it by touch without knowing its color, et cetera. So consider the simpler cognition, "That's a pot," or, "(A) pot," where there is no specifier of the qualificandumhood portion of the objecthood but only *potness* as specifying the predication content or qualifier. In this passage, Gaṅgeśa appears to say that even cognized only as a pot, with potness as the qualifier, the qualificandum would remain distinct—albeit in this case the qualificandum cannot shake loose from the universal, that is, without being destroyed (a better example would be a cognition of a cow as a cow). Gaṅgeśa intimates an epistemological reason for this broader position: the pot could be cognized as something else, as earthen, for example, and *cognition-wise* (with respect to inferences, etc.) there is all the difference in the world between being aware of something as a pot and being aware of it as earthen, although the thing cognized is one and the same.

Thus, for Gaṅgeśa there is space between the particular (the "thing cognized" most abstractly) and its properties, even those most closely bound to it, such as a pot's potness, a property the pot could never lose. Between any qualifier and qualificandum as determined by a verbalizable cognition there is a kind of mutual exclusion ("a distinctness understood as a mutual exclusion *of* blue specified *by* potness").

Nevertheless, here, as before, Gaṅgeśa accomplishes only a first step of an argument for inherence: qualifier and qualificandum cognized as distinct in any cognition of an entity as qualified means that their relation is presented as a real object. Further argument is required to show that the relation is inherence as a separate real. But the immediate task is to counter the Bhāṭṭa's appositional argument, and explain why "blue" and "pot" are used in the same case in a verbalization of a cognition of a blue pot, "The pot (is) blue" (with the "is" dropped in Sanskrit), as we see in the next passage.

Text (p. 680, Tirupati) and Translation

tathā sati nīlī ghaṭa dhīḥ syād ity uktam iti cet, nīlī ghaṭa ity atra buddhau yadi saṃbandha-viṣayatvam āpādyate, tad iṣyata eva | atha nīlo ghaṭa iti prayoge saṃbandha-vācaka-padavattvaṃ tad api iṣyate eva | matupo lopāt a-bhedôpacārād vā nīla-padam eva nīlavat-param iti |

Objection: Then this being the case, the expression should be "The pot *has* blue" (not "The pot *is* blue").

Gaṅgeśa: If the cognition, "The pot has blue," were to occur (or be expressed) showing the relation to be (part of) the cognitive object, that would be all right.

Objection: So you admit that with the usage, "The pot is blue," that there be a word expressing the relation is also desired by you. (But there is none.)

Gaṅgeśa: Well, either there is a dropping of the possessive suffix or the (use of nominatives suggesting) non-distinctness is figurative. The word "blue" in this usage means "having blue."

Comments

Again, in Sanskrit there is no word for the *is* in the English translation, "The pot is blue." The expression is more literally "Blue (is the) pot." With the expression translated, "The pot has blue"—more literally, "Blue-possessing (is the) pot"—a suffix conveys the meaning of *has*. Thus in the latter expression, there is an explicit expression of relationality.

In a broad range of cases, a simple determinate cognition "F*a*" is interpreted by Nyāya as "$F_i a$" (where 'F' is a property, '*a*' is a particular or property-bearer, and 'i' is inherence). Even in cases of self-linkage, the relational tie is presented as cognitive object, because the property and its bearer are distinct. Indeed, this ontological fact requires that linguistic expressions that might seem to be simply co-referential, such as "pot" and "blue" in the statement "(The) pot (is) blue," be interpreted as qualificative, as meaning, in effect, "The pot *has* blue," or "Blue inheres in the pot," Gaṅgeśa argues.

Here ends Gaṅgeśa's discussion of the non-distinctness/distinctness alternative. He does not explicitly counter the point made earlier that a construal of a term in its primary meaning is, *ceteris paribus*, to be preferred over a secondary or metaphorical reading. But the implication is that all things are *not* equal, that there is good reason for supposing an ellipsis or metaphorical usage, namely, the ontological requirement that qualificandum and qualifier be distinct.

Text (p. 680, Tirupati, and p. 661, Calcutta) and Translation

nanu śabda-rūpâdiṣu viśeṣaṇatā indriya-saṃbaddha-viśeṣaṇatā vā grāhikās tu kiṃ samavāyâdinā | atha viśeṣaṇatāyāṃ samavāyaḥ indriya-saṃbaddha-viśeṣaṇatāyāṃ ca saṃyukta-samavāyâdir upajīvyaḥ, tair vinā tayor a-bhāvād iti cet, viśeṣaṇatā-sva-rūpe teṣām upajīvyatvam, na tu tasyāḥ pratyāsattitve 'pi | tair vinā api samavāyâ-bhāvayor viśeṣaṇatā-sattvāt | saṃyukta-samavāyâdir api tatra asti iti cet, āstām, na tu pratyāsattiḥ, kiṃ tu viśeṣaṇatā eva, klptatvāt | saṃyukta-samavāyâdikaṃ vinā viśeṣaṇatā rūpâdau na jñāyata iti cet, mā jñāyi | na hi sā pratyāsattir jñātā, api tu sva-rūpa-satī | mā evam | śabdâdīnāṃ sākṣātkāra-viṣayatvena indriya-saṃbaddhânumitau śabdâdau samavāyâdikaṃ jñātvā eva viśeṣaṇatā-graha ity a-vaśyaṃ | prathamôpasthitatvāt samavāyâdir eva viṣayo na viśeṣaṇatā, caramôpasthitatvāt |

Objection.1: The relation "qualifierhood" (or "being a qualifier") with regard to sounds, colors, and so on, or (not simply this but) "being a qualifier related to a sense organ" is what brings about sense perception. So why postulate inherence and the others (the types of so-called operative connection in sense perception)?

Objector.2 (against objector.1): With regard to the relation of "being a qualifier," inherence is required—and with regard to "being a qualifier related to a sense organ" the required relation is "inherence in what is in contact with a sense organ"—on the grounds that without these there could not be the connections (necessary for sense perception in these cases).

Answer (by objector.1): What is required is the view that they are simply by nature "qualifierhood," i.e., types of qualifier. But qualifierhood need not also be understood as what you call an operative connection in sense perception (although the relation is crucial to bringing sense perception about). Without going so far as to admit all the types of so-called operative connection that you propose, we say that both your inherence and absence are types of qualifier.

Objector.2 (against objector.1): But there are also other relations that have to be accepted, "inherence in what is in contact with a sense organ" and so on.

Answer (by objector.1): Let them be. But they are not to be considered the "operative connection in sense perception" (as you understand it). Rather, simply "being a qualifier" fills that role; this is an accepted notion (and none other is needed).

Objector.2 (against objector.1): But "being a qualifier" without the further relations of "inherence in what is in contact with a sense organ" and so on is not cognized with colors and so on.

Answer (by objector.1): Stop thinking like that. There is no "operative connection in sense perception" that is ever cognized. Rather, "being a qualifier" is self-linking.

Gaṅgeśa: You are wrong. Sounds and so on are inferred to be in relation to the sense organs since sounds and so on are objects of immediate experience. Only after cognizing the relations of inherence and so on with regard to sounds and so on is there apprehension of the abstract, "being a qualifier." Therefore, because relations such as inherence are (epistemically prior, i.e.)

are what are first set in memory, it is just they that are the cognitive object, not "being a qualifier," which is (epistemically posterior, i.e.) set in memory afterwards.

Comments

According to objector.1, qualifierhood is the key relation in the causal process resulting in perceptual awareness. If Gaṅgeśa insists that inherence is necessary too sometimes in order to explain how particular sense perceptions come about, objector.1 says his camp can agree in that "qualifierhood" or "being a qualifier" on his view includes inherence and its function. The point is, again, that this new inherence would not be an independently real relator, but would be one of many types of qualifier, all of which work through self-linkage.

Gaṅgeśa's argument about epistemic priority is not meant as a denial that each of the sensory connections can be viewed as a type of qualifier. Each, when explicitly focused on, appears as qualifying the object cognized. His point is that their being viewed like this is an abstraction from their givenness in the simplest and most ordinary sensory awareness. There they appear as contact or conjunction, inherence in the conjoined, and so on.

Text (p. 684, Tirupati) and Translation

> nanu a-bhāva-grahe na indriya-saṃbaddha-viśeṣaṇatā pratyāsattiḥ, cakṣuṣā saṃyukte paramâṇv-ādau yogyasya jalatvâder a-bhāva-graha-prasaṅgāt | kiṃ tu sva-grāhya-saṃbaddha-viśeṣaṇatā | mahati vāyau udbhūta-rūpâ-bhāvasya, kusume saurabhâ-bhāvasya, guḍe tiktatvâ-bhāvasya vā na cakṣur-ādinā grahaḥ, api tu yogyân-upalabdhyā so 'numīyate | indriya-viśeṣaṇatā api na pratyāsattiḥ | cakṣur-ādinā sva-viśeṣaṇa-jalatvâdy-a-bhāva-graha-prasaṅgāt | yadi śabdâ-bhāvaḥ pratyakṣaḥ tadā pratyāsatty-antaraṃ kalpyam | tad-a-bhāve pratyakṣa eva na bhavati iti cet, mā evam | lāghavād indriya-saṃbaddha-viśeṣaṇatā eva pratyāsattiḥ | na ca evaṃ paramâṇau jalatvâdy-a-bhāva-graha-prasaṅgaḥ | yatra hi yat sattvam an-upalabdhi-virodhi tatra tasya a-bhāva indriya-saṃnikarṣeṇa gṛhyate | na ca paramâṇv-ādau jalatvâdi-sattvam an-upalabdhi-virodhi | yogya-saṃyukta-samavāyâ-bhāvena pṛthivītva-vad-an-upalabdhi-saṃbhavāt | mahati vāyv-ādau udbhūta-rūpâdy-a-bhāvaś cakṣur-ādi-grāhya eva | tatra udbhūta-rūpâdi-sattve 'n-upalabdhy-an-upapatteḥ | ata eva stambhe piśāca-tādātmyâ-bhāvaḥ pratyakṣaḥ stambha-tādātmye ca tasya stambhasya iva an-upalambhâ-saṃbhavāt | evaṃ śabdasya apy a-bhāvaḥ pratyakṣaḥ tadā tatra śabda-sattvasya an-upalabdhi-virodhitvād iti tatra indriya-viśeṣaṇatā eva pratyāsattiḥ | cakṣuṣi jalatvâdi-sattvaṃ ca na an-upalabdhi-virodhi iti cakṣuṣā na tad-grahaḥ |

Objection: In apprehension of an absence, it is false that the operative connection is "being a qualifier of what is related to the sense organ." Since the visual organ would be in contact with ultimate atoms (e.g., of earth) and the like, then, if you were right, there should be apprehension of an absence of wateriness and the like which are capable of being perceived. Instead, the position should be (that an absence is perceived through the relation of) "being a qualifier of what is related to the sense organ *insofar as* that is capable of being perceived by the particular sense organ."

Concerning large (perceptible) whiffs of air (and not the atoms), there is an absence of manifest color. But that is not grasped by the visual organ and so on. Rather, we know this through inference based on the fact that color is in no way perceived and that we would perceive it if it were present in air. Similarly concerning an absence of fragrance in a flower and the absence of bitter taste in sugar.

Nor is "being a qualifier of the sense organ" the operative connection. If that were right, an absence of wateriness, etc., should be (continually) grasped by the visual organ and so on, since it would stand as the organ's own qualifier.

If an absence of sound were directly perceptible (and not just inferable, as is our counterproposal), then some other operative connection would have to be dreamed up. Given that you have not come up with one, you might as well admit that these absences are not directly perceptible.

Gaṅgeśa: It is not so. Because of parsimony, it is just "being a qualifier of what is related to the sense organ" that is to be viewed as the operative connection in perception of an absence.

And you are wrong to allege that this view entails that such an absence as that of wateriness in ultimate atoms should be perceived. (There is the following concomitance:) Where the existence of something stands opposed to its non-perception, there only is its absence to be grasped through a sensory connection.

This condition is not fulfilled with respect to such an absence as that of wateriness in the likes of ultimate atoms. The existence of wateriness there does not stand opposed to its non-perception; similarly with other cases. Non-perception in such cases is possible (even though the wateriness exists) because, like earthenness (which is present in the ultimate atoms of earth where wateriness is absent), there is no inherence in something capable of being perceived when it is in contact with a sense organ (in that no ultimate atom can be perceived).

Concerning large (perceptible) whiffs of air, etc., absence of manifest color, etc., is indeed perceptible by the visual organ, etc. In such a case, there would not be an impossibility of perception if, for example, the manifest color existed. (Air, by nature, simply has no color.) Therefore, an absence of identity between a post and a demon is perceptible in the post, since if there were identity with the post it would not be impossible, as it were, that it be perceived.

In this way, absence of sound is also perceptible. The existence of sound does stand in opposition to its non-perception. So it is indeed "being a qualifier with regard to a sense organ" that is the operative connection when there is perception of no sound. And again, it is not the case that the existence of the likes of wateriness would stand in opposition to its non-perception by the visual organ. Therefore, its absence is not grasped by the visual organ.

Comments

Wateriness as absent from the atoms of earth could, the objector says, stand as "being a qualifier of what is related to the sense organ." Thus, absence of wateriness in the atoms of earth should be perceived when a sense organ is in contact with earth-composed things. But obviously this does not happen. No sense perception of atoms occurs, though a sense organ is in contact with them.

The organ of smell, unlike the visual and tactile organs, is considered incapable of apprehending a substance. It grasps qualities only. Similarly with the organ of taste. Absences are not qualities but rather qualifiers that self-link with substances. So in the case of an absence of smell or of taste, the organ, not being capable of perceiving the substance to which the qualifier would be related, would be incapable of perceiving the atoms. Thus such an absence must be known by an inference based on the rule: were a smell or taste present, it would be perceived. Gaṅgeśa's objector is maintaining—in the second paragraph—that the same type of inference would be responsible for an apprehension of an absence of color.

In the third paragraph, the objector says that if the operative connection in perception of such absences as that of color in air were "being the qualifier of the sense organ," then an absence of wateriness etc. would be continually grasped by the visual organ since such "would stand as the organ's own qualifier." Here we need to know that the visual organ is thought of as made out of fiery atoms. Thus, it is itself qualified by an absence of wateriness.

The heart of Gaṅgeśa's response is the principle he announces at the beginning: an absence of x is perceptible only if its presence is opposed—by natural law—to its non-perception (other conditions being fulfilled).

With the example of a demon and a post, Gaṅgeśa's point is that the absence is directly perceived.

Like other perceptible absences, an absence of sound is perceived through standing as a qualifier in relation to the sense organ that would grasp sound were it present.

Text (p. 692, Tirupati, and p. 669, Calcutta) and Translation

nanv a-bhāve na viśeṣaṇatā pratyāsattiḥ | kiṃ tu samavāya eva samavāya-sādhaka-viśiṣṭa-pratīter a-viśeṣāt | na ca samavetatve tasya bhāvatvâpattiḥ | bhāvasya tattve '-bhāvatvâpattir iti vaiparītya-saṃbhavāt | rūpâdau pratyāsattitvena samavāya-kalpanam a-bhāve 'pi tulyam | viśeṣaṇatā api tulyā | prāg-a-bhāva-pradhvaṃsau pratiyogyâśraye samavetau | pratiyogy-āśraya-nāśa-janya-dhvaṃso deśe samaye vā samavaiti, tatra eva nirūpaṇāt | na ca samavāyi-nāśe dhvaṃsa-nāśaḥ, ghaṭônmajjana-prasaṅgāt bhāvatvasya upādhitvāc ca | anyathā tava api tasya janyatvena nāśâpattiḥ | atha evam anyonyâtyantâ-bhāvayor nityatve 'n-eka-samavetatve ca jātitva-prasaṅgaḥ | na ca tatra bhāvatvaṃ tantram | gauravāt | na ca a-bhāvānāṃ viśiṣṭa-pratītau viśeṣaḥ, yena atra samavāya-parityāga iti cet, na | ghaṭatvâ-bhāvâder jātitve sattva-dravyatva-pṛthivītvâdinā parâpara-bhāvân-upapatteḥ | teṣāṃ vyāpyatve ghaṭe tad-a-bhāva-prasaṅgaḥ | vyāpakatve sāmānyâdau ghaṭatvâ-bhāvo na syād iti |

Objection (by objector.1): Okay, then, in the case of an absence, "being a qualifier" is not the operative connection. It is instead nothing but inherence, because the reason given for accepting inherence applies here just as much as it does elsewhere, the reason, namely, that a cognition of an absence is a cognition of an entity as qualified.

Nor does this view—that an absence is related to its locus by inherence—entail the absurdity that the absence would have to be regarded as a presence. For there would equally be the possibility of the opposite: when it is a presence that stands in that relation, it would have to be regarded as an absence. That inherence (in what is in contact with the sense organ) is the operative connection with (perception of) color and the like is equally to be imagined with (perception of) an absence (in that there, too, the relation is indirect). Also, both equally involve "being a qualifier."

Prior absences and destructional absences inhere in the substrata of their absentees. A destructional absence of *x* generated by a destruction of the substratum of *x*—with *x* as the absence's absentee—inheres in a particular location or occasion, because it is experienced there only.

And it is not the case that when the inherent cause is destroyed (e.g., when the halves of a pot are destroyed), there is destruction of the destructional absence (e.g., destruction of the destruction of a pot and so therefore preservation of the pot), because that would mean the pot's popping back into existence and it entails treating a destruction as a presence, as a positive real (*bhāva*). If somehow this move were disallowed, you too would face the difficulty of regarding a destruction as a positive real, because insofar as something is regarded as a cause of a destruction it would be regarded as a destroyer (and thus as an existent).

Objection.2 (against objector.1): Then, in this way, mutual exclusion and absolute absence would have to be counted (against accepted theory) as universals (in that both would fulfill the conditions of the traditional definition): (a) they are eternal and (b) inhere in more than one thing.

(And if they are accepted as universals) one is not also forced to view them as positive reals, because that would be more cumbersome. Nor is there (we agree) any relevant difference between cognition of an entity as qualified by an absence and cognition of something as qualified by a positive presence, such that one need reject the notion of inherence with the one and not the other.

Answer (by objector.1): No. If there were such a universal as "absence of potness," then it would be impossible to maintain the ordering of kinds among existence, substancehood, and earthenness, for example (which all inhere in a pot). With regard to the requirement that universals are pervaded by one another successively (up to the widest, existence), if these (existence, substancehood, and earthenness) pervade an absence of potness, then they would not be there in a pot. (Clearly, existence and the others are there in a pot.) With regard to the requirement that a succession of universals be pervaders, an absence of potness could not figure in the succession (for fear of cross-section).

Comments

According to Gaṅgeśa's Nyāya-Vaiśeṣika tradition, perception of color does not involve direct contact with a sense organ but an indirect relation: the color inheres in a substance that both has color and is in contact with the sense organ. Thus, to hold that the causal connection in the case of perception of an absence is inherence would be to claim no more than what is claimed with perception of color, namely, a mediated connection with a sense organ. Objector.1's chief argument is that absential awareness is cognition of an entity as qualified. But his position is shored up by the parallel he draws with color.

Objector.1's strategy is to argue that by the same considerations Gaṅgeśa would use to establish the objective reality of inherence, the relationality of absences would also be established as objectively real—and so we might as well call it inherence.

Objector.2 chimes in with Praśastapāda's definition of a universal as something eternal that inheres in more than one thing. His claim is that inherence would be a universal according to objector.1. And if mutual exclusion and absolute absence are to be counted as universals, absence would not be a seventh category or primitive, against the inherited theory.

Thus objector.2 would apparently bolster objector.1's original attack: there is no reason to separate out the relationality of absences from what inherence is supposed to accomplish. But this wrinkle is rejected by objector.1.

As pointed out, Nyāya finds a hierarchy of universals, *jāti*, based on breadth of extension, with each successive universal including the extension of an immediately narrower universal within its extension. For example, every instance of earthenness is also an instance of substancehood. The problem with counting absences as universals is that there would be "confusion of class" (or "cross-sectioning": see note 2, pp. 700–701), that would break down the natural ordering, an ordering confirmed in experience of a pot, for instance, as both earthen and a substance. An entire inclusion of the extension of a lower *jāti* in that of a higher could not be.

Text (p. 694, Tirupati) and Translation

ucyate | samavetatve dhvaṃsasya samavāyi-kāraṇa-nāśāt nāśaḥ syāt | na ca nāśyatve bhāvatvaṃ tantram, gauravāt prāg-a-bhāve '-bhāvāc ca |

Gaṅgeśa: We answer. If a destructional absence is to be taken as *inhering* in its locus, then upon the destruction of its inherent cause (i.e., the locus) it would be destroyed (resulting in a presence). And it is not the case that only positive reals can cease to exist (and so you cannot avoid the difficulty on these grounds). Not only would that be an overly cumbersome view, but there could be no ceasing of a prior absence.

Comments

A prior absence of, for instance, a pot is a relevant causal factor in the pot's production. Gaṅgeśa makes this point by way of challenging the assumption that a causal factor has to have an inherent cause. An absence may well be a causal factor, but no absence inheres in what it qualifies. It is, instead, self-linking.

The layeredness achieved by inherence is manifest in the destruction of non-eternal properties that occurs when their locus or substratum is destroyed, that is, when the thing inhered-in is destroyed, as the blue of a pot is destroyed with the destruction of the pot. But if a destructional absence inhered somewhere, for example, in the shards of a broken pot, then were they destroyed the pot would re-emerge in the destruction of its destructional absence.

Text (p. 697, Tirupati) and Translation

a-samavetatve tad-dhvaṃsasya janyatve 'pi na nāśaḥ āśraya-nāśâder a-bhāvāt | ghaṭônmajjanâpatteḥ na naśyati iti cet, na | na hi prayojana-kṣati-bhayena sāmagrī na kāryam arjayati | tasmād unmajjanâ-bhāva-nirvāhakaṃ dhvaṃsasya a-samavetatvaṃ kalpyatām | sva-samavāyi-nāśāt dhvaṃsa-paramparā-kalpane ca ghaṭa-kapālâdeḥ ā-paramâṇu nāśe ghaṭâdi-tad-dhvaṃsa-virodhī caramo dhvaṃsaḥ paramâṇu-vṛttiḥ syāt tathā ca na pratyakṣaḥ | ghaṭa-dhvaṃsasya kapāla-samavetatve ca na bhūtale nirūpaṇaṃ syāt | ubhaya-vṛttitve ca vyāsajya-vṛttitvena kapālaṃ vinā na nirūpyeta |

Objection: But if the destructional absence of something x does not inhere somewhere, then once x has arisen—and even though it has arisen (so that we expect it to perish in time)—destruction would not occur: there would be no destruction, etc., with regard to a substratum (since the destruction would not have a substratum). To avoid the difficulty of the pot popping back into existence, we would have to say that it does not perish (to begin with).

Gaṅgeśa: That's wrong. For we do not—out of fear of loss of a causal factor—say that a causal nexus sufficient to bring about an effect does not bring it about. Therefore, a destructional absence has to be considered not to inhere, in order to avoid the popping back into existence (of a destroyed pot).

Let us imagine a series of destructions occurring through a ceasing to exist of something's inherent cause so that we would have a destruction of a pot through a destruction of its halves down to its ultimate atoms or minutest parts. The problem is that this last destruction, which would stand opposed both to the pot along with the series of smaller parts and to their destructions, would obtain in the ultimate atoms (which are imperceptible). And so, therefore, it could not be perceived. Furthermore, if a destruction of a pot inhered in the halves into which it is broken, the destruction would be experienced (there in the halves), not on the floor (where it is in fact experienced). And if you were to say that it exists in both, then, because they would be so closely bound up together, the halves would be necessarily an element of all the experience.

Comments

The opponent claims that it is Gaṅgeśa's view that faces an untoward ramification, not his own, the unwanted result that something obviously destructible could not be destroyed. Only that which has a substratum can be a causal factor; thus a destructional absence must have a substratum.

Gaṅgeśa insists, in response, that neither does a destructional absence nor any absence inhere anywhere. The relationality of absences is particular to each absence. A destructional absence of a pot could not occur in its ultimate atoms. Perceiving on the floor a pot smashed to smithereens, we would not perceive its atoms but its destruction there where it occurs—on the floor.

Is, then, the *bare* floor this and other absences? To such questions we turn now in two new sections devoted to absences and how they are known. Ontological questions are for the most part postponed while the epistemic question is taken up first. Are absences perceptual or are they known in some other fashion? The *pūrvapakṣin* is a Bhāṭṭa Mīmāṃsaka.

atha an-upalabdhi-vādaḥ

NOW, **DISCOURSE ON NON-COGNITION**

Text (p. 699, Tirupati, and p. 673, Calcutta) and Translation

nanv a-bhāva-graho na indriyāt | kiṃ tu yogyân-upalabdheḥ, tad-upalambhe tad-a-bhāvâ-grahāt | na ca evaṃ bhāva-buddhir api a-bhāvân-upalabdher eva na indriyād iti vācyam | bhāva-grahe indriyânuvidhānāt | anyathā nimīlitâkṣasya api ghaṭâ-bhāvân-upalabdhyā ghaṭa-graha-prasaṅgaḥ | ata eva bhāva-grahe a-bhāvân-upalabdhiḥ pṛṣṭha-lagnā api na hetuḥ indriyeṇa anyathā-siddhatvāt | na hi indriyârtha-saṃnikarṣe sati tāṃ vinā bhāva-dhī-vilambaḥ | a-bhāva-grahe 'pi indriyaṃ hetuḥ tad-anuvidhānād iti cet, na | a-bhāvena cakṣur-ādeḥ prāpty-a-bhāvena āśraya-grahe tad-upakṣayāt |

Pūrvapakṣin (a Bhāṭṭa Mīmāṃsaka): A grasping of an absence does not result from (activity of) a sense organ (unlike a grasping of a presence). Rather, it comes about from ''non-cognition'' (*an-upalabdhi*) of something capable of being cognized. For, had it been cognized, its absence would not have been cognized.

Objection (by a Naiyāyika): If you were right, a cognition of a presence, too, should come about just from a *non-cognition* of its absence, not from (activity of) a sense organ (which is absurd).

Bhāṭṭa: That should not be said, since grasping of a presence correlates with (activity of) a sense organ. Otherwise, even someone with eyes closed would, by means of a non-cognition of an absence, grasp (e.g.) a pot—this is the difficulty.

Just for this reason, a non-cognition of an absence, however stuck to the back of (perception of a presence) it be, is not a cause of a grasping of a presence, since such non-cognition is rendered superfluous by (activity of) the sense organs. For, it is not the case that, once there is a connection between a sense organ and an object, a cognition of a presence would be retarded without it (i.e., without a non-cognition of an absence, which is, then, not a cause in the case of a cognition of a presence).

Objection (by a Naiyāyika): (If so) a sense organ would also be a cause of a grasping of an absence, since it correlates with it (too).

Bhāṭṭa: No. For (there is a difference:) in the case of an absence, the visual organ and the others exhaust themselves in grasping the substratum (for example, the bare ground where there is no pot), without any real reaching of the object.

Comments

There is no commentary by Mathurānātha on this section. However, most of the text is, according to Ramanuja Tatacharya, unproblematic.

Rucidatta identifies the *pūrvapakṣin* as a Bhāṭṭa, i.e., a member of the Mīmāṃsā subschool that follows Kumārila Bhaṭṭa. And, indeed, the positions advanced do consistently conform to that outlook. Furthermore, a quote from Kumārila appears near the section's end. And a Bhāṭṭa was Gaṅgeśa's principal adversary at the close of the preceding section.

Ramanuja Tatacharya points out that most of the Naiyāyika arguments parried by the Bhāṭṭa in the *pūrva-pakṣa* are presented by Udayana in his *Nyāya-kusumâñjali.*[1]

The Bhāṭṭa, who, like the Naiyāyika, is a realist about objects known, holds that *an-upalabdhi*, "non-cognition (of something capable of being cognized)," is a separate means of veridical cognition. There are negative facts, and none of the other recognized means—perception, inference, analogy, testimony, as admitted by Nyāya, nor an additional fifth *pramāṇa* defended by Kumārila, circumstantial implication (*arthâpatti*, "postulation")—is able to make an absence known: Kumārila provides an eliminative argument in his *Ślokavārttika* ruling out perception and the rest.[2] There are nevertheless veridical cognitions such as "The pot is not on the floor," which then have to arise out of the pot's not being there; the causal picture would be incomplete without the *pramāṇa* of non-cognition. Gaṅgeśa's position, which is ironed out in this and the following section, is that absences are known perceptually, and sometimes by inference and testimony, but not by any special cognitive means such as the Bhāṭṭa's non-cognition. There are only four *pramāṇa*, "means to veridical cognition." Thus, whereas with the absential cognition, "My glasses are not on the table," the Bhāṭṭa would find a special cognitive process, non-cognition, that, informed by a perceiving and a remembering, makes known the absence of the glasses, Gaṅgeśa would say that the absence is itself known perceptually. The two agree that the locus (the table) is given perceptually and that the absentee (the pair of glasses) is cognitively provided by memory. The disagreement concerns whether the absence itself requires a special *pramāṇa*.

In the passage at hand, the Naiyāyika's objection presumes the Naiyāyika view that some objects, a pot, for instance, can be known by more than one cognitive means, *pramāṇa-samplava*, whereas the Mīmāṃsaka position is that there must be a match, a parallelism, between cognitive objects, on the one hand, and cognitive means, on the other. Thus the Bhāṭṭa counters by denying that a non-cognition could make a presence known, for example, a pot. The parallelism—between positive facts being made known by the positive means and negative facts being known by the special negative means, with no crossovers—urges us to embrace his position. (Kumārila even uses the same word, *a-bhāva*, for both ontic "absence" and epistemic "non-cognition.") Presences are known by the cognitive means appropriate to presences, namely, activity of the sense organs. And if it were otherwise, the consequences would be ridiculous.

At the end the Bhāṭṭa explains why there should be the correlation that he proposes. Whereas with perceptions of presences at least some of the organs grasp their objects by "reaching" the things grasped, there is no such intimate sensory connection in the case of a non-cognition of an absence. There the organ exhausts itself—spends its perceptual ability—in contacting the locus, the locus where something is not. But an absential cognition has as its object an absence. So there has to be some other way of knowing it.

Text (p. 705, Tirupati, and p. 674, Calcutta) and Translation

atha adhikaraṇa-dhīr indriya-vyāpāro na ca tayā tad-anyathā-siddham | anyathā saṃnikarṣôpakṣīṇatayā indriyaṃ na hetuḥ syād iti cet, na | hetutve siddhe tad-vyāpāratvam | tad eva na asti, prāpty-a-bhāvāt | etena adhikaraṇa-grahêndriyayoḥ pṛthag-anvaya-vyatireka-grahāt daṇḍa-cakrayor iva hetutvaṃ dvayor iti nirastam | prāpty-a-bhāvena a-bhāvâ-grāhakatvāt | na ca indriyaṃ prāpta-viśeṣaṇam a-prāptam api gṛhṇāti | saṃyukta-samavāyâdy-uccheda-prasaṅgāt prāpta-caitra-gatâ-prāpta-daṇḍasya api graha-prasaṅgāt indriyasya prāpta-grāhakatvāc ca | na ca viśeṣaṇatā prāptiḥ, anyatra tad-a-kalpanāt | na ca samavāye tat-kalpanam | tasya an-upagamāt tata eva atīndriyatvād vā |

Objection (by a Naiyāyika): A cognition of a locus (is included in the activity of, i.e.) is the intermediate instrument (or "operation," *vyāpāra*) of a sense organ (with respect to a cognition of an absence). And such cognition of a locus does not render the sense organ superfluous. Otherwise, as exhausted in coming into a sensory connection, a sense organ would never be a (cognitive) cause.

Bhāṭṭa: If a sense organ's causality had been established for absential cognition, then there might be such "operation." But such causality does not occur, since there is no real reaching of the object.

By this reasoning is rejected the view that a grasping of a locus *and* a sense organ are *both* causes, like a stick and a wheel (both used to make a pot), as is shown by distinct graspings of positive and negative correlations. This is to be rejected because, since there is no real reaching, a sense organ does not give rise to a grasping of an absence.

And it is not the case that a sense organ grasps a qualifier of an object reached although the object is not really reached. For, this would land us in the predicament of a break-up of (or undermining of the motive to list sensory connections) "inherence in what is in contact with a sense organ" and so on. Moreover, there would be the unfortunate ramification that a stick that is not sensorily reached but held by (i.e., held behind the back of) Caitra who is sensorily reached would be grasped inasmuch as the sense organ would bring about a grasping of what is reached.

And (Nyāya's) "qualifierhood" is not a real reaching (i.e., not, as you have it, a real sensory connection, operative in a perception of an absence), since it is (*ad hoc*, i.e.) not postulated elsewhere (than with perception of absences). Furthermore, it is not to be postulated concerning cognition of inherence, because inherence is not accepted (by us) or because (as you should say) inherence is beyond the range of the senses just inasmuch as it is not really reached by a sense organ.

Comments

A cause of a cause of an effect is normally considered "superfluous" (*anyathā-siddha*), but this is not the case when the terminal or proximate cause is a chief cause's "employment" or "operation," *vyāpāra*. Such an operation is the required employment of a "chief" or nearly proximate instrumental cause, *karaṇa*, coming between it and the effect, so to say, and triggering the effect (see, above, in the introduction, pp. 24–5). The Naiyāyika is claiming that cognition of a locus is such an intermediate activity, and thus that it does not undermine the causal status of sense organs in cognitions of absences. The Bhāṭṭa's response is that this begs the question of the role of a sense organ in absential cognition. It remains to be shown that there is a sensory grasping of an absence. To postulate, as Nyāya does, a special sensory relation––i.e., qualifierhood—and to regard that relation as evidence for a sensory reaching are moves that are *ad hoc* and question-begging.

Furthermore, there are ridiculous consequences in supposing that without a real reaching—a real causal connection—there could be knowledge of an object brought about by the object. You cannot fudge by claiming that the absence "qualifies" the locus perceived and "reached." By perceiving Caitra, we would perceive what is hidden behind his back.

Text (p. 706, Tirupati) and Translation

atha a-bhāvasya indriya-grāhyatvena saṃyogâdi-bādhe iha eva sā kalpyate, rūpâdau saṃyukta-samavāyâdir iva iti cet, tatra an-upakṣīṇêndriyânuvidhānāt tathā eva | iha svâśraya-graha eva tad-upakṣīṇaṃ lāghavāt, na tu prāpty-antara-kalpanā, gauravāt | anyathā tvag-anuvidhānād rūpaṃ vinā api vāyu-dhīḥ pratyakṣā iti na sā sparśa-liṅga-grahe upakṣīyeta | kiṃ ca viśeṣaṇatāyāṃ indriya-grāhyatvaṃ tena sā ity anyonyâśrayatvam | api ca viśeṣaṇatā grāhya-sva-rūpam eva | na ca tayor anyonya-vyabhicārāt indriyaṃ saṃbaddhaṃ gṛṇāti ity eva vyāptir iti vācyam | dṛṣṭânte hi saṃbandhi-gataḥ saṃbandho hetuḥ gṛhītaḥ[3] cakṣuṣi, anyatra api tathā, na tu grāhya-sva-rūpam | saṃbandhasya saṃbandhi-bhinnatva-niyamāt | na hi sa eva tadvāṃs tena eva bhavati | sva-rūpa-saṃbandhasya hetutve ca rūpâdi-graho 'pi tat eva astu kiṃ samavāyâdinā | ataḥ saṃyoga-viśeṣaṇate eva pratyāsattī iti ṣoḍhā kīrtanam api viphalam | etena ālokâpeṣaṇe cakṣur apekṣā tasya tad-eka-sahakāritvād iti nirastam | prāptiṃ vinā cakṣu '-hetutvāt ālokasya ca pratiyogi-grāhakatvena yogyatā-ghaṭakatayā a-bhāva-grāhakatvāt | na ca evaṃ pratiyogy-upalambhakatvena cakṣur api hetuḥ | evaṃ hi tat-tad-vyāpyêtara-tad-upalambhaka-sākalye an-upalabdhir grāhakā bhavati iti vācyam | prāptiṃ vinā tasya a-hetutvena āśraya-grahôpakṣayāt |

Objection (by a Naiyāyika): Qualifierhood (as the sensory connection in the case of a perception of an absence) is to be postulated here, we must stress, inasmuch as an absence *is* grasped by the senses, that is to say, given (reasoned) exclusion of (the other sensory connections) contact and so on. The situation is similar to the case of color and the like, given exclusion (there, too) of contact and so on, where "inherence in what is in contact" and so on are postulated.

Bhāṭṭa: There (in the case of color and so on) it is indeed so, because correlation with (the activity of) an unexhausted sense organ is found. Here (in the case of cognition of an absence), in contrast, the sense organ is exhausted just in grasping an absence's substratum—since this is the economical position. There is to be no postulation of another real reaching, because that would be cumbersome. Otherwise, cognition of air, though without color, would be perceptual (and not, as you Naiyāyikas say, a matter of inference), since there is a correlation with touch (i.e., no cognition of air without the operation of the sense of touch). The organ of touch would not exhaust itself in the grasping of a touch that (according to you) sparks the inference.

Furthermore, given "qualifierhood" (as the sensory connection for absential cognition), you have the position that there is a sensory grasping of an absence, while also, *because of* that position, you have the other: the fallacy of circularity.

Moreover, qualifierhood (according to you) simply self-links with a thing grasped (and is not a relation distinct from the object), and no self-linking relation is a cause of (activity of) the organ of touch and so on. Rather, as the case may be, the relational cause is (to be regarded by you as) either contact or inherence (though we ourselves reject inherence).

Objection: Since contact and inherence mutually deviate (where the one is, the other is not, and vice-versa), a sense organ grasps that to which it is related (according to the relation—contact, inherence, self-linking qualifierhood—obtaining with the particular type of thing cognized). This indeed is the (pertinent) pervasion (or invariable rule).

Bhāṭṭa: That should not be said. For, in the examples given, the relation rests in the relatee. That is, the relational cause is grasped in (e.g.) the visual organ (i.e., the contact of the visual organ with an object perceived is a quality that rests in both the visual organ and the thing contacted). In the other cases, too, it is so. There is not, however, self-linkage with a thing grasped, since the rule is that a relation is something distinct from its terms, the relatees. For, it is not the case that anything x can come to be, just by itself, a *possessor* of x.

And if a self-linking relation can be a cause, let grasping of color and the like result from it, too. Why postulate inherence and the rest? Thus, contact and qualifierhood alone would be the sensory connections. Therefore, futile would be all the touting of sensory connection as sixfold!

By this reasoning is rejected the following: if cognition of an absence depends on light (as seems reasonable), there is dependency on the visual organ as well, since light is an auxiliary cause with respect to the visual organ in the one instance (namely, perception of a presence; thus, the visual organ would likewise be an auxiliary cause of an absential visual cognition). This is to be rejected, because, without a real reaching, the visual organ is not a cause, and because light brings about an absential grasping only in the sense that it would make an absentee (*pratiyogin*) grasped on the condition that the absentee is capable of being cognized. (A hare's horn is not capable of being cognized, and so there is no non-cognition making something known as bereft of the horn of a hare.)

And it is not the case that in this way the visual organ would be a cause too in that it would stand as a cause of cognition of the absentee. For, if so, *non-cognition* would be a cause of a grasping of an absence of x—this would have to be said—in that given an entirety of causal conditions (otherwise) sufficient for x's cognition (without x's being cognized)—conditions other than whatever is pervaded (or entailed) by x's being cognized (such as the presence of x)—non-cognition must be said to be the (additional) causal factor (securing awareness of the absence). For, without a real reaching, a sense organ is not a cause, since one would exhaust itself in grasping the substratum.

Comments

According to Old Nyāya and other classical schools, air is not directly perceived. Its existence is inferred as the substratum of a particular type of touch. (Gaṅgeśa presents a different view in the section, two below, devoted to air's perceptibility.) Thus, the Bhāṭṭa appears to have a relevant analogy: as the substance air is not "reached" by the organ of touch but only air's tactile quality, so an absence is not reached by any sense organ but only its substratum or locus. Air is known by inference, not perception; similarly, an absence is known by non-cognition, not perceptually.

The Bhāṭṭa also thoroughly exploits weaknesses in the Naiyāyika theory of self-linkage, the theory that so dominated the previous section. However, there is irony in the Bhāṭṭa's citing the maxim, "it is not the case that anything x can come to be, just by itself, a *possessor* of x," in that he himself rejects inherence in favor of a view of "distinctness within non-distinctness," as we have seen.

In the Bhāṭṭa view, light is a causal factor for an absential cognition only in the very weak sense that the absentee of an absential cognition has to be perceptible and, if this would be by vision, there would have to be the aid of light. No theorist admits such remotely relevant causes, and thus the sense organ is not to be regarded as a cause of an absential cognition.

Text (p. 708, Tirupati) and Translation

nanv evam andhasya tvag-indriyôpanīte nīle smṛta-pītasya an-upalabdhyā a-bhāva-graha-prasaṅgaḥ | pratiyogi-grāhakêndriya-grāhyatve tv a-bhāvasya na ayaṃ doṣaḥ, andhasya cakṣur a-bhāvād iti cet, na | a-bhāva-grāhakatvena abhimatam indriyam āśraya-grahôpakṣīṇam | tathā ca pratiyogi-grāhakêndriyeṇa āśraya-grahe an-upalabdhyā a-bhāva-grahāt | anyathā cakṣus-saṃyukte paramâṇau jalatvâ-bhāva-graha-prasaṅgaḥ |

Objection (by a Naiyāyika): In this way, a blind person would grasp by non-cognition of something remembered as yellow an absence with respect to something blue known by the organ of touch—this is the difficulty. But if (it is admitted that) an absence is grasped by the sense organ that grasps the absentee, this would not be a problem, since a blind person does not possess the organ of sight.

Bhāṭṭa: No. The sense organ that you fancy as the grasper of an absence exhausts itself in grasping the substratum. And so, given that a *substratum* is grasped by that sense organ that would grasp the absentee, an absence is grasped by (the cognitive means we call) non-cognition. Otherwise, when the visual organ comes into contact with an ultimate atom (of earth, for example), an absence of wateriness would be grasped—this is the difficulty.

Comments

According to Nyāya, by whatever sense organ something x would be grasped if grasped, by that same organ an absence of x is grasped. Thus, an absence of color cannot be grasped by the organ of touch. But according to the Bhāṭṭa a blind person grasping the substratum of something blue should know by non-cognition that it is not yellow. The Bhāṭṭa handles the difficulty by pointing out that on his view a particular kind of grasping of the substratum of an absence is required—a grasping, to wit, that occurs by the same sense organ that would grasp the absentee—before an absence can be known by the separate and distinct cognitive means, non-cognition.

Moreover, since an ultimate atom is not graspable by any sense organ, the requirement that the substratum of an absence first be grasped cannot be met, and so it is impossible to know by non-cognition an absence of wateriness in an ultimate atom of earth. However, this explanation is not available to the Naiyāyika who gives the visual organ the miraculous power to grasp absential qualifiers of the contacted. The Bhāṭṭa's proposed rule that a sense organ exhausts itself in grasping what it is capable of grasping blocks the untoward consequence facing the Naiyāyika.

Text (p. 708, Tirupati, and p. 679, Calcutta) and Translation

> atha evaṃ vāyau rūpâ-bhāvo jale tiktâ-bhāvaḥ pāṣāṇe saurabhâ-bhāvaś ca na gṛhyeta | vāyv-ādīnāṃ pratiyogi-grāhakaiś cakṣur-ādibhir a-grahāt | na ca tava api te '-bhāvāḥ kathaṃ pratyakṣāḥ, vāyv-ādīnāṃ tad-indriyâ-yogyatvād iti vācyam | liṅgena tvag-ādinā vā upanīte vāyv-ādau yogya-rūpâdy-a-bhāva-viśeṣyakaṃ pratyakṣaṃ cakṣur-ādinā eva na vāyv-ādi-viśeṣyakam, pratyakṣe yogya-viśeṣyasya hetutvād iti cet, na | vāyv-ādau rūpâdy-a-bhāva-pratītīnām an-upalabdhi-liṅgakatvāt | tava nī-rūpo vāyur iti vāyu-viśeṣyâ-bhāva-pratīti-vat |

Objection (by a Naiyāyika): An absence of color in air, an absence of bitter taste in water (which, unmixed, is by nature sweet), and an absence of fragrance in a stone could not be grasped in this way, since air and the others are not grasped by the graspers of the absentees (just mentioned), which are the visual organ and the rest (as the case may be).

And you should not say (to counter this objection) that for us, too, since air and the others are not suitable for being grasped by that particular sense organ (that grasps the absentee), there is the question of how these absences could be known perceptually. That which is perceptually known by the visual organ and the rest (as the case may be) is that whose qualificandum is not air and the like (which cannot be known by the visual organ, etc.), but rather the absence of perceptible color or the like. (That is, such an absence is the qualificandum.) Such is so known in air or the like (i.e., air as qualifier: an *airy* absence of color), air or the like that is itself knowable either by means of an inferential mark or by being presented by the organ of touch, etc. (extraordinarily, like the fragrance of sandalwood presented by the visual organ). For, a perceptible qualificandum is a cause of perception (never a qualificandum not capable of being perceived).

Bhāṭṭa: No. Cognitions of the absence of color, etc., in air, etc., arise (inferentially) with a *non-cognition* as the inferential mark—like the cognition, "Air lacks color," which for you, too, is of an absence whose qualificandum is air.

Comments

Nyāya holds that perceptual retrieval sparked by an extraordinary sensory connection is limited to qualifiers; the substrata, or qualificanda, do not appear perceptually through such a means. (See p. 125 for more on the theory of extraordinary sensory connection.) The Bhāṭṭa's alternative theory is clear: such problematic cognitions are simply not perceptual—you Naiyāyikas are mistaken about this—but rather inferential, with a non-cognition as the prover or inferential mark.

The example the Bhāṭṭa gives is particularly telling against the Naiyāyika because there the qualificandum is not the absence but rather air, the Naiyāyika's (implausible) claim to the contrary notwithstanding. (That the absence is the qualificandum and air the qualifier seems implausible initially, but it turns out to be crucial to Gaṅgeśa's position.) In any case, at least by *Old* Nyāya's lights, air is not known perceptually, but is known by inference from its perceptible touch. So, the presumed parallelism would appear to be in the Bhāṭṭa's favor.

Text (p. 709, Tirupati) and Translation

> atha bhūtale a-bhāva-dhīr indriya-janyā sākṣātkāritvāt, tata eva viśeṣaṇatā-kalpanam api | na ca sākṣātkāritvam a-siddham | parokṣatve a-jñāta-karaṇatvân-upapatteḥ | tathā hi, mandirôdare caitro nipuṇam anusṛto 'pi na ca upalabdha ity āpta-vākyâvagatân-upalabdhyā śrotā anuminoti na āsīt tatra caitra iti | evam a-bhāva-dhīḥ parokṣā cet tadā na a-jñāta-karaṇikā, parokṣatva-jāteḥ jñāta-karaṇa-prayojyatvāt | tasmāt sākṣātkāritvam a-jñāta-karaṇatvāt | na ca indriya-janyatvam upādhiḥ, tata eva tat-sādhanād iti cet, mā evam | parokṣatvaṃ hi na jātiḥ, anubhavatvena saṃkara-prasaṅgāt | kiṃ tu sākṣātkāri-bhinna-jñānatvam | evaṃ ca a-bhāva-jñānaṃ parokṣam eva smṛti-vat | yathā ca jñāta-karaṇatve 'pi śabdâdiḥ na anumitiḥ, evam a-jñāta-karaṇatve 'pi indriya-janyaṃ sākṣātkāri,[4] an-upalabdhi-janyam tad-vijātīyam an-upalabdham | yadi ca a-jñāta-karaṇatvena sākṣātkāritvaṃ tadā jñāta-karaṇatvena śābdâder anumititvâpattiḥ | jñāta-karaṇatve 'pi liṅgâdi-karaṇa-bhedāt anumity-ādi-phala-bheda iti cet, a-jñātân-upalabdhîndriya-karaṇa-bhedāt phala-bheda iha api | evaṃ ca sākṣātkāritve indriya-janyatvaṃ parokṣatve ca tad-a-janyatvaṃ prayojakam, na tu jñātâ-jñāta-karaṇa-janyatvam, gauravāt smṛtāv a-bhāvāc ca |

Objection (by a Naiyāyika putting forth an inference): An absential cognition of a floor (i.e., of an absence of a pot on a floor, for example) is sense-organ generated, *since* it is immediate. Just for this reason, qualifierhood is to be postulated (as the sensory connection), too.

And immediacy (in such cases) is not unestablished, since with the *mediately* known (*parokṣa*) it is impossible that the chief instrumental cause *not* be cognized (and, in the case of the absences we are discussing, that cause, the "trigger," is not itself cognized). For example, Caitra (let us imagine) has been thoroughly sought out in a temple but has not been seen. Someone hearing of this through an authority's statement, and understanding that he was not perceived, infers, "Caitra was not there." In this way, an absential cognition can be inferential, (and) if it is, then its chief instrumental cause would not be *un*cognized (since inference depends on an inferential mark being cognized), in that in general the mediately known is caused by a chief instrumental cause that is itself cognized. And to have a cognized instrumental cause is to have a cognition as instrumental cause, since (a cognition of an inferential mark is the chief cause of an inference, that is to say) a (mere) inferential mark, etc., does not generate an inference.

Therefore (we have in the case of some absential cognitions) immediacy, since the instrumental cause is not cognized.

And it is not the case that being-generated-by-a-sense-organ is an "undercutter" (*upādhi*, undermining the inference: "An absential cognition of, for example, a floor is sense-organ generated, *since* it is immediate). Just from that inference is it established (that some absential cognitions are sense-organ generated).

Bhāṭṭa: Don't think like that. For, the shared character of being mediately known is not a universal since it would cross-sect with the property of being experiential—this is the difficulty. Rather, to be mediately known is to be a cognition distinct from that which is immediate. And thus an absential cognition is mediate only, like a memory.

Furthermore, as a verbally mediated cognition and the like are not inferential cognitions although their chief instrumental causes are cognized, so the sense-organ generated is immediate although the chief instrumental cause is not cognized. Belonging to a different category from these is the *non-cognized* (known by non-cognition).

Moreover, if (you hold that) the immediate is known by having as chief instrumental cause something that is not itself cognized, then there is the unfortunate ramification (unfortunate for you) that verbal cognitions, etc., as known by having as chief instrumental cause something that is cognized would be inferences (that is, they could not, by that criterion, be distinguished from inferences).

Objection: Although all have as chief instrumental cause something that is cognized, results that are nevertheless distinct—viz., inferential cognitions and the others (verbal cognitions, etc.)—issue from differences of instrumental cause in an inferential mark and so forth.

Bhāṭṭa: In that case, (we can say) distinct results issue here, too, from differences of instrumental cause in uncognized non-cognitions as opposed to sense organs.

And so, for the immediate the criterion is: being generated by a sense organ. And for the mediate: not being generated like that. But these are not (what you have said) being generated by a chief instrumental cause that is cognized or not cognized. For, that thesis is cumbersome and does not apply to memory.

Comments

From the time of the original Bhāṭṭa, Kumārila himself (c. 600), examples such as the one put forth by the Naiyāyika here about Caitra and Maitra have been touchstones for rival accounts of knowledge of absences. Here Caitra's absence is not only known by Maitra at a time later than the absence's occurrence—a circumstance that in itself might make it appear that the absence is not known by perception, opening the door for the Bhāṭṭa's non-cognition—the absence, according to the Naiyāyika, is known by perception by the person who has searched the temple looking for Caitra. It is known by inference by Maitra who has been told by the authority that Caitra was not seen. (Kumārila's example eliminates the authority and the temple search: a cognizer S, having himself been in a certain house, is asked later in the day at a distant place whether a certain person A—the absentee—was in the house. Reflecting, he realizes A was not there, though this is the first time that day he has even thought about A. Kumārila argues that because of a clear lack of sensory activity as a cause of S's absential knowledge non-cognition should be considered the cognitive means.[5]) The Naiyāyika objector in the passage above is trying to take the sting out of the apparent counterexamples to his theory of perceptually known absences by himself pointing to cases that are clearly non-perceptual, in this case Maitra's inferential absential knowledge launched from a bit of testimony ("Caitra was not seen"). Although Maitra's knowledge is inferential and is itself launched from testimony, perception still plays a crucial role—in line with the standard Naiyāyika analysis of authoritative testimony—since it accounts here for the trustworthiness of the authority. (The current example is constructed to show the Naiyāyika in a good light, but later Gaṅgeśa will handle the Bhāṭṭa's own favorite version and show that it, too, lines up with the Nyāya view.)

Again, the Naiyāyika objector is able to exploit the example to make his main point, namely, that some absential cognition is immediate. It is that had by the authority, he implies. To elaborate, the chief instrumental cause (*karaṇa*) of a perceptual awareness is a sense organ, according to both camps. Sense organs are not themselves cognized in a perceptual occurrence. This is unlike the case with an inferential awareness where the *karaṇa* is a cognized inferential mark. The Naiyāyika argues that by having this type of chief cause some absential cognitions—of the absence of Maitra as known by the person who has searched for him, for instance—are perceptual.

To wind up a strong case, the Naiyāyika puts forth an inference and anticipates a proposed "undercutter" (*upādhi*) which he dismantles. The rejected undercutter does indeed pervade the probandum of his inference in that it is the same property: being-generated-by-a-sense-organ. But it also pervades the prover—since all immediate cognitions are, at least according to Nyāya, sense-organ generated—and so it is not a true undercutter. See above, pp. 160–61, for explanation of undercutters.

The Bhāṭṭa begins his response by again reminding us that according to both schools an inference is not immediate, being mediated by a cognized inferential mark. Therefore, there would be cross-sectioning between the experiential (perception) and the mediate (inference) on the Naiyāyika's proposal. Of course, this assumes that the Naiyāyika wants to uphold the experiential and the mediate as genuine universals. And though presumably he does, his commitment would not be, it seems, very heartfelt, since the issue of the natural cuts among cognitive types is, as everyone sees, extremely complex. So the argument, while a winner, is not much of a blow. (See, in this book, pp. 700–701, on cross-sectioning as "blocking" a property's counting as a true universal.)

Like an inference, which depends on an inferential mark being cognized, a verbal awareness depends on cognition of the statement of an authority. It is not immediate, like inference, but it is also supposed to be distinct from inference. Thus the Naiyāyika cognitive typology seems all the more problematic.

Memory depends on previous experience but not on a *cognized*—i.e., perceptually cognized—chief instrumental cause (triggering a remembering as the effect), since a memory-impression, *saṃskāra*, is that which directly brings a remembering about and memory-impressions do not lie within direct cognitive grasp. In sum, the Naiyāyika has misanalyzed his example, and all the cross-categorizing he indulges in makes his view a hopeless tangle.

Text (p. 712, Tirupati) and Translation

> nanv an-upalabdhir na mānam, bhāva-bhūta-māna-sahakṛtasya eva manaso bāhyânubhava-janakatvād iti cet, na | bhāvatvasya gurutvena a-prayojakatvāt | anyathā indriya-sahakṛtasya eva manaso bāhyânubhava-janakatvam ity anumānâdi na mānaṃ syāt | na ca idam a-bhāva-jñānaṃ bhāva-māna-manas-sādhyaṃ bāhyâ-bhāva-jñānatvāl liṅgâdi-janyâ-bhāva-jñāna-vad iti vācyam | ayam a-bhāvo na indriya-grāhyaḥ a-bhāvatvād a-yogyâ-bhāva-vad, iyam a-bhāva-buddhir na indriya-janyā a-bhāva-buddhitvāt liṅgâdi-janyâ-bhāva-buddhi-vat iti sat-pratipakṣāt |

Objection: Non-cognition is not a means to right cognition, because the mind (*manas*) aided only by a cognitive means that is a positive presence (e.g., a sense organ, not a non-cognition, which is an *absence* of cognition, not a positive presence) brings about awareness of an external object.

Bhāṭṭa: No. (The qualification) "being a presence" is cumbersome and is unmotivated. Otherwise, i.e., if the mind aided only by a sense organ (a positive presence) brought about awareness of an external object, then inference and the rest would not be cognitive means.

Objection (by a Naiyāyika putting forth an inference): A cognition of an absence is accomplished by the mind aided by a positive cognitive means (viz., a sense organ), *since* it is a cognition of an absence of something external, like absential cognition generated by an inferential mark or the like.

Bhāṭṭa: That should not be said. An absence is not grasped by a sense organ, *since* it is an absence (not a presence), like an absence of something incapable of being cognized. (Furthermore) there is a counterinference (showing that your prover does not cut the ice): a cognition of an absence is *not* generated by a sense organ, *since* it is an absential cognition, like an absential cognition generated by an inferential mark or the like.

Comments

The Bhāṭṭa's first retort depends on not counting absential cognition as a "positive presence." The Naiyāyika restates his argument formally: absential cognition of something external (e.g., a pot) in every instance is brought about by the *manas* aided by a sense organ, and so absential cognition in general should be regarded as so caused. Thus, whatever the *pramāṇa*, the "knowledge source," that brings it about, a sense organ would be an auxiliary cause, and a sense organ is something positive. The example or inductive basis for the conclusion is absential cognition generated by any cognitive means, such as inference. Even if we are remembering something that is a sign of something else—e.g., an absence of fire which entails an absence of smoke—the remembering has to be informed by a perception-generated memory-impression. The argument is rather weak, but it expresses Nyāya's causal realism and commitment to perception as the fundamental way we know the world.

The Bhāṭṭa's rebuttal is comprised of two inferences. First, he asserts his thesis that no absence is grasped by a sense organ. The prover: an absence of something incapable of being cognized. Surely a sense organ does not make an absence of a hare's horn known. But, of course, neither can a non-cognition make that confused sort of thing known, and the Bhāṭṭa's second counter is stronger. It is a precisely worded "counterinference," *sat-pratipakṣa*, which uses the same example as cited in the Naiyāyika inference, the same inductive basis. The lesson is that the comparison class is disputed along the same lines as the inferential subject's possessing the probandum. Thus, no conclusion may be drawn.

Text (p. 713, Tirupati) and Translation

atha pratiyogi-grāhakaṃ mānaṃ tad-a-bhāvam api gṛhṇāti yathā anumānâdi, pratiyogi-grāhakaṃ ca indriyam, ato a-bhāva-grāhakam iti cet, na | bhāva-grāhakayor eva liṅga-śabdayos tad-a-bhāvâ-grāhakatvāt | pratiyogi-grāhaka-jātīyaṃ mānaṃ tathā iti cet, na | upamāne vyabhicārāt | na ca cakṣuṣṭvâdikam a-bhāva-grāhaka-vṛtti jātitvāt, upamānatvaṃ ca na jātir iti vācyam | prāptiṃ vinā cakṣur-āder a-bhāvâ[6]-grāhakatva-sādhanāt |

Objection (by a Naiyāyika): The cognitive means that would grasp an absentee (were it present, e.g., a pot) grasps also its absence, as is the case with inference and the rest. And the grasper is a sense organ. Therefore, it grasps the absence.

Bhāṭṭa: No. For, the inferential marks and bits of verbal testimony that make known (or grasp) a positive presence do not make known their absences.

Objection: The cognitive means is the same type as that which would grasp the absentee.

Bhāṭṭa: No, because "analogy" (*upamāna*) is a counterexample.

Objection: Being-the-visual-organ and the others (viz., the universals of the sense organs, being-the-organ-of-touch, etc.) occur in those things which grasp absences, because they are universals, whereas being-analogy is not a universal (and so your counterexample is discounted).

Bhāṭṭa: That should not be said. For, it is established that, without a real reaching of the object, the visual organ and the others cannot grasp an absence.

Comments

According to Mīmāṃsā, the means of knowledge called analogy grasps a similarity but not an absence of similarity. Nyāya understands analogy somewhat differently, but agrees that analogy is not a means to absential knowledge. So this stands as a counterexample to the Naiyāyika's proposal that an absence is known by the same cognitive means whereby the absentee would be known were it present.

The entire question of the correct topography for cognitive subtypes is raised again by the objector's final move: analogy's being peculiar in not obeying the proposed rule is explained by the fact that there is no universal, analogyhood, unlike the case with the other three veridical cognitive means. Unfortunately, the question is too complex for a brief treatment. Suffice it to say that in context such ontological maneuvering is unconvincing. And the Bhāṭṭa ignores it, repeating, at the end, his basic position that an absence as a cognitive object is not "reached" by a sense organ.

Text (p. 714, Tirupati, and p. 683, Calcutta) and Translation

atha bhāva-vṛtty-a-bhāva-bhramaḥ sa ca karaṇa-doṣāt | na ca pratiyogi-smṛty-āśraya-grahân-upalabdhayaḥ sva-rūpato duṣṭāḥ, kiṃ tu indriyaṃ pittâdinā duṣṭam iti tad eva ca bhrama-hetur ity a-bhāva-pramāyām api tad eva mānam iti cet, na | indriyasya api duṣṭatvaṃ, doṣa-sāhitya-mātram, na tv anyat | tac ca an-upalabdhāv api tulyam | na ca jñāta-karaṇâ-janya-bhramatvena indriya-janyatvam | evaṃ hi a-bhāva-pramā-karaṇatvam api indriyasya tata eva astu kim anayā kusṛṣṭyā | evam astu iti cet, na | prāpty-a-bhāvena uktôttaratvāt | kiṃ ca a-saṃnikṛṣṭe 'pi doṣād upanīte '-bhāve bhrama indriyeṇa saṃbhavati, cakṣuṣā pāṣāṇaḥ surabhir iti bhrama-vat | a-bhāva-pramā na saṃbhavati prāpty-a-bhāvād ity uktam |

Objection (by a Naiyāyika): The error that presents an absence where there is a presence comes about (we both agree) from a defect in an instrumental cause. And it is not the case that (a) memory of an absentee, (b) grasping of a substratum, or (c) non-cognition are, by nature, liable to being defective. Rather, a sense organ becomes defective, as, for instance, an organ afflicted by bile (causing white things to be seen as yellow). Thus, that alone causes such an error. Thus, just that alone is the cognitive means for a veridical cognition of an absence.

Bhāṭṭa: No. A sense organ can (in a sense) be defective, but only *as associated with* a defect, not otherwise (i.e., not as defective in itself). And that holds equally, too, with a non-cognition.

Furthermore, it is not the case that (absential) error as *not* generated by an instrumental cause that is cognized *is* generated by a sense organ that is not cognized. For, a sense organ is (you hold) also in that way an instrument giving rise to a veridical awareness of an absence. So if just because of that (power of a sense organ to bring about veridical awareness you would reason as you do), well, let it be so conceived. Then enough of this imagining that it could be defective!

Objection: Let it be *so* conceived (that is, that it could be defective).

Bhāṭṭa: No. We have already given a (cogent) reply: there is no real reaching of the object. Moreover, though there be no object in sensory connection, there can come about, because of a defect, an error concerning an absence presented extraordinarily (*upanīta*) by a sense organ—like the error presented by the visual organ, "The stone is fragrant." But a veridical awareness of an absence cannot come about in that way, because there is no real reaching of the object—as we have said.

Comments

According to the Bhāṭṭa, an absential cognition comes about by, first in the process, a sensory grasping of an absence's substratum coupled with a remembering of an absentee, and, after that, a non-cognition occurring through the Bhāṭṭa's special cognitive means. The mystery in this account is brought out by the question of how absential errors are to be explained. The problem appears especially difficult given that—as is held by both Nyāya and Bhāṭṭa Mīmāṃsā—cognitive error results from a defect in a cognitive instrument. How can it be that we can have a *non*-veridical awareness of an absence? What goes wrong with which instrument on the Bhāṭṭa theory? None of the instruments identified by the Bhāṭṭa are liable to defects, the Naiyāyika objector claims. Thus, it would appear that a sense organ—which is the chief instrumental cause, *karaṇa*, for a perception—would be what goes wrong in the case of a non-veridical absential awareness, suggesting, by an economy of conception, that the sense organs bring about veridical absential awarenesses, too. "Non-cognition" would be, then, otiose.

The Bhāṭṭa, however, views all defects as *bodily* defects, and the sense organs, in his view, are not bodily organs. (One reason for their incorporeality is that they are themselves imperceptible, "beyond the senses," *atīndriya*, a position with which Nyāya agrees.) Thus, according to the Bhāṭṭa, the sense organs themselves are never defective; defects occur in auxiliary causes, such as the eyeball.

Text (p. 715, Tirupati) and Translation

> nanu adhikaraṇâ-bhāvayor viśiṣṭa-buddhir asti | sā na indriya-janyā a-bhāva-buddhitvāt, na an-upalabdhi-janyā bhāva-buddhitvāt, na ubhaya-janyā jāti-saṃkara-prasaṅgāt | ata ubhaya-grāhakam indriyam abhyupeyam iti cet, a-bhāvavad-bhūtalam ity an-upalabdhy-upanītâ-bhāva-viśiṣṭa-buddhir indriyeṇa eva cakṣuṣā candanaṃ surabhi iti-vat | bhūtale ghaṭo na asti iti ca cakṣur-upanīta-bhūtale '-bhāva-buddhir an-upalabdhyā eva, ghrāṇena candane saurabham iti-vat | yat tu vyāpārâ-bhāvān na an-upalabdhiḥ pramāṇam, vyāpāravata eva karaṇatvād iti | tan na | kriyayā a-yoga-vyavacchedena saṃbandhi karaṇaṃ na tu vyāpāravad ity api viśeṣaṇaṃ gauravād iti |

Objection: A locus and an absence are both contents of a single cognition of an entity as qualified. Such a cognition is not sense-generated (let us suppose, following your lead), because it is of an absence, and it is not generated by (your) non-cognition, because it is of a presence (the locus, namely). It is not generated by both, because, if so, there would be a cross-section of universals—this is the difficulty. Hence, that a sense organ can grasp both (an absence and a presence) must be accepted.

Bhāṭṭa: "The floor does not have *x* on it," is a cognition of an entity as qualified, with an absence (as qualifier) presented (extraordinarily) by means of a non-cognition. It is indeed by means of the visual organ (contacting the floor) that it comes about—like the cognition, "The sandalwood is fragrant" (occurring when sandalwood is only seen, not also physically smelt). (Conversely) "The pot is not on the floor" is a cognition of an absence (as qualificandum) on a floor (as qualifier) presented by the visual organ. It is indeed by means of a non-cognition (grasping the absence) that it comes about—like the cognition, "There is fragrance in the sandalwood," delivered by the organ of smell.

Objection: In lacking employment in an "operation," (your) non-cognition is not a means of knowledge (is not the chief instrumental cause of a veridical cognition). Only those things that are employed in an operation can be a *means* (i.e., the sort of instrumental cause, *karaṇa*, that any veridical cognitive means, *pramāṇa*, must be).

Bhāṭṭa: That's wrong. A relatee is the chief instrumental cause through an absence of a lack of connection with an action (i.e., through being an action, or in action), not also as the qualification (you want to add, namely) "having employment in an operation," since that is theoretically cumbersome.

Comments

The Bhāṭṭa holds that there is a single cognition involving a presence as well as an absence when an absence is cognized—and this he holds whether the absence is cognized as a qualifier, as in the first example, or as the qualificandum, as in the second. He regards as compatible the dual presentational means necessary to achieve such a cognitive synthesis—between the absence presented and the presence—albeit the one involves an "extraordinary" sensory connection and the other a sensory connection of the ordinary kind (e.g., contact).

Among New Naiyāyikas after Gaṅgeśa—in particular Raghunātha c. 1525 and later Navyas—the dominant stance, according to Ramanuja Tatacharya, rejects the position voiced by the Naiyāyika objector here, namely, that the instrumental cause most directly responsible for bringing about an effect—the *karaṇa*—requires an activity called technically an "operation" or "employment," *vyāpāra*. As noted, such an operation is a property or activity of the instrument, such as the *bringing down* of an axe, that effects a result, for instance, the felling of a tree. (See above, pp. 24–5.) Whereas Gaṅgeśa generally agrees with earlier Naiyāyikas that a true chief instrumental cause does require such employment (or he does so in this chapter), the Bhāṭṭa here suggests the later Nyāya opinion, to wit, that the so-called operation itself is the *karaṇa*. Such, in turn, does not require another employment—for fear of infinite regress among other difficulties, all summed up here as theoretic cumbersomeness.

The section's *siddhânta* begins with the next passage, where Gaṅgeśa puts forth and defends his own views. The divide is not marked in either the Asiatic Society or the Vidyapeetha edition.

Text (p. 716, Tirupati, and p. 685, Calcutta) and Translation

atra ucyate | pratiyogi-grāhakêndriyeṇa āśraya-graho na hetuḥ | prāṅ-nāstitā-grahe tu tvan-nayena vyabhicārāt | vāyvâdau ca rūpâdy-a-bhāva-dhīr indriya-janyā eva, na an-upalabdhi-liṅga-janyā, an-upalabdher a-jñānāt | āpta-vākyasya iva taj-jñāpakasya a-bhāvāt |

Gaṅgeśa: Here we answer. A grasping of a substratum by the sense organ that would grasp an absentee is not a cause of absential cognition, since there is a counterexample: a later cognition of something's not being somewhere at an earlier time can occur (without, at the time of the absential cognition, any such grasping occurring).

Further, a cognition of an absence of color, etc., in air, etc., is in fact generated by a sense organ, not by a non-cognition as inferential mark, because a non-cognition is not cognized. Similarly, there is no statement of an authority that makes such an absence known.

Comments

A bit below (pp. 429ff), Gaṅgeśa elaborates a concrete counterexample described only abstractly here, the very case cited by Kumārila (as noted above) as an instance of non-cognition as a cognitive means. Whereas Kumārila concocts his example to show absential knowledge without sensory activity, Gaṅgeśa turns the missile back to explode the Bhāṭṭa contention that there need be sensory contact with the substratum of the absence known. At the time when Maitra's absence is cognized, that is, when a cognizer, Caitra, remembers that he was not in the house, there is no sensory contact with the house, which is at the time of the remembering a long way off.

There can be no inference without an inferential mark being cognized. If, therefore, a non-cognition is not cognized, it cannot serve as such a mark. This opens a new line of debate with the Bhāṭṭa, who is committed to such inferences.

Text (p. 717, Tirupati) and Translation

> atha a-jñātā eva rūpâdy-upalambhasya an-upalabdhī rūpâdy-an-upalabdhiṃ gṛhṇāti bhūtale ghaṭâ-bhāvam iva iti cet, tvan-mate upalambhasya atīndriyatvena yogyân-upalabdhyā upalambhâ-bhāvasya grahītum a-śakyatvāt | an-upalabdhi-mātrasya a-bhāvâ-grāhakatvāt | astu tarhi jñānaṃ yogyam iti cet, na | apasiddhântāt | yogyatve 'pi bhūtalīya-ghaṭâ-bhāve 'pi jñātā eva yogyân-upalabdhir liṅgam astu, yogyâ-ghaṭôpalambhasya an-upalabdhyā graha-saṃbhavāt kṛtam an-upalabdhyā mānântareṇa |

Objection (advanced by the Bhāṭṭa): Simply remaining *uncognized*, a non-cognition of a cognition of color and the like (in air and so forth) grasps a non-cognition of color and so forth, like an absence of a pot on a floor.

Gaṅgeśa: On your view, cognition is beyond the range of the senses (being known, instead, by an inference from the property, having-been-cognized). (Therefore) a non-cognition that is "capable of being (perceptually) cognized" cannot be the means whereby such an absence of cognition is grasped (because the absentee cannot be perceptually grasped, on your view). (Also) a simple (unqualified) non-cognition (as opposed to a non-cognition qualified by the property of being capable of being perceptually cognized) cannot be the grasper of the absence.

Objection: Okay, then let it be held that cognition *is* capable of being (perceptually) cognized.

Gaṅgeśa: No, for that would amount to abandoning your view.

(Furthermore) let us assume that cognition is capable of being (perceptually) cognized—allowing, then, that a *cognizable* non-cognition, even in the case of a pot's absence on a floor, is a cognized inferential mark (i.e., a perceived non-cognition would spark an inference to the absence). (Then, it would be possible to infer, contrary to our earlier argument, that air has no color, with a non-cognition as the inferential mark. However, another problem emerges.) If this were indeed the case, then, since the grasping would occur through a non-cognition of a *cognizable* pot (i.e., a *cognized* non-cognition of a *cognizable* pot, with a *cognition* of a non-cognition triggering the inference), better give up this supposition of "non-cognition" as an additional cognitive means!

Comments

Gaṅgeśa draws out the ramification that a non-cognition (of color, etc.) would be itself an absence of a certain kind of perception, with the perception as the absentee or *pratiyogin*. Therefore, the cognition would have to be itself perceptible. But, according to Bhāṭṭa principles, no cognition is supposed to be itself perceptible—thus an internal contradiction.

The logic of Gaṅgeśa's last argument—on the presumption that a non-cognition is, as a cognition, perceptible—is difficult but clear. No problem is solved by announcing *non*-cognition as the special means whereby absences are known, since non-cognition is itself an absence (it is even called absence, *a-bhāva*, by Kumārila, as noted above). Thus the question arises: how is this second absence known? Specifically, there is no point in postulating as an additional cognitive means a non-cognition that itself needs to be known perceptually so that an absence of cognition could be inferred. Simplicity restricts us to perception and inference.

Text (p. 717, Tirupati) and Translation

ghaṭâ-bhāva-dhīr a-jñāta-karaṇikā liṅgâdy-anusandhānaṃ vinā jāyamānatvād iti cet, na | vāyvâdau rūpâdy-a-bhāva-pratītir api tathā | atha rūpâdimattayā jñātatvâ-bhāvaḥ tad-anumiti-rūpavattân-upalabdhir vā liṅgam iti cet, na | vāyâdau jñātatvâ-bhāvasya api rūpâdy-a-bhāva-tulyatayā grahītum a-śakyatvāt | vāyâdau tasya pratyakṣatve rūpâdy-a-bhāvo 'pi tathā astu | na api kāya-vāg-vyavahārâ-bhāvena an-upalabdhir anumīyate | upekṣā-jñāna-mūka-svapnayor darśane vyabhicārāt | na ca vyavahārâ-bhāva-mātraṃ liṅgam | kasyacit vyavahārâ-bhāvasya vyabhicārāt, sarva-vyavahārâ-bhāvasya grahītum a-śakyatvāt |

Objection (by the Bhāṭṭa): The reason a cognition of an absence of a pot is not brought about by a cognized instrument is that the cognition arises without knowledge of an inferential mark, etc.

Gaṅgeśa: No. (In that case) there should be, similarly, a cognition of the absence of color, etc., in air, etc. (a view you have denied).

Objection (by the Bhāṭṭa): (There) the inferential mark is an absence of a cognizedness with respect to air's having color, etc., or it is a non-cognition of a having of color inferred from that (absence of such a cognizedness).

Gaṅgeśa: No. An absence of such a cognizedness with respect to air, etc., is on a par (epistemically) with an absence of color, etc. Thus, it could not be grasped (on your assumptions). If (you say) an absence of such a cognizedness is known by perception to be in air and so on, then let the absence of color and so on be known likewise (i.e., perceptually, which is our view).

Nor also is it any good to say that a non-cognition is inferred by means of an absence of bodily and speech behavior. For, there are counterexamples (to the assumption that a lack of such behavior is probative), namely, (a) cognitions of things to which we are indifferent as well as (b) dreams of the mute. And it is not the case that merely an absence of behavior is ever an inferential mark, since anyone's (any single person's) lack of behavior could deviate (being due to something other than the desired lack of cognition), inasmuch as an absence of (the appropriate) behavior on the part of *everyone* is something that cannot be grasped.

Comments

The Bhāṭṭa cannot sort out the cognitive means responsible for knowledge of different types of absence. His final resort would be to infer certain non-cognitions (to have that cognitive means operative) from behavior or, more precisely, from a lack thereof, whether of bodily actions other than speech or of speech itself. If there is no behavior of S's indicating a cognition of color in air, for example, we can infer an appropriate non-cognition on S's part as the way the absence is known. Gaṅgeśa counters that lack of behavior is not a sign that there is not a cognition of whatever variety, since cognitions of such things as, for example, pebbles on a road or dreams of people who cannot speak, do not issue in behavior. Furthermore, such grounds are in principle suspect, Gaṅgeśa argues at the end.

Text (p. 718, Tirupati) and Translation

kiṃ ca ghaṭavattayā jñātatvâ-bhāvena tad-anumitân-upalabdhyā vā liṅgena bhūtalâdau a-bhāvânumitir iti astu, kiṃ mānântareṇa an-upalabdhyā | api ca pratiyogi-grāhakêndriya-janyam adhikaraṇa-jñānaṃ an-upalabdhi-sahakāri tadā syāt yadi tena vinā sā na a-bhāvaṃ bodhayet | na ca etad dṛṣṭam | vāyâdau rūpâdy-a-bhāve tathā dṛṣṭam iti cet, na | a-siddheḥ | na ca vyāpti-balāt sahakāritvam | evaṃ hi vāyâdau rūpâdy-a-bhāva-pratyayo 'n-upalabdher bhavaṃs tādṛśâśrayam ākṣipet an-ākṣipe vā an-upalabdher na bhavet | tato na bhavati, kiṃ tu liṅgād iti cet, liṅgam api sā eva, tac ca dūṣitam eva | kiṃ ca na an-upalabdhir liṅgam | tato hi nī-rūpo vāyur ity anumitiḥ syāt na tu vāyau rūpâ-bhāva iti |

(**Gaṅgeśa** continues:) Moreover (if you were to say) let there be an inference to the absence on the floor, etc., by means of an inferential mark—with the inferential mark as either (a) an absence having been cognized as (the floor's) pot-possessing or (b) a non-cognition inferred from that (absence)—then, what would be the point of presuming this "non-cognition" as an additional cognitive means? (Inference would suffice.)

Furthermore (according to you) a cognition of a substratum of an absence would be generated by the same sense organ that would grasp the absence's absentee. That (let us suppose, according to your view) would be, then, a non-cognition's causal auxiliary, given that no non-cognition without it could make an absence known. However, that is not found (in some cases).

Objection: It is found—as there is found a cognition of an absence of color or the like in air or the like.

Gaṅgeśa: No, it is not established (in all cases of absential cognition).

Nor is its status as an auxiliary cause derived from the force of a pervasion (wherever an absence is cognized, there such a grasping of a substratum is to be found). For, if so—there being a cognition of an absence of color or the like in air or the like, occurring by means of a non-cognition—one would (presumably, according to your view) have to cognize such a (contacted) substratum by circumstantial postulation (*ākṣepa* = *arthâpatti*). (However, formerly you said the substratum would be directly grasped; now, it is by postulation.) Or, if there is to be no such circumstantial postulation, then there would be no absential cognition resulting from non-cognition (since the preconditions for a non-cognition would not have been met; however, absential cognitions do occur).

Objection: Absential cognition does not result from non-cognition but rather from an inferential mark.

Gaṅgeśa: (According to you) the inferential mark would be just that (namely, a non-cognition), and that view has already been savaged by us.

Moreover, non-cognition is not an inferential mark. For, from that, "Air does not have color," would be an inference (presupposing what is contrary to your view, namely, that the qualificandum, air, is perceptible), in contrast to, "There is an absence of color in air" (where the absence is the qualificandum: an airy absence).

Comments

"Air does not have color," would be the form of the conclusion of an inference that had a non-cognition of color as inferential mark. Air would be the *pakṣa*, the inferential subject, the location where the absence is reasoned to occur. But such a subject must be perceptible, and, according to the Bhāṭṭa (along with Old Nyāya, too) air is not perceptible. (For more on this, see the comments at the beginning of the section on air's perceptibility, below, pp. 490–91.)

"Circumstantial postulation" (*arthâpatti* or, as here, *ākṣepa*) is an independent *pramāṇa* according to the Bhāṭṭa. By this special cognitive means we know, for example, that, given that fat Devadatta does not eat during the day, he eats at night. Naiyāyikas agree that we do have knowledge in this and similar cases, but see the examples as forms of inference.

Gaṅgeśa's main argument is that there is no reason to postulate non-cognition since perception, rightly understood, can explain a broad range of absential cognitions and since inference based on perception another broad range that is not perceptual. He supplements this with exposure of confusions internal to the Bhāṭṭa view. Now we get a new argument.

Text (p. 719, Tirupati) and Translation

api ca ghaṭavaty upalambha-prāk-kāle 'n-upalabdhyā ghaṭa-smṛtimataḥ kuto na a-bhāva-dhīḥ | ghaṭâ-bhāvâ-bhāvād iti cet, tarhi a-bhāva-rūpârtha-janyâ-bhāva-buddhir artha-janyatvena sākṣātkāriṇī indriya-janyā ca syāt | tadā ghaṭa eva pratibandhaka iti cet, tathā api tad-a-bhāvo '-bhāva-buddhau janaka eva syāt |

(**Gaṅgeśa** continues:) Furthermore, at a time prior to a perception of something having a pot on it, why is there not, by (your) non-cognition, an absential cognition on the part of someone who remembers a pot?

Bhāṭṭa: Because there is an absence of an absence of a pot.

Gaṅgeśa: Then, the absential cognition is generated by an absence in the form of something objective. (And) as generated by an object it would be immediate and sense-organ generated (which is our view).

Objection: Then, the pot itself is the blocker (of a non-veridical absential cognition generated by non-cognition—at a time before a pot perception occurs).

Gaṅgeśa: Still, in that case, too, its absence would indeed generate the absential cognition (and so, again, we would have perception as the means of absential knowledge).

Comments

Not every non-cognition (of a perceptible object) leads to knowledge of absence. There would be a non-cognition of a pot, Gaṅgeśa points out, prior to a pot's perception, albeit a pot was on the floor, and thus "knowledge" of its absence—which is absurd.

To formulate the conclusion of the current line of argument, Gaṅgeśa relies on an understanding of perception hammered out earlier: a cognition directly generated by an object is perceptual (cf., above, in the section on defining perception, pp. 332–33, definitions D^8 and D^9).

Next we are treated to an analysis of Kumārila's example of Caitra's knowledge of Maitra's absence. To counter the Bhāṭṭa's best punch completes the Naiyāyika victory.

Text (p. 721, Tirupati) and Translation

syād etat | gṛham upalabhya nirgataś caitro yatra kenacit pṛṣṭaḥ tatra maitra āsīd iti, sa ca kṣaṇam dhyātvā an-upalabdhyā tatra maitrâ-bhāvam avagamya āha na āsīt tatra maitra iti | sā iyaṃ prāñ-nāstitā-dhīḥ na smṛtiḥ purā gehe 'nubhūyamāne maitrâ-smaraṇena tad-a-bhāvân-anubhavāt | evaṃ ca tatra eva indriya-vyāpāraṃ vinā an-upalabdhyā a-bhāvânubhavāt anyatra api sā eva hetuḥ kḷptatvāt | tad āhuḥ, "sva-rūpa-mātraṃ dṛṣṭaṃ hi veśmâdy-arthaṃ smarann atha | tatra anyena astitāṃ pṛṣṭas tad eva pratipadyate ||" iti | mā evam | prāñ-na-astitāyāṃ hi na tāvad a-jñātân-upalabdhiḥ bhūtale ghaṭâ-bhāvasya iva a-bhāva-grāhikā, tadānīṃ gehasya viprakṛṣṭatvena yogyân-upalabdher a-bhāvāt | na api jñātā, an-avasthā-prasaṅgāt | an-upalabdher apy a-bhāva-rūpatayā an-upalabdhy-antareṇa grāhyatvāt | upalambhasya an-upalabdhir a-jñātā eva sva-rūpa-satī maitrân-upalabdhiṃ gṛṇāti cet, tvan-naye upalambhasya atīndriyatvena tad-a-bhāvasya yogyân-upalabdhy-a-grāhyatvāt |

Objection (by the Bhāṭṭa): That may be. (But consider the following.) Having experienced a house (from the inside), Caitra has gone out. At a certain place, he is asked by someone, "Was Maitra there?" And at that same place reflecting a moment, he knows by means of a non-cognition the absence of Maitra, and he says, "Maitra was not there." This cognition of non-existence at an earlier time is not a memory: although the house at the earlier time was being experienced, there is no remembering of Maitra (or his absence) because his absence was not experienced (and prior experience of *x*, we both agree, is a precondition for remembering *x*). And so just there (where the absential cognition occurs), *without the operation of the sense organs*, there is awareness of an absence by means of a non-cognition. So, elsewhere, too (with a cognition of an absence of a pot on a floor, etc.), just such a non-cognition is the cause, since it is an established category (of valid cognitive means, established by such examples).

So, he (Kumārila Bhaṭṭa) says (in *Ślokavārttika*), "For, remembering something such as a house that itself alone has been seen as it really is, someone asked by another about the existence of something there knows its absence just there (where he is asked)."

Gaṅgeśa: Don't think that way. For, there is not, first of all, an *uncognized* non-cognition of the non-existence at the earlier time, since such a thing would be able to cause a grasping of even a pot's absence on the floor, (and) since at the time (of the asking about whether Maitra was in the house) there is no non-cognition of something (viz., Maitra as in the house at the earlier time) that is (at that time) capable of being cognized, inasmuch as the house is far away. Nor is there a non-cognition that is *cognized*, because that would entail the predicament of an infinite regress. Since a non-cognition would have to occur in the form of an absence (an absence of cognition), its grasping would require another non-cognition (and so on without rest).

Objection: A non-cognition of a cognition which by its very nature is simply uncognized grasps the non-cognition of Maitra.

Gaṅgeśa: That's wrong, too, since, inasmuch as, on your view, cognition is beyond the range of the senses, its absence could not be grasped by a non-cognition that is capable of being grasped.

Comments

The dilemma that Gaṅgeśa uses to refute the Bhāṭṭa is: (a) if the non-cognition as the means the absence is cognized is supposed to be itself *cognized*, then there would have to be an impossible infinite series, since it itself is an absence, an absence of cognition, and so would require another non-cognition to be itself grasped, *ad infinitum*, or (b) if the non-cognition is supposed to be itself *un*cognized, then we would not know its nature and it might as well grasp an absence of a pot as of Maitra. Option (b), furthermore, is really a non-starter, since Caitra's later knowledge of the absence requires that his earlier non-cognition should have been registered or cognized.

The quotation is from the section on "absence" (in Kumārila's epistemic sense) in *Ślokavārttika*.[7]

Text (p. 723, Tirupati, and p. 689, Calcutta) and Translation

> atha gehasya yogya-maitravattayā smaraṇârhasya smaraṇâ-bhāvas tatra a-jñāta eva gehe maitrâ-bhāva-grāhaka iti cet, na | sva-rūpa-sataḥ smaraṇâ-bhāvasya grāhakatve tasmin saty a-bhāva-saṃśaya-viparyayâ-bhāva-prasaṅgāt | bhavati ca kadācit tatra āsīd iti viparyayas tatra āsīn na vā iti saṃśayaś ca | atha doṣāt saṃśaya-viparyayau | na ca a-sādhāraṇaṃ pramā-karaṇaṃ dūṣayanta eva doṣāḥ saṃśaya-hetavo bhavanti | na ca atra sva-rasa-siddhasya yogyâ-smaraṇasya kiṃcid dūṣitam iti vācyam | doṣa-sāhityam eva hi karaṇānāṃ duṣṭatā | na hi dūratvâdinā cakṣuṣaḥ kiṃcid apakriyate | kiṃ tu maṇy-āder dāha iva sva-rūpa-satām eva pratibandhakatvam iti cet, na | a-jñātād yogyâ-smaraṇāt tatra a-bhāva-dhīr ity a-siddheḥ | kiṃ tu manasā jñātād yogyâ-smaraṇāl liṅgāt pramāṇatvena kḷptāt tatra a-bhāva-pratīty-upapattau na an-upalabdhiḥ pramāṇântaraṃ kalpyate |

Objection (by the Bhāṭṭa): There is an absence of a remembering of the house as qualified by a perceptible Maitra, such a house that is (moreover) capable of being remembered. The absence there as itself uncognized causes the grasping of Maitra's absence in the house.

Gaṅgeśa: No. If the absence just by its own nature (as uncognized) caused the absence of remembering, then, that being (generally) the case, the unfortunate ramification would be that there could be no doubts or errors about absences. And sometimes there is such an error, "He was there" (when he was not), as also there is such a doubt sometimes, "Was he there or not?"

Bhāṭṭa: Such a doubt or error would result from defects. And no defects vitiating a veridical cognition's uncommon, chief instrumental cause bring about such doubt and so on (that is to say, those causes lie elsewhere—just as, on our view, the sense organs are not themselves defective, the defects lying in such auxiliary causes as the eyeball).

Furthermore, it should not be said that something has gone wrong here with (our) self-established non-remembering of something capable of being remembered and perceived. For, such chief instrumental causes can be said to have become defective only as accompanied by defects (not as intrinsically error-prone). For, no organ of sight (itself gets injured, i.e.) gets diminished because of distance (as when what is in the distance is unclear). Rather, as with fire and a jewel (jewels are fire-proof), the blockage (with distance) is intrinsic.

Gaṅgeśa: No. It is unshown that any cognition results from an *uncognized* (as you hold) non-remembering of something capable of being remembered and perceived. Rather, by the mind (by the *manas*, the internal organ, the "sixth" organ of sense) is apprehended (e.g., in the case of Caitra's knowing the absence of Maitra, an *ipso facto*) *cognized* non-remembering of something capable of being perceived, which serves as an inferential mark. The inferential mark results in (a veridical inferential cognition, explaining) the possibility of the absential cognition, insofar as there is (as indeed there is in the Maitra example) a genuine cognitive means (resulting in an absential cognition that is veridical). The inferential mark is (moreover) an established category that we are already using (*klpta*). Therefore, no non-cognition need be imagined as an additional cognitive means.

Comments

If every absence generated by its own nature a veridical cognition, there would be no room for non-veridical absential cognitions or for doubts about absences. But such do occur.

The Bhāṭṭa defends his view that a non-remembering—which is itself a type of non-cognition—as uncognized causes veridical absential cognition. In particular, he defends the plank of that view that says that no cognitive means is in itself liable to defect. He does so by drawing an analogy to defects in other types of error and by appealing to the notion that things are just one way and not another by nature, intrinsically.

Gaṅgeśa's response is perhaps his most forceful and summary rejection of the Bhāṭṭa theory as we find in the section. It constitutes a strong case for at least parts of his own view, too. For reasons already articulated—and by the very phenomenology of the Caitra and Maitra case—there is no such uncognized non-perception or even an uncognized non-remembering. Maitra's absence is known by inference from a *cognized* non-remembering; the inferentially crucial absence of cognition is cognized. An unstated premise appears to be that if Caitra had seen Maitra in the house, he would remember him when questioned; hearing the question would awaken (*udbodhaka*) the memory-impression (*saṃskāra*) which would have been formed by the perception. Gaṅgeśa's picture has Caitra noticing a non-remembering, a non-remembering of Maitra, and it is this cognized non-remembering that serves as the mark implying the absence of Maitra. In other words, Caitra infers, correctly, that Maitra was not in the house because he apperceives in himself an absence of a remembering that, given the situation, would have indicated the presence of Maitra in the house at the time. From that perceived absence of cognition, he makes his inference. This explanation is used for similar cognitive phenomena; that is to say, people make all sorts of inferences, from all sorts of inferential marks. Thus, there is no need to posit an additional cognitive means.

There remains outstanding, however, the (original) Bhāṭṭa argument that in such cases there is no sensory activity—no sensory *reaching* of the absence—and thus, according to Nyāya precepts, no possibility of a remembering because no memory-impression would have been formed. This problem is now raised again.

Text (p. 690, Calcutta) and Translation

> yogya-smaraṇâ-bhāvo na mano-grāhyaḥ pratyāsatty-a-bhāvāt jñānasya a-yogyatvād vā iti cet, na | vāyâdau rūpâdy-a-bhāva-pratīter laiṅgikatvena indriyânuvidhānena taj-janyatve siddhe indriya-saṃbaddha-viśeṣaṇatāyāḥ pratyāsattitva-kalpanāt taj-jñānaṃ pratyakṣam | jānāmi ity anubhavasya liṅgâdy-a-janyatvāt | na ca jñātatā liṅgam, nirākṛtatvāt | tava api katham a-bhāve saṃśaya-viparyayāv iti cet, na | liṅga-saṃśaya-viparyayābhyāṃ laiṅgika-saṃśaya-viparyaya-darśanāt |

Objection (by the Bhāṭṭa, claiming that the example has been misanalyzed): A lack of remembering of something graspable is not graspable by the *manas*, the mind, because no sensory connection would have occurred (as things look from your perspective), or because the cognition would not be subject to being grasped (as we hold).

Gaṅgeśa: Wrong. A cognition of an absence of color or the like in air or the like is not inferential, since a cognition's being generated by a sense organ is proved through correlation to (the absence or presence of activity of) a sense organ. Given this fact, we presume a sensory connection, namely, qualifierhood, which hooks up the sense organ (in the Caitra example, the *manas*) as a relatee. Thus, the cognition (to wit, the cognition of an absence of remembering) is perceptual.

(An apperception) "I know (a previous awareness as having such and such content)" is not generated by the likes of an inferential mark (but is itself perceptual).

And it is not the case that a "cognizedness" (set in an object by a previous awareness) is an inferential mark (for a previous awareness's having occurred), since that view has here been refuted already.

Objection: On your view, too, how can there be errors about absences? (There cannot be.)

Gaṅgeśa: You're mistaken. Inferential doubts and inferential errors occur (as is well-known) brought about by doubts about an inferential mark or by errors about a mark.

Comments

In the case of an absence grasped directly by the *manas*, the sensory connection would be the same as with other absential cognitions, qualifierhood. Gaṅgeśa fails to elaborate his response in the direction of the challenger's example, but, if we may so elaborate, the mind or *manas* would perceive, in the self, *ātman*, an absence of such and such a remembering, and thus trigger, so long as there were no intervening defects, an appropriate inference.

According to Nyāya, apperception is an awareness that occurs when the *manas* grasps a previous awareness that has occurred in the self. Apperception is itself perceptual, the result of the activity of the *manas* as a sense organ. Similarly, says Gaṅgeśa, the *manas* grasps an absence of remembering, and the resultant cognition is likewise perceptual.

The Bhāṭṭa, we should recall, sees the process of self-awareness, or awareness of awareness, as an inference from a cognizedness that, according to him, an awareness creates in an object it cognizes. Gaṅgeśa reminds us that he has already refuted that view—in case we expect the Bhāṭṭa to object to this citing of apperception.

Finally, just as there can be errors and doubts about other kinds of inferential marks, so there can be errors and doubts about an absence of memory or perception. An absence, like mist mistaken for smoke, would be presented pseudo-perceptually. From what is so presented, there can be inferential errors. A similar story can be told about doubts. Thus nothing requires special explanation. The Nyāya view handles all cases successfully.

Text (p. 691, Calcutta) and Translation

yadā tu sunipuṇena eka-jñāna-viṣayatā-yogyasya maitrasya anubhave sati smaraṇârhasya a-smaraṇam avadhāryate tadā anumitiḥ pramā | ata eva a-smaraṇa-mātrasya vyabhicāram upalabhya viśiṣṭâ-smaraṇaṃ jñātu-kāmasya praṇidhānam upayujyate | anyathā dhyānam an-upapannam, sva-rūpa-sata eva a-smaraṇasya a-bhāva-grāhakatvāt | tasmād yogyâ-smaraṇaṃ liṅgatvena eva upayujyate | prayogas tu, tad gehaṃ tadā maitrâ-bhāva-vat tat-tulya-parimāṇâdi-yogitayā smaraṇe 'pi tadvattayā a-smaryamāṇatvāt yad evaṃ tad evaṃ yathā ghaṭâ-bhāvavad-bhūtalam iti |

(**Gaṅgeśa** continues:) So when a very thorough person determines conclusively (e.g., that Maitra was not there) from a non-remembering of Maitra—who is fit to be remembered, given that he has been experienced previously and could have been the object of a single cognition—he then makes an inference, which is veridical. (And if there is no such conclusive determination, then doubt can arise.) For this precise reason, if someone wishes to be sure that it is not a mere failure to remember—given that such non-remembering has been found to admit of exceptions (it is not pervaded by the actual absence of what is not remembered)—but a specially qualified non-remembering (which establishes Maitra's past absence in the house), then one needs to reflect deeply. Otherwise, reflection would not occur, i.e., if the non-remembering were intrinsically the cause of the absence's being grasped. Therefore, a non-remembering that is capable of being grasped is alone used as an inferential mark (not an uncognized non-remembering).

But such (inferential) usage—that the house was qualified by an absence of Maitra, *since* it is not being remembered as qualified by him while it is being remembered—holds on the condition of such specifications as that the thing not remembered be of a size roughly equal to his. What is so is so, like a floor qualified by an absence of a pot.

Comments

Gaṅgeśa closes the section with a proviso about the size of the thing that is not remembered. Whereas not remembering seeing an elephant in a recently visited room would be a pretty good reason to conclude that no elephant was there (unless the room were the Astrodome!), not remembering seeing a mosquito in a room would not be good evidence that no mosquito was there.

In sum, the psychological picture that Gaṅgeśa draws with Kumārila's example is one in which the activity of the *manas*, as an internal and sixth sense, figures critically. Caitra's *manas* apperceives in himself—as he reflects on whether he saw Maitra in the house earlier that day—an absence of remembering that normally would have been sparked. Had Maitra been there, a remembering would have been sparked through an awakening of a memory-impression of him in the house, an awakening accomplished by the question and the reflection, the attempt to remember him. Finding an absence of remembering that such a memory-impression would prompt under the circumstances, Caitra *infers* from that perceptually grasped absence that Maitra was not in the house at the time. So, between direct sense perception and indirect inference, all the alleged cases of absential knowledge, current or remembered, are taken care of, with no need to postulate non-cognition as a separate knowledge source.

atha a-bhāva-vāda

NOW, DISCOURSE ON ABSENCE

Text (p. 730, Tirupati, and p. 693, Calcutta) and Translation

atha a-bhāvo bhāvâtmā eva | tatas tatra saṃyogâdir eva grāhaka iti na tatra viśeṣaṇatā pratyāsattiḥ | tatra prāñcaḥ | asti tāvad iha bhūtale ghaṭo na asti ity a-bādhitā buddhiḥ | sā ca iyaṃ na bhūtalâlambanā | ghaṭavaty api prasaṅgāt | na api kevala-tad-ālambanā, atirikta-kaivalyân-abhyupagamāt | bhūtalam eva kaivalyam iti cet, tarhi paunaruktyam adhikam | a-bhede ādhārâdheya-bhāvân-upapattiś ca | bhūtalam eva kaivalyam iti cet, tarhi paunaruktyam adhikam a-bhede ādhārâdheya-bhāvân-upapattiś ca |

Objection (by a Mīmāṃsaka): An absence is of the same nature as a presence. Therefore, just contact and so on cause grasping of absences (e.g., contact between a person's organ of sight and a floor causes a cognition of the floor as *not having a pot*). (Your) "qualifierhood" is not, in this case, the (as you say) operative connection.

Gaṅgeśa: On this topic, followers of the Old school reason as follows.

Old Nyāya: There occur, first of all, undefeated cognitions (such as), "The pot is *not* here on the floor." This is a cognition that does not have the floor as its (only) object (*ālambana*, in the sense of *viṣaya*), since if we assume otherwise we land in the predicament of (the same object as with a cognition of) the floor having a pot on it. Moreover, that the floor is *alone* its object is wrong, inasmuch as a separate and distinct category of *aloneness* is not recognized (by us).

Objection (by a Mīmāṃsaka): Aloneness is just the floor.

Old Nyāya: In that case, such repeating the same sense twice (i.e., using *aloneness* and *floor* as synonyms) is an additional fault (additional, that is, to the problem that without the category of absence the objector cannot distinguish a cognition of a floor with a pot from a cognition of a floor without a pot). Furthermore, if the floor and (its) aloneness are non-distinct, then the one (the absence) could not possibly stand in a locative relationship with the other (the floor, since they would be one and same entity; but a locative relation is indicated by the cognition, "*On* this floor, there is no pot," the floor being where the absence is located).

Comments[1]

The opening issue is the ontological nature of the causal factor responsible for an absential cognition as opposed to a non-absential cognition of the same locus or thing, e.g., a floor cognized as with and without a pot. Is the absence the mere floor or something distinct that can stand in relation to a sense organ? According to Nyāya, an absence is graspable by a sense organ, like a positive presence. But this seems mysterious. Just what does the sense organ grasp? Nothing but the bare locus, say the Mīmāṃsaka. The Naiyāyika has to establish his view against this seemingly simpler stance.

Text (p. 693, Calcutta) and Translation

atha adhikâ-bhāva-vādinā api a-bhāvaḥ sāśrayo vācyaḥ | deśâdi-niyamena vyavahārāt | tathā ca asti bhūtale viśeṣo yo '-bhāvâśrayaḥ | sa na bhūtala-mātram | ghaṭavaty api prasaṅgāt | na a-bhāva-yuktam, anyonyâśrayāt | na ca ghaṭavat, virodhād iti cet, na | viśeṣasya eva a-bhāvâśrayatvāt | sa ca an-anugata eva | ekâśrayatā tv an-anugatasya api ghaṭâśrayatā iva bhavati | kiṃ ca kutra a-bhāva iti, yatra pratīyate ity eva uttaram | kva pratīyeta ity atra, yatra asti ity eva | anyathā gotvâdhikam api na svīkriyeta | tad-āśraya-viśeṣād eva vyavahāra-saṃbhavāt | tathā api kīdṛśi bhūtale a-bhāva iti cet, a-bhāva-pūrva-samaye kīdṛśam bhūtalam iti praśne ghatavad iti uttaram | a-bhāva-samaye a-bhāva-vad iti | madhya-samayas tu na asty eva | iha bhūtale ghaṭo na asti ity ādhārâdheya-bhāva-pratīteś ca | a-bhāvâdhāratvaṃ bhūtalasya na pratīyate, kiṃ tu tan-mātra-buddhi-viṣayatvam iti cet, aho! vyākhyā-kauśalam | anubhavo 'pi vyākhyāya kathyate | tan-mātra-padârthâ-nirvacanaṃ ca | na hi bhūtala-buddhis tan-mātra-buddhiḥ | ghaṭavad-bhūtala-buddher api bhūtala-buddhitvāt | sā buddhir na bhūtalasya, kiṃ tu ghaṭa-bhūtalayoḥ, agnī-ṣomayor iva devatātvam iti cet, na | tato bhūtalâ-vyavahāra-prasaṅgāt | bhūtalasya a-viṣayatvāt | āśu-bhāvi-bhūtala-viṣayaka-jñānântarād iti cet, tarhi sā eva bhūtala-buddhis tan-mātra-buddhir iti tad-deśe ghaṭâ-bhāvasya vyavahāra-prasaṅgaḥ |

Objection (by a third party, challenging Old Nyāya): Those who see absence as an additional category (namely, you Naiyāyikas) must tell us what its substratum would be, since (absential) talk is restricted to a place, etc. (i.e., a place and time, for instance, the floor now where there is no pot). And so there is on (or qualifying) the floor (for example) a particular (*viśeṣa*) that has to be the substratum of the (pot's) absence. (What on your view is this particular, this something or other that is additional to the mere floor?) The particular is not the floor alone. Otherwise (as was pointed out) we land in the difficulty that it would be present in a case of the floor having a pot. The substratum of the absence is not the floor *as connected to* (or qualified by) the absence, because that would be circular. And it is (of course) not the floor having a pot on it, because of incompatibility.

Old Nyāya: Wrong. There is no substratum of the absence other than the particular itself (the floor). Moreover, such a particular is not uniform (a pot might be absent on a table or on a roof as well as a floor). Though not uniform or continuous, it is the same type of substratum as that which (for example) has a pot on it.

Furthermore, to the question, "*Where* does an absence occur?" the answer is, "*There* where it is cognized as occurring." "Where is it cognized (as occurring)?" "There where it occurs." Otherwise, there would be no grounds for accepting even (such natural kinds as) cowhood and the like, since our conventional speech behavior (talking about such groups as cows and the like) would issue just from (cognition of the unqualified) individuals that are their substrata.

Objection: Nevertheless, we may question what type of floor it is where there is an absence.

Old Nyāya: To the question, "What kind of floor is it that is there prior to the absence?" the answer is: "The kind of floor that has a pot on it!" (And) when (in contrast) there is the absence, it is the kind of floor where there is an absence. There is nothing between these alternatives.

Moreover, "There is not a pot here on the floor," is a cognition of a locative relationship (in that the floor is where the pot is not).

Objection (by a Mīmāṃsaka): A locative relation to an absence is not cognized for the floor. Rather, the objecthood of the cognition is a *mere that* (i e., the floor alone).

Old Nyāya: Aho! What skill at commentary! You are able to gloss experience, but you leave unexplained the meaning of the "mere that"! For, it is not the case that a cognition of the floor (as not having a pot) is a cognition of a "mere that," since a cognition of the floor with a pot on it is also a cognition of the floor.

Mīmāṃsaka: That cognition (of the presence of a pot on the floor) is not a cognition of the floor but, rather, of the pot and the floor, like Agni and Soma as (together) the fact of a (single) divinity (i.e., the single object addressed) of certain Vedic hymns.

Old Nyāya: No. For, in that case we would face the predicament that there would be no talk of the floor inasmuch as the floor would not be an object of cognition (we would talk instead of the pot *and* the floor).

Mīmāṃsaka: Talk of the floor issues from another cognition whose object is the floor, a cognition that follows quickly (after the cognition of the pot and the floor).

Old Nyāya: Then just such a cognition of the floor would be a cognition of a "mere that." Hence, there would be talk of an absence of a pot in a place where there is a pot—this is the difficulty!

Comments

The central problem for the Mīmāṃsaka opponent is to explain the difference between pot-presence and pot-absence cognitions without admitting Nyāya's category of absence. The Naiyāyika, for his part, insists that the term "mere," likewise "alone," cannot carry the explanatory weight without postulating absences as real causal factors. For, a floor with a pot on it is nevertheless just a floor, a *mere* floor, and nothing more than a floor, a floor *alone*. Furthermore, it is not cognized as a floor *and* a pot because we are able to perceive and talk about the floor independently of the pot even when a pot is there.

Text (p. 732, Tirupati, and p. 695, Calcutta) and Translation

etena bhūtalêndriya-saṃnikarṣa-ja-ghaṭavad-bhūtalêndriya-saṃnikarṣa-ja-jñānayor viśeṣo 'ṅgīkaraṇīyaḥ | sāmagrī-bhedasya kārya-bheda-niyamatvāt | tathā ca sa eva tan-mātra-padârtha iti nirastam | tato 'pi bhūtala-vyavahārāt | pratiyogi-tad-vyāpyêtara-janitā bhūtala-buddhir a-bhāva iti cet, na | ghaṭavati taj-janitā api itara-janitatvāt | tan-mātra-janitā sā iti cet, na | mātrârthasya a-bhāvatvāt tasya ca a-parijñānāt | ghaṭâ-viṣayā satī bhūtala-viṣayā iti cet, na | uktôttaratvāt |

Objection (by a Mīmāṃsaka): A particular (i.e., a difference) has to be accepted between a cognition A arising out of a sensory connection with a floor and a cognition B arising out of a sensory connection with a floor exhibiting a pot, since distinct causal complexes, by rule, result in distinct effects, and this, just such a particular (or difference), is what is meant by a *mere that.*

Old Nyāya: This argument is thrown out by reasoning already given. For, from that (cognition B of a floor with a pot on it, too, would talk of a floor result (and so B would be just like A, which you want to be an absential cognition).

Mīmāṃsaka: The absence is the *cognition* of the floor that is produced by something other than the absentee (the pot) and other than whatever is pervaded (or entailed) by that (absentee, being made of clay, for example).

Old Nyāya: No. A cognition of the floor as having a pot, which is produced (in part) by that (the pot and the entailments of its presence) is also produced from things that are other than that (e.g., a sense organ and the general causes of perception such as time and place).

Mīmāṃsaka: The absential cognition is generated by a *mere that.*

Old Nyāya: No. The term "mere" means absence, and that is not cognized (on your view that denies its reality).

Mīmāṃsaka: (What is meant is) there being no pot as object, a cognition whose object is the floor.

Old Nyāya: That's wrong for reasons already stated.

Comments

The Mīmāṃsaka's explanation shows promise; a distinct causal complex seems a good candidate indeed for the distinct result. There is, however, the lack of specificity made plain in the Naiyāyika reply. The deep problem is that the Mīmāṃsaka's proposal does not avoid reference to absences.

Text (p. 733, Tirupati, and p. 695, Calcutta, last line) and Translation

kiṃ ca pratiyogi-nirūpaṇâdhīna-nirūpaṇo '-bhāvaḥ | buddhis tu na tathā | pratiyogi-prakāśaṃ vinā api buddhi-nirūpaṇāt | vyavahārârthaṃ dṛśya-pratiyogi-jñānâpekṣā a-bhāvo jñāta eva iti cet, na | vyavahārasya vyavahartavyôpalambha-nibandhanatvena tathā a-dṛṣṭacaratvāt | yadi ca pratiyogi-smaraṇa-sāpekṣā tan-mātra-dhīr a-bhāva-padârthaḥ tadā andhakārâdau yā tan-mātra-dhīḥ sā a-bhāvo na syāt | tathā ca tatra vicaran kaṇṭakair vidhyeta | kaṇṭaka-smaraṇaṃ vinā kaṇṭakâ-bhāvâ-bhāvāt | nirjane bandha-vicchide 'pi jala-nissaraṇaṃ na syāt | tadānīṃ tan-mātra-buddheḥ sarvathā a-bhāvāt | kiṃ ca tan-mātra-dhī-nāśe ghaṭônmajjana-prasaṅgaḥ, ghaṭâ-bhāvâ-bhāvasya ghaṭatvāt | yadi ca a-bhāvo na atiriktas tadā yatra ghaṭa-saṃsṛṣṭatva-buddhir āsīt kutas tatra tan-mātra-dhīḥ | mudgara-pāta-janyâtirikta-viṣayân-aṅgīkārāt | atiriktâ-bhāve kiṃ mānam iti cet, na asti iti buddhir eva |

(The exposition of **Old Nyāya** continues:) Furthermore (you cannot say that an absence reduces ontologically to cognition, for) an absence is something whereof a discerning cognition depends on (prior) cognition of an absen*tee*. Cognition, on the other hand, is not like that, since even without (prior) cognition of an absentee cognition can be discerned (i.e., in apperception).

Objection (by the Mīmāṃsaka): To talk about an absence, one (admittedly) has to have cognized the absentee, which (then) must have been capable of being perceived. (However) an absence can be simply cognized (without being talked about and without an absentee having been cognized).

Old Nyāya: No. Inasmuch as talk is tied to what can be talked about—what we have experienced, namely—what you allege is not found.

And if the category of absence were a *cognition* of a mere that—a cognition that requires a remembering of what is absent—then a cognition of a mere that occurring in the dark, or the like, would not be an absence (because there would not be the required remembering: nothing would provoke it).

Similarly, someone walking along there in the dark would be pricked by thorns, since without a remembering of thorns there would be an absence of the thorns' absence! In a deserted place, a dam might break but there would be no outflowing of water, since in no way could there be at the time (given the place is deserted) a cognition of a mere that.

Moreover, on the destruction of a (particular) cognition of a mere that, you face the predicament of a (smashed) pot re-emerging, inasmuch as an absence of a pot's absence is a pot! And if an absence is not anything separate and distinct, then how could there be a cognition of a mere that with regard to a spot that a previous cognition took to be connected to a pot? For, you do not accept that anything separate and distinct (from that spot) could be produced by the fall of the (pot-smashing) hammer.

Objection: What is the proof for such a "separate and distinct" absence?

Old Nyāya: Simply such a cognition as, "It is not (there)."

Comments

The Nyāya view is that experience of an absence requires current or prior experience of three factors: the locus of the absence (experienced currently), what is absent (previously experienced, with a memory-impression making it available to be cognized as absent), and the absence itself (currently experienced). The absence is somehow ontologically positive, occurring independently of cognition. However, absential *cognition* depends on an absentee being furnished by memory and previous experience.

The first of the untoward ramifications drawn on the assumption that an absence is simply a certain type of cognition—a cognition of a "mere that"—assumes that we can have a cognition of a mere that, the floor, for example, without there being anything to provoke a remembering of an absentee. The principal point is that if, as the Mīmāṃsaka proposes, absences are nothing other than a certain type of cognition, then when the conditions for that type of cognition do not obtain, such as when there are no people or animals present, there would not be the absence. Thus a broken dam would not spill out its water, et cetera.

Text (p. 735, Tirupati) and Translation

> nanv[2] a-bhāva-vyavahārân-upapattir anyonyâśrayād iti | atra prābhākarāḥ | ghaṭavad-bhūtala-buddhi-bhinnā bhūtala-buddhir a-bhāva-vyavahāra-kāraṇam | na ca doṣāt ghaṭavati ghaṭavattvâ-jñāne bhūtala-jñānam a-bhāvaḥ syād iti vācyam | ghaṭavato bhūtalasya jñānād bhinnasya bhūtala-jñānasya a-bhāvatvāt tad-bhramāc ca a-bhāva-bhramaḥ |

Objection:[3] Then you are saying that absences explain talk of absences, but that commits the fallacy of circularity (that is, without a separate proof of absence as a distinct category, you are begging the question in citing absences as founding the talk).

Gaṅgeśa: On this, Prābhākaras (reason as follows).

Prābhākara: A cognition of a floor—as distinct from a cognition of the same floor with a pot on it—causes absence talk. (So there is no circularity.)

Objection: If there is no cognition of an exhibiting of a pot with respect to something (the floor) that really does exhibit a pot—all this happening because of an epistemic defect—the floor cognition would be (or entail, on your view) an absence (an absence of a pot, when in fact there is a pot present)!

Prābhākara: That should not be alleged. For, the floor cognition—*as* distinct from a cognition of the floor with a pot on it—is the absence. An error about such an absence would result from an error about a floor cognition being in that way distinct.

Comments

The key to the Prābhākara's response to the challenge based on the imagined absential error is that the Prābhākara conceives of the crucial floor cognition as not just any cognition of the floor but a cognition that is distinct-from-a-cognition-of-the-floor-with-a-pot-on-it—the long expression in dashes counting as a property or qualifier of the cognition, differentiating it from the unwanted comparisons.

Text (p. 697, Calcutta) and Translation

> vastuto 'tyantâ-bhāve pratiyogimad-adhikaraṇa-jñānasya a-prasiddheḥ pratiyogimaj-jñāna-bhinnam adhikaraṇa-jñānaṃ vyadhikaraṇâ-bhāva-vyavahāre kāraṇam | samānâdhikaraṇa-niṣedha-pratītiṣ ca pratiyogy-adhikaraṇayoḥ sva-rūpa-bhedam ālambate | tena ghaṭavattvena jñāyamāne 'pi bhūtale bhūtalaṃ ghaṭo na iti pratītiḥ |

(The **Prābhākara** continues:) In fact, absence talk when the absence is the variety that does not exist at the locus where its absentee exists (*vyadhikaraṇâ-bhāva*, e.g., an absence of a pot on a floor, where the pot is the absentee) is caused by a cognition of the locus—the cognition of the locus *as* a cognition that is distinct from a cognition of the locus exhibiting the absentee, since in the case of (what you Naiyāyikas call) an absolute absence there is no (current) cognition of the locus where the absentee really exists (e.g., the pot that is absent here is present somewhere else, with the ''somewhere else'' not currently being cognized). And (in contrast) cognition that is a denial with respect to a locus equally with both terms (i.e., a cognition of an absence that does exist at the place where its absentee exists, for instance, the mutual exclusion of a pot from a cloth, where the absence, the mutual absence, does exist at the same place), depends on an essential distinctness between two substrata (or things, two loci) of the (respective) absentees. This explains why there can be the cognition, ''The floor is *not* the pot,'' even though the floor is cognized as having a pot on it.

Comments

The Prābhākara points out that there is an important difference between absential cognitions that are (a) asymmetrical, e.g., a floor *without* a pot, and (b) symmetrical, e.g., a floor's *not being* a pot, where the cognition's absential object is matched by the pot's not being a floor. Whereas an absence of a pot *on* a floor does *not* exist where the pot exists, the distinctness, or exclusion, between a pot and a floor is mutual. Thus, there can be the one kind of absence where the other does not obtain, such that a pot can be understood as mutually distinct from a floor on which it is nevertheless present.[4]

Text (p. 737, Tirupati, and p. 698, Calcutta) and Translation

tathā ca yasya a-bhāva-jñāna-kāraṇatvaṃ pareṣāṃ tad eva a-bhāva-vyavahṛti-kāraṇam astu | na hy adhikaraṇa-buddhiṃ vinā tad-buddhiḥ | na ca bhūtala-buddhis tathā | ghaṭavaty api prasaṅgāt | na ca a-bhāvâdhikaraṇa-bhūtala-viṣayatvād buddher viśeṣaḥ | pratiyogi-sattve 'pi prāñ na āsīd idam atra iti pratīteḥ | kiṃ ca jñāna-viṣaya-bhūtalasya a-bhāvo yadi viśeṣaṇam, tadā a-bhāva-jñānam eva taj-jñāna-kāraṇam | upalakṣaṇaṃ cet, na kaścid viśeṣaḥ | pratiyogimattayā an-upalabdhir api kāraṇam iti cet, na | pratiyogimattayā upalambhe 'pi prāñ na āsīd idam atra iti pratīteḥ |

(The **Prābhākara** continues:) And so what for you others (i.e., for you Naiyāyikas) is a cause of absential cognition, let that be thought of as simply a cause of *talk* of absences. For, there is no such cognition without cognition of a locus.

And it is not the case that a floor cognition (*tout court*) is such (an "absential" cognition), because of the difficulty that a floor cognition (*tout cour*) could be also of a floor with a pot on it. (Rather, the difference is explained, as we have said, by the cognitive qualifier, being-distinct-from-a-cognition-of-a-floor-with-a-pot-on-it).

Nor is there some difference (out there on the floor) that distinguishes a cognition whose object is a floor as an absence's locus (as opposed to a cognition of a floor *with* a pot). For, even when the absentee is present, we have such (absential) cognitions as, "This was not there before."

Moreover, if an absence (cognized) were the floor's qualifier *as a cognitive object*, then the absential cognition itself (the floor cognition as qualified by the absence) would cause the absential cognition (and we would be stuck with self-dependent causality). If an absence (cognized) is (not to be a true qualifier, but only) an indicator or identifier (*upalakṣaṇa*), there is (then, in reality, as you yourself say regarding all such constructed referential devices, *upalakṣaṇa*) no (real) difference (to account for the difference between cognitions of a floor with and without a pot).

Objection: *Non-cognition* of the floor as exhibiting the absentee is also a cause (of the absential cognition, sufficient to differentiate it from the other).

Prābhākara: No. For, even when we are experiencing it as exhibiting the absentee (i.e., when we are experiencing the floor as having a pot), we can have the cognition, "This was not there before."

Comments

The Prābhākara is intent on denying absence as a separate and distinct category of cognizable object. What explains talk of absences? Certain types of cognition, reflecting certain types of fact, all describable without reference to absences. All we require is a *cognitive qualifier—a property of cognition*—to make the differentiation of the floor cognized without as opposed to with a pot. Other analyses are subject to the difficulties mentioned. (See below, pp. 641, on the distinction between qualifiers, *viśeṣa*, and indicators, *upalakṣaṇa*.)

The objection promoting the causal status of non-cognition is probably to be understood as a Bhāṭṭa's. However, it could be a Naiyāyika's. Although Nyāya denies that non-cognition is an independent *pramāṇa*, a non-cognition is required for absential perception, according to standard opinion. That is to say, an absence would be directly perceived, and the fact that the absentee is not perceived is thought of as a causal auxiliary in the process.

The Prābhākara refutes the non-cognition contention, however, by pointing out that even when we are perceiving a pot on the floor, we might have an absential cognition, e.g., "This was not there before," where no non-cognition—no current non-cognition, at least—would be a causal factor.

Text (p. 739, Tirupati) and Translation

> buddhyoś ca viśeṣaḥ sva-rūpa-viśeṣāv eva, na anyonyâ-bhāvo an-avasthānād ātmâśrayād vā | bhūtala-jñānâpekṣayā ghaṭavad-bhūtala-jñānatvam eva vā vaidharmya-bhedaḥ | na ca atiriktâ-bhāva-pakṣe 'py anyonyâ-bhāve 'tyantâ-bhāve ca nitye mānam asti | pratiyogini buddhi-sthe 'dhikaraṇa-sva-rūpasya eva an-atiprasañjakatvāt | na hi tatra adhikaraṇasya pratiyogi-tādātmyaṃ pratiyogimattvaṃ vā sambhavati | ata eva a-bhāve '-bhāvântaraṃ tvayā na svīkriyate | adhikaraṇasya tad-dvai-rūpy-a-bhāvāt[5] |

(The **Prābhākara** continues:) And the difference between the two types of cognition (the one of the floor with a pot, the other of the floor without) is that the two have essentially different natures. It is not a matter of mutual distinctness (or mutual absence, *anyonyâ-bhāva*), because that would lead to an infinite regress or involve (circularity, i.e.) self-dependence.

Alternatively, simply being a cognition of the floor with a pot is, with respect to a cognition of the floor, distinct as having different properties.

Moreover, on your view of absence as a separate and distinct category, there is no argument for (what you call) a mutual absence (or, a mutual distinctness) *or* for (what you call) an absolute absence, which are (you say) eternal, since on our explanation (of absence talk) with reference only to the essential nature of the locus—with the absentee supplied by cognition (through memory)—there is no overextension (to a case where we do *not* talk of an absence, the pot being present, whereas on your "eternal absence" view there is such overextension). For, in those cases (i.e., in the cases of what you call absolute and mutual absence, our economical explanation does not offend by overextension, since) the locus cannot possibly be identical with what is cognized as absent, nor could it have it (thus all your apparatus is otiose).

Just for this reason, you yourself do not accept that another absence could rest in (or qualify) an absence (of either of these two varieties, e.g., there is no absence of a cloth in an absence of a pot; according to you Naiyāyikas, the absence of a pot is *in itself* different from an absence of a cloth). For, a locus does not show your two types of that (relation to an absentee, namely, absence of identity and a "locative" absence).

Comments

If an absence differentiates the two cognitions—the one of the floor with a pot and the other of the floor without—then *cognition* of that absence will have to be differentiated from the other two cognitions. Thus, either there will be infinite regress, or if the cognition of the differentiating absence is thought to be identical to the cognition of the original absence, "self-dependence" would be incurred.

In the passage's second paragraph, the Prābhākara suggests that any two distinct things, including cognitions, will each have at least one property not shared by the other.

The thrust of the Prābhākara argument throughout the passage is that we have to invoke parsimony at some point. So why not stop with the nature of things as fundamentally distinct? A pot is simply not a cloth. And the mere floor just does not have a pot on it. If this seems explanationally an arbitrary stopping point, we should acknowledge that such arbitrariness is unavoidable. Nyāya, too, has its types of absence as fundamentally distinct, i.e., as by nature distinct, with no further type of absence explaining their distinctness.

Text (p. 740, Tirupati) and Translation

> nanv arthena eva viśeṣo buddheḥ | na ca artha-bhedo 'sti | mā evam | na hi tāvad-artho jñāna-kāraṇam a-vaśyam | kiṃ tu sāmagrī-viśeṣāt buddhi-viśeṣo jāyate dhārā-vāhika-buddhi-vat |

Objection (by a Naiyāyika): Just according to the object (cognized) is there a difference of cognition. And (in the case of the two floor cognitions you mention) there is no distinctness between the objects (cognized, which are in each case the floor).

Prābhākara: Don't think that way. For, the position is false that only the object causes the cognition, that only it is necessary to it. Rather, a particular cognition results from a particular causal complex sufficient to produce the effect, like a series of cognitions of the same thing.

Comments

The subjective causal factor, a necessary condition, in the case of whatever member, except the first, of a series of cognitions of the same thing would be the preceding cognition of that thing. Since objectwise one cognition in the series would be the same as the others, the immediately preceding cognition is in fact the crucial factor responsible for the distinctness of its successor. Similarly, the Prābhākara concludes, an absential cognition has its identity determined by subjective factors such as memory of an absentee. Indeed, the absence is simply the absential cognition, at least according to one of two ontological lines that Prābhākaras take (the other is introduced in the next passage). The only objective causal factor is the bare locus. The cognition itself is the absence, as is shown by its ability to explain the absential talk.

Text (p. 741, Tirupati) and Translation

> yad vā ghaṭavad-bhūtala-bhinnaṃ bhūtalam a-bhāvaḥ yatra pareṣām a-bhāvaḥ bhedaś ca sva-rūpam eva, tādātmyena a-pratitau pratītir iti tava api sva-rūpa-bheda-lakṣaṇam | idānīm idaṃ bhūtalaṃ ghaṭavad-bhūtalaṃ na bhavati iti pratīteḥ | etāvāṃs tu viśeṣo yat tava samānâdhikaraṇa-niṣedha-pratītir iyam anyonyâ-bhāva-bhedam avagāhate mama tu sva-rūpa-bhedam[6] |

(The **Prābhākara** continues:) Alternatively, the floor is the absence, the floor as distinct from the floor with a pot on it. Where you others (you Naiyāyikas) find an absence, we see a distinctness that is simply a matter of the very nature of a thing.

For you, too, the characteristic mark of essential distinctness (the distinctness, e.g., of a pot from a cloth, distinctness by something's "very nature," *sva-rūpa*) is cognition of something not cognized as identical (with something else). For, there is the cognition, "This floor is not now a floor with a pot on it" (i.e., the floor now is essentially distinct from the floor as it was, when it had a pot on it).

So far (our dispute is over) the characteristic difference that is a cognition that is a symmetrical denial with respect to a locus (e.g., "The pot is not the cloth"), which is fathomed by you as a mutual absence (a mutual distinctness) but which is for me an essential distinctness (or, a distinctness as a matter of something's very nature).

Comments

To this point, the Prābhākara had emphasized the role of a certain type of cognition in explaining what Naiyāyikas call absences. Here he focuses on objects. The change probably should not be read as a change of voice or subcamp—though that is possible—because the *eliminability* of the category of absence is the predominant Prābhākara theme. An absence is just the cognition, or, perhaps more plausibly, it's just the object cognized. It's nothing extra in any case.

We admit, says the Prābhākara, the phenomena that motivate your posits of absences. However, the posits are seen to be otiose when we understand what a thing's "own nature" involves (its "very nature," *sva-rūpa*).

Text (p. 743, Tirupati, and p. 700, Calcutta) and Translation

nanu yad eva bhūtalaṃ ghaṭavad-bhūtalâ-bhinnam āsīt tad eva kathaṃ tad-bhinnam iti cet, na | tava apy a-bādhita-samānâdhikaraṇa-niṣedha-pratīti-balena anyonyâ-bhāva-siddhau tathātvasya durvāratvāt | samaya-bhedena eva bhedâ-bhedau na virudhyete iti tu samam | yadi ca ghaṭavad-bhūtalâ-bhinnaṃ tad idānīṃ syāt tadā ghaṭavad-bhūtala-vyavahāras tatra syāt | ghaṭa-tad-a-bhāvâvacchedaka-bhedena anyonyâ-bhāva-tad-a-bhāvau bhūtale vartete iti cet, mama api bhūtala-buddher ghaṭavad-bhūtala-buddhy-avacchedena sva-rūpa-bheda-tad-a-bhāvau vartete iti gṛhāṇa |

Objection (by a Naiyāyika): Just that floor which was formerly *non-distinct* from the floor exhibiting a pot, how does it come to be *distinct* from that?

Prābhākara: No. (You face the same question:) For you, too, the force of an undefeated cognition that is a symmetrical denial with regard to a locus establishes a mutual absence (or, mutual distinctness, between two things). Such a result (viz., the change concerning a floor indicated in your question) is difficult to avoid (i.e., easy to explain).

The view, however, that just through distinctions of time (or occasion) do the distinctness and non-distinctness not oppose one another—that view is open equally to both our sides.

And if this floor that now does *not* have a pot on it were non-distinct from the floor that had a pot on it, then the talk would be of a floor that has a pot on it (which is ridiculous).

Objection (by the Naiyāyika): A mutual absence and its absence (i.e., a thing as identical with itself) exist with respect to the floor by way of distinct specifiers, namely, by way of a pot (as that from which the floor is mutually distinct) and the pot's absence.

Prābhākara: For me, too, an essential distinctness and its absence exist by way of a cognitive specifier, namely, the-floor-as-having-a-pot-on-it, as opposed to a cognition of the floor (not so specified)—grasp this (your view's explanatory equal)!

Comments

The Prābhākara seems to make a slight mistake in his last retort, in that the Naiyāyika was talking about the mutual-distinctness or symmetrical variety of absence, whereas the Prābhākara addresses the asymmetrical type of absence, a floor being bereft of a pot. Possibly, this is a slip on the part of our author. However, what are two types of absence in the Naiyāyika view are for the Prābhākara simply an object cognized in different ways.

The Prābhākara, presuming it now to be evident that his view is simpler than the Naiyāyika's, argues here that it is the other's explanational equivalent, not having an explanational fault, such as undercoverage, that the Naiyāyika view does not also incur, and having all the other's explanational merits. The explanandum is absential talk, and his approach can explain perfectly well the distinction between (a) talk of a floor as having a pot and (b) talk of it as pot-bereft.

Text (p. 744, Tirupati, and p. 701, Calcutta) and Translation

nanu bhūtale ghaṭo 'sti na vā iti saṃśayo ghaṭo na asti iti viparyayo vā kathaṃ bhavet | pratiyogini buddhi-sthe 'dhikaraṇasya taj-jñānasya ca a-bhāvasya upalambhād iti cet, na | bhūtale taj-jñāne vā ghaṭavad-bhinnatvasya ghaṭavad-bhūtala-jñāna-bhinnatvasya ca dośa-vaśena a-niścayāt | bhūtala-taj-jñāna-sva-rūpāṇām an-anugamāt katham anugata-vyavahāra iti cet, na | a-bhāve 'pi tulyatvāt | na hy a-bhāvatvaṃ sāmānyam | a-bhāvatva-gatânyonyâ-bhāvâ-vyāpakatvāt |

Objection: How can there be the doubt, "Is the pot on the floor or not?" or the wrong cognition, "The pot is not (there)" (when it is there), since (on your view) the experience of an absence is (only) of a locus or of a cognition of that, with the absentee provided by the mind?

Prābhākara: No. For, concerning the floor, whether it is distinct from the same floor as having a pot on it, or, concerning a cognition of the floor, whether it is distinct from a cognition of the same floor as having a pot on it, there can be, by the force of an epistemic defect, a lack of certainty.

Objection: Since the individual natures of floors (for instance) and of cognitions of them are not uniform (and, on your view, absences are nothing but these), how come there is the uniform (absence) talk?

Prābhākara: No. On the absence view, too, there is the same problem. For, there is no universal, "absencehood" (accounting for the uniform talk, on the Nyāya view), since such an absencehood could not include the mutual-absence type of absence, which would be entailed by the assumption that there is such an "absencehood."

Comments

Both parties agree that we do not make mistakes about a qualificandum or about a cognitive occurrence. Thus since on the Prābhākara view an absence is nothing but a qualificandum or (if you prefer) a cognitive occurrence, absential doubt and error would appear impossible—and by implication, the objector may be interpreted, *talk* of such would be impossible too (strictly speaking, the Prābhākara does not admit *cognitive* error). To the Naiyāyika's contention that they happen sometimes, the Prābhākara responds, "Yes, they do, due to the usual suspects."

Rucidatta explains (p. 744) the Prābhākara's last point. If absencehood were a universal, it would be a distinct and separate entity inhering in all individual absences. However, just in virtue of being a distinct and separate entity, it would be mutually distinct from its instances. Thus there would be the mutual-absence type of absence coming between it and any individual in which it inhered. But then that mutual-absence type of absence could not be included in the universal's instances, on pain of infinite regress. Therefore, absencehood is not a genuine universal.

Text (p. 745, Tirupati) and Translation

na ca bhāva-virodhitvam | virodhasya a-bhāva-nirūpyatvāt bhāvâ-bhāvayoḥ sahâvasthānâ-bhāvasya sva-rūpân-atirekāc ca | na api bhāva-pratiyogitvam | pratiyogitvasya a-bhāva-viraha-rūpatvāt a-bhāvâ-bhāvasya bhāvasya bhāvâ-pratiyogikatvāc ca | na api sapratiyogikatvam | samavāya-sādṛśyâdīnām api tathātvāt | na api parakīya-sva-bhāvatvam, jñānâdi-gatatvāt, sva-bhāva-śabdasya sva-rūpârthe 'n-anugamāc ca | na api sattā-śūnyatvam, sattāyām eva gatatvāt, śūnyatvasya a-bhāva-rūpatvāc ca | sattâtyantā-bhāvavattvam a-bhāvatvam, atyantâ-bhāvaś ca a-bhāvatvân-avagatāv api avagata iti cet, na | a-bhāve '-bhāvân-abhyupagamāt tathātve 'pi tatra eva tad-abhyupagamāt |

(The **Prābhākara** continues:) Nor is "absencehood" (D^1) to be the opposite of a presence. For, opposition is determined by (or presupposes) absence, and the absence of the co-presence of (a) a presence and (b) an absence (of the same thing) is nothing more than what things are by nature or in themselves (*sva-rūpa*).

Nor is it (D^2) to have a presence as countercorrelate (or absentee, *pratiyogin*). For, countercorrelateness means lack of the absence. Moreover, an absence of an absence, which is a presence, does not have a presence as its countercorrelate (and so the definition would be too narrow).

Nor is it (D^3) to have a countercorrelate. For, such relations as inherence and similarity also have countercorrelates (and so the definition would be too wide).

Nor is it (D^4) to be by nature known by something else's being cognized (as an absence of a pot is known by a pot's being remembered). For, that would include such things as cognitions (since a cognition when it is itself an object of knowledge depends on *something else's* being known, i.e., its objecthood or indication being known). Moreover, the words "by nature" in the definition mean what something is in itself, and that is not uniform.

Nor is it (D^5) to be void of beingness. For that would include beingness itself (which is said not to be a locus of beingness, for fear of infinite regress). Moreover, "to be void of" takes the form of an absence (and so there would be definitional self-dependence).

Objection (by a Naiyāyika): Absencehood is (D^6) the absolute absence of beingness. And an absolute absence can be known even when absencehood is not known (and so there is not self-dependence, since an absolute absence is distinct from absencehood).

Prābhākara: No. For (you say) you do not accept that an absence can rest in an absence (and, on the current proposal, absencehood as *an* absence, an absolute absence, would rest in other absences). Even if you did accept that an absence could rest in other absences, (you would be presupposing what is at issue, that is to say) you would be accepting an absence right there in absences (which are what need explaining).

Comments

Concerning the blue that is exhibited by a blue lotus through the relation of inherence, the blue is said to be the *pratiyogin*, "countercorrelate," and the lotus is said to be the *anuyogin*, the "correlate." In application to the similarity between the moon and the face of one's beloved, the moon is the countercorrelate and the face the correlate. An absence is, similarly, a relation between a countercorrelate—here an "absentee"—and a locus.

Matilal says that in the Prābhākara retort the term *pratiyogin* is used ambiguously.[7] Perhaps. The issue is not minor in that Gaṅgeśa's own view centers on absences' having absentees, or countercorrelates, as we shall see. (Does an absence have a countercorrelate in the same way these other relations do? What is the relational logic of an absence?) And it is noteworthy, *pace* Matilal, that Gaṅgeśa makes a comparison to "similarity" *in support of* his views. (Similarity, interestingly, is accepted by Mīmāṃsā as an additional category, and denied by Nyāya—just the reverse of the attitudes expressed in the current passage.) In any case, definition D^3 attacked here, "to have a countercorrelate," needs further specification to target absences exclusively.

The reason cognitions would be included under D^4, "to be by nature known by something else's being cognized," is that the words "something else" are subject to too wide an interpretation. From the Prābhākara perspective, every cognition is self-illumined, with the knower indicated as well as the cognition itself and an external object. So, any cognition would be known only if "*something else* were known," namely, a self and an external object.

Udayana expressly mentions the example of beingness as not inhering in itself because of the danger of infinite regress—which is one of his six blockers of candidate universals (cf., in this book, pp. 700–701).[8]

Text (p. 746, Tirupati) and Translation

sattā-bodha-vidhuratvam a-bhāvatvam | sāmānyâdau sattâvagame 'pi bādhāt sā tyajyate, a-bhāvasya tad-viruddhatayā eva pratītir iti cet, na | virodhatvasya sva-rūpân-atirekāt | sahân-avasthāna-niyamo virodha iti cet, na | an-avasthānasya avasthānâ-bhāvatvena ātmâśrayāt | bhāva-bhinnatvam iti cet, na | bhedasya sva-rūpânyonyâ-bhāva-rūpatve ukta-doṣāt | vaidharmyasya cintyamānatvāt | prāg-a-bhāvatvâder a-bhāva-nirūpyatvāt | evaṃ ced a-bhāve 'pi na anugamas tadā kiṃ adhikena | sva-rūpa-viśeṣād eva ghaṭa-vyavahāro 'py astv iti cet, na | bhūtala-vilakṣaṇa-ghaṭânubhavāt | eka eva a-bhāvo 'nugata iti cet, na | tasya nityatvena pratiyogi-kāle 'py a-bhāva-vyavahāra-prasaṅgāt | prāg-a-bhāvâdi-vyutpādana-virodhāc ca |

Objection (by a Naiyāyika): To be an absence (or, absencehood) is (D⁷) a being-bereft-of-cognition-of-(something-as-)being. Though universals and so on (ultimate differentiators, inherence, and absences, in our ontology) are commonly thought of as being, (philosophically) we reject that because of counterconsiderations (such as fear of infinite regress). An absence (in contrast) is cognized as simply incompatible with (the) being (of that which is absent).

Prābhākara: Wrong. For (as stated previously), incompatibility is nothing more than things in themselves (their *sva-rūpa*).

Objection: The rule for the incompatible is: no occurrence with the other.

Prābhākara: No, since non-occurrence is absence of occurrence, you err by self-dependence.

Objection: To be an absence is (D⁸) to be distinct from a presence.

Prābhākara: No. This commits the fault already pointed out (self-dependence), given that a distinctness is to take the form of something (separate and distinct) having its own nature, namely, a mutual absence (*anyonyâ-bhāva*). (Or, if it is to be understood differently, namely, as a difference in properties, then) "difference in properties" has to be analyzed.

(And do not say that to be an absence is to be a *prior* absence or the like, since) prior absence and the rest are determined by (or presuppose) absence.

If, though present in absences, x is not uniform, then what with this supposing it to be something additional? (No, to be an absence is just to be one or another of the multitudinous things that are distinct by nature from other things.)

Objection: Then let talk of a pot also result from just any particular thing as it is in itself!

Prābhākara: No. We experience a pot as something different from a floor.

Objection: (Then) an absence *is* just a single thing and uniform (through many occurrences).

Prābhākara: No. For (on your view) it would in that case be eternal—the difficulty is that we would have absence talk even at the time the absentee is present.

Furthermore, this proposal is incompatible with your division of the types of absence, prior absence, and so on.

Comments

The continuity and uniformity of something (normally a universal) through many instances shows that that something is eternal, according to Naiyāyika reasoning, in that individual instances can be destroyed or disappear while the something remains the same elsewhere.

The inability overall of the Naiyāyika, or anyone, to provide a proper definition is a further reason to reject, implies the Prābhākara, that there is any such thing as an absence. There are only the things that there are, each by nature distinct.

Text (Tirupati, p. 747, and p. 704, Calcutta, last line) and Translation

> yad vā a-bhāva-vādinā apy a-bhāva-jñāna-kāraṇam anugato bhūtala-buddhi-viśeṣaḥ svīkāryaḥ | tad varaṃ sa eva astu prameyaṃ pramāṇaṃ ca | sva-prakāśatvād buddhīnām | nanu tan-mātra-buddher a-bhāvatve tasyāḥ sva-kāśatvena pratiyogi-jñānâpekṣā na syād iti ced, na | na grahaṇāya tad-apekṣā, kiṃ tu vyavahārāya | jñānasya satyām icchāyāṃ na[9] vyavahārârtham adhikâpekṣā iti cet, na | dṛṣṭā hi vyavahārârtham adhikâpekṣā yathā parimāṇasya dīrghatva-vyavahāre | tathā hi adhika-saṃkhyâvacchinna-hasta-vitasty-ādy-avacchedaḥ parimāṇasya dīrghatvam | tad-viparītaṃ tu hrasvatvam | tādṛśa-parimāṇaṃ ca avayavi-graha-sama-kālam eva anubhūtam | dīrghatva-vyapadeśas tu alpa-saṃkhyâdy-avacchinna-hastâdy-avacchedya-parimāṇa-jñānam apekṣate |

(The **Prābhākara** continues:) Alternatively, let a particular type of cognition of the floor, which is continuous and uniform, be accepted by the proponent of absences (i.e., by the Naiyāyika), too, as a cause of the absential cognition. Therefore, it is the better view to let such a cognition be both what is known and the means of knowing it. For, cognitions are self-illumining.

Objection: If a cognition of a "mere that" is an absence, then (on your view), given that cognition is self-illumining, there would be no dependence on cognition of an absentee.

Prābhākara: Wrong. The dependence on that is not for cognition, but for talk.

Objection: (Then) there should not be dependence on *something else* to talk about an occurrent (absential) *cognition* (e.g., "I am *perceiving* that *the pot* is not on the floor"—whereas there obviously is such dependence).

Prābhākara: No. For, the dependence on something else is commonly experienced when it comes to talk. Similarly, there is talk of a thing's size as long. For example, delimitation by such measures as a specific number of spans of a spread hand—a comparatively large number—is (what we mean by) a size's being long, whereas being short is the opposite. And such a size (*qua* size alone) is experienced at exactly the same time as the whole thing is grasped (without a sense of comparative longness or shortness). The linguistic *expression* of something's being long, however, depends on a cognition of size which is to be made specific by such measures as a span of the hand, specifically a (comparatively) small or another number of such measures.

Comments

The Prābhākara sees cognition of a bare locus as only in part responsible for talk of an absence; prior awareness of the absentee is also involved. The behavior, the absence talk, is the ultimate explanandum, we should keep in mind, and in effect for both sides, since the Naiyāyika cannot put forward actual cognitions but only standard verbalizations.

The Prābhākara also holds that every cognition is self-illumining, having triple objecthood as discussed. Apparently, dependence on a previous awareness of an absentee would challenge the self-illumination thesis in that a cognition of an absence would be incomplete without the "outside" illumination provided by prior cognition of the absentee. However, cognition of a bare locus does indeed not include awareness of that which is absent. Only *talk* of absences is informed by a prior cognition of an absentee, according to the Prābhākara.

The Naiyāyika focuses on talk that expresses cognition of an absence, not on absences themselves, since this sharpens his sense of the incompatibility in the Prābhākara view. In reply, the Prābhākara ingeniously draws a comparison to situations where cognition presents an object in a non-relational manner, as having a certain size, for example, whereas the object is talked about relationally, as being short or long. The talk is a separate event with its own characteristic causes. That it is about a, let us say, relational property is thus affirmed by the Prābhākara while holding without contradiction that cognition is "self-illumining" in the sense at stake.

Text (p. 749, Tirupati) and Translation

tan-mātra-buddher a-bhāvatve dṛśya-pratiyogi-jñānâpekṣatayā dṛśyatā-sampatty-artham keśa-kīṭâdi-sūkṣma-jijñāsā apy arthavatī | na ca tan-mātra-buddher a-bhāvatve tad-vināśe a-bhāvâ-bhāve bhāvônmajjana-prasaṅga iti vācyam | yathā ghatâ-bhāvo buddhis tathā buddhy-a-bhāvasya api buddhy-antaratvāt | nirjane bandha-vicchede ca jala-nissaraṇaṃ na an-upapannam | manuśyâ-bhāve 'pi pakṣi-kīṭâdi-buddhi-viṣeśa-saṃbhavāt | mokṣe puruṣântarasya niyame pramāṇaṃ na asti it cet, na | kāryāt kāraṇa-kalpanāt | na ca evaṃ buddhi-nāśe punaḥ sasāritā | buddhi-dhārā-sattvāt | na ca sarva-muktiḥ pramāṇâ-bhāvāt | pratiyogimad-adhikaraṇa-bhinnâdhikaraṇa-sva-rūpasya a-bhāvatve sarvam samañjasam eva iti pūrva-pakṣaḥ |

(The **Prābhākara** continues:) On our view of an absence as a cognition of a "mere that," a person desiring to know whether there are very small things such as hairs or insects (in rice, for instance, so that, knowing that there are *not* such things there, he might proceed to eat) would—in searching them out to ascertain (the presence or absence) of something perceptible—depend on a cognition of a *perceptible absentee*. (In this superior way is explained the importance you attribute to cognition of a perceptible absentee.)

Objection: If an absence is a cognition of a "mere that," there would be the untoward ramification of a re-emergence of a presence, there being an absence of the absence upon the cognition's destruction.

Prābhākara: That should not be said. For, as the "absence" of a pot is a cognition, so too is the "absence" of a cognition (merely) another cognition.

Prābhākara: And it is not impossible (on our view) that when a dam breaks in a place when there are no people around there would be an outflowing of water. For, it is possible that, in the absence of humans, birds, insects, and so on would have the (absential) cognition.

Objection: (Given that "liberation," *mokṣa*, is an absence of cognition, such an absence would have to be cognized by another person, but) there is no reliable evidence (*pramāṇa*) that liberation requires another person.

Prābhākara: No. According to the effect is the cause to be postulated (and liberation's etiology need not be understood in your way). And (even if it is) there would not be in this way a liberated person's becoming again a transmigrating soul through the destruction of the other's (absential) cognition. For, there is the cognitive stream (one cognition following another, either of the same person or of others). Moreover, there is no liberation for everyone (and so we do not have to face the problem of whose cognition would grasp all those absences), since there is no reliable evidence (for such a possibility).

(In sum) on the view that an absence is the very nature of a locus as distinct from the (same) locus exhibiting the absentee, all indeed is unimpeachable.

Gaṅgeśa: Here ends the *pūrva-pakṣa* (exposition of an opponent's position).

Comments

The Prābhākara again vacillates about that to which an absence reduces. And his views and arguments on liberation—as on other problems here—seem weak. A better presentation, focusing on absential talk, is made in other Prābhākara passages still to come. The claims here are refuted or parried pretty easily in Gaṅgeśa's *siddhânta*. And there is an entire section devoted to the topic of liberation within the chapter on inference. So let us withhold comment for the moment.

Thus ends a Prābhākara-dominated *pūrva-pakṣa*. Next Gaṅgeśa's *siddhânta*. The break is not marked by either the Asiatic Society or the Vidyapeetha edition.

Text (p. 751, Tirupati, and p. 707, Calcutta) and Translation

siddhântas tu, sapratiyogiko '-bhāvo 'nubhūyate | ghaṭo na paṭo na ity anubhavāt na tu tan-mātram | ato '-bhāva-vitti-vedyatvaṃ pratiyoginaḥ pratiyogi-jñānâdhīna-jñānatvaṃ ca a-bhāvasya anubhava-sākṣikaṃ go-sādṛśya-vat | na ca kevalaṃ adhikaraṇam taj-jñānaṃ vā a-bhāvaḥ | pratiyogi-jñānaṃ vinā api tad-vitteḥ, tad-vittau pratiyogino '-viṣayatvāc ca | sapratiyogikatvâ-bhāve ca kasya pratiyogī ghaṭaḥ |

Gaṅgeśa: But the following is the right view. An absence is experienced as having a countercorrelate (or "absentee," *pratiyogin*). For, there is the awareness, "No pot (is there on the floor)," and "No cloth (is there)," (and so on). An absence is *not* experienced as a "mere that." Therefore, a countercorrelate is cognized in every cognition of an absence. Furthermore, experience testifies that a cognition of an absence is dependent (i.e., causally dependent) on cognition of a countercorrelate, like (cognition of) similarity to a cow (on the part of a gayal, a kind of buffalo).

And it is false that only a locus, or a cognition of one, is an absence. For, each of these is (sometimes) cognized without a cognition of a countercorrelate. And the cognitive object need not involve a countercorrelate.

Moreover, if an absence did not have a countercorrelate, (one might well wonder about) a pot (cognized as absent: it) is a countercorrelate of what?

Comments

Since Gaṅgeśa draws an analogy to similarity as a relation having a countercorrelate, it seems more precise to translate *pratiyogin* here as "countercorrelate" as opposed to "absentee."

Gaṅgeśa's knock-down argument against the Prābhākara is that neither a "mere that" nor a mere cognition invariably involves cognition of a countercorrelate whereas a cognition of an absence does. However, it is not until the next passage that Gaṅgeśa begins to deal with the real strength of the Prābhākara approach, its targeting of absential *talk* as explanandum. The cognition of a "mere that" is less of the story than has been presumed. The Prābhākara does not deny that absential talk requires cognition of the countercorrelate or absentee. Prior cognition of the pot and current cognition of the floor are all that are needed to explain the talk, "The pot is not on the floor," and no absence need be imagined as an additional ontological category.

Gaṅgeśa's argument at the end of the passage is obscure. But apparently he is emphasizing that we experience an absence as a relation between a correlate or locus and a countercorrelate or absentee. If taken by the Prābhākara account we closed our eyes to the relational factor, we would still have absential experiences and wonder about—in the case of a particular pot that we know is not on a floor—what relation it has to the floor.

Text (p. 751, Tirupati, and p. 708, Calcutta) and Translation

atha kevalam adhikaraṇaṃ taj-jñānaṃ vā a-bhāvaḥ | sa ca a-pratiyogika eva | a-bhāva-vyavahāras tu pratiyogi-jñānam apekṣata iti tasya pratiyogī ghaṭaḥ, ghaṭa-tad-a-bhāva-vyavahārayor virodhād iti cet, na | iha ghaṭo na iti nañ-arthasya pratiyogī ghaṭo 'nubhūyate | na tv a-bhāva-jñānântara-bhāvino a-bhāva-vyavahārasya | tasya a-bhāvânubhava-samaye '-pratīteḥ | vyavahriyate 'sau na tv anubhūyata iti cet, na | tādṛśânubhavaṃ vinā tathā vyavahārâ-bhāvāt | vyavahāre pratiyogi-jñānâpekṣā ity api na yuktam | vyavahartavya-jñānasya satyāṃ icchāyāṃ vyavahāre 'dhikâpekṣāyā a-dṛṣṭacaratvāt, lāghavād iha tathā kalpyate na tv a-bhāva iti cet, na | vyavahāra-mātre tathā kāraṇatvân-avadhāraṇāt[10], vyavahāra-viśeṣasya an-anugatatvāt |

Objection (by the Prābhākara): An absence is only a locus; alternatively, a cognition of one. And such simply does not have a countercorrelate. Absence *talk*, however, does depend on cognition of a countercorrelate. Thus, a pot would be the countercorrelate inasmuch as there is natural opposition between talk of a pot and talk of its absence.

Gaṅgeśa: No. "Here the pot is not"—(with such a cognition) the pot as the countercorrelate (or, negatum) is *experienced* as belonging to the meaning of the *not*. But it is not experienced as belonging to talk of an absence, talk coming right after the absential cognition, since the talk is not cognized at the time of the experience of the absence.

Objection: An absence is not *experienced*; rather, it is *talked about*.

Gaṅgeśa: No. For, without such an experience, there could be no such talk.

Furthermore, the thesis that there is dependence on cognition of a countercorrelate in absential talk is not correct. For, given a desire to express verbally a cognition (that has occurred) about a thing to be expressed, (it is normally immediately expressed; that is to say) no dependence on anything else is seen to occur.

Objection: Such a dependence should be imagined here because of economy, as opposed to an absence.

Gaṅgeśa: No. Such has not been determined to be a cause of such talk in general, since particular instances of such talk are not (in that way) uniform.

Comments

The impasse between Gaṅgeśa and the Prābhākara over whether an absence is experienced or merely talked about prompts Gaṅgeśa to shift our focus to the relation between experience and talk. He points out that if we wish to speak about something that we are cognizing, then nothing more is normally necessary. The talk follows on the heels of the desire, given the cognition, presuming no relevant defect. Gaṅgeśa's view is that a cognition of an absence is directly informed by cognition of an absentee or countercorrelate through memory. Talk about that follows immediately only if one so desires. A desire would trigger effort then talk, not an absential cognition. The Prābhākara account suggests that cognition of an absentee would come between the occurrence of the absential cognition (i.e., the cognition of a "mere that") and the talk, whereas, to repeat, common experience shows that another cognition is not needed. Given a desire to speak, normally nothing intervenes. Once we wish to talk about something we have cognized, or are cognizing, we can do so directly, immediately. Though at the end of the passage Gaṅgeśa seems to admit that there could be cases of some kind of extra dependence such that there could be gaps, under special circumstances, between desire and expression, that is not to be regarded as holding in general, whereas it would have to be, he implies, on the Prābhākara analysis.

Next Gaṅgeśa responds to the comparisons to size, etc., drawn earlier by the Prābhākara.

Text (p. 753, Tirupati, and p. 709, Calcutta) and Translation

> hrasvatva-dīrghatve ca parimāṇântare eva | tava apy alpâdhika-saṃkhyâvacchinna-hastâdy-avacchedyatvaṃ parimāṇasya hrasvatvaṃ dīrghatvaṃ ca alpâdhikâvadhi-jñānâdhīna-jñānam | ato dravya-sama-kālaṃ parimāṇânubhave 'pi na anubhūtam iti na tadā tad-vyavahāraḥ | go-sādṛśyaṃ yady api gavaya-gatāni sāmānyāni taj-jñāna-sama-kālam eva anubhūtāni, tathā api go-vṛttitve sati gavaya-vṛttitvaṃ go-sādṛśyatvaṃ go-jñānâdhīna-jñānam iti na tadā sādṛśya-vyavahāraḥ |

(**Gaṅgeśa** continues:) Furthermore, shortness and longness are simply two sizes. For you, too, shortness of size is to be specified by such measures as a small number of spans (of a spread hand), and longness of size by a large number. (Thus) such cognition is dependent (and not only the talk) on a cognition of limitation to a small or large number. Hence, although something's size is experienced at the same time as the substance itself, longness or shortness is not experienced. For this reason, there is not, at that time, talk of longness or shortness.

Similarity to cows (on the part of a gayal is to be understood as follows). Although the common characteristics that a gayal has (i.e., shares with cows) are experienced at just the same time as a cognized gayal, the being similar to a cow, which as occurring in cows is occurring in the gayal, is cognized in dependence on cognition of cows. (However) there is no talk of similarity (or need not be) at that time (i.e., at the time of the similarity cognition).

Comments

Gaṅgeśa's main point, with each of the two rebuttals here of earlier Prābhākara arguments, is that the cognitions, and not only the talk, are informed by cognition of something else. To speak of a specific size, one has to be aware of a specific delimiter or measure. And to speak of a similarity in something G, then one must have had prior cognition of things F that the G is similar to and the respects in which they are similar. A memory-impression would be a causal auxiliary in the production of a similarity cognition.

Text (p. 755, Tirupati) and Translation

> syād etat | asti tāvat kasyacit jñānāt kvacit a-bhāva-pada-prayogaḥ sarva-siddhaḥ | tatra prayogâlambanaṃ bhūtalâdy eva ghaṭa-vad-atiriktâ-prakāśāt | tataś ca yad-apekṣaṃ yasya a-bhāva-pada-prayoga-viṣayatvaṃ tat tasya a-bhāva ity upeyate | tad-buddhi-janitâ-bhāva-pada-prayoga-viṣayatvam eva ghaṭa-bhūtalayoḥ pratiyogy-anuyogi-rūpaḥ saṃbandhaḥ | ata eva bhūtalasya sapratiyogikatvam, tad-buddhi-janitâ-bhāva-pada-prayoga-viṣayatvena tad-buddhiṃ vinā a-bhāva-pada-prayogâ-viṣayatvāt | anena eva upādhinā ghaṭâ-bhāvâdi-pada-vyutpatti-graha iti cet | tan na | a-bhāva-pada-prayogâlambanaṃ na bhūtalam | na hi bhūtalaṃ ghaṭâ-bhāva iti pratīti-prayogau, api tu bhūtale ghaṭâ-bhāva iti | bhūtale ghaṭa iti-vat bhūtale ghaṭo na asti iti bhūtalâdhikaraṇâtirikta-nañ-artha-prakāśāt |

Objection (by the Prābhākara): That may be. (But let me try to get at the truth here.) There is, first of all, as everyone admits, use of the word "absence," which results from cognition of something or other somewhere. The use of the word is based on such things as floors by themselves, since the absential cognition does *not* reveal anything else such as something with a pot on it.

And, therefore, the following principle is to be honored: a (verbal) objecthood's dependence on a *y* (i.e., reference to a *y*), which is the objecthood of the usage of the words "absence of *x*," is (what we mean by) an absence of *x* at (or on) *y*. The relation is between a countercorrelate and a correlate, between, for example, a pot and a floor. (And) the relation is simply (the floor as) the object of usage of the word "absence," usage produced (to be sure in part) by cognition of a countercorrelate.

Just for this reason, the floor may be thought of as having a countercorrelate (in the following sense): the objecthood of a usage of the word "absence" depends on (prior) cognition of a countercorrelate inasmuch as without cognition of that there would be no such objecthood of such usage (there would be no such usage). Grasping the reference of the words "absence of the pot" or the like is bought about by just this characteristic (namely, again, the obtaining of this dependence, not by any absence as a separate and distinct reality).

Gaṅgeśa: That's wrong. The basis of usage of the word "absence" is not the floor (in our example). For, the floor is not the absence of the pot. This holds for both the cognition and the verbal usage. Rather, the absence of the pot is *on* the floor. For, the meaning of the *not* with such cognitions as, "On the floor, the pot is not"—which is like "On the floor, there the pot is"—is known as something other than the floor, the floor being its locus.

Comments

Near the very beginning of the section, Gaṅgeśa asserts in the voice of Old Nyāya that the veridical cognition "The pot is not on the floor" presumes a locative relationship, *ādhāra-ādheya*, that the Mīmāṃsaka cannot explain as a matter of a *mere* floor (above, p. 436). Here that such a relationship is presupposed by the veridicality of certain absential cognitions is again invoked by Gaṅgeśa to refute now more specifically the Prābhākara stance. However, the argument has weaknesses: the locution, in Sanskrit the seventh or locative case in syntactical relation to the first or nominative, (x is not *in* or *at* y), is assumed to express the cognitions correctly, and the cognitions, as so expressed, are assumed to reflect reality. Both of these assumptions could be challenged, and it is not until later, after Gaṅgeśa deals with further Prābhākara protests, that he nails down this, let us say, locative argument.

That argument aside, the Prābhākara articulates here in the current passage a pretty clear picture of promptings of absential talk with no role for absences. So it seems appropriate that Gaṅgeśa proceed, as he does in the next passage, to draw out a few untoward ramifications of the Prābhākara's approach. Later, as indicated, he fills out his contention about the locative relationship constituting certain absences.

Text (p. 756, Tirupati, and p. 711, Calcutta) and Translation

api ca ghaṭa-buddhi-janitâ-bhāva-pada-prayoga-viṣayatvaṃ bhūtalasya ghaṭâ-bhāvatvam | tathā ca ghaṭâ-bhāvatve tasya avagate ghaṭâ-bhāva-pada-prayoga-viṣayatvam | ghaṭâ-bhāva-pada-prayoga-viṣayatve ca jñāte ghaṭâ-bhāvatvam iti anyonyâśrayaḥ | pada-pravṛtti-nimitte 'vagate pada-prayoga-niyamāt | ghaṭâ-bhāvatvaṃ ca ghaṭâ-bhāva-pade pravṛtti-nimittam | yadi ca bhūtalaṃ sapratiyogikaṃ tadā pratiyoginaṃ vinā kevalaṃ na bhāseta sādṛśyâdi-vat | ghaṭâ-bhāva-pada-prayoga-daśāyāṃ tat sapratiyogikaṃ na anyadā iti cet, tarhi ghaṭa-pratiyogikatve tasya ghaṭa-buddhi-janitâ-bhāva-pada-prayoga-viṣayatvam, sati ca tasmin ghaṭa-pratiyogikatvam ity anyonyâśrayaḥ, kevalasya a-pratiyogikatvāt | evaṃ ca go-buddhi-janita-sādṛśya-pada-prayoga-viṣayatvaṃ gavayasya go-sādṛśyam astu, kṛtam atirikta-sādṛśyena iti sapratiyogika-padârthâpalāpaḥ |

(**Gaṅgeśa** continues:) Moreover (you say) the pot's absence is the floor as the objecthood of a use of the word "absence," usage generated by (prior) cognition of the pot. And if this were the case, given that it is understood that the floor is the absence of the pot, there would be such objecthood of such usage. And given that it is understood that the objecthood of a use of the words "the absence of the pot" is it (the floor), there it would be as the absence of the pot! Thus here we have the fallacy of mutual dependence. For, rules about word usage rely on what provokes a person's effort to use certain words. And (according to you, the floor's) being (ontologically) the absence of a pot causes—or is the occasion for—effort to use the words "the absence of the pot."

Furthermore, if the floor is to have a countercorrelate, then without the countercorrelate it should not appear by itself alone—like similarity and so on.

Objection (by the Prābhākara): On an occasion of a use of the words, "the absence of the pot," that is (known as) having a countercorrelate, not at other times.

Gaṅgeśa: Then (again) we have mutual dependence: given that the floor has the pot as countercorrelate, the floor is the objecthood of the use of the word "absence," a usage that is generated by a (prior) cognition of the pot; and given that such is so, it has the pot as countercorrelate. For, alone it does not have a countercorrelate.

And in this way let similarity to a cow be a gayal as the objecthood of a use of the word "similar," usage generated by (prior) cognition of cows. What (then) would be the point of a separate and distinct category of similarity? Thus we would find outright denial of reference to anything that has a countercorrelate.

Comments

The Prābhākara has to see the floor at a particular time as both having the countercorrelate and not having it. He differentiates the two by way of the absential cognition, as he indicates in his objection. But it begs the question to explain away the absential cognition as nothing but the floor with the countercorrelate inasmuch as we suppose that the floor is without the countercorrelate only on the basis of the absential cognition (reversing *explanans* and *explanandum*). Gaṅgeśa adds a wrinkle about verbal usage. The absential cognition provokes use of the words indicating a floor without a pot; the floor's being without a pot is the truth-maker for the cognition and thus a causal factor prompting the usage. But the floor is without a pot only given the absential cognition.

The comparison that Gaṅgeśa draws between absences and similarities has, in addition to its polemical punch, a rhetorical sting or irony: the Prābhākara accepts similarity as a separate category of object, like Naiyāyikas with absence.

Text (p. 757, Tirupati) and Translation

api ca na kevalaṃ bhūtalam a-bhāvaḥ, bhūtalâ-bhāvayoḥ ādhārâdheya-bhāvânubhavāt a-bhede tad-an-upapatteḥ | duḥkhavad-ātma-bhinnasya ca ātmano duḥkhâ-bhāvatve mokṣasya a-puruṣârthatva-prasaṅgaḥ, ātmano '-sādhyatvāt | atha ghaṭavad-bhūtala-jñāna-bhinnaṃ bhūtala-jñānam a-bhāvaḥ | tasya ca bhūtalâdhāratā sva-rūpa-saṃbandhena anubhūyata iti cet, na |

tasya niṣpratiyogikatvena a-bhāvatvân-upapatteḥ ity uktatvāt | api ca taj-jñānaṃ kiṃ sva-rūpa-sad eva a-bhāva-vyavahāra-kāraṇam, bhūtalâdhikaraṇaka-niṣedha-rūpatayā anubhūyamānaṃ vā | na ādyaḥ, sva-rūpa-sato bhūtalâdheyatayā pratīty-an-upapatteḥ | na dvitīyaḥ, ghaṭavad-bhūtala-jñānasya tadānīm an-upasthiteḥ tad-bhinna-jñānasya pratyetum a-śakyatvāt | kiṃ ca yadi ghaṭavad-bhūtala-jñānāt bhinna-bhūtala-jñānam a-bhāvaḥ tadā ghaṭavati doṣāt ghaṭavattvâ-jñāne bhūtala-jñānam a-bhāvo bhavet | tathā ca tad eva tadā eva ghaṭavat ghaṭâ-bhāvavac ca syāt, na syātāṃ ca ghaṭâ-bhāva-jñāna-tad-vyavahārau visaṃvādinau viṣayâ-bādhāt |

(**Gaṅgeśa** continues:) Furthermore, the floor alone is not the absence, since a locative (contained/container) relationship is experienced between the floor and the absence. If the two were non-distinct, that would not be possible.

And if a self—a self as distinct from the same self as endowed with suffering—were itself an absence of suffering, then liberation would not be a goal of human endeavor—this is the difficulty. For, a self is not itself something to be achieved or accomplished.

Objection: (Not the floor but) the *cognition* of the floor—as distinct from cognition of the floor with a pot on it—is the absence. And this cognition of the floor *is* "located on" (or contained by) the floor (and so do not hurl this logic of location in our faces).

Gaṅgeśa: Wrong, for a reason already stated: if such a cognition does not have a countercorrelate, then it could not possibly be an absence.

Furthermore, is this cognition of the floor (including—we wonder—the qualifier, "as distinct from cognition of the floor with a pot on it") to be a cause of the absential talk simply by its own nature, or, is it to be such a cause inasmuch as it occurs in the form of a *denial*, a denial that has the floor as the locus? (On either alternative, there is insuperable difficulty.) The former is wrong because, if it is simply by its own nature located (or contained by) the floor, then cognition would not be necessary (to provoke absential talk; the mere existence of the floor would cause talk of the absence). The latter is wrong because (if you include the qualifier, "as distinct from cognition of the floor with a pot on it") cognition of the floor *with* a pot on it is not, at the time (of the talk), situated in memory (or it might not be). (In that case) it would not be possible to cognize the cognition as distinct from that (other cognition and so no such absence could be cognized).

Moreover, if the absence is a cognition of the floor, a cognition distinct from cognition of the floor as having a pot on it, then when *because of a defect* cognition of the floor does not occur as having a pot on it when in fact one is there, cognition of the floor (erroneous cognition of a bare floor) would result in an actual absence. And so one and the same thing (at one and the same spot) at one and the same time would have and not have a pot on it, while neither the cognition of the absence of the pot nor the absence talk would be erroneous (on your account), since there would be nothing at odds with the "object."

Comments

Gaṅgeśa astutely points out that the Prābhākara needs to describe the floor cognition that is supposed to be an absence by saying that it is distinct from a cognition of the floor with a pot. But what, in that case, is the absentee? If it is to be the differentiator, "as distinct from cognition of the floor with a pot on it," the problem is that that might well not be situated in memory and thus not be cognitively available. We can be aware that a pot on the table is not on the floor without having previously experienced it as on the floor.

Furthermore, the Prābhākara cannot avoid the problem of error that Gaṅgeśa brings up, partly because he holds that all cognition is veridical but also because there is no objective basis, on his account, whereby such an error could be accounted for. The absential "error" would make it true that there was the absence, and so it would not be an error.

But Gaṅgeśa's chief argument is the first one given, about the locative relationship. To this, the Prābhākara's response is to switch back to the absential cognition away from the floor as what the absence reduces to, claiming that the locative relationship holds between the cognition and the floor. This seems particularly lame, though Gaṅgeśa takes the trouble to refute the suggestion through pointing out the trouble with countercorrelate availability, as we have seen. He elaborates the point in the next passage.

Text (p. 758, Tirupati, and p. 713, Calcutta) and Translation

atha vastuto ghaṭavato bhūtalasya jñānād bhinnaṃ bhūtala-jñānam a-bhāvaḥ, na ca ghaṭavati bhūtala-jñānam tathā |[11] vyavahāras tu visaṃvādī | tathā-vidha-bhramâ-darśanād iti cet, tarhi ghaṭavato bhūtalasya jñānāt bhinnatvena jñātaṃ[12] bhūtala-jñānam a-bhāva-vyavahṛti-hetuḥ | na ca tat saṃbhavati | sva-prakāśena anuvyavasāyena vā adhikaraṇa-jñāne tad-a-prakāśāt bheda-pratiyogino 'n-upasthiteḥ | na ca jñānântareṇa tathā anubhavaḥ | yogyân-upalabdhyā ghaṭâ-bhāva-niścayaṃ vinā tathā niścetum a-śakyatvāt |

Objection (by the Prābhākara): In fact, the absence is a cognition of the floor *as distinct* from cognition of the floor with a pot. And a floor cognition occurring with respect to the floor's having a pot is not like that. But the absential talk does not bring this out; it fails in this regard. For, such (*cognitive*) error is not found (but only *verbal* error).

Gaṅgeśa: Then, a cognition of the floor, cognition cognized *as distinct* from cognition of the floor with a pot, would cause the absence talk. But that is not possible. For, whether by self-illumination or by apperception, such distinctness could not be illumined within a cognition of the locus, since the countercorrelate of the distinctness would not (at the time) be set in awareness. Nor could another cognition bring it into experience. For, without certainty about *an absence* of the pot there—occurring because what is perceptible (namely, the pot) is not perceived—it would be impossible to be certain about such a distinctness.

Comments

Here Gaṅgeśa argues that the Prābhākara's qualification centering on the distinction between the two types of floor cognition requires "certainty about an absence" to make the distinction. There is an impossible circularity in this, and no way that the Prābhākara can get the required awareness of the countercorrelate into the mix. Furthermore, we are often certain about such distinctions, and so the Prābhākara proposal that the absential talk misrepresents the distinction may be ignored.

Text (p. 759, Tirupati) and Translation

> api ca adhikaraṇa-taj-jñānānām an-anugatatvena anugatâ-bhāva-vyavahārân-upapattiḥ | na ca atiriktâ-bhāva-pakṣe 'pi tathā a-bhāvatvasya anugatasya a-bhāvād iti vācyam | anugatâ-bhāvatvaṃ vinā api ghaṭâdir na paṭa iti samānâdhikaraṇa-niṣedhād anugata-vyavahāraḥ paṭânyonyâ-bhāvena ekena, evaṃ ghaṭâdau na gotvam ity anugata-vyavahāra ekena atyantâ-bhāvena, kapāleṣu bhūtaleṣu idānīṃ ghaṭo vinaṣṭa ity anugata-vyahāro dhvaṃsena ekena, ghaṭân-utpāda-daśāyām eteṣu ghaṭo na asti ity anugata-vyavahāra ekena prāg-a-bhāvena, evaṃ catvāro 'nugata-niṣedha-vyavahārāś catasṛbhir eva vyaktibhiḥ kriyante | tava tu a-bhāva-catuṣṭayaṃ tat-tad-adhikaraṇa-tat-tad-buddhīnām an-anugatatvān na sambhavati, anugatâ-bhāva-catuṣṭaya-vyavahārasya pratyekâ-bhāvena upapādayitum a-śakyatvād ity atiriktâ-bhāva-vyakti-catuṣṭaya-siddhiḥ | tasya ca yathā a-bhāvatvena ekena eka-padârthatvaṃ tathā anupadam eva vakṣyāmaḥ |

(**Gaṅgeśa** continues:) Moreover, if there were no uniformity among absential locations nor among cognitions of the locations, no uniform absential talk would arise (and of course it does).

Objection: On your view, too, on your view of absence as a separate and distinct category, there is the same problem, since there is (on your view) no uniform absencehood.

Gaṅgeśa: That cannot be alleged. Even without a uniform absencehood, (four types of absence giving rise to four types of absential cognition resulting in four types of uniform talk are found:) uniform absence talk results from (cognitions such as), "The cloth is not the pot and so on," which involve symmetrical negation with regard to a locus, (cognitions) brought about by something unitary, namely, *mutual distinctness* (or, "mutual absence," *anyonyâ-bhāva*). In the same way, (from cognitions like) "There is no cowhood in a pot and so on," brought about by something unitary, namely, *absolute absence*, uniform talk results. (Cognitions like) "The pot is now destroyed, smashed into potsherds on the floor," brought about by something unitary, namely, posterior or *destructional absence*, result in uniform talk. At times previous to the production of a pot, (cognitions like) "There is no pot there in those things," brought about by something unitary, namely, *prior absence*, result in uniform talk. In this way, four uniform ways of expressing denial come about just by way of four particulars (without a uniform absencehood).

But on your view, in contrast, this absential quadruplet would not be possible, because this and that locus or this and that cognition are not uniform. The uniform talk conforming to the quadruplet of absences could not possibly arise as a result of each individual absence (you find). Therefore, the thesis of a quadruplet of particular absences as separate and distinct (from the six other basic types of thing) is proved. And very shortly we shall explain how they all can be absences designated by the same word.

Comments

The Prābhākara view entails that there be an infinite variety of absences, since an infinity of distinct things could be a bare locus or an absential cognition.

The predominant Navya view of *absencehood* is—according to Ramanuja Tatacharya—that it is an "unanalyzable surplus property" (*a-khaṇḍôpādhi*). This is the common meaning of "absence" with the four types. Unlike black-cow-hood, this imposed property, though not a universal, recurs and cannot be further analyzed.[13]

B. K. Matilal points out that Raghunātha and Gadādhara make important contributions to later Navya thinking about the kind of "consecutive character" (*anugama*, uniformity) found with the four types of absence, that is, about how to understand it without seeing it as manifesting a universal.[14] Here Gaṅgeśa promises to say more "very shortly" on the ontological issue. And he does, but with a shift of focus down a level such that we get disappointingly little about the status of absencehood as opposed to absences.

But first, having now refuted the Prābhākara views of absences as bare loci and as certain types of cognition, Gaṅgeśa considers a new variation and third expression of the Prābhākara eliminative spirit.

Text (p. 761, Tirupati) and Translation

syād etat | yasmin samaya-viśeṣe yatra bhūtale '-bhāvaḥ paraiḥ svīkriyate, tat-samaya-viśeṣa-yoga eva bhūtalasya ghaṭâ-bhāvaḥ | evaṃ ca iha bhūtale ghaṭo na asti ity ādhārâdheya-bhāva-pratītir apy upapadyate | samaya-viśeṣa-yogasya bhūtala-vṛttitvāt | na ca samaya-viśeṣa-yogasya a-bhāvatve an-anugamo doṣaḥ | atiriktâ-bhāva-pakṣe 'pi tulyatvāt | a-bhāvatvasya jāter upādher vā a-sattvāt | yadi ca a-bhāva-pratīti-prayogânugamârthaṃ tatra dharmântaraṃ svīkriyate, tadā samaya-viśeṣa-yoga-vṛtty eva tad astu, lāghavād iti | tan na | samaya-viśeṣa-yogasya niṣpratiyogikatvena a-bhāva-vyavahārâ-sāmarthyāt | kiṃ ca bhūtala-vat samaya-viśeṣo 'pi a-bhāvâdhāratayā anubhūyate idānīṃ bhūtale ghaṭo na asti iti pratīteḥ | na ca tat-samaya-viśeṣe tat-samaya-viśeṣa-yogaḥ | a-bhede saṃbandhân-upapattau ādhārâdheya-bhāvâ-bhāvāt | api ca samaye kim a-bhāvâśrayatā eva viśeṣaḥ, tat-tat-samaya-sva-rūpaṃ vā | ādye '-bhāva-svīkāraḥ | dvitīye 'n-anugamaḥ | mama tu ekâ-bhāva-vyakter eva tathā, nānā-samaya-vṛttitvāt | kiṃ ca samaya-viśeṣa-yogād idānīṃ bhūtalam iti pratīti-prayogau syātām, viśeṣaṇasya sva-prakāraka-viśiṣṭa-pratyaya-janakatvāt na tu bhūtale ghaṭâ-bhāva iti | yadi ca tat-tat-samaya-viśeṣa-yogād bhūtale ghaṭâ-bhāva-vyavahāras tadā yādṛśa-saṃsthāna-viśeṣa-viśiṣṭe kapāle ghaṭo vartate tādṛśa-kapālâdikam eva tat-tat-samaya-viśeṣa-yogāt ghaṭâdi-vyavahāra-janakam astu kiṃ ghaṭâdinā | pratītiś ca tulyā |

Objection: That may be. (But consider the following, better view.) Where you others (you Naiyāyikas) accept an absence, namely, at (for example) a particular period of time on a floor, precisely the *connection* of the floor with the particular time-period is the absence of the pot. And in this way it *is* possible (contrary to your earlier objection) to have too a cognition of a locative relationship such as "The pot is not here *on* the floor." For, the connection with the particular time-period occurs *on* the floor (i.e., it obeys the logic of "occurrence on," *vṛtti*).

Nor do we face the fault (which you alleged against previous essays of our Prābhākara side, namely) of "lack of uniformity" with respect to the absencehood exhibited by (all the various things that have) connections with a particular time-period. For, the same problem is not solved on your view of absences as separate and distinct. Absencehood is neither a universal (*jāti*) nor a "surplus property" (as you would have it, *upādhi*). (Either way, you are accepting something as a further property, and) if for the purpose of accounting for uniformity among absential cognitions and among verbal expressions a further property is accepted in that regard, then it may as well be (our) "occurrence of a connection with a particular time-period," since this is the economical view.

Gaṅgeśa: That's wrong. A connection with a particular time-period could not generate absence talk inasmuch as (while an absence has a countercorrelate) a connection with a particular time-period has no countercorrelate.

Furthermore, cognitions occur such as, "Right now (or, *at* this time) *on* the floor there is no pot," where the time-period as well as the floor are experienced as location. And there is no connection with a particular time-period *at* (or *on* or *in*) a connection with a particular time-period. For, given that no relation is possible in the case of (identity or) non-distinctness, there could be no locative relationship.

Moreover, does the particular rest in the time-period which would be its substratum, or is the relation with this and that time-period self-linking (*sva-rūpa*)? On the first alternative, you are accepting absence (as a distinct and separate category). On the second, you cannot account for uniformity. On my view, in contrast, a unitary absence individual is like this (i.e., is uniform, etc.), since it occurs at various time-periods.

Further, the cognition and verbal expression resulting from a connection with a particular time-period would be, "Right now the floor," instead of "On the floor, the pot is not," since a qualifier ϕ generates a cognition having ϕ as predication content.

And if we are to view talk of an absence of a pot on the floor as resulting from (the floor's) connection to this or that particular time-period, then let us view talk of a pot and the like as generated by just the particular configuration of potsherds that make up the pot, that is, (we should hasten to add) pot talk and the like "resulting from (the configured potsherds') connection to this or that time-period"! What then would be the point of the pot? (We would have explained it away.) And (not only would this insane logic apply to pot talk, etc., but also) the same would apply to the cognition.

Comments

The locative relation touted by the Prābhākara would be between a particular occasion—which would occur at or on a locus—and the particular thing or locus that it would occur on. Gaṅgeśa points out that we commonly talk about absences as occurring *at* a particular time (*idānīṃ* = *asmin samaye*). Thus in this way too the Prābhākara reductive candidate does not conform to the logic of absential talk and cognition.

When Gaṅgeśa says, "a qualifier ϕ generates a cognition having ϕ as predication content," he means in the default case of veridical cognition.

The last paragraph of the passage is comprised of counterfactual reasoning intended to show the absurdity of the latest Prābhākara proposal. Segments of time are, in a sense, containers of phenomena. But that relationship is hardly sufficient to deem otiose the separate reality of the contained. A pot, as a whole, rests in its potsherds; it is located in them. And the potsherds are configured in a certain way during a particular time-period, the period, to be precise, when the pot exists! Such awkward substitutes are better dispensed with, not pots or the like.

The Prābhākara, like all Mīmāṃsakas, tends to be realist about wholes. Thus the counterfactual argument is particularly biting in the context of the Nyāya/Prābhākara debate that has dominated the section. But next Gaṅgeśa takes up not this but the Buddhist view that denies that there is a distinct reality of wholes over the parts that make them up.

Text (p. 763, Tirupati) and Translation

etena, "dṛṣṭas tāvad ayaṃ ghaṭo 'tra ca patan dṛṣṭas tathā mudgaro / dṛṣṭā kharpara-saṃhatiḥ param ito '-bhāvo na dṛṣṭo '-paraḥ | tena a-bhāva iti śrutiḥ kva-nihitā kiṃ ca atra tat-kāraṇaṃ / svâdhīnā kalaśasya kevalam iyaṃ dṛṣṭā kapālâvalī ||'' iti nirastam | mudgara-pātād vinaṣṭo ghaṭaḥ iti pratītyā[15] atirikta-vināśânubhavāt | na ca kevala-bhūtalaṃ tad-buddhir vā taj-janyā, tena vinā api tayoḥ sattvāt | tvan-mate ca tayor a-bhāva-mātratvena vināśatvâ-yogāt | yoge vā a-bhāva-mātrasya vināśitvâpattiḥ | atha tvan-mate yad vināśakaṃ tad eva tat-sahitaṃ bhūtalaṃ jñānaṃ vā vināśa iti cet, na | mudgara-pāta-janyo hi vināśo 'nubhūyate | na ca tasya eva taj-janakatvam | sapratiyogikaś ca vināśo 'nubhūyate | na ca mudgara-pātas tathā |

(**Gaṅgeśa** continues:) By this reasoning the following is refuted.

Buddhist (Jñānaśrī in a verse): First here a pot is seen, and then seen is a hammer falling./Seen is a heap of sherds, but other than these an ''absence'' is not seen./Thus where does your ''absence'' testimony direct us? And what is its cause?/Only this is seen, a pot's potsherds in a self-dependent stream.

Gaṅgeśa: (This is to be thrown out.) For, there is experience of a separate and distinct destruction, as is shown by such a cognition as, ''By the fall of the hammer, the pot is destroyed.''

Furthermore, it is not the case that the floor alone or a cognition of it are generated by the destruction, since those two occur without it occurring. And since, on your (Prābhākara) view (which does not distinguish types of absence), the two would be simply absences, neither could be connected to the destruction (the connection would be to another absence). Or, if there is to be a connection, then any absence would be destructible (and the floor would be destroyed by a pot's being present and could not be cognized)—this is the difficulty.

Objection: That which, on your view, is the *instrument* of destruction, is itself—or the floor *and* it, or the cognition *and* it—the destruction.

Gaṅgeśa: No. For, the destruction is experienced as *produced* by the hammer. And nothing is a producer of itself. Furthermore, a destruction is experienced as having a countercorrelate (viz., that which is destroyed), and the fall of the hammar is not like that.

Comments

In the Buddhist view, universal flux is ''self-dependent'' in that it is impossible to trace external causal sequences. We project shape and form according to our wants and needs. The phenomenal display is mind-dependent, but there are no external causal processes. Everything is self-created and self-destroyed at every moment. Pragmatically, we take potsherds configured in a certain fashion to be a pot. When we say it is destroyed, we are taking successor sherds to lie on the floor in a different configuration. Where then is an ''absence?'' The presence itself was our own projection. And we project onto positive ''event atoms'' (the *sva-lakṣaṇa*-s), not somehow on gaps.

Gaṅgeśa's refutation proceeds ''by the same reasoning'' effective against the Prābhākara, to wit, that veridical absential experience cannot be explained except by presuming absences.

The verse belongs to the eleventh-century Buddhist eclectic, Jñānaśrī, and the rhetorical effect of the citing seems mainly to damn the Prābhākara by association.[16]

In the middle of the passage, Gaṅgeśa again brings out that the Prābhākara attempts at reduction are insensitive to the precise varieties of absence. If the Prābhākara sees the mere floor bereft of the pot—or as a cognition of that—as simply an absence like any other, he will have to face the destructive dilemma one horn of which leads to the re-emergence of a destroyed pot (this untoward ramification lurks in the bushes but is not expressly mentioned) and the other to destruction of the floor by even the gentlest setting down of ever so tiny a pot!

The final proposal is defeated by the chief argument given earlier, by the logic of absences, so to say, as involving a countercorrelate, as well as by the principle that nothing is self-caused.

Text (p. 764, Tirupati, and p. 718, Calcutta) and Translation

> nanv a-bhāvena samaṃ bhūtalasya saṃbandhâ-bhāvāt kathaṃ bhūtale ghaṭâ-bhāva-pratyayaḥ | sva-rūpa-saṃbandhād iti cet, tarhi ghaṭavad-bhūtalasya api catvarīyâ-bhāvena sva-rūpa-saṃbandho 'sti | bhūtalam a-bhāvaś ca ity adhikasya sva-rūpa-saṃbandhasya a-bhāvāt | pratiyogy-āropa eva sva-rūpa-saṃbandhaḥ | ata eva āropya niṣidhyata ity ucyata iti cet, na | tatra a-bhāva-saṃbandhe saty āropaḥ sa eva ca a-bhāva-saṃbandha ity anyonyâśrayāt iti cet, na | saṃbandhântaram antareṇa viśiṣṭa-pratyaya-janana-yogyatvasya sva-rūpa-saṃbandhatvāt | na ca ghaṭavad-bhūtala-catvarīyâ-bhāvayoḥ paras-paraṃ viśiṣṭa-pratyayaḥ | jñāna-viṣayoḥ samavāya-samavāyinor iva saṃbandhântarâbhyupagame ca an-avasthā-bhiyā tat-saṃbandha-sambandhinor api tādṛśa-saṃbandha-svīkārād iti siddho 'tirikto '-bhāva iti tad-grāhikā viśeṣaṇatā iti siddham etat |

Objection: Since (on your view) there is no relation between the floor and the absence, how can there be a cognition of a pot's absence *on* the floor? If you say (as Naiyāyikas do say) that such a cognition results from self-linkage (*sva-rūpa-saṃbandha*), then the floor having a pot on it will stand also in a self-linking relation with the absence of another pot that it is the courtyard! For there is no self-linkage in addition to that constituted by the floor and an absence (you yourself hold).

If you were to answer that the self-linking relation amounts to an (imaginative or illusory) superimposition of a countercorrelate (as silver is superimposed on mother-of-pearl in the erroneous perception)—thus first superimposing would one be able to deny anything—you would still be wrong. For, you would have a superimposition on the condition that you have to explain a relation to an absence, while the superimposition would turn out to be just that very relation to the absence: the fallacy of "mutual dependence" would be incurred.

Gaṅgeśa: No. For, self-linking relations are capable of generating a cognition of an entity as qualified without another relation. And there arises no cognition of an entity as qualified that would be a cognition both of a floor with a pot on it and of an absence of another pot that is in a courtyard, the two as mutually qualificative. Furthermore, like a cognition and its object (or indication) and like inherence and its terms where acceptance of another relation would invite fear of infinite regress, the relation of an absence to its relatee is also to be accepted as such a relation (namely, as self-linking).

Thus is absence proved to be a separate and distinct category. Hence the thesis that "qualifierhood" brings about a grasping of an absence is proved (too).

Comments

Gaṅgeśa does not say why there does not arise cognition of an entity as somehow qualified both by the presence of one pot and by the absence of another pot that is far away in a courtyard. Surely such is possible. Apparently, the reason is that the one cannot stand as the substratum of the other, at least not in a perceptual situation. Neither could stand as perceptual qualificandum relative to the other as qualifier.

In closing, Gaṅgeśa again invokes self-linkage as the way to avoid infinite regress. As with inherence and its terms, the relation between an absence and its locus is self-linking. The relation is called "qualifierhood" (*viśeṣaṇatā*) apparently to stress that it gives rise to cognition of an entity as qualified, e.g., a cognition of a pot-absence as qualifying a floor—or vice-versa, with the pot-absence as the qualificandum and the floor as the qualifier.

atha viṣayâloka-saṃnikarṣa-vādaḥ

NOW, DISCOURSE ON THE CONNECTION OF THE SENSE OBJECT AND LIGHT

Text (p. 770, Tirupati, and p. 720, Calcutta) and Translation

ṣodhā saṃnikarṣaḥ pratyakṣa-viśeṣe kāraṇam | viṣayeṇa āloka-saṃyoga-viśeṣaś ca tatra kāraṇam, na tu cakṣuṣā | prakāśa-sthena andhakāra-sthasya a-grahaṇāt vaiparītye ca grahaṇāt | nanv evaṃ para-bhāgâvacchedena āloka-saṃyukto 'pi ghaṭo gṛhyeta | na ca avayavi-graha-sāmagryāḥ svâvayava-sāmagrī-niyamāt para-bhāgâvacchinno na gṛhyata iti vācyam | try-aṇuke vyabhicārāt, pratyakṣâvayave ca sāmagrī-bheda-kalpane mānâ-bhāvāt |

Gaṅgeśa: Six kinds of sensory connection are causes of particular types of perception (as has been explained). A particular type of contact of light with an object (perceived) is also a cause of a type of perception, but not contact of light with the visual organ. For, something situated in the dark is not grasped by someone in the light, and in the reverse case there is perception.

Objection: If what you say were right, a pot would be grasped (visually) even when its contact with light was limited to its back portion (relative to a perceiver, a notion that is obviously false). And it should not be said that (this can be ruled out) according to the principle, "A causal complex sufficient to make a whole grasped is a causal complex sufficient to make (some) parts grasped," such that (there being no contact with an object's back which is not perceived while other parts are perceived) the object specifically in its back portion would not be grasped. For (that principle is wrong in that) there is a counterexample in the triad (which as the smallest thing visible is visible as a whole while its parts are not visible). Furthermore, there is no reason to imagine distinct causal complexes for those things whose parts are perceptible (i.e., this way to eliminate what you see as a troublesome counterexample would be *ad hoc*).

Comments

This section, which is another on which there is no extant commentary by Mathurānātha, is full of dubious readings in the manuscripts according to Ramanuja Tatacharya. He has suggested several changes beyond those indicated in the Vidyapeetha edition. These, as always, are marked by notes.

The Asiatic Society edition lumps this and the following two sections together as the "Discourse on Causes of Perception," *pratyakṣa-kāraṇa-vāda*.

A brief commentary by Jayadeva is included—for these sections and the rest of the perception chapter.

Ramanuja Tatacharya informs us that many of the positions and arguments that Gaṅgeśa presents here can be found in Śrīdhara's *Nyāya-kandalī* commentary on Praśastapāda.[1]

Gaṅgeśa begins by summarizing the discussion of the previous four sections. With regard to perceptions as end results, there are six fundamental types of sensory connection. The principal causal factors are the object perceived and the sense organ, though it is only the sense organ that is identified as the chief cause, the *karaṇa*. (Objects do, after all, exist unperceived; sense-organ activity *triggers* perception.) But there are other causal factors to be identified, too, and of course not every proposal proffering a candidate cause can survive scrutiny. In this new section and the next three to follow, we are concerned with a variety of auxiliary causes that help to bring about one or another type of perception.

Perhaps what is most interesting throughout this new discussion is simply the attempt to picture the physical processes involved in perception, an attempt at a kind of cognitive science. Alternatively, the effort could be viewed as in spite of its immature science valuable as philosophic phenomenology, closely tied—as it is—to the way people talk about their perceptions. Nyāya's physical theory is decidely pre-modern, limited to five material elements, four of which, we may remind ourselves, are atomic, compounding to form material things, solid, fluid, luminous, odiferous, and so on. And the sense organs operate in peculiar fashions according to the natures of these elements, which are the, so to say, perceptual media. We shall fill in further background as we proceed.

Gaṅgeśa's opening argument is clear. A person standing in the dark can see something in the light. But nothing itself not in the light can be visually perceived. Contact between light and an object perceived is a necessary condition for veridical visual perception. Contact between light and the visual organ, however, is not required, since a person standing in the dark can see an illumined object. Below, Gaṅgeśa will resist a series of proposals motivated by the consideration that if light has to be in contact with an object seen along with the visual organ (which "reaches" the object by travelling out of the eyes), there should be postulated this additional contact, too.

Another perplexity concerns the relation of perception of parts of a compound object to perception of the object as a whole. When we perceive a thing as a whole, do we necessarily perceive all of its parts, or some, or none? The smallest thing perceptible is thought to be a mote in a sunbeam, which is also considered a triad. A triad is composed of three dyads, which are in turn each made up of two ultimate atoms. Dyads are thought to be imperceptible. Thus, the smallest perceptible thing has imperceptible parts. How, then, does

Gaṅgeśa propose to make specific his rule about contact with light? Just where, with which parts, etc., is the contact supposed to occur?

But before addressing this problem about light and the perceived object, Gaṅgeśa turns to *pūrvapakṣin* proposals about the organ and contact with light.

Text (p. 720, Calcutta) and Translation

atha abhimukhâvayavâvacchedena ghaṭâloka-saṃyogaḥ kāraṇam, tarhi abhimukhâvayavâvacchedena cakṣur-āloka-saṃyogo 'pi hetur astu | yadi ca āloka-saṃyogâvacchinne cakṣus-saṃyogas tathā samāna-deśatā-virodhaś ca nibiḍayor eva, anyathā paṭa-mahārajatayor paṭôdakayoś ca a-graha-prasaṅgaḥ | tarhi ghaṭa-saṃyogâvacchinne cakṣur-āloka-saṃyogaḥ kāraṇam astu |

(A further) **objection**: (It seems you want to hold that) there is a (cognitive) cause in light's contact with a pot, specifically with the parts facing the perceiver. So, let a cause also be light's contact with the visual organ, contact restricted to the parts (of the thing perceived) facing the perceiver. And if the visual organ's contact with something (e.g., a pot perceived) restricted to the precise spots where there is contact with light is a cause, then the incompatibility that holds with respect to one and the same place would be only between two solid things (i.e., no two solid things can be at the same place at the same time, but light and the visual organ are not solid). Otherwise, a gold cloth or a piece of cloth soaked in water would not be grasped. So let there be a cause in light's contact with the visual organ at the location specified by contact with (the object seen, e.g.) a pot.

Comments

Cloth can apparently be soaked in liquid gold such that the two things can occupy the same location, like water and cloth. The thesis that the visual organ requires in its operation the presence of light—light in contact with it—is no more ruled out by a one-thing-at-one-spot principle than is ruled out that the object seen has to be in contact with light. Only two solid things cannot be at the same location, and light is not solid. Light's presence does not preclude the presence of something else. It precludes darkness, the absence of light, but nothing else.

Text (p. 771, Tirupati) and Translation

atha cālinī-nyāyena āloka-saṃyoga-saṃnihite cakṣur-ghaṭa-saṃyogaḥ kāraṇam tadā ghaṭa-cakṣus-saṃyoga-saṃnihite cakṣur-āloka-saṃyogo hetur astv iti cet, na evam | anvaya-vyatirekābhyāṃ viṣayâloka-saṃyogasya kāraṇatve niścite tena eva upapattau na cakṣur-āloka-saṃyogaḥ kāraṇaṃ kalpyate |

(Still another) **objection**: There is a (cognitive) cause in the visual organ's contact with the pot at the location of the connection where there is also contact with light. So by the maxim of the "strainer," let there (also) be a cause in light's contact with the visual organ at the location of the connection where there is also contact between the pot and the visual organ.

Gaṅgeśa: No, it's not so. By the method of agreement (or positive correlation) and disagreement (or negative correlation), it is definitely settled that light's contact with the object is a (cognitive) cause. That being the case, the possibility of perception is explained. No contact of light with the visual organ need be imagined as an additional cause.

Comments

The "strainer" (*cālinī*) maxim draws an analogy: a *cālinī* is a sieve that allows what's on top to pass through several holes simultaneously. No single hole is alone a cause of something's getting strained. Similarly, or so it is claimed, contact between light and an object seen is not alone the relevant cause. Contact between light and the visual organ is also required for something to be seen.

Gaṅgeśa's argument is that once light's contact with the object is admitted as a cause of visual perception, the objector's proposal is otiose. There are other causal factors identifiable by the method of positive and negative correlation, but not that proposed.

Text (p. 771, Tirupati, and p. 721, Calcutta) and Translation

anye tu dvayor apy āloka-saṃyogayoḥ kāraṇatve viṣayâloka-saṃyogaḥ kāraṇam eva iti | nanv abhimukhâvayavâvacchedena viṣayâloka-saṃyogasya kāraṇatve[2] āvaśyakatvāt[3] avayavâloka-saṃyoga eva hetur astu iti cet, na | avayava-saṃyoga-mātrasya atiprasakteḥ svâvayava-saṃyogo vaktavyaḥ | tathā ca sva-saṃyoga eva lāghavāt | avayava-saṃyogena ca anyatha-siddhau kāraṇatā eva na syāt saṃyogasya ity uktam |

(**Gaṅgeśa** continues:) But others (i.e., other Naiyāyikas, reason as follows).

A **Naiyāyika faction**: Light's contact with an object seen is (in all instances) a cause (of sight of an object), given that (in some instances) there occur two contacts with light that are causes (a contact with the object and a contact with the visual organ).

Objection: If such an (invariable) cause is conceived as light's contact with the object restricted to the parts that face the perceiver—(as it should be conceived) since that is necessary (for the object to be seen)—let contact alone between such parts and light be the relevant cause.

Naiyāyika faction: No. Mere "contact with such parts" would have too wide an application (since, with light in contact with a *cloth's* part, a *pot* could be seen, according to this formulation): contact with *its own* parts is what has to be said.

Gaṅgeśa: (Yes.) And so light's contact with a thing itself (i.e., with a whole) is *alone* a cause (not also with its parts), because this is the economical position. Furthermore, it has been said (above, in the section on sensory connection, pp. 344–47) that if contact with a whole is rendered superfluous (as a cause) by contact with its parts, contact would not be a cause at all. (And so light's contact with a whole is not rendered superfluous.)

Comments

Gaṅgeśa endorses the law as amended by the Naiyāyika faction. And we need not multiply causal factors. To target light's contact with a thing perceived—the whole that would be picked out by an appropriate verbalization, e.g., "A pot," referring to a pot being perceived visually—is to target a relevant causal factor when the visual perception is the effect to be explained. Such targeting is identifying a cause that is not rendered irrelevant by a more proximate causal factor.

Next we are presented another controversial causal factor, and another by Gaṅgeśa endorsed.

Text (Tirupati, p. 772) and Translation

> ālokasya udbhūta-rūpam api vyañjakam anvaya-vyatirekitvāt | nanu[4] tejaḥ-kāraṇatâvaccedakaṃ tat ūśmâdīnāṃ cākṣuṣa-janakatvâ-[5] bhāvāt | na ca svātantryeṇa anvaya-vyatirekitvāt dvayor api hetutvam | anyathā daṇḍâder api cakrâvacchedakatvaṃ syād iti vācyam | udbhūta-tejo-mātrayoḥ samavadhāne kāryân-udayād iti cet, mā evam | udbhūta-rūpasya tejastvam, tejasaś ca udbhūta-rūpatvaṃ vā avacchedam iti vinigamakâ-bhāvād ubhayor api hetutvāt, daṇḍa-cakrayor iva eka-ekaṃ vihāya aparasya anvaya-vyatirekâ-bhāvāt |

(**Gaṅgeśa** continues:) The manifest color of light is also a cause (making a visual perception come about, *vyañjaka*)—by an inference based on both positive and negative correlations.

Objection.1: Manifest color is a cause in that it qualifies the causal role of the fiery element (*tejas*, the element of which the sun is made as well as light). For, the (properties of) heat and so on (belonging to *tejas*) do not generate visual perceptions.

Objection.2 (against objector.1): Since both light and manifest color are, by positive and negative correlations, independently established, both should be regarded as causes. Otherwise, we would say that a stick and so on, *as qualified by the wheel*, is (alone) a cause (of a pot, whereas clearly both stick and wheel are causes).

Answer (by objector.1): That should not be said. For, if manifest color by itself (as a property of a pot) and the fiery element (*tejas*) by itself (in the form of heat at night that does not have manifest color) were to be present at the same place (but without the one qualifying the other), the effect would come about (according to this conception, given the rest of the factors in the causal complex—but we do not see a pot at night).

Gaṅgeśa: Don't think like that. Is the specifier the manifest color's being fiery or the fiery element's being manifestly colored? Since there is no way to choose between the two alternatives, both should be regarded as causes. Like the case of a stick and a wheel (both used to make a pot), leaving aside either the other would not conform by positive and negative correlations (with production of the effect).

Comments

An important piece of background information is that sometimes at night one can feel the heat of the sun. This occurs, just as in daytime, because the sun's rays—which are made of the fiery element, *tejas*—carry heat, which is, however, considered to be something separate from the rays and also to be made of *tejas*. The word *tejas* is rendered here as "the fiery element," but it should be kept in mind that fire is just one of the things made of *tejas* atoms. Light is another. Now, whereas we can we see light, we cannot see heat. Therefore, the manifest color of light has also to be counted a cause of visual perception. Heat has non-manifest color.

Since by the end of the passage it has been cogently objected that without qualifying one another manifest color and fire are not causes, presumably Gaṅgeśa in his response means that the fiery element *as qualified by* manifest color and manifest color *as qualified by* the fiery element are causes. Rucidatta points this out (p. 773: *paras-parâvaccinnasya eva paras-parasya tathātvāt*).

Text (p. 773, Tirupati) and Translation

evaṃ cakṣuṣo rūpam api vyañjakaṃ vyañjaka-tejo-rūpatvāt āloka-rūpa-vat |
rūpasya vyañjakatve udbhūta-rūpatvaṃ tejo-gatôdbhūta-rūpatvaṃ vā na upādhiḥ,
vyabhicāreṇa gauraveṇa ca a-prayojakatvāt |

(**Gaṅgeśa** continues:) In this way, the (non-manifest) color of the visual organ also makes something (visually) grasped, *since* the visual organ has the color of the fiery element that makes something (visually) grasped, like the color of light.

Neither being-manifest-color nor being-manifest-color-residing-in-*tejas* is an "undercutter," *upādhi*, for this inference, since, because of deviation and cumbersomeness, such is not a cause (of something being grasped).

Comments

Just as it is has been established that the color of light is one of the causes of visual perception, so the color of the visual organ, although non-manifest, must also be considered such a cause. For, as stated in the inference, it has the color of the fiery atoms that make it up, while those atoms are themselves a cause of visual perceptions. A visual organ is very small, but is made of fiery atoms, and thus has color although non-manifest and not visible to another visual organ.

The proposed undercutter, *upādhi*, is ruled out on the following grounds. A true undercutter must pervade the probandum but not pervade the prover. Naiyāyikas consider fiery atoms to have *manifest* color; such color is not seen because the atoms are too small to be seen, not because the color is not manifest. The same holds for dyads, though not for triads (a triad is composed of three dyads). Thus, while it might seem that being-manifest-color pervades the probandum (wherever a making something grasped visually, there manifest color), the manifest color of the dyad is a counterexample.

Text (p. 777, Tirupati) and Translation

kiṃ tu vyañjaka-rūpam eva tathā, lāghavāt | viṣaya-stham api rūpam udbhūtaṃ sahakāri | tad-udbhave ca mānam, indriyâlokâdi-pratyāsannaṃ mahad-avayavivāyûpanīta-surabhi-śītôṣma-cakṣur-ādikaṃ sākṣātkāra-kāraṇa-bhūta-kiṃcit-samavadhāna-śūnyam a-pratyakṣatvāt andhakāra-stha-ghaṭa-vad iti | tac ca kāraṇaṃ lāghavād anugataṃ sāmānyaṃ rūpâdi-vṛtti na dravya-gatam | ūṣmâdau sparśa-grahe rūpasya, prabhâdau rūpa-grahe sparśasya graha-prasaṅgāt, udbhavatva-ekârtha-samavāyâ-viśeṣāt | anyathā sparśa-rūpayor a-graha-prasaṅgāt | na apy ubhaya-vṛtti, rūpâdi-vṛttitvena eva upapatteḥ | rūpa-sparśayos tu tan nānā, eka-grahe 'py aparasya a-grahāt | na ca rūpatvâdinā parâpara-bhāvân-upapattiḥ, tāratvâdi-van nānātvāt | rūpâdi-pratyakṣe eka-ekôdbhavasya eva prayojakatvāt |

(**Gaṅgeśa** continues:) Rather, just the color (of *tejas* or of anything made of the atoms of the fiery element) is so (i.e., is a cause of something being visually grasped), because this is the economical position.

(**Old Nyāya**:) The manifest color situated in the object is *also* an auxiliary cause (of a visual perception). And there is the following proof of the causality of its being manifest. Something fragrant (e.g., an invisible particle of a flower), cold (e.g., a tiny bit of water), or hot (e.g., a tiny bit of *tejas*) can be brought into contact with the visual organ and the like by a large-sized whole, for instance, a puff of wind. That is to say, things can be brought into relation to the sense organ, light, and so on, but not be immediate causes of a perception if the things are not seen, like a pot in the dark.

And this cause (namely, being-manifest or manifestness) is, for considerations of economy, to be considered a uniform and continuous universal that rests in colors and so on (in qualities, that is) but not in substances. For (if it rested in substances) we would have the unfortunate ramification that in grasping heat and the like (which are substances) color would be grasped, and in grasping light and the like (which are also substances) a touch would be grasped, since manifestness would, without distinction, inhere in a single object (that would be manifest). Otherwise (contrariwise, i.e., if although exhibiting manifestness an object need not be grasped, all the other causal conditions obtaining), we would be in the predicament that neither color nor touch (etc.) would be grasped.

Nor does it rest in both (qualities and substances). For, taken to rest only in color and so on (i.e., in qualities), perception can be explained (thus the additional supposition is otiose).

Now, manifestness is distinct in (the distinct qualities) color and touch, because one is grasped without the other's being grasped. And it is not the case that it is impossible to have a relation of pervaded and pervading (characteristic of the hierarchy of universals, without cross-section), since, like shrillnesses and so on (shrillness is a universal that rests in more than one type of shrill sound, "ka," "kha," "ga," and so on), it is multiple. Just the respective manifestness (respective, that is, according to the quality perceived) is what brings about perception of color and the rest.

Comments

It might seem as though colorhood does not pervade manifestness, since there are manifest qualities other than colors. But, according to the Old school, the hierarchy has a more complex structure: as the shrillness that rests in one sound is different from that in another, so there are distinct universals, distinct manifestness-es, that rest in distinct qualities. Colorhood does rest in every instance of manifest color, and of unmanifest color, too, as does touchhood in every manifest touch, et cetera.

Text (p. 779, Tirupati) and Translation

> nanu mahattva eva udbhavatvam astu | tad eva pratyakṣatve tantram, lāghavāt | na rūpe 'pi gauravād iti cet, na | āśraya-mahattvôdbhavâ-bhāve 'pi gandha-sparśayoḥ pratyakṣatvena udbhavatvam iti pratyakṣa-mūrta-viśeṣaṇa-guṇatvena rūpe 'py udbhavatvāt na mahattve, sāmānya-guṇatvāt |

Objection: Why not let this "manifestness" be (the relevant cause of perception) of just those things that are of appreciable size? (Thus) being-of-appreciable-size is that which allows perception—this is the economical position. Being-of-appreciable-size (*mahattva*) does not rest in color, too, because that would be cumbersome (i.e., it rests only in things that are in this way large, because that is the economical position).

Old Nyāya: No. Given that manifestness can be absent in something whose substratum *has* appreciable size (e.g., a triad that can be grasped by the organ of smell but not by sight), smell and touch are perceptible (because of an object's having *distinct types* of appreciable size, a size that makes one or the other quality, a smell or a touch, perceptible). Thus (by the principle that this fact implies) there must be manifestness with respect to a thing's color, too, inasmuch as color is a *specific quality* appropriate to things having the minimal size required to be "formed" (*mūrta*). But this does not hold of things with appreciable size (*tout court* or in general), since that is a *generic quality*.

Comments

Manifestness as a perceptual cause is not reducible to something's being of appreciable size, because "being-of-appreciable-size" varies according to the qualities perceived—sights, sounds, and so on—by the several sense organs. Some triads (a triad is composed of three dyads) can be smelled but not seen. Thus they would have appreciable size in one way and not in another.

A "specific quality" is a property common to a certain natural grouping of things and to nothing not of the group. For example, smell is a specific quality of things earthen. Non-earthen things appearing to have smell are to be understood as composites, having earthen atoms in their composition. Thus smelly water would not be pure. Color is a specific quality because things having color make up, according to natural divisions, a tidy group: things made of earth, water, and/or *tejas*, the fiery element. "Generic qualities" are exhibited across fundamental types, such as conjunction, *samyoga* ("contact"). Various things can be conjoined, i.e., exhibit the quality and be in contact, ocean and shore, for example, tree and monkey, or an earthen and a fiery atom. Fundamentally different types of thing similarly all have size and weight.

Manifestness is a generic quality, and so does little to explain why objects are perceptible by one organ, two organs, or three, or four, as the case may be, and not the rest. In fact, something that has form—or is "formed," *mūrta*—will have visible color, which is a specific quality of the group of things perceptible by sight. In other words, Naiyāyikas say that something having the minimal size and form to be visible is *mūrta*, "formed," and Gaṅgeśa, presenting here views of the Old school, uses the term to make plain that one way requirements for perceptibility vary is according to the specific qualities of the things perceived, such as color for things perceptible by sight.

Text (p. 780, Tirupati) and Translation

atha an-udbhavatvam eva jātiḥ, a-pratyakṣatva-prayojakatvena sākṣād eva tat-kalpanāt tad-a-bhāvāt pratyakṣatvam iti cet, na | a-pratyakṣatāyāḥ pratyakṣa-kāraṇa-viraha-prayojyatvena pratyakṣa-kāraṇasya lāghavena jāteḥ kalpanāt | na tu pratibandhakatvena an-udbhavatvaṃ kalpayitvā tad-a-bhāvaḥ kāraṇaṃ gauravād iti saṃpradāya-vidaḥ |

Objection: Just *non*-manifestness is the (relevant) universal. Inasmuch as it directly causes *non*-perception, it is to be postulated. From its absence, perceptions occur.

Old Nyāya: No. Non-perceptions occur because of a lack of one or another cause of perception (not because of non-manifestness). It is more economical to postulate universals for causes of perception (as opposed to anything as a cause of a non-perception). Non-manifestness is not to be supposed a preventer such that its absence would be a cause, because that is a cumbersome view.

Gaṅgeśa: So say those who know the tradition (i.e., those of the Old school).

Comments

In the next passage, Gaṅgeśa endorses non-manifestness, against the Old Nyāya view voiced here. His argument is economy, as we shall see.

At this point we may pause to remark that while modern commentators regularly claim that Gaṅgeśa blindly follows tradition in his physical theory and in ontological matters in general, his innovations being restricted to epistemology, this and the next few sections show him in a different light. Of course, our author works within a pretty tightly confined problem space formed by his tradition, and, from the distant perspective of current science, his speculations may not appear innovative. He does, nevertheless, work to make his views conform to what were apparently prevalent arguments and accepted evidence. Moreover, some interesting features of physical reality are identified in several places in upcoming text—perhaps most notably in speculation that gold might be made not of atoms of *tejas*, the fiery element, but of atoms of an entirely unique element (a conclusion suggested after the exhaustion of numerous possibilities, below, p. 536). However, in the next stretch of text it is also all too plain that the Naiyāyika theory of universals is inadequate to the explanatory role it is called to play. Gaṅgeśa tries to get too much out of it as he applies it to physical processes responsible for experience of colors and to color phenomenology to boot.

Text (p. 781, Tirupati) and Translation

vayaṃ tu brūmaḥ | śuklatvâdinā kāraṇa-rūpâgni-saṃyoga-prayojyābhyāṃ jātibhyāṃ parâpara-bhāvân-upapattyā rūpa-vṛtty-udbhavatvam an-ekaṃ vācyam | tathā ca udbhūtatvena kāraṇatve 'n-anugamaḥ | tasmād an-udbhavatvaṃ śuklatvâdi-vyāpyaṃ nānā-jātiḥ tad-a-bhāva-kūṭas tu pratyakṣatve prayojakaḥ | anyathā anugata-pratyakṣân-upapatteḥ | evaṃ sparśâdāv api |

Gaṅgeśa: But we say the following. The manifestness that rests in colors would have to be (on the view of Old Nyāya) multiple (which invites the charge of ontological cumbersomeness), because otherwise (if it were not multiple) the hierarchy (characteristic of universals) would not be possible: two universals would come into play (namely, two manifestness-es) as appropriate to (a) two effects of fire contact (with, e.g., two species of clay), or as appropriate to (b) the color of the causes (one batch of clay might be paler than another) such as whiteness and the rest—this would have to be said. And so there would not be the uniformity (characteristic of universals) in the causes being manifest. Therefore, *non*-manifestness, which is pervaded by (the universals of the individual colors) whiteness and the rest, is the universal throughout the variety. (Visual) perceptions have a cause in the absences of non-manifestness as a (unified) group. Otherwise, it would be impossible to explain (visual) perception as uniform (following the principle, "from similar causes come similar effects"). The same holds as well for touch and so on.

Comments

The force of a dilemma appears to move Gaṅgeśa to a new position. If there is a single manifestness in all colors, then the hierarchy we expect would break down, i.e., there would be "cross-section" of kinds. But if each color has its own universal of manifestness, then there would be cumbersomeness, a peopling, so to say, of the world of color with too many abstract entities. Not-being-manifest apparently faces neither problem, though Gaṅgeśa fails to address the cross-section issue and it is far from evident just how non-manifestness would avoid the difficulty. More clearly, however, non-manifestness does seem unitary, such that we could say that whatever color is perceived, an absence of non-manifestness of color is a cause of the perception; similarly for smell and touch.

But Gaṅgeśa is not himself convinced that this is the right position. In the next passage, he provides an alternative picture.

Text (p. 781, Tirupati, and p. 725, Calcutta) and Translation

> atha vā udbhūtatvam an-udbhūtatvaṃ vā na jātiḥ | kiṃ tu rūpatva-vyāpya-vyāpya-[6]jātimattvam eva udbhūtatvaṃ tad-a-bhāvo 'n-udbhavatvam | pratyakṣe rūpe śuklataratamattvâdi-jātimattvāt | ūṣma-cakṣur-ādi-rūpe tu śuklatva-mātram eva, tad-vyāpya-jātau mānâ-bhāvād utkarṣâ-bhāvāt | na ca rūpatvam eva mānam | lāghavena tasya prayojakatve pratyakṣatva-prasaṅgāt | evaṃ sparśâdāv api iti | ito 'pi mahattve na udbhavatvaṃ prayojakam | vāyâdau mahattvôtkarṣe 'py a-pratyakṣatvāt |

(**Gaṅgeśa** continues:) Alternatively, neither manifestness nor non-manifestness is a universal. Rather, manifestness is just the fact that some things exhibit a universal that is pervaded by those (universals such as whiteness, yellowness, blueness, etc.) that are pervaded by colorhood. Its absence is non-manifestness. The reason for this is that there are (degrees of whiteness) the more and the most white, which rest in the visible color.

But in the (non-manifest) color of heat, the visual organ, and so on, (the universal is) simply whiteness in general (or, mere whiteness, which is negated or prevented), because there is no evidence of a universal that is pervaded by it, since (with non-manifest color) there is no increasing (or degrees).

And is not the case that colorhood is itself the evidence (in that colorhood pervades lower-order universals such as whiteness). It is simpler to assume colorhood as a cause to avoid the unfortunate ramification that heat and the like should be visually perceived. So, too, for touch and the rest. It is also the case, therefore, that manifestness as lying in things of appreciable size is not a cause (of perception of touch or the like). For, we also do not perceive any enhancement of manifestness with respect to air or the like.

Comments

Within the range of color identifiable as white, there are, apparently, degrees, from the least to the most white. The most manifest would be the most white, and the least manifest would be the least white. Thus, manifestness would correspond to a range of color. The same could be said for other perceptible qualities. Manifestness would not be, then, a distinct universal; similarly, non-manifestness.

Text (p. 783, Tirupati) and Translation

nanu bharjana-kapāla-gato vahniḥ vāri-stha-ghaṭa-vyañjaka-sūra-tejaś ca gṛhyeta, vāri-kapālayoḥ pratyakṣatvena udbhūta-rūpavattvāt | tayoḥ saṃyoga-viśeṣa eva pratibandhaka iti cet, na | jala-kapālâdīnām āloka-vyaṅgyatayā tad-grahe pratibandhakatvâ-bhāvāt | pratibandhakatve vā bharjana-kapāla-vāri-saṃyogi-vahni-saurâlokayor a-graha-prasaṅgaḥ | saṃyoge ca na viśeṣo jāti-kṛtaḥ anyatara-karma-jatvâdinā saṃkara-prasaṅgāt | tāratva-van nānātve gauravāt | na api tat-saṃyoga-bhedaḥ, an-anugamād iti | mā evam | jala-sthaṃ tu tejo gṛhyata eva | ubhayoḥ svacchatayā vivicya graho na bhavati | bharjana-kapāle ca an-udbhūta-rūpam udbhūta-sparśam anyad eva tejas tādṛśair avayavair vahni-sahacaritair ārabhyate | atitapta-tailâdau kadācit udbhūta-rūpâvayava-praveśād vahny-ārambho 'pi | na ca evaṃ dugdha-sahacarita-dadhi-paramāṇubhir eva dadhy-ārambhaḥ | dugdha-dhvaṃsa-janya-dravyatvena khaṇḍa-dugdha-vad dadhno dugdhôpādānôpādeyatvāt |

Objection.1: The fire within a pot-half being baked and dried out (before being put together with another half to make a pot, that is to say, fire that is not seen but inferred on the basis that the pot-half is hot), and the fiery element (*tejas*) from the sun (i.e., rays of the sun) that make known a pot submerged in water (with the *tejas* not seen but only the pot)—these should be perceptually grasped (if what you say were correct), since the water and the pot-half are (visually) perceptible in that they have manifest color.

Objection.2 (against objector.1): Just the particular type of contact in both cases prevents perception (of the fire in the pot-half and the *tejas* in the water).

Answer (by objector.1): No. For, light makes perceptible such things as water and pot-halves. When they are grasped, it (or its contact with them) is not prevented. Or, if there is to be prevention, then there would be the unfortunate ramification that a pot-half being baked and dried out or water as the relatum in contact with the light of a fire or of the sun would not be perceived (while of course they are visually grasped).

Moreover, a contact is not an individual included as an instance of a universal, because (if it were) we would have the unfortunate ramification of cross-section with such contacts as those born of the movement of one of the two relata (in contrast with contacts born of contacts and contacts born of movement on the part of both relata). (And) the view that there are various universals of contact, as there are of shrillness, is cumbersome. Nor is one contact (simply) distinct from those other contacts, since in that case there would be no uniformity (to account for uniform usages of the word "contact").

Gaṅgeśa: Don't think like that. When the fiery element is situated in water, it can be (visually) grasped (i.e., rays of the sun can be seen in water). However, the grasping does not come about after each of the two has been, in its pure form, differentiated (rather, water and rays are seen mixed together). And in a pot-half being baked and dried out, there is simply another form of the fiery element (different from ordinary fire), which has *non*-manifest color and manifest touch, and which is constituted by parts like that (i.e., parts that have non-manifest color and manifest touch) *in accompaniment to* (ordinary) fire. Sometimes, in such a case as overheated oil, fire is started, too, because of the presence of the (fiery) parts that do have manifest color.

And it is not the case that curd is constituted similarly just by curd atoms in accompaniment to milk. For, curd—which is a substance that arises (only) upon the destruction of milk, like milk reduced by a pouring into separate parts—comes to be out of the same material cause (i.e., out of the same atoms) as milk.

Comments

The counterproposal to the original objection is that a particular kind of contact of fire with clay in a pot-half would make the fire invisible. But, in that case, the same type of contact that is supposed to be responsible for making the pot-half visible (a pot is, after all, visible when lit by fire) would be responsible for blocking the visibility of the fire.

Contact is of three kinds: (a) born of contact (*saṃyoga-ja*), for instance, contact between someone's hand and a book, which is also a contact between the person's body and the book; (b) born of movement on the part of one or the other of the relata (*anyatara-karma-ja*), for instance, contact between a stationary book and a hand placed on it; (c) born of movement on the part of both of the relata (*ubhaya-karma-ja*), for instance, a clap of two moving hands.

Gaṅgeśa does not respond to the entanglement in the Naiyāyika theory of universals that objector.2 provokes from objector.1 with respect to contact. Rather, he takes the different tact of admitting distinct kinds of *tejas*, one with manifest color, as in the case of ordinary fire, and another with non-manifest color, as in the case of a hot pot-half being baked and dried out. Indeed, light is a kind of *tejas*, too: unlike fire, it has no manifest touch, but also, unlike heat, it has manifest color. Rays of the sun are still another subvariety: like ordinary fire, they have manifest color and manifest touch (they are warm), but, unlike fire, they do not consume fuel.

This strand of Gaṅgeśa's thought (and of others before and after him) appears to be a movement towards expansion of the traditional Vaiśeṣika chemistry through openness to new fundamental elements. However, Gaṅgeśa never goes quite so far as to admit a new element, and here we have, in sum, not a new element proposed but another variety of an old one, *tejas*, the "fiery" element.

Finally, whereas different configurations of the four types of atoms (earthen, watery, fiery, and airy) occur as naturally distinct subtypes that conjoin or accompany one another in giving rise to perceptible objects, milk and curd are not comprised of atoms in configurations that can be conjoined. Only upon the destruction of the configuration that gives rise to milk does curd arise, since curd is made of the same atoms as milk, Gaṅgeśa implies. A prominent view in earlier Indian philosophy—opposed by Gaṅgeśa's Vaiśeṣika—is that milk and curd pre-exist in the same stuff—or as the same stuff—and may accompany one another in this sense. They pre-exist, that is to say, as non-manifest effects in material that manifests the one or the other according to various factors. This causal doctrine writ large is a linchpin of the early classical philosophy known as Sāṃkhya, which finds a infinitely aspected but unified "Nature," *prakṛti*, to make manifest one or another particular property perceived (*guṇa*), or groups of properties, holding back at every time and place all others in non-manifest potentiality within herself. Vaiśeṣika and Nyāya authors proposed a much more complex view of causal relations from the earliest texts. Gaṅgeśa lines up with this opposition to the Sāmkhya doctrine and holds that curd arises as an entirely new thing upon the destruction of milk (although there are no new ultimate atoms). Apparently, he makes the point in fear that his view of conjoining types of *tejas* will be misunderstood as an endorsement of the Sāmkhya position.

Text (p. 784, Tirupati, and p. 727, Calcutta) and Translation

> nanv evam udbhūta-rūpa-vahny-ādau udbhūta-sparśo na asti | tat-sahacarita-tejo 'ntara-niyamena tatra ūṣma-buddher upapatteḥ | udbhūta-rūpôdbhūta-sparśa-sāmagryor ūṣmaṇi prabhâdau virodhâvadhāraṇād iti cet, na | yaṃ vahnim adrākṣaṃ taṃ spṛśāmi ity a-bādhita-pratyabhijñāna-vaśāt darśana-sparśanābhyāṃ vahnau rūpa-sparśayor upalambhāt | na ca tejastvaṃ bādhakaṃ | udbhavân-udbhavayor nimitta-bheda-saṃsarga-prayojyatvāt, tejastvasya rūpavad-vṛtti-dravyatva-sākṣād-vyāpya-jātitvena udbhūta-rūpa-sparśavad-vṛttitvāt | na ca udbhūta-rūpa-sparśayor virodhaḥ, jala-pṛthivyor ubhaya-sattvāt | tejasi virodhasya nimitta-bhedôpādhikatvād iti |

Objection: If what you say were right, there would be no manifest touch in fire and the like that have manifest color (or, there would be no need for such a conception). By the law of an auxiliary *tejas* accompanying that (of which ordinary fire is made), experience of heat there (in ordinary fire) is explained (i.e., as ordinary fire accompanies the *tejas* in things heated but not burning and is responsible for the flaring up of overheated oil, so, that second *tejas* is responsible for the heat of ordinary fire). For, you find incompatibility between the causal complexes sufficient to produce, on the one hand, manifest color, and, on the other, manifest touch, with respect to heat (which has no manifest color) and light (which has no manifest touch).

Gaṅgeśa: Wrong. For, by the force of an undefeated recognition, "I am touching the fire that I saw," there is, with respect to a fire (i.e., with respect to a single object), experience of both color and touch through seeing and touching.

And it is not the case that there is a defeater (i.e., a cogent counterconsideration) in (fire's) being (composed of) the fiery-element (such that, like heat and light, which are also composed of *tejas*, it could have only one of the pair, manifest color and manifest touch). For, the the reason why there is a manifest or non-manifest quality is a difference of instrumental cause. Being-the-fiery-element (the universal of *tejas*) rests in things that have manifest color and touch inasmuch as it is a universal that is immediately pervaded by (the higher-order universal) being-a-substance that rests in things that have color. Manifest color and touch are not incompatible since both are present in water and earth (and things made of either of these elements). The incompatibility occurring in something made of the fiery element (such as light, which has no heat, and heat, which has no color) is due to distinct instrumentality (of unseen force).

Comments

Rucidatta glosses *nimitta-bheda*, "difference of instrumental cause," as *a-dṛṣṭa-bheda*, "difference with respect to unseen force." Apparently, "unseen force" is a last resort for explaining accidents of nature, explanatory refuge failing all else. Note, however, that Gaṅgeśa says only "difference of instrumental cause," a vague expression, and does not explicitly say *a-dṛṣṭa*, "unseen."

Here the relevant hierarchy of substance universals involving firehood, lighthood, and heathood has these as all lower-order universals each of which is pervaded by *tejastva*, the universal of *tejas*. ("Pervaded" is philosophic shorthand for "every instance of the lower-order universal is an instance of the higher-order, pervading universal.") Earthhood, waterhood, and *tejastva*, along with other lower-order universals of substance, are, of course, pervaded by being-a-substance. But only things that are earthen (i.e., in which earthhood inheres), things composed of water, or things composed of *tejas* have color and are instances of the universal, being-a-substance.

A pot, which is something earthen, can, therefore, be both seen and touched.[7] All things in which earthhood inheres—except atoms and dyads—can be both touched and seen. Moreover, instances of other fundamental types of substance, such as selves and space and time, have no color. In addition to earth, water, and *tejas*, there are two more "material" substances, air and ether, both of which apparently have no color, though whether air has *non-manifest* color (on the grounds that it can be touched) is an issue. Thus, there is no reason to suppose that everything in which *tejastva* is present could not, by that fact, have both color and touch, since we have the examples of things that are earthen or watery having both color and touch. If so, why there is the division among the three lower-order universals that are pervaded by *tejastva*—namely, (a) firehood, (b) lighthood, and (c) heathood—cannot be explained other than by reference to some sort of hidden instrumental cause or "unseen force."

Text (p. 785, Tirupati) and Translation

udbhūta-rūpa-sahacaritayor mahattvân-eka-dravyavattvayoḥ yuga-naddha-vāhitayā anvaya-vyatireka-tulyatve 'pi dravya-cākṣuṣatve na an-eka-dravyavattvam ubhayaṃ vā tantram, kiṃ tu mahattvam eva lāghavāt | an-eka-dravyôtkarṣaṃ vinā api tūlakâdau pracaya-janyôtkṛṣṭa-parimāṇāt pratyakṣôtkarṣa-darśanāc ca | dūra-stha-keśa-rāśau dravyân-utpādena mahattvâ-bhāve 'py eka-keśasya sajātīya-saṃyogena an-eka-dravyavattvāt dravya-pratyakṣatā ity an-eka-dravyavattvaṃ tatra tantram iti cet, na | an-eka-dravya-saṃbandhitvasya samavāyena prayojakatvāt, na tu saṃyogena, atiprasaṅgāt | tathā ca dūra-grahaṇe sajātīya-saṃyogasya an-eka-dravyavattve sahakāritā vācyā | sā mahattva eva astu |

(**Gaṅgeśa** continues:) Along with manifest color, (a) something's being of appreciable size and (b) something's being composed of a substance plurality (anything perceptible is composed of a plurality of atoms) are, by positive and negative correlations, found together regarding substance visibility, like a pair (of oxen) pulling by way of a single yoke stick. But although equally established by that method, neither being-composed-of-a-substance-plurality, nor both (that *and* the other universal, being-of-appreciable-size) together comprise the causal arrangement we accept. Rather, it is simply being-of-appreciable-size, since that is the economical position.

Furthermore, with no increase in the number of substance components, there can be enhancement of (visual) perception due to an increase in size, as with a ball of cotton or the like by spreading it wider (i.e., by pulling at its sides, one makes it more easily seen).

Objection: (Consider:) a collection of hairs that stands at a distance (but is seen) is not something that originates a new composite substance. (That is to say, the hair ball is not a new composite but only a collection of individual hairs.) Because it is not so, it is not a locus of being-of-appreciable-size (since being-of-appreciable-size is said only of things that are wholes with parts, not of a collection). But an individual hair in *conjunction* (*saṃyoga*, "contact") with things that are alike in kind brings about something (a collection of hairs) that is something "composed" of a substance plurality ("composed" in the sense of *conjoined* parts and not only in the sense of a whole's inhering it in its parts; that is to say, a single hair, which is in itself, up close, of appreciable size, is in this case *not* a cause of the visual perception—only the mass of hair is, rather, since only the mass of hair, and not the individual hairs, is seen in the distance). Being-composed-of-a-substance-plurality is, therefore, (part of) the relevant causal arrangement regarding (visual) perceptibility of substances. (That is, it is an *additional* factor; being-of-appreciable-size, though necessary to explain the enhanced visibility of an expanded ball of cotton, does not eliminate the need for this additional factor.)

Gaṅgeśa: No. The way the world is that is caually relevant here is that the relation binding together anything "composed of a substance plurality" is *inherence*, not contact, since the latter would apply to too much. And so, in the case of seeing such a thing in the distance (viz., a mass of hair), the being-composed-of-a-substance-plurality brought about by the relation of contact among things alike in kind (the individual hairs) has to be understood as requiring a causal auxiliary. Let that auxiliary be nothing other than being-of-appreciable-size. (That is, being-of-appreciable-size is also causally relevant in the example of a visual perception of a distant mass of hairs in that each hair conjoined in the mass is of appreciable size. Thus there is no counterexample.)

Comments

The objector is saying that the aggregation relation holding among the individual hairs is perceptually relevant, and he implies that, in this case, being-of-appreciable-size is irrelevant. Gaṅgeśa retorts that inherence, not contact, is the relation with causal efficacy with respect to visual perception of substances. A *conjoined* collection of invisible things like atoms is not seen, but rather only a whole that *inheres* in a plurality of atoms. To say that contact is a causal factor for substance visibility would be to say that it is necessarily present when any substance is seen. But that is false. The relevant relation is inherence. What about the objector's apparent counterexample? Well, if each hair conjoined in the mass of hair did not itself have appreciable size, then the mass of hair would not be seen. We do not see heaps of atoms. The individual hairs inhere in their parts, in the atoms that make them up. Increase by conjunction is, to be sure, relevant to the visibility of the mass of hairs. But that is no causal factor relevant to substance visibility *in general*. Rather, only a perceived object's being-of-appreciable-size is a causal factor in the case of every visual perception.

Text (p. 786, Tirupati, and p. 729, Calcutta) and Translation

> nanu yady udbhūta-rūpavattvaṃ mahattvaṃ ca dravya-pratyakṣatāyāṃ sva-rūpa-yogyatā tadā daṇḍatva-vat tayoḥ kāraṇatā na syād iti cet, na | tad-utkarṣāt pratyakṣôtkarṣeṇa tayoḥ kāraṇatvāt | na hy a-kāraṇôtkarṣam kāryam[8] anuvidhatte | daṇḍatvâdau na evam, prakāra-bhedena ubhaya-rūpatvāc ca cākṣuṣa-dravya-jñāne viṣayatvena tayoḥ kāraṇatvam, dravye 'nugatatvena kāraṇatâvacchedakatvam iti |

Objection: If having-manifest-color and being-of-appreciable-size constitute intrinsic eligibility with respect to substance perceptibility, then, like stickhood (which is a specifier of a type of causality relevant to production of a pot, but which is not itself a cause in bringing a pot about; only individual sticks are such causes), neither of the two would be a cause (in this instance). (And they are such specifiers.)

Gaṅgeśa: Wrong. The two *are* causes because there is enhanced perceptibility with increase of either. For, an (enhanced) effect does not follow regularly an increase in what is not its cause. (Rather, an enhancement of an effect follows regularly an increase in one or more causes.) Stickhood and the like are not like this (pots are not somehow enhanced by an increase in stickhood).

With respect to substance visibility, the two (having-manifest-color and being-of-appreciable-size) are causes by way of being objects (of visual perceptions), since, with a difference in predication content, the two can be both causes and specifiers. As resting in substances (that is to say, looking at having-manifest-color and being-of-appreciable-size as properties that rest in substances), the two are causal specifiers.

Comments

The three abstracts, (a) being-a-substance, (b) having-manifest-color, and (c) being-of-appreciable-size, specify a relevant type of cause regarding any substance that is visually perceived. Being-a-substance is only such a specifier, not also ever itself a direct causal factor in that, like stickhood with pots being produced, individual substances, like sticks, give rise to visual perceptions, not the universal, substancehood. The other two, in contrast, (b) having-manifest-color and (c) being-of-appreciable-size, are also direct causes, since an increase along either dimension results in enhanced visibility.

atha vāyu-pratyakṣa-vādaḥ

NOW, DISCOURSE ON THE PERCEPTIBILITY OF AIR

Text (p. 788, Tirupati, and p. 730, Calcutta) and Translation

nanu na udbhūta-rūpavattvam tatra tantram, vāyoḥ pratyakṣatvāt | tathā hi, vāyuḥ pratyakṣaḥ pratyakṣa-sparśâśrayatvāt mahattve saty udbhūta-sparśavattvād vā ghaṭa-vat | ūṣmâdau pratyakṣatvān na vyabhicāraḥ | na ca a-prayojakam | spārśana-pratyakṣatve mahattve saty udbhūta-sparśavattvaṃ prayojakam, na udbhūta-rūpavattvam api, gauravāt | na ca pakṣa-dharmâvacchinna-sādhya-vyāpakaḥ sādhanâvacchinna-sādhya-vyāpakaś ca udbhūta-rūpavattvam upādhiḥ | spārśana-pratyakṣatve tasya a-prayojakatvāt, tvag-indriya-vyāpārân-antaraṃ vāyur vāti iti pratītes ca | na ca sparśa-liṅga-grahe[1] tad-upakṣayaḥ | ghaṭe 'pi tathātvâpatteḥ |

Pūrvapakṣin: Having-manifest-color is *not* a cause of substance perception, since air is perceptible.

For so it is (established by the following inference): air is perceptible, *since* it is a substratum of a perceptible touch—or, *since* it has, when it has appreciable size, a manifest touch—like a pot.

Heat and the like (which might be thought to be counterexamples because heat is a substratum of touch but is not visible) *are* perceptible (by touch). So, there is no deviation (in that way).

Nor is the (second) prover "misleading" (and to be suspected of deviation as would be shown by counterfactual considerations). Given something having appreciable size, its having manifest touch is a cause of its being perceptible tactually. Having-manifest-color is not a cause as well, since that is theoretically cumbersome.

And it is not the case that having-manifest-color is (with respect to this inference) the sort of "undercutter," *upādhi*, that (a) pervades the probandum as specified by a (relevant) property of the subject (here, being-a-substance), or (b) pervades the probandum as specified by the prover. For, having-manifest-color is (simply) not a cause of something being tactually perceptible, and, moreover, immediately following the operation of the tactile organ, there occurs (in the appropriate circumstances) the cognition, "The air (or wind) is blowing" (without any color being manifest).

Furthermore, it is not the case that the organ of touch exhausts itself in grasping (air's) touch as an inferential mark (for inferring, not perceiving, air). For, if that were the case, there would be the difficulty that such should also apply to a pot (and the like, which clearly are perceptible by touch—a pot is tactilely perceptible as a substance; not only its touch or "feel" as a quality is perceptible).

Comments

This section is dominated by the view of Old Nyāya that having-manifest-color is a causal factor when an *external* substance is perceived (thus excluding the question of the perceptibility of *manas* and selves, which are *internal* substances, though the perceptibility of selves is addressed at the very end of the section). Several alternative positions are debated and shown deficient, including views of "New Vaiśeṣikas" and of a faction of New Naiyāyikas that is not Gaṅgeśa's own. According to Old Nyāya, since air does not have color, it can be known only by inference. Gaṅgeśa undermines a nexus of views surrounding this stance, but only gradually, in examining several competing positions. The *pūrvapakṣin* in the section is, moreover, less of a foil and a set-up for Gaṅgeśa's own position than a refuter of the Old Nyāya view. Thus would the way be prepared for Gaṅgeśa's new view. Or, taking as evidence the fact that Gaṅgeśa's own position is not much elaborated or defended, we might say that airing the issues—forgive the pun—is the main point. However, Gaṅgeśa does put forth a carefully crafted statement of his own view (below, p. 498), albeit without much directly supportive argument.

"Inferential undercutters," *upādhi*, are not limited to those that pervade a probandum without pervading its putative prover. The stock example of *wet fuel* does conform to that logic: "wherever fire, there smoke" is a putative pervasion to be rejected because of wet fuel which is present wherever there is smoke but not in an hot iron ball where there is fire (see above, pp. 160–61). But as Gaṅgeśa explains in the next chapter, there can be a veritable undercutter (U) that fails to pervade a probandum (S) so long as it pervades everything that exhibits both some other property (P) of a certain character and the probandum (S)—the condition is, that is, that everything that is both an S and a (relevant) P be a U.[2] In a first variation, the undercutter is said to pervade the probandum as specified by a property of the subject, a *relevant* property of the subject in that it has to pervade the prover (H).

1. $(x)\ ((Px \,.\, Sx) \rightarrow Ux)$ (The undercutter U pervades the probandum S as delimited by a relevant property P of the inferential subject.)

2. $(x)\ (Hx \rightarrow Px)$ (A *relevant* property P of the inferential subject pervades the prover H.)

3. $(\exists x)\ (Hx \,.\, {\sim}Ux)$ (The undercutter U fails to pervade the prover H).

4. Therefore, $(\exists x)\ (Hx \,.\, {\sim}Sx)$. (There is something that exhibits the prover without exhibiting the probandum.)

In a second variation, the undercutter pervades the probandum (S) as specified by the prover (H).

1. (x) ((Hx. Sx) → Ux) (The undercutter U pervades the probandum S as delimited by the prover H.)

2. (∃x) (Hx.~Ux) (The undercutter U fails to pervade the prover H.)

3. Therefore, (∃x) (Hx.~Sx). (There is something that is an H but not an S.)

In other words, given the undercutter in both cases—albeit restricted in its relation to the probandum relative to the standard case of a pervading of the entire probandum—it is provable that the putative prover is not pervaded by the probandum, that something H is not an S.

Now one worry in the current passage is whether there is an *upādhi* of one of these exotic varieties. The inference is to be broken down as follows: *air* is the inferential subject, *being-perceptible* is the probandum, and *being-a-substratum-of-perceptible-touch* is the prover—or, in an alternative formulation that is for the moment ignored, the prover is comprised of the combination of two properties, *having-perceptible-touch* and *being-of-appreciable size.* A candidate relevant property of the subject is: being-a-substance, since air is a substance and everything that is a substratum of a perceptible touch is a substance. And as an example of the second exotic type of undercutter, we have things that are perceptible and exhibit touch. Do these show that the inference is wrong?

Another issue is whether having-manifest-color is a cause of perception of a substance, or, again, in a more precise version which will be introduced, a causal factor for any perception of an *external* substance by an *external* organ of sense. Air does not have color, at least not manifest color, and if color is required for touch, air itself cannot be known by touch but only inferred from the feel of its tactile qualities.

Two questions are, then, whether all perceptible substances have manifest color, and whether all things perceptible and exhibiting touch have manifest color. The answer is *no* in both cases, for the reasons stated in the text, disputable though they may be. Air, or wind, is presumed to be both (a) a substance that is directly perceived (as in sensing a "puff of wind" or being prompted to say, "The wind is blowing") and (b) a substratum of a perceptible touch, though it has no manifest color. The organ of touch is capable of feeling through the presentation of a tactile property to grasp the property-bearer itself, as when we know by touch a pot. Its sensory activity is not exhausted in feeling the pot's tactile quality.

Text (p. 792, Tirupati) and Translation

> laiṅgikatve ca sparśo vāyu-vṛttir iti dhīḥ syāt, na tv an-uṣṇâ-śīta-sparśo vāyur iti, sparśâ-grahe 'pi śīto vāyur iti pratītes ca | na ca śīta-dravyôpanāyakatvena anumite vāyau tathā dhiḥ | bādhakâ-bhāvāt viśeṣa-darśane saty āropâ-bhāvāc ca |

(The **pūrvapakṣin** continues:) And if air were known (only) inferentially, we would have the cognition, "Touch (or feel) is *in* air," not, "The air *has* a touch that is (in itself) not hot and not cold" (which is a cognition that sometimes we do have). Nor, if that touch were not grasped, would we have the cognition, "The air is cold."

Nor would there be such a cognition ("The air is cold") about air known inferentially as presented (as cold) by a cold substance (mixed therein), since this is no cogent counterconsideration (showing that the cognition is not perceptual). Moreover, given experience of details (as with experience of hands and feet confirming the presence of a human being), there is no superimposition.

Comments

Air and earth are thought to have a, so to say, neutral touch, neither hot nor cold. Hot air is due to admixture of bits of *tejas*, the fiery element, and cold air due to admixture of watery particles. But while the hot and cold feels may be illusory, still the form of the experiential report, "That wind *is* cold," remains evidence that the wind—or air—is directly perceived. We do not say, "I perceive some coldness *in* the wind," and in the case of a pot, "The pot is smooth," we do know the pot itself and not only its smoothness.

Rucidatta refutes (p. 792) a further reason why air must be known perceptually—a bit of background worth reviewing. He says that it may be thought there can be no inference where the subject is not previously known. So, air could not be known only inferentially. However, air need not be the subject of the inference, he points out in line with the standard Old Nyāya view, but its probandum, that which is to be proved. The model is the *sāmānyato dṛṣṭa* type of inference, "on the basis of a general principle holding for all things experienced (as of such a kind)." This is explained in *Nyāya-sūtra* commentaries with the example of the existence of the self as a substance inferred from the fact that pleasure and the like are qualities that require a substance in which to inhere, like other perceptually known qualities.[3] Since pleasure and the like are known only by an *internal* perception—directly by the internal organ or *manas*—the self, which is something interior and not anything external, has to be their locus or substratum. According to Old Nyāya, touch is similarly a quality, though belonging to external things, that has to have a substratum, air, namely, air that is in itself imperceptible and thus knowable only by an inference—of the *sāmānyato dṛṣṭa* type. (The traditional argument thus has two steps. Touch inheres in a substance, *since* it is a quality, like color. That substance is air.)

About the current passage, Rucidatta is also helpful, taking the perspective of the *pūrvapakṣin* against the Old Nyāya advocate of a *sāmānyato dṛṣṭa* inference to air. In the case of the cognition, "That wind is cold," to admit illusoriness about the cold qualifier not only does not mean having to admit that the wind itself is not felt, but also to accept such illusoriness does mean that the property, coldness, would not be projected or superimposed through the revival of memory. Rucidatta says that air as known inferentially to have been presented as cold by a cold substance mixed therein has to be known to be distinct from the cold substance. This implies that air would have to be known as having a feel of its own—as, indeed, is borne out, "The air temperature is perfect, neither hot nor cold." Again, the view is that air itself has a neutral touch, neither hot nor cold, with any heat felt explained by admixture with tiny bits of *tejas* and any cold felt by bits of water. The point is that as something to be admixed, air has to be separately known; it is has to be conceptually available as a substance to be conjoined.

Text (p. 793, Tirupati) and Translation

> atha a-cākṣuṣatvaṃ spārśanatve bādhakam | cākṣuṣā an-upalabhyamānasya tvacā an-upalambhād iti cet, tarhi cakṣur eva dravya-grāhakam | tvacā sparśa-mātraṃ pratīyeta, vāyāv iva pratyabhijñā api tad-vad eva | atha anubhavasya durapahnavatvāt tvacā āśraya-rahita eva sparśa upalabhyate, tadā vāyāv api tulyam | atha dośâ-bhāve sati dravya-grahe tad-gata-saṃkhyâdi-graha-niyamāt vāyau sarvathā tad-a-grahāt na sa pratyakṣa iti cet, na | na ca tāvad ayaṃ vyaktau niyamaḥ | pṛṣṭha-lagna-vastrâdeḥ saṃkhyā-parimāṇā-grahe tvacā grahaṇāt | taj-jātīye tu phūt-kārâdau saṃkhyā-parimāṇâdīnāṃ vāyv-abhighātasya ca śarīre pratyakṣatvāt |

Objection: Something's not being visually grasped prevents it from being tactually grasped. For, if something is not being experienced by the visual organ, it is not experienced by the organ of touch.

Pūrvapakṣin: In that case, only the visual organ would (directly) grasp (external) substances. Merely touch (as a quality) would be cognized by the tactile organ (not the substance that has touch). (And) as would be the case with air (namely, that we seem to feel it but in fact feel only its touch), so too the recognition (e.g., "This pot that I am touching is the pot that I saw") would be merely like that (i.e., an error).

Objection: (Yes, that is right, though you fail to see it.) Since it is difficult to deny experience, (let us admit, as you imply, though not as an error) touch is cognized by the organ of touch precisely as lacking a substratum.

Pūrvapakṣin: Then it would also be the same in the case of air (i.e., that air, like touch, is directly grasped—which is our view).

Objection: Given no defects (in the perceptual process), when a substance is grasped, its number and size are invariably also grasped. Since these are not grasped in the case of air, air is not perceptible.

Pūrvapakṣin: No. First of all, there is no rule that applies (only) to a single individual (here, air). (Furthermore) there is no grasping of number and size when (a handful of) cloth hanging behind the back is grasped by the tactile organ (i.e., one does not know precisely how many undergarments there are nor the overall size of clothes grasped behind one's back). On the other hand, in the same category there is perception of number and size with a "whoot" (or "puff" blown out once, twice, or thrice, according to the count, just to a certain distance and not further, by someone out of his mouth), as well as in the case of air (i.e., wind) striking the body (a gust from one direction, another from another, and so on, as the case may be).

Comments

If the organ of touch does not grasp substances, the other organs, including sight, should be regarded as not grasping substances but, like touch, only qualities. This is the *pūrvapakṣin*'s principal counterargument. It is held on all sides (except certain Buddhist camps) that the visual organ does grasp substances directly. Thus the *pūrvapakṣin* draws out an untoward ramification of the objector's proposal: recognitions such as "This pot that I am touching is the pot that I saw" would have to be doubly erroneous. For not only is one not touching it (but only its feel), one did not see it too.

The "whoot" blowing is perceived as a puff of air of a definite size normally felt no more than a short distance beyond the mouth. We are able to count its occurrences. So we are able to count "airs"—further evidence that we do perceive them as substances.

Text (p. 793, Tirupati) and Translation

syād etat | bahir-indriya-ja-dravya-sākṣātkāre mahattve saty udbhūta-rūpavattvaṃ prayojakam | sati saṃbhave tyāgâ-yogāt | na tu janyêndriya-grāhya-viśeṣa-guṇavattvam, kārya-mahattva-samānâdhikaraṇa-viśeṣa-guṇavattvaṃ vā | rasana-gata-pitta-dravyasya udbhūta-tikta-rasasya vāyûpanīta-surabhi-dravyasya ca pratyakṣatâpatteḥ | mā evam | na udbhūta-rūpavattvaṃ tathā, nayana-gata-pitta-dravyasya ca pratyakṣatâpatteḥ |

Objection: That may be. But given that something is of appreciable size, its having manifest color *is* a cause of its being immediately perceived *as a substance* through an external organ of sense. There being this possibility, it is inappropriate to reject the causal principle (in a single case, namely, with respect to air).

But neither (a) exhibiting a specific quality (e.g., color) graspable by a created sense organ nor (b) exhibiting a specific quality that rests in the same locus as an effected appreciable size is a cause of such perception. For (if these were accepted as causes) we would land in the predicament of the perceptibility (1) of bile, which is a substance (although not in fact directly perceived), on the tongue, a substance whose bitter taste is manifest, and (2) of a substance whose fragrance is carried and presented by the wind.

Pūrvapakṣin: Don't think that way. Exhibiting manifest color is not the way you propose (i.e., is a not a cause of perception of external substances), since that also would land us in the predicament of the perceptibility of bile as a substance in the eye (since someone afflicted with bile has a yellow eyeball, with the yellow as manifest color but without, at least on your view, the bile itself being directly grasped, since its number and size are not grasped).

Comments

Since a self does not have manifest color, the objector says "through an *external* organ of sense," thereby excepting the internal organ of sense, *manas*, which can grasp the self. Similarly, the word "created" is used to exclude *manas*, which is considered to be uncreated (remaining with a self through rebirth). And "effected appreciable size" excludes a self, which has appreciable size that is non-effected or eternal.

Rucidatta explains why the perceptibility of bile on the tongue would be a problem, namely, that its size and number should be grasped according to the *pūrvapakṣin* and they are not.

Text (p. 794, Tirupati) and Translation

astu vā udbhūta-sparśavattvaṃ tatra tantram | na ca evaṃ prabhāyām a-pratyakṣatvam | prabhā hi tejaso rūpaṃ na dravyam | tad-āśraya-tejaḥ-pratītiḥ pratyakṣa-rūpa-liṅgâdhīnā eva, yathā tava ūṣmâdi-pratītiḥ | tatra saṃyoga-karmâdi kathaṃ pratyakṣam iti cet, cāndra-saura-dīpa-prabhâdau tu na kathaṃcit | indranīlâdi-prabhāyā rūpasya pūrva-deśân-upalambhena uttara-deśôpalambhena liṅgena tad-āśraya-tejaḥ-saṃyoga-vibhāgâdy-anumānam iti | tvan-naye yathā tvacā sparśa-mātra-grahân-antaraṃ phūt-kāre saṃyogâdīnām | etena dhūma-bāṣpayor a-spārśanatvena udbhūta-sparśâ-bhāve 'pi cākṣuṣatvam, anyathā tad-gata-saṃyoga-vibhāga-karmaṇāṃ pratyakṣatā na syāt liṅgâ-bhāvād iti nirastam |

(The **pūrvapakṣin** continues:) Or, let exhibiting a manifest *touch* be a cause of perception of external substances.

And it is not the case that in this way light should be imperceptible. For, light is the color of the fiery element (*tejas*); it is not (itself) a substance. Cognition of the fiery element as its substratum is dependent on perceptible color as an inferential mark (i.e., cognition of the substratum is inferential), as is the case, on your view, of cognition of heat and so on (which are known inferentially by taking certain qualities, being hot and so on, as inferential marks).

Objection: In the case of light, how are its movements, etc., perceptible (if light is a quality and not a substance; how is it that light has perceptible movements) bringing about contacts (as in light's contact with an external object)?

Pūrvapakṣin: Not in any way whatsoever. Consider the light and so on of the moon, the sun, or a lamp (imperceptible *tejas* moves, not light, which is a quality). Through not cognizing in one place the color of the "light" of, for instance, an emerald (which is made of earth and is not in itself luminous), and then cognizing it in another place (e.g., on a wall)—with this as inferential mark, one infers contacts and disjunctions, etc., on the part of the fiery element that is the substratum. This is like the "whoot" case where, on your view, contacts and so on (with air) are inferred immediately following a grasping just of touch by the tactile organ (without the substance being grasped).

Objection: Smoke and steam, which are not tactile, are visible even though they have no manifest touch. Otherwise (if they were not counted as directly perceptible), contacts, disjunctions, and movements resting in them (contacts with air as the smoke or steam particles rise) would not be perceived, (nor could they be inferred) since there would be no inferential mark.

Pūrvapakṣin: This is rejected by the reasoning just given. (That is to say, their movements, etc., are inferred.)

Comments

The *pūrvapakṣin* opened the section with a denial, a denial of manifest color as a cause in every case of substance perception. Now he asserts (mockingly?) that manifest touch *is* such a cause. The disparateness of the two positions is one reason why we said at the beginning that the *pūrvapakṣin* has an unusual role in the section, which, as a whole, has an exploratory atmosphere, unlike sections where battle lines are clearly drawn. Also, by the end of the next passage the *pūrvapakṣin* has apparently relinquished this view in favor of the (more reasonable!) view that manifest touch is a cause of substance perception by the organ of touch and manifest color of substance perception by the organ of sight.

But according to the current proposal, light, which has no manifest touch, would not be a counterexample in that light would not be a substance. The light of the moon, for instance, would be a peculiar color of an underlying *tejas*; the light of the sun would be another, much brighter. The color would be visible, but not the *tejas* itself. The *tejas*'s movement and contact with a pot, for example, would make the pot visible. This would accord with the view that no quality but only a substance can be the substratum of a movement or action. Similarly, the further phenomena brought up by the objector at the end, the rising of smoke and steam, would be movements known by inference.

Text (p. 795, Tirupati, and p. 733, Calcutta) and Translation

> na ca bahir-indriya-yogyân-eka-viśeṣa-guṇavattvaṃ tantram | tava trasa-reṇu-prabhayor a-pratyakṣatâpatteḥ, gauravāc ca | nanv evaṃ vinigamakâ-bhāvād ubhayor api tathātvam astu | tathā api vāyur a-pratyakṣa iti cet, evaṃ bahir-indriya-ja-dravya-sākṣātkāre cākṣuṣatve spārśana-pratyakṣatve ca pratyeka-udbhūta-rūpavattve saty udbhūta-sparśavattvaṃ prayojakaṃ paryavasyati iti gauravam |

(The **pūrvapakṣin** continues:) And it is not the case that there is a cause (of substance perception) in the having of multiple specific qualities that are amenable to being grasped by an external organ of sense. For, that would land us in the predicament that a mote in a sunbeam, and light as well, should be imperceptible. Moreover, that view is cumbersome.

Objection: Since there is no way to decide between the alternatives, why not let both (having manifest color and having manifest touch) be causes? Nevertheless, air would not be perceptible (but rather known by inference).

Pūrvapakṣin: (No.) If so, it would have to be concluded that, given a having of manifest color, having manifest touch would be a cause of both the visual and the tactile when a substance is immediately perceived by an external organ of sense—this is cumbersome. (Therefore, manifest color is a cause of visual perception of substances, and manifest touch of tactile substance perception.)

Comments

The proposal rejected by the *pūrvapakṣin* concerning multiple specific properties is quite condensed, requiring a deep dive into Nyaya-Vaiśeṣika physics to bring out all that is implied. Here is the gist. Earth has multiple "specific qualities" (on this notion, see above, p. 478): smell (which only things earthen have), taste (which only things earthen and watery have, along with their compounds), color (things earthen, watery, and fiery), and others. Some of the other elements obviously have multiple specific properties, too (though not ether). Selves have a particularly long list of specific properties, the psychological properties of pleasure, pain, cognition, and so on. The external organs of sense are the five commonly known sense organs, smell, etc., and thus not the internal organ, *manas*, which is responsible for grasping psychological qualities (among other tasks). Substances (including compounds) that are both (a) amenable to perception by an external organ of sense and (b) have multiple specific properties would be things earthen, watery, and fiery. Air and things airy would not be on the list. The *pūrvapakṣin* points out that the proposal is cumbersome (a judgement with which we may agree without reservations). Furthermore, a mote in a sunbeam is perceptible (as is proved by sight) but does not have multiple specific properties, and, similarly, he states, light.

Then at the end the *pūrvapakṣin* reverses his previous declaration and denies that manifest touch is required for all substance perception. His final statement suggests the eminently more reasonable view that having a manifest touch is a cause only for tactile substance perceptions, while having a manifest color is restricted to visual substance perceptions.

Next we are treated to Gaṅgeśa's own views. While neither the Vidyapeetha nor the Asiatic Society edition marks the discourse break, the combination of content and the word "mine" (*mama*) signal that what follows is Gaṅgeśa own position.

Text (p. 795, last line, Tirupati, and p. 733, Calcutta) and Translation

> mama tu cākṣuṣatve udbhūta-rūpavattvaṃ, spārśanatve udbhūta-sparśavattvam | yasya viśeṣe prayojakatvaṃ tasya anugatena rūpeṇa sāmānya-prayojakatvam iti dravya-grāhaka-bahir-indriya-vyavasthāpakôdbhūta-viśeṣa-guṇavattvaṃ[4] sāmānya-prayojakam iti lāghavam | viśeṣasya sāmānyasya ca bhinna-prayojyatva-niyamān na ekaṃ prayojakam |

Gaṅgeśa: But my own view is as follows. Having manifest color is a cause of visual perceptions; having manifest touch is a cause of tactile perceptions. (To this much, we both agree. But such is not the economical way to state the causal principle with respect to the perceptibility of external substances in general.) The economical view is that there is a cause in general, namely, *having a manifest specific quality*, on the basis of which the (activity of a specific) external organ of sense grasping a substance is inferred—in that whatever is a cause of a particular type of (substance) perception is (also), in its (appropriately abstract or) uniform and continuous form, a cause (of external substance perception) in general. (Having manifest color is a cause of, in particular, visual perception of substances, and having a manifest specific quality is a cause of external substance perception in general.) Moreover, by the rule that the particular and the general are distinct effects, they do not have the same causes.

Comments

Considering the entire section, we may say that Gaṅgeśa debates many competing opinions, some, in an unusual ordering, after having stated this his own view. Many of the positions appearing from this point on have been mistakenly read as by him endorsed.[5] Note how reasonable is this Gaṅgeśa's true *siddhânta*, given the context. It is a position formulated at an appropriate level of generality in order to identify, along the lines discussed, a cause in general (a necessary condition) of the perceptibility of external substances.

This cause is the having of a specific quality (color, touch, etc.) appropriate to our knowledge of an individual sense organ. Now the sense organs are themselves imperceptible. We infer the organ of sight because only it is capable of perceiving color. Similarly, we infer the organ of touch because of a certain uniformity in our tactile experiences. And so on. Thus, according to Gaṅgeśa, having a manifest touch is a necessary condition for perceptions of things knowable by touch, things that are by the tactile organ perceived, as is having manifest color a necessary condition for visual perceptions of substances. We should not say that having manifest color is a general condition for substance perceptibility, but, again, only the having of an appropriate specific quality. In sum, the effects that are types of perception differentiated according to the operative sense faculty—the external organs generating perceptions visual and so on—have a cause in an appropriate specific quality's being manifest.

A few words now about the discourse divisions of *siddhânta* and *pūrva-pakṣa*, since this is admittedly an unusual section. No single word is sufficient to make a determination of a discourse break, not even such a usually clear indicator as *mama*, "mine" ("my own view"). A cumulative case establishes all discourse divides, as was explained in the preliminaries, including, in particular, the determinations made here.

Furthermore, we may note, Gaṅgeśa suggested his departure from Old Nyāya on the perceptibility of air above in the section on inherence (see, in this text, pp. 401–02). There he declared the absence of color in air to be directly perceptible, and that would not be possible by his lights were air itself not directly perceived.

Text (p. 796, Tirupati) and Translation

atha vāyur yadi bahir-indriya-janya-sākṣātkāra-viṣaya-dravyaṃ spārśana-sākṣātkāra-viṣaya-dravyaṃ vā syāt udbhūta-rūpaḥ syāt | na ca evam, tasmān na[6] tathā | tādṛśa-sākṣātkāra-viṣaya-dravyasya rūpa-janakatva-niyamād iti cet, na | rūpavat-samavetatvena hi dravyasya rūpa-janakatvaṃ, na tu tādṛśa-sākṣātkāra-viṣaya-dravyatvena, tasya rūpa-jananôttara-kālīnatvāt | ghaṭo yadi cakṣur-itarêndriya-grāhya-dravyaṃ syāt a-rūpam a-sparśam a-cākṣuṣâdi syāt | tvag-indriyaṃ yadi dravya-grāhaka-bahir-indriyaṃ syāt rūpavat syāt sparśa-grāhakaṃ vā na syāt rūpa-grāhi vā syāt cakṣur-vat | na ca evam, tasmān na tathā iti ghaṭo 'pi na tvag-indriya-grāhyaḥ syāt, tad-gata-saṃkhyâdi-jñānaṃ phūt-kārâdāv iva iti syāt, spṛśāmi ity anuvyavasāyaś ca ghaṭa-vad vāyāv api |

Old Nyāya (advocating the view that having manifest color is a cause of all external substance perception and consonantly that air is not known by perception): If air were a substance and an object of immediate experience generated by an external organ of sense, or if it were a substance and an object of an immediate tactile experience, then it would have manifest color. It is not so (i.e., it does not have manifest color). Therefore, it is not like that.

Objection: A substance that is an object of such an immediate experience does, by rule, *give rise to* a color (in the sense that it would be a color's inherent cause: this is the appropriate sense of "having," not, as you seem to imply, having actually visible color).

Old Nyāya: No. For, a substance "gives rise to" (in your sense) a color only if it is an inherent cause that has color (and not all do), not (just) if it is a substance that is an object of such an experience, since such a substance (i.e., a substance as experienced) happens at a later time than its (having) color (i.e., a thing exists as colored before it exists as experienced). (According to your view) if a pot were a substance graspable by a sense organ *other than* sight, then it would not be colored, nor tactile, nor an object of the visual organ, and so on. If the organ of touch were an external sense organ that grasped substances, then it would (itself) be colored, or it would not grasp touch, or it would grasp color, like sight. It is not so. Therefore, it is not like that. Hence (on your view), a pot, too, would not be grasped by the tactile organ; cognition of its number, etc., would be (inferential only) like with "whoot" sounds, etc; and the apperception, "I am touching (something)" would be in the case of a pot even as it is with air (an error, on your view, since, like air, the pot would not itself be felt; howver, apperceptions are generally infallible).

Comments

The Old Nyāya exposition begins with a *modus tolens* inference. Simplifying slightly: if air were perceptible, then it would be colored. It is not colored. Therefore, it is not perceptible. On our reading, Gaṅgeśa would deny the conditional statement that is the central premise.

Some atoms have color and in combination give rise to colored composites. But there are substances, e.g., selves, which do not have color and do not give rise to anything colored.

Gaṅgeśa's main purpose in the passage is to make clear just what Old Nyāya is committed to and on what grounds. Air fails the tests of pertinent comparisons. The organ of touch is not like sight. Hence, air's touch or feel is perceptible but not air as a substance.

Text (p. 797, Tirupati) and Translation

atha spārśanatve udbhūta-sparśa-vad udbhūtaṃ rūpam api tantram | udbhūta-rūpavattve cākṣuṣatva-vat spārśanatva-darśanād iti cet, na | udbhūta-rūpavattve saty apy prabhāyāṃ na spārśanatvam iti udbhūta-sparśasya āvaśyakatvena udbhūta-rūpasya anyathā-siddhatvāt | na hy udbhūta-sparśe saty udbhūta-rūpâ-bhāvāt spārśanatvâ-bhāvaḥ | nanv evaṃ sparśa-gata udbhavaḥ kāraṇam astu | na tu rūpam a-kāraṇam iti cet, tathā api sparśas tad-a-bhāvaś ca kāraṇam, na tu rūpam api | tasmin dvaye sati tad-a-bhāvena tad-a-bhāvâ-darśanāt | vastuto rūpa-sparśa-gate udbhavatva-jātī kāraṇatâvacchedike na tu kāraṇe iti |

Objection: Like manifest touch with respect to the tactile, manifest color is *also* a cause (of substance perception, but its causality does not exclude that of manifest touch). For, when there is something that has manifest color, such as anything visual, it is found that it is tactile (too).

Gaṅgeśa: No. For, when something has color—for example, light—it may not be tactile. Hence, manifest touch, which is necessarily to be accepted as a cause (of a tactile perception), shows manifest color to be causally irrelevant (for tactile perception). For, it is not the case that, presuming something has manifest touch, there could be no tactile perception unless there were (also) manifest color.

Objection: That a touch's being manifest is a cause, let us grant. But this is not to say that color is not (also) a cause.

Gaṅgeśa: (It is in the case of visual perceptions.) Still, a touch (as an objective quality) and its being manifest are causes (of a tactile perception), *not* a color, too. For, given the two (viz., a touch and its being manifest), an absence of color is compatible with *not* finding an absence of tactile perception of some substance.

In fact, the two universals—the two manifestness*es*—resting in color and resting in touch are specifiers of types of causality. The two are not themselves causes.

Comments

Gaṅgeśa argues that there is no reason to assume that an object's having color is causally relevant to its being tactilely perceived. Our side may lack examples (other than air, which is at issue). But why should air itself be considered *not* to be graspable by touch? What is the basis of the proposed incompatibility? A puff of air (or wind) to be perceptible must, of course, have a manifest touch. But why should not it itself be grasped along with its touch, instead of, as Old Nyāya would have it, only the quality? A pot, though it has manifest touch and color, can be grasped as a substance solely through the organ of touch (with one's eyes closed, for instance) and solely through the organ of sight. Our simpler view does not overextend the causal role of having-a-manifest-color to tactile perceptions.

With regard to the last paragraph of the passage, let us recall the stock example of such causal specification: stickhood specifies a type of cause, things that are sticks, in the production of pots (a potter uses a stick, not stickhood). Similarly, manifestness of color is a causal specifier, not itself a cause of visual perception. Likewise, manifestness of touch.

Next, a party of Vaiśeṣika innovators picks up the gauntlet and provides examples of properties that, counterintuitively, would have to be regarded as perceptible unless having-manifest-color be granted the wider causal status, and, similarly, having-manifest-touch, deemed now also a causal factor in all perception of external substances.

Text (p. 797, Tirupati) and Translation

ucyate | dravyasya spārśanatve udbhūta-sparśa-mātraṃ na tantram | nidāghôṣmaṇi vāyûpanīta-śītôṣṇa-dravye ca pratyakṣatvena tad-gata-saṃkhyā-parimāṇa-saṃyoga-vibhāga-karmaṇāṃ pratyakṣatva-prasaṅgāt | yogya-vyakti-vṛttitvena teṣāṃ yogyatayā dravya-grāhaka-sāmagrī-grāhyatvâvadhāraṇāt | na ca ūṣmâdi-jātīye doṣâ-bhāve 'pi ghaṭâdāv iva kara-parāmarṣe kadācit kena api saṃkhyā gṛhyate | tathā udbhūta-rūpavattva-mātrasya tathātve cāndrâdy-udyotasya nayana-gata-pitta-dravyasya ca pratyakṣatve tad-gata-saṃkhyā-graho 'pi syāt | na ca ghaṭâdāv iva nipuṇaṃ nibhālayanto 'pi tad-gata-saṃkhyā-dvitvâdi hasta-vitasty-ādi-parimāṇaṃ karma vā vīkṣāmahe ity eka-eka-vyabhicārād vinigamakâ-bhāvāt ubhayam api bahir-indriya-dravya-pratyakṣatve prayojakam iti vāyur a-pratyakṣaḥ | na ca evam apasiddhântaḥ | pītaḥ śaṅkha ity ādau nayana-pitta-pītimā eva gṛhyate na tu pitta-dravyam, viṣaktâvayavatvāt prabhāyām iva tejasa iti ṭīkā-kṛtām abhidhānād iti navīnāḥ |

New Vaiśeṣikas: We can answer. Manifest touch alone (without manifest color) is not a cause of tactile perceptions of substances. For, if summer heat (as a substance), or the cold or hot substance presented by the wind (when the wind seems cold or hot) were perceptible (as opposed to inferable on the basis of perceived qualities), then the number, size, contacts, disjunctions, and motions that rest in them should be perceptible (too)—this is the difficulty.

For, as occurring in individuals that could be perceived, those qualities (number, etc.) would be capable of being perceived in that the causal complex responsible for making a substance grasped secures such graspability. (Thus, since those qualities are not grasped, a causal factor has to be missing, which would be manifest color.)

And no perceiver ever grasps through a relation to the hand number (or count as a quality) belonging to things in the class of heat and the like, although no defect obtains, as in contrast one does with the likes of a pot.

Similarly, if merely having manifest color were such, then the light of the moon and so on, and bile, which is a substance, in the eye (of someone with defective vision), would have—as things perceptible do have—a number (or count) that could be grasped. And it is not the case that we ever perceive, as we do with the likes of a pot, however clever or skilled we be, such numbers (or counts) as a two exhibited by this sort of thing (e.g., two heats), or a size, such as the length of a span of the hand, or a motion, though we be closely watching and attentive.

Therefore, since with each (having-manifest-color and having-manifest-touch), there is deviation (when we consider the one alone without the other to be a cause), and since there is no way to choose between the two, simply both are to be deemed causes of the perceptibility of a substance by an external organ of sense.

Hence, air is not perceptible.

And by viewing it in this way, we are not contradicting our stated positions. With such a cognition as, "The shell is yellow" (when it is really white), only yellowness is grasped, the yellowness of the bile in the eye (of the person with deficient eyesight), not also bile as a substance. (For) this is like the result that occurs in the case of light (which as a visual phenomenon is to be understood as the color of an underlying *tejas*), because particles of *tejas* have become very closely bound together—according to what the commentator (on Praśastapāda) explicitly states.

Gaṅgeśa: So say certain New (Vaiśeṣikas).

Comments

Phenomenologically, heat is not denumerable or countable—it does not appear in discrete units—although, of course, it can be measured gradiently.

Visual illusions brought about by bile in the eye are brought about, it seems, by a close connection between bile particles and the visual organ. This would be like the phenomenon of visible light, whose intensity, it seems, would vary with the closeness of the *tejas* particles.

It is unclear, so far as we know, to whom Gaṅgeśa is referring when he says "the commentator" (*ṭīkā-kṛt*), although Praśastapāda's *Padârtha-dharmasaṃgraha* is most probably his subject.

Text (p. 798, Tirupati, and p. 739, Calcutta) and Translation

sampradāya-vidas tu, calati pakṣi-kāṇḍâdau pūrva-deśa-vibhāgôttara-deśa-saṃyogayoḥ pratyakṣatā na syāt, pūrvôttara-deśasya prabhā-maṇḍalasya an-udbhūta-sparśatvena a-pratyakṣatvāt | tathā ca pareṣāṃ calati iti pratītir api tal-liṅgikā na syāt | asmākam api candra-tārâdau saṃyoga-vibhāga-liṅgaka-gaty-anumānaṃ na syāt | na ca pūrvôttara-deśe upalambhân-upalambhābhyāṃ saṃyoga-vibhāgāv anumāya tābhyām eva gaty-anumānam | pūrvôttara-deśayor a-pratyakṣatvena liṅgâ-siddheḥ | tasmād udbhūta-rūpavattvaṃ tatra prayojakam iti vāyur a-pratyakṣaḥ |

(**Gaṅgeśa** continues:) But the knowers of tradition (i.e., Nyāya tradition) say the following.

Old Nyāya: (The position just stated is wrong. If it were right) neither a moving (i.e., flying) bird's nor an arrow's conjunctions and disjunctions with one place after another would be perceptible, since the prior and posterior place would belong (not to the ether, which does not have parts, but) to the sun, the globe of light, which as not having manifest touch (but only color) would be (on the view of the New Vaiśeṣikas) imperceptible. And so, on the view of these others (the New Vaiśeṣikas), even the cognition, "It is moving," could not be inferred on the basis of a perceived inferential mark (because no connection with prior and posterior place could be perceived).

Nor, too, would the inference be possible that we make, on our view, to the movement of the moon, stars, and so on, on the basis of (perception of) conjunctions and disjunctions as inferential mark. And it is not the case that inference to such movement proceeds from conjunctions and disjunctions having themselves been inferred from cognition and non-cognition of prior and posterior places. For, since prior and posterior places would not be perceived (on that view), no inferential mark would be known.

Therefore, having manifest color is a cause of the perceptibility of external substances. Hence, air is imperceptible (and is known by inference).

Comments

According to the New Vaiśeṣikas, if either manifest color or manifest touch is absent, there will be no direct perception. How then is the flight of a bird, for example, to be grasped? From perceptions of conjunctions and disjunctions (*saṃyoga* and *viyoga*, "contacts" and "separations")? But conjunctions and disjunctions with what? The sun has no manifest touch. Therefore, it cannot be directly grasped. No conjunction or disjunction with something imperceptible can be perceived. The sun, however, as the Naiyāyikas conceive it, creates a sphere of light with extended particles of light or *tejas*. These being directly perceptible, a bird's conjunctions and disjunctions with them are perceptible—wherefrom, the bird's flight or movement is inferred. The Vaiśeṣikas' view, in contrast, would not allow the inference. Hence, since we do veridically infer such a movement, that view is wrong. Having manifest color is alone the relevant causal factor. Therefore, air, which has no manifest color, is not directly graspable by an external organ of sense.

The next passage centers on the cognition, "The air is cold," and it is important to keep in mind that everyone agrees that air, however it is known (whether directly by perception or indirectly by inference), possesses a feel or touch that is neither hot nor cold—a "neutral" touch. Thus the cognition, "The air is cold," is an illusion concerning the qualifier, *cold*. But it appears to be also, according to Old Nyāya, an illusion concerning the qualificandum, that is, if the cognition is taken to be perceptual, since air, on the Old Nyāya view, is not directly perceived.

Text (p. 803, Tirupati) and Translation

> nanu śīto vāyur ity āropo na spārśanaḥ, viśeṣyasya a-yogyatvāt | na ca prāmāyāṃ[7] tathā | sāmānye bādhakâ-bhāvāt | na apy anumānôpanīte vāyau tvag-indriyôpanītaḥ

śītâropaḥ śīta-dravyâ-bhedâropo vā | manasā tal-liṅga-sparśādi-catuśkasya a-grahaṇāt śīta-sparśasya a-tal-liṅgatvāt | na ca śīta-dravyôpanāyakatvena anumite vāyau manasā śītâropaḥ | śītân-āśrayatvena anumite vāyau tad-an-āropāt | na api pītaḥ śaṅkha iti-vat bahir-indriya-janyo 'yaṃ bhramaḥ, yena anumānika-viśeṣa-grahe 'pi doṣa-māhātmyāt bhavet | śīta-dravyôpanayana-janaka-praṇālīm a-viduṣo 'pi śīto vāyur iti pratyayāc ca | na api liṅgâbhāsa-janyânumiti-rūpo bhramaḥ | tad-a-pratīteḥ, śīta-sparśasya vāyu-liṅgatvena bhramâ-viṣayatvāt | na ca śīta-sparśânumite dravye smṛta-vāyv-a-bhedâropaḥ | vāyu-viśeṣyaka-śīta-pratyayāt | ata eva śīta-sparśo 'yaṃ vāyor iti bhrama-śarīram apāstam | na ca svapna-vibhrama-vat svôtprekṣita-padârtha-saṃsargâropa-vac ca mānaso 'yam | tvag-indriya-vyāpārânuvidhānād iti | ucyate | yathā vāyu-vaidharmyeṇa jala-vṛttitayā gṛhītasya śīta-sparśasya vāyāv āropo diṅ-moha-vad doṣa-māhātmyāt tathā śīta-sparśe vāyu-liṅgatvâropāt vāyavīyatvânumānam | na ca evaṃ śīto vāyur iti pratītiḥ na syād iti vācyam | śīto 'yaṃ vāyavīya iti jñānântaraṃ śīto 'yaṃ vāyur iti ca manasā āropāt, an-uṣṇo vāyur iti-vat |

Objection: "The air is cold" is (on your view) a superimposition (an illusion) that is not a tactile cognition, since the qualificandum (the air, namely) is not subject to being perceived. (The problem is, then, the nature of the superimposition in the case of cognized cold air.) And this problem would not occur if it were a veridical awareness, since the general principles for perceptual cognition would not be undermined.

The cognition ("The air is cold") is not, first of all, a superimposition where the superimposed cold would be presented by the organ of touch and superimposed on a mass of air that has been set in awareness by an inference. Nor is it a superimposition of the non-distinctness variety, where a cold substance would be superimposed. For, the four inferential marks of air—touch and the rest (sound, holding aloft, and shaking or causing movement)—would not be (in either case) grasped by the mind or internal organ (*manas*), since a cold touch is not one of those marks (or, is not a mark of air).

Further, (the error is not due to the *manas* making a mistake about an inferential mark, i.e.) the *manas* does not bring about a superimposition of cold on a mass of air that has been inferred as the vehicle of presentation of a cold substance. For, given (by the very inference whereby the mass of air would be inferred) that the inferred mass of air is not the substratum of the cold, the cold could not be superimposed on it.

Nor is this an error produced by an external organ of sense, like "The shell is yellow" (when it is in fact white), such that, even though the difference would be known inferentially (between the yellow and the true white, or the cold air and the true air that is neutral to touch), the perceptual illusion would nevertheless occur due to the peculiar extent of a defect (of the sense organ). For, the cognition, "The air is cold," also occurs when the cognizer does not know the channel or instrument whereby the presentation of the cold substance has been generated.

Nor is it an inferential error resulting from an apparent (but false) inferential mark. For, a cognition of such an apparent mark does not occur inasmuch as a cold touch is not erroneously taken to be an inferential mark of air.

Nor is it a superimposition of non-distinctness (i.e., identity) between a substance (other than air) that is inferred as the substratum of the cold touch and a remembered mass of air. For, the cognition of cold (with "The air is cold") is a cognition whose qualificandum is a mass of air (not a substance inferred as the locus of the cold touch).

For these same reasons, the view is rejected that the error takes the following form, "This cold touch *belongs* to the air."

Further, the cognition ("The air is cold") is not the hallucinating of a dream, nor like the self-modification (or self-imagining) of the mind, the *manas* (working independently of the external organs) superimposing things and relations. For, there is a correlation between the cognition ("The air is cold") and the operation of the organ of touch.

(What, then, is this superimposition that your view would commit us to?)

Old Nyāya: We can answer. The cold touch that is superimposed on a mass of air (or, at least, as so it seems) is grasped as a quality different from those of air, a quality that rests in water. Like (perceptual) confusion about direction, the cognition results from a peculiar extent of epistemic defect. But insofar as this can be said, so also can it be said that an inference to an *airiness* results from a superimposition of air taken (erroneously) to be an inferential mark, a superimposition *on a cold touch*. (That is to say, cold is not superimposed on a mass of air. Rather, airiness is the attribute superimposed—on the cold touch, the qualificandum of the error, which, then, takes the following form: "Airy is the cold touch.")

Objection: If so, the cognition, "The air is cold," would not occur.

Old Nyāya: That should not be alleged. For, immediately after the (mistaken, inferential) cognition, "This cold (touch) is airy," there can follow, "Cold is this air," as a result of a mental superimposition, like the cognition, "The air is not hot."

Comments

Praśastapāda finds four inferential marks of air: (1) touch, as in the feel of the wind, (2) sound, as in the chime-like sound of wind blowing, (3) holding aloft, as in the holding aloft of clouds or leaves, and (4) causing movement, as in the movement of branches of trees.[8]

A qualificandum that by nature is not subject to being perceived (*a-yogyatva*) is of course not perceived. Air, according to Old Nyāya, is such a qualificandum. The problem is, then, how it can be the subject or qualificandum of a perceptual illusion, since such a cognition, like a veridical cognition, has, on the Nyāya view, a qualificandum that is directly grasped. For example, mother-of-pearl is directly grasped in a silver illusion. Old Nyāya solves the problem by stressing, first, that airiness is mistakenly inferred, and, second, that the cold, which is directly perceived, is the qualificandum of the perceptual illusion, with airiness as the qualifier. The *manas* converts from "The cold is airy" to "The air is cold."

Text (p. 805, Tirupati) and Translation

> atha tvag-vyāpārân-antaraṃ kathaṃ vāyur vāti iti pratītiḥ, tal-liṅga-saṃyoga-vibhāgayor a-pratyakṣatvāt | na ca śarīre vāyv-abhighāta eva tal-liṅgam | abhighātasya saṃyogatvena a-pratyakṣatvād iti cet, na | abhighāta-janya-sukha-duḥkha-viśeṣeṇâbhighātam unnīya tasya sparśavad-vegavaj-janyatvam anumāya vegena karmânumānāt | evaṃ praṇālīm a-viduṣas tat-pratyayâ-siddheḥ | atha vāyuḥ śīto vāti iti kathaṃ viśiṣṭa-vaiśiṣṭya-pratītir ekā, śīta-viśiṣṭa-pratīteḥ mānasatvena karma-pratīter ānumānikatvena jāti-saṃkara-prasaṅgād iti cet, na | śīta-viśiṣṭatvena smṛte vāyau karmânumānād viśiṣṭa-vaiśiṣṭyam, na tu ubhayaṃ viśeṣaṇam ekadā bhāsate | na ca evaṃ kalpanā-gauravaṃ doṣāya, pratyakṣatve balavad-bādhaka-sattvāt |

Objection: How can the cognition, "The wind (or air) is blowing," follow immediately upon an operation of the organ of touch? For, the conjunctions and disjunctions that (apparently) would be the inferential mark (generating the cognition) would themselves be imperceptible (on your view of air as imperceptible, and if either relatee is imperceptible, no conjunction or disjunction could be perceived).

And it is not the case that an inferential mark is presented only upon a collision between the wind (or air) and the body (of the person making the inference). For, the collision, which is a conjunction, would be imperceptible (on your view of air as imperceptible).

Old Nyāya: No. One infers the collision by means of an (immediately grasped) qualifier, pleasure or pain, that is generated by the collision. Then, that the air responsible for the collision possesses touch and velocity is inferred. From the velocity, the air's movement is inferred. For a person who does not know, in this way, the channel, the route (to the cognition, "The wind (or air) is blowing"), the cognition does not occur.

Objection: How then can there be the single cognition, "A *cold* wind (or air) is blowing," which is a cognition of something as qualified that is again qualified (*viśiṣṭa-vaiśiṣṭya*)? For, there would be a confusion of class (i.e., cross-section of universals) between (1) a cognition of an entity as qualified (again) as qualified by cold, which would be *mental* (a superimposition accomplished by the *manas*, as you have just explained), and (2) a cognition of movement, which would be *inferential.*

Old Nyāya: No. Once the air has been remembered—the air that is cognized as qualified by cold—there occurs a cognition of something as qualified that is again qualified as a result of an inference to its movement. Both qualifiers (the cold and the movement) are not *presented* simultaneously (and so there is no confusion of class between the mentally superimposed and the inferential).

And it is not the case that a cumbersomeness of the conception here makes for a theoretical fault, since the view that air is perceptible has against it more forceful counterconsiderations.

Comments

It seems implausible that "for a person who does not know . . . the route (to the cognition, 'The wind (or air) is blowing'), the cognition does not occur." This implausibility is not addressed. But other difficulties pointed out by the objector force complexities in the overall causal picture: these are summed up as "cumbersomeness." That charge is answered with the retort that the competing view, to wit, that air is grasped immediately, faces still greater difficulties. Thus the apparent falsity of someone's needing to know the inferential route to know "The wind is blowing" seems motivated by the overall picture including the untenability of the alternative. "Again, just what are these greater difficulties?" one wants to ask. The alleged difficulties obtain only on the assumption of certain parallelisms, we hazard. That Gaṅgeśa's own position maintains weightier symmetries is, we would argue, the implication.

Next, a challenge left outstanding against the Old Nyāya perspective is taken up: whether or not having manifest color is a necessary condition for the perceptibility of a substance by an external organ of sense. If air cannot be directly grasped, Old Nyāya's stance that it is such a condition, or cause, would not be ruled out on account of air's colorlessness.

Text (p. 805, Tirupati, and p. 742, Calcutta) and Translation

> evaṃ bahir-indriya-ja-dravya-pratyakṣatve udbhūta-rūpavattvasya prayojakatve vyavasthite pratyakṣatva-sādhyakânumāne pakṣa-dharmâvacchinnasya sādhyasya sādhanâvacchinnasya vā vyāpakam udbhūta-rūpavattvam upādhiḥ | na ca viśiṣṭasya vyabhicāra-vyatirekayoḥ sādhane 'rthântaram | viśeṣya-vyabhicāra-vyatireka-siddhir paryavasānāt ity upādhau vakṣyāmaḥ |

(The exposition of **Old Nyāya** continues:) In this way, given that having-manifest-color has been established as a cause of the perceptibility of a substance by an external organ of sense, the inference (stated earlier) to show the perceptibility of air is undercut. The undercutter (*upādhi*) is: having-manifest-color. This pervades the (restricted) probandum (viz., being perceptible), (a) as specified by a relevant property of the subject, or (b) as specified by the prover. (And while it pervades in this way a pertinently restricted probandum, it fails to pervade the prover, namely, those things that are substrata of a perceptible touch, and is thus a true undercutter.)

Furthermore, the fallacy, "equivocation" (*arthântara*, "introducing new meaning"), does not apply to this argument either through the undercutter's deviating from (and thus failing to pervade) the probandum as qualified (viz., being not just perceptible but a perceptible external substance) or in being negated (through an equally well-founded counterinference) with respect to the probandum as (in that way) qualified. For, it is to be concluded that what gets qualified (namely, the probandum, being perceptible) can be shown to deviate in the same way or to be negated in the same way—as will be spelled out in the section on the undercutter (in the chapter on inference).

Comments

The section opened with an inference given by a *pūrvapakṣin* purporting to show that air is perceptible: air is perceptible, *since* it is a substratum of a perceptible touch . . . , like a pot. (See above, p. 489.) However, not everything that is a substratum of a perceptible touch also has manifest color. Thus, since everything that is a perceptible external substance has manifest color—according to Old Nyāya—having-manifest-color undercuts the inference—contrary to the *pūrvapakṣin*'s precisely contradictory statement, above, p. 489). See the comments made there for explanation of the types of undercutter mentioned again here. The forward reference is to the undercutter section of the inference chapter, where, as outlined above, it is indeed shown that pervading of a restricted probandum can satisfy one of the two criteria for undercutter status.

Finally, to close the section, we have a passage of extraordinary interest. Recall our discussion, at section's opening, of the *sāmānyato dṛṣṭa* type of inference and the example of a self being inferred from psychological properties. A deep problem can be seen in the connection between this inferential view of how a self is known and a perceptual view also endorsed. The Naiyāyika understanding of apperception, as expressed in such statements as, "I am cognizing a pot," has it that the self is immediately known, thus prompting the "I" part of the verbalization. But now the conclusion that air is not perceptible but knowable only by inference would seem to urge a parallel view about selves, and the doctrine of apperception would have to be revised rather thoroughly.

Text (p. 805, Tirupati, and p. 743, Calcutta) and Translation

atha vāyu-vad ātmā api na pratyakṣaḥ, dravya-pratyakṣatve udbhūta-rūpavattvasya tantratvāt | na ca liṅga-jñānaṃ vinā eva ahaṃ jānāmi iti pratyayāt na laiṅgikatvam |

jñānam a-viduṣo jānāmi iti viśiṣṭa-pratyayâ-bhāvena jñānasya liṅgatvāt | na ca ghaṭam ahaṃ jānāmi iti vartamāna-pratyayo na syāt, ghaṭa-jñānasya anumiti-pūrva-tṛtīya-kṣaṇe vināśād iti vācyam | sthūla-samayôpādhim ādāya vartamāna-pratyayāt | yathā kulāle ceṣṭā-darśanena karoti ity anumitir iti | ucyate | yo 'haṃ ghaṭam adrākṣaṃ so 'ham ghaṭaṃ spṛśāmi ity a-bheda-pratyabhijñānād ātmā pratyakṣaḥ | na ca etat spārśanêndriya-janya-jñānâśrayo 'haṃ tad-darśana-jñānâśrayâ-bhinnaḥ madīyâhaṃ-pratyaya-viṣayatvāt tad-darśana-jñānâśrayavad ity ātmâ-bheda-pratyaya iti vācyam | mad-aṃśasya a-pratyakṣatvena anumāna-liṅgâ-siddheḥ | na ca jñānena ātmânumānaṃ tatas tatra jñāne ātmīyatvânumānaṃ tato madīyâhaṃ-pratyaya-viṣayatva-jñānam ātmani iti vācyam | evaṃ praṇālīm a-viduṣo 'pi yo 'haṃ so 'ham iti pratyayāt | na ca vāyau pratyabhijñānam asti | sadā-gatimattvena gatasya punar a-jñānāt | sa eva punaḥ puro-vāta iti pratiteḥ taj-jātīyânumiti-rūpatvāt | tasmād vāyuḥ bahir-indriyâ-pratyakṣaḥ nīrūpatvāt ākāśa-vat | na ca sādhanâvacchinna-sādhya-vyāpakam udbhūta-sparśân-āśrayatvam upādhiḥ | udbhūta-sparśasya tatra a-hetutvena upādheḥ sādhyâ-vyāpakatvāt |

Objector.1 (against Old Nyāya): Like air, a self, too, is not perceptible, since (as you say) having-manifest-color is to be accepted as a cause of the perceptibility of substances.

Objector.2 (against objector.1): Since the cognition, "I am cognizing," occurs entirely without a cognition of an inferential mark, cognition of self cannot be inferential.

Answer (by objector.1): That's wrong, because cognition (itself as a psychological property) is the inferential mark, since, without knowing cognition, no one has the cognition of the qualified entity, "I am cognizing" (which is a cognition of a self as qualified by a cognition).

Objector.2 (against objector.1): (On your view) the cognition, "I am aware of a pot," would not occur in the present, since the awareness of the pot would have passed away before the inference (to the self), i.e., would have passed away by the third instant (after arising).

Answer (by objector.1): That should not be alleged. For, cognition of the present is to be understood as conditioned by gross (or "thick," *stūla*) divisions of time (lasting more than three instants, *kṣaṇa*). For example, seeing a certain type of activity carried on by a potter, one infers, "He is making (a pot)."

Old Nyāya: We answer. "I, who saw the pot, am now touching it," is a recognition of non-distinctness (or identity), a recognition that shows a self to be presented perceptually.

Objection: That "I," the substratum of a cognition generated by an external organ of sense, the organ of touch (in the part of your so-called recognition, "*I* am now touching the pot"), is cognized as non-distinct from the substratum of a visual cognition of the pot. (Your cited recognition, then, is nothing but an *inference* to a self.) It is so, *since* a self is the object of an indexical "I" (*madīyâham*), like the substratum of the visual cognition of the pot. In this way (i.e., inferentially), the cognition of an identical (i.e., enduring) self is arrived at.

Old Nyāya: That should not be said. For, if the "I" portion (of the recognition) were not perceptual, then an inferential mark necessary for such an inference would not be known.

Objection: From occurrence of a cognition (that as a quality has to have a substratum), a self is inferred. After that, it is inferred that cognition (in general) belongs to a self. After that, that a self is the object of an indexical "I" (and is one and the same over time) is inferred.

Old Nyāya: Again, that should not be said. For, someone who has no knowledge of such a channel, of such an (inferential) route, still has the cognition, "I am he who" (i.e., "I, who saw the pot, am now touching it").

But there is no such recognition with respect to air, which, as always moving, is not, once gone, cognized again.

Objection: (No. There is the cognition) "This is the same air (or wind) that was blowing formerly."

Old Nyāya: That cognition is an inference to a similar wind.

Therefore, air is not perceptible by an external organ of sense, *since* it lacks color, like ether.

And it is not the case that there is an "undercutter," *upādhi* (for this inference), in the property, not-being-a-substratum-of-a-manifest-touch, as pervading the probandum as specified by the prover. For, inasmuch as manifest touch is not a cause there (such that it is not the case that what lacks it would be imperceptible by an external organ of sense), this (putative) undercutter does not pervade the probandum (and is thus not a genuine undercutter).

Comments

In the background is the view that a single cognition corresponds to the smallest increment of time, an "instant" or "moment," *kṣaṇa* (cognition is "momentary" according to Buddhist camps and at least short-lived according to Nyāya). Thus, at a first instant, there would be awareness of a pot, an awareness that could serve as an inferential mark of a self. At a second instant, an apperception would occur, an awareness of an awareness of a pot, i.e., a cognition of the inferential mark. Then, at a third, an inferential cognition of one's self as qualified by the initial awareness would arise. Objector.2 alleges that, by the time of this third instant, the original cognition of the pot would have passed away. Thus, the present tense used with the verbalization of the cognition, "I am aware of a pot," would stand in tension with such an inferentialist analysis. Objector.1, championing the inferentialist view, responds in the usual Naiyāyika fashion to this type of problem (which occurs in various contexts), claiming that "present time" has to be understood as a larger unit than the instant. There is some overlap, and cognitive moments have spread. We shall return to the thesis in the section on apperception, in connection with Gaṅgeśa's own view.

Now Gaṅgeśa does agree that a self is knowable both perceptually and inferentially, and may be taken to endorse the Old Nyāya reasoning here on how a self is known. Elaboration is to be provided in the section on apperception, as mentioned. And there is no bar to interpreting him as accepting the argument, voiced here, that a self is known directly through a recognition of the form, "I who am touching X did formerly see it." That this is a veridical perception is a key Naiyāyika argument against the Buddhist position that there is no enduring self, and it is rehearsed in the current passage to show not enduringness but just that there are perceptual routes, in addition to the inferential, to knowledge of self. Elaboration of recognition as genuinely perceptual dominates the final section below, on determinate cognition.

But Gaṅgeśa does not agree that air is not perceptible. His view—stated above in terms of manifest qualities specific to different substances and different sense media matching the operations of the several sense organs—is that a substance has to have, for instance, only a manifest touch in order to be perceptible by the organ of touch, like a pot known tactilely. Similarly, a pot seen as blue has only to be blue to be veridically cognized by the organ of sight, to whose operation its having manifest touch is irrelevant.

Note that the Old Nyāya rejoinders here (a) about those ignorant of the epistemic route or channel still having the self-perception, "I am he who," and (b) about air "which, as always moving, is not, once gone, cognized again," jibe better with the reasoning leading to Gaṅgeśa's own view than they do with the Old Nyāya position that air is not known perceptually. The implausibility of the Old position about the inferential route to the cognition, "The wind (or air) is blowing," having to be known for the cognition to occur stood out, we saw just above, and if air is known perceptually, then the cognition, "This is the same air (or wind)," would not have to be explained away as an illusion.

To be sure, Gaṅgeśa's treatment of undercutters in the next chapter (in the *upādhi-prakaraṇa*) draws on a common stock of inferences about air which may seem to urge attributing to him the Old Nyāya view of air's imperceptibility. However, the point there is to analyze logical relations against familiar background assumptions (including wrong ones), not to fight out all over again the right view about the *pramāṇa* of our knowledge of air.

Finally, one might think—assuming the Old Nyāya perspective—that in the case of the last inference of the current passage the putative undercutter (U) does pervade the probandum (S) as specified by the prover (H), contrary to what the text says at the very end. The Old Nyāya inference:

a = air
S = not-perceptible-by-an-external-organ-of-sense

H = lacks-color

And the proposed undercutter:

U = not-a-substratum-of-a-manifest-touch

The putative undercutter meets, first of all, the existential condition that it not pervade the prover, since air, the inferential subject itself, is (~U) not not-a-substratum-of-a-manifest-touch while it does of course exhibit the prover.

$$(\exists x)\ (Hx . {\sim}Ux)$$

And, to consider the first or generality condition for a true undercutter, the property, not-a-substratum-of-a-manifest-touch, while not pervading the "pure" (*śuddha*) probandum, would meet the weaker condition of one of the exotic undercutters already discussed. It does not pervade the pure probandum because heat, which is a form of *tejas*, as in a recently baked pot-half, is not itself perceptible by an external organ of sense (S) but is (~U) a substratum of a touch (according to Old Nyāya, we feel the hot quality of the heat of the pot-half). But heat does not "lack color" (H); it has a *non-manifest* color. Thus it does not exhibit the prover (H), and it does not stand as a counterexample to the restricted pervasion:

$$(x)\ ((Sx . Hx) \rightarrow Ux)$$

Thus, the putative undercutter, though exotic (see above, pp. 490–91.), would indeed defeat the inference. Furthermore, the example, ether, which exhibits both the probandum and the prover, is not a substratum of a manifest touch. (Ether is not known perceptually but is inferred as the substratum of sound.) Thus, it would seem as though we are faced with a true undercutter. Old Nyāya's response to this problem is weak, repeating without argument (in an ironic parallel to the attitude about having-manifest-color) simply that having-manifest-touch is no cause of external substance perception and so not-having-manifest-touch could not pervade the probandum.

Note also that the current inference is nothing other than a counterinference relative to the inference with which the section opened—air is perceptible (by an external organ of sense), *since* it is a substratum of a manifest touch, like a pot—a counterinference constructed from Old Nyāya's *upādhi* alleged against that original inference, the *upādhi*, having-color (or being-colored), namely. Does, then, having-color qualify, air excluded, every substance that is perceptible by an external organ of sense? What again about heat? According to Old Nyāya, heat, like air, is not perceptible but only inferable from its touch. Furthermore, it has color, non-manifest color. Heat is, then, indecisive, and no decisive example seems to be known. So here the rebuttal argument would seem to be that having-manifest-touch is not a candidate for a universal cause of the perceptibility of external substances, unlike having-color, because there is a counterexample in the case of light. But this leaves it open whether having-manifest-touch might be, as Gaṅgeśa himself holds, on our reading, a cause of the perceptibility of substances that are perceptible by touch (including, presumably, those that do not have color, such as air). In the absence of a concrete example of a substance (other than the disputable cases of air and heat) that is both *not* perceptible by an external organ of sense (S) and lacks color (H) but *is* (~U) a substratum of a manifest touch, the question of the undercutter's being appropriately pervasive should be regarded as open—which is, all in all, further support for our reading.

suvarṇa-taijasatva-vādaḥ

DISCOURSE ON THE FIERY CHARACTER OF GOLD

Text (p. 808, Tirupati, and p. 745, Calcutta) and Translation

kiṃ ca udbhūta-sparśavattvasya bahir-indriya-janya-sākṣātkāra-prayojakatve suvarṇa-rūpaṃ tejo-dravyaṃ pratyakṣaṃ na syāt prabhā-vat tasya an-udbhūta-sparśavattvāt | rūpaṃ tu tasya udbhūtam eva | kiṃ tu upaṣṭambhaka-pīta-rūpâbhibhūtam | abhibhavaś ca balavat-sajātīya-saṃbandhaḥ | evam andhakāre pītâ-grahaṇe 'py abhibhūtam | na ca evam andhakāre suvarṇôpalambhâpattiḥ, abhibhūtasya api tejaso grahāt | na ca tejaṣi tejo 'ntaraṃ vyañjakam iti vācyam | rūpe gṛhyamāṇa eva cakṣuṣā dravya-grahāt | suvarṇa-rūpam abhibhavād eva na upalabhyate, upaṣṭambhaka-rūpaṃ ca ālokâ-bhāvāt |

Old Nyāya (in particular, Udayana): Moreover, if having manifest touch were a cause of immediate experience of substances by way of an external organ of sense, then the fiery substance, *tejas*, in the form of gold would not be perceptible, since, like light, *tejas* does not have manifest touch. Its color, on the other hand, is indeed manifest. However, (in the case of gold) that color is eclipsed (or obstructed) by the yellow color of (another element, earth, that is intermingled with *tejas* in gold's composition) its co-support.

The eclipse, furthermore, is a relation with something dominant of the same category (viz., the color of the co-support). Thus, when gold's yellow color is not grasped in the dark, the eclipse is still in place. And for this reason (i.e., that the eclipse remains in place) we do not have to face the following difficulty: that since, though (at other times) eclipsed, (the color would not be eclipsed in the dark and) the fiery element should be grasped and gold perceived in the dark.

Furthermore, it should not be said that another bit of the fiery element could (overcoming the eclipse) make the fiery element (in gold) manifest. For, only when a color is grasped is a substance grasped by the visual organ. Just because of the eclipse, the color of (the *tejas* in) gold is not perceived. And when there is no light, the color of the co-support is not perceived.

Comments

According to the Asiatic Society edition, there is no section divide between this and the preceding section. But though the voice (Udayana's) is continuous with that at the end of the last section, there is a marked change of topic. Our focus is moved from the perceptibility of air to the composition of gold. As mentioned in the preliminaries, section divides are open to question. Most likely, breaks were inserted by early copyists or editors.

More important overall (including for our reading of the last section) is the evidence provided early on for discourse divides between *pūrva-pakṣa* and *siddhânta*. The determination is made difficult, to be sure, by Gaṅgeśa's lengthy rehearsing of views of Udayana's. But explicit reference is made to Udayana, below, p. 521. Then Gaṅgeśa presents—without endorsing—four Navya positions each distinct from Udayana's.

The section is concerned with the phenomenon of gold's not changing color when placed in contact with extreme heat. Gold is also not destroyed by even the hottest fire. All things made of earth, however, seem both to change color and finally to burn up and turn to ashes. Is, then, gold not earthen? But things made of the fiery element—a second-best candidate stuff—are by and large luminous (though heat is not). Near the section's end, a Navya Nyāya faction suggests that gold is an additional substance, presumably an additional atomic substance, an element not on the usual list comprised of earth, water, *tejas*, and air. But until that point in the text the discussion proceeds under the presupposition that atoms of these four types are the only candidates for what gold is composed of.

This section is especially interesting for several general points made about the relation of perception and inference, including questions of comparative evidential weight and what counts as a defeater and when.

With regard to the opening passage, we should know that the color native to *tejas*, the fiery element, is white. The yellow of the earthen co-support obstructs its visibility, so it is proposed. The hardness of gold is accounted for by the "co-support," the earth atoms that are intermingled with atoms of *tejas*.

Text (p. 808, Tirupati) and Translation

atha yathā aruṇa-kapilâdi-rūpâbhibhūtam api vahni-rūpaṃ param ātmānaṃ ca prakāśayati, tathā kanakam api prakāśeta prakāśayec ca iti cet, na | tatra hi abhibhūta-rūpa-vahni-saṃbaddhân-abhibhūta-rūpā vahni-madhyâdi-vyāpinī prabhā eva vyañjikā | yad vā vahnau rūpa-bhāsvaratve na abhibhūte kiṃ tu śuklatva-mātram, suvarṇe tu rūpam abhibhūtam | tena tad-gata-śuklatva-bhāsvaratve an-abhibhūte api vyakty-a-grahān na gṛhyete iti phala-balāt kalpyate | na ca pītama-gurutvâśrayâtiriktaṃ tad-a-siddham | asti hi suvarṇasya atyantânala-saṃyoge 'pi pītaṃ rūpaṃ na tad-vijātīyam | tad-an-upapannam a-sati drava-dravya-saṃbandhe, pārthive atyantâgni-saṃyogasya pūrva-rūpa-vijātīya-rūpa-janakatva-niyamāt | jala-saṃbandhe tad-apagame ca paṭâdau dāhâ-dāha-darśanāt | tad idaṃ dhmāyamānaṃ kanakaṃ yady atyantâgni-saṃyogi-pārthivatve sati vijātīya-rūpa-pratibandhaka-drava-dravya-saṃyuktaṃ na syāt, pūrva-rūpa-vijātīya-rūpavat syāt vahni-saṃbaddha-ghaṭa-vat | anyathā pārthivaṃ na syāt jalaṃ vā syāt agni-saṃyogi vā na syāt |

Objection: As a fire's (native) color eclipsed by reddish, brownish, or another color (depending on what is being burned) nevertheless illumines both other things and itself, so gold, too, should be luminous (itself) and illumine (other things).

Udayana: No. For, in the case of fire, light—whose color is *not* eclipsed by being in contact with the fire whose color *is* eclipsed and which pervades the fire from bottom to top—is itself that which makes itself and other things manifest. (However, the kind of *tejas* present in gold does not involve light.)

Alternatively, the color and radiance of fire are not eclipsed but only the white*ness* (the universal of the native color of fire). With gold, in contrast, the color (itself) is eclipsed. Thus, the whiteness and the radiance resting in the color, though themselves not (directly) eclipsed, are not grasped because the individual in which they rest is not grasped—so it should be supposed according to (observed) result.

And it is not established that there is anything separate from the (earth-composed) substratum of (gold's properties of) yellowness and heaviness. For, gold's yellow color does not change even when in contact with an extreme (very hot) fire. That would be impossible if there were not conjoined a liquid substance (namely, *tejas*, which would be in this case accidentally liquid). With something made of earth, contact with extreme fire does, lawfully, cause a change from a previous color to a different color. For, we see that such things as a cloth burn or do not burn according to whether the cloth is in contact with water or not. This (our topic) gold, being blown upon (in melting), would not—if it were (solely) earth-composed and in contact with extreme fire—be of the character that a conjoined fluid substance (viz., *tejas*) would be able to block a change of color. It would (instead) have a color different from its previous color (before being melted), like a pot conjoined with fire (a pot that changes from black to red in being baked). Otherwise, there would be no earthen substance (composing it at all). Or it would be water. Or it would be such that it could not come into contact with fire.

Comments

As a general rule, when something's substratum is destroyed, it itself is destroyed. So, if the *tejas*'s color is eclipsed, then the two qualities inhering in the color—the radiance and the universal—would be eclipsed, too.

Text (p. 809, Tirupati) and Translation

> tad ayaṃ prayogaḥ, atyantâgni-saṃyogi pītaṃ vijātīya-rūpa-pratibandhaka-drava-dravya-saṃyuktam, atyantâgni-saṃyogitve sati pūrva-rūpa-vijātīya-rūpân-adhikaraṇa-pārthivatvāt jala-madhya-sthitâgni-saṃyukta-pīta-paṭa-vat | yad vā

pītaṃ suvarṇaṃ pīta-rūpâtirikta-rūpôtpatti-pratibandhaka-drava-dravya-saṃyuktam, naktaṃ-divam agni-saṃyoge 'pi pīta-rūpâtirikta-rūpân-āśrayatvāt tāvat-paryantam agni-saṃyukta-jala-madhya-stha-pīta-paṭa-vat | na ca a-prayojakam, virodhi-drava-dravya-saṃbandhaṃ vinā pārthive 'tyantâgni-saṃyogasya vijātīya-rūpa-janakatvāt | tac ca drava-dravyaṃ na jalam, svābhāvika-dravatvân-āśrayatvāt | na ca an-udbhūtaṃ tat, śītala-śilā-tale 'gni-saṃyogād dāha-darśanena an-udbhūta-dravatvasya dāhâ-virodhitvāt naimittaka-dravatvāc ca | na api tata eva pārthivatvam, druta-pārthivasya vijātīya-rūpa-pratibandhakatve ghṛtâdāv api tathātvâpatteḥ, tatra api rūpa-parāvṛtti-prasaṅgāc ca | upaṣṭambhakasya api pārthivatvena vijātīya-rūpâ-pratibandhakatvāt |

(Gaṅgeśa continues expositing the position of **Udayana**): Then there are the following formal inferences.

Something yellow in contact with extreme (very hot) fire is (also) in contact with a fluid substance preventing a change of colors, *since*, given contact with extreme fire, it is something composed of earth that is not the substratum of a color different from its previous color—like a yellow cloth that is both in water and in contact with fire.

Alternatively, gold, which is yellow, is something to which a fluid substance is conjoined preventing the production of a color separate from the color yellow, *since*, though there be contact with fire night and day, it is not the substratum of a color that is separate from the color yellow—like a yellow cloth that is both in water and in contact with fire for however long a time.

And it is not the case that these inferences are unsupported or ineffectual (*a-prayojaka*, as shown by counterfactual reasoning), for, without a relation to an incompatible fluid substance, contact with extreme fire would produce a different color in something made of earth.

Furthermore, the fluid substance is not water, since the fluid substance here is not by nature a substratum of fluidity (unlike water, which is by nature fluid). Nor is the fluidity non-manifest (when gold is heated, such that water could be its substratum, with fire required to make a native fluidity apparent and actual). For, since we find that, from contact with fire, (even) a cold stone burns (i.e., explodes and becomes fluid), a non-manifest fluidity is not incompatible with burning (whereas gold never burns). Moreover, gold's fluidity (it bears repeating) is accidental.

For the same reason, the fluid substance is not made of earth. If something fluid and earth-composed were proposed as what prevents a change of color (with gold), then the same should occur with such things as ghee, too (but ghee when heated does change color)—there is this problem. Furthermore, there is the difficulty that a change of color should occur there, too, in that the co-support, as (*ex hypothesi*) something also made of earth, could not prevent a change of color.

Comments

The variety of *tejas* composing gold is not by nature fluid, but requires another variety, fire, namely, to make it fluid.

On the hypothesis that the fluid substance that prevents gold from changing colors is something made of earth, there would have to be another earthen substance to prevent that fluid earthen substance from changing colors, since earth-composed things are seen to undergo color changes—and so on infinitely! Or, perhaps, since it is already accepted that the substratum of gold's yellow color is something earthen, we should suppose that that earthen substance prevents the co-support's color from changing while the co-support prevents its color from changing—a balance of mutual preventing!

Text (p. 810, Tirupati, and p. 748, Calcutta) and Translation

> yady api tejo-antaraṃ na naimittika-dravatvâdhikaraṇam, na api vijātīya-rūpa-pratibandhakam, kiṃ tu taj-janakam, tathā api pratyakṣa-dravyatvena tasya rūpavattve pṛthivī-jalânyatvena tejastvāt dharmi-grāhaka-māna-siddhaṃ tathātvam | pīta-bhāga-dravatvam api agni-saṃyoge na naśyati, druta-tejaḥ-pratibandhād eva jala-madhya-sthâgni-saṃyukta-ghṛta-vad iti |

(**Udayana**:) Even though other forms of *tejas* (the fiery element) are not substrata of an accidental fluidity nor prevent a change of color but rather generate one, still gold-composing *tejas*, although a perceptible substance and thus itself colored, has to be other than earth and water (as has just been shown) and therefore is (indeed) *tejas*. It is thus different from the others in these ways, as is shown by the arguments that apprehend it as the property-bearer (of the two properties, accidental fluidity and preventing a change of color). Even the fluidity of the yellow portion is not destroyed in contact with fire. That is prevented precisely by a fluid form of *tejas*, like ghee in the middle of water (that does not separate) when fire is applied (and the water heated).

Comments

The worry addressed is why the gold-composing form of *tejas* should be so different from other forms, fire, light, etc. The current proposal seems not only *ad hoc* but to fly in the face of accepted theory about the general nature of *tejas*-composed things. However, when a property-bearer is inferred to explain certain phenomena, it has to be supposed to have the properties appropriate to those phenomena. For example, God is inferred to explain world appearance—as its creator—and is considered omniscient and omnipotent to be able to play the explanatory role. Similarly, once we have grounds for ruling out water and earth, we have to suppose that gold-composing *tejas*—*tejas* being the only element that cannot be ruled out—has the properties necessary to account for the phenomena that are the basis for inferring it in the first place. Otherwise, any inference of the *sāmānyato dṛṣṭa* type would be illicit.

The ghee of the comparison class does indeed change color in the circumstances identified. But the water in which it would stand, like the inferred *tejas*, would prevent a change of properties: a blob of ghee apparently does not run in hot water but remains a coherent mass.

Text (p. 811, Tirupati) and Translation

atha yadi druta-tejaso vijātīya-rūpa-pratibandhakatvaṃ tadā jala-stha-paṭa-vat druta-suvarṇa-madhya-sthita-paṭâder api rūpa-parāvṛttir na syād iti, na | loke suvarṇatvena anubhūyamāne pīta-dravye a-vinirbhāga-vartiny upaṣṭambhake drutaṃ tejo vijātīyaṃ rūpaṃ pratibadhnāti na anyatra, tathā eva anvaya-vyatirekāt | tarhi upaṣṭambhakatvam anubhava-siddhaṃ suvarṇasya ity asya āvaśyakatvāt, tasya eva sva-rūpa-parāvṛttau pratibandhakatvam astu, kṛtaṃ dṛṣṭa-vijātīya-tejaḥ-kalpanayā iti cet, na | upaṣṭambhaka-mātre hi vijātīya-rūpa-pratibandhaka-sva-bhāvatvaṃ druta-tejaso dharmi-grāhaka-māna-siddhatvāt tasya tena eva rūpeṇa siddheḥ | yadi drutaṃ tejo rūpa-parāvṛtti-pratibandhakaṃ syāt paṭâdi-rūpa-parāvṛttim api pratibadhnīyād iti tarkasya tad-viparyayasya ca siddhy-a-siddhi-vyāhatatvāt | anubhūyamāna-suvarṇasya ca upaṣṭambhaka-rūpa-parāvṛtti-pratibandhaka-sva-bhāvatvaṃ na dharmi-grāhaka-mānād anyato vā siddhaṃ yena pārthive a-sati virodhi-drava-dravya-saṃbandhe agni-saṃyogasya rūpa-parāvartakatvam anvaya-vyatireka-siddhaṃ paribhūyeta ity ācāryāḥ |

Objection: If the fluid *tejas* prevents a change of color (with gold), then, like a cloth submerged in water, there should be no change of color in things like a cloth when they are put in the midst of fluid gold. (However, such things not only change color, they burn right up.)

Udayana: Wrong. There is in the world a yellow substance that is experienced. That substance is gold. The fluid *tejas* (that in part composes it) can prevent a different color (from emerging when gold is brought into contact with fire) only if there is a co-support that is tightly bound up with the *tejas* (the relation being so tight that the two are inseparable), not in any other case. For, our finding positive and negative correlations urges just such a conception.

Objection: In that case, that gold has a co-support would be established by experience inasmuch as the co-support would be necessary (to explain what you need to explain). (Now) why not just let that co-support itself prevent itself from changing color? What's the point of dreaming up a *tejas* that is so different from the types that we know?

Udayana: No. For, (your argumentation, which is as follows, is defeated:) the co-support (you say) by itself prevents by its nature the change of color, since it is shown to be just like that by the proof that establishes a fluid *tejas*, the fluid *tejas* that is proved by the arguments that apprehend it as the property-bearer (of the properties in question). (And) if the fluid *tejas* were what prevents the change of color, then it should prevent a change of color with such a thing as a cloth, too. (However) such counterfactual reasoning (*tarka*), and its opposite (namely, if there were no prevention of a change of color with such a thing as a cloth, then there should be no prevention of change of color with gold, too), is defeated by the (very) establishment (of a fluid *tejas*) and non-establishment (of prevention of change of color in the case of a cloth or the like).

And in the case of gold, which is commonly experienced, there is by nature prevention of a change of color of its supports (or co-supports). This is not a position that results from arguments that prove a property-bearer (of a certain variety, as we have arguments to prove that there is a *tejas* that bears certain properties). Nor does it result from any other argument whereby (let us again think counterfactually) a change of color would be established, by positive and negative correlations, as caused by contact with fire—given, that is, *no* earth-composed thing as incompatible with a change of color in relation to the fluid substance. The proof that there (ever) occurs change of color because of contact with fire would (itself) be defeated (which is absurd)!

Gaṅgeśa: So reasons our revered teacher (Udayana).

Comments

The final argument in this passage is convoluted. The point is that there is no other way to explain why gold does not change color than that the co-supports as tightly intermingled block such change given that we have established that a peculiar kind of *tejas* accounts for the fluidity that occurs when gold is heated. The arguments that establish the existence of the *tejas* do not themselves directly establish the existence of the earthen co-support nor its role in the blocking of a change of color. But once the *tejas* is proved, there is no option for explaining the fact that gold does not change color when heated other than by supposing such a contingently preventional co-support that can only be earthen (by eliminative argument).

The mention of the ''revered teacher'' Udayana at this point is helpful in establishing the discourse segments of the section, and of the preceding section, too, as was commented earlier.

Text (p. 812, Tirupati) and Translation

navīnās tu, atyantâgni-saṃyogena an-ucchidyamāna-pratyakṣa-dravatvâdhikaraṇaṃ taijasaṃ jala-pṛthivībhyām anyatve sati rūpavattvād vahnivat | na ca a-siddhiḥ, pratyakṣa-dravatvâdhikaraṇatvena tasya rūpavattvāt | na ca taj jalam, sāṃsiddhika-dravatvân-āśrayatvāt naimittika-dravatvâdhāratvāt sneha-

śūnyatvād vā lākṣā-vat | snehe sati sneha-dravatvâdhīna-saṃgraha-prasaṅgāt | na ca pārthivam, atyantâgni-saṃyoge 'py an-ucchidyamānaṃ yad-dravatvaṃ tad-adhikaraṇatvāt jala-paramâṇu-vat | a-sati virodhi-drava-dravya-saṃbandhe iti viśeṣaṇam, tena kvathyamāna-jala-stha-ghṛtena na vyabhicāraḥ | na ca a-prayojakatvam, atyantânala-saṃyogena lākṣâdi-ghṛtâdi-pṛthivī-dravatvôcchede pṛthivī-dravatvatvam eva prayojakam, a-sati bādhake anugatasya prayojakatve saṃbhavati tyāgâ-yogāt | na ca ghṛta-dravatvatvâdikam, an-anugamāt | na api naimittika-dravatvatvam, dravatvatvam eva vā, suvarṇe dravatvôccheda-prasaṅgāt |

Gaṅgeśa: But there are philosophers of the New school who reason as follows.

A **Navya Nyāya faction** (putting forth an inference): The substratum of a perceptible fluidity that is not destroyed by extreme fire is made of the fiery element (*taijasa*), *since* such a substratum—which is different, as is demonstrable, from water and earth—exhibits color, like fire (i.e., the campfire variety).

And this inference does not suffer from the fallacy, *a-siddhi*, the "unshown" (where a putative prover is not known to obtain in the locus at issue), since any perceptible substratum does have color.

(Now to consider the reasons for the qualification stated, "which is different from water and earth":) the substratum is not water-composed because it is not the substratum of a natural fluidity—since it is (instead) the support of a fluidity that is accidental—or because it lacks viscosity (*sneha*), like lac (a kind of red dye). If gold is presumed to be in fact viscous (and made of water), then there would be the unfortunate ramification that gold's beading (when heated) would be dependent on its viscous and fluid character.

And the substratum is not earthen (either), because it is the substratum of something that, as a substance (i.e., as an individual), is not destroyed even in contact with extreme fire, like a watery ultimate atom. A qualification has to be added, to wit, "that there be no direct relation to a fluid substance that is incompatible (with destruction by fire)," such that ghee (which *is* an earthen substance) situated in boiling water (which is incompatible with such destruction) is not a counterexample.

Nor is the inference "unsupported" (*a-prayojaka*). Given that the fluidity of earthen substances such as lac as well as ghee is destroyed by contact with extreme fire, that very fluidity of earthen substances provides support, since, without prevailing counterconsiderations, a uniform cause is to be supposed in that it would be inappropriate to renounce one (i.e., to renounce a good explanation).

Nor is the cause (of being liable to destruction by extreme fire) the likes of ghee's being a substance, for there is no uniformity (in such a conception). Nor is it the fact that there is accidental fluidity, nor just the fact that there is fluidity, since this would land us in the difficulty that the fluidity of gold could be destroyed. (Therefore, anything that is earthen and fluid is destructible by contact with extreme fire.)

Comments

The larger explanation being defended—of which so far we have only hints among the arguments—is that the fluidity of gold is accounted for by a propensity to fluidity on the part of the kind of *tejas* that composes gold in part. Tiny bits of a yellow earthen material, the co-support, have a solid form that remains intact (according to this first Navya faction, not according to a second) because conjunctions with the gold-composing kind of *tejas* prevent the earthen bits from being destroyed by contact with extreme heat. When the connections are tight, we shall learn, the gold is solid, and when, through contact with extreme heat, the connections become loose, the gold liquifies. This holds true although the color, shape, weight, solidity, and so on of earthen things in general are destroyed by contact with extreme heat.

The Vaiśeṣika tradition presents viscosity (*sneha*) as a specific quality of things watery. All things watery flow more or less freely, with degrees of viscosity determined, apparently, by distinct configurations among watery particles (triads, dyads, atoms), not by admixture with another element.

Text (p. 812, Tirupati) and Translation

> atha a-pārthivam api sāṃsiddhika-dravatvaṃ taile janya-jalântare ca atyantâgni-saṃyogād ucchidyate | ato 'n-anugatam[1] eva tṛnâraṇi-maṇi-nyāyena dravatvôccheda-prayojakam iti cet, na | pṛthivī-dravatvôcchede ca janya-rasavad-dravatvaṃ prayojakam | etena vivāda-viṣayaḥ pṛthivī naimittika-dravatvâśrayatvāt ghṛta-vad iti sat-pratipakṣatvam apāstam | anukūla-tarkâ-bhāvena, agni-saṃyogād dravatvôccheda-prasaṅga-lakṣaṇa-pratikūla-tarkeṇa ca hīna-balatvāt |

Objection: Some things that are *not* earthen but that are also naturally fluid are destroyed from contact with extreme fire, vegetable oil (for example, which is in part water-composed) and anything that is a watery composite. Therefore, your cause of destruction of fluidity is in fact *not* uniform, by the maxim of "straw, a tinder stick, and a jewel" (all of which are used to make fire but which are not uniform in the ways they have such causal capacity).

Navya Nyāya faction: No. With respect to the destructibility of the fluidity of things earthen, *earthen* fluidity is a cause; with respect to the destructibility of the fluidity of things made out of water (or the watery element), *watery-composite* fluidity is a cause, and a cause of the destruction of fluidity in general is the fluidity of composite things that exhibit (the quality) *taste*.

Objection: (There is a counterinference.) The subject of dispute (i.e., the substratum of a perceptible fluidity that is not destroyed by extreme fire) is earthen, *since* it is the substratum of an accidental fluidity, like ghee.

Navya Nyāya faction: That this is a successful counterinference is thrown out by the considerations just given. For, the argument has no cogency (on two counts): (1) it has no supportive counterfactual reasoning in its favor and

(2) it has undermining counterfactual reasoning against it—to wit, that characterized by the absurdity of a destruction of *x*'s fluidity through contact with fire (an absurdity that does not obtain on the assumption that *x* is earthen, since it is not absurd that something earthen is liable to destruction through contact with fire).

Comments

To exclude ultimate atoms, which are indestructible, the word *janya*, "composite" or "generated," is used in the opening inference.

The Navya Nyāya faction presents a textured view but not one that is so unruly or non-uniform as the maxim about starting a fire in different ways would suggest. Note that only things at least in part made of earth or water exhibit taste as a quality. Air and *tejas* have no taste (nor, needless to say, does ether). And so having taste lines up with being capable of fluidity.

If we were to suppose—to suppose counterfactually—that the substratum of a perceptible fluidity that *is* destroyed by extreme heat were earthen, then we would expect to be faced with absurdity. But things earthen that become fluid in contact with extreme heat are also, we find, eventually destroyed by heat. Thus there is no absurdity, and the counterfactual attack on the Navya Nyāya faction's inference is repelled.

Text (p. 813, Tirupati) and Translation

atha naimittika-dravatve pṛthivītvaṃ samavāyi-kāraṇatâvacchedakam a-sati bādhake tyāgâ-yogād iti cet, na | ghaṭâdāv api naimittika-dravatva-prasaṅgāt | na ca ghṛta-lākṣâdiṣu pṛthivītvâvantaraṃ kiñcid ekam anugataṃ naimittika-dravatva-samavāyi-kāraṇatâvacchedakam asti | pṛthivī-niyata-naimittika-dravatvaṃ katham a-pṛthivyām iti cet, na tāvat tiryag-gamanôrdhva-jvalana-vat tat jāti-niyatam, ghaṭâdāv a-bhāvāt | na api pṛthivītvâvantara-jāti-viśeṣa-niyatam, ghṛtaṃ vihāya lākṣâdiṣv api bhāvāt |

Objection: Being earthen specifies the nature of the inherent causality of (gold's) accidental fluidity, in that (as you say) without prevailing counterconsiderations it would be inappropriate to renounce it (as such a specifier).

Navya Nyāya faction: No. For that would land us in the predicament that such things as a pot would also exhibit accidental fluidity.

And there is no specifier of inherent causality with respect to accidental fluidity; that is say, there is nothing that is a less extensive universal than being-earthen that at the same time is uniform and continuous in such things as ghee and lac.

Objection: How, then, would there be in anything non-earthen an accidental fluidity that is, by rule, concomitant with things earthen? (There couldn't be.)

Navya Nyāya faction: No. First of all, like a fire (naturally) flaming upwards (but) running sideways (when blown by wind), that (what you propose, viz., a universal, being-accidentally-fluid, which you presume is pervaded by being-earthen, such that anything accidentally fluid would be earthen) is not concomitant with that universal (being-earthen), since it does not exist in such (earthen) things as a pot. Nor is it restricted to particular less extensive universals each of which would be pervaded by being-earthen (e.g., being-ghee, being-lac, and so on) because being-accidentally-fluid would apply in the other cases too, such as lac, in addition to ghee.

Comments

The last point made is that no intermediate or less extensive universal, such as being-ghee, is the exclusive province of being-accidentally-fluid such that only ghee clumps have a fluidity that is accidental. We can make out no law about fluidity with respect to things earthen.

Text (p. 813, Tirupati) and Translation

atha upaṣṭambhake pītima-gurutvâśraye pārthive atyantâgni-saṃyogena an-ucchidyamāna-dravatvâdhāratvam an-aikāntikam | na hi tejo-dravatva-daśāyāṃ tad-a-dravam eva āste | pītaṃ drutam iti pratīter iti cet, na | tatra dravatvâ-bhāvāt | pārthiva-dravatvasya atyantâgni-saṃyogena ucchitty-āpattyā bādhakena druta-pratīter bhramatvāt | jala-madhya-sthita-masī-kṣodâder iva tad-avayavānāṃ drava-dravya-saṃbandhena praśithila-saṃyogâśrayatvāt, na tu teṣām | na ca evaṃ ghṛtâdāv api tathā, dravatve tatra bādhakâ-bhāvāt |

Objection: On the assumption that the earthen thing that is gold's co-support (i.e., co-support along with *tejas*) is the substratum of gold's yellowness and weight, the prover term in your inference is deviant (that is to say, it is found in instances where the probandum is not), namely, *being the support of a fluidity that is not destroyed by contact with extreme fire*. For, it is not the case that when the *tejas* turns liquid there would be no liquidity there (too, in the earthen co-support), since we do have the cognition (regarding melted gold), "The yellow thing is fluid."

Navya Nyāya faction: No, because there is (with gold) no fluidity in the earthen stuff. (Taking the cognition you mention to be veridical faces) a cogent counterconsideration in the predicament of (what happens in fact, namely) destruction of earthen things' fluidity when they come into contact with extreme fire. That is to say, there is no fluidity there, since the cognition of the yellow thing as fluid is an error.

Like such phenomena as tiny bits of ink spread in water, the earthen stuff's parts are, in relation to the (truly) fluid substance, substrata of loose connections. But they are not themselves fluid. And so this does not apply to such things as ghee too, since with respect to their fluidity there is no cogent counterconsideration.

Comments

Therefore, gold is composed of two substances: (1) tiny bits of yellow earthen stuff that give rise to solids, such as a gold bracelet at room temperature, insofar as there are tight conjunctions with bits of the second co-support, and (2) a peculiar variety of *tejas*, the fiery element, that exhibits the key property of having accidental fluidity. Upon being heated, the tiny bits of yellow stuff spread out and are only loosely connected with the fluid *tejas*.

Next, another Naiyāyika faction denies that the earthen stuff does not liquify when, under conditions of extreme heat, the gold it partly composes becomes liquid.

Text (p. 814, Tirupati, and p. 753, Calcutta) and Translation

anye tu, upaṣṭambhake dravatvam utpadyata eva, anubhavasya durapahnavatvāt | atyantâgni-saṃyogena tad-ucchedas tu na bhavati, drava-dravyasya tejasaḥ pratibandhakatvāt | na ca evaṃ druta-tejasi mānâ-bhāvaḥ | tathā hi pītaṃ dravatvâdhikaraṇaṃ dravatvôccheda-pratibandhaka-drava-dravya-saṃyuktam atyantâgni-saṃyoge 'py an-ucchidyamāna-dravatvâdhāra-pārthivatvāt kvathyamāna-jala-madhya-sthita-ghṛta-vat | na ca a-prayojakatvam, atyantâgni-saṃyogena virodhi-drava-dravya-saṃbandhâ-saṃbandhe pārthiva-dravatvôcchedân-uccheda-darśanāt |

Gaṅgeśa: But (still) others say the following.

A second **Navya Nyāya faction**: Fluidity does arise in the (earthen) co-support, for it is difficult to deny experience. But that co-support's fluidity is not destroyed by contact with extreme fire because destruction is prevented by the fluid *tejas* (that is the second co-support).

And it is not the case that, if our view were right, there would be no argument for a fluid *tejas*. For instance (there is the following inference:) the yellow thing that is the substratum of the fluidity is conjoined with a fluid substance that prevents the destruction of the yellow thing's fluidity even when in contact with extreme fire, *since* it is something earthen that is the support of a fluidity that is not destroyed, like ghee in the midst of boiling water. Furthermore, this inference is not "unsupported" (*a-proyojaka*) inasmuch as an earthen fluidity would not be found to be destroyed (when the earthen things that have it are) connected to a fluid substance incompatible (with such destruction), while such destruction would occur were there no connection to such a substance.

Comments

Apparently other Naiyāyika contemporaries of Gaṅgeśa's say that both of the substances that compose gold exhibit accidental fluidity. The earthen support's fluidity, which normally would be destroyed by extreme heat, is not destroyed, on this view, because of its conjunction with the gold-composing kind of *tejas*.

In the next passage, Gaṅgeśa presents another inference in support of this second Navya view. Then he launches into expatiation of conditions governing a certain type of logical fallacy whose applicability becomes the principal issue in focus, the fallacy, namely, of an inference's prover term having "no comparison class," or "no similar instance," *a-sādhāraṇya*. As in a stock example, "Sound is eternal, *since* it exhibits soundhood," the fallacy occurs where the prover (soundhood, the universal of sound) is present nowhere except in the inferential subject. In technical terms, there is no supportive *sapakṣa*, no set of things known to be examples of the probandum where the prover also occurs.

Text (p. 814, Tirupati) and Translation

atha vā rūpavattve jalânyatve ca sati taijasatva-pārthivatva-saṃdehe vivādâdhyāsitaṃ dravatvâdhikaraṇaṃ taijasam, a-sati drava-dravya-saṃyoge atyantâgni-saṃyoge 'py an-ucchinnâ-nitya-dravatvâdhāratvāt yan na evaṃ tan na evaṃ yathā a-jalaṃ ghṛtaṃ vā iti vyatirekī | na ca a-sādhāraṇyam, a-gṛhyamāṇa-viśeṣa-daśāyāṃ tasya doṣatvāt | tathā hi, yathā sādhyâ-bhāvavad-vyāvṛttatvena pakṣe tasya sādhya-sādhakatvaṃ tathā sādhyavad-vyāvṛttatvena sādhyâ-bhāva-sādhakatā api syād iti sat-pratipakṣôtthāpakatayā tasya doṣatvam | na ca sādhyâ-bhāva-sādhakasya pṛthivītva-siddhi-paryavasāyinas tulya-balatvam, anukūla-tarkâ-bhāvena hīna-balatvāt | yadi idaṃ pārthivaṃ syāt a-sati virodhi-drava-saṃbandhe atyantâgni-saṃyogena ucchidyamāna-dravatvâdhikaraṇaṃ syāt taila-vad iti pratikūla-tarkeṇa hīna-balatvāt | yadi idaṃ jalânyatva-rūpavattve sati taijasaṃ na syāt pārthivaṃ syāt, yadi ca pārthivaṃ syāt, atyantâgni-saṃyogena ucchidyamāna-dravatvâdhikaraṇaṃ syād ity anukūla-tarka-sad-bhāvena pratikūla-tarkâ-bhāvena ca taijasatva-sādhakasya adhika-balatvāt | yadi ca a-sādhāraṇasya sādhya-tad-a-bhāva-vyāvṛttatvena tad-ubhaya-saṃśaya-janakatayā doṣatvaṃ tathā api viśeṣâ-darśana-sahitasya saṃśāyakatvam, prakṛte ca anukūla-tarka-viśeṣa-darśana-sahakṛtasya vyatireki-bhāvena sādhakatvam | tasmād yadā sādhya-tad-a-bhāva-koṭau na viśeṣa-darśanaṃ tadā a-sādhāraṇyasya doṣatvam | na ca evaṃ śabdo '-nityaḥ śabdatvād ity-ādikam api hetuḥ syāt, viśeṣa-darśana-daśāyām iṣṭatvāt |

(The second **Navya Nyāya faction** continues:) Or, there is another inference, one based on negative correlations: given that gold has color and that it is other than water, the substratum of its fluidity—over which there is dispute because of doubt about that substratum's fieriness or earthenness—the substratum is (in fact) fiery, *since*, were it not in conjunction with a fluid substance, it would nevertheless be the support of a fluidity that is not destroyed even in contact with extreme fire, although it is also a fluidity belonging to non-eternal things (i.e., not to atoms). What is not so is not so, like water or ghee (which *are* destroyed by such contact).

And this is not an instance of the fallacy, "no similar instance" (*a-sādhāraṇya*). For, that is a fault on the condition that no (doubt-resolving) particulars are grasped (whereas in this case there are such particulars).

To be precise, "no similar instance" is a fault (of the prover) through its giving rise to an opposite conclusion. An inference suffering such a prover would (purport to) establish its probandum by excluding those things that do not exhibit the probandum and so would also "establish" the negation of the probandum by excluding those things that do exhibit it.

And yet (here, with our inference establishing that the substratum of gold's accidental fluidity is fiery) there is no equal forcefulness of a prover establishing the negation of the probandum in showing, as a conclusion, that the substratum's being earthen is (equally) proved. For, that opposite inference has less force since it has no supportive counterfactual reasoning in its favor (whereas there is counterfactual reasoning that supports our fieriness conclusion). (Moreover) that opposite inference is less forceful because it has counterfactual reasoning against it: If the substratum of gold's accidental fluidity were earthen, then, were it *not* connected to a substance whose fluidity is incompatible (with gold's fluidity's being destroyed), it would be the substratum of a fluidity that *would* be destroyed by contact with extreme fire, like vegetable oil.

Given that the substratum is other than water and that it has color, if it were not fiery, then it would be earthen. And if it were earthen, then it would be the substratum of a fluidity that *would* be destroyed by contact with extreme fire: because of this favorable counterfactual reasoning together with there being no unfavorable counterfactual reasoning, the inference that establishes the fieriness of the substratum is more forceful.

And if this were (truly) a prover "without a similar instance" (*a-sādhāraṇya*), which excluded both things that exhibited the probandum and things that did not, it would be faulty inasmuch as it would generate doubt about both possibilities, and so it would remain dubious as accompanied by no finding of (doubt-resolving) particulars. But in the case at issue here, the prover is accompanied by a finding of (doubt-resolving) particulars in the form of favorable counterfactual reasoning. It establishes the probandum—by an inference based on negative correlations.

Therefore, so long as there is no finding of (doubt-resolving) particulars either on the side of the probandum or on the side of its absence, then a "prover with no similar instance" would be a fault. (However, that is not the case here.) Moreover, such inferences as "Sound is non-eternal, *since* it exhibits soundhood," would not, in this way, have such a prover too (i.e., a faulty prover, subject to the charge of "no similar instance"), since, given that there is a finding of (doubt-resolving) particulars (such as favorable counterfactual reasoning), such a prover is what is desired.

Comments

The inference put forth to open this passage is extremely complex and daunts analysis. A couple of clarifications. The fallacy of "no similar instance" is—at least in the instance suspected here (there are varieties of the fallacy)—closely similar to the fallacy of making an inference that is matched by an equally forceful counterinference, *sat-pratipakṣa*. The difference is that, unlike the *sat-pratipakṣa* fallacy, the prover having no similar instance would itself, not a different prover, prompt the predicament. That is, with no instance of the prover discovered in places (*sapakṣa*) where the probandum is known to be—bracketing the case at issue—there would be suspicion that the prover may be present in places (*vipakṣa*) where the probandum is known definitely not to be. Or, there at least would be doubt about whether the prover occurs in the one set of places, where the probandum occurs, or the other, where it does not occur. However, with the current inference, so the overall argument goes, there are doubt-resolving particulars; that is to say, there is reason to conclude that at least in some places where the probandum is not, the prover fails to be, too. Certain bits of counterfactual reasoning (*tarka*) match what we expect about these places of absence. All things considered, the case is a good one.

The answer to the charge that *exhibiting-soundhood* has "no similar instance" undercores Gaṅgeśa's view of inference as non-monotonic in character. As remarked, judgment of the cogency of an inference at issue cannot be separated from a concern with truth overall. That sound exhibits the universal of soundhood absolutely cuts no ice by itself: it is, as pointed out, the stock example of a faulty prover "with no similar instance," since only sounds exhibit soundhood and there is no comparison class. However, Gaṅgeśa suggests that this prover is not faulty *given* that there is counterfactual reasoning in favor of the thesis of sound's non-eternality (earlier Naiyāyikas had argued this too). Thus, exhibiting-soundhood is not a faulty prover for that inference. This then nicely shows that inferences for Nyāya are defeasible and open-ended, open to correction or support from other things known and shareable through testimony and public reasoning.

Text (p. 816, Tirupati, and p. 757, Calcutta) and Translation

> anye tu, tejastvaṃ na a-druta-rūpavad-mātra-vṛtti rūpavad-vṛtti-dravyatva-sākṣād-vyāpya-jātitvāt pṛthivītva-vat | yad vā tejastvaṃ druta-vṛtti rūpavad-vṛtti-dravyatva-sākṣād-vyāpya-jātitvāt jalatva-vat | na ca rasavad-vṛttitvam upādhiḥ, rasavattvaṃ dravatva-samānâdhikaraṇâtyantâ-bhāva-pratiyogi a-druta-vṛtti-

dravyatva-vyāpya-dharmatvāt paṭatva-vad iti druta-tejas-siddhau sādhyâ-vyāpakatvād iti sāmānyato-dṛṣṭena tejasi dravatvaṃ prasādhya, vivādâdhyāsitaṃ drutaṃ taijasam atyantâgni-saṃyogena an-ucchidyamānâ-nitya-dravatvâdhikaraṇatvāt na yad evaṃ na tad evaṃ yathā jalam iti vadanti |

Gaṅgeśa: But (still) others say the following.

A third **Navya Nyāya faction**: Fieriness does not rest only in non-fluid things that have color, *since* it is an (intermediate) universal that is pervaded by (i.e., whose instances all exhibit) the substancehood that rests in things that have color, like earthenness (which rests in some things that are fluid as well as in some things that are not fluid). Alternatively, fieriness rests in (some) fluid things, *since* it is an (intermediate) universal that is pervaded by the substancehood that rests in things that have color, like wateriness (which rests in some things that are not fluid—ice, for instance—as well as in some things that are fluid).

And these inferences are not defeated by the (putative) undercutter, resting-in-things-that-have-taste. For, that fails to pervade the probandum (namely, not-resting-only-in-non-fluid-things-that-have-color), in that a fluid fiery element is proved (by another inference): the fiery element is the absentee with respect to an absolute absence that rests in the same things as fluidity (i.e., it is not excluded from all things that are fluid), *since* it is a property that is pervaded by the substancehood that rests in non-fluid things, like being-a-cloth. Hence, that there is fluidity in something fiery having been demonstrated by a *sāmānyato-dṛṣṭa* type of inference (an inference by analogy), it is proved that the fluid thing over which there is dispute is fiery, *since* that fluid thing is the substratum of a non-eternal fluidity (i.e., not the eternal fluidity that belongs to certain atoms) that is not destroyed by contact with extreme fire. What is not so is not so, like water.

Comments

According to this third Naiyāyika faction, apparently gold would be composed only of *tejas*. There is no mention of an earthen "co-support."

All earthen things have taste, as do all things composed of water. Thus the candidate "undercutter," *upādhi*, having-taste, seems to pass the first test—according to the standard definition of an *upādhi* (see above, pp. 160–61)—pervading the probandum, at least as instanced in the cited examples. It passes the second test of a genuine undercutter with respect to both inferences, in that things fiery do not have taste: the *upādhi* indeed fails to pervade the prover in the very case of subject of both inferences, fieriness, or, more precisely, things that exhibit fieriness. The dismantling of the challenge is indirect in that another pair of inferences is put forth, inferences that show the failure of the undercutter to pervade the original probandum (which is the same in both inferences though formulated differently).

The *sāmānyato-dṛṣṭa* type of inference has—let us remind ourselves—a probandum that is nowhere perceived in conjunction with the prover, but is, instead, established by analogy. An occurring pleasure is a quality; all qualities have substrata; therefore, a pleasure has a substratum—albeit no pleasure and its particular substratum being perceived together counts as evidence (as we might argue against Buddhists who refuse to agree with us Naiyāyikas that we do sometimes perceive a self and its properties). With this stock example, the inference is supplemented by elimination of candidate substrata, such that a self (*ātman*) emerges as the only remaining candidate inherent cause. Similarly, as we shall see by the end of the section, the conclusion that the substratum of gold's peculiar fluidity is a kind of *tejas* turns out to hinge on an eliminative argument.

Text (p. 818, Tirupati, and p. 758, Calcutta) and Translation

> atha prathamânumāne tejo-mātrâ-vṛttitvam upādhiḥ | na ca pakṣêtaratvam | pradīpatvâder api vyāvartyatvād iti cet, na | balavad-vipakṣa-bādhakena vivāda-viṣaye druta-taijasatva-siddhāv upādheḥ sādhyâ-vyāpakatvāt | evaṃ ca vivādâdhyāsite pārthivatva-taijasatva-sādhakāni yady api bahūny anumānāni santi, tathā api vipakṣa-bādhaka-tarkāt taijasatva-sādhakasya balavattvam iti dhyeyam |

Objection: There is an undercutter for the first inference given above, namely, not-resting-in-the-entirety-of-things-fiery. And this is not a case of being-other-than-the-subject (when that fails to be a true undercutter). For, our undercutter excludes such properties as being-light, too.

Third **Navya Nyāya faction**: No. For, your (candidate) undercutter does not pervade the probandum inasmuch as a fluid fieriness is established for gold, the subject of dispute, (by another argument, i.e.) by forceful (counterfactual reasoning, to wit, that if gold were not fiery—if it were earthen even in part—then it would be destroyed by contact with extreme fire) ruling out counterinstances (namely, non-fiery gold).

And, in this way, although there are many inferences purporting to show either the earthen or fiery character of that over which there is dispute, still the proving that gold is fiery is to be deemed more forceful because of counterfactual reasoning that defeats the alternative.

Comments

The sense of the objection is difficult to translate because the objector corrects a possible misunderstanding of the Sanskrit word rendered here as "entirety" that depends on a homonymic, a double meaning, not occurring in English. Just above, the word *mātra* is used, within the expression of the probandum of the first inference of the current Navya Nyāya faction, to mean "only." Here that meaning is not operative, as is brought out by the denial that the undercutter proposed is an example of being-other-than-the-subject. It would be if *mātra* meant "only" instead of, as must be the case, "entirety," since the inferential subject is fieriness. As explained above (pp. 161–62), being-other-than-the-subject is a cooked-up undercutter that is valid only under the circumstances where it is known in advance that an inferential subject does not exhibit a proposed probandum. The objector tells us explicitly that his undercutter is not to be understood in that way. And with the word read in the sense of "entirety," the proposed undercutter encapsulates the view of those who would find an earthen co-support, in opposition to the current Naiyāyika faction.

The proposed undercutter, not-resting-in-the-entirety-of-things-fiery, obviously fails to pervade the prover inasmuch as the inferential subject itself, fieriness (where the prover is admitted as residing), does rest in everything that is fiery. The question is, then, whether it pervades the probandum, which is: not-resting-only-in-non-fluid-things-that-have-color. This strikes at the heart of the third faction's proposal, and there is no easy analogy whereby to rule the pervading out. But, says the third faction, there is another argument that supports our inference and shows that the proposed undercutter does not pervade our probandum. Unfortunately, the argument is not explicitly stated, but it appears to be the counterfactual one we have indicated in parentheses: if gold were not fiery—if it were earthen even in part—then it would be destroyed by contact with extreme heat.

In overview, the current faction is claiming that it is better not to tamper with the thesis that things earthen are all subject to destruction when brought into contact with extreme heat and to view the fiery element as present not only in non-fluid things like light and campfires but also, in one special instance, in gold brought into contact with extreme heat.

Next, a key presupposition is challenged, to wit, that even the hottest fire would not destroy gold.

Text (p. 818, Tirupati) and Translation

atha druta-drutatarâdeḥ kramaśaḥ pratīteḥ prabalânala-saṃyogena suvarṇa-nāśāt tad-dravatvaṃ naśyati ity a-siddho hetuḥ | na ca dravatva-prāg-a-bhāvâ-samānâdhikaraṇa-dravatva-dhvaṃsa-rūpa ucchedo na suvarṇe, dravatva-nāśe 'py agrima-dravatvena utpādāt ghṛte ca tathā iti vācyam | suvarṇe dravatva-nāśe sati vinaṣṭâśraye dravatvântarasya an-utpādena dravatva-prāg-a-bhāvâ-samānâdhikaraṇa-dravatva-dhvaṃsasya sattvād iti cet, na | suvarṇa-dravatvaṃ hi āśraya-nāśād vinaśyati na tv agni-saṃyogāt | yadi ca agni-saṃyogāt vinaśyet tadā ghṛta-van na dravatvântaram utpadyeta, dravatvôcchedakâgni-saṃyogasya dravatvântara-pratibandhakatvāt | tathā ca agni-saṃyogitve sati tad-dhetuka-nāśâ-pratiyogi-dravatvâdhikaraṇatvād iti hetv-arthaḥ | athavā ghṛte dravatvôccheda-samaye samānâdhikaraṇa-dravatva-sāmagrī-samavadhānaṃ na asti, suvarṇe tv asti |

evaṃ ca samānâdhikaraṇa-dravatva-sāmagrī-samavahitâgni-saṃyoga-janya-dhvaṃsa-pratiyogy-a-vṛtti-dravatvatvâvāntara-[2] sāmānyavad-dravatvaṃ hetv-arthaḥ |

Objection.1: Gradually things become fluid and then more fluid and so on through contact with intense fire. Because of the (eventual) destruction of gold, then, its fluidity *is* destructible. Hence, your prover is not established (as qualifying the inferential subject).

Objection.2 (against objector.1): Not in gold does there reside the destructibility that takes the form of a fluidity-destruction (that is final, that is to say) that does not share a locus with a prior absence of (another) fluidity. (In other words, in the case of gold, unlike ghee, if one degree of fluidity is destroyed, another emerges, such that there is always one degree or another of fluidity.) For, gold shows the next (degree of) fluidity arising on the destruction of a (prior) fluidity. And in ghee (in contrast), there is such a final destructibility.

Answer (by objector.1): That should not be alleged. For, there is in gold (a possibility of) a fluidity-destruction (that is final, that is to say) that does not share a locus with a prior absence of (another) fluidity, in that another fluidity does not arise when the substratum has been destroyed—as would happen in the destruction of gold's fluidity.

Third **Navya Nyāya faction**: No. For, the fluidity of gold would be destroyed in the destruction of its substratum, but not from contact with fire.

And if it could be destroyed from contact with fire, then, like ghee, another (degree of) fluidity would not arise, since the fire contact that destroys the fluidity would prevent another (degree of) fluidity from arising.

And so (the prover you attacked is a good one, i.e.) the meaning of (what we implied by way of stating) the prover is: (*tejas* composes gold) *since* it is the substratum of a fluidity that is not (what would be destroyed by contact with fire, i.e., it is the substratum of a fluidity that is not) the countercorrelate to a destruction caused by contact with fire, given contact with fire. Alternatively, the presence of a collection of causal factors sufficient to produce a fluidity that would rest in the same substratum as that destroyed on the occasion of a destruction of a (prior) fluidity does not (continually) exist in ghee. But it does in gold.

And thus the meaning of the prover comes to: (*since tejas* is the substratum of) a fluidity that accompanies a causal complex sufficient to produce a fluidity in its same substratum (were it to be destroyed), or (*since* being-fiery is) a lower-order universal with respect to the fluidity that does not rest in a countercorrelate (e.g., ghee) to a destruction generated by contact with fire.

Comments

To experiment with the hottest fire one has available and find out whether gold eventually burns would not decide the question, since one could imagine a hotter fire.

Silver is another thing that becomes fluid but is not destroyed by contact with extreme heat. Thus, the "lower-order universal" would be the indestructible fluidity presumed to inhere in gold, silver, and similar things.

Text (p. 820, Tirupati, and p. 760, Calcutta) and Translation

yad vā ghṛta-paramâṇau agni-saṃyoga-daśāyāṃ dravatva-nāśe sati dravatvântaraṃ na utpadyate tad-ārabdha-bhasmani dravatvâ-bhāvāt | evaṃ suvarṇa-paramâṇu-dravatvam agni-saṃyogāc ca yadi vinaśyet tadā tad-ārabdha-suvarṇam a-dravaṃ syāt | tathā suvarṇârambhakāḥ paramâṇavo na pārthivāḥ atyantâgni-saṃyogena an-ucchidyamāna-dravatvâdhikaraṇatvāt jala-paramâṇu-vat | taijasā vā tata eva yan na evaṃ tan na evaṃ yathā ghṛta-paramâṇur iti vyatirekī vā | evam a-pārthivârabdhaṃ vā suvarṇam a-pārthivaṃ taijasaṃ vā atyantânala-saṃyoge 'pi an-ucchidyamāna-dravatvâdhikaraṇa-paramâṇv-ārabdhatvād ity anyava-vyatirekī ca iti |

(The third **Navya Nyāya faction** continues:) Alternatively, on an occasion of contact with fire, another (degree of) fluidity does not arise—given a destruction of a (prior degree of) fluidity—in the ultimate atoms of ghee, since there is no fluidity in the ashes composed of such atoms. And so if the fluidity of gold's ultimate atoms were destroyed from fire contact, then the gold that is composed of such atoms would not be fluid. Therefore, the ultimate atoms of which gold is composed are not earthen atoms, *since* they are the substratum of a fluidity that is not destroyed by contact with extreme fire, like the ultimate atoms of water. Or, they are fiery ultimate atoms, for the same reason. What is not so is not so, for example, the ultimate atoms of ghee—here we have, as an alternative, an inference based on negative correlations.

In this way, there is an inference based on both positive and negative correlations and another based on negative correlations: gold is non-earthen, or, it is fiery, that is, it is composed of non-earthen atoms, or, it is composed of fiery atoms, *since* it is composed of ultimate atoms that are the substratum of a fluidity that is not destroyed even in contact with extreme fire.

Comments

The proposition that ghee exposed to extreme heat leaves ashes that are solid is empirically established. And though not directly experienced, ultimate atoms are hypothesized to have the characteristics necessary to explain the empirical properties that they are postulated to explain. Watery atoms have a certain character, as do fiery atoms and so on.

So far, the eliminative nature of the reasoning that, in the end, would establish the fiery character of gold has been implicit or suppressed. But in the next passage it is made explicit, as a fourth Naiyāyika faction argues that gold is a separate and distinct element, not a form of *tejas* or of any other substance commonly recognized. To this point it has been presupposed that gold must be one or the other of the known elements, and *tejas* has been arrived at as the only uneliminated candidate. In the next passage, the final of the section, that presupposition is jettisoned.

Text (p. 822, Tirupati) and Translation

> eka-deśi tu dravatvâdhikaraṇaṃ na tejaḥ pītatvāt[3] | na ca a-siddhiḥ, pītaṃ drutam iti pratīteḥ | pītatve pārthivatvâpattyā bādhakena pīta-pratītir bhrama iti cet, na | śuklatve 'py a-pārthivattva-vat pītatve 'py a-pārthivatve bādhakâ-bhāvāt | yathā naimittaka-dravatve pṛthivītvaṃ na tantram atiprasaṅgāt, tathā pītatve 'pi |[4] gandha-niyatatvam api naimittaka-dravatva-vad eva | pṛthivī-jalânyatve sati rūpitvena teja iti cet, na | a-prayojakatvāt | anyathā jala-tejo-'nyatve sati sparśavattvena vāyor api pṛthivītvâpatteḥ | atha rūpa-rasa-gandhānām a-bhāvāt na tathātvam, teṣām an-udbhave ca pṛthivī udbhūta-rūpa-rasa-gandhâdy-anyatamavatī ity-ādi-bahu-vidha-vyāpti-virodha iti cet, na | tejo '-dravam eva pratyakṣam, tejaḥ pratyakṣa-rūpa-sparśâdi-anyataravad eva, sva-para-prakāśakam eva ity-ādi-vyāpti-virodhasya tejasy api sattvāt | dravatvâdhikaraṇaṃ ca na pṛthivī iti tvayā eva sādhitam, ato naimittika-dravatvâdhikaraṇaṃ pītaṃ suvarṇaṃ dravyântaram eva ity āha |

Gaṅgeśa: But another faction (of Navya Nyāya) says the following.

Fourth **Navya Nyāya faction**: The substratum of the fluidity is not *tejas*, since it is yellow. And it is false that its yellowness is not shown, since there is the cognition, "The yellow thing is fluid."

Objection: If its substratum were yellow, we would face the predicament of its being earthen—a predicament that is a defeater. Therefore, the cognition of yellow must be an error.

Fourth **Navya Nyāya faction**: No. For, there is no reason not to suppose that although it is yellow it is not earthen, as some things (viz., watery things) are not earthen although they are white. As there is no causal principle demanding that accidentally fluid things be earthen, so too there is none concerning the yellow. There is also no invariable rule that things yellow have smell. Just like that is the case of the accidentally fluid.

Objection: Given that gold's substratum is neither earth or water, then it is *tejas*, *since* it is colored.

Fourth **Navya Nyāya faction**: No. For that argument is "unsupported" (*a-prayojaka*). Otherwise, given that air is neither water or *tejas*, it would be earthen too, since it has touch—this is the difficulty.

Objection: Air is not so (i.e., is not earthen), because it has no color, taste, or smell. And if it were held that those (qualities) were (present but) unmanifest, then several types of incompatibility would emerge with respect to such rules as that anything earthen has one or the other of (the qualities) color, taste, smell, etc., as manifest.

Fourth **Navya Nyāya faction**: No. That *tejas* simply is not fluid is perceptual. (The rule is that) the fiery element (*tejas*) has precisely one or the other of (the qualities) perceptible color, touch, and so on. For (if *tejas* were gold's substratum) *tejas* would also be in opposition to such pervasions or rules as that it always illumines itself and other things.

Furthermore, the thesis that the substratum of the fluidity is not earthen has been proved by you (above). Therefore, that which is the substratum of the accidental fluidity—something yellow, i.e., gold—is simply another substance.

Comments

According to Ramanuja Tatacharya, the seventeenth-century Naiyāyika, Dinakara̱, calls this Nyāya faction, *antyanta-navya*, "extremely New."

An eliminative argument would be cogent if we could presume (a) that there are only nine substances (earth, water, *tejas*, air, *ākāśa*, time, space, *manas*, and self) and (b) that *tejas* did not have strikes against it. But we should not so presume, this fourth faction proposes. In other words, the reasons why none of the nine known substances compose gold outweigh the economy (*lāghava*!) of having a smaller number. Gold is a distinct element.

The proposal for a tenth substance is not so different from the proposal that there is a special type of *tejas*, unlike all other types. Rucidatta says, however, that scripture favors the latter thesis, such as the Vedic text: *agner apatyaṃ prathamaṃ hiraṇyam* ("Gold is the first offspring of fire").

atha mano-'ṇutva-vāda

NOW, **DISCOURSE ON THE MIND'S ATOMICITY**

Text (p. 823, Tirupati, and p. 763, Calcutta) and Translation

nanu indriya-janyatvaṃ sukhâdi-pratyakṣâ-vyāpakaṃ pratyakṣa-lakṣaṇam iti cet, na | jñāta-karaṇâ-janyaḥ sukhâdi-anubhavaḥ indriya-janyaḥ janya-pratyakṣatvāt | rūpa-pratyakṣa-vat janya-sākṣātkārasya indriya-janyatvād iti tatra api tal-lakṣaṇa-sattvāt | sparśâdy-a-viṣayatvena tvag-ādinā na arthântaram | gandha-rūpa-rasa-sparśeṣv eka-eka-mātra-sākṣātkārâ-janakatvena pṛthivy-ādi-bheda-siddhau niḥsparśaṃ lāghavān niravayavaṃ ca manaḥ |

Objection: The definition (or "characterization," *lakṣaṇa*) of perception as generated by a sense organ (is too narrow in that it) does not include perceptions of pleasure and the like (qualities specific to selves).

Pūrvapakṣin (a Mīmāṃsaka): No. Experience of pleasure or the like, which is (unlike inference) not generated by a cognized instrument, is generated by a sense organ, *since* it is a generated perception, like a perception of color—at least this is true assuming that a generated immediate experience is sense-organ generated. Thus, there too (i.e., with perceptions of pleasure and the like) the characterization applies.

No fallacy of "equivocation" is committed (with this inference), since pleasure and the like are not (presumed to be) objects—like touch and so on—grasped by the tactile organ and the rest (of the external organs of sense). Pleasure and so on are not generated by the organs that generate, severally, immediate experiences of smell, color, taste, and touch, which are experiences that establish distinctions among earth and the rest. Therefore, there exists an internal organ (*manas*, "mind") that is intangible and without parts. This is the economical position.

Comments[1]

Several considerations motivate the supposition of a mental intermediary, called *manas*, which is intermediate to a self and its organs of sensing objects outside the body to which it is conjoined. Sanskrit *manas* as used in Nyāya and other philosophies is sometimes translated "mind" and sometimes "internal organ"; in this case it seems better to use the Sanskrit word. The *manas* of the classical Indian schools is a very peculiar entity, and there is little like it in Western thought. And the reasons Nyāya puts forth for positing, as it does, an individual *manas* as belonging to each and every individual self are complex and systematic—some shared by the Mīmāṃsaka *pūrvapakṣin* Gaṅgeśa introduces here and some not.

Probably the clearest appears to be as old as the *Nyāyasūtra*. In his commentary on *NyS* 1.1.15, Vātsyāyana gives it, and it is repeated in the current passage: perception of a self's "specific qualities" such as pleasure and pain and of cognition itself—in apperception—is analogous to perception of objects external to the body.[2] Thus we have a reason to suppose the operation of an internal sense organ that is like sight, hearing, and the external organs, each of which, we might add, has its own cognitive rights or range: colors, sounds, tastes, and so on. But a *manas* is not only an internal sense organ; it has other functions, reflecting other reasons to postulate an internal instrument.

The conception of a *manas* ties up with the Naiyāyika idea of self. A self, which endures, is, in the person of Devadatta and so on, connected with a body, which does not endure. So just what is the connection, and what is the role of each, body and self, in the occurrence of cognition?

Naiyāyikas have views about this that are apparently influenced by sacred tradition, teachings, in particular, about the possibility of liberation, *mukti* or *mokṣa*. But Gaṅgeśa worries less, as we shall see, about the nature or extent of the self's conjunction with the body as with the serial nature of cognition. Cognitions occur one at a time as well as in particular areas of the conjoined self/body. This is shown by the phenomena of exclusive concentration, or focus, as well as in a progressive revealing of properties of something. Thus, requirements of both temporal and spatial specificity—beyond that afforded by the body as a whole—demand the postulation of a sensory funnel, a delivery channel for the flow of sensory information to a self in the form of a series of cognitions comprising an individual's conscious life. The nature of the *manas* accounts for focus and exclusivity of awareness as when a loud sound commands one's attention no matter what else is going on. And the *manas* is a two-way intermediary, funneling a self's desires into effort and action, including voluntary focus, and not only information delivered to a self willy-nilly from the operations of the organs of sense.

The main point of atomicity being attributed to *manas* is, then, not like the atomicity of the material elements, earth and the rest. For, there the motivation is to account for increases in size and heaviness by talking about combinations of atoms, as well as to halt a regress of divisibility. With the *manas* atomicity means that only one bit of information can be channeled at a single instant. (Cognition, by the way, does not have a size, since it is a property. But, interestingly, information is thought to flow through the smallest imaginable entity, an entity of atomic dimension.) Gaṅgeśa takes much pains to elaborate and defend this correlate denial of sensory simultaneity.

Nyāya-sūtra 1.1.16 states that cognitive non-simultaneity is an inferential mark establishing *manas*'s existence, and *NyS* 3.2.59 adds that for this reason the mind must be atomic (*aṇu*).[3] Since the concept of *manas* is central to the overall Naiyāyika picture of cognitive psychology, the considerations that impinge on its postulation and atomic character become, let me repeat, complex and systematic. Indeed in the *Nyāya-sūtra* itself and the early commentaries, the nature of *manas* is discussed in several extensive passages.[4]

Like other sense organs, *manas* is listed as a substance, though it is otherwise *sui generis* and not a subcategory. That is to say, it has a high position in the ontological taxonomy, numbering among nine primary substances. Now, every substance has a size, and so how big is a *manas*? Sizes are in a primary division, (a) infinite or ubiquitous, (b) intermediate, and (c) atomic. The intermediate is the size of every finite, measurable dimension larger than that of an atom. Gaṅgeśa sees stronger reasons against the two sizes, the ubiquitous and the intermediate, than against the atomic, and by eliminative argument concludes that *manas* is atomic. This line of reasoning coalesces with the positive consideration of accounting for the exclusivity of cognitive focus and action, as will become clear below.

As mentioned, the *pūrvapakṣin* is a Mīmāṃsaka whose opinions coalesce with Nyāya on many points. Especially the two camps agree that the *manas* is intangible and without parts. The central disagreement concerns its atomicity or ubiquity. (Both atoms and ubiquitous substances, such as selves, do not have parts.) In other words, the central issue is how to characterize partless *manas*, whether as ubiquitous or atomic.

Nevertheless, psychological facts concerning focus are so much discussed along with arguments that hinge on them that they may be said to force themselves on our attention as readers, practically to the exclusion of the question about *manas*'s size. The mix of psychological and phenomenological evidence makes the section engaging.

God's cognitions are ungenerated or eternal. They are excluded from the prover term of the *pūrvapakṣin*'s opening inference by the use of the word "generated" ("since it is a *generated* perception").

The fallacy of "equivocation" (*arthântara*) does not occur since the term "generated cognition" is used univocally in the statement of the inference without implying generation by an external organ of sense.

Thus the force of the argument is clear. All perceptions of external objects are sense-organ generated. Perceptions of pleasures and pains are not generated by an external organ. And so there must be an internal organ, *manas*, that grasps them.

Text (p. 823, Tirupati) and Translation

tac ca vibhu jñānâ-samavāyi-kāraṇa-saṃyogâdhāratvāt nityêndriyatvāt nityatve sati dravyân-ārambhaka-dravyatvāt viśeṣa-guṇa-śūnya-dravyatvāt ātmâdi-vat | na ca mahattvam upādhiḥ, sādhana-vyāpakatvād iti |

(The Mīmāṃsaka **pūrvapakṣin** continues, proffering a new inference with a disjunctive series of provers): And a *manas* is ubiquitous (*vibhu*), *since* it is a support (along with a self) of a contact that is an emergent cause (*a-samavāyi-kāraṇa*) of a cognition; (or, it is so) *since* it is an eternal sense organ; (or, it is so) *since*, given its eternality, it is a non-composite substance; (or, it is so) *since* it is a substance in which rests no specific quality. (The confirming example for the first prover:) like a self (and for the others:) et cetera.

And (regarding this inference or these inferences) being-of-appreciable-size is not an undercutter, since the probandum does pervade the provers.

Comments

As mentioned in the introduction, emergent, inherent, and instrumental causes are three fundamental types of cause in the Nyāya-Vaiśeṣika system. (The term "emergent" may not be the best choice to render *a-samavāyi-kāraṇa*, but two translations standardly used, "non-inherent" and "co-inherent," are both misleading.) A quality or motion that invariably precedes an effect x in a relevant (or "non-irrelevant," *an-anyathā-siddha*) fashion is an emergent cause of x on the condition that (a) it inheres in an inherent cause of x or, down a level, (b) it inheres in an inherent cause of an inherent cause of x. A commonly cited example of the second type (b): the color of threads that make up a cloth is an *emergent cause* of the color of the cloth. Here the effect, the color of the cloth, inheres in the cloth that (down a level) inheres in its threads, the same threads in which the emergent cause, the color of the threads, inheres. An example of the first type (a): the contact between two threads that help to make up the cloth is an *emergent cause* of the cloth. Here the effect, the cloth, inheres in its threads, two of which are that in which the emergent cause, the contact, inheres. (There are of course as many emergent causes of the cloth as there are contacts among its threads.) Now, any cognition will, according to Nyāya, have a contact between a self and its *manas* as an emergent cause, a contact that inheres in the two loci simultaneously, that is, in both the self and its *manas*. Mīmāṃsakas appear to accept as much, too. (The nature of this extraordinary contact will be addressed shortly.)

Also common to both camps, or at least to the dominant factions of both camps, is the view that each individual self has a single *manas* that is, like a self, eternal, staying with a self through death and reincarnation. Further, the *manas* funnels all sensory information to consciousness, external data as well as internal. That is, while the *manas* is responsible for bringing psychological qualities such as pleasure and pain to awareness without the aid of external organs, it also turns external sensory data into cognitions of external objects. As noted, the *manas* acts in the reverse direction as well, channeling the effort of a self into attention, or focus, attention to specific, individual sense presentations and into bodily acts.

A few words now about selves. Naiyāyikas grant, along with Mīmāṃsakas, that selves have a ubiquitous size. If a self had an intermediate size, then it would have parts and therefore be destructible. Other reasons rule out atomicity, leaving ubiquity, by an eliminative argument, as the only possibility.

The term *ādi* in the above inferences' "example," which translates "et cetera," permits supplying a different example for the second, third, and fourth provers. According to Ramanuja Tatacharya, we can take the auditory organ for the second (which is ether delimited to the earhole but nonetheless ether, therefore eternal); for the third, time, which is a non-composite substance; and for the fourth also time.

Since the Mīmāṃsaka *pūrvapakṣin* holds that a *manas* is ubiquitous, he holds that it has appreciable size. So the proposed "undercutter," *upādhi*, is an undercutter only from the Naiyāyika perspective.

Text (p. 824, Tirupati) and Translation

> nanu sukhâdikaṃ mūrta-saṃyogâ-samavāyi-kāraṇaka-guṇa-vṛtti-guṇatvâvantara-jāti-yogi nitya-vṛtti-nitya-viśeṣa-guṇatvāt śabda-vat pāka-ja-rūpavac ca iti cet, na | an-ātma-vṛttitvasya śabda-bhinna-viśeṣa-guṇa-grāhakêndriyâ-janyatvasya śabdasya dravyatvena mūrta-vṛtti-guṇatvasya ca upādhitvāt a-prayojakatvāc ca | kāraṇe mūrtatvasya gurutvāt | astu vā śarīrâtma-saṃyoga-janyatvena an-arthântaram |

Objection (by a Naiyāyika proffering a counterinference): Pleasure and company are instances of an intermediate universal (pleasurehood and company) that is pervaded by (the universal) being-a-quality and that rests in qualities each of which has something of finite form (*mūrta*) as a term in a contact that is an emergent cause of it, *since* pleasure and company are non-eternal, specific qualities that rest in things that are eternal (namely, selves), like sound and like (atoms') color due to baking, too.

Pūrvapakṣin: No. Resting-in-a-non-self is an undercutter (for your inference, considering the first example given, namely, sound, in that resting-in-a-non-self pervades the probandum while it fails to pervade your prover, and in your very own example): sound is not generated by those sense organs that grasp specific qualities (color, etc.) that are distinct from sound inasmuch as it is a substance (sound is a substance on our Mīmāṃsaka view). Being-a-quality-resting-in-something-of-finite-form is also an undercutter (considering the second example given, namely, color due to baking, since atoms have finite form). Furthermore, your inference is unsupported (in that the probandum occurs where the prover does not occur).

(Moreover, your proposal contains as a qualification that one term of the contact be) something of finite form as a cause (of pleasures and company)—this is cumbersome (compared to our Mīmāṃsaka theory). Or, if what you mean is production of pleasure and company through contacts between self and body (which is a plank of our view), then your inference suffers from the fallacy of proving something other than what was (apparently) intended.

Comments

A sound is a quality resting in ether, *ākāśa*, which is an eternal substance, like a self. Sounds are non-eternal, at least according to Nyāya (Mīmāṃsā denies this), and each sound has an emergent cause in a contact—a contact with a drum, for example—a contact that has something of finite form—the drum—as a term of the relation. Similarly, the color of an atom that has changed due to baking is a quality that rests in something eternal—the atom—but is itself non-eternal, having as emergent cause a contact between the atom and fire of finite form. (Atoms are also of finite form.) Similarly, pleasure and company, which are non-eternal, rest in a self, which is eternal. They are in fact specific qualities, qualifying only selves. A pleasure's emergent cause is invariably a contact of a person's *manas* with the person's self. And such contact has to have one term that is of finite form—the Naiyāyika objector reasons—by the principle implicit in the analogies cited. Since selves are infinite, i.e., ubiquitous, the internal organ has to be of finite size and is therefore not ubiquitous.

The intuition guiding the Naiyāyika inference is that, since pleasure and company are limited qualities but are also qualities of selves which are unlimited, there has to be something that accounts for the limitations. The *manas* seems the best candidate. That the *manas* is of finite form—a proposition embedded in the probandum—is what is at stake. The *pūrvapakṣin*'s undercutters, resting-in-a-non-self and being-a-quality-resting-in-something-of-finite-form, connect with the Mīmāṃsaka reasoning that because a self is ubiquitous its *manas* must be so, too.

Whether Kumārila really holds that sound is a substance is debatable. The issue is tied up with that of the eternality of sound understood as individual sounds or words or letters, and Mīmāṃsaka opinion ranges over several theses that bear on the eternality question. But clearly we are supposed to presume that our Mīmāṃsaka *pūrvapakṣin* regards sound as an eternal substance. Soundhood would be, then, an intermediate or less extensive universal pervaded not by being-a-quality, but by being-a-substance.

Text (p. 825, Tirupati) and Translation

atha a-samavāyy-adhīno vibhu-kāryāṇāṃ prādeśikatva-niyama iti vibhu-mano-yogād ātma-mātre sukhâder utpattau niyata-deśatā na syāt, ataḥ aṇu mana iti | mā evam | kim a-samavāyi-kāraṇaṃ svâvacchinne vibhu-kāryaṃ janayati iti niyamaḥ, svâvacchinne janayaty eva iti vā, svâvacchinna eva janayati iti vā | ādye sukhâder adhika-deśatve āpādakâ-bhāvaḥ | dvitīye 'ṇu-manas-saṃyoge 'pi svâvacchinne adhika-deśe ca janayet niyāmakâ-bhāvāt | antye tava api sukhâder aṇu-mātra-deśatâpattiḥ | mano-vaibhave 'pi a-virodhaś ca |

Objection (by the Naiyāyika): For effects resting in something ubiquitous (such as a self), the rule determining their precise location depends on the emergent cause (specifically, on its location). Thus, if there is to be production—simply in a self—of pleasure and company from contact with a *ubiquitous manas*, there could be no restriction to place (and a particular pleasure, for example, would be felt ubiquitously). Therefore, the *manas* has to be atomic.

Pūrvapakṣin: Don't think like that. What's the rule? Is it that the emergent cause (contact of self and *manas*) brings about (or, helps to bring about along with other necessary factors) an effect in something ubiquitous in any spot demarcated (or specified) by that very emergent cause (i.e., helps to bring it about in any spot within its overall range)? Or, is it that it necessarily brings it about in a spot demarcated by itself? Or, is it that it brings it about only in the spot demarcated by itself? On the first alternative, there would be no contrary ramification were pleasure and the like to arise in places other than where they do (since the body comprises the *manas*'s range). On the second, even if the contact (that is the operative emergent cause) were with an *atomic manas* (as one of its terms), the contact could also give rise to pleasure and company in places other than where they actually occur (since the range of an atomic *manas* would still be the body). This would be true because the self-demarcated spots could include such places, since there is (as formulated) no (further) restriction. On the last alternative, you face the difficulty that the place where pleasure and the like would be felt would be itself exclusively atomic.

And on our view of a ubiquitous *manas*, there is no such incompatibility (with the facts).

Comments

Here Gaṅgeśa uses *tarka*, dialectical or counterfactual reasoning, in support of the Mīmāṃsaka position, trading on the opacity of the notion that psychological properties have a bodily location and, more generally, that a ubiquitous self and a finite body are conjoined. The Naiyāyika objector tries to make hay out of the specificity of location of certain pleasures and pains, which requires more than simple self-body conjunction in that some of these are felt only in specific bodily parts. But just what does the proposed rule say? Three distinct interpretations are outlined: (1) the operative emergent cause happens to bring about the effect-in-something-ubiquitous—e.g., a bit of pleasure occurring in a self—in some particular locus of self-body conjunction that is specified by that emergent cause, but it could bring it about, depending on other factors, elsewhere, in some other bodily part or in the body as a whole; (2) it itself is in every instance the crucial factor bringing the effect about as restricted to a certain place; and (3) an atomic *manas* brings about the effect only in the place where it itself is located at a particular time. On the first and second interpretations, which are both too loosely formulated, self-*manas* contact could occur in the elbow while the pain was in the toe! Finally, on the third alternative, there is the problem of some pain being not a pinpoint (atomic) prick but as having a certain spread in a bodily area.

Text (p. 765, Calcutta) and Translation

> atha nimitta-candanâdy-anurodhena sukhâdau nyūnâdhika-deśatā nimitta-vāyu-saṃyogād iva śabde na tu a-samavāyy-anurodhāt | tathā ca sukhâdikaṃ tad-avacchinna eva utpadyata iti cet, hanta! tarhi vaibhave 'pi tathā astu | na ca vibhu-kāryâ-samavāyī svâcchinne kāryaṃ janayaty eva bhery-ākāśa-saṃyoga iva śabdam iti candanâdy-an-avacchinne[5] 'pi sukhâdikam utpadyeta iti vācyam | tad-deśīya-candana-sukhe hi tad-deśīya-candana-saṃbandha-sāpekṣo a-samavāyī hetur iti kathaṃ tan-nirapekṣas tat kuryāt | candanaṃ ca svâvacchinnaṃ sukha-janakaṃ kathaṃ svâvacchinne 'pi tad utpādayet, kathaṃ vā tad-deśīya-candana-sukhaṃ tad-deśa-candana-saṃbandha-janyaṃ tena vinā eva utpadyeta |

Objection (by the Naiyāyika): Whether it is a smaller or larger place where pleasure and the like are felt conforms to such *instrumental* causes as (the extent of) sandalwood paste (applied to the body, i.e., in a smaller or larger area), not to an emergent cause—like a sound whose nature is due to an instrumental cause, contact-with-air (not to the emergent cause, contact-with-ether). And so pleasure and the like are produced in a spot specified by such *instrumental* causes.

Pūrvapakṣin: Come on! Then the same could happen with a ubiquitous *manas*, too. (You have given no reason to prefer an atomic *manas*.)

Objection: The emergent cause of an effect in something ubiquitous would bring the effect about only in a spot specified by it, as contact between ether and a drum brings about a sound. Hence, pleasure and the like can (in some instances) come about not restricted to an area determined, e.g., by the spread of sandalwood paste (and we do sometimes feel pleasure all over the body from sandalwood paste spread limitedly).

Pūrvapakṣin: That should not be said. For, your claim is that, in a case of pleasure due to sandalwood paste spread in a certain area, the emergent cause (i.e., contact between self and *manas*) would depend on the relation that the sandalwood paste has to that area. How, then, would it, *independently* of that relation, bring about pleasure? And (if you say) "The sandalwood produces pleasure restricted to its own location"—how would it produce it also in places not restricted like that (as, we agree, sometimes happens)? Or, how is it, if the pleasure of sandalwood paste at a certain spot is to be generated by the relation to the sandalwood paste at that spot, that even without such a relation pleasure can be produced (as also happens on occasion)?

Comments

The phenomenology of pleasure due to sandalwood ointment presents a squadron of theoretical difficulties, and frustrates the Naiyāyika's attempts to find a reason favoring an atomic *manas*. Pleasure from sandalwood paste is not easier to understand on the atomic hypothesis. Both theories require complex supplementation with reference to the body. Yet sometimes pleasure occurs even without bodily stimulus, as when we imagine sandalwood paste spread over a certain part of our skin. We can feel it a few inches up the arm from its actual extent which is, say, restricted to a small area just under the wrist.

Text (p. 826, Tirupati) and Translation

> atha mano-vaibhave sukhâdy-utpattau niyata upādhir vācyaḥ | tena nānā-nimitta-samavadhāne 'pi tad-avacchedena ekadā sukha-duḥkhâdiṣv ekam eva utpadyate na nānā | ekâvacchedena ekadā eka eva vibhu-viśeṣa-guṇa utpadyata iti niyamāt | nimittasya tv avacchedakatve nānā-sukhâdikam utpadyeta śabda-vad iti cet, na | śrotre karṇa-śaṣkuly-avacchedena nānā-nimittād an-eka-śabdôtpādāt | anyathā kolāhala-graho na syāt | nānâvacchedena ekadā candana-dahanâdi-saṃbandhe sukha-duḥkhayoś ca ekadā anubhava-siddhatvena iṣṭâpādanāt | na ca yaugapadya-pratyayo bhramaḥ, bādhâ-bhāvāt | na ca anyatra kramād atra api kramânumānam, anyatra kramasya nimitta-kramâdhīnatvāt | evaṃ ca vivāda-viṣaya-sukha-duḥkhāni yugapad-utpannâ-samavāyi-kāraṇakāni yugapad-utpadyamānatvāt yugapad-utpanna-ghaṭâdi-vat | a-bādhitânubhavāc ca na a-siddhiḥ | etena caraṇa-duḥkhaṃ yadi śarīrâvacchinnâ-samavāyi-hetukaṃ syāt śarīra-vyāpakaṃ syād iti nirastam | nimitta-samavadhānasya tantratve 'sya a-prayojakatvāt | anyathā aṇutva-pakṣe śarīra-vyāpakaṃ sukhâdi na syāt | ābhimānikâbhyāsika-mano-rathika-sukheṣu jñānêcchā-prayatna-dveṣeṣu ca deśâ-niyamaḥ | śarīrâvayaveṣu yat-kriyāyām icchā tad-avacchedena prayatna iti tatra eva ceṣṭā āvaśyakatvāt a-niyata-deśa-jñānêcchâdau laghutvāc ca | anyathā aṇutva-pakṣe prayatnasya aṇu-deṣatvaṃ śarīra-mātra-deśatvaṃ vā syāt |

Objection: On your view of the ubiquitousness of *manas* (as well as of a self) a factor regulating the production of pleasure and the like has to be identified. Due to that factor, simply a single occurrence—not various pleasures and pains—would, at a single time, be produced, even though occasioning conditions of many possible pleasures and pains be present. This single pleasure, or pain, would be produced through specification of precisely which instrumental cause (comes into play)—and all this albeit various potential instrumental causes are present. By a single such specification, just one specific quality resting in an ubiquitous self (i.e., a pleasure or a pain) is, on a single occasion, produced—this is the rule.

In contrast, if (your thesis is that only) the instrumental causality (all the instrumental causes in the overall set of causes sufficient to produce the effect) is appropriately delimited (by self-*manas* conjunction), then many various pleasures and pains could be produced (on a single occasion), like tumultuous noise (*kolāhala*, conflicting sounds arising from different sources, a hedonic chaos).

Pūrvapakṣin: No. For, a plurality of sounds arises from a plurality, and variety, of instrumental causes—in the organ of hearing through a delimitation to the earhole. Otherwise, tumultuous noise would not be grasped. The fact that by means of a variety of specifiers present at a single time both pleasure and pain come about on the same occasion is a desired consequence of our view: there does sometimes occur a (simultaneous) relation with sandalwood paste (on one part of the body) and fire (with another), as is established by experience.

And it is not the case that such a simultaneous cognitive occurrence would be an error (i.e., non-veridical), since there are no prevailing considerations to that effect. Furthermore, it is not the case that, from serial orderings witnessed elsewhere, here too a series is to be inferred, since elsewhere a serial ordering (among effects) is dependent on a serial ordering among instrumental causes.

And so, pleasures and pains, which are the topic of our dispute, can have emergent causes that bring them about simultaneously, *since* they do arise simultaneously, like simultaneous production (by many potters, etc.) of many pots, etc.

Moreover, because experience (of simultaneous pleasures and pains) is not defeated or overridden, our inference does not suffer from the fallacy of an unestablished prover (i.e., simultaneity of pleasures and pains is experiential and not to be explained away as an error as Naiyāyikas are wont to try).

Objection: If pain in the foot can have an emergent cause occurring in the area of the head (i.e., a conjunction of self and *manas*), then the pain should pervade the body.

Pūrvapakṣin: This is rejected by reasoning already provided. For, given that an entirety of instrumental causes (including, for instance, a thorn in the foot) is what the causality would amount to (for any particular effect)—pain throughout the body would not (necessarily) be caused. Otherwise, on your view of the atomicity of *manas*, pleasure and the like that does (on occasion) pervade the body could not be. The pleasures of pride of accomplishment, of skill through practice and repetition, and of fancy or imagination are not restricted to an area (of the body), nor are cognitions, desires, efforts, and aversions.

Desire that a certain action occur in just certain parts of the body results in effort specifically in those parts (e.g., a movement of an arm or a hand).

Hence, movement occurs just there—because this is an unavoidable position and because it is economical to hold that cognition and desire are not limited to one area (of the body). Otherwise, on your view of the atomicity of *manas*, effort would occur in an atomic place, or the place would simply be the body (without a possibility of restricted occurrences of pleasure and so on).

Comments

If the special regulating factor that is self-*manas* conjunction is as ubiquitous as the self that feels, then there would be *hedonic chaos*, a great tumult (*kolāhala*) of conflicting pleasures and pains all over the body. Absorption in a very specific sensation of pleasure or pain would then be impossible. But selective pleasure/pain is the rule. Hedonic chaos is exceptional.[6]

The current passage brims with this and other excellent countering of theory by phenomenological observation, the remainder of which is left to others to mine. Note, however, that the *pūrvapakṣin* has done little to defend his own view, as opposed to parrying Naiyāyika arguments.

Now we are treated to new voices, belonging presumably to other Mīmāṃsakas.

Text (p. 827, Tirupati, and p. 768, Calcutta) and Translation

anye tu sukhâdau tan-nimittâvacchedena ātma-manas-saṃyogo '-samavāyī tan-mātra-sukhâdy-upalambhāt, na tv ātma-manas-saṃyoga-mātram atiprasaṅgād ity āhuḥ | yāvati yat-sukhâdi-prāg-a-bhāvas tāvaty eva tat-sukhâdikam utpadyata ity apare | yat tu tad-itara-hetu-sākalye tad-vyāpakatvena prāg-a-bhāvasya āvaśyakatvam iti | tan na | prāg-a-bhāvasya a-hetutvâpatteḥ | tad-itara-hetu-sākalye tad-a-bhāvena kāryâ-bhāvâ-bhāvāt |

Gaṅgeśa: There are others who say the following.

A third view (a Mīmāṃsaka faction): Contact between a self and its *manas* is an emergent cause of a pleasure and the like *through* some particular instrumental cause or causes that specify (the nature of the effect), since our experience is of a pleasure or the like restricted according to such specification. Contact between a self and its *manas* does not stand on its own as an emergent cause, because that would apply to too much.

Gaṅgeśa: (Still) others (hold a different view).

A fourth view (another Mīmāṃsaka faction): In that portion of the body where there stood a prior absence of such and such a pleasure or the like, just there there arises precisely such and such a pleasure or the like.

Objection (to the fourth view): When an entire group of causes is present, each different from the prior absence (of the effect), the prior absence, as invariably occurring (with the production of the effect), necessarily comes about.

Answer: That's wrong. For, in that case the prior absence would not be a cause (whereas prior absence is generally admitted to be a causal factor)—this is the difficulty. When there is present the entire group of causes that are different from the prior absence, an absence of an absence of the effect comes from an absence of the prior absence of the effect.

Comments

The view labeled third seems promising. It is not, however, examined.

The fourth view tries to exploit the logic of prior absences. But since an absence of a prior absence occurs along with every (positive) effect, no prior absence could carry the causal weight that needs to be borne. That is, none could explain why pleasure and pain occur just where they do on a given occasion.

Next we return to views expressed previously.

Text (p. 827, Tirupati) and Translation

etena vyāpakam an-avacchinnaṃ na indriyam atiprasaṅgād ity ākāśe karṇa-śaṣkulī-vat niyata upādhir vācyaḥ | sa ca na śarīram, tad-avayava-mātraṃ vā niyatas tad-avayavī vā, ceṣṭâśraya-mātraṃ vā | nānâvayavâvacchedena a-vyāpya-vṛtti-sukhâdy-upalabdheḥ | evaṃ ca sūkṣmam indriyam upādhitvena kalpanīyam | tathā ca tad eva manaḥ, kim upadheyena vibhunā | tatra ca sarva eva hetavo dharmi-grāhaka-māna-bādhitā iti nirastam | indriyatve[7] tasya śarīra-mātrasya upādhitve 'pi nimitta-vaśāt sukhâder niyata-deśatôpapatteḥ | na ca ekadā an-eka-viṣayêndriya-saṃbandhe yugapaj-jñānân-utpattyā indriya-sahakāritayā anumitaṃ mano 'ṇu, tad eva sukha-grāhakam indriyam lāghavād iti tad-vaibhava-hetavo bādhitā iti vācyam | bubhutsā-vaśāt karaṇa-dharmatvād vā, aṇutva-pakṣe śrotre an-eka-śabda-samavāye 'pi bubhusita-mātra-śabda-graha-vat vyāsaṅga-daśāyāṃ yugapaj-jñānân-utpatteḥ upapatteḥ anyatra dīrgha-śaṣkulī-bhakṣaṇâdau yugapaj-jñānôtpatter iṣṭatvād iti |

(Mīmāṃsaksa) **pūrvapakṣin**: (And) by reasoning already given the following is to be thrown out.

(Naiyāyika) **objection**: There is no all-pervading, undelimited sensory organ, since that would have implications that are too wide. As with (ether and) the earhole, a restricting factor has to be identified. And the restricting factor is not the body, nor is it merely bodily parts, nor is the factor restricted to the whole as specified by parts, nor is it restricted merely to those portions of the body where there is movement. For, our experience of pleasure and so on is not invariably demarcated by a variety of parts or by a part (or by the whole).

And so we have to imagine a subtle sense as the limiting factor. And, therefore, *manas* is just such a limiting factor. What's the point (then) of manufacturing something ubiquitous? Furthermore, given this, every reason that was earlier identified is overridden by this argument that establishes *manas* and its character.

Pūrvapakṣin: (By our previous reasoning, what *you* have just said is rejected) for, given that the *manas* is a sense organ, the possibility of a pleasure or pain being restricted to a place is explained by the force of the *instrumental causes*, even assuming that just the body provides the (chief) limiting factor. (That is to say, instrumental causes, such as the extent of a smear of sandalwood paste, have much to do, though not all, with determining the nature of pleasures and pains including where they occur.)

Objection: Given that at a single time a plurality of objects are in relation to the sense organs whereas simultaneity of cognition is impossible, an *atomic* internal organ is inferred. Just that (*manas*) is the organ that grasps pleasure, since this is the economical position. Hence, the reasons given to show its ubiquity are defeated and overridden.

Pūrvapakṣin: That cannot be said. By the force of a desire to know or to focus (on something particular) or through the character of the instruments (what you point to is explained, namely, that sometimes there is no cognitive simultaneity). As, according to your atomicity view (too), there can be grasping of a sound that is alone desired to be heard amidst a plurality of sounds present in the organ of hearing (i.e., a grasping and a focus that are due simply to the desire), (so) non-arising of cognitive simultaneity is explained with reference to the occasion being one of distraction.

On other occasions, cognitions do arise simultaneously, for example, in the eating of a long pastry (where there is simultaneously its touch, its sight as long and so on, its smell, taste, and the sound of chewing)—this is a desired ramification of our position.

Comments

The same consideration that establishes the existence of *manas* according to the Naiyāyika urges us to regard it as atomic in character: lack of cognitive simultaneity. As mentioned, this reasoning appears in the *Nyāya-sūtra*. Here our Mīmāṃsaka counters by contending that appearances of lack of cognitive simultaneity can be explained by a subject's being distracted, by a lack of alertness. Not only do simultaneous cognitions occur sometimes, such simultaneity is the natural state and deviations can be explained by special circumstances.

Before we dig into the issues, however, raised by all this, let us attend to Gaṅgeśa's own view. The *pūrva-pakṣa* of the section ends here. Next comes Gaṅgeśa's *siddhânta*.

Text (p. 828, Tirupati, and p. 771, Calcutta) and Translation

atra ucyate | vyāsaṅga-daśāyām indriyāṇāṃ sva-sva-viṣaya-saṃbandhe 'py ekasmāt jñānaṃ na anyasmād ity anubhava-siddham | ato yasya a-saṃbandhāt na yugapat jñānāni tad-indriya-sahakāri krameṇa tad-adhiṣṭhāyakaṃ manaḥ tad eva sukhâdi-grāhakam iti tasya dharmi-grāhaka-māna-bādhitaṃ vibhutvam | tathā hi, cākṣuṣa-jñānavato maitrasya sva-sva-viṣaya-saṃbaddhāni ghrāna-rasana-tvak-śrotrāṇi sva-sva-viṣaya-sākṣātkāra-hetu-saṃyoga-śūnyāni, tadādīṃ sva-viṣaya-sākṣātkārâ-janakatvāt indriyâ-saṃbaddha-ghaṭa-vat | eka-ekaṃ vā pakṣaḥ, anyathā hetu-sākalye yugapat-jñānôtpatti-prasaṅgaḥ | na ca vaibhave 'py a-dṛṣṭa-vilambād vilambaḥ | tad-itara-hetu-sākalye tasya api sattvāt indriyântara-vilopa-prasaṅgāc ca | na ca bubhutsā-vaśāt kramaḥ, dṛśyate hi nṛtya-darśanavato bubhutsāto 'bhimata-viṣayântara-jñānam iti vācyam | sā hi na sva-viṣaya-jñāne hetuḥ, a-bubhutsite 'pi jñānôdayāt | na apy anya-jñāna-pratibandhikā, ghaṭa-bubhutsāyām api paṭa-jñānôdayāt | bubhutsā ca kriyā-hetu-mano-gocara-prayatna-dvārā indriyântarād ākṛṣya abhimatârtha-grāhiṇîndriyântare mano niveśayantī bubhutsita-grahe hetur anya-grahe pratibandhikā ca, na sākṣāt | ata eva bubhutsā-sattve 'pi mano-gocara-praṇidhānâ-bhāve sā na kiṃcit-karī |

Gaṅgeśa: We answer. Experience shows that, (even) on an occasion of distraction (as well as at other times), a cognition arises from one—and not another—among the objects that are related, severally, to the respective sense organs. Therefore, that with which a lack of connection results in no simultaneous cognition is an auxiliary to the sense organs by way of a (cognitive) series (it determines). It is *manas*, the overseer of the external senses. It alone grasps pleasure and the like. Hence, the ubiquity view is defeated by the argument that establishes its existence and character.

For example, Maitra, who is having (let us say) a visual cognition, has (at the same time) organs of smell, taste, touch, and hearing that are related, severally, to their own objects, and that are devoid of the contact (with the *manas*) that causes immediate experience of their respective objects, *since* at that time (the time of Maitra's visual experience) such immediate experience of their respective objects is not being caused, like a pot that is not in relation to a sense organ.

Alternatively, take any other mix of cognitions as the subject of the inference (e.g., a tactile cognition, instead of a visual cognition, as the cognition assumed to be occurring).

On any other view, the difficulty is that cognitions should arise simultaneously when the entirety of causal factors is present (all the causal factors other than connection with *manas*, that is).

And it is wrong to hold that, although the *manas* is ubiquitous, delay (in perception of other sense-related objects) is due to a delay in unseen force (i.e., a person's *karman*). For, when an entire group of causes other than unseen force is in place, that too is in place. Moreover, this view would mean that the sense organs and other causes (would be unnecessary, that they) would drop out.

Objection: Cognitive series come about by force of a desire to know or focus. For, it is found that someone whose sight is on a dancer can have cognition of another, fancied object through a desire to focus (through a special cognitive interest).

Gaṅgeśa: That should not be said. For, desire to focus is not a cause of every (perceptual) cognition with respect to the cognitive object, since (sometimes) cognition arises of objects though there is no desire to focus on them. Nor does a desire to focus (i.e., to have a certain cognitive interest) block the occurrence of other cognitions, since, although there is a desire to focus on a pot, a cognition of a cloth arises (given, that is, the presence of a cloth). Furthermore, a desire is a cause (of perception, but only indirectly): by means of effort that is within the province of a *manas* and that causes a (bodily) act, a desire to focus pulls the *manas* away from one sense organ and directs it to another that grasps the desired object—in this way is it a cause of a grasping of an object that was desired to be known. And in the same way it blocks graspings of other things. It is not directly a cause.

Just for this reason, though there be a desire to focus on something, a *manas* does not bring about the knowledge unless there is an effort at attention that lies within the *manas*'s domain.

Comments

In order to appreciate Gaṅgeśa's stance, we have to feel the weight of his assumption that simultaneous cognitions are impossible. He acknowledges that the several sense organs are active simultaneously. Moreover, there is no limit in principle to how much information can be contained in the indeterminate stage of perception, which is unverbalizable. But determinate cognition is verbalizable, and verbalization requires focus. Focus, in turn, is a matter of looking at, actively grasping, one definite thing, or group of things, at a time, albeit focus can change *very* quickly. Walking along, I have eyes and ears that are picking up diverse information at any given moment, but I am watching only a single butterfly skirting off to the right.

Gaṅgeśa and Nyāya are not ambivalent about the thesis that only one determinate cognition occurs at a time, but a single cognition can have multiple objects, as in a *samūhâlambana-jñāna*, "cognition of a group of things." And the group can be indefinitely large. Focus is exclusionary, but it does not have to be on only a single thing. For example, visually we can look at, or watch, many things simultaneously, three butterflies, for instance, or even a hundred clustering, given an appropriate perspective and gaze.

Cognitive delimitation cannot be merely a matter of being interested in knowing one particular thing, or group of things, rather than another. Sometimes an object, despite our lack of interest, forces its way into our attention, and we see or hear only it. So, focus, or interest, is not the only way cognition becomes circumscribed—this is a key point for countering the Mīmāṃsaka position, as we see in the passage above. We should also recall that Mīmāṃsakas hold that cognitions are acts, not qualities, as in the Nyāya view. So, an object's forcing us to notice it seems impossible on the Mīmāṃsaka view.

Gaṅgeśa implies that available sensory information and bodily movement are the domain of the *manas*'s activity. A *manas* is impelled by a self to contact one sense or another or to move one limb or another. Thus, the psychological series that Gaṅgeśa suggests at the end of the passage would be: first, a desire to focus occurring as a quality in a self, second, effort directing the *manas*, third, movement of the *manas* away from one sense presentation to another organ of sense, fourth, the *manas*'s presentation of the new, desired sensory information to the self in the form of a cognition of that which was desired to be known. The point of Gaṅgeśa's final statement seems to be that the series can be broken, that it is not inevitable that once there is a desire to focus there will be the necessary effort and so on.

Next, a Mīmāṃsaka objector proposes another way that the particularity, or circumscribed definiteness, of determinate cognition can be accounted for in those cases where a self's desiring to focus would be implausible, as in hearing a deafening sound.

Text (p. 831, Tirupati) and Translation

> nanu indriya-manas-saṃyoga-viśeṣa eva viṣaya-viśeṣa-grahe hetuḥ kalpyatām | na ca evaṃ siddha-kāraṇa-bhāvasya viśeṣa-kalpane hetv-antarôcchedaḥ, tasya apy anvaya-vyatirekitvād iti cet, na | indriya-manas-saṃyoge hi viśeṣo na jāti-rūpo 'nugata-hetv-a-bhāvāt jāti-saṃkara-prasaṅgāc ca | na api sahakāri-rūpaḥ, tasya eva hetutâpatteḥ | atha astu karaṇa-dharmatvena kriyā-kramaḥ | ekaṃ karaṇam ekatra ekadā ekâvacchedena tulya-deśe vā eka-jātīyām an-ekāṃ kriyāṃ na karoti, kiṃ tu ekām eva | ekatra ity-ādi-viśeṣaṇāt kuṭārâgni-saṃyoga-śabdeṣu na vyabhicāra iti cet, tarhi cakṣur-ādy-avacchedena bhinna-deśīya-śabda-vat paramâṇāv iva vijātīyām agni-saṃyoga-vad an-ekāṃ kriyāṃ kuryād eva |

Objection (by a Mīmāṃsaka): Okay, let a specific factor in the contact of a (ubiquitous) *manas* and a (delimited, finite) sense organ be viewed as a cause of a specific object's being grasped.

So viewing, we may add that there is not, for anything whose causality has been proved, a breakup of its status as an additional cause, on this view of a specific factor (in the contact between *manas* and sense organ as responsible for cognitive delimitation; analogously, both a stick and a wheel are necessary to make a pot). For, any second cause (such as a sensory contact with the object perceived) would also be established by a finding of positive and negative correlations.

Gaṅgeśa: Wrong. For, this "specific factor" (as you say) in the contact between a sense organ and the *manas* would not take the form of a universal, since there is no recurrent experience urging its adoption and since the proposal would mean a "cross-sectioning" of kinds. Nor would it take the form of an auxiliary cause, since that view would land us in the predicament of taking it alone as (potentially) the cause (of cognitive delimitation).

Objection (by the Mīmāṃsaka): Let the order of activity (of the sense organs) be according to the essential nature of the (sense organs each as an) instrument: a single instrument at a single place on a single occasion does not set off multiple actions by being (in these ways) singly restricted; nor does it, in one and the same place, set off multiple actions of one type. Rather, it performs one action only.

Actions set off by contact with an axe, or fire, or by a sound are not counterexamples to the qualifications stated, "in a single *place*" and so on.

Gaṅgeśa: In that case, you would indeed allow multiple (cognitive) acts (to occur at the same time) as specified by (the several sense organs) the visual organ and the rest—like sounds occurring in different places (though with a single origin), or like ultimate atoms in (simultaneous) contact with fire.

Comments

Perhaps the Mīmāṃsaka could interpret his "specific factor" in the contact between sense organ and *manas* ontologically as something other than a universal and avoid the onslaught that Gaṅgeśa mounts against its fitting into cognitive theory in that manner. Not only is there no recurrent experience in its favor, it would involve a "cross-sectioning" of kinds. Such cross-sectioning indicates that we are failing to find the natural divisions among things (see, in this volume, pp. 22 and 211). The cross-sectioning that Gaṅgeśa mentions here would be not only among kinds of sensory presentation—visual, auditory, and so on—but also, presumably, among kinds of contact as well.

Gaṅgeśa finds three kinds of contact (above, pp. 482–83): (a) born of contact, (b) born of movement on the part of one or the other of the conjoined, and (c) born of movement on the part of both conjuncts. The Mīmāṃsaka proposal would demand confusing variety of contacts, contacts for feeling pleasure or pain in all the various parts of the body where we do feel pleasures or pains, contacts between the visual organ and the *manas*—and different types of contact here to account for visual focus and other peculiarly visual/mental phenomena—other contacts in the case of hearing and so on. Contact, which is a quality we know best from its exhibition by external things (e.g, "The man is holding a staff" where there is contact between the staff and the man's hand) would thus involve "cross-section" in several different ways.

We see that, after the objector's reply, Gaṅgeśa apparently agrees that the singleness of each individual sense organ and of its relation to its immediate environment could account for the definiteness of a particular type of sense presentation. However, the different sense organs all operate simultaneously, and this new proposal about a mysterious "specific factor" in the contact between *manas* and an individual organ of sense still does not show, given the assumption that both *manas* and self are ubiquitous, how a person's attention could be exclusively occupied by a single sense presentation. There are, moreover, other problems with this proposed "specific factor."

Gaṅgeśa's last response is directed to drawing out an impossibility in the Mīmāṃsaka theory. There cannot be multiple cognitive acts occurring simultaneously. One thing at a time is all that anyone can do. Here we have to suspect that while Gaṅgeśa, like the *Nyāya-sūtra*, claims to establish the atomicity of *manas* on the basis of cognitive and volitional non-simultaneity, a prior commitment to that atomicity leads him to deny these phenomenological facts.

Text (p. 832, Tirupati, and p. 773, Calcutta) and Translation

atha jñāna-karaṇam ekatra ātmany ekadā ekam eva jñānaṃ karoti samūhâlambana-karaṇa-vat | katham anyathā nānā-sāmagrī-sattve samūhâlambanam ekam | yat tu, apara-jñāna-sāmagrī yadi tadā kāryâvaśyaṃ-bhāvaḥ | tad-a-sattve kiṃ karaṇa-dharmatvena, tasya sahakāry-antara-paryavasāyitvād iti, tan na | samūhâlambana-sāmyāt | karaṇasya ekadā eka-mātra-janakatvena aparâ-janakatayā tatra kāraṇâ-bhāvena eva sāmagry-a-sattvād iti cet, tarhi pañcasu yad ekaṃ janayati na aparāṇi, tatra niyāmikam āstheyam | anyathā jñāna-janane teṣāṃ kalahaṃ kaḥ samādadhyāt | kiṃ ca evaṃ yugapaj-jñānāni mā bhūvan yugapaj-jñānaṃ tu kena vāryate, eka-samūhâlambana-vat | na ca cākṣuṣatvâdi-jāti-saṃkarâpatteḥ na eka-jñānam iti vācyam | evaṃ hi phala-virodhena ekam api jñānaṃ na janayet a-viśeṣāt | utpadyatāṃ vā cākṣuṣâdi-vijātīyaṃ jñānaṃ sāmagrī-sattvāt citra-rūpa-vat | phala-balāt tatra tathā iti cet, tarhi atra phalâ-bhāve hetuḥ kalpyatām, anyonya-pratibandhakasya tattve vā jñānam eva na syāt na tv eka-jñānam ity uktam |

Objection.1 (by a Mīmāṃsaka): A cognitive instrument (such as the visual organ) brings about at a single place, in a self on a single occasion just one cognition, like the instrument that brings about awareness of a group of things. Otherwise (i.e., on your view) how could a single awareness of a group of things come about, given the variety of causal complexes in place (each sufficient to produce a separate and distinct cognition)?

Objection.2 (against the Mīmāṃsaka, by a Naiyāyika): If a causal complex sufficient to produce another cognition is in place, then necessarily does the effect come about. If it is not in place, what's the point of the talk of an "essential nature of the instrument," since all that amounts to is that there is another auxiliary (i.e., another necessary but insufficient condition for the occurrence of a particular cognitive effect).

Answer (by the Mīmāṃsaka): That's wrong, for the same reasoning would apply to an awareness of a group of things.

Objector.2 (the Naiyāyika, against the Mīmāṃsaka): (No, it would not) for there would be no causal complex in place sufficient to produce such an awareness. One of its causes would be absent inasmuch as the instrument bringing about on a single occasion just something single would not be bringing about something else.

Answer (by the Mīmāṃsaka): Then what needs to be spelled out is the rule or principle governing the fact that a single sense organ, out of five, is productive (on a certain occasion) and not the others. Otherwise, who would be able to resolve the "dispute" that would break out among the sense organs about the generating of cognition (about, that is, whether this or that sense organ, all five being simultaneously active, gets to deliver its information to consciousness)?

Furthermore, let there be in this way no cognitions occurring simultaneously (i.e., on some occasions; we admit that attention sometimes is exclusively absorbed by a single sensory presentation). However (tell me) what is to prevent a simultaneous cognition (at other times, i.e., a synthesis of sensory information)? It would be like a cognition of a group of things (which you Naiyāyikas admit).

It cannot be held that, to avoid the predicament of kinds overlapping among the visual and so on, there cannot be such a single cognition. For, if that were right, *no* cognition would be produced inasmuch as—any effect being incompatible with any other—there would be no distinctive reason why one and not another should be produced.

Alternatively, let us assume that there arises a cognition that is distinct from the (merely) visual and so on, (a cognition that is a synthesis of the visual, the auditory, and so on) because the causal complex sufficient for such a complex cognition is in place—like (among visual cognitions, a cognition of) variegated color (*citra-rūpa*).

Objector.2 (the Naiyāyika against the Mīmāṃsaka): In the case of a cognition of variegated color, the fact of the effect (namely, such a cognition) urges a similar view (of the cause. However, the case at issue is simultaneous content from distinct sense organs, and there is no such synthetic cognition or one would occur all the time and exclusive psychological absorption would be impossible).

Answer (by the Mīmāṃsaka): Then, here, when that effect does not occur (i.e., on those occasions when there is no such synthetic cognition), let a cause be assumed (such as distraction). Or, assuming a principle of mutual prevention (among the various sense organs), there would be no cognition at all, not the single cognition (that we describe)—as has already been pointed out.

Comments

Philosophers raised on Immanuel Kant are likely to have sympathies in line with the Mīmāṃsaka. Since Kant, philosophers in the West have largely assumed a sensory synthesis running through and holding together sensory data. The question has been how to explain it.

Nyāya does admit multiple cognitive content in cognition of a group (*samūhâlambana-jñāna*) including visual experience of variegated color as well as in the very nature of qualificative cognition—cognition of an entity as qualified—which can be multiply qualified cognition, such as "This is a blue pot." There is also apperception and the "cognitively extraordinary sensory connection," *jñāna-lakṣaṇa-pratyāsatti*, with time-lapsed or state sense-experience, more about which below. What is not allowed is truly simultaneous presentation of information through distinct sensory modalities, auditory, visual, and so on. Otherwise, the reasoning goes, focus and exclusive absorption become impossible to explain.

A strength of the Mīmāṃsaka ubiquity view is that sensory operations and objects perceived are called upon to carry the greatest causal responsibility for perceptions. Look to nature, to physical processes that result in sensory awareness, not to the atomicity of a *manas*, is a call heard from their camp. The physical processes will explain why one bit of presentation rather than another comes about. And on the Naiyāyika view, it is argued, the same in the end will have to be said. Moreover, it is implied, the very simultaneity of presentation in distinct perceptual modes is a *good reason*—in contrast with Naiyāyikas' *bad* reason in thinking about their dubious sensory series—for postulating a *manas* to begin with, a true sensory "overlord" and not just a sixth sense.

Gaṅgeśa will repeat the arguments aired here when he presents his conclusion, in the next passage, below. First, there is another round of wrangling with Mīmāṃsaka subtleties.

Text (p. 833, Tirupati) and Translation

nanu cakṣur-ādi na saṃbhūya-janakam anya-viṣaye 'nyasya a-sāmārthyāt | śītaṃ surabhi śubhraṃ candanam ity atra iva kāraṇântarân-upanayanāc ca | na ca sva-sva-viṣaya-jñānāya udyatam indriyaṃ kāraṇântara-sahakārāt tat-tad-viṣayam ādāya eva sva-sva-viṣayaṃ jñāpayed iti vācyam | bhinna-viṣaya-pramāṇānāṃ saṃbhūyâ-janakatva-niyamāt | tat-tad-indriyaṃ tat-taj-jñānâṃśe janakam ity api na, viṣayasya aṃśatvād iti cet, mā evam | na hi indriyāṇāṃ saṃbhūya-kāritvaṃ, kiṃ tv ārthaḥ samājaḥ | pratyeka-jñāna-sāmagrī-sattvāt ekadā nānā-jñāna-prasaktau karaṇa-dharmatvena manaṣ tāvat-gocarām ekām eva jñāna-kriyām utpādayet | samūhâlambana-vat | na ca eka-kriyā-janana-daśāyām apara-viṣaya-kriyāyāṃ mano na samartham iti kathaṃ tāṃ janayet iti vācyam | bhinna-kriyāyām a-sāmarthye 'py eka-kriyāyāṃ sāmarthyāt | vastutas tu viśeṣâ-bhāvād ekām iva aparām api buddhiṃ janayed a-viśeṣāt na ca ekām api ity an-eka-jñānôtpattir vā na tv eka-viṣayajñānôtpattir iti niyāmakam āstheyam | samūhâlaṃbane phala-balena paras-parâpekṣitatvena ekā eva sāmagrī |

Objector.2 (the Naiyāyika against the Mīmāṃsaka): The visual organ and the rest do not produce in mutual collaboration, since none of them has a productive capacity with respect to an object grasped by any of the rest. Furthermore, in the present case (where we are imagining causal complexes in place sufficient to produce visual, auditory, tactile, etc., perceptions, and where you say, but not I, that a single synthetic cognition would arise), there is no "extraordinary sensory connection" with the other causes, as occurs with the cognition (presented through a single sense medium), "The sandalwood paste is cool, fragrant, white."

Objection.3 (by a Mīmāṃsaka against objector.2): A sense organ that is active for the sake of producing a cognition of its very own type of object (e.g., sound by the organ of hearing) makes known, with the help of auxiliary causal factors, its very own object (in the case we are imagining) *only if* the very own objects (of the other sense organs) are taken in as well (into a synthetic cognition).

Answer (by objector.2, the Naiyāyika): That should not be said. For, the rule is that the individual cognitive means (perception, inference, and so on, and thus similarly vision, hearing, and so on), whose cognitive objects are distinct, do not function through first having come together (for a unitary production).

Objector.3 (against the Naiyāyika): This and that sense organ contribute this and that cognitive portion (of the synthetic cognition).

Answer (by objector.2, the Naiyāyika): That also is wrong. For, it is the object that has portions (not cognition).

Answer (by objector.1, the Mīmāṃsaka): Don't think like that. For, (on my view) the sense organs do not have to come together to produce an effect; rather, the (cognitive) assembly is occasional. On a single, specific occasion, a case of a (perceptual) cognition with multiple or various objects arises because the causal complexes are in place for each type of cognition (produced by an individual sense organ): the *manas*, operating in its characteristic nature as a (cognitive) instrument, achieves an absolutely single cognitive act whose content ranges just so far (as the activity of all the operative organs and thus synthesizes their information), like what happens (you yourself admit) with (your) "cognition of a group of things" (*samūhâlambana-jñāna*).

Objector.2 (the Naiyāyika against the Mīmāṃsaka): On the occasion of a *manas*'s generating one type of cognitive act (e.g., an act of seeing), it is not capable of generating a cognitive act with different content (e.g., an act of hearing). So how could it produce that single act which you describe?

Answer (by objector.1, the Mīmāṃsaka): That should not be asked. For, it is capable of generating such a single act although it is (of course) not capable of generating distinct acts (at the same time).

Gaṅgeśa: But in reality (there is a difficulty that your view cannot surmount:) in the absence of a distinctive reason (which you have failed to give) a *manas* might as well give rise to another cognition as to the one it gives rise to, in that there would be no difference (in the conditions that give rise to one cognition rather than another). Or, if it would not give rise to the one cognition, then either (a) it would not give rise to the other or (b) no cognition would arise at all. But there would not be (so far as the story goes on your theory) a cognition with single (synthetic) object in that regulative conditions would have to be stated (and you have provided none).

Regarding our "cognition of a group of things" (a phenomenon that you say we understand in the same way that you understand your synthetic cognition): according to the nature of the effect, the causal complex is, simply, multiple (e.g., multiple sounds being grasped in a single auditory cognition because multiple sounds have been produced, etc.). A causal complex works through mutual co-operation of all the causal factors (within the complex).

Comments

Nyāya has the resources to admit a synthetic cognition: the "cognitively extraordinary sensory connection," *jñāna-lakṣaṇa-pratyāsatti*, which explains how the cognition verbalized as, "The sandalwood paste is cool, fragrant, and white," can arise. Remembered contents can get projected or revived in current perception. But this would not be a cognitive synthesis of separate immediate sense presentations by the organs of touch (with the sandalwood's coolness), smell (fragrance), and sight (whiteness). Rather, there is only one sensory contact that is informed by the other sensory modalities through an extraordinary sensory relation involving memory. Here the point is that invariably each separate sense organ delivers its simple or complex information independently of the activity of the others. The advantage of this thesis is that thereby we are able to understand how we can be absorbed in a single sense presentation—which the Mīmāṃsaka cannot do.

The Mīmāṃsaka's sensory synthesis challenges the atomicity theory in that an atomic *manas* could not grab up simultaneously a range of inputs restricted, as they are, to different areas of the body—hearing to the earholes, etc. But there is, Gaṅgeśa takes great pains to argue, no reason to presume that such a cognition occurs.

The unstated alternative explanation for the appearance of such a synthesis is that attention—like *manas*—can move *very* rapidly from one sensory modality to another. To make the point, *Nyāyasūtra* 3.2.58 draws an analogy to an illusory circle of fire created by a torch whirled around to render an impression of a circle of flame, a false appearance of fiery simultaneity.[8] We know we do not in fact see a circle of fire but rather only the torch in a series of spots. A general principle governing postulation of hypothetical entities—and *manas* is hypothetical in the sense that there is no direct experience of it—is that the entity is to be postulated as having the properties it needs to fulfill its explanatory role. Thus, for example, God, who is postulated to explain the origin of the universe and its design, is to be conceived as having a consonant power and intelligence. The *manas* has to be similarly understood as capable of rapid motion, contacting the several sense organs and conjoining with the self extremely fast.

Gaṅgeśa claims here that the Mīmāṃsaka has failed to tell us why the *manas* would sometimes grasp a cognitive synthesis and at other times be absorbed in a single sensory modality. In other words, the Mīmāṃsaka does not provide a story about why the one and not the other would occur. Without something about this, we have no reason to accept a putative occurrence the appearance of which we can explain on different assumptions. In the case of a cognition of a group of things, the multiplicity of the cognitive object or objects—multiple sounds, colored things, a single thing variegated in color, etc.—explains cognitive multiplicity, which is nonetheless restricted to a single modality. Thus, on the Nyāya view, we are able to pick up the gauntlet cast. Regulative conditions are given by us; our explanation is adequate.

Next we have a Mīmāṃsaka query about how precisely the Naiyāyika understands focus. This attacks the heart of the Naiyāyika argument in that allowing us to understand focus appears to be the decisive advantage of the atomic theory.

Text (p. 834, Tirupati) and Translation

nanu mano-'ṇutve kathaṃ mando 'pi bubhutsitaḥ śabdo gṛhyate na anyaḥ | atha śabde bubhutsā eva itara-graha-pratibandhikā a-grahasya tad-anuvidhānāt | an-anya-gatika-kārya-darśanāt bubhutsita-śabda-graha-sāmagry eva vā balavatī iti yadi manyase, tadā vaibhave 'pi tata eva yugapaj-jñānân-utpattir iti cet, mā evam | bubhutsā na rūpâdi-grahe hetuḥ na vā itara-grahe pratibandhakā ity uktatvāt | kiṃ ca rūpâdi-sakala-bubhutsāyāṃ paras-para-pratibandhakād a-jñānaṃ bubhutsâdhīna-sāmagrī-balavattvād vā sarveṣāṃ jñānaṃ syāt na tv ekasya pañcâvadhānasya | sarveṣāṃ jñānaṃ bhavaty eva cet, na | tatra api kramânumānāt | anyathā sarva-bubhutsâdhīna-praṇidhāne 'py anyeṣāṃ kathaṃ na syāt |

Objection.1 (by the Mīmāṃsaka): If *manas* is atomic, how is it that a single low sound that is desired to be known is the sound that is grasped and not another?

Objection.2 (against objector.1): A desire to grasp the one sound is itself the blocker, is itself what prevents the others from being grasped, since its presence correlates with the non-graspings. Alternatively, a collection of causal factors sufficient to make grasped an object that is desired to be known is, as a matter of fact, the most potent complex (overriding alternative causal complexes), since no other explanation is forthcoming concerning an effect that we do find (hearing, for instance, only a single low sound among many sounds available to be heard).

Answer (by objector.1, the Mīmāṃsaka): If this is what you think, then, on our ubiquity view, too, the same explanation is available. We say that it is just for such a reason (a desire to know or focus) that simultaneous cognition (sometimes) does not arise.

Gaṅgeśa: It is not so. Desire to focus is not (invariably) a cause of graspings of color and so forth. Nor does it prevent the grasping of other things. These points have already been made. Furthermore, if a person desired to know altogether something's color and so on, then, because of mutual preventing, he would have no cognition at all. Or, since the causal complex that included the desire to focus would be the most potent, a person who was focusing on the five (sensory presentations) would have cognition of it all but never of anything single (no single sensory quality).

Objection: The cognition would indeed be of it all (if that is what the cognizer desired to focus on).

Gaṅgeśa: No. For, we infer there too a (rapidly occurring) series. Otherwise, why is it that some other things are not known when the effort at attention is in response to a desire to know it all?

Comments

Our cognition does not regularly follow our desire to know or focus. Only on the atomic hypothesis are we able to understand phenomena of exclusive attention. We have already pointed out that effort or exertion does not invariably follow a desire to focus. But why should not a person who desires to know everything about, for example, a long pastry, and who tries to attend to everything about it, in fact know everything? In fact, there would always be bits of information available sensorily that would *not* be cognized ("some other things are not known"). You Mīmāṃsakas still owe us a story about this. Finally, according to our Nyāya view, an appearance of simultaneity occurs because a cognitive series can happen very fast. In fact, we infer such a series on the basis of such appearances.

Text (p. 834, Tirupati, and p. 777, Calcutta) and Translation

nanv aṇutve 'pi daśabhiḥ pathyamānāsu gāthāsu tāvad-gocara-bubhutsāyāṃ praṇidhāne ca ukta-rītyā sarveṣāṃ jñānam a-jñānaṃ vā, na tv eka-jñānam iti cet, atra kaścit | śrotra-manas-saṃyoge ātma-manas-saṃyoge vā kaścid viśeṣaḥ kāryôneyaḥ | kiṃcic-chabda-grahe hetuḥ tad-anya-grahe pratibandhaka iti | tan na | vaibhave 'pi indriya-manas-saṃyoga-viśeṣasya tathātve vyāsaṅgôpapatteḥ | anugata-rūpâ-bhāvena prativyakti pratibandhakatve hetutve ca vyabhicārāt |

saṃyoge ca viśeṣasya jātitve jāti-saṃkaraḥ | upādhitve sa eva hetur na manaḥ |

Objection: How can it be on the atomic view that when verses are being recited out loud by ten persons and both a desire to know with precisely that scope and the necessary effort to attend are in place, there can be, according to your way of thinking, either cognition of all ten or no cognition at all but not of one person (reciting, although that happens)?

Gaṅgeśa: On this question, some say the following.

Naiyāyika faction: Something distinctive, a "specific factor," is to be inferred from the nature of the effect (cognition of one or ten or none), something distinctive in the contact between the organ of hearing and the *manas*, or in that between the self and the *manas*. What causes a grasping of a particular sound (or group of sounds) prevents graspings of others.

Gaṅgeśa: That's wrong. For, distraction (a failure to notice all the sensory input in a cognitive synthesis that is the normal result of perceptual processes) can be explained in such a way, too, on the ubiquity theory. A distinctive contact between *sense organ* and *manas* could be similarly cited. Moreover, the view faces a counterexample in that there would be no recurrent experience of color and the like given that both a bringing about and a preventing would occur according to the "specific factor."

Furthermore, if there are to be particular instances of contact as a universal, then we would face a "cross-sectioning" of kinds. If the "something distinctive" is to be an additional factor (*upādhi*), then it would be the (relevant) cause, not *manas* (and there would be no need to suppose that a *manas* has in this regard at all a causal role).

Comments

The challenge is to explain just why it is that we can hear only one sound of many available to be heard. On the Naiyāyika theory, the *manas* could be directed by the self—or be forced by an object (e.g., the loudness of a sound)—into contact with the organ of hearing such all the sounds available to be heard would be heard. But how is it, on the Nyāya view, that sometimes, if we so desire, we can focus on one sound to the exclusion of other sounds available? The challenge is not to explain focus on sounds rather than on sights, etc., but to explain focus within a single sensory modality given that many objects on a given occasion are in that modality perceptible. Thus the theoretic equivalent of hypocrisy lies in the Naiyāyika position that focus shows the explanatory superiority of the atomic view. Properly focused, focus shows the Naiyāyika theory's inadequacy.

Before definitively answering the challenge by giving us his own view, Gaṅgeśa elaborates and rejects two Naiyāyika responses. The first occurs in the passage at hand, the second in the following passage. Gaṅgeśa gives two reasons for rejecting the first Naiyāyika response that "something distinctive" between the *manas* and the sense organ accounts for the focusing: (a) the Mīmāṃsaka could say the same thing, and (b) the view would face the dilemma of either an unwanted cross-section of kinds or the eliminability of *manas* in favor of the additional "specific factor." We have already seen the argument about contact cross-section. The second horn of the dilemma shows perhaps most of all just how theoretical a posit *manas* is in the first place as well as that Gaṅgeśa is aware of this. He says we might as well stop talking about *manas* and talk instead about that "something distinctive."

Text (p. 835, Tirupati) and Translation

apare tu, pratyakṣânukūlêndriya-manas-saṃyoga-dvārā bubhutsā praṇidhānaṃ ca pratyakṣa-hetur iti cākṣuṣâdi-bubhutsita-grahe klptatvāt tābhyāṃ śrotre bubhutsita-śabdâvacchedena manaḥ saṃyujyata iti sa gṛhyate na anyaḥ | kvacit praṇidhānaṃ vinā eva tathā | anyatra praṇidhānâdhīna-kriyayā a-śruyamāna-śabdâvacchinnâtmano vibhajya bubhutsita-śabdâvacchedena manaḥ saṃyujyata iti tad-graho na sarvasya iti | tat tuccham | yugapad-utpadyamānāsu viṃśatau gāthāsu tāvad-gocara-bubhutsāyāṃ praṇidhāne ca tāvad-gāthâvacchedena manas-saṃyogād yugapat tāsām upalambha-prasaṅgāt, pratyeka-sāmagrī-sattvāt, nikaṭâhanyamāna-ḍhakkâdi-śabdānāṃ śrotra-vyāpakatva-niyamāc ca | atha yatra kolāhale śruyamāṇa eva bubhutsita-śabda-grahaḥ tatra ubhaya-śabdâvacchedena manas-saṃyogād ubhaya-grahaḥ kolāhale tu upekṣā-jñānaṃ tad iti tathā atra api iti cet, tarhi kṛtam anayā kusṛṣṭyā | a-bubhutsite upekṣā-jñānam eva astu | na ca tad api | ito na śabdântaram aśrauṣam ity anubhavāt | anythā vaibhave 'pi vyāsaṅga-daśāyām itareṣām upekṣā-jñānam eva iti |

(**Gaṅgeśa** continues:) But still others say the following.

Second Naiyāyika faction: Desire to focus and effort to attend (on the part of a self) are causes of perception through the instrumentality of a contact between a sense organ and the *manas*, a contact favorable to the occurrence of a perception. For, such causes are well-known (i.e., are established by positive and negative correlations) regarding something visual, etc., that is desired to be known. The *manas* becomes conjoined (with a sense organ) according to the specification accomplished by these two, desire to focus and effort to attend—thus does one thing get grasped and not another. Sometimes even without an effort to attend (etc.) such occurs. At other times, the *manas*, through separating out by an action dependent on (a self's) effort to attend those things to be characterized as sounds that are *not* being heard, comes into a (sensory) contact specified according to which sound is desired to be known. Hence, *it* is grasped, not all the sounds available.

Gaṅgeśa: That's an empty proposal. When twenty (distinctive) verses are simultaneously being recited out loud, and there is in place a desire to know with precisely that scope along with the necessary effort to attend to all that, all the verses would be experienced simultaneously (which does not in fact happen: no one can make out twenty different verses being recited at the same time). This would be because of (the nature of the contact as a cause, according to you, i.e.) the contact with the *manas* according to a specification that (in the terms of the example we are imagining) would have precisely that scope (namely, to hear all the different verses simultaneously). This is the difficulty. For, a causal complex sufficient to produce cognition of each would be in place (i.e., all twenty would be available).

Moreover, such sounds as those of a tambourine being struck nearby (i.e., right next to one's ear) do, by rule, come into contact with one's organ of hearing (whether one has any desire to hear them or not).

Objection: When chaotic noise (*kolāhala*) is being heard, a sound that is desired to be known (e.g., a son's voice) can be grasped. And wherever there is such a situation, there would be, due to a contact with the *manas* as specified by (let us say) a pair of sounds (or voices, each desired to be heard), a grasping of both. Regarding chaotic noise, however, the cognition would be indifference. Here, too (concerning the case at issue, namely, why one, or a group of sounds, can be heard when other available sounds are not), the case would be likewise.

Gaṅgeśa: Then, enough with this bad creative theorizing! To explain (on this view) that which is *not* desired to be known, let it simply be indifference as a cognition. And, to boot, that does not do the work. For, the experience is: "Other than this, another sound I did not hear." Otherwise, on the ubiquity view, too, could an indifference cognition alone be cited to explain (what we have argued is not explained on the Mīmāṃsaka view, namely) the others (the bits of sensory information that do not come into focus or grab our attention), when there is (not their default "perceptual synthesis" but) distraction (a failure to notice some of the sensory information available).

Comments

On Mīmāṃsaka premises, indifference would be a good candidate for explaining why sometimes cognitive synthesis does not occur, why sometimes we fail to be aware of, for example, auditory information while attending to something visual. Thus, if the Nyāya camp uses indifference to explain why we hear one sound or a group of sounds throughout a range of circumstances, Nyāya will have to grant Mīmāṃsā just the factor it needs and no longer be able to make the charge of explanatory inadequacy.

Next, Gaṅgeśa presents his own view, his own response to the challenge about why just some sounds are heard on certain occasions and others on other occasions although a variety of sounds be available.

Text (p. 836, Tirupati) and Translation

atra ucyate yady api bubhutsā-praṇidhāne na śabda-graha-mātre sahakāriṇī na vā itara-graha-pratibandhake | tathā api nānā-śabda-samavāya-daśāyāṃ yaḥ śabda-grahas tatra tayos tathā-bhāvaḥ tathā eva tayor anvaya-vyatireka-niyamāt | yad vā kolāhale śruyamāṇa eva bubhutsita-śabda-graha ity anye 'pi kolāhalatvena tad-viṣayā eva | bahūnāṃ ca ekadā samavāye yugapat-saṃnidhāne vā vyakti-grahe tad-gata-gatva-katvâdi-graho na bhavati | a-gṛhīta-katvâdi-nānā-śabdasya kolāhala-buddhi-viṣayatvāt | tasyāṃ daśāyāṃ bubhutsita-śabda-katvâdi-jāti-grahe bubhutsā eva śaraṇam | eka-kālīna-bahu-śabda-bubhutsā ca na hetur vyabhicārāt | yat tu kolāhalāt anyatra ekadā nānā-śabda-grahe śrotraṃ na samartham, kiṃ tu eka-śabda-grahe vinigamikā bubhutsā eva iti | tan na | eka-gīyamānâpekṣayā ekadā nānā-gīyamāna-sajātīya-gâdiṣu sukhâdi-vailakṣaṇyânubhavāt |

Gaṅgeśa: Here we answer. Desire to focus and effort to attend are not auxiliary causes of sound perception in general, nor are they what prevent other sounds from being grasped. They do, nevertheless, have such a status occasionally, that is, with respect to the grasping of a sound grasped when a variety of sounds inhere (in the organ of hearing). For, the two are indeed established as such by the principle of positive and negative correlation.

Alternatively, only when chaotic noise (*kolāhala*) is being heard is that which is desired to be known grasped (that is to say, only on such an occasion is desire to focus a causal factor). Hence, other sounds that also become objects of such (a perception guided by a prior desire to focus) are so only as occurring within chaotic noise.

And when a single individual (noise) is grasped when many sounds are at the same time inhering (in the organ of hearing), or when nearby sounds are simultaneously present, (the universals present in the sounds are not recognized, i.e.) the *ga*-ness, *ka*-ness, and so on that are contained in those (sounds not identified) are not grasped. For, the various sounds would be, without their *ka*-ness and so on being grasped, the object of the chaotic-noise cognition. On such an occasion, a desire to focus is indeed a cause—and our explanatory refuge—with respect to the grasping of the *ka*-ness and so on in the sound desired to be known (which is in fact heard). But a desire to know many sounds at the same time is not a cause (of grasping many sounds simultaneously), since there are counterexamples (i.e., occurrences of such a desire without many sounds being simultaneously discerned).

Objection: Other than chaotic noise (which can be heard without aid from a desire to focus), a variety of sounds cannot be grasped by the organ of hearing at the same time. A desire to focus is indeed a determiner—contrary to what you say—of a single sound's being grasped.

Gaṅgeśa: That's wrong. For, in comparison with one person singing, several singing on a single occasion the same song or the like results in such experiences as unusual pleasure (which should be impossible if the organ of hearing were restricted in that way).

Comments

The double meaning of the word *śabda* in Sanskrit—both "sound" and "word"—makes this passage more suggestive than comes across in translation.

To use another example to express what is probably Gaṅgeśa's best point: a stranger may hear the sound of a foreign language and not recognize individual words, the sound being, in effect, noise. Or, one may see letters of a foreign alphabet and not recognize line configurations as tokens of types. One may hear music and not recognize a melody. Such recognitions depend on perceiving—in Naiyāyika terms—certain universals, that is, on seeing individuals *as* instances of types.

Thus does Gaṅgeśa put here to good use the Nyāya theory of universals, a theory that on some topics, as we have seen, carries him into greater difficulty and obscurity, not as here greater clarity.

Another feature of his explanation of why one sound rather than another is heard on certain occasions is that sometimes both a prior desire to focus and consonant effort to attend are causal factors, but not all the time for every auditory perception. We might interpret this as the arresting thesis that when perception is of *meaningful* sounds, as opposed to mere noise, its causes include such psychological factors as *effort to attend*—which involves a kind of perceptual training, as, for example, having learned the musical score or the letters of the foreign alphabet.

Next, Gaṅgeśa tries to deal with the phenomenological difficulty of an apparent simultaneity of sensory presentation in the example of a person eating a long piece of pastry. The challenge is formidable in that, as mentioned, Naiyāyikas acknowledge that the several sense organs are active simultaneously. Nyāya's cognitive non-simultaneity is not a doctrine concerning the availability of sensory information. The following example seems to show, then, that it is untenable.

Text (p. 837, Tirupati, and p. 779, Calcutta) and Translation

atha dīrgha-śaṣkulī-bhakṣaṇe katham pañca jñānāni | kramas tatra iti cet, na | jñānānāṃ yaugapadya-pratyayasya bādhakaṃ vinā pramātvāt | vyāsaṅgo bādhaka iti cet, tarhi mano-'vayavy astu | tena saṃkoca-vikāsābhyām ubhayam upapadyata iti kecit | tan na | yadi hi saṃkoca-vikāsa-hetur a-dṛṣṭaṃ tarhi tata eva tad-ubhayam astu, kṛtaṃ manasā | na apy eka-pañca-bubhutsayā tau bhavataḥ, tasyā a-hetutvāt | hetutve vā astu vibhu manaḥ, avayavito laghutvāt | atha yathā kvacit bubhutsayā kvacit tīvra-viṣayêndriya-saṃnikarṣāt indriya-manas-saṃyogaḥ, evaṃ manas-saṃkoca-vikāsayoḥ bubhutsâdikaṃ hetur iti cet, tarhi pañca-bubhutsāyāṃ praṇidhāne ca sarvadā sarveṣāṃ pañca jñānāni jāyeran | pañcāvadhāna-jñāne krama eva | etena aṇuḥ manaḥ pañcatayam astu avayavito laghutvāt, bubhutsâdi-vaśāt teṣām eka-pañcêndriya-saṃbandhād ubhayam upapadyata iti nirastam | pañca-bubhutsāyāṃ sarveṣāṃ pañcêndriya-saṃbandhe vyāsaṅgân-upapatteḥ |

Objection: How can there be (on your view) five (simultaneous) cognitions, as we find with the eating of a long pastry (where at the same time there is the pastry's touch, its sight, smell, taste, and the sound of chewing)?

Gaṅgeśa: The five would occur in (quick) succession.

Objection: No. For, without a prevailing counterconsideration, our sense of the simultaneity of the cognitions is (to be counted) veridical.

Gaṅgeśa: Attention (to one thing specifically) is a counterconsideration, a defeater of apparent simultaneity.

Objection: Then, let the *manas* be (not eternal and partless but) something composite. Thus, both (cognitive simultaneity and cognitive focus) would be possible, through the *manas*'s contraction and expansion.

Gaṅgeśa: So some say. But the view is wrong. For, if (nothing other than) unseen force is to be the cause of contraction or expansion, then just from that would both of those occur—thus enough with this *manas* (i.e., it would be causally and explanationally otiose—and for both cognitive focus and simultaneity). Nor through a desire to know one, or five, would there be the two (the contraction or expansion, such that unseen force could be eliminated as a cause), for then such a desire would have no cause. Or, if there is to be a cause, then let *manas* be ubiquitous, since, in comparison with the view of a composite *manas*, that would be theoretically simpler.

Objection: As on some occasions due to a desire to focus and on other occasions from an intense contact of sense organ and object there is contact between the *manas* and a sense organ (or organs), so desire to focus *and so on* would cause contraction or expansion of the *manas*.

Gaṅgeśa: In that case, given a desire to focus on all five sensory presentations, and (consonant) effort to attend to all that, there would be generated, on all occasions, for everyone, five (simultaneous) cognitions. (However, there are countless counterexamples to the rule.) There is simply a (very quick) series when there appears to be attention to all five (at the same time).

Objection: Let an atomic *manas* be conceived (not as a single thing) but as fivefold (i.e., five "internal organs," each atomic), since that is, in comparison to a composite *manas*, theoretically simpler. By force of a desire to focus and the like would there be a sensory connection to one (at the one extreme) or five (at the other extreme) *manas*es. Thus would both (extremes) be possible (i.e., both simultaneous cognition and cognitive focus).

Gaṅgeśa: By the reasoning given just above is this to be rejected too. For, if there were a desire to know or focus on all five, then, for everyone, with a relation to the five sense organs being given, distraction (a failure to notice some of the desired information) would be impossible.

Comments

Disappointingly, Gaṅgeśa does not develop his theory of a quickly moving *manas* (in what does it move? does it rest? how fast does it move? does it move always at the same rate? what are the laws of its movement?), but, perhaps feeling the weakness of the hypothesis, turns to debunk rival explanations of attention and focus.

Whatever would cause a desire to move the *manas* to expand to take in all five modes of sensory information simultaneously, or to contract to attend to one sensory presentation alone would indirectly be a cause of cognitive simultaneity or focus, and so the *manas* might as well be thought of as ubiquitous, following Mīmāṃsā, since that is the simpler thesis—in comparison with a composite *manas* capable of expansion and contraction. The contraction and expansion would be eliminable in favor of a single ubiquitous *manas* given this extra factor.

Furthermore, contraction and expansion are not caused by a desire to focus and effort to attend, since sometimes a person fails to perceive what he would like to, concentrating on taking in everything available to be perceived but getting distracted instead. This same phenomenon rules out the "five *manas*es" theory.

In broad overview, however, it seems that Gaṅgeśa's very willingness to consider such divergent theses suggests that the atomicity of *manas* was not, as I have now several times indicated, viewed by him as an entirely satisfactory solution to the problems of how (apparent) cognitive simultaneity and focus come about.

Next Gaṅgeśa considers another thorny example, an apparent *apperception* of simultaneous cognition. One senses Gaṅgeśa's own feeling for the power of the pastry example. And since an apperception presumably would be not only veridical but immune from doubt if such simultaneous content were apperceived, simultaneous awareness within all five sensory modes would have to be accepted as an actual fact. The upcoming discussion, moreover, provides transition to the following section, which concerns the mechanics of apperception as a cognitive process. And the next passage is especially noteworthy for Gaṅgeśa's willingness, as we shall see, to question "apperceptive evidence," entertaining the possibility that like a pseudo-perception that seems to be the result of perception as a "knowledge source," *pramāṇa*, but is in fact non-veridical, there can also be pseudo-apperception.

Text (p. 838, Tirupati, and p. 780, Calcutta) and Translation

> kathaṃ tarhi dīrgha-śaṣkulī-bhakṣaṇe gandha-rasa-rūpa-sparśa-śabdān pratyemi ity anuvyavasāyaḥ kramika-jñāna-pañcatayena yugapat manas-saṃnikarṣâ-bhāvād iti cet, na | anuvyavasāyasya ekatvâ-siddheḥ anuvyavasāyāḥ pañca eva, samaya-saukṣmyāt teṣāṃ kramo na gṛhyate | atha vā kramikânuvyavasāyâhita-saṃskārāt pañca-jñāna-viṣaya-smṛtāv anubhavatvâropāt yugapat pratyemi ity anuvyavasāyaḥ |

Objection (by a Mīmāṃsaka): How then (on your view) can there be the apperception, "I am (simultaneously) cognizing a smell, taste, color, touch, and sound," as with the eating of a long pastry (as apperceived)? For (on your view) the fivefold cognition would be serial such that there could be no simultaneous sensory connection with the *manas*.

Gaṅgeśa: No. The unity of your "apperception" is not demonstrated. There would be (in the pastry case) precisely five apperceptions ("I am cognizing a smell," "I am cognizing a taste," and so on). Because of the subtlety (or indistinctness) of (separate apperceptive) occasions, the series or order among them is (sometimes) not grasped.

Alternatively, due to a memory-impression left behind by (five) apperceptions that have occurred sequentially, a memory whose object is those five (past) cognitions occurs. When that memory gets misinterpreted through superimposition of (the property) experiencehood (i.e., when it is mistaken for an experience), the (pseudo) apperception, "I am cognizing (five sensory presentations) simultaneously" occurs.

Comments

The apperceptive cognition cited in the objection if honored at its face value would show that at the bottommost level of sensory experience a synthesis of information from different sensory modalities occurs. There would be simultaneity of awareness in distinct sensory modes. Gaṅgeśa's first response is to deny that such an apperception occurs. There can be pseudo-apperceptions. What then, we may ask, about the thesis of apperceptive infallibility? The answer is that infallibility is restricted to the objecthood of the apperceived; an apparent apperception can be in error about duration and other factors. These include, we might stress, whether a target is in fact a perception, an inferential awareness, etc., or only a pseudo-perception, pseudo-inferential awareness, etc., seeming to be veridical and the result of one of the "knowledge sources" but in fact not. Thus it is possible to mistake a remembering for a perceiving and to think we are having an apperception of simultaneous content but be wrong. Clearly Gaṅgeśa does not accept the position that a cognition of cognition need be in every way veridical. The apparent apperception cited could be in fact a remembering informed by five previous apperceptions. And, as mentioned, while apperception may be an infallible guide to *what* has been cognized, it is not unerring about *when* it has been cognized. (This point is also important in the final section of the chapter, on recognition and "determinate perception"; see below.)

Next, Gaṅgeśa draws out another untoward ramification of the Mīmāṃsaka ubiquity view. His broader argument appears to be that overall less severe difficulties face his theory than face the Mīmāṃsaka's.

Text (p. 838, Tirupati) and Translation

vibhutve hetv-a-bhāvāt ātma-manas-saṃyogâ-bhāvāt na ātma-sukhâdy-upalambhaḥ syāt | dravyatvena ātma-saṃyogitva-sādhane tv a-ja-saṃyoga-siddhau tata eva tad-vibhāgitve 'pi sarvadā tayoḥ paras-para-viruddha-saṃyoga-vibhāga-prasaṅgaḥ |

(**Gaṅgeśa** continues:) On the ubiquity view, no experience of a self's pleasure or the like would occur, since nothing would cause it because there could be no self-*manas* contact. In proving that a *manas* comes into contact with a self—in that it is a substance ("A *manas* comes into contact with a self, *since* it is a substance, like a pot")—if a contact between two things (ubiquitous and) unborn were proved, then, by the very same reasoning, if the two were disjoined, they would always be so. Thus we would face the predicament of a mutually incompatible contact and disjunction (the two both joined and disjoined forever).

Comments

A central reason for supposing the existence and functions of a *manas* is to explain internal perceptions such as pleasures and pains. Pleasures and pains are transitory, in this way unlike an eternal and ubiquitous self, *ātman*. The current problem is not how pleasures and pains can be related ontologically to a self but how epistemically. Ontologically, we have a model in eternal universals standing in relation to their non-eternal instances, e.g., cowhood in Bessie, Flossie, and so on. Similarly (though in reverse relation), an eternal self can be the substratum of non-eternal properties. But epistemically the problem is to account for the serial delivery of pleasure and the like to consciousness. This is said to happen through self/*manas* contact. But if, as on the Mīmāṃsaka ubiquity view, *manas* and self are both eternal and ubiquitous substances, they could *be* in contact (forever) but they could not *come* into contact. In the passage above, Gaṅgeśa nails down the incompatibility by a bit of counterfactual reasoning—though misleadingly he says "unborn" (*a-ja*) where he should say "ubiquitous." Nyāya, too, holds *manas* to be "unborn" in the sense of "eternal," in this way like a self. An atomic substance, though unborn or unproduced, can move around, and thus come into contact at a specific spot not only with other atoms but with something ubiquitous.

Simultaneity, however, remains a problem for Gaṅgeśa, and not only in the direction of sense organ, *manas*, self, but also in reverse, in the direction of self to body or bodily movement. For we do seem to be able to move more than one limb at a time, and the *manas*, according to Nyāya, is responsible for channeling a self's effort into action. The problem is made dramatic in the next passage, which is a long objection, the last of the section, where the Mīmāṃsaka attack is brought to a high point peppered with examples highly unfavorable to Nyāya.

Text (p. 781, Calcutta) and Translation

nanu aṇutve '-samavāyy-anurodhāt ceṣṭā-hetu-prayatnasya aṇu-deśatvaṃ śarīra-deśa-mātratvaṃ vā syāt, na tu śarīra-tad-avayava-deśatvaṃ yena kriyā-niyamo bhavet, niyāmakâ-bhāvāt | na ca nodanâbhighātād iva a-vyāpino 'pi prayatnāt śarīrâdi-kriyā, atiprasaṅgāt | evam ekadā viṃśati-prayatnâ-bhāvāt katham aṅgulīṣu viṃśatiḥ kriyāḥ | na ca yaugapadya-bhramaḥ, bādhakâ-bhāvāt | yugapat-saṃnikarṣâ-bhāvena aṅgulyaś calanti iti samūhâlambanân-upapatteḥ | viṃśati-jñānānām ekadā anuvyavasāyâ-saṃbhavāt agra-paścād-bhāve vinigamakâ-bhāvāc ca | kramôtpāde ca bhrū-nayana-kara-caraṇâdi-sakala-śarīrâvayavānāṃ yugapad-vicitra-nānā-karma-samūha-rūpaṃ nṛtyaṃ na pratyakṣaṃ syāt | tathā ca pratyeka-karma-janya-sukhāt vilakṣaṇa-sukha-viśeṣo na anubhūyeta iti |

Objection (by the Mīmāṃsaka): On the atomicity view, effort that causes bodily action (or movement, *ceṣṭā*) would be confined to an atomic locality in accordance with the effort's *emergent cause* (namely, a contact between an atomic *manas* and an individual self). Or (perhaps) such effort would be confined to the body as a whole (the contact would be with the body as a whole, as one touches and picks up a whole pot, not just its handle). But it would not be confined to the body as a whole (in the fuller sense of, for example, a pot being submerged in water or a whole body in motion) *or* one or another part (or group of parts in combination). This (the right) rule about action, therefore, could not hold, since (on the atomic view) there would be no regular confinement (as is found in the movement of a hand or foot by itself).

Nor is there an effort that, although not pervasive, is capable of resulting both in action of the body (as a whole) and (on different occasions) in action of its parts, like pushing or striking (where the whole moves in response to a contact with some of its parts, like a wagon being pulled by its handle), because that would have "too wide an application," *atiprasaṅga* (in that always, even with movements of individual parts of the body by themselves, we would have to suppose the contact to be with the body as a whole).

(Moreover) if the atomic view were true, then how could there be all at once twenty actions in the bodily digits (fingers and toes), since there could not be twenty (simultaneous) efforts? Nor could the simultaneity be an error, because there is no counterconsideration (to defeating our sense that they do all move at once).

Because there would be (on the atomic view) no simultaneous sensory contact, there could be no group cognized, as in "Moving digits (fingers and toes)." Moreover, since there could be no apperception of twenty cognitions occurring at once, there would be no way to tell which digit was moved before or after which other.

And if there is to be a serial production, then a dance would not be perceptible—a dance, that is, that takes the form of a group of simultaneous actions of various, and variegated, parts of the body—of the eyebrows, eyes, hands, feet, and the like, as well as of the whole body. And, likewise, given a serial production, there would be no experience (contrary to what occurs in fact) of the particular pleasure (produced by the dance) that exceeds the pleasure which would be produced from each single action alone.

Comments

Both the Naiyāyika and Mīmāṃsaka views rely on bodily delimitation in explaining how the *manas* works in generating cognition and in channeling effort into action. But such delimitation is not really imaginable on the atomicity view, so the objector opens, because effort would have to be confined to an atomic locality.

A response harking back to the *Nyāya-sūtra* about a whole being moved through contact with a part—like a wagon[9]—is rejected as having "too wide an application." Rucidatta (p. 839) explains why this would be so—as suggested by the long expression in parentheses at the very end of the second paragraph—namely, that action isolated to a single bodily part would be unintelligible. A human body is not like a wagon, it is implied. We can move one limb alone.

The next perplexity exposed is movement of all one's fingers and toes simultaneously, which is an example of limbs moving not in unison but, it seems, separately. The problem is not only the *manas*'s role in producing what seems to be twenty simultaneous but distinct actions but also, in the reverse direction, its capacity to receive information. We are able to count the moving toes, to take them in all in a sweep, in a "cognition of a group," apparently through a sensory connection with all of them at once. But on the Naiyāyika view, there is no group available to be perceived but only a twenty-membered temporal series ("moving thumb, moving forefinger, etc."). In other words, the objector sees the cognition, "Moving digits (fingers and toes)," as a counterexample to the atomic thesis because the movement of twenty fingers and toes would have to be cognized serially and analyzed as twenty things moving in quick succession. And even serial counting, he adds, does not make sense given the Naiyāyika picture. No idea about the particular order of movements among the twenty could be generated, since there would be no possibility of an apperception whose object was twenty separate cognitions produced by the twenty separate movements.

To make matters worse, it is very difficult to understand, on the atomic hypothesis, how we can perceive such a thing as a dance, in particular the pleasure that we feel upon perceiving a dance, which is a complex and multiple-qualitied object, mediated diversely through diverse sensory presentations. The dance gives rise to pleasure distinct from that resulting from viewing exclusively any of its parts. In other words, we get more pleasure from such a complex witnessing than we would get from, as on the Nyāya view, an experience isolated to a single sensory mode. Thus we have a phenomenon that is a ramification of simultaneous cognition in different sensory modes, an excess of pleasure that otherwise would not occur.

Against Buddhist proponents of a momentariness and "point-instant" view of the self, Naiyāyikas use such examples as that of the dance spectator to show that the self is unified both over different sensory modalities and over time. But here the example is used against them since the *manas*-as-atomic thesis implies that only diachronic unity would be possible, not, counterintuitively, synchronic unity too.[10]

Gaṅgeśa closes the section by trying to answer this last round of Mīmāṃsaka challenge. On the cognitive side, most of his view has already been given. But as the current objection also focuses on the *manas*'s role in originating movement—the apparently simultaneous movement of all twenty of one's fingers and toes—so, targeting the effort and movement, Gaṅgeśa talks now about a causal factor not previously introduced, *cikīrṣā*, "desire to do (or act)."

Text (p. 839, Tirupati) and Translation

> atra brūmaḥ | sukhe candanâdi-vat cikīrṣā eva niyāmikā | yat-kriyāyāṃ cikīrṣā sā kriyā tac-cikīrṣā-janyāt prayatnād bhavati | tatra śarīra-kriyā api tac-cikīrṣā-janyād aṇu-mātra-deśād api prayatnād bhavati | atha vā yasya kriyāyāṃ cikīrṣā tad-avacchedena prayatna utpadyate | tena śarīrâvacchedena utpanna-prayatnād eva śarīra-kriyā | evaṃ viṃśati-kriyā-cikīrṣā-janyād aṇu-mātra-deśād api prayatnād viṃśati-kriyā yugapad utpadyante athavā aṅgulī-viṃśati-kriyāyāṃ cikīrṣā iti viṃśaty-avacchedena viṃśati-prayatnād viṃśati-kriyā-hetava utpadyante | evaṃ nṛtyâdāv api etac-cikīrṣânuvidhānāt kriyā-prayatnayor adhyavaseyam | tad evam aṇu-manas-siddhau tad-grāhyā ātma-viśeṣa-guṇā buddhi-sukhâdaya iti na a-vyāpakaṃ pratyakṣa-lakṣanam |

Gaṅgeśa: On these matters, we say the following. As sandalwood paste and such things regulate the arising of pleasure, precisely *desire to do* regulates bodily movement. An action for which there is a desire to do is the action that comes about, due to effort that is generated by the desire to do that. Even an action of the body (as a whole)—among the things to which this rule applies—comes to be because of effort that is generated by a desire to do that action, albeit the effort is restricted (in accordance, indeed, with its emergent cause) to an atomic locality.

Alternatively, that which exhibits an action for which there is a desire to do is that whereby there is specification of the effort that arises (e.g., a desire to move one's left thumb generates effort restricted to the left thumb). Thus, due precisely to effort that has arisen as restricted to the body (as a whole) is there action of the body (as a whole).

In this way, from effort that is generated from a desire to do twenty actions, twenty actions are produced simultaneously—albeit the effort is restricted to an atomic locality. Or, there would be a desire for movement of the twenty digits (fingers and toes). Hence, due to effort restricted to the twenty digits to do twenty acts, causes of the twenty acts would be produced.

Similarly is it to be concluded in such a case as the dance (used as an example against us): in accordance with a desire to do that (simultaneous movement "of the eyebrows, eyes, hands, feets, and the like, as well as of the whole body") would there be the actions and effort.

Therefore, an atomic *manas* being in this way established, the specific qualities of selves—cognition, pleasure, and so on—are grasped by it. Hence, it is not the case that our definition of perception fails to include them (contrary to what was alleged at the beginning of the section).

Comments

Gaṅgeśa's own view appears to depend on the analogy, suggested in the preceding objection, of an entire object—a whole—being pushed by contacting merely a part. (This is the thesis of *Nyāya-sūtra* 2.1.35.) In this way, despite the atomic dimension of a person's *manas*, it could channel desires into efforts and acts involving more than one bodily part at the same time. This may seem satisfactory, but let us look at the objection again.

Effort, it was said, that was not pervasive could not move the body or its parts—*unlike* what goes on in cases of "pushing or striking (where the whole moves in response to a contact with some of its parts)." The reason given to reject the analogy was that the rule would be "too wide" that proposed that non-pervasive things could cause such effects. Rucidatta, we pointed out, explained that even isolated movements of individual bodily parts would have to be regarded as due to a contact delimited to (*avacchinna*) the body as a whole. It is difficult to see how Gaṅgeśa's current proposal avoids the problem.

Regarding movement, just how does the *manas* do its work? Gaṅgeśa shows in several ways that he is not confident about this, not confident, we could say, about how an effort gives rise to bodily motion. One indication is that he gives disjunctive answers: note the use of "alternatively" to begin the second paragraph and the use of "or" in the third. Note also how he shifts the focus from *manas* to a "desire to do" in the first paragraph, along with an apology for the "atomic locality" at the paragraph's end, and how in the second there is no reference to *manas* at all.

Puzzles and counterintuitive cases supposedly disappear when we understand the causal role of a "desire to do" (*cikīrṣā*). This is a kind of desire that invariably precedes a voluntary act. (All desires are psychological qualities,

qualities that inhere in individual selves.) In other words, any imaginable voluntary bodily act, x, is generated by an effort that flows from a psychological quality known as a desire to do x. And (somehow) a desire to do x, where x is a complex action involving many different bodily parts, is not prevented by the atomicity of the *manas* medium, though, again, just how the transmission works is not explained.

Now cognition is sometimes similarly voluntary, i.e., indirectly, as in the case of focus, although a cognition is not an act. It results from a desire to know or focus on something in particular. Sometimes, in contrast, cognition is involuntary, as when a loud sound dominates, willy-nilly, one's attention. Mīmāṃsakas see cognitions as acts, and though Gaṅgeśa seems willing to concede some ground in that direction in admitting that a desire to focus can determine what one sees, cognitions are qualities that inhere in selves and different cognitions have different causal histories. Many perceptual cognitions are not in any way caused by "a desire to do x," in particular, not by "a desire to know something or other." An object or objects and a sensory connection, not a desire, play the dominant roles.

It is open to interpretation precisely which causes Gaṅgeśa has in mind when he says, ". . . *causes* of the twenty acts would be produced." He has not indicated that he sees anything standing between an effort and an act (having the same object). This may be another indication that he himself views his current proposals as dubious. On the other hand, he may simply mean the role of the bodily parts involved, the twenty fingers and toes.

The section opened with the complaint that the definition of perception as *generated by a sense organ* does not include perceptions of pleasure and the like. Hence, by showing that there is an atomic *manas*—an internal sensory organ—that grasps these, the "specific qualities" of selves, that complaint is put to rest.

atha anuvyavasāya-vādaḥ

NOW, DISCOURSE ON APPERCEPTION

Text (p. 841, Tirupati, and p. 784, Calcutta) and Translation

> nanu vartamānaṃ jñānaṃ na mānasam, kiṃ tu svayam eva sva-vyavahāra-hetuḥ, svasmin saty eva sva-vyavahārāt, na tu jñānântaram apekṣate, tad-anvaya-vyatirekân-anuvidhānāt |

A **Prābhākara** Mīmāṃsaka: A current cognition (even one having as its object a psychological property, a perceiving, etc.) is not mediated by the *manas*, the inner sense (as you Naiyāyikas hold), but is just in itself sufficient to account for its own verbalization (e.g., "I *am cognizing* such and such"). For, all that is required for the linguistic expression is simply the cognition itself (which is self-illumining). That does not depend on another cognition, in that there is no correlation, either positive or negative, of the sort.

Comments

Throughout this *pūrva-pakṣa* section, the principal opponent expresses Prābhākara views. But note that Buddhists and Vedāntins as well as Mīmāṃsakas of the Kumārila camp subscribe to many of the Prābhākara theses.

Every cognition, according to Prābhākara Mīmāṃsā, is self-cognized or self-aware. Indeed, a cognition simultaneously takes notice of three things, the cognition, the object cognized, and the subject cognizing. Gaṅgeśa's Nyāya, on the other hand, insists that a cognition is absorbed in its own object (however complex). And among objects to be known are cognitions themselves as properties of selves. A person sometimes, in a distinct mental episode, becomes aware of his own cognizing, noting, for example, that he was seeing such and such, with the seeing as the cognitive object. Of course, this is an object with its own objecthood, the such and such seen, but as the target of the scoping cognition it is an object nonetheless. The scoping cognition, which is exclusively preoccupied with its object too, is called *anuvyavasāya*, "apperception" or "after-cognition," a type of cognition defined by having an internal object not mediated by an external organ of sense. For example, the perceptual cognition expressible as "That's a pot" can become the object of an apperception expressed as "I am aware of a pot." These two linguistic expressions are used by both sides of the dispute (in

Sanskrit, *ghaṭam iti* and *ghaṭam jānāmi iti*). In other words, the cognition (verbalized as) "I am aware of a pot" is taken by Naiyāyikas to have as object a distinct cognition (verbalized as) "A pot," whereas the Prābhākara opponent takes the two expressions, "I am aware of a pot" and "A pot," to express the same cognition in different ways.

This section connects with several earlier discussions. Many of the arguments here have been anticipated in the sections on knowing veridicality and on error where, in each case, the Prābhākara view of self-illumination figured prominently.

This opening passage connects to the immediately preceding section in that the *manas* has a role in generating apperception according to Nyāya. A cognition as a quality of an individual self cannot become the object of an external organ of sense; one cannot visually perceive, for instance, the cognition expressible as "That's a pot." Similarly, the *manas* cannot directly grasp the pot, which is grasped, instead, by the visual organ. But a cognition can through the operation of the *manas* unaided by the external senses perceive a cognition that has occurred just previously. We can notice our own awareness. This reasoning is challenged here by the Prābhākara in pointing to the greater simplicity of the Prābhākara theory.

In other words, the Prābhākara opens by implying that his theory of self-illumining cognition gets rid of Nyāya's cumbersome hypothetical apparatus concerning cognition of cognition, with no need here to talk about an "inner sense" or *manas* at all.

The Prābhākara also exploits the presumed Nyāya inference that would be based on the fact that in all cases of "apperception" (a) a cognition known correlates with (b) a knowing awareness. But, he avers, no such correlation is established. How could it be? How could the Nyāya doctrine be known? Do we stand outside both the cognition known and the knowing awareness and observe a pervasion relationship?

Text (p. 784, Calcutta) and Translation

> jñānântara-viraha-daśāyāṃ sva-virahād eva sva-vyavahāra-virahāt, svata eva sva-vyavahāra-upapattau jñānântara-kalpane gauravāc ca | ghaṭâdi-vyavahāre jñānânvaya-vyatirekād astu tad-apekṣā | svīyam atītam an-āgataṃ parakīyaṃ ca jñānaṃ sva-vyavahāre jñānântaram apekṣata eva, vyavahāra-kāle tad-a-bhāvāt jñānântarânvaya-vyatirekânuvidhānāc ca |

(The **Prābhākara** continues:) (Moreover) when a particular cognition (C) does not occur, nor some other cognition (C^c, let us say, what you Naiyāyikas would call an apperception of C), to imagine that an absence of linguistic behavior that would express the particular cognition (C) is due to the non-occurrence of that other cognition (C^c) is cumbersome, given that the absence can be explained simply by the non-occurrence of (C) the particular cognition itself. Granted, with regard to a pot, for example, linguistic usage does depend on a cognition of a pot, because there both positive and negative correlations are found. Also, cognition of one's own past or future cognition, or cognition of another person's cognition, does require a second cognition to be expressed, since at the time of the expression the first cognition would be absent and since there both positive and negative correlations do ground (a view of) dependence on a second cognition. (But with regard to one's own current cognition, the cognition itself is sufficient to account for self-referential linguistic expressions.)

Comments

The Prābhākara challenges the Naiyāyika to show, in the case of "I am aware of a pot," the dependence on another cognition evident elsewhere, for instance, in someone's talking tomorrow about what he or she is cognizing now. Since there is no such correlation, self-referential expressions are more economically explained by the self-illumination thesis. Naiyāyika views are by comparison cumbersome, as shown when a lack of expression is targeted as explanandum: for Nyāya two cognitions would have to be absent (C and C^c) to explain what the Prābhākara explains by an absence of one.

Text (p. 785, Calcutta) and Translation

> nanv evam icchâdikam api sva-vyavahāra-jñānaṃ na apekṣeta, jñāna-tulyatayā svayam eva sva-vyavahāra-śaktatvād iti cet, na | vyavahārasya jñāna-janyatva-niyamena icchâdi-vyavahāre jñānâpekṣaṇāt | atha jñāna-mātraṃ na vyavahāra-hetuḥ atiprasaṅgāt | kiṃ tu vyavahartavya-viṣayam iti jñāna-vyavahāro 'pi tad-viṣaya-jñānântarād bhaved iti cet, satyam | svasya eva sva-viṣayakatvāt | yad-vyavahārânukūla-śakti-yogi yaj-jñānaṃ tasya eva tad-viṣayakatvāt | śaktiś ca padārthântaraṃ na kāraṇatā iti na anyonyâśrayaḥ | sva-vyavahāre jñānaṃ śaktam iti sva-viṣayakam | vyavahāra-śakti-samavāyâdayaś ca sva-bhāvata eva tadīyāḥ saṃbandhântare 'py an-avasthānāt sva-bhāva eva śaraṇam |

Objection (by a Naiyāyika): On this view, (not only cognition but) also desire and the like would not depend on cognition to express it (which is absurd). Inasmuch as desire is similar to cognition (as a psychological quality), a desire would have to be capable just in itself to account for the verbal usage ("I desire such and such").

Prābhākara: No. Cognition brings about usage; this is an invariable rule. So, concerning usage expressive of desire or the like, cognition (of the desire) would be necessary.

Objection (by the Naiyāyika): Don't tell us cognition alone is sufficient for usage because that would have too wide an application. (Then, a cognition of a cloth, for example, as a cognition—aside from all content or objecthood—could produce the verbal expression, "A pot.") Rather, a cognition whose object is the thing to be talked about (whether a cloth or a cognition) results in the linguistic usage. Therefore, talk about a (first) cognition also comes about from another cognition that has the first as object.

Prābhākara: That's true (to an extent), since a selfsame cognition has just itself as object. A cognition of *x* (whatever *x* be, including that very cognition) is what has power to produce conforming linguistic usage about *x*, because it is indeed its object.

And this power is a distinct type of entity, a distinct category. It is not a cause. Therefore, there is no "mutual dependence" here.

That a cognition has productive power with regard to the linguistic usage expressive of it is what we mean when we say that it has itself as object.

And the power of cognition with regard to linguistic usage is, along with inherence and the like, "self-linking," because each of these functions through itself alone. If an additional relation were required, there would be an infinite regress. Refuge (from this unwanted consequence) is provided by the view that they link up through themselves alone.

Comments

The Prābhākara does not assimilate awareness of desire to awareness of cognition. The two are simply different on his view, and we should not be led to expect that a desire could be expressed without cognition of it. An awareness is self-aware, but a desire is not, according to Prābhākara Mīmāṃsā.

A cognition, which is thought of as an act, is an expression of itself in a sense, according to the Prābhākara. Verbalizing is inseparable from the cognitive act. Perception is saturated by language. Thus the duality of "cause and effect" is inapplicable. If the "power" to produce such-and-such linguistic behavior were thought of in those terms, there would occur the fallacy known as "mutual dependence": no effect can be a cause of itself. But the fallacy does not occur on our Prābhākara view in that the power is not a cause but rather a special category to itself, with its own nature and logic.

In upcoming text, the Prābhākara will repeatedly complain against the Naiyāyika posit of apperception that it cannot avoid infinite regress. Here his argument concerns his own position: since (a) cognition, (b) content or objecthood, and (c) expression are all bound up together through self-linkage, no infinite regress is incurred.

Text (p. 842, Tirupati) and Translation

etena bheda-niyato viṣaya-viṣayi-bhāvaḥ katham a-bhede iti nirastam | sva-vyavahāra-śaktatvasya sva-viṣayatvasya a-bhede 'pi saṃbhavāt | astu vā jñānasya sva-bhāva-viśeṣa eva sva-viṣayatvam | saṃbandhaṃ vinā eva sva-bhāva-viśeṣāt yathā jñānaṃ ghaṭīyaṃ ghaṭa-vyavahāra-janana-yogyaṃ svīyam api tathā | ko 'sau sva-bhāva-viśeṣa iti cet, na | ākhyātum a-śakyatve 'py anubhava-siddhasya sva-bhāva-viśeṣasya mādhuryâdi-viśeṣa-vat pratyākhyātum a-śakyatvāt | yady api sva-bhāva-viśeṣa iti vākyena ākhyāyate eva, tathā api padena ākhyātum a-śakyatvāt |

Objection: On your theory that cognition is its own object, how can there be a relation between consciousness and its objects? The two are, by rule, distinct, while you claim there is no distinctness.

Prābhākara: This objection is thrown out by the reasoning just given. What we mean by the "own object" plank in our position is that a cognition has power with respect to its own characteristic linguistic expression. That is possible though there is non-distinctness.

Or, let this do: "own object" amounts to viewing a cognition as having a special nature. As a pot-formed cognition (a "pot-ish" presentation, so to say) is capable by its own special nature—without reliance on an (external) relation—of producing "pot" expression, so also (with cognition).

Objection: What is a "special nature?"

Prābhākara: Although it is impossible to say what a special nature is, it is established by experience, like such particularities as sweetness that are impossible to explain (to someone who has not had the experience). If you object that simply by using the expression "special nature" we have (contradicted ourselves and) said what it is, (you miss the point because) it remains impossible to put in words.

Comments

The Prābhākara softens his position and makes it more plausible first by stating that linguistic behavior stands as the "effect" (or second term) in the empowerment relation he gives to cognition, and second by citing the private or first-person sense of the experiential—the ineffably experiential—which Bertrand Russell and followers call "knowledge by acquaintance." A person "directly acquainted with" a potish presentation is able to express it, "There is a pot there," without being able to describe the experiential nature of the cognition that "empowers" it. So also are we able to say that we are aware.

The logic of the ineffability claimed does not mean that certain objects, such as the color red, cannot be designated, but that one oneself has to have had experience of red to know what it is. Thus, we are supposed to know the "special nature" of cognition by having cognitions—and also to see that cognition is self-illumining.

Text (p. 842, Tirupati) and Translation

atha vyavahāro vyavahartavya-bhinna-jñāna-sādhyaḥ kathaṃ tena vinā syād iti ced, na | vyavahāraṃ prati vyavahartavya-jñānatvena hetutvāt, na tu vyavahartavya-bhinna-jñānatvena gauravāt | samūhâlambanaṃ ca eka-eka-vyavahāra-janakatvād eka-eka-viṣayakam api, na tu samūha-viṣayakam eva, atiriktasya tasya a-sattvena saṃnikarṣâ-bhāvāt | bhrama-sthale rajata-vyavahārânukūlā śaktir asty eva rajata-jñāne | kiṃ tu doṣāt abhibhūtā eva sā jāyata iti na tayā rajate vyavahāraḥ | rajata-jñānaṃ na śuktau pravartakam, kiṃ tu indriya-janyam idaṃ-jñānam eva | rajatârthi-pravṛtty-arthaṃ tu upasthita-rajata-bhedâ-graham apekṣata iti rajata-jñānaṃ kāraṇatâvacchedakam | evaṃ ca sva-viṣayatvaṃ sva-prakāśatvam, na tu sva-vyavahāre jñānântarân-apekṣatvam, gauravāt | anyathā jñānasya svâ-viṣayatvena saṃskārâ-bhāvāt smaraṇaṃ na syāt |

Objection: Linguistic usage (referring to something) is produced by a cognition distinct from that which is referred to. So how without such distinct entities (when cognition itself is that which is referred to) could there be reference?

Prābhākara: No. Only as a cognition of what is to be expressed is a cognition a cause of the linguistic usage, not as a cognition "distinct from" what is to be expressed, since the latter formulation (adding the qualification "as distinct from") is unnecessarily cumbersome.

Also, (analogously) a cognition of a group of things has each of the individual items as object in that it generates linguistic usage with respect to each item. The collection *qua* group is not the object because nothing extra (over and above the individual items) exists in that there is no sensory connection (with anything like that).

With respect to occasions of error (or, so-called perceptual illusion), expressive power concordant with silver linguistic usage (for example) exists precisely in silver cognition. But because of a defect (or deviation from normal cognitive operations), the silver-usage power, though (in a sense) defeated, still arises, and thus through it no linguistic usage is directed to (real) silver. Silver cognition is not an instigator of effort to act toward a piece of mother-of-pearl (in front of a deluded subject). Rather, simply the cognition of a "this" (as in, "This is silver," said of mother-of-pearl in front) is the instigator, i.e., the cognition produced by the sense organ.

But the (unattained) goal of one seeking silver depends on the person's failure to apprehend the distinctness (of a current perceptual awareness) from remembered silver. In this way, cognition of silver delimits the causal process.

And so a cognition takes itself as (part of its) objecthood and is self-illumining. It is false that to express a cognition *as* a cognition another cognition is required, for that is unnecessarily cumbersome.

Otherwise, if a cognition did not have itself as object, then, since there could be no memory-impression (*saṃskāra*), there could be no remembering (of a prior cognition).

Comments

The opening objection is sustained by a use/mention lag that seems generalizable: to refer to Bessie, you use her name, not the cow herself which is a distinct entity. Similarly, cognition of the cow would provoke mentioning of it, not the cow itself. So, referring to cognition depends on awareness of the cognition referred to.

The Prābhākara responds by claiming his view achieves an economy in causal formulations. The opponent's picture of the causal relations are needlessly cumbersome. This is supported by an analogy to cognition of a group of things where nothing other than the individual items need be posited ontologically. Nothing other than a cognition C itself, not a cognition of C, is required to explain the usage, "I know such-and-such," where what is known is not only such-and-such but also the knowing and the "I."

The passage continues with a rehearsal of now familiar Prābhākara positions on error and failed effort. We shall pass these by and reconstruct the argument introduced at the end.

As explained in the introduction, the Sanskrit term *anubhava*—translated "awareness" and sometimes "experience"—connotes presentation of *new* information in contrast to a second species of cognition, "remembering," *smaraṇa*, which presents *old* information. A remembering depends on an enlivening of a subliminal memory-impression, and would not occur in its absence. That is, awarenesses create subliminal traces of their objects, traces that are dispositional vehicles for rememberings, and no object not previously experienced can be remembered. Thus, if an awareness or cognition did not have itself as object, it could not be remembered. But we do remember having had previous cognitions. Thus, cognition must be self-illumining.

This counterfactual argument, or *tarka*, about remembering previous experiences is not, of course, the Prābhākara's argumentative mainstay. Cognition itself, e.g., perception, directly attests to the truth of the self-illumination thesis, as we are told in the passage coming up.

Text (p. 843, Tirupati) and Translation

yat tu sva-vyavahāre jñānântarân-apekṣatvam uktam, tat sva-prakāśatva-nirvāhakatayā | pramāṇaṃ ca sva-prakāśe pratyakṣam eva | sarvāḥ pratītaya idam ahaṃ jānāmi ity evam ākārāḥ jñātāraṃ jñānaṃ jñeyaṃ ca ullikhantyo jāyante | tatra ātmā kartṛtvena jñeyaṃ karmatayā jñānaṃ kriyātvena bhāsate | ato jñātṛ-jñeya-sva-viṣayaṃ jñānam anubhūyata iti tri-puṭī-pratyakṣa-vādinaḥ |

(The **Prābhākara** continues:) But what has been stated—namely, that in order to express itself a cognition is not dependent on another cognition—this view follows from the fact that cognition is self-illumining. And the proof (*pramāṇa*) for self-illumination is perception itself.

All cognitions arise in the form "I cognize this," with the cognizer, the cognition, and the cognized as all explicitly mentionable. Among these, a self appears as the agent (the cognizer), a cognized as the object, and the cognition itself as the (cognitive) act (and according to the structure of the articulation, these would be the nominative, the accusative, and the verb respectively). Thus the position of those who hold that perception is threefold (in its objecthood): a cognition is experienced with a cognizer, a cognized, and itself as object.

Comments

Here we have a summary statement of the Prābhākara position. Every cognition illumines itself as well as a cognizer (or "I") and a thing. And there is a match between each word in the verbalization, "I am-cognizing this" (*idam ahaṃ jānāmi*), and an item expressed: 'this' and thing, 'I' and self, and 'am-cognizing' and cognitive act.

Next, the Prābhākara defends his position by attacking alternative views, claiming his theory is not only the more economical but also the only one for which there is any "proof" or *pramāṇa*. The Bhāṭṭas are wrong because some cognitions could not be known by the inferential mark the Bhāṭṭas presume, and the Nyāya position flounders with its theorizing about *manas*, the internal organ.

Text (p. 789, Calcutta) and Translation

nanu idam iti vyavasāyaḥ tad uttaram idam ahaṃ jānāmi ity anuvyavasāyo mānasa iti cet, na | sva-prakāśatvena upapattau jñānântara-kalpane gauravāt pariśeṣāc ca sva-prakāśatvam | para-prakāśatve hi jñānam eva na sidhyet mānâ-bhāvāt | na hi jñātatā liṅgam | atītân-āgatayos tad-a-bhāvāt | na api mānasaṃ pratyakṣam | a-jijñāsitasya mānasatve jñānâ-virāmād an-avasthānāt viṣayântarâ-saṃcārāc ca | jijñāsitasya grāhyatve jñānaṃ na mānasaṃ jijñāsā-grāhyâtma-dharmatvāt saṃskāra-vad ity anumāna-pratirodhaḥ | ata eva jijñāsāṃ vinā eva sukhâdīnāṃ mānasatvam | jijñāsā api jñāna-sādhyā ity an-avasthā, dharmi-jñāna-icchâdibhir jñānasya nāśāc ca na pratyakṣam |

Objection (by a Naiyāyika): An original (or scoped) cognition (*vyavasāya*) is (e.g.) "This." Afterwards, an apperception, *anuvyavasāya*, "I am cognizing this," occurs mediated by the inner sense (*manas*).

Prābhākara: No, that's wrong. Given the possibility of the self-illumining view, to imagine another cognition (to account for self-cognition) is the more cumbersome position. By that argument, and because of an eliminative argument too, self-illumination stands. For, on the other-illumination view, no cognition could be itself established (as objectively real), because there would be no proof.

For, it is not the case that a "cognizedness" is an inferential mark (of a cognition's occurrence), because this (property) is not exhibited by things past or future (whereas a cognition can have past and future things as object).

Furthermore, a supposed apperceptive cognition could not be perceptual as mediated by the inner sense (*manas*). If such a "mental" cognition could occur without there being a desire to cognize it, then there would be (a) no cessation of such cognition, (b) an (impossible) infinite series, or (c) no transition to another object. If, on the other hand, it is to become cognizable on the condition of its being desired to be cognized, then the cognition could not be mediated by the *manas*, in that, like a memory-impression (*saṃskāra*, which is a property resting in a self), the cognition would be both a property of a self and that which is to be grasped by the desire to cognize. Thus, a counterinference (can be constructed, namely, that a cognition is not known through mediation of a *manas*, *since* it is a psychological property to be grasped by a desire to cognize).

Just for this reason, we hold that pleasure and company are known through mediation of a *manas* even when there is no desire to cognize them (i.e., when they force their way into awareness).

Moreover, since a desire to cognize is to be brought about by a cognition (in that there is no desire about something that has not in general been experienced), there would be an infinite regress (on a view that requires another cognition for a target cognition to be known). And, because a cognition (as a member of a series of cognitions occurring one at a time) would perish through (the arising of) a desire to cognize it, i.e., the cognition as the propertied thing (desired to be cognized) or the like, the cognition (your supposed apperceptive cognition) could not be perceptual.

Comments

Voicing an argument that Gaṅgeśa has already aired, the Prābhākara attacks the Bhāṭṭa position that a cognition could be known by an inference from a "cognizedness" perceived. As explained, the problem is that while we cognize past and future objects in the present, the past and future objects are not available in the present to exhibit the feature "having been cognized." Thus we could not know a cognition about the past or the future.

The Prābhākara proceeds to criticize the Naiyāyika cognitive psychology according to which a desire to cognize—or doubt or concern (*jijñāsa*)—would be responsible, presumably, for making a particular cognition apperceived. If an apperception could occur without a prior desire to cognize it, there would be one or the other of the three untoward ramifications listed. The deep problem is that there would be no regulation of apperceptive occurrence.

Furthermore, says the Prābhākara, it is impossible to understand how an apperception could be prompted by a desire to cognize a cognition and at the same time be mediated by a *manas*. The target cognition would be a property of a self, like a memory-impression. But a memory-impression is not known by a *manas*; it itself prompts a *manas* to an act of remembering. The disanalogy tells against the Naiyāyika view. The *manas* has to be moved by a psychological property, the desire to cognize C, and directed toward another psychological property, C, the target cognition that is already implicated in the desire. This is at a minimum confusing if not not also impossible. That's one reason we say that pleasure and company prompt a *manas* to a cognitive act though there is no desire to cognize them. (Another is that if to cognize pleasure and the like there had to be a desire to cognize them, then we would not feel pain when stepping on a thorn unless we wanted to.)

But there is an even deeper incoherence in the Naiyāyika picture. Consider a desire to cognize something in the distance that is only vaguely seen. The vague perception, or, as Naiyāyikas say, a perception of something according to a general feature, is a precondition for the desire to cognize, to cognize the thing in its full particularity. Similarly, with experiences that we wish to have again, such as pleasure, the desire is dependent on previous cognition. The Prābhākara alleges that all this invites the charge of infinite regress, since a cognition would be both a prior condition as well as the effect of such a desire. Then since such an order may well seem not only possible but natural to the Naiyāyika, he nails his refutation down by pointing out that the cognition that would be the object of a desire to cognize would be unavailable to be apperceived since by the time the apperception occurred as an event in the cognitive flow the target cognition would have perished. Thus the apperception could not grasp a current object and therefore could not be perceptual, contrary to what Nyāya tells us. Gaṅgeśa has special difficulty with this ''availability'' problem, as we shall see at the end of the section.

Text (p. 844, Tirupati) and Translation

atha jñānaṃ mānasa-pratyakṣaṃ pratyakṣâtma-guṇatvāt ātma-viśeṣa-guṇatve sati kṣaṇa-mātra-sthāyitvāt sukha-vat, jñānaṃ pratyakṣa-janakêndriya-saṃnikarṣâśrayaḥ pratyakṣatvāt sukha-vad iti cet, na | mānasatve 'n-avasthānāt | ata eva cakṣur-janyaṃ jñānaṃ na cakṣur-janya-jñāna-viṣayaḥ pratyakṣatvāt rāsana-vat, na etaj-jñāna-viṣayo vā, etaj-janakêndriya-saṃnikarṣân-āśrayatvāt gagana-vat | cakṣur na cākṣuṣa-jñāna-grāhakaṃ bahir-indriyatvāt rasana-vat iti pratipakṣânumānam apāstam | para-prakāśatve 'n-avasthayā jñānâ-siddhāv āśrayâ-siddheḥ | sva-prakāśatvena tat-siddhau dharmi-grāhaka-māna-bādhāt | kiṃ ca sva-vyavahāra-śaktatvaṃ sva-viṣayatvaṃ, tac ca sva-saṃnikarṣâ-janyatve svâ-janyatve ca na viruddham | na ca sva-vyavahāre śaktatvasya a-bhāva eva sādhyaḥ, a-prayojakatvāt | sva-saṃnikarṣâ-janye svâ-janye vyavahāra-śakte ghaṭâdau[1] vyabhicārāc ca |

Objection (by a Naiyāyika): Then consider the following argument. A cognition is perceivable mentally (i.e., is perceptible by a *manas*), *since* it is a perceptible psychological quality (*ātma-guṇa*, "quality of the self or soul"). (Or) it is so, given that it is a *specific* quality of a self, *since* it lasts only an instant. Pleasure is the confirming example. (Alternatively) a (target) cognition is a relatum or locus of a sensory connection productive of a perception (i.e., an apperception), *since* it is perceptible, like a pleasure.

Prābhākara: No. On the view that a cognition is mentally perceptible, there is a (vitiating) infinite regress.

For this very reason, a cognition that is generated by the visual organ is not (itself) the object of a cognition generated by the visual organ, *since* it is perceptible, like an object of taste. Nor is a cognition an object of a cognition of anything whatsoever, *since* it is not a locus that could stand in a sensory connection that would generate anything, like the sky (or ether, which does not have a locus). The visual organ does not grasp a visual cognition, *since* it is an external organ, like the organ of taste.

Therefore, your inference to the opposite conclusion is rejected: no locus (i.e., no cognition) can be established (and thus your inference suffers from the fallacy of having an inferential subject that is unknown) because, on the other-illumination view, there would be an infinite regress such that no cognition could be established (as a reality and thus as the subject of the inference). As self-illumining (however), a cognition *is* established, since the need for a means that would grasp (cognition as an inferential subject, i.e., as) an object with properties is blocked.

Moreover, something's "being capable of producing everyday usage expressing itself" is tantamount to its "being its own object." And that is not an impossible contradiction—whether with respect to the fact that nothing can generate a sensory connection with itself, or to the fact that nothing can produce itself. No absence of such capability can be shown with respect to expression of self-manifesting cognition, for there is no support for the position. There would be deviation, too, in the instance of (self-)cognition of a pot (a cognition whose object is itself as well as a pot), etc., a cognition that could be expressed although it was neither generated by itself nor in sensory connection with itself.

Comments

Gaṅgeśa puts forth rather different arguments from the Naiyāyika's here: see below in the *siddhânta*, p. 593.

The principal new point that the Prābhākara makes here is that a cognition cannot be the object of another cognition because that would require an impossible sensory connection. No such impossibility occurs on the self-illumination view. But, as we shall see, it is precisely the requirement that any *perception* be generated by a sensory connection that sinks the Prābhākara view, or so Gaṅgeśa will try to show.

Text (p. 846, Tirupati) and Translation

ata eva sva-prakāśatvena pūrvânubhava-viṣayatā tattânubhūta-mātra-viṣaye smaraṇe utsargato bhāsate jñānântarasya an-āvaśyakatvāt | svasya svâ-janyatve kathaṃ sva-karmatā iti cet, na | atītân-āgatayor iva sva-viṣayatvaṃ na tu karmatvam | viṣayatvaṃ ca a-bhede 'pi | sva-vyavahāra-śaktatvasya jñāna-sva-bhāva-viśeṣasya vā viṣayatvāt | na ca adhīkarmatayā śaśa-śṛṅga-vad a-sattvam | tasya kadā apy a-prakāśāt | dhī-janya-vyavahāra-bhāgitvaṃ karmatvaṃ sva-prakāśe 'pi, tad-anya-phala-bhāgitvaṃ ca ghaṭe 'py a-siddham, jñātatā-niṣedhāt | jñānân-apekṣêndriya-saṃnikarṣa-jaṃ jñānaṃ pratyakṣam, ataḥ sarvaṃ jñānaṃ jñānân-apekṣâtma-manas-saṃnikarṣa-janyatvena svâtmani pratyakṣam | viśiṣṭa-pratyakṣaṃ ca na viśeṣaṇa-jñāna-janyam, nirvikalpaka-niṣedhāt | savikalpakatvena jñānâ-janya-jñānaṃ vā pratyakṣam | tena nirvikalpaka-janyaṃ jāti-viśiṣṭa-jñānaṃ pratyakṣam, na tv a-sādhāraṇêndriyâdi-karaṇakam, tena vinā api anumity-ādau svâtma-prakāśāt | indriyâdikaṃ tu artha-prakāśa eva hetuḥ, tasya eva tat-pratibaddha-hetu-janyatvād iti |

(The **Prābhākara** continues:) For the same reason, the rule is that the object of a previous experience as known self-illuminingly appears in a remembering whose object is nothing other than that which has been experienced previously. This holds because another cognition is not necessary.

Objection: Given that this view finds that a self-aware cognition is not generated by itself, how is it that it would be its own object (*karman*, the "object" of a cognitive act, as is typically expressed in the accusative case)?

Prābhākara: No, the question is misdirected. As with (cognition of) things past and future, there is cognition with itself as object ("cognitive object," *viṣaya*), but not cognition with itself as (verbal) object (*karman*, as is typically expressed in the accusative case).

Moreover, although in fact cognition and object are not distinct, objecthood (*viṣayatva*, "intentionality") is possible. For, objecthood is to be understood as (a cognition's being) "capable of self-expression," or as "a peculiarity essential to a cognition."

And it should not be objected that, like a hare's horn, something that is not an object (*karman*) of a cognition does not exist. Sometimes what exists is not illumined.

There is, nevertheless, a sense in which there is (the other type of) "objecthood" (as is typically expressed in the accusative case, *karmatva*): a cognition is "suitable to be itself expressed" by the expression it generates, even though cognition is self-illumining. (The expression serves to articulate the cognitive occurrence as well as the thing cognized such that the cognition is elliptically to be construed as verbal object and the sense of the accusative case.) And suitability for an effect other than such expressibility does not occur (with cognition), even in the case of (a cognition of) a pot, for that would violate our position on the property "cognizedness" (which does not qualify a cognition but only a thing known, such as a pot).

A cognition born of a connection (of an object) with a sense organ independently of another cognition is a *perceptual* cognition. Thus, every cognition that is generated by a connection between self and *manas* independently of another cognition is a perception with respect to itself.

And (contrary to what you Naiyāyikas hold) a perception of an entity as qualified is not produced by cognition of the qualifier. For, that would violate our position concerning "indeterminate perception" (which we do not accept).

Alternatively (as a concession to your Naiyāyika position, let us say that) perception is a cognition that is not generated by another cognition that is (adding the qualification you desire) a determinate cognition. Thus, a cognition of an entity qualified by (e.g.) a universal—i.e., a cognition generated (according to you) by a (preceding) indeterminate cognition—would be a perception. But (then) a perception would not be (by definition) a cognition that has as its chief instrumental cause (*karaṇa*) a sense organ, etc., because even without that (sensory cause) there is self-illumination in the case of inferential cognitions and the like. Having a sense organ, etc., as a cause is, nevertheless, a cause of precisely a *thing*'s illumination (not also of a cognition itself), since only in that respect is there generation through such a relational cause.

Comments

Cognitions of things past and future have objects only in the sense of presentational content. Clearly, these are not objects of acts. Cognitions are acts, according to our reading of the Prābhākara in this stretch of Gaṅgeśa's text. But a cognition is not directed toward itself as object of an act, though it is its own object in the sense of including itself as presentational content. Thus we have a first line of response to the alleged predicament that on the Prābhākara view a cognition, as something illumined, should be an "object," *karman*, in the sense of an object of a cognitive act, as would typically be expressed in the accusative case (also called *karman*, the "objective case").

But there is a connection, the Prābhākara continues, between being a "cognitive object" (*viṣaya*) and being a "verbal object" (*karman*) in the sense of being appropriately expressed in the accusative case, even for the cognition itself: every cognition as cognitive object of itself is "suitable for expression" and, indeed, at least elliptically expressed in whatever verbalization the cognition results in. Thus when someone looking at a flower says, "That's a lotus," the fact that the person is cognizing not only the locus but also the lotus-cognition is understood. This point connects with that about the possibility of memory: being self-illumined makes it possible to remember a cognition as it does also to talk about it.

Now, normally an act, e.g., cooking, alters its object, e.g., rice. Cognitive acts do alter objects such as a pot, generating a new attribute, namely, cognizedness. But that new property, cognizedness, does not come to qualify the cognition, too. Cognitions are different. Cognition is responsible equally for the suitability of self-expression subject-wise ("*I* am cognizing a pot"), thing-wise ("I am cognizing a *pot*), and even act-wise ("I *am cognizing* a pot"). But cognition does not alter itself as known, whereas it does alter a pot in establishing the attribute, "having been cognized."

The Prābhākara rejects indeterminate cognition, holding that an individual property-possessor and one or more properties possessed are simultaneously cognized. The Nyāya view, in contrast, is that (in the appropriate circumstances) an indeterminate perception of a property, e.g., cowhood, is a causal factor in generating a a determinate perception of an entity as qualified, e.g., "That is a cow." Here the Prābhākara exploits asymmetries in the Naiyāyika posit relative to other planks of the Nyāya theory, such as the definition of perception. The Prābhākara then takes the opportunity to explain perception in his own terms.

A final note. The relation between apperception and indeterminate perception is an obscure area of Nyāya. Indeterminate perception is the main topic of the following section, and Gaṅgeśa tries to explain the relation at the end of the *siddhânta* of this one, which commences now. Gaṅgeśa will now defend his own position by rebutting most of the arguments put forth in support of the self-illumination view.

Text (p. 847, Tirupati, and p. 793, Calcutta) and Translation

> atra ucyate | pratyakṣaṃ na sva-prakāśe pramāṇam, vyavasāyānām idam ahaṃ jānāmi ity-ākārâ-siddheḥ | na ca evam anubhava-virodhaḥ, artha-niścayena pravṛtty-ādi-darśanāt | vyavasāyasya artha-viṣayatva-mātram anubhūyate na tu sva-viṣayatvam api, gauraveṇa tasya sva-viṣaya-bhānatayā pravṛtty-a-hetutvāt | anubhavo 'pi idaṃ rajatam ity-ādy eva | na ca evam idam ahaṃ jānāmi ity-anubhavâpalāpe upekṣaṇīyatā | vyavasāyôttara-kālaṃ tad-upagamāt, idaṃ rajataṃ ity-ādi-laukikânubhavāt vyavasāyasya tad-ākāratāṃ niṣedhāmo na tv anuvyavasāyasya |

Gaṅgeśa: Here we answer. Perception does not prove self-illumination, because it has not been shown that first or non-apperceptive cognitions (*vyavasāya*) take the form, "I am cognizing this."

And there is not in this way opposition to experience, since it is seen that effort and the like occur upon a clear determination of an object (as goal). Only so much is experienced, namely, that a first (or non-apperceptive, ordinary, determinate) cognition has a thing (*artha*) as object (*viṣaya*), not its having itself as object (*viṣaya*), too. The more cumbersome position is to hold that a cognition's illumination includes itself as object, since having itself as object is not a cause of effort to act. The experience, moreover, is simply "This is silver" and the like (not, "I am cognizing silver").

Nor is this (our Nyāya contention) to be ignored because we neglect to talk about the experience, "I am cognizing this." Since we accept that (only) at a time after a cognition has occurred is its occurrence known, we deny that ordinary cognition has that form: the common experience is, "This is silver," etc. (with no mention of cognition). But we do not deny that an apperception (*anuvyavasāya*) is like that (namely, typically expressed as "I am cognizing this"—and so we do not neglect to talk about this sort of experience and statement).

Comments

Gaṅgeśa first attacks the proposition that perception establishes cognitive self-illumination by questioning the Prābhākara position phenomenologically: it has not been shown that every perceptual awareness—no matter what its object—would be properly and precisely expressed using the first-person pronoun and a cognitive verb, "I am cognizing such and such." The point draws on the feeling we have of being absorbed in objects with no awareness that we are aware. Thus, "This is a pot," can express a perceptual awareness where there is no awareness of awareness but only of a pot.

Gaṅgeśa supplements the phenomenological appeal with an argument about effort to act. Awareness of an object is all we need to make effort toward it, not also awareness of awareness or awareness of self. Thus the Naiyāyika position is also the more economical view.

Next we have a counterargument to the effect that Gaṅgeśa and Nyāya are overlooking the evidence of people's (quite commonly) saying, "I *am cognizing* such and such." This is fended off through the reminder that it is precisely an apperception that is verbalized like that according to Nyāya.

Text (p. 847, Tirupati) and Translation

nanu bhinnânuvyavasāye 'n-avasthānāt vyavasāya eva anuvyavasāya iti cet, tarhi para-prakāśe bādhakāt sva-prakāśatva-siddhau sarva-pratītīnām idam ahaṃ jānāmi ity-ākāratā-siddhiḥ | tathā ca sva-prakāśatvâ-siddhau sarva-pratītīnām idam ahaṃ jānāmi ity-ākāratvam a-siddham iti na sā pratītiḥ sva-prakāśe pramāṇam | api ca kriyāyāḥ kṛter vā samavāyitvaṃ kartṛtvam, para-samaveta-kriyā-phala-śālitvaṃ karaṇa-vyāpāra-viṣayatvaṃ vā karmatvam, dhātv-arthatvam anyad vā kriyātvam, idam ahaṃ jānāmi iti vyavasāye na bhāsate, tad-bodhakêndriya-saṃnikarṣâbhāvāt | kiṃ tu idaṃ-viṣayaka-jñānatva-viśiṣṭasya jñānasya vaiśiṣṭyam ātmani bhāsate | na ca sva-prakāśe vyavasāye tādṛśaṃ svasya vaiśiṣṭyaṃ bhāsitum arhati, pūrvaṃ viśeṣaṇasya tasya a-jñānāt | tasmād idam ahaṃ jānāmi iti na vyavasāyaḥ, kiṃ tva anuvyavasāyaḥ |

Objection (by a Prābhākara): Since, given a distinct apperception (distinct from a previous cognition understood as its object), there would be an infinite regress, every cognition is to be understood as itself an apperception.

Gaṅgeśa: Then, self-illumination being established by this ruling out of other-illumination, it would be established that all cognitions have to be of the form, "I am cognizing this." And, by the same token, if self-illumination is not established, then that all cognitions have to be of the form, "I am cognizing this," would not be established. Therefore, this cognition (the cognition or thesis that cognitions take such a form) is not itself proof of self-illumination.

Furthermore (on your view) to be a (cognitive) agent is to be that in which a (cognitive) action, or will to act, inheres. To be an "object" (*karman*, of a cognitive act as expressible as the direct object of a cognitive verb) is to have the character of being the fruit (or effect) of the action that inheres in the other (the agent). Or, it is to be an object (*viṣaya*) of the employment of a chief instrumental cause (*karaṇa*). The meaning of the verb (that would be used to express the act) is the (cognitive) action, or it is something else—(on your view where every cognition would be properly and precisely verbalized as) "I am cognizing this." But all this does not appear in a first or ordinary cognition, because no sensory connection could make it known.

Moreover, the being (doubly) qualified on the part of a cognition—its being qualified both by its being a cognition and by its having a "this" as an object—would have to appear in a self. And such qualifiedness as a relation with itself cannot appear in a first or ordinary (non-apperceptive) awareness understood as self-illumining, because previously those qualifiers have not been cognized. Therefore, "I am cognizing this" is not a first awareness, but rather a subsequent apperception.

Comments

Gaṅgeśa dispatches the Prābhākara's best arguments, with the exception of the infinite-regress charge. He will answer that a bit below.

His first argument is that it begs the question to argue that the thesis that all cognitions take a self-illumining form ("I am cognizing this") proves self-illumination. To be sure, that thesis would have to be true given the truth of self-illumination. But it is no separate argument. Thus there is only the infinite-regress eliminative argument in favor of the Prābhākara view.

Just beneath the surface of Gaṅgeśa's opening response there is sarcasm about the Prābhākara argumentation. The fact that the Prābhākara is *arguing* for self-illumination means that at least one cognition does not have the form, "I am cognizing this." The position is itself obviously not self-illumined if that would entail "self-proved." Though only suggested, the parody recalls the rout of the intrinsic-veridicality view in the opening section on veridicality, and such self-refutation will be charged explicitly a little later.

The Mīmāṃsaka terms of analysis that Gaṅgeśa uses in his second paragraph can be clarified with a less controversial example. In the case of the true statement, "Caitra is going to the village," Caitra is the agent, the going is the action, and the village the object of the action, all according to Mīmāṃsaka ontology as well as Sanskrit grammatical categories. The Prābhākara tries to assimilate a view of perception to this structure of agent-act-object (self-cognizing-thing) as properly and precisely expressed as "I am cognizing this." However, there can be no *sensory connection* of an action with itself as inhering in the agent, the self. So how could a cognizing be a perceiving with respect to itself?

Perhaps, then, the Prābhākara takes the "self" or "I" part of the cognitive object to be what the cognition as chief instrumental cause (*karaṇa*) works on. That a cognition is its own *pramāṇa* would be understood on analogy to the stock example of a forester cutting wood with an axe. The *karaṇa*, the axe, has the cutting as its operation, and the object of the operation is the wood. For cognitive presentation of "self," a cognition would be its own *karaṇa*, and it would itself be the object of itself as such an operation. Nevertheless, the basic problem remains, for, again, how could there be sensory connection with all that? The process of perception begins in the world, with stimulation of a sensory organ.

Finally, neither of a perception's putative cognitive qualifiers, (a) its presenting-of-a-particular-this and (b) its being-a-cognition, can be known to qualify an occurrent perception because until the cognition occurs they are not available. As qualifiers through which a qualificandum would be known they are unavailable in advance of their qualificandum which would be the knowing itself. They need to be have been cognized indeterminately, but they arise only with the determinate knowing and so cannot be its objects. This is an important and contentious point, and in the next passage the Prābhākara responds by giving a slightly different analysis of qualifiedness.

Text (p. 848, Tirupati) and Translation

> syād etat | kartṛtvâdi-jñāna-vaiśiṣṭyam ātmani mā jñāyi, vyavahārasya sva-viṣayaka-jñāna-sādhyatva-siddhau tad eva jñānaṃ sva-viṣayakaṃ kalpyate lāghavāt | jñāna-vitti-vedya ātmā api tad-viṣaya ity ātma-viṣayatvaṃ sarva-vittīnām iti cet, na | sva-janakêndriya-saṃnikarṣân-āśrayatvena svasya svâ-viṣayatvāt, viṣayatva-niyāmakêndriya-saṃnikarṣâder a-bhāve sva-viṣayatvân-upapatteḥ, kāraṇaṃ vinā kāryân-utpādāt, pratyakṣa-janakasya pratyakṣa-viṣayatvân-upapatteś ca | ātma-dharma-pratyāsatty-an-āśraye pratyakṣa-viṣayatāyā janakatva-vyāptatvāt | jñānasya pratyakṣatvena indriya-saṃnikarṣâśrayatvāt manas-saṃnikarṣa-janyatvena mānasatvam |

Objection (by the Prābhākara): That may be. So don't think of the qualifiedness as appearing in a self, that is, don't think that way of a cognition's being qualified by its being-a-cognition-with-an-agent-etc. What should be held is the simpler position that a cognition has itself as object—in the sense required by the established fact that conventional expression can be explained by a cognition having itself as object.

Let me add that "self" is to be known as cognition of cognition. Thus is it an object of that. Self is an object, therefore, of every cognition.

Gaṅgeśa: No, your view is wrong. A cognition is not a locus of a sensory connection generating itself. So, a cognition does not have itself as object (*viṣaya*, that to which a cognition's intentionality is directed). In the absence of anything like a sensory connection regulating cognitive objecthood, self-objecthood is impossible. Without a cause, an effect is not produced. And perceptual objecthood cannot occur without something being produced perceptually. For, given that a cognition is no locus of a sensory relationality with psychological properties (among which would number cognition itself), being-a-perceptual-object is co-extensive with being-a-(perception)-generator.

Inasmuch as a (target) cognition is perceptible in being able to stand as a locus of a sensory connection, apperception is mediated by the *manas* in that an apperception would be produced by a sensory connection with a *manas* (the "internal organ").

Comments

Gaṅgeśa's opponent responds that the subtleties of his view are unappreciated. And he tries to show that his commitments are narrower than Gaṅgeśa has alleged. In particular, it is misleading to imply that "self" would be a locus whose cognition would require a mysterious sensory connection. It is, rather, "cognition of cognition." An ambiguity in "self-illumination"—"self" as (a) cognition or (b) the self, the person or agent—is thus resolved in favor of the former, and the Prābhākara has in effect reduced his "threefold" objecthood view down to a twofold view.

But Gaṅgeśa insists that causal requirements cannot be met in the case of a perceptual "self-presentation" or self-objecthood even so understood. All veridical perceptual objecthood arises out of a connection with a sense organ. Indeed, all perceptual objecthood so arises since the non-veridical is parasitic on the veridical (through the operation of memory which is itself formed by previous perception), as we have seen. The point cuts all the more sharply against the Prābhākara who does not accept the possibility of cognition that is non-veridical. So *a fortiori* "perceptual objecthood cannot occur without something being produced perceptually" by that very thing, or objective complex (an "entity as qualified"), that the objecthood is about or directed to. This passage draws on the heart of Gaṅgeśa's causal realism. The Prābhākara theory not only fails to show what the connection is in the case of the "I" or cognitive-act objecthood presumed; the Prābhākara must fail in that the logic of sensory connection precludes perceptual self-objecthood. For, nothing can be its own cause. There is an information flow, so to say, through the sensory connection, and cognition of *x* is a result of connection with *x*. A target cognition is a cause of an apperception by being the value of the variable, by being that with which there is sensory connection. An apperception is therefore said to be *manas*-mediated, the *manas* being the sense organ.

Text (p. 849, Tirupati) and Translation

tad ayaṃ prayogaḥ, vivādâdhyāsitam indriya-janyaṃ jñānaṃ na etaj-jñāna-viṣayam[2] etaj-janakêndriya-saṃnikarṣân-āśrayatvāt etad-a-janakatvād vā a-saṃnikṛṣṭa-vat | na etaj-jñāna-viṣayakaṃ vā ātma-dharma-pratyāsatty-an-āśrayatve sati etad-a-janyatve ca sati sākṣātkāritvāt | pratyakṣa-viṣayo jñānaṃ sva-pratyakṣa-janakêndriya-saṃnikarṣâśrayaḥ pratyakṣa-viṣayatvād iti manas-saṃnikarṣa-grāhyam | cākṣuṣaṃ jñānaṃ na cakṣur-janya-jñāna-viṣayaḥ, cakṣur-a-saṃnikṛṣṭatvāt ghaṭa-vat | jñānaṃ prameyam eva iti vyāpti-jñānaṃ jñānatva-pratyāsattyā sva-viṣayam | īśvara-jñānam a-hetukatvena sarva-viṣayatvāt sva-prakāśam |

(**Gaṅgeśa** continues:) Therefore, the inferential demonstration is as follows. A cognition *C* which is produced by the senses—the subject of our dispute—is not the object of *C* (alternatively, is not the locus of the objecthood of *C*[3]) that very cognition, *since C* could not be a locus of a sensory connection productive of *C*, that very cognition, or *since C* does not produce that, like anything not standing in a sensory connection.

Or, given that *C* is not a locus of a perceptual connection with any psychological property—as well as that *C* is not to be produced by *C*—*C* does not have *C*, that very cognition, as object, *since* it is an immediate experience.

A cognition becomes a perceptual object (*viṣaya*) by being a locus of a sensory connection that produces perception of itself, because (sometimes) a cognition is a perceptual object. Therefore, such a cognition would itself be grasped through a sensory connection with the internal organ (*manas*).

A visual cognition cannot be the object of a cognition generated by the visual organ, *since* it cannot be in connection with the visual organ, (un)like a pot.

(There are some cognitions that do include themselves as object. They are exceptions. For example) "Cognition is knowable in every instance," is a cognition of a pervasion (between cognition and knowability) that has itself as object, through the (special) connectiveness (characteristic of knowledge of unexperienced instances of universals, in this case) of (the universal) cognitionhood. (And) God's cognition as uncaused is self-illumining, since it has everything as object.

Comments

Here Gaṅgeśa formalizes his arguments that center on perception requiring connection with a sense organ. Parallels, similar cases, he implies, urge us to take his side. All perception involves sensory connection. A visual cognition cannot apperceive visual cognition, because a cognition is never in the appropriate contact with the organ of sight. We do not see seeings as we see pots. Different sense organs are involved and different types of connection, but sensory connection there is in every case. Therefore, no cognition can grasp itself perceptually—with two very special exceptions—because an impossible sensory connection would have to stand as a cause.

Gaṅgeśa does acknowledge a couple of cases of cognition having itself as object, specifically (a) the cognition that every cognition is knowable and (b) God's cognition. The sensory connectedness known as *sāmānya-lakṣaṇā*, operative with respect to unexperienced instances of a universal, is what he refers to in the first case. The cognizing cognition, which is itself a knowable, would be self-cognized as an instance of knowability. God's omniscience, in the second case, is said to be exempt from the causal requirement, and is self-aware.

Next, Gaṅgeśa responds to the infinite-regress argument which is also given a clever twist.

Text (p. 850, Tirupati) and Translation

> nanu para-prakāśakatve jñānam eva na sidhyet an-avasthānād iti dharmi-grāhaka-mānāt sva-prakāśatva-siddhau an-anya-gatikatayā svasya a-saṃnikṛṣṭasya api pratyakṣa-viṣayatvam, ato dharmi-grāhaka-māna-bādhitās tvadīya-hetava iti cet, na | vitter a-vaśya-vedyatvâ-bhāvena an-avasthā-vigamāt | saṃyukta-samavāyena mano-vedyatvâ-bhāvād apekṣanīyântarâ-bhāvāc ca utpannā eva kuto na a-vaśya-vedyā iti cet, na | sukhâdi-tad-buddhy-ādi-sāmagryā pratibandhāt, viṣayântara-saṃcāra-darśanena tasyā balavattvāt anubhavād iti kecit |

Objection: On the other-illumined view, because of (attendant threat of) infinite regress no cognition could be known or established, inasmuch as other-illumination would require a grasping of (cognition as) a property-bearer (i.e., cognition would have to be grasped as an inferential subject for "other-illumination" to proceed). Therefore, the self-illumining view is proved as the only available option—in spite of the fact that a cognition as its own perceptual object is not sensorily connected with itself. Hence, your reasons are blocked (or defeated) by the evidence that there is grasping of cognition as a property-bearer (i.e., by the thesis, which you accept, that cognition is itself known).

Gaṅgeśa: No, that's wrong. For, the (alleged) infinite regress is avoided due to the fact that a cognition need not necessarily be cognized.

Objection: (On your view) a cognition, which is not necessarily cognized, arises through inhering in that which is in contact with a *manas* (namely, a self). But it does so in the absence of another cognition being necessarily depended upon. So why is it not necessarily cognized (as we say) just then (when it arises)?

Gaṅgeśa: No. Awareness of a cognition may be prevented by a collection of causal conditions productive of pleasure or the like or awareness of it and so forth (dominating one's attention). Also, some say (simply) that such awareness of a (prior) cognition does not arise because (some other) causal conditions are stronger, as is commonly seen in distraction towards some other object.

Comments

The alleged regress does not get started because apperception following a perception is strictly optional or circumstantial and often there is no call to apperceive. And it would be the rare apperception where there would be a push for it to be apperceived. In the background is the supplementary argument that a non-apperceived cognition is sufficient, nevertheless, to guide action.

Pleasure seems a good example of a cognitive object the strength of whose presentation could prevent apperception. Pleasure can be so thoroughly absorbing that we are aware of nothing else. Thus the example helps us to see that it is simply not the case that our cognitions are always self-aware.

Text (p. 851, Tirupati, and p. 799, Calcutta) and Translation

> yogyâtma-viśeṣa-guṇatvāt jñānatvāt jñānaṃ pratyakṣam eva iti vyāpteḥ vitter a-vaśya-vedyatvena sva-prakāśatvam iti cet, na | vyāpter a-siddheḥ, para-prakāśakatve 'n-avasthānāt | sva-prakāśe kāraṇân-upapatteḥ saṃnikṛṣṭam eva pratyakṣaṃ tad-viṣaya-janyam eva pratyakṣam iti vyāpteś ca | anyathā kāraṇaṃ vinā kāryân-utpatti-vyāpter vinigamakaṃ kāraṇa-sattve 'pi pratibandhāt kāryân-utpāde kāraṇatvam a-pratyūhyam | kḷpta-kāraṇaṃ vinā kāryôtpāde kāraṇatā-bhaṅgaḥ kāryân-utpādaś ca | api ca para-prakāśe 'n-avasthānāt pariśeṣânumānena jñānasya sva-prakāśatvaṃ | tathā ca sva-prakāśatvânumiter api sva-prakāśatvam anumity-antara-gamyam evaṃ tasya api ity an-avasthā sva-prakāśatvânumiti-paramparā-dvārā tava api syāt | viṣayântara-saṃcārasya pratibandhakatvaṃ yāvaj-jijñāsaṃ vā sva-prakāśatvânumitir iti yadi, tulye para-prakāśatve 'pi | na ca jñānaṃ sva-prakāśam ity anumityā sva-prakāśatvam api sāmānya-pratyāsattyā viṣayīkṛtam iti vācyam | parataḥ-pakṣe 'pi tulyatvāt tvayā tad-an-abhyupagamāc ca |

Objection: Inasmuch as a cognition is a specific quality of a self—a quality fit to be perceived—a cognition is indeed perceived, *since* it is a cognition. Because of this pervasion relationship, a cognition, as necessarily cognized, is self-illumining.

Gaṅgeśa: No. Such pervasion is not established, since, if such (self-)illumination would occur through another, there *would be* an infinite regress. And if it would be illumined through itself, it could have no cause. Only that which stands in a sensory relation is perceptual. Only that which is produced "having that" (object that stands in a sensory relation) as object is perceptual—there is such pervasion, too. Otherwise, (if there could be self-illumination as an effect without a sensory relation as cause, then) since no effect occurs without a cause—which is another pervasion—the option (for you) would be (no better than) a view of interrupted causality, such that an effect would not arise upon the occurrence of its causes because of (unexplained) blockage. Furthermore, if an effect is to arise without its usual causes, then causality becomes a hopeless mess and (known) effects would not arise.

And you have argued that an eliminative inference establishes cognition as self-illumining, with our "other-illumining" view falling to an infinite regress. And (yet) likewise, because there is also (on your side you yourself say) an inferential awareness of self-illumination, self-illumination is inferred *by another*, by an inferential awareness. Thus, it too (would need to be known by another inferential awareness). So, an infinite regress would occur according to your own lights, by way of a series of inferential awarenesses required to establish self-illumination.

If you were to say that the series could be blocked by distraction towards another object, or that inferential awareness of self-illumination would occur only insofar as there were (a question about it and thus) a desire to know it, then we would reply that these positions are equally available to us on our other-illumination view (to disarm the regress you allege).

Objection: Through an inferential awareness to the effect that a cognition is self-illumining, self-illumination, too, is becomes an object by way of the sensory relationality operative in the case of (unexperienced) instances of a universal.

Gaṅgeśa: That move should not be tried. For, it, too, is available to us on our other-illumination view, whereas you (Prābhākaras) do not accept such a relation.

Comments

The infinite-regress argument is a two-edged sword—or one-edged, injuring not the Naiyāyika but the Prābhākara, since the Naiyāyika can explain why some cognitions are not cognized and nevertheless guide action. If the Prābhākara would avoid the regress on psychological grounds R, that same R would be available as part of the Naiyāyika's explanation why some cognitions are not themselves cognized.

Moreover, the Prābhākara view, not the Naiyāyika, makes a mess of how we think about perception causally, as has been stressed all along.

In his second paragraph of response, Gaṅgeśa repeats an earlier argument, this time with a different yet still telling example. How would the cognition, "Cognition is self-illumining," be proved? It is not, by the very occurrence of our dispute, self-established, says Gaṅgeśa. If it is to be established by argument, then it is *by another* established.

Text (p. 851, Tirupati) and Translation

kiṃ ca anumity-ādau jāti-saṃkarān na tava pratyakṣatvam | na ca jñāna-sāpekṣaṃ mano janakam ity anumiti-viṣaya-vad ātmani na tat pratyakṣam | tasya sva-viṣayatve jñânân-apekṣā iti cet, na | jñānaṃ jñāna-janyaṃ, tac ca sva-viṣaye svâtmany ekam eva iti kathaṃ tad-apekṣaṃ tad-an-apekṣam ca viruddhatvāt | na ca jñāna-bhinna-viṣayatvaṃ sāpekṣam, tathātve bahir-jñānaṃ pratyakṣaṃ na syāt |

(**Gaṅgeśa** continues:) Moreover, with regard to inferential and other non-perceptual awarenesses, (one and same awareness would have to be both perceptual and non-perceptual, i.e.) there would be a cross-sectioning of universals (between, e.g., between being-a-perception and being-an-inferential-awareness). Thus, there could be no (genuine) being-a-perception (on your account).

And an internal organ (*manas*) in generating (a perceptual awareness of an inferential cognition) cannot operate *depending on* a (prior) cognition (since it would have to do two things at once). Thus, like the object of an inferential awareness, the cognition generated could not be perceptual with respect to itself.

Objection (by a Prābhākara): (That's right in part.) Concerning itself as object, an inferential awareness works making itself known independently of another cognition.

Gaṅgeśa: No. Such cognition (inferential awareness) is produced by another cognition. Given (on your view) both its own object (e.g., something as fiery) and itself as object, it is (nonetheless) to be just a single cognition. How, then, is it to be both dependent on another and not dependent? The two are incompatible.

Furthermore, it is not dependent (only) in the sense that it has as object something that is distinct from cognition. On such a view, no cognition of an external thing would be perceptual.

Comments

According to the Prābhākara, every cognition *qua* cognition is perceptual in the sense that it itself is immediately cognized. Gaṅgeśa uses the word *pratyakṣa* in the sense of both awareness and *pramāṇa*, but in all usages the word carries a sense, from its etymology, of the presence of the object "before the eyes." The contrast is with the inferential object which is said to be *parokṣa*, "beyond the eyes," i.e., not present in the immediate environment. Gaṅgeśa argues that the Prābhākara view of self-illumination involves in this way a confusion of a basic cognitive division (a "cross-sectioning of universals," a confusion of kinds) in that a single inferential awareness would have to be viewed as having as object both something known "right here" and something not.

Concerning inferential awarenesses, the Prābhākara holds that of the three factors cognized—an object (e.g., fire on a mountain), a cognition (the inferential awareness itself), and a self—the object is, of course, not known immediately. Only the inferential awareness, *qua* a cognitive act, along with a self, is known immediately. Gaṅgeśa responds that even in that restricted sense an inferential awareness could not be self-illumined, since its having an object cannot at once be dependent on a cognition—a perceptual presentation that sparks the inference—and independent.

On the Prābhākara view, the triply faceted inferential cognition is said to be perceptual with respect to itself and non-perceptual insofar as it depends on a prior perception, e.g., of smoke, or, more precisely, of a locus exhibiting a property as pervaded by another. But how is such dependence on another cognition to be characterized? Not in terms of having an object distinct from the cognition itself—though the "thing" part seems to be in this way different from the "I" and the "cognizing" parts—because, if the *inferential* part of the cognition were to be differentiated in that manner, there would be, properly speaking, no *perception* of external objects, since of course an external object cognized is distinct from the cognizing cognition. The predicament is that no external-object cognition could be counted perceptual.

Text (p. 852, Tirupati, and p. 801, Calcutta) and Translation

> atha anyasya anya-viṣayatve saṃnikarṣâdir niyāmakaḥ, sva-viṣayatve kiṃ tena, an-atiprasaṅgāt saṃnikarṣasya an-anugamāc ca | vyavahāre śaktatvaṃ viṣayatvam a-bhede saṃnikarṣaṃ vinā api iti cet, na | anyatra pratyakṣa-mātre saṃnikarṣasya hetutvāt, anyathā an-anugamâpattiḥ | atha yā vittiḥ na vedyā sā pramāṇâ-bhāvād a-satī iti tad-adhīna-sattvasya viṣaya-paryantasya a-sattvaṃ syād iti cet, na | a-virala-lagna-tad-vitti-vitti-dhārā na abhyupeyate | kiṃ nāma kenacit kadācit kācid vittir vyavahāra-smaraṇa-liṅgâdinā pratīyata iti sarvā pramāṇa-siddhā eva ity abhyupagamāt |

Objection (by the Prābhākara): Look, sensory connections et cetera regulate cognition in cases of one thing (a cognition) having another (an external object) as object. But with respect to a cognition's having itself as object, what would be the use of that? For, not only is there no untoward ramification on our view, there is also no correlation (between being an immediate or perceptual presentation and being dependent on a sensory connection). With respect to common linguistic usage, a cognition's "having power" (to generate and ground usage about itself as well as about an exterior object) is no different from a cognition's "objecthood," whether or not there is sensory connection.

Gaṅgeśa: No. For, a sensory connection (invariably) stands as a cause of, specifically, perception of (what you call) "another" (namely, awareness of something other than the cognizing cognition itself). Otherwise, there would be the problem of lack of uniformity (in nature and in theory).

Objection (by the Prābhākara): A cognition that is not cognized does not (or, is not to be taken to) exist, because there would be no evidence. Non-existence would hold for that whose existence would depend on such (evidence), reaching as far as its objects (if the cognition were not itself cognized).

Gaṅgeśa: No. We do not accept an uninterrupted series of cognitions of cognitions of something or other. Rather, by someone, sometimes, *some* cognitions are cognized through such characteristic marks as a linguistic expression or a remembering (indicating a prior awareness). It is only in such ways that every cognition (that is shown by evidence) is shown by evidence—this is our view.

Comments

Gaṅgeśa occasionally uses the term *anugama*, "uniformity"—often rendered as "experience of a consecutive character"—for a law of nature. Perception depends invariably on a sensory connection. There can be no sensory connection on the Prābhākara view of cognition of cognition, which, therefore, could not rightly be called perception. Jayadeva says that this as Gaṅgeśa's principal argument (p. 801: *mūla-yukti*).

In his second response of the passage, Gaṅgeśa repeats his phenomenological contention that often a person is not aware of being aware (of whatever). He also suggests an analogy through his reference to such inferential "marks as a linguistic expression": as speech and other behavior are objective signs of another's cognition which is only sometimes by others cognized, so also only given certain circumstances is a person herself provoked to an awareness of her own awareness. As another's cognition need not be cognized or shown by evidence, so, indeed, one's own cognition need not be apperceived.

Text (p. 853, Tirupati) and Translation

> atha syād eva yadi ghaṭo 'yaṃ ghaṭam ahaṃ jānāmi ity ato 'dhikā ghaṭavad-vitti-dhārā-vāhi-viṣaya-śata-bhāra-mantharā kācid vittir asmad-āder utpadyamānā anubhūyate | na ca evam, iti cet, na | anuvyavasāyo viṣaya-mātra-nirūpyaḥ, na tu tad-viṣaya-paraṃ-parā-nirūpyo gauravāt | tathā ca jñāna-jñānatvena sarvā vittir asmad-āder utpadyamānā anubhūyata eva | na ca evam a-nirmokṣaḥ | yoga-ja-dharma-pratyāsattyā sāmānya-lakṣaṇayā vā vyāpti-jñāna-rūpasya an-anuvyavasāyasya api sva-viṣayatvâbhyupagamāt |

Objection (by the Prābhākara): That may be, if a cognition arising of the following sort were to be experienced by us, you, or anyone: a cognition exceedingly slow (to arise), burdened by hundreds of objects in carrying along a series of previous cognitions with (say) a pot as indicated and more, in this fashion, "This is a pot," "I am cognizing a pot," ("I am aware that I am cognizing a pot," etc.). However, it is not so.

Gaṅgeśa: No (this response is ill-conceived). An apperception is determined by its object alone. It is not determined by a series of objects of such (previous cognitions). For, that would be a cumbersome view.

And, likewise, all such cognition (i.e., all apperception) arising is indeed experienced by us, you, or anyone, as cognition of cognition (not as self-illumining or as cognition of cognition of cognition, etc.).

Moreover, there is not in this way an infinite regress. For (among the reasons why there is no regress) we accept that there can be (in certain cases) self-inclusive cognitive objecthood even with non-apperceptive cognitions in the form of a cognition of a (self-inclusive) pervasion (that is perceptual) either by way of an (extraordinary) sensory connection involving cognitive abilities born of yogic practice or by way of that characteristic of cognition of unexperienced instances of universals.

Comments

Gaṅgeśa generalizes one of the exceptions he gave above to the Nyāya position of "other-illumination," here in the context of yet another way a cognitive regress may be avoided. "Everything is knowable" and other self-referential cognitions have an *extraordinary* connection as a cause, not one of the six types of *ordinary* sensory connection. On extraordinary connections, see the glossary entry, *a-laukika-saṃnikarṣa*, p. 685.

Text (p. 854, Tirupati) and Translation

na ca tad-vyavahāra-śaktatvaṃ tad-viṣayatvam | tad-viṣayatvena tad-vyavahāra-kāraṇatva-grahe sati tac-chaktatva-jñānam, tac-chaktatvaṃ ca tad-viṣayatvam ity anyonyâśrayāt, kāraṇatva-grahaṃ vinā śakter a-grahāt, tvan-mate 'pi rajata-jñānasya śukti-viṣayatvâpatteś ca | rajatârthi-pravṛttau rajata-jñānaṃ hetuḥ, na tu tad-avacchedakam ity uktatvāt | lāghavena sva-viṣaye pravartakatvam, sarvair eva ādya-pravṛttau tathâvagamād iti cet, hanta evam anyathā-khyātir astu, na tu anyathā-siddhi-rajata-jñānasya a-pravartakatvam iti |

(**Gaṅgeśa** continues:) And "having x as object" (x-objecthood) is not equivalent to "being empowered to express x." For, (you say) grasping what causes an expression of x is to have x as object—given this, there would be (you say) a cognition empowered to express x, while the empowerment to express x is to have x as object: thus you commit the fallacy of mutual dependence, since, without a grasping of what stands as the cause, there would be no grasping of the empowerment.

And also, on your view, there is the difficulty that an (illusory) cognition of silver can have mother-of-pearl as object. With respect to the effort of someone intent on picking up a piece of silver, cognition of silver is a cause, as has been explained, not a specifier of the causality (contrary to what you Prābhākaras say).

Objection (by the Prābhākara): It is simpler to hold that a cognition provokes effort to act with respect to its own object, since in every instance it is so understood with respect to an initial effort.

Gaṅgeśa: Look here, what you have said, well, it may as well be called (the view of error we Naiyāyikas espouse, namely) that of "presentation of something as other than it is." But it is not the case (in fact it is a howler to say) that the impelling on the part of a cognition of silver holds only with that cognition as causally irrelevant.

Comments

Having ϕ as object may be necessary but it is not sufficient for empowerment to express ϕ (in the appropriate sense of "express"), since very young children and the mute, who have cognitions, lack necessary physical skills for expression. Furthermore, the Prābhākara view suffers from the "mutual dependence" that Gaṅgeśa makes plain.

Perceptual illusion presents the Prābhākara with the difficulty, regarding his self-illumination thesis, of a divorce between cognitive objecthood and the direction of effort to act, as we saw in the earlier section. On the Prābhākara analysis, a mother-of-pearl presentation is self-illuminingly known—mother-of-pearl (a mere "this" in front), the cognition itself, and a self as all made known therein or thereby—with the silver mistake due to a separate cognition, a remembering of silverness, and a failure to notice the difference between the two. However, as here Gaṅgeśa again points out, effort flows out of a cognition of silver taken to be perceptual, in that one who desires silver mistakenly reaches out to pick up mother-of-pearl.

Text (p. 803, Calcutta) and Translation

etena yathā tad-guṇa-saṃvijñāna-bahuvrīhi-siddhaṃ kuṭâdi-padam a-śakyam api kuṭam ādāya eva pradhānam anya-padârthaṃ bodhayati tathā jñānam a-viṣayam apy ātmānam ādāya eva sva-viṣaye vyavahāraṃ karoti saṃskāraṃ ca | sva-janya-vyavahāra-viṣaye jñānasya saṃskāra-janakatvāt | sva-janya-vyavahāra-viṣayaḥ svâtmā viṣayaś ca iti prācīnaṃ guru-matam apāstam | anyatra lāghavena jñānasya sva-viṣaye vyavahāra-saṃskāra-janakatva-kalpanāt sva-viṣaye svâtmani vyavahāra-saṃskārâ-janakatvāt | vyavahāra-saṃskārayoḥ sva-viṣaya-jñāna-sādhyatvena svâ-viṣayaka-jñānâ-sādhyatvāt |

Objection (by the Prābhākara): The word *kuṭ-ādi* (appearing in Pāṇiṇi) is known as an example of the type of *bahuvrīhi* compound whose meaning includes the property mentioned. While the word is incapable of expressing (the meaning of the verbal root *kuṭ* directly), still, taking *kuṭ* as the (verbal) class, which is the compound's primary or principal meaning, it makes known that other sense (namely, *kuṭ* as the particular verbal root, "to break"). Just likewise, a cognition, although not having itself as (cognitive) object, does indeed, taking itself (as verbal object), produce speech about itself as object, and it produces a memory-impression as well. For, a cognition generates a memory-impression of an object of the speech that is generated by itself.

Gaṅgeśa: By previous reasoning, this the Old Prābhākara view is rejected.

Taking other considerations into account, we see that the simpler view is to imagine that a cognition produces speech and a memory-impression (only) with respect to its object (not with respect to itself). A cognition is not productive of either speech or a memory-impression of itself as object. Speech and a memory-impression are established (only) though a cognition with respect to its object, since what is not a cognition's object cannot be established by the cognition.

Comments

The *sūtra* from Pāṇini is: 1.2.1 (*kuṭ-ādi*).

Another example of a *tad-guṇa-saṃvijñāna bahuvrīhi* compound is: "the long-eared," *lamba-karṇa*, more literally, "he whose ears are long." The compound consists of two words, *lamba*, "long," and *karṇa*, "ear," thus the usage, "a long-eared person." The primary meaning or reference of this as of any *bahuvrīhi* compound would lie outside the individual meanings of the component words. Neither "long" nor "ears" is meant by *lamba-karṇa*. The word is used to refer to a particular person who has long ears. Now the property, having-long-ears, not only is picked out to indicate the person, there is an attributive sense, too. Thus, the indicator property (unlike the typical "indicator," *upalakṣaṇa*: see below, pp. 642ff) is not just an indicator but also a qualifier. Mentioning the property fixes the referent. In this way there is a contrast with other *bahuvrīhi* compounds. As qualifying the person, the long ears are also meant when he is referred to. The Prābhākara would thus have a rough analogy for his double or triple faceted type of cognitive self-illumination.

In brief, the view of the older Prābhākara faction—as Gaṅgeśa labels it here—is that cognition produces speech behavior about itself as well as its object without having itself as *cognitive* object. There is, then, no need to posit an apperception to explain *talk* about cognition. Gaṅgeśa says he disagrees—principally, it seems, for reasons of theoretical economy but also, he says, because typically we do not remember cognitions but objects, the indications of prior cognitions, not the cognitions themselves, and, by implication, cognitions only when they have been previously apperceived. (The phenomenon of ''blind sight''—a person's ability to recognize something he or she does not remember experiencing—appears to favor the Nyāya position. The fact that we can remember so much experience shows only that often we do apperceive. Indifference and other cognitive attitudes seem responsible for blind sight.)

Text (p. 854, Tirupati) and Translation

> nanu jñānasya mānasatve kathaṃ jānāmi iti viśiṣṭa-buddhiḥ jñānatva-nirvikalpaka-janya-jñāna-kṣaṇe viśeṣyâ-bhāvena pratyakṣân-utpatter iti cet, na | jñāna-nāśa-kṣaṇa eva jñāne jñānatva-viśiṣṭa-buddhiḥ viśeṣyasya pūrva-kṣaṇa-sattvāt | pratyakṣe sva-samaya-vartitayā gauraveṇa viśeṣyasya a-hetutvāt | jānāmi iti vartamānatvena sthūla upādhir bhāsate na tu kṣaṇaḥ, tasya atīndriyatvāt | tato jñāna-viśiṣṭa-buddhir ātmani viśeṣaṇa-jñānasya pūrva-sattvāt | viśeṣaṇaṃ ca na viśiṣṭa-pratyaya-hetuḥ gauravāt, kiṃ tu taj-jñānam, āvaśyakatvāt | ata eva tattāṃ vinā api tad-buddheḥ pratyabhijñā |

Objection: If a cognition is cognized through the mediation of the *manas*, how could the cognition, ''I am cognizing,'' arise as a qualificative cognition? The (qualifier) cognitionhood, which would be indeterminately grasped, would produce (according to you) the cognition (the apperceptive perception). Cognitionhood at the time of the (later, apperceptive) cognition would be without a (locus or) qualificandum (since the previous cognition would be gone). Thus, no such perception could arise.

Gaṅgeśa: No. Even though the (target) cognition has been destroyed at the time (of the apperception), a cognition of an entity qualified by cognitionhood can occur because that qualificandum (the cognition that is apperceived) exists at the preceding moment. For, it would be cumbersome to hold that a qualificandum not existing at the (precise) time of a perception could not be a cause of the perception (as in general it would be cumbersome to require a cause to exist at the same time as its effect, as opposed to immediately before).

(Furthermore) the present time that figures in ''I am cognizing'' (with the verb in the present tense) appears as a ''thick'' time interval (to be broadly construed), not as the precise current instant (*kṣaṇa*). For, the latter is beyond the range of what can be sensed.

After that (after a first apperception, a second, i.e.) a cognition of an entity (a self) qualified by (the first apperception, i.e., by) a cognition occurs, because cognition (the first apperception) of the qualifier (viz., the original, non-apperceptive cognition) exists in the self (immediately) previously. And the qualifier (the original, non-apperceptive cognition with its objecthood) is not a cause of the (second apperceptive) cognition of an entity as qualified, as that would be a cumbersome view. Rather, cognition (the first apperceptive cognition) of the qualifier is a cause, since it is required.

Thus, indeed, even without a thatness (as a cause), recognition of a that occurs (as in "This is *that* Devadatta I saw yesterday") through a *cognition* of the that (as a cause).

Comments

A cognitionhood qualifier could not have the requisite grounding in something cognized, says the objector, because an indeterminate cognition, on the Nyāya view, would stand between a supposedly apperceived cognition and an apperception. Cognition is momentary, and only one cognition occurs at a time. So there would be no target cognition available to be apperceived—other than the indeterminate cognition, which, Nyāya holds, is the one type of cognition that cannot be apperceived. In other words, since even an apperception begins as an indeterminate cognition—as a direct awareness of a qualifier, to wit, cognitionhood—the problem is that there would be available no qualificandum to be cognized, no locus of the cognitionhood. The determinate cognition can arise only after the indeterminate cognition,

But a time-lag in perceptual processes is acceptable, Gaṅgeśa responds. With causal relationships in general, an effect does not require its causes to exist at the same time it does but only immediately before. Thus, there is no rule that an object of a perception, which is one of its causes, and the perception itself have to occur at exactly the same time. Moreover, cognition endures for more than a point instant: a target cognition passes away as an indeterminate cognition arises, with an instant of overlap. The apperceived and the apperception do not overlap, but they are contiguous. In sum, there is no causal problem.

Again, the momentariness of cognition is not to be interpreted literally. For, a point instant of time, *kṣaṇa*, is an imperceptible interval, whereas a cognition can be perceived (i.e., apperceived). There is, so to say, cognitive spread. Nevertheless, perception is immediate. It occurs in the present. But in pointing this out, we refer not to an infinitesimal interval but to gross or "thick" time, as Gaṅgeśa says.

Then our author announces a rather surprising thesis. Such an apperception as "*I* am cognizing such and such" is, Gaṅgeśa implies, dependent on a prior *ap*perception that, strictly speaking, would take the form, "Such and such is being cognized" (with no *I* as explicitly an object). "*I* am cognizing such and such" expresses a second apperception. Thus there would be the following series: first, a non-apperceptive cognition, "A pot," second, an indeterminate cognition of its cognitionhood, third, an apperception of the original, non-apperceptive cognition as a cognition qualified by its object, "A pot is being cognized,'' and fourth and finally, a second apperception with a self as explicitly its object, ''I am cognizing a pot.'' The qualificandum portion of the objecthood of the first apperception would be the original, non-apperceptive cognition, and the qualificandum portion of the objecthood of the second would be a self, an entity that endures, the locus of the entire cognitive stream.

But now there are two cognitions standing between the final apperception and that part of its objecthood that is the original, non-apperceptive cognition of, e.g., a pot. This problem is resolved by a view of the causal sequence that is much like the story told with recognition. Recognition is prompted in its ''thatness'' porition not by the reality that is the qualifier but by a cognition of the qualifier; similarly, an original target cognition, though destroyed, would be a qualifier cognized by a first apperceptive cognition that gives rise to a second and becomes its object complete with its objecthood, carrying along its objecthood, so to say. Thus the fourth cognition, ''I am cognizing a pot,'' is able to present the objecthood of the first, the original non-apperceptive cognition, ''A pot,'' by means of a cognitive intermediary.

Text (p. 855, Tirupati) and Translation

> yat tu vyavasāya-nāśa-kṣaṇôtpanna-vyavasāyântare jñānatva-viśiṣṭa-buddhir iti | tan na | tad-dhetor a-bhāvāt | anuminomi ity-ādāv anuvyavasāye anumititvâ-bhāvāc ca | yad vā jñānaṃ jñānatvaṃ ca nirvikalpake bhāsate tato jñānatva-vaiśiṣṭyaṃ jñāne jñāna-vaiśiṣṭyaṃ ca ātmani bhāsate | viśeṣye viśeṣaṇam, viśeṣaṇe viśeṣaṇântaraṃ ca bhāsata ity eva hi viśiṣṭa-vaiśiṣṭyârthaḥ |

Objection: (The problem of the perceptual availability of cognitionhood is to be solved differently, since, as you imply, a cognition lasts for two instants.) Given another first-level, non-apperceptive cognition, produced at the moment of the destruction of a (prior) non-apperceptive cognition, then there can occur (with an indeterminate cognition intervening, overlapping the last instant of the first non-apperceptive cognition and the first of the second) a cognition of an entity qualified by cognitionhood.

Gaṅgeśa: Wrong. For, one of the causes of such a cognition would be absent (namely, cognition of the qualifier). And, with respect to the apperception, ''I *infer* (such and such),'' or the like, there would be no inferencehood (available to be apperceived).

Or (according to some) a cognition and cognitionhood are (both) presented in an indeterminate awareness (without their relationality being presented, at a second instant, immediately following the target cognition). Thereafter (at a third instant), qualificative relationality to the cognitionhood is presented in an (apperceptive) cognition as well as a self's qualificative relationality to the cognition (such that a self, a cognition, and its object would all appear in a first apperception, "I am cognizing such and such," as opposed to a second apperception being required). A qualifier (a target cognition as a cognition) appears as occurring in a qualificandum (a self), and another qualifier (the objecthood of the target cognition) appears in the qualifier (the target). For thus, indeed, would we have the meaning of a qualified entity as again qualified.

Comments

The objector's picture would have the virtue of an immediately preceding non-apperceptive cognition—presumably identical to a first non-apperceptive cognition except for its place in the series—standing as the required locus for the cognitionhood that is grasped. Gaṅgeśa's response is brief but telling. He finds a cognitive stream, running: target cognition$_1$ (C_1), indeterminate cognition$_2$ of C_1's cognitionhood, apperceptive cognition$_3$ of C_1, apperceptive cognition$_4$ of C_3 as a qualifier of a self as qualificandum. There is a thick temporal link analyzable as a first instant of C_3 overlapping the last instant of C_2 and contiguous with C_1 whose last instant overlaps the first instant of C_2. Both C_1 and C_2 are causes of C_3. A similar story is to be told for C_2 through C_4, except that C_3, being an apperception with C_1 as object, preserves, so to say, the presentational objecthood of C_1 into C_4. The main problem with the objector's proposal is that such objecthood would be lost, since there would be no apperceptive link in a series that ran from C_1 to C_4.

A second refutation trades on a distinction between perception and inferential awareness. A series of perceptions of the same thing, "Pot," "Pot," "Pot," and so on, are each veridical cognitions, according to Nyāya. There is, however, no similar series of veridical inferential cognitions, "Fire on the mountain," and so on, since the second concluding would commit the fallacy of "establishing what is already proved," *siddha-sādhana*. (One doesn't want to waste one's time or another's. And one does not need to make a second inference to proceed to act.) The second rejoinder that Gaṅgeśa makes in the passage at hand is that the objector's cognitive picture would not allow apperception of an inferential awareness, "I am inferring such and such," because the second non-apperceptive cognition could not be an inferential awareness, unlike the case with perception. Thus having another first-level cognition available might help for the availability of cognitionhood, also of perceptionhood, but not of inferencehood.

Just how Gaṅgeśa himself looks at the matter of apperception of an inferential awareness is, however, not clear. And he himself asserts, in the next passage, the unavailability of inferencehood.

The alternative view presented in the last paragraph does not receive Gaṅgeśa's endorsement, but neither is it refuted (at least not explicitly). An indeterminate cognition would grasp a prior cognition itself as well as its cognitionhood, but the qualificative relationality—of the prior cognition's cognitionhood to the cognition itself—would not be cognized until a following apperception arose. Thus the verbalization of a first apperception, occurring as the third member of a series, not the fourth, would appropriately include a reference to an I, as in "*I* am cognizing such and such."

Text (p. 856, Tirupati) and Translation

vastutas tu jñānam a-bhāva iva viśiṣṭa-jñāna-viṣaya eva, anuvyavasāyasya viṣaya-rūpa-viśeṣaṇa-viṣayaka-vyavasāya-sādhyatvena viśiṣṭa-jñāna-sāmagrī-sattvāt | jñānatvam api tatra bhāsate taj-jñāna-sāmagrī-sattvāt | aṃśe tat saprakārakaṃ niṣprakārakaṃ ca iti nara-siṃhâkāram | tatra eva viśiṣṭa-jñāne jñānatva-vaiśiṣṭyaṃ bhāsate | anuminomi ity-ādau tu na tathā, anuvyavasāye 'numititvâ-bhāvād iti |

(**Gaṅgeśa** continues:) But in fact a cognition (as identified by its objecthood), like an absence, can only be an object of a cognition of an entity as qualified (i.e., it cannot be the object of an indeterminate cognition). An apperception is produced by a non-apperceptive cognition (enduring for two instants) whose object is (for the apperception) the cognition's qualifier taking the form of the object (of the non-apperceptive cognition) inasmuch as the causal complex sufficient to produce such a qualificative cognition includes it. Cognitionhood is also presented there (in the apperception), in that an (indeterminate) cognition of cognitionhood is among the causes in the complex sufficient to produce the (determinate) cognition of it. In part, an apperception's object is (determinate in that it is) possessed of predication content, and (in part) it is (indeterminate in that it is) lacking predication content (as simply an occurrent cognition grasped as a cognition). Thus, it is (dual in nature as though it were) in form the man-lion (manifestation of Viṣṇu). There indeed in the (apperceptive) cognition of (a cognition as) a qualified entity, a qualificative relationality with cognitionhood appears.

But regarding such (apperceptions) as "I am inferring (such and such)," the case is different. In such apperception (there would be no such cognition of inferencehood because) inferencehood would be unavailable.

Comments

An absential perception may be fed by an indeterminate cognition of a qualifier, such as *on-the-floor*, but there is no indeterminate cognition of an absence itself. The absence, e.g., of a pot on the floor, would be, properly speaking, the qualificandum that the absential perception determined. (The mind converts "on-the-floor" from qualifier to locus.) Similarly, the qualificandum determined by an apperception—the thing it cognizes, a determinate cognition, namely—is not cognized indeterminately although its cognitionhood is cognized indeterminately.

The cognitionhood, which is not an object of the cognition itself, appears in the apperception along with the original cognition's objecthood. Thus, an apperception is dual in nature, having a target with its objecthood as apperceptive object, and having the same target simply as a cognition as apperceptive object as well. Gaṅgeśa suggests the criticism of a confusion of kinds ("cross-sectioning") when he uses the image of the "man-lion" form of Viṣṇu. But apparently that is not a fault when a dual nature is arrived at, as here, by cogent reasoning. The point gets elaborated at the end of the next section, on indeterminate cognition: see, below, p. 639.

However, there is an outstanding problem, which is mentioned in the last line of the text. Consider the cognitive series where an original cognition_1 is an inferential awareness (C_1), "Fire on the mountain": C_1, then indeterminate cognition_2 of C_1's inferencehood, and then apperceptive cognition_3 of C_1. But, unlike the case with perception and its perceptionhood or any cognition and its cognitionhood where there can be a perceptual or cognitive stream, a second inference would commit the fallacy of "proving what is already established." So, by the time we got to C_4, which could be verbalized as "*I* am inferring fire on the mountain," C_1 would have entirely passed away and could not be grasped. As we saw just above, the qualificandum that C_4 would determine would be a self, an entity that endures. But whereas C_3, which is the qualifier that C_4 would cognize as belonging to a self, would be a cognition such that its cognitionhood could stand in for the cognitionhood of C_1, C_3 in an inferential apperceptive series would not be another inferential awareness but just a cognition, indeed, a perception, a mental perception of an inferential awareness. The original inferential awareness's objecthood could be passed on through the apperception, C_3. But the nature of the cognition as an inferential awareness, which would appear to be an object of C_4 ("I am *inferring* such and such"), would be simply unavailable. Probably, the brief remark on inferencehood here at the end should be read as an acknowledgement of the problem with no solution implied.

atha nirvikalpaka-vāda

NOW, **DISCOURSE ON INDETERMINATE PERCEPTION**

Text (p. 857, Tirupati, and p. 809, Calcutta) and Translation

> tac ca pratyakṣaṃ dvi-vidham nirvikalpakaṃ savikalpakaṃ ca iti | tatra nāma-jāty-ādi-yojanā-rahitaṃ vaiśiṣṭyân-avagāhi niṣprakārakaṃ nirvikalpakam |

Gaṅgeśa: And perception is of two sorts, indeterminate and determinate.

Of the two, the indeterminate does not have (as object) the tie to name, universal, and so on (having which a perception is determinate); it does not grasp a qualificative relationality; and it is without predication content.

Comments[1]

In wide perspective, the purpose of the theory of indeterminate perception seems to be to maintain the position that, despite illusion (and the arguments of Buddhist subjectivists), there are perceptual instances where *all* the information presented comes from the object perceived, that nothing comes from the side of the subject, such that the view of cognition as "having form of itself" (*sākāra-vāda*) is clearly wrong. To find an instance of this for purposes of refutation of subjectivism, we cannot turn to recognitions ("This is that Devadatta") or to complex perceptions ("The person is a staff-bearer") where, albeit the perceptions are veridical, a prior determinate perception (of Devadatta or the staff) provides content through the workings of memory or of a special cognitive relationality. For we, too, admit that recognitions are infused with content by activation of a latent memory-impression, *saṃskāra*, which is something seemingly "subjective," on the side of the subject. And complex perceptions (including illusions or errors) also, we admit, require subjective elements to be explained. But with a first-time perception of, for example, a cow, nothing on the side of consciousness could provide the object. Cowhood is provided by a direct sensory connection with the thing as it is in the world. Cowhood causes an indeterminate perception that has it as its object.

There is, however, no direct, apperceptive evidence for *nirvikalpaka pratyakṣa*. Rather, by force of the following inference as the first step of a two-step argument it is to be *postulated*: "The perceptual cognition, 'A cow' (for example), is generated by a cognition of the qualifier, *since* it is a cognition of an entity as qualified (by that qualifier appearing), like an inferential awareness.'' The second step takes a person's first perception of an individual (Bessie, let us say) as a cow (i.e., as having some such property) as the perceptual cognition figuring as the inference's subject such that the cognizer's memory not informed by previous cow experience could not possibly provide the qualifier, cowhood. The qualifier has to be available, and the best candidate is its perception in the raw, a qualifier (cowhood), that is to say, not (as some are wont to misinterpret the point) as divorced from its qualificandum (Bessie) but rather as neither divorced nor joined, and, furthermore, not as qualified by another qualifier (such as, being-a-heifer) but rather just the plain, unadorned entity. In the particular example, the entity is the universal, cowhood, or being-a-cow, though, again, it would not be grasped as a universal or as anything except itself.

Gaṅgeśa's argument would maintain a causal uniformity among *pramāṇa*-generated cognitions of an entity as qualified. A law strikes us as we survey veridical cognitions and the processes that generate them: a cognition of an entity as qualified has a prior cognition of the qualifier counting among its causes, among the conditions individually necessary and together sufficient for bringing it about. But this presents a problem: if anything that is known through a qualifier presented as predication content requires a prior cognition of the qualifier, will there not be a vicious regress of prior cognitions required? The answer is no. Indeterminate perception blocks such a threat. The qualifier itself is not known through another qualifier, *ad infinitum*, but is grasped directly. In indeterminate perception, the qualifier is not cognized as a qualifier. Indeterminate perception is not a cognition of an entity as qualified, where a qualificandum is cognized as qualified by a qualifier. It has no predication content.

Finally, we may mention a distinct line of reflection that though not much developed by Gaṅgeśa in this section feeds the view that determinate perception is a cognizing of a qualificandum qualified by a qualifier where the qualifier is provided by a prior cognition: things have multiple properties some of which normally go undetected on any given occasion of experience. If I can touch what I saw, for example, then when I am only touching the thing, I normally will not be aware of the thing's color perceptually. If the ontological layering of things and their qualifiers were not reflected in the causal ordering that has the qualificandum known through knowledge of one or more of its properties, properties that are already known, then perception of a qualificandum should entail that the ''thick'' particular be presented, the thing with all of its properties, and, as Gaṅgeśa pointed out in the section on inherence—above, pp. 391—92—a blind person in touching a yellow cloth would know its yellow color.

These considerations notwithstanding, indeterminate perception is acknowledged by Gaṅgeśa to be a theoretical posit for which the evidence is indirect and systemic. It is worth repeating that it is not itself perceptible; indeed, it is the only type of cognition that cannot be apperceived. This section is consumed by examination of the reasons for the posit, against the backdrop of a *pūrvapakṣin* rejection of it. Apparently, all perception is, in this opponent's view, determinate, i.e., of an entitied as qualified (*savikalpaka-jñāna* = *viśiṣṭa-jñāna*).[2]

The evidence suggests that Gaṅgeśa has a Prābhākara in mind as his *pūrvapakṣin*, specifically the view of error indicated. Moreover, at the end of the distinctly Prābhākara *pūrva-pakṣa* of the last section, on apperception, a rejection of indeterminate cognition was announced (above, pp. 586ff), as it is again in the next chapter's section on the sensory relationality operative in knowledge of particulars through perception of a universal (the *sāmānya-lakṣaṇā-prakaraṇa*, Tirupati II, pp. 234–35). However, there is a historical source for attributing to the Prābhākara school an acceptance of a kind of indeterminate perception, namely, Śālīkanātha Miśra,[3] though elsewhere, in the heat of refuting Buddhists (who hold that all perception is indeterminate) Śālīkanātha exclaims that that there is no raw perception and implies that all perception is determinate.[4] Probably this was a disputed topic among Prābhākaras, with different groups taking different positions and offering different arguments. All things considered, Gaṅgeśa does pretty clearly identify rejection of indeterminate perception—and acceptance of all perception as determinate—with the Prābhākara camp in general. On the other hand, here, unlike in a dozen *pūrva-pakṣa*s elsewhere approximately, he does not mention the Mīmāṃsaka faction by name or by epithet (the *guru*, etc.). And at places this Prābhākara sounds very much like a renegade Naiyāyika citing positions central to Nyāya to argue that there is no perception that is indeterminate. All perception is of an entity as qualified; all cognition is of an entity as qualified.

That the *pūrvapakṣin* could be a renegade or reform-minded Naiyāyika finds further support from the fact that within Nyāya tradition indeterminate perception is a latecomer. Gautama, the *sūtra* author, Vātsyānana, and Uddyotakara, whose writings form the core of the Old school, do not recognize an indeterminate type of perception. Vācaspati Miśra (c. 950) introduces the notion into the system. Gaṅgeśa is clearly aware of this history, for he opens his discussion by echoing Vācaspati's commentary on *Nyāya-sūtra* 1.1.4 where, as discussed in the section on defining perception, Vācaspati takes the two words *a-vyapadeśyam* ("non-verbal") and *vyavasāyâtmakam* ("definite") as indicating two types of perception, indeterminate and determinate. Udayana and later Naiyāyikas follow him, but there seems to have been some dissension.

Text and Translation

nanu jñānatvaṃ savikalpaka-bhinna-vṛtti ity atra kiṃ mānam | na pratyakṣam, asiddheḥ, atīndriyatvâbhyupagamāc ca | na ca vyavahāraḥ, tasya savikalpaka-sādhyatvāt | na api na vivecitaṃ pūrvam adhunā vivecayāmi ity-anubhava-pramāṇakāv ālocana-vikalpau, bahu-viśeṣaṇa-jñānâ-jñānābhyāṃ tad-upapatteḥ |

Pūrvapakṣin: What is the evidence that a cognition can be anything other than determinate? It is not perception, for it is not established that perception can do that and your own position is that indeterminate perception is beyond the range of the senses.

Moreover, it is not the way we talk (that establishes indeterminate perception), since that (verbalization) is accomplished through determinate awareness (alone).

Also, the (common introspective) experience, "I now discern distinctly this (qualifier) not previously discerned (by me just previously)," which shows two cognitions (in succession), is no evidence that there is a bare looking at (*ālocana*) and then a determinate perception. For that (introspective datum) can be explained by cognition or non-cognition (of a particular qualifier) of something with many qualifiers.

Comments

According to Nyāya, indeterminate cognition is a posit made for systemic reasons, as mentioned, and it is held that perceptually founded verbalization requires determinate perception. So, indeterminate perception is founded neither in perception nor in everyday speech.

The last argument rejected is not obviously a failure. Something perceived, e.g., a pot, has properties that go unnoticed on any given occasion. Without a change in perception—without new sensory activity—one notices a qualifier not previously distinctly discerned. This suggests that the qualifier was formerly perceived indistinctly, i.e., indeterminately. The *pūrvapakṣin* rebuts the argument by pointing out that not all of a thing's qualifiers are perceived. That is, the phenomenon of previously unnoticed information can be accounted for by the fact that no (determinate) cognition grasps all the qualifiers of an object. That there be non-cognition of one qualifier belonging to an object is compatible with cognition of another belonging to the same object. Other causes are to be identified for changes in the sensory flow of information, such as attention and focus.

Text (p. 809, Calcutta) and Translation

nanu gaur iti pratyakṣaṃ viśeṣaṇa-jñāna-janyam, viśiṣṭa-jñānatvāt anumiti-vad iti | atha viśeṣaṇa-viśeṣya-jñāna-sāmagrītaḥ sākāṅkṣôbhaya-viṣayam ekaṃ viśiṣṭa-jñānam | tatra pratyakṣe yogyêndriya-saṃnikarṣāt, anumitau pakṣa-dharmatā-balāt vyāpakatvâvacchedaka-prakāreṇa, śābde yogyatâdi-vaśāt padârthatâvacchedaka-rūpeṇa a-pūrvam eva viśeṣaṇaṃ bhāsate, upamitāv apy eva iti na kvâpi viśeṣaṇa-jñānaṃ janakam | na ca pratyabhijñāyāṃ tattânubhavas tathā | tattânubhave 'pi saṃskārasya an-udbodhāt, vilopād vā pratyabhijñānân-utpādena udbuddhaḥ saṃskāra eva pratyāsattitayā viśeṣaṇa-jñānârtham indriya-sahakārī | surabhi candanam ity-ādāv api viśeṣaṇa-jñānârthaṃ taj-jñānaṃ pratyāsatti-sthānīyam indriya-sahakāri | bhramo viśiṣṭa-jñānam eva na asti iti cet |

Objection (by a Naiyāyika proponent of indeterminate perception, presenting an inference that Gaṅgeśa accepts): The perceptual cognition, "A cow," is generated by an (indeterminate) cognition of the qualifier, *since* it is a cognition of an entity as qualified, like an inferential awareness.

Pūrvapakṣin: (No.) Cognition of an entity as qualified—which comes about as the result of the totality of causes of cognition of the qualifier and what it qualifies—is single and unified, and has as object both (the qualifier and what it qualifies) in a relation of mutual expectation (each requiring the other). Concerning it (i.e., concerning subtypes of cognition of an entity as qualified), perception arises from a sensory connection with an object that is fit (to be perceived). Inferential awareness arises by force of an (inference-provoking) property possessed by (a locus that is) the subject of the inference—predication content that is specified by being pervaded (by another property, namely, that which is to be inferred). Knowledge acquired from trustfully understood words involves a qualifier, not previously cognized (as qualifying a particular object), being made manifest by force of semantic fitness and so forth (present in a speech act), as specifying the meaning of the words. And analogical comprehension as well involves such indeed (i.e., both a qualifier and what it qualifies). Nowhere is there an (independent) cognition of a qualifier that is generative (of a cognition of an entity as qualified by that qualifier, and thus nowhere a preceding indeterminate perception).

Moreover, experience of thatness in the case of a recognition (as in "This is *that* Devadatta") is not so (i.e., does not have an indeterminate perception as a cause). Since a recognition does not arise if the memory-impression is not awakened or if it is destroyed even though an experience of thatness has occurred, the awakened memory-impression is the sensory connector and a causal auxiliary coördinate with the sense organ (an indeterminate perception does not play this role).

Also in the case of such cognitions as, "Fragrant sandalwood" (known by vision alone), the requirement that there be cognition of the qualifier is (satisfied by) a cognition of that (the fragrance, without, however, an indeterminate perception); the cognition (itself) would function as the (extraordinary) operative connection; it would be an auxiliary cause aiding the sense organ.

(Finally) error is not a cognition of an entity as qualified at all (but rather a failure to cognize two cognitions as distinct).

Comments

The *pūrvapakṣin* contends that the causal complex that gives rise to a cognition of a cow as an individual property-possessor is the same causal complex that gives rise to cognition of cowhood. And this surely seems plausible on Naiyāyika premises: a sense organ would be in contact with an individual in which cowhood inhered. Furthermore, the *pūrvapakṣin*'s analysis of the cognitive qualification relation seems tidier than Gaṅgeśa's own. That is, the predication content and the qualificandum portions of a cognition carry "mutual expectation" (*ākāṅkṣā*). Neither can be independently cognized since each requires a complement, like a transitive verb that requires a direct object. This would be something like the syntactical "expectation" recognized as an "excellence" for testimony as a knowledge source.

Another argument is that no other type of veridical cognition has indeterminate cognition as a cause. In fact, not just all varieties of veridical cognition conform to the (Prābhākara) *pūrvapakṣin*'s analysis, all cognitions do. Error, or illusion, may appear to be an exception, since the qualifier and qualificandum portions being divorced—their objecthoods residing in no single qualified entity—would seem to be cognized separately (with, therefore, no "mutual expectation"). But error is not a cognition at all—on the Prābhākara "omission" view. It is a certain type of failure to cognize.

Text (p. 858, Tirupati) and Translation

ucyate | sādhya-prasiddhi-padârthôpasthiti-vācyatva-jñāna-tattânubhavānām anumity-ādi-hetutvam | sādhya-prasiddhy-ādikaṃ vinā anumity-āder a-saṃbhavāt | sādhyâdikaṃ ca viśeṣaṇam iti taj-jñānam anumity-ādi-hetuḥ | yady api anumity-ādikaṃ prati sādhyâdi-viśeṣaṇa-jñānatvena na kāraṇatā | tathā api viśiṣṭa-jñāna-mātraṃ prati viśeṣaṇa-jñānatvena kāraṇatā, bādhakâ-bhāvāt |

Gaṅgeśa: We answer. Inferential awareness and so on (verbal knowledge, analogy, and recognition) have causes (severally) in a familiarity with a probandum (as pervading a prover given perceptually), memory of the meaning of words, cognition of significance, and experience of thatness. For, without familiarity with a probandum and so on, inferential awareness and so on would be impossible. Moreover, the probandum and so on stands as the qualifier (through which a qualificandum is cognized throughout this entire range of cognition). Therefore, a cognition of that (the qualifier) is a cause of inferential awareness and so on (and thus we expect this regularity to occur with perception, too).

Cognition of the probandum and so on as the qualifier (through which a qualificandum is known) need not be taken as a cause of inferential awarenesses and so on (when such cognitions are known or regarded in some other way than as a cognition of an entity as qualified, to wit, when they are known simply as occurrent cognitions). Nevertheless, concerning precisely (an inferential awareness and so on regarded as) cognitions of entities as qualified, a cognition of the qualifier is a cause. For, there are no countercon- siderations prevailing.

Comments

All cognition of an entity as qualified by a qualifier (F) is generated, in part, by a cognition of the qualifier (F). The examples that Gaṅgeśa clearly means to include are, in addition to (1) the inferential cognitions that he mentions, (2) recognitions (which are a kind of perception), (3) bits of knowledge based on trustfully understood words, and (4) analogical comprehensions. In each case, a prior cognition of the qualifier (F) appearing as predication content is required and thus is identified as a causal factor, a condition that though insufficient in itself to bring about a later determinate cognition with F as predication content is needed for the determinate cognition to occur. "For," as Gaṅgeśa says, "without familiarity with a probandum and so on, inferential awareness and so on would be impossible."

But non-veridical cognitions, too, have a cognition of the qualifier presented as a cause. Indeed, *every* determinate cognition is found to have a cognition of the qualifier as one of its causes. Sometimes in veridical experience memory clearly informs the perception such that the memory-forming prior experience would be a causal factor, such as when we see a piece of distant sandalwood as fragrant without the involvement of the organ of smell. Similarly, in the case of an illusory experience of a rope as a snake ("*a* is a snake"), the snakehood is furnished by memory and previous experience of snakes. In the case of recognitions, too, there is a cognitive causal factor in a remembering of the thing now experienced again. Indeterminate perception of the qualifier is to be posited to maintain causal uniformity in a case when nothing else is able to make the qualifier available. As will be indicated below, an experience of something *a* as an F for the very first time requires indeterminate perception of the qualifier F. Much perception is informed by memory but not all.

So, as a second step in Gaṅgeśa's argument that begins with the observation that a (determinate) perception is a cognition of an entity as qualified, we expect that a first-time perception ("[That's a] cow") to be both caused by a preceding cognition of the qualifier and to differ from the other types of veridical cognition in the precise role the preceding cognition has in the determinate perception's characteristic causal complex. An indeterminate perception of the qualifier provides the qualifier that emerges in the determinate perception as its predication content in some cases. Perceptions of entities as doubly qualified, it will be brought out, also have a cognition of the qualifier as a cause, a determinate cognition. But a perception of a singly qualified entity not previously known in that way requires a prior indeterminate cognition of the qualifier.

In the last paragraph of the passage, Gaṅgeśa makes a disclaimer, reminding us of a principle of causal explanation. Just as an individual may be rightly cognized through any of many diverse properties, one and the same cognition may be viewed differently. And it makes a difference how one is viewed if we are interested in what causes it. It is a central plank of Gaṅgeśa's theory of causal law that cause and effect relationships are specified cognitively. As cooked rice viewed as food has different causes than the same rice viewed as a substance, so also an inferential awareness, for example, viewed as a cognition of an entity as qualified will have a cognition of the qualifier as a cause, while the same cognitive event viewed differently—as a cognition exhibiting cognitionhood—would not be explained in this manner.

Text (p. 859, Tirupati) and Translation

> syād etat | vahnimān ity-ādi-jñānaṃ prati vahni-jñānasya na viśeṣaṇa-jñānatvena kāraṇatā, dravyatvena vahni-jñāne 'pi vahnimān iti jñānâ-bhāvāt | kiṃ tu viśeṣaṇatâvacchedaka-prakāraka-jñānatvena, ato na viśiṣṭa-jñāne viśeṣaṇa-jñānaṃ hetuḥ | viśeṣaṇa-jñānam api tatra asti iti cet, na | tasya atiprasaktatvāt anyathā-siddheś ca | na ca tādṛśa-viśeṣaṇa-jñāna-janyatvaṃ sādhyam, bādhād iti |

Pūrvapakṣin: That may be. (But) such a cognition as "(The mountain is) fire-possessing" is not caused by a cognition of fire as a cognition of the qualifier, since, when fire is (cognized merely as) a substance, no cognition "(The mountain is) fire-possessing" occurs even though there is cognition of fire. Rather the cognition ("The mountain is fire-possessing) is caused by a cognition whose predication content specifies what the qualifier is. Hence, a cognition of the qualifier is not a cause of cognition of an entity as qualified (and your inference to indeterminate perception is flawed).

Should you argue that a cognition of the qualifier is also (a cause) there, you would be wrong. Your thesis would let in too much, and your cause would be irrelevant, too. Further, the probandum (portion of a generated inferential cognition) is not what is generated by a cognition of such and such a qualifier, because of overriding counterconsiderations.

Comments[5]

The generated inferential awareness, "The mountain is fire-possessing," requires a prior cognition of fire. But how precisely is that requirement to be formulated? According to the *pūrvapakṣin*, it should not be formulated by saying so loosely as does Gaṅgeśa that a cognition of the qualifier is a causal factor. Here the mountain is the qualificandum and fire its qualifier as the object of the cognition. But the fire that is actually on the mountain, qualifying it, can be cognized merely as a substance. In that case "cognition of the qualifier" would not stand as a causal factor in the generation of the inferential awareness, "The mountain is *fire*-possessing." So the *pūrvapakṣin* proposes that the principle be formulated so that cognition of fire as fire gets targeted. We say that the causal factor at issue is the cognition whose predication content specifies what the qualifier is in the resultant inferential awareness (it "specifies what the qualifier is"). This is the cognition required for the inferential awareness to arise. Thus a cognition of the qualifier *tout simplement* does not play a causal role, and Gaṅgeśa's inference for indeterminate cognition is not based on proper analogues.

Gaṅgeśa cannot reply that all this is true but a cognition of the qualifier can also be said to be a cause. For, that would overextend to cognitions of fire as a substance, for example. Furthermore, cognition of the qualifier, being-a-substance, is causally irrelevant to the arising of an inferential cognition of a mountain as fire-possessing.

In sum, with the causes of inferential awareness understood differently, the force of Gaṅgeśa's prover, "*since* it is a cognition of an entity as qualified," does not get support from, as claimed, "inferential awareness and the others."

Text (p. 860, Tirupati, and p. 812, Calcutta) and Translation

> tan na | viśiṣṭa-vaiśiṣṭya-jñānaṃ prati hi viśeṣaṇatâvacchedaka-prakārakaṃ jñānaṃ kāraṇam ubhaya-siddham | ato viśiṣṭa-jñāna-mātraṃ prati viśeṣaṇa-jñānaṃ hetuḥ | yad viśeṣayoḥ kārya-kāraṇa-bhāvas tat-sāmānyayor api bādhakaṃ vinā kārya-kāraṇa-bhāva-niyamāt, anyathā sāmānya-kāryôcchedaḥ | na ca atiprasaṅgaḥ, viśeṣa-sāmagrī-viraheṇa tat-tat-kārya-viśeṣân-udayāt | na ca parokṣatvam upādhiḥ | pratyabhijñāyāṃ sādhyâ-vyāpakatvāt | na api viśiṣṭa-viśeṣaṇakatvam, pakṣêtaratvād iti |

Gaṅgeśa: That is incorrect. For, we both accept that a cognition of an entity as qualified by a qualified qualifier (for instance, "A staff-bearer") has as a cause a cognition whose predication content specifies what the qualifier is (for instance, the staff-bearer cognized as a bearer of a staff because of a prior cognition of the staff). (But) then in general a cognition of an entity as qualified has a cognition of the qualifier as a cause.

What holds as a relation of effect and cause between two particulars also holds in general—given no counterconsiderations—because of the regularity of effect-cause relationships. Otherwise, there would be a rupture in the general (train of) effects.

Furthermore, this view does not have too wide an application, since this or that particularly characterized effect does not arise in the absence of its particularly characterized collection of causes.

And *non-immediacy* (or, being-mediate, as an inference is not immediate whereas a perception is) is not an undercutter (*upādhi*) for the inference (given above: "The perceptual cognition, 'A cow,' is generated by an (indeterminate) cognition of the qualifier, *since* it is a cognition of an entity as qualified, like an inferential awareness"). For, with respect to recognitions (which are perceptual and immediate), it (non-immediacy) does not pervade the probandum (and a true undercutter must pervade the probandum).

Nor is having-a-qualified-qualifier an undercutter, since that is an instance of being-other-than-the-subject (when a being-other-than-the-subject is not a genuine undercutter).

Comments

"(That's a) staff" is a cognition of an entity as singly qualified. An object is cognized through the property, or qualifier, staffhood. "(That man is a) staff-bearer" is a multiply qualificative cognition where the qualifier is itself cognized as qualified: a person is cognized not only through the property, or qualifier, of a holding of something but a holding of something that is known as a staff. The *pūrvapakṣin* has admitted that in such cases the predication content of the effect specifies a bit of relevant causality. Well, then, we should say the same thing more generally, to wit, that a prior cognition of a qualifier is a cause. Thus, since some perceptual cognitions are cognitions of an entity as singly or simply qualified, for instance, "A cow," or "(That's a) cow," the same causal principle should be operative, and an indeterminate perception of the qualifier, cowhood, would be a cause—clearly in cases where no cow had been experienced before (such that the qualifier could not be provided by memory) and presumably in other cases, too, as will be explained. "Otherwise, there would be a rupture in the general train of effects."

The inference that Gaṅgeśa has in mind is, again, that any cognition of an entity as qualified has a cognition of a qualifier as a cause, like an inferential awareness. A second step is required to justify a posit of indeterminate perception, namely, that a first-time perceptual determinate cognition of an entity as singly qualified, e.g., "A cow," has an indeterminate cognition of a qualifier as a cause. This second step, partially explicated in the current passage, will be amplified as we proceed.

Now granting that Gaṅgeśa has identified a causal regularity, we may nevertheless wonder whether he has made the appropriate distinctions. In his inference, he cites inferential awareness as a supporting example, but inferential awareness differs from perceptual awareness in not being immediate. Indeed, all of the analogues—testimonial awareness, etc.—seem to contrast with perception in just this way, being non-immediate, such that non-immediacy appears to undercut the inference: it pervades the probandum "has a cognition of the qualifier as a cause'' and fails to pervade the prover in the instance of the inferential subject itself, which is a perceptual cognition.

Gaṅgeśa responds that non-immediacy is not an undercutter (*upādhi*), since a recognition, which is an immediate cognition (''*This* is that Devadatta''), also has a cognition of the qualifier (namely, of the ''that'') as a cause. Thus everything that has a cognition of the qualifier as a cause is not non-immediate; that is to say, the proposed undercutter fails to pervade the probandum. On conditions governing undercutters, see, above, pp. 160–61.

Every cognition of an entity as qualified is a cognition of what is in fact a qualified qualifier: all qualifiers have further qualifiers, minimally, Navyas say—looking at the qualification relation as, in a way, symmetrical—the qualificandum that it qualifies. Therefore, the last proposed undercutter is bogus as equivalent to a particular type of apparent but false *upādhi*. See, above, pp. 161–62, for discussion of the being-other-than-the-subject type of putative undercutter.

Text (p. 860, Tirupati) and Translation

mā evam | tava api smṛti-vat pūrvânubhavasya saṃskāra-dvārā janakatvāt siddha-sādhanāt | na ca a-vyavahita-viśeṣaṇa-jñāna-janyatvaṃ sādhyam, a-prayojakatvāt pratyabhijñā-vat smṛtyā eva upapatter vā | na api tata eva a-vyavahita-viśeṣaṇânubhava-janyatvaṃ sādhyam, a-prasiddheḥ pratyabhijñānâdau vyabhicārāc ca | atha tat-kālôtpanna-rūpâdi-viśiṣṭa-pratyakṣe saṃskārâ-bhāvena smaraṇâ-bhāvāt pakṣa-dharmatā-balena nirvikalpaka-siddhau anyatra api sāmagrī-taulyāt tat-siddhir iti cet, na | pratyutpanna-viśeṣaṇa-sthale hi śuklatvâdi-viśiṣṭa-śukla-vaiśiṣṭya-bodho vā a-viśiṣṭa-tad-viśiṣṭa-bodho vā, ādye śuklatvâdi-smaraṇaṃ prathamam, tataḥ pratyakṣeṇa tad-viśiṣṭa-bodhaḥ tataḥ śuklatvâdi-viśiṣṭa-śukla-vaiśiṣṭya-bodhaḥ dravya iti kim an-upapannam | śuklatvâdi-jāti-smaraṇam eva vā sāmānya-lakṣaṇayā sakala-rūpâdi-viṣayam astu | dvitīye 'n-anubhavaḥ | na hi śuklatvâdi-pratyaya-vilakṣaṇaṃ śukla-rūpâdi-viśiṣṭa-bodhaṃ kaścid anubhavati |

Pūrvapakṣin: It is not so. On your view, too, previous experience is productive (of a recognition) *by means of* a memory-impression, as with memory. Thus (with your inference) you would commit the fallacy of trying to establish what is already accepted (by us who nonetheless do not accept an inference to indeterminate cognition).

And the probandum (in your inference) could not be the (general) productivity of an unmediated cognition of a qualifier, since that is not causative, or the causal role is accounted for simply by memory as with recognition (where an awakened memory-impression formed by a previous experience is directly causative, not such a memory-impression *and* the previous experience, too). Nor (should we think that) for this very reason is productivity by an unmediated experience of a qualifier the probandum (of the inference). For, such productivity is not known, and recognition and the like are counterexamples.

Objection: By force of the (prover) property being possessed by the subject of the inference, indeterminate cognition is proved regarding a perception of an entity as qualified by the likes of color produced at the time (of a particular color perception, not earlier), since (in such a case) there can be no remembering—in that no memory-impression would have been formed. (Then) in other cases, too, it is proved (to have a causal role) in that the total collection of causal factors is similar.

Pūrvapakṣin: No. For, on an occasion of a qualifier so produced, (what would arise would have to be) either (a) a cognition of a bit of white as qualified by whiteness and the rest (being-colored, being-a-quality, and so on), or (b) a cognition of a bit of white not qualified like that.

On the first alternative, a remembering of whiteness, for example, would occur first. From that (i.e., with the remembering as a causal factor), a cognition of white as so qualified would occur by means of perception. (And) from that would occur a cognition of a substance, that is to say, a cognition presenting something as qualified by a bit of white as qualified by whiteness and the rest. What here is impossible (without, that is, an indeterminate perception having a causal role)? Or, let the remembering of a universal, whiteness or the like, have as its object the entirety of such color (all the bits of white in the world) through the relationality characteristic of (knowledge of unexperienced instances of) universals. (A perception of a particular bit of white would normally follow; otherwise. it could not be seen as white.)

On the second alternative (which is a non-starter), there would be no experience (of, e.g., a bit of white). For, no one without cognition of, for example, whiteness has an experience of a cognition of an entity qualified by the color white.

Comments

By concocting an example where apparently memory could not be a causal factor, the *pūrvapakṣin*'s opponent (who is in Gaṅgeśa's camp) would appear to prove that, if a perceptual cognition, e.g., "Something white," is generated by prior cognition of the qualifier, then that prior cognition must be itself indeterminate. For there is no other option. However, the *pūrvapakṣin* retorts that without appreciating the universal we could not see a white thing *as* white, as like other white things we know. And this can be explained either through the causal role of a memory-impression or through the sensory relationality characteristic of knowledge of unexperienced instances of universals (as in knowing, for example, that Bessie's as yet unborn calf will have a dewlap). One of these two factors would fill the causal role posited for an indeterminate perception, with, therefore, no need to assume any such thing.

Text (p. 861, Tirupati, and p. 814, Calcutta) and Translation

atha jāgarâdya-viśiṣṭânubhavo viśeṣaṇa-jñāna-janyo viśiṣṭa-jñānatvāt | na ca tatra saṃskāra-dvārā pūrva-viśeṣaṇânubhavaḥ taj-janya-viśeṣaṇa-smaraṇaṃ vā sambhavati | udbodhakaṃ vinā saṃskārasya smaraṇe viśiṣṭa-bodhe vā sāmarthyâbhāvād ity udbodhakaṃ vaktavyam | udbodhakaṃ ca anyatra jñānaṃ dṛṣṭam iti tad eva vācyam | na ca tad viśiṣṭa-jñānam eva, tatra api viśeṣaṇa-jñānâpekṣāyām an-avasthâpatter ity ālocana-siddhir iti | tan na | saty api jñāne saṃskārân-udbodhāt | yasmāt phalaṃ bhavati sa jñāna-viśeṣas tathā iti cet, na | an-anugatatvāt | yad an-antaraṃ phalaṃ dṛśyate tad eva an-anugatam apy udbodhakaṃ kalpyate phala-balād iti ced, tarhi jāgara-kāraṇân-antaraṃ saṃskārôdbodhe na niyato hetur iti | "sadṛśâ-dṛṣṭa-cintâdyāḥ smṛti-bījasya bodhakā" ity āhuḥ | evaṃ ca praṇidhānâdi-sūtram api saṃgacchate | api ca viśiṣṭa-jñānatvād ity atra vyavacchedyam a-viśiṣṭa-jñānam | tac ca a-prasiddham | siddhau vā vyartham anumānam | jñānatvam ca svato '-siddha-vyāptikaṃ nirvikalpake vyabhicārād an-avasthâpātāc ca |

Objection: An experience of an entity as qualified had at the first moment of waking from sleep is produced by an (indeterminate) cognition of a qualifier, *since* it is a cognition of an entity as qualified.

And in such a case no prior experience of the qualifier (as delivered) by means of a memory-impression is possible, nor in such a case is a remembering generated by a memory-impression possible. For, without a stimulator (or exciter) a memory-impression (lies dormant and) does not have the capacity to produce a remembering or a cognition of an entity as qualified. Hence a stimulator has to be identified. Moreover, in other cases a *cognition* has been found to be the stimulator. Thus, a cognition is precisely that which is to be identified (here). And the stimulator is not a cognition of an entity as qualified, since, given dependence there too on cognition of a qualifier, an infinite regress would be the unfortunate consequence. Hence the establishment of indeterminate perception.

Pūrvapakṣin: That's wrong. For, there is (sometimes) no exciting of a memory-impression although a cognition is present (thus, cognition does not cause such excitation).

Objection: That from which the result ensues is a particular cognition. Such (is then the exciter in the cases where there is the result: it is a necessary but not a sufficient causal factor).

Pūrvapakṣin: No. For, there is no uniformity.

Objection: Just that which is seen immediately to precede a result is to be imagined as—by force of the effect—the stimulator, although it is not uniform.

Pūrvapakṣin: Then, inasmuch as a memory-impression gets excited immediately after whatever causes a person to awake from sleep, let just that be (the stimulator, i.e.,) what causes exciting of memory-impressions (too), since the position is already established. Just for this reason, there is no fixed cause of memory-impressions becoming revived.

(And so) they say, "Similarity, unseen force (i.e., *karman*), thinking, and the like are stimulators of the causes of memory."

Moreover, the *sūtra*s (of the *Yoga-sūtra*) which concern concentration and the like are also in accordance with such (a view, namely, that memory-impressions are excited in a variety of ways).

Furthermore, when you say (in giving your inference), "*since* it is a cognition of an entity as qualified," cognition of an entity as *not* qualified is what is excluded there. But cognition of an entity as not qualified is nowhere found. Or, if it is known, (we would not be debating the matter and) your inference would be pointless. (So, let us reconsider the inference bereft of the useless qualifier, "of an entity as qualified": the prover would be expressed simply as, "*since* it is a cognition.") And being-a-cognition (as the prover) is not by itself pervaded (by the probandum, being-generated-by-a-cognition), because (assuming, as you do, that there is indeterminate perception) there would be a counterexample in indeterminate perception (itself, which is a type of cognition but which is not itself generated by a cognition, according to you) and because there would be the unfortunate ramification of an infinite regress (if indeterminate perception were considered itself to require a cognitive cause).

Comments

Ramanuja Tatacharya says the quotation ("Similarity, unseen force . . .") is to be located somewhere in the vast *alaṃkāra-śāstra*, classical literary criticism, but we have not found it. Among the memory exciters or stimulators mentioned by the *pūrvapakṣin*, similarity is generally said to be the most important for poetry.

Rucidatta elaborates the reference to the *Yoga-sūtra* (p. 862): repetition and other yogic practices destroy *saṃskāra*s, "memory-impressions," which are obstacles to enlightenment. The overall point is that arousal of a memory-impression is triggered by a wide variety of things. Thus, it will not do to focus on a first moment of waking from sleep as a moment free from the possibility of a memory-impression having a causal role in perception. That possibility cannot be ruled out so easily. This exchange is only an opening volley, and Gaṅgeśa will find a better way to eliminate the unwanted possibility by explaining just what could excite a *saṃskāra*.

The *pūrvapakṣin* argues that the expression, "of an entity as qualified," in the disputed inference (viz., "The perceptual cognition, 'A cow,' is generated by an (indeterminate) cognition, *since* it is a cognition *of an entity as qualified*, like an inferential cognition") is useless since its contrary fails to refer anything. And if, on the other hand, we understand it to refer, then we would be wasting everyone's time with the inference: cognitions of entities as not qualified is precisely what indeterminate perceptions are supposed to be.

However, the matter is obviously not already known.

To try to reformulate the inference without the qualifier would be to no avail. For, the pared-down prover would be "being-a-cognition," and not all cognitions have a cognition, according to present company, as a cause. Indeterminate perception itself is precisely the kind of cognition that does not have a cognition in its causal complex, so we are told. And if Naiyāyikas change their minds and say that indeterminate cognitions do too, they are faced with an impossible regress.

Gaṅgeśa will defend the relevance of the qualifier, as we shall see. The remainder of this subsection is focused on the meaning of the expression "a cognition of an entity as qualified" (*viśiṣṭa-jñāna*) as it is used in the crucial inference. Gaṅgeśa's *siddhânta* begins after the *pūrvapakṣin* rejects six attempts at definition—the *pūrvapakṣin* has also one last argument that is new. Then Gaṅgeśa defends the inference, and eventually paries the attacks on the meaningfulness of the expression, "a cognition of an entity as qualified."

Text (p. 862, Tirupati) and Translation

> kiṃ ca viśiṣṭa-jñānatvaṃ na tāvat vastu-gatyā viśeṣaṇa-viśeṣya-viṣayaka-jñānatvam, ālocanena vyabhicārāt | na api viśeṣaṇatva-viṣayakatvam | a-tad-vyāvṛtta-bodha-janaka-jñāna-viṣayatvasya viśeṣaṇatvasya tatra a-prakāśāt | na api vaiśiṣṭya-viṣayaka-jñānatvam | tathā sati gaur iti vikalpe vaiśiṣṭyaṃ viśeṣaṇam ity ālocanasya api tad-viṣayatvena viśiṣṭa-jñānatve an-avasthâpātād iti |

(The **pūrvapakṣin** continues:) Moreover, to be a cognition of an entity as qualified (*viśiṣṭa-jñāna*, i.e., a determinate cognition, *savikalpaka-jñāna*) is not, first of all, to be in effect (D^1) "a cognition that has a qualifier and a qualificandum as object," since (on your own view) indeterminate perception would be a counterexample (since both a qualificandum and a qualifier are objects of indeterminate perception albeit not as related).

Nor is it to be (D^2) "a cognition that has as object something as a qualifier." For, there (in determinate perceptual awareness) nothing is known as a qualifier in the sense that cognition of it generates cognition of exclusion of what is not that (qualifier).

Nor is it to be (D^3) "a cognition whose object is a qualificative relation." If that were the case, the qualificative relation would be the qualifier in a determinate cognition such as, "(That's a) cow." Then (according to you) indeterminate perception would also have that as object. The difficulty is that there would have to be an impossible infinite series of qualificative cognitions (since the qualificational relationality would make any "indeterminate" cognition relational and thus would require, *ex hypothesi*, another "indeterminate" cognition to generate it).

Comments

The reason D[1] fails is apparent. It does not state that a thing cognized (a qualificandum) and what it is cognized as (a qualifier) have to be cognized as related qualificationally. Note that the *pūrvapakṣin*'s rejection of D[1] presupposes a view of indeterminate perception that seems at odds with Gaṅgeśa's own. As he says below, Gaṅgeśa does not himself view any qualificandum as an indeterminate perception's object. Only a qualifier thereby is grasped. But it is a common Navya opinion to view both qualificandum and qualifier as grasped in indeterminate perception, though of course not in relation.[6]

D[2] is obscure but apparently is to be taken to imply that a qualifier must be cognized as a qualifier if there is be cognition of an entity as qualified, (*viśiṣṭa-jñāna*, sometimes translated "qualificative cognition"). The *pūrvapakṣin* rejects the definition by asserting that the point of being aware of a qualifier as the particular qualifier it is is to provoke awareness of exclusion of something that is not that. However, when we cognize a cow as a cow, in a determinate perception, we do not thereby become aware of something that is not a cow. Such an exclusion is a relation known by inference, not by perception.

D[3] proposes that the qualificational relation be viewed as intrinsic to the qualifier, such that a cognition of an entity as qualified would present a qualifier as qualifying a qualificandum. The problem is that, according to standard Nyāya theory, the qualificational-relation-cum-qualifier would be directly grasped in indeterminate cognition, thus making it relational and determinate. Thus it would require, again according to the theory, a further cognition to make the qualifier known, *ad infinitum*.

Text (p. 815, Calcutta) and Translation

na api saprakāraka-jñānatvam, prakāraś ca viṣayatā-viśeṣaḥ iti vācyam | jñāna-viṣaya-sva-rūpâtiriktāyā viṣayatāyā a-bhāvāt | na ca viśeṣaṇa-jñāna-janyatvaṃ saprakāratvam | yad-viśeṣaṇa-jñāna-janyaṃ yat sa eva prakāra iti gaur iti vikalpe tasya eva sādhyatvāt, īśvara-jñānasya niṣprakārakatvâpātāc ca | na apy a-tad-vyāvṛtti-viṣayatvaṃ viśiṣṭa-jñānatvam | apoha-vāda-nirāsena gaur iti vikalpe tathātvâ-siddheḥ | na apy a-tad-vyāvṛtti-bodha-janakatvaṃ tat | ālocana-vyāvṛttânugata-rūpam antareṇa a-tad-vyāvṛtta-bodha-janakatvasya grahītum a-śakyatvāt | na ca gaur iti jñānam etad-anya-savikalpakânya-jñāna-bhinnaṃ prameyatvāt, yad vā cakṣuḥ cākṣuṣa-vikalpaka-jñānâtirikta-jñāna-janakam indriyatvād iti tat-siddhiḥ | a-prayojakatvāt, ubhayatra savikalpaka-padân-antaraṃ nirvikalpakâdi-pada-prakṣepeṇa tṛtīyâdi-jñāna-siddhi-prasaṅgāc ca iti |

(The **pūrvapakṣin** continues:) Nor should it be said (that D[4] is an acceptable definition of a cognition of an entity as qualified:) "a cognition having predication content, with predication content as a particular kind of objecthood." For, (ontologically) there is no objecthood over and above what a cognition is by nature along with what its object is by nature.

Objection: (D^4 is an acceptable definition, since you misunderstand what it is to have predication content.) To have predication content is to be generated by a cognition of the qualifier (that appears as predication content).

Pūrvapakṣin: (Then, for you, a determinate cognition, a cognition of an entity as qualified, is) a cognition that is *generated by a cognition of the qualifier* (which term is the probandum of the inference you have been defending, "The perceptual cognition, 'A cow,' is generated by a cognition of the qualifier, *since* it is a cognition of an entity as qualified, like an inferential awareness"). The qualifier that does the generating is (you say) that which appears there as predication content. (With this understanding of a cognition of an entity as qualified) the prover in your inference, which has the determinate cognition "A cow" as its subject, is just the same as the probandum (thus you fallaciously assume what's at issue). Furthermore, you face the difficulty that God's cognitions (which are not generated, according to you) would be without predication content.

Nor is a cognition of an entity as qualified to be (D^5) "a cognition whose object excludes what is not that (qualifier cognized in indeterminate cognition)." Because of our rejection of (Buddhist) *apoha-vāda* (the "concepts-as-exclusionary" view), the prover in your inference, which has the determinate cognition "A cow" as its subject, is not established as like that (that is, it has not been shown that the qualifier known in a cognition of an entity as qualified is to be understood in the Buddhist fashion).

Nor (for the purposes of your inference) is a cognition of an entity as qualified (D^6) "a cognition that produces awareness of exclusion of what is not that (qualifier)." For, it is impossible to understand "a producing of awareness of what's excluded as other than that (qualifier)" except as that which is common to what is *not* indeterminate perception.

Moreover, it would be wrong to argue that, *since* the cognition, "A cow," is a cognitive object, the cognition is distinct from an (indeterminate) cognition that is other than determinate cognitions that are different from that cognition ("A cow") itself (and in this way smuggle indeterminate perceptions into acceptance). To argue in this way, one might as well try to establish indeterminate perception by arguing that, *since* the visual organ is a sense organ, the visual organ generates a cognition that is different from cognitions that are determinate and visual! For, this reasoning is "ineffectual" (i.e., the prover is not confined to the probandum as shown by counterfactual considerations). And in both cases (the original and the mock inferences), one could insert the words "indeterminate and so on" immediately after the word "determinate" (in the statement of the probandum, to get, in effect: "is distinct from both determinate and indeterminate cognitions"), and land in the predicament of proving (too much, namely) a third kind of cognition and so on.

Comments

If a cognition of an entity as qualified is defined as a cognition having predication content and having predication content is defined, in turn, as a cognition's being generated by a cognition of a qualifier (the qualifier that appears as predication content), then the Naiyāyika inference that has been championed as the main reason to posit indeterminate perception ("The perceptual cognition, 'A cow,' is generated by a cognition of a qualifier, *since* it is a cognition of an entity as qualified, like an inferential awareness") will suffer from having identical probandum and prover terms. Given that the context prior to inference is uncertainty about a probandum, an assumption that the prover belongs to the inferential subject would beg the question.

Furthermore, God's cognitions, according to Nyāya, are not generated, and so the Naiyāyika objector's definition of *having predication content* as being generated by an indeterminate perception would mean that God's cognitions would not have predication content—which is absurd.

The prover of the crucial inference is *being a cognition of an entity as qualified*, which we are supposed to know actually qualifies the subject, namely, the perceptual cognition, "(That's a) cow." The problem with D^5 is that it requires new argument to motivate the view that "(That's a) cow," or any such cognition, is to be understood as fitting the description proposed. Earlier Naiyāyikas and Mīmāṃsakas have roundly trounced Buddhist views—including D^5, which is endorsed by Buddhists—as anyone would know who was familiar with Sanskrit philosophical literature. Thus failing presentation of a new argument, D^5 can be ruled out.

A difficult stretch of text commences with D^6, the rejection of which seems gimicky. D^6 is rejected because it involves such a general description—applying, at least by certain lights, to all cognitions—that it cannot meaningfully be used to differentiate—and thereby establish—an otherwise dubious cognitive indeterminacy. Indeterminacy would apply to a class of posited cognitions, whereas cognitive determinacy would apply to all the cognitions with which we are familiar. It is unilluminating to differentiate the indeterminate and determinate on such grounds. However, why this criticism applies in particular to D^6 as opposed to other candidates is open to interpretation.

The *pūrvapakṣin*'s last pair of sentences—Sanskrit text rendered by the last paragraph above—brings a shift of focus, a stepping back from the difficulty of defining *cognition of an entity as qualified* to a different inference meant to establish indeterminate cognition.[7] The wider point appears to be that the new inference contains an understanding of determinate cognition that depends only on contrasts among determinate cognitions. Thus, apparently, it would not fall to the previous criticism. But there are problems with the reasoning both with the formulation of the probandum ("is distinct from an (indeterminate) cognition that is other than determinate cognitions that are different from that cognition itself'') as well as a laughable prover (''is a cognitive object''). The problem with the formulation of the probandum can be seen by the word insertion spelled out, but it would be too tedious to explain to readers not knowing Sanskrit. The point is that by such reasoning one could prove an absurd third, fourth, fifth type of cognition by adding the second, the third, the fourth and so on types of cognitions as that which the cognition ''(That's a) cow'' is distinct from. The problem with the prover is obvious, since everything nameable is a ''cognitive object,'' *prameya*. Being a cognitive object does not entail anything worth our attention here.

Thus ends the *pūrva-pakṣa* of the section.

Text (p. 863, Tirupati, and p. 817, Calcutta) and Translation

> atra ucyate | prāthamikaṃ gaur iti pratyakṣaṃ jñānaṃ janya-viśeṣaṇa-jñāna-janyaṃ janya-viśiṣṭa-jñānatvāt anumiti-vat | na ca smaraṇaṃ tatra saṃbhavati | taj-janmani tena gotvasya an-anubhavāt |

Gaṅgeśa: We answer. When a person for the first time in his life has the perceptual cognition, ''(That's a) cow,'' that cognition is generated by an (indeterminate) cognition of a qualifier, a cognition that is itself generated, *since* it is a generated cognition of an entity as qualified, like an inferential awareness.

And it is not the case that a remembering could be the (prior) cognition with this example. For he has not had in this life any experience of cowhood.

Comments

Gaṅgeśa excludes God's cognitions from the prover—and from the probandum as well—by using the term ''generated.''

An inferential awareness is generated by a prior cognition of a very precise informational type, namely, in the stock example, a cognition of a mountain (the qualificandum) as possessed-of-smokiness-pervaded-by-fieriness (the qualifier). In Gaṅgeśa's inference, the subject is a cognition that is like an inferential awareness in being about an individual (Bessie, the qualificandum) as exhibiting a certain property (cowhood, the qualifier). Thus we expect that here too the cognition is generated by a prior cognition of a precise informational type, a cognition that is responsible for Bessie being perceived as a cow and not, say, as a horse or even as a non-horse. Now because of the impossibility of memory-impressions in cases like the one cited, the generating cognition is not a remembering. Nor is it a previous determinate cognition as in the case of multiply qualificative cognition such as ''(That's a) staff-bearer.'' Nor is it any other kind of cognition with qualificative content because of the foundational character of perception and the threat of an infinite regress, more about which in a moment. The only possibility, then, is that the required cognition is indeterminate in the sense that the qualifier (cowhood) that emerges as predication content is provided "in the raw," that is to say, not as playing a relational role, not as qualifying the qualificandum, but just, so to say, as a pure datum.

Whatever is known determinately requires the availability of a qualifier—a property—through which a qualificandum—a property-bearer—is known. To perceive a cow as a cow requires not so much acquaintance with cowhood (in the Russellian sense of "acquaintance") but the cognitive availability of cowhood. Does this availability require a thoroughly conscious grasping of the qualifier, a cognizing it as itself something or other? Definitely not. If it did, an infinite regress would loom.

For all determinate cognitions, perceptual, inferential, and so on, a qualificandum appears to be known through a qualifier that itself has been made available by some sort of prior cognition. But precisely how has the qualifier been made available in the case that Gaṅgeśa cites? In cases of doubly qualificative cognition, a qualifier can be furnished by a prior determinate cognition. And in many cases of even singly qualificative cognition, the qualifier can be furnished by way of the awakening of a memory-impression. But with a first-time perceptual cognition of a singly qualified entity, such as "(That's a) cow," an indeterminate prior "grasping" of the qualifier has to be posited to avoid an infinite regress. There are no other candidates. The mediation of memory-impressions is excluded by the stipulation that the perceiver has had no prior experience of cows. And determinate cognition is blocked by the regress consequence. Hence cowhood is directly known without "cowhood-ness" being cognized. In indeterminate awareness, a qualifier is directly cognized and no further cognition is required.

Though it has been suggested that an indeterminate perception would be a kind of "glance," *ālocana* (see the *pūrvapakṣin*'s statement, above, p. 612), it is important to keep in mind that this could be no more than a metaphor. For, as Gaṅgeśa will say explicitly, indeterminate perceptions cannot be apperceived; there is no phenomenological evidence for their existence or character.

Gaṅgeśa will make even more plain the role of regress dread within his overall argument after he rebuts a couple of objections to the way he understands the example of a first-time perception of a cow.

Text (p. 817, Calcutta) and Translation

atha yathā bālasya ādya-pravṛtti-balāt prāg-bhavīya-saṃskārād vyāpti-smaraṇam tathā iha api janmântarīya-saṃskārāt gotva-smaraṇam astu, prāthamika-viśiṣṭa-jñāna-balād iti cet, na | jīvanâ-dṛṣṭena tatra saṃskārôdbodhāt tathā astu | iha tu na vilakṣaṇam udbodhakam asti | ato gotvâ-saṃnikarṣe 'pi gotva-smaraṇa-prasaṅgaḥ |

ya eva gotvêndriya-saṃnikarṣas tava nirvikalpake hetuḥ sa eva saṃskārôdbodhaka iti cet, tarhi anyatra[8] kḷpta-kāraṇa-bhāvāt gotvêndriya-saṃnikarṣāt gotvânubhava eva syāt, smaraṇa-sāmagrīto 'nubhava-sāmagryā balavattvāt | na ca tad viśiṣṭa-jñānam, pūrvaṃ viśeṣaṇa-jñānâ-bhāvād ity arthān nirvikalpakam | ata eva na tatra jñānatvena viśiṣṭa-jñānânumānam, kāraṇa-bādhena bādhāt | yadi ca anubhava-sāmagrītaḥ smaraṇaṃ tadā nityānāṃ vaidikârthānāṃ ca smaraṇaṃ syāt na tv anubhavaḥ |

Objection: By force of (our need to account for) the effect, namely, the initial effort to act (of a newborn child in reaching for its mother's breast), the child (in your example, who sees a cow for the first time) remembers pervasions (such as being-a-cow and not-being-a-horse) because of memory-impressions formed in a previous life. Here, too, the case would be similar: let there be a remembering of cowhood because of a memory-impression formed in a previous birth, by force of (our need to account for) the effect, (namely, in your example) the occurrence of a first-time cognition of an entity as qualified (e.g., something as a cow).

Gaṅgeśa: No. (What *excites* the memory-impression?) Let the stimulator be, in the case you imagine (of an infant's first effort to act), unseen force (or instinct) necessary for life. But in the case that we imagine (of a first-time perception of a cow as a cow), in contrast, there is no stimulator of any type. If there were, then, even when no sensory connection to cowhood (or a cow) obtained, (a cognition of a cow could arise, i.e., there would be) a remembering of cowhood—this is the difficulty.

Objection: That which, according to you, causes the indeterminate cognition—(namely) a sensory connection to cowhood—itself awakens the memory-impression.

Gaṅgeśa: In other cases a sensory connection with cowhood is established as causal; thus in the (current) case (too) of experience of cowhood it should indeed (play a causal role—but according to you it does not, but rather a memory-impression does). For, a collection of causal factors sufficient to produce an *experience* (of x) outweighs a collection of causal factors (otherwise) sufficient to produce a *remembering* (of x).

And (in our example of a first-time perception of a cow as a cow) no cognition of an entity as qualified is a causal factor. There is no prior (determinate) cognition of the qualifier. Hence, by implication, indeterminate perception is a causal factor.

Just for this reason, there can be no inference to conclude that here (too, with so-called indeterminate cognitions) we have cognitions of entities as qualified in that we have cognitions. For, such is prevented (or, the thesis is defeated) by a defeating (out of fear of unwelcome regress) of the causality (this would involve).

And if a remembering (of x) could occur when conditions sufficient to produce an experience (of x) were in place, then the eternal words and meanings of the Veda would be a matter of remembering, not of awareness (contrary to opinion on both sides, specifically, that a person's understanding the Veda would be an *awareness* brought about by trustfully understood words).

Comments

Gaṅgeśa cogently responds to the alternative proposal that a first-time perception of cowhood would be caused by a memory-impression formed in previous births: why should the excitation, or lack thereof, be different in this case than in others? Of course, there can be no awakening of a memory-impression if there is no memory-impression to begin with. If there is to be one in this case, then why doesn't occasionally a person who has never seen a cow before remember cows?

In larger perspective, Gaṅgeśa's counterattack centering on memory-stimulators is an important argument against a subjectivist stance that can be sensed in the background. Here with a first-time perception and an indeterminate cognition of a qualifier there is no contribution from the side of the subject, not even from memory. Perception originates in the world.

Gaṅgeśa also invokes the natural law, which is generally admitted, that perception wins out over remembering when it would be the same thing that would be remembered or perceived. In the last paragraph of the passage, he adds some counterfactual reasoning: there would be no reason to view Vedic understanding as a matter of a verbal and testimonial awareness generated by Vedic sentences as opposed to remembering generated by memory-impressions if remembering could trump perception. Testimony presupposes that a testifier, or the first in a chain of testifiers, knows the truth testified to by means of experience, not memory, and there are "seers" of Vedic truths, not just a tradition sustained by memory.

In sum, in the typical case of a first-time perceptual awareness of a cow, there is a prior stage in the causal process that is an indeterminate perception, indeterminate in that cowness is cognized but not as related to the particular cow, the qualificandum of the ensuing determinate perception. All other cases of cognition of an entity as qualified have a prior cognition of the qualifier as a cause. It is thus reasonable that the case of a first-time perception does too. But since here clearly we do not have a memory-impression as a causal factor, indeterminate cognition has to be posited.

Text (p. 864, Tirupati) and Translation

na ca gotva-jñānaṃ gotva-jñāna-janyaṃ janya-jñāna-janyaṃ janya-viśeṣaṇa-jñāna-janyaṃ ca ity anyatra darśanāt prathamaṃ na gotvânubhavaḥ iti vācyam | ekasya eva janya-janakatvân-avacchedakatvāt an-avasthâpātāc ca | nanu gaur ity atra gotva-vaiśiṣṭyaṃ gavi bhāsate | tathā ca tad-viṣayakaṃ jñānaṃ syāt, tac ca nirvikalpakam iti cet, gotvaṃ hi tatra viśeṣaṇam, na tu tad-vaiśiṣṭyam | nanu tathā-bhūta-viśeṣaṇa-dhī-janya-viśiṣṭa-jñāne viśeṣaṇaṃ sva-dharma-viśiṣṭaṃ kathaṃ bhāseta, pūrvaṃ tasya an-avagamāt | avagame vā tasya api viśeṣaṇam iti an-avasthā iti cet, na | gaur iti viśiṣṭa-jñāne viśiṣṭasya gotvasya a-bhānāt | atha sarvaṃ viśeṣaṇaṃ viśeṣaṇavad eva | gotvâdāv api vyakty-āder viśeṣaṇatvād iti cet, astu tathā | kiṃ tu viśeṣaṇam viśeṣaṇavad eva bhāseta iti na niyamaḥ | anyathā gaur iti jñāne viśeṣaṇa-tad-viśeṣaṇân-antara-paraṃ-parā-viṣayatve viṣayâ-paryavasāna-prasaṅgaḥ | kvacin nirviśeṣaṇasya api bhāne prathamato 'pi tathā syād a-viśeṣāt |

Objection: A cognition of cowhood is generated by a cognition of cowhood. It is generated by a generated cognition. And it is generated by a generated cognition of the qualifier. Because cognition of cowhood is found like this elsewhere (we can generalize and conclude that) there is no first-time experience of cowhood.

Gaṅgeśa: That should not be said. For, one and the same thing does not specify both being-an-effect and being-a-cause (within a causal relationship). Moreover, there would be an infinite regress.

Objection: With "(That's a) cow," cowhood qualificative relationality appears in the cow. And so (according to you) there has to be a (prior) cognition with *that* as object, which would (also) be indeterminate.

Gaṅgeśa: (No.) For, there cowhood is the qualifier, not cowhood qualificative relationality.

Objection: The qualifier that appears in a cognition of an entity as qualified is generated (you say) by (indeterminate) cognition of just such a qualifier. (But) since it would not be cognized previously, how is it to appear as qualified by its own properties (as cowhood is qualified by cowhood-ness or, as Navyas say, by cows)? Or, if it is cognized previously, then, as possessing another qualifier, it too would exhibit another qualifier (that would have to have been cognized previously)—hence, an infinite regress.

Gaṅgeśa: No. With the cognition of an entity as qualified, "(That's a) cow," cowhood does not appear as qualified.

Objection: Every qualifier does possess some qualifier. For (such universals as) cowhood and the like have individuals (individual cows) and the like as qualifiers.

Gaṅgeśa: We'll let that stand. But there is no invariable rule that a qualifier has to *appear* as possessing some qualifier. Otherwise, with the cognition, "(That's a) cow," the qualifier and its qualifier would, without end, mutually present themselves as objective content, and there could be no final determination of what the object is like—this is the difficulty. If at any point there is to be an appearance of an unqualified qualifier, then it might as well be at the first point, since there is no (discernible) difference (between the first, second, and so on as being such an unqualified qualifier).

Comments

The passage opens with expression of the alternative view that memory does invariably play a role in the perception of something *a* as an F, as, for example, a cow: elsewhere we see that cognition of cowhood is caused, in part, by a prior cognition of cowhood, a cognition that has itself been generated. Thus, we may assume that such is involved in a "first-time" perception, too.

Gaṅgeśa replies that the opponent's theory is, first of all, badly formulated. Nothing can specify both what it is to be a cause and what it is to be an effect within the same causal relationship—here cowhood specifying the cognition as an effect as well as specifying one of the cognition's causes. Furthermore, there would be an infinite series of required cognitions of the cowhood. However, it is not clear that this would be a vicious regress—the comparable regress of seed, sprout, seed, sprout, and so on is viewed as benign—though Rucidatta argues that on such a view death would be impossible.

Gaṅgeśa flatly states that the qualificative relation between qualifier and qualificandum is not what emerges as predication content, though this position gets modified below in consideration of absential cognition. In the case of a self-linking qualifier, the self-linkage, the qualificative relation, is viewed as part of the qualifier presented as predication content.

Gaṅgeśa also insists, in reply to a further objection, that indeterminate perception is capable of grasping a *naked* qualifier that emerges as predication content with such a cognition as "A cow." A qualifier does not have to be grasped as clothed. Otherwise, there would be an epistemic regress.

The objector misunderstands the reply as asserting that there are qualifiers that are ontologically unqualified, and argues that this is false. The objection draws on an understanding of a qualifier as being different from other qualifiers partly in virtue of what it qualifies. Cowhood is distinct from horsehood since it exists in cows and horsehood does not. From the bottom up, in contrast, an individual cow is distinct from a horse because of its cowhood. A logic of ontological layeredness is implicit in the differentiation intrinsic to being a qualifier, but it can be indicated from either of two directions: a universal (or the like) qualifying an individual or an individual qualifying a universal (or the like). The qualification relation is asymmetrical nonetheless. For certain purposes in certain contexts, the normal order of the relation may be reversed. Thus, at a minimum in such a sense, every qualifier does possess some qualifier. Nevertheless—and this is Gaṅgeśa's main point—a qualifier does not have to *appear* as qualified. In indeterminate awareness, we grasp a property but not as belonging to anything. We get pure cowhood information without knowing not only not further properties, such as being-a-universal, but not even that the cowhood belongs to the individual Bessie which in the next moment we perceive determinately as a cow.

Text (p. 865, Tirupati) and Translation

na ca viśiṣṭa-jñānatvād ity atra hetor vyartha-viśeṣaṇatvam | yena viśeṣaṇena vinā vyāptir grahītuṃ na śakyate tasya eva sārthakatvāt | vyabhicāra-vārakasya api sārthakatve etad eva mūlam | iha api jñānatva-viśeṣaṇa-jñāna-janyatvayoḥ viśeṣaṇaṃ vinā vyāptiḥ grahītuṃ na śakyate, an-avasthānāt sāmānyato vyabhicārâvagamāt | ata eva cakṣus-taijasatvâdi-sādhane rūpâdiṣu madhye rūpasya eva vyañjakatvād ity-ādau a-siddhi-vārakam api viśeṣaṇaṃ sārthakam | tena vinā rūpasya eva vyañjakatvād ity asya a-prasiddher vyāpty-a-grahāt | viśeṣaṇaṃ vinā api yatra vyāpti-grahas tatra vyartha-viśeṣaṇatvam, yathā nīla-dhūmatva-śarīrâ-janyatvâdau |

(**Gaṅgeśa** continues:) And it is not the case that here the prover—*since it is a generated cognition of an entity as qualified*—employs insignificant qualification (in the inference given: "A first-time perceptual cognition, 'A cow,' is generated by a cognition of the qualifier, a cognition that is itself generated, *since* it is a generated cognition of an entity as qualified, like an inferential awareness," with the expression "of an entity as qualified" suspected as pointless or insignificant). A qualification (such as is achieved by the expression "of an entity as qualified") without which a pervasion could not be grasped is entirely significant. Just this is at the very bottom of the significance of a qualification's preventing deviation (in a context ripe for right inference). Here, too, without the qualifications (a) that there is a cognition and (b) that there is something generated by a cognition of a qualifier, the pervading (the probandum's pervading the prover) could not be grasped, because there would be an infinite regress and because a general deviation would be found.

Just for this reason, concerning the inference where the visual organ's fieriness, etc., is to be shown (and the prover is) "*since* the visual organ makes known only color among (the perceptible qualities) color and the like"—here and in other inferences there is significant qualification that avoids the fallacy of an unshown prover (i.e., not known to qualify the inferential subject, *a-siddhi*). For, without such qualification (the purported prover would be:) "*since* the visual organ makes known only color" (while in fact the visual organ makes known *colorhood* as well as color). The (relevant) pervasion would not be grasped because the prover would not be known (as qualifying the inferential subject).

Pointless or insignificant qualification occurs when without the (added) qualification the pervasion would still be grasped, as in such cases as being *blue* smoke (in an inference to fire) and *not being produced by a body* (in an inference to God).

Comments

Precision in mentioning qualifiers—i.e., qualification by adding adjectives—is important with respect to the probandum and prover terms of an inference. Without the qualification, *of an entity as qualified*, the prover in the inference proving indeterminate cognition would be: being a cognition. Thus, not only would there be obvious deviation—no pervasion—an unwelcome regress of cognitions as causes would be set up by the implication that any cognition (cognition *tout court*, the prover, including indeterminate cognition) would be generated by a cognition of a qualifier (the probandum).

Because the visual organ makes known universals such as colorhood as well as colors such as red, the statement that put together a pared-down prover with the subject in the inference referred to would be false: the visual organ (the subject) does not make known color only. But it does make known only color among perceptible qualities (universals are not qualities).

Gaṅgeśa pretty clearly explains why adding terms in the statement of a prover or probandum is significant or insignificant with potential for being worse. Being *blue* smoke is irrelevant to inferring fire, and we might miss an opportunity to infer fire if we thought we needed to see something blue. If we wished to know not just fire, but what kind of fire, or the fuel being burned, then the blue might be relevant. With the theological inference based on the fact that the earth and the like are artifacts (like a pot), to add that they are effects *not produced by a body*, is unnecessary and obfuscating to boot. Those are examples of wrong qualification. There is no such example here with our inference, says Gaṅgeśa.

Next, Gaṅgeśa turns to the issue of the nature of the qualificative relation presented in a cognition of an entity as qualified.

Text (p. 866, Tirupati, and p. 821, Calcutta) and Translation

yasya yatra yaḥ saṃbandhaḥ sa eva tatra tasya vaiśiṣṭyam | tena hi svâ-saṃbaddhebhyo vyāvṛtto bodhyate | yathā daṇḍī puruṣa iti jñāne daṇḍa-saṃbandhaḥ puruṣe avagata iti tena ayam a-daṇḍa-vyāvṛtto bodhyate tathā gaur iti vikalpe 'pi | tathā ca viśeṣaṇavad-viśeṣya-jñānatvaṃ viśiṣṭa-jñānatvam | etad eva a-tad-vyāvṛtta-bodha-janakatâvacchedakam |

(**Gaṅgeśa** continues:) When ϕ is in x by the relation R, then R is the qualificative relationality (*vaiśiṣṭya*) of ϕ with respect to x. For, by it is known what's excluded from not being so related. As with the cognition, "Staff-bearing is the person," where a relation to a staff being cognized with respect to a person makes known the person as excluded from all those things not related to staffs, so also in the case of the determinate cognition, "(That's a) cow," (a cognized relation is what makes the cow known as excluded from all those things that are not cows).

And, therefore, to be a cognition of an entity as qualified is to be a cognition of a qualificandum possessing a qualifier. This characterization alone specifies what it is to generate a cognition of exclusion of the *not-that* (i.e., exclusion of what does not have the qualifier that is the predication content).

Comments

The definition of a cognition of an entity as qualified is given to show that none of the terms of the qualificative relation is grasped in qualificative cognition as an isolated and unrelated item. The Sanskrit of the opening sentence is elegantly compact, a series of three correlative pronouns (*yasya yatra yaḥ*) bound to three others (*sa . . . tatra, tasya*) defining the qualificative relation. Gaṅgeśa's point is that all three march together or none marches at all. A second point is similar: exclusion of a qualificandum from the class of things that do not possess the qualifier appearing as predication content is available to be immediately inferred by an inference that relies on taking all three items together. The relation may be taken as the excluder, but only insofar as it is understood as a relation *binding* the qualifier to its qualificandum.

Thus does Gaṅgeśa's view tie the logic of double negation to an ontological "qualifiedness." As Buddhist logicians of the Yogācāra school stressed, all verbalizable cognition—all determinate cognition—obeys the principle of double negation. Gaṅgeśa finds the principle grounded ontologically in a relation that is implicit in whatever we determinately perceive.

Text (p. 821, Calcutta) and Translation

> nanu daṇḍa-puruṣa-saṃbandhā ity atra api daṇḍa-saṃbandhaḥ puruṣe 'vagata iti apy a-daṇḍa-vyāvṛtta-puruṣa-bodhaḥ syād iti cet, bhavaty eva daṇḍa-saṃbandhaḥ eva puruṣe daṇḍa-jñānaṃ vinā na jñāyate iti brūmaḥ | yatra viśiṣṭa-jñāna-sāmagrī na asti tatra nirvikalpakam, jñāna-karaṇa-janye sarvatra viśeṣaṇa-jñāna-janyatvān na tad iti pratyakṣam eva etad iti |

Objection: Even with such a (conjunctive) cognition as, "A staff, a person, and a relation," the staff's relation would be grasped with respect to the person. Hence, also from that the person would be cognized as excluded from things not related to staffs.

Gaṅgeśa: He would indeed (but only if the relation is understood as taking the other two items as terms, like "Staff-bearing is the person"). We assert that without cognition of the staff with respect to the person (the relation's second term), a relation to the staff alone is not cognized.

When the conditions sufficient to produce a cognition of an entity as qualified are not in place, an indeterminate perception can occur.

All cognitions that are generated through a (determinate) cognition as chief instrumental cause are, in being generated by a cognition of a qualifier, *not* perceptions, which are only that (namely, having something else, a sense organ, as chief instrumental cause).

Comments

The first three quarters of the passage are clear. Gaṅgeśa drives home the logic of qualifiedness and its difference from conjunction. The circumstances giving rise to the cognition of a group of things, "A staff and a person," are distinct from those giving rise to the cognition of an entity as qualified, "A staff-bearer." However, the last line is obscure.

Gaṅgeśa seems to be fleshing out the second step in the proof of indeterminate perception. Inferential awarenesses and other non-perceptual veridical cognitions have a cognition of an entity as qualified as a cause (e.g., a cognition of a mountain as qualified by smokiness-pervaded-by-fieriness). Indeed, *non*-perceptual veridical cognitions have a determinate cognition of a qualifier not only as a cause but as their chief cause, *karaṇa*, their "trigger." No perception is like that, having, instead, a sense organ in action as the *karaṇa*. Nevertheless, a perception as a cognition of an entity as qualified should be presumed to have a cognition of the qualifier as a cause. But in some cases a simple perceptual cognition (of an entity as singly qualified) is unlike others in not having a *determinate* cognition of a qualifier as a cause, as is shown by the example of a first-time experience of a cow. Therefore, indeterminate perception has to be posited as a cause.

Moreover, to take the last statement against different background, the definition of perception can stand that says that a perception does not have a cognition as its chief instrumental cause. A sense organ, not a cognition, not even an indeterminate perception, is the *karaṇa* of perception whether determinate or indeterminate. Though Gaṅgeśa does not fill out the causal picture, he seems to be thinking of the sense organ as generating an indeterminate cognition as part of the overall process that results in an awareness of an entity as qualified by the qualifier that is indeterminately grasped. Thus a sense organ is the *karaṇa* in all instances of perception.

Text (p. 866, Tirupati) and Translation

ata eva a-bhāve na nirvikalpakam | tad-buddhau pratiyogy-adhikaraṇa-jñānayoḥ kāraṇatvena tad-ubhaya-viśiṣṭa-jñāna-sāmagrī-niyamāt | yadi a-bhāve na nirvikalpakam, tadā ghaṭâ-bhāvavad-bhūtalam iti jñānam na syāt, viśeṣaṇa-jñānaṃ vinā tad-a-bhāvāt | bhāve vā na nirvikalpaka-siddhiḥ | viśiṣṭa-jñānatvasya tatra eva vyabhicārād iti cet, na | prathamaṃ bhūtale ghaṭo na asti iti buddhiḥ | tatra bhūtalaṃ viśeṣaṇam, a-bhāvo viśeṣyaḥ | viśeṣya-jñānaṃ ca na kāraṇam | paścād-bhūtala-viśeṣyakaṃ ghaṭâ-bhāvavad iti jñānam | nanu indriya-saṃbaddha-viśeṣaṇatayā a-bhāvo gṛhyata ity uktam | ataḥ kathaṃ sa viśeṣya iti cet, bhūtala-viśeṣaṇatayā sva-bhāva-pratyāsattyā gṛhyata iti tad-arthaḥ | na tv a-bhāvasya viśeṣaṇatayā bhānam iti | ata eva vāyau rūpâ-bhāva iti pratītes cākṣuṣatvam uktam ācāryaiḥ | a-yogya-viśeṣye indriyasya a-sāmarthyāt |

Objection: Just for this reason, there is (you say) no indeterminate perception of an absence. For, as causes of an absential cognition, both a cognition of the countercorrelate (or absentee) and a cognition of the locus are cognitions of entities as qualified, by the rule of, in both cases, a collection of causal factors sufficient to produce a cognition of an entity as qualified being in place. (Then) if there is no indeterminate perception of an absence, then (by your lights) there should be no such (perceptual) cognition as, "The floor has (or shows) an absence of a pot," since (according to you) there should be nothing like that without a (prior) cognition of the qualifier. Or, if (you admit) there is, then there is no proof of indeterminate perception, since there would be a counterexample (your prover deviating from your probandum) in just such a case, inasmuch as it is a cognition of an entity as qualified.

Gaṅgeśa: No. First there occurs the cognition, "The pot is not on the floor," where the floor is the qualifier, the absence the qualificandum. And a (prior) cognition of a qualificandum is not a causal factor (for a cognition of an entity as qualified). Later there occurs (as an immediate inference) the cognition that has the floor as the qualificandum exhibiting the absence of the pot.

Objection: You have declared that an absence is grasped through (the sensory relation of) a *qualifierhood* connecting a sense organ (to what is grasped). Thus, how can an absence be the qualificandum (cognized in a perception)?

Gaṅgeśa: It is grasped through the qualifierhood relation to the floor, that is to say, through a sensory connection that is self-linking—this is what we mean (by our talk of qualifierhood as the sensory connection in perception of absences). We do not mean that an absence appears (perceptually) as a qualifier.

Just for this reason, our revered teacher (Udayana) has said that the cognition, "There is an absence of color in air," is a visual perception (that is, in that the absence is a qualificandum fit to be perceived by the visual organ because of the perceptibility, or visibility, of the absentee, color). For a sense organ has no capacity to grasp a qualificandum that is not fit to be perceived (by that particular organ).

Comments

Absential perception presents a problem for Gaṅgeśa's proof of indeterminate cognition in that all cognitions of entities as qualified are supposed to be "produced by a cognition of the qualifier." If an indeterminate perception of the qualifier is necessary for a first-time perception of a cow, then the same factor should play a causal role with absential perceptions. But then does an indeterminate cognition grasp an absence? An absence requires prior familiarity with the absentee (the pot) and, typically, perception of the locus (the floor where the pot is not). But does it require prior familiarity with the absence itself? Something seems wrong with the picture.

Gaṅgeśa replies that in perceiving an absence of a pot on the floor, there is indeed a prior indeterminate cognition of the *floor* as the qualifier, which feeds one of the slots in the ensuing determinate perception of the absence, whose second slot is fed by memory of the absentee. (An absence is by nature a relational entity—having an absentee and occurring at a precise spot—an absence of *x*, the absentee, at *y*, the locus.) Thus, the rule is not broken that any perception of an entity as qualified has a cognition of the qualifier as a cause.

Admittedly, there occur absential cognitions to be analyzed as having the floor not as qualifier but as qualificandum, with an *absence of a pot* as the qualifier. But these are not perceptual. They are the results of one-step inferences from perceptual cognitions, such as from a perception where the qualifier is the floor and the qualificandum the absence of a pot.

With the last paragraph of the passage, Gaṅgeśa uses Udayana's view of the visibility of air's having no color to tie up nicely several loose ends. For Udayana, air is not perceptible at all and indisputably not visible. How, then, could the absence of color in air be grasped by the visual organ, as the text says? Air, the locus, is invisible, and the absentee, color, is furnished by memory. So, only the absence itself could be visible. And the rule there is that an absence is perceptible by a particular organ of sense if and only if its absentee is perceptible by that faculty. Its perceptibility does not depend on the perceptibility of its locus. And color is visible. And so air's absence of color is visible, Udayana reasons.

In the next and final passage of the section, apperception and the question of natural subkinds of perception are revisited, as Gaṅgeśa shows the unity of diverse parts of his theory. He also adds one last wrinkle to the argument for indeterminate perception.

Text (p. 868, Tirupati) and Translation

> jñānatve ca nirvikalpakaṃ viṣaya-viśiṣṭatvâṃśe savikalpakam api | anuvyavasāyasya vyavasāya-janyatvena niyamataḥ pūrvaṃ viṣaya-rūpa-viśeṣaṇa-bhānāt tatra eva jñāne tad eva jñānaṃ niṣprakārakaṃ saprakārakaṃ ca iti na viruddham, aṃśa-bhedam ādāya a-virodhāt | ata eva nirvikalpakatva-savikalpakatve na jātī, cākṣuṣatvâdinā saṃkarâpatteḥ | gaur iti savikalpakam api gotvâṃśe nirvikalpakam eva, tatra prakārâ-bhānāt, bhāne vā an-avasthā nirvikalpakâ-siddhiś ca |

(**Gaṅgeśa** continues:) We may add that a cognition is perceived as a cognition indeterminately and also determinately in its aspect (or "portion") where it is qualified by (i.e., is known as presenting) its object. The rule is that an apperception is generated by its target. So there is a prior perception of a qualifier as the (apperceptive) object. Because of the illumination of a qualifier previously as an object, just such an (apperceptive) cognition of just such a (target) cognition both has and does not have predication content. This is not an impossible contradiction, since when one considers distinctions of portion (or aspect) there is no incompatibility.

Just for this reason, being-indeterminate and being-determinate are not universals or natural kinds (*jāti*). To regard them that way faces the difficulty of an (illicit) "cross-sectioning" with (other candidate kinds, such as) the visual and the like.

The cognition, "(That's a) cow," is determinate. Still, concerning the cowhood presented, it is indeterminate only, since no predication content appears (with respect to cowhood). Or, if there is to be such an appearance, there would be (the insuperable difficulty of) infinite regress and no proof of indeterminate perception.

Comments

Gaṅgeśa's talk of "portions" of cognitions is strictly metaphoric, cognitive delimiters or "specifiers" (*avacchedaka*) being the correct technical language. But the portion talk here ties in nicely with the Naiyāyika view of universals as locus-pervading. Whenever we are forced to speak of a property as applying only to a portion of a thing, the property is not a universal, since it does not pervade its locus.

At the end of the last section, Gaṅgeśa used the figure of the man-lion form of Viṣṇu as an analogue for the dual nature of a cognition as an apperceptive object: (a) as a locus of the property, cognitionhood, which is grasped indeterminately, and (b) as having its own object, a qualificandum presented as qualified by a qualifier. Here a similar point is made concerning apperception as both determinate and indeterminate: with respect to the cognitionhood that it presents it is indeterminate but with respect to a target presented as being of an object—or, as Gaṅgeśa says, as being qualified by its object—the selfsame apperception has predication content.

Gaṅgeśa usually speaks as though any indeterminate perception would be a separate cognitive event preceding and in part bringing about a determinate perception. But here it seems he is thinking about perception as a process with an indeterminate strand. The nature of the causal relation depends on how we are conceiving the effect. "(That's a) cow" is a cognition that can be regarded as indeterminate insofar as we are looking at it as presenting cowhood. But when we look at that qualifier as being cognized qualificatively, it becomes a bit of predication content cognized in relation to Bessie and the cognition is determinate. We infer about the cognition that "cowhood" is there indeterminately. Thus, if we consider only the qualifier, we apprehend it as there indeterminately, i.e., as unqualified. If we did not, we would have to live with a regress. And we would have no reason to posit an indeterminate stage, or strand, of the perceptual process.

One has to wonder, however, whether avoidance of infinite regress, mentioned again here at the very end, is made to bear too much weight. Hopefully, this is not the only reason to make the controversial posit. And, indeed, we know it is not. Gaṅgeśa's retort is aimed at bringing out the foundational nature of perception, its ability to grasp properties in a way unsullied by relations or qualification. The overall argument is the place of indeterminate cognition within a broadly externalist cognitive theory and in particular the causal analogues in inferential awarenesses et cetera.

atha viśeṣôpalakṣaṇa-vādaḥ

NOW, **DISCOURSE ON QUALIFIERS VERSUS INDICATORS**

Text (p. 869, Tirupati, and p. 824, Calcutta) and Translation

> prakāraś ca dvi-vidhaḥ, viśeṣaṇôpalakṣaṇa-bhedāt | nanu vyāvartakatvâ-viśeṣe kathaṃ tayor bhedaḥ | vyāvartakatve sati sat viśeṣaṇam, a-sad upalakṣaṇam, yathā daṇḍī puruṣa kuruṇā kṣetram iti cet, na | kākavad devadatta-gṛhaṃ jaṭābhis tāpasaḥ ity-ādāv upari bhrāmyataḥ kākasya jaṭâdeḥ sattve[1] 'py a-viśeṣaṇatvād upalakṣaṇatvāc ca | etena vyāvṛtti-bodha-kāle vyāvartakaṃ sad viśeṣaṇam, a-sad upalakṣaṇam | tena kākâdīnāṃ vyāvṛtti-bodha-samaye satāṃ viśeṣaṇatvam eva, vyāvṛtti-bodha-samaye '-satām upalakṣaṇatvam | ata eva kākaiḥ jaṭābhiḥ kuruṇā ity-ādāv itthaṃ-bhūta-lakṣaṇe tṛtīyā iti nirastam | vyāvṛtti-bodha-samaye sato 'py upari bhramataḥ kākâder a-viśeṣaṇatvāt upalakṣaṇatvāc ca |

Gaṅgeśa: And predication content is of two sorts, since a qualifier (*viśeṣaṇa*) is different from an indicator (*upalakṣaṇa*).

Objection (by a *pūrvapakṣin*, who proceeds to refute a series of definitions): How can there be a difference between the two, given that both are differentiators?

Objector.2 (answering the *pūrvapakṣin*): Presuming (cognitive) differentiation (as accomplished by each), we have (D^1) a qualifier if the thing exists (i.e., resides in that which it differentiates) and an indicator if it does not exist (there). For example (we have a qualifier with) a person as a staff-bearer (given that the person is really bearing a staff) and (an indicator with) the field as the Kurus' (the Kurus of the *Mahābhārata* war, who are no more).

Pūrvapakṣin: No. Concerning the likes of (the stock examples of) Devadatta's house having crows and an ascetic as known by his matted hair, the crow roaming above and the matted hair might *exist* (just as indicated; i.e., the circling crow might be right above Devadatta's roof, and the ascetic might still have his matted hair). Nevertheless, these are not instances of qualifiers but rather of indicators.

Objector.2: (Then, D^2) if a differentiator exists (i.e., resides in that which it diifferentiates) at the time it makes known a distinction, it is a qualifier; if it does not exist (there at that time), it is an indicator. Thus, the crows that are there at the time of the awareness of the distinction (between the house with crows as opposed to things without) would indeed be a qualifier. If they are not there at the time one becomes aware of the difference, they are an indicator.

Just for this reason, the crows, the matted hair, the Kurus, and so forth are expressed through use of the instrumental case to mean a mark that is a way something has been.

Pūrvapakṣin: This is rejected by the previous reasoning. Though the crow roaming above exists at the time a person becomes aware of the distinction (between Devadatta's house and things without such crows), this and the like are indicators. They are not qualifiers.

Comments

The Asiatic Society edition includes this section as part of the previous one, the *nirvikalpaka-vāda*.

The topic provides transition to the final section, on "determinate cognition," the *savikalpaka-vāda*, through the worry that only indeterminate perception presents the world as it is, all determinate cognition being infected with human concepts, human inventions, not grasping things as they are. It is "imagination" (*vikalpa*) enriched—a Yogācāra Buddhist contention. According to Nyāya, a determinate cognition has "predication content," a "way," *prakāra*, that an object is cognized. But these ways include, Naiyāyikas concede, presentations that are tools of human reference having the remotest relationship to what an object indicated really is—as with crows pointed to to indicate Devadatta's house. Expressions prompted by "predication content" can utterly fail to reveal something's nature ("It's where the crows are hovering"). How then are we to differentiate truly perceptual cognition determinate in presenting a thing as it is, i.e., cognition of a property-bearer as qualified by a property that it has naturally, independently of human cognitions and purposes? What is this kind of "predication content" that merely "fixes the referent"—to use the language of a similar discussion in contemporary analytic philosophy—that differentiates but does not really qualify the thing differentiated and picked out?[2]

Gaṅgeśa opens the section in his own voice, and claims that indicators and qualifiers are distinct. But then others' views of how they are distinct are aired for several pages, as a *pūrvapakṣin* refutes a series of definitions that would show the difference.

The *pūrvapakṣin* opposes a series of definitions—twelve in all—of a qualifier (*viśeṣaṇa*) in contrast to an indicator (*upalakṣaṇa*), but he nevertheless intuitively distinguishes cases using the terms. His counterexamples, with perhaps one exception, are assumed to be clear instances of indicators or qualifiers that are not themselves to be questioned. (The exception is the ascetic and his matted hair, about which more below.) Thus the central presupposition of the section is that one can refer to something by means of a mark or sign—an indicator—that does not relate to the thing indicated in the same way that a true qualifier would. The indicator is a tool to fix reference, to direct an interlocutor's attention to a certain thing, i.e., to a property-bearer, without remotely appearing to be one of thing's true properties. An indicator is not a feature that really qualifies the thing helping to determine what it is. Note that unclassified properties, *upādhis*, i.e., "surplus (or extracategorial) properties," are qualifiers (*viśeṣaṇa*) just as much as properties sorted in the conventional Vaiśeṣika fashion—as "qualities" (*guṇa*), "motions" (*kriyā*), "universals" (*jāti*), etc. That is, even an *upādhi* such as blue-cowhood would as presented in a perception ("Bessie is a blue-cow") be cognized in a way grounded in the thing's nature (Bessie really is a cow and blue) despite the property's getting ontologically analyzed as a composite with no reality independent of its parts. Thus qualifiers are presented perceptually as (somehow!) tightly bound up with whatever is cognized, whereas the indicator is merely a reference tool. The aim of the definitional project is to reveal the epistemic and ontological grounds of the distinction in precise statements. The *pūrvapakṣin*'s rejections pave the way for Gaṅgeśa's definitions below.

In overview, the realist assumption that perceptual predication content hits real features of things in a world external to and causally determinant of a cognition's intentionality is challenged by our ability to, e.g., indicate Devadatta's house by referring to crows hovering above. Just how is it that we know Devadatta's house through properties much more crucial to the nature of a house? In particular, many of the house's true properties seem causally relevant to our perception of the thing as a house. But indicators, such as the hovering crows, have little relevance to what the thing is, and yet they are perceived and do distinguish that which is indicated from other things. The problem is that indicators seem not to be determined by the thing but by our purposes. Some predication content turns out to arise solely through accidental cognitive and communicational circumstance; its objecthood is located in something that indicates something else but does not qualify it. How, then, in precise terms are we to distinguish true qualifiers from mere indicators?

The discussion often presupposes a conversational context. An indicator may be given perceptually as predication content, but testimony is just as much the knowledge source in focus. We are to imagine that one of two people looking for Devadatta's house sees crows hovering above it, and says to the companion, "Where the crows are hovering." The crows serve to differentiate Devadatta's house. Thus one can indicate Devadatta's house, given an appropriate setting, without, it seems, mentioning a true qualifier. The relation of the crows to the house seems adventitious and arbitrary in comparison with true qualification. What could account for the difference?

Pāṇini's *sūtra* 2.3.21 defines a predicative usage of the instrumental case that is alluded to in objector.2's final statement and the expression, "a mark that is a way something has been." But objector.2 trades on the pastness expressed by the past passive participle used in Sanskrit (*ittham-bhūta*), a stress that is not present in the Pāṇinian *sūtra*.

Text (p. 824, Calcutta) and Translation

na api viśeṣya-vṛttitve sati pratyāyya-vyāvṛtti-samānâdhikaraṇatve sati vyāvartakaṃ viśeṣaṇam | yad vā yatra viśeṣyatvâvacchedena vyāvṛttyā vā yat samānâdhikaraṇatvena pratīyate tatra tad viśeṣaṇam | viśeṣyatvaṃ ca pratyāyya-vyāvṛtty-adhikaraṇatvam iti | jaṭābhis tāpasa ity-ādau jaṭâdāv atiprasaṅgāt | na hi tāpase na jaṭā vartate | na api viśeṣya-samāna-vibhaktikatvaṃ viśeṣaṇatvam | kākavat devadatta-gṛham ity-ādāv upalakṣaṇe 'pi gatatvāt | an-abhidhāna-daśāyām a-viśeṣaṇatvâpātāc ca |

(The **pūrvapakṣin** continues:) Nor are the following definitions correct. (D^3) A qualifier is a differentiator that resides in its qualificandum, that is to say, that has the same locus as a differentiation to be made known. (D^4) A ϕ that is cognized as having the same locus x as that which specifies x's being a qualificandum, alternatively, a ϕ that is cognized as having the same locus as the differentiation (that ϕ accomplishes with respect to x), is a qualifier with respect to x—where what is meant by a qualificandum is a locus of a differentiation that is to be made known. These definitions are wrong, for they overextend to include cases such as an ascetic known by matted hair, since it is false that the matted hair does not *reside in* the ascetic.

Nor (D^5) to be a qualifier is to be expressed by a word in the same case as the word that expresses the qualificandum. For, that would include such indicators as obtain with Devadatta's house having crows (since "having crows" is in the same case as "house"). Moreover, this faces the difficulty that a qualifier would not be a qualifier when it is not named.

Comments

Our ability to indicate Devadatta's house by referring to crows challenges the Nyāya stress on the importance of perceptually given predication content. We can also refer to Devadatta's house by pointing to a property relevant to our perception of the house as a house, as the crows are not. Even a transitory property F would be causally relevant to our perception of something as an F. But an indicator is accounted for by our purposes, namely, in our example, to point out Devadatta's house. This is the frame, as explained, and should be kept in mind.

D^3 and D^4 almost exactly match definitions Gaṅgeśa endorses at the section's end, and so should pretty clearly capture his sense of the difference between qualifiers and indicators. Thus, the *pūrvapakṣin*'s counterexample is particularly interesting, the matted hair. The hair does have the same locus, the ascetic, namely, as the thing cognized (the ascetic). The matted hair *resides in*, in the specified sense, the ascetic. Perhaps, then, having-matted-hair is causally relevant to perception of the ascetic as an ascetic.

Of the examples given so far, the staff-bearing of a person bearing a staff is expressed by a predicate adjective, a word in the same case as that used to mean "person" in the characteristic expression, whereas the matted hair and the Kurus are expressed by words in Sanskrit in the instrumental case, with what they indicate—an ascetic and a particular plot of land—being expressed by words in Sanskrit in the nominative case. D[5], however, confuses word with thing, denoter and denoted. A qualifier exists without being named. Furthermore, when Devadatta's house is indicated as that having crows, "having-crows" is in the same case as "house" (in Sanskrit a possessive suffix expresses the having and the word "having-crows" is a predicate adjective).

Text (p. 870, Tirupati, and p. 825, Calcutta) and Translation

atha vyāvartakatve sati viśiṣṭa-dhī-viṣayatvaṃ viśeṣaṇatvam | viśiṣṭa-buddhiś ca na viśeṣaṇatva-gocarā gauravāt, kiṃ tu viśeṣaṇa-viṣayā | viśeṣaṇôpalakṣaṇa-saṃdehân-upapatteḥ | ata eva cākṣuṣatvâdi-virodhaḥ | upalakṣaṇatve tu upalakṣitaṃ saṃsthānâdi viśiṣṭa-dhī-viṣayo na kākavattvam, tad-a-bhāve 'pi tad-gṛha-pratītes tādrūpyāt | anyathā bhramatvâpatteḥ | na ca śabdôpasthāpitasya kathaṃ śābda-jñāna-bahir-bhāva iti vācyam | tathā eva vyutpatteḥ | na hi gaṅgāyāṃ ghoṣa ity atra pravāho 'pi tīrâvacchedakatayā bhāsate | kiṃ tu tīratvena tīra-viśeṣa eva | anyathā a-jahat-svârthâ-sāmyāt | na ca evam upalakṣaṇa-padasya lākṣaṇikatvam, a-śakyasya saṃsthānâder upasthityā tad-anvaye tātparyād iti | mā evam | tathā vyutpatter a-siddheḥ na hy upalakṣaṇa-padâtiriktam upalakṣyôpasthāpakam asti ity upalakṣaṇa-padaṃ svârtham upasthāpya, upalakṣyam upasthāpayati iti lakṣaṇā eva syāt | anyathā lakṣaṇôcchedaḥ | ghaṭo na asti ity atra upalakṣaṇasya pratiyogino '-bhāva-dhī-viṣayatvāt niyatôpalakṣyâ-bhāvāc ca |

Objection.1: Then (D[6]) to be a qualifier is to be an object of a cognition of an entity as qualified so long as the qualifier differentiates.

And a cognition of an entity as qualified does not have as object a qualifier *known as* a qualifier, because that would be cumbersome. Rather, (let us say simply that) it has a qualifier as object. Otherwise, doubt whether there is a qualifier or an indicator would not be possible. Just for this reason, awareness of a qualifier as a qualifier is incompatible with being a visual perception or the like.

With indicators, in contrast, that which is indicated, something (e.g., Devadatta's house) that has a particular shape, etc., is the object of the cognition of an entity as qualified, not as *having crows*. For, even when it does not have crows, the house is cognized as taking that form (the particular shape, etc.). Otherwise, the difficulty would be that the cognition (of the house provoked by the indication) would be an error.

Objection.2 (against objector.1): Why (on your view) is that which is set in awareness by an utterance (e.g., about crows) outside the verbal cognition (generated, namely, a cognition of Devadatta's house as having a certain shape, etc.)?

Answer (by objector.1): Since the meaning is just that (i.e., since the crows are not an object of the cognition), your question should not be asked. For, with "The village is on the Gaṅgā," what appears (designated by the words, "on the Gaṅgā") is not the river, the flow of the water, made specific with respect to the banks. Rather, a particular bank alone (is made known), a bank as a bank. Otherwise, the case would not be similar to a (compounded) word's keeping (in compound) its own meaning (in that "crows" means crows in the expression, "By the crows, that is Devadatta's house").

Objector.2 (against objector.1): If your view were right, the indicatory word must have a metaphoric or secondary sense. For, it (in the case of "crows") has no capacity to designate (i.e., to take the word in its primary sense) the shape and so on (of the house) that gets set in awareness.

Answer (by objector.1): That, too, should not be alleged. For (the meaning is not secondary or metaphoric; rather) through the (house's) shape being set in awareness through another cause (of cognition, for example, the roof over which the crows are circling) being set in awareness by the indicatory cognition—with such a construal—is there the meaning.

Pūrvapakṣin (rejecting D^6): Do not think in that way. That the meaning is as you say is unproved. For, no word other than the indicatory word sets in awareness the thing indicated. The indicatory word sets in awareness its own meaning (crows), which sets in awareness the thing indicated (Devadatta's house). Hence, this *is* secondary meaning. Otherwise, the way we understand secondary meaning would be destroyed.

Furthermore, with (the cognition) "The pot is not (here)," the countercorrelate (or absentee, the pot), which is an indicator, is an object of the absential cognition, and there is (with an absential cognition) nothing regularly indicated (comparable to the shape, etc., indicated by the crows).

Comments

Among the twelve definitions considered by the *pūrvapakṣin*, D^6 is given by far the most attention. It draws on a picture of an indicator as known separately and outside the cognition it provokes. Thus, every cognition of a qualificandum as qualified by a property would present the property as a qualifier.

Just how this proposal is wrestled with in the text is, however, difficult to see. Also, since several issues are broached, let us look at the passage closely.

To begin not with the definition but with the second paragraph of the translation—about a qualifier's not being known as a qualifier when it is an object of a cognition of an entity as qualified—we might elaborate, sympathetically, that just about anything can be cognized through anything else. If Devadatta's house is cognized as having crows on it, the crows would be cognitively appearing as a qualifier. We cannot tell simultaneously with a cognition's occurrence, generally speaking, whether the predication content's object is a qualifier or an indicator. That would be determined later when we realize that a cognition provoked does not have as object the thing used to provoke its having the objecthood that it does. For example, the crows would be an indicator when they are used to provoke a cognition that does not in any way have them as object, but something else, for instance, Devadatta's house as having a certain shape. Whether a qualifier, upon reflection, or, to be precise, apperception, is cognized as qualifying the qualificandum of the cognition apperceived would be the test of qualification differentiating it from the mere indication. Recall that an apperception is required to see a qualifier as a qualifier, and an apperception is a type of perception distinct from those mediated by the external organs that grasp qualifiers, at least those external qualifiers, blue, a staff, and so on, that have been our focus. (Thus objector.1 says "incompatible with being a visual perception or the like.")

Objector.1 wants to stave off the objection that D^6 begs the question, ruling that all cognitive presentation is a matter of qualifier and qualificandum, with no indicators at all. Thus, the next paragraph gives an account of indicators as provoking cognitions of entities as qualified, i.e., of entities both indicated and cognized in a fashion other than that of the indicator (Devadatta's house not as having crows but as having a certain shape).

Objector.2 then hones in on the central problem with this view, namely, the mystery of an indicator's lying entirely outside of the cognition of the indicated. We are to imagine that the cognition of the indicated is generated by a bit of testimony, testimony that includes such words as "crow." What then does, for example, the word "crow" mean? And why should its meaning lie outside the cognition generated in S's companion T when S says to T, "By the crow (hovering there), you can make out Devadatta's house." Objector.1's answer in the fifth paragraph engages the issue of secondary meaning.

Secondary meaning is a large topic, one which Gaṅgeśa explores in the fourth and final chapter of the *TCM*. Objector.1's grammatical analogue—viz., a compounded word's (such as the word "king," *rāja*) keeping its own meaning in compound, "a king and a person" as opposed to "a policeman" ("a king's man") as the meaning of the Sanskrit compound, *rāja-puruṣa*—is an abstruse way of saying that the word "crow" would mean the hovering crow. But the cognition provoked does not involve the crow.

Objector.1 resists the claim that he is committed to a view of secondary meaning for the usage of "crow." On the one hand, he sees the phenomenon of indication as like the standard example of secondary meaning—"The village is on the Gaṅgā (the river)"—where the village cannot, in the directly referential and primary sense of the phrase, be "*on* the Gaṅgā," since no village is built on water. He wants to use this analogy to prove the possibility that an indicatory word can provoke a cognition of something very different from what it means in its primary sense. But, on the other hand, if objector.1 admitted that the indicatory word had a secondary sense, the cognition of the crow would be intrinsic to the cognition of the house. So he argues that an indicatory word has a literal or primary sense in picking out a thing, a crow, that then figures—in part perceptually, in part as represented verbally—as provoking a cognition of Devadatta's house. In the penultimate paragraph, the *pūrvapakṣin* pins him on this analysis, claiming that the word "crow" has a secondary sense *as explained by* objector.1. Later, in refuting D^{10}, the *pūrvapakṣin* insists that "crow" has a primary significance. Thus, from the *pūrvapakṣin*'s perspective, objector.1 goes astray by presenting an analysis that requires resort to secondary significance.

In the final paragraph, the *pūrvapakṣin* points out that the absentee of an absence is regarded as an indicator, not a qualifier—this is, by the way, presumably Gaṅgeśa's own view—whereas an absentee is also an object of an absential cognition. Therefore, D^6 is too broad.

Text (p. 872, Tirupati) and Translation

na api vyāvartakatve sati kriyânvayi viśeṣaṇam, anyad upalakṣaṇam | kriyā-hīne subhago 'yaṃ daṇḍī mahā-bāhur ity-ādau daṇḍâder a-viśeṣaṇatvâpātāt | paraṃ-parayāupalakṣaṇe 'pi kriyânvayitvāc ca | atha a-tad-vyāvṛttir vaiśiṣṭyam | tathā ca viśiṣṭa-jñāne a-tad-vyāvṛtti-viṣayo na viśeṣaṇaṃ upalakṣaṇaṃ vā | tathā ca viśiṣṭa-dhī-kāraṇa-jñāna-viṣayatve sati pratyāyya-vyāvṛtti-samānâdhikaraṇaṃ viśeṣaṇam iti | tan na | nīlam utpalam ity-ādāv a-nīlân-ullekhe a-tad-vyāvṛtty-an-ullekhāt, nīlaṃ jānāmi ity anuvyavasāya-virodhāt apohâpātāc ca |

(The **pūrvapakṣin** continues:) Nor (the following definition, D^7:) a qualifier is a differentiator that is connected to the meaning of the verb (used to express the distinction); what is other than that is an indicator. (D^7 is wrong) for, with, "Fortunate this staff-bearer, with big arms," there is no verb, a fact entailing that the staff and so on would not be qualifiers—this is the difficulty. Furthermore, though there be a (candidate) indicator (in that there is apparently no connection with the verb), still successively (through however long a chain of mediation) a connection would be involved.

Objection: The qualificative relation (implicit in a cognition of an entity as qualified) is the exclusion of what is not that (qualifier presented as predication content). And so a cognition of an entity as qualified has as its object the exclusion of what is not that (qualifier), an exclusion that is neither a qualifier nor an indicator. And so, given that there is a cognitive object (viz., such an exclusion to be made known) that causes a cognition of an entity as qualified, (D^8 is a satisfactory definition:) a qualifier is that which has the same locus as the exclusion made known.

Pūrvapakṣin: That's wrong. In the case of a cognition such as, "(That's a) blue lotus," there would be no mention of the non-blue (in the characteristic expression), in that there is no mention of "exclusion of what is not that." (Mentioning of the non-blue is not the proper expression) for that would be incompatible with the apperception, "I am cognizing something blue." Furthermore, this view runs the risk of being reducible to the (Buddhist) exclusion theory (of generality, *apoha-vāda*).

Comments

Apperception can show the content of a target cognition, which hardly need be negative in form whereas an exclusion is negative. A perceptual presentation of something blue does indeed exclude the non-blue, and the presentation can prompt cognition of the exclusion. But here the knowledge means would be inference. The exclusion is not explicit predication content. Furthermore, such issues have been thoroughly aired by Naiyāyikas of the Old school in refuting the Buddhist *apoha-vāda*, the exclusion theory of concepts.

Text (p. 873, Tirupati, and p. 829, Calcutta) and Translation

> atha vyāvartakaṃ sākṣāt-saṃbaddhaṃ nīlâdi, paraṃ-parā-saṃbaddhaṃ gṛhôpari bhramat kākâdi, tatra vyāvartanīyam adhitiṣṭhati yad dhi sākṣād eva tad viśeṣaṇam, ato viparītam anyat | daṇḍī pumān iti viśeṣaṇam, atra daṇḍaḥ puṃso, na jātiḥ anu daṇḍam asau ca tasya iti saṃbandhi-dvayâtirikta-saṃbandha-ghaṭakâ-bhāve sati saṃbandha eva sākṣāt-saṃbandhaḥ | sa ca saṃyoga-samavāya-sva-rūpa-saṃbandha-sādhāraṇe jñāne viṣayasya adhikaraṇe a-bhāvasya saṃbandhini samavāyasya asti iti teṣām api viśeṣaṇatvam iti śivādityamiśrāḥ | tan na | gaur a-nityo, rūpavān calati, rūpavati rasa ity-ādau jāte rūpasya ca sākṣāt-saṃbandhe 'pi upalakṣaṇatvāt | lohitaḥ sphaṭika ity-ādau paraṃ-parā-saṃbandhe 'pi lohitatvasya viśeṣaṇatvāt |

Objection: Blue or the like is a differentiator that is related directly (to what it qualifies, e.g., a lotus); crows or the like hovering above a house are related indirectly (to the house). For, among these two (in a statement by Śivāditya, we have, D[9]:) a qualifier *directly* occupies (or stands in) that which is to be differentiated. Thus, the other would be the opposite (i.e., an indicator would be a differentiator standing *indirectly* in a thing cognized). In the case of "The man is a staff-bearer," the man's staff is a qualifier (in that it is directly related to the man by the relation of contact). And the universal (staffhood) does not come along after (*anu*) the staff that is his. Hence, a direct relation is a relation that occurs when there is no relational factor other than its own two relatees. Contact, inherence, and self-linkage have this in common—self-linkage, that is, which obtains between a cognition and its object, an absence and its locus, and inherence and its relatees. Therefore, these (contact, etc.) all involve qualifiers.

Gaṅgeśa: This is the view of Śivāditya Miśra.

Pūrvapakṣin: It is wrong. For, in the case of cognitions such as, "The cow is not eternal" (where the universal, cowhood, which is eternal, is an indicator), "Something colored is moving" (where the color is an indicator), "There is taste in the colored thing" (where the color is again an indicator), we have indicators although the universal or the color is related *directly* (to the thing cognized). (And) in the case of cognitions such as (the erroneous cognition), "The crystal is red" (the red being due to a flower behind it), the red is a qualifier although the relation is *indirect*.

Comments

Gaṅgeśa rarely mentions philosophers by name. Śivāditya, who lived in the twelfth century, wrote a lucid exposition of the Vaiśeṣika system, *Sapta-padârthī*, whose title translates, "The Seven Categories."[3]

Direct (*sākṣāt*) relations have no intermediary, whereas indirect (*param-parā*) or chain relations work through one or more objects that serve as intermediate links. For example, conjunction or contact directly relates a hand and a staff, whereas grandparenthood is an indirect relation, having the grandparent's child, the parent of the grandchild, as intermediate link.

It bears repeating that the *pūrvapakṣin*'s definitional counterexamples are presumably accepted instances of indication as opposed to qualification. But the ones given here seem much more system-related than the hovering crows and company. Apparently, in the case of the non-veridical perception, "The crystal is red," the red is a qualifier because it helps to give rise to a cognition of an entity as qualified. In the other cases, an indicator rests objectwise in the thing cognized by a direct relation, but cognitionwise it is not in focus, so to say, functioning only to indicate something or other about which something else is expressly predicated. "The cow is not eternal" is about a cow that is directly qualified by the universal cowhood, but the cognition is not about the cow as instancing cowhood but about the individual who dies. We cognize the universal, cowhood, as related to mortality only through the intermediary of the cow. We cognize a color as related to a movement through the colored thing that moves, and a color to a taste through the tasty morsel. The most interesting example is the last, the illusion, "The crystal is red." Again, the cognitive connection between the red bit of objecthood and the crystal as qualificandum is said to be direct, although ontologically the relation is not direct, being mediated by the transparency of the crystal and the location of the flower. But cognitively the relation between redness and the crystal is direct. Cognitively, there is no intermediary, and we are prompted to describe the crystal as red.

Text (p. 873, Tirupati) and Translation

> atha anvaya-pratiyogy-upasthāpakatayā anvitam upalakṣaṇam, sākṣād-anvitaṃ viśeṣaṇam | kākâdeḥ saṃsthānâdy-upasthāpakatayā upayogāt, a-tathātve daṇḍâdivad viśeṣaṇatvam eva iti cet, na | upalakṣaṇasya lākṣaṇitvâpatteḥ, pratiyogino '-bhāve dharmântarân-upanayāc ca | atha vyāvṛtti-buddhi-samaye viśeṣya-saṃbaddhaṃ vyāvartakaṃ viśeṣaṇam, tadānīṃ viśeṣyâ-saṃbaddhaṃ vyāvartakam upalakṣaṇam | na ca jaṭā yadā yatra asti tadā tatra upalakṣaṇam | ata eva tatra eva tad eva saṃbandha-samaye viśeṣaṇam, a-saṃbandha-samaye upalakṣaṇam iti | tan na | rūpavati ghaṭe rasa ity-ādau rūpasya viśeṣaṇatva-prasaṅgāt | daṇḍy āsīd ity-ādāv atīte daṇḍasya a-viśeṣaṇatvâpātāc ca | etena yatra yad viśeṣyatâvacchedaka-dharmeṇa vyāvṛttyā vā samānâdhikaraṇatvena pratīyate tatra tad viśeṣaṇam ity api pratyuktam |

Objection: An indicator is that which is connected (to a thing cognized) through its setting the correlate to the connection in awareness. (D[10]) A qualifier is what is directly connected. The crows and so on are used to indicate (a house) by way of setting the (house's) shape in awareness. Having a staff or the like is not so. There we have in fact qualifiers.

Pūrvapakṣin: Wrong, since an indicator (as expressed) would have a secondary significance (whereas "crows" is used in its primary sense to refer to crows)—this is a difficulty. There is also (a difficulty in how the correlate that is to be set in awareness according to your definition gets targeted by the indicator, which is an apparent requirement of) a lack of a setting of another property in awareness (i.e., another property of the thing indicated) in the absence of the correlate (required according to the definition).

Objection: (D[11]) A qualifier is a differentiator that is related to the qualificandum at the time of cognition of differentiation. An indicator is a differentiator that is not related to the qualificandum at that time.

And it is not the case that whenever matted hair (for example) is cognized with respect to someone, the matted hair is an indicator (the ascetic cognized may indeed have matted hair at the time). Just for this reason, when there is the relation—when it (the matted hair or whatever) is indeed there—we have a qualifier. If there is no relation on the occasion, we have an indicator.

Pūrvapakṣin: That's wrong. For there would be the untoward ramification that with a cognition such as, "There is taste in the colored pot," the color would be a qualifier. Moreover, with "He *was* a staff-bearer" and the like, which are cognitions about something in the past, we face the difficulty that the staff would not be a qualifier.

By this reasoning is refuted too (D[12]) that a qualifier is that which is cognized, with respect to its locus, as having the same locus as the property that specifies the qualificandum (determined by the particular cognition), or the same locus as the exclusion (of the thing cognized from things that are not that qualifier).

Comments

The implication that an indicatory word would have to have a secondary sense is unfavorable, as explained in connection with D^6. The second reason given by the *pūrvapakṣin* against D^{10} reveals a problem of fixing the correlate's identity. Let us change the example to the roof of Devadatta's house. Arguably, the house remains a house without a roof (imagine the roof being replaced, and the house roofless for a couple of days).

In advancing D^{11}, the objector challenges the standard interpretation of the example of an ascetic's matted hair as an indicator. As mentioned, matted hair is thought of as something that one might lose very easily. But if an ascetic referred to really has matted hair at the time of the reference, the matted hair would be a true qualifier, not a mere indicator.

The *pūrvapakṣin* does not rebut the interpretation of the matted hair example, but focuses on other examples of indicators instead. In contrast with, "There is taste in the colored pot," we would have, "Taste *and* color are in the pot," if the color were a qualifier as opposed to an indicator. But D^{11} would have the former cognition presenting color as a qualifier. The second counterexample to D^{11}, "He *was* a staff-bearer," presumes that the staff-bearer is not now—not at the time of a cognition of differentiation from things that are not staff-bearers—being cognized as bearing a staff. Thus, the staff would be, by D^{11}, an indicator, whereas our intuitions are that it is a qualifier, at least a qualifier for the time at which the person is being cognized as bearing a staff. ("Staff-bearer" is also a synecdoche-like designation of an ascetic inasmuch as it is a common ritual requirement for an ascetic to carry a staff but not much else in his wandering.)

D^{12} is defeated by the reasoning given against D^{11}. In the case of, "There is taste in the colored pot," the color is intuitively an indicator but it also meets the terms of D^{12}.

Here ends the *pūrva-pakṣa* of the section. Next, Gaṅgeśa presents a series of definitions that he accepts.

Text (p. 874, Tirupati, and p. 833, Calcutta) and Translation

> atra ucyate | daṇḍī puruṣa iti jñānân-antaraṃ daṇḍavaty a-daṇḍa-vyāvṛttir avagamyata iti pratyāyya-vyāvṛtty-adhikaraṇatā puruṣasya daṇḍena avacchidyate na puruṣatvena, ativyāpteḥ | upalakṣaṇe tu gṛha-tāpasâdi-niṣṭha-pratyāyya-vyāvṛtty-adhikaraṇatā na kāka-jaṭâdibhir avacchidyate, tad-a-bhāvavaty api vyāvṛtti-pratīteḥ | kiṃ tu saṃsthāna-viśeṣavattvâdinā | evaṃ ca pratyāyya-vyāvṛtty-adhikaraṇatâvacchedakatve sati vyāvartakaṃ viśeṣaṇam, tad-anya-vyāvartakam upalakṣaṇam |

Gaṅgeśa: We answer. Immediately following the cognition, "The person is a staff-bearer," exclusion of things that do not have staffs with respect to the staff-bearer is inferred (on occasion). Hence, the person is the locus of an exclusion to be made known, an exclusion that is specified by the staff, not by being-a-person, since that would include too much (namely, other persons who are staff-bearers). In the case of an indicator, in contrast, an exclusion to be made known, which resides in the house, the ascetic, or the like, is not specified by the crows, the matted hair, and so on, since cognition of exclusion occurs even in their absence. Rather, it is specified by, for example, the having of a particular shape.

And so, (D^{13}) a qualifier is a differentiator that specifies a locus of an exclusion to be made known. A differentiator that is other than this is an indicator.

Comments

An indicator functions to draw attention to something else, to make one aware of a distinct property in some other locus. Nothing further about, e.g., the crows is "to be made known." A qualifier, in contrast, gives rise to a cognition of its own locus, its qualificandum, which would appropriately be known as distinct from all things that are not that qualifier. Cognition of a qualifier F is not itself a cognition of an exclusion of those things that are not-F. But, Gaṅgeśa says, there would be nothing abnormal about our immediately inferring, by a one-step inference, from a cognition of *a* as F that *a* is not not-F. Strictly speaking, the same may be said when F is an indicator: Devadatta's house is not something that does not have crows hovering above. But that is not how our focus is directed; pragmatic circumstances determine what is to be made known. Gaṅgeśa's overall context is epistemic, and we are talking about qualifiers and indicators as factors in the acquisition of knowledge. Psychological causes such as desire-to-know-X sometimes determine focus. It is to be understood as given that we are interested in the house, perhaps to go there and meet Devadatta. We have no interest in the crows. Thus we are interested in the house's more intrinsic features, its shape, its precise location, and so on. This suggests that crucial to indication are psychological facts about focus and intention and the relation of cognition to acts. We cannot read off from the nature of a perceptual or testimonial awareness whether a differentiator presented is a qualifier or an indicator. That depends on what we are interested in, including a contextual determination of a locus intended, e.g., a mentioning or focusing on crows for the purpose of making someone cognize Devadatta's house.

Gaṅgeśa does not explain here how the locus gets fixed, though it is clearly with reference to a fixed locus that qualifiers and indicators are to be distinguished. Technically, however, we can distinguish indicators and qualifiers in relation to negations to be inferred from a qualificandum brought into focus by either as a bit of predication content. That Devadatta's house does not have the shape of the house across the street is an inferendum specified by a qualifier presented as predication content (the shape of Devadatta's house), whereas it is not an inferendum specified by an indicator presented (the hovering crows).

Text (p. 877, Tirupati) and Translation

vyāvṛtty-ullekhân-antaram eva viśeṣaṇatva-buddhiḥ | tad āhur ācāryāḥ, "sad a-sad vā samānâdhikaraṇaṃ vyacchedakaṃ viśeṣaṇam, vyadhikaraṇam upalakṣaṇam" iti | asya arthaḥ svâdhikaraṇa-mātra-vṛtti-vyāvṛtti-bodhakatvaṃ svâvacchinnâdhikaraṇatāka-vyāvṛtti-bodhakatvaṃ svân-adhikaraṇâdhikaraṇaka-vyāvṛtty-a-bodhakatve sati vyāvṛtti-bodhakatvaṃ vā iti | upalakṣaṇaṃ tu svân-adhikaraṇe 'pi vyāvṛttiṃ bodhayati |

(**Gaṅgeśa** continues:) Cognition that something is a qualifier occurs only just after a mentioning of (or, an explicit awareness of) an exclusion. So, our revered teacher (Udayana) has said (D^{14}), "Whether an existent or a non-existent, a qualifier is a differentiator that has the same locus as the thing cognized. An indicator has a different locus." What he means is as follows. A qualifier makes known an exclusion occurring in precisely the locus of that qualifier. That is to say, a qualifier makes known an exclusion whose locus is specified by that qualifier. Alternatively, (D^{15}) a qualifier makes known an exclusion on the condition that this is no making known of an exclusion whose locus is not the locus of that qualifier. An indicator, in contrast, makes known an exclusion even when the exclusion's locus is not its own.

Comments

Gaṅgeśa's gloss centers on what Udayana means by a differentiator and a sharing of the same locus. After being cognized, both qualifiers and indicators make known a differentiation that obtains at a particular locus. But crows mentioned to point out Devadatta's house do not distinguish Devadatta's house with respect to things that do not have crows but rather with respect to things that are not houses. The staff carried by a staff-bearer, in contrast, does differentiate the staff-bearer from those things that are not staff-bearers.

Gaṅgeśa does not explain what he takes Udayana to mean by the phrase in D^{14}, "whether an existent or a non-existent," but Ramanuja Tatacharya interprets him as saying that absences as well as presences can be qualifiers.

The quotation, which is slightly altered from the original, occurs in Udayana's *Tātparyaṭīkapariśuddhi* commentary on *Nyāya-sūtra* 1.1.4.[4]

Text (p. 877, Tirupati, and p. 835, Calcutta) and Translation

athavā vivakṣitânvaya-pratiyogitâvacchedakaṃ viśeṣaṇam | daṇḍinam ānayet ity-ādau daṇḍas tathā | tad-an-avacchedakaṃ upalakṣaṇam, kākena devadattasya gṛhā ity-ādau kāko na gṛhasya devadattânvaya-pratiyogitâvacchedakaḥ, tad-viraha-daśāyām api devadattânvayâvagamāt | kiṃ tu gṛha-viśeṣa eva upalakaṣaṇaparicitaḥ | ata eva anvayâ-pratiyogitve 'pi na upalakṣaṇa-vaiyarthyam | yad vā yad-anvitatayā jñāta eva viśeṣye tātparya-viṣayêtarânvaya-dhīḥ tad vyavacchedakaṃ viśeṣaṇam, an-evaṃ-bhūtaṃ tad upalakṣaṇam | upalakṣaṇân-avacchinne 'py upalakṣye tātparya-viṣayī-bhūtânvaya-bodhāt | ayam eva kāryânvayi viśeṣaṇaṃ tad-an-anvayy upalakṣaṇam ity asya arthaḥ, na tu tātparya-viṣayī-bhūta-viśeṣyânvaya-bodha-viṣayatvaṃ viśiṣṭa-jñāna-viṣayatvaṃ vā, pratiyogy-a-bhāva-buddhi-viṣaya iti mate tad-a-bhāvāt | yad vā viśeṣyânvayinā yasya a-vaśyam anvayaḥ tad-avacchedakaṃ viśeṣaṇam, tad-anyad upalakṣaṇam iti | tatra upalakṣya[5]-viśeṣya-mātrânvayāt | yad vyāvartakaṃ viśeṣyânvayinā anvīyate | tad viśeṣaṇam, tad-anyad upalakṣaṇam iti vā | yad vā tātparya-viṣayânvaya-pratiyogī uddeśyânvaya-pratiyogī vā dharmo viśeṣaṇaṃ tad-anyad upalakṣaṇam ity alaṃ vistareṇa |

(**Gaṅgeśa** continues:) Alternatively, (D[16]) a qualifier specifies the correlate to an *intended* connection, as does a staff with respect to, "Bring the staff-bearer," or the like (where the action of bringing, which is the statement's intended sense, has as its correlate a person qualified by a staff, and the staff as the specifier of the correlateness). An indicator is not such a specifier. With the likes of, "By the crow (hovering overhead), it's Devadatta's dwelling" (or, "The hovering crow marks Devadatta's dwelling"), the crow does not specify the correlate of the connection of the house to Devadatta. For, the connection to Devadatta can be understood even when it is not there. On the contrary, precisely a particular house is made known by the (crow as) indicator.

Just for this reason it is false that indication is useless, in that it is appropriately used when the correlate of an intended relation is not (set in awareness, being thus unlike qualification where the correlate would be the qualifier and would be set in awareness).

Alternatively, (D[17]) when a cognition arises of connection with (x, a staff, for instance, as) something other than (a qualificandum, a staff-bearer, as) an intended object (of a statement, "Bring the staff-bearer"), x as the distinguisher is a qualifier on the condition that its qualificandum is cognized as connected with x. That which is not so is an indicator, since (by an indicator) a connection would be made known with an intended object (of a statement) when the thing indicated is not specified by the indicator.

(In such circumstances of an intended object) just that is a qualifier which is connected to the effect (e.g., a staff-bearer being brought); an indicator is not connected to that—this is its (D[17]'s) meaning. But being the object of a cognition of a connection with a qualificandum that is the intended object (of a statement), or, being the object of a cognition of an entity as qualified, is not its meaning (i.e., these are not adequate characterizations of a qualifier). For, there is (in fact) no qualifier where some find one, namely, in an absentee as object of an absential cognition (i.e., the pot mentioned in "The pot is not on the floor" is, for example, an indicator, not a qualifier, contrary to the opinion of some).

Alternatively, (D^{18}) a qualifier is a distinguisher that is connected to a qualificandum (that a cognition determines) by a connection that is necessary (or invariable, *a-vaśyam*). An indicator is otherwise (the crow, for example, is not necessarily connected to the house). For, in such a case the connection is simply that a qualificandum is indicated (with no necessity at all).

Alternatively, (since D^{18} is too narrowly conceived, as a replacement, D^{19}) a qualifier is a distinguisher that connects to a qualificandum by the relation (whether necessarily obtaining or not) to the qualificandum (that a cognition determines). An indicator is otherwise.

Alternatively, (D^{20}) a qualifier is a property that is correlate to a connection to an object that is intended by a statement; or, a property that is correlate to a connection to a thing (explicitly) designated.

But now with details enough!

Comments

When S says to T "By the crow" etc., Devadatta's house is the intended object of the statement. It is the object to which T's attention is directed, and what S intends to talk about. "Intention," *tātparya*, sometimes translated, "what a speaker means to say," may be controversial in the the context of testimonial knowledge.[6] But Gaṅgeśa's meaning in the current context is pretty clear. Indication is primarily a speaker's tool to determine a qualificandum. It becomes a term of art in analogue analyses. Indication hinges on a qualificandum being determined by a speaker's intention, by a combination of his cognition and desire, what he means to say. A qualifier constrains our understanding of its qualificandum; an indicator is extraneous to its "indicated," being used only to fix attention on that which is to be made known.

An absence, such as a pot's absence on the floor, is a qualifier with respect to its locus (the floor) and a pot a locus of the mutual absence or distinctness it has from a cloth. The pot is not a cloth, and its not being one constrains how it is known. In an absential statement such as, "The pot is not on the floor," the absentee mentioned (the pot) is an indicator. In discussing D^{17}, Gaṅgeśa says that some philosophers see, wrongly, the absentee as a qualifier.

Before considering the remaining definitions, let us again take a broad perspective on Gaṅgeśa's efforts in this section. In addition to its importance for philosophy of language, the qualifier/indicator distinction has polemical punch in various ontological controversies in late classical Indian philosophy. Qualification presented cognitively is taken (by Naiyāyikas and others) to be evidence for the way the world is, whereas indication may involve a relation between two things that is nothing more than a human construct, a referring to one thing merely to point to another. In other words, predication content involves either a qualifier or an indicator, and if a bit of predication content can be ruled an indicator, we would have therein no evidence about the nature of the indicated—unlike an experience of a qualifier.

At the end of the first paragraph, Gaṅgeśa suggests the contradictoriness test of referential as opposed to attributive usages as these terms are sometimes employed by philosophers now: Devadatta's house, though referred to by the expression "having hovering crows" may be perceived, rather immediately, as not having hovering crows, for the expression is merely indicatory or referential, whereas picked out by "having a certain shape" it cannot be known as not having that shape—unless, of course, there intervened something dramatic and relevant to the attributed property such as Devadatta adding a room. The Nyāya law is that a perception with contradictory objecthood cannot be a direct successor cognition: no perception that *a* is F can be followed by a cognition that *a* is not-F, understanding F to be a qualifier. But we can know immediately that Devadatta's house is without crows. ("Smith's murderer did not murder Smith.") Provoked to cognition C through indication as opposed to her own perception of a qualified object, a subject does not expect that the object indicated has the indication-vehicle as a true property, as anything to know it as.

Yet however intuitive the distinction, it is not easy to say precisely what it amounts to. As pointed out in my *Classical Indian Metaphysics*, Gaṅgeśa's son Vardhamāna complains outright about its slipperiness,[7] and Gaṅgeśa, too, has trouble. More or less obvious problems face the one or the other of his definitions (does not the staff direct attention to the person in the same way as the crow directs attention to the house? could not the person cease to be a staff-bearer in the same sense as the house could cease to have the crow? is the qualification relation in any sense necessary? what does "connection" mean? is not the color *connected* to the pot referred to with, "There is taste in the colored pot"?). It is possible that Gaṅgeśa is not to be read as presenting a list of adequate definitions (as is his usual practice) but a list of further candidates—the examination of which is too detailed to continue now. In particular, the opposition between D^{18} and D^{19} supports this interpretation.

But whatever the merits, or failings, of the definitions, Gaṅgeśa has a good point in advancing the practical usefulness of indication. In certain contexts, we do not have to mention a true qualifier to bring something into focus. We can indicate it by whatever is appropriate in the context, by mentioning something that may have the feeblest of relations, practically no relation, to the thing to which we refer. Indication is noncommittal—a feature taken to heart by philosophers other than Naiyāyikas. Certain Advaitins, for example, say that their statements about Brahman, the Absolute, are only indicators, meant to direct our attention to Brahman in our own meditative experience, not to say what Brahman is. Thus they would avoid certain predicaments.[8]

atha savikalpaka-vādaḥ

NOW, DISCOURSE ON DETERMINATE COGNITION

Text (p. 881, Tirupati, and p. 839, Calcutta) and Translation

savikalpakaṃ ca viśiṣṭa-jñānaṃ yathā gaur ayam iti | tac ca sāmānyâdīnāṃ paramârtha-sattvena arthajatvād indriyajatvāc ca pratyakṣam | kvacit saṃskāra-sahakāri-vaśena tattā-viśiṣṭasya idantā-viśiṣṭâ-bhedôllekhī aindriyako vikalpaḥ |

Gaṅgeśa: And determinate (as opposed to indeterminate perception) is cognition of an entity as qualified, for example, "This is a cow." And this would be a perception inasmuch as it would be produced both by an object—such as a universal, which is an ultimately real existent—and by a sense organ.

In some cases (viz., recognition, e.g., "This is that Devadatta"), the determinate cognition is sensory with an identity manifest between that which is qualified by thisness and that which is qualified by thatness, inasmuch as a memory-impression serves as an auxiliary cause.

Comments[1]

Gaṅgeśa begins this final section of the chapter by alluding to the Buddhist exclusion view of generality (*apoha-vāda*), according to which universals are not objects in the world but fabrications of the mind. In contrast, Gaṅgeśa says, ". . . a universal, which is an ultimately real existent." The allusion is interesting in the context of a metaphysical debate about identity, or endurance over time, more about which shortly.

A perception that is a simple cognition of an entity as qualified such as, "This is a cow," is relatively unproblematic compared to a recognition such as, "This is that Devadatta," taken to be perceptual. The apparent co-intentionality of the "this" and the "that" presented—or the co-referentiality of the two terms used in the characteristic verbalization—is mysterious since the two terms are not synonyms. Furthermore, the "that" seems dubiously perceptual. Gaṅgeśa's strategy is to argue that a recognition is a single perceptual cognition with a memory-impression, *saṃskāra*, playing an auxiliary causal role. Thus *a fortiori* "This is a cow" would be perceptual even though, unlike the example in the *nirvikalpaka-vāda*, cows have been experienced previously and a cowhood memory-impression plays an auxiliary causal role. Error, e.g., "This is silver," is similarly analyzed. Its predication content (silverhood) appears to be presented perceptually with a *saṃskāra* as an auxiliary causal factor—in contrast to the Prābhākara "two cognition" analysis. The Prābhākara also sees recognition as two cognitions, but, unlike the case with error, we are not unaware of their difference. The Prābhākara view seems to make an epistemically relevant distinction, since memory seems to have less authority than perception. So, is a recognition a single determinate perceptual cognition—the Nyāya position—or two cognitions, a perception (accounting for the "this") and a remembering (accounting for the "that")—the Prābhākara view? Or, as Buddhists hold, do the "this" and the "that" indicate distinct realities? Furthermore, does the role of memory make a recognition's veridicality suspect? Does it make identification of a cow suspect when memory-impressions inform our categorization of Bessie? What is the epistemic value of remembering and the significance of *saṃskāras* playing a causal role?

In the discussion that follows, it is again helpful to imagine a conversational context. In Gaṅgeśa's verbalization of a typical recognitional cognition, "This is that Devadatta," the term "that" may be construed as an anaphor for a definite description of a certain type (answering the question, "Which Devadatta?"). The usage implies, in particular, that Devadatta has been perceived before. In effect, "this" and "that" function as variables, and the debate concerns restrictions of use and range. We may imagine a cognizer S telling a companion T, "This is that Devadatta whom I saw yesterday," substituting for the "that" the description capturing some such property as "being seen yesterday by me." The cognition that Gaṅgeśa focuses on, "This is that Devadatta," is to be thought of, nevertheless, as S's own, and as verbalizable but as non-testimonial not necessarily verbal in form.

Gaṅgeśa gives the core of his view right here at the beginning: recognition is a perception informed by a memory-impression as an auxiliary cause. The problem of how an object's thatness can be perceptually presented is solved through the theory of extraordinary sensory connection that we have encountered before, *a-laukika-saṃnikarṣa*, the three kinds of which are: (a) connection characteristic of knowledge of unexperienced instances of a universal, (b) connection mediated by cognition, i.e., memory, and (c) connection born of yogic merit. The second, *jñāna-lakṣaṇā-pratyāsatti*, has a role in recognition, as Gaṅgeśa says here. A current sensory encounter with Devadatta, who has been previously perceived by the person now recognizing him, sparks memory to project into the perception the "thatness." It is to be stressed that, for Gaṅgeśa and other realists, Devadatta is thought of as qualified by thatness in fact. Like an absence that exists independently of cognition but whose cognition depends on memory to furnish the absentee, a recognition depends on memory for the "thatness" cognitively though the thing recognized is the that in fact. The presentation of the "that" qualifier has a memory-impression as an auxiliary cause and is thus extraordinary, not the fact that Devadatta has thatness.

As was particularly clear in the debate about error in the *anyathā-khyāti-vāda* (above, p. 308), the of recognition is an issue central to the Prābhākara/Naiyāyika dispute over perception in general. The Prābhākara uses recognition as a model for his omission view of error (i.e., as two cognitions whose difference goes unnoticed), and, as we have seen, the ties to other areas of theory are, in each case, multiple and tight.

Text (p. 839, Calcutta) and Translation

nanv eka-kārya-sahakāritvam anyatra, pratyabhijñānaṃ tu na ekaṃ jñānam tad-aṃśe pārokṣasya idam-aṃśe ca a-pārokṣasya anubhavena viruddha-dharma-saṃsargāt | na ca idaṃ yathârtham | an-eka-deśa-kāla-sambandhasya ekatra bādhāt | eka-kālâdi-saṃsarga-tad-a-bhāva-vyavacchedavat tad-a-vinā-bhūta-kālântarâdi-saṃbandha-vyavacchedāt | tad a-yathārthatve bahu viplaveta iti cet, na | pārokṣyâ-pārokṣyayor iha a-siddheḥ, indriya-janyatvena a-parokṣatva-niyamāt, tattâṃśasya ca smṛty-upanītatvāt indriya-saṃbaddha-viśeṣaṇatā-pratyāsatteḥ | na ca eka-kāla-saṃbandhaḥ kālântara-saṃbandhâ-bhāvâ-vinā-bhūtaḥ, ekasmin nānā-dik-saṃbandhasya jñāne 'n-eka-viṣayatvasya ca vyāghātâpatteḥ | sākṣāt karomi ity anuvyavasāye bādhakâ-bhāvāc ca |

Objection (by a Prābhākara): There are cases of auxiliary causes of a single effect elsewhere. But recognition is not a single cognition, since (if it were) there would be a union of incompatible properties—in that there would be an experience of something not present, with respect to the "that" portion (of the cognition), as well as of something present, with respect to the "this" portion.

Moreover (if it were a single cognition) a recognition could not correspond to the object (*yathârtha*, i.e., could not be correct). For, multiple places and times cannot (simultaneously) relate to a single thing. Something connected to a single time and so on excludes (by nature) an absence of that (time and so on), since such a connection invariably excludes a relation to another time and so on.

But if there is no correspondence, unwanted consequences flood in. (Therefore, a recognition is comprised of two cognitions, a perception and a remembering.)

Gaṅgeśa: No. It has not been shown that the (temporally) distant and the immediate converge here. For, as generated by a sense organ, a recognition is a cognition that is tied, by rule, to the immediate. Furthermore, the "that" portion is presented extraordinarily through memory in that it serves to connect the qualifier with the object in relation to the sense organ.

And it is not true that a relation to one time invariably excludes a relation to another time. For, the difficulty would be that a single thing's relationship (at different times) to various directions (east, south, etc.) would be impossible, as well as a cognition's having multiple objects.

Moreover, there is no counterconsideration to the (evidence of) apperception (whose target is a recognition), "I am immediately aware" (i.e., "I am immediately aware that this is that Devadatta," as opposed to, "I am remembering Devadatta").

Comments

The Prābhākara presumes that the two Sanskrit pronouns translated "this" and "that" are used to make a temporal distinction: "that" meaning something past and "this" something present. Indeed, Gaṅgeśa himself seems to presume as much throughout the section. Now, the English correlative pronouns, "this" and "that" have roughly the same range of meaning as the Sanskrit, *idam* and *tat*: use of the former implies that its referent is *close* to the speaker, and the latter that it is *distant*. With the examples we shall see here, the distance relation is assumed to be temporal and tied to the thesis that perception presents something contemporaneous (in a loose sense) and memory something past. Gaṅgeśa would not dispute, we may presume, that the two pronouns—so frequently employed (like "this" and "that" in English)—could be used to express other relations, such as relative spatial distance from a perceiver. But the current focus is the type of cognition called recognition, and, in particular, assumptions about the temporality of a recognition's object. The meaning of "this" and "that" in verbalizations of recognitions such as "This is that" is our topic.

On a realist view about enduring objects, there is no impossibility—Gaṅgeśa implies, denying the Prābhākara's argument—that a single thing be connected to multiple times. A single thing can be at different places at different times. It can have, at different times, properties that it could not have at the same time, such as being black and being red. Therefore, the Prābhākara complaint about incompatible properties is unfounded.

Furthermore, apperception of recognition shows recognition to be an immediate experience, not a remembering, since there is no defeater countering its default epistemic force.

Of course, ontologically there must be something that grounds the intentionality of the presentation of what is verbalized as "that" in, e.g., "This is *that* Devadatta"—unless the cognition is non-veridical. In a series of passages below, a *pūrvapakṣin*, who has the dominant voice, refutes purported ways to understand such thatness. Gaṅgeśa's own view of thatness follows, pp. 670ff.

Possibly the *pūrvapakṣin* is to be understood not as a Prābhākara but as a Buddhist advocating momentariness. Through centuries of debate recognition is the principal evidence cited by Naiyāyikas to show enduring entities, against the Buddhist position. Recognition proves that Devadatta has endured from the time of a first encounter to the time of the recognitional event. It also proves the endurance of the perceiver, the self who recognizes, as Vātsyāyana himself makes plain.[2] Buddhists deny the evidence. The metaphysical debate may to taken to inform our *pūrvapakṣin*'s stance. The *pūrvapakṣin* appears opposed to any attempt to account for the "thisness" and "thatness" putatively manifest in a recognition, offering no account of his own. On the other hand, it is hard to identify any particular statement of his as marking a Buddhist view uniquely, and there is, as mentioned, reference to the Prābhākara view of illusion.

Text (p. 882, Tirupati) and Translation

> nanu kā iyaṃ tattā, na tāvad atīta-samaya-saṃbandhaḥ, an-āgata-gocara-smṛti-pratyabhijñayos tattôllekhāt, pratyakṣânubhūyamāna-ghaṭâdau atīta-samayâvacchedânumāne tattā-dhī-vyapadeśayor a-bhāvāt, atīta-samaya-saṃbandhâvagame 'pi so 'yaṃ na vā saṃśayāt, sa na ayam iti viparyayāt, tad-a-bhāvâvagame 'pi so 'yam iti pratīteḥ, atīta-samaya-viśiṣṭaḥ sa iti saha-prayogāt, kāle tad-a-bhāvāc ca | etena jñāta-dharmântara-vaiśiṣṭyaṃ tattā iti nirastam |

Objection (by a *pūrvapakṣin*): But what is this thatness (purportedly perceived in a recognition, e.g., "This is *that* Devadatta")?

It is not, first of all, (D^1) "relation to a past occasion." For, the thatness cognitively manifest in (or, mentioned on the basis of) a memory or recognition could include something future (as were someone to say, "This is *that* Devadatta whom I shall see tomorrow"). (Furthermore) with respect to something being experienced in the present perceptually, such as a pot, which is inferred to be qualified by or connected to a past occasion (as in "By the water mark, this pot was full yesterday upto this point"), there need be neither cognition of nor reference to thatness. (Furthermore) although a relation to a past occasion is cognized, there can still be the doubt, "Is *that* (person whom I saw) this (person) or not?" as well as the error, "This is not *that*." (And) although an absence of such (a relation to a past occasion) be cognized, the cognition "This is *that*" occurs (as in "This pot being made now is *that* pot which I shall use tomorrow"). (Furthermore, there should be no) usage together (of the term "that" and "connection with a past occasion," but there is, viz.) "That is connected to a past occasion." And (finally, we do find, "This is *that time*," whereas on the current proposal) "that" (as meaning a relation to a past occasion) should not occur with respect to a time (since times do not have times).

By this reasoning (because the doubt and so on can and do occur) is the view rejected that thatness is (D^2) "something's being qualified by another property previously known."

Comments

In this highly elliptical passage, several reasons are given for rejecting the naïve view that any "that" used to express a recognition means in some way a past occasion. The first reason trades on a predictive usage, showing that recognizing or mentioning a "that" does not guarantee reference to the past. The second is that mentioning a "that" is unnecessary: we can make inferences to a past state of an object without using a "that." Third, if the "that" is to mean only something as past, no doubt or error would be expressed, for instance, "Is *that* this?" or "This is not *that*," for the connection with the past would be apparent. However, these do occur. Conversely, fourth, when we understand there to be no relation to a past occasion, we may still legitimately say, "This is *that* (pot which I shall use tomorrow)." Fifth, D^1 would imply that "that" and "connection with a past occasion" are synonyms, and so, like synonyms, the two would not normally be used in apposition. However, there is nothing exceptional about that usage. Finally, we could not use "that" with regard to a time, because a time would then have to endure and have a past. But we do legitimately cognize and say, "*That* time."

The same reasons refute the stricter view, D^2, that the recognitional "that" picks out not just a relation to a past occasion but something's being qualified by a property known on a previous occasion. A supposition of a rigid tie or identity between a presentational "that" and something past seems to lie at the bottom of the deficiencies.

Text (p. 840, Calcutta) and Translation

> na ca tad-vṛtti-guṇâdikam eva tattā, tad-avagame 'pi tad-an-avagamāt, tad-an-avagame 'pi tad-avagamāc ca | na apy atīta-jñāna-vaiśiṣṭyam, pareṇa jñāta iti jñāne 'pi sa iti prayogâ-bhāvāt | na apy etaj-janmâtīta-sva-jñāna-vaiśiṣṭyam | tad-avagame 'pi tattā-saṃśaya-viparyaya-darśanāt, atīta-jñāna-viśiṣṭaḥ sa iti saha-prayogāt, atītânubhava-viṣayatvasya anubhavâ-viṣayatvena smṛtyā tad-ullekhân-upapatteś ca |

(The **pūrvapakṣin** continues:) And it is wrong to hold that the thatness is (D^3) "the qualities, etc., occurring in it." For, even when those are known, the thing may not be known, and even when those are not known, the thing may be known.

Nor is it (D^4) "to be qualified by a past cognition." For, there may be such a cognition, for instance, (Devadatta) cognized by another (person), while there is no usage of "that" (on one's own part).

Nor is it (D^5) "to be qualified by a past cognition belonging to oneself in this lifetime." For, even when such qualification is known, doubt and error about the thatness can occur. Furthermore, "that" and "qualified by a past cognition (etc.)" are used together (and true synonyms would not be used in apposition). And it would be impossible for a that to be mentioned in connection with a memory, inasmuch as a (remembering requires the remembered to have been experienced and) past experience as an object cannot be the object of an experience (since a past experience is over and gone and unavailable for a current experience).

Comments

D^3 fails because no set of properties exhausts what a particular is; the bare particular transcends its qualities, motions, and so on. A package of properties might be known and the thing that the "that" picks out not be known, and conversely. D^4 suffers from vagueness: a past cognition as specified by the definition could belong to another person. Later, Gaṅgeśa will endorse a view of the recognitional "that" that ties it to a previous cognition—assuming that the person who is using "that" now is the person who had the previous cognition. Such a requirement is made explicit with D^5, which, however, still fails. For, "Is it *that* or not?" is a doubt that arises sometimes even when the thing is known as having been perceived before, the "that" referring to the thing at some third occasion. Furthermore, the definition would provide a synonym for the thatness expressed in a recognition, but the two terms are sometimes used together in apposition—breaking, we may say, a pragmatic rule. Finally, one might use "that" simply to express what one remembers, but D^5 would tie the usage to the pastness of a past experience, which could not possibly have been the object of an awareness and thus which could not be remembered.

Text (p. 882, Tirupati, and p. 840, Calcutta) and Translation

yat tu atītânubhava-viṣayatvaṃ tattā | tac ca anubhava-viṣayatvena[3] yadā jñānântareṇa gṛhyate tadā sa ghaṭa iti smaraṇam, no cet pramuṣṭa-tattākaṃ ghaṭa iti | tan na | atītânubhava-viṣayatvasya anumitau bhāne 'pi sa iti dhī-vyapadeśayor a-bhāvāt, atītânubhava-viṣayatva-niścaye 'pi tattā-saṃśaya-viparyaya-darśanāt saha-prayogân-upapatteḥ, jñānântareṇa atītânubhava-viṣayatva-grahe tattôllekhâpatteś ca | atha atīta-dharma-vaiśiṣṭyaṃ tattā | sa dharmaḥ kvacit samayaḥ kvacit jñānâdiḥ | na ca atīta-dharma-viśiṣṭaḥ sa iti saha-prayogân-upapattiḥ | dharma-viśeṣam ādāya tad-upapatteḥ | tad-a-pratītāv api sa iti pratītir a-siddhā eva | na ca atīta-dharma-viśiṣṭa-pratītāv api sa na vā iti saṃśayāt sa na ayam iti viparyayāc ca na evam iti vācyam | niścita-dharmêtara-dharma-viśeṣa-viśayatvena tayor upapatter iti cet | mā evam | yadi vastu-gatyā yo 'tīto dharmas tad-vaiśiṣṭyaṃ tattā, tadā anubhave 'pi tad-viṣayatvāt tattôllekhâpattiḥ | na apy atītatvena yo bhāsate dharmas tad-vaiśiṣṭyam, bhāsamāna-dharmasya atītatvena anubhavâ-viṣayatvāt pratyuta vartamānatvena anubhavāt smṛtau tad-ullekhân-upapatteś ca |

Objection: Then to be a that is (D^6) "to be a past experience's object." And when (the thing, i.e.,) the that is, as an object of a (past) experience, grasped by another cognition, then (e.g.) "*That* pot" would be a remembering. Or, on the other hand, if a that is not explicitly remembered, a cognition can have a that "stolen away," (thus, the cognition) "(The) pot." (Therefore, the thing does not have to be expressly presented or verbalized as "that.")

Pūrvapakṣin: The view is wrong. For, sometimes no cognition or usage, "That," is to be found although an inference to an object of a past experience occurs ("By this mark, this is yesterday's pot"). And even when a clear determination occurs of an object as of a past experience, there can still be the doubt ("Is *that* this?") as well as the error ("This is not *that*"). Further, there should not be usage together (of synonyms, but there would be). And (finally) when an object of a past experience has been grasped by another cognition, the difficulty would be that mention (or explicit presentation) of thatness should occur (but sometimes does not).

Objection.1: Thatness is (D^7) "something's being (or having been) cognized as qualified by a past property." The property is sometimes an occasion or context, sometimes a cognition or the like.

And (on this view) it is not inappropriate to use the terms together, namely, "that" and "cognized as qualified by a past property." Such would be (possible and) appropriate presuming (the one to pick out) a particular property (while the other term would pick out another property).

Objection.2 (against objector.1): Even when such is not cognized, there can be a cognition, "That."

Answer (by objector.1): Such a cognition simply does not occur.

Objector.2 (against objector.1): Your view is wrong, because even when something is cognized as having been cognized as qualified by a past property there can be the doubt, "Is it *that* or not?" as well as the error, "This is not *that*."

Answer (by objector.1): Such should not be alleged. For, such doubt and error are possible insofar as a cognition has as object some particular property that is other (relative) to the specifically and clearly cognized property (that is the object of "that").

Pūrvapakṣin: Don't think that way. If the thatness is to be something taken as having been cognized as qualified by a *thingwise* property that is past, then there would be the difficulty that "that" should be mentioned (and explicitly presented) even when there is (current) awareness (of the property, as in, "This is such-and-such") since the that would be the object (of the current experience).

Objection: (Then) thatness is (D^8) "something's having been cognized as qualified by a property that is *presented* as past."

Pūrvapakṣin: No, that's wrong, too. For, on the contrary, a property that is appearing as past is not an awareness's object (but, rather, a remembering's). Moreover, inasmuch as there would be awareness of something as occurring currently, there would be no mention (or explicit presentation) of the that in a remembering (since awareness blocks remembering).

Comments

D^6 expresses a position reminiscent of the Prābhākara view of illusion: awareness of the distinctness between an awareness (of something in front) and a remembering (of, e.g., silver) is, by an epistemic defect, omitted or "stolen away." Similarly, when we fail to express the fact that an object was experienced before, saying simply "Book" (or "The book," *pustakam*, referring to a book in front), instead of, "*That* book" (*tat pustakam*), we do know and mean to imply that this is the same book that we saw yesterday. The *pūrvapakṣin* retorts that when we are aware of something as an object of a past experience by, for example, an inference, we need not say "that" when we express what we cognize. And there are the other difficulties mentioned.

D^7 is subtler, and draws our attention to things having multiple properties. Devadatta would have had in the past many properties that would not have endured to the present. These may or may not have been cognized by us. Thus, operating by the logic of D^7 we might still legitimately question whether Devadatta cognized as F is the Devadatta we cognized as G.

The proponent of D^7 also suggests that something can be referred to as *that* while the particular property through which it is being cognized or picked out varies with context. This would allow usage together of D^7 and a "that" ("*That* is something cognized as qualified by a past property"). The *pūrvapakṣin*, we see here, catches the equivocation. However, below we shall find Gaṅgeśa making the same move. D^7, moreover, is not far from a definition that Gaṅgeśa accepts, D^9.

The problem with D^8 seems to be that no experience endures to be an object of a current awareness (niceties about apperception notwithstanding).

Text (p. 883, Tirupati) and Translation

> na ca anubhavântaraṃ yadā jñānântareṇa atīta-dharma-vaiśiṣṭya-bhānaṃ tadā smṛtau tattôllekho na anyadā iti vācyam | atīta-dharmasya anumitau tattôllekhâpatteḥ |

Objection: Thatness is mentioned (is presented explicitly) in a remembering just on occasions when—*following* an awareness, not otherwise (i.e., not when there is a direct awareness of a property that has endured from the past)—there occurs a presentation of a cognitive relation to a past property (grasped) by another cognition.

Pūrvapakṣin: That should not be said. The difficulty (with restricting "that" to memory) is that with an inferential awareness of a past property there can be mention of thatness.

Comments

That can be the object of an inferential awareness of a past property. But such an inferential awareness "follows an awareness," too. Thus, since an inferential awareness is not a remembering, the current proposal is too broad.

Text (p. 883, Tirupati) and Translation

> idantā api na tan-mātra-vṛtti-guṇâdikam, anumānâdinā tad-avagame 'pi ayam iti vyapadeśâ-bhāvāt | pratyakṣeṇa tad-avagame ayam iti vyapadeśa iti cet, na | vācasya pramāṇa-gocaratayā vyapadeśasya niyantum a-śakyatvāt | guṇâdāv api tan-nirvacane an-anugamāt |

(The **pūrvapakṣin** continues:) *Thisness* (as is evident in a recognition, "*This* is that), too, is not (E^1) "qualities, etc., occurring only in the thing." For, when those are known through, for instance, inference, as can happen, too (there being no restriction to perception), the expression "this" may not be used.

Objection: When the thing is known by perception, the expression "this" is used.

Pūrvapakṣin: No. Usage of "this" cannot be restricted according to a designatum's being made known by a particular knowledge source (perception or any other). (Moreover) since the word is used to refer to qualities and so on, too (and not just to a thing as uniquely possessing certain qualities, etc.), there would be no uniformity (of thisness and thus no uniformity of meaning).

Comments

The first proposal about thisness, E^1, is a variation of D^3 given above as a definition of thatness. E^1 is not taken seriously until it is expanded and qualified as restricting usages of "this" to things known perceptually. Now there may be limitations to what the various sources can make known, but these do not translate, according to the *pūrvapakṣin*, into restrictions governing what can be a this. The proof is linguistic practice. Anything known through any *pramāṇa* can be the indication of a "this."

The problem is not only lack of correlation to knowledge source but also the difficulty that qualities, motions, etc.—picked out without awareness of that in which they occur—can be meant by a "this." We can point to qualities. Our verbal practices are not circumscribed in the way implied.

Text (p. 884, Tirupati) and Translation

na ca etad-vyakty-āśrayatvam, idam-etadoḥ paryyāyatvāt | na api pratyakṣa-jñāna-gocaratvam, a-cākṣuṣatvâpattcḥ atīte tad-anumāne 'yam iti-buddhi-vyapadeśâ-bhāvāt smṛtyā api tad-ullekhâpatteś ca |

(The **pūrvapakṣin** continues:) And (thisness is) not (E^2) "that whose substratum is that individual." For "this" and "that" would be synonyms (which is absurd).

Nor (is thisness, E^3) "an object of perceptual cognition." For (replacing the terms of the definition, a this would be grasped by, e.g., the visual organ, and so being an object of the visual organ would be grasped by the visual organ, but) there is the difficulty that it (an object as exhibiting "being an object of the visual organ") is not an object of the visual organ. Furthermore, when by inference a past object is known to have been an object of perception, neither the cognition nor the name "this" need occur ("that" typically being used instead). Finally, there is the difficulty that "this" would also be used in connection with remembering (since a past object remembered would be "an object of perception"—otherwise it would be unavailable for remembering).

Comments

Rucidatta says there would be definitional circularity (*ātmâśraya*) with E^2, with "this" needed to define "that" as well as vice-versa.

As we shall see, Gaṅgeśa himself takes usage of "this" to be normally restricted to or connected to objects being known perceptually, while usage of "that" is normally to suggest pastness or temporal distance and connection to memory. Nevertheless, the objections to E^3 are cogent, since the definition is too imprecise, suggesting that being an object of visual perception is a property that could be visually perceived. There are also the further difficulties mentioned.

Text (p. 884, Tirupati, and p. 842, Calcutta) and Translation

atra kecid āhuḥ | tattêdante smṛty-anubhava-bhāsinyau a-khaṇḍe eva upādhī kḷpta-dharmâtirekhiṇau | evaṃ ca idantā-saṃskāreṇa idantā eva tattayā smaryate | na ca tattāyāḥ kvacid an-ārope katham āropa iti vācyam | pratyabhijñāyāṃ tattâṃśe yathârthatvāt | idantân-ullekhy-anubhava-prabhava-smaraṇe dharmântaram eva tattayā bhāsate | ata eva ayaṃ ghaṭa iti na smaraṇam | ata eva sarvā smṛtir a-yathârthā a-yathârthânubhavā ca | hari-harâdy-anucintanaṃ ca kavi-kāvya-mūla-jñāna-vat mano-ratha-jñāna-vac ca sākāṅkṣa-padārtha-jñāna-prabhavam anubhava-rūpam eva iti | tan na | smṛteḥ pūrvam idantôpasthitiṃ vinā tatra tattāropâ-saṃbhavāt | kiṃ ca tattâṃśe 'n-anubhūta-gocaratvena smṛteḥ saṃskāra-sīmā-laṅghane idantā tattayā smaryata ity atra mānâ-bhāvāt | ghaṭa eva tattayā smaryata ity astu lāghavāt iti |

(The **pūrvapakṣin** continues:) Here some hold the following view.

Innovator (proposing novel ontological categories): Thatness and thisness, which are presented by memory and awareness, are just unanalyzable "surplus properties" (*upādhi*), properties that are not subsumable under the well-known and established properties (according to the Nyāya-Vaiśeṣika system).

And so, a this itself is (in any particular case) remembered as a that by way of a thisness memory-impression.

Objection (against the innovator): How then could there be superimposition (of a that, an illusory projection of a thatness), in that there could be no superimposition of thatness anywhere (since only that which has been cognized previously can be superimposed)?

Innovator: That should not be asked. For (the thatness would be previously known:) the thatness portion of a recognition conforms to its object (i.e., is veridical in that it is in "object-conformity," *yathârthatva*).

A remembering arises by force of an awareness wherein a thisness was not explicitly an object (e.g., "Pot"): in the remembering (e.g., "That pot") just another property appears as a that. Precisely for this reason, "*This* is a pot," is not a remembering (but a perceptual awareness). Therefore, *all memory fails to be in object-conformity* (period)—in addition to falling outside of object-conforming awareness (in that remembering is distinct from awareness).

And (this view is not irreligious:) recalling Hari (Viṣṇu), Hara (Śiva), and so forth—like the root cognition of a poet for his poetry and like fancy—(is not remembering, not a cognitive error but) simply takes the form of an awareness born of verbal cognition founded in (fulfilled) syntactic expectancy (etc.).

Pūrvapakṣin: This view is wrong. Without a (corresponding) thisness having been set in experience previously, superimposition of thatness is not possible.

Furthermore, there is no evidence in support of the view that a this is remembered as a that—that is, there is none unless you (illicitly) jump over the boundary of a memory's requiring a memory-impression—inasmuch as there would be—concerning a thatness portion—nothing that had been experienced before. (Not, as you say, a this is erroneously remembered as a that, but) just the pot is remembered as a that—let this be the position, since it is simpler.

Comments

The ontological innovator views recognition as a perception and as a veridical awareness even in its thatness portion. A thing cognized in a recognition, "This is that," is in fact both a this and a that. A remembering, on the other hand, fails to conform to the object cognized, presumably because an experience of something as a *this* would have been converted, through a memory-impression, into a remembering of a *that*. The cognitive law that frames the discussion is that nothing that has not been previously experienced can be either (a) remembered or (b) superimposed and presented non-veridically. The innovator is able to answer the objection that his view is impossible because thatness would be unavailable (not having been veridically apprehended in an awareness) by reminding us that recognition does, on his view, constitute veridical experience of thatness.

The innovator's view about the non-veridicality of remembering, which foreshadows Udayana's view discussed at the end of the section, is not simply the point that since a remembering is not an awareness (and only awarenesses can be veridical) a remembering is not veridical. Rather, his position is that remembering is constitutionally non-veridical, or, to use a less technical term, not in "object-conformity," *yathârthatva*. Just why is not made very clear at this point, but Udayana's arguments to the same conclusion do get aired below.

Testimonial cognitions, all of which arise out of comprehending a string of words fulfilling conditions for meaningfulness, are awarenesses, not rememberings. Thus, the innovator is not stuck with the position that recalling God (meditating "Hari, Hara, and so on") would be erroneous.

The *pūrvapakṣin* does not accept the purported perceptual status of recognition. But, of course, there are the common practices of people saying, "This is that," and the cognitions—the recognitions—which such usages seem to express. It seems that such cognitions and usages occur, moreover, only when there has been an experience of a this. Now, we might suppose that the *pūrvapakṣin* as a Buddhist (an anti-intellectualist) might refuse to offer a substitute explanation of the linguistic practice were he asked. However, there is offered the barest bones of an alternative theory when it is indicated at the end that, for instance, the remembering "That pot" has not a this but a pot as its object. And the *pūrvapakṣin* defends the view, saying it is simpler.

Text (p. 885, Tirupati, and p. 843, Calcutta) and Translation

atra ucyate | anubhave kālo dharmântaraṃ yo vā vartamānatvena viṣayaḥ sa eva smaraṇasya, anubhava-smaraṇayor eka-viṣayatve 'pi smaraṇe tatra tac-chabda-prayogaḥ, saṃskāra-ja-jñānasya eva tac-chabda-prayoga-hetutvāt | ata eva pratyabhijñāne tatra tac-chabda-prayogaḥ, pratyakṣânubhave tatra eva idaṃ-śabda-prayogaḥ na tu viṣaya-kṛto 'nubhava-smaraṇayor viśeṣaḥ | ata eva ayaṃ ghaṭa ity anubhavād ayaṃ ghaṭa iti na smaraṇam, sa ghaṭa iti smaraṇa-kāraṇaṃ sa ghaṭa iti na anubhavaḥ |

Gaṅgeśa: Here we answer. Whatever object—whether a time interval or any property—appears as current in experience, just that (and not something else) is remembered. Although an experience and a remembering can have the same object, "that" would be used in connection with a remembering of it, since a cognition born of a memory-impression prompts usage of the word "that."

Just for this reason, the word "that" is used for a recognition's object. The word "this" is used for the same object when the object is experienced perceptually (e.g., "This pot"). There is not, however, a difference that is object-based between (usages in connection with) an awareness and a remembering.

Just for this reason, the remembering that arises out of the awareness, "This pot," (nevertheless) is not "This pot" (but rather "That pot"). The awareness that gives rise to the remembering, "That pot," (nevertheless) is not "That pot" (but rather "This pot").

Comments

Gaṅgeśa holds that the information contained in "That pot" (*sa ghaṭaḥ*) includes the fact that the expression is of a remembering. The meaning or indication of a "That" includes the fact that a remembering is its cognitive ground. What is indicated with a "That" is the same thing ontologically as with a "This." But the information in a "This" includes the fact that its source is a perception.

Concerning a recognition, "This is that," Gaṅgeśa's view is that the cognition is perceptual with the thatness presented—presented extraordinarily—through memory (*jñāna-lakṣaṇā-pratyāsatti*). The property is presented through a perceptual connection that works through memory.

In the current passage, the concern is primarily to explain why "that" and "this" have a different meaning or intentionality although their referent is the same. In the next paragraph, the ontological problem comes into focus. What is the object of a "This" and of a "That"? Are thisness and thatness properties? And what about the cognitive law that all the material of memory is supplied by experience? This is the consideration that defeated several earlier attempts to characterize thatness. How can "This" and "That" have the same object given that the former as tied to perception indicates something current and the latter as tied to remembering indicates something past?

Text (p. 886, Tirupati) and Translation

yad vā ayaṃ ghaṭa ity atra yad dharma-vaiśiṣṭyaṃ bhāsate tasya atītatvaṃ tattā | tad-vaiśiṣṭyaṃ an-anubhūtam api smṛti-viṣayaḥ | idantā-viśiṣṭa-gocara-saṃskārāt kathaṃ tattā-smṛtir iti cet, na | sa ghaṭa iti smṛtiṃ praty anubhavasya hetutva-nirvāhakatayā saṃskārasya tathā eva kalpanāt | ayaṃ ghaṭa iti smṛteḥ sa ghaṭa ity anubhavasya a-darśanāc ca | samāna-viṣayatvena smṛter ayaṃ ghaṭa iti smṛtiḥ na sa ghaṭa iti na anubhavaś ca syāt | na ca evaṃ smṛtir an-anubhūta-tattâṃśe anubhavaḥ syāt | saṃskārâ-sādhāraṇa-kāraṇakatvena smṛtitvāt | saha-prayogaś ca dharma-viśeṣam ādāya pratividheyaḥ | ata eva saṃskāra-hetv-anubhava-prāmāṇya-pāratantryeṇa yathârthatve 'pi smṛtir a-pramā iti sarva-tantra-siddhāntaḥ |

(**Gaṅgeśa** continues: What is thatness?) One alternative is that a being-cognized-as-qualified-by-a-certain-property is, with "*This* pot," presented; (and so, D^9) "a being-cognized-as-qualified (i.e., the relational complex cognized as a this-having-ϕ) as past" is thatness. Although the being-cognitively-relational is (as past) not experienced, it is the object of memory.

Objection: If cognition of thatness is supposed to be through a memory-impression of an object as qualified by thisness, why is the memory of thatness?

Gaṅgeśa: No. The memory-impression is to be imagined as just so, inasmuch as, with a memory (such as) "That pot," experience carries the causal load. Furthermore, "This pot" as a memory is not found, nor "That pot" as an experience. If memory had (precisely) the same object, the memory would be "This pot" and it would not be the case that "That pot" would not be an experience.

Objection: On your view, a memory would have to be (in part) an experience, that is, with respect to the previously unexperienced thatness portion (as with "That pot").

Gaṅgeśa: Wrong. For, a memory's uncommon (or chief) instrumental cause is a memory-impression.

Moreover, taking (in the appropriate cases "that" to indicate) a particular property (different from another also cognized), (the problem of) usage together (of our definition, D^9, "a being-cognized-as-qualified as past," and "that") is resolved (since two different properties would be meant).

Just for this reason is the following position accepted by all the schools: (correct) memory, even if it is (granted to be) in conformity with its object, is not a veridical cognition in that it is parasitic on the veridicality of the experience that creates the memory-impression.

Comments

Thatness—which would be indicated by the qualifier portion of the objecthood of a correct remembering "That"—is no particular property in that a "That" could indicate a qualificandum as qualified by any of several properties belonging to the thing as it had been previously experienced. Whatever gave rise to a perception of thisness in the past, that same thing with the properties that were experienced—except now in some respect past, i.e., past with respect to a particular property or properties cognized—is what a cognition "That" would point to. Or, if we are worried about the difficulty, already discussed, of synonymy between "that" and D[9] as *definiens*, "a cognitively relational complex as past," we can pick another property had by the thing that had also been previously perceived. Propertywise, "that" has an indefinite range considering the various ways something has been previously known. The point is that "This" and "That" can have objectwise the same meaning, or indication, qua qualificandum-as-cognized-as-having-certain-properties. As already brought out, the difference between a "This" and a "That" is to be explained by an intentional tie to perception and remembering respectively.

The causal capability of a memory-impression (*saṃskāra*) is both Gaṅgeśa's problem and solution to the conundrum about how thatness can be remembered when, evidently, it is not experienced. (We remember the pot as past, as having been seen by us in the house. But we did not experience it as past, and so no pastness *saṃskāra* could have been formed.) The conversion from an experience of a this to a remembering of a that is accomplished by a memory-impression (which of course has also other rioles). To have a that as an object is, we might say, constitutive of a remembering. An experience of a this gives rise to, through creating a memory-impression, a remembering of a that, although its pastness was not then predication content. Note that in taking this view Gaṅgeśa appears to admit that a remembering does not derive absolutely all of its objecthood from the relevant memory-forming experience. However, the additional objecthood, the pastness, does in a sense derive from the experience in that to be a remembering is to have a memory-impression as proximate or chief cause, a memory-impression formed by the previous experience. The additional objecthood is, so to say, a surface grasping of the causal process that originated with the perception. Furthermore, there is no difficulty differentiating remembering from perceiving—we do it by apperception. The one is characterized by perception-hood (a fundamental cognition subtype) and the other by memory-hood (another subtype).

Now, in broader perspective, memory is generally—with a few exceptions, mostly Jainas—not counted among classical philosophers as a knowledge source, as a *pramāṇa*. A prominent explanation is that a knowledge source has to make something known for the first time whereas memory is by nature not such an originator. However, Naiyāyikas reject the requirement of freshness: a series of perceptions of the same thing can all be veridical, for example, and a "desire to infer" can generate a veridical inferential awareness whose objecthood is the very same as that of a perception already had. Gaṅgeśa suggests here that the telling point is that a remembering is causally dependent on prior experience. Epistemically, this fact has an important consequence, namely, that the (in)correctness of a (pseudo-)remembering reflects, normally, the (in)correctness of an earlier (pseudo-)perception. I will be wrong in appearing to remember a rope as a snake if I erroneously perceived it that way. However, a deficiency in the causal process resulting in a pseudo-remembering could lie in the operation of the memory-impression that is normally the causal link between an original perceiving and a remembering with the same object. Furthermore, the object may have changed. A pot we remember as black may now be red without our knowing about its emergence from the kiln. To be correct, memory has to result in the right way from the experience. It must be "in conformity with the original experience" (*yathânubhava*).[4] But meeting that criterion, it could still mislead, i.e., it could be correct and mislead if the experience to which it conformed were itself non-veridical. For these reasons, whether or not one grants that a remembering can be in "object-conformity" (*yathârtha*)—some Naiyāyikas take this position, others do not—remembering does not have the same epistemic weight as perceiving and does not get the highest epistemic commendation, which is reserved for *pramāṇa*-generated awareness.

Finally, at the very beginning of the passage, the Sanskrit *yad vā*, which is translated, "One alternative is that," is misleading. It should not be taken to indicate that D[9] is only one of a series of positions acceptable to Gaṅgeśa. For, no further alternative is laid out. In other *TCM* passages where a plurality of acceptable views is put forth, the expression *yad vā* is indeed used to indicate inclusiveness. Thus we expect that here too a disjunctive *siddhânta* on the ontology of thatness is forthcoming. However, Gaṅgeśa gives us a plurality of analyses not of the ontological issue but of the epistemology of remembering. D[9] does stand as the only position on thatness by him endorsed.

To close the section and the perception chapter, Gaṅgeśa takes up Udayana's view that no remembering could be in conformity with its object. In his *Pariśuddhi* commentary cited by Gaṅgeśa at the very end, Udayana explains his views about the epistemic status of remembering.[5]

Text (p. 887, Tirupati) and Translation

yad vā na iyaṃ yathârthā | tathā hi smṛtiḥ sva-viṣaya-vartamānatva-viṣayā atītân-āgatâ-gocara-pratītitvād pratyabhijñā-vat | pratītitvād vā ghaṭo 'sti iti pratīti-vat | pratīteḥ samaya-viśeṣa-viṣayatva-niyamāt jñāna-sāmagrī-mahimnā ca an-anubhūte 'pi samayâṃśe smṛtiḥ, na tatra saṃskāra-vyāpāro 'nyathā-siddhatvāt | ata eva pāka-rakto śyāmo 'yam iti dhiyo '-yathârthatva-vyavahāraḥ laukikānāṃ śyāmatvasya vartamānatvena avagamāt | etena śyāma-dhīs tatra yathârthā eva ghaṭe kadācit tat-sattvāt idānīm ayaṃ śyāma ity-ākāra eva na ity apāstam | ata eva atītân-āgata-vahny-a-gocaratve vidyamāna-dhūmena parvate vahnir ity anumiteḥ vartamāna-vahni-viṣayatvād idānīṃ vahni-niścayena vahny-arthi-pravṛttiḥ | anyathā idānīṃ tat-saṃdehe pravṛttir na syāt | yadā dhūmas tadā vahnir iti vyāptāv api tad-a-jñāna-daśāyāṃ pravṛtter anyathân-upapatteḥ |

(**Gaṅgeśa** continues:) Alternatively (as Udayana holds), remembering is not (even) "in conformity with the object" (*yathârtha*). For (there is an inference that supports this position:) a remembering has as object the presentness of its object, *since* it is a cognition whose presentation is neither past nor future, like a recognition—or (simply) *since* it is a cognition, like the cognition, "It's a pot." For, there is the general rule that an objecthood occurs on a particular occasion because of the weight of a collection of causal factors. And remembering concerns intervals of particular occasion even though they are not experienced. There is in this matter (i.e., the parts of time) no operation of a memory-impression, since such a supposition would be superfluous.

Just for this reason, the cognition, "Black (is) this," indicating a pot now red from baking, is regarded, in popular practice, as *not in object-conformity* (though indeed being-black is a quality that it possessed). For, the being-black would be understood as present.

Objection: There, a cognition of black would indeed be *in object-conformity*, concerning a pot, since at one time it was true. It would be only a cognition that has (explicitly temporal) form, "*Now* this (is) black," that would be false.

Gaṅgeśa (voicing Udayana's view): This is thrown out by that (argument already given).

Just for this reason, past and future fire are outside the scope of the inferential awareness, "There is fire on the mountain," (that is provoked) by (sight of) currently existing smoke, since the object (of the resultant inferential cognition) is currently existing fire. From certainty about fire now is there effort by someone concerned (to put it out, etc.). Otherwise, given doubt about whether the fire were now (or at some other time), there would be no effort to act, since, even though a pervasion "Where smoke, there fire" (had been grasped), given the circumstance that the fire (as current) would not be known, effort to act would be otherwise inexplicable.

Comments

A conversational default is suggested here. The common Sanskrit locution where the copula (*is*, *was*, etc.) is understood or suppressed ("A pot" as ambiguous between "This is a pot" and "That was a pot" etc.) is by conversational default to indicate that the object is current.

Like all cognitions, a remembering occurs in the present. But the information it presents concerns a past state of affairs, one now gone (*atīta*), a bit of the flow of time that, qua delimited interval relative to the present moment of remembering, cannot have been experienced, since of the past or future there is no immediate experience. The best a remembering can do is to be faithful to the experience that formed the memory-impression whose awakening is its proximate cause. But the original experience, though now in the past, was then not of the past but the present. Thus, in this regard a remembering cannot be said to be in conformity with its object. In other words, Udayana holds, says Gaṅgeśa, beyond the common devaluation of remembering as causally dependent on a perceiving and the memory-impression it formed, that a remembering cannot be "in object-conformity" since it is conflicted in the temporality of its objecthood.

The usefulness of veridical cognition lies in its power to guide effort and action, which of course are current when they occur. Not only do we reach to pick up a pot on the basis of a current pot-perception, inferential awareness, such as, "There is fire over there," which is not immediate but dependent on a perceiving as informed by memory (of the relationship between a prover and probandum property), guides current action, such as to form a bucket brigade. The usefulness, too, of remembering is to help us get we want in acting. But a remembering's intentionality is tied to the past—it indicates a qualificandum as it *was*--while we are disposed—such is the nature of all cognition—to take the thing to be like that in the present. Otherwise, the cognition could not guide action. Thus remembering is by nature conflicted in the temporality of its objecthood. Thus it is not "in object-conformity."

This judgment should not be construed, however, as extreme skepticism on Udayana's part about remembering. Gaṅgeśa in offering alternative theories means to highlight agreements rather than differences, and though unstated there is overall accord among Naiyāyikas that remembering is normally worthy of trust, prompting unhesitating effort and action. In his *Pariśuddhi* commentary, Udayana glosses correct remembering as "in *experience*-conformity," though he refuses the higher rating, "in *object*-conformity."[6] He does not see object-conformity as the appropriate epistemic grade, but memory's score is still positive.

Now the view Gaṅgeśa has just previously sketched may be taken to conflict with this judgment of Udayana's about object-conformity. Gaṅgeśa did not say there that a remembering has currentness of any sort as part of its objecthood, though he did admit the other half of Udayana's antinomy, the tie to the past. Two other statements made earlier also contrast sharply with what Udayana says here. First, whereas on the earlier view a memory-impression is held to be responsible for the pastness in a remembering's objecthood, Udayana says that to suppose *saṃskāra*-operation would be superfluous. Second, there was the odd mention of a "time interval" at the beginning of the *siddhânta* just above. It seems that on the alternative view a time interval could be, *pace* Udayana, an object of experience. The order of the two views would seem to indicate on Gaṅgeśa's part a preference for the former. But all he says explicitly is that there are alternatives (*yad vā*). And on the main point there is the agreement already suggested: memory, although a cognitive resource with positive value, is no *pramāṇa*. We can see pretty clearly two reasons why this is so, (1) the causal dependence and (2) the problematic nature of the intentional tie to the past.

Text (p. 887, Tirupati, and p. 844, Calcutta) and Translation

yad vā sa ghaṭa iti smṛtau tattā-viśiṣṭasya vartamānatā bhāsate | saṃskārasya vartamāna-jñāna-sāmagrī-sahitasya eva hetutvāt, so 'yam idānīm ity-ādau tathā kalpanāt, gehe sa ghaṭa iti smaraṇān niḥśaṅka-pravṛtteś ca | anyathā tattā-viśiṣṭasya idānīṃ saṃdehe sā na syāt | na ca vartamānatvâṃśe 'n-anubhūta-viṣayatvam | vartamānatvena an-āgata-vartamānasya pūrvam anubhavāt | evaṃ ca smṛtes tathā-bhūtasya vartamānatā viṣayaḥ, tatra viśeṣyasya viśeṣaṇasya vā vartamānatvâ-bhāvāt smṛtir a-yathârthā eva | na ca pūrvaṃ tathā āsīd artha iti tad yathârthatvaṃ | pāka-rakte śyāmo 'yam iti jñānasya yathârthatva-prasaṅgāt | pramuṣṭa-tattâṃśe ca smaraṇe a-vidyamāna-dharmâvacchedaḥ na bhāsate | tad āhur ācāryāḥ | "smṛter yāthârthyam api kutaḥ" iti |

(**Gaṅgeśa** lays out another argument of Udayana's:) Alternatively, (remembering is invariably not in object-conformity because) the *being current* of something qualified by thatness is presented in a remembering such as "That pot." For, a memory-impression is causally efficacious only if it is accompanied by the full collection of causal factors necessary for a *current* cognition. For example, "That (is) this (thing here) now," is to be imagined as such a remembering (entailing that the thing, the "that," is current).

Furthermore, we do make unworried effort to act based on remembering (i.e., presuming that the remembered object is current:) "That pot is in the house." Otherwise, given doubt about whether a thing qualified by thatness exists now, there would be no such effort to act (e.g., to go into the house for the pot).

Objection: (Remembering cannot have as object currentness.) With respect to the currentness portion, no objecthood has been experienced.

Gaṅgeśa (voicing Udayana): Wrong. For, something that will be current in the future has been, insofar as its being current is concerned, previously experienced.

And so, a remembering, which is as indicated, has a being-current as (in part) its object. There, since either the qualificandum (the thing remembered) or the qualifier (what it is remembered as) would be absent in the present, remembering is indeed not in object-conformity.

Objection: Formerly the object was like that. Thus there is the conformity.

Gaṅgeśa (voicing Udayana): No. For, the difficulty would be that the cognition, "This (is) black," indicating a pot now red from baking, would be in object-conformity.

And in a remembering whose thatness portion is suppressed (as with the remembering, "Pot," which is equivalent to, "That pot"), the connection to the unknown properties (of earlier time and place) are not presented. Therefore, our revered teacher (Udayana) has said, "How of memory is there even object-conformity?"

Comments

Again, Udayana's view is not an outright skepticism about memory, for, as he says, we make unworried effort on its basis. Nevertheless, the pot we remember as being in the house may no longer be there. Correct memory does not guarantee the object's continued presence, whereas if a perceiving is veridical its object has to be as it is cognized.

Among the worries of Udayana's expressed here, the most serious seems to be the problem about time. "That" indicates a pastness that stands in tension with the currentness not only of the cognition as occurrent but also with a currentness presumed for the object-as-formerly-cognized. The claim, "That pot is in the house"—where there is an intentional tie between the "that" presentation and a pot as experienced in the past—is about the pot that is in the house currently, which, we are to imagine, is not being directly perceived or recognized. While the remembering is able to prompt action, the pot may well have changed. It necessarily will have changed with respect to temporal qualification in addition to numerous ways it may have changed (including having been completely smashed). Viewing the objecthood of a cognition "That" to include somehow both a currentness and a pastness—the particular time, namely, when the memory-impression was formed—Udayana concludes that a "That" would be necessarily erroneous, even if the formational perceiving was veridical and nothing untoward has occurred in the remembering-prompting causal chain.

In other words, Udayana may be taken to say that, since remembering prompts action in the present, a remembering is to be understood as entailing, at least normally, the currentness of its object. A less radical position is, as above, that an epistemic rank, being-in-object-conformity, which is lower than veridicality but not so low as Udayana says, accrues to right remembering. A remembering's correctness depends on the veridicality of the perception that generated the memory-impression that is the remembering's chief instrumental cause and on the *saṃskāra*'s functioning properly. Sometimes remembering is indeed misleading for reasons peculiar to memory. Because of a later destruction of a qualifier previously perceived—the black of a remembered pot now red by baking—or because of the pot itself, the qualificandum, no longer existing, a remembering could be correct but still guide us incorrectly. However, the possibility of being disappointed in finding the pot smashed does not mean that the remembering is not to be deemed "in object-conformity." The memory was good but something happened of which we were unaware.

Udayana's position goes further in downgrading memory's worth. Udayana argues that either a qualifier as indexed according to the time of the formation of the triggering memory-impression or a qualificandum as so indexed would be indicated by a remembering. But it would also indicate that the object is still that way currently (a claim not shared by the more moderate position), and flux, though not universal, occurs at least with respect to temporal indexing. There is guaranteed this amount of change. Thus remembering is not just sometimes wrong but constitutionally erroneous. The memory-forming cognition occurred at a precise moment of consciousness and of the thing cognized, a moment that, as past, cannot be re-presented. We may wonder if Udayana, famed for his refutations of Buddhist positions including momentariness, may not have capitulated to a Buddhist position. However, we must keep in mind, Udayana sees recognition as a perception, not a remembering, and he offers the substitute honor of "in experience-conformity" that we discussed.

Gaṅgeśa does not bring up recognition here at the end of the section. It is nevertheless useful to contrast the supposition that a recognition is perceptual and veridical with the derogatory remarks made about remembering here. A mere remembering—with no perceptual evidence—that an object is in the house has some significant probability of being wrong (even if the remembering itself is maximally correct), whereas a recognition of the pot, "This is that pot," comes sealed with perceptual certainty.

To sum up, there are several reasons, as our revered teacher Udayana has pointed out, why remembering is much to be debunked epistemologically. Remembering involves a causal complex centering on a memory-impression formed by a perceptual cognition that might not have been veridical. The time between formation of a memory-impression and the prompting of a remembering is, moreover, a period not only wherein something could go wrong with the impression but also wherein the impression, as fixed, would depart from the objective course of the thing that originally gave rise to it. We may remember a black pot that is now red and may well be unaware of the change. Then, to boot, there are the problems that Udayana points out with currentness as part of a remembering's objecthood.

The quote from Udayana occurs in his *Tātparya-pariśuddhi* commentary on *Nyāya-sūtra* 1.1.1.[7]

• •

iti śrīmad-gaṅgeśopādhyāya-viracite tattva-cintā-maṇau pratyakṣa-khaṇḍe savikalpaka-vādaḥ pratyakṣa-khaṇḍaś ca samāptaḥ

Here end the Perception Chapter and the Discourse on Determinate Cognition within the Perception Chapter of the *Tattvacintāmaṇi* composed by the professor and luminary, Gaṅgeśa.

SANSKRIT GLOSSARY

1. Proper Names

(philosophic schools and important Sanskrit authors and texts)

Advaita Vedānta: a prominent school of classical philosophy subscribing to an Upanishadic monism: "All is Brahman," including—and especially—the seemingly individual consciousness or self.

Bhāṭṭa: a follower of the Mīmāṃsaka philosopher Kumārila Bhaṭṭa or a view belonging to or deriving from Kumārila (q.v.).

Dharmakīrti: (c. 650) Buddhist logician and epistemologist of the Yogâcāra school, author of *Pramāṇavārttika* along with other works of Buddhist philosophy

Dharma-śāstra: see *dharma-śāstra*.

Gadādhara: (c. 1650) Nyāya author famous for his linguistic theorizing and analysis of the concept of "intentionality," *viṣayatā*, "objecthood."

Gaṅgeśa: (c. 1325) recognized founder of "New Logic," *navya nyāya*, author of the *Tattvacintāmaṇi* (*TCM*).

Gautama: (c. 200) legendary author of the *Nyāyasūtra*, Nyāya's founding text.

Jaina philosophy: commencing with Mahāvīra (c. 450 BCE) with dozens of texts in all periods, famous for an ethics of *a-hiṃsā*, "non-injury."

Jayadeva: (c. 1485) author of a *TCM* commentary part of which is published in the Asiatic Society edition (see the bibliography).

Kaṇāda: (c. 150 CE) legendary author of the *Vaiśeṣikasūtra*, Vaiśeṣika's founding text.

Kiraṇāvalī: the long commentary by Udayana on Praśastapāda's central Vaiśeṣika text, the *Padârthadharmasaṃgraha*.

Kumārila: (c. 650) prominent Mīmāṃsaka philosopher whose views or those of his followers (called Bhāṭṭas, from "Kumārila Bhaṭṭa") Gaṅgeśa often disputes.

Lakṣaṇamālā: "Garland of Definitions," a text by Udayana providing a series of interlocking definitions, or characterizations, principally within Vaiśeṣika ontology.

Lakṣaṇāvalī: "Row of Definitions" by Udayana.

Mādhyamika: the Buddhist school of skeptical philosophy founded by Nāgārjuna; sometimes called Buddhist Mysticism or Buddhist Absolutism.

Maṇikaṇṭha Miśra: (c. 1300) author of *Nyāyaratna*, an early "New Logic" text that precurses several of Gaṅgeśa's positions, particularly concerning inference, and that is sometimes cited by Gaṅgeśa.

Manu: legendary author of *Mānavadharmaśāstra*

Mānavadharmaśāstra: (c. 100 BCE in its final form) an important law book and manual of conduct within Vedic or Hindu society attributed to a legendary Manu.

Mathurānātha: (c. 1650) author of an influential commentary on Gaṅgeśa's *TCM* published in the Asiatic Society edition (see the bibliography).

Mīmāṃsā: a long-running realist school famous for its Vedic interpretation, principles of interpretation, philosophy of language, and epistemology (Mīmāṃsā epistemology is a prime target of Gaṅgeśa's); the *Mīmāṃsāsūtra* (c. 100 BCE) is the root text, and Kumārila Bhaṭṭa (c. 650) and Prabhākara (c. 700) the chief proponents.

Mīmāṃsaka: an advocate of Mīmāṃsā (q.v.).

Mīmāṃsāsūtra: (c. 100 BCE), the founding text of Mīmāṃsā.

Murāri Miśra: (c. 1200) a Mīmāṃsaka who follows neither Kumārila nor Prabhākara and holds that a cognition is not self-aware and requires an apperception to be known, an apperception that grasps both the target and its veridicality.

Nāgārjuna: (c. 150) prominent Buddhist philosopher understood by Naiyāyikas to be a skeptic about "knowledge sources," *pramāṇa*; founder of the Mādhyamika school of Buddhist philosophy.

Naiyāyika: an advocate of Nyāya (q.v.).

Navya Nyāya: "New Logic"; the revolutionary Nyāya (q.v.) of, preëminently, Gaṅgeśa and his followers, pioneered in part by Udayana and others.

Nyāya: "Logic"; a school of realism and externalist epistemology prominent throughout the classical period, from the *Nyāyasūtra* (c. 200) on, developing out of canons of debate and informal logic; explicitly combined with Vaiśeṣika in later centuries beginning with Udayana (c. 1000) and sometimes called Nyāya-Vaiśeṣika; focused on issues in epistemology but having positions on a wide range of philosophical topics; see also *nyāya*.

Nyāya-Vaiśeṣika: see "Nyāya."

Nyāyakusumāñjali: ("Flower-Offering of Arguments") a text by Udayana where he collects and defends numerous arguments for the existence of God.

Nyāyaratna: ("Jewel of Nyāya") a long text by Maṇikaṇṭha that precurses some of Gaṅgeśa's *TCM* particularly concerning inference.

Nyāyasūtra (*NyS*): (c. 200) Nyāya's foundational text.

Padârthadharmasaṃgraha (*PDS*): "Compendium of the Properties of the Fundamental Types of Things or Categories") the sole work of Praśastapāda (c. 575) and the central text as far as Gaṅgeśa and other New Logicians are concerned for the topic of Vaiśeṣika categories, although there are a few lines of separate development.

Pāṇini: (c. 450 BCE) author of a systematic grammar for Sanskrit, sometimes referred to as Pāṇini's sūtras, which inaugurated the long and rich grammarian tradition of classical India including "grammarian philosophy."

Prabhākara: (c. 700) prominent Mīmāṃsaka philosopher whose views, or those of his followers (called Prābhākaras), are assumed by Gaṅgeśa in a majority of the sections of the *TCM* to be the primary competitors to his own views; commonly called "Guru" (sometimes sarcastically) throughout classical philosophy.

Prācīna Nyāya: "Old Logic"; the philosophy of the *Nyāyasūtra* and its commentaries—including Udayana's—and of a few independent treatises; see "Nyāya."

Praśastapāda: (c. 575) author of *Padârthadharmasaṃgraha*, the reformulation and explanation of the *Vaiśeṣikasūtra* that comes to be the central or defining text of the Vaiśeṣika tradition.

Raghunātha: (c. 1500) prominent Gaṅgeśa commentator who further revolutionized Nyāya.

Rāmakṣṇa Adhvarin: (c. 1650) the author of the subcommentary (on Rucidatta) published in the Tirupati edition of the *TCM*; see the bibliography.

Rucidatta: (c. 1500) author of an important commentary on Gaṅgeśa's *TCM* published in the Tirupati edition; see the bibliography.

Śālīkanātha Miśra: (c. 900): author of *Prakaraṇapañcikā*, a good (and available) presentation of Prābhākara Mīmāṃsaka views.

Sāṃkhya: "Analysis"; an early school of metaphysical dualism analyzing nature (*prakṛti*, q.v.) in the interests of psychological disidentification.

Śaṅkara: (c. 725) the most prominent philosopher of the Advaita Vedānta school, espousing a radical monism of the sole reality of Brahman, the Absolute.

Ślokavārttika: a principal text by Kumārila commenting on a portion of the *Mīmāṃsāsūtra*.

Śrīdhara: (c. 1000) author of the *Nyāyakandalī* commentary on Praśastapāda.

Śrīharśa: (c. 1100): famous Advaita dialectician, whose *Khaṇḍanakhaṇḍakhādya*, "Sweetmeats of Refutation," is directed principally against Nyāya and in particular Udayana.

Tātparyapariśuddhi: Udayana's commentary on the *Nyāyasūtra* and its earlier commentaries.

Tattvacintāmaṇi (*TCM*): "Jewel of Reflection on the Truth (about Epistemology)," Gaṅgeśa's sole extant text.

Udayana: (c. 1000) the Nyāya philosopher whom Gaṅgeśa counts as, more than all others, his teacher; a prolific author of both commentaries and independent texts, Udayana unified Nyāya epistemology and logic with the ontology of Vaiśeṣika (q.v.); his *Kiraṇāvalī*, *Lakṣaṇamālā*, *Nyāyakusumāñjali*, and *Tātparyaṭīka-pariśuddhi* are mentioned in this chapter of Gaṅgeśa's *TCM*.

Uddyotakara: (c. 600) author of the earliest extant commentary on Vātsyāyana's *Nyāyasūtra* commentary; Uddyotakara combats, principally, Buddhist views.

Upaniṣad: "secret doctrine"; various prose and verse texts (appended to the Vedas, q.v., over many centuries) with mystic themes centered on an understanding of the self and its relation to the Absolute or God, called Brahman; the primary sources for classical Vedānta philosophy.

Vācaspati Miśra: (c. 950) major Naiyāyika figure within the Old School on whose *Tātparyaṭīka* commentary on the *Nyāyasūtra* Udayana wrote his subcommentary (which is, in turn, probably the philosophic text most closely followed by Gaṅgeśa).

Vaiśeṣika: "Atomism"; a classical philosophy focusing on ontological issues ("What kinds of things are there?") and defending a realist view of material things as composed of atoms; explicitly combined by Udayana with Nyāya with practically no separate literature during the Navya-Nyāya period.

Vaiśeṣikasūtra: (c. 100 CE) of Kaṇāda, the oldest extant Vaiśeṣika text, recast by Praśastapāda (c. 575) and thereafter largely ignored.

Vardhamāna: (c. 1350) Gaṅgeśa's son and author of a dozen influential commentaries mainly on the works of Udayana.

Vātsyāyana: (c. 400) author of the oldest extant commentary on the *Nyāyasūtra*.

Veda: "revealed Knowledge"; the four Vedas, comprised principally of hymns to various indo-european gods and goddesses, are the oldest texts composed in Sanskrit (some hymns are possibly as early as 1500 BCE); the Vedas are the holiest texts of Hinduism, though their Sanskrit is pre-classical and during the classical period they seem not to have been read widely.

Vedānta: originally an epithet for Upaniṣads; in the classical period, the philosophy of the *Brahmasūtra* and of several subschools defending Upaniṣadic views often in an idealist or illusionist spirit and opposed to Nyāya's realism.

Yogācāra: Buddhist Idealism; late Buddhist Idealists (Dignāga, Dharmakīrti, and their followers) propose a pragmatic epistemology which is a principal rival of Old Nyāya.

Yogasūtra: (c. 400 CE in its final redaction): a textbook on meditation and yogic practices by Patañjali utilizing much Sāṃkhya metaphysics and psychology.

2. Terms

a-bhāva: absence, negative fact; an absence invariably has a locus and an absentee; e.g., an absence of a pot on the floor has the floor as its locus and the pot as its absentee; absences come in four varieties, prior (as of a pot before its production), posterior (as of a pot after it is destroyed), absolute (as of a pot on the floor), and mutual (as between a pot and a cloth).

adhikārin: a "qualified" person; in the context of prescriptions about sacrificial rites, someone "fit" to undertake a sacrifice, or, in Vedānta, to read the sacred texts.

adhyāsa: superimposition.

a-dṛṣṭa: "unseen force," i.e., *karman* (q.v.).

ākāṅkṣā: "expectation"; syntactic expectation, a condition governing the intelligibility of a statement, according to Naiyāyikas and others; to cite a classical example, no single word appearing in the accusative case can be understood as a statement (excepting verbal ellipsis)—somewhat like "to the cow'' standing alone in English—because of a violation of ''syntactic expectation.''

ākāśa: ''ether,'' the medium of sound, the only non-atomic substance among five that are material, according to Nyāya-Vaiśeṣika and other classical views.

a-khaṇḍa upādhi: unanalyzable ''surplus property'' (see *upādhi*), contrasting with *sakhaṇḍa upādhi* (q.v).

a-laukika-saṃnikarṣa: ''extraordinary sensory connection'' which, according to Nyāya, comes in three types: (a) connection mediated by a universal, as in cognition of an unobserved instance of a universal (''The calf to be born will have a dewlap''), (b) connection mediated by memory, as in cognition of sandalwood in the distance as having a certain smell, recognition of something perceived previously, and perceptual illusion—see below, the entry, *jñāna-lakṣaṇa-saṃnikarṣa*—and (c) connection mediated by yogic power. (See also the entry, *laukika-saṃnikarṣa*, below.)

an-anyathā-siddha: relevant causally (''not irrelevant''); see *anyathā-siddha*.

an-avasthā: infinite regress, a defeater and conceptual predicament revealed by *tarka* (q.v.).

anubhava: awareness, experience; according to Navya Nyāya, perceptual, inferential, and other veridical awarenesses—*pramā* as the result of the respective *pramāṇa*—are all *anubhava*, as are also their non-veridical counterparts; a remembering is a ''cognition,'' *jñāna*, but not an ''awareness.''

anugama (anugata): uniformity, consecutive character; one of the criteria of a true universal or natural kind, *jāti*, whose uniformity is taken to prompt recurrent experience.

anumāna: inference, the inferential process; one of four *pramāṇa* (q.v.) or generators of veridical cognition, according to Nyāya.

anumiti: inferential awareness, the result of inference.

an-upalabdhi: ''non-cognition,'' the means of knowledge whereby an absence is known, according to the Bhāṭṭa branch of Mīmāṃsā.

anuvyavasāya: apperception, ''after-cognition,'' introspection.

anuyogin: relational correlate to a countercorrelate, *pratiyogin* (q.v.).

anvaya: positive correlations (things both H and S) entailed by a natural pervasion, *vyāpti* (q.v), constituting positive evidence for the pervasion; see also *vyatireka*.

anvaya-vyatireka : positive correlations (things both H and S) and negative correlations (things not-S and not-H) entailed by a natural pervasion, *vyāpti* (q.v), constituting both positive and negative evidence for a pervasion.

anvaya-vyatirekin : (1) a property with both a positive and a negative range, i.e., both occurring in some places and not occurring at others; (2) an inference based on both positive and negative correlations; cf. *kevalânvayin* and *kevala-vyatirekin*.

anvayin : see *kevalânvayin*.

anvīkṣā : (= *ānvīkṣikī*) "critical investigation," a term used by Naiyāyikas and others to refer to the enterprises of philosophy in general and Nyāya in particular.

anyathā-khyāti : the view of perceptual error endorsed by Gaṅgeśa that finds a property-bearer presented perceptually as "other than what it is" due to an epistemic deficiency (*doṣa*, q.v.) such as a departure from the normal workings of the sense organs, etc., and involving a retrieval of previous perceptual information through excitation of a "memory-impression" (*saṃskāra*).

anyathā-siddha : "causally irrelevant," not regulative; a thing or property that accidentally precedes an effect in focus or in another way is not relevant to its production as captured by causal laws; an ass invariably used to carry the clay out of which a particular kind of pot is made is a stock example.

anyonyâśraya : "mutual dependence" as a logical, conceptual, or argument flaw (as in *a* conceived as required for the production of *b* and *b* as required for the production of *a*); "circular reasoning" (*cakraka*).

a-prāpta-kāla : the "mistimed," a debate error explained by Vātsyāyana as putting the members of an argument in the wrong order.

a-prayojaka : the "ineffectual" fallacy or defeater of assuming a pervasion without consideration of counterfactual instances such that the putative prover is "misleading" and fails to be pervaded by the probandum; a prover that deviates from its probandum—see *vyabhicāra*.

ārambhaṇīyā : a subordinate or minor Vedic sacrifice performed immediately prior to a principal or major one.

arthântara : "switching meaning" (or "introducing new meaning"), a fallacy or defeater in a debate context (*nigraha-sthāna*, q.v.) explained by Vātsyāyana as "irrelevance."

arthâpatti : "postulation," "presumption," "circumstantial implication," an independent *pramāṇa* according to Mīmāṃsakas and some other classical philosophers, a knowledge source viewed as a form of inference by Naiyāyikas; an argument that something would otherwise be impossible or inexplicable (*anyathā-an-upapatti*); e.g., from the information that fat Devadatta does not eat during the day, we know by "postulation" that he eats at night.

a-sādhāraṇya : "no similar instance," a "fallacy of the prover," *hetv-ābhāsa*, where there is no comparison class, no extrapolative basis for presuming a pervasion or general rule on which a genuine inference would depend.

a-samavāyi-kāraṇa : "emergent" or "co-inherent" cause, e.g., the blue color of the treads of a blue piece of cloth is an emergent cause of the blue of the cloth.

a-siddha : the "unshown," "unestablished," or "unproved," a "fallacy of the prover," *hetv-ābhāsa*, that may be likened to an unwarranted premise, normally, the prover's being "unestablished" as qualifying the inferential subject, but also, in some usages, the inference-grounding pervasion's being "unestablished" (*vyāpyatvâ-siddhi*); subvarieties include *sva-rūpâ-siddhi*, the prover's being "unestablished" as exhibited by the subject by way of what each by nature is (e.g., smoke as "unestablished" as qualifying a lake), and several other types.

ātman : individual self, one of nine basic types of substance, according to Nyāya-Vaiśeṣika; in Vedānta, self or soul, the Upanishadic term for an individual's true consciousness.

ātmâśraya : "self-dependence"; the defeater of any thesis proposing (impossible) self-causation or self-qualification; definitional circularity.

avaccheda : specification, delimitation, "paring down to"; techniques used by Gaṅgeśa and other Naiyāyikas to remove vagueness and over-extension.

avacchedaka : specifier, delimiter.

bādha : (1) the fallacy or defeater of "patent falsehood," where the inferential subject is "known in advance" not to exhibit the probandum; (2) experiential "sublation," as when one sees a real rope previously mistaken for a snake.

bādhaka : counterconsideration, epistemic "defeater," blocker of a cognitive effect of a specified type under specified conditions.

bhūyo-darśana : "wide experience"; the key condition leading to knowledge of a natural pervasion (*vyāpti*, q.v.) of things H by things S, according to Nyāya.

brahman : the "Absolute" or "God," the central concern of Vedānta philosophy.

bhrama (bhrānti) : perceptual illusion; erroneous awareness opposed to veridical awareness, *pramā* (q.v.).

cakraka : "circularity," the epistemic defeater of any thesis that proposes an impossible circular chain of causation or qualification.

darśa : a Vedic sacrifice undertaken at the time of a new moon.

darśana : a "seeing," a perspective on the truth, a philosophy; the discipline of philosophy understood as holistic and concerned with the most important truiths and values (sometimes contrasted with "critical inquiry," *anvīkṣā*, q.v.).

dharma : (1) property; (2) right religious and moral practice.

dharma-śāstra : judicial literature in Sanskrit; jurisprudence comprised of law books and code-of-conduct manuals.

dharmin : property-bearer.

doṣa : "fault," "epistemic defect," a veridicality-undermining causal condition responsible for the generation of a non-veridical awareness, according to Gaṅgeśa and Navya Nyāya.

dravya : substance, one of seven ontic primitives or categories (*padârtha*, q.v.) of Nyāya-Vaiśeṣika; nine fundamental types of substance are earth, water, fire (or the "fiery element," *tejas*), air (these are the four atomic elements), ether (the fifth "material" element, non-atomic and the medium of sound), time, space, *manas* (q.v., the "mind" or "internal organ"), and self.

dṛṣtânta : a pervasion-supportive "example," a basis for induction, typically a locus known to exhibit both the prover and the probandum (i.e., an instance of *sapakṣa*, q.v., that exhibits the prover), e.g., a kitchen hearth where both smoke and fire are known to have occurred; providing an example suggests that proper inductive procedure has been followed (cf., *anvaya-vyatireka*) and that the "pervasion" or *vyāpti* which a proffered inference presumes is properly evidenced.

gauravatva : "heaviness," theoretic cumbersomeness (usually alleged comparatively).

guṇa : (1) "excellence," "epistemic excellence," a veridicality-grounding causal condition with respect to awareness, according to Gaṅgeśa and Navya Nyāya; (2) quality; one of seven fundamental categories (*padârtha*, q.v.) in traditional Nyāya-Vaiśeṣika ontology.

guru : teacher.

hetu : inferential mark, "prover," synonymous with *sādhana* (q.v.).

hetvābhāsa : false or misleading prover or inferential mark, "fallacy of the prover" or sometimes simply "fallacy."

indriya-saṃnikarṣa : (= *indriya-pratyāsatti*) connection between a sense organ and an object perceived; see, in this book, p. 343; cf., *a-laukika-saṃnikarṣa.*

īśvara : God, "Lord"; an individual self or *ātman* responsible for the creation of the world but not of other selves, such as human selves, which are eternal but also subject to spiritual ignorance and other weaknesses whereas God is not.

jāti : universal, natural kind, a property occurring in more than a single instance or locus.

jāti-bādhaka : a "blocker," defeater, or counterconsideration against taking a property to be a true universal, *jāti*, generating an "infinite regress," for example, which blocks cowhood-hood; see Udayana's list, pp. 700–701.

jñāna : "cognition"; awareness and remembering (remembering is a *jñāna* but not an "awareness," *anubhava*); an episodic psychological quality, according to Nyāya-Vaiśeṣika, that has an object or objecthood, *viṣayatā* (q.v.), and that guides voluntary action.

jñāna-lakṣaṇa-saṃnikarṣa : (*jñāna-lakṣaṇa-pratyāsatti*) cognitively mediated connection with a cognized object that enables perception of something not in direct connection with the operative sense organ; for example, the recognition, "This is that Devadatta," is perceptual with the "thatness" provided—"retrieved" (*upanīta*)—by memory; see also the entries, *saṃnikarṣa* and *upanīta.*

jyeṣṭha-pramāṇa : perception as the fundamental ("eldest") *pramāṇa* (q.v.), according to Nyāya; non-perceptual *pramāṇa* are each said to depend in some way on perception.

karaṇa : (sometimes) "trigger" or "proximate instrumental cause," (usually) "chief instrumental cause," a necessary condition that on being met an effect regularly comes about; see, in this book, pp. 24–25.

kāraṇa : "cause," a necessary and regulative condition for an effect, by default of the subtype called "instrumental cause," *nimitta-kāraṇa* (q.v.) but including causes called "inherent," *samavāyin*, and "emergent," *a-samavāyin* (q.v.); see also *sāmagrī*, "sufficient causality."

kārīrī: a Vedic sacrifice performed for rain.

karman: (1) action, motion; (2) psychological dispositions to act in a certain manner accrued through previous actions; habits; sometimes conceived metaphysically as an environmental influence (i.e., *a-pūrva* = *a-dṛṣṭa*, "unseen force").

kevalânvayin: (1) "universally positive," a property with no negative range, nowhere, that is, where it is not; (2) "only positive," an inference whose inductive support consists only of instances of co-presence between the prover (H) and probandum (S), with no instances of co-absence, i.e., things S and H but not things not-S and not-H.

kevala-vyatirekin: "only negative," an inference whose inductive support consists only of instances of co-absence between the prover (H) and probandum (S), with no instances of co-presence, i.e., things not-S and not-H but not things S and H.

kṣaṇa: "point-instant," the smallest increment of time, too small to be perceptible, according to Nyāya.

lāghavatva: "lightness," parsimony, theoretic simplicity.

lakṣaṇa: characterization, definition.

manas: the mind or internal organ, the sense-mind, the sense organ operative in the perception of psychological properties sush as pleasure and pain, and the conduit of sensory information to the perceiving self, according to Nyāya and several classical schools; also, the sensory instrument responsible for apperception according to Nyāya.

maṅgala: "doing something auspicious," a religious practice performed at the beginning of an enterprise, for example, an author's praising his "chosen deity," as Gaṅgeśa praises Śiva in opening the *TCM*.

mīmāṃsā: (1) science of interpretation; (2) a philosophic school, see "Mīmāṃsā."

mukti: (*mokṣa*) liberation from rebirth, salvation, the *summum bonum* according to several schools.

nigraha-sthāna: "grounds for rebuke" in a debate; informal fallacy (several are identified in the *Nyāya-sūtra*).

nimitta-kāraṇa: instrumental cause, necessary condition, such as a potter, wheel, etc., for a pot.

nirākāra: "without form," said of cognition by Naiyāyikas who see cognitions as given shape or form by their objects or object-determined intentionality (*viṣayatā*), a view contrasting with Buddhist *sākāra-vāda* (q.v.).

nirvikalpaka: "indeterminate"; indeterminate perception grasps a qualifier "in the raw," not as qualifying a qualificandum; indeterminate perception is not apperceptible and not directly verbalizable, in Gaṅgeśa's view.

niścaya: certainty, warrant, sufficient epistemic confidence to act unhesitatingly.

nyāya: (1) the philosophic school, see "Nyāya"; (2) philosophical examination and argument; (3) maxim or principle.

padârtha: category, primitive, "type of thing to which words refer"; there are seven fundamental categories according to Nyāya-Vaiśeṣika, (1) substance, (2) quality, (3) motion, (4) universal, (5) final particularizer, (6) inherence, and (7) absence.

pakṣa: the "inferential subject," a locus where the prover is known or presumed to reside (e.g., the mountain in the stock example).

pakṣêtaratva: being-other-than-the-inferential subject, a property that is "universally positive," i.e., present everywhere, with the sole exception of the inferential subject itself.

parāmarśa: "reflection" or "consideration" necessary to the generation of inferential awareness; a cognitive putting together, so to say, of the evidence of the prover as qualifying the subject with that of the prover's being pervaded by the probandum.

para-prāmāṇya: cognition as "certified through another," "extrinsic justification," i.e., by means of an inference; Nyāya's doctrine of certification as requiring an inference to establish the truth of a target cognition; an epistemological thesis opposed to self-certification (*sva-prāmāṇya*).

prakāra: as a technical term "predication content," more generally, "way," a way something appears; e.g., a cognition F*a* has F-hood as its "predication content," as the way something, *a*, is being cognized, provoking, in appropriate circumstances, the cognizer to say, "It's F," or "It's an F," or the like; a qualifier (*viśeṣaṇa*) as cognized.

prakṛti: "nature" in Sāṃkhya philosophy, the uniform bosom of all phenomena, of everything material as presented in experience, all effects being transformations of a common material cause in which they in a sense pre-exist.

prakarana: topic; section of a text.

pramā: veridical awareness (see Gaṅgeśa's definitions, in this book, pp. 236ff).

pramāṇa: "knowledge source," means to veridical awareness; according to Nyāya, there are four *pramāṇa*, perception, inference, analogy, and testimony.

prāmāṇya: (1) veridicality, a cognition's being true of its object; (2) the condition of being generated by a knowledge source, i.e., a true cognition's being generated by a genuine knowledge source, *pramāṇa*.

prameya: object of veridical awareness; the knowable.

prāpya-kāri: a doctrine concerning a sense organ such as touch which is said to "work by reaching" its object through a direct contact at the object's own locus; contrasting with *a-prāpya-kāri*, "not reaching its object," said of a sense organ such as hearing in relation to an object that is not grasped simply through contact at the object's own locus; see, in this book, p. 346.

prasaṅga: dialectical difficulty, predicament drawn out by *tarka* (q.v.), "counterfactual reasoning," such as contradiction or infinite regress.

pratibandhaka: preventer, blocker.

pratibandhī: *tu quoque*, "two wrongs don't make a right," the ineffective rejoinder that an opponent's view commits a fault or mistake that the opponent has already identified in one's own view.

pratiyogin: (1) Navya-Nyāya term for the countercorrelate or relatum of a dyadic relation, i.e., the second term of a relation, the *anuyogin* being the first (e.g., the *pratiyogin* of "objecthood," *viṣayatā*, is cognition and the object of cognition is the *anuyogin*; the *pratiyogin* of "subjecthood," *viṣayitā*, is the object of cognition and the cognition is the *anuyogin*); (2) counterpositive of an absence (e.g., with an absence of a pot on the floor, the pot is the *pratiyogin*), "absentee."

pratyāsatti: see *saṃnikarṣa*.

pratyakṣa: (1) perception or perceptual awareness, the veridical result of perception as a knowledge source; (2) the source itself, the "knowledge source, *pramāṇa* (q.v.), that generates perceptual awarenesses. (See Gaṅgeśa's definitions, in this book, pp. 330ff.)

puṇya: religious or moral merit, good karma.

pūrva-pakṣa: a *prima facie* position, the opponent's position; a portion of a text devoted to exploring views and arguments not accepted by the author who will express his own views in an upcoming and correlate *siddhânta* (q.v).

pūrva-pakṣin: an opponent or first-level interlocutor in relation to a *siddhântin* (q.v.) who is normally the author himself.

śabda: (1) "testimony" as a *pramāṇa* (q.v.) according to Nyāya and some other Indian schools; (2) "sound," the quality grasped by the organ of hearing.

śābda-bodha: knowledge from trustfully understood words, veridical awareness generated by testimony.

sādhana: "prover" in relation to a probandum within an inference (e.g., smoke or smokiness, in an inference to fire or fieriness).

sādhya: "probandum," the property to be proved by a prover in an inference (e.g., fire or fieriness, in an inference from sight of smoke to the presence of fire).

sākāra-vāda: a Buddhist doctrine about awareness "taking form internally," not depending on external things, as opposed to Nyāya's view that awareness is in itself "without shape or form," *nirākāra* (q.v.).

sakhaṇḍa upādhi: a surplus property that is ontologically composite and analyzable, e.g., "blue-cow-hood," which is a composite of the quality, blue, and the universal, cowhood.

sāmagrī: a collection of causal factors sufficient to produce an effect of a certain type.

sāmānyato dṛṣṭa: a type of inference, discussed in the *Nyāya-sūtra* commentaries on *NyS* 1.1.5 and elsewhere, an inference proceeding "on the basis of a general principle holding for all things experienced (as of such a kind)" to an inferred analogue in a case at issue; e.g., "Pleasure and the like have a substratum, *since* they are qualities, like color" (which is the key step to inferential knowledge of the self, which is to be identified with the substratum proved).

samavāya: "inherence"; ontic glue, according to Nyāya, relating certain types of things to their loci, such as true universals, *jāti*; e.g., cowness inheres in cows.

samavāyi-kāraṇa: "inherent cause," a substratum in relation to a superstratum, e.g., a property-bearer in relation to its properties.

saṃnikarṣa: see *indriya-saṃnikarṣa*.

saṃśaya: doubt, uncertainty.

saṃskāra : memory-impression, disposition; impetus.

samūha-ālambana-jñāna : cognition of a group of things, of a group of two or more qualificanda in a sweep, for example, taking in perceptually four butterflies in a single glance.

saṃyoga : contact, conjunction.

sapakṣa : loci where the probandum is known to occur, e.g., a kitchen hearth. etc., with respect to an inference from smoke to fire.

śāstra : an individual science or craft; a scientific textbook.

sat-pratipakṣa : the "counterinference" fallacy and defeater of a putative inference, where a first thesis to be proved (S*a*) is countered by an opposite thesis (~S*a*), each with a prover counterbalanced by another prover equally well supported by correlations, e.g., "Sound is non-eternal, *since* it is produced," countered by, "Sound is eternal, *since* it has soundhood (the universal).'

savikalpaka : "determinate"; determinate perception is a relational cognition, "propositional" cognition, verbalizable cognition, cognition of an entity as qualified; according to Gaṅgeśa and Navya Nyāya, paradigmatically an awareness of a qualificandum (*viśeṣya*, q.v.) qualified by a qualifier (*viśeṣaṇa*, q.v.) or property, thus having an objecthood or intentionality (*viṣayatā*) with the structure *a*-as-ϕ; opposed to *nirvikalpaka* (q.v.).

siddhânta : the "right view" answering a correlate "*prima facie* view" or *pūrva-pakṣa* (q.v.); an author's "own position" or that of his school; a portion of a text devoted to elaborating an author's own views in relation to a previous *pūrva-pakṣa*.

siddhântin : the "proponent of the right view" answering a correlative *pūrva-pakṣin* (q.v.); the *siddhântin* is normally the author himself.

siddha-sādhana : the fallacy of trying to prove what is already known or generally admitted.

smṛti : second-order of sacred texts designated "remembering" in epistemological contrast with the first order, or *śruti*, "direct hearing or revelation"; *smṛti* is usually considered to include certain epics, Purāṇas (poems about divine incarnations), and *dharma-śāstra* or law books.

śruti : the Veda, the highest order of "revelation."

sūtra : "thread"; an aphorism or summary statement meant to express succinctly a position or argument which is to be explained and fleshed out by commentary whether in written form or orally by a teacher or expert.

sva-prāmāṇya: cognition as "self-authenticating," a Mīmāṃsaka (and Vedāntic) view of cognitive confirmation contrasting with the Naiyāyika view that a cognition is certified or known to be true "through another," *para* as opposed to *sva*; see also *para-prāmāṇya*.

sva-rūpa: "own nature," "own form."

sva-rūpa-sambandha: self-linking relation.

svayam-prakāśamāna: "irreflexively self-illuminating": an Upanishadic doctrine of the nature of self-consciousness championed by, among others, the Prābhākara Mīmāṃsaka.

tarka: "counterfactual reasoning"; according to Nyāya and other classical schools, a hypothetical argument that is capable of revealing fallacies and defeaters with respect to a position *~p* opposed to another position *p* that is to be accepted so long as *p* has some additional evidence in its favor; (in some contexts) "indirect proof," proof by refutation of a counterthesis.

tarkâbhāsa: apparent or fallacious instance of counterfactual reasoning, *tarka* (q.v.).

tātparya: "intention," what a speaker or author means to say; an "excellence" (*guṇa*) for all testimonial knowledge according to some Naiyāyikas though not Gaṅgeśa.

tejas: the "fiery element," one of four atomic elements; *tejas* is found in distinct varieties according to Vaiśeṣika physics, for instance, atoms of *tejas* comprising both light and fire, which are visible, and another configuration or variety comprising heat, which is not visible, and still another gold which is in part composed of *tejas* though it is naturally felt as cool (a phenomenon explained by an earthen, "co-support," according to some Navyas).

upādhi: in Nyāya, (1) the inferential *upādhi*, the inferential "undercutter," a special condition awareness of which undercuts an inference, blocking or preventing the occurrence of genuine inference through bringing about reasonable suspicion of deviation from a rule or pervasion (*vyāpti*); standardly defined as something that pervades the probandum of a targeted inference while failing to pervade its prover (all things S, the probandum, are U, the undercutter, but some things H, the prover, are not U); defined by Gaṅgeśa (*TCM* II, p. 282) as "that which a (putative) prover as deviating from means the prover deviates from its probandum"; (2) the ontological *upādhi*, a "surplus property," an "imposed property" contrasting with a genuine universal, *jāti* (q.v.).

upalakṣaṇa: "indicator"; a feature presented, or referred to, to indicate something else; a "differentiator" that determines reference having little or nothing to do with what that referendum is, i.e., not one of its genuine qualifiers, e.g., hovering crows pointed to or mentioned to pick out Devadatta's house.

upamāna: "analogy"; analogical acquisition of vocabulary, a *pramāṇa* (q.v.) according to Nyāya and some other classical schools.

upanīta: "retrieved," "revived"; memory-impressions, *saṃskāra*, can be provoked to project previous perceptual content or objecthood into a current experience, as happens in perceptual illusion and in several further types of sensory cognition according to Nyāya.

vāda: "discourse," enquiry undertaken to discover the truth on a topic or issue of concern.

vipakṣa: loci where the probandum is known to be absent, e.g., a lake with respect to an inference from smoke to fire.

virodha: "incompatibility" or "contradiction," a fallacy and defeater of a putative inference where the prover proves not the probandum but its absence or negation.

viṣaya: (a) object, thing, cognized object; (b) object of cognition, cognitive presentation.

viṣayatā: "objecthood," intentionality, one side of the relation between a cognition and its object, with the other as *viṣayitā* (q.v.), according to Navya Nyāya.

viṣayitā: "subjecthood," intentionality, one side of the relation between a cognition and its object, with the other as *viṣayatā* (q.v.).

viśeṣa: distinction, difference, particular; individualizer, particularizer, or numeralizer, one of seven ontic primitives or categories according to much Nyāya-Vaiśeṣika.

viśeṣaṇa: qualifier; qualities (e.g., blue), universals (e.g., cowhood), motions, along with unclassified properties (*upādhi*) all count as qualifiers that qualify a qualificandum, *viśeṣya*, according to Nyāya.

viśeṣaṇatā: "being-a-qualifier," "qualifierhood"; the relation (or *saṃnikarṣa*, q.v.) between an absence and a sense organ that is operative in perception of an absence; for example, it is in virtue of being a qualifier of a floor that a pot-absence grasped there can be known.

viśeṣya: the qualificandum as determined by a cognition of an entity as qualified; the thing cognized, the bearer of qualifiers (= *dharmin*).

viśiṣṭa : an entity as qualified; a qualificandum together with one or more of its qualifiers as known by a qualificative cognition (*viśiṣṭa-jñāna*, "cognition of an entity as qualified").

vyabhicāra : "deviation" of the occurrence of a putative prover from the occurrence of its probandum such that there is no pervasion (*vyāpti*, q.v.) of the probandum by the prover.

vyākaraṇa-śāstra : the science of grammar.

vyāpāra : "operation," "employment in causal operation," which is said to be required of "triggers" (*karaṇa*, q.v.) in relation to effects; e.g., the activity of an axe being used to fell a tree is the "causal employment" of the axe as a cause with respect to the tree's being cut down.

vyāpti : "pervasion," a factual relation that grounds inference (according to Nyāya) such that everything exhibiting a prover (H) would also exhibit a probandum (S), e.g., wherever smoke, there fire: (x) (Hx $\rightarrow$ Sx).

vyatireka : negative correlations (things not-S and not-H) entailed by a natural pervasion, *vyāpti* (q.v), constituting negative evidence for a pervasion; see also *anvaya-vyatireka*.

vyavahāra : common experience and linguistic practice, what people commonly do and say, taken by Naiyāyikas and other philosophers as *prima facie* evidence, i.e., as claims having positive epistemic weight; convention, agreement.

yathârtha : matching or corresponding to an object, cognition "as something is (or was)."

yogyatā : semantic fitness, a condition or "excellence" (*guṇa*) governing the intelligibility of a statement and the acquisition of knowledge through testimony, according to Naiyāyikas and others; e.g., "He is sprinkling with fire," is unintelligible in a non-metaphoric sense, because the logic of "sprinkling with" precludes fire as object (one "sprinkles" only with water).

NOTES

Preliminaries

1. Many of the following remarks were read by me at a conference in Pondicherry, India, January 1997, sponsored by École Française d'Extrême Orient and the French Institute of Pondicherry, "Ellipsis and Propositional Anaphora in Gaṅgeśa's *Tattvacintāmaṇi*." A revised version appears in *Time and Sources*, ed. F. Grimal (2002), pp. 173–86.

2. The paragraph breaks in the Tirupati edition of the *TCM* are also key. We may note, then, that N. S. Ramanuja Tatacharya as the editor responsible is, along with his guiding me, doubly to blame for the precise cuts.

Introduction

1. *Gaṅgeśa on the Upādhi, the "Inferential Undercutting Condition"*, by Ramanuja Tatacharya and myself (2002), contains a somewhat richer explanation of inference that I draw on here: pp. 8–22.

2. The Nyāya theory of generality is explained in my *Classical Indian Metaphysics* (Chicago: 1995; Delhi: 1996), pp. 57–63. For amplification, see, in this book, pp. 210–11 and 700–701, in particular, .

3. The conflict between Advaita Vedānta and Nyāya is the primary topic of *Classical Indian Metaphysics*.

4. We may grant Toshihiro Wada's contention that among several innovators Udayana gets the prize as the genius most responsible for the changes that differentiate the views of the New school from the *Nyāya-sūtra*'s and its commentaries: "The Origin of Navya-nyāya and Its Place within the History of Indian Logic" (2000). My point is that in Gaṅgeśa's usage of the terms "Old" and "New," likewise that of later Naiyāyikas', Udayana is counted as representing Old Nyāya.

Auspicious Performance (*maṅgala-vāda*)

1. Gaurinath Sastri, *Maṅgalavāda* (1979), pp. 23–24.

2. *Mīmāṃsāsūtra* 1.1.10.

3. *Gītā* 13.33.

4. *Kiraṇāvalī*, pp. 8–32 on "auspicious performance"; p. 20 for the line Gaṅgeśa quotes.

5. *Mānavadharmaśāstra* 4.146, p. 84.

6. For instance, *Bṛhadāraṇyaka* 3.7.1.

7. John Stuart Mill, *Utilitarianism*, p. 23.

Knowing Veridicality (*prāmāṇya-jñapti-vāda*)

1. Both the Asiatic Society and Vidyapeetha editions indicate that the perception chapter begins with the "Discourse on Auspicious Performance," the *maṅgala-vāda*. However, as explained in the introduction, the perception chapter begins here. The *maṅgala-vāda* is preamble to the entire *TCM*, not to this chapter alone.

2. This section has been translated by Jitendranath Mohanty, *Gaṅgeśa's Theory of Truth* (2nd ed., 1989). Ramanuja Tatacharya and I have discussed and read together most of the section, including all apparently ambiguous passages, some of which we read differently from Mohanty. But this is the one section of the perception chapter that he did not explain to me in its entirety. Thus Mohanty's translation has been particularly helpful. Mohanty's comments, moreover, which are extensive, are invaluable for students of Navya Nyāya. Nevertheless, he renders *prāmāṇya* ("veridicality") as "truth" infelicitously; "cognition" is much better than "knowledge" for *jñāna* in my opinion; there are other differences. But my debt to Mohanty is large, including several renderings of technical terms.

There is, however, one major misreading by him. Led astray by the ambiguity of a collection of words meaning "first" or "initial," Mohanty misunderstands an issue that frames a relatively long discussion. As will be elaborated (pp. 102–105, in this book), Gaṅgeśa is not addressing the problem of how anything is known for the very first time as Mohanty thinks. Instead, our author is talking about a first-time cognition occurring in unfamiliar circumstances (*an-abhyāsa-daśāyām* glossing *prathame*). As we shall see, the topics are Gaṅgeśa's contention that doubt about the veridicality of such a cognition shows the error of a Mīmāṃsaka position and then an argument that the veridicality of a veridical cognition arising in unfamiliar circumstances, though doubted at first, can come to be known.

3. Mohanty, pp. 84–96.

4. The idea for a chart comes from Arindam Chakrabarti.

5. Mohanty, pp. 110–11.

6. ibid., p. 125.

7. *Nyāyakusumāñjali* 2.1, ed. Goswami, p. 220, and ed. Dravid, p. 113. The attributed inference is worded somewhat differently in the original.

8. Here we follow the Asiatic Society edition, p. 241, reading 'a-prāmāṇya-saṃśayâ-janya-saṃśaya-viṣayatvād' instead of 'a-prāmāṇya-saṃśayâ-janya-saṃśayâ-viṣayatvād'.

9. Reading 'tad-āśrayâ-grāhyatve' instead of 'tad-āśrayâ-grāhyatvena'. Although neither the Vidyapeetha nor the Asiatic Society edition has this reading, it is suggested by Mathurānātha and accepted by Mohanty, p. 150.

10. Mohanty, pp. 152–56.

11. Mohanty's reading leads him to protest, p. 155: "Gaṅgeśa is obviously making the rather questionable assumption that though truth has not yet been known falsity has been."

12. Mohanty misreads the word *prathama*, "first," which Gaṅgeśa uses to indicate the example of a cognition arising in unfamiliar circumstances whose type is later found out to be veridical.

13. *TCM*, vol. 2, pt. 1 (Tirupati: 1982), pp. 463–515.

14. ibid.

15. Mohanty, pp. 171–72.

16. ibid., p. 172.

17. Here we follow the Asiatic Society edition, deleting 'grāhyatvān na'.

18. *Nyāyadarśana* (the *Nyāyasūtra* with four commentaries), ed. Taranatha and Amarendramohan, 1985 reprint, pp. 1ff.

19. *anumānasya tu pravṛtti-sāmarthya-liṅga-janmano . . . nirasta-samasta-vyabhicāra-śaṅkasya svata eva prāmāṇyam anumeyâ-vyabhicāri-liṅga-samutthatvāt*, ibid., p. 9.

Production of Veridical Cognition (*utpatti-vāda*)

1. *Classical Indian Metaphysics*, pp. 142–46.

2. *Nyāyakusumañjali* 2.1, ed. Dravid, p. 105, and ed. Goswami, p. 219.

3. Here we follow the Asiatic Society edition and read 'kāraṇa-janyaṃ' instead of 'kārya-janyaṃ'.

4. *TCM*, vol. 2, pt. 1 (Tirupati: 1982), p. 254. Here Gaṅgeśa follows Maṇikaṇṭha's *Nyāyaratna*. See our discussion in *Gaṅgeśa on the Upādhi* (2002), pp. 43–45.

5. Though both editions read, 'tad-darśana-janyaṃ', not 'tad-darśanâ-janyaṃ', Ramanuja Tatacharya makes the emendation.

6. With the Asiatic Society edition instead of 'visaṃvādāt'.

7. The Asiatic Society edition adds 'a-yathârtha-' to read 'a-yathârtha-yathârthatve', and Mathurānātha accordingly gives a slightly different interpretation than Rucidatta.

8. Here the Tirupati edition has incorrectly 'a-gṛhīta-saṃsarga'.

Characterizing Veridical Awareness (*pramā-lakṣaṇa-vāda*)

1. Previous versions of this section appeared in the *Journal of Indian Philosophy* (June 1993) and *Classical Indian Metaphysics*. Unknown to me unfortunately until after the latter had been typeset, Nandita Bandopadhyay translated the first part of this section, the *pūrvapakṣa* (as she says), text up to the first definition that Gaṅgeśa endorses (p. 236, in this book): *Definition of Valid Knowledge* (1989). Bandopadhyay's renderings aıe good, and her accompanying explanations insightful. She has helped me correct mistakes.

2. Paraphrasing *Classical Indian Metaphysics*, pp. 60–61 (trimming the commentary), let me list Udayana's six *jāti-bādhaka*, "blockers" that unmask pseudo-universals. (1) No universal has only one instance; thus "spaceness" is not a true universal because there is only one space. (2) Two apparently distinct universals having the same instances are one and the same universal; thus mankind and humanity are the same entity. (3) There are no cross-sectional kinds (*jāti-saṃkara*). If two candidates have an instance in common without one lying in every instance of the other, then neither is a true universal. (We see here Gaṅgeśa presenting an argument supporting this third *bādhaka*.) (4) No true universal generates an infinite series of entities. Thus "universalhood" is not a true universal. (5) There is no universal "individualizerhood," since an individualizer only particularizes—the ultimate atoms, for instance—and such a universal would make that work impossible. (6) There is no universal "inherencehood." This is the "non-relation" blocker—inherence as a connector would apparently implode if inherencehood were not ruled out.

3. Reading with the Asiatic Society edition 'atyantâ-bhāva-sāmānâdhikaraṇyaṃ' instead of 'antâ-bhāva-sāmānâdhikaraṇyaṃ'.

4. Fuller discussion of definition from the Nyāya point of view can be found in *Classical Indian Metaphysics*, pp. 63–64, in particular concerning the flaws of (a) overextension, (b) underextension, and (c) missing altogether what is to be defined.

5. Cf., *Classical Indian Metaphysics*, pp. 164ff.

6. *Nyāyadarśana* (the *Nyāyasūtra* with four commentaries), ed. Taranatha and Amarendramohan, pp. 1–24.

7. *Lakṣaṇamālā* (1963), p. 1.

8. Gadādhara's *Viṣayatāvāda* has been translated by Sibajiban Bhattacharyya (1990).

9. Sibajiban Bhattacharyya, *Gadādhara's Theory of Objectivity*, pt. 1 (1990), pp. 75–78 and 177–79.

10. *Nyāyakusumañjali* 4.5, ed. Goswami, p. 539, and ed. Dravid, p. 353.

11. *Nyāyadarśana*, pp. 110–20, where Vācaspati defends his interpretation of *a-vyapadeśyam* ("non-verbal") as indicating indeterminate perception, contrasting with determinate perception, *vyavasāyâtmakam* ("definite"), the two being the fundamental types of perception and thus targeted in the *Nyāyasūtra* definition.

12. *Ātmatattvaviveka*, ed. Dvivedin and Dravida, p. 508: *sa (viṣaya-viṣayi-bhāva) ca prakāśasya satas tadīyatā-mātra-rūpaḥ sva-bhāva-viśeṣaḥ.*

"Presentation Otherwise" (*anyathā-khyāti-vāda*)

1. A previous version of our translation of this section appeared in the

Journal of Indian Philosophy 28 (December 2000), pp. 567–650.

2. In ''Analysis of Perceptual Illusion,'' a section of B. K. Matilal's *Perception* (1986), arguments of the classical disputants are reconstructed most admirably. Matilal makes plain the strength of the Prābhākara position with respect to subjectivist views: pp. 180–220. The comments that follow are pretty much in accord with his points.

3. Instead of 'jñāta-bhedasya', the Asiatic Society edition has 'jñātâ-bhedasya', and both Rucidatta and Mathurānātha understand 'jñātâ-bhedasya'. But the line reads better without the negation.

4. The Vidyapeetha edition has, incorrectly, 'a-bhedâ-grahāt'.

5. For a similar problem in Advaita Vedānta, see my ''Padmapāda's Illusion Argument'' (1987).

6. B. K. Matilal explains the verse, and shows the cost to the realist of maintaining a positive account of error: ''A Realist View of Perception,'' *The Philosophy of P. F. Strawson* (ed. Sen and Verma, 1995), pp. 316–17.

7. *Prakaraṇapañcikā*, p. 53.

8. Here we read 'idaṃ-jñānaṃ' instead of 'idaṃ jñānaṃ', although both editions have the latter.

9. Reading 'an-anyathā-siddhāv' instead of 'anyathā-siddhāv', though both editions have the latter.

10. Reading 'rajatatvâ-saṃsargâ-saṃsargâ-graha-rūpaṃ' instead of 'rajatatvâ-saṃsargâ-graha-rūpaṃ', with the Asiatic Society edition.

11. Reading, with the Asiatic Society edition, 'rajata-bheda-saṃsargâ-saṃsargâ-grahād' instead of 'rajata-bheda-saṃsargâ-saṃsarga-grahād'.

12. Reading 'bheda-grahān' instead of 'bhedâ-grahān'.

13. Reading 'bhedâ-grahe', with the Asiatic Society edition, instead of 'bheda-grahe'.

14. Emending from 'pūrvaṃ bādhâtmakam' to 'pūrva-bādhâtmakam'.

15. John Pollock, *Contemporary Theories of Knowledge* (1986), p. 185.

16. *Tantravārttika*, p. 819, according to Ramanuja Tatacharya's reference, *TCM*, Tirupati, p. 889.

17. *Nyāyadarśana*, p. 73, a verse that is slightly altered by Gaṅgeśa (who has at the end 'matam' instead of the 'ca tat' of the original).

Characterizing Perception (*pratyakṣa-lakṣaṇa-vāda*)

1. *Nyāyadarśana*, pp. 110–20.

2. *Lakṣaṇamālā*, p. 13: *indriya-ja-pramā-sādhakatamaṃ pratyakṣam*. Udayana goes on to explain that what he means by *sādhakatama* is that a cognition is not the trigger or chief instrumental cause.

3. Reading 'taj-jñānasya' instead of 'tatra jñānasya'.

Sensory Connection (*saṃnikarṣa-vāda*)

1. Reading 'anugata', not 'an-anugata', with the Asiatic Society edition.

2. Reading 'karaṇatvena' with the Asiatic Society edition, instead of 'kāraṇatvena'.

Inherence (*samavāya-vāda*)

1. A previous translation of this section was published in my *Classical Indian Metaphysics*. The principal improvement is rendering *viśiṣṭa-jñāna* as "cognition of an entity as qualified," as opposed to "relational cognition." The new phrase makes the central arguments of the section much clearer.

2. *Padārthadharmasaṃgraha*, pp. 774–75.

3. Reading 'indriya-saṃbaddha-viśeṣaṇa-viśeṣaṇatā' for 'indriya-saṃbaddha-viśeṣaṇatā'. While both the Vidyapeetha and Asiatic Society editions have the latter, we presume that Gaṅgeśa would formulate his adversary's proposal accurately.

4. Reading with the Asiatic Society edition 'a-vyāpya-vṛtti-vṛtti' for 'a-vyāpya-vṛtti'.

5. Reading with the Asiatic Society edition 'nityâ-bhāva-vṛtty-a-bhāvatva-sākṣād-vyāpya-dharmatvāt' for 'nityâ-bhāvavad-vṛtty-a-bhāvatva-sākṣād-vyāpya-dharmatvāt'.

Non-Cognition (*an-upalabdhi-vāda*)

1. See in particular *Nyāyakusumañjali* 3.20, ed. Goswami, pp. 464–66, and ed. Dravid, pp. 308–11.

2. *Ślokavārttika*, the *a-bhāva-pariccheda*, pp. 335–49.

3. Here we remove the *daṇḍa* or full stop found in the Tirupati edition, and add a comma after 'cakṣuṣi'.

4. Here we change the punctuation, adding a comma at this point and removing the comma after the next compound, *an-upalabdhi-janyam*.

5. *Ślokavārttika*, pp. 342–43. Other versions of the case occur in Vācaspati's *Nyāyavarttikatātparyaṭikā*, p. 89, and in Udayana's *Pariśuddhi* commentary, p. 132.

6. Here we correct the wrong reading of a short 'a'.

7. *Ślokavārttika*, verse 28, *a-bhāva-pariccheda*, p. 343.

Absence (*a-bhāva-vāda*)

1. There is no published commentary by Mathurānātha on the section. The brief commentary in the Asiatic Society edition is by Jayadeva Pakṣadhara Miśra (c. 1500). The section has been translated by B. K. Matilal along with

his own commentary, *The Navya-Nyāya Doctrine of Negation* (1968). Professor Matilal wrote widely on Navya Nyāya and other classical systems, and was throughout his career a brilliant exponent of Nyāya philosophy. Probably there will never be another scholar of his ability. However, the book on absences is an early work of Matilal's, and we shall only occasionally refer to it. We shall not note variant readings. Ramanuja Taṭacharya and I did not plan at first to read this section together. But as we noticed how many sentences we read differently from Matilal, we decided to start afresh. My debts to Professor Matilal are nevertheless great.

The most serious problem with Matilal's work is too easy use of Western logical terms that do not carry the ontological commitments of the corresponding Naiyāyika usages. The same may be said of some of Matilal's epistemological terminology in English, where again he fails to do justice to Gaṅgeśa's objectivism and realism. For example, not "contradiction" or "self-contradiction" for *virodha*, but "incompatibility," when what Gaṅgeśa has in mind are not logical oppositions but natural incompatibilities, like fire and water or a pot and its absence.

2. Restoring the original reading, pace Jayadeva and Matilal (p. 175, last line).

3. As just noted, Matilal corrects the text adding a "not" ('na'), contrary to both the Asiatic Society and Vidyapeetha editions. Thus he finds an argument for the Nyāya position: there is no circularity because such talk of absences would not be possible otherwise (p. 115). Jayadeva seems to read the text in the same way, and this is, though different from ours, a possible reading.

4. Matilal, we may note, though he makes a small error (concerning what is not known and why), gives on the whole here a good translation, albeit one different from ours. Matilal finds (1) an absence whose expression uses words for the locus and the absentee in the same grammatical case, usually the nominative—"The pot is not the cloth," with the corresponding nouns in Sanskrit both in the nominative case—distinguished from (2) an absence whose expression uses terms that are in different cases, usually the nominative and the locative—"The pot in not on the floor." See, ibid., pp. 115–17. Matilal translates *vyadhikaraṇâ-bhāva* as "locative absence," and *samānâdhikaraṇâ-bhāva* as "nominative absence." Ramanuja Tatacharya says this is a viable interpretation. Note that however one reads the words *vyadhikaraṇâ-bhāva* and *samānâdhikaraṇâ-bhāva*, the distinction is between "relational absence" (*samsargikâ-bhāva*, which comes in three varieties, prior, posterior, and absolute) and "mutual absence" or "mutual distinctness" (*anyonyâ-bhāva*).

5. Reading 'tad-dvai-rūpy-a-bhāvāt' instead of 'tad-vairūpy-a-bhāvāt'.

6. Adding 'bhedam'.

7. Matilal, p. 122.

8. Matilal has a particularly good discussion, p. 123.

9. Adding 'na'.

10. Reading 'kāraṇatvân-avadhāraṇāt' instead of 'karaṇatvân-avadhāraṇāt', with the Asiatic Society edition.

11. Here we change the punctuation, moving the *daṇḍa* back one word.

12. Reading 'jñātaṃ' instead of 'jñānaṃ'.

13. See also *Classical Indian Metaphysics*, pp. 142–46.

14. Matilal, pp. 136–37.

15. Reading 'pratītyā', instead of 'pratīti' in compound, with the Asiatic Society edition.

16. Matilal discusses the Buddhist verse both astutely and amply: see, esp., p. 141. But he mistakes the following text as voicing arguments directed against the Buddhist, whereas they pretty clearly seem to be directed against the Prābhākara.

Light's Sensory Relationality (*viśayâloka-saṃnikarṣa-vāda*)

1. *Nyāyakandalī, pratyakṣa-prakaraṇa*, pp. 442ff.

2. Here instead of 'nanv abhimukhâvayavâvacchedena viṣayâloka-saṃyogayoḥ kāraṇatve' or the following long expression in parentheses, we read, with the Asiatic Society edition (for the most part), 'nanv abhimukhâvayavâvacchedena viṣayâloka-saṃyogasya kāraṇatve'.

3. Reading 'āvaśyakatvāt' for 'āvaśyaka' and adding 'avayavâloka-' immediately afterwards.

4. Reading 'nanu' for 'na tu', with the Asiatic Society edition.

5. Reading 'cākṣuṣa-janakatvâ-' instead of 'cākṣuṣa-'.

6. Here we add the second 'vyāpya'.

7. A single pot at a single moment can be touched and seen—through "retrieval" of previous perceptual content and its projection into current perception through awakening of memory (recall the example of distant sandalwood visually contacted and perceived as fragrant, in this text, p. 125). Here the point, however, is ontological, or causal, to explain how such objecthood could arise.

8. Reading 'kāryam' instead of 'a-kāryam'.

The Perceptibility of Air (*vāyu-pratyakṣa-vāda*)

1. Reading 'liṅga-grahe' in place of 'liṅgâ-grahe'.

2. *TCM*, vol. 2, pt. 1 (Tirupati), pp. 253ff and 282ff, and vol. 2 (Calcutta), pp. 299ff and 336ff. See our discussion in *Gaṅgeśa on the Upādhi*, pp. 38–41 and 80–82.

3. See in particular the commentaries on the *anumāna sūtra*, *NyS* 1.1.5: *Nyāyadarśana*, pp. 132ff.

4. Reading 'viśeṣa-guṇavattvaṃ' instead of 'viśeṣaṇa-guṇavattvaṃ'.

5. For example, Kisor Chakrabarti in his summary of the section—Karl Potter and Sibajiban Bhattacharyya, eds., *Encyclopedia of Indian Philosophies* VI, pp. 144–45—ascribes a *siddhânta* to Gaṅgeśa that is in this way wrong. Correspondence from Professor Chakrabarti has shown me that a case can be made for giving this passage to the previous *pūrvapakṣin* and aligning Gaṅgeśa in this instance with Old Nyāya and the view that air is not perceptible. However, I find his arguments comparatively weak. Our reasons for our reading are stated in the main text.

6. Here 'na' is added.

7. Reading 'prāmāyāṃ' instead of 'prābhāyāṃ', with the Asiatic Society edition.

8. *Padārthadharmasaṃgraha*, pp. 114–15.

The Fiery Character of Gold (*suvarṇa-taijasatva-vāda*)

1. Reading 'an-anugatam' instead of 'anugatam'.

2. Reading 'dravatvatva' as opposed to 'dravatva'.

3. Reading 'pītatvāt' instead of 'pītavat', with the Asiatic Society edition.

4. Here we change the punctuation.

The Mind's Atomicity (*mano-'ṇutva-vāda*)

1. Some of the comments to this section derive from a conference paper of mine (later published) and remarks by Mark Siderits and Kisor Chakrabarti. "Two Problems about Perception and Mental Intermediaries in the Nyāya Dualism: Focus and 'Extraordinary' Sensory Connections with Perceived Properties" (2000).

2. *Nyāyadarśana*, p. 215.

3. ibid., pp. 215 and 899.

4. *NyS* 1.1.4 itself, the "perception sūtra," leads Vātsyāyana—and all later commentators—to talk about *manas*; ibid., pp. 98ff.

5. Reading 'an-avacchinne' instead of 'avacchinne'.

6. These observations are due mainly to Arindam Chakrabarti.

7. Reading 'indriyatve' for 'indriyatvena'.

8. *Nyāyadarśana*, p. 897.

9. *NyS* 2.1.35, ibid., p. 498.

10. Good papers on the point are Arindam Chakrabarti, "I Touch What I Saw" (1992), and Jonardon Ganeri, "Cross-modality and the Self" (2000).

Apperception (*anuvyavasāya-vāda*)

1. Rucidatta reads 'ātmâdau' as what Gaṅgeśa means here.

2. The superiority of this reading, which follows a variant noted in both the Tirupati and Calcutta editions, was pointed out by Arindam Chakrabarti: 'etaj-jñāna-viṣayam' instead of 'etaj-jñāna-viṣayâśrayaḥ'. If the word 'āśrayaḥ' is used, the text should read: 'etaj-jñāna-viṣaya**tâ**śrayaḥ'.

3. The alternative reading follows the text emendation required with use of the word 'āśrayaḥ': see the preceding note.

Indeterminate Perception (*nirvikalpaka-vāda*)

1. Sibajiban Bhattacharyya published a translation of this section, *Gaṅgeśa's Theory of Indeterminate Perception*, vol. 2 (1993), facilitating my effort here. But a Sanskrit tape-recording I made of a reading by Ramanuja Tatacharya completed in 1991 has been my principal guide, and we have reread together several problematic passages. Among the many merits of Sibajiban's book is his bringing the main points out from Rucidatta's and Jayadeva's commentaries, a depth not aimed at here.

Some of the comments repeat remarks made in a paper of mine, "There's Nothing Wrong with Raw Perception" (2001), written in response to Arindam Chakrabarti (see the following note).

2. This position is championed by Arindam Chakrabarti in "Against Immaculate Perception: Seven Reasons for Eliminating *Nirvikalpaka* Perception from Nyāya" (2000). Several of Chakrabarti's seven reasons, however, are different from the *pūrvapakṣin*'s.

3. *Prakaraṇapañcikā*, p. 162.

4. ibid., p. 142.

5. Sibajiban (1993) following Jayadeva explains this passage in a particularly helpful manner: pp. 22–24. However, we read the last sentence not in a Naiyāyika objector's voice but in the *pūrvapakṣin*'s.

6. Sibajiban Bhattacharyya, *Gadādhara's Theory of Objectivity*, pt. 1 (1990), pp. 172–76, discusses this among other prominent Navya views.

7. Sibajiban (1993), following Rucidatta, reconstructs an implicit argument in four steps, pp. 52–3.

8. Reading 'anyatra' instead of 'atra'.

Qualifiers versus Indicators (*viśeṣaṇôpalakṣaṇa-vāda*)

1. Reading 'sattve' instead of 'a-sattve' and changing the *saṃdhi*.

2. Sukharanjan Saha connects Gaṅgeśa's thought with a distinction between referential and attributive usages, in his *Meaning, Truth and Predication* (1991), chapter nine, where he discusses at length this section of

Gaṅgeśa's text; see, esp., p. 259. Arindam Chakrabarti remarks that the distinction as employed in contemporary analytic philosophy is due to Keith Donnellan, "Reference and Definite Descriptions," anthologized in *Naming, Necessity, and Natural Kinds*, ed. Stephen Schwartz (1977), pp. 42–65. To use Donnellan's examples, 'Smith's murderer' is used referentially when it is said (perhaps at Smith's trial), "Smith's murderer is innocent," whereas in "Smith's murderer deserves punishment" the phrase 'Smith's murderer' is used attributively.

3. The passage referred to is *Saptapadārthī*, p. 87.

4. *Nyāyavārttikatātparyapariśuddhi*, p. 145.

5. Reading, with the Asiatic Society edition, 'tatra upalakṣya' instead of 'tattôpalakṣya'.

6. An important argument is that in a context of a speaker desiring to communicate to a hearer and a hearer desiring to understand, a hearer faced with an ambiguous statement typically will ask the speaker what he intended to say in an effort to disambiguate and acquire the information at hand. This is taken to show that speaker's intention does determine a qualificandum in certain circumstances, in the sense of "that which is to be talked about." However, there are contrary cases such as a truth-telling parrot and a deluded deceiver, as we saw (pp. 180 and 182). And whether the speaker's intention need be considered, more strictly, a causal factor for a hearer's testimonial knowledge as opposed to, more parsimoniously, the statement under the interpretation of the hearer—the speaker's interpretation being normally irrelevant—is an issue for Gaṅgeśa and other Naiyāyikas, as was remarked.

7. *Classical Indian Metaphysics*, p. 366, note 90.

8. Cf., ibid., p. 347, note 35.

Determinate Perception (*savikalpaka-vāda*)

1. A portion of this section was published in "The Error of 'That': Gaṅgeśa on the Epistemology of the Memory Cognition 'That' " (1996).

2. *NyS-bhāṣya* 1.1.10; *Nyāyadarśana*, p. 188.

3. Reading 'anubhava-viṣayatvena' instead of 'anubhavâ-viṣayatvena'.

4. Udayana, right after declaring that memory is *not* to be considered in "object-conformity" (for reasons that Gaṅgeśa is about to rehearse), uses this term, saying that it can be "in conformity with its (originating) experience": *Nyāyavārttikatātparyapariśuddhi*, p. 53.

5. ibid., pp. 52–3.

6. As noted, Udayana uses the term 'yathânubhava', "in conformity with experience," implying that remembering normally gets positive epistemic weight though it has the counts mentioned against it: ibid., p. 53.

7. ibid., p. 52.

BIBLIOGRAPHY

Ātmatattvaviveka of Udayana. Ed. Vindhyesvariprasada Dvivedin and Lakshmana Sastri Dravida. Bibliotheca Indica 170. Reprint, the Asiatic Society, Calcutta, 1986.

Bagchi, Sitansusekhar. *Inductive Reasoning.* Calcutta: Munishchandra Sinha, 1953.

Bandopadhyay, Nandita. *Definition of Valid Knowledge.* Calcutta: Sanskrit Pustak Bandar, 1989.

Bhattacharya, Dinesh Chandra. *History of Navya-nyāya in Mithilā.* Darbhanga: Mithila Institute, 1958.

Bhattacharya, Gopinath. *Tarkasaṃgraha-dīpikā on Tarkasaṃgraha by Annaṃbhaṭṭa.* Calcutta: Progressive Publishers, 1976.

Bhattacharyya, Sibajiban. *Doubt, Belief and Knowledge.* New Delhi: Indian Council of Philosophical Research and Allied Publishers, 1987.

———. Introduction, pt. 1 of *Gadādhara's Theory of Objectivity.* New Delhi: Indian Council of Philosophical Research, 1990.

———. Gadhādara's *Viṣayatāvāda,* pt. 2 of *Gadādhara's Theory of Objectivity.* New Delhi: Indian Council of Philosophical Research, 1990.

———. *Gaṅgeśa's Theory of Indeterminate Perception.* Vol. 2. New Delhi: Indian Council of Philosophical Research, 1993.

Chakrabarti, Arindam. "Telling as Letting Know." *Knowing from Words.* Ed. Arindam Chakrabarti and B. K. Matilal. Dordrecht: Kluwar, 1994.

———. "Against Immaculate Perception: Seven Reasons for Eliminating *nirvikalpaka* Perception from Nyāya." *Philosophy East and West* 50, no. 1 (January 2000).

———. "I Touch What I Saw." *Philosophy and Phenomenological Research* 52, no. 1 (March 1992).

Chakrabarti, Kisor. *Classical Indian Philosophy of Mind.* Albany, New York: 1999.

Donnellan, Keith. "Reference and Definite Descriptions." *Naming, Necessity, and Natural Kinds.* Ed. Stephen Schwartz. Ithaca, New York: Cornell University Press, 1977.

Dravid, N. S., trans. *Ātmatattvaviveka by Udayanācārya.* Shimla: Indian Institute of Advanced Study, 1995.

———. *Nyāyakusumāñjali of Udayanācārya*. Vol. 1. New Delhi: Indian Council of Philosophical Research: 1996.

Ganeri, Jonardon. "Cross-modality and the Self." *Philosophy and Phenomenological Research* (October 2000).

Gaṅgeśa: see *Tattvacintāmaṇi*.

Gangopadhyay, Mrinalkanti, trans. *Nyāya-Sūtra with Vātsyāyana's Commentary*. Calcutta: Indian Studies, 1982.

Gettier, Edmund. "Is Justified True Belief Knowledge." *Analysis* 23 (1963).

Goekoop, C. *The Logic of Invariable Concomitance in the Tattvacintāmaṇi*. Dordrecht: D. Reidel, 1967.

Goldman, Alvin. *Epistemology and Cognition*. Cambridge: Harvard University Press, 1986.

Hamblin, C. L. *Fallacies*. London: Methuen, 1970. Reprint, Newport News, Virginia: Vale Press, 1993.

Jha, Ganganatha, trans. *The Khaṇḍanakhaṇḍakhādya of Śrīharṣa*. Reprint, Delhi: Sri Satguru, 1986.

———. *The Nyāyasūtra of Gautama* (with the commentaries of Vātsyāyana and Uddyotakara). 4 vols. 1912–19. Reprint, Delhi: Motilal Banarsidass, 1984.

———. *Padārthadharmasaṃgraha of Praśastapāda*. Reprint, Varanasi: Chaukhamba Orientalia, 1982.

———. *Ślokavārtika*. Reprint, Delhi: Sri Satguru, 1983.

Jha, V. N., trans. *Viṣayatāvāda of Harirāma Tarkālaṅkara*. Pune: University of Poona, 1987.

Jhalakikar, Bhimacarya, compiler. *Nyāyakośa* (*Dictionary of Technical Terms of Indian Philosophy*). Ed. and rev. Vasudev Shastri Abhyankar. Poona: Bhandarkar Oriental Research Institute, 1978.

Khaṇḍanakhaṇḍakhādya of Śrīharṣa. Ed. Navikanta Jha, Kashi Sanskrit Series 197. Varanasi: Chowkhamba, 1970.

Kiraṇāvalī of Udayana. Ed. Jitendra S. Jetly. Gaekwad Oriental Series 154. Baroda: Oriental Institute, 1971.

Kiraṇāvalī of Udayana. With the commentary of Vardhamāna. Fasc. I - 111. Ed. Siva Chandra Sarvvabhouma. 1911. Reprint, Calcutta: Asiatic Society, 1989.

Kumārila: see *Ślokavārttika*.

Lakṣaṇamālā of Udayana. Ed. Sasinatha Jha. Mithila Institute Series 13. Darbhanga: 1963.

Lakṣaṇāvalī of Udayana. Ed. Sasinatha Jha. Mithila Institute Series 14. Darbhanga: 1963. See also Musashi Tachikawa.

Madhavananda, Swami, trans. *Bhāṣā-pariccheda of Viśvanātha.* Calcutta: Advaita Ashrama, 1977.

Mānava Dharmaśāstra. Ed. J. Jolly. Reprint. New Delhi: Orientalist, 1993.

Maṇikaṇṭha Miśra: see *Nyāyaratna.*

Mathurānātha: see *Tattvacintāmaṇi.*

Matilal, B. K. *The Character of Logic in India.* Ed. Jonardon Ganeri and Heeraman Tiwari. Albany, New York: State University of New York Press, 1998.

———. *The Navya-Nyāya Doctrine of Negation.* Cambridge, Massachusetts: Harvard University Press, 1968.

———. *Nyāya-Vaiśeṣika.* Wiesbaden: Otto Harrassowitz, 1977.

———. *Perception: An Essay on Classical Indian Theories of Knowledge.* Oxford: Oxford University Press, 1986.

———. "A Realist View of Perception." *The Philosophy of P. F. Strawson.* Ed. Sen and Verma. New Delhi: Indian Council of Philosophical Research, 1995.

Manu-dharma-śāstra.

Mill, John Stuart. *Utilitarianism.* Indianapolis: Hackett, 1979.

Mīmāṃsā-sūtra: see Mohan Lal Sandal.

Mishra, Umesha. *History of Indian Philosophy.* 2 vols. Allahabad: Tirabhukti, 1966.

Mohanty, Jitendranath. *Gaṅgeśa's Theory of Truth.* Reprint, Delhi: Motilal Banarsidass, 1989.

Mukhopadhyay, P. K. *Indian Realism.* Calcutta: K. P. Bagchi, 1984.

Mullati, L. C. *The Navya-Nyāya Theory of Inference.* Dharwad: Karnatak University, 1977.

Nyāyadarśana: see *Nyāyasūtra.*

Nyāyakandalī commentary by Śrīdhara on Praśastapāda: see *Padārtha-dharma-saṃgaha.*

Nyāyakośa: see Bhimacarya Jhalakikar.

Nyāyakusumāñjali of Udayana. Ed. Mahaprabhulal Goswami. Mithila Institute Ancient Texts Series 23. Darbhanga, 1972.

Nyāyakusumāñjali of Udayana: see N. S. Dravid.

Nyāyalīlāvatī of Vallabha. With the *Nyāyalīlāvatīprakāśa* commentary of Vardhamāna. Ed. Dhundhiraj Sastri, Chowkhamba Sanskrit Series 407. Benares: 1927–34.

Nyāyaratna of Maṇikaṇṭha Miśra. Ed. V. Subrahmanya Sastri and V. Krishnamacharya. Madras: Madras Government Oriental Series, 1953.

(*NyS*) *Nyāyasūtra* (Nyāyadarśanam). With four commentaries, the *Nyāyasūtra-bhāṣya* of Vātsyāyana, the *Nyāyasūtra-vārttika* of Uddyotakara, the *Nyāyasūtravārttika-tātpāryaṭīkā* of Vācaspati Miśra, and the *Vṛtti* of Viśvanātha. Ed. A. M. Tarkatirtha, Taranatha Nyayatarkatirtha, and H. K. Tarkatirtha. Calcutta Sanskrit Series 18. 1936–44. Reprint, New Delhi, Munshiram Manoharlal, 1985.

Nyāyavārttikatātparyapariśuddhi of Udayanācārya. Ed. Anantalal Thakur. New Delhi: Indian Council of Philosophical Research, 1996.

(*PDS*) *Padārthadharmasaṃgraha* of Praśastapāda (*Praśastapādabhāṣyam*). With the *Nyāyakandalī* commentary of Śrīdhara. Ed. with a Hindi translation by Durgadhara Jha. Varanasi: Sampurnanand Sanskrit Vishvavidyalaya, 1977.

Phillips, Stephen H. *Classical Indian Metaphysics*. Chicago: Open Court, 1995. (Indian edition) Delhi: Motilal Banarsidass, 1996.

———. "The Error of 'That': Gaṅgeśa on the Epistemology of the Memory Cognition 'That.' " *Journal of Indian Philosophy and Religion*, vol. 1 (Oct. 1996).

———. "Padmapāda's Illusion Argument." *Philosophy East and West* 37, no. 1 (January 1987).

———. "There's Nothing Wrong with Raw Perception: A Response to Chakrabarti's Attack on Nyāya's *Nirvikalpaka Pratyakṣa*." *Philosophy East and West* 51, no. 1 (January 2001).

———. "Two Problems about Perception and Mental Intermediaries in the Nyāya Dualism: Focus and 'Extraordinary' Sensory Connections with Perceived Properties." *Journal of Indian Philosophy and Religion*, Vol. 5 (Oct. 2000).

Phillips, Stephen H. and N. S. Ramanuja Tatacharya, *Gaṅgeśa on the Upādhi, the "Inferential Undercutting Condition": Introduction, Translation and Explanation*. New Delhi: Indian Council of Philosophical Research, 2002.

———. "From Gaṅgeśa's *Tattvacintāmaṇi*: Discourse on Perceptual Presentation of Something as Other Than What It Is." *Journal of Indian Philosophy*, Vol. 28 (December 2000).

Pollock, John. *Contemporary Theories of Knowledge*. Lanham, Md: Rowman & Littlefield, 1986.

Potter, Karl H., ed. *Encyclopedia of Indian Philosophies.* Vol. 2. *Nyāya-Vaiśeṣika.* Delhi: Motilal Banarsidass, 1977.

Potter, Karl H. and Sibajiban Bhattacharyya, eds. *Encyclopedia of Indian Philosophies.* Vol. 6. *Indian Philosophical Analysis: Nyāya-Vaiśeṣika from Gaṅgeśa to Raghunātha Śiromaṇi.* Delhi: Motilal Banarsidass, 1993.

Prakaraṇa Pañcikā of Śalikanātha Miśra. Ed. A. Subrahmanya Sastri. Banaras Hindu University Darśana Series 4. Varanasi: 1961.

Ramanuja Tatacharya, N. S. *Pratyakṣatattvacintāmaṇi Vimarśa: A Comprehensive and Evaluative Study of the Pratyakṣakhaṇḍa of the Tattvacintāmaṇi.* Tirupati: Rashtriya Sanskrit Vidyapeetha, 1992.

——— "Upādhi-Vimarśa." *P. N. Pattabhirama Sastri Commemoration Volume.* Tirupati: Rashtriya Sanskrit Vidyapeetha, 1993.

Rucidatta Miśra: see *Tattvacintāmaṇi.*

Saha, Sukharanjan. *Meaning, Truth and Predication.* Calcutta: Jadavpur University: 1991.

Śalikanātha: see *Prakaraṇa Pañcikā.*

Sandal, Mohan Lal, trans. *Mīmāṃsā Sūtras of Jaimini.* 2 vols. Reprint. Delhi: Motilal Banarsidass, 1980.

Saptapadârthi of Śivāditya. Ed. J. S. Jetly. Ahmedabad: Lalbhai Dalpatbhai Bharatiya Sanskriti Vidya Mandira, 1963.

Sastri, Gaurinath. *Maṅgalavāda.* Calcutta: Asiatic Society, 1979.

Ślokavārttika of Kumārila. Ed. Dvarikadas Sastri. Varanasi: Tara Publications, 1978. See also Ganganatha Jha.

Solomon, Ester. *Indian Dialectics.* 2 vols. Ahmedabad: Gujarat Vidya Sabha, 1976.

Śrīharṣa: see *Khaṇḍanakhaṇḍakhādya.*

Staal, J. F. "The Concept of Pakṣa in Indian Logic." *Journal of Indian Philosophy* 2, no. 2 (August 1973).

———. "Negation and the Law of Contradiction in Indian Thought." *Bulletin of the School of Oriental and African Studies* 25 (1962).

Swartz, Stephen P., ed. *Naming, Necessity, and Natural Kinds.* Ithaca, New York: Cornell University Press, 1977.

Tachikawa, Musashi. *The Structure of the World in Udayana's Realism,* including editions and translations of Udayana's *Lakṣaṇāvalī* and a portion of his *Kiraṇāvalī.* Dordrecht: D. Reidel, 1981.

Tarkabhāṣā of Keśava Miśra. Ed. Devadatta Ramakrishna Bhandarkar and Pandit Kedarnath. Bombay Sanskrit and Prakrit Series 84. Bombay, 1937.

(*TCM*) *Tattvacintāmaṇi* of Gaṅgeśa, vol. 1, *pratyakṣa-khaṇḍa*. With the *Prakāśa* commentary by Rucidatta Miśra and a subcommentary by Rāmakṛṣṇādhvarin. Ed. N. S. Ramanuja Tatacharya. Kendriya Sanskrit Vidyapeetha Series 20. Tirupati, 1972.

Tattvacintāmaṇi of Gaṅgeśa, vol. 2, *anumāna-khaṇḍa*. With the *Prakāśa* commentary by Rucidatta Miśra and a subcommentary by Dharmarājādhvarin. Ed. N. S. Ramanuja Tatacharya. Kendriya Sanskrit Vidyapeetha Series 33. Tirupati: 1982.

Tattvacintāmaṇi of Gaṅgeśa, *anumāna-khaṇḍa*, part two. With the *Prakāśa* commentary by Rucidatta Miśra and a subcommentary by Dharmarājādhvarin. Ed. N. S. Ramanuja Tatacharya. Kendriya Sanskrit Vidyapeetha Series. Tirupati: 1999.

Tattvacintāmaṇi of Gaṅgeśa, vol. 1, *pratyakṣa-khaṇḍa*. With the *Māthurī* commentary of Mathurānātha. Ed. Kamakhyanath Tarkavagish. Asiatic Society. Calcutta, 1884–1901. Reprint, 1991.

Tattvacintāmaṇi of Gāṅgeśa, vol. 2, pt. 1, *anumāna-khaṇḍa*. With the commentary of Mathurānātha. Ed. Kamakhyanath Tarkavagish. Asiatic Society. Calcutta, 1884–1901. Reprint, 1991.

Udayana: see *Ātmatattvaviveka*, *Kiraṇâvalī*, *Lakṣaṇamālā*, *Lakṣaṇāvalī*, *Nyāyakusumāñjali*, and *Nyāyavārttikatātparyapariśuddhi*; see also N. S. Dravid.

Vaiśeṣikasūtra of Kaṇāda. With the commentary of Candrānanda. Ed. Muni Sri Jambuvijayaji. Gaekwad Oriental Series 136. Baroda: Oriental Institute, 1961.

Vasu, S. C. *Aṣṭādhyāyī of Pāṇini*. 2 vols. 1891. Reprint, Delhi: Motilal Banarsidass.

Vattanky, John. *Gaṅgeśa's Philosophy of God*. Madras: Adyar, 1984.

Vātsyāyana: see *Nyāyasūtra*.

Wada, Toshihiro. *Invariable Concomitance in Navya Nyāya*. Delhi: Sri Satguru, 1990.

———. "The Origin of Navya-nyāya and Its Place within the History of Indian Logic." *Three Mountains and Seven Rivers: Prof. Musashi Tachikawa's Felicitation Volume*, ed. S. Hing and T. Wada, pp. 439–62. Delhi: Motilal Banarsidass, 2000.

INDEX